WORLD HISTORY
THE HUMAN EXPERIENCE

NATIONAL GEOGRAPHIC SOCIETY

Mounir A. Farah
Andrea Berens Karls

GLENCOE
McGraw-Hill

New York, New York   Columbus, Ohio   Woodland Hills, California   Peoria, Illinois

About the Authors

The **National Geographic Society**, founded in 1888 for the increase and diffusion of geographic knowledge, is the world's largest nonprofit scientific and educational organization. Since its earliest days, the Society has used sophisticated communication technologies and rich historical and archival resources to convey knowledge to a worldwide membership. The Educational Media Division supports the Society's mission by developing innovative educational programs—ranging from traditional print materials to multimedia programs including CD-ROMs, videodiscs, and software.

Mounir A. Farah, Ph.D. is a research historian and Associate Director of the Middle East Studies Program at the University of Arkansas, Fayetteville. Dr. Farah taught history and social science at New York University and Western Connecticut State University and has lectured at many teachers' conferences and workshops in the United States and abroad. He was a consultant to the Ministry of Education in Jordan and served as Coordinator of Social Studies in the Monroe, Connecticut public schools. Named Outstanding History Scholar-Teacher in New England and a recipient of the Connecticut Social Studies Annual Award, Dr. Farah is a past president of the Connecticut Council for the Social Studies and of the Middle East Outreach Council and a board member of the Arkansas Council for Social Studies. He is a contributing writer to several books and has authored numerous articles and reviews. Dr. Farah also is coauthor of Glencoe's *Global Insights.*

Andrea Berens Karls is an educator and coauthor of Glencoe's *Global Insights.* Educated at Wellesley College and Harvard University, she has taught at both the elementary and secondary levels. Ms. Karls was formerly Program Associate at Global Perspectives in Education, Inc., where she edited and wrote curriculum materials and worked with teachers. She is a member of the National Council for the Social Studies and the American Historical Association.

About the Cover

The temple of Amon-Ra—ancient Egypt's most important god—was the major building in Thebes, a city of Egypt. Between the 1300s B.C. and the 1100s B.C. Egyptian builders constructed the temple at the site of the present-day city of Luxor.

The part of the temple shown is an outer court, decorated with colossal images of the great Egyptian pharaoh Ramses II. A pair of granite obelisks covered with hieroglyphics also graced the outer court. One obelisk (shown in the cover photo) still stands. The other was removed to the Place de la Concorde in Paris, France, in 1831.

Glencoe/McGraw-Hill

A Division of The **McGraw-Hill** Companies

Design and Production: DECODE, Inc.
Cover photograph: Temple of Amon-Ra, Luxor, Egypt; Mark D. Phillips/Photo Researchers, Inc.

Send all inquiries to:
Glencoe/McGraw-Hill
8787 Orion Place
Columbus, OH 43240

ISBN 0-02-821576-1 (Student Edition) ISBN 0-02-821578-8 (Teacher's Wraparound Edition)

Printed in the United States of America.
8 9 10 11 12 13 071/043 06 05 04 03

Academic Consultants

Richard G. Boehm, Ph.D.
Professor of Geography
Southwest Texas State University
San Marcos, Texas

William Brinner, Ph.D.
Professor of History
Department of Near Eastern Studies
University of California
Berkeley, California

Stephen Chicoine
Author/Lecturer, World Affairs
Vice President
Bechtel Energy Resources Corporation
Houston, Texas

Paula Fredriksen, Ph.D.
Aurelio Professor of Scripture
Boston University
Boston, Massachusetts

Madhulika S. Khandelwal, Ph.D.
Research Historian
Asian/American Center
Queens College
City University of New York
New York City, New York

George Demetrius Knysh, Ph.D.
Associate Professor of Political Studies
University of Manitoba
Winnipeg, Manitoba
Canada

Frances Malino, Ph.D.
Professor of History
Wellesley College
Wellesley, Massachusetts

Shabbir Mansouri
Founding Director
Council on Islamic Education
Fountain Valley, California

Ali A. Mazrui, Ph.D.
Professor of History
State University of New York
Binghamton, New York

Jesus Mendez, Ph.D.
Associate Professor of History
Barry University
Miami Shores, Florida

Brendan Nagle, Ph.D.
Associate Professor
University of Southern California
Los Angeles, California

Al Naklowycz, Ph.D.
President, Ukrainian-American Academic
    Association of California
Carmichael, California

Donald Niewyk, Ph.D.
Professor of History
Southern Methodist University
Dallas, Texas

Boniface Obichere, Ph.D.
Professor of History
University of California
Los Angeles, California

Sayyid M. Syeed, Ph.D.
Secretary General
The Islamic Society of North America
Plainfield, Indiana

Frank De Varona
Region 1 Superintendent
Dade County Public Schools
Hialeah, Florida

Bluma Zuckerbrot-Finkelstein
Director, Special Projects
Middle Eastern Affairs
Anti-Defamation League of B'nai B'rith
St. Louis, Missouri

Teacher Reviewers

Christine Allen
North Salem High School
Salem, Oregon

John M. Arevalo
Harlandale High School
San Antonio, Texas

Mattie Collins
Pine Bluff High School
Pine Bluff, Arkansas

Janice Darley Dreyer
Vines High School
Plano, Texas

Louis Gallo
West High School
Knoxville, Tennessee

Mary Helen Haines
Richardson High School
Richardson, Texas

Mark Heinig
Reitz Memorial High School
Evansville, Indiana

Paul Horton
Williamsville East High School
East Amherst, New York

Jim Lloyd
Department Chair, History-Social Science
Bullard High School
Fresno, California

Patti Long
Forrest City High School
Forrest City, Arkansas

Willis M. Overton III
Warren Central High School
Indianapolis, Indiana

TABLE OF CONTENTS

TABLE OF CONTENTS

TABLE OF CONTENTS

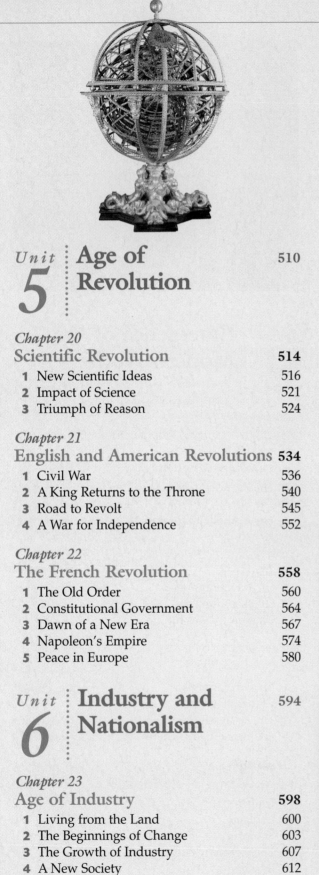

TABLE OF CONTENTS

TABLE OF CONTENTS

The Spread of Ideas

Literature
Bridge to the Past

Images of the Times

TABLE OF CONTENTS

CONNECTIONS To...

Geography

Economics

Science and Technology

The Arts

AROUND THE WORLD

Footnotes to History

Multimedia Activity

Turning Points in World History

Surfing the "Net"

SKILLS

Social Studies Skills

TABLE OF CONTENTS

Maps

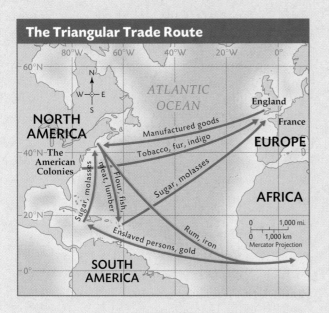

The Triangular Trade Route

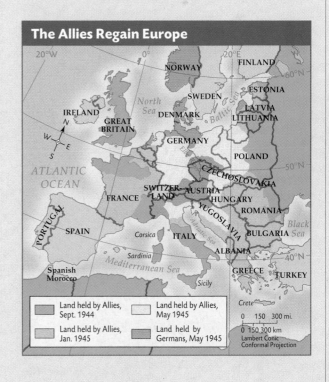

The Allies Regain Europe

TABLE OF CONTENTS

Population Density of Africa

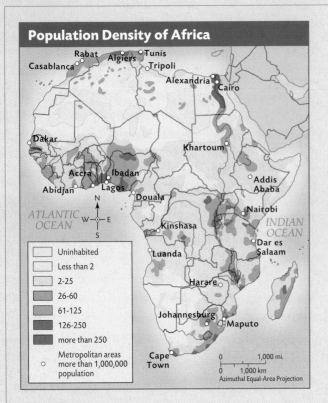

Population Density of Africa

Charts, Graphs, and Diagrams

Major Oil Producers in the Middle East

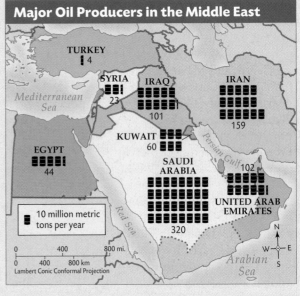

Major Oil Producers in the Middle East

Reference Atlas

Atlas Key

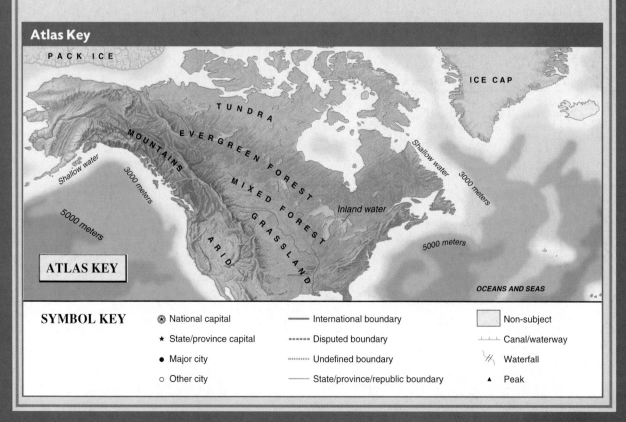

ATLAS KEY

SYMBOL KEY

⊚ National capital	—— International boundary	☐ Non-subject
★ State/province capital	------ Disputed boundary	⊥⊤⊥ Canal/waterway
● Major city	.... Undefined boundary	⅄ Waterfall
○ Other city	—— State/province/republic boundary	▲ Peak

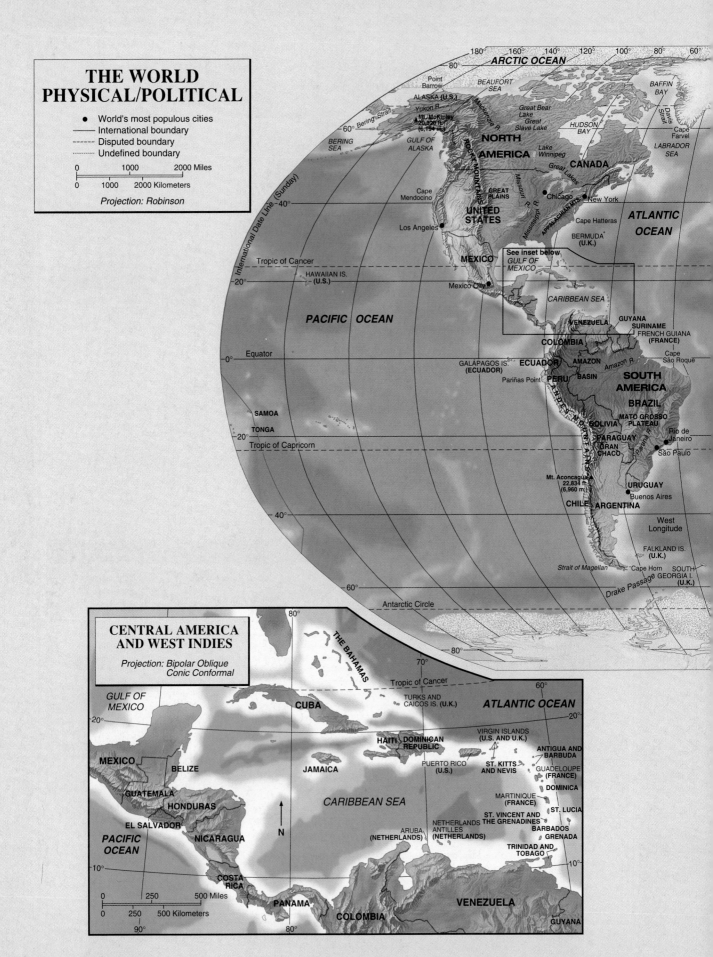

THE WORLD PHYSICAL/POLITICAL

- ● World's most populous cities
- —— International boundary
- ----- Disputed boundary
- ········ Undefined boundary

| 0 | 1000 | 2000 Miles |
| 0 | 1000 | 2000 Kilometers |

Projection: Robinson

CENTRAL AMERICA AND WEST INDIES

Projection: Bipolar Oblique Conic Conformal

| 0 | 250 | 500 Miles |
| 0 | 250 | 500 Kilometers |

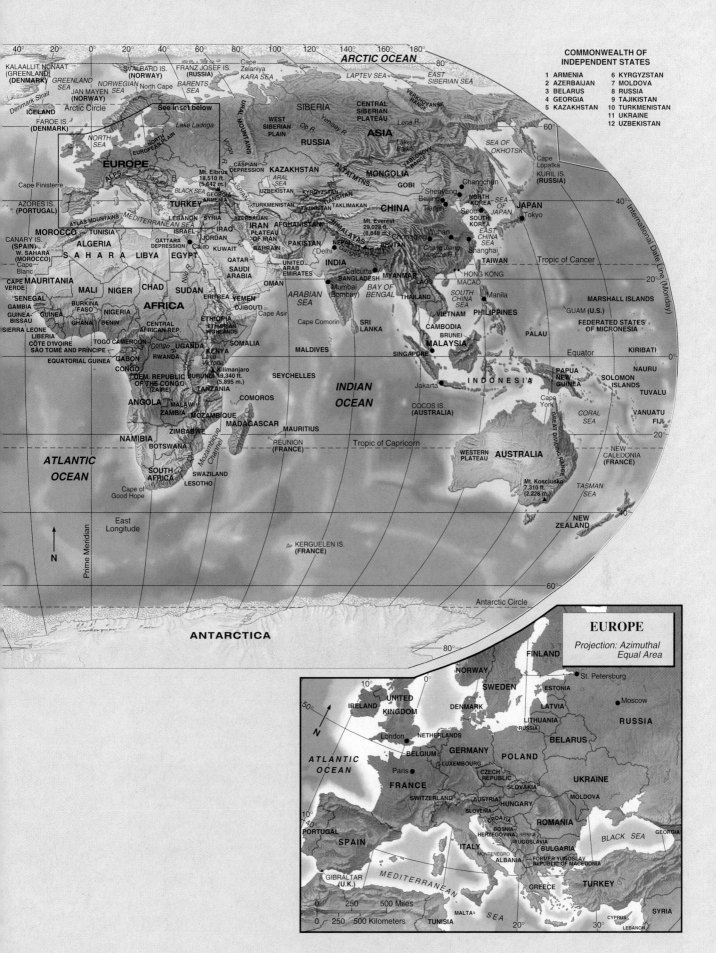

COMMONWEALTH OF
INDEPENDENT STATES

1	ARMENIA	6	KYRGYZSTAN
2	AZERBAIJAN	7	MOLDOVA
3	BELARUS	8	RUSSIA
4	GEORGIA	9	TAJIKISTAN
5	KAZAKHSTAN	10	TURKMENISTAN
		11	UKRAINE
		12	UZBEKISTAN

EUROPE

Projection: Azimuthal Equal Area

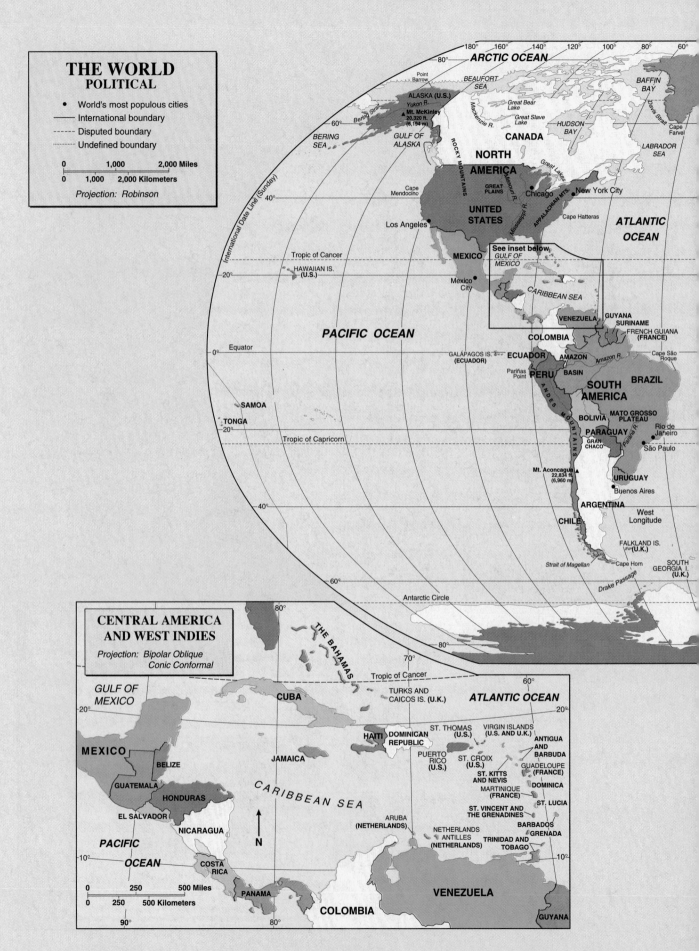

THE WORLD
POLITICAL

- • World's most populous cities
- —— International boundary
- - - - Disputed boundary
- ······ Undefined boundary

| 0 | 1,000 | 2,000 Miles |
| 0 | 1,000 | 2,000 Kilometers |

Projection: Robinson

ARCTIC OCEAN

BEAUFORT SEA

BAFFIN BAY

Point Barrow

ALASKA (U.S.)
Yukon R.
Mt. McKinley
20,320 ft.
(6,194 m)

Bering Strait

Great Bear Lake

Mackenzie R.

Great Slave Lake

HUDSON BAY

Davis Strait

Cape Farvel

BERING SEA

GULF OF ALASKA

CANADA

NORTH

ROCKY MOUNTAINS

LABRADOR SEA

AMERICA

Cape Mendocino

GREAT PLAINS

Missouri R.

Great Lakes

Chicago

New York City

UNITED STATES

Mississippi R.

APPALACHIAN MTS.

Cape Hatteras

ATLANTIC OCEAN

Los Angeles

MEXICO

See inset below
GULF OF MEXICO

Tropic of Cancer

HAWAIIAN IS.
(U.S.)

20°

Mexico City

CARIBBEAN SEA

VENEZUELA

GUYANA
SURINAME
FRENCH GUIANA
(FRANCE)

COLOMBIA

PACIFIC OCEAN

GALÁPAGOS IS.
(ECUADOR)

ECUADOR

AMAZON

Amazon R.

Cape São Roque

0° Equator

Pariñas Point

PERU

BASIN

BRAZIL

SOUTH

SAMOA

ANDES MOUNTAINS

BOLIVIA

MATO GROSSO PLATEAU

AMERICA

TONGA

20°

PARAGUAY

GRAN CHACO

Paraná R.

Rio de Janeiro

São Paulo

Tropic of Capricorn

Mt. Aconcagua
22,834 ft
(6,960 m)

URUGUAY

Buenos Aires

ARGENTINA

West Longitude

40°

CHILE

FALKLAND IS.
(U.K.)

Strait of Magellan

Cape Horn

SOUTH GEORGIA I.
(U.K.)

Drake Passage

60°

Antarctic Circle

International Date Line (Sunday)

180° 160° 140° 120° 100° 80° 60°

80°

60°

40°

20°

CENTRAL AMERICA
AND WEST INDIES

*Projection: Bipolar Oblique
Conic Conformal*

GULF OF MEXICO

THE BAHAMAS

80°

CUBA

TURKS AND CAICOS IS. (U.K.)

ATLANTIC OCEAN

70°

Tropic of Cancer

60°

20°

20°

HAITI

DOMINICAN REPUBLIC

ST. THOMAS
(U.S.)

VIRGIN ISLANDS
(U.S. AND U.K.)

ANTIGUA AND BARBUDA

MEXICO

BELIZE

JAMAICA

PUERTO RICO
(U.S.)

ST. CROIX
(U.S.)

GUADELOUPE
(FRANCE)

GUATEMALA

CARIBBEAN SEA

ST. KITTS AND NEVIS

DOMINICA

HONDURAS

MARTINIQUE
(FRANCE)

ST. LUCIA

EL SALVADOR

ST. VINCENT AND THE GRENADINES

PACIFIC

NICARAGUA

ARUBA
(NETHERLANDS)

BARBADOS

OCEAN

10°

NETHERLANDS ANTILLES
(NETHERLANDS)

GRENADA

TRINIDAD AND TOBAGO

10°

COSTA RICA

N

| 0 | 250 | 500 Miles |
| 0 | 250 | 500 Kilometers |

PANAMA

VENEZUELA

90°

COLOMBIA

80°

GUYANA

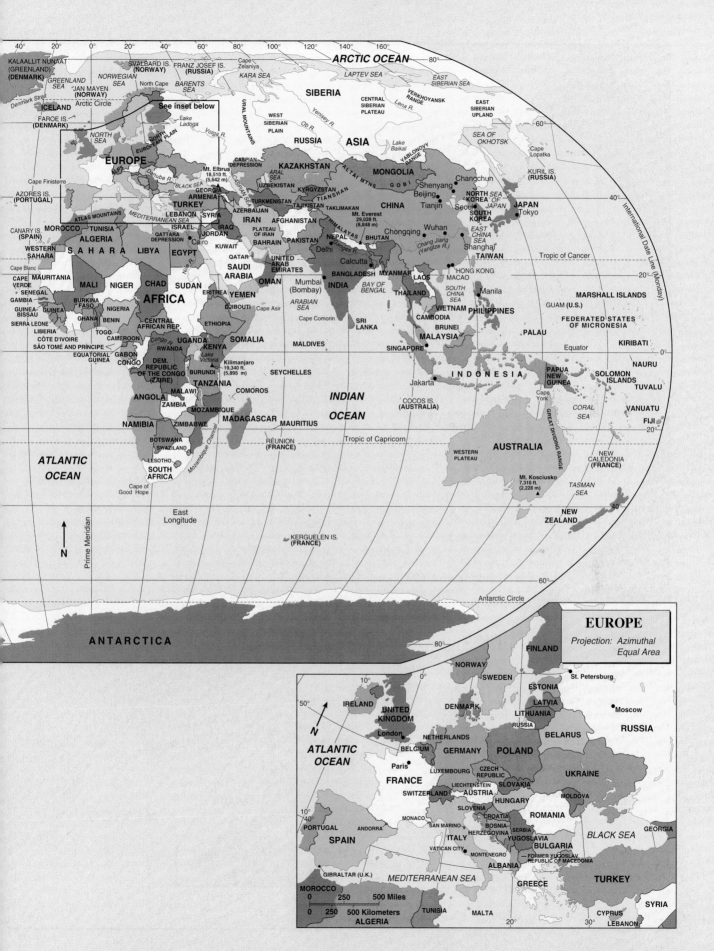

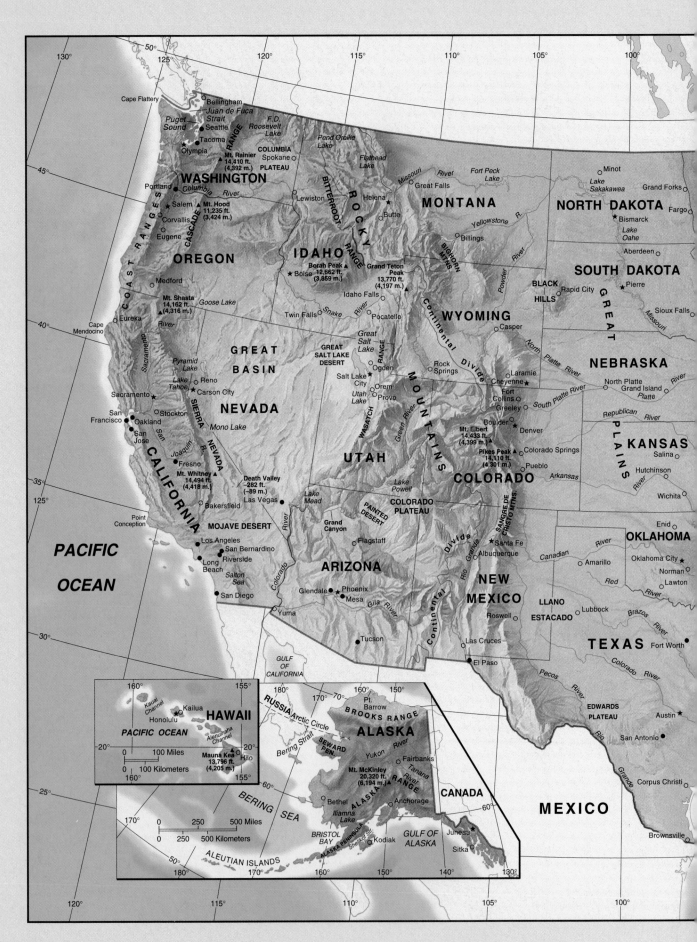

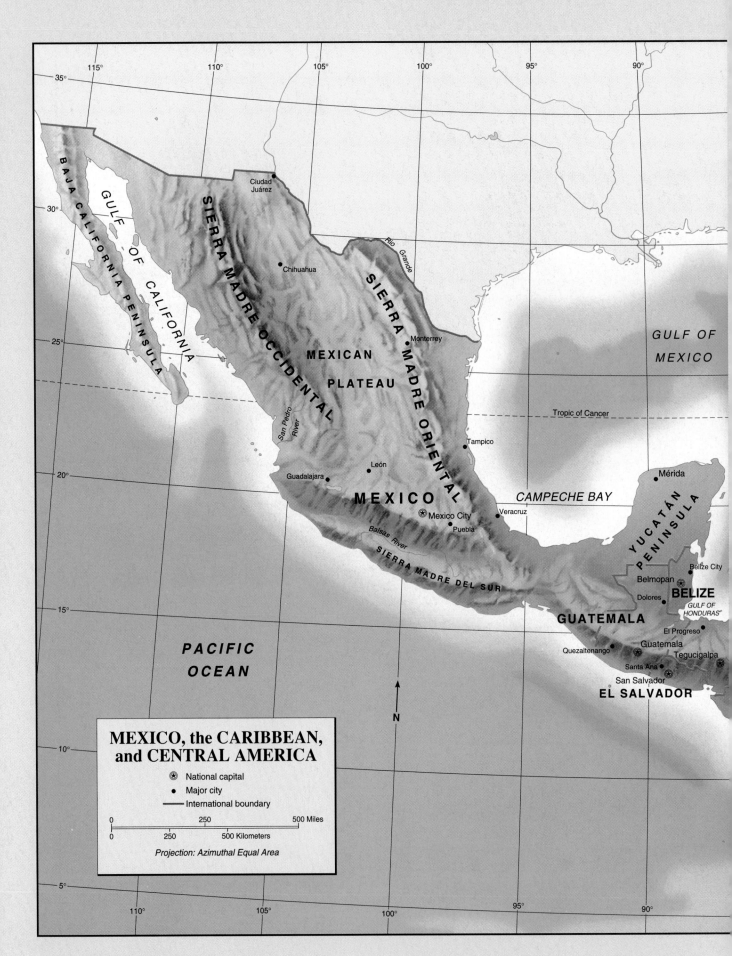

MEXICO, the CARIBBEAN, and CENTRAL AMERICA

⊛ National capital
• Major city
— International boundary

0   250   500 Miles
0   250   500 Kilometers

Projection: Azimuthal Equal Area

Labels on map:

BAJA CALIFORNIA PENINSULA

GULF OF CALIFORNIA

SIERRA MADRE OCCIDENTAL

Ciudad Juárez

• Chihuahua

MEXICAN PLATEAU

SIERRA MADRE ORIENTAL

Río Grande

• Monterrey

GULF OF MEXICO

Tropic of Cancer

San Pedro River

• Tampico

• León

• Guadalajara

MEXICO

⊛ Mexico City
• Puebla

Balsas River

Veracruz

CAMPECHE BAY

• Mérida

YUCATÁN PENINSULA

SIERRA MADRE DEL SUR

Belize City

Belmopan ⊛

BELIZE

• Dolores

GULF OF HONDURAS

GUATEMALA

El Progreso

Guatemala ⊛

Tegucigalpa ⊛

Quezaltenango

Santa Ana •

San Salvador ⊛

EL SALVADOR

PACIFIC OCEAN

N

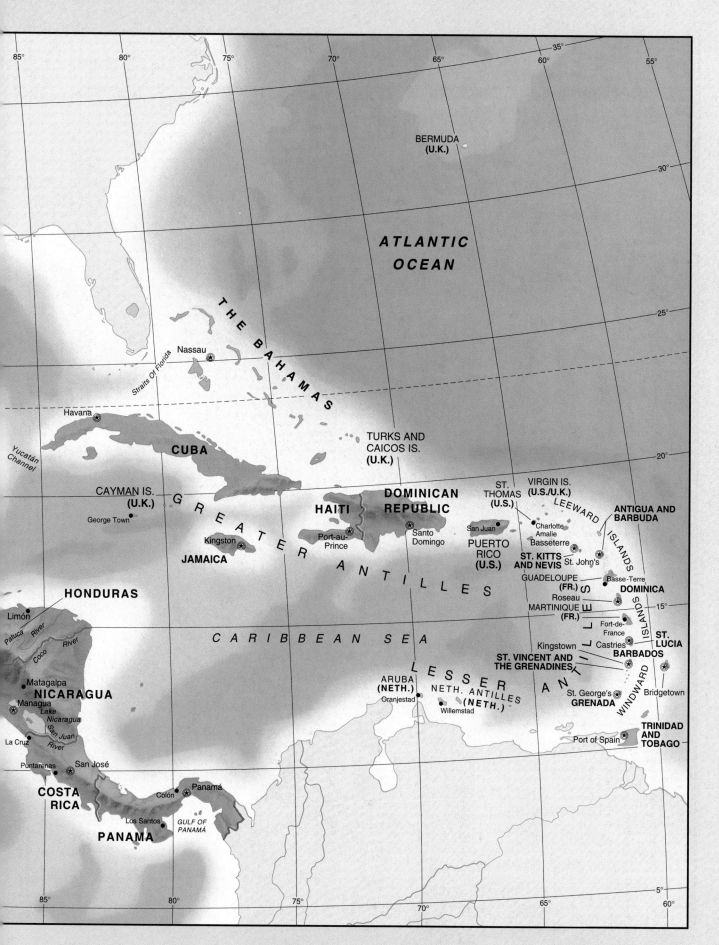

BERMUDA
(U.K.)

*ATLANTIC
OCEAN*

85° 80° 75° 70° 65° 60° 35°
30°
25°
20°
15°
5°

THE BAHAMAS

Nassau

Straits Of Florida

Havana

*Yucatán
Channel*

CUBA

TURKS AND
CAICOS IS.
(U.K.)

CAYMAN IS.
(U.K.)

George Town

GREATER

DOMINICAN
REPUBLIC

HAITI

Port-au-
Prince

Santo
Domingo

PUERTO
RICO
(U.S.)

San Juan

ST.
THOMAS
(U.S.)

VIRGIN IS.
(U.S./U.K.)

LEEWARD

ANTIGUA AND
BARBUDA

Charlotte
Amalie
Basseterre

ST. KITTS
AND NEVIS

St. John's

ISLANDS

Kingston

JAMAICA

ANTILLES

GUADELOUPE
(FR.)

Basse-Terre

Roseau

DOMINICA

MARTINIQUE
(FR.)

HONDURAS

Limón

Patuca River

Coco River

Fort-de-
France

CARIBBEAN SEA

ANTILLES

Kingstown

Castries

ST.
LUCIA

BARBADOS

Matagalpa

NICARAGUA

Managua

*Lake
Nicaragua*

San Juan River

La Cruz

ST. VINCENT AND
THE GRENADINES

ARUBA
(NETH.)

Oranjestad

LESSER

NETH. ANTILLES
(NETH.)

Willemstad

St. George's

GRENADA

Bridgetown

WINDWARD

Puntarenas

San José

COSTA
RICA

Colón

Panamá

Port of Spain

TRINIDAD
AND
TOBAGO

Los Santos

*GULF OF
PANAMÁ*

PANAMA

85° 80° 75° 70° 65° 60°

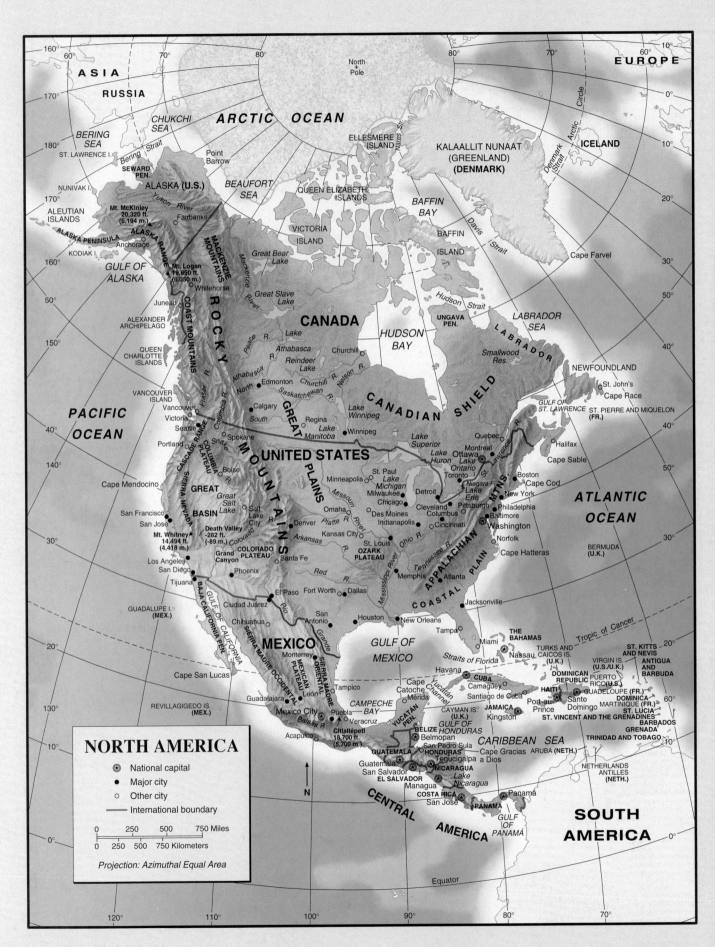

NORTH AMERICA

⊛ National capital
● Major city
○ Other city
━━━ International boundary

| 0 | 250 | 500 | 750 Miles |
| 0 | 250 | 500 | 750 Kilometers |

Projection: Azimuthal Equal Area

SOUTH AMERICA

⊚ National capital
● Major city
○ Other city
⎯ International boundary

0   250   500 Miles
0   250   500 Kilometers

Projection: Azimuthal Equal Area

EUROPE

- ⊛ National capital
- ● Major city
- ○ Other city
- International boundary
- Republic boundary
- ╫ Canal

| 0 | 100 | 200 | 300 Miles |
| 0 | 100 | 200 | 300 Kilometers |

Projection: Azimuthal Equal Area

ICELAND
Reykjavik

Arctic Circle

NORWEGIAN SEA

SCANDINAVIAN HIGHLANDS

Trondheim

NORWAY
Galdhöpiggen 8,097 ft. (2,468 m.)

GULF OF BOTHNIA

Bergen

Oslo

SWEDEN
Lake Vänern

ÅLAND I.

Uppsala

Stockholm

HIIUMAA I.
SAAREMAA I.
GOTLAND I.

Lake Vättern

ÖLAND I.

BALTIC SEA

FAROE IS. (DEN.)

Prime Meridian

SHETLAND IS. (U.K.)

OUTER HEBRIDES IS.

Cape Wrath

ORKNEY ISLANDS

N

SCOTLAND

NORTH SEA

Skagerrak

Kattegat

Göteborg

NORTHERN IRELAND (U.K.)

Glasgow

Edinburgh

PENNINE RANGE

UNITED KINGDOM

JUTLAND

Copenhagen
DENMARK

Malmö

BORNHOLM I.

RUSSIA

Belfast

IRISH SEA

Manchester

Gdańsk

Szczecin

NORTH

Dublin

ISLE OF MAN

Liverpool
Leeds
Sheffield

Kiel Canal

Rostock

POLAND

IRELAND

Cork

ENGLAND

ELba R.

Hamburg

Bremen

Berlin

Poznań

Vistula

Warsaw

Łódź

Cape Clear

St. George's Channel

WALES

Birmingham

NETHERLANDS
Amsterdam

Mittelland Canal

Hannover

Magdeburg

Oder R.

Wrocław

Katowice

Cardiff

Bristol

London

The Hague
Rotterdam

Antwerp

Essen
Dortmund

Cologne

Leipzig

Dresden

Prague

Ostrava

Kraków

English Channel

Strait of Dover

BELGIUM
Brussels

Liège

Bonn

GERMANY

Chemnitz

CZECH REPUBLIC

Brno

GUERNSEY I. (U.K.)
JERSEY I. (U.K.)

Le Havre

Seine River

Paris

LUXEMBOURG
Luxembourg

Frankfurt

Marne-Rhine Canal

Rhine R.

Stuttgart

Vienna

SLOVAKIA

Bratislava

ATLANTIC OCEAN

BRETON PEN.

Marne R.

Nantes

Loire

FRANCE

Strasbourg

Danube River

Munich

Bodensee

Linz

Salzburg

AUSTRIA

Innsbruck

Budapest

Miskolc

HUNGARY

Lausanne
Geneva

Zürich

SWITZERLAND

Bern

L. Geneva

Mt. Rosa 12,203 ft. (4,634 m.)

LIECHTENSTEIN
Vaduz

Graz

L. Balaton

Pécs

CANTABRIAN MTNS.

Bilbao

Bordeaux

Garonne R.

Lyon

Mt. Blanc 15,771 ft. (4,807 m.)

ALPS

Ljubljana

SLOVENIA

Zagreb

Novi Sad

Tisza

BAY OF BISCAY

Cape Finisterre

Porto

Valladolid

Duero River

CENTRAL MASSIF

Toulouse

Midi Canal

Rhône R.

Turin

Milan

PO VALLEY

Venice

Genoa

DINARIC ALPS

CROATIA

Sava R.

Belgrade

PYRENEES

Montpellier

Nice

Bologna

SAN MARINO
San Marino

BOSNIA-HERZEGOVINA

Sarajevo

Aneto Peak 11,168 ft. (3,404 m.)

ANDORRA
Andorra la Vella

Marseille

GULF OF LION

Monaco
MONACO

Florence

APENNINES

ADRIATIC SEA

Split

PORTUGAL

IBERIAN

Zaragoza

Madrid

Barcelona

CORSICA (FR.)

VATICAN CITY

MONTENEGRO

FORMER YUGOSLAV REPUBLIC OF MACEDON

Lisbon

Setúbal

Tagus

River

PENINSULA

Rome

ITALY

Tirané

Guadiana

River

SPAIN

Valencia

Palma

BALEARIC IS. (SP.)

Naples

Bari

ALBANIA

SIERRA MORENA

Seville

Murcia

SARDINIA (IT.)

TYRRHENIAN SEA

G. OF TARANTO

Cape St. Vincent

Málaga

Granada

Cagliari

Strait of Gibraltar

GIBRALTAR (U.K.)

MEDITERRANEAN

Strait of Sicily

Palermo

SICILY

Catania

IONIAN

KEFALLINIA I.

SEA

PANTELLERIA (IT.)

AFRICA

MALTA
Valletta

SEA

40° 60° 30° 20° 10° 70° 10° 20°

30°

50°

20°

40°

30°

10° 0° 10° 20°

North
Cape
30°   40°   50°   70°
*BARENTS
SEA*

• Murmansk

TIMAN
RIDGE
*Pechora
R.*

60°

**KOLA
PENINSULA**

*WHITE
SEA*

U
R
A
L

• Arkhangel'sk

*White Sea-
Baltic
Waterway*

*N.
Dvina
River*
*Vychegda
River*

Mt. Konzhakovskiy ▲
5,147 ft.
(1,569 m.)

M
O
U
N
T
A
I
N
S

A S I A

FINLAND

*Lake
Onega*

Sukhona River

*Kama
R.*

• Perm

70°

• Tampere
*Lake
Saimaa*
• Turku
• Helsinki
• Espoo
GULF OF FINLAND
⊛ Tallinn
ESTONIA

*Lake
Ladoga*

*Volga-Baltic
Waterway*

• St. Petersburg

*Chudskoye
Lake*

*Rybinsk
Reservoir*

• Yaroslavl

Kazan •

Kama River

Ufa •

Ural River

50°

GULF
OF
RIGA
LATVIA
⊛ Riga
W.

Volga River
*Volga-Baltic
Waterway*

• Nizhniy
Novgorod

*Kuybyshev
Reservoir*

• Samara

BALTIC
PLAIN
*Dvina
River*

⊛ Moscow

River

Orenburg •

Ural River

LITHUANIA
• Kaunas
⊛ Vilnius

E
U
R
O
P
E
A
N

P
L
A
I
N

• Smolensk

Oka • Tula

RUSSIA

V
O
L
G
A

U
P
L
A
N
D

Volga River

Saratov •

• Minsk

C
E
N
T
R
A
L

R
U
S
S
I
A
N

U
P
L
A
N
D

• Kursk

Don
• Voronezh

KAZAKHSTAN

BELARUS

Pripet River

*Desna
R.*

River

*Volgograd
Reservoir*

Ural River

70°

50°

40°

60°

30°

*ARAL
SEA*

⊛ Kiev
*Kremenchug
Reservoir*

• Kharkov

Volgograd •

Volga River

D
E
P
R
E
S
S
I
O
N

• Lvov
DNIEPER UPLAND
Dniester R.

UKRAINE

• Lugansk

*Tsimlyansk
Reservoir*

Astrakhan •

• Dnepropetrovsk
• Krivoy Rog
• Zaporozhye

• Donetsk

Don River

• Rostov

C
A
S
P
I
A
N

*Delta of
the Volga*

CARPATHIAN MTNS.

MOLDOVA
⊛ Chisinau
Prut River

**DNIEPER
LOWLAND**

*Kakhovka
Res.*

*Dniepr
River*

*SEA
OF
AZOV*

C
A
S
P
I
A
N

S
E
A

• Debrecen

• Odessa

CRIMEA

• Krasnodar

Grozny •

• Cluj-Napoca

ROMANIA
• Timişoara   • Braşov

**WALLACHIA
PLAIN**
⊛ Bucharest
Danube River

C A U C A S U S   M T N S.

Mt. Elbrus
18,510 ft.
(5,642 m.)

SERBIA
• Constanţa
• Ruse

• Niš

BULGARIA
⊛ Sofia   • Burgas
• Plovdiv

• Varna

B L A C K   S E A

⊛ Skopje   Musala Peak
9,536 ft.
(2,926 m.)

Bosporus

TURKEY

B
A
L
K
A
N

PENINSULA

• Salonika

Dardanelles — *SEA OF
MARMARA*

A S I A

• Larissa

*AEGEAN
SEA*

GREECE

• Patras   • Athens
• Piraeus

**PELOPONNESE
PEN.**

30°

40°

50°

RHODES

CRETE (GR.)
• Iráklion

30°

ARCTIC
OCEAN

BARENTS SEA

FRANZ JOSEF
ISLANDS

Cape Zelaniya

NOVAYA ZEMLYA

KARA SEA

EUROPE

BALTIC SEA

GULF OF FINLAND

(RUSSIA)

Murmansk

KOLA
PENINSULA

WHITE
SEA

Arkhangel'sk

TIMAN RIDGE

Kara Strait

YAMAL
PEN.

GYDAN
PENINSULA

St.
Petersburg

Lake
Ladoga

Baltic-
White Sea
Canal

Lake Onega

Volga-Baltic
Waterway

N. Dvina R.

Yenisey
River

VALDAI HILLS

Minsk

BELARUS

Lvov

DNIEPER
UPLAND

Kiev

UKRAINE

DNIEPER
LOWLAND

MOLDOVA

Chisinau

Odessa

Nikolayev

Krivoy Rog

Dnepropetrovsk

Zaporozh'ye

Donetsk

Lugansk

Mariupol

Rostov

SEA OF
AZOV

Kharkov

Dnieper R.

Rybinsk Res.

Vologda

Yaroslovl

Moscow

Ivanovo

Tula

Ryazan'

Nizhniy Novgorod

NORTHERN HILLS

Volga

Sukhona R.

Vychegda

Pechora River

Don River

Kama

Kazan

Izhevsk

Perm

Mt. Konzhakovskiy
5,147 ft.
(1,569 m.)

URAL MOUNTAINS

Ob

Ob

Urengoy

WEST
SIBERIAN
PLAIN

Vakh

River

Kuybyshev Res.

Ul'yanovsk

Kamsk Res.

VOLGA UPLAND

Penza

Saratov

Tol'yatti

Samara

Ufa

Yekaterinburg

Chelyabinsk

Tobol R.

Irtysh River

River

Tomsk

Voronezh

Don River

Volga R.

Volgograd
Reservoir

Volgograd

Tsimlyansk
Res.

Volga R.

Ural R.

Orenburg

Ishim R.

L. Chany

Omsk

Novosibirsk

Novosibirsk Res

Kemerovo

Novokuznetsk

BLACK
SEA

Krasnodar

CASPIAN DEPRESSION

Astrakhan

KYRGYZ

TURGAY

STEPPE

PLATEAU

KAZAK
UPLAND

Karaganda

Semipalatinsk

Barnaul

Mt. Belukha
14,783 ft.
(4,506 m.)

CAUCASUS

Mt. Elbrus
18,510 ft.
(5,642 m.)

MTNS.

GEORGIA

Tbilisi

ARMENIA

Yerevan

AZERBAIJAN

AZERBAIJAN

Baku

CASPIAN
SEA

KARA BOGAZ
GOL GULF

USTYURT
PLATEAU

ARAL
SEA

PLAINS OF TURAN

KAZAKHSTAN

Kzyl-Orda

Syr Darya

BETPAK-DALA
DESERT

L. Zaysan

Lake Balkhash

Ili R.

L. Alakol

TURKMENISTAN

KARAKUM

DESERT

Amu Darya

UZBEKISTAN

Samarkand

Tashkent

Darya

Almaty

Bishkek

KYRGYZSTAN

L. Issyk-Kul

ASIA

Ashkhabad

ALAY MOUNTAINS

Dushanbe

TAJIKISTAN

Communism Pk.
24,590 ft.
(7,495 m.)

A14   Reference Atlas

North Pole

ARCTIC
OCEAN

Cape Arkticheski
SEVERNAYA
ZEMLYA

Vil'kitskiy Strait

BYRRANGA
MTNS.

TAYMYR
PEN.

L. Taymyr

CENTRAL SIBERIAN

Noril'sk

Kotuy R.

Lowet

PLATEAU

Tura   Tunguska

River

Yenisey River

Angara   R.

Krasnoyarsk

Krasnoyarsk
Reservoir

Bratsk

Bratsk
Reservoir

SAYAN
MOUNTAINS

ALTAI MTNS.

RUSSIA

Oleněk

R.

Markha

R.

Vilyuysk
Reservoir

Vilyuy   R.

Vilyuy

LENA PLATEAU

Lena

River

Lena

STANOVOY
UPLAND

YABLONOVY RANGE

Lake
Baikal

Vitim

R.

R.

Irkutsk   Ulan-Ude

Chita

Shilka

R.

Shilka

NEW SIBERIAN
ISLANDS

Sannikov Strait

Laptev Strait

LAPTEV SEA

VERKHOYANSK

RANGE

R.

CHERSKIY   RANGE

Verkhoyansk

Indigirka

Aldan

Yakutsk

S   I   B   E

ALDAN
MTNS.

STANOVOY RANGE

R.

Aldan

River

EAST SIBERIAN
SEA

WRANGEL
ISLAND

Long Strait

KOLYMA
PLAIN

Kolyma

Cherskiy

R   I   A

Kolyma

River

River

DZHUGDZHUR RA.

Uda R.

Komsomol'sk

Bering Strait

CHUKCHI
SEA

CHUKOTSK
PEN.

Anadyr R.

KOLYMA

RANGE

Evensk

Magadan

BERING   SEA

Cape
Navarin

KORYAK

MTNS.

KARAGIN
ISLAND

SHELIKHOV
GULF

KAMCHATKA

SREDINNY

RA.

PENINSULA

▲ Mt. Klyuchevsk
15,584 ft.
(4,750 m.)

KOMANDORSKIY
ISLANDS

Petropavlovsk-
Kamchatskiy

SEA   OF   OKHOTSK

Cape Lopatka

KURIL ISLANDS

Cape Yelizavety

SAKHALIN

ISLAND

Terpeniya Point

Tatar

Strait

Amur

River

Khabarovsk

Ussuri River

SIKHOTE-ALIN   RA.

L. Khanka

La Pérouse
Strait

ASIA

Vladivostok

SEA   OF   JAPAN

RUSSIA AND
THE EURASIAN REPUBLICS

⊛   National capital

●   Major city

○   Other city

——   International boundary

0	250	500 Miles

0	250	500 Kilometers

Projection: Two-Point Equidistant

80°   70°   60°   170°   180°   170°   160°   50°   150°   40°   140°   30°

90°   100°   110°   120°   130°

KALAALLIT NUNAAT
(GREENLAND)
(DEN.)

ARCTIC OCEAN

FRANZ JOSEF IS.
(RUSSIA)

Cape
Zelaniya

SVALBARD
(NOR.)

NOVAYA ZEMLYA

KARA SEA

YAMAL
PEN.

JAN MAYEN
(NOR.)

NORWEGIAN
SEA

BARENTS SEA

LAPLAND

Arctic Circle

Murmansk

KOLA PEN.

Arkhangel'sk

WEST

ICELAND

Reykjavík

SWEDEN

FINLAND

North Cape

North Dvina R.

Mt. Konzhakovskiy
5,147 ft.
(1,569 m.)

SIBERIAN

FAROE IS.
(DEN.)

NORWAY

SCANDINAVIA

L. Saimaa

Tampere

Helsinki

Lake
Ladoga

Perm

Yekaterinburg

Irtysh

PLAIN

Bergen

Oslo

Stockholm

Tallinn

L. Onega

St. Petersburg

Rybinsk Res.

Nizhniy Novgorod

Chelyabinsk

Omsk

ATLANTIC
OCEAN

NORTH
SEA

DENMARK

L. Vänern

Göteborg

Copenhagen

BALTIC

Riga

ESTONIA

LATVIA

Kuybyshev Res.

URAL MTNS.

Moscow

Samara

Orenburg

Karaganda

KAZAKHSTAN

UNITED
KINGDOM

Dublin

Manchester

Sheffield

NETHERLANDS

LITH.
(RUSSIA)

Vilnius

Minsk

BELARUS

VOLGA UPLAND

Volga River

Ural R.

Lake Balkhash

IRELAND

Liverpool

London

Amsterdam

Berlin

Poznań

Warsaw

EUROPE

Kiev

NORTH EUROPEAN PLAIN

Volgograd

KYRGYZ STEPPE

Birmingham

Brussels

Hamburg

GERMANY

Elbe

Dresden

POLAND

Kraków

Lvov

DNIEPER
LOWLAND

UKRAINE

ARAL
SEA

Syr Darya

Almaty

BELGIUM

LUX.

Luxembourg

Paris

Bern

SWITZ.

Munich

Danube

Prague

CZECH REPUBLIC SLOVAKIA

Vienna

Bratislava

AUSTRIA HUNGARY

Budapest

MOLDOVA

Chisinau

Odessa

CASPIAN
DEPRESSION

SEA OF
AZOV

CASPIAN SEA

UZBEKISTAN

Tashkent

Bishkek

KYRGYZST.

FRANCE

Loire

Lyon

LIECH.

Zagreb

ROMANIA

Brasov

Belgrade

Bucharest

BLACK SEA

Mt. Elbrus
18,510 ft.
(5,642 m.)

CAUCASUS MTNS.

GEORGIA

Tbilisi

Baku

PLAINS OF
TURAN

Amu Darya

Communism Pk.
24,590 ft.

Kongur Pk.
25,324 ft. (7,719 m.)

MON.

Monaco

Toulouse

Marseille

SLO.

S.M.

Sarajevo

SERBIA

Sofia

BULGARIA

Istanbul

Ankara

ARMENIA

Yerevan

AZERBAIJAN

TURKMENISTAN

Ashkhabad

Dushanbe (7,495 m.)

TAJIKISTAN

PAMIR
KNOT

SPAIN

Cape
Finisterre

Pyrenees

ANDORRA

San
Marino

MONT.

Tiranë

Skopje

F.Y.R.O.M.

Bursa

TURKEY

Van

Tabriz

ELBURZ MTNS.

Mashhad

Godwin Austen
Pk. (K2)
28,251 ft.
(8,611 m.)

Zaragoza

Aneto Pk.
11,168 ft.
(3,404 m.)

Andorra
la Vella

Rome

Naples

ITALY

ALBANIA

GREECE

Athens

ANATOLIA

Konya

Adana

Mosul

Kirkuk

L. Urmia

Tehran

GREAT SALT
DESERT

HINDU KUSH

Kabul

Islamabad

Rawalpindi

KARAKORAM
RANGE

PORTUGAL

Madrid

Valencia

Palermo

Nicosia

CYPRUS

SYRIA

Aleppo

Euphrates

Tigris

Estahan

IRAN

PLATEAU
OF
IRAN

AFGHANISTAN

Lahore

Lisbon

Tagus R.

IBERIAN
PEN.

Seville

MEDITERRANEAN SEA

MALTA

Valletta

Tel Aviv-Yafo

Beirut

LEBANON

Damascus

Baghdad

IRAQ

Ahvaz

Abadan

Shiraz

Kandahar

Helmand

PAKISTAN

BALUCHISTAN

THAR
DESERT

New Delhi

Jaipur

INDIA

Jerusalem

ISR.

Amman

JORDAN

SYRIAN
DESERT

Al Basrah

KUW.

Kuwait

PERSIAN GULF

Strait
of
Hormuz

Indus

Sutlej

Delhi

ALBAN. —Albania
BAH. —Bahrain
B.H. —Bosnia and Herzegovina
CR. —Croatia
ISR. —Israel
KUW. —Kuwait
LIECH. —Liechtenstein
LITH. —Lithuania
LUX. —Luxembourg
F.Y.R.O.M. —Former Yugoslav
Republic of Macedonia
MON. —Monaco
MONT. —Montenegro
S.M. —San Marino
SL. —Slovenia
SWITZ. —Switzerland
U.A.E. —United Arab Emirates

DEAD SEA
DEPRESSION

AN NAFUD
DESERT

SAUDI

Riyadh

Madinah

Manama

BAH.

Doha

QATAR

Abu Dhabi

U.A.E.

GULF OF
OMAN

Muscat

OMAN

Karachi

Hyderabad

Narmada R.

Ahmadābād

Nagpur

DECCAN
PLATEAU

Tropic of Cancer

AFRICA

RED
SEA

ARABIA

NAJD
PLATEAU

ARABIAN PENINSULA

RUB AL
KHALI

ARABIAN
SEA

WESTERN GHATS

Mumbai
(Bombay)

Poona

HINDU-
STAN

Hyderabad

EASTERN GHATS

Godavari R.

Makkah

Chennai (Madras

Bangalore

Calicut

Palk Str.

Cape Comorin

SRI LANKA

Colombo

Dehiwala-Mt.
Lavinia

Cape Dondra

San'a

YEMEN

Shu'ayb
Mt. Nabi
12,336 ft.
(3,760 m.)

Aden

Bab el
Mandeb

GULF OF
ADEN

SOCOTRA
(YEMEN)

Male

MALDIVES

EURASIA

⊛ National capital
● Major city
○ Other city

——— International boundary
- - - - Disputed boundary
········· Undefined boundary

| 0 | 500 | 1000 Miles |
| 0 | 500 | 1000 Kilometers |

Projection: Robinson

Equator

INDIAN OCEAN

N

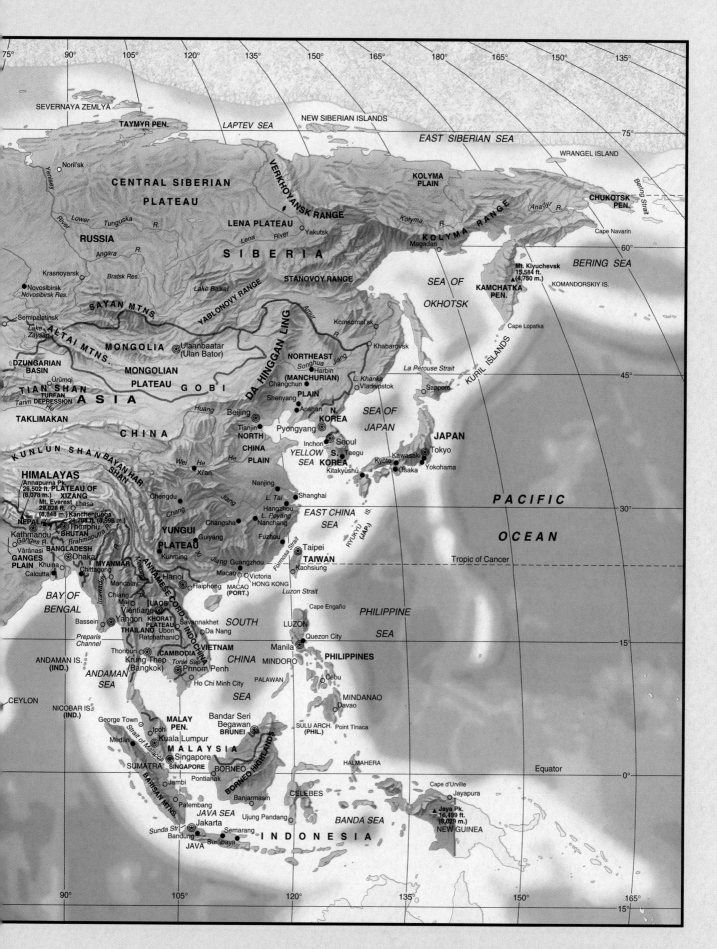

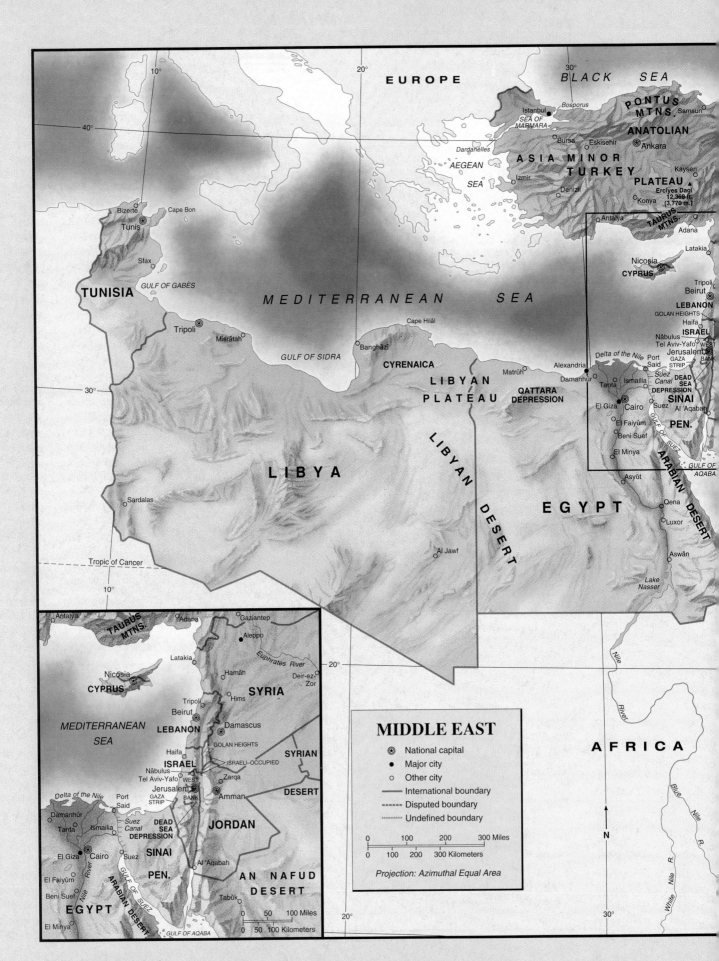

EUROPE

BLACK SEA

PONTUS MTNS.
Samsun
Istanbul
Bosporus
SEA OF MARMARA
ANATOLIAN
Bursa
Eskisehir
Ankara
ASIA MINOR
TURKEY
Dardanelles
Kayseri
AEGEAN SEA
Izmir
PLATEAU
Erciyes Daği
12,369 ft.
(3,770 m.)
Denizli
Konya
Antalya
TAURUS MTNS.
Adana

Latakia

Bizerte
Cape Bon
Tunis
Nicosia
CYPRUS
Tripoli
Beirut
LEBANON
GOLAN HEIGHTS
Haifa
TUNISIA
Sfax
GULF OF GABÈS
Nâbulus
ISRAEL
Tel Aviv-Yafo
WEST
Jerusalem
BANK
GAZA
STRIP
DEAD
SEA
DEPRESSION

MEDITERRANEAN   SEA

Cape Hilâl
Tripoli
Misrâtah
GULF OF SIDRA
Banghâzi
CYRENAICA
Matrûh
Alexandria
Delta of the Nile
Port Said
Suez Canal
Ismailia
SINAI
Al 'Aqabah
PEN.
Damanhûr
Tanta
LIBYAN PLATEAU
QATTARA DEPRESSION
El Giza
Cairo
Suez
El Faiyûm
Beni Suef
GULF OF SUEZ
El Minya
GULF OF AQABA

30°

LIBYA
LIBYAN DESERT
EGYPT
ARABIAN DESERT
Sardalas
Asyût
Qena
Luxor

Tropic of Cancer

Al Jawf
Aswân
Lake Nasser

Antalya
TAURUS MTNS.
Adana
Gaziantep
Aleppo
Latakia
Euphrates River
Deir-ez-Zor
Nicosia
CYPRUS
Hamâh
SYRIA
Hims
Tripoli
Beirut
LEBANON
Damascus
MEDITERRANEAN SEA
GOLAN HEIGHTS
SYRIAN
Haifa
ISRAELI-OCCUPIED
Nâbulus
ISRAEL
Tel Aviv-Yafo
WEST
Zarqa
Jerusalem
BANK
DESERT
Amman
Delta of the Nile
Port Said
GAZA
STRIP
DEAD SEA DEPRESSION
JORDAN
Damanhûr
Suez Canal
Ismailia
Tanta
SINAI
El Giza
Cairo
Suez
PEN.
Al 'Aqabah
AN NAFUD
El Faiyûm
GULF OF SUEZ
DESERT
Beni Suef
ARABIAN DESERT
Tabûk
EGYPT
El Minya
GULF OF AQABA

0   50   100 Miles
0   50 100 Kilometers

MIDDLE EAST

⊛ National capital
● Major city
○ Other city
— International boundary
---- Disputed boundary
⋯⋯ Undefined boundary

0   100   200   300 Miles
0 100 200 300 Kilometers

Projection: Azimuthal Equal Area

N

AFRICA

Nile River
Blue Nile R.
White Nile R.

20°

30°

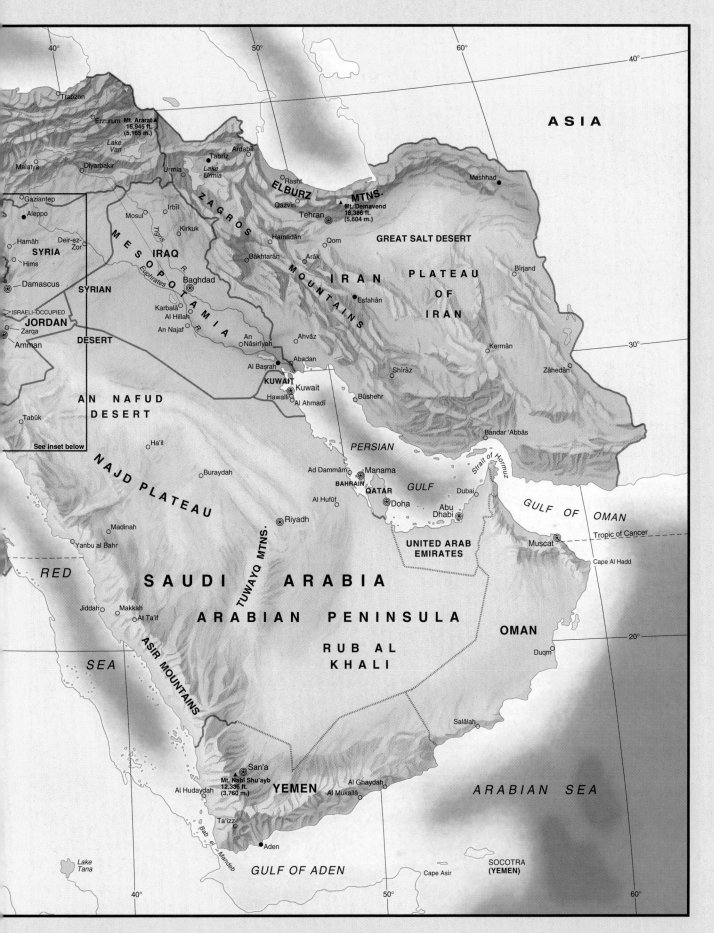

40°

50°

60°

40°

○ Trabzon

ASIA

Erzurum Mt. Ararat ▲
16,945 ft.
(5,165 m.)

Malatya

Lake Van

○ Diyarbakir

Ardabīl ○

● Tabrīz

Lake Urmia

Urmia ○

Rasht ○

● Mashhad

○ Gaziantep

ZAGROS

ELBURZ MTNS.

● Aleppo

Mosul ○

Irbīl ○

Qazvin ○

Mt. Demavend ▲
18,386 ft.
(5,604 m.)

Hamâh ○

Deir-ez-Zor ○

Tigris

Kirkuk ○

Tehran ◎

Hims ○

SYRIA

IRAQ

Hamadān ○

◎ Damascus

Euphrates

Bâkhtarân ○

Arāk ●

Qom ○

GREAT SALT DESERT

ISRAELI-OCCUPIED

SYRIAN

Baghdad ◎

M E S O P O T A M I A

Karbalā ○

IRAN

PLATEAU

○ JORDAN

Al Hillah ○

● Esfahān

OF

Zarqa ○

An Najaf ○

Bīrjand ●

Amman ●

DESERT

An Nâsirîyah ○

Ahvāz ●

IRAN

Ahvāz ●

Kermān ○

30°

Abadan ●

Shīrāz ●

Zāhedān ○

○ Tabūk

AN NAFUD

Al Başrah ○

KUWAIT ■

● Kuwait

Hawalli ○

Al Ahmadî ○

Bûshehr ○

DESERT

See inset below

Ha'il ○

Bandar 'Abbās ●

N A J D P L A T E A U

Buraydah ○

PERSIAN

Strait of Hormuz

○ Madinah

Ad Dammām ○

◎ Manama

GULF OF OMAN

● Riyadh

BAHRAIN

GULF

○ Yanbu al Bahr

Al Hufūf ○

QATAR

Dubai ●

Tropic of Cancer

RED

Doha ◎

Abu Dhabi ●

Muscat ◉

● Muscat

SAUDI   ARABIA

UNITED ARAB
EMIRATES

Cape Al Hadd ○

○ Jiddah

Makkah ○

A R A B I A N   P E N I N S U L A

OMAN

20°

SEA

At Ta'if ○

ASIR MOUNTAINS

TUWAYQ MTNS.

RUB AL
KHALI

Duqm ○

Salālah ●

Mt. Nabî Shu'ayb ▲
12,336 ft.
(3,760 m.)

● San'a

Al Ghaydah ○

ARABIAN   SEA

Al Hudaydah ○

YEMEN

Al Mūkallā ○

Ta'izz ○

● Aden

Lake Tana

GULF OF ADEN

Cape Asir ○

SOCOTRA
(YEMEN)

40°

50°

60°

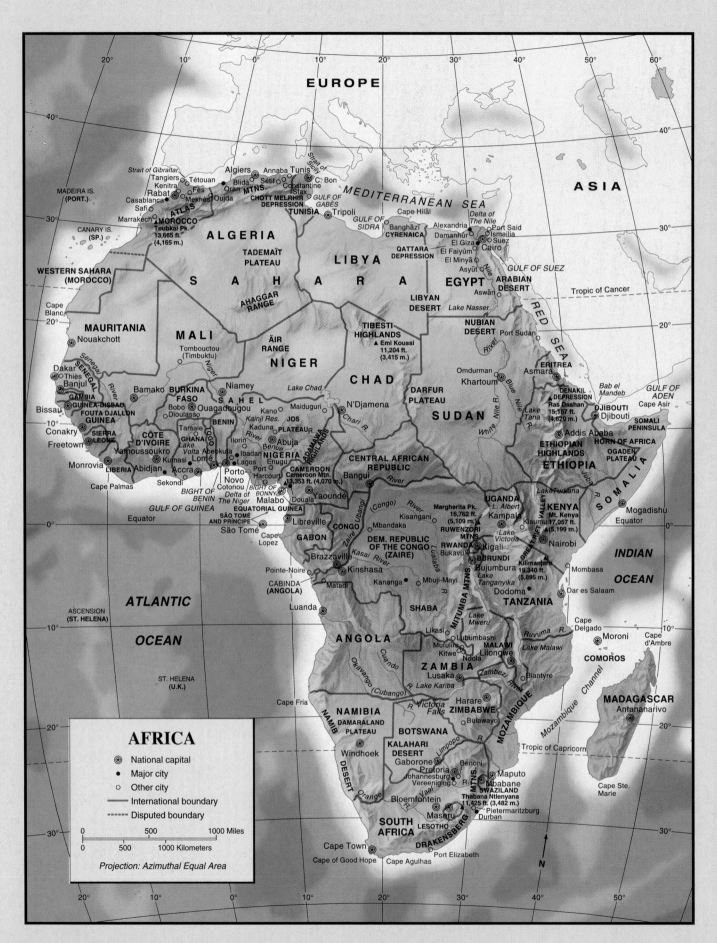

EUROPE

ASIA

MEDITERRANEAN SEA

Strait of Gibraltar Tangiers · Algiers · Annaba · Tunis · C. Bon
MADEIRA IS. (PORT.)
Tétouan · Blida · Sétif · Constantine
Kenitra · Oran · MTNS. · Sfax
Fès · Meknes · Oujda
Casablanca **MOROCCO** · CHOTT MELRHIR DEPRESSION · Tripoli · **GULF OF GABÈS** · Cape Hilāl · **Delta of The Nile** · Port Said
Safi **TUNISIA**
ATLAS · Toubkal Pk. 13,665 ft. (4,165 m.) · **GULF OF SIDRA** · Banghāzī **CYRENAICA** · Alexandria · Damanhūr · Ismailia
Marrakech

CANARY IS. (SP.) · **ALGERIA** · **LIBYA** · **EGYPT** · El Giza · Suez · Cairo
WESTERN SAHARA (MOROCCO) · TADEMAÏT PLATEAU · El Faiyūm · El Minyā
S A H A R A · **QATTARA DEPRESSION** · **ARABIAN DESERT** · Tropic of Cancer
Cape Blanc · **LIBYAN DESERT** · Asyūt · **GULF OF SUEZ**
AHAGGAR RANGE · Aswān · **RED SEA**

MAURITANIA · **MALI** · **ÄIR RANGE** · **NUBIAN DESERT** · Lake Nasser · Port Sudan
Nouakchott · Tombouctou (Timbuktu) · **NIGER** · **TIBESTI HIGHLANDS** · Emi Koussi 11,204 ft. (3,415 m.) · Omdurman · Khartoum · Asmara **ERITREA** · **Bab el Mandeb** · **GULF OF ADEN** · Cape Asir
Niger · **SAHEL** · **CHAD** · **DARFUR PLATEAU** · **DENAKIL DEPRESSION** Ras Dashan 15,157 ft. (4,620 m.) · **DJIBOUTI** · Djibouti · **SOMALI PENINSULA**
Dakar **SENEGAL** · Bamako **BURKINA FASO** · Niamey · Lake Chad · Maiduguri · N'Djamena · **SUDAN** · Lake Tana · Addis Ababa · **HORN OF AFRICA**
Thiès · Banjul · Bobo Dioulasso · Ouagadougou · Kano · **JOS PLATEAU** · Chari R. · **CENTRAL AFRICAN** · **ETHIOPIAN HIGHLANDS** · **OGADEN PLATEAU**
GAMBIA · **BENIN** · Kaduna · **ADAMAWA HIGHLANDS** · **REPUBLIC** · White Nile · **ETHIOPIA**
Bissau **GUINEA-BISSAU** · **FOUTA DJALLON** · Tamale **GHANA** · Ilorin · Abuja · Benue R. · Bangui · River
GUINEA · Kainji Res. · Ibadan · **NIGERIA** · **CAMEROON** · Cameroon Mtn. 13,353 ft. (4,070 m.)
Conakry · Freetown **SIERRA LEONE** · **CÔTE D'IVOIRE** · Kumasi · Abeokuta · Enugu · Yaoundé · **UGANDA** · L. Albert · **KENYA** · Mogadishu
Monrovia **LIBERIA** · Yamoussoukro · Lake Volta · Lagos · Port Harcourt · Douala · Margherita Pk. 16,762 ft. (5,109 m.) · Kampala · Mt. Kenya 17,057 ft. (5,199 m.) · **SOMALIA**
Cape Palmas · Abidjan · Accra · Lomé · **Porto-Novo** · **BIGHT OF BONNY** · Kisangani · **RUWENZORI MTNS.** · Lake Victoria · Nairobi
Sekondi · **BIGHT OF BENIN** · Cotonou · **Delta of The Niger** · Malabo · Libreville · **CONGO** · Mbandaka · **DEM. REPUBLIC** · **RWANDA** · Kigali · Kilimanjaro 19,340 ft. (5,895 m.) · Mombasa · **INDIAN OCEAN**
GULF OF GUINEA · **EQUATORIAL GUINEA** · **GABON** · (Congo) · River · **OF THE CONGO (ZAIRE)** · Bukavu **BURUNDI** · Bujumbura · Lake Tanganyika · Dodoma
SÃO TOMÉ AND PRÍNCIPE · São Tomé · Cape Lopez · Zaire · Kasai River · Brazzaville · Kananga · Mbuji-Mayi · **TANZANIA** · Dar es Salaam
Equator · Equator · **MITUMBA MTNS.** · Lake Mweru · Cape Delgado · Moroni · Cape d'Ambre
Pointe-Noire · Kinshasa · **SHABA** · Likasi · Lubumbashi · **COMOROS**
ATLANTIC · **CABINDA (ANGOLA)** · Matadi · Mufulira · Kitwe **MALAWI** · Lilongwe
OCEAN · Luanda · Lumumbashi · Ndola · Lake Malawi · **MADAGASCAR**
ASCENSION (ST. HELENA) · **ANGOLA** · **ZAMBIA** · Lusaka · Blantyre · Antananarivo
ST. HELENA (U.K.) · Okavango (Cubango) · Lake Kariba · Zambezi R. · **MOZAMBIQUE**
Cape Fria · Cuando · Victoria Falls · Harare **ZIMBABWE** · **Mozambique Channel**
NAMIBIA · **DAMARALAND PLATEAU** · Bulawayo · Cape Ste. Marie
NAMIB · **BOTSWANA** · Limpopo R.
KALAHARI DESERT · Gaborone · Benoni · Maputo · Tropic of Capricorn
Windhoek · Pretoria · Johannesburg · Mbabane **SWAZILAND**
DESERT · Vereeniging · Thabana Ntlenyana 11,425 ft. (3,482 m.)
Orange R. · Bloemfontein · **DRAKENSBERG** · Pietermaritzburg · Durban
SOUTH AFRICA · Maseru **LESOTHO**
Cape Town · Port Elizabeth
Cape of Good Hope · Cape Agulhas

AFRICA

⊚ National capital
• Major city
○ Other city
— International boundary
······ Disputed boundary

0 · 500 · 1000 Miles
0 · 500 · 1000 Kilometers

Projection: Azimuthal Equal Area

N

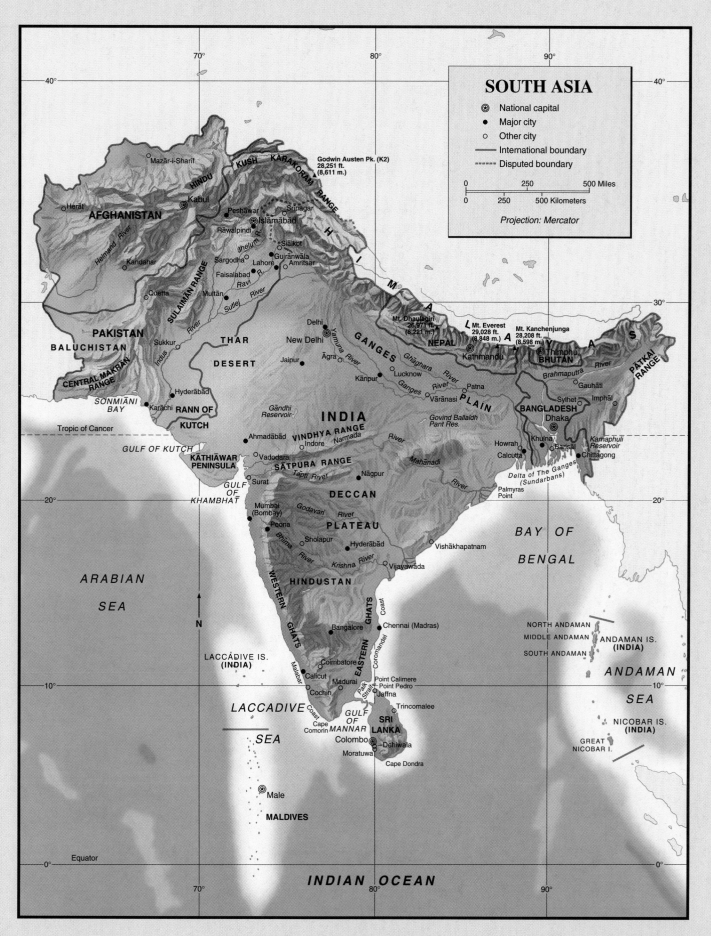

SOUTH ASIA

⊛ National capital
● Major city
○ Other city
— International boundary
----- Disputed boundary

| 0 | 250 | 500 Miles |

| 0 | 250 | 500 Kilometers |

Projection: Mercator

Godwin Austen Pk. (K2)
28,251 ft.
(8,611 m.)

HINDU KUSH

KARAKORAM RANGE

Mazār-i-Sharīf

Herāt

Kabul ⊛

AFGHANISTAN

Peshāwar

Islāmābād ⊛

Srinagar

Rāwalpindi

Jhelum

Siālkot

Sargodha

Gujrānwāla

Lahore

Amritsar

Faisalabad

Ravi R.

Multān

Quetta

Sutlej River

PAKISTAN

BALUCHISTAN

Sukkur

Indus

River

THAR

DESERT

Delhi

New Delhi

Jaipur

Yamuna River

Āgra

GANGES

Mt. Dhaulagiri
26,971 ft.
(8,221 m.)

NEPAL

Mt. Everest
29,028 ft.
(8,848 m.)

Mt. Kanchenjunga
28,208 ft.
(8,598 m.)

Kathmandu ⊛

Ghāghara

HIMALAYAS

Thimphu ⊛

BHUTAN

PĀTKAI RANGE

River

Brahmaputra

Gauhāti

Sylhet

Imphāl

CENTRAL MAKRĀN RANGE

SULAIMĀN RANGE

Kānpur

Lucknow

Ganges

River

Patna

Vārānasi

PLAIN

BANGLADESH

Dhaka ⊛

SONMIĀNI BAY

Karāchi

RANN OF KUTCH

Hyderābād

Tropic of Cancer

GULF OF KUTCH

KĀTHIĀWAR PENINSULA

Ahmadābād

Gāndhi Reservoir

INDIA

VINDHYA RANGE

Indore

Narmada

River

Govind Ballaldh Pant Res.

Howrah

Khulna

Calcutta

Barisāl

Karnaphuli Reservoir

Chittagong

Vadodara

SĀTPURA RANGE

Tapti River

Nāgpur

Mahānadi

Delta of The Ganges
(Sundarbans)

GULF OF KHAMBHAT

Surat

DECCAN

River

Palmyras Point

Mumbai
(Bombay)

Poona

Godavari

River

Bhima

Sholapur

PLATEAU

Hyderābād

Krishna River

Vijayawāda

Vishākhapatnam

BAY OF BENGAL

ARABIAN

SEA

N

HINDUSTAN

WESTERN GHATS

Bangalore

EASTERN GHATS

Coromandel Coast

Chennai (Madras)

NORTH ANDAMAN

MIDDLE ANDAMAN

SOUTH ANDAMAN

ANDAMAN IS.
(INDIA)

LACCĀDIVE IS.
(INDIA)

Coimbatore

Calicut

Malabar

Madurai

Cochin

Point Calimere

Point Pedro

Jaffna

Palk Strait

Trincomalee

ANDAMAN

SEA

LACCADIVE

SEA

Coast

Cape Comorin

GULF OF MANNAR

SRI LANKA

Colombo ⊛

Dehiwala

Moratuwa

Cape Dondra

NICOBAR IS.
(INDIA)

GREAT NICOBAR I.

Male ⊛

MALDIVES

Equator

INDIAN OCEAN

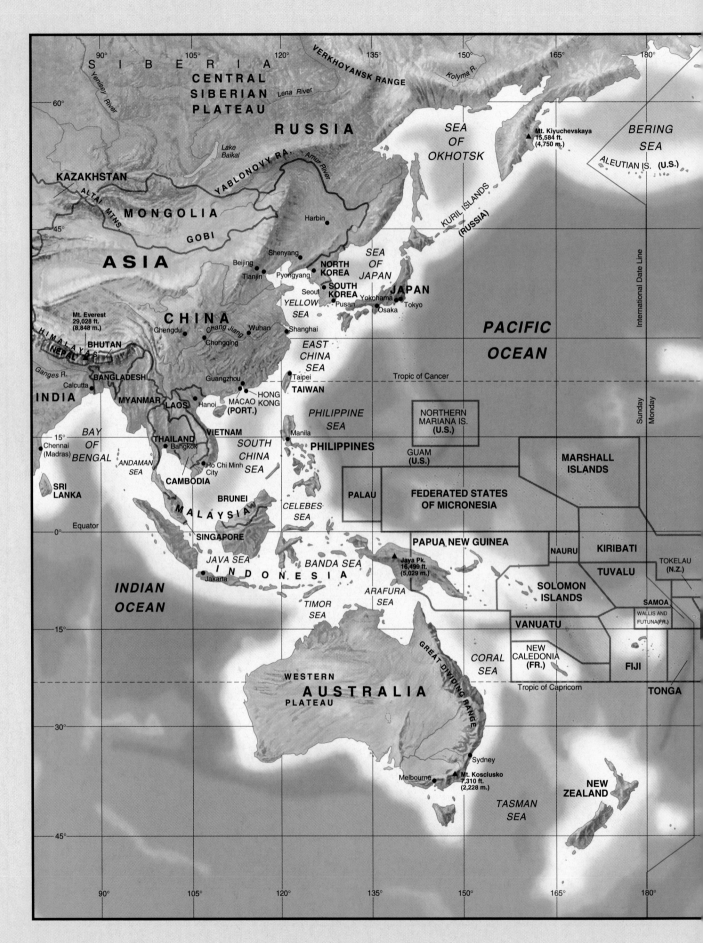

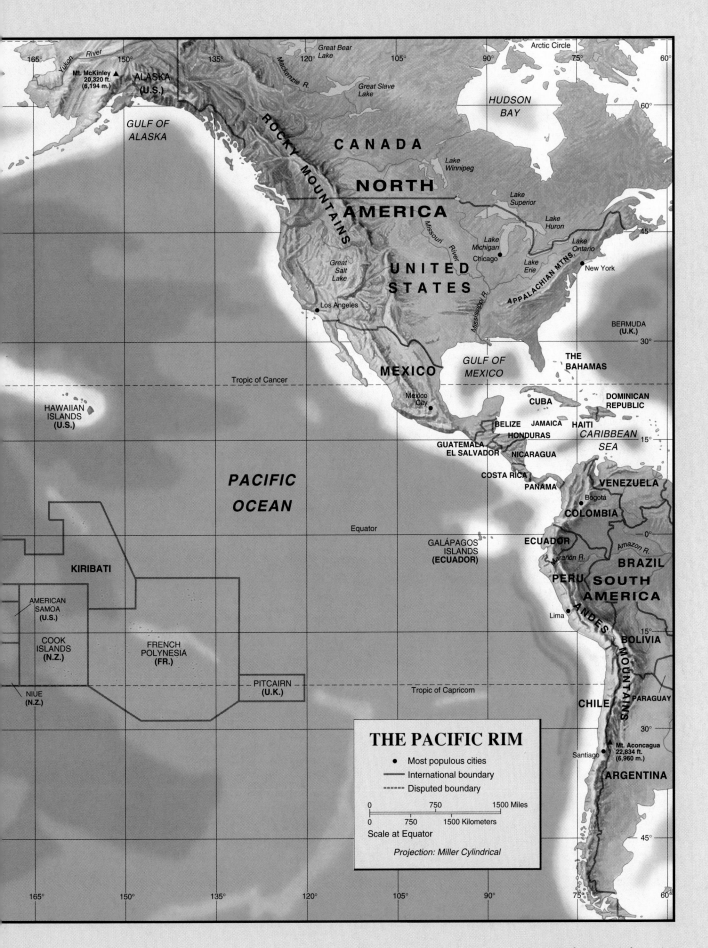

THE PACIFIC RIM

- • Most populous cities
- —— International boundary
- ---- Disputed boundary

| 0 | 750 | 1500 Miles |
| 0 | 750 | 1500 Kilometers |

Scale at Equator

Projection: Miller Cylindrical

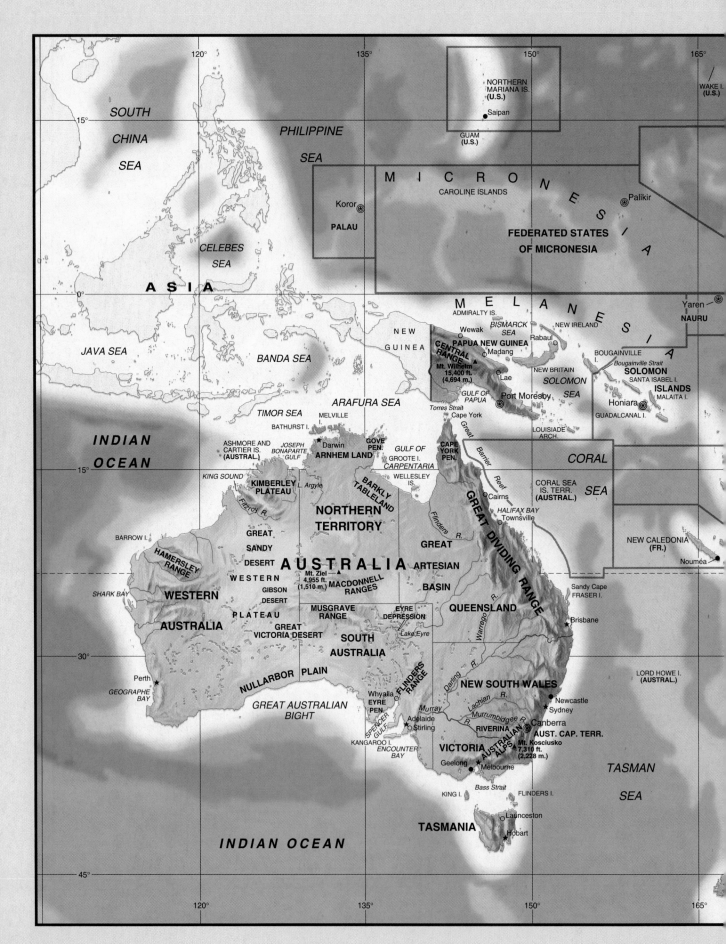

SOUTH

CHINA

SEA

PHILIPPINE

SEA

15°

120°   135°

NORTHERN
MARIANA IS.
(U.S.)

Saipan

GUAM
(U.S.)

150°   165°

WAKE I.
(U.S.)

M I C R O N E S I A

CAROLINE ISLANDS

Koror

PALAU

Palikir

FEDERATED STATES
OF MICRONESIA

JAVA SEA

CELEBES

SEA

A S I A

BANDA SEA

0°

M E L A N E S I A

Yaren

NAURU

ADMIRALTY IS.

NEW IRELAND

Wewak

BISMARCK
SEA

NEW CALEDONIA
(FR.)

INDIAN

OCEAN

TIMOR SEA

ARAFURA SEA

NEW

GUINEA

PAPUA NEW GUINEA
CENTRAL
RANGE
Mt. Wilhelm
15,400 ft.
(4,694 m.)

Madang

Lae

Rabaul

BOUGAINVILLE

Bougainville Strait

SOLOMON
ISLANDS

SANTA ISABEL I.

MALAITA I.

NEW BRITAIN

SOLOMON

SEA

Honiara

GUADALCANAL I.

LOUISIADE
ARCH.

GULF OF
PAPUA

Port Moresby

Torres Strait

Cape York

MELVILLE
I.

BATHURST I.

ASHMORE AND
CARTIER IS.
(AUSTRAL.)

JOSEPH
BONAPARTE
GULF

Darwin

ARNHEM LAND

GOVE
PEN.

GROOTE I.

GULF OF

CARPENTARIA

WELLESLEY
IS.

CAPE
YORK
PEN.

CAPE YORK

Great

Barrier

Reef

CORAL

SEA

CORAL SEA
IS. TERR.
(AUSTRAL.)

15°

KING SOUND

L. Argyle

KIMBERLEY
PLATEAU

BARKLY
TABLELAND

NORTHERN

TERRITORY

Flinders

R.

HALIFAX BAY

Townsville

Cairns

BARROW I.

Fitzroy R.

HAMERSLEY
RANGE

GREAT

SANDY

DESERT

AUSTRALIA

GREAT

ARTESIAN

BASIN

GREAT DIVIDING RANGE

Sandy Cape
FRASER I.

NEW CALEDONIA
(FR.)

Nouméa

SHARK BAY

WESTERN

GIBSON

DESERT

Mt. Ziel
4,955 ft.
(1,510 m.)

MACDONNELL
RANGES

WESTERN

AUSTRALIA

PLATEAU

GREAT
VICTORIA DESERT

MUSGRAVE
RANGE

SOUTH

AUSTRALIA

EYRE
DEPRESSION

Lake Eyre

QUEENSLAND

Warrego

R.

Brisbane

30°

Perth

GEOGRAPHE
BAY

NULLARBOR   PLAIN

GREAT AUSTRALIAN

BIGHT

Whyalla
EYRE
PEN.

FLINDERS
RANGE

SPENCER
GULF

Adelaide

Stirling

KANGAROO I.

ENCOUNTER
BAY

Darling

R.

Murray

Lachlan

R.

Murrumbidgee R.

RIVERINA

VICTORIA

Geelong

Melbourne

AUSTRALIAN ALPS

NEW SOUTH WALES

Newcastle

Sydney

Canberra

AUST. CAP. TERR.

Mt. Kosciusko
7,310 ft.
(2,228 m.)

LORD HOWE I.
(AUSTRAL.)

TASMAN

SEA

KING I.

Bass Strait

FLINDERS I.

INDIAN OCEAN

TASMANIA

Launceston

Hobart

45°

120°   135°   150°   165°

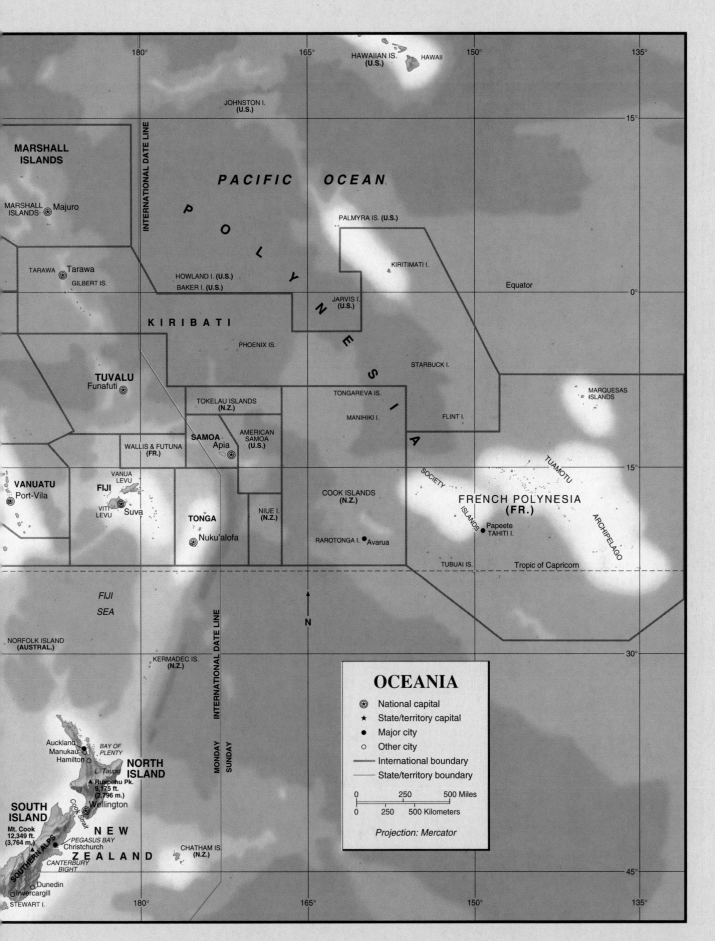

MARSHALL
ISLANDS

180°

165°

150°

135°

HAWAIIAN IS.
(U.S.)

HAWAII

15°

JOHNSTON I.
(U.S.)

P A C I F I C   O C E A N

MARSHALL
ISLANDS ⊛ Majuro

PALMYRA IS. (U.S.)

INTERNATIONAL DATE LINE

P
O
L
Y
N
E
S
I
A

TARAWA ⊛ Tarawa
GILBERT IS.

HOWLAND I. (U.S.)
BAKER I. (U.S.)

KIRITIMATI I.

Equator

0°

KIRIBATI

JARVIS I.
(U.S.)

PHOENIX IS.

STARBUCK I.

TUVALU
Funafuti ⊛

TOKELAU ISLANDS
(N.Z.)

TONGAREVA IS.

MARQUESAS
ISLANDS

MANIHIKI I.

FLINT I.

WALLIS & FUTUNA
(FR.)

SAMOA
Apia ⊛

AMERICAN
SAMOA
(U.S.)

15°

VANUATU
Port-Vila ⊛

VANUA
LEVU

FIJI

SOCIETY

TUAMOTU

COOK ISLANDS
(N.Z.)

FRENCH POLYNESIA
(FR.)

ISLANDS

ARCHIPELAGO

VITI
LEVU ⊛ Suva

TONGA

NIUE I.
(N.Z.)

Papeete
TAHITI I.

Nuku'alofa ⊛

RAROTONGA I. ● Avarua

TUBUAI IS.

Tropic of Capricorn

FIJI
SEA

N

INTERNATIONAL DATE LINE

NORFOLK ISLAND
(AUSTRAL.)

30°

KERMADEC IS.
(N.Z.)

OCEANIA

⊛ National capital
★ State/territory capital
● Major city
○ Other city
— International boundary
— State/territory boundary

MONDAY

SUNDAY

Auckland
Manukau ○
Hamilton ○

BAY OF
PLENTY

NORTH
ISLAND

L. Taupo
▲ Ruapehu Pk.
9,175 ft.
(2,796 m.)
○ Wellington

0   250   500 Miles

0   250   500 Kilometers

Projection: Mercator

SOUTH
ISLAND

N E W

Mt. Cook
12,349 ft.
(3,764 m.) ▲

PEGASUS BAY
Christchurch

Z E A L A N D

SOUTHERN ALPS

CANTERBURY
BIGHT

CHATHAM IS.
(N.Z.)

45°

○ Dunedin
○ Invercargill
STEWART I.

180°

165°

150°

135°

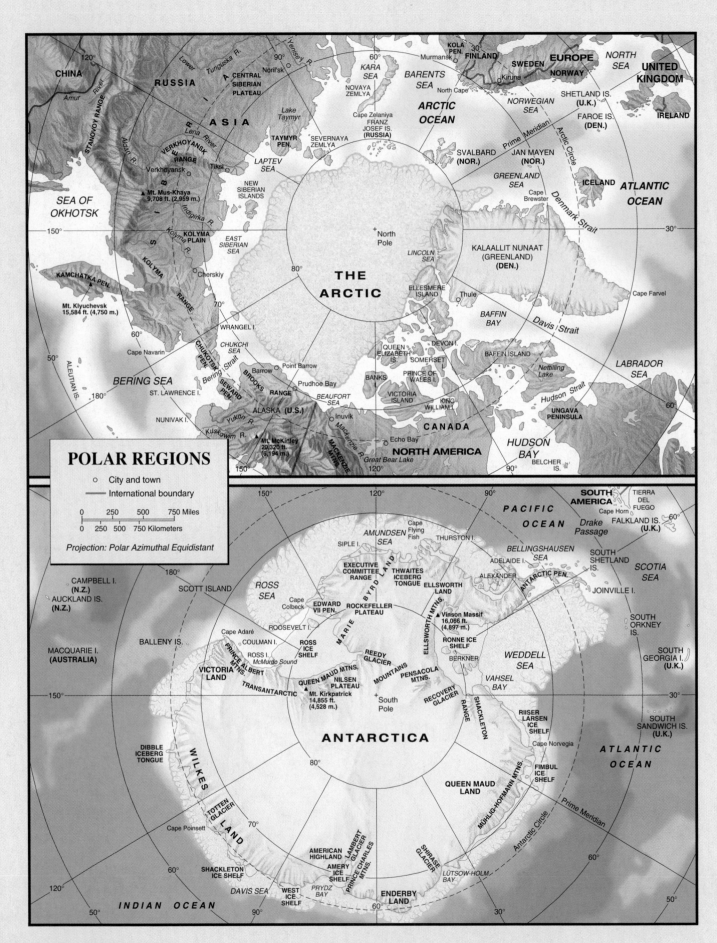

POLAR REGIONS

○ City and town
═══ International boundary

0   250   500   750 Miles
0 250 500 750 Kilometers

Projection: Polar Azimuthal Equidistant

THE ARCTIC

+ North Pole

CHINA · RUSSIA · ASIA · CENTRAL SIBERIAN PLATEAU · Lower Tunguska R. · Yenisey R. · Noril'sk · Amur River · Aldan R. · STANOVOY RANGE · VERKHOYANSK RANGE · Verkhoyansk · Lena River · Tiksi · TAYMYR PEN. · Lake Taymyr · SEVERNAYA ZEMLYA · LAPTEV SEA · Mt. Mus-Khaya 9,708 ft. (2,959 m.) · Indigirka R. · NEW SIBERIAN ISLANDS · SEA OF OKHOTSK · KOLYMA R. · KOLYMA PLAIN · EAST SIBERIAN SEA · KOLYMA RANGE · Cherskiy · KAMCHATKA PEN. · Mt. Klyuchevsk 15,584 ft. (4,750 m.) · Cape Navarin · CHUKOTSK PEN. · CHUKCHI SEA · WRANGEL I. · Bering Strait · BERING SEA · ALEUTIAN IS. · ST. LAWRENCE I. · SEWARD PEN. · BROOKS RANGE · Barrow · Point Barrow · Prudhoe Bay · BEAUFORT SEA · NUNIVAK I. · ALASKA (U.S.) · Yukon R. · Kuskokwim R. · Mt. McKinley 20,320 ft. (6,194 m.) · MACKENZIE MTNS. · Mackenzie R. · Inuvik · Echo Bay · Great Bear Lake · NORTH AMERICA · CANADA

KOLA PEN. · Murmansk · FINLAND · SWEDEN · NORWAY · Kiruna · EUROPE · North Cape · NORTH SEA · UNITED KINGDOM · IRELAND · BARENTS SEA · KARA SEA · NOVAYA ZEMLYA · Cape Zelaniya · FRANZ JOSEF IS. (RUSSIA) · ARCTIC OCEAN · NORWEGIAN SEA · SHETLAND IS. (U.K.) · FAROE IS. (DEN.) · Prime Meridian · Arctic Circle · SVALBARD (NOR.) · JAN MAYEN (NOR.) · GREENLAND SEA · Cape Brewster · ICELAND · ATLANTIC OCEAN · Denmark Strait · LINCOLN SEA · KALAALLIT NUNAAT (GREENLAND) (DEN.) · ELLESMERE ISLAND · Thule · Cape Farvel · BAFFIN BAY · Davis Strait · DEVON I. · QUEEN ELIZABETH IS. · SOMERSET · BAFFIN ISLAND · Cape Farvel · PRINCE OF WALES I. · BANKS · VICTORIA ISLAND · KING WILLIAM I. · Nettilling Lake · Hudson Strait · LABRADOR SEA · UNGAVA PENINSULA · HUDSON BAY · BELCHER IS. · 30° · 60° · 80° · 70° · 90° · 120° · 150° · 180° · 60° · 30° · 90°

ANTARCTICA

+ South Pole

CAMPBELL I. (N.Z.) · AUCKLAND IS. (N.Z.) · MACQUARIE I. (AUSTRALIA) · BALLENY IS. · SCOTT ISLAND · ROSS SEA · Cape Colbeck · EDWARD VII PEN. · ROCKEFELLER PLATEAU · ROOSEVELT I. · Cape Adaré · COULMAN I. · ROSS ICE SHELF · ROSS I. · McMurdo Sound · PRINCE ALBERT MTNS. · VICTORIA LAND · TRANSANTARCTIC · Mt. Kirkpatrick 14,855 ft. (4,528 m.) · QUEEN MAUD MTNS. · NILSEN PLATEAU · REEDY GLACIER · MARIE BYRD LAND · EXECUTIVE COMMITTEE RANGE · SIPLE I. · AMUNDSEN SEA · Cape Flying Fish · THWAITES ICEBERG TONGUE · THURSTON I. · ELLSWORTH LAND · ELLSWORTH MTNS. · Vinson Massif 16,066 ft. (4,897 m.) · RONNE ICE SHELF · BERKNER · PENSACOLA MTNS. · MOUNTAINS · RECOVERY GLACIER · SHACKLETON RANGE · DIBBLE ICEBERG TONGUE · WILKES LAND · TOTTEN GLACIER · Cape Poinsett · SHACKLETON ICE SHELF · WEST ICE SHELF · DAVIS SEA · PRYDZ BAY · LAMBERT GLACIER · AMERY ICE SHELF · PRINCE CHARLES MTNS. · AMERICAN HIGHLAND · SHIRASE GLACIER · ENDERBY LAND · QUEEN MAUD LAND · MÜHLIG-HOFMANN MTNS. · FIMBUL ICE SHELF · RIISER LARSEN ICE SHELF · Cape Norvegia · VAHSEL BAY · WEDDELL SEA · LÜTSOW-HOLM BAY · Antarctic Circle · Prime Meridian · ATLANTIC OCEAN · SOUTH SANDWICH IS. (U.K.) · SOUTH GEORGIA I. (U.K.) · SOUTH ORKNEY IS. · SCOTIA SEA · JOINVILLE I. · SOUTH SHETLAND IS. · ANTARCTIC PEN. · ADELAIDE I. · ALEXANDER I. · BELLINGSHAUSEN SEA · PACIFIC OCEAN · SOUTH AMERICA · Cape Horn · TIERRA DEL FUEGO · FALKLAND IS. (U.K.) · Drake Passage · INDIAN OCEAN

Historical Atlas AND World Data Bank

Early Civilizations 3500 B.C —1700s B.C.

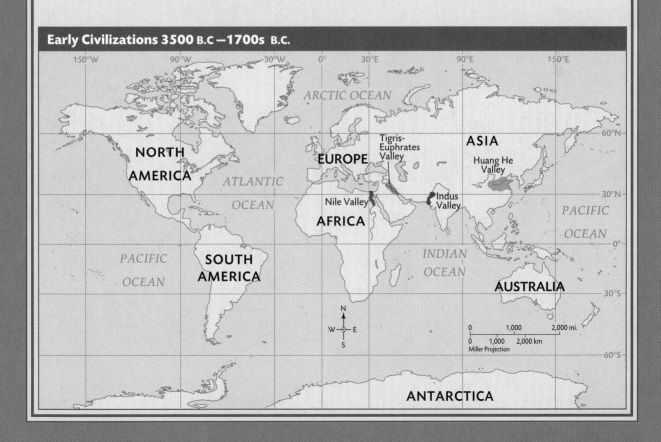

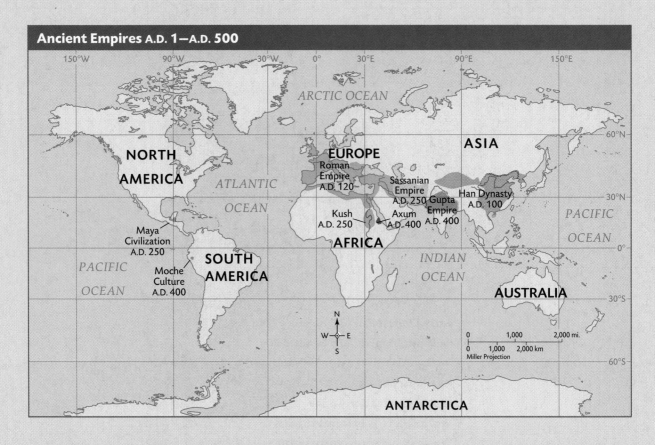

Ancient Empires A.D. 1—A.D. 500

150°W 90°W 30°W 0° 30°E 90°E 150°E

ARCTIC OCEAN

60°N

NORTH AMERICA

ATLANTIC OCEAN

EUROPE

ASIA

Roman Empire A.D. 120

30°N

Sassanian Empire A.D. 250

Han Dynasty A.D. 100

PACIFIC OCEAN

Kush A.D. 250

Gupta Empire A.D. 400

Maya Civilization A.D. 250

Axum A.D. 400

0°

PACIFIC OCEAN

AFRICA

SOUTH AMERICA

INDIAN OCEAN

Moche Culture A.D. 400

30°S

AUSTRALIA

N
W   E
S

0   1,000   2,000 mi.
0   1,000   2,000 km
Miller Projection

60°S

ANTARCTICA

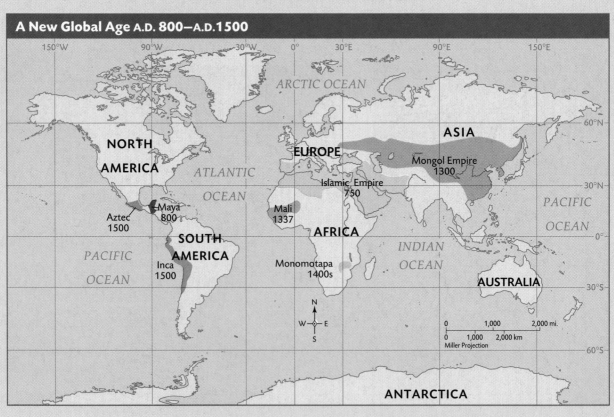

A New Global Age A.D. 800—A.D.1500

150°W 90°W 30°W 0° 30°E 90°E 150°E

ARCTIC OCEAN

60°N

NORTH AMERICA

ATLANTIC OCEAN

EUROPE

ASIA

Mongol Empire 1300

30°N

Islamic Empire 750

PACIFIC OCEAN

Maya 800

Mali 1337

Aztec 1500

SOUTH AMERICA

AFRICA

INDIAN OCEAN

0°

PACIFIC OCEAN

Inca 1500

Monomotapa 1400s

AUSTRALIA

30°S

N
W   E
S

0   1,000   2,000 mi.
0   1,000   2,000 km
Miller Projection

60°S

ANTARCTICA

Age of Imperialism 1870–1914

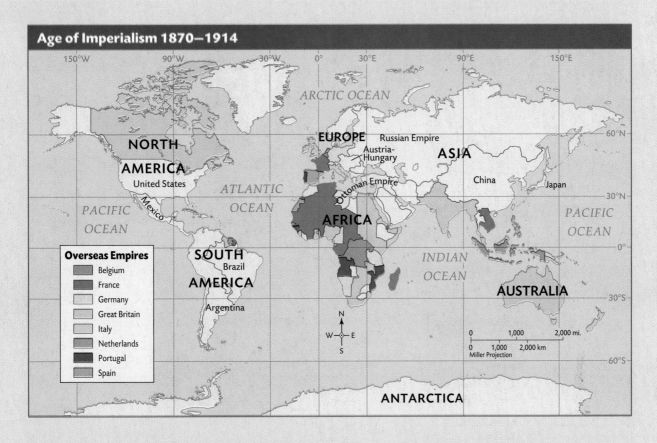

ARCTIC OCEAN

NORTH AMERICA
United States
Mexico

EUROPE
Russian Empire
Austria-Hungary
Ottoman Empire

ASIA
China
Japan

AFRICA

PACIFIC OCEAN

ATLANTIC OCEAN

PACIFIC OCEAN

SOUTH AMERICA
Brazil
Argentina

INDIAN OCEAN

AUSTRALIA

ANTARCTICA

Overseas Empires
- Belgium
- France
- Germany
- Great Britain
- Italy
- Netherlands
- Portugal
- Spain

N
W—E
S

| 0 | 1,000 | 2,000 mi. |
| 0 | 1,000 | 2,000 km |
Miller Projection

Global Civilization Today

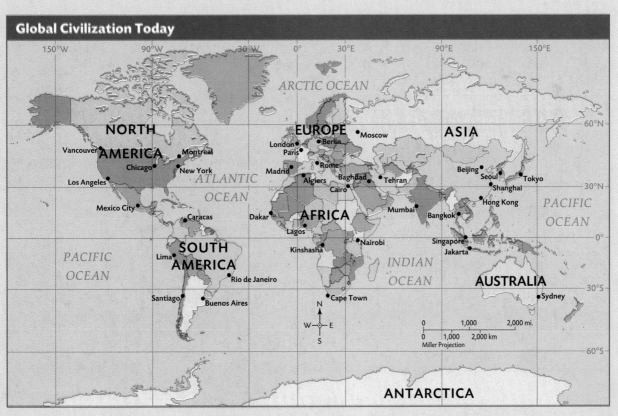

ARCTIC OCEAN

NORTH AMERICA
Vancouver
Montreal
Chicago
New York
Los Angeles
Mexico City

EUROPE
London
Paris
Berlin
Moscow
Madrid
Rome
Algiers
Baghdad
Tehran
Cairo

ASIA
Beijing
Seoul
Tokyo
Shanghai
Hong Kong
Bangkok
Mumbai

AFRICA
Dakar
Lagos
Kinshasha
Nairobi
Cape Town

SOUTH AMERICA
Caracas
Lima
Rio de Janeiro
Santiago
Buenos Aires

Singapore
Jakarta

ATLANTIC OCEAN

PACIFIC OCEAN

PACIFIC OCEAN

INDIAN OCEAN

AUSTRALIA
Sydney

ANTARCTICA

N
W—E
S

| 0 | 1,000 | 2,000 mi. |
| 0 | 1,000 | 2,000 km |
Miller Projection

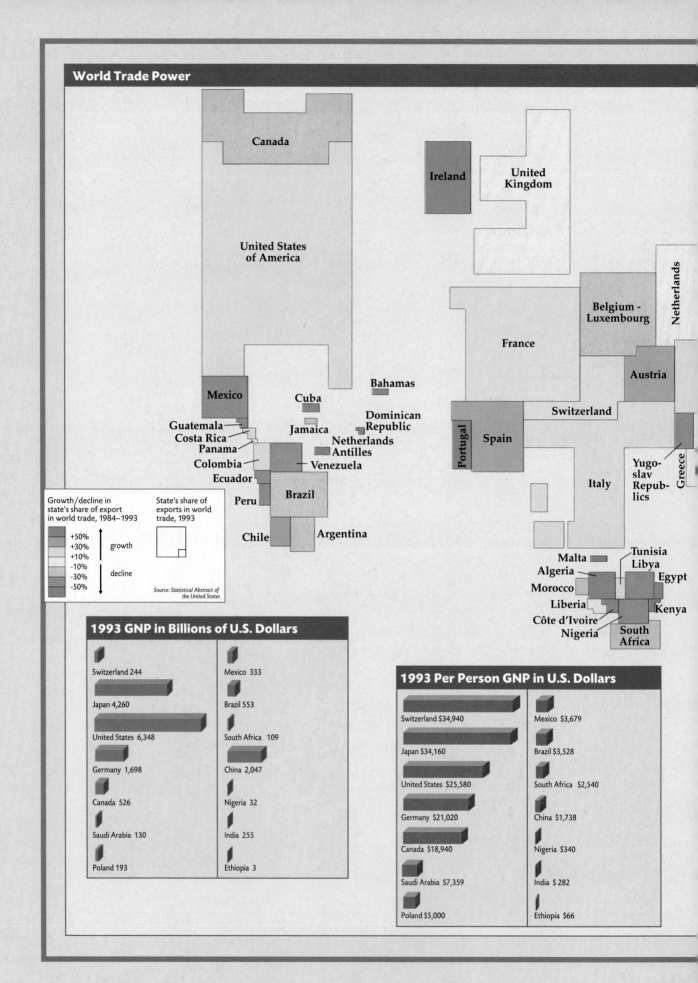

Canada

United States
of America

Ireland

United
Kingdom

Netherlands

Belgium -
Luxembourg

France

Austria

Mexico

Bahamas

Cuba

Dominican
Republic

Jamaica

Switzerland

Netherlands
Antilles

Portugal

Spain

Guatemala
Costa Rica
Panama
Colombia
Ecuador

Venezuela

Yugo-
slav
Repub-
lics

Greece

Peru

Brazil

Italy

Chile

Argentina

Malta

Tunisia
Libya

Algeria

Egypt

Morocco

Liberia

Kenya

Côte d'Ivoire

Nigeria

South
Africa

Growth/decline in
state's share of export
in world trade, 1984–1993

State's share of
exports in world
trade, 1993

+50%
+30%
+10%   growth
-10%
-30%   decline
-50%

Source: Statistical Abstract of
the United States

1993 GNP in Billions of U.S. Dollars

Switzerland 244

Mexico 333

Japan 4,260

Brazil 553

United States 6,348

South Africa 109

Germany 1,698

China 2,047

Canada 526

Nigeria 32

Saudi Arabia 130

India 255

Poland 193

Ethiopia 3

1993 Per Person GNP in U.S. Dollars

Switzerland $34,940

Mexico $3,679

Japan $34,160

Brazil $3,528

United States $25,580

South Africa $2,540

Germany $21,020

China $1,738

Canada $18,940

Nigeria $340

Saudi Arabia $7,359

India $ 282

Poland $5,000

Ethiopia $66

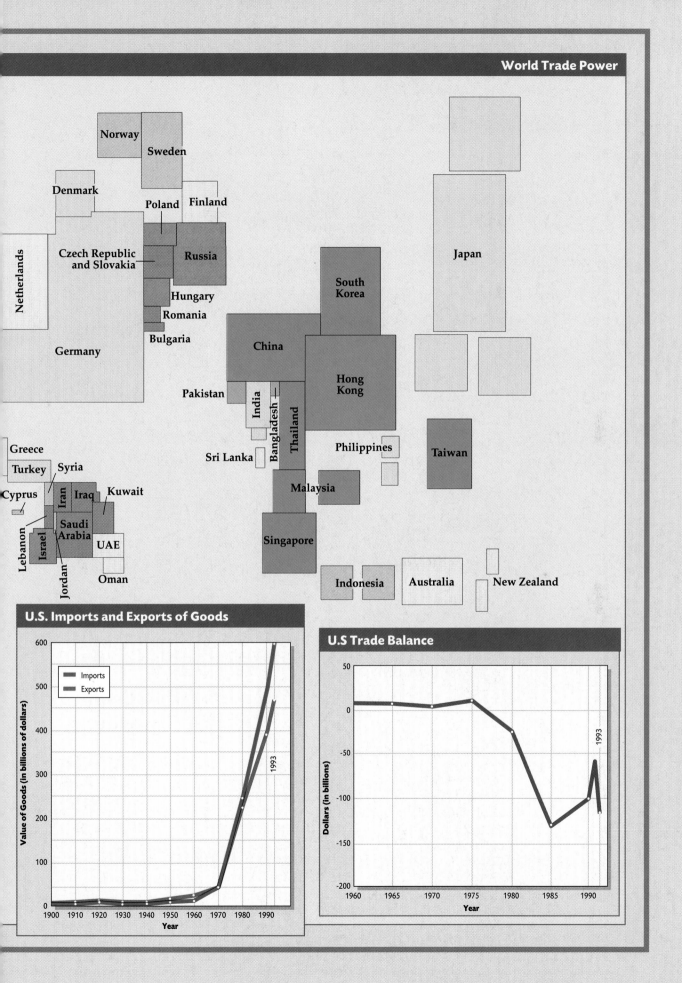

Norway

Sweden

Denmark

Poland   Finland

Netherlands

Czech Republic
and Slovakia   Russia

Hungary

Romania

Germany   Bulgaria

China

South
Korea

Japan

Pakistan

India

Bangladesh

Thailand

Hong
Kong

Sri Lanka

Philippines

Taiwan

Greece

Turkey   Syria

Cyprus

Iran   Iraq   Kuwait

Lebanon

Israel

Saudi
Arabia

Jordan   UAE

Oman

Malaysia

Singapore

Indonesia   Australia   New Zealand

U.S. Imports and Exports of Goods

Imports
Exports

Value of Goods (in billions of dollars)

600

500

400

300

200

100

1993

1900 1910 1920 1930 1940 1950 1960 1970 1980 1990

Year

U.S Trade Balance

Dollars (in billions)

50

0

-50

-100

-150

-200

1993

1960 1965 1970 1975 1980 1985 1990

Year

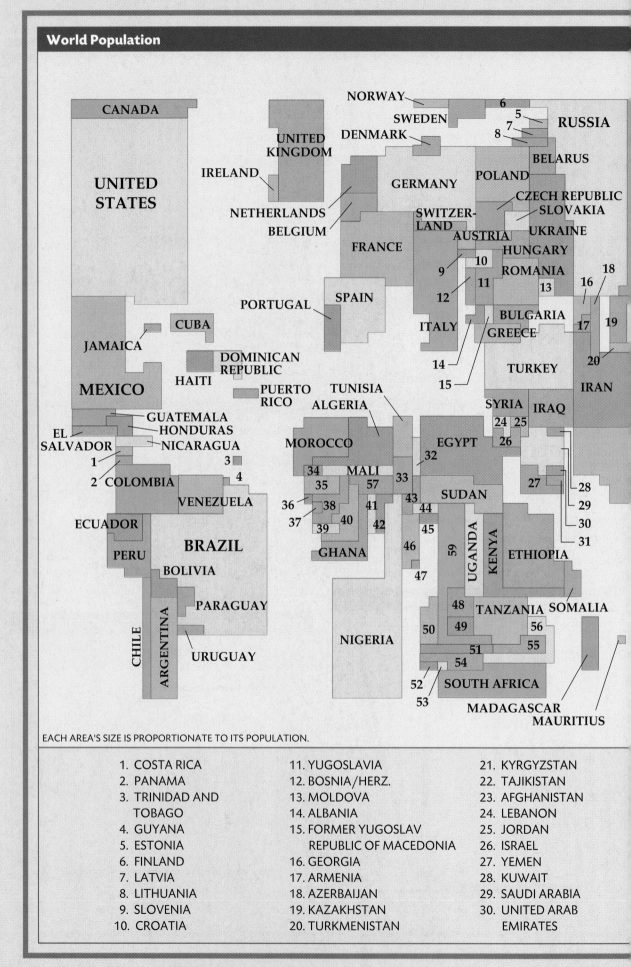

EACH AREA'S SIZE IS PROPORTIONATE TO ITS POPULATION.

1. COSTA RICA	11. YUGOSLAVIA	21. KYRGYZSTAN
2. PANAMA	12. BOSNIA/HERZ.	22. TAJIKISTAN
3. TRINIDAD AND TOBAGO	13. MOLDOVA	23. AFGHANISTAN
	14. ALBANIA	24. LEBANON
4. GUYANA	15. FORMER YUGOSLAV REPUBLIC OF MACEDONIA	25. JORDAN
5. ESTONIA		26. ISRAEL
6. FINLAND	16. GEORGIA	27. YEMEN
7. LATVIA	17. ARMENIA	28. KUWAIT
8. LITHUANIA	18. AZERBAIJAN	29. SAUDI ARABIA
9. SLOVENIA	19. KAZAKHSTAN	30. UNITED ARAB EMIRATES
10. CROATIA	20. TURKMENISTAN	

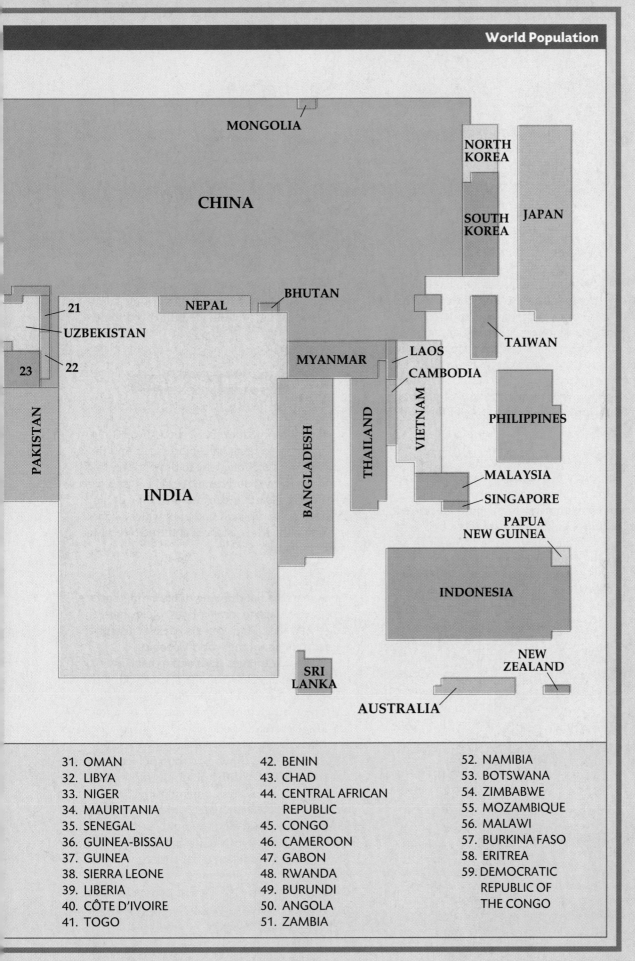

MONGOLIA

CHINA

NORTH
KOREA

SOUTH
KOREA

JAPAN

21

UZBEKISTAN

23

22

NEPAL

BHUTAN

TAIWAN

PAKISTAN

MYANMAR

LAOS

CAMBODIA

PHILIPPINES

INDIA

BANGLADESH

THAILAND

VIETNAM

MALAYSIA

SINGAPORE

PAPUA
NEW GUINEA

INDONESIA

SRI
LANKA

NEW
ZEALAND

AUSTRALIA

31. OMAN	42. BENIN	52. NAMIBIA
32. LIBYA	43. CHAD	53. BOTSWANA
33. NIGER	44. CENTRAL AFRICAN	54. ZIMBABWE
34. MAURITANIA	REPUBLIC	55. MOZAMBIQUE
35. SENEGAL	45. CONGO	56. MALAWI
36. GUINEA-BISSAU	46. CAMEROON	57. BURKINA FASO
37. GUINEA	47. GABON	58. ERITREA
38. SIERRA LEONE	48. RWANDA	59. DEMOCRATIC
39. LIBERIA	49. BURUNDI	REPUBLIC OF
40. CÔTE D'IVOIRE	50. ANGOLA	THE CONGO
41. TOGO	51. ZAMBIA	

What Is Geography?

The story of humanity begins with **geography**—the study of the earth in all of its variety. Geography concerns the earth's land, water, and plant and animal life. It also tells you about the people who live on the earth, the places they have created, and how these places differ. The earth is a planet of diverse groups of people. A study of geography can help you see why the people of the earth are so diverse.

The Five Themes of Geography

The study of geography can be organized around five themes: **location**, **place**, **human/environment interaction**, **movement**, and **region**. Geographers use these five themes to study and classify all parts of the earth and its variety of human activity.

Geography and World History

World geography is especially important to the study of world history. Historians use geography to explain connections between the past and the present. They study how places

looked in the past, how places and patterns of human activity have changed over time, and how geographic forces have influenced these changes.

Globes

Photographs from space show the earth in its true form—a great ball spinning around the sun. The only accurate way to draw the earth is as a globe, or a round form. A globe gives a true picture of the earth's size and the shape of the earth's landmasses and bodies of water. Globes also show the true distances and true directions between places.

Maps

A map is a flat drawing of the earth's surface. People use maps to locate places, plot routes, and judge distances. Maps can also display useful information about the world's peoples.

What advantages does a map have over a globe? Unlike a globe, a map allows you to see all areas of the world at the same time. Maps also show much more detail and can be folded and more easily carried.

Maps, however, have their drawbacks. As you can imagine, drawing a round object on a flat surface is very difficult. Cartographers, or mapmakers, have drawn many **projections**, or kinds of maps. Each map projection is a different way of showing the round earth on a flat map. This is because it is impossible to draw a round planet on a flat surface without distorting or misrepresenting some parts of the earth. As a result, each kind of map projection has some distortion. Typical distortions involve distance, direction, shape, and/or area.

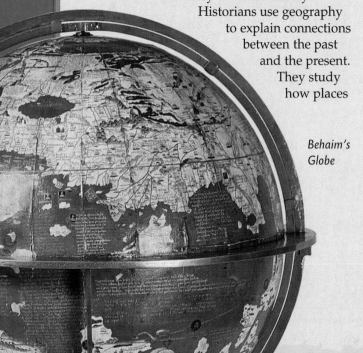

Behaim's Globe

The Hemispheres

To determine location, distance, and direction on a map or globe, geographers have developed a network of imaginary lines that crisscross the earth. One of these lines, the **Equator**, circles the earth midway between the **North Pole** and the **South Pole**. It divides the earth into "half spheres," or **hemispheres**. The Northern Hemisphere includes all of the land and water between the Equator and the North Pole. The Southern Hemisphere includes all of the land and water between the Equator and the South Pole.

Another imaginary line running from north to south divides the earth into half spheres in the other direction. This line is called the **Prime Meridian**. Every place east of the Prime Meridian is in the Eastern Hemisphere. Every place west of the Prime Meridian is in the Western Hemisphere.

Latitude and Longitude

The Equator and the Prime Meridian are the starting points for two sets of lines used to find any location. The two sets measure distances north or south of the Equator, and east and west of the Prime Meridian.

One set of lines called **parallels** circle the earth and show **latitude**, which is distance measured in degrees (°) north and south of the Equator at 0° latitude. The letter *N* or *S* following the degree symbol tells you if the location is north or south of the Equator. The North Pole is at 90° North (*N*) latitude, and the South Pole is at 90° South (*S*) latitude.

Two important parallels in between the poles are the **Tropic of Cancer** at 23 1/2°N latitude and the **Tropic of Capricorn** at 23 1/2°S latitude. You can also find the **Arctic Circle** at 66 1/2°N latitude and the **Antarctic Circle** at 66 1/2°S latitude.

The second set of lines called **meridians** run north to south from the North Pole to the South Pole. These lines signify **longitude**, which is distance measured in degrees east (*E*) or west (*W*) of the Prime Meridian at 0° longitude. On the opposite side of the earth is the International Date Line, at about the 180° meridian.

The Grid System

Lines of latitude and longitude cross one another in the form of a **grid system**. You can use the grid system to find where places are exactly located on a map or globe. Each place on Earth has an address on the grid. This grid address is the place's **coordinates**—its degrees of latitude and longitude. For example, the coordinates of the city of San Francisco are 38°N latitude and 122°W longitude. This means that San Francisco lies about 38 degrees (°) north of the Equator and 122 degrees (°) west of the Prime Meridian. Where those two lines cross is called the **absolute location** of the city.

Map Symbols

Maps can direct you down the street, across the country, or around the world. There are as many different kinds of maps as there are uses for them. Being

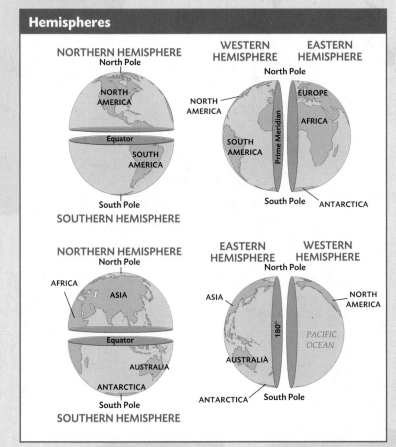

Hemispheres

NORTHERN HEMISPHERE
North Pole
NORTH AMERICA
Equator
SOUTH AMERICA
South Pole
SOUTHERN HEMISPHERE

WESTERN HEMISPHERE   EASTERN HEMISPHERE
North Pole
NORTH AMERICA
EUROPE
AFRICA
SOUTH AMERICA
Prime Meridian
South Pole
ANTARCTICA

NORTHERN HEMISPHERE
North Pole
AFRICA
ASIA
Equator
AUSTRALIA
ANTARCTICA
South Pole
SOUTHERN HEMISPHERE

EASTERN HEMISPHERE   WESTERN HEMISPHERE
North Pole
ASIA
NORTH AMERICA
180°
PACIFIC OCEAN
AUSTRALIA
ANTARCTICA
South Pole

able to read a map begins with learning about its parts.

The **map key** explains the symbols used on the map. On a map of the world, for example, dots mark cities and towns. On a road map, various kinds of lines stand for paved roads, dirt roads, and interstate highways. A pine tree symbol may represent a state park, while an airplane is often the symbol for an airport.

An important first step in reading any map is to find the direction marker. A map has a symbol that tells you where the **cardinal directions**—north, south, east, and west—are positioned. Sometimes all of these directions are shown with a **compass rose**.

A measuring line, often called a **scale bar**, helps you find distance on the map. The map's **scale** tells you what distance on the earth is represented by the measurement on the scale bar. For example, 1 inch on a map may represent 100 miles on the earth. Knowing the scale allows you to visualize how large an area is, as well as to measure distances. Map scales are usually given in both miles and kilometers, a metric measurement of distance.

purpose maps are physical maps and political maps. **Physical maps** show natural features, such as rivers and mountains. **Political maps** show places that people have created, such as cities or the boundaries of countries and states.

Special Purpose Maps

Special purpose maps show information on specific topics, such as climate, land use, or vegetation. Human activities, such as exploration routes, territorial expansion, or battle sites, also appear on special purpose maps. Colors and map key symbols are especially important on this type of map.

LANDSAT Maps

LANDSAT maps are made from photographs taken by camera-carrying LANDSAT satellites in space. The cameras record millions of energy waves invisible to the human eye. Computers then change this information into pictures of the earth's surface. With LANDSAT images, scientists can study whole mountain ranges, oceans, and geographic regions. Changes to the earth's environment can also be tracked using the satellite information.

TYPES OF MAPS

Maps of many different kinds are used in this text to help you see the connection between world geography and the history of humanity.

General Purpose Maps

Maps that show a wide range of general information about an area are called **general purpose maps**. Two of the most common general

LANDSAT map of
San Francisco Bay area

San Francisco

San Francisco
(38°N, 122°W)

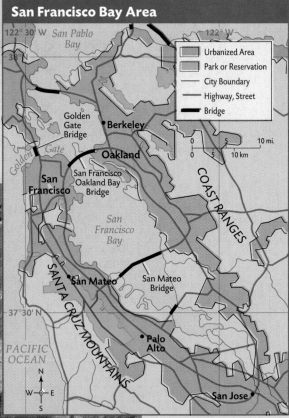

San Francisco Bay Area

122° 30′ W   San Pablo Bay
38°N

Urbanized Area
Park or Reservation
City Boundary
Highway, Street
Bridge

122° W

Golden
Gate
Bridge   Berkeley

Golden Gate   Oakland

San
Francisco   San Francisco
Oakland Bay
Bridge

0   5   10 mi.
0   5   10 km

San
Francisco
Bay

COAST RANGES

SANTA CRUZ MOUNTAINS

San Mateo   San Mateo
Bridge

37°30′ N

PACIFIC
OCEAN

Palo
Alto

N
W   E
S

San Jose

CONTINENTS

Geographers divide most of the earth's land surface into seven large landmasses called **continents**. The continents are North America, South America, Europe, Africa, Asia, Australia, and Antarctica. Asia is the largest continent in size, and Australia is the smallest.

LANDFORMS

Landforms cover about 30 percent of the surface of the earth. **Landforms**, or the natural features of the earth's surface, include **mountains**, **hills**, **plateaus**, and **plains**. Geographers describe each landform by its **elevation**, or height above sea level, and by its **relief**, or changes in height.

Mountains

Mountains are the highest of the world's landforms. They rise from about 2,000 feet (610 m) to more than 20,000 feet (6,100 m) above sea level. One of the peaks in the Himalaya mountain ranges of central Asia is Mount Everest, the world's highest mountain. It towers 29,028 feet (8,848 m) above sea level. Other mountains, such as the Appalachians in eastern North America, are not as high. Mountains generally have high relief.

Hills, Plateaus, and Plains

Hills are lower than mountains and generally rise from about 500 to 2,000 feet (152 to 610 m) above sea level. They generally have moderate relief.

Plateaus are raised areas of flat or almost flat land. Most plateaus have low relief and vary in elevation from about 300 to 3,000 feet (91 to 914 m) above sea level. The world's largest plateau area is the Tibetan Plateau in central Asia. It covers about 715,000 square miles (1,852,000 sq. km) and has an average altitude of 16,000 feet (4,877 m) above sea level.

Plains are large areas of flat or gently rolling land that generally rise less than 1,000 feet (305 m) above sea level and have low relief. The world's largest plain is the North European Plain, which stretches for more than 1,000 miles (1,609 km) from the western coast of France to the Ural Mountains in Russia.

BODIES OF WATER

About 70 percent of the earth's surface is covered with water. Geographers identify bodies of water by their shapes and sizes. The major types include oceans, seas, bays, gulfs, lakes, and rivers.

Oceans and Seas

The largest bodies of water in the world are the four saltwater **oceans**—the Pacific, the Atlantic, the Indian, and the Arctic. The Pacific Ocean is the largest ocean, covering about 64 million square miles (165,760,000 sq. km)—more than all the land areas of the earth combined.

Seas are smaller bodies of salt water that are usually in part surrounded by land. The world's largest sea is East Asia's South China Sea, with an area of 1,148,500 square miles (2,975,000 sq. km).

Bays and Gulfs

Still smaller bodies of salt water are gulfs and bays. **Bays** are extensions of a sea usually smaller than a **gulf.** The largest bay in the world measured by shoreline is Hudson Bay, Canada, with a shoreline of 7,623 miles (12,265 km) and an area of 476,000 square miles (1,233,000 sq. km). Measured by area, the Bay of Bengal, in the Indian Ocean and bordering South Asia and part of Southeast Asia, is larger at 839,000 square miles (2,173,000 sq. km).

Lakes and Rivers

Other water features of the earth include lakes and rivers. A **lake** is a body of water completely surrounded by land. The world's largest freshwater lake is Lake Superior, one of the five Great Lakes between the United States and Canada. It has an area of 31,820 square miles (82,414 sq. km). The world's largest inland body of water, however, is the Caspian Sea, often considered a saltwater lake. Lying between Europe and Asia and east of the Caucasus Mountains, the Caspian Sea has a total area of 143,550 square miles (371,795 sq. km).

A **river** is a waterway flowing through land and emptying into another body of water. The world's longest river is the Nile River in Africa, which flows into the Mediterranean Sea from the highlands of East Africa. The Nile's length is about 4,160 miles (6,690 km).

GEOGRAPHY HANDBOOK

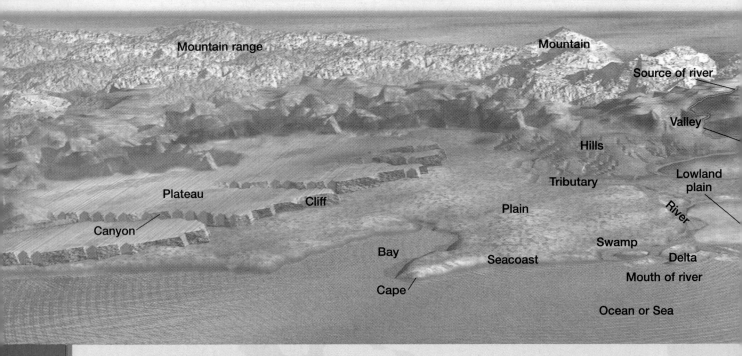

Mountain range
Mountain
Source of river
Valley
Hills
Lowland plain
Tributary
Plateau
Cliff
River
Plain
Canyon
Swamp
Bay
Delta
Seacoast
Mouth of river
Cape
Ocean or Sea

GEOGRAPHIC DICTIONARY

As you read about the world's geography and history, you will discover most of the terms listed and explained below. Many of the terms are pictured in the diagram above. Others you learned earlier in this Geography Handbook.

absolute location–exact location of a place on the earth described by global coordinates

basin–area of land drained by a given river and its branches; area of land surrounded by lands of higher elevations

bay–part of a large body of water that extends into a shoreline

canyon–deep and narrow valley with steep walls

cape–point of land surrounded by a body of water

channel–deep, narrow body of water that connects two larger bodies of water; deep part of a river or other waterway

cliff–steep, high wall of rock, earth, or ice

continent–one of the seven large landmasses on the earth

cultural feature–characteristic that humans have created in a place, such as language, religion, and history

delta–land built up from soil carried downstream by a river and deposited at its mouth

divide–stretch of high land that separates river basins

downstream–direction in which a river or stream flows from its source to its mouth

elevation–height of land above sea level

Equator–imaginary line that runs around the earth halfway between the North and South Poles; used as the starting point to measure degrees of north and south latitude

glacier–large, thick body of slowly moving ice, found in mountains and polar regions

globe–sphere-shaped model of the earth

gulf–part of a large body of water that extends into a shoreline, larger than a bay

harbor–a sheltered place along a shoreline where ships can anchor safely

highland–elevated land area with sloping sides such as a hill, mountain, or plateau, smaller than a mountain

island–land area, smaller than a continent, completely surrounded by water

isthmus–narrow stretch of land connecting two larger land areas

lake–a sizable inland body of water

latitude–distance north or south of the Equator, measured in degrees

longitude–distance east or west of the Prime Meridian, measured in degrees

lowland–land, usually level, at a low elevation

map–drawing of all or part of the earth shown on a flat surface

meridian–one of many lines on the global grid

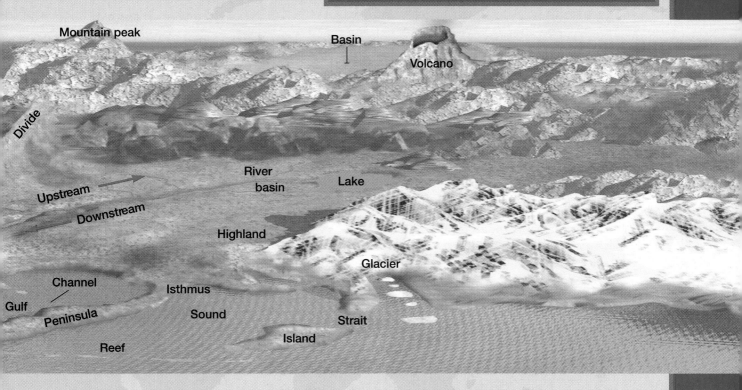

Mountain peak

Basin

Volcano

Divide

River basin

Lake

Upstream

Downstream

Highland

Glacier

Channel

Isthmus

Gulf

Peninsula

Sound

Strait

Island

Reef

running from the North Pole to the South Pole, used to measure degrees of longitude

mesa–area of raised land with steep sides; smaller than a plateau

mountain–land with steep sides that rises sharply from surrounding land; larger and more rugged than a hill

mountain peak–pointed top of a mountain

mountain range–a series of connected mountains

mouth–(of a river) place where a stream or river flows into a larger body of water

ocean–one of the four major bodies of salt water that surrounds a continent

ocean current–stream of either cold or warm water that moves in a definite direction through an ocean

parallel–one of many lines on the global grid that circle the earth north or south of the Equator; used to measure degrees of latitude

peninsula–body of land almost surrounded by water

physical feature–characteristic of a place occurring naturally, such as a landform, body of water, climate pattern, or resource

plain–area of level land, usually at a low elevation

plateau–area of flat or rolling land at a high elevation

Prime Meridian–line of the global grid running from the North Pole to the South Pole at Greenwich, England; used as the starting point for measuring degrees of east and west longitude

relative location–position of a place on the earth in relation to other places

relief–changes in elevation, either few or many, that occur over a given area of land

river–large stream of water that runs through the land

sea–large body of water completely or partly surrounded by land

seacoast–land lying next to a sea or ocean

sea level–average level of an ocean's surface

sound–body of water between a shoreline and one or more islands off the coast

source–(of a river) place where a river or stream begins, often in high lands

strait–narrow stretch of water joining two larger bodies of water

tributary–small river or stream that flows into a large river or stream; a branch of the river

upstream–direction opposite the flow of a river; toward the source of a river or stream

valley–area of low land between hills or mountains

volcano–mountain created as liquid rock or ash are thrown up from inside the earth

CLIMATE

Climate is the usual pattern of weather events that occurs in an area over a long period of time. Climate is determined by distance from the Equator, by location near large bodies of water, and sometimes by positions near mountain ranges.

The world's climates can be organized into four major regions: **tropical**, **mid-latitude**, **high latitude**, and **dry**. Some of these regions are determined by their latitude; others are based on the vegetation that grows in them.

Tropical Climates

Tropical climates get their name from the tropics, the areas along the Equator. Temperatures in the tropics change little from season to season. The warm tropical climate region can be separated into two types: tropical rain forest and tropical savanna.

The tropical rain forest climate region is wet in most months, with up to 100 inches (254 cm) of rain a year. In these areas, rain and heat produce lush vegetation and **rain forests**, dense forests that are home to millions of kinds of plant and animal life. The Amazon River basin in South America is the world's largest rain forest area.

The tropical **savanna** climate has two seasons—one wet and one dry. Savannas, or grasslands with few trees, occur in this region. Among the leading tropical savanna climate areas are southern India and eastern Africa.

Mid-Latitude Climates

Mid-latitude, or moderate, climates are found in the middle latitudes of the Northern and Southern Hemispheres. Most of the world's people live in this climate region. The mid-latitude region has a greater variety of climates than other regions. This variety results from the mix of air masses—warm air coming from the tropics and cool air coming from the polar regions. In most places, temperatures change with the seasons.

High Latitude Climates

High latitude, or polar, climate regions lie in the high latitudes of each hemisphere. Climates are cold everywhere in the high latitude regions, some more severe than others.

High latitude climate regions also include highland or mountainous regions even in lower

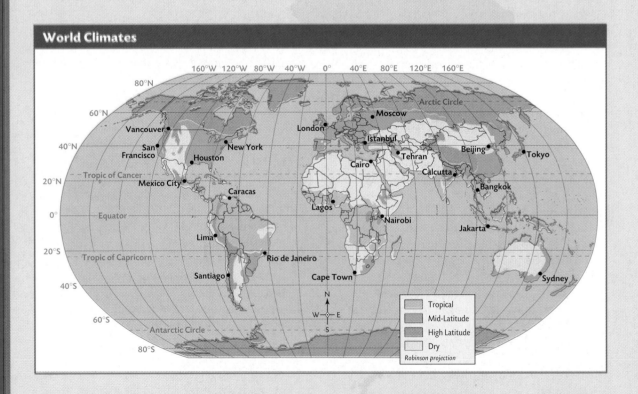

World Climates

Robinson projection

Tropical
Mid-Latitude
High Latitude
Dry

World Land Use and Resources

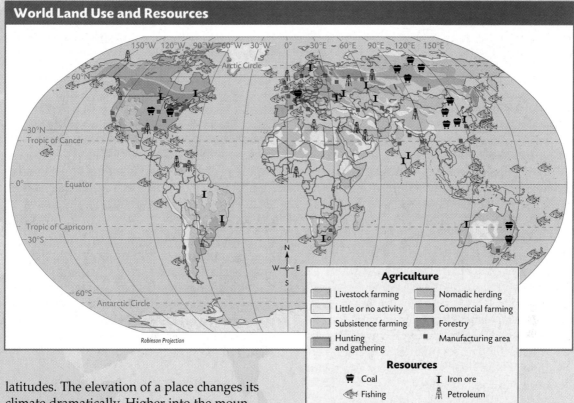

Agriculture

- Livestock farming
- Little or no activity
- Subsistence farming
- Hunting and gathering
- Nomadic herding
- Commercial farming
- Forestry
- Manufacturing area

Resources

- Coal
- Fishing
- Iron ore
- Petroleum

Robinson Projection

latitudes. The elevation of a place changes its climate dramatically. Higher into the mountains, the air becomes thinner. It cannot hold the heat from the sun, so the temperature drops. Even in the tropics, snow covers the peaks of high mountains.

Dry Climates

Dry climate refers to dry or partially dry areas that receive little or no rainfall. Temperatures can be extremely hot during the day and cold at night. Dry climates can also have severely cold winters.

Nearly an eighth of the world's land surface is dry, with a rainfall of less than 10 inches (25 cm) per year. The Sahara in North Africa is the largest desert in the world. The area covered by the Sahara—3,579,000 square miles (9,270,000 sq. km)—is about the size of the United States.

NATURAL RESOURCES

Natural resources refer to anything from the natural environment that people use to meet their needs. Natural resources include fertile soil, clean water, minerals, trees, and energy sources. Human skills and labor are also valuable natural resources.

Renewable Resources

Some natural resources can be replaced as they are used up. These renewable resources can be replaced naturally or grown fairly quickly. Forests, grasslands, plant and animal life, and rich soil all can be renewable resources if people manage them carefully. A lumber company concerned about future growth can replant as many trees as it cuts. Fishing and whaling fleets can limit the number of fish and whales they catch in certain parts of the ocean.

Nonrenewable Resources

Metals and other minerals found in the earth's crust are nonrenewable resources. They cannot be replaced because they were formed over millions of years by geologic forces within the earth.

One important group of nonrenewable resources is fossil fuels—coals, oil, and natural gas. Industries and people depend on these fuels for energy and as raw materials for plastics and other goods. We also use up large amounts of other metals and minerals, such as iron, aluminum, and phosphates. Some of these can be reused, but they cannot be replaced.

ENVIRONMENTAL CHALLENGES

When people use natural resources to make a living, they affect the environment. The unmanaged use of resources is a threat to the environment. Many human activities can cause pollution—putting impure or poisonous substances into the land, water, and air.

Land and Water

Only about 11 percent of the earth's surface has land good enough for farming. Chemicals that farmers use may improve their crops, but some also may damage the land. Pesticides, or chemicals that kill insects, can pollute rivers and groundwater, or water that fills tiny cracks in the rock layers below the earth's surface.

Other human activities also pollute soil and water. Oil spills from tanker ships threaten ocean coastal areas. Illegal dumping of dangerous waste products causes problems. Untreated sewage reaching rivers pollutes lakes and groundwater as well. Salt water can also pollute both soil and groundwater.

Air

Industries and vehicles that burn fossil fuels are the main sources of air pollution. Throughout the world, fumes from cars and other vehicles pollute the air. The chemicals in air pollution can seriously damage people's health.

These chemicals combined with precipitation may fall as acid rain, or rain carrying large amounts of sulfuric acid. Acid rain eats away the surfaces of buildings, kills fish, and can destroy entire forests.

Energy

All of the world nations need safe, dependable sources of energy. Fossil fuels are most often used to generate electricity, heat buildings, run machinery, and power vehicles. Fossil fuels, however, are nonrenewable resources. In addition, they contribute to air pollution. So today many countries are trying to discover new ways of using renewable energy sources. Two of these ways are hydroelectric power, the energy generated by falling water, and solar energy, or energy produced by the heat of the sun.

GEOGRAPHY'S IMPACT ON WORLD HISTORY

Geographic factors have shaped the outcome of historical events. Landforms, waterways, climate, and natural resources all have helped or hindered human activities. In many cases, people have learned either to adapt to their environment or to transform it to meet their needs.

Throughout the units of your text, you will discover how geography has shaped the course of events in world history. Here are some examples of the role that geographic factors have played in the story of humanity.

Unit 1 The Rise of Civilizations

Rivers contributed to the rise of many of the world's early civilizations. By 3000 B.C. the Sumerians of the Middle East had set up 12 prosperous city-states in the Tigris-Euphrates River valley. The Fertile Crescent, as the area is often called because of its relatively rich topsoil and its curved shape, was able to support city-state populations ranging from 20,000 to 250,000 people.

Unit 2 Flowering of Civilizations

Landforms and waterways also affected the political relationships of the world's ancient peoples. For example, the rugged landscape of Greece divided the ancient Greeks into separate city-states instead of uniting them into a single nation. Furthermore, closeness to the sea caused the Greek city-states to expand their trade, culture, and sense of civic pride to other parts of the Mediterranean world.

Unit 3 Regional Civilizations

From about A.D. 400 to A.D. 1500, regional civilizations developed at the crossroads of trade between different areas of the world. The city of Makkah (Mecca), in the Middle East's Arabian Peninsula, was a crossroads for caravans from North Africa, Palestine, and the

Persian Gulf. The religion of Islam established a firm base in Makkah, from which it spread to other areas of the Middle East, North Africa, South Asia, and Southeast Asia.

Unit 4 Emergence of the Modern World

The desire to control or to obtain scarce natural resources has encouraged trade and stimulated contact among the world's peoples. At the dawn of the modern era, Asians and Europeans came into contact with one another partly because Europeans wanted Asia's spices and silks. When the Asiatic people known as the Mongols could no longer guarantee safe passage for traders on overland routes, Europeans were forced to consider new water routes to Asia. This opened a new global age that brought the peoples of Europe, Asia, Africa, and the Americas into closer contact with each other.

Unit 5 Age of Revolution

Climate often affects the way a country behaves toward its neighbors. For example, many of Russia's harbors stay frozen during much of the year. In the past, Russia has often gone to war with other countries to capture land for warm water ports. Climate was also one reason why the Russians were able to stop the invasions of French ruler Napoleon Bonaparte in 1812 and the German dictator Adolf Hitler in 1941. The Russians were used to the bitter cold and snow of their country's winter, whereas the invaders were not.

Unit 6 Industry and Nationalism

Exploiting natural resources, such as coal and iron, was an important factor in the growth of the Industrial Revolution. Modern industry started in Great Britain, which had large amounts of coal and iron ore for making steel. Throughout Europe and North America, the rise of factories that turned raw materials into finished goods prompted people eager for employment to move from rural areas to urban centers.

Also, the availability of land and the discovery of minerals in the Americas, Australia, and South Africa caused hundreds of thousands of Europeans to move to these areas in hope of improving their lives. These mass migrations were possible because of improvements in industrial technology and transportation that enabled people to overcome geographic barriers.

Unit 7 World in Conflict

Environmental disasters during the first part of the 1900s affected national economies in various parts of the world. For example, during the 1930s, winds blew away so much of the soil in the Great Plains of central North America that the area became known as the Dust Bowl. Ruined by the drought, many farmers packed up their belongings and headed west. It took many years of normal rainfall and improved farming techniques to transform the Great Plains from a Dust Bowl into productive land once again.

Unit 8 The Contemporary World

The world's peoples have become more aware of the growing scarcity of nonrenewable resources. Oil takes millions of years to form, and the earth's supply is limited. Industrialized countries like the United States consume far more oil than they produce and must import large amounts. Many experts believe that the world's fossil fuels will be used up if steps are not taken to limit their consumption and to find alternative sources of energy.

Geography and History Journal

You are about to journey to the past to learn about the people and events that have shaped the world you live in today. Throughout your course of study, keep a record of the events discussed above and any other events in world history that have been affected by geography. When you come to the last unit, you may also want to explore how geography impacts current events or issues: For example, how has geography influenced peacekeeping missions in Bosnia and other parts of the world, or what would happen to Canada geographically if the province of Quebec were to separate and form an independent nation? On a world map locate the places where these historical events have occurred, and identify the units of study in your text in which they are discussed.

THE Five THEMES OF GEOGRAPHY

To help illustrate the link between history and geography, geographers have identified five themes that can be used to examine the role that geography plays.

1 **Location** serves as a starting point by asking, "Where is it?" To be more specific, there are two types of location. **Absolute location** refers to the exact location on the earth's surface as measured by latitude (lines north and south of the Equator) and longitude (lines east and west of the Prime Meridian). Every location on the earth can be found in this way.

   Relative location is less precise. It helps you orient yourself to a location that is relative to something else. Relative location has been important historically as people decided where to build their cities and establish their civilizations.

Modern mapmaking uses photography as a tool. A LANDSAT satellite provided data for this image of Miami, Florida.

This village in Tunisia, North Africa, is at the northern edge of the Sahara. Stone and mud brick buildings give the village and its surroundings a sense of place.

2 The idea of **Place** includes more than just where something is located. It includes those features and characteristics that give an area its own identity or personality. These can be *physical* characteristics—such as landforms, weather, plants, and animals—or *human* characteristics—language, religion, architecture, music, politics, and way of life.

3 **Human/Environment Interaction** focuses on how people respond to and alter their environment. To live comfortably or even to survive in many parts of the world, people must make changes in the environment or adapt to conditions they cannot change, or both.

How people choose to change their environment depends on their attitude toward the natural setting and on the technology they have available to change it.

Fishing is a major industry in Denmark, a small European nation nearly surrounded by water.

4 The **Movement** of people and things between places means that events in other places can have an impact on you personally. Transportation routes, communication systems, and trade connections link people and places throughout the world. Products, ideas, and information are sent around the globe, either slowly by ship or almost instantaneously by electronics.

The movement of people is particularly important because they can spread ideas and cultural characteristics from one place to another. Sometimes those ideas or characteristics are accepted in the new location, and the culture is changed by that linkage.

On the southern coast of China is Hong Kong, one of Asia's busiest ports.

Street signs and buildings in a historical area of Montreal reveal the French character of the Canadian province of Quebec.

5 A **Region** is an area that is unified by some feature or a mixture of features. It is used to generalize about parts of the earth's surface in either physical or human terms. A neighborhood is an example of a small region, while a cultural region that shares a common language would be a larger region. Other regions could be economic, where a particular economic activity is dominant, or political, where the same type of political system is followed.

> ### Geography's Impact on History
>
> While studying the history of the world, you will be learning about the people and events that have shaped the past and provide the framework for the future. As you read *World History: The Human Experience*, pay special attention to the ways in which geography has influenced history and fashioned the world in which you live.

The Five Themes of Geography   11

Themes IN WORLD HISTORY

Relation to Environment
The ancient Egyptians develop a civilization in northeastern Africa's Nile River Valley.

Bust of infant sun god

Uniformity
Early Chinese dynasties establish and maintain a strong central government in East Asia.

Terra-cotta warriors—Qin dynasty

Change
Early modern Europe enjoys a cultural awakening based on ancient Greek and Roman ideas as well as on Christianity and Judaism.

Renaissance musicians

The Gas Factory

Cultural Diffusion
The Industrial Revolution begins in Great Britain and gradually spreads to other parts of the world.

Innovation
New technology transforms many aspects of life in the modern world.

Space shuttle lift-off

orld history is a record of the adventures of humankind—both the famous and the ordinary—throughout thousands of years. By studying world history—by gazing across time—you can understand the past and recognize its contribution to the present and the future. World history tells of significant people and events. It also encompasses broad historical themes that happen again and again, providing meaning for events in the past and showing how they affect contemporary life.

World History: The Human Experience introduces 9 key historical themes. Each chapter highlights and develops several of these themes that demonstrate the interconnectedness of ideas and events. These events help organize your study of world history and make connections across time.

Cooperation/Conflict focuses on how people relate to each other throughout history—sometimes in cooperation, working together to accomplish a common goal, at other times in conflict, struggling against one another.

Revolution/Reaction deals with revolution, or the sudden overthrow of long-established ideas and organizations, contrasted with reaction, or the efforts to oppose new ideas and preserve traditional ways.

Change includes political, social, religious, cultural, and economic transformations that influence human activities throughout the centuries.

Diversity/Uniformity focuses on the diversity or variety of world peoples and customs, contrasted with the desire for uniformity or commonality in some societies.

Regionalism/Nationalism deals with a sense of loyalty and belonging, expressed in ties to a region, to a nation, or to the world as a whole—to the global community.

Innovation includes cultural, scientific, and technical breakthroughs that increase knowledge and impact the way people live and think.

Cultural Diffusion focuses on the spread of cultural expressions through a variety of means across nations, regions, and the world.

Movement involves the movement of people throughout history, including patterns of migration, exploration, and colonization as well as imperialism—people in one place on the globe exercising control over people in another place.

Relation to Environment emphasizes human-environment interchange—how people are affected by their environment and, in turn, how they affect that same environment.

Horn player, Benin

Rise of Civilizations

Then & Now *Scholars have divided history into periods according to environmental changes on Earth and cultural developments of humanity. The Paleolithic period or Old Stone Age began about 2 million years ago and lasted until about 12,000 B.C. The earliest evidence of human cultural development was discovered by four teenagers, quite by accident. Jacques Marshal and three young friends entered a cave near Lascaux, France, in 1940 and found the most spectacular cave paintings from Ice Age Europe, created some 17,000 years ago. Cave paintings have been discovered in many parts of the world, but the Lascaux paintings provide the most dramatic and best preserved "snapshots" of early human life yet to be discovered.*

A Global Chronology

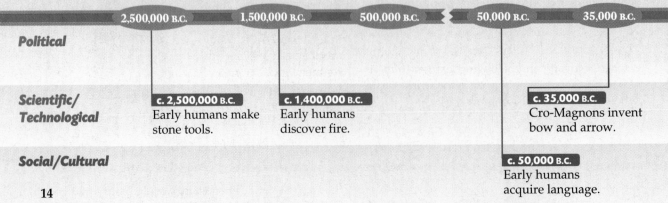

	2,500,000 B.C.	1,500,000 B.C.	500,000 B.C.	50,000 B.C.	35,000 B.C.
Political					
Scientific/ Technological	**c. 2,500,000 B.C.** Early humans make stone tools.	**c. 1,400,000 B.C.** Early humans discover fire.			**c. 35,000 B.C.** Cro-Magnons invent bow and arrow.
Social/Cultural				**c. 50,000 B.C.** Early humans acquire language.	

14

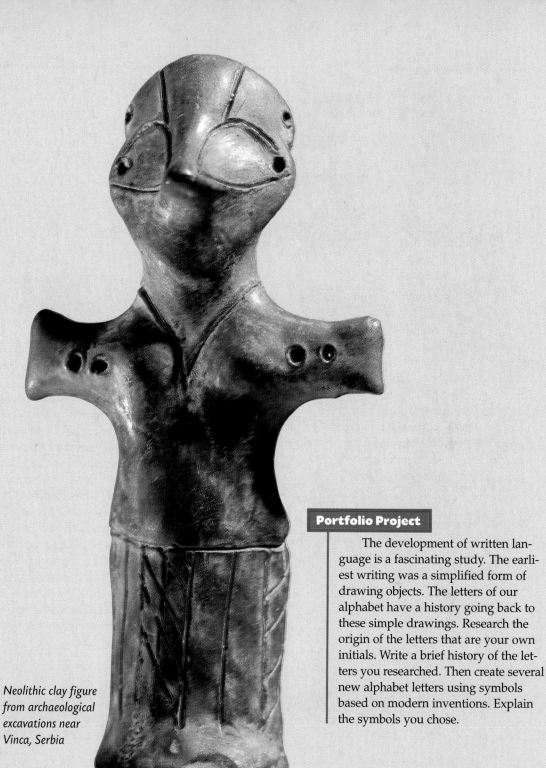

Neolithic clay figure from archaeological excavations near Vinca, Serbia

Portfolio Project

The development of written language is a fascinating study. The earliest writing was a simplified form of drawing objects. The letters of our alphabet have a history going back to these simple drawings. Research the origin of the letters that are your own initials. Write a brief history of the letters you researched. Then create several new alphabet letters using symbols based on modern inventions. Explain the symbols you chose.

4000 B.C.   **3000 B.C.**   **2000 B.C.**   **1000 B.C.**

c. 3500 B.C. Sumerians build first cities.

c. 3000 B.C. Narmer unites Upper Egypt and Lower Egypt.

c. 1150 B.C. Olmec civilization begins in Mexico.

c. 3400 B.C. Corn and beans cultivated in the Americas.

c. 1700 B.C. Stonehenge monument is built.

c. 2000 B.C. Chinese write on oracle bones.

15

The Spread of Ideas

Farming and Civilization

etween 8,000 and 10,000 years ago, a quiet revolution took place. In scattered pockets of the Middle East, Asia, Africa, and the Americas, people learned to cultivate food-producing plants for the first time. As knowledge of farming gradually spread, it dramatically changed human culture. Farming encouraged the growth of permanent communities, which in turn became the seedbeds for the world's first civilizations.

The Middle East
Breadbasket of the Ancient World

Today only sparse vegetation covers the foothills of Iran's Zagros Mountains. Erosion and overgrazing by sheep and goats have taken their toll. Around 8000 B.C., however, wild wheat known as emmer covered the hills. Experts believe it was here that the world's first farmers may have watched seeds fall to earth and sprout. This observation led these ancient wanderers to plant seeds.

Over time, knowledge of farming spread in a broad arc of fertile land that curved from the Persian Gulf to the Mediterranean Sea. Farmers gradually added other foods to their diets—barley, chickpeas, lentils, figs, apricots, pistachios, walnuts, and more. A hunger for these foods kept people in one place. Hunting and gathering lifestyles changed as people began to develop new ideas and skills. Slowly—very slowly—farming settlements grew into cities. Known by names such as Ur, Babylon, and Jericho, these cities were the centers of Earth's oldest civilizations.

Greek grain storage jar

Foothills of the Zagros Mountains

The Americas
Mexico and Peru: Farming and Diversity

For much of world history, distance separated the Americas from the rest of the world. But the independent invention of farming in the areas of present-day Mexico and Peru created cities as sophisticated as those in other regions. The crops that spurred their growth, however, differed from crops elsewhere. Few of the wild grains found on other continents grew in the Americas. The first farmers in the Americas used the seeds of other plants, especially squash and beans. They also developed two high-yield foods unknown to the rest of the world—potatoes and maize (corn). When distant civilizations made contact, ideas about agriculture accompanied the wide distribution of foods that early peoples had developed and cultivated.

Corn Dance *by Frank Reed Whiteside*

Asia and Africa
Expansion of Earth's Gardens

The farming revolution did not happen just once. It occurred several times in widely separated regions. More than 6,000 years ago, farmers along the upper Huang He in present-day northern China started planting millet. About 5,000 years ago, farmers near the mouth of the Chang Jiang in southern China learned to grow rice. At roughly the same time, farmers along the Nile River in the northern part of Africa harvested their first crops of wheat and barley.

Like the gardens of the Middle East, the gardens of China and northern Africa grew more diverse. By 3000 B.C., farmers cultivated soybeans, bananas, and sugarcane. Supported by the harvests, people had more time to think and dream. Soon they created things that were used by the civilizations of the Middle East—calendars, systems of writing, forms of art and government.

Wood relief of farming activities, Yoruba peoples

LINKING THE IDEAS

1. How do experts think farming probably began?
2. Why is farming considered one of the most important inventions of human history?

Critical Thinking

3. **Cause and Effect** What is the connection between farming and the rise of ancient civilizations?

Prehistory–1000 B.C.

Human Beginnings

Chapter Themes

▶ **Movement** Migrations of prehistoric peoples result in their spread throughout the world. *Section 1*

▶ **Innovation** Early humans produce tools and domesticate animals and crops. *Section 2*

▶ **Change** The earliest civilizations begin with the evolution of farming settlements into the first cities. *Section 3*

S*toryteller*

On the coast of southern Africa, in caves and rock shelters, lived some of the world's first communities of prehistoric people. The region enjoyed a mild climate and abundant food from both the land and the sea. Women gathered supplies, while men made longer journeys inland, hunting for big animals such as antelope, buffalo, and wildebeest. Both men and women searched the coast at each low tide for small sea animals.

The cave dwellers preserved food for times of scarcity by drying leftover meat in smoke from fires. They did not know that more than 70,000 years later scientists and other people exploring the same area would uncover the remains of their long-vanished way of life.

Historical Significance

How did early peoples develop skills that became the basic elements of human ways of life? What developments led to the rise of the world's first civilizations?

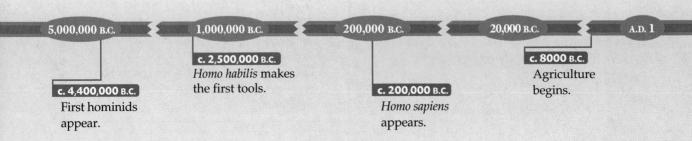

| 5,000,000 B.C. | 1,000,000 B.C. | 200,000 B.C. | 20,000 B.C. | A.D. 1 |

c. 2,500,000 B.C.
Homo habilis makes the first tools.

c. 8000 B.C.
Agriculture begins.

c. 4,400,000 B.C.
First hominids appear.

c. 200,000 B.C.
Homo sapiens appears.

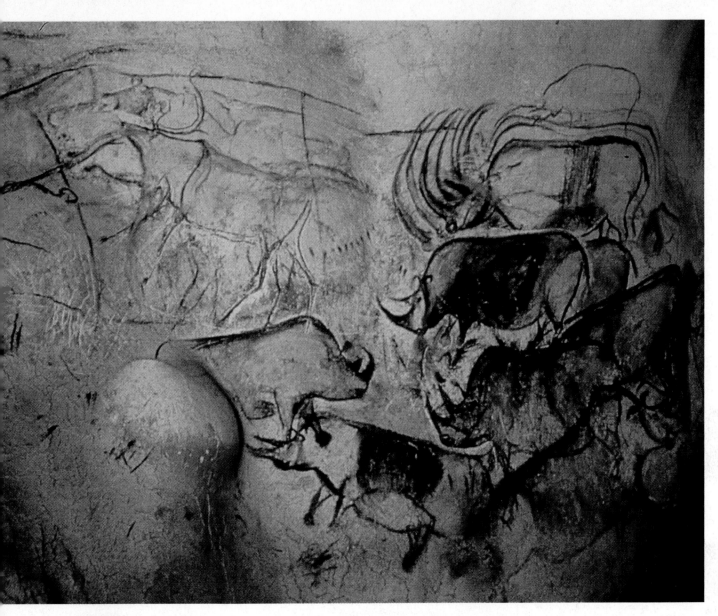

History & Art Cro-Magnon cave paintings from Vallon-Pont-d'Arc
near Avignon, France

Your History Journal

Imagine that you and a friend are stranded on a large uninhabited island. You have no tools except a pocket knife. There are many species of small animals, a stream of fresh water, a sandy beach, and a dense forest. You must survive until rescued, perhaps a month later. Write a journal account of your first seven days.

5,000,000 B.C.		3,000,000 B.C.		1,000,000 B.C.

c. 4,400,000 B.C.
Earliest known human ancestor lives in East Africa.

c. 2,500,000 B.C.
Homo habilis develops first stone tools.

c. 1,700,000 B.C.
Homo erectus reaches Asia.

Section 1

Discovery of Early Humans in Africa

Setting the Scene

▶ **Terms to Define**
prehistory, hominid, anthropologist, paleontologist, archaeologist, artifact, radiocarbon dating, nomad, culture, technology

▶ **People to Meet**
Gen Suwa, Tim D. White, Donald C. Johanson, Louis Leakey, Mary Leakey

▶ **Places to Locate**
Aramis, Hadar, Olduvai Gorge

 **ind Out** How have recent archaeological finds contributed to our understanding of human origins?

The Storyteller

On the slab lies the shriveled corpse of a man…. Alongside him lies a long wooden stave with a fibrous end. Laid out on the slab … are the other finds—the axe with its elbow-shafting and metal blade, a stone bead with a strange tassel of twisted hide thongs, the small dagger … a wooden stick with holes in it, a scrap of leather, and a nut-sized stone…. Archaeologist Konrad Spindler's assessment: 'Roughly four thousand years old … [or] even earlier.'

—adapted from *The Man in the Ice*,
Konrad Spindler, 1994

Excavation of an ancient site in Lake Kinneret, Galilee

History tells the story of humankind. Because historians mostly use written records to gather information about the past, history is said to begin with the invention of writing about 5,500 years ago. But the story of humankind really begins in the time *before* people developed writing—the period called prehistory.

Using the best available evidence, scientists have traced the existence of the first humanlike creatures back to about 4.4 million years ago in Africa. Human beings and the humanlike creatures that preceded them together belong to a group of beings named hominids (HAH•muh•nuhds). The scientific study of hominids—their physical features, development, and behavior—is called anthropology. Physical anthropologists (AN•thruh•PAH•luh•jihsts) compare hominid bones and other fossil remains, looking for changes in such features as brain size and posture. Anthropologists work closely with other scientists. Paleontologists (PAY•lee•AHN •TAH•luh•jihsts), for example, study fossil remains to determine the characteristics of various prehistoric periods. Archaeologists (AHR•kee•AH•luh •jihsts) investigate prehistoric life by unearthing and interpreting the objects left behind by prehistoric people. These artifacts include any objects that were shaped by human hands—tools, pots, and beads—as well as other remains of human life, such as bits of charcoal.

Dating Early Artifacts

As they carefully unearth the remains of prehuman and human settlements, archaeologists and physical anthropologists face the additional problem of dating what they find. It is easy to determine the relative sequence in which events happened.

More recent remains are usually found above older ones. The problem lies in assigning a definite age to fossil bones, tools, and other remains.

Among the techniques for determining age is radiocarbon dating. Once-living things contain small amounts of radioactive carbon. Because radioactive carbon decays at a known rate, archaeologists can measure how much the radioactive carbon has decayed in organic remains and figure out when the animal or plant died. In recent years, they also have used a dating technique that measures the rate of decay for chemical elements other than carbon.

Scientists have increased our understanding of the age of prehistoric peoples through the use of genetic evidence. They obtain genetic material called DNA from living people and compare it with DNA from other people and from living animals. Using computers, they calculate and analyze the rate of change in DNA over time. Although not error free, these studies have produced valuable information about the links between people today and their prehistoric ancestors.

Prehistoric Finds in Africa

On December 17, 1992, a paleontologist from Japan named **Gen Suwa** walked across the rugged desert landscape of Ethiopia in East Africa. At a site called **Aramis**, an object in the ground caught Suwa's eye. It turned out to be one of the oldest hominid teeth ever found—a link to the origins of our human ancestors!

The Oldest Human Ancestor

Over the next two years, Suwa, his colleague **Tim D. White** of the University of California, and a 20-person team uncovered additional remains. They came up with teeth, arm bones, and parts of a skull and jaw that belonged to 17 individuals. Analyzing the fossils, the scientists determined that they were about 4.4 million years old and came from the oldest direct human ancestor known. The small creatures would have weighed about 65 pounds (30 kg) and stood 4 feet (1.2 m) tall. Scientists have yet to determine whether they walked upright.

Discovery of Lucy

About 45 miles (73 km) north, at **Hadar**, two scientists—**Donald C. Johanson** and Tom Gray—in 1974 had uncovered the 3.2 million-year-old skeleton of a hominid nicknamed "Lucy." Lucy received her name from a popular Beatles song of the period,

"Lucy in the Sky with Diamonds." Hers was the most nearly complete skeleton of any erect-walking prehuman found up to that time.

Since then, Johanson and his team of researchers have made further discoveries. In 1994 they assembled, from other fossils found at the Hadar site, the first reasonably complete skull of a Lucy-like hominid. The scientists claimed that the skull provided evidence that males and females in this early hominid group were of significantly different sizes. The evidence also indicated that Lucy-like hominids spent some time climbing in trees and could also walk upright.

The earliest known direct evidence of upright walking comes from Kenya, where archaeologists in 1995 discovered a fossilized hominid shinbone about 4 million years old. The shape and size of the bone indicate upright walking.

Human Origins

Scientists disagree about many aspects of the story of human beginnings. As scientists unearth more clues, newer evidence may require them to reinterpret older evidence.

HISTORY AND SCIENCE
Human Origins: Differing Points of View

People disagree about the interpretation of the available data on human origins. The following are some examples of these differences.

Fossil record Fossils provide insights into human origins, but they do not give a complete or conclusive history of human development. Many gaps are present in the record, and fossils showing changes from one life-form to another are sometimes absent.

Fossil dating Scientists analyze many different samples, using as many different methods as possible because samples may not provide consistent results. Dating methods are constantly being refined to provide more accurate data.

Varying viewpoints A variety of ideas exist about the source of life. Many religions claim that a supreme being or a supernatural force created humans and other life-forms. Current scientific theories focus on chemical reactions in which organic materials have come together to form complex life-forms.

The First Hominids

According to one of the generally accepted theories, the first prehuman hominids, of whom the discoveries in Ethiopia are an example, date back about 4.4 million years. Known as *Australopithecus* (aw•STRAY•loh•PIH•thuh•kuhs), or "southern ape," they stood about 3.5 to 5.0 feet (1.1 to 1.6 m) tall and walked on two legs. They had large faces that jutted out. The brain was small, the nose flat, and the teeth large. The back teeth were suitable for grinding food.

Australopithecus lived in the humid forests of eastern and southern Africa, where they fed on fruits, leaves, and nuts. They probably also ate fish caught in streams and meat from animals killed by lions or other predators. *Australopithecus* were most likely nomads—moving constantly in search of food. They probably had few, if any, possessions and may have shared food with one another. Fossil evidence shows that family groups lived in temporary camps. Perhaps they lived together for protection from large animals. No evidence exists showing that *Australopithecus* made or used tools. They may have used grass stems and twigs as tools and sticks or bones to dig roots, however.

Hominid Groups

Scientists use the Latin word *Homo*, which means "human," to name these hominids and all later human beings as well. Anthropologists today are still not certain whether a direct relationship connected *Australopithecus* and human beings or exactly when hominids became truly human. Scientists divided *Homo*—the genus of humans—into three species that differ somewhat in body structures. These three human or humanlike species arose at different times in prehistory. The earliest of the three was *Homo habilis*, or "person with ability," who lived until about 1.5 million years ago. After *Homo habilis* lived the second type

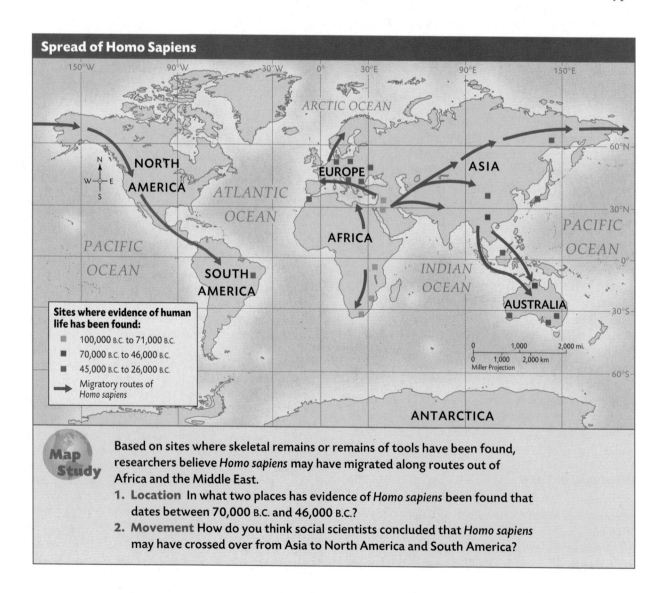

Spread of Homo Sapiens

Sites where evidence of human life has been found:

- 100,000 B.C. to 71,000 B.C.
- 70,000 B.C. to 46,000 B.C.
- 45,000 B.C. to 26,000 B.C.
- → Migratory routes of *Homo sapiens*

Map Study Based on sites where skeletal remains or remains of tools have been found, researchers believe *Homo sapiens* may have migrated along routes out of Africa and the Middle East.

1. **Location** In what two places has evidence of *Homo sapiens* been found that dates between 70,000 B.C. and 46,000 B.C.?
2. **Movement** How do you think social scientists concluded that *Homo sapiens* may have crossed over from Asia to North America and South America?

© Bob Campbell

Hominid Hunter

Kenneth Garrett

Meave Leakey, daughter-in-law of famed fossil hunters Mary and Louis Leakey, sifts through the soil near Lake Turkana in northern Kenya, a site in the East African Rift System famous for its treasury of the fossils of early humans. In recent years a wide range of scholars have continued to push back the date for the origin of the earliest humans. Molecular biologists, through the study of human, chimpanzee, and gorilla genes and blood proteins, speculate that hominids, or early humans, originated somewhere between five and seven million years ago. One of a number of scientists influenced by this research, Meave Leakey and her team began exploring for new evidence. They now theorize that a jawbone found near Lake Turkana in 1994 may be 4.1 million years old. Before that discovery there was little evidence of hominids older than 3.6 million years. Some researchers believe that a 5.6 million-year-old jaw fragment (left) discovered in 1967 may be the oldest hominid fossil yet found. ⊕

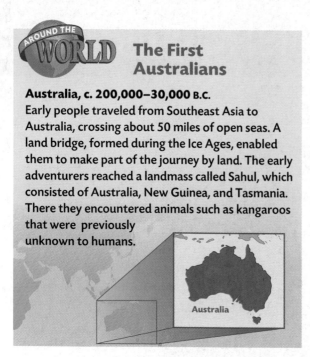

The First Australians

Australia, c. 200,000–30,000 B.C.
Early people traveled from Southeast Asia to Australia, crossing about 50 miles of open seas. A land bridge, formed during the Ice Ages, enabled them to make part of the journey by land. The early adventurers reached a landmass called Sahul, which consisted of Australia, New Guinea, and Tasmania. There they encountered animals such as kangaroos that were previously unknown to humans.

Australia

of early human—*Homo erectus*, or "person who walks upright"—who was, in turn, followed between 100,000 and 200,000 years ago by *Homo sapiens*, or "person who thinks." All people living today belong to the species *Homo sapiens*.

The Ice Ages

Climatic changes played an important part in the development of early humankind. Between 2 million and 10,000 years ago, Earth experienced four long periods of cold climate, known as the Ice Ages. During each such period, average temperatures in many parts of the world fell to below freezing, and massive glaciers spread out from the Poles, scarring the landforms over which they crept. The northern glaciers covered large portions of Europe, Asia, and North America, and the ice fields of Antarctica stretched over wide regions in the Southern Hemisphere. Only the middle latitudes remained warm enough to support human and animal life. Between glacial periods, Earth's climate warmed overall, and abundant rains brought lush plant growth—until the next glacial period began.

As the sheets of ice formed, the level of the oceans dropped more than 300 feet (90 m). As a result, some areas that are now separated by water were connected then by bridges of land. One such land bridge joined Japan and mainland Korea, another connected Great Britain and Ireland to western Europe, a third led from the Malay Peninsula through the Indonesian islands almost

all the way to Australia, and a fourth connected Asia and North America at the Bering Strait.

Early human beings responded to the environmental changes of the Ice Ages in several ways. Some migrated to warmer places. Others found strategies for keeping warm, such as clothing and fire. Those who could not adapt died from starvation or exposure.

Human Culture

Clothing and fire had become part of the culture, or way of life, of prehistoric people. Culture also includes the knowledge a people have, the language they speak, the ways in which they eat and dress, their religious beliefs, and their achievements in art and music.

Toolmaking

One of the earliest aspects of culture that people formed was the use of tools. At first they dug roots and tubers out of the ground with wooden digging sticks. Later, they made crude tools of stone, which enabled them to skin small animals and cut off pieces of meat. Improving their technology—the skills and useful knowledge available to them for collecting material and making the objects necessary for survival—early people began to create specialized tools, such as food choppers, skin scrapers, and spear points.

The Stone Age

The use of stone tools by early people led historians to apply the name Stone Age to the period before writing became established. Scholars divided the Stone Age into three shorter periods, depending on differences in toolmaking techniques. The earliest period, the Paleolithic (PAY•lee•uh•LIH•thihk) or Old Stone Age, began about 2.5 million years ago with the first toolmaking by *Homo habilis* and lasted until about 12,000 B.C. The Mesolithic (MEH•zuh•LIH•thihk) period or Middle Stone Age is usually dated from 12,000 B.C. to about 8000 B.C. The Neolithic (NEE•uh•LIH•thihk) period or New Stone Age lasted from about 8000 B.C. to 5000 B.C.

Paleolithic Hunter-Gatherers

Archaeologists as yet do not know a great deal about the culture of the early humans called *Homo habilis* and *Homo erectus*. Their knowledge, however, widens as new discoveries are made.

Homo Habilis

Homo habilis lived during the first quarter of the Paleolithic period. It seems probable, however, that these prehistoric people are the oldest hominids known to manufacture tools. They lived in Africa from about 2.5 million to 1.5 million years ago, alongside *Australopithecus*. Their larger brains indicate that they were more physically and mentally advanced. Much of the evidence for *Homo habilis* has come from research by **Louis and Mary Leakey**, and later their son Richard, at **Olduvai** (OHL•duh•VY) **Gorge** in Tanzania and other sites in the eastern part of Africa.

Homo Erectus

Scientists have gathered much more information about *Homo erectus* than about *Homo habilis*. *Homo erectus* first appeared in Africa and lived from 1.8 million years ago to about 30,000 years ago. Their living areas covered a variety of environments from woodlands and grasslands in Africa to forests and plains in Europe and Asia.

Homo erectus at first were mostly food gatherers. Scientists think the females gathered fruits, nuts, and seeds, and the males scavenged for meat—either searching for an animal that had died of natural causes or yelling and waving their arms to frighten carnivores away from a kill. By about 500,000 years ago, however, the males had become hunters, using spears and clubs to kill such small prey as deer, pigs, and rabbits. The females, whose movements were restricted by the constant demands of child care, continued to forage close to home for vegetable food.

Meanwhile, these early humans also had learned how to make fire. This discovery allowed them to keep warm, cook food, and scare away threatening animals. It also enabled them to live in caves. Before, they had protected themselves from the weather by digging shallow pits and covering these with branches. Now, they could drive animals out of caves and use the caves themselves.

Homo erectus by this time not only had fire but also made clothing. Initially they simply wrapped themselves in animal skins, having first scraped hair and tissue off the inner side of the skins. Later, they laced the skins together with strips of leather.

Migrations

Scientists disagree on when prehistoric peoples left Africa and moved to other parts of the world. Some experts believe that *Homo habilis* may have been the earliest to migrate to Europe and Asia; however, clear evidence to support this view is lacking. Scientists do know, however, that *Homo erectus* migrated from their native Africa to Europe and Asia. Skeletal remains found in Java have led anthropologists to conclude that *Homo erectus* reached the Indonesian islands about 1.6 to 1.8 million years ago. *Homo erectus* was clearly well established in China by 460,000 years ago, and the earliest skeletal traces in Europe may also date back around 400,000 years.

Language

To communicate, *Homo erectus* may have used little more than gestures and grunts. By 50,000 B.C., however, prehistoric peoples had developed speech. Language was one of humanity's greatest achievements. It enabled individuals to work with one another—to organize a hunting group, for example, or to give specific instructions about where to find a spring of fresh water. It allowed individuals to exchange ideas, such as how the world began or what caused animals to migrate across the plains. Individuals could sit around a hearth fire, eat together, and talk about the day's events. They could talk about the best way to fell a tree or build a shelter. Perhaps most significantly, spoken language made it possible for the older generation to pass its culture on to the younger generation, enabling new generations to build upon the knowledge of the past.

SECTION 1 REVIEW

Recall
1. **Define** prehistory, hominid, anthropologist, paleontologist, archaeologist, artifacts, radiocarbon dating, nomad, culture, technology.
2. **Identify** Gen Suwa, Tim D. White, Donald C. Johanson, Louis Leakey, Mary Leakey.
3. **Locate** each of these prehistoric sites and explain their importance: Aramis, Hadar, Olduvai Gorge.

Critical Thinking
4. **Making Comparisons** Compare and contrast the culture of *Homo habilis* and *Homo erectus*. Consider housing, technology, and mobility.

Understanding Themes
5. **Movement** How did changes in climate affect the migration of early peoples from one part of the world to another?

100,000 B.C.　　　　75,000 B.C.　　　　50,000 B.C.　　　　25,000 B.C.

c. 100,000 B.C. Neanderthals spread from Africa into Europe and Asia.

c. 50,000 B.C. Modern humans originate in Africa.

c. 15,000 B.C. World population reaches about 2 million.

Section 2

The Appearance of *Homo Sapiens*

Setting the Scene

▶ **Terms to Define**
   domesticate, deity

▶ **People to Meet**
   Neanderthals, Cro-Magnons

▶ **Places to Locate**
   Neander Valley, Lascaux, Vallon-Pont-d'Arc, Jericho, Çatal Hüyük

 **ind Out** What were the achievements of the earliest humans?

The Storyteller

The first sign of animal domestication we have discovered, at some of the earliest human settlements, is not of something that pulled a plow, or was eaten; it is the dog. This creature, which willingly chooses a human as the leader of its lifelong pack, was humankind's first friend, it seems, as well as its best. Certain species began to thrive under human care; and humans rearranged their lives to care for the animals that now came to depend on them.

—adapted from *Women's Work: The First 20,000 Years*, Elizabeth Wayland Barber, 1994

Paleolithic scraper

Homo erectus discovered, used, and improved upon numerous aspects of culture that are basic to present-day life. These accomplishments occurred extremely slowly, however, taking place over many thousands of years. When *Homo sapiens*, the modern human species, appeared, cultural changes began occurring with much greater frequency and took on greater sophistication. In 1995 archaeologists uncovered in the Democratic Republic of the Congo, a number of 80,000-year-old barbed points and blades. This find indicates that humans made the first sophisticated tools in Africa and at a much earlier date than had been believed.

The Neanderthals

Evidence of early *Homo sapiens* dates back about 200,000 years. The first *Homo sapiens* probably were the **Neanderthals** (nee•AN•duhr•TAWLZ). Anthropologists named them after the **Neander Valley** in Germany where their remains were first discovered in the A.D. 1850s. Fossil evidence indicates that Neanderthal people may have originated in Africa and began spreading into Europe and Asia about 100,000 years ago.

Neanderthals stood about 5.5 feet (1.7 meters) tall. Their brains were slightly larger than those of modern human beings, and their bodies were stocky, with thick bones and very muscular necks and shoulders. Some scientists today believe that these distinctive physical characteristics enabled Neanderthals to adapt to colder climates.

Technological Skills

Like their predecessors, Neanderthals were nomadic hunter-gatherers who used fire for warmth and for cooking their food, but their toolmaking ability was more sophisticated than that of *Homo erectus*. Neanderthals skillfully crafted stone knives, spear points, and bone tools. Hide-cleaning and food-preparing tools were made of flakes struck from flint or whatever other kind of stone was available. The flakes were delicately shaped by chipping away small pieces from one or more edges of the stone.

Ways of Life

Most Neanderthals lived in small groups of 35 to 50 people. Because they were nomads, Neanderthals did not live in permanent homes. In good weather or warm climates, they lived in open-air camps along the shores of lakes or rivers. In several places, archaeologists have found the remains of Neanderthal shelters built of branches and animal skins. In colder climates, Neanderthals lived together in caves or under the overhangs of cliffs. Heavy clothing made from animal skins must have been worn to fight off the cold.

Culture and Beliefs

The Neanderthals were advanced culturally. They cared for their sick and aged, and may have been the first to practice medicine. A number of Neanderthal fossils show signs of serious injuries that had completely healed before death. Neanderthals also apparently had a belief in life after death. They covered the bodies of their dead with flowers and buried them in shallow graves with food, tools, and weapons.

Homo Sapiens Sapiens

Most scientists believe that modern humans, or *Homo sapiens sapiens*, originated in Africa about 50,000 years ago. Within 20,000 years, this new group dominated almost every continent in the world, including Australia and North America and

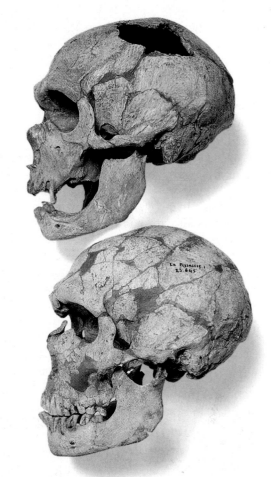

Visualizing History *Homo neanderthalensis* **fossil skulls found in caves in France resemble the original fossil skull from the Neander Valley in Germany. Neanderthals were short, sturdy hunter-gatherers.** *How did Neanderthals adapt to cold weather?*

South America. Many scientists believe that as *Homo sapiens sapiens* appeared in various places, they may have come into contact with Neanderthals and even *Homo erectus*. With the extinction of the Neanderthals and *Homo erectus*, *Homo sapiens sapiens* became the only hominids left on Earth.

The Cro-Magnons

The earliest *Homo sapiens sapiens* in Europe are called **Cro-Magnons**, after the rock shelter in France where their remains were first found in the A.D. 1860s. Since then, a wealth of Cro-Magnon remains have been found in other parts of Europe and in eastern and central Asia. Similar forms of modern humans have been discovered in Russia, China, Southeast Asia, and all over Africa.

The Cro-Magnons were taller but less robust than the Neanderthals. They brought with them improved technology and a more sophisticated

Footnotes to History

The First Razors
Archaeologists have unearthed evidence that prehistoric men were shaving as early as 18,000 B.C. Some Cro-Magnon cave paintings portray beardless men, and early Cro-Magnon grave sites contain sharpened shells that were the first razors. Later, people hammered razors out of bronze, and eventually, out of iron.

culture. Although they still made their living by hunting and gathering, their methods of food gathering were more efficient, and their hunting techniques were more effective than those of earlier groups.

Cro-Magnon Technology

The many advances the Cro-Magnons made in their toolmaking technology transformed human life. Their blades were thinner and had sharper cutting edges than those of the Neanderthals. The Cro-Magnons used bone, antler, and ivory to make new kinds of tools—hammers, hoes, and pincers. Soon they were fishing with bone fishhooks and using bone needles to sew fitted leather clothes.

With the invention of the stone ax, Cro-Magnons could chop down trees and shape them into canoes. Soon they were traveling down rivers and along seacoasts. They may have used rafts to cross 50 miles (80 km) of sea to reach Australia.

Cro-Magnon hunters also invented long-distance weapons—the spear-thrower and the bow and arrow. Now they could hunt several animals at once and larger animals, too, such as woolly mammoths and bison. The food supply increased and with it the number of people on Earth. Anthropologists estimate that by 15,000 B.C., the world population of human beings stood at a little more than 2 million.

Social Life

The Cro-Magnons' increased food supply had political and social consequences as well. Because it was not possible for a lone band of Cro-Magnons to carry out a big-game hunt, it became necessary for four or five unrelated bands to cooperate, often for weeks at a time. The cooperating bands probably needed formal rules in order to get along, giving rise in turn to leaders who devised and enforced the rules. The evidence for Cro-Magnon leaders consists of high-status burials. Archaeologists have discovered certain Cro-Magnons buried with ivory daggers, amber beads, and other signs of high rank.

Cro-Magnons at first lived in a variety of temporary structures. Some lived inside cave

Images of the Times

Early Human Technology

Although they are difficult to date precisely, ancient artifacts provide important clues to early human life.

Discovered in France, this bison licking its flank was carved from bone during the Mesolithic period–12,000–8000 B.C.

A Paleolithic scraper, c. 70,000–50,000 B.C., flaked by repeated blows, helped ancient people dig up roots, shape wood, and cut meat.

entrances, while others built huts in forested areas. As better hunting methods developed, Cro-Magnons built more permanent homes. Long houses holding many families were made of stone blocks. There is archaeological evidence that communities of 30 to 100 people lived together.

Cave Paintings

To their technological advances, the Cro-Magnons added accomplished artistry. They created cave paintings like those found at **Lascaux** (la •SKOH) and **Vallon-Pont-d'Arc** (vah•YOHN pohn DAHRK), both in France, as well as those at numerous other cave sites in Spain and Africa. Researchers so far can only speculate on the purpose behind the mysterious wall images. Perhaps the hunting scenes were educational, designed to teach young hunters how to recognize prey. On the other hand, the Cro-Magnon painters may have been reaching out to the spiritual world, creating images meant to have mystical powers that would help the hunters.

Archaeologists have discovered some Cro-Magnon figures sculpted from clay or carved from reindeer antlers. They have also found figures of ivory and bone decorated with animal drawings and abstract designs. Some of these artifacts may well have been used in magic rituals.

The Neolithic Revolution

During the Neolithic period and immediately after, humanity made one of its greatest cultural advances. New environments had developed with the end of the last Ice Age, and forests and grasslands appeared in many areas. Over some 5,000 years, people gradually shifted from gathering and hunting food to producing food. Because new agricultural methods led to tremendous changes in peoples' lifestyles, this period is usually called the Neolithic Revolution.

Sumerian cuneiform laid the foundation of writing about 3000 B.C.

REFLECTING ON THE TIMES

1. What clue to early human life does the bison licking its flank provide?
2. How did people store information about the past before writing began?

In a sense, the Mesolithic period was a forerunner of the Neolithic Revolution. Most of the cultural changes of the Mesolithic period came in methods of obtaining food. People domesticated, or tamed for human purposes, the dog and used it to help them hunt small game. They also domesticated the goat to use for meat and milk. Early farmers invented the sickle for cutting wild grains so that they could eat the seeds. Pottery, made from sun-hardened clay, was far more effective for carrying and storing food and water than the pouches of animal skin people had used previously.

The Dawn of Agriculture

The Neolithic Revolution not only took place slowly, but also began at different times in different parts of the world. Archaeologists have found evidence of agriculture in the Middle East dating as far back as 8000 B.C. In contrast, China and the Americas did not have agriculture until between 5000 B.C. and 4000 B.C.

The crops that Neolithic people domesticated varied from place to place, depending on the varieties of wild plants and on the crops best adapted to the region's climate—wheat and barley in the Middle East, rice in Southeast Asia, and corn in the Americas. Farmers in Africa cultivated bananas and yams, and farmers in South America grew potatoes. Neolithic people also domesticated animals. They used cattle, pigs, and sheep for meat and sometimes milk. Chickens provided eggs as well as meat.

Farming in many ways made life easier. It brought a steady food supply and enabled people to stay longer in one place. However, farmers had to work harder and longer than earlier hunters and gatherers.

Early Humans

	Homo Habilis	Homo Erectus	Homo Sapiens	
Years B.C.	**2.5–1.5 million**	**1.8 million–30,000**	**200,000–35,000**	**40,000–8,000**
			Neanderthal	**Cro-Magnon**
TECHNOLOGICAL INNOVATIONS	• Crude stone tools	• Hand axes and other flaked stone tools • Caves used and pits dug • Clothing of animal skins • Fire controlled for warmth, protection, and cooking	• Spear points and hide scrapers • Shelters built or caves improved • Skins laced for clothing	• Knives, chisel, spear-thrower, bow and arrow • Bone tools: needle, fish hook, harpoon • Fish nets, canoes • Sewed leather clothing • Sun-hardened pottery
SOCIAL BEHAVIORS	• Limited speech • Food gathering and scavenging	• Beginnings of language • Nomadic bands • Hunting-gathering	• Planned burials of dead • Care for disabled members of the community	• Cooperative big-game hunts • Status burials for leaders • Possible magic rituals with cave painting and carved, sculpted artifacts

Chart Study The category "Technological Innovations" describes items found in archaeological digs and dated to a specific period. Interpretation of likely prehistoric social behaviors, however, depends mostly on inferences made by archaeologists and anthropologists.

What evidence do researchers have to support the theory that the social behaviors listed above really existed?

The First Villages

Now that they could produce food, many more people survived. Anthropologists estimate that by 4000 B.C. the world population had risen to 90 million. Once they had agriculture, people could also settle in communities instead of wandering as nomads. Soon, agricultural villages of about 200 or so inhabitants began to develop where soil was fertile and water abundant. Archaeologists date one of the earliest such villages—**Jericho**, in the modern West Bank—back to 8000 B.C. Another village, **Çatal Hüyük** (CHAH•tuhl hoo• YOOK), in present-day Turkey, dates from 7000 to 6300 B.C.

Çatal Hüyük is one of the largest Neolithic villages that archaeologists have so far discovered. Its people built rectangular, flat-roofed houses of mud bricks placed in wooden frames. Houses of several related families made up a compound with shared walls. People had to walk across roofs. The villagers of Çatal Hüyük also painted the interior walls of their windowless houses with vivid scenes of hunting and other activities.

Technological Advances

Neolithic farmers eventually made their agricultural work easier and more productive by inventing the plow and by training oxen to pull it. They also learned how to fertilize their fields with ashes, fish, and manure.

The relatively steady food supply quickened the pace of technological advance. Neolithic villagers invented the loom and began weaving textiles of linen and wool. They invented the wheel and used it for transportation. They found a way to bake clay bricks for construction. They learned how to hammer the metals copper, lead, and gold to make jewelry and weapons. In 1991, for example, the frozen body of a late Neolithic Age man was discovered in the Italian Alps. The 5,000-year-old "Iceman" wore well-made fur and leather clothing and shoes stuffed with grass. He carried a wooden backpack, a copper ax, a bow, and arrows.

The agricultural way of life led to many other changes. People created calendars to measure the

Visualizing History This Neolithic flint knife and these cooking utensils are from Çatal Hüyük. *What evidence tends to show that these people enjoyed art?*

seasons and determine when to plant crops. Because their food supply depended on land ownership, people now cared about such matters as boundary lines and rules of inheritance. Warfare probably came into being as villages competed for land and water.

Neolithic people also believed in many deities, or gods and goddesses. The spirits that supposedly surrounded them throughout nature were transformed into humanlike gods and goddesses with the power to help or hurt people. The people of Çatal Hüyük, for example, set up shrines at which they offered gifts in honor of their deities.

SECTION 2 REVIEW

Recall
1. **Define** domesticate, deity.
2. **Identify** Neanderthals, Cro-Magnons, Neolithic Revolution.
3. **List** the innovations made during the Neolithic period.

Critical Thinking
4. **Evaluating Information** Does the use of agriculture by Neolithic peoples deserve to be called a revolution? Give reasons.

Understanding Themes
5. **Innovation** Discuss how technological developments affected the food supplies of early peoples in various parts of the world.

c. 10,000 B.C.
Last Ice Age ends.

c. 8000 B.C.
Agriculture begins
in various places.

c. 3500 B.C.
Cities develop
along the Tigris
and Euphrates Rivers.

c. 1500 B.C.
First urban
communities in
East Asia appear.

Section 3

Emergence of Civilization

Setting the Scene

▶ **Terms to Define**
civilization, economy, artisan, cultural
diffusion, myth

▶ **People to Meet**
the Sumerians

▶ **Places to Locate**
Nile, Tigris-Euphrates, Indus, and Huang
River valleys

Find Out ▶ What economic, political, and social
changes resulted from the rise of cities?

The Storyteller

*Archaeological evidence leaves little doubt
that women played key roles in every aspect of life
in Old Europe. "In the temple workshops …
females made and decorated quantities of various
pots appropriate to different rites. Next to
the altar of the temple stood a vertical loom on which were probably
woven the sacred garments…. The
most sophisticated creations of Old
Europe—the most exquisite vases,
sculptures, etc. now extant—were
women's work."*

*—from The Early
Civilizations of Europe,
(Monograph for Indo-
European Studies,
UCLA, 1980), Marija
Gimbutas*

Mohenjo-Daro mother goddess

Over thousands of years, some of the
early farming villages evolved slowly
into complex societies, known as
civilizations. The people of a civilization lived in a
highly organized society with an advanced knowledge of farming, trade, government, art, and science. The word *civilization* comes from the Latin
word *civitas*, meaning "city," and most historians
equate the rise of civilizations with the rise of cities.
Because most city dwellers learned the art of writing, the development of cities also marks the beginning of history.

River Valley Civilizations

As with agriculture, cities formed at different
times in different parts of the world. Many of the
earliest civilizations, however, had one thing in
common: They rose from farming settlements in
river valleys like that of the **Nile** River in northeastern Africa. The earliest cities that archaeologists
have uncovered so far lie in the valley of the **Tigris
and Euphrates** (yoo•FRAYT•eez) Rivers in present-
day Iraq and date back to about 3500 B.C. Cities
arose in the **Indus** River valley in South Asia some
1,000 years later. The first urban communities in
East Asia appeared about 1500 B.C. in the **Huang
He** (HWONG HUH) valley. By about 1000 B.C.
cities were flourishing in Europe and in the
Americas, and by 750 B.C. in East Africa.

Early river valley civilizations also shared several other basic features. People's labor was specialized, with different men and women doing different jobs. The civilization depended on advanced
technology, such as metalworking skills. Each civilization always had some form of government to
coordinate large-scale cooperative efforts such as
building irrigation systems. The people in each

Behind high baked-brick walls the people of the ancient city of Mohenjo-Daro, near the Indus River in Pakistan, used four-wheeled carts to carry grain to a large granary. *What was the value of surplus food to the development of a civilization?*

civilization also shared a complex system of values and beliefs.

Not all societies formed civilizations, however. Some people continued to live in small agricultural villages, while others lived by hunting and gathering. Some nomadic people built a specialized culture that relied on moving herds of domesticated animals in search of good pasture.

The Economy of a Civilization

The ways in which people use their environment to meet their material needs is known as an economy. The economy of early civilizations depended on their farmers' growing surplus food. With extra food, fewer men and women had to farm and more could earn their living in other ways.

First Irrigation Systems

A major reason that farmers could produce surpluses of grain crops was that early civilizations built massive irrigation systems. Neolithic farmers had relied at first on rainfall to water their crops. Later, farmers transported water to grow the crops by digging ditches from a nearby river to their fields. Then they began building small canals and simple reservoirs.

Farmers also built earthen dikes and dams to control flooding in their valley by the river itself. They could now count on a reasonably steady flow of water and prevent destructive flooding.

Specialization of Labor

As men and women continued to specialize in ways of earning a living, artisans—workers skilled in a craft—became increasingly productive and creative. The longer they worked at one task, such as producing storage vessels, the more they learned about how to handle available materials, such as different types of clay. Gradually they turned out larger quantities of goods and improved the quality of their products.

Jewelry, eating utensils, weapons, and other goods were made by hammering copper, lead, and gold. Later, metalworkers in the early civilizations learned to make alloys, or mixtures of metals. The most important alloy was bronze, a reddish-brown metal made by mixing melted copper and tin. Historians refer to the period that followed the Stone Age as the Bronze Age, when bronze replaced flint and stone as the chief material for weapons and tools.

Bronze, harder than either copper or tin alone, took a sharper cutting edge. Artisans also found it much easier to cast bronze, or shape the liquid metal by pouring it into a mold to harden. Because the copper- and tin-containing ores needed to make bronze were scarce, however, the metal was expensive and therefore used only by kings, priests, and soldiers.

Long-Distance Trade

The search for new sources of copper and tin is an example of the long-distance trade that accompanied the rise of early civilizations. At first farmers and artisans traded within their own communities. They eventually began traveling to nearby areas to exchange goods. After a while merchants, a specialized class of traders, began to handle trade, and expeditions soon were covering longer routes.

Some long-distance trade moved overland by means of animal caravans. Some goods were transported by water. People made rafts and boats for travel on rivers. After a time, people learned how to harness the force of the wind, and rivers and seacoasts became filled with sailing ships.

Along with goods, ideas were actively shared. This exchange of goods and ideas when cultures come in contact is known as cultural diffusion. Although early civilizations developed many similar ideas independently, other ideas arose in a few areas and then spread throughout the world by cultural diffusion. When ancient peoples learned about the technology and ideas of different civilizations, the new knowledge stimulated them to improve their own skills and way of life.

The Rise of Cities

Civilizations grew both more prosperous and more complex. Early cities had from 5,000 to 30,000 residents. A population of this size could not function in the same way that a Neolithic village of 200 inhabitants had.

Planning and Leadership

Ancient cities faced several problems unknown in the Neolithic period. Because city residents depended on farmers for their food, they had to make certain that farmers regularly brought their surplus food to city markets. At the same time, farmers could not build dams, dig irrigation ditches, and maintain reservoirs on their own. As civilizations prospered, they drew the envy of nomadic groups, who would repeatedly raid and pillage farms and attack caravans. In short, the first cities needed a way of supervising and protecting agriculture and trade.

The early city dwellers found two solutions to these problems. First, ancient cities organized a group of government officials whose job it was to oversee the collection, storage, and distribution of farming surpluses. These officials also organized and directed the labor force needed for large-scale construction projects, such as irrigation systems and public buildings. Second, ancient cities hired professional soldiers to guard their territory and trade routes.

Government leaders, military officials, and priests belonged to a ruling class often led by a king, although women also held positions of authority. The ruling class justified its power by means of religion. According to ancient beliefs, the land produced food only if the gods and goddesses looked on the people with favor. One of the king's main functions, therefore, was to assist priests in carrying out religious ceremonies to ensure an abundant harvest. The first kings were probably elected, but in time they inherited their positions.

Levels of Social Standing

Archaeological evidence for the position of the ruling class can be found both in the treasures with which they were buried and in the physical layout of the ancient cities. At the city's center was an area that held the most imposing religious and government buildings. Nearby stood the residences of the ruling class. Next to these came the houses of the merchants. Farther out, the shops and dwellings of specific groups of artisans—such as weavers or smiths—were established in special streets or quarters. Farmers, as well as sailors and fishers, lived on the city's outskirts. Archaeological evidence suggests too that slaves, who were probably captured in battle, lived in many parts of the city.

Invention of Writing

Many archaeologists think that writing originated with the records that priests kept of the wheat, cloth, livestock, and other items they received as religious offerings. At first the priests used marks and pictures, called pictograms, to represent products. After a time they used the marks and pictures to represent abstract ideas and, later still, to represent sounds. Priestly records listed the individual men and women who were heads of households, landowners, and merchants. Soon the priests were also recording such information as the king's battle victories, along with legal codes, medical texts, and observations of the stars.

Systems of Values

Among the materials recorded by the priest-hoods in early civilizations were myths, traditional stories explaining how the world was formed, how people came into being, and what they owed their creator. The priests of **the Sumerians** in the Tigris-Euphrates River valley wrote their myth of creation, for example, on seven clay tablets.

According to the Sumerian story, before creation there were two gods, Apsu the First Father and Tiamat the First Mother. They married and had many children. "But each generation of gods grew taller than its parents … [and] the younger gods could do things their parents had never tried to do." Eventually Apsu's great-grandson Ea made a

magic spell and killed Apsu. Ea's son Marduk killed Tiamat. Then:

66 Marduk turned again to the body of
Tiamat.
He slit her body like a shellfish into two parts.
Half he raised on high and set it up as sky.…
He marked the places for the stars.…
He planned the days and nights, the months and years.
From the lower half of Tiamat's body, Marduk made the earth.
Her bones became its rocks.
Her blood its rivers and oceans.…
'We need creatures to serve us,' he said.
'I will create man and woman who must learn to plow land to plant, and make the earth bring forth food and drink for us.
I will make them of clay.'… 99

—"Enuma Elish," Sumerian account
of creation from *The Seven Tablets
of Creation*, date unknown

After relating how the people drained marshes

One of the land bridges that formed during the Ice Ages joined Siberia, the easternmost part of Asia, with Alaska, the westernmost part of the Americas. Modern historians have named this land bridge Beringia, after the shallow Bering Strait that covers it today.

Approximately 40,000 years ago, groups of Cro-Magnons may have crossed Beringia from Asia to the Americas. According to some anthropologists, these groups were nomadic hunting bands in search of migrating herds of animals. We do not know whether the migrants crossed all at once or in successive waves.

From the north the migrants gradually moved south into new territory. Anthropologists estimate that their journey all the way to the southernmost tip of South America took about 600

generations. This equals a rate of migration of about 18 miles (29 kilometers) per generation, over 18,000 years.

Today, the availability of fast, safe, and mechanized transportation—by air and by water—makes migration easier and quicker from one place to another. As in the past, war, persecution, and disasters—such as famines and epidemics—have forced people to flee their homelands. At the same time, people have also been attracted to new places by economic opportunity—a better job and higher standards of living.

Linking Past and Present   ACTIVITY

Research and write a brief essay comparing and contrasting prehistoric and modern migrations. Focus on methods and routes of travel, reasons for migrating, and the challenges faced in the new homeland.

Little Diomedes Island, Bering Strait

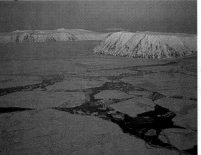

for farmland, built walled cities, learned to make bricks, and built a great temple at the center of their biggest city, the myth continues:

> 66 Daily they sang praises to Marduk,
>   supreme among the gods
> He who created the vast spaces and fashioned earth and men;
> He who both creates and destroys; who is god of storms and of light;
> He who directs justice; a refuge for those in trouble;
> From whom no evil doer can escape;
> His wisdom is broad. His heart is wide. His sympathy is warm. 99

Creation myths have been found in every civilization. Because these myths vary from place to place, historians often examine them for evidence of a people's customs and values. For example, the seven Sumerian clay tablets could easily imply information about Sumer's values and beliefs. The clay tablets reveal that Marduk, though not the first god, had become—at the time the tablets were recorded—the leading one by supplanting the goddess Tiamat. The Sumerians seemed to believe too that evil should—and would—be punished. Apparently they also thought it was effective to praise and worship Marduk. Of course, the inferences an archaeologist can reasonably make from a myth are often limited and leave many unanswered questions.

SECTION 3 REVIEW

Recall
1. **Define** civilization, economy, artisan, cultural diffusion, myth.
2. **Identify** the Sumerians.
3. **Name** the four river valleys in which the world's earliest civilizations developed.

Where are these river valleys located?

Critical Thinking
4. **Synthesizing Information** Imagine that you rule a city in an early civilization. What instructions would you give to your government officials to

improve the living conditions of your people?

Understanding Themes
5. **Change** How did technological changes of the first civilizations improve toolmaking skills and the transportation of trade goods?

Understanding Map Projections

Greenland appears to be a larger landmass than Australia on some maps, yet Australia actually has a larger land area than Greenland. Have you ever wondered why?

Learning the Skill

When mapmakers attempt to transfer the three-dimensional surface of Earth to a flat surface, some inaccuracies occur. To accomplish this mapmakers use *projections*—an image produced when light from within the globe projects the globe's surface on a flat paper. These projections may stretch or shrink Earth's features, depending on the map's intended use.

Projections create two major kinds of maps. A *conformal map* shows land areas in their true shapes, while distorting their actual size. An *equal-area map* shows land areas in correct proportion to one another, but distorts shapes.

The map on this page is a *Cylindrical Projection (Mercator)*. Imagine wrapping a paper cylinder around the globe. A light from within projects the globe's surface on the paper. The resulting conformal projection makes Alaska appear larger than Mexico. Distortion is greatest near the Poles.

A *Conic Projection* is formed by placing a cone of paper over a lighted globe. This produces a cross between a conformal and an equal-area map. This projection is best to show areas in middle latitudes.

To understand map projections use the following steps:
- Compare the map to a globe.
- Determine the type of projection used.
- Identify the purpose of the projection.

Practicing the Skill

Turn to the map of the world in the Atlas. Compare the sizes and shapes of the features on this map to those on a globe. Based on this comparison, answer the following questions:
1. What is the map's projection?
2. How does the map distort Earth's features?
3. In what way does the map accurately present Earth's features?
4. Why did the mapmaker use this projection?

Applying the Skill

Compare the size of Antarctica as it appears on a map with Antarctica on a globe.

For More Practice

Turn to the Skill Practice in the Chapter Review on page 43 for more practice in understanding map projections.

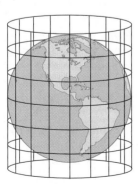

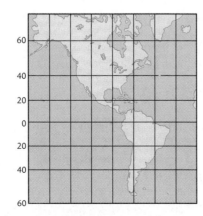

Cylindrical Projection *(Mercator): This projection is accurate along the line where the cylinder touches the globe, with great distortions near the Poles.*

Sygma

The Iceman

O n September 19, 1991, Helmut and Erika Simon, a German couple hiking near the border between Austria and Italy, wandered slightly off the trail. Suddenly Erika Simon caught sight of a small head and pair of shoulders emerging from the ice. The Simons thought they had stumbled across a discarded doll. In fact, they had found the solitary prehistoric traveler now known around the world as the Iceman.

At first the Iceman was thought to be 4,000 years old—which would have made the discovery remarkable enough. Scientists later discovered that the Iceman was at least 5,000 years old! In comparison, Tutankhamen, Egypt's boy-king, was born some 2,000 years later.

The Iceman is the oldest body ever retrieved from an Alpine glacier; the next-oldest was only 400 years old. At 10,530 feet (3,210 m),

▣ **Overcome by fatigue and cold, a mountaineer (above) lies down to die high in the Alps. Some 5,000 years later, the discovery of his well-preserved body, along with clothes and a copper ax, offers startling clues about how humans greeted the metal age in Europe.**

▣ **The Iceman (top) emerges from under a melting glacier.**

Greg Harlin/Wood Ronsaville Harlin, Inc.

Sygma

NGS Cartographic Division

Map labels:

FEET
0 5
NGS CARTOGRAPHIC DIVISION

DAGGER AND SHEATH

ICEMAN

GRASS CAPE FRAGMENT

QUIVER

BIRCH-BARK CONTAINER

AX

BOW

BACKPACK FRAME

AUSTRIA

SWITZ.

SITE ENLARGED

ITALY

the site where the Iceman lay is the highest elevation in Europe in which prehistoric human remains have been found. Not even traces of a campfire have ever been discovered at that height.

The body of the Iceman was preserved through sheer luck. Shortly after he died, the rocky hollow where he lay filled with snow. For thousands of years a glacier covered this pocket of snow, only a few yards over the Iceman's head. More commonly, a body caught in a glacier would be crushed and torn by the movement of the ice. Instead, the Iceman was naturally mummified.

In the four days following the discovery, many well-meaning hikers and officials tried to free the Iceman from the glacier. They took turns hacking and prodding around the body with ice axes and ski poles. Unfortunately, they damaged the Iceman and the artifacts found with him—in ways that 5,000 years of glaciation had not. One of the "rescuers" seized a stick to dig with, breaking it in the process; the stick turned out to be part of the hazel-wood-and-larch frame of the Iceman's backpack, a type of ancient artifact never seen before. Workers also snapped off the top

■ *The local coroner (above) and an assistant remove the corpse from his icy grave.*

■ *The Iceman was found at an elevation of 10,530 feet (3,210 m) on the Austrian-Italian border. His tools and backpack frame were located near his body.*

end of the Iceman's six-foot-long bow. What remained of the Iceman's clothing was torn off, as were parts of his body, and an officer using a jackhammer left a gaping hole in the Iceman's hip. To be sure, none of the salvagers suspected how old the Iceman was.

Not until five days after the discovery did an archaeologist examine the Iceman's body. Basing his estimate on the style of the ax found with the body, the archaeologist guessed that the Iceman was 4,000 years old.

Once officials knew the Iceman's approximate age, a rigorous effort to stabilize his condition began. The mummy was placed in a freezer, where the temperature was kept at a constant 21°F (-6°C) and the humidity at 98 percent—conditions much the same as those of the ice in which he had lain. The Iceman was not removed from the freezer for more than 20 minutes at a time, and then only for the most important scientific research. Part of that research was carbon-dating the Iceman to verify how old he was. Further chemical analysis revealed that the blade of his ax was not bronze, but nearly pure copper. He was, in fact, unique: a mummy from the Copper Age, which lasted in central Europe roughly from 4000 to 2200 B.C. Two different laboratories concluded that he was 5,000 to 5,500 years old.

&

THE ICEMAN'S DOMAIN was the Alps, stretching from southeast France to the Swiss-German border, and from Austria to northern Italy. Five thousand years ago these mountains were a vast wilderness. In the Copper Age, hardy voyagers trekked these ranges, and the goods they traded traveled even farther. We know from his tools and clothes that the Iceman was one of these

Iceman's artifacts photographed by Kenneth Garrett

rugged mountaineers.

The first half of the Copper Age was an era of climatic warming, when humans penetrated higher than ever into the Alps. The tree line climbed during the warming, game followed the forests, and hunters followed the game. Meadows above the tree line offered the best pastures for sheep, goats, and cattle and contained great green veins of a newly valued metal—which today we call copper. Copper changed the Alpine world forever, leading to the development of major trade routes between isolated valleys. Earlier, wealth was made through cattle or wheat. Copper was not only a form of portable wealth but also a stimulus for the development of specialized occupations. Men became smelters, axmakers, possibly even salesmen. The world's earliest known man-made copper objects—beads, pins,

A fragment of the Iceman's plaited-grass cape (above) was found next to his head.

This stone disk threaded with a leather thong (inset, top right) may have been worn to protect against evil.

The Iceman's copper ax is the oldest ever found in Europe with its bindings and handle intact (inset, bottom right).

A fungus on a string may have been a first-aid kit (inset, above left).

and awls—were made about 8000 B.C. in Turkey and Iran. There is evidence of copper mining in the Balkans by 5000 B.C. From there the technology spread west, reaching the Alps a thousand years later.

copper ax may tell us most. Its yew-wood handle ends in a gnarled joint, where a notch holds the blade. Dark birch gum held the blade firmly in position beneath a tightly wrapped thong of rawhide. It is a ribbed ax, rather than the more primitive flat ax that archaeologists would have expected to find.

Researchers who reconstructed what remained of the Iceman's clothing observed that his garment had been skillfully stitched together with sinew. Cruder repairs had been made, probably by the Iceman himself on his travels. This led researchers to believe that the Iceman had been part of a community, although he was used to fending for himself. Also, tiny pieces of a wheat that grew only at low altitudes, and bits of charcoal from a variety of trees found throughout the Alps were discovered with the Iceman, indicating that he may have come from southern Tirol (in Austria).

Included among the Iceman's possessions were a stick with a tip of antler used to sharpen flint blades; a deerskin quiver that contained 14 arrows; and an unfinished bow. His small flint dagger was similar to those found at other Copper Age sites, but no one had ever seen the kind of delicately woven sheath that held the dagger.

Central Europe's oldest known plow is more than a thousand years younger than the Iceman. Yet Copper Age artists cut images of plows on rocks. Rows of furrows have been found preserved at a major Copper Age religious complex excavated in northwest Italy, though experts believe plowing was ritualistic rather than agricultural.

The Iceman also had tattoo-like marks that might imply something about his spiritual life. Located on normally hidden places—his lower back, behind his knee, and on his ankle—the marks were not for

The Iceman's head was reconstructed by John Gurche, an anthropologically trained artist. He first sculpted a replica of the skull by using computer images, X rays, and CT scans of the Iceman. Gurche then added clay to duplicate the Iceman's mummified face, complete with smashed nose and lip. Next, he added muscles and fatty tissue, nasal cartilage, and glass eyes. Finally he made a new model of the head with soft urethane, tinted to suggest wind-burned skin. He completed the replica of the Iceman's head by adding human hair.

show. Perhaps they were meant to confer supernatural power or protection. So might the pair of fungi he carried, each pierced by a leather thong. Archaeologists have never seen anything like this artifact from that period. The fungi contain chemical substances now known to be antibiotic. If the Iceman used them to counteract illness, perhaps they also seemed magical to him.

We may never know what drew the Iceman to the mountain pass where he died. Perhaps he was a shepherd, a trader, or an outcast. But, in the late 20th century, it is our good fortune to have the opportunity to learn from this ambassador of the Copper Age.

The work of many researchers over the past 30 years tells us much about life during the Copper Age. Excavations have yielded bones that indicate that by around 5000 B.C. Alpine people had domesticated five animals: dogs, which were originally more important for food than companionship, cattle, sheep, goats, and pigs. Horses and chickens were still unknown in the Alps. Villagers grew wheat and barley and made linen clothes from flax. They had only recently discovered how to milk a cow and how to make cheese and butter. Their sheep may have been used for meat but not yet for wool. Many staple foods of today were still unknown, including potatoes, onions, and oats.

EVENTUALLY, THE ICEMAN'S possessions may tell us more than his body will. Of those possessions, his

Connections Across Time

Historical Significance Prehistoric people created the basics of human culture—for example, tools, language, and religious belief. In time, increased food supplies and a diverse labor force led to the rise of cities and civilizations. In ancient times, cities enabled large numbers of people to live together, to cooperate with each other, and to carry out many cultural activities. Today the populations of many cities are more than 100 times that of these first cities. Modern cities serve as complex economic, cultural, and political centers in a world that has become, in many ways, one global civilization.

Using Key Terms

Write the key term that completes each sentence. Then write a sentence for each term not chosen.

a. technology
b. artisan
c. myth
d. civilization
e. nomad
f. economy
g. anthropologist
h. prehistory
i. radiocarbon dating
j. archaeologist
k. artifact
l. cultural diffusion
m. culture

1. The period of time before people developed writing is called _____.
2. Among the techniques used by scientists for determining the age of organic remains is _____.
3. Over thousands of years, some of the early agricultural villages evolved into highly complex societies, known as _____ .
4. The exchange of goods and ideas when different peoples come in contact is known as _____.
5. _____ includes the skills and useful knowledge available to people for collecting materials and making objects necessary for survival.

Technology Activity

Using a Word Processor Search the Internet for information on recent discoveries about early humans. Narrow your search by using words such as *archaeology* and *anthropology*. On your word processor, create a chart to organize your information. Include headings such as location, date of discovery, results of discovery, and approximate time period of remains. Then in a paragraph, theorize about what caused the extinction of early humans.

Using Your History Journal

Evaluate your journal account of being stranded on a deserted island. What skills and knowledge, known to early humans but not to you, may have helped you survive?

Reviewing Facts

1. **Geography** Name the four land bridges used by prehistoric people during the Ice Ages.
2. **Geography** Locate the two places in which Cro-Magnons seem to have originated before spreading into other parts of the world.
3. **Culture** Explain why language is one of humanity's greatest achievements.
4. **Technology** Describe how the invention of the spear-thrower and the bow and arrow changed the Cro-Magnons' food supply.
5. **Culture** Explain the social, economic, and geographic factors that led to the rise of the world's first civilizations.
6. **History** State the ways archaeologists, anthropologists, historians, and geographers analyze limited evidence.

Critical Thinking

1. **Apply** What do you think are the three basic characteristics of a civilization?
2. **Analyze** What were the major cultural features of each period in the Stone Age?
3. **Synthesize** How do you think the invention of the stone ax might have changed the culture of a people who lived along the banks of a navigable river?

4. Evaluate What do you think was the most valuable skill that prehistoric people learned during the Paleolithic period? What was the most valuable skill learned during the Neolithic period?

Geography in History

1. Location Refer to the map below. What is the relative location of Mesopotamia?

2. Human/Environment Interaction Where in this area would ancient peoples have likely begun farming?

3. Human/Environment Interaction Why did early farmers build dikes and dams in the river valleys where they raised their crops?

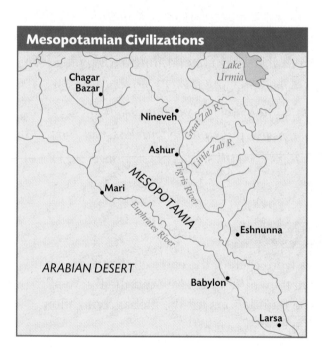

Mesopotamian Civilizations

Chagar Bazar
Lake Urmia
Nineveh
Great Zab R.
Ashur
Little Zab R.
Mari
MESOPOTAMIA
Tigris River
Eshnunna
Euphrates River
ARABIAN DESERT
Babylon
Larsa

Understanding Themes

1. Movement Describe the migrations of human beings from their places of origin to other parts of the world.

2. Innovation How did improvements in tool-making affect the way in which prehistoric people lived?

3. Change How did city life differ from village life in early civilizations?

Linking Past and Present

1. Many aspects of human culture are passed down from generation to generation. What cultural achievements of *Homo erectus*—from more than 200,000 years ago—do people still use today?

2. Government officials 5,000 years ago directed large-scale building projects, such as irrigation systems, and oversaw the collection, storage, and distribution of agricultural surpluses. Evaluate the effectiveness of their activities. How do government officials' activities in early civilizations compare with those of government officials in your community?

Skill Practice

Using a small tennis ball, place a dot on each side directly opposite one another to represent the North and South Poles. Cut paper strips in such a way that they could completely cover this "globe." (See the example below.)

1. Why are the cut strips shown on the example below wider at the middle than at each of the ends?

2. If the strips are laid down side-by-side on a flat surface, what object do they resemble or what pattern do they form?

3. What does this show about the problem of creating an accurate map of a round object on a flat surface?

4. The earth is a sphere, but it is somewhat pear-shaped—not a perfect sphere. What additional problem does this create for the cartographer who wants to make a very accurate map of the world?

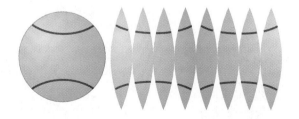

Chapter

2

4000–1000 B.C.

Early Civilizations

Chapter Themes

▶ **Relation to Environment** The Egyptians learn to control the floodwaters of the Nile River upon which their agriculture relies. *Section 1*

▶ **Cooperation** The peoples of the Fertile Crescent work together to build irrigation systems and cities. *Section 2*

▶ **Cultural Diffusion** Cities in early India develop close trading and cultural ties with the Fertile Crescent area. *Section 3*

▶ **Innovation** Early Chinese civilization excels in metal-casting skills. *Section 4*

The Storyteller

Under the blazing sun, a gigantic stone structure began to take shape on the desert sands of Egypt in northeastern Africa. A hundred thousand men toiled together, building a burial pyramid for Khufu, a king of Egypt about 2500 B.C. Gangs of laborers dragged huge blocks of limestone up winding ramps of dirt and brick to pile layer upon layer of stone. Farmers during the rest of the year, these laborers were compelled to work for the 3 or 4 months during which the annual flooding of the Nile River made farming impossible. It would take 20 years of their forced labor and more than 2 million blocks of stone before the Egyptians completed the massive pyramid. Today, the Great Pyramid built almost 5,000 years ago still stands at Giza, near the city of Cairo.

Historical Significance

In what ways were each of the early civilizations unique? How were they different? How did the river valley civilizations lay the foundations for the global civilization that we know today?

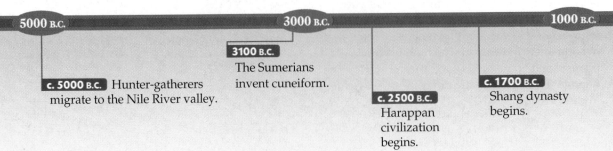

5000 B.C.	3000 B.C.	1000 B.C.

3100 B.C.
The Sumerians invent cuneiform.

c. 5000 B.C. Hunter-gatherers migrate to the Nile River valley.

c. 2500 B.C.
Harappan civilization begins.

c. 1700 B.C.
Shang dynasty begins.

Fowling scene from a tomb at Thebes
along the Nile River, Egypt

Your History Journal

Sumerian scribes studied at special schools called eddubas. There they learned cuneiform writing. After reading Section 2, write a short creative account of a scribe's day at an edduba.

3000 B.C.   2000 B.C.   1000 B.C.

c. 3000 B.C.
King Narmer unifies Egypt.

c. 1700s B.C.
The Hyksos
invade Egypt.

c. 1480 B.C.
Queen Hatshepsut
comes to power.

c. 945 B.C.
Egypt enters
long period of
foreign rule.

Section 1

The Nile Valley

Setting the Scene

▶ **Terms to Define**
monarchy, dynasty, theocracy, bureaucracy, pharaoh, empire, polytheism, hieroglyphics

▶ **People to Meet**
Narmer, Hatshepsut, Thutmose III, Akhenaton, Ramses II

▶ **Places to Locate**
Nile River valley, Memphis, Thebes

Find Out Why was Egypt called the "gift of the Nile"?

The Storyteller

Live for today; the afterlife will come soon enough! The following message about the brief pleasures of this life demonstrates that Egyptian poets sometimes sang what their wealthy patrons liked to hear:

"The pharaohs, those ancient gods, rest now in their pyramids. The people who built houses; their walls have crumbled, as if they had never been! Listen! Put perfume upon your head, wear fine linen. Make holiday! … No one who has died has ever returned."

—freely adapted from "Song of the Harper," *Journal of Near Eastern Studies 4*, 1945, translated by Miriam Lichtheim

King Narmer

One of the world's first civilizations developed along the banks of the Nile River in northeastern Africa. The **Nile River valley**'s early inhabitants called their land *Kemet*, meaning "black land," after the dark soil. Later, the ancient Greeks would name the Nile area *Egypt*. Of the four early river valley civilizations, people today probably know the most about the ancient Egyptian civilization. People still marvel at its remains in modern Egypt—especially the enormous Sphinx, the wondrous pyramids, and the mummies buried in lavish tombs.

A River Valley and Its People

Running like a ribbon through great expanses of desert, the Nile River for thousands of years has shaped the lives of the Egyptians. The land of Egypt receives little rainfall, but its people have relied instead on the Nile's predictable yearly floods to bring them water.

At 4,160 miles (6,690 km) in length, the Nile River is the world's longest river. Several sources in the highlands of East Africa feed the Nile. The river then takes a northward route to the Mediterranean Sea. On its course through Egypt the Nile crosses six cataracts, or waterfalls. Because of the cataracts the Nile is not completely navigable until it reaches its last 650 miles (1,040 km). Before emptying into the Mediterranean, the Nile splits into many branches, forming a marshy, fan-shaped delta.

The Gifts of the River

The green Nile Valley contrasts sharply with the vast desert areas that stretch for hundreds of miles on either side. Rich black soil covers the river's banks and the Nile Delta. From late spring through summer, heavy tropical rains in central Africa and melting mountain snow in East Africa add to the Nile's volume. As a result the river overflows its banks and floods the land nearby. The floodwaters recede in late fall, leaving behind thick deposits of silt.

As early as 5000 B.C., nomadic hunter-gatherers of northeastern Africa began to settle by the Nile. They took up a farming life regulated by the river's seasonal rise and fall, growing cereal crops such as wheat and barley. The Nile also provided these Neolithic farmers with ducks and geese in its marshlands and fish in its waters. The early Egyptians harvested papyrus growing wild along the banks of the Nile, using the long, thin reeds to make rope, matting, sandals, baskets, and later on, sheets of paperlike writing material.

Uniting Egypt

Protected from foreign invasion by deserts and cataracts, the early farming villages by the Nile prospered. In time a few strong leaders united villages into small kingdoms, or monarchies, each under the unrestricted rule of its king. The weaker kingdoms eventually gave way to the stronger. By 4000 B.C. ancient Egypt consisted of two large kingdoms: Lower Egypt in the north, in the Nile Delta, and Upper Egypt in the south, in the Nile Valley.

Around 3000 B.C., **Narmer**, also known as Menes (MEE•neez), a king of Upper Egypt, gathered the forces of the south and led them north to invade and conquer Lower Egypt. Narmer set up the first government that ruled all of the country. He governed both Lower Egypt and Upper Egypt from a capital city he had built at **Memphis**, near the border of the two kingdoms.

Narmer's reign marked the beginning of the first Egyptian dynasty, or line of rulers from one family. From 3000 B.C. until 332 B.C., a series of 30 dynasties ruled Egypt. Historians have organized the dynasties into three great periods: the Old Kingdom, the Middle Kingdom, and the New Kingdom.

The Old Kingdom

The Old Kingdom lasted from about 2700 B.C. to 2200 B.C. During the first centuries of the unified kingdom, Upper Egypt and Lower Egypt kept their separate identities as kingdoms. In time, however, Egypt built a strong national government under its kings. It also developed the basic features of its civilization.

CONNECTIONS

Geography

Stemming the Flood

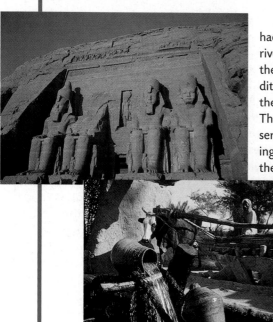

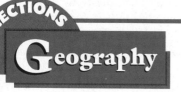

Ancient Egyptians had to take control of their river environment. Over the years farmers built ditches and canals to carry the floodwaters to basins. There the silt settled and served as fertilizer for planting crops. Machines, such as the shadoof, lifted water to cultivated land. Farmers eventually built dams and reservoirs, making year-round irrigation possible.

Built in the 1960s, the Aswan High Dam in southeastern Egypt trapped the waters of the Nile in a huge reservoir for later irrigation. When the rising waters of the Nile behind the dam threatened to destroy statues of Ramses II, engineers had to move the statues to higher ground. Today, the dam generates electrical power and protects against flooding. Because the dam prevents the Nile from flowing over the valley land, however, the floodwaters no longer deposit fertile silt annually. Farmers must add expensive chemical fertilizers to their fields. The absence of silt has also increased land erosion along the Nile.

Linking Past and Present ACTIVITY

Describe ancient ways of controlling rivers. How are the Nile and other rivers "tamed" today? Why might people object to some modern methods of river control?

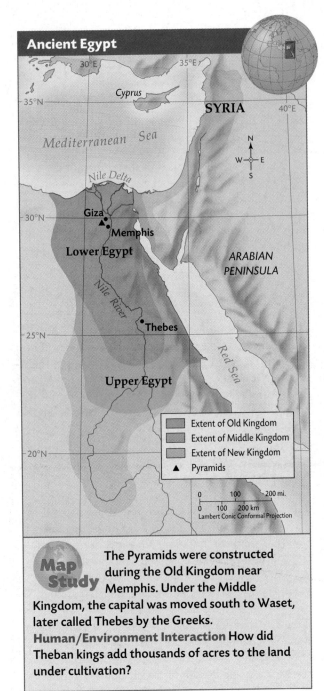

Ancient Egypt

Extent of Old Kingdom
Extent of Middle Kingdom
Extent of New Kingdom
▲ **Pyramids**

0   100   200 mi.
0 100 200 km
Lambert Conic Conformal Projection

Map Study The Pyramids were constructed during the Old Kingdom near Memphis. Under the Middle Kingdom, the capital was moved south to Waset, later called Thebes by the Greeks.
Human/Environment Interaction How did Theban kings add thousands of acres to the land under cultivation?

The Egyptian Monarchy

The Egyptian people regarded their king as a god who ruled over all Egyptians. Such a government, in which the same person is both the religious leader and the political leader, is called a theocracy. As a god, the king performed many ritual acts believed to benefit the entire kingdom, such as cutting the first ripe grain to ensure a good harvest. As political leader, the king wielded absolute power, issuing commands regarded as the law of the land.

Unable to carry out all official duties himself,

the king delegated many responsibilities to a bureaucracy, a group of government officials headed by the king's vizier, or prime minister. Through the vizier and other bureaucrats the king controlled trade and collected taxes. He also indirectly supervised the building of dams, canals, and storehouses for grain—all crucial to survival for an agriculture-based civilization.

The Pyramids: A Lasting Legacy

To honor their god-kings and to provide them with an eternal place of rest, the Egyptians of the Old Kingdom built lasting monuments—the Pyramids. The Step Pyramid was built for King Djoser in the mid-2600s B.C. Overlooking Memphis, it was the first large, all-stone building in the world. Later the Egyptians constructed the three Pyramids at Giza, which stand today as testimony to Egyptian engineering skills. The Great Pyramid, the largest of the three, stands 481 feet (147 m) high. Long, narrow passageways lead to the king's burial chamber deep within the pyramid.

The Egyptians believed that a king's soul continued to guide the kingdom after death. Before entombing a dead king in his pyramid, they first preserved the king's body from decay by a procedure called embalming. Next they wrapped the dried, shrunken body—called a mummy—with long strips of linen and placed it in an elaborate coffin. Only then could the coffin lie in the burial chamber of the pyramid along with the king's clothing, weapons, furniture, and jewelry—personal possessions the king could enjoy in the afterlife.

The Middle Kingdom

Around 2200 B.C., the kings in Memphis began to lose their power as ambitious nobles fought each other for control of Egypt. The stable, ordered world of the Old Kingdom entered a period of upheaval and violence. Then, around 2050 B.C., a new dynasty reunited Egypt and moved the capital south to **Thebes**, a city in Upper Egypt. This new kingdom, known as the Middle Kingdom, would last until after 1800 B.C.

In time Theban kings became as powerful as the rulers of the Old Kingdom and brought unruly local governments under their control. They supported irrigation projects that added thousands of acres to the land already under cultivation. The Theban dynasty seized new territory for Egypt, setting up fortresses along the Nile to capture Nubia (part of modern Sudan) and launching military campaigns against Syria. Theban kings also ordered construction of a canal between the Nile and the Red Sea, and as a result, Egyptian ships traded along the coasts of the Arabian Peninsula and East Africa.

In the 1700s B.C., local leaders began to challenge the kings' power again, shattering the peace and prosperity of the Middle Kingdom. At the same time, Egypt also faced its first serious threat—invasion by the Hyksos (HIHK•SAHS), a people from western Asia. The Hyksos swept across the desert into Egypt with new tools for war—bronze weapons and horse-drawn chariots. So armed, they easily conquered the Egyptians, who fought on foot with copper and stone weapons. The Hyksos established a new dynasty that ruled for about 110 years.

The New Kingdom

The Egyptians despised their Hyksos masters. To overthrow Hyksos rule, the Egyptians learned to use Hyksos weapons and adopted the horse-drawn chariots of their conquerors. About 1600 B.C. Ahmose (ah•MOH•suh), an Egyptian prince, raised an army and drove the Hyksos out.

The Great Pyramid (left), built for King Khufu (Cheops), rises on the Nile River's west bank in northern Egypt. The smaller pyramid (right) was constructed for King Khafre (Chephren). *Why did the Egyptians build pyramids for their kings?*

Pharaohs Rule an Empire

Ahmose founded a new Egyptian dynasty—the first of the New Kingdom. He and his successors assumed the title pharaoh, an Egyptian word meaning "great house of the king." Ahmose devoted his energies to rebuilding Egypt, restoring abandoned temples, and reopening avenues of trade. The pharaohs who followed him, however, used large armies to realize their dreams of conquest. They pressed farther to the east and into the rest of Africa than had the kings of the Middle Kingdom.

Around 1480 B.C. Queen **Hatshepsut** (hat•SHEHP•soot) came to power in Egypt. She first ruled with her husband and then ruled on behalf of her stepson **Thutmose** (thoot•MOH•suh) **III**, who was too young to govern. Finally she had herself crowned pharaoh. Hatshepsut assumed all the royal trappings of power, including the false beard traditionally worn by Egyptian kings. Hatshepsut carried out an extensive building program, which included a great funeral temple and a tomb built

into the hills of what is now called the Valley of the Kings.

Thutmose III did reclaim the throne at Hatshepsut's death and soon after marched with a large army out of Egypt toward the northeast. He conquered Syria and pushed the Egyptian frontier to the northern part of the Euphrates River. In a short time, Thutmose III had conquered an empire for Egypt, bringing many territories under one ruler.

The Egyptian Empire grew rich from commerce and tribute from the conquered territories. The capital of Thebes, with its palaces, temples, and carved stone obelisks, reflected the wealth won by conquest. No longer isolated from other cultures, Egyptians benefited from cultural diffusion within their empire.

Akhenaton Founds a Religion

A new ruler, Amenhotep (AH•muhn•HOH•TEHP) IV, assumed power about 1370 B.C. Supported by his wife, Nefertiti, Amenhotep broke with the Egyptian tradition of worshiping many

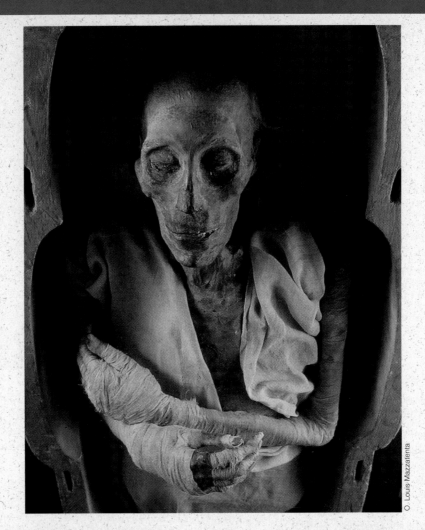

O. Louis Mazzatenta

Ramses the Great

O. Louis Mazzatenta

The mummy of Ramses the Great (above) lies in a display case on the second floor of the Egyptian Museum in Cairo. For many centuries before Ramses was brought to Cairo, the great pharaoh lay in his tomb near Luxor in a richly decorated coffin (left), embellished with symbols of Osiris, god of the afterlife. Ramses was nearly 90 when he died in 1237 B.C. His mummy has remained intact for the last 3,000 years.

Egyptians believed strongly in the afterlife and took great care to preserve the bodies of their pharaohs. Embalmers spent 70 days preparing the corpse of Ramses the Great. First they removed the internal organs and placed them in sacred jars. The heart was sealed in the body because Egyptians believed that it was the source of intellect as well as feeling and was needed in the afterlife. The brain, on the other hand, was thought to be useless, and embalmers drew it out through the nose and threw it away. The body was then dried with salt, washed, coated with preserving resins, and wrapped in hundreds of yards of linen. Recent medical tests show that Ramses suffered from arthritis, dental abscesses, gum disease, and poor circulation. ⊕

deities. He declared that Egyptians should worship only Aton, the sun-disk god, as the one supreme deity. Claiming to be Aton's equal, Amenhotep changed his royal name to **Akhenaton** (AHK•NAH•tuhn), which means "spirit of Aton." To stress the break with the past, Akhenaton moved the capital from Thebes to a new city in central Egypt dedicated to Aton.

These controversial changes had an unsettling effect on Egypt. Many of the common people rejected the worship of Aton, a god without human form, and continued to believe in many deities. The priests of the old religion resented their loss of power. At the same time, the army was unhappy about Egypt's loss of territories under Akhenaton's weak rule.

After Akhenaton's death, the priests restored the old religion. They also made Akhenaton's successor, Tutankhamen, move the capital back to Thebes. Shortly thereafter, the head of the Egyptian army overthrew the dynasty and created a new one.

Recovery and Decline

During the 1200s B.C., the pharaohs worked to restore Egypt's prestige. Under **Ramses II**, or Ramses the Great, the Egyptians fought their neighbors, the Hittites, for control of Syria. The conflict, however, led to a standoff at the Battle of Kadesh in 1285 B.C. Later the two empires concluded a treaty—unique for its time—pledging to keep permanent peace with each other and to fight as allies against any enemy.

In Egypt, Ramses, who ruled for 67 years, erected large statues of himself and built many temples and tombs. In A.D. 1995, archaeologists uncovered one of the most significant Egyptian discoveries: a vast underground tomb believed to be the burial place of 50 of Ramses' 52 sons.

After the death of Ramses II in 1237 B.C., Egypt weakened under the attacks of Mediterranean sea raiders, and entered a period of decline. Beginning in 945 B.C., it came under the rule of foreigners—among them the Libyans from the west and the Kushites from the south.

Life in Ancient Egypt

At the height of its glory, ancient Egypt was home to some 5 million persons, most of whom lived in the Nile Valley and the Nile Delta. Even though Egyptian society was divided into classes, ambitious people in the lower classes could improve their social status somewhat.

Levels of Egyptian Society

Royalty, nobles, and priests formed the top of the social order. They controlled religious and political affairs. Members of the wealthy upper class lived in the cities or on estates along the Nile River. There they built large, elaborately decorated homes surrounded by magnificent gardens, pools, and orchards.

Below the upper class in social rank was the middle class. Its members—artisans, scribes, merchants, and tax collectors—carried out the business activities of Egypt. Middle-class homes—mostly in the cities—were comfortable but not elegant.

The majority of Egyptians belonged to the poor lower class. Many were farmers. For the land they farmed, they paid rent to the king—usually a large percentage of their crop. Farmers also worked on building projects for the king, and some members of the lower class served the priests and the nobles. They lived in small villages of simple huts on or near the large estates along the Nile.

Egyptian Families

In the cities and in the upper class the husband, wife, and children made up the family group.

Visualizing History Ramses II holds an offering table—one of many great monuments erected to honor the pharaoh and Queen Nefertari. *What recent discovery yielded more information about the reign of Ramses II?*

Outside the cities, especially among farmers and laborers, a family also included grandparents and other relatives, who took an active part in the life of the household. An Egyptian child was taught great respect for his or her parents, with a son particularly expected to maintain his father's tomb.

The status of Egyptian women changed somewhat as the centuries passed. Literature of the Old Kingdom portrayed women as the property of their husbands and as valued producers of children. Wise men reminded children to cherish their mothers for bearing them, nourishing them, and loving and caring for them. By the time of the empire, documents indicate that women's legal rights had improved. Women could buy, own, and sell property in their own names, testify in court, and start divorce and other legal proceedings. The lives of Hatshepsut and some of the queens of the later pharaohs, like Nefertiti, suggest that privileged women of the royalty could attain prominence.

The falcon god Horus served both as a protector and symbol of the pharaoh. Horus was the son of the deities Osiris and Isis. *What was the major role of Osiris and Isis?*

Worshiping Many Deities

Religion guided every aspect of Egyptian life. Egyptian religion was based on polytheism, or the worship of many deities, except during the controversial rule of Akhenaton. Gods and goddesses were often represented as part human and part animal—Horus, the sky god, had the head of a hawk. The Egyptians in each region worshiped local deities, but rulers and priests promoted the worship of specific gods and goddesses over all of Egypt. These deities included Ra, the sun god, whom the Theban pharaohs joined with their favorite god Amon to make one god, Amon-Ra.

The popular god Osiris, initially the powerful god of the Nile, became the god responsible for the life, death, and rebirth of all living things. The Egyptians worshiped Osiris and his wife, the goddess Isis, as rulers of the realm of the dead. They believed that Osiris determined a person's fate after death.

Because their religion stressed an afterlife, Egyptians devoted much time and wealth to preparing for survival in the next world. At first they believed that only kings and wealthy people could enjoy an afterlife. By the time of the New Kingdom, however, poor people could also hope for eternal life with Osiris's help.

Writing With Pictures

In their earliest writing system, called hieroglyphics, the Egyptians carved picture symbols onto pieces of slate. These picture symbols, or hieroglyphs, stood for objects, ideas, and sounds. For everyday business, however, the Egyptians used a cursive, or flowing, script known as hieratic, which simplified and connected the picture symbols.

Few people in ancient Egypt could read or write. Some Egyptians, though, did prepare at special schools for a career as a scribe in government or commerce. Scribes learned to write hieratic script on paper made from the papyrus reed.

After the decline of ancient Egypt, hieroglyphs were no longer used, and their meaning remained a mystery to the world's scholars for nearly 2,000 years. Then in A.D. 1799 French soldiers in Egypt found a slab of stone dating to the 200s B.C. near the town of Rosetta. The stone was carved with Greek letters and two forms of Egyptian writing. In A.D. 1822 a French archaeologist named Jean-François Champollion (shahn•pawl•YOHN) figured out how the Greek text on the Rosetta stone matched the Egyptian texts. Using the Greek version, he was able to decipher the Egyptian hieroglyphics.

Some of the oldest writings from the Old Kingdom were carved on the inner walls of the Pyramids. Scribes also copied many prayers and hymns to deities. The Book of the Dead collected texts telling how to reach a happy afterlife, recording more than 200 prayers and magic formulas.

The ancient Egyptians also wrote secular, or nonreligious, works such as collections of proverbs. One vizier gave this advice: "Do not repeat slander; you should not hear it, for it is the result of hot temper. Repeat a matter seen, not what is heard." The Egyptians also enjoyed adventure stories, fairy tales, and love stories, as this excerpt shows:

> 66 Now I'll lie down inside
>   and act as if I'm sick.
> My neighbors will come in to visit,
>   and with them my girl.
> She'll put the doctors out,
>   for she's the one to know my hurt. 99
>
> –a love poem by a young Egyptian,
> date unknown

Achievements in Science

Pyramids, temples, and other monuments bear witness to the architectural and artistic achievement of Egyptian artisans. These works, however,

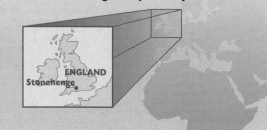
would not have been possible without advances in disciplines such as mathematics. The Egyptians developed a number system that enabled them to calculate area and volume, and they used principles of geometry to survey flooded land.

The Egyptians worked out an accurate 365-day calendar by basing their year not only on the movements of the moon but also on Sirius, the bright Dog Star. Sirius rises annually in the sky just before the Nile's flood begins.

Egyptians also developed medical expertise, having first learned about human anatomy in their practice of embalming. Egyptian doctors wrote directions on papyrus scrolls for using splints, bandages, and compresses when treating fractures, wounds, and diseases. Other ancient civilizations would acquire much of their medical knowledge from the Egyptians.

SECTION 1 REVIEW

Recall
1. **Define** monarchy, dynasty, theocracy, bureaucracy, pharaoh, empire, polytheism, hieroglyphics.
2. **Identify** Narmer, the Hyksos, Ahmose, Hatshepsut, Thutmose III, Akhenaton, Ramses II.
3. **Explain** how a bureaucracy became part of government in ancient Egypt.

Critical Thinking
4. **Evaluate**
Which pharaoh—Thutmose III or Ramses II—was more successful in handling conflict with neighboring peoples? Support your opinion.

Understanding Themes
5. **Relation to Environment**
How did geography and climate affect where people lived in ancient Egypt? How did the ancient Egyptians make use of the environment to meet their economic and cultural needs?

The Egyptians

The Valley of the Kings has seen more than its share of visitors. For thousands of years, travelers, warriors, and more recently, archaeologists have descended on this area on the outskirts of what is now Luxor to marvel at the magnificence of ancient Egypt. It was thought that most of what there was to discover had been found after British explorer Howard Carter opened up the tomb of Tutankhamen in 1922.

Then in 1988, plans were made to build a parking lot over the site of Tomb 5, which had been discovered—and looted—years earlier. Wanting to make sure that the parking facility would not seal off anything important, Egyptologist Kent Weeks of the American University of Cairo decided to make one last exploration of the tomb. To his surprise, beyond a few debris-choked rooms, he opened a door that led to the mostly unexcavated tomb of perhaps 50 of the sons of Ramses II, the powerful pharaoh who ruled Egypt from 1279 to 1212 B.C.

Though the tomb was emptied of valuables long ago, archaeologists consider Weeks's discovery a major find. Scientists and researchers hope

Kenneth Garrett

Illustration by C.F. Payne

that artifacts found in the tomb will provide clues about Egyptian civilization during Egypt's last golden age.

For students of Judeo-Christian history, any information on Ramses' oldest son, Amen-hir-khopshef, would be a most important discovery. Ramses was in power when, in retribution for the enslavement of the Israelites, according to the Book of Exodus, the Lord "...smote all the firstborn in the land of Egypt, from the firstborn of Pharaoh that sat on his throne unto the firstborn of the captive that was in the dungeon."

The tomb and pyramids of

ancient Egypt hold many answers: These stone monuments have certainly established the immortality of the pharaohs. But what about the commoners, who vastly outnumbered the royalty? What of the men and women who gave their strength, sweat, and lives to create Egypt's lasting monuments? The widespread fame of the Sphinx and the Pyramids at Giza make it easy to forget that basic questions about Egyptian history have remained unanswered. Only recently have Egyptologists begun to fill in those gaps.

✂

SEVERAL YEARS AGO, archaeologists began to excavate two sites—located about half a mile from the Sphinx—searching for signs of the

 Offerings of food are carved in relief on an official's tomb (left).

Another pyramid nears completion about 2500 B.C. (above). Limestone facing blocks were quarried across the Nile and ferried to the work site. Teams then dragged the blocks to ramps made of rubble that were built around the pyramid during construction. Some experts believe that it took only 10,000 men—far below earlier estimates of up to 100,000—and 25 years to lay 5 million tons of rock. Half lion, half pharaoh, the Sphinx (in the foreground) is carved from an outcropping left unexcavated in a U-shaped quarry.

ordinary people who built the pyramids. Within months they uncovered the remains of many mud-brick buildings, including the oldest bakery yet discovered in Egypt.

This was a significant find. While the pyramids built Egypt by drawing its provinces together in a unified effort, it can be said that bread built the pyramids. For thousands of workers, a loaf of emmer–wheat bread—washed down with beer—was most likely the dietary staple.

At about the time the bakery was discovered, searchers also unearthed a cemetery of 600 graves of workers. Their skeletons revealed years of hard labor: Vertebrae were compressed and damaged from years of carrying heavy loads. Some skeletons were missing fingers and even limbs. A few of the tombs were adorned with mini-pyramids several feet high, made of mud brick. Nothing like these tiny pyramids had been found before. In the past, scholars believed that the pyramid form was invented as the shape for a royal tomb. However, Zahi Hawass, director general of the Giza Pyramids, thinks that the pyramid form actually may have arisen among the common people. He believes that the mini-pyramids evolved from sacred rectangular mounds found in tombs even older than the pharaohs' pyramids.

Life for most ancient Egyptians was hard. Society was built around a preoccupation with the pharaohs' immortality. But perhaps there were spiritual rewards for the common people in this devotion to their pharaohs. Some scholars think that ancient Egyptians believed not so much that the pharaoh was divine,

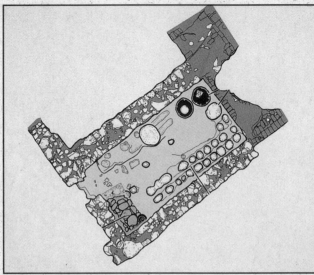

Hosul Kang, based on a drawing by Mark Lehner

Kenneth Garrett

A drawing of an ancient bakery (top) was used to build this replica of an ancient Egyptian bakery near Saqqara, Egypt (bottom).

but that through the pharaoh the divine nature of their society was expressed. Building a pyramid might have been an act of faith much as building a cathedral was in the Middle Ages.

Such recent discoveries about the life of the common people may lead to a new way of seeing ancient Egypt: not only as a brilliant civilization of the elite trickling down to the masses but also as a culture built

from the bottom up—a culture that stood on the daily toil of the workers and the beliefs of ordinary men and women.

Much of the emerging picture of daily life in ancient Egypt is one of arduous toil. The villages were crowded and dirty. Huts were made of thatch and mud brick. Men wore loincloths; women dressed in long sheaths with wide shoulder straps; and children went naked. On wooden sledges workers hauled the giant granite blocks that built the pyramids. Egypt created a vast agricultural empire, yet all the irrigation was done by hand. Farmers filled two heavy jars from the canals, then hung them from a yoke over their shoulders. Oxen dragging wooden plows tilled the fertile soil along the Nile, followed by lines of sowers who sang in cadence as they cast grains of emmer wheat from baskets.

There is much still to be learned and understood about daily life in ancient Egypt. The discovery of the bakery has provided insight into what sustained the masses; the bones in the commoners' graveyard tell us that life was not easy; the mini-pyramids illustrate that art, culture, and faith may have developed up from the average man and woman, rather than down from the royalty. For years Egyptologists have focused on the grandiose—and thereby disregarded most of Egyptian society. Eventually, however, our view of ancient Egyptian culture is broadening to encompass those responsible for creating it.

Kenneth Garrett

Kenneth Garrett

Kenneth Garrett

▨ *A potter was hired to make replicas of the old baking pots. A local worker (top left) heats the tops in a wood fire in preparation for baking.*

▨ *A kind of wheat known as emmer was supplied by a Californian who collects and grows ancient grains. The wet flour made from the emmer was left outside to collect free-floating native yeast spores and bacteria. (Store–bought yeast was not known to ancient Egyptians.) On baking day, the dough was placed into the pot bottoms and allowed to rise (bottom left). A hole for each pot was dug in the hot coals. The heated pot tops were then placed on the heated bottom halves and were placed in the coals to bake.*

▨ *Success! For perhaps the first time in more than 4,000 years, a loaf of emmer bread popped out of an Old Kingdom-style pot. Edward Wood (above), who has been baking ancient breads for 50 years, holds up a perfect loaf.*

Chapter 2 *Early Civilizations* **57**

c. 3000 B.C.
Sumerians set up city-states.

c. 2300 B.C.
Akkadian king
Sargon I begins
conquests.

c. 1700 B.C.
Hammurabi develops
code of laws.

Section 2

The Fertile Crescent

Setting the Scene

▶ **Terms to Define**
city-state, cuneiform

▶ **People to Meet**
the Sumerians, Sargon I,
the Akkadians, Hammurabi

▶ **Places to Locate**
Fertile Crescent, Mesopotamia, Tigris and
Euphrates Rivers

 **Find Out** How did Sumer's achievements
enrich the early culture of the Middle East?

The Storyteller

*Sumerians honored the sun god Shamash as a
defender of the weak, giver of life, and even as a
judge of business deals, as in this hymn:*
"The whole of mankind bows to you,
Shamash the universe longs for your light....
As for him who declines a present, but
nevertheless takes the part of the weak,
It is pleasing to Shamash, and he will prolong
his life....
The merchant who practices
trickery as he holds the
balances...
He is disappointed in the matter
of profit and loses his capital.
The honest merchant who holds
the balances and gives good
weight—
Everything is presented to him in
good measure."

*Sumerian
board game*

—from *Babylonian Wisdom
Literature,* W. B. Lambert, in
Readings in Ancient History
(2nd ed.), N. Bailkey

round 5000 B.C.—at about the same
time as Egyptian nomads moved
into the Nile River valley—groups of
herders started to journey north from the Arabian
Peninsula. Rainfall in the area had declined over
the years, and the lakes and grasslands had begun
to dry up. Other peoples—from the highlands near
present-day Turkey—moved south at this time.
Driven by poor weather, they also fled war and
overpopulation.

Both groups of migrants headed into the crescent-shaped strip of fertile land that stretched from
the Mediterranean Sea to the Persian Gulf, curving
around northern Syria. Called the **Fertile Crescent**,
this region included parts of the modern nations of
Israel, Jordan, Lebanon, Turkey, Syria, and Iraq.

Many of the peoples migrating from the north
and south chose to settle in **Mesopotamia** (MEH
•suh•puh•TAY•mee•uh), the eastern part of the
Fertile Crescent. Located on a low plain lying
between the **Tigris and Euphrates Rivers**, the name
Mesopotamia means "land between the rivers" in the
Greek language. The two rivers begin in the hills of
present-day eastern Turkey and later run parallel to
each other through present-day Iraq on their way to
the Persian Gulf. In this region, the newcomers
built villages and farmed the land.

The Twin Rivers

Beginning with Neolithic farmers, people used
the Tigris and Euphrates Rivers to water their
crops. Unlike the Nile River, however, the twin
rivers did not provide a regular supply of water. In
the summer no rain fell, and the Mesopotamian
plain was dry. As a result, water shortages often
coincided with the fall planting season. By the
spring harvest season, however, the rivers swelled
with rain and melting snow. Clogged with deposits
of silt, the Tigris and Euphrates Rivers often over-
flowed onto the plain. Strong floods sometimes

swept away whole villages and fields. The time of year of such flooding, however, was never predictable, and the water level of the rivers often varied from year to year.

The early Mesopotamian villages cooperated in order to meet the rivers' challenges. Together they first built dams and escape channels to control the seasonal floodwaters and later constructed canals and ditches to bring river water to irrigate their fields. As a result of their determined efforts, Mesopotamian farmers were producing food, especially grain crops, in abundance by 4000 B.C.

The Sumerian Civilization

Around 3500 B.C. a people from either central Asia or Asia Minor—**the Sumerians**—arrived in Mesopotamia. They settled in the lower part of the Tigris-Euphrates river valley, known as Sumer. Sumer became the birthplace of what historians have considered the world's first cities.

The Sumerian City-States

By 3000 B.C. the Sumerians had formed 12 city-states in the Tigris-Euphrates valley, including Ur, Uruk, and Eridu. A typical Sumerian city-state consisted of the city itself and the land surrounding it.

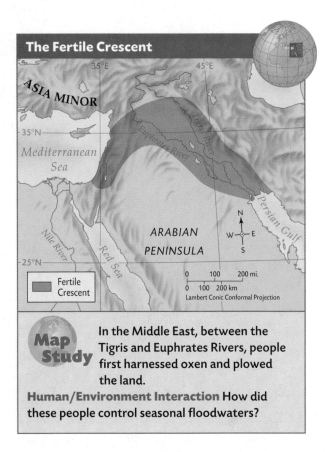

The Fertile Crescent

Map Study In the Middle East, between the Tigris and Euphrates Rivers, people first harnessed oxen and plowed the land.

Human/Environment Interaction How did these people control seasonal floodwaters?

Visualizing History **Restored ziggurat at Ur, c. 2100 B.C.** *What was the purpose of a ziggurat?*

The population of each city-state ranged from 20,000 to 250,000.

The people of Sumer shared a common culture, language, and religion. Sumerian city-states also shared some physical features. A ziggurat (ZIH •guh•RAT), or temple, made of sun-dried brick and decorated with colored tile, was built in each city-state. Sumerians built a ziggurat as a series of terraces, with each terrace smaller than the one below. A staircase climbed to a shrine atop the ziggurat. Only priests and priestesses were allowed to enter the shrine, which was dedicated to the city-state's chief deity. In form a ziggurat resembled a pyramid—both being massive stepped or peaked structures—but the feeling and emphasis of the two differed. A pyramid hid an inner tomb reachable only through passageways. A ziggurat raised a shrine to the sky, reached by mounting outer stairs.

Sumerian Government

Each Sumerian city-state usually governed itself independently of the others. In the city-state of Uruk, for example, a council of nobles and an assembly of citizens ran political affairs at first. But later, as city-states faced threats of foreign invaders and began to compete for land and water rights, the citizens of each city-state typically chose a military leader from among themselves. By 2700 B.C. the

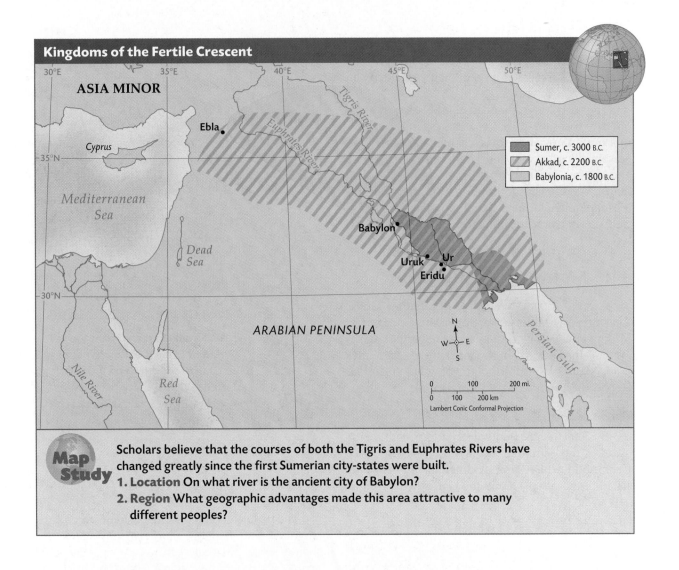

ASIA MINOR

Ebla

Cyprus

Mediterranean
Sea

Dead
Sea

Babylon

Uruk • Ur
Eridu

ARABIAN PENINSULA

Nile River

Red
Sea

Tigris River

Euphrates River

Persian Gulf

	Sumer, c. 3000 B.C.
	Akkad, c. 2200 B.C.
	Babylonia, c. 1800 B.C.

N
W—E
S

0   100   200 mi.
0   100   200 km
Lambert Conic Conformal Projection

Map Study Scholars believe that the courses of both the Tigris and Euphrates Rivers have changed greatly since the first Sumerian city-states were built.
1. **Location** On what river is the ancient city of Babylon?
2. **Region** What geographic advantages made this area attractive to many different peoples?

leaders of several city-states ruled as kings. Soon after, the kingships became hereditary.

A Sumerian king served not only as military leader but as the high priest, who represented the city-state's deity. Thus the governments of the city-states were not only monarchies but theocracies. Because the Sumerians believed that much of the land belonged to a city-state's god or goddess, a king and his priests closely supervised farming. A king also enforced the law and set penalties for law-breakers. Most punishments consisted of fines and did not involve bodily injury or loss of life.

The Roles of Men and Women

Sumerian law extensively regulated family life and outlined the roles of men and women. As the heads of households, men exercised great authority over their wives and children. According to Sumerian law codes, a man could sell his wife or children into slavery if he needed the money to pay a debt. He could also divorce his wife for the slightest cause. For a Sumerian woman, in contrast, the

law codes made divorce much more difficult. Women did enjoy some legal rights, however. Like Egyptian women, they could buy and sell property. They could also operate their own businesses and own and sell their own slaves.

Writing on Clay Tablets

Commerce and trade dominated the Sumerian city-states. The Sumerians developed a system of writing so they could keep accounts and prepare documents. Archaeologists believe that the writing system the Sumerians invented is the oldest in the world, dating to about 3100 B.C. The cuneiform (kyoo•NEE•uh•FAWRM) system began with pictograms—as did Egyptian hieroglyphics—and consisted of hundreds of wedge-shaped markings made by pressing the end of a sharpened reed on wet clay tablets. Then the Sumerians dried or baked the tablets until they were hard. Eventually the pictograms developed into symbols representing complex ideas. In this way, cuneiform influenced later Mesopotamian writing systems.

Medical remedies are inscribed on this Sumerian clay tablet—a cuneiform writing tablet that was baked until hard. *How did cuneiform develop as a writing system?*

Sumerians wishing to learn cuneiform and become scribes studied for many years at special schools called *eddubas*. As educated professionals, scribes rose to high positions in Sumerian society. They produced business records, lists of historical dates, and literary works.

One of these literary works, the epic poem *Gilgamesh*, was written down about 1850 B.C. Scholars believe that the *Gilgamesh* epic may be the oldest story in the world. The scribes probably based the stories of Gilgamesh, a godlike man who performs heroic deeds, on an actual king of the city-state of Uruk.

Sumer's Many Deities

The Sumerians, like the Egyptians, practiced a polytheistic religion. Each Sumerian deity presided over a specific natural force—rain, moon, air—or over a human activity—plowing or brick making, for example. An, the highest Sumerian deity, was responsible for the seasons. Another important god—Enlil, god of winds and agriculture—created the hoe. Although Sumerians honored all the deities, each city-state claimed as its own one god or goddess, to whom its citizens prayed and offered sacrifices.

The Sumerians pictured their gods and goddesses as unpredictable, selfish beings who had little regard for human beings. The Sumerians believed that if deities became angry, they would cause misfortunes such as floods or famine. To appease their temperamental gods and goddesses, Sumerian priests and priestesses performed religious ceremonies and rituals.

Unlike the Egyptians, the Sumerians felt that humans had little control over their daily lives and could not look forward to a happy life after death. Only a grim underworld, without light or air, awaited them—an afterlife where the dead were only pale shadows.

Sumerian Inventions

Historians credit the Sumerians with numerous technological innovations. The Sumerians developed the wagon wheel, for example, to better transport people and goods, the arch to build sturdier buildings, the potter's wheel to shape containers, and the sundial to keep time. They developed a number system based on 60 and devised a 12-month calendar based on the cycles of the moon. The Sumerian civilization also was the first to make bronze out of copper and tin and to develop a metal plow. They produced an abundance of finely crafted metal work, some of which has been discovered in the Royal Cemetery at Ur. These and other Sumerian achievements have prompted one scholar to observe that "history begins at Sumer."

First Mesopotamian Empires

After a long period of conquest and reconquest, the Sumerian city-states eventually fell to foreign invaders in the 2000s B.C. The invaders of Sumer, like the Egyptians of the New Kingdom, were inspired by dreams of empire.

Footnotes to History

The Umbrella
1400 B.C.—Umbrellas actually originated under the sunny skies of Mesopotamia. Sumerians used palm fronds or feather umbrellas to shield their heads from the harsh rays and scorching heat of the Middle Eastern sun.

Sargon Leads the Akkadians

The first empire builder in Mesopotamia—**Sargon I**—may have been born a herder or a farmer's son. According to legend his mother abandoned him as a baby, setting him out on the Euphrates River in a reed basket. Downstream a farmer irrigating his fields pulled Sargon ashore and raised him as his own.

Sargon's people, **the Akkadians**, were Semites, one of the nomadic groups that had migrated from the Arabian Peninsula to the Fertile Crescent around 5000 B.C. The Akkadians established a kingdom called Akkad (AH•KAHD) in northern Mesopotamia. When Sargon assumed power in Akkad around 2300 B.C., he immediately launched a military campaign of expansion. Sargon's conquests united all of the city-states of Mesopotamia in one empire, which predated the empire of the Egyptian New Kingdom by more than 800 years.

Under Sargon's rule the people of Mesopotamia began to use the Akkadian language instead of Sumerian. But the Akkadians adopted various Sumerian religious and farming practices. After Sargon's death and the successful rule of his grandson, however, the Akkadian Empire disintegrated.

The Kingdom of Ebla

No one really knows how far Sargon's empire extended. Historians do know, however, that Ebla, a kingdom located in what is now northern Syria, fought unsuccessfully against Sargon for control of the Euphrates River trade. When Sargon's grandson captured Ebla, he burned the royal archives. Yet fire did not destroy the thousands of clay tablets stored there. These tablets and other finds from Ebla have convinced historians that highly developed Semitic civilizations prospered in that area of Syria earlier than previously believed.

The overland trade that passed between Egypt and Mesopotamia made Ebla a wealthy and powerful city-state. Ebla controlled a number of neighboring towns, from which it exacted tribute.

The kings of Ebla were elected for seven-year terms. In addition to their political role, they looked

Images of the Times

Mesopotamia

For many centuries, beginning about 4000 B.C., enterprising civilizations rose and fell in the fertile valley of the Tigris and Euphrates Rivers.

The Royal Standard of Ur is an oblong decorated box with panels that represent scenes of war and peace. The war panel celebrates a military victory by the Sumerian city of Ur.

after the welfare of the poor. If the kings failed, they could be removed by a council. After 2000 B.C., Ebla declined and eventually was destroyed by the Amorites, a Semitic people from western Syria.

Hammurabi's Babylonian Empire

The Amorites also expanded beyond Syria. Their military forces poured into Mesopotamia, which was in decline after a short period of prosperity under the kings of Ur. The Amorites overran many Sumerian centers, including Babylon. The dynasty that they founded at Babylon later produced a ruler who would dominate Mesopotamia: **Hammurabi**.

Hammurabi used his might to put down other Mesopotamian rulers. He eventually brought the entire region under his control, reorganizing the tax system and ordering local officials to build and repair irrigation canals. Hammurabi organized a strong government and worked to increase the economic prosperity of his people. Under Hammurabi's rule, Babylon became a major trade center. Merchants from as far away as India and China paid gold and silver for the grain and cloth the Babylonians produced.

POINT

Hammurabi's Law Code

Historians consider Hammurabi's greatest achievement his effort "to make justice appear in the land." Hammurabi collected laws of the various Mesopotamian city-states and created a law code covering the entire region. When completed, Hammurabi's code consisted of 282 sections dealing with most aspects of daily life. It clearly stated which actions were considered violations and assigned a specific punishment for each. Hammurabi's code penalized wrongdoers more severely than did the old Sumerian laws. Instead of fining violators, it exacted what the Bible later expressed as "an eye for an eye, and a tooth for a tooth." According to the harsh approach of Hammurabi's code:

This goddess, one of many similar preserved relics, along with discovered temple sites, reveals the significance of religion in early Mesopotamian civilizations.

The Kassite stela fragment shows animals that were important to a vigorous agricultural people, the Kassites, who emerged as a dominant force after 2000 B.C.

REFLECTING ON THE TIMES

1. What evidence reveals the importance of religion in Mesopotamian cities?
2. What role might gods and goddesses have in times of war?

63

King Hammurabi stands in front of the sun god Shamash at the top of the stone slab upon which is inscribed Hammurabi's code of laws. Shamash—the supreme judge—delivers the laws to the king. *Why were Hammurabi's laws carved in stone for public display?*

❝ If a builder has built a house for a man and has not made his work sound, so that the house he has made falls down and causes the death of the owner of the house, that builder shall be put to death. If it causes the death of the son of the owner of the house, they shall kill the son of that builder. ❞

Other sections of Hammurabi's code covered the property of married women, adoption and inheritance, interest rates on loans, and damage to fields by cattle. Some laws were attempts to protect the less powerful—for example, protecting wives against beatings or neglect by their husbands. The development of written law in Mesopotamia was a major advance toward justice and order. Before this achievement, people who had been offended or cheated often acted on their own and used violence against their opponents. Now, crimes against people or property became the concern of the whole community. Government assumed the responsibility of protecting its citizens in return for their loyalty and service. ◣

Babylonian Society

Historians have been able to infer from Hammurabi's code a threefold division of Babylonian social classes—the kings, priests, and nobles at the top; the artisans, small merchants, scribes, and farmers next; and slaves as the lowest group. His laws varied according to the class of the person offended against, with more severe penalties for assaulting a landowner than for hurting a slave. Most slaves had been captured in war or had failed to pay their debts.

The Babylonians borrowed heavily from Sumerian culture. They used the cuneiform script for their Semitic language and wrote on clay tablets. Babylonian literature was similar to that of Sumer.

Decline and Fall

After Hammurabi's death, the Babylonian Empire declined, and Mesopotamia was again divided into a number of small states. Hammurabi's dynasty finally ended and his empire fell apart when the Hittites, a people from Asia Minor, raided Babylon about 1600 B.C. Babylon, however, would again play a role in Mesopotamian civilization in the 600s B.C. as the capital of a new empire under the Chaldeans.

SECTION 2 REVIEW

Recall
1. **Define** city-state, cuneiform.
2. **Identify** the Sumerians, Gilgamesh, Sargon I, the Akkadians, Hammurabi.
3. **Explain** the purpose of the religious ceremonies and rituals performed by Sumerian priests and priestesses.

Critical Thinking
4. **Making Comparisons** Contrast Hammurabi's code with modern American law. Which do you think serves justice better? Explain your answer.

Understanding Themes
5. **Cooperation** Identify an economic or cultural achievement of one of the civilizations of the Fertile Crescent region that must have required skillful planning and organization of many people.

Critical Thinking SKILLS

Classifying Information

Imagine shopping in a store where shoes, rugs, dishes, and books are all mixed together in piles. To find the item you need, you would have to comb through each pile. How frustrating!

Dealing with large quantities of information about a subject likewise can be frustrating. It is easier to understand information if you put it into groups, or classify it.

Learning the Skill

In classifying anything, we put together items with shared characteristics. Department stores group items according to their uses. For example, shoes and boots are in the footwear department, while pots and pans are in the kitchen department.

We can classify written information in the same way.

1. As you read about a topic, look for items that have similar characteristics. List these items in separate columns or on separate note cards.
2. Label these categories with an appropriate heading.
3. Add facts to the categories as you continue reading.
4. Review the groups. If necessary, subdivide the categories into smaller groups or combine categories that overlap.

Once you have classified the material, look for patterns and relationships in the facts. Make comparisons, draw conclusions, and develop questions or hypotheses for further study.

Practicing the Skill

Use the information in the following passage to answer these questions:
1. The passage describes two groups of children in ancient Egypt. What are these groups?
2. Classify the educational opportunities available to each group.

3. Classify the occupations available to each group.
4. From your classifications, what conclusions can you draw about Egyptian society?

❝ The royal children ... were privately tutored ... frequently joined by the sons of great noble families.... The most sought-after profession in Egypt was that of scribe.... The most important subjects were reading and writing ... history, literature, geography, [and] ethics. Arithmetic was almost certainly part of the curriculum.... Boys who were to specialize in medicine, law or religious liturgy would perhaps have devoted some of their time to elementary studies in these fields.

Formal education for [a son from] the lower classes ... was not selected for him because he wished to become an artist or goldsmith or a farmer ... he entered a trade because it was his father's work. The sons of artists and craftsmen were apprenticed and went to train at one of the temples or state workshops ... the sons of peasants would have joined their fathers in the field at an early age. ❞
—A. Rosalie David, *The Egyptian Kingdoms*, 1975

Applying the Skill

Find two newspaper or magazine articles about a topic that interests you. Classify the information on note cards or in a chart.

For More Practice

Turn to the Skill Practice in the Chapter Review on page 77 for more practice in classifying information.

2500 B.C.	2000 B.C.	1500 B.C.

c. 2500 B.C.
Settlements develop in the Indus River valley.

c. 2300 B.C. Harappan people trade with Mesopotamia.

c. 1500 B.C.
Indus Valley civilization declines.

Section 3

Early South Asia

Setting the Scene

▶ **Terms to Define**
  subcontinent, monsoon

▶ **People to Meet**
  the Harappans

▶ **Places to Locate**
  Indus River valley, Harappa, Mohenjo-Daro

Find Out How did people of the Indus River valley civilization build cities?

The Storyteller

For a long time, it had been known that the mounds of Mohenjo-Daro and Harappa contained archaeological remains. But neighborhood construction workers actually used the ancient mounds as sources for bricks, until practically none remained above ground. As Sir Alexander Cunningham, the first Director General of the Archaeological Survey records, "Perhaps the best idea of the extent of the ruined brick mounds of Harappa may be formed from the fact that they have more than sufficed to furnish brick ballast for about 100 miles of Lahore and Multan Railway."

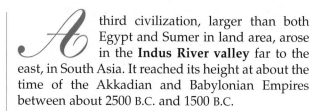

—adapted from *Indus Valley Civilization*, Ashim Kumar Ron N.N. Gidwani (Cunningham, 1875), 1982 and *Harappan Civilization*, Gregory Possehl, 1982

Harappan jar lid

A third civilization, larger than both Egypt and Sumer in land area, arose in the **Indus River valley** far to the east, in South Asia. It reached its height at about the time of the Akkadian and Babylonian Empires between about 2500 B.C. and 1500 B.C.

The Subcontinent

Three modern nations—India, Pakistan, and Bangladesh—trace their roots to the Indus Valley civilization. These countries lie on the subcontinent of South Asia, a large, triangular-shaped landmass that juts into the Indian Ocean.

Bounded by Mountains

Natural barriers separate the South Asian subcontinent from the rest of Asia. Water surrounds the landmass on the east and west. To the north rise two lofty mountain ranges—the Himalayas and the Hindu Kush. Throughout history, invaders entering the subcontinent by land have had to cross the few high mountain passes of the Hindu Kush.

Plains sweep across the landscape to the south of the mountains. Across the plains flow three rivers, fed by rain and melting mountain snows. The Indus River drains into the Arabian Sea, and the Ganges (GAN•JEEZ) and Brahmaputra (BRAH•muh•POO•truh) Rivers join and empty into the Bay of Bengal, forming a wide delta. The Ganges-Brahmaputra Delta and the Indus-Ganges plain are formed from soils left by the rivers. Like the Nile Valley and Delta and the Tigris-Euphrates plains, fertile river areas of South Asia have supported vast numbers of people over the ages.

Seasonal Winds

The northern mountains ensure generally warm weather in South Asia. Like a wall, they block blasts of cold air from central Asia. Two seasonal winds called monsoons affect the climate,

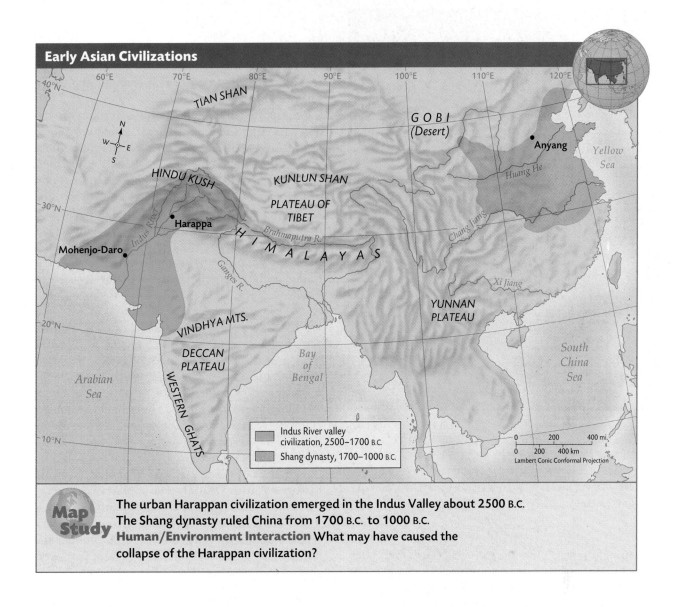

GOBI
(Desert)

TIAN SHAN

HINDU KUSH

KUNLUN SHAN

PLATEAU OF TIBET

Harappa

H I M A L A Y A S

Brahmaputra R.

Indus River

Ganges R.

Mohenjo-Daro

VINDHYA MTS.

DECCAN PLATEAU

Bay of Bengal

Arabian Sea

WESTERN GHATS

Anyang

Huang He

Chang Jiang

Xi Jiang

YUNNAN PLATEAU

Yellow Sea

South China Sea

Indus River valley civilization, 2500–1700 B.C.

Shang dynasty, 1700–1000 B.C.

0   200   400 mi.
0   200   400 km
Lambert Conic Conformal Projection

Map Study The urban Harappan civilization emerged in the Indus Valley about 2500 B.C. The Shang dynasty ruled China from 1700 B.C. to 1000 B.C. **Human/Environment Interaction** What may have caused the collapse of the Harappan civilization?

however, and shape the pattern of life on the subcontinent.

The northeast, or winter, monsoon blows from November to March; the southwest, or summer, monsoon from June to September. The northeast wind brings dry air from the mountains, and the average winter temperatures of the Indus-Ganges plain remain mild—about 70°F (21°C). By June, temperatures have soared, sometimes exceeding 100°F (38°C), and South Asians welcome the rain-bearing southwest wind blowing off the ocean.

Because of the heavy downpours of the southwest monsoon, the rivers swell rapidly, then widen across the flat plains and rush to the sea. The flooding enriches the soil, but in some years unusually heavy rains drown people and animals and destroy whole villages. In other years the monsoon arrives late or rainfall is light; then crops are poor and people go hungry. The people of the plains are dependent on the monsoons.

The Indus Valley Civilization

Less than a century ago, archaeologists working in the Indus River valley first identified an ancient civilization in South Asia. They dated this early civilization to about 2500 B.C.

Centrally Planned Cities

Archaeologists named the Indus Valley settlements "the Harappan civilization" after one of its major cities, **Harappa** (huh•RA•puh), located in present-day Pakistan. **Mohenjo-Daro** (moh •HEHN•joh DAHR•oh), another important Harappan city, lay nearer the Arabian Sea.

The ruins of Harappa and Mohenjo-Daro are outstanding examples of urban planning. A citadel, or fortress, built on a brick platform overlooked each city—possibly serving as a government and religious center. Below the citadel Harappan engineers skillfully laid out each city in a grid pattern of

Chapter 2 *Early Civilizations* **67**

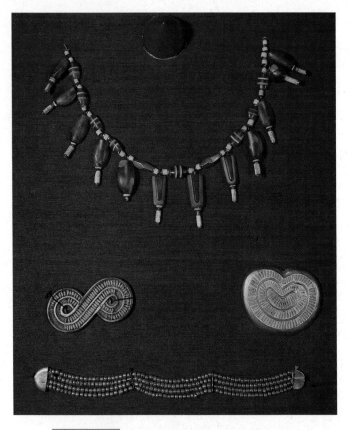

Some fine jewelry crafted by Harappan artisans has survived. **These pieces are now in the National Museum at New Delhi, India.** *Why is less known about Harappan civilization than about Egypt and Mesopotamia?*

straight streets crossing each other at right angles. **The Harappans** used oven-baked bricks to build houses with flat wooden roofs, and some houses rose to several stories and enclosed courtyards. Almost every house had at least one bathroom, with drains and chutes connected to a brick sewer system beneath the streets.

Harappan Life

Most of the Harappan people worked the land. In the fields of the Indus Valley floodplain they grew wheat, barley, rice, and cotton. Farmers planted at the beginning or end of the flood season and relied on the drenched land to provide the necessary water for their crops.

Supported by a food surplus, Harappan city dwellers engaged in industry and commerce. Some artisans worked bronze and copper into tools, while others made silver vessels and gold, shell, and ivory jewelry. The Harappans also mass-produced clay pots, and they spun and wove cotton cloth. Merchants who handled these goods used soapstone seals to identify bundles of merchandise. The discovery by archaeologists of Harappan seals in Mesopotamia indicates that Indus Valley people traded with the people of Mesopotamia as early as 2300 B.C.

Language and Religion

The Harappans inscribed pictograms on the seals they placed on packages of goods. Scientists have yet to decipher these inscriptions—almost the only known examples of the written language of the Harappan civilization. Some believe that the Harappans made their pictograms after adopting the idea of writing from the people of Mesopotamia.

The lack of written records has made it difficult to learn as much about the Harappan civilization as is known about Egypt and Mesopotamia. Artifacts found in the ruins, however, have provided archaeologists with some clues. For example, animal and humanlike figures suggest that the Harappans worshiped gods associated with natural forces.

Collapse of a Civilization

By 1500 B.C. the Harappan civilization had disappeared. Historians have many theories for what caused this collapse. Evidence of floods, for example, suggests possible climate changes. In the Mohenjo-Daro ruins are signs that some of its people may have met a violent end, possibly at the hands of invaders.

SECTION 3 REVIEW

Recall
1. **Define** subcontinent, monsoon.
2. **Identify** the Harappans.
3. **Name** three modern nations of South Asia that trace their roots to the Indus Valley civilization. In what present-day nation were the cities of Harappa and Mohenjo-Daro located?

Critical Thinking
4. **Analyzing Information** What do archaeological clues suggest about the decline and collapse of the Indus Valley civilization?

Understanding Themes
5. **Cultural Diffusion** How might the Indus Valley civilization at Mohenjo-Daro and the civilization at Harappa have been influenced by the Mesopotamian city-states and empires?

c. 2500 B.C. Lung-shan culture begins in China.

c. 2000 B.C. Yu founds the legendary Xia dynasty.

c. 1700 B.C. Tang establishes the Shang, the first historical dynasty.

c. 1000s B.C. The Zhou dynasty comes to power.

Section 4

Early China

Setting the Scene

▶ **Terms to Define**
  mandate

▶ **People to Meet**
  Yu the Great

▶ **Places to Locate**
  Huang He valley, Anyang

Find Out ➤ What were the major contributions of early Chinese civilization?

The Storyteller

What would the oracle say this time? Tang tried not to lean too far forward to watch as the fortune-teller began to apply red-hot coals to the turtle shell. A man of his station should not appear too anxious: his confidence in divine support should be seen by all. On the shell was inscribed a question known only to him: "Shall I attack before harvest?" So much depended on the answer. There was nothing to do now but wait for the fire to work on the brittle shell covered with scratchings, containing the destiny of China.

—adapted from *Ancient Records of Assyria and Babylon*, Volume 1, edited by Daniel David Luckenbill, 1968

A tortoise shell oracle bone from the Shang Dynasty

Even as the Harappans were meeting their mysterious fate, China's first dynasty had begun to assert its power over another river valley. This fourth river valley civilization has endured to the present day.

For many centuries the Chinese lived in relative isolation from the rest of the world. They called their homeland *Zhong Guo* (JOONG GWAH), or "the Middle Kingdom." To them it was the center of the whole world and the one truly supreme civilization. The lack of outside contacts allowed the Chinese to develop one culture across many regions and a strong sense of national identity as well. As a result, China has the oldest continuous civilization in the world.

China's Geography

China's varied geography has affected its historical development. Mountains make up about one-third of China's area. The Himalayas close off China to the southwest, and on the western border rise the Kunlun Shan and Tian Shan ranges. To the east of the Tian Shan lie the vast desert wastes of the Gobi. These rugged physical features hindered cultural diffusion both into and out of China for many centuries.

On the east, China's coastline touches the Pacific Ocean. Although some Chinese became devoted seafarers, they mostly focused on developing the agriculture of eastern China's fertile river valleys and plains. Unlike the land to the west with its forbidding terrain, the east welcomed life. For centuries large numbers of Chinese have farmed in the region's North China Plain.

Three major rivers drain eastern China: the Huang He (HWONG HUH); the Chang Jiang (CHAHNG JYAHNG), known also as the Yangtze (YANG•SEE); and the Xi Jiang (SHEE JYAHNG), also called the West River. The Huang He flows more than 2,900 miles (4,640 km) from the northern

Oracle bones used to obtain advice about military campaigns were often inscribed with the question and answer and preserved as part of the king's records. *Why were such oracle bones stored by the rulers?*

highlands eastward to the Yellow Sea. On its way it cuts through thick layers of loess (LEHS), a rich yellow soil. The river carries away large amounts of loess, which it deposits farther downstream. The abundance of yellow soil in the Huang's waters gives it its name—Yellow River. The Chinese sometimes call the Huang He "the Great Sorrow" because of the tragedy brought by its floods. However, the silt deposits brought by the flooding river have made the North China Plain a rich agricultural area.

A favorable climate also contributes to successful farming on the North China Plain. Melting snow from the mountains and the monsoon rains between July and October feed the Huang He. Farmers of the region have long depended on the seasonal rhythm of temperature and rainfall.

The Shang Dynasty

Very little is known about the origins of Chinese civilization. In the A.D. 1920s, archaeologists in the Huang He valley uncovered traces of Neolithic life in China. The magnificent painted pots of the Yang-shao (YAHNG•SHOW) culture found by the archaeologists date back to 3000–1500 B.C. Archaeologists have discovered that the Lung-shan culture, from about 2500–2000 B.C., used a potter's wheel to make delicate pots and goblets. These and other Neolithic finds dated to earlier than 5000 B.C. make it clear that the **Huang He valley**, like the river valleys of Egypt, the Fertile Crescent, and South Asia, invited settlement from very early times.

Chinese Myths

Over the centuries the Chinese developed many myths to explain their remote past. One myth tells how the universe was created from the body of a giant named Pan Gu (PAHN GOO), who hatched from an egg. Other legends celebrate the deeds of hero-kings. These larger-than-life rulers included Yao (YOW), a person in the form of a mountain, and Shun, the master of elephants. Another, **Yu the Great**, was a miraculous engineer. According to a myth about Yu:

❝ When widespread waters swelled to Heaven and serpents and dragons did harm, Yao sent Yu to control the waters and to drive out the serpents and dragons. The waters were controlled and flowed to the east. The serpents and dragons plunged to their places. ❞

The myth about Yu—written much later than the first oral tellings—may reflect stories about the attempts of one or many early rulers to channel the floodwaters of the Huang He.

According to tradition, Yu the Great founded China's first dynasty, named Xia (SYAH), around 2000 B.C. Archaeologists, however, have yet to find evidence of the legendary Xia. The first dynasty to be dated from written records in China is the Shang (SHAHNG). The Shang ruled China from about 1700 B.C. to 1000 B.C.

Early Religion

Though the Shang kings were political leaders, they also performed religious duties. As high priests, they could communicate with nature deities on behalf of the people. They prayed, made offerings, and performed sacrifices to gain a good harvest, a change in the weather, or victory in battle. Kings also had special powers for calling upon their ancestors. To do so, they had a priest scratch a question on an animal bone or sometimes on a

(AHN•YAHNG). Their excavations reveal the general layout of Anyang. A palace and temple stood at the center of the city, as in the cities of other early civilizations, and public buildings and homes of government officials circled the royal sanctuary. Beyond the city's center stood various workshops and other homes.

Expansion and Decline

Shang kings at first ruled over a small area in northern China. Later, their armies, equipped with bronze weapons and chariots, conquered more distant territories and finally took over most of the Huang He valley.

The Shang dynasty lacked strong leaders, however, and in time grew weak. Around 1000 B.C., Wu, a ruler of a former Shang territory in the northwest, marshaled his forces and marched on the capital. Wu killed the Shang king and established a new dynasty. Wu's dynasty, known as the Zhou (JOH), ruled China for 800 years.

Many Centuries of Dynasties

From the beginning of its recorded history until the early 1900s, dynasties ruled China. When writing about China's past, Western historians have followed the Chinese practice of dividing Chinese history into periods based on the reigns of these ruling families.

The Chinese believed that their rulers governed according to a principle known as the Mandate of Heaven. If rulers were just and effective, they received a mandate, or authority to rule, from heaven. If rulers did not govern properly—as indicated by poor crops or losses in battle—they lost the mandate to someone else who then started a new dynasty. The principle first appeared during the Zhou dynasty. Indeed the Zhou, as did later rebels, probably found the Mandate of Heaven a convenient way to explain their overthrow of an unpopular dynasty.

tortoise shell. The priest then applied intense heat to the bone. The bone would crack, and the priest would interpret the splintered pattern of cracks as the answer to the king's question. The bones helped the kings to predict the future. The scratchings on the oracle bones, as they are called, are the first known examples of writing in China.

Important Achievements

The priests writing on the oracle bones used a script with many characters. These characters represented objects, ideas, or sounds and were written in vertical columns. To use the script with ease, a writer had to memorize each character. Because only a small percentage of the population could master all the characters, few people in ancient China could read and write.

Not only did the Chinese of the Shang period develop a written script, but they also perfected their metal-casting skills and produced some of the finest bronze objects ever made. These included bronze daggers, figurines, and ritual urns. They built massive ceremonial cauldrons that stood on legs. Bronze fittings adorned hunting chariots, and warriors carried bronze daggers. Artisans also carved beautiful ivory and jade statues. They wove silk into elegantly colored cloth for the upper class and fashioned pottery from kaolin, a fine white clay.

The Chinese built their first cities under the Shang. Archaeologists today have identified seven capital cities, including the city of **Anyang**

SECTION 4 REVIEW

Recall

1. **Define** mandate.
2. **Identify** Yu the Great, Xia dynasty, Shang dynasty, Mandate of Heaven.
3. **Use** the map on page 67 to list the major physical features of China. Explain how these physical features affected the development of Chinese civilization.

Critical Thinking

4. **Making Comparisons** Compare the Mandate of Heaven with the way Egyptian kings justified their rule.

Understanding Themes

5. **Innovation** Explain the basic features of the Chinese writing system as it developed in early times. How widespread was the use of this method of writing in China under the early dynasties?

from

Gilgamesh

retold by Herbert Mason

*L*ike people today, ancient Sumerians loved adventure tales featuring extraordinary heroes battling the forces of evil. Many Sumerian myths featured a king, Gilgamesh, who lived around 2700 B.C. The earliest known written accounts of Gilgamesh's adventures date from about 1850 B.C., making them the oldest surviving examples of epic poetry. An epic is a long poem recalling the exploits of a legendary hero. Gilgamesh, after the death of his friend Enkidu, searched for the secret of eternal life, which he hoped to share with his departed friend. In the following excerpt, Gilgamesh, hoping to learn how to escape death, listens to a mysterious elderly man, Utnapishtim, recount how he survived a great flood.

*T*here was a city called Shurrupak
  On the bank of the Euphrates.
It was very old, and so many were the gods
Within it. They converged in their complex
    hearts
On the idea of creating a great flood.
There was Anu, their aging and weak-minded
    father,
The military Enlil, his adviser,
Ishtar, the sensation-craving one,
And all the rest. Ea, who was present
At their council, came to my house
And, frightened by the violent winds that filled
    the air,
Echoed all that they were planning and had said.
Man of Shurrupak, he said, tear down your
    house
And build a ship. Abandon your possessions
And the works that you find beautiful and crave,
And save your life instead. Into the ship
Bring the seed of all living creatures.

I was overawed, perplexed,
And finally downcast. I agreed to do
As Ea said, but I protested: What shall I say
To the city, the people, the leaders?

Tell them, Ea said, you have learned that Enlil
The war god despises you and will not
Give you access to the city anymore.
Tell them for this Ea will bring the rains.

This is the way gods think, he laughed. His tone
Of savage irony frightened Gilgamesh
Yet gave him pleasure, being his friend.
They only know how to compete or echo.
But who am I to talk? He sighed as if
Disgusted with himself; I did as he
Commanded me to do. I spoke to them,
And some came out to help me build the ship
Of seven stories, each with nine chambers.
The boat was cube in shape, and sound; it held
The food and wine and precious minerals
And seed of living animals we put
In it. My family then moved inside,
And all who wanted to be with us there:
The game of the field, the goats of the steppe,
The craftsmen of the city came, a navigator
Came. And then Ea ordered me to close
The door. The time of the great rains had come.
O there was ample warning, yes, my friend,
But it was terrifying still. Buildings
Blown by the winds for miles like desert brush.
People clung to branches of trees until
Roots gave way. New possessions, now debris,
Floated on the water with their special
Sterile vacancy. The riverbanks failed
To hold the water back. Even the gods
Cowered like dogs at what they had done.
Ishtar cried out like a woman at the height
Of labor: O how could I have wanted
To do this to my people! They were *hers*,
Notice. Even her sorrow was possessive.
Her spawn that she had killed too soon.
Old gods are terrible to look at when
They weep, all bloated like spoiled fish.
One wonders if they ever understand

That they have caused their grief. When the
    seventh day
Came, the flood subsided from its slaughter
Like hair drawn slowly back
From a tormented face.
I looked at the earth and all was silence.
Bodies lay like alewives [a type of fish], dead
And in the clay. I fell down
On the ship's deck and wept. Why? Why did they
Have to die? I couldn't understand. I asked
Unanswerable questions a child asks
When a parent dies—for nothing. Only slowly
Did I make myself believe—or hope—they
Might all be swept up in their fragments
Together
And made whole again
By some compassionate hand.
But my hand was too small
To do the gathering.
I have only known this feeling since
When I look out across the sea of death,
This pull inside against a littleness—myself—
Waiting for an upward gesture.

O the dove, the swallow and the raven
Found their land. The people left the ship.
But I for a long time could only stay inside.
I could not face the deaths I knew were there.
Then I received Enlil, for Ea had *chosen* me;
The war god touched my forehead; he blessed
My family and said:
Before this you were just a man, but now
You and your wife shall be like gods. You
Shall live in the distance at the rivers' mouth,
At the source. I allowed myself to be
Taken far away from all that I had seen.
Sometimes even in love we yearn to leave mankind.
Only the loneliness of the Only One
Who never acts like gods
Is bearable.

Visualizing History Gilgamesh subdues a lion. By the 700s B.C. Gilgamesh had become a mythological hero. The real Gilgamesh ruled over ancient Uruk. *What blessing did the war god give Gilgamesh and his family?*

I am downcast because of what I've seen,
Not what I still have hope to yearn for.
Lost youths restored to life,
Lost children to their crying mothers,
Lost wives, lost friends, lost hopes, lost homes,
I want to bring these back to them.
But now there is you.
We must find something for you.
How will you find eternal life
To bring back to your friend?
He pondered busily, as if
It were just a matter of getting down to work
Or making plans for an excursion.
Then he relaxed, as if there were no use
In this reflection. I would grieve
At all that may befall you still,
If I did not know you must return
And bury your own loss and build
Your world anew with your own hands.
I envy you your freedom.

As he listened, Gilgamesh felt tiredness again
Come over him, the words now so discouraging,
The promise so remote, so unlike what he sought.
He looked into the old man's face, and it seemed changed,
As if this one had fought within himself a battle
He would never know, that still went on.

Connections Across Time

Historical Significance The world's first civilizations developed along the banks of river valleys—the Nile, Tigris-Euphrates, Indus, and Huang. They faced similar challenges in explaining the mysteries of nature, using their resources, and providing for defense. They all sought answers through cooperation, government, technology, and religion. They built cities, created dynasties, developed writing systems, and devised laws. Their political ideas, social institutions, and cultural achievements were inherited by later peoples and became the foundation of the civilization we know today.

Using Key Terms

Write the key term that completes each sentence. Then write a sentence for each term not chosen.

a. bureaucracy
b. city-state
c. cuneiform
d. dynasty
e. empire
f. hieroglyphics
g. mandate
h. monarchy
i. monsoon
j. pharaoh
k. polytheism
l. theocracy

1. In ancient China, the first historical _____, or line of rulers from one family, was called the Shang.
2. The ancient Egyptians carved onto pieces of slate a variety of picture symbols, or _____, that stood for objects, ideas, and sounds.
3. The Sumerian form of writing, _____, consisted of hundreds of wedge-shaped markings made by pressing the end of a sharpened reed on wet clay tablets.
4. A typical Sumerian ____ included the city itself and surrounding land.
5. Sargon I united all of the Mesopotamian city-states in a single ____, which consisted of many different territories under one ruler.

Technology Activity

Using E-mail Search the Internet for the E-mail address of an Egyptologist from an international museum or university. Compose a letter requesting information about various aspects of ancient Egyptian culture such as architecture, religion, hieroglyphics, or medicine. From your response, write a short report of your findings. Share your report with the class.

Using Your History Journal

Choose one event from this chapter. Describe the event in picture-writing (cuneiform). Exchange your description with other students and try to guess what each person's event is.

Reviewing Facts

1. **Technology** Explain how the early Mesopotamians controlled the Tigris and Euphrates Rivers.
2. **Culture** Describe the major difference between the pyramids of Egypt and the ziggurats of Mesopotamia.
3. **Economics** Explain why archaeologists believe that there was contact between Mesopotamian and Harappan cultures.
4. **Culture** List the achievements of the ancient Chinese that show their artistic innovation.
5. **Geography** Describe how the Himalayas affected two early river valley civilizations.
6. **History** Identify one event from each of the following periods: the Old Kingdom, the Middle Kingdom, and the New Kingdom.
7. **Government** Name the capital of Upper Egypt that was established in 2050 B.C.
8. **Government** Explain why Amenhotep changed his royal name to Akhenaton.
9. **Government** Describe the main powers and responsibilities of a typical king of a Sumerian city-state around 2700 B.C.
10. **Government** List four examples of the kinds of laws found in Hammurabi's code. Explain why the code was a significant development.

Critical Thinking

1. **Apply** What clues do artifacts found in the ruins at Harappa and Mohenjo-Daro provide about the Harappan religion?
2. **Compare** How did the powers of the Egyptian kings differ from those of the Shang kings? How were their powers the same?
3. **Synthesize** What reaction would you have had to Akhenaton's reforms if you had been a priest of Amon-Ra?
4. **Compare** How did life along the Tigris and Euphrates Rivers in Mesopotamia differ from life along the Nile River in Egypt?

Geography in History

1. **Location** Refer to the map below. What is the relative location of the Sinai Peninsula? Find this peninsula on the Middle East map in the Atlas. What is its absolute location?
2. **Place** Why was most agricultural production in ancient Egypt and in that nation today found along the Nile River?
3. **Movement** Why would travel in ancient Egypt have been easier for a person who was going from south to north than for a person going from east to west? What might make travel from east to west less difficult today?

Egypt

Mediterranean Sea
Nile Delta
QATTARA DEPRESSION
SINAI PENINSULA
Gulf of Aqaba
Gulf of Suez
LIBYAN DESERT
EGYPT
Nile River
ARABIAN DESERT
Red Sea
Lake Nasser
SAHARA

Skill Practice

Read about life in Harappan civilization in the Indus River valley on pages 67 and 68 in Section 3. Use this information to complete the following chart.

Harappan Life		
Occupations	**Artifacts**	**Theories of Decline**

Understanding Themes

1. **Relation to Environment** What flood-control methods of the ancient Egyptians and other river valley peoples are still in use today?
2. **Cooperation** In what areas of city life today is cooperation as important as it was when the Sumerians built the earliest cities?
3. **Cultural Diffusion** What advances in the twentieth century have made cultural diffusion easier and faster than in ancient times?
4. **Innovation** Why would you consider each of the following developments in ancient China an innovation: a writing script with many characters, bronze vessels and tools, pottery, and silk cloth?

Linking Past and Present

1. Examine Hatshepsut's role as a ruler of Egypt. How does her position and its influence compare with those of modern women holding high political office?
2. Why was early China largely isolated from the rest of the world? Do these same factors still affect modern China? In what ways have the modern Chinese increased contacts with other cultures? To what extent are they still isolated?

Kingdoms and Empires in the Middle East

Chapter Themes

▶ **Cultural Diffusion** Aramaean and Phoenician merchants spread ideas throughout the Middle East. *Section 1*

▶ **Innovation** The Israelites contribute to the world the concept of monotheism. *Section 2*

▶ **Conflict** A series of empires—Hittite, then Assyrian, then Chaldean, then Persian—each conquers the previous one. *Section 3*

The Storyteller

Ashurbanipal, the last great Assyrian king, reigned in the mid-600s B.C. The dim rooms were almost still in Ashurbanipal's great palace at Nineveh, the splendid capital of his empire. Men with shoulder-length hair and squared-off beards glided in their tunics and sandals through the vast hallways. But the stone reliefs that decorated the palace walls told a less peaceful story. In intricately carved scenes, the impassive hunter in his chariot lets fly with a volley of arrows into a staggering lion, and the valiant general on the battlefield proudly waves his sword above the defeated enemy legions. Ashurbanipal followed a long line of ruthless Assyrian conquerors who boasted of their military exploits and cruelty.

Historical Significance

How did traders, religious thinkers, and empire builders shape the development of the ancient Middle East? How have their achievements influenced cultural and religious life today?

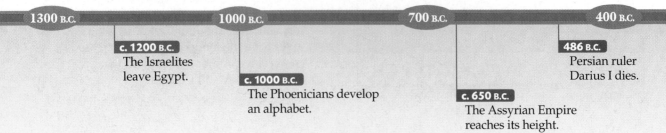

1300 B.C.	1000 B.C.	700 B.C.	400 B.C.

c. 1200 B.C.
The Israelites leave Egypt.

c. 1000 B.C.
The Phoenicians develop an alphabet.

c. 650 B.C.
The Assyrian Empire reaches its height.

486 B.C.
Persian ruler Darius I dies.

 Ashurbanipal hunting on horseback. Relief from the NW Palace at Nineveh, c. 640 B.C.

Your History Journal

Early Middle Eastern accounts deal with the themes of peace and justice. Read the quotes on pages 86 and 93, and write similar verses describing events in the chapter that relate to these themes.

1200 B.C.	1000 B.C.	800 B.C.	600 B.C.

c. 1200 B.C.
Aramaeans settle
in central Syria.

c. 1100 B.C.
Phoenicians reach Spain and
western Africa.

c. 600s B.C.
Lydians develop a
wealthy kingdom
in Asia Minor.

Section 1

Trading Peoples

Setting the Scene

▶ **Terms to Define**
confederation, alphabet, colony, barter

▶ **People to Meet**
the Aramaeans, the Phoenicians, the Lydians

▶ **Places to Locate**
Syria, Damascus, Tyre

Find Out How did trading peoples influence
the development of the Middle East?

The Storyteller

*King Hiram was pleased. Tyre, his capital city,
was a bustling seaport: sophisticated, cosmopoli-
tan, and rich. Not only did the kings of Egypt and
Babylon send ambassadors to Hiram's court, they
also brought business to his land. Gold, copper,
ivory, and linen from Egypt; precious stones from
Babylon; silver from Asia Minor; and pottery from
Crete enriched Tyre. In return, Tyre exchanged
cedar, cut from the nearby mountains, and a vivid
purple dye, harvested from murex shells found in
the seas near the rocky coast. Hiram's people were
Phoenicians, the people of the purple, the color—
beautiful, costly, and rare—which throughout the
ancient world marked an individual as one of
immense wealth and high rank.*

—adapted from
*The Bible as
History*, Werner
Keller, translated
by William Neil,
1969

Phoenician ship

The magnificent civilizations of
Mesopotamia and Egypt greatly influenced neighboring peoples in the
Fertile Crescent—among them **the Aramaeans**
(AR•uh•MEE•uhnz) and **the Phoenicians** (fih
•NEE•shuhnz). In turn, these trading peoples
helped to spread their own cultures throughout the
region and into much of the ancient world.
Traveling on sailing ships and by caravan, traders
from the Fertile Crescent brought languages, customs, and ideas along with their trade goods.

The Aramaeans

One of the most active peoples in early Middle
Eastern trade, the Aramaeans settled in central
Syria around 1200 B.C. Although Aramaean kings
established a capital at **Damascus**, provincial leaders frequently challenged their authority. Despite
political weaknesses, the Aramaeans gained control
of the rich overland trade between Egypt and
Mesopotamia.

Because Aramaean caravans crossed and
recrossed the Fertile Crescent on business, people
throughout the region learned Aramaic, the language of the Aramaeans. Until the A.D. 800s, the
majority of the people living in the Fertile Crescent
spoke Aramaic, a language closely related to
Hebrew and Arabic. In addition, some parts of the
Bible were written in Aramaic.

The Phoenicians

Between ancient Egypt and Syria lay the land of
Canaan, today made up of Lebanon, Israel, and
Jordan. The Phoenicians, one of the Semitic groups
that migrated from the Arabian Peninsula about
3000 B.C., settled in the northern part of Canaan.
Their neighbors in Canaan, the Philistines, came
from the eastern Mediterranean. The Romans would

Lloyd K. Townsend

Merchants of the Mediterranean

In this illustration sturdy cargo boats dock in their North African home port of Carthage, and war galleys in the harbor lie in wait for any rivals caught in Phoenician waters. A captain bargains over the price of a bale of purple cloth for the next voyage as his crew unloads grain from Sardinia and cedar logs from North Africa. Above deck sit clay jars of olive oil and wine; below, silver, tin, gold, and ivory are stored. Departing vessels take on terra-cotta figurines, decorated ostrich eggshells, metal utensils, and perfume vials.

From their cities nestled along the coast of the eastern Mediterranean Sea, Phoenicians launched a trading empire. They soon became middlemen for their neighbors in Mesopotamia, Arabia, and Egypt. By 800 B.C., Phoenician trade had spread into the western Mediterranean. From Carthage and other Mediterranean cities, the Phoenicians manned supply depots, guarded sea lanes, and expanded their trading empire. ⊕

later call southern Canaan *Palestine*, meaning "land of the Philistines."

In contrast to the Aramaeans, who trekked overland to reach their markets, the Phoenicians sailed the seas. On a narrow strip of land between the mountains of western Syria and the Mediterranean Sea, Phoenicia lacked enough arable land for farming, and many Phoenicians turned to the sea to earn a living. They harvested timber from the cedar forests on nearby slopes to build strong, fast ships.

By 1200 B.C. the Phoenicians had built a string of cities and towns along their coast. Many of these scattered ports grew to become city-states, the largest of which were **Tyre**, Byblos, Sidon, and Berytus (modern Beirut). The city-state of Tyre often provided the leadership for what remained a confederation, or loose union, of independent Phoenician city-states. According to the Bible:

> ❝ Who was like Tyre…. In the midst of the sea? When your wares were unloaded from the seas, You satisfied many peoples; With your great wealth and merchandise You enriched the kings of the earth. ❞
>
> —Ezekiel 27:32-33

The Phoenicians sailed from their coastal city-states throughout the Mediterranean. Expert navigators, they learned to plot their voyages with great accuracy by means of the sun and the stars. By 1100 B.C. Phoenicians reached the southern coast of Spain and the western coast of Africa. Some historians believe they even ventured as far as the British Isles in northwestern Europe.

Astute traders and businesspeople, the Phoenicians soon took charge of Mediterranean shipping and trade. At ports of call, they exchanged cedar logs, textiles dyed a beautiful purple, glass objects, and elegant jewelry for precious metals. They also brought new business practices, such as bills of sale and contracts.

An advantage that Phoenician merchants held over their competitors when keeping track of complex business deals was an improved alphabet—a series of written symbols that represent sounds. Phoenicians developed their efficient alphabet about 1000 B.C. from earlier, more complicated systems from southern Canaan and northwest Syria. The concise Phoenician alphabet used just 22 characters, each character representing a consonant sound. Readers mentally supplied vowels in the proper places.

The Phoenician system later became the foundation of several alphabets, including Greek, which in turn became the basis of all Western alphabets. Because the Phoenician alphabet did not require years of study to master, merchants no longer needed the services of specially trained scribes to keep records.

To protect and resupply their ships, Phoenician sailors and traders set up along the coasts of the Mediterranean a network of temporary trading posts and colonies, or settlements of Phoenician emigrants. For example, about 814 B.C., people from Tyre founded a colony named Carthage on the coast of present-day Tunisia. Carthage eventually became the most powerful city in the western Mediterranean.

The Lydians

The Lydians (LIH•dee•uhnz) lived in Asia Minor—the peninsula jutting westward between the Mediterranean, Aegean, and Black Seas. Lydian merchants and artisans were well situated to prosper in the growing regional trade. By the late 600s B.C., the Lydians had developed a wealthy and independent kingdom famous for its rich gold deposits.

Most traders from neighboring cultures still relied on a system of barter for their transactions, exchanging their wares for other goods. The Lydians, however, began to set prices and developed a money system using coins as a medium of exchange. Soon Greek and Persian rulers began to stamp their own coins, and the concept of money spread beyond Lydia.

SECTION 1 REVIEW

Recall
1. **Define** confederation, alphabet, colony, barter.
2. **Identify** the Aramaeans, the Phoenicians, the Lydians.
3. **Describe** the bodies of water

bordering the regions of Canaan and Asia Minor.

Critical Thinking
4. **Evaluating Information** What geographic factors enabled the Phoenician city-

states to remain independent and to prosper?

Understanding Themes
5. **Cultural Diffusion** Why was the Phoenician alphabet a significant development?

2000 B.C.   1500 B.C.   1000 B.C.   500 B.C.

c. 1900 B.C.
Abraham settles in Canaan.

c. 1200 B.C.
The Israelites
first celebrate
Passover.

c. 1000 B.C.
David sets up
capital at
Jerusalem.

c. 530s B.C.
Jews rebuild the
Temple in Jerusalem.

Section 2

Early Israelites

Setting the Scene

▶ **Terms to Define**
monotheism, prophet, covenant, exodus, Diaspora

▶ **People to Meet** the Israelites, Abraham, Moses, Deborah, David, Solomon

▶ **Places to Locate** Canaan, Jerusalem

Find Out What part do slavery, exile, and return play in the history of the Israelites?

The Storyteller

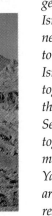

This battle would be decisive, Jael was certain. Before the sun set, the Israelites would be recognized as Yahweh's chosen people. Unlike the nomads who had passed through Canaan for generations, the 12 tribes of Israel now sought permanent settlement. However, to remain and prosper, the Israelites had to join together and defeat the threatening Canaanites. Several tribes of Israel, held together only by their common covenant with Yahweh, were sending armed men to battle. Jael, resolving to take action herself, if necessary, was sure that Yahweh would muster the heavens themselves to confound the enemies of the covenant, give victory to the Israelites, and bring peace to the land.

Mount Sinai

—adapted from the *Holy Bible,* Judges

Most cultures of the ancient world worshiped many deities. The Phoenicians, for example, worshiped a chief god known as El, Baal, or Melqart; an earth-mother goddess called Astarte; and a young god of rebirth named Adonis.

The Israelites—another people living in **Canaan**—were an exception. They adhered to monotheism, the belief in one all–powerful God whose commands were revealed by prophets, or holy messengers. The Israelites believed that God, whom they called Yahweh, determined right and wrong and expected people to deal justly with each other and to accept moral responsibility for their actions. The teachings of the Israelites exist today as the religion of Judaism, which shares many beliefs with two other monotheistic religions— Christianity and Islam.

The Land of Canaan

The Bible remains one of the main sources of ancient history in the Fertile Crescent. As a record of the early Israelites, the Bible traces their origins to **Abraham**, a herder and trader who lived in the Mesopotamian city of Ur. Around 1900 B.C. Abraham and his household left Ur and settled in Canaan at the command of Yahweh, or God. The Israelites believed that God made a covenant, or agreement, with Abraham at this time. "I will make of you a great nation" was God's promise to bless Abraham and his descendants if they would remain faithful to God.

According to the Bible, once in the land of Canaan, the descendants of Abraham shared the land with other peoples, such as the Phoenicians and Philistines. Canaan contained rocky hills and desert, fertile plains and grassy slopes, with the best farming in the valley of the Jordan River. Many people lived as nomads herding sheep and goats.

The Exodus From Egypt

Abraham's grandson Jacob, also known as Israel, raised 12 sons in Canaan, and each son led a separate family group, or tribe. These groups became the 12 tribes of Israel. To escape a severe famine, the Israelites migrated to Egypt. There they lived peacefully for several generations, until the Egyptians decided to enslave them.

In the 1200s B.C., the Israelite prophet **Moses** led his people out of Egypt in an exodus, or departure, into the Sinai Desert. Every year during the festival of Passover, Jews today retell the story of the Exodus from Egypt.

According to the Bible, during the long trek across the desert of the Sinai Peninsula, God renewed the covenant made with Abraham. Moses and the Israelites pledged to reject all gods other than the one true God and to obey God's laws, the most important of which would be called the Ten Commandments:

> ❝ I the Lord am your God who brought you out of the land of Egypt, the house of bondage: You shall have no other gods beside Me.
> You shall not make for yourself a sculptured image....
> You shall not swear falsely by the name of the Lord your God....
> Remember the sabbath day and keep it holy....
> Honor your father and your mother, that you may long endure on the land that the Lord your God is giving you.
> You shall not murder.
> You shall not commit adultery.
> You shall not steal.
> You shall not bear false witness against your neighbor.
> You shall not covet … anything that is your neighbor's. ❞
>
> —Exodus 20:2–14

In return for their loyalty, God promised the Israelites a safe return to the land of Canaan.

Settling the Land

Moses died before reaching Canaan, but his successor, Joshua, led the Israelites across the Jordan River into Canaan. For about 200 years, the

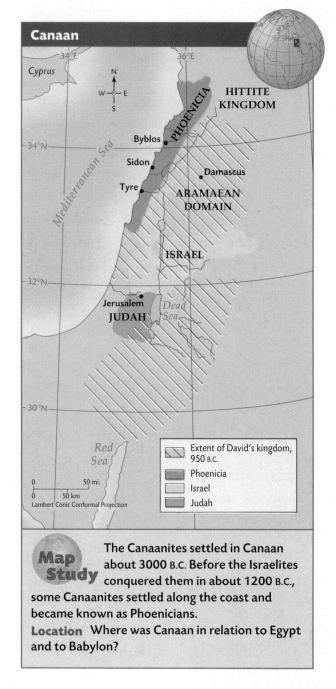

Canaan

The Canaanites settled in Canaan about 3000 B.C. Before the Israelites conquered them in about 1200 B.C., some Canaanites settled along the coast and became known as Phoenicians.
Location Where was Canaan in relation to Egypt and to Babylon?

Israelites fought the Philistines and the Canaanites who now occupied the land.

The Fighting Judges

Lack of unity among the 12 tribes of Israel prolonged the campaign to acquire Canaan. Leaders known as "judges" ruled each tribe. Serving as both judicial and military leaders, some of the judges attempted to rally the Israelites. The Bible relates how **Deborah**, a judge widely admired for her wisdom, planned an attack on a Canaanite army camped near Mount Tabor. The Israelites believed that through God's help, they won the battle.

The Davidic Monarchy

Around 1020 B.C. continual warfare led most of the Israelite tribes to unite under one king, Saul. Although he was popular at first, Saul's power waned when he proved unable to defeat the Philistines. **David**, who had once fought the Philistine Goliath on Saul's behalf, took the throne in 1012 B.C. and ruled for the next 40 years. King David set up a capital at **Jerusalem**, organized a central government, and enlarged his kingdom's borders. During his reign, the Israelites enjoyed economic prosperity.

David's son **Solomon** succeeded his father in 961 B.C. Solomon founded new cities and lavished money on the construction of a magnificent temple to God in Jerusalem. The Israelites resented Solomon's high taxes and harsh labor requirements. After Solomon's death in 922 B.C., the 10 northern tribes broke away from the 2 tribes in the south. The northern tribes continued to call their kingdom Israel. The 2 southern tribes called their kingdom Judah, and kept Jerusalem as their capital. The word *Jew* comes from the name *Judah*.

Exile and Return

Although split politically, the people of Israel and Judah continued to share one religion. The 2 kingdoms, however, were too weak to resist invasions by powerful neighbors. In 722 B.C. the Assyrians of Mesopotamia swept in and conquered Israel, scattering the people of the 10 northern tribes throughout the Assyrian Empire. Then, in 586 B.C., another Mesopotamian people, the Chaldeans (kal•DEE•uhnz), gained control of Judah and destroyed the Temple in Jerusalem. They enslaved some of the city's residents and carried them off to exile in the Chaldean capital city of Babylon.

Exile in Babylon

During this difficult period, a series of prophets arose among the Israelites, who were called Jews after the Babylonian exile. Some prophets, such as Jeremiah, condemned abuses in society and blamed the exile on the Jews' forgetting their duties to God and to one another. The prophets also helped the Jews retain their religious culture during the exile.

While in Babylon, the Jews no longer had a temple. Instead, small groups of Jews began to meet on the Sabbath, the holy day of rest, for prayer and study. The rise of synagogues developed from these gatherings.

Rebuilding Jerusalem

Many Jews hoped to return to Jerusalem. Finally, in 539 B.C., the Persians conquered the

Chaldeans. The Persian king, Cyrus II, allowed the Jews to return to Judah and to rebuild the Temple. In the 400s B.C., Jewish holy writings were organized into the Torah, made up of the first five books of the Bible: Genesis, Exodus, Leviticus, Numbers, and Deuteronomy.

Although a new Jewish community arose in Jerusalem, many Jews remained in Babylon, and some migrated to other areas in the Middle East. Ever since this time, communities of Jews have existed outside their homeland in what is known as the Diaspora, a Greek word meaning "scattered."

A Lasting Legacy

Their troubled history—with cycles of slavery, exile, and return—made the Jews keenly aware of their past. Seeing events as having a God-directed purpose, the Jews recorded their history and examined it for meaning. The Jewish Scriptures begin with the Torah, which states that God created the universe and that humans have infinite worth:

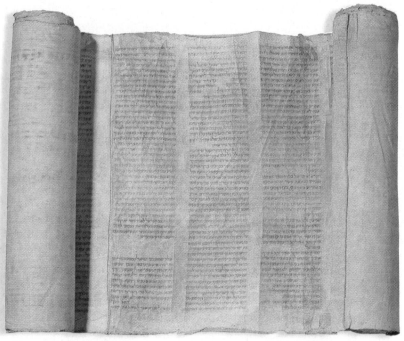

Visualizing History Scribes recopied the Torah carefully, comparing each letter and word to the original copy. *What was the prophet Micah's vision for the world?*

❝ God created humankind in his image,
in the image of God did he create it,
male and female did he create them.
God blessed them,
God said to them:
Bear fruit and be many and fill the earth
and subdue it!
Have dominion over the fish of the sea, the
fowl of the heavens, and all living things
that crawl upon the earth! ❞
                    –Genesis 1:27–28

The Jewish Scriptures also include the writings of the prophets. The prophetic teachings state that humans work in partnership with God, striving to achieve a perfect world, and this link makes people accountable for what happens in the world. The prophet Micah expressed his vision for the world as follows:

❝ And they shall beat their swords
    into plowshares,
And their spears into pruning hooks.
Nation shall not take up
Sword against nation;
They shall never again know war;
But every man shall sit
Under his grapevine or fig tree
With no one to disturb him. ❞
                    –Micah 4:3–4

As the Jews scattered beyond Canaan, they took their sacred writings with them. Jewish religious beliefs and ethical principles became an important part of the heritage of the West.

SECTION 2 REVIEW

Recall
1. **Define** monotheism, prophet, covenant, exodus, Diaspora.
2. **Identify** the Israelites, Abraham, Moses, Deborah, David, Solomon.
3. **Locate** Jerusalem on the map on page 84. What was the significance of Jerusalem to Jews in exile in Babylon?

Critical Thinking
4. **Analyzing Information** Create a chronology of the migrations of the Israelites.

Understanding Themes
5. **Innovation** What religious beliefs set the Israelites apart from other ancient peoples? How have these beliefs helped the Jews to survive in spite of exile and persecution?

Problem Solving

You have just done poorly on a geography exam. You wonder why you can't do better since you always go to class, take notes, and study for exams. In order to improve your grades, you need to identify the specific problem, and then take actions to solve it.

Learning the Skill

There are six key steps you should follow that will help you through the problem-solving process.

1. Identify the problem. In this case, you know that you are not doing well on geography exams.

2. Gather information. You know that you always go to class and take notes. You study by yourself for about two hours each day for two or three days before the exam. You also know that as you are taking the exam, you sometimes forget details or get confused about things.

3. List and consider options. For example, instead of studying by yourself, you might try a study group, or study with a friend.

4. Consider the advantages and disadvantages of each option.

5. Choose and implement a solution to the problem. Now that you have listed and considered the options, you need to choose the best option.

6. Evaluate the effectiveness of the solution. This will help you determine if you've solved the problem. If, on the next few geography exams, you earn better scores, you know that you have solved your problem.

Practicing the Skill

Reread the material in Section 1 on pages 80–82 about the trading peoples of the Middle East. Use that information to answer the following questions.

1. What problem did the Phoenicians encounter as they tried to farm the land of Phoenicia?

2. Summarize information the Phoenicians might have gathered after finding that they couldn't rely on farming as a means of survival.

3. List some of the options available to the Phoenicians. What were the advantages? What were the disadvantages?

4. Explain the solution the Phoenicians implemented to solve their problem.

5. Evaluate the effectiveness of their solution. Was it successful? How do you determine this?

Applying the Skill

The conservation club at your school has no money to continue its recycling project. The school district allocated money to the club at the beginning of the year, but that money has been spent. As a member of the club, you have been asked to join a committee to save the conservation club and its projects. Write an essay describing the problem, the list of options and their advantages and disadvantages, a solution, and an evaluation of the chosen solution.

For More Practice

Turn to the Skill Practice in the Chapter Review on page 95 for more practice with problem solving.

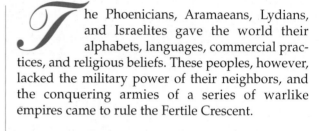

2000 B.C.   1500 B.C.   1000 B.C.   500 B.C.

c. 1600 B.C.
Hittite Empire reaches
its height.

c. 605 B.C.
Nebuchadnezzar
begins reign in
Babylon.

525 B.C.
Persian armies
conquer Egypt.

Section 3

Empire Builders

Setting the Scene

▶ **Terms to Define**
satrap

▶ **People to Meet**
the Hittites, the Assyrians, the Chaldeans,
Nebuchadnezzar, the Persians, Cyrus II,
Darius I, Zoroaster

▶ **Places to Locate** Anatolia, Babylon, Nineveh,
Persepolis

ind Out How did a series of powerful
empires extend their rule throughout the
Middle East?

The Storyteller

*The scribe carefully recorded King
Ashurbanipal II's proclamation. The royal
archives would preserve an accurate
account of the actions taken against
the cities that had dared to revolt.
The king dictated: "With the
fury of my weapons I stormed
the city. I flayed all the chief
men who had revolted, and I
covered a pillar with their skins.
Some I impaled on the pillar on
stakes.... I fashioned a heroic
image of my royal self, my
power and my glory I inscribed
thereon...." Ashurbanipal called
the gods to destroy all who
opposed him, overthrowing their
kingdoms and blotting out their
names from the land.*

Giant winged bull

—from *Ancient Records of Assyria and
Babylonia*, Volume 1, edited by Daniel
David Luckenbill, 1968

The Phoenicians, Aramaeans, Lydians,
and Israelites gave the world their
alphabets, languages, commercial prac-
tices, and religious beliefs. These peoples, however,
lacked the military power of their neighbors, and
the conquering armies of a series of warlike
empires came to rule the Fertile Crescent.

The Hittites

Around 2000 B.C., **the Hittites**—perhaps coming from areas beyond the Black Sea—conquered
the local people of Asia Minor. The Hittites set up
several city-states on a central plateau called
Anatolia, and by about 1650 B.C., they had built a
well-organized kingdom. Archaeologists have deci-
phered the writing on some of the clay tablets
found in the ruins of Hattusas, the Hittite capital.
Other information about the Hittites comes from
records of peoples they confronted as they expanded their empire. An Egyptian source, for example,
described the Hittites' custom of wearing their hair
in a long, thick pigtail that hung down in the back.

Hittite kings assembled a fearsome army—the
first in the Middle East to wield iron weapons
extensively. The army used light, spoked-wheel
chariots that could carry two soldiers and a driver.
This gave the Hittites a decided advantage in battle,
because they were able to field twice as many
troops as their foes in two-person chariots.
Overwhelming any army that stood in their way,
the Hittites pushed eastward and conquered the
city of **Babylon** about 1595 B.C. The Hittite
Empire—spanning Asia Minor, Syria, and part of
Mesopotamia—lasted until about 1200 B.C.

The Hittites largely borrowed their culture
from Mesopotamia and Egypt. However, they did
contribute to Middle Eastern civilization a legal
system considered less harsh than Hammurabi's
code. Hittite law emphasized payments for damages rather than harsh punishments.

The Assyrians

The Assyrians, a people living in northern Mesopotamia, had faced constant invasions from adjoining Asia Minor—including those by the Hittites. About 900 B.C. the Assyrians finally became strong enough to repel attacks from the west. They also began to launch their own military campaigns to subdue their Mesopotamian neighbors.

A Powerful Army

The Assyrian army earned a reputation as the most lethal fighting force in the Middle East. The Assyrians organized their warriors into units of foot soldiers, charioteers, and fast-moving cavalry fighting on horseback. They were described as fighters "whose arrows were sharp and all their bows bent, the horses' hooves were like flint, and their [chariot] wheels like a whirlwind." The Assyrians fought with iron weapons and used battering rams against the walls of the cities they attacked.

The Assyrians treated conquered peoples cruelly. They burned cities and tortured and killed thousands of captives. The Assyrians routinely deported entire populations from their homelands. Resettling the land with people from other parts of the empire, the Assyrians forced these settlers to pay heavy taxes.

The Assyrian Empire

By about 650 B.C., the Assyrian kings governed an empire stretching from the Persian Gulf to Egypt and into Asia Minor. They divided their empire into provinces, each headed by a governor directly responsible to the king. Officials sent from the central government collected taxes to support the army and to fund building projects in **Nineveh**, the Assyrian capital. To improve communication, the Assyrians built a network of roads linking the provinces. Government messengers and Aramaean merchants traveled these roads, protected by soldiers from bandits.

In spite of these links, the Assyrian Empire eventually began to fracture as conquered peoples continually rebelled. In 612 B.C. **the Chaldeans**, who lived in the ancient city of Babylon, formed an alliance with the Medes from the east. The alliance captured Nineveh and brought down the Assyrian Empire.

The Chaldeans

Soon after the Assyrians fell, the Chaldean Empire succeeded in dominating the entire Fertile Crescent. Most of the Chaldeans—sometimes called the New Babylonians—were descended from people of Hammurabi's Babylonian Empire of the 1700s B.C.

The Chaldeans reached the height of their power during the reign of one of their greatest

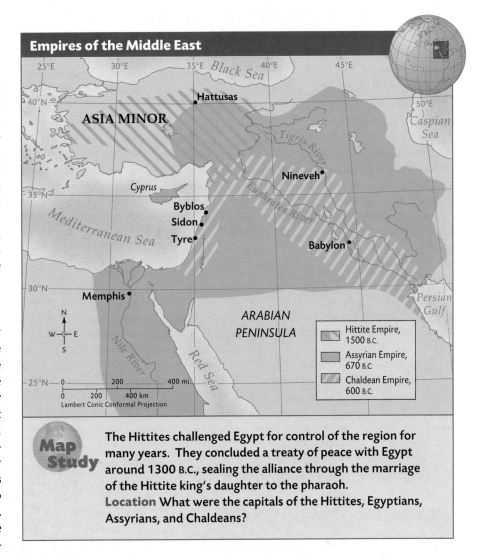

Empires of the Middle East

Hittite Empire, 1500 B.C.
Assyrian Empire, 670 B.C.
Chaldean Empire, 600 B.C.

Map Study

The Hittites challenged Egypt for control of the region for many years. They concluded a treaty of peace with Egypt around 1300 B.C., sealing the alliance through the marriage of the Hittite king's daughter to the pharaoh.
Location What were the capitals of the Hittites, Egyptians, Assyrians, and Chaldeans?

rulers, King **Nebuchadnezzar** (NEH•byuh•kuhd •NEH•zuhr), from 605 B.C. to 562 B.C. He extended the boundaries of the Chaldean Empire as far west as Syria and Canaan, conquering the city of Jerusalem and the Phoenician city-state of Tyre and forcing the people of the kingdom of Judah into a Babylonian exile in 586 B.C. Nebuchadnezzar also amassed great wealth and rebuilt Babylon into one of the most beautiful cities of the ancient world.

Historians of the time counted a feature of Babylon among the so-called Seven Wonders of the World—its Hanging Gardens. Nebuchadnezzar created the Hanging Gardens for his wife. Constructed on several levels and designed to be visible from any point in Babylon, the elaborate park was fed by water pumped from a nearby river. Another landmark of Babylon was an immense wall that snaked around the city, stood 50 feet (15 km) high, and bristled with watchtowers every 100 yards (90 m).

The Chaldeans were also noted for their interest in astrology. They recorded their observations of the stars and made maps that showed the position of the planets and the phases of the moon. Their studies laid the foundations for the science of astronomy.

After Nebuchadnezzar's death, a series of weak kings held the throne. Poor harvests and slow trade further sapped the strength of an empire whose people had been severely taxed and plundered. Then, in 539 B.C., **the Persians** under **Cyrus II** came from the mountains to the northeast, seized Babylon, and then conquered the rest of the Chaldean Empire.

The Persians

The Persians originated from a larger group of people now called Indo-Europeans. As warriors and cattle herders in search of new grasslands, the Persians and the Medes, another Indo-European group, left central Asia about 2000 B.C. They settled on a plateau between the Persian Gulf and the

Images *of the* Times

Ancient Persepolis

The most luxurious palace of Darius was built at Persepolis. Completed by Xerxes, the palace was a monument to the king's power.

Alexander the Great destroyed most of the palace in 331 B.C., but the stone monumental gateways and terraces survived.

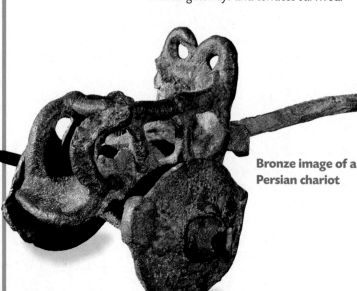

Bronze image of a Persian chariot

Caspian Sea, in the area of present-day Iran.

Cyrus's Conquests

During the 540s B.C., Cyrus had developed a strong army, conquered the Medes, and advanced into neighboring lands. He added northern Mesopotamia, Syria, Canaan, and the Phoenician cities to his empire. Cyrus also took over the kingdom of Lydia and the Greek city-states in Asia Minor. In 525 B.C. Cyrus's son Cambyses (kam•BY•seez) conquered Egypt, bringing all of the Middle East under Persian control.

The Persian Empire, then second to none, stretched from the Nile River to the Indus River, a distance of 3,000 miles (4,800 km). Within this immense empire, the Persians ruled more than 50 million people.

Darius's Empire

The best organizer among the Persian kings was **Darius I**, who reigned from 522 B.C. to 486 B.C. To administer his empire, Darius effectively divided the realm into provinces and assigned satraps, or provincial governors, to rule. Military officials and tax inspectors, chosen by the king from among the conquered people themselves, assisted the satraps in carrying out the king's decrees in the provinces. In addition, inspectors called "Eyes and Ears of the King" made unannounced tours of the provinces and reported directly to the king on the activities of officials. In this way, the king's court was able to keep watch on local government.

In contrast to the Assyrians, the Persians were tolerant rulers who allowed conquered peoples to retain their own languages, religions, and laws. The Persians won the loyalty of conquered peoples by respecting local customs. They believed that this loyalty could be won more easily with fairness than by fear or force. When faced with rebellion, however, the Persians did not hesitate to take extreme military measures.

Commerce and Roads

Darius brought artisans from many of his

Persian god and goddess protecting a palm tree

More than 1,000 years after Alexander destroyed Persepolis, the first curious travelers rediscovered the impressive remains of the city. The Apadana hall at the northern end of the palace contains stairways with beautiful reliefs of Persian nobles, guards, and tribute bearers.

REFLECTING ON THE TIMES

1. About what year did travelers rediscover Persepolis?
2. What ruins reveal the wealth of Persian kings?

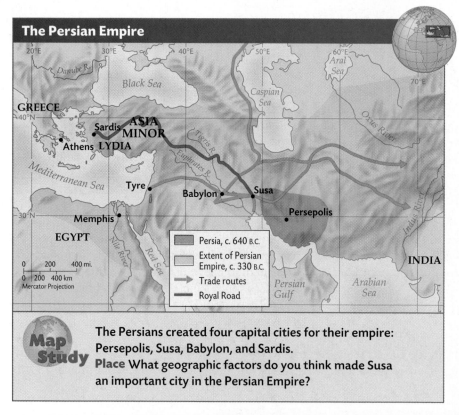

The Persian Empire

Legend:
- Persia, c. 640 B.C.
- Extent of Persian Empire, c. 330 B.C.
- → Trade routes
- — Royal Road

0 200 400 mi.
0 200 400 km
Mercator Projection

Map Study
The Persians created four capital cities for their empire: Persepolis, Susa, Babylon, and Sardis.
Place What geographic factors do you think made Susa an important city in the Persian Empire?

Persian Religion and Culture

The Persians followed a strict moral code that stressed bravery and honesty. They taught their sons to "ride horses, to draw a bow, and to speak the truth." Before the 500s B.C., the Persian people worshiped many deities associated with the sky, sun, and fire. Then, about 570 B.C., a prophet named **Zoroaster** (ZOHR•uh•WAS•tuhr) began to call for reform of the Persian religion. Zoroaster preached that the world was divided by a struggle between good and evil. The god Ahura Mazda led the forces of good, and a lesser deity, Ahriman, represented the spirit of darkness. At the end of time, Ahura Mazda would triumph over Ahriman.

Zoroaster also taught that humans were caught up in this struggle and had to choose between good and evil. All humans who fought on the side of Ahura Mazda against evil would be rewarded with eternal life. Those who chose Ahriman would be condemned after death to eternal darkness and

conquered lands to build **Persepolis**, the most magnificent city in the empire. The Persians themselves did not engage in trade, which they considered an indecent occupation. However, they did encourage trade among the peoples of their empire. To advance trade throughout the empire and aid the movement of soldiers, Darius had Persian engineers improve and expand the network of roads first laid down by the Assyrians. Royal messengers also journeyed on the roads allowing "neither snow, nor rain, nor heat, nor the darkness of night to hinder them in the prompt completion of their ... tasks."

The Royal Road, the most important thoroughfare in the Persian Empire, stretched more than 1,500 miles (2,400 km) from Persia to Asia Minor. Every 14 miles (22.4 km), stations along the Royal Road provided travelers with food, water, and fresh horses. Royal messengers could travel the length of the road in just seven days, a journey that had taken three months before the road was built.

A Persian Disaster

During his reign, Darius waged war against the Greeks over the control of city-states in Asia Minor. After Darius died, his son Xerxes (ZUHRK •SEEZ) led the forces of Persia in a disastrous campaign to conquer Greece in 480 B.C. Xerxes' defeat stopped Persian expansion into Europe.

AROUND THE WORLD Spread of Celtic Culture

Central Europe, c. 600 B.C.
The Hallstatt Celts spread their influence from Austria to the British Isles. They were among the first people in northern Europe to make iron. Their warlike chieftains relied on horses and slept on animal skins in crude houses. Their weapons and artifacts, however, were decorated with elaborate patterns. Celtic art featured highly stylized plants and animals.

Central Europe

This relief of King Darius and Xerxes is one of many at the palace of King Darius. *What do you think the appearance of these figures reveals about the Persian royal court?*

misery. These teachings were contained in a book called the Avesta.

Persian rulers believed that they ruled by the power of Ahura Mazda and were responsible to him alone. Darius I had the following statement carved on a cliff:

❝ On this account Ahura Mazda brought me health…. Because I was not wicked, nor was I a liar, nor was I a tyrant, neither I nor any of my line. We had ruled according to righteousness. ❞

Zoroaster's teachings were eventually linked to the glorification of the Persian monarchy. Because the monarchy was viewed as a sacred institution, Persian kings commanded great respect and were surrounded by pomp and pageantry. This style of kingship later shaped the development of monarchies in the Western world.

Zoroaster's beliefs also may have shaped beliefs in the Mediterranean world. Some scholars believe that Zoroaster's teachings about paradise, hell, and the Last Judgment—or the separation of good and evil at the end of time—may have influenced Judaism, Christianity, and Islam. Other aspects of Persian culture lived on as well, and mixed with Greek culture when Alexander the Great absorbed the Persians into his own empire in the 300s B.C.

SECTION 3 REVIEW

Recall
1. **Define** satrap.
2. **Identify** the Hittites, the Assyrians, the Chaldeans, Nebuchadnezzar, the Persians, Cyrus II, Darius I, Zoroaster.
3. **Locate** the Hittite, Assyrian, Chaldean, and Persian Empires on the maps on pages 89 and 92. Rank them in order of approximate size.

Critical Thinking
4. **Evaluating Information** Why might other religions have adopted features of the Zoroastrian religion?

Understanding Themes
5. **Conflict** How did the military exploits of the Hittites and the Assyrians both change the way peoples of the time fought military battles and the way in which they dealt with conquered peoples?

Connections Across Time

Historical Significance Trading peoples and empire builders both enriched the culture of the ancient Middle East and strongly influenced later civilizations. One of the most significant innovations, for example, was the concise and easy-to-learn Phoenician alphabet, which spread communication, enhanced trade, and eventually evolved into the alphabet used to spell the words on this page.

Spiritual life also evolved dramatically, through the adherence of the Israelites to a belief in one God, who required people to live justly. The concepts of monotheism and ethical laws have endured in the modern religions of Judaism, Christianity, and Islam.

Using Key Terms

Write the key term that completes each sentence. Then write a sentence for each term not chosen.

a. alphabet
b. monotheism
c. colony
d. covenant
e. barter
f. satraps
g. exodus
h. prophets
i. Diaspora
j. confederation

1. In the 1200s B.C., the Israelite leader Moses rallied his people and led them out of Egypt in a(n)_____ into the Sinai Desert.
2. The Phoenicians were organized into a(n) _____ of independent city-states along the coast of northern Canaan.
3. Israelite _____ condemned abuses in society and urged people not to forget their duties to God and to one another.
4. Persian kings appointed a number of a(n)_____ to govern the provinces of the Persian Empire.
5. Jewish communities existing outside of their homeland have become known as the _____, after a Greek word meaning "scattered."

Technology Activity

Using a Word Processor
Search the Internet or your local library for information about the early Israelites and the Phoenicians. Using a word processor, create a chart comparing the two cultures. Include heads such as major contributions, cultural achievements, location, and time period. After comparing the contributions of both cultures, write a paragraph explaining how these contributions have affected your life.

Using Your History Journal

Choose one of the verses that you have written for your journal dealing with an event mentioned in the chapter. After research expand the verse into an epic poem about the event.

Reviewing Facts

1. **Culture** Explain how Aramaic came to be spoken throughout the Fertile Crescent.
2. **Technology** Identify the practices that the Phoenicians introduced to business and trade. What advantage did the Phoenicians have over their competitors?
3. **Culture** Describe how the Israelites interpreted and applied monotheism.
4. **History** List the peoples with whom the Israelites came into conflict after the Exodus from Egypt and the return to Canaan.
5. **Culture** Describe the role of Deborah in helping the Israelites settle Caanan.

Critical Thinking

1. **Apply** What natural resource supported the Lydians' development of a money system to replace the barter system?
2. **Analyze** How were the deities and beliefs of the Phoenicians, the Israelites, and the Persians different from one another?
3. **Analyze** What actions taken by Darius I made his rule so effective?

4. Evaluate Why was the Exodus important to the Israelites? In what way did it shape the development of religion in the Western world?

Geography in History

1. Movement What event led to the establishment of a large Jewish community in Babylon after 586 B.C.?

2. Human/Environment Interaction How did the people of Babylon provide water to various locations inside the city walls?

3. Human/Environment Interaction How did the people of Babylon fortify the city against attack from outsiders?

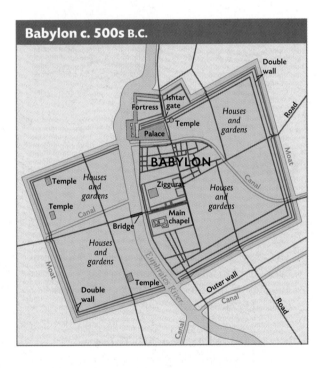

Babylon c. 500s B.C.

Understanding Themes

1. Cultural Diffusion Based on your knowledge of the ancient trading peoples of the Middle East, what kinds of ideas might people be likely to adopt from other cultures?

2. Innovation From a modern perspective, do you see any advantages or disadvantages to the development of a religious belief system based on monotheism?

3. Conflict Make a list of what aims might have motivated conquerors such as the Hittites, Assyrians, Chaldeans, and Persians to incorporate their neighbors into empires.

Linking Past and Present

1. Does the legal system of our country parallel Hittite law or Hammurabi's code? Provide a brief explanation of your view.
2. The Persian Empire was made up of many different peoples. Evaluate the ways in which the Persians ruled their empire. How does the Persian experience compare or contrast with that of modern nations, such as the United States, that have diverse populations?
3. Solomon built a magnificent temple at Jerusalem. The last Jewish temple on the Temple Mount was destroyed in A.D. 70. What building stands on that site now?

Skill Practice

Reread pages 91-92 in Section 3 about Darius and his empire. Use that information to answer the following questions about the Persian Empire.

1. What problem hindered the expansion of the Persian Empire?
2. Write a short summary of the information the Persians might have gathered after deciding that trade was an indecent occupation in which to engage.
3. List the options that were available to the Persians. What were the advantages? What were the disadvantages?
4. What kind of solution did the Persians find to help in the expansion of the empire?
5. Evaluate and discuss the effectiveness of the solution. Why do you think it was, or was not, successful?

ABCNEWS INTERACTIVE™ # Turning Points in World History

The Rise of Cities

Setting up the Video

Work with a group of your classmates to view "The Rise of Cities" on the videodisc *Turning Points in World History*. Many historians believe that the Sumerians arrived in Mesopotamia around 3500 B.C. They settled in the lower part of the Tigris-Euphrates river valley, known as Sumer. Scholars credit the Sumerians with being the first to create cities. This program highlights the contributions and innovations of the people of Sumer.

Side One, Chapter 3

View the video by scanning the bar code or by entering the chapter number on your keypad and pressing Search. (Also available in VHS format.)

Hands-On Activity

Design a bulletin board illustrating Sumerian technological advances and contributions to culture and government. Include examples of what Sumerian innovations have evolved into today. Write captions to go with the illustrations.

Surfing the "Net"

Ancient Cultures

To honor their god-kings and to provide them with an eternal place of rest, the Egyptians of the Old Kingdom built lasting monuments called pyramids. To learn about other ancient cultures and their monuments, look on the Internet.

Getting There

Follow these steps to gather information.

1. Go to a search engine. Type in the phrase *ancient cultures*.
2. After typing in the phrase, enter words like those below to focus your search:
   - *monuments*
   - *temples*
   - *structures*
   - *pyramids*

3. The search engine should provide you with a number of links to follow. Links are "pointers" to different sites on the Internet and commonly appear as blue underlined words.

What to Do When You Are There

Click on the links to navigate through the pages of information and gather your findings. Use a word processor to create an information pamphlet about your findings. Include information such as the purpose of the monument, its location and the time period it was created, illustrations, and the culture of the people. Draw a world map and indicate the location of each monument.

1 Digest

The bones of early human beings as well as other fossil remains, archaeological artifacts, and written records hold many clues for researchers studying the past. Although historians consider history to have begun about 5,500 years ago, when early peoples began writing, the human story extends much further into the past—into millions of years of prehistory.

Chapter 1
Human Beginnings

Using research techniques such as radiocarbon dating to date plant and animal matter, anthropologists and archaeologists have been able to establish a time frame for prehistoric human life. Scientists do not agree about all aspects of how or when the first human beings became truly human, but fossil evidence suggests that the first prehuman hominids lived about 4.4 million years ago. Over the next few million years, hominids gradually migrated to other areas and adapted to changes in their environment, such as a colder climate, in various ways. Some hominids evolved larger brains.

Early Humans

Two large-brained hominids, *Homo habilis* and *Homo erectus*, as well as all modern human beings, are scientifically classified in the genus, or group, *Homo*—human. Around 200,000 years ago, the modern human species, *Homo Sapiens*, appeared. Two major groups of early *Homo Sapiens* were the Neanderthals and the Cro-Magnons.

In prehistoric times, early human beings set many cultural patterns that continued into historic times. They cooperated with one another to obtain food and came into conflict over land and water. They developed techniques for staying warm, for hunting, and for defense and attack. Clothing and fire became part of the culture of prehistoric people, as did the use of stone tools and weapons. Prehistoric peoples also developed many social skills, including spoken language, and adopted from one another new methods and ideas.

Civilizations

Between 8,000 and 10,000 years ago, early peoples in various parts of the world shifted from hunting and food gathering to farming. The development of agriculture was an essential stepping-stone to civilization. Initially farming allowed people to give up their nomadic life and settle in communities. Eventually, with a relatively steady food supply, many men and women could devote their time to economic activities other than farming. As time passed, some of the early agricultural villages grew into the first cities, which were home to highly organized societies, or civilizations.

All early civilizations shared some basic features. They had specialized labor; cooperative methods for producing surplus food, such as irrigation; and metalworking technology. Under an organized government they formed social classes and maintained an army. They undertook long-distance trade. With a system of values and religious beliefs, they were sophisticated enough to have written records.

Visualizing History **Archaeologist working at a grave site in Jerusalem.** *What allowed people to give up their nomadic life and settle in cities?*

Chapter 2
Early Civilizations

Cities and civilizations arose at different times in different parts of the world. Many of the earliest civilizations had one thing in common, however: they grew out of agricultural settlements in river valleys. Civilization appeared around 3500 B.C. in the Tigris-Euphrates River valley in the Fertile Crescent, but it also arose soon thereafter in the Nile River valley of Egypt, and again later in the Indus River valley of the South Asia and in the Huang He valley in China.

Ancient Egypt and Mesopotamia

In northeastern Africa, villages along the Nile banded together in small kingdoms, which were later united under a king. The ruling monarch was a religious and political leader and head of a government bureaucracy, or a group of government officials.

With innovative irrigation and flood control methods, the Egyptians used the seasonally fluctuating Nile waters and the river's rich soil deposits to grow crops. They undertook ambitious building projects, such as the Pyramids, which required new engineering skills. The writing system that early Egyptians invented as well as the script that was later formed from it were used both for everyday purposes and for decorating their massive monuments.

Egypt's prosperity encouraged later Egyptian rulers, or pharaohs, to expand the frontiers of their country and to build an empire, or group of territories under a single ruler or government. The Egyptian Empire led to an exchange of ideas, goods, and customs among different cultures. This cultural diffusion further enriched Egyptian civilization.

In Mesopotamia, the land between the Tigris and Euphrates Rivers, peoples fleeing war and overpopulation, as well as poor climate, settled on the fertile river plain. Although the early Mesopotamians, unlike the Egyptians, could not depend on a regular supply of water, they managed to meet the challenges of the twin rivers by cooperating with one another and devising methods of irrigation and flood control. An innovative Mesopotamian people known as the Sumerians built city-states, invented the wheel, and created cuneiform, perhaps the world's oldest writing system. The prosperous Sumerians eventually fell to empire-builders, first the Akkadians and later the Babylonians.

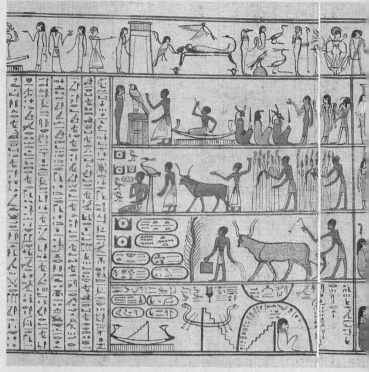

Visualizing History — **A funeral papyrus from the *Book of the Dead*, Egypt.** *Along what river are most ancient Egyptian monuments found?*

South Asian and East Asian Civilizations

While empires rose and fell in Mesopotamia, a third river valley civilization to the east, the Harappans, reached its peak. Adapting to the unique seasonal wind and floods patterns of their environment, the people of the South Asian subcontinent prospered in the Indus River valley. They produced a surplus of food and various goods, which they traded with the Mesopotamians, among others. Although the remains of Harappan cities such as Mohenjo-Daro indicate that people of the Indus Valley were expert urban planners, why the cities were destroyed and what caused the end of their civilization remains a mystery.

The fourth river valley civilization, which began in ancient China, has continued to the present day. Isolated from other cultures for many centuries by formidable landforms, the Chinese formed a strong sense of national identity. From late prehistoric times, people settled and flourished in the Huang He valley. The Shang dynasty, or ruling family controlled the river valley from about 1700 B.C. to 1000 B.C. Under Shang rule, the Chinese built their first cities, created a complex writing system, and perfected their skill in casting bronze. The replacement of the Shang dynasty by the Zhou dynasty was the first of many transitions between the dynasties that successively governed China.

Visualizing History Shang ritual vessel in the form of a tiger protecting a man. *In what river valley did the Shang dynasty flourish?*

Chapter 3
Kingdoms and Empires in the Middle East

A region of the Middle East known as the Fertile Crescent continued to be home for diverse peoples after the earliest river valley civilizations fell. Many people in the Fertile Crescent were active in trade and made lasting cultural and economic contributions to later civilizations.

Traders and Herders

Prominent among the trading peoples of the Middle East were the Phoenicians. They navigated the Mediterranean Sea and beyond, founded overseas settlements, and created an alphabet that became a model for later alphabets. Among the other trading peoples in the region, the Aramaeans spread their Aramaic language, making it the primary language of trade and everyday speech in the Middle East. The Lydians left a lasting mark on the economies of other civilizations by using coins as a medium of exchange.

The Israelites also made lasting cultural contributions. Foremost among these was monotheism—the belief in one all-powerful, merciful, and just God—an idea that formed the basis of Judaism, Christianity, and Islam. During their long history, the Israelites several times came into conflict with neighboring peoples. Although they were enslaved and exiled, they kept close ties to their homeland.

Empire Builders

Many peoples in the Fertile Crescent suffered as warlike empires successively dominated the region and neighboring regions as well. In spite of their emphasis on war, these empires also advanced trade, created new methods of government, and carried out building projects. The Hittites were the first of the empire builders, coming to Asia Minor from Europe or central Asia. With many advantages in military tactics, the Hittites conquered an empire spanning Asia Minor, Syria, and part of Mesopotamia.

The Assyrians, a Mesopotamian people, were the next conquerors in the Middle East. They too had powerful armies, and cruelly treated the peoples they conquered. They controlled an empire stretching from the Persian Gulf to Egypt and into Asia Minor.

The well-organized and extensive Assyrian Empire fell to the Chaldeans (descendants of the Babylonians). The Chaldeans built their capital, Babylon, into one of the largest, most stunning cities of the ancient world. In less than 100 years, however, the Chaldean Empire was in turn overthrown by the Persians.

The Persians, who originated in central Asia and settled in the area of present-day Iran, built an empire that stretched from the Nile River to the Indus River. The Persians surpassed their predecessors in governing a vast area and in tolerating the languages, religions, and customs of subject peoples. When faced with rebellion, however, they did not hesitate to use military force. Persian rulers, such as Cyrus and Darius I, developed a well-organized government and surrounded themselves with pomp and pageantry. Their style of kingship later shaped the development of monarchies in the Middle East and the Western world.

SURVEYING UNIT I

1. **Chapter 1** Why was the development of agriculture a stepping-stone to the rise of the first civilizations?
2. **Chapter 2** How did early river valley civilizations, such as the Egyptian and the Sumerian, meet the challenges of their environments?
3. **Chapter 3** What major contribution was made by each of the following peoples: the Phoenicians, the Israelites, and the Persians?

Flowering of Civilizations

Then & Now

As people developed agricultural technology, nomadic life gave way to living in communities. Emerging cities became centers of trade and commerce, characterized by highly organized social structures and governments. Commerce brought wealth that allowed more people time for leisure and study. Ancient civilizations contributed much that remains in the modern world. China developed a civil service system based on merit. The city of Alexandria in Egypt had a great library. The Greeks refined geometry to calculate the size of the earth. Architecture, theater, and education all have their roots in ancient civilizations.

* In A.D. 532, a Christian monk started a system of dating events, beginning with the year he believed Jesus was born. The years before Jesus' birth were called *B.C.* (before Christ). The years after this event were called *A.D.*, an abbreviation for *anno Domini*, which is Latin for "in the year of the Lord." Today, some publications use *B.C.E.* (before the common era) instead of *B.C.*, and *C.E.* (common era) instead of *A.D.* Note that unlike *A.D.*, *C.E.* follows the year.

A Global Chronology

	2000 B.C.	1500 B.C.	1000 B.C.
Political		**c. 1500 B.C.** Aryans cross the Hindu Kush into South Asia.	
Scientific/ Technological		**c. 1700 B.C.** Babylonian Empire adopts Sumerian calendar.	
Social/Cultural			**c. 1200 B.C.** Vedic Age begins in India.

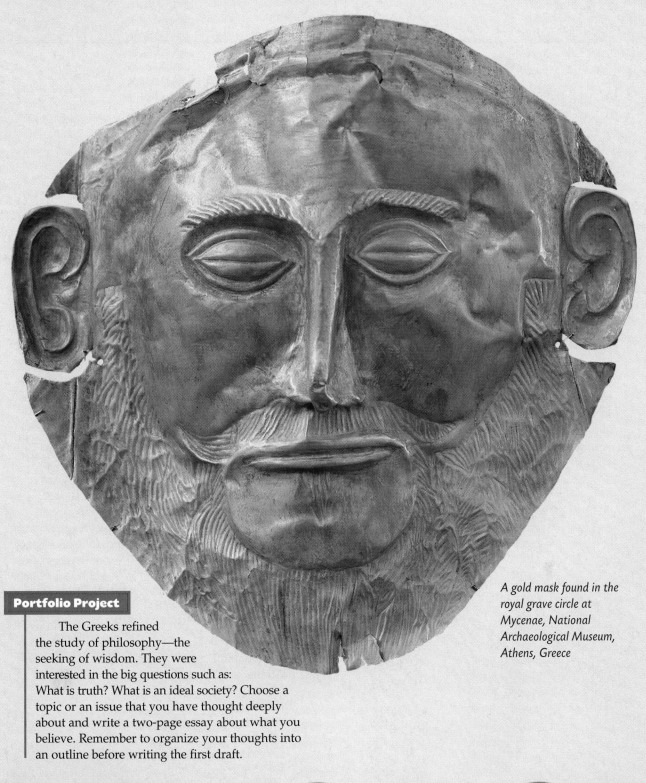

A gold mask found in the royal grave circle at Mycenae, National Archaeological Museum, Athens, Greece

Portfolio Project

The Greeks refined the study of philosophy—the seeking of wisdom. They were interested in the big questions such as: What is truth? What is an ideal society? Choose a topic or an issue that you have thought deeply about and write a two-page essay about what you believe. Remember to organize your thoughts into an outline before writing the first draft.

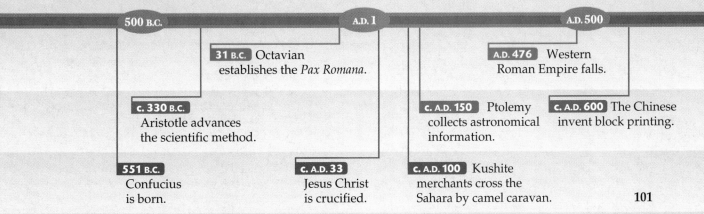

500 B.C.   **A.D. 1**   **A.D. 500**

31 B.C. Octavian establishes the *Pax Romana*.

A.D. 476 Western Roman Empire falls.

c. 330 B.C. Aristotle advances the scientific method.

c. A.D. 150 Ptolemy collects astronomical information.

c. A.D. 600 The Chinese invent block printing.

551 B.C. Confucius is born.

c. A.D. 33 Jesus Christ is crucified.

c. A.D. 100 Kushite merchants cross the Sahara by camel caravan.

The Spread of Ideas

Systems of Law

L aw is a code of conduct and rights accepted or formally recognized by a society. Law provides social control, order, and justice. It enables people to know their rights and responsibilities. Law also forms the cornerstone of constitutional government. A constitutional government based upon law helps ensure justice, or the fair treatment of all citizens. "Where law ends, tyranny begins," said William Pitt, an English leader, in A.D. 1770.

Roman Empire
Laying the Foundation

Sometime around 451-450 B.C., a group of judges posted 12 tablets in Rome's main forum, or marketplace. According to legend, the common people of Rome had demanded that the laws be written down for all to see. People would then know their rights. The tablets listed the unwritten laws that guided judges. They also included penalties imposed on people who broke the law.

Although a group of invaders smashed the so-called Twelve Tables in 390 B.C., the basic code of law remained in effect for almost 1,000 years. When Roman armies marched out to conquer a huge empire, they carried their belief in law with them. By A.D. 120 Roman law governed the entire Mediterranean world and much of western Europe.

In theory, Roman law applied to all people, regardless of wealth or power. Not everyone honored Roman legal ideals. Nonetheless, the Romans developed an important democratic principle. They believed people should be ruled by law rather than by the whims of leaders. In A.D. 533-534 the Byzantine emperor Justinian consolidated all Roman law into a single written code. The Justinian Code became the foundation of the present civil law system. Civil law and common law, which originated in England, are two of the major legal systems in the world today.

Cicero

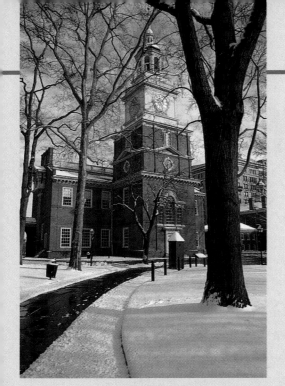

The United States
A Model for Constitutional Government

The Founders of the United States knew about and admired the Romans. They understood what the Roman orator Cicero meant when he spoke of the need to limit the power of government. When it came time to draw up a plan of government, they wrote a constitution that balanced the powers of government among three branches.

To ensure that rulers did not place themselves above the law, the Framers included a provision that made the Constitution "the supreme law of the land." The Framers used the example of Rome to defend the Constitution. "The Roman republic attained ... the utmost height of human greatness," declared Alexander Hamilton. He then explained how government under the Constitution would do the same.

A second system of legal justice, common law, evolved in England. Trial by jury, the right to petition the government, and many other rules governing trials originated in this system. Common law is not a written code but rather is based on written judicial decisions. Common law was established in the American colonies and continued to develop when the colonies became states of the United States.

Independence Hall, Philadelphia

France
Unifying the Law

In A.D. 1799 a French general named Napoleon Bonaparte set out to build an empire even larger than Rome's. By A.D. 1802 he had conquered much of Europe. Napoleon then tried to extend his reach into the Americas.

In seeking to rule this empire, Napoleon followed the Roman example. He took part in a commission to draw up a uniform code of laws. This code, known as the Napoleonic Code, was completed in A.D. 1804.

Although Napoleon ruled as emperor, the code named in his honor reaffirmed the principle that the same laws should be used to govern all people. In drafting these laws, Napoleon drew upon many of the legal precedents first introduced by the Romans. Under Napoleon, this code became applied in lands as far-flung as present-day Belgium, Quebec, Spain, and some Latin American nations.

Assemblée Nationale, Paris

LINKING THE IDEAS

1. What important democratic principle did the Romans develop?

Critical Thinking

2. How did the United States hope to ensure that rulers would not place themselves above the law?

The Rise of Ancient Greece

Chapter Themes

▶ **Relation to Environment** Closeness to the sea helps make the early Greeks seafarers. *Section 1*

▶ **Movement** The Greeks establish colonies throughout the area of the Mediterranean and Black Seas. *Section 2*

▶ **Regionalism** Two leading Greek city-states—Athens and Sparta—differ greatly from each other in their values, cultures, and achievements. *Section 3*

▶ **Conflict** Greek city-states together fight the Persians; then the city-states, led by rivals Athens and Sparta, fight each other. *Section 4*

The Storyteller

An eager crowd gathered in the sun-drenched sports arena just outside King Minos's palace at Knossos on the Aegean island of Crete. According to legend, Minos ruled over the Minoan civilization in the 2000s B.C. The Minoans' favorite event—bull leaping—was about to begin. The crowd gasped as a raging bull, representing the earthquakes that shook Crete, charged a young male gymnast who stood motionless. Just before the collision, the gymnast grabbed the bull's horns and somersaulted onto the bull's back. Then his body arched into the air, and he completed a back flip, landing in the arms of his female partner waiting nearby. The crowd cheered at the end of this spectacle, part sport and part religious ritual. By leaping over the bull, the gymnast had shown that no matter how much the earth trembled, the Minoans would stay on Crete.

Historical Significance

What kinds of governments and societies developed in ancient Greece? How have Greek political ideas shaped the development of Western civilization?

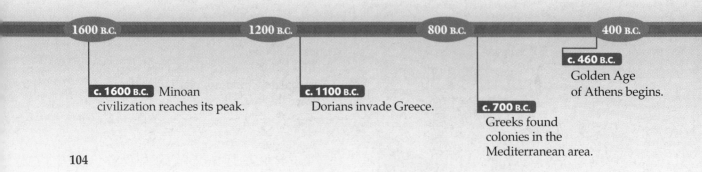

1600 B.C.   **1200 B.C.**   **800 B.C.**   **400 B.C.**

c. 1600 B.C. Minoan civilization reaches its peak.

c. 1100 B.C. Dorians invade Greece.

c. 700 B.C. Greeks found colonies in the Mediterranean area.

c. 460 B.C. Golden Age of Athens begins.

Minoan wall painting (fresco) of bull leaping.
Archaeological Museum, Heraklion, Crete, Greece

Your History Journal

Athens laid the foundation for the Western concept of democratic government. After reading about Athenian democracy, write an essay entitled "What Democracy Means to Me."

Section 1

Beginnings

Setting the Scene

▸ **Terms to Define**
  labyrinth, bard

▸ **People to Meet**
  Sir Arthur Evans, the Minoans, the Mycenaeans, Homer, Heinrich Schliemann

▸ **Places to Locate**
  Crete, Mycenae

Find Out Where and how did the early civilizations of Greece develop?

The Storyteller

The hero Sarpedon was a son of Zeus, but destined to die in the Trojan War. He held before him the perfect circle of his shield, a lovely thing of beaten bronze, which the bronze-smith had hammered out for him. On its inward side were stitched ox-hides in close folds with golden staples all around the circle.... And now Sarpedon spoke to Glaukos, son of Hippolochos: "Glaukos, why are we honored before others with the best seats, choice cuts of meat, brimming wine cups, and the best plots of land? Because we stand in the front line of blazing battle. Friend, if we could escape, and live forever ageless and immortal, I would not go on fighting, or encourage you to fight. But now, since the spirits of death stand close by us, let us go win glory for ourselves, or yield it to others."

Entrance to the ancient silver mines at Siphnos, Greece

—adapted from *The Iliad of Homer*, translated by Richmond Lattimore, 1951

The ancient Greeks became the people who set their stamp on the Mediterranean region and who also contributed greatly to the way we live today. Every time you go to the theater or watch the Olympic Games on television, you enjoy an activity that has its roots in ancient Greece. Modern public buildings often reflect Greek architectural styles. Above all, the ancient Greeks developed the Western concept of democracy.

The Aegean Area

Ancient Greece included the southern part of Europe's Balkan Peninsula and a group of small, rocky islands, most of which dot the Aegean (ih•JEE•uhn) Sea near Asia Minor. Low-lying, rugged mountains make up about three-fourths of the Greek mainland. Between the mountain ranges and along the coast lie fertile plains suitable for farming. Short, swift rivers flow from the interior to the sea, and the long, indented coastline provides many fine harbors. The climate is mild, with rainy winters. Afternoon breezes carrying cooler air from the sea offset the hot, dry summers.

The mountains both protected and isolated Greeks on the mainland. Besides making attacks by foreigners difficult, the mountains limited travel and communication between communities. The Greek people, therefore, never united under one government, although they spoke one language and practiced the same religion.

Because of the numerous harbors and since no place in Greece is more than 50 miles (80 km) from the coast, many Greeks turned to the sea to earn their living. They became fishers, traders, and even pirates.

In addition, the mild climate allowed the ancient Greeks to spend much of their time outdoors. People assembled for meetings in the public square, teachers met their students in public gardens, and actors performed plays in open-air theaters.

Chalices such as these are evidence that Mycenaean kings were rich and powerful.

What evidence suggests that these kings were meticulous about collecting taxes?

Aegean Civilizations

Greek myths referred to an early civilization on the island of **Crete**, southeast of the Greek mainland, but for a long time historians disputed this claim. Then, about A.D. 1900, British archaeologist **Sir Arthur Evans** unearthed remains of the Minoan civilization, which flourished from about 2500 B.C. to 1450 B.C.

The Minoans

At Knossos (NAH•suhs) on Crete, Evans uncovered the palace of legendary King Minos. Throughout the palace, passageways twist and turn in all directions to form a labyrinth, or maze. Brightly colored murals that decorate palace walls show that **the Minoans**—both men and women—curled their hair, bedecked themselves with gold jewelry, and set off their narrow waists with wide metal belts. The murals also show that they were fond of dancing and sporting events, such as boxing matches.

Minoan women apparently enjoyed a higher status than women in other early civilizations. For example, Minoan religion had more goddesses than gods. The chief deity of Crete was the Great Goddess, or Earth Mother, whom the Minoans believed caused the birth and growth of all living things.

The Minoans earned their living from sea trade. Crete's oak and cedar forests provided wood for ships. In addition, the island's location enabled Minoan traders to reach Egypt and Mesopotamia. By 2000 B.C., Minoan fleets dominated the eastern Mediterranean, carrying goods and keeping the seas free from pirates. The ships also guarded Crete

against outside attack, which explains why the Minoans did not build walls around their cities.

Minoan civilization reached its peak around 1600 B.C. About 250 years later it collapsed. Some historians think its cities were destroyed by huge tidal waves resulting from an undersea earthquake. Others think that a people from the Greek mainland, **the Mycenaeans** (MY•suh•NEE•uhnz), succeeded in invading Crete.

The Mycenaeans

The Mycenaeans originated among the Indo-European peoples of central Asia. About 2000 B.C., as a result of the rapid growth of their population, the Mycenaeans began moving out from their homeland. Upon entering the Balkan Peninsula, they gradually intermarried with the local people——known as Hellenes (HEH•leenz)—and set up a group of kingdoms.

Each Mycenaean kingdom centered around a hilltop on which was built a royal fortress. Stone walls circled the fortress, providing a shelter for the people in time of danger. Nobles lived on their estates outside the walls. They would turn out in armor when the king needed them to supply horse-drawn chariots. The slaves and tenants who farmed the land lived in villages on these estates.

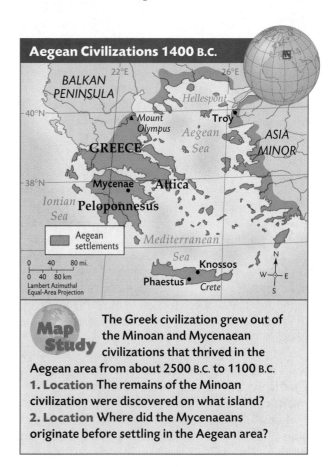

Aegean Civilizations 1400 B.C.

Aegean settlements

0 40 80 mi.
0 40 80 km
Lambert Azimuthal Equal-Area Projection

Map Study
The Greek civilization grew out of the Minoan and Mycenaean civilizations that thrived in the Aegean area from about 2500 B.C. to 1100 B.C.

1. Location The remains of the Minoan civilization were discovered on what island?

2. Location Where did the Mycenaeans originate before settling in the Aegean area?

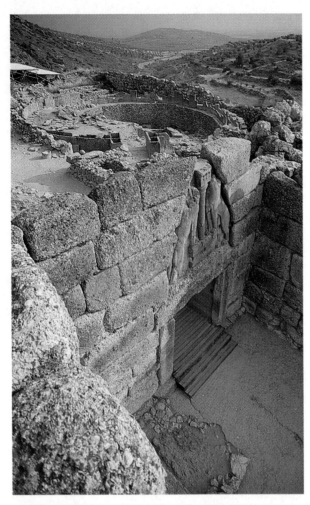

Heinrich Schliemann discovered six tombs at the royal grave circle near the lion gate at Mycenae. They contained 16 skeletons and a large hoard of gold. *What events ended Mycenaean civilization?*

The palaces in the city of **Mycenae** served as centers of both government administration and production. Inside, artisans tanned leather, sewed clothes, fashioned jars for storing wine and olive oil, and made bronze swords and ox-hide shields. To help in collecting taxes, government officials kept records of the wealth of every person in the kingdom. They collected taxes in the form of wheat, livestock, and honey, which were stored in the palace.

Minoan traders visited the Greek mainland soon after the Mycenaeans set up their kingdom. Gradually, the Mycenaeans adopted many elements of Minoan culture—metalworking and ship-building techniques and navigation by the sun and stars. The Mycenaeans worshiped the Minoan Earth Mother as well.

By the mid-1400s B.C., the Mycenaeans had conquered the Minoans and controlled the Aegean area. By 1100 B.C., however, fighting among the Mycenaeans had destroyed the great hilltop fortresses. Soon after, a new wave of invaders, the Greek-speaking Dorians, entered Greece from the north. Armed with iron weapons, the Dorians easily overran the mainland.

Historians call the next 300 years of Greek history a "dark age." During this period, overseas trade stopped, poverty increased, and people lost skills such as writing and craft making. Thousands of refugees fled the mainland and settled in Ionia—the west coast of Asia Minor and its adjoining islands.

By 750 B.C. the Ionians had reintroduced culture, crafts, and skills to their homeland, including the alphabet used by Phoenician traders. The "dark age" of the Dorians ended, and a new Greek civilization with Mycenaean elements emerged. The new civilization—called Hellenic, after the original people of Greece—flourished from about the 700s B.C. until 336 B.C.

Poets and Heroes

During the "dark age," bards, or singing story-tellers, had kept alive Mycenaean traditions. With their new ability to write, the Greeks began to record the epic poems that the bards had passed from generation to generation.

The *Iliad* and the *Odyssey*

According to tradition, a blind poet named **Homer** who lived during the 700s B.C. composed the two most famous Greek epics—the *Iliad* and the *Odyssey*. Homer set the *Iliad* and the *Odyssey* during and after the legendary Trojan War. The Mycenaeans had supposedly fought the people of Troy in the mid-1200s B.C. In A.D. 1870 **Heinrich Schliemann**, a German archaeologist, claimed that Troy actually existed and was a major trading city in Asia Minor.

The *Iliad* begins when a Trojan prince named Paris falls in love with Helen, the wife of a Mycenaean king, and takes her with him to Troy. To avenge Helen's kidnapping, the Mycenaeans lay siege to Troy for 10 years, but they cannot capture the city. Finally, they trick the Trojans by building a huge, hollow wooden horse. The best Mycenaean soldiers hide inside the horse, while the rest board their ships and pretend to sail away. The joyful Trojans, thinking themselves victorious, bring the gift horse into the city. That night, the Greeks creep out of the horse, slaughter the Trojan men, enslave

Erich Lessing, Magnum

Trojan Horse

On this Greek vase from the 600s B.C. the Trojan horse of myth and epic stands tall. According to the Greek poet Homer—who described the Trojan War in his epic poem the *Iliad*—for ten long years the Mycenaeans of Greece battled their enemies who lived within the walls of the Turkish city of Troy. The two sides were so well matched that only a clever strategy of war could produce victory. So the Greeks came up with one: They built a great wooden horse, so large that a cargo of soldiers could hide in its belly. Then they set the horse on wheels and gave it to Troy as a "gift." Having tricked their way into Troy, the Greek soldiers leapt out of the horse and conquered their foe.

While time has blurred the line between historic fact and Homeric epic (written centuries after the struggle), an important war did take place in which a loose federation of Greek kings set out to conquer the city-state of Troy. Homer's epic reveals that piracy and plunder were part of that era's commerce. Archaeologists have uncovered the ruins of a mighty Turkish fortress that once commanded the narrows of the Hellespont. Modern opinions, however, differ as to whether or not this was the site of Homer's Troy. ●

the women and children, and burn the city to the ground.

The *Odyssey* describes the homeward wanderings of the Mycenaean king Odysseus after the fall of Troy. Because it took him 10 years to return to Greece, people refer to any long, adventure-filled journey as an *odyssey*.

Teaching Greek Values

Eventually, schools in ancient Greece used the *Iliad* and the *Odyssey* to present to students many of the values of Hellenic civilization. For example, in an exciting description of men marching to war, the *Iliad* taught students to be proud of their Greek heritage and their heroic ancestors:

> **❝** As a ravening fire blazes over a vast forest and the mountains, and its light is seen afar, so while they marched the sheen from their forest of bronze [spears] went up dazzling into high heaven.
> As flocks of wildfowl on the wing, geese or cranes or long-necked swans fly this way and that way over the Asian meadows, proud of the power of their wings, and they settle on and on honking as they go until they fill the meadow with sound: so flocks of men poured out of their camp onwards over the Scamandrian plain, and the ground thundered terribly under the tramp of horses and of men. **❞**
>
> —Homer, from the *Iliad*, mid-700s B.C.

The *Iliad* and the *Odyssey* also represented other values of Hellenic civilization, such as a love for nature, the importance of husband-wife relationships and tender feelings, and loyalty between friends. Hellenic schools also used the two epics to teach students to always strive for excellence and to meet with dignity whatever fate had in store.

A Family of Deities

In Greek religion, the activities of gods and goddesses explained why people behaved the way they did and why their lives took one direction rather than another. The Greeks also believed that their powerful deities caused the events of the physical world to occur—such as the coming of spring or violent storms with thunder and lightning.

Most ancient peoples feared their deities. They believed that people were put on the earth only to obey and serve the gods and goddesses. The Greeks were the first people to feel differently. They placed

importance on the worth of the individual. Because they believed in their own value, the Greeks had a great deal of self-respect. This allowed them to approach their gods with dignity.

Much more than other civilizations did, the Greeks humanized their deities. Unlike the half-animal gods and goddesses of Egypt, Greek deities had totally human forms. They behaved like humans, too—marrying, having children, lying, and murdering. Frequently jealous of one another, the Greek deities quarreled and sometimes played tricks on one another. They also possessed superhuman powers. Since the Greeks saw their deities as sources of power, both physical and mental, they tried to be like them by doing everything to the best of their ability.

Gods and Goddesses

The gods and goddesses of ancient Greece combined features of both Minoan and Mycenaean deities. For example, different Greek goddesses took over different aspects of the Earth Mother. Athena became the goddess of wisdom and art, Demeter became the goddess of agriculture, and Aphrodite became the goddess of love and beauty. Each community chose a particular god or goddess as its patron and protector, but all Greeks worshiped as their chief deity the Mycenaean god Zeus.

 Visualizing History The Greek poet Homer (below) wrote of the ancient Mycenaean king Agamemnon. Nineteenth-century discoveries raised Homer's work from the rank of myth to that of history. *Who was Helen of Troy?*

Dionysus shown riding a leopard. Greek tragedy was developed from the odes sung by choruses in honor of the god Dionysus. *Where were Greek dramas performed?*

Greeks believed that the 12 most important Greek deities lived on high Mount Olympus, an actual mountain in Greece. Each of the deities controlled a specific part of the natural world. For example, Zeus, the chief god, was thought to rule the sky, weather, and thunderstorms. His brother Pluto was thought to rule the underworld, where the dead spent eternity.

Zeus's son Apollo, the god of light, drove the sun across the sky every day in his chariot. Because the Greeks also considered Apollo to be the god of prophecy, they would bring gifts to the oracle at Delphi—a holy place to honor Apollo—and ask to have hidden knowledge revealed. Like the Shang in ancient China, the Greeks believed that oracles could predict the future. At the Delphic oracle, they would ask questions, and the priests and priestesses would interpret Apollo's replies.

Festivals

As Hellenic civilization developed, certain religious festivals became an important part of Greek life. Every four years the Greeks held a series of athletic contests "for the greater glory of Zeus." Because these contests were held at the city of Olympia, they were called the Olympic Games. The Greeks also originated the play—a celebration in honor of Dionysus, the god of wine and fertility. At these events, the audience sat on a hillside around an open space, where a chorus chanted a story about Dionysus and danced to the sound of a flute. As the years passed, cities began building permanent theaters, carving a hillside into a semicircle, adding rows of stone seats, and paving the stage area. Actors began to recite poems explaining the songs and dances of the chorus. The words they recited eventually evolved into dialogue.

SECTION 1 REVIEW

Recall
1. **Define** labyrinth, bard.
2. **Identify** Sir Arthur Evans, the Minoans, the Mycenaeans, Homer, Heinrich Schliemann.
3. **Describe** the routes the Mycenaeans would have taken to reach Troy and Knossos from their home city of Mycenae.

Critical Thinking
4. **Applying Information** Using Zeus, Athena, and Apollo, illustrate how the Greeks viewed their gods and goddesses.

Understanding Themes
5. **Relation to Environment** How did the geography and climate of Greece and the Aegean islands affect the development of the Minoan and Mycenaean civilizations?

700 B.C.	600 B.C.	500 B.C.

c. 700s B.C. Greek kings lose power to aristocrats.

c. 600s B.C. Greeks learn coinage from the Lydians.

c. 500 B.C. The rule of tyrants in Greek city-states ends.

Section 2

The Polis

Setting the Scene

▶ **Terms to Define**
polis, citizen, aristocrat, phalanx, tyrant, oligarchy, democracy

▶ **Places to Locate**
Athens, Sparta

Find Out How did economic prosperity bring significant political and social changes to the Greek city-states?

The Storyteller

An Athenian ruler had to be careful of plots hatched by jealous nobles. The tyrant Hippias, the once-mild ruler of Athens, learned this lesson. He was with his bodyguard, arranging a citywide parade, when two assassins approached. Pretending to take part in the procession, they had daggers ready, hidden behind their shields. Suddenly, seeing one of their accomplices casually talking with Hippias, they halted, thinking that he had betrayed the plot to the tyrant. Turning, they rushed within the gates, met Hippias's brother, and killed him. Afterward, Athenians found Hippias harsher, ever fearful of revolt.

The Parthenon on the Acropolis

—adapted from *The Peloponnesian War*, Thucydides, Crawley translation revised by T.E. Wick, 1892

The English language offers evidence of how ancient Greeks have influenced modern life. Words such as *police* and *politics*, for example, derive from the Greek word *polis*. The **polis**, or city-state, was the basic political unit of Hellenic civilization. Each polis developed its own pattern of life independently but shared certain features with other city-states.

The Typical Polis

A typical polis included a city and the surrounding villages, fields, and orchards. At the center of the city on the top of an acropolis (uh•KRAH•puh•luhs), or fortified hill, stood the temple of the local deity. At the foot of the acropolis the agora, or public square, served as the political center of the polis. Citizens—those who took part in government—gathered in the agora to carry out public affairs, choose their officials, and pass their laws. Artisans and merchants also conducted business in the agora.

The citizens of a polis had both rights and responsibilities. They could vote, hold public office, own property, and speak for themselves in court. In return, the polis expected them to serve in government and to defend the polis in time of war.

Citizens, however, made up only a minority of the residents of a polis. In Athens, slaves and those who were foreign-born were excluded from citizenship, and before 500 B.C. so were men who did not own land. Greek women had no political or legal rights.

Greek Colonies and Trade

The return of prosperity after the "dark age" led to an increase in Greece's population. By 700 B.C. Greek farmers no longer grew enough grain to feed everyone. As a result, each polis sent out groups of people to establish colonies in coastal areas around the Mediterranean and Black Seas.

Colonies

Each colony kept close ties with its metropolis, or "parent city." A colony supplied its metropolis with grain—wheat and barley. Farmers on the Greek mainland produced wine, olive oil, and other cash crops for export. Because vineyards and olive groves needed fewer workers than did grain fields, many farmers moved to the cities, where they learned crafts. With more goods to sell, Greek merchants began trading throughout the Mediterranean region.

Economic Growth

During the 600s B.C. the Greeks replaced their barter system with a money economy, and their overseas trade expanded further. Merchants issued their own coins, but eventually individual city-states took over this responsibility.

The cities of Ionia in Asia Minor assumed leadership in a growing textile industry. Sheep in the interior of Asia Minor furnished the raw material. Purple dye obtained from mollusks, a type of shellfish, gave the woven materials color.

Pottery developed as a local industry wherever sufficient clay was found. Pottery made in Ionia was the earliest Greek pottery to be exported. Ionian pottery styles were based on Mycenaean and Middle Eastern influences. The artists who made and decorated the vases painted figures of birds and humans interspersed with line or geometric decorations.

Political and Social Change

Economic growth changed Greek political life. Greek communities at first were ruled by kings. By the 700s B.C., however, the kings had lost power to landholding **aristocrats,** or nobles, who as members of the upper class provided cavalry for the king's military ventures.

By 650 B.C. disputes arose between the aristocrats and the common people. Farmers often needed credit until harvest time. To obtain loans from the wealthy aristocrats, they had to pledge their fields as security. When they could not repay the loans, many farmers lost their land to the aristocrats and became either sharecroppers or day laborers in the cities. Some even had to sell themselves into slavery. In protest, farmers demanded political reforms.

CONNECTIONS

Geography

Sailing the Aegean

Because of their many natural harbors, the Greeks transported most goods by sea. Sea travel made good sense, given the rugged mountains of the Greek mainland. Besides, pack animals could carry only small loads short distances. Merchants found sea transport of bulky cargo—grain, timber, and even jugs of olive oil—to be practical and inexpensive.

Greek sailors could sail easily only when the wind was behind them. The prevailing northerly winds made the voyage from Athens to the Black Sea slow and difficult, but the return trip was quick and easy. Likewise, Greek ships could coast to Egypt, but they had to struggle to get home. Most ships managed only one round-trip per year.

Pottery jar showing a merchant ship

The typical Greek freighter was broad—about 25 feet (7.5 m) wide compared to a length of 80 feet (24 m). Rigged with a large square sail, this sturdy ship averaged only about 5 knots with the wind. Merchant ships usually sailed in fleets escorted by warships—galleys propelled by oarsmen.

Compare the ancient ships with today's diesel-driven giants. A container ship makes the round-trip between the United States and Europe in 21 days. It holds cargo in 1,000 containers—four of which are the size of one Greek freighter. Some things have not changed, however. The Greek merchant fleet of today ranks among the largest in the world.

Linking Past and Present ACTIVITY

Explain why the ancient Greeks relied on the sea for the transport of goods. In what kind of vessels did they sail? How has cargo transport changed since ancient times?

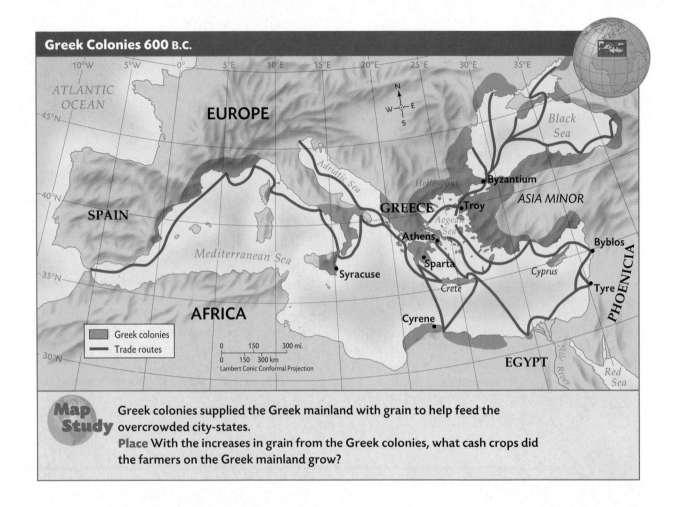

Greek Colonies 600 B.C.

Map Study Greek colonies supplied the Greek mainland with grain to help feed the overcrowded city-states.

Place With the increases in grain from the Greek colonies, what cash crops did the farmers on the Greek mainland grow?

The farmers, who were foot soldiers, were becoming more valuable to Greek armies than the aristocrats, who were cavalry. As Greek armies came to rely on the phalanx—rows of foot soldiers closely arrayed with their shields forming a solid wall—aristocrats began to lose influence. Middle-class, non-landowning merchants and artisans, thus far excluded from citizenship, wanted a voice in the government and joined the farmers in their demands. Merchants and artisans also wanted the polis to advance their interests by encouraging industry and by protecting profitable overseas trade routes.

As a result of the unrest, tyrannies arose. A tyranny was created when one man, called a tyrant, seized power and ruled the polis single-handedly. Although most tyrants ruled fairly, the harshness of a few gave *tyranny* its present meaning—rule by a cruel and unjust person.

Tyrants ruled various Greek city-states until about 500 B.C. From then until 336 B.C., most city-states became either oligarchies or democracies. In an oligarchy, a few wealthy people hold power over the larger group of citizens. In a democracy, or government by the people, power lies in the hands of all the citizens. The democracy of **Athens** and the oligarchy of **Sparta** became the most famous of the Greek city-states.

SECTION 2 REVIEW

Recall
1. **Define** polis, citizen, aristocrat, phalanx, tyrant, oligarchy, democracy.
2. **Identify** Athens, Sparta.
3. **Describe** the social and politi-cal functions of an acropolis and an agora in a Greek polis.

Critical Thinking
4. **Synthesizing Information** What arguments might a citi-zen of a polis present for or against changing citizenship?

Understanding Themes
5. **Movement** What kind of rela-tionship existed between a Greek colony and its metropo-lis on the Greek mainland?

c. 650 B.C.
Slaves revolt
in Sparta.

621 B.C.
Draco enacts code
of laws in Athens.

594 B.C. Solon becomes
leader of Athens.

507 B.C.
Athens becomes
a democracy.

Section 3

Rivals

Setting the Scene

▶ **Terms to Define**
constitution, rhetoric

▶ **People to Meet**
Draco, Solon, Peisistratus, Cleisthenes

▶ **Places to Locate**
Peloponnesus, Attica

Find Out What different Greek values did
Athens and Sparta each represent?

The Storyteller

*Pausanias darted among the bushes to avoid
the moonlight. Finally, stumbling, he plunged
behind a large rock, his lungs heaving. Having
managed to steal just one loaf of fresh bread, he
knew that he must ration it out for at least two
days. The ephors had declared that those caught
with stolen food would be beaten severely. But, if
he could just survive for two more days, he
would finish the initiation and join the
other young men in the barracks. He
shivered quietly, trying to imagine
where he might spend the next two
cold nights.*

—adapted from *The Ancient
World*, edited by Esmond
Wright, 1979

Spartan female athlete

The two leading city-states in ancient
Greece—Sparta and Athens—stood in
sharp contrast to each other. Though
citizens of both Sparta and Athens participated in
polis government, the two city-states differed greatly
from each other in their values, cultures, and accomplishments.

Sparta

The descendants of the Dorian invaders of the
dark age founded Sparta. It was located in the
Peloponnesus (peh•luh•puh•NEE•suhs), a peninsula of southern Greece. Like other city-states, Sparta
based its economy on agriculture.

Instead of founding overseas colonies, the
Spartans invaded neighboring city-states and
enslaved the local people. The polis of Sparta owned
many slaves, known as helots (HEH•luhts), who
farmed the estates of individual Spartans. In addition, a group of free individuals called *perioeci*
(peh•REE•ee•sy)—artisans and merchants from the
conquered territories—worked for the Spartans.
Helots and *perioeci* together outnumbered Spartans
by about 200,000 to 10,000.

Around 650 B.C., the helots revolted against their
Spartan masters. It took 30 years, but the Spartans
managed to suppress the revolt. They then decided
that the only way they could maintain power was to
establish a military society.

A Military Society

All life in Sparta revolved around the army.
Spartan men strove to become first-rate soldiers, and
Spartan women aspired to become mothers of soldiers. Spartans despised the other Greeks who lived
behind city walls, believing that a city defended by
Spartan soldiers did not need walls.

In Sparta, government officials examined newborn infants to see if they were healthy. If not, an official left the sickly infant on a hillside to die. At the age
of 7, Spartan boys were taken away from their homes

and placed in military barracks. Their training included learning to read, write, and use weapons.

At age 20, Spartan men became soldiers and were sent to frontier areas. At age 30, they were expected to marry. But Spartan men could not closely supervise their family affairs. Instead, they spent their days in military drill until age 60, when they could retire from the army.

The Role of Women

The Spartans brought up women to be, like the Spartan men, as healthy and strong as possible. Female infants received as much food as their brothers, which was not the case elsewhere in Greece. Young Spartan girls trained in gymnastics, wrestling, and boxing. The women in Sparta married at age 19 rather than at 14—the average marrying age in most of Greece—which increased the likelihood that their children would be healthy.

Sparta gave its women more personal freedoms than the women of other Greek city-states received.

Spartan women could go shopping in the marketplace, attend dinners at which nonfamily members were present, own property, and express opinions on public issues. They could not, however, take part in government.

Sparta's Government

According to tradition, Sparta's government was set up by a lawmaker named Lycurgus during the 800s B.C. Two kings, who ruled jointly, officially governed Sparta. Except for leading the army and conducting religious services, however, Spartan kings had little power. The Assembly, made up of all male citizens over the age of 30, passed laws and made decisions concerning war and peace. Each year the Assembly elected five overseers, or ephors (EH•fuhrs), to administer public affairs. The ephors could also veto legislation. A Council of Elders, consisting of 28 men over the age of 60, proposed laws to the Assembly and served as a supreme court.

Images *of the* Times

The Glory of Greece

Archaeological treasures and architectural remains remind the world of the achievements of Greek civilization.

The Parthenon crowns the Acropolis at Athens.

Greek sculptors in the classical period depicted living and moving people in natural poses.

Results of Militarism

The Spartans succeeded in maintaining control over their subject peoples for nearly 250 years. They paid a price, however. Suspicious of any new ideas that might bring change, the Spartans lagged far behind other Greek city-states in economic development. For example, Sparta used heavy iron bars instead of coins as currency. In this way, it hoped to discourage trade and to remain self-reliant. The Spartans also shunned philosophy, science, and the arts, while Athens and other city-states advanced in these fields. The Spartans, however, were exceptional Olympic athletes, and their soldiers played key roles in defending Greece against invaders.

Athens

Northeast of the Peloponnesus—on a peninsula of central Greece named **Attica**—people descended from the Mycenaeans established the city-state of Athens. They named their polis after the goddess Athena. Like the early rulers of the other city-states, Athenian kings and aristocrats in the 600s B.C. faced demands by small farmers, merchants, and artisans for economic and political reforms.

Around this time, the governing methods of Athens and Sparta diverged. Athens gradually expanded its definition of citizenship to encompass more people. Initially, only a man whose father and maternal grandfather had been citizens could be a citizen; however, non-landowning citizens could not participate in Athens's Assembly. Athenians called the many free (non-enslaved) foreigners who lived in Athens *metics*. These people could not own land or participate in government. By 507 B.C., however, the constitution, or plan of government, of Athens stated that all free, Athenian-born men were citizens regardless of what class they belonged to, and that they could participate in the Assembly regardless of whether they owned land. This political change reduced much of the friction between social classes and enabled Athens to forge ahead.

The goddess Athena, according to Greek tradition, won the contest for control of Athens over the sea god Poseidon.

REFLECTING ON THE TIMES

1. What innovation did Greek sculptors introduce in the classical period?
2. Why was Athena's name rather than Poseidon's given to the city of Athens?

117

Draco

Four successive leaders brought most of the changes in Athenian government. **Draco**, the first of these leaders, issued an improved code of laws in 621 B.C. The penalties given to offenders were extremely harsh. Even minor offenses, like stealing a cabbage, were punishable by death.

Over time, the word *draconian* has come to describe something that is very cruel and severe. On the other hand, because Draco's laws were written down, everyone knew exactly what the laws were. Aristocrats could no longer dictate what was legal and what was not.

Solon

The next series of reforms took place under the poet-lawmaker **Solon**, who became the leader of Athens in 594 B.C. To improve economic conditions, Solon canceled all land debts and freed debtors from slavery. He also placed limits on the amount of land any one individual could own. By urging farmers to grow cash crops rather than grain, Solon promoted trade. He also promoted industry by ordering fathers to teach their sons a skill and by extending citizenship to foreigners who would settle in Athens as skilled artisans.

Next, Solon introduced political reforms that moved Athens toward democracy while preserving some aristocratic control. He allowed citizens of all classes to participate in the Assembly and public law courts. An aristocratic Council of 400 was also established to draft measures that then went to the Assembly for approval.

Peisistratus

In 546 B.C. **Peisistratus** (pih•SIHS•truh•tuhs) took over the government of Athens. Peisistratus pushed reforms in an even more radical direction than had Solon. He divided large estates among landless farmers and extended citizenship to men who did not own land. Peisistratus provided the poor with loans and put many of them to work building temples and other public works.

Athenian Democracy

Cleisthenes (KLYS•thuh•NEEZ), the fourth leader to help reform Athens, came to power in 508 B.C. The following year he introduced a series of laws that established democracy for Athens. Through his reforms, Cleisthenes sought to end local rivalries, break the power of the aristocracy, and reorganize the structure of Athenian government.

Under Cleisthenes' constitution, the Assembly won increased powers and fully emerged as the major political body. All citizens could belong to the Assembly, in which they were considered equal before the law and guaranteed freedom of speech. In addition to passing laws, the Assembly served as a supreme court and appointed generals to run the military. A Council of 500, whose membership was open to any citizen, carried out daily government business.

Each year in a lottery, Athenian citizens chose members of the Council. They favored a lottery over a ballot, believing that all citizens were capable of holding public office. Elections, in their view, would unfairly favor the rich, who had the advantage of fame and training in public speaking. Besides, all citizens were supposed to take part in government.

Athenian democracy included a jury system to decide court cases. Juries contained from 201 to

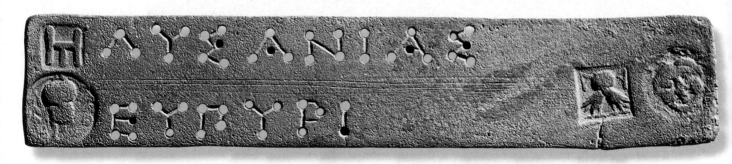

Visualizing History A juror's token is shown above. Athenian courts demonstrated faith in the ordinary man's ability. Groups of hundreds of citizens sat on panels called *dicasteries* and decided cases by majority vote. *Why were juries so large?*

1,001 members, with a majority vote needed to reach a verdict. The Athenians reasoned that the large size of their juries would keep jurors from being influenced by threats and bribes.

Athenian democracy also included a system called ostracism. Each year, citizens could write the name of an undesirable politician on a piece of baked clay called an ostracon. If a person's name appeared on 6,000 ostraca, he could be exiled.

Cleisthenes' democracy transformed Athens, but it affected only those 20 percent of Athenians who were citizens. Non-citizens—women, foreign-born males, and slaves—were still excluded from political life. In spite of these limitations, ancient Athens nevertheless laid the foundation for the Western concept of democratic government.

Athenian Education

The training an Athenian received depended on social and economic status. About a week after being born, a male child received a name and was enrolled as a citizen. Because Athens expected every citizen to hold public office at some time in his life, it required Athenian citizens to educate their sons. With few exceptions, Athenian girls—who would not participate in governing the democracy of Athens—did not receive a formal education. Instead, a girl learned household duties, such as weaving and baking, from her mother.

Private tutors educated the boys from wealthy upper-class families, while other students paid a small fee to attend a private school. Much of their education was picked up in the agora, through daily conversations and debates in the Assembly.

Athenian boys entered school at age 7 and graduated at age 18. Their main textbooks were the *Iliad* and the *Odyssey*, and students learned each epic by heart. They studied arithmetic, geometry, drawing, and music in the morning and gymnastics in the afternoon. When boys reached their teens, they added rhetoric, or the art of public speaking, to their studies. Because lawyers did not represent

AROUND THE WORLD

Zapotec Temple Complex at Monte Albán

Mexico, c. 500 B.C.
Monte Albán in the valley of Oaxaca in southern Mexico became an important center of Zapotec culture. The Zapotecs flattened the mountaintop to create a large plaza, around which they designed a temple complex. They carved the slopes of the mountain into terraces for agriculture and housing. An estimated 5,000 people, or about 50 percent of the valley's population, lived at Monte Albán.

Monte Albán • MEXICO

participants in a court case, an Athenian needed to be accomplished in rhetoric to argue his own position.

When young Athenian men reached 18, they left for two years of military service. Before entering the army, however, they went with their fathers to the temple of Zeus, where they swore the following oath:

> 66 I will not bring dishonor upon my weapons nor desert the comrade by my side. I will strive to hand on my fatherland greater and better than I found it. I will not consent to anyone's disobeying or destroying the constitution but will prevent him, whether I am with others or alone. I will honor the temples and the religion my forefathers established. 99
>
> —oath of enrollment in Epheboi corps, early 400s B.C.

SECTION 3 REVIEW

Recall
1. **Define** constitution, rhetoric.
2. **Identify** Draco, Solon, Peisistratus, Cleisthenes.
3. **Locate** Athens and Sparta on the map on page 121. In which peninsula was each located?

Critical Thinking
4. **Evaluating Information** Do you think the reasons the Athenians gave for choosing government officials by lottery were good reasons? What other method would you propose if you were an Athenian reformer?

Understanding Themes
5. **Regionalism** Contrast Athens and Sparta in their idea of citizenship, type of education, and position of women.

550 B.C.		500 B.C.		450 B.C.		400 B.C.

546 B.C. Persian armies conquer Ionia.

490 B.C. Athenians and Persians fight the Battle of Marathon.

447 B.C. Pericles begins rebuilding of Athens.

431 B.C. Peloponnesian War begins.

Section 4

War, Glory, and Decline

Setting the Scene

▶ **Terms to Define**
symposium, mercenary

▶ **People to Meet**
Darius I, Xerxes, Themistocles, Leonidas, Pericles, Aspasia

▶ **Places to Locate**
Marathon, Thermopylae, Salamis, Delos

Find Out How did the Persian Wars and the Peloponnesian War affect democracy in the Greek city-states?

The Storyteller

The Greek historian Herodotus reported that during the Persian Wars, some Greek deserters approached the Persian king Xerxes. Questioned about what the Greeks were about to do, they told him the truth: The Olympic Games were being held. They were going to watch the athletic competitions and chariot races. When asked what the prize was for such contests, they responded that the Olympic prize was an olive wreath. Upon hearing this, a Persian noble cried out in fear: "What kind of men are these? How can we be expected to fight against men who compete with each other for no material reward, but only for honor!"

—adapted from *The Histories*, Herodotus, translated by Aubrey de Selincourt

Themistocles

As the 400s B.C. opened, the Persian Empire—then the strongest military power in the ancient world—stood poised to extend its influence into Europe. Surprisingly, the Greek city-states not only cooperated with each other in resisting the Persian attack, but they also succeeded in throwing Persia's armed forces back into Asia.

After their victory against Persia, the Greeks—especially the Athenians—enjoyed a "golden age" of remarkable cultural achievements. Then, the Greek city-states began to fight among themselves. This bitter and devastating war lasted for more than 27 years.

The Persian Wars

In 546 B.C. the Persian armies, led by Cyrus II, conquered the Greek city-states of Ionia, in Asia Minor. Despite the mildness of Persian rule, the Ionians disliked the conquerors. The Ionians considered the non-Greek-speaking Persians to be barbarians. In addition, an all-powerful king ruled the Persian Empire, whereas the Greek population of Ionia believed that citizens should choose their own government.

Finally, in 499 B.C., the Ionians revolted against the Persians. Even though Athens and another mainland polis sent some warships to help the Ionians, **Darius I** of Persia soon defeated the Ionians. Darius then decided to punish the mainland Greeks for helping the rebels.

Marathon

Darius first tried to send an army around the northern coast of the Aegean Sea. However, a storm destroyed his supply ships, forcing him to turn back. Two years later, in 490 B.C., Darius tried again.

This time he sent his fleet directly across the Aegean to the coastal plain of **Marathon**, about 25 miles (40 km) north of Athens. For several days the Persians awaited the Athenians. However, the Athenians, outnumbered 20,000 to 10,000, did nothing. Finally, the Persians decided to attack Athens directly. They loaded their ships with the cavalry—the strongest part of their army—and then began loading the infantry.

Not waiting for the Persians to take the offensive, the Athenians struck. The Athenian general ordered his well-disciplined foot soldiers to charge down the hills above Marathon at the Persian infantry, which stood in shallow water waiting to board the ships. This tactic astounded the Persians, who believed that infantrymen would fight only with the support of horsemen and archers. Marathon was a terrible defeat for the Persians, who reportedly lost 6,400 men compared to only 192 Greek casualties.

Salamis

After Marathon, the Persians withdrew to Asia Minor, but they returned 10 years later. In 480 B.C. Darius's son and successor, **Xerxes**, invaded Greece from the north, this time with 200,000 soldiers. Because so huge an army could not live off the land, offshore supply ships accompanied them.

Once again the Greeks, this time under the leadership of Sparta, faced the Persians. A few years before, the oracle at Delphi had said that Greece would be safe behind a "wooden wall." The Athenian general **Themistocles** (thuh•MIHS•tuh •KLEEZ) tried to convince his Greek allies that a "wooden wall" meant a fleet of ships and that the way to defeat the Persians was to challenge them at sea.

To do this, the Greek army had to set up a delaying action on land. They chose **Thermopylae** (thuhr•MAH•puh•lee) as the place—a mountain

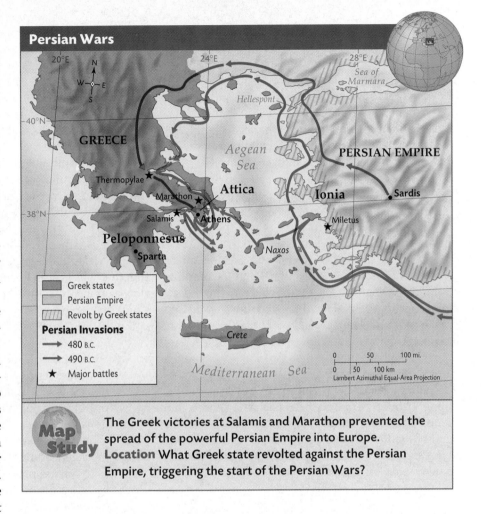

Persian Wars

Greek states
Persian Empire
Revolt by Greek states
Persian Invasions
→ 480 B.C.
→ 490 B.C.
★ Major battles

Map Study The Greek victories at Salamis and Marathon prevented the spread of the powerful Persian Empire into Europe. **Location** What Greek state revolted against the Persian Empire, triggering the start of the Persian Wars?

pass north of Athens. There, 7,000 Greeks led by King **Leonidas** of Sparta stood firm against the Persians for three days. Then a Greek traitor showed the enemy a trail over which they could attack the Greeks from the rear. Realizing that he would soon be surrounded, Leonidas sent off most of his troops. But he and 300 fellow Spartans remained obedient to the law of their polis—never

Footnotes to History

Marathon
According to legend, a messenger named Pheidippides (fy•DIH•puh•DEEZ) carried the news of the victory at Marathon back to Athens. Because Pheidippides had previously run 280 miles (448 km) in four days, he barely managed to reach the city and deliver his message before he fell to the ground, dead from exhaustion. Ever since, people have used the word *marathon* to describe a long-distance race.

surrender on the battlefield, but fight until victory or death.

> **❝** They [the Spartans] defended themselves to the last, such as still had swords using them, and the others resisting with their hand and teeth; till the barbarians [Persians] … overwhelmed and buried the remnant left beneath showers of missile weapons. **❞**
>
> —Herodotus, from *History*, 400s B.C.

The heroic stand of Leonidas and the Spartans gave Themistocles time to carry out his plan. He drew the Persian fleet into the strait of Salamis, a narrow body of water between Athens and the island of **Salamis**. Themistocles reasoned that the heavy Persian ships would crowd together in the strait and make easy targets for the lighter but faster and more maneuverable Greek ships. The plan worked, and the outnumbered ships of the Greek navy destroyed almost the entire Persian fleet.

After the battle at Salamis, the Greeks gained the upper hand. By 479 B.C., the Persians had once again retreated to Asia Minor, this time for good. With the end of the Persian Wars, Athens emerged as a powerful and self-confident city-state, ready to embark on a new age of expansion.

The Golden Age of Athens

Greek culture reached its peak after the Persian Wars. Most historians refer to the period from 461 B.C. to 429 B.C. as the Golden Age of Athens because most Greek achievements in the arts and sciences took place in Athens during this time.

Pericles in Charge

The Athenian general **Pericles**, beginning in the 450s B.C., led Athens through its Golden Age. The Persians had burned Athens during the Persian Wars, but beginning in 447 B.C., Pericles was determined to rebuild the city. When the rebuilt temples and palaces crowned its acropolis, Athens became the most beautiful city in Greece. The most famous structure built under Pericles, the Parthenon (the temple of Athena), still stands.

Pericles wanted the polis of Athens to stand for all that was best in Greek civilization. A persuasive speaker, he expressed his ideas in a famous funeral oration quoted by the Greek historian Thucydides (thoo•SIH•duh•DEEZ):

> **❝** We are called a democracy [because power] is in the hands of the many and not the few.… When it is a question of putting one person before another in positions of public responsibility, what counts is not membership of a particular class, but the actual ability which the man possesses.… We are prevented from doing wrong by respect … for the laws.… We are lovers of the beautiful, yet simple in our tastes, and we cultivate the mind without loss of manliness.… To avow poverty with us is no disgrace; the true disgrace is in doing nothing to avoid it.… Athens is the school of Hellas [Greece]. **❞**

Athenian Daily Life

Athenians lavished money on public buildings, but they kept their individual homes simple. The typical Athenian house contained two main rooms and several smaller ones built around a central courtyard. In one main room, the dining room, the men entertained guests and ate while reclining on couches. An Athenian woman joined her husband for dinner only if company was not invited. In the other main room, the wool room, the women spun and wove cloth. In the courtyard stood an altar, a wash basin, and sometimes a well. The courtyard also contained the family's chickens and goats.

Athenian men usually worked in the morning as farmers, artisans, and merchants. Then they spent the afternoon attending the Assembly or exercising in the gymnasium. Slaves—who were mostly foreigners and prisoners of war and who made up one-third of the population—did most of

Visualizing History Pericles held virtual control over Athenian affairs for the last 15 years of his life, being elected each year as one of the 10 city generals. *How did Pericles identify his faith in democracy?*

the heavy work in craft production and mining. Many slaves also worked as teachers and household servants. Most Athenian women spent their time at home, cooking and making wool cloth, but poor women worked in the open-air markets as food sellers and cloth weavers.

Upper-class Athenian men—as well as citizens from other city-states—enjoyed the symposium as a form of recreation. Wives were excluded from a symposium, which was a drinking session following a banquet. The men at a symposium were entertained by female dancers and singers as well as by acrobats and magicians. The guests also spent much of the evening entertaining each other, telling riddles and discussing literature, philosophy, and public issues.

Athenian Women

In spite of restrictions, many Athenian women were able to participate in public life—especially in city festivals—and learned to read and write. Public opinion allowed greater freedom to women of the *metic* class than to those of other groups. The most famous of *metic* women was **Aspasia**, who was known for her intelligence and personal charm. To her house came many of the women of Athens, and she apparently gave advice on home life while attempting to gain more education and greater freedom for Athenian women. Her views aroused great opposition among some Athenians of both sexes, and she was prosecuted on a charge of "impiety," or disloyalty to the gods. Aspasia was finally acquitted after an impassioned plea to the jury by Pericles himself.

The Peloponnesian War

Even after the Persian Wars ended, the Persian threat remained. Athens persuaded most of the city-states—but not Sparta—to ally against the enemy. This alliance became known as the Delian League because the treasury was kept on the sacred island of **Delos**. Athens provided the principal naval and land forces, while the other city-states furnished money and ships. Over the next several decades, the Delian League succeeded in freeing Ionia from Persian rule and sweeping the Aegean free of pirates. Overseas trade expanded, and Greece grew richer.

The Athenian Empire

Athens gradually began to dominate the other city-states. Pericles, for example, used part of the Delian League's treasury to build the Parthenon.

Visualizing History A Spartan soldier poised for battle. The Spartans developed a chain of orders to be shouted above the din of battle. *How did Sparta attain a navy?*

He insisted that criminal cases be tried only in Athens and that other city-states adopt the Athenian coinage system. He also sent Athenian troops to support revolts by commoners against aristocrats in other city-states. In short, the policies of Pericles more or less transformed the Delian League from what had been an anti-Persian defense league into an Athenian empire.

As Athens's trade and political influence grew, several city-states reacted by forming an alliance opposed to Athens. Sparta, a long-standing Athenian rival, became the leader of the anti-Athens alliance. Since Sparta was located in the Peloponnesus, historians have called the war against Athens and its allies the Peloponnesian War.

The Conflict

The Peloponnesian War lasted from 431 B.C. to 404 B.C., excluding one brief period of peace. At first it seemed as if Athens could hold out indefinitely, since Sparta had no navy. Sparta's fear and jealousy of Athens, however, were so strong that the Spartans made a deal with the Persians to return Ionia to Persian control. In exchange, Sparta received gold to build its own fleet. Then, in 430 B.C., a disastrous plague—probably typhus—weakened Athens. More

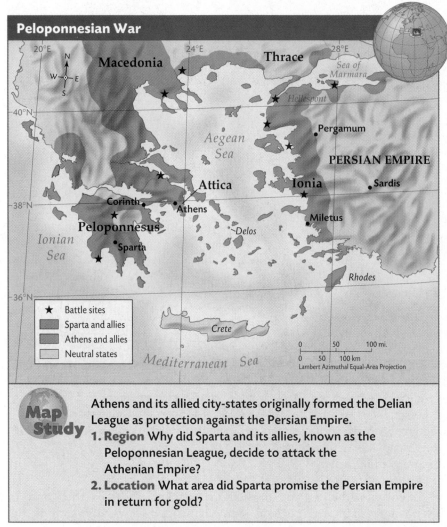

Peloponnesian War

Battle sites ★
Sparta and allies
Athens and allies
Neutral states

Map Study

Athens and its allied city-states originally formed the Delian League as protection against the Persian Empire.

1. **Region** Why did Sparta and its allies, known as the Peloponnesian League, decide to attack the Athenian Empire?
2. **Location** What area did Sparta promise the Persian Empire in return for gold?

fleet. After the Spartans laid siege to Athens itself, the Athenians finally surrendered in 404 B.C.

Effects of the War

The Peloponnesian War brought disaster to the Greek city-states, both victors and vanquished. Many city-states declined in population. Fighting had destroyed many fields and orchards. Unemployment became so widespread that thousands of young men emigrated and became mercenaries, or hired soldiers, in the Persian army.

Worst of all, the Greeks lost their ability to govern themselves. The length and cost of the war made people forget about the common good of their polis and think only about making money. Feelings between aristocrats and commoners grew increasingly bitter. Many Greeks, losing faith in democracy, even came to look down on free political discussion and began to believe that

than a third of its population died, including Pericles.

After Pericles died in 429 B.C., some Athenians wanted to make peace with Sparta and its allies, while other Athenians wanted to keep on fighting. No decision was made, and the war continued deadlocked for many more years. Eventually, several allies of Athens switched sides and joined the Spartan-led alliance. Then, with their Persian-financed navy, the Spartans destroyed the Athenian

might makes right.

For a time, Sparta tried to rule the other city-states. Then, in 371 B.C., a new alliance of city-states led by Thebes overthrew the harsh, incompetent Spartan rulers. The Thebans, however, also made poor rulers and were also overthrown. As a result of almost continual fighting, the city-states became weaker than ever. When a new invader, the Macedonians, threatened Greece in the 350s B.C., the city-states were unable to resist.

SECTION 4 REVIEW

Recall

1. **Define** symposium, mercenary.
2. **Identify** Ionia, Darius I, Marathon, Xerxes, Themistocles, Thermopylae, Leonidas, Salamis, Pericles, Aspasia.

Critical Thinking

3. **Compare** the daily activities of an Athenian husband with those of an Athenian wife.
4. **Evaluating Information** Judge whether Pericles' rule

was a "golden age" for Athens. Support your answer.

Understanding Themes

5. **Conflict** What was the significance of the outcome of the Persian Wars?

Critical Thinking SKILLS

Making Comparisons

In shopping for athletic shoes, you have narrowed your selection to two pairs. Which pair should you buy? To decide this question, you must make a comparison.

Learning the Skill

Making comparisons means finding similarities and differences. In the above example, you might first notice the similarities between the shoes. Both pairs are the same price and the same color. Then, you would look for differences. One pair extends above the ankle, the other pair does not. One pair is designed for jogging, the other for aerobics. Once you have compared the shoes, you can draw a conclusion about which pair will best suit your needs.

Apply the same method in comparing any two objects, groups, or concepts. First, determine the purpose of your comparison. What question do you want to answer? Then determine the bases for comparison. In the shoe example, we compared on the bases of price, color, style, and athletic function. Then identify similarities and differences in each of these categories. Finally, use the comparison to draw conclusions or to answer your question.

Practicing the Skill

The excerpts on this page discuss the military strength of Sparta and Athens. Read the excerpts and answer the questions below.

1. Identify three bases for comparing the military strength of Athens and Sparta.
2. Do both city-states have armies and navies?
3. What are two differences in the military strength of Athens and Sparta?
4. Based on this comparison, which city-state has greater military strength? Why?

“ We [Spartans] have many reasons to expect success,—first, superiority in numbers and in military experience, and second, our general and unvarying obedience in the execution of orders. The naval strength which they [Athens] possess shall be raised by us from ... the monies at Olympia and Delphi. A loan from these enables us to seduce their foreign sailors by the offer of higher pay.... A single defeat at sea is in all likelihood their ruin. ”

—Thucydides, account of a Corinthian envoy to the Congress at Sparta, 432 B.C.

“ Personally engaged in the cultivation of their land, without funds either private or public, the Peloponnesians [Spartans] are also without experience in long wars across the sea.... Our naval skill is of more use to us for service on land, than their military skill for service at sea. Even if they were to ... try to seduce our foreign sailors by the temptation of higher pay ... none of our foreign sailors would consent to become an outlaw from his own country, and to take service with them. ”

—Pericles, account to Athenian Ecclesia, 432 B.C.

Applying the Skill

Choose a topic or activity that interests you, such as baseball, rock music, politics, etc. Research and compare two individuals, groups, or organizations involved in this activity. Write a short essay or make a chart outlining at least five similarities and five differences.

For More Practice

Turn to the Skill Practice in the Chapter Review on page 127 for more practice in making comparisons.

Connections Across Time

Historical Significance Ancient Greece provided the world with its first example of democratic government. Because the limited number of citizens in a Greek polis permitted direct participation by all citizens, Athens can be described as a *direct* democracy. In the United States today, where we elect senators and representatives who are responsible to us, the form of government is called a *representative* democracy. In contrast to citizenship in ancient Greece, United States citizenship has broadened to include women and people of all races, as well as naturalized foreign-born citizens.

Using Key Terms

Write the key term that completes each sentence. Then write a sentence for each term not chosen.

a. aristocrats
b. citizen
c. democracy
d. oligarchy
e. mercenary
f. polis
g. rhetoric
h. tyrant
i. symposiums
j. labyrinth
k. phalanx
l. bards
m. constitution

1. The _____, the basic political unit of ancient Greece, included a city and the surrounding villages, fields, and orchards.
2. A woman in ancient Greece was not considered to be a full _____ with the right to take part in political affairs.
3. By the 700s B.C., kings in Greece had lost power to landholding members of the upper class known as _____.
4. Athenian men entertained each other at _____, telling riddles and discussing literature, philosophy, and public issues.
5. _____, or singing storytellers, kept alive Mycenaean literary traditions during Greece's "dark age."

Technology Activity

Using a Spreadsheet Search the Internet or your local library for additional information about Greek gods and goddesses. Organize your findings by creating a spreadsheet. Include headings such as name of god or goddess, purpose of their existence, types of powers, and relationships to other gods or goddesses. Research further to find out and list the corresponding Roman names for Greek gods and goddesses.

Using Your History Journal

Democracy is not easy to achieve or to maintain. Make a list of the issues that challenge democracy in America. Write a paragraph entitled "Maintaining Democracy" or "Achieving Democracy" that responds to this issue.

Reviewing Facts

1. **Culture** List the elements of Minoan culture that were adopted by the Mycenaeans.
2. **Culture** State the values of the *Iliad* and the *Odyssey*.
3. **Culture** Explain how Greek attitudes toward their deities differ from those of the Egyptians.
4. **History** Explain how Sparta's response to the problems of increased population and a shortage of arable land differed from the response of most other Greek city-states.
5. **Citizenship** Trace the development of democracy in Athens, and describe citizens' rights and responsibilities. What groups were excluded from citizenship?

Critical Thinking

1. **Apply** How did Sparta's values affect its educational system?
2. **Analyze** How did the reforms of Cleisthenes in Athens affect the future development of government in the Western world?
3. **Synthesize** What might have been the outcome of the Persian Wars if Themistocles had not convinced the Greeks to build a fleet of ships?

4. Analyze Shown below, the south porch of the Erechtheum near the Parthenon has figures of maidens in place of conventional columns. The buildings on the Acropolis are examples of early classical architecture and sculpture. What might these figures suggest about the role of women in Athenian life?

Understanding Themes

1. **Relation to Environment** What aspects of Crete's environment enabled the Minoans to become skilled seafarers?
2. **Movement** What role did trade play in the development of Greek civilization?
3. **Regionalism** What effect did Sparta's emphasis on military values have on its development as a city-state?
4. **Conflict** How did the Peloponnesian War affect Athens, Sparta, and the other Greek city-states?

Linking Past and Present

1. Why did tyrants seize power in ancient Athens during times of unrest? Do you think a tyrant could establish a dictatorship today in the United States in a time of crisis? Explain your answer.
2. Why might students at the United States Naval Academy study the Persian Wars?

Skill Practice

Reread Section 3 and compare the two leading city-states in ancient Greece.

1. What are two similarities in the education of young people in Athens and Sparta?
2. What are two differences in their educations in these two city-states?
3. What are two similarities in the political structure of Athens and Sparta?
4. What are two differences that can be identified in the political structure of these two Greek city-states?
5. What are two differences in the roles of women in Athens and Sparta?
6. What are two similarities in women's roles in these two city-states?

Geography in History

1. **Place** Although it is a small island without much land area, Crete contains what two distinct, but neighboring, landforms?
2. **Location** Refer to the map on page 124. What is the relative location of Crete? What is Crete's absolute location?
3. **Location** Where was the palace of the legendary king Minos?
4. **Human/Environment Interaction** Geography has an impact on how people live from day to day. How did the early people of Crete earn their living?

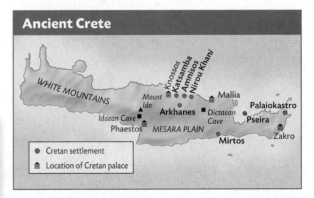

Ancient Crete

- ● Cretan settlement
- 🏛 Location of Cretan palace

WHITE MOUNTAINS · Mount Ida · Idaean Cave · Phaestos · MESARA PLAIN · Knossos · Katsamba · Ammisos · Nirou Khani · Arkhanes · Dictaean Cave · Mallia · Palaiokastro · Pseira · Mirtos · Zakro

The Height of Greek Civilization

Chapter Themes

▶ **Innovation** The ancient Greeks develop a culture that becomes one of the foundations of Western civilization. *Section 1*
▶ **Innovation** Ancient Greek thinkers believe in reason and the importance of the individual. *Section 2*
▶ **Cultural Diffusion** Alexander's empire brings about a mix of Greek and Middle Eastern cultures. *Section 3*

The Storyteller

An outwardly unimpressive man, Socrates was nonetheless an intellectual giant in the Athens of the late 400s B.C. One of his devoted followers described Socrates' day: "At early morning he was to be seen betaking himself to one of the promenades or wrestling grounds; at noon he would appear with the gathering crowds in the marketplace; and as day declined, wherever the largest throng might be encountered, there was he to be found, talking for the most part, while anyone who chose might stop and listen." Socrates was a supreme questioner who succeeded in getting people to analyze their own behavior. Today, Socrates' reputation lives on as one of the greatest teachers of all time.

Historical Significance

What were the principal beliefs and values of the ancient Greeks? How did their achievements in art, philosophy, history, and science shape the growth of Western civilization?

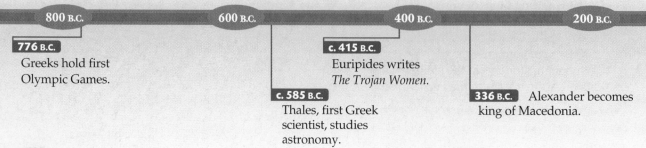

| 800 B.C. | 600 B.C. | 400 B.C. | 200 B.C. |

776 B.C.
Greeks hold first Olympic Games.

c. 585 B.C.
Thales, first Greek scientist, studies astronomy.

c. 415 B.C.
Euripides writes *The Trojan Women.*

336 B.C. Alexander becomes king of Macedonia.

Plato's School, a mosaic from the Hellenistic period. National Museum Naples, Italy

Your History Journal

The word thespian, *meaning "actor," derives from the Greek dramatist Thespis. Many Greek innovations in staging productions are still used today. Research the history of early Greek drama. Write a comparison with modern theater.*

Section 1

Quest for Beauty and Meaning

Setting the Scene

▶ **Terms to Define**
  classical, sanctuary, perspective, amphora, tragedy, comedy

▶ **People to Meet**
  Myron, Phidias, Praxiteles, Aeschylus, Sophocles, Euripides, Aristophanes

▶ **Places to Locate**
  Olympia

Find Out How did the Greeks express their love of beauty and meaning?

The Storyteller

An early Greek actor remembers performing in his first tragedy: "I put on the robe of Zeus for the prologue, a lovely thing, purple worked with golden oak leaves.... The next thing I remember is sitting enthroned down center on the god-walk, eagle on left fist, scepter in right hand ... and all the eyes of Athens skinning me to the bone." The actor felt as though he had sleepwalked into the scene. Gripped by fear, he tried to remember his lines: "My father would die of shame.... He was twice the artist I am. At once my lines came back to me. I started my speech...."

—adapted from *The Mask of Apollo,* Mary Renault, 1974

Vase depicting actors preparing for a play

During the mid-400s B.C., Greek civilization reached its cultural peak, particularly in the city-state of Athens. This period of brilliant cultural achievement has been called ancient Greece's Golden Age. Artists of the Golden Age excelled in architecture, sculpture, and painting. They created works characterized by beautiful simplicity and graceful balance, an artistic style now called **classical**.

Classical Greek art, copied soon after in Roman artistic styles, set lasting standards of beauty still admired today. The writers and thinkers of ancient Greece also made enduring achievements in literature and drama, creating works read through the centuries and still considered classics today. Many cultural traditions of Western civilization—the civilization of Europe and those parts of the world influenced by Europeans—began with Greece's Golden Age.

Building for the Gods

The Greeks, wrote the Athenian leader Pericles, were "lovers of the beautiful." Each Greek city-state tried to turn its acropolis into an architectural treasure.

The Parthenon—the temple to Athena built on the summit of the Acropolis in Athens—best exemplified classical Greek architecture. It was begun in 447 B.C. and finished in 432 B.C., under the rule of Pericles. Because the Greeks worshiped either in their homes or at outdoor altars, they did not need large **sanctuaries**, or places of worship. Instead, they built temples as places where their deities would live.

The Parthenon has an ingeniously simple design. It is a rectangle surrounded by 46 fluted columns. At the same time, the Parthenon is extremely beautiful. In the right light, because of

iron in its white marble, the Parthenon gleams a soft gold against the blue sky.

The Parthenon's graceful proportions perfectly balance width, length, and height. To the Greeks the Parthenon represented the ideal of "nothing to excess," an ideal sometimes called the "golden mean," or the midpoint between two extremes.

The architects of the Parthenon also understood optical illusions and perspective, or the artistic showing of distances between objects as they appear to the eye. Thus, they made the temple's columns thicker in the middle and thinner at the top so that the columns appeared straight when viewed from a distance. The steps leading up to the Parthenon, actually lower in the center than at either end, likewise appear straight. The Athenians wanted to create the impression of perfection—and they succeeded.

Greek Arts

The Greek love of beauty was expressed in the fine arts as well as in architecture. In both painting and sculpture, the Greeks—because they emphasized the individual—excelled at portraying the human form.

Painting on Vases

Although the Greeks painted murals, as had the Minoans, no originals have survived. We know of Greek murals only from written descriptions or Roman copies. But today we can still see examples of their work in the paintings on Greek vases.

The Greeks designed their pottery with different shapes that were suited for different functions. For example, Greek potters gave the *krater*—a small

two-handled vase—a wide mouth in which it was easy to mix wine with water. On the other hand, they gave the *leythos* a narrow neck so that oil could be poured out slowly and in small quantities.

Most pottery remaining from ancient Greece is either red on a black background or black on a red background. The varied subjects of the paintings depended on the size and use of the vase. Potters usually decorated an amphora—a large vase for storing oil and other bulk supplies—with scenes from mythology. In contrast, a *kylix*—a wide, shallow two-handled drinking cup—showed scenes of everyday life: children attending school, shoemakers and carpenters plying their trades, a farmer guiding the plow behind a team of oxen, a merchant ship braving the winds. Greek potters skillfully adapted their designs and decorations to the curves and shape of the vase.

Sculpting the Human Body

Greek sculpture, like Greek architecture, reached its height in Athens during the time of Pericles. **Myron**, one of the greatest sculptors of Greece's Golden Age, portrayed in his statues idealized views of what people *should* look like rather than actual persons. When Myron sculpted his *Discus Thrower* poised to hurl the discus, he carved the lines of the body to indicate an athlete's excellent physical condition as well as his mental control over what he was doing.

The great sculptor **Phidias** (FIH•dee•uhs) was in charge of the Parthenon's sculptures. Phidias himself carved the towering statue of Athena that was placed inside the Parthenon. The statue, made of gold and ivory plates attached to a wooden framework, showed the goddess in her warlike aspect, carrying a shield, spear, and helmet.

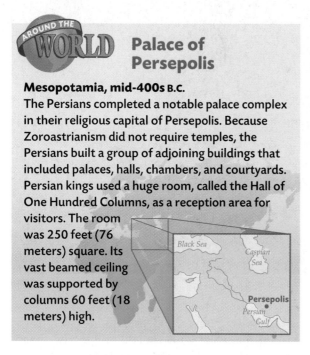

Mesopotamia, mid-400s B.C.
The Persians completed a notable palace complex in their religious capital of Persepolis. Because Zoroastrianism did not require temples, the Persians built a group of adjoining buildings that included palaces, halls, chambers, and courtyards. Persian kings used a huge room, called the Hall of One Hundred Columns, as a reception area for visitors. The room was 250 feet (76 meters) square. Its vast beamed ceiling was supported by columns 60 feet (18 meters) high.

A hundred years after the Golden Age of Athens, the work of another famous Greek sculptor—**Praxiteles** (prak•SIH•tuhl•EEZ)—reflected the changes that had occurred in Greek life. The sculptures of Myron and Phidias had been full of power and striving for perfection, as befitted a people who had defeated the mighty Persian Empire. By the time of Praxiteles, the Greeks had suffered through the Peloponnesian War and had lost their self-confidence. Accordingly, Praxiteles and his colleagues favored life-sized statues rather than massive works. They emphasized grace rather than power. The sculptors of the Golden Age had carved only deities and heroes, but the sculptors of the 300s B.C. carved ordinary people too.

Drama and Theater

The Greeks also explored the human condition through theatrical dramas. They were the first people to write and perform plays, which they presented twice a year at festivals to honor Dionysus, the god of wine and fertility.

Aeschylus

The earliest Greek plays were tragedies. In a tragedy, the lead character struggles against fate only to be doomed—after much suffering—to an unhappy, or tragic, ending. **Aeschylus** (EHS•kuh •luhs), the first of the great writers of tragedies in the 400s B.C., wrote 90 plays. Seven have survived. His *Oresteia* is a trilogy—a set of three plays with a related theme—and is famous for the grandeur of its language.

The *Oresteia* shows how the consequences of one's deeds are carried down from generation to generation. The first play in the trilogy tells about the return of King Agamemnon from the Trojan War and his murder by his wife Clytemnestra in revenge for Agamemnon's sacrifice of their daughter Iphigenia before the Greeks sailed for Troy. The second play describes how Agamemnon's son Orestes in turn avenges his father's death by killing his mother. The third play has Orestes standing trial in Athens for his bloody deed. When the jury splits six to six, the goddess Athena intervenes and casts the deciding vote in favor of mercy. The moral of the trilogy is that the law of the community, not personal revenge, should decide punishment.

Sophocles

The next great tragedian, **Sophocles** (SAH•fuh •KLEEZ), had served as a general in the Athenian army and had lived through most of the Peloponnesian War. Sophocles accepted human suffering as an unavoidable part of life. At the same time, he stressed human courage and compassion.

In one of his most famous plays, *Oedipus Rex*, Sophocles deals with the plight of Oedipus, a king who is doomed by the deities to kill his father and marry his mother. Despite Oedipus's efforts to avoid his fate, the deities' decree comes true. When Oedipus discovers what he has done, he blinds himself in despair and goes into exile.

Euripides

The last of the three great Greek tragedians—**Euripides** (yu•RIH•puh•DEEZ)—rarely dealt with the influence of the gods and goddesses on human lives. Instead, he focused on the qualities human beings possess that bring disaster on themselves.

Euripides also hated war, and many of his 19 surviving plays show the misery war brings. In *The Trojan Women*, the Trojan princess Cassandra explains why the Greeks, despite their victory, are not better off than the Trojans:

  ❝ And when [the Greeks] came to the banks
     of the Scamander those thousands died.
     And why?
  No man has moved their landmarks or
     laid siege to their high-walled towns.
  But those whom war took never saw their
     children.
  No wife with gentle hands shrouded them
     for their grave.
  They lie in a strange land. And in their

Fulvio Rizzo

Liberto Perugi

Greek Soldier

A Greek warrior, sculpted in bronze, gazes at the world with a determined stare. For more than 1,500 years, the soldier rested under the waters of the Mediterranean Sea. Then in 1972 an Italian chemist from Rome, diving off the coast of southern Italy, found this statue and a companion bronze of an older Greek soldier. The statues were probably lost at sea en route to Rome—perhaps thrown overboard to lighten a storm-tossed ship. Rescued by divers (upper left) and carefully restored, the statues now stand guard in an Italian museum.

The Greeks began casting statues in bronze in the mid-500s B.C. Within a century ancient Greek civilization entered its Golden Age, the era in which Plato (427–347 B.C.) and Aristotle (384–322 B.C.) laid the foundations of Western philosophy; Sophocles (495–405 B.C.) wrote tragedies; Thucydides (471–c. 400 B.C.) recorded Greek history; and Phidias of Athens (500–431 B.C.) created statues—perhaps even these rare examples. It was an age in which sculptors created new modes of artistic expression and began to depict the human body with precision. ⊕

Visualizing History The Greek sculptor Myron honored the Olympic discus thrower, shown here in a Roman marble copy. *How did the Greeks honor winners of the Olympic Games?*

about issues of his day. In his play *The Clouds*, Aristophanes had a character named Strepsiades ask where Athens was on a map. When the polis's location was pointed out to him, Strepsiades replied: "Don't be ridiculous, that can't be Athens, for I can't see even a single law court in session."

The Olympic Games

Believing that healthy bodies made the best use of nature's gifts, the ancient Greeks stressed athletics in their school curriculum. Greek men who could afford the leisure time usually spent all or part of their afternoons practicing sports in their polis's gymnasiums.

The ancient Greeks held the Olympic Games—their best-known sporting event—in **Olympia** every four years. Because the Olympic Games were a religious festival in honor of Zeus, trading and fighting stopped while they were going on. The Greek calendar began with the supposed date of the first Olympic Games: 776 B.C.

Athletes came from all over the Greek-speaking world to compete in the Olympics. Only male athletes, however, were allowed to take part, and women were not permitted even as spectators. Games that honored the goddess Hera were held at a different location than Olympia and gave Greek women an opportunity to participate in races.

In line with the Greek emphasis on the individual, Olympic competition took the form of individual rather than team events. These consisted at first of only a footrace. Later other events—the broad jump, the discus throw, boxing, and wrestling—were added. An activity called the pentathlon (pehn•TATH•luhn) combined running, jumping, throwing the discus, wrestling, and hurling the javelin.

The Greeks crowned Olympic winners with wreaths of olive leaves and held parades in their honor. Some city-states even excused outstanding athletes from paying taxes.

> homes are sorrows, too, the very same.
> Lonely women who died, old men who
>   waited for sons that never came—no
> son left to them to make the offering at
>   their graves.
> That was the glorious victory they won. **"**
>
> ——Euripides, from his tragedy
> *The Trojan Women*, c. 415 B.C.

A Comedy Tonight

Eventually the Greeks also wrote comedies, plays with humorous themes and happy endings. **Aristophanes** (ar•uh•STAH•fuh•NEEZ), the most famous writer of comedies, created imaginative social satire. In his works he made witty comments about leading figures—such as Euripides—and

---

SECTION 1 REVIEW

Recall
1. **Define** classical, sanctuary, perspective, amphora, tragedy, comedy.
2. **Identify** Myron, Phidias, Praxiteles, Aeschylus, Sophocles, Euripides, Aristophanes.
3. **Describe** how worship of Greek deities influenced architecture, art, and athletics.

Critical Thinking
4. **Applying Information** Show how the Greek emphasis on the individual was demonstrated both in the Olympic Games and in the fine arts.

Understanding Themes
5. **Innovation** How was the ancient Greeks' emphasis on reason and individuality revealed in their arts? Cite examples from architecture, sculpture, and drama.

c. 500s B.C.
Pythagoras develops
mathematical theories.

435 B.C.
Herodotus
writes history of
the Persian Wars.

399 B.C.
Athenians try
Socrates for
treason.

335 B.C.
Aristotle opens
the Lyceum in
Athens.

Section 2

The Greek Mind

Setting the Scene

▶ **Terms to Define**
   philosopher, logic, hygiene

▶ **People to Meet**
   Sophists, Socrates, Plato, Aristotle, Herodotus,
   Thucydides, Thales, Pythagoras,
   Hippocrates

Find Out What did the ancient Greeks
achieve in philosophy, history, and science?

The Storyteller

*Socrates was on trial for his life, for crimes
against religion and for corrupting the youth of
Athens. He spoke in his own defense: "I have done
nothing but try to persuade you all, young and
old, not to be concerned with body or property
first, but to care chiefly about improvement of the
soul. I tell you that virtue does not come from
money, but that money comes from virtue, as does
every other good of man, public and private. This
is my teaching, and if this corrupts the youth,
then I am a mischievous person. O men of
Athens, either acquit me or convict me; but
whichever you do, understand that I shall never
alter my ways, not even if I have to die many
times."*

—adapted from
*The Apology of
Socrates*, Plato

Socrates

The Greeks believed the human mind
capable of understanding everything.
As a result, the **philosophers**, or
thinkers, of ancient Greece produced some of the
most remarkable ideas the world has ever known.
Through philosophy—which means "the seeking of
wisdom"—they laid the foundations for such disciplines as history, political science, biology, and
logic, or the science of reasoning.

The Sophists

In the 400s B.C. higher education was provided
by professional teachers known as **Sophists**.
Although Sophists traveled from polis to polis,
many gathered in Athens, possibly for the freedom
of speech allowed there. Sophists, meaning "know-
ers," claimed that they could find the answers to all
questions.

Many Sophists rejected the belief that the gods
and goddesses influenced human behavior. They
also did not believe in absolute moral and legal
standards. Instead, they asserted that "man is the
measure of all things" and that truth is different for
each individual.

Not only did Sophists challenge certain traditional Greek beliefs, they also took money for their
teaching. Many of them seemed most intent on
teaching young men how to win a political argument and get ahead in the world. Many Greeks,
including two of Greece's greatest philosophers—
Socrates (SAH•kruh•TEEZ) and his pupil **Plato**—
criticized the Sophists severely.

Socrates

Socrates was born to a poor Athenian family in
470 B.C. Athough a sculptor by trade, he spent most
of his time teaching. Unlike the Sophists, Socrates
believed in absolute rather than relative truth. His

main interest did not lie in teaching rhetoric or in imparting information. Rather, Socrates was attracted to the process by which people learned how to think for themselves.

To encourage his students to clear away mistaken ideas and discover the truth, Socrates developed a teaching technique known as the Socratic method. He would ask students pointed questions without giving them answers and then oppose the students' answers with clear logical arguments. Through this method, he forced his students to defend their statements and to clarify their thinking. For example, in discussing the topic of justice, Socrates proceeded as follows:

> **❝** Socrates: Does falsehood then exist among mankind?
> Euthydemus: It does assuredly.
> Socrates: Under which head [justice or injustice] shall we place it?
> Euthydemus: Under injustice, certainly.
> Socrates: Well then … if a father, when his son requires medicine, and refuses to take it, should deceive him, and give him the medicine as ordinary food, and, by adopting such deception, should restore him to health, under which head must we place such an act of deceit?
> Euthydemus: It appears to me that we must place it under [justice].… I retract what I said before. **❞**
>
> —Xenophon, from *Memorabilia*, early 300s B.C.

Some prominent Athenians viewed Socrates' teachings as a threat to the polis. In 399 B.C. they accused him of "corrupting the young" and of "not worshiping the gods worshiped by the state" and had him brought to trial.

Socrates argued in his own defense that a person who *knew* what was right would always *do* what was right and that the intellectual search for truth was the most important thing in the world. "A man who is good for anything ought not to calculate the chance of living or dying; he ought only to consider whether … he is doing right or wrong."

Despite Socrates' eloquence, a jury of citizens found him guilty and sentenced him to death. Although Socrates had the right to ask for a lesser penalty, such as exile, he refused to do so. He had lived his life under the laws of his polis, and he would not avoid obeying them now.

Socrates carried out the sentence of his fellow citizens himself. He drank poisonous hemlock juice and died quietly among his grieving followers.

Plato

Born an Athenian aristocrat, Plato thought at first of entering politics. However, after Socrates' death, Plato—at age 40—became a teacher and opened his Academy, a school that remained in existence until A.D. 529.

From memory Plato recorded dialogues, or conversations, between Socrates and fellow Athenians, and he also wrote the earliest book on political science, *The Republic*. In this book, he presented a plan for what he considered would be the ideal society and government.

Plato disliked Athenian democracy and preferred the government of Sparta. He gave more importance to the state than to the individual. Like the Spartans, he believed that each person should place service to the community above strictly personal goals. Plato also believed that the result of people having too much freedom is social disorder. He distrusted the lower classes and wanted only the most intelligent and best-educated citizens to participate in government. As he explained in *The Republic*:

> **❝** Until philosophers are kings, or the kings and princes of this world have the spirit and power of philosophy, and political greatness and wisdom meet in one, and those commoner natures who pursue either to the exclusion of the other are compelled to stand aside, cities will never have rest from their evils, no, nor the human race. **❞**

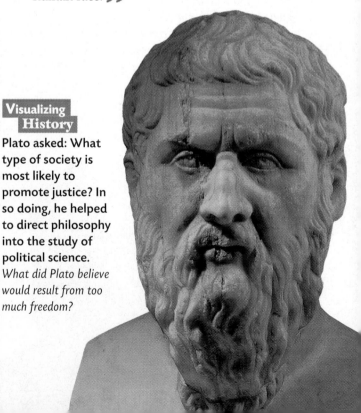

Visualizing History

Plato asked: What type of society is most likely to promote justice? In so doing, he helped to direct philosophy into the study of political science. *What did Plato believe would result from too much freedom?*

Plato's political views were part of an all-embracing philosophy by which he tried to search for "truth." Plato rejected the senses—seeing, hearing, touch, smell, and taste—as a source of truth, believing that the many things that could be perceived by these senses were only "appearance." Reality, the "real" world, was constructed from ideas, or ideal "forms," which could be understood through logical thought and reasoning.

Aristotle

The third great philosopher of ancient Greece was **Aristotle** (AR•uh•STAH•tuhl), who wrote more than 200 books on topics ranging from astronomy to political science. At his Athenian school known as the Lyceum, Aristotle taught the golden mean, an ethical principle that affirmed living moderately and avoiding extremes in one's actions.

Aristotle influenced later philosophers with his work on logic. He developed the syllogism, a means for presenting an argument in such a way that one can determine whether or not the conclusion follows logically from the premises, or basic statements.

Aristotle and Science

Aristotle also influenced scientific work. Unlike Plato, he stressed the value of knowledge gained through the senses. In his work *Physics*, Aristotle stated that the physical world's most striking feature is change, and that change basically consists of the same matter taking on new form. He was also the first person to observe facts, then classify them according to their similarities and their differences, and finally develop generalizations from his data. Some of his specific beliefs—notably, that Earth is the center of our solar system—were incorrect. Aristotle's views and his method of inquiry, however, would continue to dominate European scientific thinking for centuries.

Aristotle and Government

Many of Aristotle's writings focused on political science. Unlike Plato, he did not theorize about idealized principles of government. Instead, he examined the political structure of various city-states, analyzing their advantages and disadvantages. Only then did he spell out his conclusions in a book called *Politics*. Aristotle believed that the ideal form of government balanced monarchy, aristocracy, and democracy in one system. He preferred, however, to have power rest with the middle class, because they knew both how to command *and* obey.

Writers of History

The Greeks also used their intellectual skills in writing history. Until the 400s B.C. the Greeks had considered literary legends as history. **Herodotus** (hih•RAH•duh•tus), the first Greek historian, decided to separate fact from legend. Historians still consider him "the father of history."

Herodotus

Herodotus chose as his subject the Persian Wars and called his work the *Historia*, or "investigation." Herodotus traveled throughout the Persian Empire and also visited many Greek colonies. Everywhere he went, he asked questions, recorded answers, and checked the reliability of his sources. However, he accepted some statements that were not true, especially exaggerated numbers—such as how many Persians died at Marathon. He also sometimes offered supernatural explanations of events.

Herodotus did not limit himself to describing military and political events. He also wrote about outstanding individuals, social customs, and religious beliefs and practices. Later historians have learned a great deal from the *Historia* about the culture of the period and about the civilizations that Herodotus visited.

Thucydides

The second noted historian of ancient Greece, **Thucydides** (thoo•SIH•duh•DEEZ), wrote about the Peloponnesian War. Thucydides is regarded as the first scientific historian because he completely rejected the idea that the deities played a part in human history. Only human beings make history, Thucydides said. He also was as accurate and impartial as possible. He visited battle sites, carefully examined documents, and accepted only the evidence of actual eyewitnesses to events.

Footnotes to History

The Atom

The Greek thinker Democritus came up with the idea of a solid particle of matter so small that it was both invisible and not divisible. He named this particle *atom*, meaning "indivisible." Today scientists know that atoms are in fact divisible and include many separate and smaller types of matter. But the basic idea of atomic physics can be traced back to Democritus.

Greek physicians observed the many symptoms of disease and concluded that illnesses are not caused by evil spirits, but have natural causes. *What three prescriptions for health did Hippocrates suggest?*

guish mathematics as a pure science apart from everyday practical uses. They constructed systematic methods of reasoning to prove the truth of mathematical statements. Through the study of mathematics, Greek thinkers believed that they could find absolutely certain and eternal knowledge.

The first prominent Greek scientist was **Thales** (THAY•leez) of Miletus, a Greek city-state in Ionia. Born in the mid-600s B.C., Thales studied astronomy at Babylon and mathematics in Egypt and could foretell a solar eclipse. He also formulated a theory that water was the basic substance of which everything in the world is made.

During the 500s B.C., **Pythagoras** (puh •THA•guh•ruhs) tried to explain everything in mathematical terms. He explored the nature of numbers, especially whole numbers and their ratios. Students of geometry still learn the Pythagorean theorem about the relationship of sides of a right-angled triangle. Pythagoras also taught that the world was round and revolved around a fixed point.

Greek Medicine

Greek scientists also contributed to the field of medicine. Called "the father of medicine," the physician **Hippocrates** (hih•PAH•kruh•TEEZ) believed that diseases had natural, not supernatural, causes and that the body could heal itself. He was the first doctor to view medicine as a science separate from religious beliefs or mythological explanations.

Basing his work in the late 400s B.C. on observation, he traveled all over Greece diagnosing illnesses and treating sick people. He urged fellow doctors to keep records of their cases and to exchange information with one another. He strongly advocated proper hygiene, or health care, a sound diet, and plenty of rest.

According to tradition, Hippocrates drafted a code for ethical medical conduct that has guided the practice of medicine for more than 2,000 years. Many doctors today recite the Hippocratic oath when they receive their medical degree.

Thucydides did not simply recite facts, however. He also offered explanations for why events took place and what motivated political leaders. He believed that future generations could learn from the past.

The First Scientists

The ancient Greeks passed on a great scientific heritage. They believed that the world is ruled by natural laws and that human beings can discover these laws by using reason. Lacking scientific equipment, the Greek scientists made most of their discoveries by observation and thought. They then went on to develop general theories or statements about the workings of nature.

Greek Mathematicians

The Greeks became the first people to distin-

SECTION 2 REVIEW

Recall

1. **Define** philosopher, logic, hygiene.
2. **Identify** Sophists, Socrates, Plato, Aristotle, Herodotus, Thucydides, Thales, Pythagoras, Hippocrates.

3. **Explain** how Plato, Socrates, and Aristotle were related as philosophers.

Critical Thinking

4. **Making Comparisons** Compare the political views of Plato and Aristotle and their

attitudes regarding observations made through the senses.

Understanding Themes

5. **Innovation** How did Socrates and Hippocrates each contribute to the intellectual life of ancient Greece?

Finding Exact Location on a Map

Your new friend invites you to her house. In giving directions, she says, "I live at the northwest corner of Vine Street and Oak Avenue." She has pinpointed her exact location. We use a similar system to identify the exact location of any place on Earth.

Learning the Skill

Over many centuries, cartographers developed a grid system of imaginary lines—the lines of latitude and lines of longitude. Lines of latitude run east and west around the earth. Because they always remain the same distance from each other, they are also called parallels. The parallel lines of latitude measure distance north and south of the Equator, located at 0° latitude. Each line of latitude is one degree, or 69 miles (110 km), from the next. There are 90 latitude lines between the Equator and each Pole. For example, New York City lies 41° north of the Equator, or 41° N.

Lines of longitude, or meridians, run north and south from Pole to Pole. Unlike lines of latitude, lines of longitude are not always the same distance from each other. Lines of longitude are farthest apart at the Equator and intersect at each Pole. Longitude measures distance east and west of the Prime Meridian, located at 0° longitude. That line runs through Greenwich, England, in western Europe and through western Africa. Longitude lines increase east and west of the Prime Meridian to 180°. This meridian runs through the Pacific Ocean. New York City, for example, lies 74° west of the Prime Meridian, or 74° W.

With this system, we can pinpoint the "grid address" of any place on Earth. On a map, find the nearest line of latitude to the designated place. Then follow along this line until it crosses the nearest line of longitude. The point where the lines intersect is the grid address. For example, New York City has this grid address: 41° N, 74° W.

Practicing the Skill

Use the map below to answer the following questions:
1. What is the approximate grid address of Babylon?
2. What city is located at approximately 30° N, 31° E?
3. What is the approximate grid address of Nineveh?
4. What is the approximate grid address of Tyre?

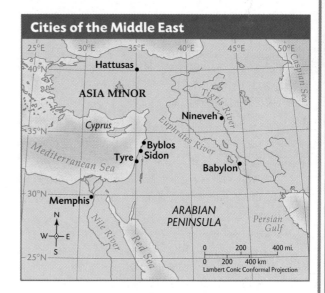

Cities of the Middle East

Applying the Skill

Create a travel itinerary for a tour of the ruins of ancient Egypt, Greece, or the Middle East. Choose at least 10 locations you would like to visit. Draw a map of the region, including grid lines. On the map, identify the approximate grid location of each place.

For More Practice

Turn to the Skill Practice in the Chapter Review on page 151 for more practice in finding exact location on a map.

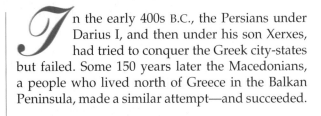
359 B.C. Philip II becomes king of Macedonia.

331 B.C. Alexander the Great defeats the Persians in the battle of Gaugamela.

250 B.C. Jewish scholars translate the Hebrew Bible into Greek.

c. 150 B.C. Rome conquers Greece.

Section 3

Alexander's Empire

Setting the Scene

▶ **Terms to Define**
domain

▶ **People to Meet**
Philip II, Demosthenes, Alexander the Great, Zeno, Menander, Eratosthenes, Euclid, Archimedes

▶ **Places to Locate**
Macedonia, Alexandria

Find Out What were Alexander's goals for his empire, and how successful was he in achieving them?

The Storyteller

Hellenistic poets who lived in bustling cities loved to tell simple fables about love in a countryside setting:

*A bee once stung the god of love [Cupid]
as he was stealing honey.
His fingertips began to smart,
and he blew upon his hand,
stamped and danced.
When he showed his wound to his mother,
she laughed. "Aren't you just like the bee,
so small, yet inflicting great pain?"*

—adapted from *The Idylls of Theocritus,* (no. 19, "The Honey-Thief"), in *Greek Pastoral Poetry,* Anthony Holden, 1974

Cupid, wall painting, Pompeii, Italy

In the early 400s B.C., the Persians under Darius I, and then under his son Xerxes, had tried to conquer the Greek city-states but failed. Some 150 years later the Macedonians, a people who lived north of Greece in the Balkan Peninsula, made a similar attempt—and succeeded.

Rise of Macedonia

The Macedonians, like the Spartans, were descended from the Dorians, and the Macedonian language incorporated many Greek words. The Greeks, however, looked down on the Macedonians as backward mountaineers.

In 359 B.C. **Philip II** became king of **Macedonia**. During his youth he had been a hostage for three years in the Greek city-state of Thebes. There he had learned to admire both Greek culture and military organization. As king, Philip determined to do three things: create a strong standing army, unify the quarreling Greek city-states under Macedonian rule, and destroy the Persian Empire.

Philip increased his army's fighting power by organizing his infantry into Greek-style phalanxes. Arrayed in close formation 16 rows deep, Philip's lance-bearing foot soldiers fought as a single unit.

For the next 23 years, Philip pursued his ambition. Sometimes he conquered a polis or bribed a polis's leaders to surrender. Sometimes he allied a polis through marriage; Philip had a total of six or seven wives.

The Greek city-states, weakened by the Peloponnesian War, would not cooperate in resisting Philip. The great Athenian orator **Demosthenes** (dih•MAHS•thuh•NEEZ) appealed to his fellow citizens to fight for their liberty. But Demosthenes' words were to no avail. By 338 B.C. Philip had conquered all of Greece except Sparta.

Philip then announced that he would lead the Greeks and Macedonians in a war against Persia. But in 336 B.C., just as he was ready to carry out his

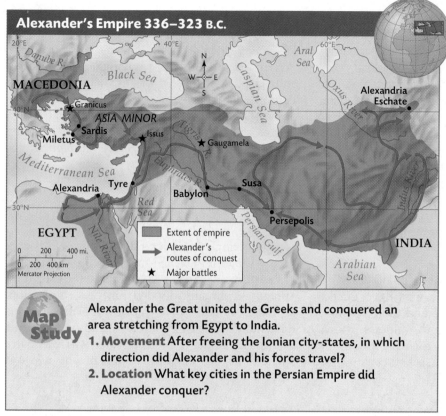

Alexander's Empire 336–323 B.C.

Extent of empire
Alexander's routes of conquest
★ Major battles

0 200 400 mi.
0 200 400 km
Mercator Projection

Map Study Alexander the Great united the Greeks and conquered an area stretching from Egypt to India.
1. **Movement** After freeing the Ionian city-states, in which direction did Alexander and his forces travel?
2. **Location** What key cities in the Persian Empire did Alexander conquer?

plans, Philip was murdered—either by a Persian agent or by an assassin hired by his first wife, Olympias. Olympias' son Alexander, later known as **Alexander the Great**, became king.

POINT

Alexander's Conquests

Alexander was only 20 when he became the ruler of Macedonia and Greece. A commander in the Macedonian army since he was 16, Alexander was highly respected by his soldiers for his courage and military skill. He was also extremely well educated, for his father had him tutored by Aristotle.

Conflict With Persia

In 334 B.C. Alexander led 30,000 soldiers and 5,000 cavalry into Asia to open his campaign of "West against East." The first major encounter with the Persians took place at the Granicus River in western Asia Minor. Alexander's forces won, and he sent 300 suits of Persian armor to Athens as an offering to the goddess Athena. He then marched along the coast of Asia Minor, freeing the Ionian city-states from Persian rule.

The second major battle between the Greeks

and Persians took place in 333 B.C. at Issus, Syria. Once again, Alexander's superb tactics resulted in victory, forcing the Persian king Darius III to flee.

Instead of pursuing Darius, Alexander and his troops moved south along the Mediterranean coast. First they captured the seaports of Phoenicia and cut off the Persian fleet from its main supply bases. The fleet soon surrendered. Next, turning west, they invaded Egypt where the people, discontented under Persian rule, welcomed them and declared Alexander a pharaoh. In Egypt, Alexander established a new city and named it **Alexandria** after himself.

Final Campaigns

In 331 B.C. Alexander again turned his attention eastward. He invaded Mesopotamia and smashed Darius's main army in the battle of Gaugamela near the Tigris River. He

Alexander the Great

went on to capture the key cities of the Persian Empire: Babylon, Persepolis, and Susa. When Darius was killed by one of his own generals, Alexander declared himself ruler of the Persian Empire.

Even this success was not enough for the young conqueror. In 327 B.C. he led his soldiers into India, and after three years they reached the Indus River valley. Alexander hoped to go farther yet, but his Macedonian veterans refused. Alexander therefore reluctantly turned around and went to Babylon, which he had made the capital of his empire. But the hardships of the journey had undermined his health, and he fell ill with a fever, probably malaria. In 323 B.C. Alexander the Great died at the age of 33.

Imperial Goals

When Alexander first set out with his army, his goal was to punish Persia for its invasion of Greece 150 years earlier. But as more and more territory came under his control, Alexander's views changed. His new vision was to create an empire that would unite Europe and Asia and combine the best of Greek and Persian cultures.

Alexander tried to promote this goal by example. He wore Persian dress and imitated the court life of Persian kings. He married a daughter of Darius III and encouraged 10,000 of his soldiers to marry Persian women. He enrolled 30,000 Persians in his army. He also founded about 70 cities that served both as military outposts and as centers for spreading the Greek language and culture throughout his empire.

Divided Domain

Following Alexander's death, three of his generals—Ptolemy (TAH•luh•mee), Seleucus (suh•LOO•kuhs), and Antigonus (an•TIH•guh•nuhs)—eventually divided his vast empire into separate **domains**, or territories. Ptolemy and his descendants ruled Egypt, Libya, and part of Syria. The most famous Ptolemaic ruler was Cleopatra VII, who lost her kingdom to the Romans in 31 B.C.

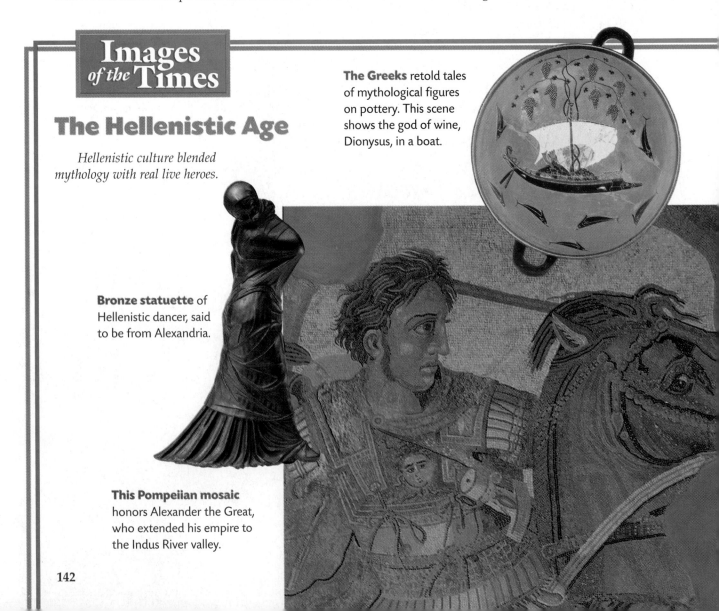

Images
of the Times

The Hellenistic Age

Hellenistic culture blended mythology with real live heroes.

The Greeks retold tales of mythological figures on pottery. This scene shows the god of wine, Dionysus, in a boat.

Bronze statuette of Hellenistic dancer, said to be from Alexandria.

This Pompeiian mosaic honors Alexander the Great, who extended his empire to the Indus River valley.

Seleucus and his descendants—the Seleucids (suh•LOO•suhds)—at first controlled the rest of Syria, as well as Mesopotamia, Iran, and Afghanistan. After a while, however, they were forced to give up their eastern territory and withdraw to Syria. In 167 B.C. Jewish guerrillas led by Judah Maccabee challenged the Seleucid control of Palestine. The Seleucid Antiochus IV had ordered the Jews to worship the Greek deities, but many Jews refused to abandon their religion. In 165 B.C. Judah Maccabee succeeded in reoccupying Jerusalem and rededicating the Temple, an event commemorated by the Jewish festival of Hanukkah. The kingdom of Judah would remain independent until its defeat by Rome in 63 B.C. The Seleucids likewise ruled in Syria until the Romans came.

The domain of Antigonus and his heirs consisted at first of Macedonia and Greece. But the Greek city-states soon declared their independence and once again began fighting with each other. In the 100s B.C., the growing Roman Empire would conquer Macedonia and Greece.

Hellenistic Culture

The political unity of Alexander's empire disappeared with his death, but the Greek language and culture continued to spread and flourish in the lands he had conquered. There, Hellenic ways of life mixed with elements of Middle Eastern culture to form a new culture, called Hellenistic.

City Life

Hellenistic culture was concentrated in cities. The largest and wealthiest of these was Alexandria in Egypt. Alexandria's straight streets intersected each other at right angles, in contrast to the crooked streets of older cities. Its white stucco stone palaces and temples gleamed brilliantly in the sun.

The city's economic position benefited from a double harbor that could hold 1,200 ships at a time. Another asset to trade was the city's lighthouse, which was visible from 35 miles (56 km) out at sea.

Alexandria also was a major intellectual center. Its museum was the first ever and included a

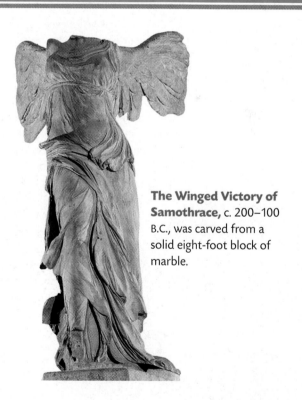

The Winged Victory of Samothrace, c. 200–100 B.C., was carved from a solid eight-foot block of marble.

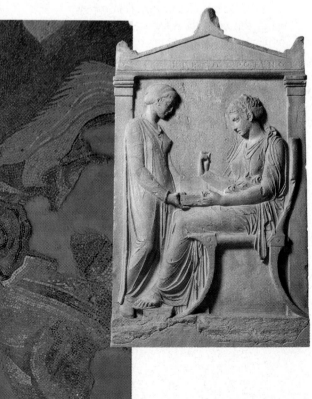

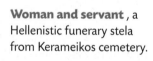

Woman and servant, a Hellenistic funerary stela from Kerameikos cemetery.

REFLECTING ON THE TIMES

1. How did Greek pottery promote popular myths?
2. How are humans portrayed in Hellenistic art?

library of nearly a million volumes, an institute for scientific research, a zoo, and a botanical garden. Scientists came from all over the Hellenistic world. Around 250 B.C. Jewish scholars in Alexandria translated the Hebrew Bible into Greek. This translation, known as the Septuagint (sehp•TOO •uh•juhnt), was later used by the apostle Paul and is still used in the Eastern Orthodox Church.

During Hellenic times, the Greeks had been intensely involved with their particular polis. In Hellenistic society, however, the Greeks formed the upper class of Alexandria and other cities in the Middle East and Asia Minor that were ruled by kings. Rather than being loyal to their king or kingdom, professional Greek soldiers and bureaucrats moved from place to place, wherever job opportunities were best.

In Alexandria and other Hellenistic cities, the social status of upper-class Greek women improved over their traditional status in Athens. No longer secluded, women could move about freely. They learned how to read and write and entered such occupations as real estate, banking, and government. Such opportunities were not, however, available to commoners.

Hellenistic Philosophers

Hellenistic philosophers focused on personal behavior, especially the question of how to achieve peace of mind. Three systems of thought attracted most Hellenistic intellectuals: Cynicism, Epicureanism (EH•pih•kyu•REE•uh•NIH•zuhm), and Stoicism.

The best known Cynic was Diogenes (dy•AH •juh•NEEZ). He criticized materialism and asserted that people would be happy if they gave up luxuries and lived simply, in accord with nature. The scholar Epicurus started the philosophy of Epicureanism. He argued that people should avoid both joy and pain by accepting the world as it was, ignoring politics, and living simply and quietly with a few close friends.

Zeno founded Stoicism. The name *Stoicism* comes from the *Stoa Poikile*, or "painted porch," in which Zeno lectured. The Stoics believed that what happened to people was governed by natural laws. Accordingly, people could gain happiness by ignoring their emotions, and instead following their reason. In this way, they were able to accept even the most difficult circumstances of life and do their duty. Stoicism later affected both Roman intellectuals and early Christian thinkers.

CONNECTIONS
Economics

An Economic Region

Geographers, historians, and economists often divide the world into regions based on economic factors, such as trade routes and uniform currency. The empire of Alexander the Great came to be one economic region.

Alexander and his successors used vast sums of gold and silver captured in Persia to finance public works projects, road construction, and harbor development. Extensive land routes helped maintain close economic links among the cities built by Alexander. A uniform currency also developed that held the empire together economically. International sea trade expanded greatly under Alexander's empire and its successor domains. Hellenistic sailors used monsoon winds to sail directly across the Indian Ocean between Africa and Asia

instead of hugging the coast. As a result, luxury items from India and Arabia became common in Mediterranean cities. As in ancient times, the world today is made up of many different economic regions. For example, the American Midwest can be classified as an economic region because one of its economic characteristics is the production of corn, hogs, and cattle. Another example of an economic region is a large metropolitan area—such as that of Johannesburg, South Africa—in which a central urban area is joined to surrounding areas by transportation links, or by people's wants and needs, such as jobs, shopping, or entertainment.

Coin bearing the face of Alexander the Great

Linking Past and Present ACTIVITY

List three economic characteristics of Alexander's empire. Then, identify an economic region in which you live and list its characteristics.

History & Art Actors preparing for a performance, a mosaic from the House of the Tragic Poet, Pompeii. National Museum, Naples, Italy *Why might people have had a work like this in their home?*

Hellenistic Art and Literature

During the Hellenistic era, artists departed from Hellenic styles. Instead of carving idealized individuals, Hellenistic sculptors showed people in the grip of powerful emotions. They also carved portrait heads, because art had become a business.

Hellenistic playwrights usually wrote comedies rather than tragedies. Like Hellenistic philosophers, they ignored the problems of the outside world as much as possible. **Menander,** the most renowned Hellenistic playwright, specialized in comedies about everyday life. Well-known lines from his works include "Whom the gods love die young" and "We live not as we will, but as we can."

Science, Medicine, and Mathematics

Although limited by their simple instruments, Hellenistic scientists performed many experiments and developed new theories. Aristarchus (AR•uh•STAHR•kuhs) of Samos concluded that the sun is larger than the earth, that the earth revolves around the sun, and that the stars lie at immense distances from both heavenly bodies. **Eratosthenes** (EHR•uh•TAHS•thuh•NEEZ) estimated the earth's circumference to within 1 percent of the correct figure. Hellenistic doctors dissected corpses in order to learn more about human anatomy. They discovered the body's nervous system, studied the brain and the liver, and learned how to use drugs to relieve pain.

The Hellenistic period also saw great developments and breakthroughs in mathematics and physics. **Euclid** of Alexandria wrote *The Elements of Geometry,* a book that organized all information about geometry. **Archimedes** (AHR•kuh•MEE•deez) invented the compound pulley, which moves heavy objects easily, and the cylinder-screw, which is still used to lift water for irrigation. He also discovered the principle of buoyancy and demonstrated the principle of the lever.

SECTION 3 REVIEW

Recall
1. **Define** domain.
2. **Identify** Philip II, Demosthenes, Alexander the Great, Zeno, Menander, Eratosthenes, Euclid, Archimedes.
3. **Locate** Macedonia and Alexandria on the map on page 141. What does Alexandria owe to the Macedonians?

Critical Thinking
4. **Making Comparisons** Compare and contrast Alexander the Great's original goal and the goal he finally chose for his empire. Why did his goals change?

Understanding Themes
5. **Cultural Diffusion** Explain how and why Hellenistic arts differed from Hellenic arts.

Chapter 5 *The Height of Greek Civilization* **145**

Literature

Bridge to the Past

from

Antigone
by Sophocles

The Greek playwright Sophocles, who lived from about 495–405 B.C., wrote about the conflict between conscience and authority in his play Antigone. After Antigone's two brothers died battling each other for the throne of Thebes, her uncle, Creon, became king. Creon allowed one brother, Eteocles, an honorable burial. He declared, however, that the other brother, Polyneices, was a traitor whose body should be left for the "birds and scavenging dogs." Anyone attempting to bury Polyneices, he warned, would be stoned to death. Antigone's sister, Ismene, obeys Creon. Antigone, however, out of respect for her brother, buries him.

Creon [*slowly, dangerously*]. And you, Antigone, You with your head hanging—do you confess this thing?

Antigone. I do. I deny nothing.

Creon [*to* SENTRY].   You may go.
[*Exit* SENTRY] [*To* ANTIGONE] Tell me, tell me briefly:
Had you heard my proclamation touching this matter?

Antigone. It was public. Could I help hearing it?

Creon. And yet you dared defy the law.

Antigone.   I dared.
It was not God's proclamation. That final justice
That rules the world below makes no such laws.
Your edict, King, was strong,
But all your strength is weakness itself against
The immortal unrecorded laws of God.
They are not merely now: they were, and shall be,
Operative forever, beyond man utterly.

I knew I must die, even without your decree:
I am only mortal. And if I must die
Now, before it is my time to die,
Surely this is no hardship: can anyone
Living, as I live, with evil all about me,
Think death less than a friend? This death of mine
Is of no importance; but if I had left my brother
Lying in death unburied, I should have suffered.
Now I do not.
                    You smile at me. Ah Creon.

Think me a fool, if you like; but it may well be
That a fool convicts me of folly....
Creon, what more do you want than my death?

Creon.   Nothing.
That gives me everything.

Antigone.   Then I beg you: kill me.
This talking is a great weariness: your words
Are distasteful to me, and I am sure that mine
Seem so to you. And yet they should not seem so:
I should have praise and honor for what I have done.
All these men here would praise me
Were their lips not frozen shut with fear of you.
[*Bitterly*] Ah the good fortune of kings,
Licensed to say and do whatever they please!

Creon. You are alone here in that opinion.

Antigone. No, they are with me. But they keep their tongues
in leash.

Creon. Maybe. But you are guilty,
and they are not.

Antigone. There is no guilt in reverence for the dead.

Creon. But Eteocles—was he not
your brother too?

Antigone. My brother too.

Creon.   And you
insult his memory?

Antigone [*softly*]. The dead man
would not say that I insult it.

Creon. He would: for you honor a
traitor as much as him.

Antigone. His own brother, traitor or
not, and equal in blood.

Creon. He made war on his country.
Eteocles defended it.

Antigone. Nevertheless, there are
honors due all the dead.

History & Art Actors preparing for a performance
(detail), the House of the Tragic Poet,
Pompeii. National Museum, Naples, Italy
What is the theme of Antigone?

Wall painting of a Greek woman with flowers. National Museum, Naples, Italy

The Greeks admired beauty and virtue. *Does Ismene regain virtue by confessing a share in the crime?*

Creon. But not the same for the wicked as for the just.

Antigone. Ah Creon, Creon.
Which of us can say what the gods hold wicked?

Creon. An enemy is an enemy, even dead.

Antigone. It is my nature to join in love, not hate.

Creon [*finally losing patience*]. Go join them, then; if you must have your love,
Find it in hell!

Choragos [*leader of a group of 15 citizens*]. But see, Ismene comes:
[*Enter Ismene, guarded.*] Those tears are sisterly, the cloud
That shadows her eyes rains down gentle sorrow.

Creon. You too, Ismene,

Snake in my ordered house, sucking my blood
Stealthily—and all the time I never knew
That these two sisters were aiming at my throne!
                                        Ismene,
Do you confess your share in this crime, or deny it?
Answer me.

Ismene. Yes, if she will let me say so. I am guilty.

Antigone [*coldly*]. No, Ismene. You have no right to say so.
You would not help me, and I will not have you help me.

Ismene. But now I know what you meant; and I am here
To join you, to take my share of punishment.

Antigone. The dead man and the gods who rule the dead
Know whose act this was. Words are not friends.

Ismene. Do you refuse me, Antigone? I want to die with you:
I too have a duty that I must discharge to the dead.

Antigone. You shall not lessen my death by sharing it.

Ismene. What do I care for life when you are dead?

Antigone. Ask Creon. You're always hanging on his opinions.

Ismene. You are laughing at me. Why, Antigone?

Antigone. It's a joyless laughter, Ismene.

Ismene.   But can I do nothing?

Antigone. Yes. Save yourself. I shall not envy you.
There are those who will praise you; I shall have honor, too.

Ismene. But we are equally guilty!

Antigone.   No more, Ismene.
You are alive, but I belong to death.

RESPONDING TO LITERATURE

1. Explain what Antigone means when she says to Creon, "But all your strength is weakness itself against the immortal unrecorded laws of God."
2. Quote a passage that demonstrates Antigone's bravery.
3. Explain whether you would like to live in a society in which individuals followed only their consciences.
4. **Making Inferences** Predict whether Creon actually would have Antigone stoned to death.

Connections Across Time

Historical Significance Greek culture has influenced Western civilization in many ways. The ancient Greeks developed classical models on which later architects, artists, and playwrights have relied. Their thinkers also laid the foundation for the disciplines of history, political science, and logic.

The Founders of the United States took inspiration from ancient Greek ideals, such as belief in the worth and importance of the individual. The Founders' belief in a democratic form of government—as the one best suited to enabling people to enhance their abilities—also has its roots in ancient Greece.

Using Key Terms

Write the key term that completes each sentence. Then write a sentence for each term not chosen.

a. classical
b. comedies
c. logic
d. philosophers
e. tragedies
f. domains
g. hygiene
h. sanctuaries
i. amphora
j. perspective

1. The architects of the Parthenon in Athens understood _____, the artistic representation of distances between objects as they appear to the eye.
2. Greek potters usually decorated an _____— a large vase for storing bulk supplies—with scenes from their mythology and legends.
3. Greek artists and architects created works characterized by a _____ style known for its beautiful simplicity and graceful balance.
4. After Alexander's death in 323 B.C., his large multicultural empire was divided into several _____.
5. Greek thinkers, or _____, developed the foundations for disciplines such as history, political science, and logic.

Using Your History Journal

The Greeks liked to relive historic events through drama. Each actor would wear a large mask to show the age, sex, and mood of each character. Write a short scene for a drama depicting an event from the chapter.

Reviewing Facts

1. **Geography** Locate where the Parthenon was built and explain for what purpose.
2. **Culture** Describe the main philosophical differences between the Sophists and Socrates.
3. **Science** Name the main steps in the scientific method of inquiry developed by Aristotle.
4. **History/Culture** Explain why Thucydides is considered the first scientific historian.
5. **History** Discuss the ways in which Alexander's conquests changed Greek life.
6. **Culture** Identify the two major cultural areas that contributed to Hellenistic civilization.
7. **Science** State the contributions of Pythagorus, Archimedes, and Eratosthenes.

Technology Activity

Building a Database Search the Internet or your local library for additional information about the Olympic Games. Build a database by collecting information about recent Olympic Game results of both summer and winter sporting events. Include headings such as name of the event, when it first became an event, if participated in by both sexes, and the number of medals each country obtained.

Critical Thinking

1. **Apply** How did the Peloponnesian War affect Greek drama and philosophy?
2. **Evaluate** Whose political ideas does the United States government more closely follow, those of Plato or those of Aristotle?
3. **Analyze** Why did conflicts develop in Alexander's empire after his death? Could they have been resolved peacefully? Why or why not?

Geography in History

1. **Place** Refer to the map "Alexander's Empire Divided." Who controlled the area of Macedonia?
2. **Location** What present-day countries make up the part of Alexander's empire ruled by Ptolemy?
3. **Place** Which of the Hellenistic lands do you think was the most difficult to govern, based on geographic factors? Explain.

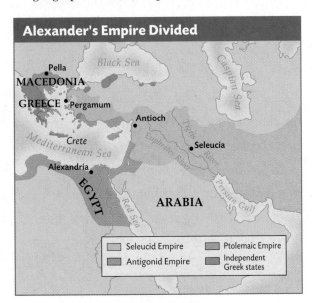

Alexander's Empire Divided

Pella
MACEDONIA
GREECE • Pergamum
Antioch
Crete
Seleucia
Alexandria
EGYPT
ARABIA

☐ Seleucid Empire   ☐ Ptolemaic Empire
☐ Antigonid Empire ☐ Independent Greek states

Linking Past and Present

1. The Olympic Games were revived in 1896. In what ways do the modern Olympic Games resemble those of ancient Greece? In what ways do they differ?
2. The inclusion of diverse territories in Alexander the Great's empire led to widespread cultural diffusion. Besides military conquests, what factors promote cultural diffusion today?
3. Ideas of Greek civilization have affected much of American culture. Choose one area such as medicine, philosophy, politics, art, or architecture. Reread information about that area in your chapter. Then list as many examples of influences on American culture as you can. Ask friends, parents, or other family members to help complete the list.

Understanding Themes

1. **Innovation** What might contemporary theater be like if such great Hellenistic playwrights as Aristophanes and Menander had not lived and written about Greek society?
2. **Innovation** Do you think Herodotus deserves to be called the "father of history"? Explain your answer.
3. **Cultural Diffusion** How did Alexander the Great's founding of cities throughout his empire help spread Greek culture?

Skill Practice

Use the map "Greece and Persia" to answer the following questions.

1. What is the approximate location of Athens with regard to latitude and longitude?
2. Which body of water lies entirely north of 40° N latitude?
3. What is the approximate location of Sparta with regard to latitude and longitude?
4. What is the approximate location of Sardis with regard to longitude and latitude?
5. What is the relative location of Sardis?
6. What Mediterranean island lies along the 35th parallel?

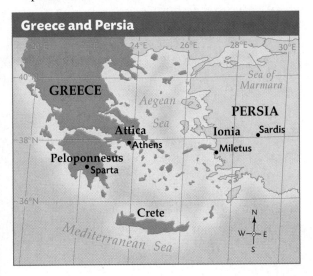

Greece and Persia

GREECE
Aegean Sea
Sea of Marmara
PERSIA
Attica
Athens
Ionia   Sardis
Miletus
Peloponnesus
Sparta
Crete
Mediterranean Sea

Ancient Rome and Early Christianity

Chapter Themes

▶ **Change** The Roman political system evolves as Rome allows more of its people to participate in government. *Section 1*

▶ **Conflict** Roman armies conquer most of the Mediterranean world. *Section 2*

▶ **Cultural Diffusion** The Romans build an empire and spread Latin culture. *Section 3*

▶ **Innovation** Christianity becomes the dominant religion in the West. *Section 4*

▶ **Change** Germanic invasions and cultural weaknesses destroy the Roman Empire. *Section 5*

The Storyteller

War trumpets rang over the cheers of the people of Rome who gathered to view the triumphal grand parade. Then sweating horses jerking at their harnesses rattled the victor's chariot over the paving stones, and the people's cries became louder. On this day in 146 B.C., the Romans were celebrating their conquest of the last of the free Greek city-states.

Ironically, however, over the next several centuries Greek culture would come to form the base of Roman culture and society. Texts written by Greeks would shape Roman knowledge in many areas of study. Even after years of Roman rule, the eastern Mediterranean world would retain Greek as its primary language.

Historical Significance

How did the small city-state of Rome become the center of a vast, diverse empire that spanned the Mediterranean world? What were Rome's last legacies to Europe, Africa, the Middle East, and other parts of the world?

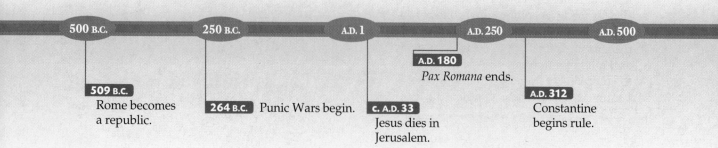

500 B.C.	250 B.C.	A.D. 1	A.D. 250	A.D. 500

509 B.C.
Rome becomes a republic.

264 B.C. Punic Wars begin.

c. A.D. 33
Jesus dies in Jerusalem.

A.D. 180
Pax Romana ends.

A.D. 312
Constantine begins rule.

Woman playing the cithera, painted on the east wall of a room in the villa of Publius Fannius Synistor, Pompeii, Italy

Your History Journal

The European cities of Bonn, Vienna, London, and Paris were each founded by the Romans. Research the early history of one of these cities and describe the Roman influence on its early architecture and lifestyle.

Chapter 6 *Ancient Rome and Early Christianity* **153**

c. 753 B.C.
Romulus
founds Rome.

c. 620 B.C.
Etruscans
gain control
of Rome.

451 B.C.
The patricians of
Rome enact the
Twelve Tables.

287 B.C.
The plebeians
begin to make
laws for Rome.

Section 1

The Roman Republic

Setting the Scene

▶ **Terms to Define**
   patrician, republic, plebeian, consul, dictator, tribune

▶ **People to Meet**
   the Etruscans, the Latins, Romulus, the Tarquins

▶ **Places to Locate**
   Italy, Sicily, Rome

Find Out How was Rome governed as a republic? How did the Roman Republic change over the years?

The Storyteller

The Forum

The city of Rome was besieged by Lars Porsena, king of Clusium, and the time had come for decisive action. One young Roman hoped to break the siege by killing Porsena. After laying his plan before the Senate, he set out alone toward enemy lines. However, he was seized as a spy and dragged by guards before the very man he had hoped to kill—Porsena. He spoke boldly: "I am a Roman, my name is Gaius Mucius. I came here to kill you—my enemy. I have as much courage to die as to kill. It is our Roman way to do and to suffer bravely."

—adapted from *Early History of Rome*, Titus Livy, in *The Global Experience, Readings in World History to 1500, 1987*

The peoples of **Italy** first came into contact with the Greeks around 900 B.C., when Greek traders sailed up both the east and west coasts of the Italian Peninsula. From about 750 B.C. to 500 B.C., the Greeks set up farming communities in southern Italy and in **Sicily**, an island southwest of the Italian Peninsula. These Greek colonists planted olive trees for the oil yielded and grapevines from which they could produce wine, thus introducing these two major products to Italy. The Greeks also introduced the Greek alphabet to the Italians.

The Italian Peninsula

The Greeks were interested in colonizing Italy for several reasons, one of which was Italy's central location in the Mediterranean. A narrow, boot-shaped peninsula, Italy extends from Europe toward the shores of Africa, dividing the Mediterranean almost in half. Thus, Italy was ideally situated to be the center of trade among three continents: Asia, Europe, and Africa. Italy's rich soil and mild, moist climate also attracted the Greek colonists. Beyond the mountains and foothills that covered three-quarters of the peninsula lay plains with soil enriched by the silt deposits of mountain streams.

However, the silt washing down Italy's short and shallow rivers blocked the mouths of many rivers, creating mosquito-infested swamps. The people of Italy suffered recurrent epidemics of malaria and other diseases carried by mosquitoes.

Because of Italy's mountains, the early inhabitants of the peninsula generally traded among themselves. Italy's only land connection—to the north—was cut off by the Alps. Furthermore, Italy's rocky and marshy coastline lacked good harbors. To increase trade, the Italians eventually turned to the sea, but until that time came, they remained attached to the land.

Early Peoples

Archaeological evidence suggests that people lived in Italy long before the Greeks arrived or Roman civilization began. The remains of human settlements reveal that Neolithic cultures may have begun to form in Italy as early as about 5000 B.C. Early peoples in the Italian Peninsula built villages and farms, moving on whenever they had exhausted the land around their settlements.

Indo-Europeans

Between 2000 B.C. and 1000 B.C., waves of Indo-European immigrants arrived and overwhelmed these Neolithic peoples. By the time Greek colonists came to Italy, many peoples inhabited the peninsula—including Umbrians in the north, Latins in the central plain called Latium (LAY•shee•uhm), and Oscans in the south. Like the Greeks, most of these people spoke Indo-European languages.

The Etruscans

From about 900 B.C. to 500 B.C., one of these peoples, **the Etruscans**, ruled northern Italy from the plains of Etruria. Little is known about their origins, although the Etruscans did not speak an Indo-European language as did many of the peninsula's other inhabitants. The Etruscan alphabet came from the Greeks, but modern scholars have been able to decipher only a few Etruscan words.

Although Etruscan writings still baffle our understanding, Etruscan art is expressive, needing no translation. In wall paintings, Etruscan figures dance and play music, enjoying a rich and pleasant life. In Etruscan sculpture, men and women feast and converse, triumphant soldiers revel in their victories, and hauntingly beautiful deities smile and gesture.

Such sculptures ornamented the homes of the Etruscan upper classes. Historians believe that Etruscan society probably consisted of wealthy overlords, aristocratic priests, and a slave labor force made up of conquered peoples. Wealthy overlords enslaved these peoples to provide themselves with comforts, and aristocratic priests sacrificed prisoners of war or forced them to duel to the death to appease angry gods.

After repeated revolts, the Etruscan lower classes and the other Italian peoples under

---

CONNECTIONS

The Arts

Murals: Etruscan and Modern

Although archaeologists have unearthed the remains of some Etruscan cities, these tell little about Etruscan culture. Murals unearthed in burial chambers, however, have provided significant clues about the Etruscans.

Etruscan mural

The murals show colorful and lively scenes of Etruscan daily life. Particularly popular subjects are scenes of wrestling matches, religious ceremonies, and people enjoying music and feasts.

Today, the desire to beautify urban areas has produced many

striking murals in cities from Sydney, Australia, to Caracas, Venezuela. The boldly colored works appear on office, apartment, and supermarket walls. They usually are sponsored by municipal officials or businesses, and the artists employed draw inspiration from sources as varied as fashion magazines, cartoons, and modern art. Among their subjects are movie, TV, and sports celebrities as well as ordinary people involved in daily activities, such as shopping on a busy street or playing basketball at a neighborhood playground.

Linking Past and Present **ACTIVITY**

What subjects are popularly shown in Etruscan murals? Modern urban murals? What do Etruscan murals reveal about Etruscan life? What do urban murals today reveal about modern life?

Etruscan rule finally freed themselves from domination by these wealthy overlords and priests. Chief among those who overthrew the Etruscans were **the Latins**, whose center was the city of **Rome** in the central plain of Latium.

The Rise of Rome

According to legend, in 753 B.C., a stocky man named **Romulus** was building the wall of a city on a hill overlooking the Tiber River. His twin brother, Remus, came over from the hillside opposite, where he too had been laying the foundations for a city. The Roman historian Livy tells what happened next:

> 66 Remus, by way of jeering at his brother, jumped over the half-built walls of the new settlement, whereupon Romulus killed him in a fit of rage, adding the threat, 'So perish whoever else shall over-leap my battlements.' 99
> —Livy, *Ab Urbe Condita*, 29 B.C.

Setting more stone on the stains of his brother's blood, Romulus is said to have continued his building. In time, his namesake city—Rome—grew to include his brother's hill and the other nearby hills. Romulus was so effective a military ruler, the myth tells us, that Rome became the greatest city in that part of the peninsula.

In fact, the origins of Rome were probably much less violent. At some time between 800 B.C. and 700 B.C., the Latins huddled in straw-roofed huts in the villages on the seven hills apparently agreed to join and form one community. It was this community that came to be called Rome.

Etruscan Rule

About 620 B.C. the Etruscans gained control of Rome. A wealthy Etruscan family, **the Tarquins**, provided kings to rule over the Romans. The Tarquins taught the Latins to build with brick and to roof their houses with tile. They drained the marshy lowlands around Rome and laid out city streets. At the center of the city they created a square called the Forum, which became the seat of Roman government. The Tarquins also built temples, taught the Romans many of the Etruscans' religious rituals, and elevated Rome to a position among the wealthiest cities in Italy.

Then in 534 B.C. Tarquin the Proud came to the throne. This king's cruelties so angered the Romans that in 509 B.C. they drove the Tarquins out. Skilled Etruscan artisans stayed on in Rome, however, helping the city continue to prosper.

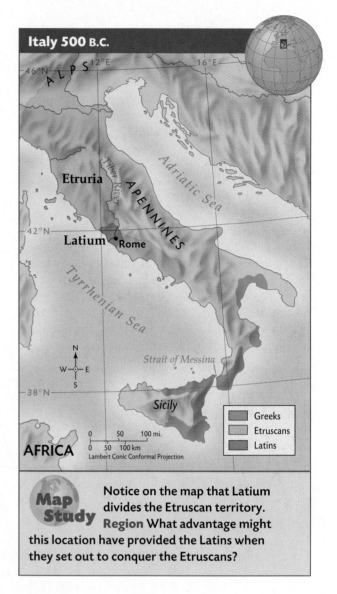

Italy 500 B.C.

Greeks
Etruscans
Latins

Map Study Notice on the map that Latium divides the Etruscan territory. **Region** What advantage might this location have provided the Latins when they set out to conquer the Etruscans?

Social Groups

Under Etruscan rule, a new wealthy aristocratic class had come into being in Rome—Latin nobles called patricians. Once the Etruscan rulers were driven out, the patricians declared Rome a republic, a community in which the people elect their leaders.

Most of Rome's inhabitants, however, were plebeians (plih•BEE•uhns), who included wealthy, nonaristocratic townspeople and landowners as well as merchants, shopkeepers, small farmers, and laborers. As citizens, both the plebeians and the patricians had rights, such as the right to vote, and responsibilities, such as paying taxes and serving in the military. Plebeians, however, could not hold public office as patricians could.

The Roman Republic

The patricians organized Rome's government into executive and legislative branches. The

Roman legislative branch at first consisted of the Assembly of Centuries and the Senate, both under patrician control. Members of the Assembly of Centuries (named for a military formation of 100 soldiers) elected officials of the executive branch. However, the power of the Senate—a group of 300 patrician men who served for life—outweighed the Assembly of Centuries. The senators advised the consuls, debated foreign policy, proposed laws, and approved contracts for constructing roads, temples, and defenses.

The executive branch was headed by two patrician officials elected for one-year terms. These officials were called **consuls** because they had to consult each other before acting. They understood that either consul could veto the other's decisions. The word *veto* is Latin for "I forbid." The consuls oversaw other executive officials, such as praetors, or judges, and censors, or keepers of tax and population records. Only a **dictator**, a leader whose word was law, could overrule the consuls. But dictators were temporarily appointed to lead the Romans only in time of crisis.

The most admired Roman dictator was the legendary hero Cincinnatus (SIHN•suh•NA•tuhs). In 458 B.C., a powerful rival threatened Rome, and the Senate sent messengers to tell Cincinnatus that he had been named dictator to meet this emergency. The messengers found him plowing his fields. Always loyal to Rome, Cincinnatus immediately joined the army and led his forces into battle. He defeated the enemy, marched his army back to Rome, and then resigned as dictator. He returned to his plowing 16 days after taking command.

Plebeians Against Patricians

The plebeians resented their lack of power in the new republic—especially because they knew that the patricians could not maintain the republic without them. In 494 B.C., many plebeians refused to fight in the Roman army unless the patricians yielded to their demands for change.

Plebeian Victories

Frightened at the loss of their military forces, the patricians finally agreed to reforms. They recognized the plebeians' chosen representatives, the **tribunes**, granting them legal protections and the right to veto government decisions. The patricians also recognized the Assembly of Tribes, the body of plebeians who elected the tribunes. Eventually, the Assembly of Tribes even won the right to make laws.

In addition to political rights, the plebeians improved their social standing. Enslavement for debt was ended, and marriage between patricians and plebeians was allowed. In spite of these benefits for the common people, the republic's social structure was still dominated by a small group of powerful and wealthy citizens. However, through their struggles, the plebeians slowly moved Rome closer to democracy.

The Twelve Tables

The most significant plebeian victory was the creation of a written law code. Roman law rested largely on unwritten traditions that patrician judges often interpreted to favor their class. To make sure that the judges applied the laws fairly, the plebeians insisted that the government write down the laws.

In 451 B.C. the patricians finally engraved the laws on 12 bronze tablets and set them in the Forum for all to see. The Twelve Tables, as these tablets were called, became the basis for all future Roman law. Although sometimes harsh, the Twelve Tables established the principle that all free citizens had a right to the law's protection.

Religion

Early Romans worshiped nature spirits. Under Etruscan influence, they came to think of these spirits as gods and goddesses. They also adopted the practice of foretelling the future. Priests known as soothsayers believed that they could gain knowledge of future events by observing the flight of birds or the intestines of animals.

For almost 500 years, Rome thrived as a republic. During this time, the Romans were influenced by Greek culture. They borrowed Greek deities, giving them Roman names. Aphrodite, the Greek

A Roman Dinner Party
In ancient Rome, dinner guests of wealthy Romans would recline on couches while slaves served them delicacies. Main course dishes might include boiled stingray garnished with hot raisins; boiled crane with turnips; roast hare in white sauce; leg of boar; wood pigeon baked in a pie; or roast flamingo cooked with dates, onions, honey, and wine.

An Etruscan farmer and his animals, c. 300 B.C. Etruscan literature, music, painting, metalwork, and jewelry were admired by the Romans. *Why did the Romans drive the wealthy Etruscan family, the Tarquins, from the city?*

goddess of love, became the Roman goddess Venus. Ares, the Greek god of war, became Mars. They also made their old gods look Greek, giving the Etruscan god Jupiter the characteristics of the Greek Zeus.

Roman life remained distinctly Roman, however. Families privately worshiped their ancestral spirits and their storeroom guardians, as well as Vesta, goddess of the hearth.

Family

The family was the basic unit of Roman society. Roman households were large and close-knit. They included all unmarried children, married sons and their families, all dependent relatives, and household slaves.

In Roman families the father was absolute head of the household. He conducted the religious ceremonies, controlled property, and supervised the education of his sons. He also had the power to sell family members into slavery, or even kill them. However, fathers also felt a deep sense of responsibility for the welfare of all family members.

Roman wives had few legal rights, but they had more freedom than Greek women. They acted as hostesses for parties, did their marketing, and ran their households with little or no interference. Occasionally, however, they did acquire their own property and businesses. Wealthy women, with slaves to do their work, could study Greek literature, arts, and fashions. Lower-class women spent their time at household tasks and in family-run shops.

Roman children grew up with firm discipline and had to give complete loyalty to their family. In early Rome, parents taught their children reading, writing, and moral standards. Boys were trained by their fathers to be good farmers and soldiers. Mothers taught their daughters how to run households.

Rich or poor, most Romans held the same values: thrift, discipline, self-sacrifice, and devotion to the family and the republic. Long after the Roman Republic ended, nostalgic reformers saw these as traditional Roman values.

SECTION 1 REVIEW

Recall

1. **Define** patrician, republic, plebeian, consul, dictator, tribune.
2. **Identify** the Etruscans, the Latins, Romulus, the Tarquins.

3. **Locate** Etruria, Latium, and Rome on the map on page 156. How were the people of these three places connected?

Critical Thinking

4. **Evaluating Information** Did the struggle between patricians and plebeians strengthen or weaken Rome? Give examples to support your case.

Understanding Themes

5. **Change** Why did political change occur in the Roman Republic?

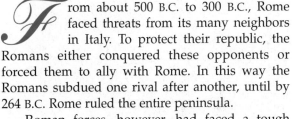

300 B.C.	200 B.C.	100 B.C.	A.D. 1

C. 264 B.C. Rome rules the entire Italian Peninsula.

202 B.C. Roman forces defeat Carthage at the battle of Zama.

133 B.C. The reformer Tiberius Gracchus becomes tribune.

44 B.C. Group of senators assassinate Julius Caesar.

Section 2

Expansion and Crisis

Setting the Scene

▶ **Terms to Define**
  indemnity, triumvirate

▶ **People to Meet**
  Hannibal, Scipio, Tiberius Gracchus, Gaius Gracchus, Marius, Sulla, Julius Caesar, Octavian, Marc Antony

▶ **Places to Locate**
  Carthage

 How did economic and social problems bring down the Roman Republic?

The Storyteller

The government of Rome had become cumbersome and corrupt. Maecenas, the richest man in Rome, was about to propose a radical change. Called before Mark Anthony, Marcus Lepidus, and Octavian, the most powerful men in Rome, he spoke persuasively. "Ever since we were led outside the peninsula, filling the whole earth with our power, nothing good has been our lot. Our city, like a great ship manned with a crew of every race and lacking a pilot, has been rolling and plunging as it has drifted in a heavy sea." Maecenas looked at his hearers. One of them must assume all authority. Rome had to cease being a republic.

—from *Roman History*, Dio Cassius, in *Readings in Ancient History from Gilgamesh to Diocletian*, 1969

Marc Antony

From about 500 B.C. to 300 B.C., Rome faced threats from its many neighbors in Italy. To protect their republic, the Romans either conquered these opponents or forced them to ally with Rome. In this way the Romans subdued one rival after another, until by 264 B.C. Rome ruled the entire peninsula.

Roman forces, however, had faced a tough challenge from the Greek colonies in southern Italy. In 282 B.C. the Greek colonists received help from Pyrrhus (PIHR•uhs), a ruler in western Greece. Twice Pyrrhus's armies threw back the Romans, but each time suffered terrible losses. In 275 B.C. Roman forces finally pushed Pyrrhus's exhausted troops back to Greece. Since then, a victory won at too great a cost has been called a "Pyrrhic victory."

Roman Legions

Rome's success in war was due to its strong army. In the early days of the republic, every male citizen had to serve in the military when needed. Early Roman armies also used the tactics of Greek phalanx warfare. Roman generals, however, learned that phalanxes were too large and slow to be effective. They reorganized their troops into legions of 6,000 men and divided these further into small, mobile units of 60 to 120 soldiers. With this new organization, the Romans could shatter the phalanxes of their enemies.

Roman soldiers—called legionaries—were well trained, and deserters were punished by death. With such iron discipline, the legionaries would conquer an empire. In a time when victors routinely slaughtered or enslaved whole cities, Rome treated conquered foes remarkably well. Some conquered peoples were allowed to keep their own governments if they helped fight Rome's wars.

Roman legionaries are shown in a mosaic, or picture made from bits of stone. *Why were legionaries so successful in their conquests?*

Rome gave other peoples partial rights, and to some peoples even granted citizenship.

The Romans set up permanent military settlements—called *coloniae*—throughout Italy to defend strategic heights and river crossings. To link these *coloniae*, the legions forged a chain of roads up and down the Italian Peninsula. As war yielded gradually to peace, some of these roads became major trade routes.

Rome Against Carthage

In Chapter 3 you read how **Carthage** became the Mediterranean area's wealthiest city. To expand their commerce, the Carthaginians had then gone on to conquer the Spanish coast and most of Sicily by about 300 B.C. The Romans decided to check the expansion of the Carthaginians—the *Punici*, as the Romans called them.

The First Punic War

In 264 B.C. Carthage threatened to seize the Strait of Messina, a narrow passage between Sicily and Italy. When the Romans sent a force to secure the strategic waterway, a full-scale war erupted.

The Romans' strong army conquered most of Carthage's colonies in Sicily. However, the Carthaginians lashed out at the Romans with their huge and powerful fleet. For a time this naval superiority gave Carthage the advantage.

Undaunted, the Romans built a larger fleet. In a battle off the African coast, they stunned the Carthaginians with a new tactic. They snared the enemy's ships with grappling hooks, boarded them, and defeated the enemy in hand-to-hand combat. This enabled the Romans to fight on sea as well as they did on land. Thus, they were able to force the Carthaginians to retreat.

The war raged on until 241 B.C., but the Carthaginians never regained control of Sicily or the sea. Threatened with invasion of their homeland, they agreed to hand the Romans a huge indemnity, or payment for damages.

The Second Punic War

In 221 B.C. a young soldier named **Hannibal** became general of the Carthaginian army in Spain. In 219 B.C. Hannibal grabbed one of Rome's allied cities in Spain. His next move was even more audacious—to take the war into Italy itself. Leading 40,000 soldiers and about 40 elephants, he marched out of Spain, crossed southern Gaul, and started up the Alps. His soldiers, however, were terrified by the sight of those chilly heights, and their fears were well-founded. Before they reached Italy, cold, snow, hunger, sickness, and attacks by mountain peoples killed half of Hannibal's army and most of the elephants.

Although outnumbered, Hannibal's troops defeated the Roman armies sent against them. By 216 B.C., in a battle at Cannae in southeastern Italy, Hannibal's soldiers had nearly destroyed the Roman army. But the Romans rallied, refusing to admit defeat, and raised dozens of new volunteer legions. Their general, **Scipio** (SIH•pee•OH), attacked Carthage and forced Hannibal's recall to Africa.

In 202 B.C. Scipio's forces defeated Hannibal's army at Zama, near Carthage. At Scipio's demand, the Carthaginians gave up their lands in Spain, handed over most of their warships, and agreed to another indemnity.

The Third Punic War

After 50 years of peace, Carthage regained its prosperity but posed no threat to Rome. The Romans, however, decided to force war on

Carthage. The most vindictive foe of Carthage was the Roman senator Cato, who always ended his speeches with the statement: *"Carthago delenda est"* (Carthage must be destroyed). In 146 B.C. the Romans burned Carthage, and sold its surviving population into slavery. Legend states that they even sowed salt in Carthage's soil so that no crops would grow. This victory gave Rome complete control of the western Mediterranean.

The Republic in Crisis

While Rome was fighting the Punic Wars in the west, its forces were also engaged in the east. Between 230 B.C. and 130 B.C., Rome brought the entire eastern Mediterranean area under its influence. As a result of this conquest, Romans began referring to the Mediterranean as *mare nostrum*— "our sea."

Rich, Poor, and Slavery

Although the Romans had triumphed militarily, they faced growing social discontent in their new empire. The conquered provinces, which paid tribute to Rome, complained of corrupt Roman officials stealing provincial wealth for personal gain. In Italy and throughout the empire, wealthy Romans acquired or seized land from war-ravaged small farmers who found it difficult to rebuild their farms, homes, and villages. Turning agriculture into a profitable business, these landowners created large estates called latifundia (LA•tuh•FUHN•dee •uh) that provided grain, sheep, olives, and fruits for urban markets. Labor for the latifundia was cheap because Rome's conquests brought thousands of captives and prisoners of war to work as slaves. By 100 B.C., slaves formed about 30 percent of Rome's people.

As slave labor replaced paid labor, thousands of small farmers and rural workers poured into the cities seeking employment. Jobs, however, were not readily available, and the new arrivals gradually formed into a class of urban, landless poor. Angry and without hope, the urban poor eked out a meager living and supported any politician who promised "bread and circuses," cheap food and free amusements.

As the gap between rich and poor steadily widened, upper-class Romans lived with the constant danger of revolts. To quell mounting unrest, Rome stationed legions in most provinces. Even Italy was not safe from uprisings. From 73 B.C. to 71 B.C., an army of 70,000 slaves led by the slave Spartacus plundered the Italian countryside in an effort to win freedom. With great difficulty, the Romans finally crushed the uprising and killed about 6,000 of Spartacus's followers. Putting down revolts cost Rome troops and money and placed a strain on its resources.

Rome's legions put down revolts in the provinces, but not without cost. Here, women funeral dancers mourn losses. *Why were the provinces not an endless source of wealth to Rome?*

Reformers and Generals

Feuding among Rome's leading families also weakened the republic. As violence increased, some Romans proposed reforms to narrow the social gap and to stabilize society. In 133 B.C. the tribune **Tiberius Gracchus** proposed limiting the size of the latifundia and distributing land to the poor. But the Senate, made up of the wealthiest Romans, opposed him, and Tiberius was killed in street fighting. Ten years later, his brother **Gaius Gracchus** proposed the same reforms and was also murdered.

Crowding the Cities

After the death of the Gracchi, army leaders came to power in Rome. The first, the general **Marius**, became a consul in 107 B.C. after saving Rome from attack by Germanic tribes. Because the dwindling number of small farmers had made a citizen army obsolete, Marius turned to the unemployed urban poor to build a new army. Unlike the citizen soldiers, Marius's recruits were paid, given uniforms and equipment, and promised land when they were discharged. As a result of Marius's action, Rome for the first time had a professional army in which soldiers owed allegiance to their commander, not to the republic.

To advance their political ambitions, rival military and political leaders formed their own separate armies and used them against each other. From 88 B.C. to 82 B.C., Marius and a rival general named **Sulla** fought for control of Rome. Sulla finally drove Marius into exile and had himself appointed dictator. This practice of using the army to gain political power was copied by a rising young politician named Julius Caesar.

Julius Caesar

Born in Rome in about 100 B.C. of an aristocratic family, **Julius Caesar** became one of Rome's greatest generals and political leaders. Skillfully maneuvering himself through Rome's tumultuous game of politics, Caesar gradually rose to power. In 60 B.C. the ambitious aristocrat allied himself with the general Pompey and the politician Crassus. A year later, with their help he was elected consul. For the next decade, the three men ruled Rome as a *triumvirate*, or group of three persons with equal power. Through force and bribery, the triumvirate silenced government critics, bending senators and tribunes alike to its will.

Caesar's Military Campaigns

While serving as consul, Caesar realized he needed military victories to advance his political career. In 59 B.C. he took a military command in Gaul, which was inhabited by Indo-Europeans known as Celts (KEHLTS). Caesar conquered the Celts and brought them under Roman rule. He also crossed the Rhine River to fight Germanic tribes and twice invaded Britain.

As a result of his victories, Caesar was hailed as a military hero by Rome's lower classes. But senators, alarmed at Caesar's growing popularity, regarded him as a political threat. By 50 B.C. the triumvirate itself had fallen apart: Crassus was dead, killed in battle while leading Roman forces in Asia, and Pompey had become Caesar's political rival.

In 49 B.C. the Senate, with Pompey's backing, ordered Caesar to give up his army and return to Rome. Caesar, however, had no intention of turning himself over to his enemies. He assembled 5,000 loyal troops and crossed the Rubicon, a stream that

Visualizing History Political strife following the murders of the Gracchi aided the rise of the young Julius Caesar, sculpted here in a heroic pose. *How do you think Roman sculpture differed from the Greek models on which it was based?*

divided his military provinces from Roman Italy. According to legend, Caesar had seen a vision that encouraged him to cross, and exclaimed to his troops, "Let us accept this as a sign from the gods, and follow where they beckon, in vengeance on our double-dealing enemies. The die is cast." By defying the Senate's order, Caesar realized there was no turning back; and a civil war was unavoidable. Ever since, "crossing the Rubicon" has meant making a decision that cannot be undone.

Caesar's army swiftly captured all of Italy and drove Pompey and his allies out of the country. The fighting eventually spread eastward, with Caesar's troops finally defeating Pompey's forces at Pharsalus, Greece, in 48 B.C.

Caesar in Power

In 45 B.C. Caesar took over the government as dictator for life, to rule very much like a monarch. As absolute ruler, Caesar granted Roman citizenship to many people in the provinces outside of Italy. He added to the Senate representatives from the provinces who were loyal to him. In making these reforms, Caesar not only made the central government more responsive to Rome's newly conquered territories, he also strengthened his own power at the expense of the old patricians.

Caesar also carried out social reforms aimed to benefit the poor. To provide jobs for the unemployed, he set up public works programs and ordered slave-owning landowners to hire more free laborers. Colonies were founded throughout Rome's territories to provide land for the city's landless poor. Under Caesar, the government also continued its long-standing practice of distributing free grain but reduced the number of people eligible for it.

Caesar's most lasting reform was a new calendar based on the work of scholars in Alexandria. Replacing the old Roman lunar calendar, this new solar calendar counted 365 days in a year and 1 extra day every fourth year. Caesar's calendar, later named Julian in honor of him, was used in western Europe until early modern times.

Caesar's Death

Many Romans believed that Caesar was a wise ruler who had brought order and peace to Rome. Others, however, considered him to be a tyrant who meant to make himself a king. According to ancient Roman law, anyone who plotted to become king could be killed without trial. Acting on this law, a group of senators, led by the chief conspirators Brutus and Cassius, stabbed Caesar to death as he entered the Senate on March 15, 44 B.C.

End of the Republic

After the death of Julius Caesar, his 18-year-old grandnephew **Octavian** joined forces with **Marc Antony** and Marcus Lepidus, two of Caesar's top government officers. Together this second triumvirate defeated Caesar's assassins in 42 B.C. Then, while keeping up the appearance of republican government, these three generals divided the Roman world among themselves. Octavian took command in Italy and the west, Antony ruled in Greece and the east, and Lepidus took charge of North Africa.

The second triumvirate did not last long, however. Octavian forced Lepidus to retire from political life. When Antony married Cleopatra, the queen of Egypt, Octavian persuaded the Romans that Antony intended to rule them with his foreign queen by his side, and so Octavian declared war on Antony in Rome's name. In 31 B.C. Octavian scattered the forces of his enemies in a critical naval battle at Actium in Greece. A year later, to evade capture by Octavian, Antony and Cleopatra committed suicide in Egypt. With Antony dead, Octavian became the undisputed ruler of Rome. Octavian's period of rule would mark the beginning of the Roman Empire.

SECTION 2 REVIEW

Recall
1. **Define** indemnity, triumvirate.
2. **Identify** Hannibal, Scipio, Tiberius Gracchus, Gaius Gracchus, Marius, Sulla, Julius Caesar, Octavian, Marc Antony.
3. **Locate** Carthage and Gaul on the map on page 165. What was the importance of each place in the military history of the Roman Republic?

Critical Thinking
4. **Analyzing Information** How did Julius Caesar's crossing of the Rubicon help destroy the Roman Republic and create a dictatorship?

Understanding Themes
5. **Conflict** Explain how Roman conquests overseas affected Rome's development.

A.D. 1	A.D. 50	A.D. 100	A.D. 150	A.D. 200

A.D. 14
Augustus Caesar dies.

A.D. 79
Volcanic eruption destroys Pompeii.

A.D. 96 Rule of the Good Emperors begins.

A.D. 180
Pax Romana ends.

Section 3

The Roman Empire

Setting the Scene

▶ **Terms to Define**
aqueduct

▶ **People to Meet**
Augustus, Tiberius, Claudius, Nero, Marcus Aurelius, Galen, Ptolemy, Virgil, Livy

▶ **Places to Locate**
Appian Way

 **ind Out** What was life like in the Roman Empire during the *Pax Romana*?

The Storyteller

The visitor, Aelius Aristides, an educated and well-travelled man, had never seen anything to rival Rome. And it was not just the city—it was everything that Rome represented: military might, sensible government, and an elegant lifestyle. Who could help but admire an empire that commanded vast territories and diverse peoples, a military that conquered both armed forces and selfish ambition, a government where officials ruled not through arbitrary power but by law. Romans "measured out the world, bridged rivers, cut roads through mountains, filled the wastes with posting stations, introduced orderly and refined modes of life." They were, he declared, natural rulers.

Augustus Caesar

—adapted from *Oration on the Pax Romana*, Aelius Aristides, reprinted in *Sources of the Western Tradition*, Marvin Perry, 1991

Under the Roman Republic, laws had proven too weak to control social changes, while generals had taken power away from elected officials. Thus, Octavian believed that Rome needed one strong leader. The Senate agreed and appointed Octavian consul, tribune, and commander in chief for life in 27 B.C. Octavian gave himself the title *Augustus*, or "Majestic One."

The First Emperors

Augustus claimed to support the republic, but he actually laid the foundation for a new state called the Roman Empire. In practice, he became Rome's first emperor, or absolute ruler.

Augustus Caesar

In the 40 years of his reign—from 27 B.C. to A.D. 14—Augustus rebuilt the city of Rome and became a great patron of the arts. He also introduced many reforms to the empire. Proconsuls could no longer exploit the provinces. Publican tax collectors were replaced with permanent government employees. Grain was imported from North Africa so that all in Rome would be fed. New roads were built and old ones repaired. Magnificent public buildings were constructed throughout the empire. Augustus boasted that he had "found Rome a city of brick and left it a city of marble."

In 31 B.C. there began the *Pax Romana*, or Roman Peace, which lasted about 200 years. The only major disturbances during those years occurred when new emperors came to power. For, although Augustus chose his own successor carefully, he failed to devise any law for the selection of later emperors.

The Julio-Claudian Emperors

Historians call the four emperors who ruled from A.D. 14 to A.D. 68 the Julio-Claudians because

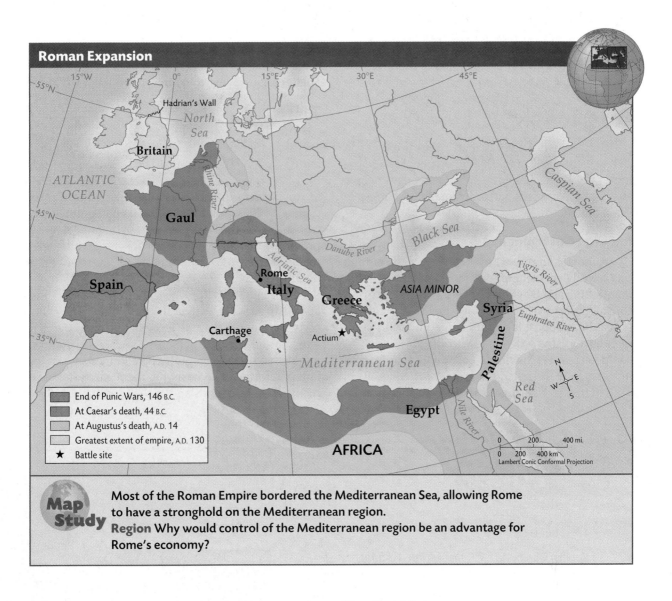

End of Punic Wars, 146 B.C.
At Caesar's death, 44 B.C.
At Augustus's death, A.D. 14
Greatest extent of empire, A.D. 130
★ Battle site

Map Study Most of the Roman Empire bordered the Mediterranean Sea, allowing Rome to have a stronghold on the Mediterranean region.
Region Why would control of the Mediterranean region be an advantage for Rome's economy?

each was a member of Augustus's family, known as the Julio-Claudians. Each showed promise when he became emperor, but later revealed great faults.

Augustus's adopted son **Tiberius**, who succeeded Augustus Caesar as emperor, spoiled his able leadership by accusing many innocent people of treason against him. Caligula, Tiberius's grandnephew and successor in A.D. 37, became mentally disturbed and was killed by a palace guard in A.D. 41. Caligula's uncle, **Claudius**, was a renowned scholar, but as he grew older he had difficulty focusing on affairs of state.

Nero, Claudius's stepson, who became emperor in A.D. 54, was cruel and probably insane. Nero was willing to bankrupt Rome to pay for his twin pleasures—horse racing and music. Suspecting others of plotting against him, he killed his wife and his mother and executed many senators. In A.D. 68 the Senate sentenced Nero to death for treason. Before he committed suicide, reportedly he cried, "What a loss I shall be to the arts!"

The Good Emperors

For 28 years following Nero's death, Rome was governed by a number of emperors who were backed by the army. Then, in A.D. 96 the Senate chose its own candidate for emperor: Nerva. Historians consider Nerva the first of the so-called Good Emperors; the others were Trajan, Hadrian, Antoninus Pius, and **Marcus Aurelius** (aw•REE •lee•uhs). The Good Emperors were known for their skills as effective administrators and their support of large building projects.

The Emperor Trajan increased the empire to its greatest size. Hadrian then strengthened Rome's frontiers, building Hadrian's Wall in Britain and other defense positions. Antoninus Pius succeeded him, maintaining the empire's prosperity. The philosopher-ruler Marcus Aurelius brought the empire to the height of its economic prosperity. All of these Good Emperors lived by the principle of Stoic philosophy best expressed by Marcus Aurelius in *Meditations*: "Every moment think steadily as a

Roman and a human being how to do what you have in hand with perfect and simple dignity."

Roman Rule

By the time Augustus had come to power in 27 B.C., between 70 and 100 million people were living in the Roman Empire. To rule so many people effectively, Augustus had to make many changes in government.

Imperial Government

Augustus improved the working of the empire by carefully choosing professional governors rather than letting the Senate appoint inexperienced proconsuls every year. In some provinces, such as Judea, he left local kings in charge under his command. Augustus ordered new roads built so that he could keep in touch with all parts of the empire, and he personally inspected the provinces frequently.

Augustus also dignified his own position by serving as *pontifex maximus*, or chief priest of Rome. Thus he and each later emperor became the head of a national, unifying religion.

The Law

As the Romans won more provinces, they found that they needed a new kind of law that would apply to noncitizens. They therefore created the *jus gentium*, or law that dealt with noncitizens, as opposed to the *jus civile*, or citizen law. By the early A.D. 200s, however, emperors had granted citizenship to the peoples of so many nearby provinces that all free males in the empire had been made full citizens of Rome, and the two laws became one.

In their laws Romans generally stressed the authority of the state over the individual. They also accorded people definite legal rights, one of which was that an accused person should be considered innocent until proven guilty. The Roman system of law has formed the basis for the legal systems of many Western nations and of the Christian Church.

Images *of the* Times

Pompeii, A.D. 79

On August 23-25, A.D. 79, the volcano Vesuvius erupted in southern Italy. The city of Pompeii was buried in a single day.

A detail from the Villa of the Mysteries shows that life for many in Pompeii offered many comforts and pleasures.

An Imperial Army

Augustus and later emperors maintained the professional army. As conditions became more peaceful, however, Augustus reduced the number of legions and supplemented this fighting force with troops recruited from the provincial peoples. Even with forces combined, the emperor could count on having only about 300,000 troops, which was not enough to defend a border with a length of about 4,000 miles (6,440 km). Therefore, by A.D. 160, invasions by peoples outside the empire had become a continuing problem.

Roman Civilization

From about 31 B.C. to A.D. 180, the Roman world enjoyed a period of prosperity known as the *Pax Romana*, or Roman Peace. The stability of the *Pax Romana* boosted trade, raised standards of living, and generated many achievements in the arts. The Latin author Tertullian described this time:

66 Everywhere roads are built, every district is known, every country is open to commerce … the [fields] are planted; the marshes drained. There are now as many cities as there were once solitary cottages.… Wherever there is a trace of life, there are houses and human habitations, well-ordered governments, and civilized life. 99

—Tertullian, *Concerning the Soul*, c. A.D. 180

The Empire's Economy

Tertullian's description of economic growth under the empire was not exaggerated. In the first century A.D., artisans in Italy made pottery, woven cloth, blown glass, and jewelry for sale throughout the empire. The provinces in turn sent to Italy luxury items, such as silk cloth and spices, gathered in trade with China, India, and Southeast Asian countries. Dockworkers at Rome's harbor, Ostia, unloaded raw materials such as tin from Britain,

Citizens of Pompeii were almost instantly overwhelmed by volcanic ash and fire. A plaster cast of victims serves as a stern reminder of Vesuvius's power.

REFLECTING ON THE TIMES

1. Why were so many artifacts from Pompeii so well preserved?
2. What do Roman wall paintings in Pompeii reveal about the lifestyles of upper-class Romans?

iron from Gaul, and lead from Spain. Soon skillful Greek traders within the empire were doing business in distant areas, such as eastern Africa, Southeast Asia, and China.

Life During the *Pax Romana*

These economic changes brought changes in lifestyles. The family gradually became less significant than it had been during the republic. Romans had fewer children and were likely to divorce and remarry several times. Fathers lost some of the absolute power they had during the republic, and wives gained some legal rights. Society became less stable. Patricians might go bankrupt, wealthy military officers might sit in the Senate, and a poor man might even make a fortune in manufacturing.

Within each class, a consistent pattern of life formed. The wealthy often held public office, owned large farms outside the cities, ran factories, or directed trading firms. They lived comfortably in luxurious homes with marble walls, mosaic floors, running water, and baths.

The prosperity of the *Pax Romana* sometimes reached people of average means—shopkeepers and artisans. Although fewer people became very rich, more became moderately well off. The majority in Rome, however, were still poor. There were no private baths for them; instead they bathed at crowded public areas built under Augustus and later emperors. Most Romans lived in flimsy wooden apartment buildings of six or seven stories that readily collapsed or caught fire.

Public Amusements

Despite these trying conditions, the poor did not rebel against the government, because it offered them both free bread and free entertainment. By A.D. 160, Romans were celebrating 130 holidays a year. On some days, teams of charioteers competed in races in the Circus Maximus, an arena seating more than 150,000. On other holidays, crowds could watch gladiators fight each other to the death or battle wild animals in stadiums like the Colosseum.

Architecture, Engineering, and Science

The Romans erected many impressive buildings during the *Pax Romana* besides the Circus Maximus and the Colosseum. Between A.D. 118 and A.D. 128, Hadrian rebuilt the Pantheon, a temple for all the deities, with a soaring dome and a huge skylight. To build the Pantheon, the Romans mixed concrete—a new building material—with various kinds of stone.

The Romans also excelled in road building. The first major Roman road was the **Appian Way**. Constructed in the 300s B.C., it connected Rome and southeastern Italy. During the *Pax Romana*, a network of roads was built to link Rome with the provinces. Reaching a total length of 50,000 miles (80,000 km), the road network contributed to the empire's unity.

As they constructed public buildings and a vast network of roads, the Romans engineered aqueducts, or artificial channels for carrying water.

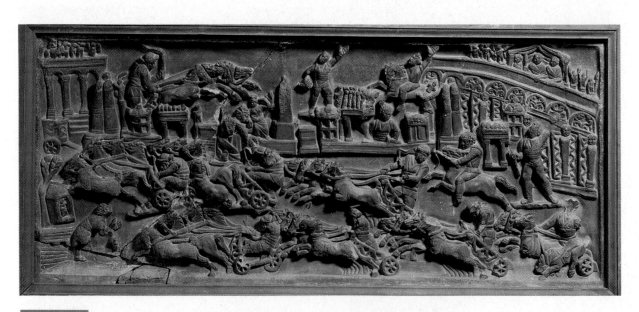

Visualizing History Entertainment at the giant arena Circus Maximus, depicted in this bas-relief, was free to Roman citizens. *What new building material did the Romans use to construct the Pantheon?*

© Sonia Halliday Photographs

Roman Forum

The ruins of the Roman Forum are a major tourist attraction of modern Rome. In ancient times, the Forum was the center of both politics and commerce. The Forum contained a number of separate buildings: In the foreground the Temple of Castor and Pollux, built in the 400s B.C., honored Roman gods. Behind is the Arch of Titus, the ruler whose military victory is enshrined in the arch built about A.D 80. Beyond the Arch stand the walls of the Colosseum. The largest amphitheater built in ancient Rome, the Colosseum took a decade to construct and could seat 50,000. Here the Romans watched gladiators battle lions and later vanquish Christians.

The rise of the Roman state began with the city of Rome itself hundreds of years before the birth of Christ. Slowly the Romans consolidated control over Italy and built a great army. By 200 B.C. Rome had become a vast empire. Power brought wealth and great monuments such as these in the Forum. ⊕

These lofty arches built out of stone enabled water to flow into Rome from as far away as 57 miles (about 92 km). One Roman-built aqueduct in Segovia, Spain, was so well constructed that it is still used today—nearly 1,900 years after it was completed.

The Romans excelled at adapting the discoveries of others and using them in new and more practical ways. They made use of the Etruscan arch and dome to build aqueducts and the Pantheon, and borrowed the Greek design for columns to support porches built around city squares.

Roman scientists also relied upon information that had been gathered from other cultures. The medical ideas of the ancient world compiled by the Greek physician **Galen** formed the basis of Roman medical science. Likewise, the observations of the Egyptian astronomer **Ptolemy** formed the foundation of Roman astronomy. Galen's works influenced medical science for many centuries, and Ptolemy's work made it possible for later astronomers to predict with accuracy the motion of the planets.

Roman Education

The Romans studied their borrowed knowledge avidly. Wealthy boys and girls received private lessons at home. Young men from wealthy families went on to academies—where former Greek slaves often taught—to learn geometry, astronomy, philosophy, and oratory. The daughters of the wealthy did not attend academies. Many upper-class women continued to study at home, however, and often became as well educated as Roman men. People in the lower classes usually had at least the basic knowledge of reading, writing, and arithmetic they needed to conduct business.

Language and Literature

Latin, Rome's official language, had a vocabulary far smaller than that of Greek or modern English; thus, many words expressed several meanings. Nevertheless, Latin remained the *lingua franca*, or common language, of Europe as late as the A.D. 1500s. Latin also forms the basis of the so-called Romance languages, such as Italian, French, Spanish, Portuguese, and Romanian, and supplies the roots for more than half of English words.

Although Romans learned from Greek literature, during the reign of Augustus Latin literature achieved an elegance and power of its own. Cicero, a Roman senator, published beautifully written speeches. Ovid wrote the *Metamorphoses*, verses based on Greek mythology. Horace, a poet, wrote about the shortness of life and the rewards of companionship in his *Odes*. Horace's friend **Virgil** wrote the *Aeneid*, an epic poem comparable to those of Homer. In one passage of this poem, Virgil expresses both the humility and pride of Romans:

> 66 Others, no doubt, will better mould the bronze
> To the semblance of soft breathing, draw, from marble,
> The living countenance; and others plead
> With greater eloquence, or learn to measure,
> Better than we, the pathways of the heaven,
> The risings of the stars: remember, Roman,
> To rule the people under law, to establish
> The way of peace, to battle down the haughty,
> To spare the meek. Our fine arts, these, forever. 99
>
> —Virgil, the *Aeneid*, c. 20 B.C.

Livy, a later writer, wrote a monumental history of Rome that glorified the early Romans. The historian Tacitus, in contrast, condemned the tyranny of the Julio-Claudian emperors with subtle but scathing irony. In *Germania*, Tacitus contrasted the robust life of the Germans with what he felt was the weak and pleasure-loving life of the Romans.

SECTION 3 REVIEW

Recall

1. **Define** aqueduct.
2. **Identify** Augustus, *Pax Romana*, Tiberius, Claudius, Nero, Marcus Aurelius, Galen, Ptolemy, Virgil, Livy.
3. **Use** the map on page 165 to identify Roman expansion. When did the empire reach its greatest extent?

Critical Thinking

4. **Synthesizing Information** The expression "bread and circuses" has been used to describe hasty measures taken by a government to prevent discontent among the poor. Explain whether you believe this expression applies to any aspects of life in the modern United States. If so, to what aspects does it apply?

Understanding Themes

5. **Change** How did Roman family life change from the time of the republic to that of the *Pax Romana*?

Section 4

The Rise of Christianity

Setting the Scene

▶ **Terms to Define**
sect, messiah, disciple, martyr, bishop, patriarch, pope

▶ **People to Meet**
Jesus, Paul, Peter, Constantine, Theodosius, Augustine

 **Find Out** What did Jesus of Nazareth teach, and how did the early Christians influence the later Roman Empire?

The Storyteller

How could Justin, a man well versed in philosophy and intellectual pursuits, explain to the emperor why he had embraced Christianity? He had opened a school to teach others about this religion, although most educated people dismissed it as a dangerous superstition. He had to convince the emperor that, just as the ancient philosophers had sought truth, Christians sought it too. Since both scholars and Christians shared this quest, following Christian teachings could only help in the search for understanding. He set his pen to paper and began to write a defense of the Christian faith.

—from *Apology*, Justin, reprinted in *Readings in Ancient History from Gilgamesh to Diocletian*, Nels M. Bailkey, 1969

Mosaic of Jesus as shepherd

The early Romans worshiped nature spirits. Under Etruscan influence they came to think of these spirits as deities. Later, the Romans adopted much of Greek religion, identifying Greek deities with their own. Beginning with Augustus, the government also expected people to honor the emperor as Rome's chief priest. Nevertheless, the empire's people were still allowed to worship freely, and a variety of religions flourished.

Meanwhile, a new monotheistic religion called Christianity began to be practiced by some of the Jews in the eastern Mediterranean. At first, both the Romans and the earliest Christians thought of the new religion as a sect, or group, within Judaism. As Christians won over non-Jewish followers, however, the faith diverged from its Jewish roots and became a separate religion.

Judaism and the Empire

In A.D. 6 the Emperor Augustus turned the kingdom of Judah into the Roman province of Judea. The Romans in Judea still allowed the Jews to practice their religion, but they treated them cruelly. Many Jews therefore strengthened their hope that a messiah, or a deliverer chosen by God, would help them regain their freedom. The coming of a messiah had long been foretold by Jewish prophets.

Believing that God would intervene on their behalf, some Jews took matters into their own hands. In A.D. 66 they rebelled against the Romans and overpowered the small Roman army in Jerusalem. But only four years later, in A.D. 70, the Romans retook Jerusalem, destroying the Temple and killing thousands of Jews.

Then, after another unsuccessful rebellion in A.D. 132, the Romans banned the Jews from living

Chapter 6 *Ancient Rome and Early Christianity* **171**

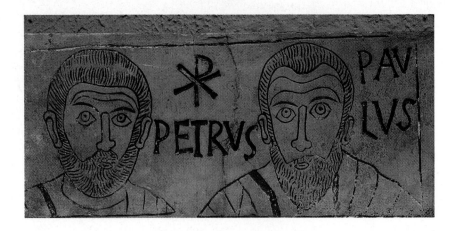

An engraving of the apostles Peter and Paul decorates the sepulchre of the child Asellus. *Why did the apostles form churches?*

in Jerusalem. The Jews were forced to live in other parts of the Mediterranean and the Middle East. In their scattered communities, the Jews continued to study the Torah, the entire body of Jewish religious law and learning. They set up special academies called yeshivas to promote its study. Furthermore, between A.D. 200 and A.D. 500, rabbis—scholars trained in the yeshivas—assembled their various interpretations of the Torah into a book known as the Talmud. To this day the Talmud remains an important book of Jewish law.

Jesus of Nazareth

A few decades before the Jewish revolts, a Jew named **Jesus** grew up in the town of Nazareth. With deep spiritual fervor, Jesus traveled through Galilee and Judea from about A.D. 30 to A.D. 33, preaching a new message to his fellow Jews and winning disciples, or followers.

Proclaiming that God's rule was close at hand, Jesus urged people to turn away from their sins and practice deeds of kindness. He said that God was loving and forgiving toward all who repented, no matter what evil they had done or how lowly they were. In his teaching, Jesus often used parables, or symbolic stories. With the parable below, Jesus urged his followers to give up everything so that they would be ready for God's coming:

> **❝** The kingdom of heaven is like treasure lying buried in a field. The man who found it, buried it again; and for sheer joy went and sold everything he had, and bought that field. **❞**
>
> —Matthew 13:44-46

Jesus' disciples believed that he was the messiah; other Jews, believing that the messiah had yet to come, disputed this claim. The growing controversy over Jesus troubled Roman officials in Palestine. They believed that anyone who aroused such strong public feelings could endanger Roman rule in the region. In about A.D. 33, the Roman governor Pontius Pilate arrested Jesus as a political rebel and ordered that he be crucified—hung from a cross until dead. This was a typical Roman way of punishing criminals.

The Spread of Christianity

After Jesus' death, his disciples proclaimed that he had risen from the dead and had appeared to them. They pointed to this as evidence that Jesus was the messiah. His followers began preaching that Jesus was the Son of God and the way of salvation. Small groups in the Hellenistic cities of the eastern Mediterranean world accepted this message. Jews and non-Jews who accepted Jesus and his teachings became known as Christians—*Christos* was Greek for "messiah." They formed churches—communities for worship, fellowship, and instruction.

A convert named **Paul** aided Christianity's spread, especially among non-Jews. He traveled widely and wrote on behalf of the new religion. Paul's letters to various churches were later combined with the Gospels, or stories about Jesus, and the writings of other early Christian leaders. Together, these works form the New Testament of the Bible.

Meanwhile, other apostles, or Christian missionaries, spread Christianity throughout the Roman world. It is believed that **Peter**, the leader of the group, came to Rome and helped found a church in that city. Other churches were set up in Greece, Asia Minor, Egypt, and later in Gaul and Spain.

Persecution and Competition

Christians taught that their religion was the only true faith. They refused to honor the emperor as a god and rejected military service. As a result, many Romans accused them of treason.

The Romans feared that Christian rejection of their deities would bring divine punishment. Therefore, although they did not hunt out the Christians, if local officials thought Christians were causing trouble, they might have the Christians killed. The Romans frequently threw these Christian martyrs—people who chose to die rather than give up their beliefs—into the stadiums to be killed by wild beasts in front of cheering crowds.

Such persecution, which lasted until the early A.D. 300s, kept many people from becoming Christians. To win converts, Christians had to overcome this obstacle. Christianity also had to compete for followers with polytheistic religions and mystery religions—so named for their mythical heroes and secret rituals—and with Judaism.

During the A.D. 200s and 300s, Christianity flourished in the Mediterranean world along with these other religions. Like Judaism, Christianity was mainly a religion of the cities, while traditional Roman religions retained their hold in the countryside. Even though the number of Christians was relatively small during this period, their strength in the cities of the Roman Empire gave Christianity an influence that was far beyond its size.

Romans Adopt Christianity

According to legend, in A.D. 312, as the Roman general **Constantine** led his army into battle, a flaming cross appeared in the sky and beneath it in fiery letters appeared the Latin words *In hoc signo vinces*: "With this as your standard you will have victory." Apparently because of this vision, Constantine ordered his soldiers to paint the Christian symbol of the cross on their shields. When his army won the battle, Constantine credited the victory to the Christian God.

Named emperor of Rome in A.D. 312, Constantine thus became a protector of Christianity. A year later, he issued the Edict of Milan, which decreed that all religious groups in the empire, including Christians, were free to worship as they pleased. Constantine attended meetings of Christian leaders and ordered churches to be built in Rome and Jerusalem.

Because of effective missionary work and growing government support, Christianity further increased in size and influence throughout the entire Roman world. It became as important in the western part of the empire as it was in the eastern part. In A.D. 392 the Emperor **Theodosius** (THEE•uh •DOH•shuhs) made Christianity the official religion of the Roman Empire. At the same time, he banned the old Hellenistic and Roman religions.

The Early Church

From early times Christians recognized that their organization, the Church, would prosper only if it was united. They also felt that Christian teachings had to be stated clearly to avoid differences of opinion that might divide the Church. Consequently, Christians turned to important religious thinkers who attempted to explain many Christian beliefs. Between A.D. 100 and A.D. 500, various scholars known as Church Fathers wrote books explaining Christian teachings. They greatly influenced later Christian thinkers.

Teachings of Augustine

Christians in the western part of the empire especially valued the work of **Augustine**, a scholar born in North Africa in A.D. 354. Augustine is considered to have written one of the world's first great autobiographies. In this work called *Confessions*, Augustine describes how he was converted to Christianity:

> ❝ I heard from a neighboring house a voice, as of a boy or girl, I know not, chanting, and oft repeating, 'Take up and read; Take up and read.'… So … I arose, interpreting it to be no other than a command from God, to open the book [the Bible], and read the first chapter I should find. ❞
>
> —Augustine, *Confessions*, c. A.D. 398

 Constantine became a defender of Christianity. *How did the status of Christians living in the Roman Empire change under the rule of Constantine?*

Roman mural of Christian disciples

Characteristics of Christianity

- Christians acknowledge the God of the Jews as their God. The Christian Bible includes both the Jewish Scriptures (the Old Testament) and the New Testament.

- Most Christians believe that in one God are three Persons —the Father, the Son, and the Holy Spirit (the Trinity).

- Christianity affirms that Jesus is God the Son who became a human being, died, and rose from death to save humanity from sin. According to Christian belief, people receive eternal life by believing in Jesus and following his teachings.

- Christianity has had a major impact on the West, especially in the arts, philosophy, politics, and society.

- Today, Christianity, with more than 1.5 billion followers, is the world's largest religion. It is the major faith in Europe, the Americas, and Australia.

- Most Christians today belong to one of three major groups— Roman Catholic, Protestant, or Eastern Orthodox.

So powerful was Augustine's influence that he became a leading church official in North Africa. In this post he wrote books, letters, and sermons that shaped Christian thought during his own time and afterward. For instance, he wrote *City of God*—the first history of humanity from the Christian viewpoint.

Church Structure

By Augustine's time, Christian leaders had organized the Church as a hierarchy—into levels of authority, each level more powerful than the level below it. Local gatherings of Christians, called parishes, were led by priests. Priests conducted worship services and supervised parish activities. Several parishes together formed a diocese, each overseen by a bishop. Bishops interpreted Christian beliefs and administered regional church affairs. The most powerful bishops governed Christians in the empire's larger cities. The bishops of the five leading cities—Rome, Constantinople, Alexandria, Antioch, and Jerusalem—were called patriarchs.

The bishops of the Christian Church met in councils to discuss questions and disputes about Christian beliefs. The decisions they reached at these councils, such as that at Nicaea in A.D. 325, came to be accepted as doctrine, or official teachings. The points of view the council did not accept were considered heresy, or false doctrine.

During the A.D. 400s, the bishop of Rome began to claim authority over the other patriarchs. Addressed by the Greek or Latin word *papa*, his name today is rendered *pope* in the English language. Latin-speaking Christians in the West regarded the pope as head of all of the churches. Greek-speaking Christians in the East, however, would not accept the authority of the pope over their churches. The bishops of Alexandria and Antioch claimed to exercise a paternal rule equal to that of the pope. Eventually these churches and those of the Latin West separated from each other. In time, the Latin churches as a group became known as the Roman Catholic Church. The Greek churches as a group became known as the Eastern Orthodox Church.

SECTION 4 REVIEW

Recall
1. **Define** sect, messiah, disciple, martyr, bishop, patriarch, pope.
2. **Identify** the Talmud, Jesus, Paul, Peter, Constantine, Theodosius, Augustine.
3. **Use** a chart to describe the hierarchy of the Christian Church by the time of Augustine. What were the functions of bishops? Of priests?

Critical Thinking
4. **Evaluating Information** Why might the Romans in Judea especially have responded harshly toward anyone arousing strong feelings among the Jewish people?

Understanding Themes
5. **Innovation** List some of the ways in which Christianity diverged from Judaism to become a distinct religion rather than a sect.

A.D. 284 Diocletian becomes Roman emperor.

A.D. 330 Constantine moves capital to Byzantium, renamed Constantinople.

A.D. 395 Theodosius divides Roman Empire.

A.D. 476 German soldier Odoacer seizes Rome.

Section 5

Roman Decline

Setting the Scene

▶ **Terms to Define**
   inflation

▶ **People to Meet**
   Diocletian, Constantine, Theodosius I, Alaric, Attila

▶ **Places to Locate**
   Constantinople

Find Out What caused the decline of the western Roman Empire?

The Storyteller

The old world had ended. There was no longer any doubt of that. Gregory, whose family had for countless generations served Rome as Senators and consuls, looked out the window at the city which had once ruled the world. Now it was in the hands of warlike tribes who had no appreciation for Roman virtue, achievements, or culture.

"Cities are destroyed," he mused, "fortifications razed, fields devastated. Some men are led away captive, others are mutilated, others slain before our eyes." The pride of Rome was reduced to memories of a vanished glory.

—from *Homiliarum in Ezechielem*, Pope Gregory I, reprinted in *Sources of the Western Tradition*, Marvin Perry, Joseph Peden, and Theodore Von Laue, 1991

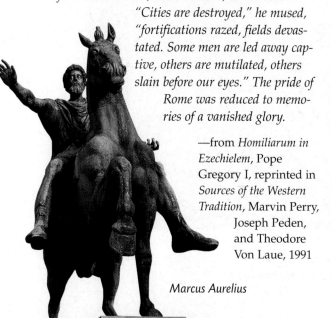

Marcus Aurelius

During the A.D. 200s, while Christianity was spreading through the Roman Empire, Germanic tribes began to overrun the western half of the empire. Many inhabitants in this area reported widespread devastation and chaos. The Germanic tribes had always been a threat to the empire. Why were they so much more successful now than they were during the times of Marcus Aurelius?

The Empire's Problems

The Romans had a brief rest from political violence during the reign of the five Good Emperors. When Marcus Aurelius died in A.D. 180, however, a new period of violence and corruption brought the *Pax Romana* to an end.

Political Instability

The time of confusion began with the installation of Emperor Commodus, Marcus Aurelius's son. Like Nero, he spent so much state money on his own pleasures that he bankrupted the treasury. In A.D. 192 Commodus's own troops plotted to kill him.

From A.D. 192 to A.D. 284, army legions installed 28 emperors, only to kill most of them off in rapid succession. During this time of political disorder, Rome's armies were busier fighting each other than they were defending the empire's borders. Germanic tribes such as the Goths, the Alemanni, the Franks, and the Saxons repeatedly and successfully attacked the empire.

Economic Decline

Political instability led to economic decline. Warfare disrupted production and trade. For artisans and merchants, profits declined sharply, forcing many out of business. Warfare also destroyed farmland, causing food shortages that sent food prices soaring.

Chapter 6 *Ancient Rome and Early Christianity* **175**

To cope with falling incomes and rising prices, the government minted more coins. It hoped the increase would make it easier to pay its soldiers. However, because the government had already drained its stores of gold and silver, the new coins contained less of the precious metals—cutting their value. To continue getting the same return for their goods, merchants raised prices. Thus, the government's policy sparked severe inflation—a rise in prices corresponding to a decrease in the value of money.

The spiraling decline in wealth affected almost all parts of the empire. To sustain a fighting force, the Roman government had to continually raise soldiers' wages. Taxing landowners heavily seemed the only way to meet this expense, but as increased taxes made farming less profitable, more and more farmers abandoned their lands. As a result, the output of crops shrank even more, worsening the food shortage.

Unsuccessful Reforms

During the late A.D. 200s and early A.D. 300s, two emperors—**Diocletian** (DY•uh•KLEE•shuhn) and later, **Constantine**—struggled to halt the empire's decline. Their reforms preserved the government in the eastern part of the empire for more than 1,000 years. In the west, they succeeded only in briefly delaying the Germanic tribes' invasion of Rome.

Diocletian

General Diocletian came to power in A.D. 284 by slaying the murderer of the preceding emperor. To hold back invasions, he raised the number of legions in the army and spent his time traveling throughout the empire to oversee defenses. Recognizing, however, that the empire was too large for one person to govern, Diocletian divided the empire into two administrative units. Diocletian set himself up as coemperor of the eastern provinces and set up General Maximian as coemperor of the western provinces.

Diocletian also tried to stop the empire's economic decline. To slow inflation, he issued an order called the Edict of Prices. In this edict, Diocletian froze wages and set maximum prices for goods. Yet, even though the penalty for breaking the law was death, his effort failed completely. Citizens merely sold their goods through illegal trade. To stop farmers from leaving their lands and heavily taxed people from changing their

Visualizing History As this relief sculpture shows, tax collectors in Roman times were very visible. *Why did the Roman government have to increase taxes?*

professions to avoid taxation, Diocletian required farmers who rented land never to leave their property and all workers to remain at the same job throughout their lives.

Constantine

When Diocletian retired in A.D. 305, civil wars broke out again. They continued until Constantine came to power in A.D. 312.

Constantine worked to stabilize the empire once more by reinforcing Diocletian's reforms. He made it legal for landowners to chain their workers to keep them on the farm. He declared most jobs hereditary; sons had to follow their fathers' occupations. In A.D. 330 he moved the capital of the eastern empire to the Greek town of Byzantium —an ideal site for trade and well protected by natural barriers—and re–named it **Constantinople**.

Theodosius

After Constantine's death in A.D. 337, civil war flared anew until **Theodosius I** succeeded Constantine. During Theodosius's rule, the empire still suffered internal problems, and again the western half suffered more. To lessen the problems, Theodosius willed upon his death that the eastern and western parts should be separate empires. In A.D. 395 this division came to pass. To distinguish the two, historians refer to the eastern empire as the Byzantine Empire—after Byzantium, the town that became the capital—and the western empire as the Roman Empire.

Barbarian Invasions

Germanic tribes entered the Roman Empire for many reasons. Beginning in the late A.D. 300s, large numbers of Germanic peoples migrated into the empire because they sought a warmer climate and

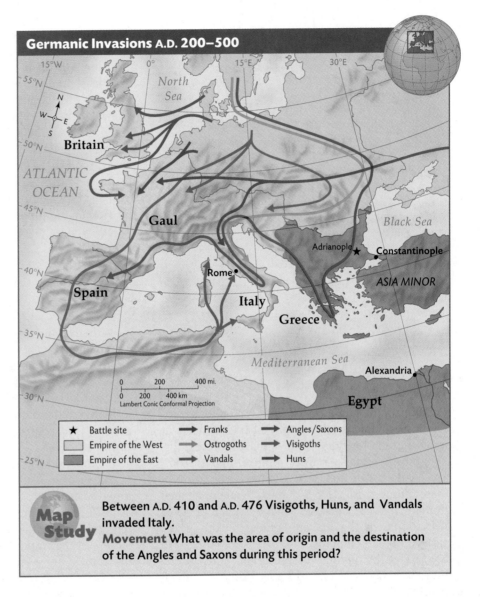

Germanic Invasions A.D. 200–500

Legend:
★ Battle site
▢ Empire of the West
▨ Empire of the East
→ Franks
→ Ostrogoths
→ Vandals
→ Angles/Saxons
→ Visigoths
→ Huns

Map Study

Between A.D. 410 and A.D. 476 Visigoths, Huns, and Vandals invaded Italy.
Movement What was the area of origin and the destination of the Angles and Saxons during this period?

better grazing land. Others crossed the empire's borders wanting a share of Rome's wealth. Most, however, came because they were fleeing the Huns, fierce nomadic invaders from central Asia.

Warrior Groups

Germanic warriors lived mostly by raising cattle and farming small plots. Despite their interest in the empire's goods, they themselves had little surplus to trade and were poor compared to the Romans. Each warrior group consisted of warriors, their families, and a chief. This chief governed the group and also led the warriors into battle. As the bands of warriors were numerous, so too were the chiefs. Often the only unifying factor among these Germanic groups was their language, which to the Romans sounded like unintelligible babbling. The Romans labeled the Germanic peoples barbarians, a reference to the sounds they made.

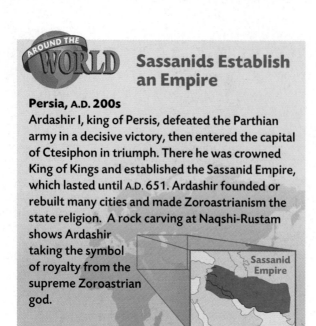

AROUND THE WORLD

Sassanids Establish an Empire

Persia, A.D. 200s
Ardashir I, king of Persis, defeated the Parthian army in a decisive victory, then entered the capital of Ctesiphon in triumph. There he was crowned King of Kings and established the Sassanid Empire, which lasted until A.D. 651. Ardashir founded or rebuilt many cities and made Zoroastrianism the state religion. A rock carving at Naqshi-Rustam shows Ardashir taking the symbol of royalty from the supreme Zoroastrian god.

Sassanid Empire

The Visigoths

During the late A.D. 300s and A.D. 400s, a variety of Germanic groups extended their hold over much Roman territory. They were the Ostrogoths, Visigoths, Vandals, Franks, Angles, and Saxons. The Visigoths, at first, were the most important of these groups. In A.D. 378 they rebelled against Roman rule and defeated a large Roman army at Adrianople in the Balkan Peninsula, killing the eastern Roman emperor. His successor managed to buy peace by giving the Visigoths land in the Balkans. Then in A.D. 410 the Visigothic chief, **Alaric**, led his people into Italy, capturing and sacking Rome. After Alaric's death the Visigoths retreated into Gaul.

The Huns

The next threat to the empire was invasion by the Huns. This nomadic group streamed westward from the grasslands of central Asia. Led by their chief, **Attila**, the Huns raided the eastern empire; then they moved north into Gaul. In A.D. 451 the Romans and the Visigoths combined to fight and stop the Huns in central Gaul. Foiled in the provinces, Attila turned upon Italy. There his horde plundered the larger cities and terrified the people. Eventually plague and famine took their toll on the Huns. After Attila died in A.D. 453, they retreated to eastern Europe.

The end of the empire of the Huns brought new troubles to the Romans. Wandering Germans, Persians, Slavs, and Avars battered continually at the Roman Empire's eastern frontier. Diplomacy, bribery, and warfare kept them at bay for only a short time.

End of the Western Empire

With the Huns gone and Italy devastated, nothing remained to prevent Germanic tribes from taking over. The Vandals raided and thoroughly sacked Rome in A.D. 455. Franks and Goths divided Gaul among themselves. Finally, in A.D. 476, a German soldier named Odoacer (OH•duh•WAY•suhr) seized control of Rome and overthrew the young emperor, Romulus Augustulus. Odoacer then named himself king of Italy.

Because Odoacer called himself king and never named a substitute emperor, people today refer to A.D. 476 as the year in which the Roman Empire "fell." However, this event no more signifies the collapse of the empire than any other event. Its end was caused by a complex interaction of events between A.D. 200 and A.D. 500.

More accurately, the western Roman Empire ended in the late A.D. 400s. Yet it did not mean the end of Roman culture, for the new Germanic rulers accepted the Latin language, Roman laws, and the Christian Church. In the Byzantine Empire, however, aspects of Roman culture were gradually supplanted by Hellenistic culture. By the A.D. 700s, Greek had even replaced Latin as the language of the Byzantine Empire.

SECTION 5 REVIEW

Recall
1. **Define** inflation.
2. **Identify** Diocletian, Constantine, Theodosius I, Alaric, Attila, Odoacer.
3. **Locate** Adrianople on the map on page 177. What significant event occurred there during the time of the "fall" of the Roman Empire?

Critical Thinking
4. **Synthesizing Information** Which do you think had a greater impact on the fall of the Roman Empire, internal difficulties or outside invaders? Why?

Understanding Themes
5. **Change** How did warfare both create and destroy the Roman Empire?

Decision Making

Suppose you have been given the choice of taking an art class or a music class during your free period at school. How will you decide which class to take?

Learning the Skill

When you make a decision, you are making a choice between alternatives. In order to make that choice, you must be informed and aware. There are five key steps you should follow that will help you through the decision-making process.
1. Identify the problem. What are you being asked to choose between?
2. Identify and consider various alternatives that are possible.
3. Determine the consequences for each alternative. Identify both the positive and the negative consequences.
4. Evaluate the consequences. Consider both the positive and negative consequences for each alternative.
5. Ask yourself: Which alternative seems to have more positive consequences? Which seems to have more negative consequences? Then make your decision.

Practicing the Skill

Decisions throughout history have affected the outcome of events, and defined history as we know it today. Identify the alternatives and describe their consequences for each of the following events that occurred during the time of ancient Rome. Each of these events took place as a result of a decision made by a person or a group of people.
1. The Twelve Tables became the basis for all future Roman law in 451 B.C.
2. During the Third Punic War, in 146 B.C., the Romans burned Carthage.
3. In 27 B.C., Augustus Caesar became Rome's first emperor.
4. The Emperor Theodosius made Christianity the official religion of the Roman Empire in A.D. 392.
5. Beginning in the late A.D. 300s, large numbers of Germanic peoples migrated into the Roman Empire.

Applying the Skill

Use a newspaper or magazine to find a current issue that directly affects your life. Identify the issue, and then review the facts and what you already know about the issue. Identify various alternatives, and then determine the consequences for each alternative. Use this information to evaluate both positive and negative consequences. Make a sound decision about which alternative would be best for you.

For More Practice

Turn to the Skill Practice in the Chapter Review on page 181 for more practice in decision making.

Connections Across Time

Historical Significance The Romans established a common culture among the diverse peoples of the Mediterranean world. Their legal system, forms of government, engineering feats, and arts formed the foundation of many provincial cities. Frequent civil wars triggered a chain of events that ultimately led to the Roman Empire's economic and political ruin.

The lasting legacies of the Roman Empire, however, are its Latin language, which provided the root of the Romance languages; its engineering skills; its transmission of Greek culture; and Christianity. Today, the city of Rome is still the center of the Roman Catholic Church.

Using Key Terms

Write the key term that completes each sentence. Then write a sentence for each term not chosen.

a. indemnity
b. bishop
c. plebeians
d. sect
e. inflation
f. aqueducts
g. republic
h. patricians
i. triumvirate
j. messiah
k. pope
l. consul
m. dictator

1. After years of rule by kings, the Romans declared their city-state a _____, a form of government in which people elect their leaders.
2. In 60 B.C. Pompey, Crassus, and Julius Caesar formed a _____, a group of three persons with equal power, to control the government.
3. After their defeat, the people of Carthage agreed to pay the Romans a huge _____, or payment for damages.
4. Early Christianity was thought of as a _____, or group, within Judaism.
5. The majority of people in the Roman Republic were _____ —nonaristocratic landowners, merchants, shopkeepers, small farmers, and laborers.

Technology Activity

Creating a Multimedia Presentation Search a computerized card catalog or the Internet for information about the early Etruscans. Using multimedia tools, create a short presentation about the Etruscan culture. Incorporate images from the Internet. Before you begin, plan the type of presentation you want to develop and the steps you will take to make the presentation successful. Indicate tools you will need and cite all electronic resources.

Using Your History Journal

Imagine that you are either a young Roman legionary stationed in a remote outpost of the empire in A.D. 130 or you are a friend of the legionary, awaiting his return to Rome. Write a letter describing what you have been doing in the past week.

Reviewing Facts

1. **Science** Identify Roman achievements in science and engineering, and discuss their impact.
2. **Government** Describe how Rome's political system changed under Augustus Caesar.
3. **Citizenship** Trace the development of Roman law and its influence on Western civilization.
4. **Government** Discuss how Roman governors made provincial cities more like Rome.
5. **Geography** Explain the geographic factors that helped Rome to dominate the Mediterranean.

Critical Thinking

1. **Apply** In what ways did the Roman Republic, in its structure and growth, affect later governments in western Europe and America?
2. **Analyze** What evidence suggests that Roman society was more stable during the republic than during the time of the empire?
3. **Evaluate** In what ways did the Romans' treatment of the peoples they conquered differ from the ways in which other victors usually treated the peoples they conquered? How might Roman attitudes have strengthened the empire?

4. Analyze The vase shown here incorporates the Etruscan alphabet. Why have scholars been unable to tell the full story of Etruscan history?

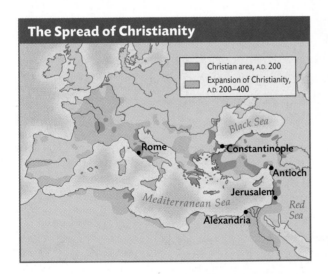

Geography in History

1. Location Refer to the map below. Which area (east or west) was more heavily influenced by Christianity by A.D. 200?

2. Movement What major body of water did many early missionaries cross in their efforts to spread Christianity?

3. Place According to the map below, which city in western Europe had the largest concentration of Christians by A.D. 200?

The Spread of Christianity

Christian area, A.D. 200
Expansion of Christianity, A.D. 200–400

Rome
Constantinople
Antioch
Jerusalem
Alexandria
Black Sea
Mediterranean Sea
Red Sea

Understanding Themes

1. Change How did the Roman government change from the time of the Etruscans to Augustus Caesar?

2. Conflict Evaluate a conflict between nations that has occurred in the recent past, and analyze the ways in which it is similar to conflicts between the Romans and other peoples of the Mediterranean region.

3. Cultural Diffusion How might Roman roads have helped to foster cultural diffusion?

4. Innovation In what way did Constantine's victory in battle in A.D. 312 change the religious life of the Roman Empire? How did his religious policies later shape the future course of religion in Western civilization?

5. Change How did Roman architecture reflect the political and social changes that transformed Rome from a republic into an empire?

Linking Past and Present

The United States government operates on the system of checks and balances, in which each branch of government limits the power of the other branches. Did this system operate in the Roman Republic? Why or why not? Use examples from Roman history to support your answer.

Skill Practice

Reread page 160 about the Punic Wars. For each of the three wars, identify the decision that affected the outcome of each. Explain the consequences of each decision, and how they affected the outcome. Examining the decisions and final outcomes of each war will help you see alternatives that might have been available to the decision makers at the time. Discuss some of the alternatives and their consequences for each war. How would history have changed if different decisions had been made?

1500 B.C.–A.D. 1500
Flowering of African Civilizations

Chapter Themes

▶ **Movement** Migrations of Bantu-speaking people influence Africa's cultural development. *Section 1*

▶ **Cultural Diffusion** Africa's trade contacts with Europe and Asia affect African cultures. *Section 2*

▶ **Innovation** East African city-states develop a new culture based on African and Arab cultures. *Section 3*

The Storyteller

The Yoruba—West Africans living by the Niger River—gather each winter to hear storytellers recount a legend that tells of how their ancestors struggled to clear their land with tools made of wood and soft metal. Even orishas, *or gods, could not cut through vines or trees with these tools until the god Ogun appeared, carrying his bush knife.*

"He slashed through the heavy vines, felled the trees and cleared the forest from the land.... So [the people] made [Ogun] their ruler.... He built forges for them and showed them how to make spears, knives, hoes, and swords."

Legends such as this describe experiences that early people valued most. Early Africans built civilizations that have left rich traditions for today's peoples.

Historical Significance

How did early Africans use the natural resources of their environment to develop trade networks? What impact did their cultures have on other lands?

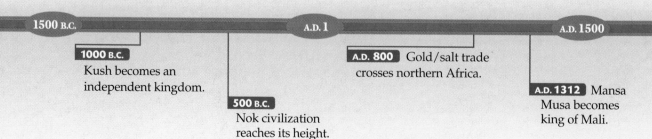

1500 B.C.		A.D. 1		A.D. 1500
1000 B.C. Kush becomes an independent kingdom.	**500 B.C.** Nok civilization reaches its height.	**A.D. 800** Gold/salt trade crosses northern Africa.	**A.D. 1312** Mansa Musa becomes king of Mali.	

Prehistoric cave art from
Tassili N'Ajjer Plateau, Algeria

Your History Journal

*Consult a historical atlas, and draw
an outline map of Africa showing early
African kingdoms, the dates when they
existed, and major trade routes. Write
and answer questions based on the map's
data.*

2000 B.C.	1000 B.C.	A.D. 1	A.D. 1000

c. 750 B.C. Kushite kings rule over Egypt.

c. 250 B.C. Merchants from Egypt, Rome, Persia, and India trade with Axum.

A.D. 330 Christianity becomes Axum's official religion.

Section 1

Early Africa

▶ **Terms to Define**
oral tradition, plateau, savanna, matrilineal, age set

▶ **People to Meet**
Piankhi, Ezana, the Nok

▶ **Places to Locate**
Nubia, Kush, Axum

 **ind Out** What kinds of societies emerged in early Africa?

The Storyteller

African oral tradition contained stories full of wisdom, to be enjoyed by all. For example, where did death come from? A myth from Madagascar gave this answer. One day God asked the first couple what kind of death they wanted, one like that of the moon, or that of the banana? The couple was puzzled. God explained: The banana creates young plants to take its place, but the moon itself comes back to life every month. After consideration, the couple prayed for children, because without children they would be lonely, would have to do all the work, and would have no one to provide for. Since that time, human life is short on this earth.

—freely adapted from
The Humanistic Tradition,
Gloria K. Fiero, 1992

Kilimanjaro

Africa's earliest civilizations left few written records of their existence. It was through oral traditions—legends and history passed by word of mouth from one generation to another—that early African peoples communicated knowledge about their culture. Thus, archaeologists and historians have had to rely on legends and artifacts to learn about the culture of African civilizations between 1100 B.C. and A.D. 1500.

Archaeologists have discovered that early African cultures developed technologies and trade based on regional natural resources. Civilizations rose and declined, and were influenced by the movement of people and by the way in which natural resources were developed.

Geography and Environment

Africa's geography and climate are a study in contrasts. Africa, the world's second-largest continent, is three times larger than the United States. Within its huge expanse lie desolate deserts, lofty mountains, rolling grasslands, and fertile river valleys.

Regions of Africa

The African continent can be divided into five regions based on location and environment: North Africa, East Africa, West Africa, Central Africa, and Southern Africa.

North Africa consists of a thin coastal plain, bordering the Mediterranean Sea, and an inland desert area. Coastal North Africa has mild temperatures and frequent rainfall. In contrast, the area south of this green belt is a vast expanse of sand: the Sahara, the world's largest desert. Extending more than 3,500 miles (5,630 km) across the continent, the Sahara is a region of shifting dunes and jagged rock piles.

Wall painting from the Metropolitan Museum of Art, New York City, New York. **Four late Bronze Age Nubian princes offer rings and gold to an Egyptian ruler.** *In what ways did Nubian culture resemble Egyptian culture?*

The Sahel

South of the Sahara, the continent of Africa is dominated by a great central plateau—a relatively high, flat area known as the Sahel. This region receives moderate rainfall to sustain the savannas, or treeless grasslands, that cover the plateau. The savannas south of the Sahara constitute about 40 percent of Africa's land area.

In East Africa, the Sahel descends into a deep crack known as the Great Rift Valley. The valley extends 40 miles (65 km) in width and 2,000 feet (610 m) in depth. It runs 3,000 miles (4,827 km) from the Red Sea in the north all the way to Southern Africa. Rising above the Sahel plateau east of the valley are two mountain peaks—Mount Kenya and Kilimanjaro. Kilimanjaro is Africa's highest mountain, with an elevation of 19,340 feet (5,895 m).

In West Africa, the Sahel descends to a narrow coastal plain that has a relatively unbroken coastline. The major rivers that do flow through the coastal plain—the Niger and the Zaire (Congo)—are navigable only for short distances. The few natural harbors and limited river travel isolated early African civilizations and made foreign invasions difficult in some areas.

Central Africa near the Equator has lush tropical rain forests so thick that sunlight cannot reach the forest floor. Although the rain forest climate is hot and humid, 1,500 miles (2,413 km) farther south the land again turns into a desert—the Kalahari. Still farther south, the Kalahari gives way to a cool, fertile highland in Southern Africa.

The African continent has provided rich resources for its people. Early cultures developed where rainfall was plentiful, or near lakes or along rivers like the Nile.

Nubia and Kush

By 3000 B.C., a people called the Nubians established a kingdom called **Nubia** in the southern part of the Nile River valley in present-day Sudan. The Nubian people mastered the bow and arrow and became warriors. With their military skills, they conquered smaller neighboring communities in the Nile Valley.

The Nubians maintained close contacts with Egypt to the north. Archaeologists have uncovered the tombs of Nubian kings, which contained precious stones, gold, jewelry, and pottery. These are as ornate as those found in Egypt from the same period. Some scholars believe that political ideas, such as monarchy, and various objects, like boats and eating utensils, reveal the early beginnings of the close cultural links between Nubia and Egypt.

By 2000 B.C., the Nubian river civilization had developed into the kingdom of **Kush**. After defeat in warfare, Kush was under Egyptian rule for 500 years. Egyptian pharaohs stationed soldiers in Kush to collect duties on goods moving through the region.

The people of Kush used their location along the Upper Nile River to develop a strong trade economy. The Kushite cities of Napata and Meroë stood where trade caravans crossed the Nile, bringing gold, elephant tusks, and timber from the African interior. This strategic location brought wealth to the merchants and kings of Kush.

Around 1000 B.C. Kush broke away from Egypt and became politically independent. In time Kush grew strong enough that a Kushite king named **Piankhi** (pee•AHNK•hee) in 724 B.C. led a powerful army from Kush into Egypt and defeated the Egyptians. After this victory, Kushite kings ruled over both Egypt and Kush from their capital at Napata. The city boasted white sandstone temples, monuments, and pyramids fashioned in styles similar to those of the Egyptians.

In 671 B.C. the Assyrians invaded Egypt, easily defeating the Kushites, whose bronze weapons were no match against Assyrian iron swords. The Kushites were forced to leave Egypt and return to their home territory at the bend of the Upper Nile. In spite of their defeat, the Kushites learned from their enemies the technology of making iron. They built a new capital at Meroë that became a major center for iron production. Kush merchants traded iron, leopard skins, and ebony for goods from the Mediterranean and the Red Sea regions. They also conducted business throughout the Indian Ocean area. Meroë's merchants used their wealth to construct fine houses built around a central courtyard and public baths modeled after ones they had seen in Rome.

For about 150 years, the Kushite kingdom thrived. Then a new power—**Axum**, a kingdom located near the Red Sea—invaded Kush and ended Kushite domination of northeastern Africa.

Axum

Because of its location along the Red Sea, Axum also emerged as a trading power. During the 200s B.C., merchants from Egypt, Greece, Rome, Persia, and India sent ships laden with cotton cloth, brass, copper, and olive oil to Axum's main seaport at Adulis. Traders exchanged their goods for cargoes of ivory that the people of Axum hauled from Africa's interior.

Through trade Axum absorbed many elements of Roman culture, including a new religion:

Visualizing History **Church of St. Mary of Zion.** According to tradition, this church contains the original tablets of Moses, brought by King Menelik I to Axum. Menelik, the legendary founder of Axum's monarchy, was reputed to be the son of the Israelite king Solomon and the Arabian queen of Sheba. *How did Christianity come to Axum?*

Christianity. A remarkable event led to the conversion of Axum's King **Ezana** to Christianity. Shipwrecked off the coast of Ethiopia, two Christians from Syria were picked up and brought to King Ezana's court, where they lived for several years. The young men convinced Ezana that he should become a Christian. About A.D. 330 the king made Christianity the official religion in Axum. During this time, Christianity also became dominant in other areas of northeastern Africa—Kush and Egypt.

Axum declined after the rise of the religion of Islam during the A.D. 600s. Its Red Sea ports lost their importance as links to the Mediterranean world, and Axum's rulers—confined to the remote interior of East Africa—set up the Christian kingdom of Ethiopia.

South of the Sahara

Between 700 B.C. and 200 B.C., during Axum's rise to power, a West African culture called **the Nok** had already established itself in the fertile Niger and Benue River valleys. In the 1930s archaeologists working in present-day central Nigeria found terra-cotta, or baked clay, figurines that provided evidence of the Nok culture. Working in the Nok sites and other areas of West Africa, archaeologists also unearthed iron hoes and ax-heads. This latter discovery provided evidence that metal production had enabled African cultures south of the Sahara to farm their land more effectively.

As West African farmers used their iron tools to produce more food, the population increased. In time, arable land became scarce, causing widespread food shortages. Small groups of Africans began to migrate from West Africa to less populated areas. Other groups followed. Over about a thousand years a great migration took place.

Bantu Migrations

Historians call this mass movement the Bantu migrations because descendants of the people who migrated throughout the continent share elements of a language group known as Bantu. The Bantu migrations did not follow a single pattern. Some villagers followed the Niger or other rivers, settling in one spot to farm for a few years and moving on as the soil became less fertile. Other groups penetrated the rain forests and grew crops along the riverbanks. Still others moved to the highland savannas of East Africa and raised cattle. Groups that settled on the

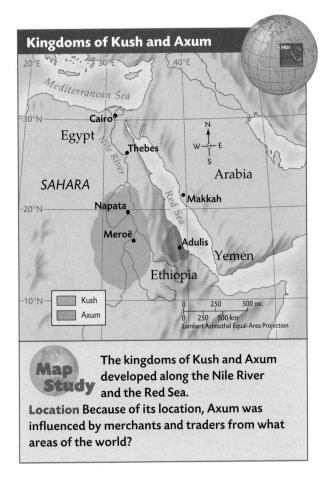

Kingdoms of Kush and Axum

Kush
Axum

0   250   500 mi.
0   250   500 km
Lambert Azimuthal Equal-Area Projection

Map Study The kingdoms of Kush and Axum developed along the Nile River and the Red Sea.
Location Because of its location, Axum was influenced by merchants and traders from what areas of the world?

eastern coastal plain grew new crops, such as bananas and yams that had been brought to East Africa by traders from Southeast Asia.

As people pushed into new areas, they met other African groups that adopted their ways of life. In time, Bantu-speaking peoples became the dominant group in Africa south of the Sahara.

Village Life

Africans who spoke Bantu languages became divided into hundreds of ethnic groups, each with its own religious beliefs, marriage and family customs, and traditions. Ethnic groups living around A.D. 1000 formed close-knit communities where most families were organized into large households that included descendants of one set of grandparents.

Many villages were matrilineal societies in which villagers traced their descent through mothers rather than through fathers. However, when a girl married, she became a member of her husband's family. To compensate the bride's family for the loss of a member, the husband's family gave the bride's family gifts of iron tools, goats, or cloth.

Even before marriage, specific jobs were assigned to groups of males and females of a similar

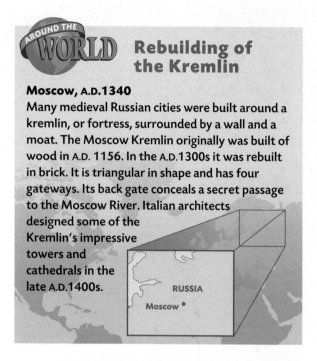

age, called age sets. Boys younger than 10 or 12 herded cattle; girls of the same age helped their mothers plant as well as tend and harvest crops. At about 12 years old, boys and girls took part in ceremonies initiating them into adulthood. A boy remained with his age set throughout his life. After marriage, a girl joined an age set in her husband's village.

Religious Beliefs

To most Africans, marriage customs and all other social laws and traditions were made by a single supreme god who created and ruled an orderly universe. The god rewarded those who followed social rules with abundant harvests and the birth of healthy children, and punished those who violated tradition with accidents, crop failures, or illness.

Beneath the supreme god were many lesser deities who influenced the daily affairs of men and women. These deities were present in natural phenomena such as storms, mountains, and trees.

Many Africans also believed that spirits of dead ancestors lived among the people of the village and guided their destiny.

The religious beliefs and family loyalties of most Africans maintained stability and support within villages. Most communities expected their members to obey the social rules they believed to have come from the supreme god.

Although African communities relied heavily on religious and family traditions to maintain a stable social structure, outside influences through trade and learning still affected them. North Africans absorbed influences from the Arab world, whereas African people south of the Sahara adapted to Persian, Indian, and later, European influences. From these outsiders, African communities adopted many new customs, ideas, and languages.

The Arts

Various arts developed throughout Bantu-speaking Africa. Sculpture was an important art form. African sculpture included figures, masks, decorated boxes, and objects for ceremonial and everyday use. Most of these items were made of wood, bronze, ivory, or baked clay. The wearing of masks at ceremonial dances symbolized the link between the living and the dead. Those wearing the masks and performing the dances called upon ancestral spirits to guide the community.

Music rich in rhythm was interwoven with the fabric of everyday African life. It included choral singing, music performed at royal courts, and songs and dances for ceremonies. In villages, where many activities were performed by groups, music often provided the motivation and rhythm for various tasks, such as digging ditches or pounding grain. African musicians used a variety of drums as well as harps, flutes, pipes, horns, and xylophones.

Early Africa excelled in oral literature passed down from one generation to another. The stories included histories, fables, and proverbs. Oral literature not only recorded the past but also taught traditions and values.

SECTION I REVIEW

Recall
1. **Define** oral tradition, plateau, savanna, matrilineal, age set.
2. **Identify** Sahel, Nubia, Kush, Piankhi, Axum, Ezana, the Nok, Bantu.
3. **Locate** the Nile River valley on

the map on page 187. Why did the Nubians settle in the Upper Nile Valley?

Critical Thinking
4. **Applying Information** Explain how Mediterranean trade influenced the economy

of the kingdom of Axum.

Understanding Themes
5. **Movement** How do the Bantu migrations in early Africa compare with the Aryan migrations in early South Asia?

A.D. 300 Ghana begins to build a trading empire.

c. A.D. 1275 Mali conquers surrounding territory.

A.D. 1493 Askia Muhammad begins rule in Songhai.

Section 2

Kingdoms in West Africa

Setting the Scene

▶ **Terms to Define**
monotheism, ghana, mosque

▶ **People to Meet**
Sundiata Keita, Mansa Musa, Askia Muhammad

▶ **Places to Locate**
Ghana, Mali, Timbuktu, Songhai

Find Out How was trade carried out in West Africa?

The Storyteller

The poets of Mali preserved the history of their people. Hear one speak: "I teach kings the history of their ancestors so that the lives of the ancients might serve them as an example, for the world is old, but the future springs from the past. My word is pure and free of all untruth…. Listen to my word, you who want to know, by my mouth, you will learn the history of Mali. By my mouth you will get to know the story of the ancestor of great Mali, the story of him who … surpassed even Alexander the Great…. Whoever knows the history of a country can read its future."

—from *Sundiata: An Epic of Old Mali* in *The Humanistic Tradition*, Gloria K. Fiero, 1992

Horn player, Benin

A diverse environment provided rich natural resources for the early kingdoms of West Africa. Africans living in this region between A.D. 300 and A.D. 1500 mined gold and other mineral resources. An active trade developed between them and peoples outside West Africa who practiced a religion called Islam. Islam preached monotheism, or the belief in one God, and spread throughout the Middle East, North Africa, and Spain during the A.D. 600s and A.D. 700s. Through their trade contacts with Muslims, the followers of Islam, African cultures gradually adopted Islamic cultural elements such as language and religion.

Kingdom of Ghana

The kingdom of **Ghana** became one of the richest trading civilizations in West Africa due to its location midway between Saharan salt mines and tropical gold mines. Between A.D. 300 and A.D. 1200 the kings of Ghana controlled a trading empire that stretched more than 100,000 square miles (260,000 sq. km). They prospered from the taxes they imposed on goods that entered or left their kingdom. Because the ghana, or king, ruled such a vast region, the land became known by the name of its ruler—Ghana.

There was two-way traffic by caravan between cities in North Africa and Ghana. Muslim traders from North Africa sent caravans loaded with cloth, metalware, swords, and salt across the western Sahara to northern settlements in Ghana. Large caravans from Ghana traveled north to Morocco, bringing kola nuts and farming produce. Ghanaian gold was traded for Saharan salt brought by Muslim traders.

Salt was an important trade item for the people of Ghana. They needed salt to preserve and flavor their foods. Using plentiful supplies of gold as a medium of exchange, Ghanaian merchants traded the precious metal for salt and other goods from Morocco and Spain.

Masudi, a Muslim traveler, writing about A.D. 950, described how trade was conducted:

> **❝** The merchants … place their wares and cloth on the ground and then depart, and so the people of [Ghana] come bearing gold which they leave beside the merchandise and then depart. The owners of the merchandise then return, and if they are satisfied with what they have found, they take it. If not, they go away again, and the people of [Ghana] return and add to the price until the bargain is concluded. **❞**

Ghana reached the height of its economic and political power as a trading kingdom in the A.D. 800s and A.D. 900s. The salt and gold trade moving through Ghana brought Islamic ideas and customs to the kingdom. Muslim influence increased and many Ghanaians converted to Islam.

At the end of the A.D. 1000s, an attack on the Ghanaian trade centers by the Almoravids, a Muslim group from North Africa, led to the decline of Ghana as a prosperous kingdom. Groups of Ghanaians broke away to form many small Islamic states.

Kingdom of Mali

Mali, one of the small states to break away from Ghana, became a powerful kingdom that eventually ruled much of West Africa. The word *Mali* means "where the king resides" and is an appropriate name for a kingdom that gained much of its power and influence from its kings. **Sundiata Keita**, one of Mali's early kings, defeated his leading rival in A.D. 1235 and began to conquer surrounding territories. By the late A.D. 1200s, Mali's territory included the old kingdom of Ghana.

Images *of the* Times

Africa's Religious Heritage

Religion played a central role in the development of African cultures. Islam became the dominant religion in the north.

The Great Mosque at Timbuktu
Founded around A.D. 1100, the city of Timbuktu became a major center of trade and site of an important Islamic school.

Altar of the Hand, Benin
Beginning in the A.D. 1200s the kingdom of Benin emerged as a wealthy trading state. The *oba*, or king, became the political, economic, and spiritual leader of the people.

Sundiata worked to bring prosperity to his new empire. He restored the trans-Saharan trade in gold and salt that had been interrupted by the Almoravid attacks and he restored agricultural production. Sundiata ordered soldiers to clear large expanses of savanna and burn the grass that had been cleared to provide fertilizer for crops of peanuts, rice, sorghum, yams, beans, onions, and grains. With the benefit of rainfall, agriculture flourished in Mali. With larger tracts of land under cultivation, farmers produced surplus crops that Mali's kings collected as taxes.

Mali's greatest king was **Mansa Musa**, who ruled from A.D. 1312 to A.D. 1332. By opening trade routes and protecting trade caravans with a powerful standing army, Musa maintained the economic prosperity begun by Sundiata. He also introduced Islamic culture to Mali.

A Muslim himself, Musa enhanced the prestige and power of Mali through a famous pilgrimage to Makkah in A.D. 1324. Arab writers report that Musa traveled in grand style. He took with him 12,000 slaves, each dressed in silk or brocade and carrying bars of gold. Musa gave away so much gold on his journey that the world price of gold fell. At Makkah, Musa persuaded a Spanish architect to return with him to Mali. There the skilled architect built great mosques—Muslim houses of worship—and other fine buildings, including a palace for Musa in the capital of **Timbuktu** (TIHM•BUHK•TOO). Timbuktu became an important center of Muslim art and culture mainly through the efforts of Mansa Musa, who encouraged Muslim scholars to teach at his court. Two hundred years later, the North African scholar and traveler Hassan ibn Muhammad (known in the West as Leo Africanus) described Timbuktu's continuing intellectual brilliance:

66 Here are great store of doctors, judges, priests, and other learned men that are bountifully maintained at the king's cost and charges. And hither are brought diverse manuscripts or written books out of [North Africa], which are sold for more money than any other merchandise. 99

Terra-cotta heads, c. early 1600s, commemorate the deceased members of the royal family among the Akan peoples of southern Ghana.

REFLECTING ON THE TIMES

1. How did religion influence the arts and other aspects of culture in Africa?
2. In what ways did Africans honor royalty?

James L. Stanfield

West African Empire

This turreted mosque in Djenné, Mali, harks back to the A.D. 1300s, when the town thrived as a center of trade and Islamic learning. A masterpiece of African-Muslim architecture, the great mosque boasts massive mud ramparts broken by patterns of protruding beams. Its tall spires are crowned not with the traditional Islamic crescent but with ostrich eggs, symbol of fertility and fortune. Every year, after the rainy season, the town turns out 4,000 people to replaster the walls of the mosque with their bare hands. The job is done in a day.

Almost two centuries before Columbus set off for the Americas, an Arab traveler and author named Ibn Battuta began his travels in A.D. 1325 to the far corners of the Islamic world—from North Africa to China and back. He returned home three decades later as one of history's great travelers and travel writers. His journeys totaled 75,000 miles (121,000 km)—three times the distance logged by his European predecessor, Marco Polo. Ibn Battuta's final journey brought him here to the West African empire of Mali where he praised the piety of the Muslims. Battuta sought out the ruler, Mansa Sulayman, at his capital but was not impressed with the king's generosity. Mansa Sulayman, he wrote, "is a miserly king." Battuta also traveled to Timbuktu—about a hundred years before the city really started to prosper. At its height, in the A.D. 1500s, the city could boast three universities and perhaps 50,000 residents. ⊕

After Mansa Musa died in A.D. 1332, the empire came under attack by Berbers, a people living in the Sahara region to the north. They raided Mali and captured Timbuktu. From the south, warriors from the rain forest also attacked Mali. Inside the kingdom, people living in the **Songhai** region of the Niger River valley resented losing control over their region and rebelled against the empire. By the middle of the A.D. 1500s, Mali had split into several independent states.

Kingdom of Songhai

The rebellious Songhai, who were skilled traders, farmers, and fishers, were led by strong leaders. During the late A.D. 1400s their ruler, Sunni Ali, fought many territorial wars and managed to conquer the cities of Timbuktu and Djenné, expanding his empire to include most of the West African savanna. Sunni Ali was a Muslim ruler, but when he died, rule fell to his son, a non-Muslim. The Muslim population of Songhai overthrew Ali's son and brought a Muslim ruler to the throne.

Under the new ruler, **Askia Muhammad**, the Songhai Empire reached the height of its glory. Ruling from A.D. 1493 to A.D. 1528, Askia Muhammad divided Songhai into five huge provinces, each with a governor, a tax collector, a court of judges, and a trade inspector—very much like the government structure of China in the A.D. 1400s. The king maintained the peace and security of his realm with a cavalry and a navy. Timbuktu was a center of Muslim learning.

Devoted to Islam, Muhammad introduced laws based on the teachings of the holy book of Islam, the Quran (kuh•RAHN). Lesser crimes were sometimes overlooked, but those who committed major crimes such as robbery or idolatry received harsh punishments. Askia Muhammad appointed Muslim

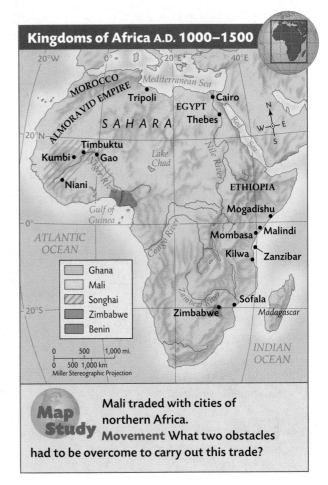

Kingdoms of Africa A.D. 1000–1500

Ghana
Mali
Songhai
Zimbabwe
Benin

Map Study Mali traded with cities of northern Africa.
Movement What two obstacles had to be overcome to carry out this trade?

judges, assuring that Islamic laws would be upheld.

In A.D. 1528 Askia Muhammad was overthrown by his son. A series of struggles for the throne followed, leading to a weakened central government. Around A.D. 1589 the rulers of Morocco sent an army across the Sahara to attack Songhai gold-trading centers. Moroccan soldiers, armed with guns and cannons, easily defeated the Songhai forces fighting with only swords, spears, and bows and arrows. By A.D. 1600 the Songhai Empire had come to an end.

SECTION 2 REVIEW

Recall
1. **Define** monotheism, ghana, mosque.
2. **Identify** the Almoravids, Sundiata Keita, Mansa Musa, Askia Muhammad.
3. **Locate** Timbuktu on the map on this page. How did Timbuktu become an important center of Islamic art and learning during the A.D. 1300s?

Critical Thinking
4. **Analyzing Information** Why was trade vital to the economies of the West African kingdoms?

Understanding Themes
5. **Cultural Diffusion** What goods were traded, and how did trade between West Africa and the Islamic world influence the development of West African cultures between A.D. 900 and A.D. 1500?

A.D. 900   Arab and Persian merchants trade in East Africa.

c. A.D. 1200   Kilwa thrives as East African coastal city-state.

c. A.D. 1300   People of Karanga build stone-walled fortresses.

Section 3

African Trading Cities and States

Setting the Scene

▶ **Terms to Define**
monopoly, multicultural

▶ **Places to Locate**
Kilwa, Malindi, Mombasa, Sofala, Zanzibar, Karanga, Great Zimbabwe

Find Out   How did areas in East, Central, and Southern Africa develop as a result of inland and overseas trade?

The Storyteller

The first trained engineer ever to see the ruins of the Great Zimbabwe reported: "For fifty miles I saw the ruins.... The ruins are principally terraces, which rise up continually from the base to the apex of all the hills.... The terraces are all made very flat and of dry masonry.... The way the ancients seem to have levelled off the contours of the various hills around which the water courses are laid is very astonishing, as they seem to have been levelled with as much exactitude as we can accomplish with our best mathematical instruments."

Ruins of the Great Zimbabwe

—from *The Mystery of the Great Zimbabwe,* Wilfrid Mallows, 1984

During the same time that West African kings ruled their empires, important trading communities developed along the coast of East Africa and in the interior of Central and Southern Africa. Inland African kingdoms mined copper and iron ore and traded these minerals and ivory with city-states that had developed along the East African coast. There Muslim traders brought cotton, silk, and Chinese porcelain from India and Southeast Asia to exchange for the products from Africa's interior. As in West Africa, trade contacts with the Muslim world enabled East African coastal areas to adopt the religion of Islam and Islamic cultural practices.

East Africa

As early as 500 B.C., coastal areas of East Africa were trading with the Arabian Peninsula and South Asia. Using dhows (Arab sailboats), East Africans sailed with the monsoon winds across the stretch of Indian Ocean separating Africa from India. By the A.D. 900s Arab and Persian merchants had settled on the East African coast and controlled the trade there. Traders from the interior of Africa brought ivory, gold, iron, and rhinoceros horn to the east coast to trade for Indian cloth and Chinese porcelain.

Coastal City-States

By A.D. 1200 small East African trading settlements had become thriving city-states taxing the goods that passed through their ports. The port of **Kilwa** had a virtual **monopoly**, or sole control or ownership, of the gold trade with the interior. **Malindi** and **Mombasa**, both ports farther north on the coast, were also important centers, as was **Sofala**, a port in what is present-day Mozambique. The iron mined in the surroundings of these three city-states was widely used in the Arabian Peninsula and South Asia.

The island of **Zanzibar** was also an important center of trade. Sailors from the islands of Southeast Asia as well as India and China came to Zanzibar in search of ivory and gold, which was brought to Zanzibar ports from the coastal city-states of East Africa.

Blending of Cultures

By the A.D. 1300s, the city-states of East Africa had reached the height of their prosperity. They had become truly multicultural centers—populated by a variety of cultural groups. Within each city-state, Islamic and African cultures blended. For the most part, Arab and Persian merchants ruled the trading states. They converted many Africans to Islam.

Arab merchants married local women who had converted to Islam. Families having members with African and Islamic cultural backgrounds began speaking Swahili, a Bantu language that included Arabic and Persian words. The people of the East African coastal city-states also developed an Arabic form of writing that enabled them to record their history.

East African rulers were either Arab governors or African chieftains. They used coral from Indian Ocean reefs to build mosques, palaces, and forts.

The Bantu Kingdoms

The Indian Ocean trade was not limited to the coastal trading states. It reached far inland, contributing to the rise of wealthy Bantu kingdoms in Central and Southern Africa. The inland kingdoms mined rich deposits of copper and gold. During the A.D. 900s, traders from the East African coast made their way to the inland mining communities in Central Africa and began an active trade among the people living there. The traders brought silk and porcelain from China, glass beads from India, carpets from Arab lands, and fine pottery from Persia. They traded these goods for minerals, ivory, and coconut oil. They also acquired enslaved Africans for export.

Great Zimbabwe

The people of **Karanga**, a Bantu kingdom located on a high plateau between the Zambezi and Limpopo Rivers, built nearly 300 stone-walled fortresses throughout their territory between A.D.

East African Trading Cities

In the A.D. 700s Arab immigrants arrived on East Africa's coast to set up a flourishing trade in gold, ivory, and tortoise shells. Descendants of the Arab immigrants and the local African inhabitants became known as the Swahili (an Arabic word for "people of the coast"). By the late A.D. 1100s, thriving Swahili port cities, such as Kilwa, Malindi, and Mombasa, served as trading links between the gold and ivory producers of East Africa's interior and traders from India, Ceylon (Sri Lanka), and China. Cotton, porcelain, and pottery were the major imports. By the 1500s China's withdrawal from foreign trade and the coming of European rule to East Africa contributed to a serious decline in East Africa's international trade.

Today, the East African coast has become an important link in the global trading network. While preserving its old town and traditions, the modern city of Mombasa ranks as one of Africa's busiest seaports and the second-largest city in the nation of Kenya. It handles most of the international shipping of Kenya as well as that of the neighboring, land-locked nations of Uganda, Rwanda, and Burundi, to which it is linked by rail. East African agricultural products, such as coffee, tea, sisal (a plant fiber used for twine), cotton, sugar, and coconuts are exported from Mombasa, as well as petroleum products produced from the foreign oil refined at Mombasa's refinery.

Port of Mombasa, Kenya

ACTIVITY

Compare and contrast Mombasa's trade in the A.D. 1200s with that of the city today. What factors have contributed to any changes?

This view shows the circular stone ruins of the Great Zimbabwe with an exterior wall more than 800 feet in circumference.
What functions did this "stone house" serve?

1000 and A.D. 1500. The largest was called the **Great Zimbabwe**—meaning "stone house"—and served as the political and religious center of the kingdom. The oval stone wall of the Zimbabwe enclosure was 30 feet (9.15 m) high. Within the wall was a maze of interior walls and hidden passages that protected the circular house of the Zimbabwe chief. Near the house, archaeologists have uncovered a platform with several upright stones that may have been the place where the chief held court.

Territorial Divisions

For nearly five centuries, Karanga and the other Bantu states grew wealthy from their control of the chief routes between the gold mines and the sea. However, during the A.D. 1400s, Bantu states in Southern Africa struggled in civil wars that brought disorder to the kingdoms and disrupted trade.

The Changamire Empire became stronger than the Monomotapa Empire. Changamire rulers took over Great Zimbabwe and built the fortress's largest structures. At the same time, European explorers arrived along the African coasts. Eager to control the sources of gold, ivory, and copper, the Europeans posed challenges to the survival of the African civilizations in the continent's interior.

SECTION 3 REVIEW

Recall
1. **Define** monopoly, multicultural.
2. **Identify** Kilwa, Malindi, Mombasa, Sofala, Zanzibar, Karanga, Great Zimbabwe.
3. **Explain** why the Bantu kingdoms of Central and Southern Africa prospered.

Critical Thinking
4. **Synthesizing Information** Imagine that you are an Arab merchant visiting an East African coastal city-state in the A.D. 1300s. What aspects of the people's culture would be familiar to you? What parts might seem different?

Understanding Themes
5. **Innovation** What new aspect of cultural life developed in the city-states of East Africa as a result of African and Middle Eastern contacts?

Interpreting Point of View

Suppose you are interested in seeing a new science fiction movie, but you are hearing mixed reviews from your friends. Opinions range from "terrific" to "boring." People often have different opinions about the same people, events, or issues because they look at them from different points of view.

Learning the Skill

A point of view is a set of beliefs and values that affects a person's opinion. Many factors affect an individual's point of view, including age, sex, racial or ethnic background, economic class, and religion. In order to determine the accuracy of a description or the objectivity of an argument, first you must identify the speaker's point of view.

To interpret point of view in written material, read the material to identify the general subject. Then gather background information on that author that might reveal his or her point of view. Identify aspects of the topic that the author chooses to emphasize or exclude. Look for emotionally charged words such as *cruel, vicious, heartrending, drastic*. Also notice metaphors and analogies that imply an opinion such as, "If this budget can work, then pigs can fly."

If you are uncertain of an author's point of view, read a selection on the same topic by another author with a different background. By comparing works on the same subject, both points of view may become clear. This may not always be an easy task.

Practicing the Skill

Read the following excerpt from Ross E. Dunn's book *The Adventures of Ibn Battuta* and then answer these questions.

1. What is the general subject of the excerpt?
2. What do you know about Ibn Battuta that might reveal his point of view?
3. What emotionally charged words and phrases indicate his point of view?
4. Which aspects of Islamic leadership are praised and which are not?

&& Sulayman came close to matching his brother's [Mansa Musa's] reputation for Islamic leadership and piety. Moreover, he ruled Mali in prosperity and peace. He was the sort of king from whom Ibn Battuta had come to expect an honorable and large-hearted reception. . . . Later, when Ibn Battuta had returned to his house, one of the scholars called to tell him that the sultan [Sulayman] had sent along the requisite welcoming gift.

'I got up, thinking that it would be robes of honor and money, but behold! It was three loaves of bread and a piece of beef fried in *gharti* [shea butter] and a gourd containing yoghurt. When I saw it I laughed, and was long astonished at their feeble intellect and their respect for mean things.' &&

According to Dunn, Ibn Battuta found Sulayman to be "a miserly king from whom no great donation is to be expected," while Mansa Musa had been "generous and virtuous."

Applying the Skill

In a newspaper, find an editorial, column, or a letter to the editor that expresses a point of view that conflicts with your own. Write a brief paragraph analyzing the author's point of view and compare it to your point of view. Explain why you agree or disagree with the viewpoint of the author.

The Columbus Dispatch

An Independent Newspaper Serving Ohio Since July 1, 1871.

JOHN F. WOLFE, Publisher, President and CEO
MICHAEL F. CURTIN, Editor

EDITORIALS

Ballot issue
Workers' comp to steal thunder from schools

For More Practice

Turn to the Skill Practice in the Chapter Review on page 199 for more practice in interpreting point of view.

Connections Across Time

Historical Significance Throughout the early history of Africa, civilizations developed religious beliefs, agriculture, and trade networks in harmony with their environment. Some African peoples mined gold, iron, and other minerals from the land and then turned the raw ores into trade items. Others grew surplus crops to sell at local markets.

Trade networks brought Africa, Europe, the Middle East, South Asia, and East Asia into contact with each other and encouraged the exchange of ideas and practices. This set the stage for the later development of global trading links.

Using Key Terms

Write the key term that completes each sentence. Then write a sentence for each term not chosen.

a. multicultural
b. matrilineal
c. plateau
d. savanna
e. ghana

f. oral traditions
g. monopoly
h. age sets
i. monotheism
j. mosque

1. Africa south of the Sahara includes a large central _____—a relatively high, flat area called the Sahel.
2. Early African peoples communicated knowledge about their culture through _____ —legends and history passed by word of mouth from one generation to another.
3. Much of Africa's landscape is covered by ____, or treeless grasslands.
4. The city-state of Kilwa had a near _____, or sole control, of the gold trade along the East African coast.
5. A society is said to be _____ when it has people of many different cultural backgrounds.

Technology Activity

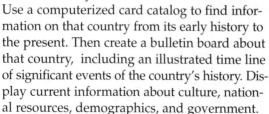

Using a Computerized Card Catalog Choose a modern-day African country to research.
Use a computerized card catalog to find information on that country from its early history to the present. Then create a bulletin board about that country, including an illustrated time line of significant events of the country's history. Display current information about culture, national resources, demographics, and government.

Using Your History Journal

On your map of Africa draw in the modern states where each ancient kingdom that you identified was located. Use the map of Africa in the Atlas of your text.

Reviewing the Facts

1. **Geography** List the five major regions of Africa.
2. **History** Discuss how archaeologists and historians have learned about early Africa.
3. **Culture** Identify the Nok people, their location, and their major cultural achievements.
4. **Economics** Explain Ghana's wealth.
5. **History** Summarize the major accomplishments of Mansa Musa in Mali.
6. **Culture** Name the city that became a major center of trade and learning in Mali.
7. **Government** Explain how Askia Muhammad kept order and control over his huge empire.
8. **Economics** List the products traded in the coastal city-states of East Africa.
9. **Culture** State how the language of Swahili originated.
10. **Geography** Name the three areas of Africa that prospered from the Indian Ocean trade.
11. **Culture** Identify Great Zimbabwe and discuss its importance to Karanga.

Critical Thinking

1. **Apply** How do climate and geography affect the development of a civilization?

2. **Evaluate** The Bantu languages changed as people moved into central, eastern, and southern regions of Africa. Why do you think this happened?

3. **Making Comparisons** Compare the causes for the decline of each of the three West African kingdoms.

4. **Synthesize** Discuss how family and social life in a typical Bantu-speaking village was organized around A.D. 1000.

5. **Analyze** What two cultural values does this artifact of a West African horn player reveal?

*Horn player,
Benin*

Understanding Themes

1. **Movement** How did population movements affect the development of early Africa?

2. **Cultural Diffusion** What were major political and cultural developments in each of the following early African territories: Nubia, Axum, Songhai, Kilwa, and Karanga?

3. **Innovation** What two examples can you give that illustrate how the peoples of coastal East Africa and of the interior of Central Africa and Southern Africa made creative use of their resources?

Linking Past and Present

1. Gold helped make Ghana a powerful empire. Name another natural resource that has made African countries wealthy today.

2. Ancient peoples adapted to their environments in order to survive. Explain ways we adapt today.

3. How do strong central governments affect a nation's economic and social structures? What factors often lead to a weakening of central governments?

Skill Practice

Read the following African proverbs carefully. Then answer the questions for each proverb.

- Familiarity breeds contempt; distance breeds respect.
- When you follow in the path of your father, you learn to walk like him.

1. What is the general subject of each proverb?

2. Describe the point of view expressed in each proverb.

3. Do you agree with the point of view? Make sure you are able to support your answer.

Geography in History

1. How does the continent of Africa compare with the United States in land area?

2. Refer to the map below. Why has communication and travel always been difficult between the northwest African interior and northeast Africa?

3. Why has Egypt had nearly continual contact with peoples of Asia and Europe?

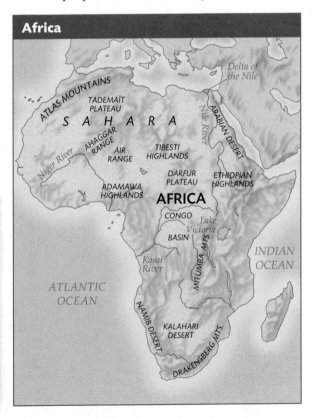

Africa

India's Great Civilization

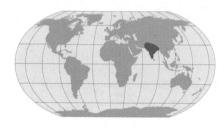

Chapter Themes

▶ **Movement** Aryans invade the Indian subcontinent and bring new ideas and practices. *Section 1*

▶ **Innovation** Hinduism and Buddhism emerge and become the dominant religions in much of Asia. *Section 2*

▶ **Cultural Diffusion** Mauryan and Gupta rulers bring unity to northern India and encourage cultural achievements. *Section 3*

The Storyteller

The Mahabharata, *an epic poem of ancient India, relates an amazing event. A battle raged, but the prince Arjuna did not want to fight. After all, among his foes were relatives. Arjuna took his case to the god Krishna: "O Krishna, when I see my own people … eager for battle, my limbs shudder, my mouth is dry, my body shivers, and my hair stands on end…. I can see no good in killing my own kinsmen."*

Krishna answered, "As a [warrior], your duty is to fight a righteous battle…. Arise, O Arjuna, and be determined to fight. Get ready for battle without thought of pleasure and pain, gain and loss, victory and defeat."

As a warrior, Arjuna understood Krishna's words. A warrior must fight. It was his duty.

Historical Significance

What were the achievements of India's early civilization? What religions emerged from early India that have shaped the cultures of Asia and, in many ways, the rest of the world?

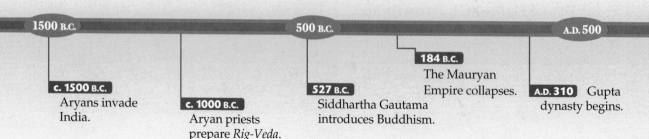

1500 B.C.	**500 B.C.**		**A.D. 500**

c. 1500 B.C. Aryans invade India.

c. 1000 B.C. Aryan priests prepare *Rig-Veda*.

527 B.C. Siddhartha Gautama introduces Buddhism.

184 B.C. The Mauryan Empire collapses.

A.D. 310 Gupta dynasty begins.

Visualizing History Hindus communicated their beliefs through poems, tales, songs, and art. This painting of Vishnu on a bird honors one of the three main gods of Hinduism.

Your History Journal

Using a recent edition of an almanac, make a chart of the world's major religions, including the number of people who today are adherents of each religion.

Section 1

Origins of Hindu India

Setting the Scene

▶ **Terms to Define**
   rajah, epic, *varna*, *jati*, dharma, reincarnation, karma, ahimsa

▶ **People to Meet**
   the Aryans

▶ **Places to Locate**
   Hindu Kush, Ganges Plain

 **ind Out** How did the cultures of the Aryans and the peoples they conquered develop into the culture of Hindu India?

The Storyteller

The bleeding warrior lay helpless with a broken arm. Only proper words and medicines could save him now. The priest, sprinkling him with water and herbs chanted: "He who drinks you, medicine, lives. Save the man. You are mender of wounds inflicted by club, arrow, or flame. Mend this man. O most beautiful one, go to the fracture." Next would come the grass and termite mud mixture to drink, then water in a cow's horn, and

pepper-corns to eat. The warrior breathed quietly, thankful that he had found a healer who knew the ritual.

—adapted from *Religious Healing in the Veda*, Kenneth Zysk, 1985

Hindu Kush

I nto the Indus River valley raced horse-drawn chariots carrying tall, light-skinned warriors. These warriors, known as **the Aryans**, were an Indo-European group from areas north of the Black and Caspian Seas. The invasion began around 1500 B.C. For several generations, waves of Aryans swept through passes in the mountains known as the **Hindu Kush** into the Indus River valley and from there into northern India.

Aryans

After conquering the people of the Indus River valley, the Aryans moved southeast into the **Ganges Plain**. There they subdued the local inhabitants and developed a new civilization that eventually spread over much of South Asia. Aspects of this civilization endure today.

Ways of Life

The Aryans were loosely organized into tribes of nomadic herders. Each tribe was led by a rajah, or chief. Ancient Aryan legends and hymns describe people who delighted in waging war, gambling on chariot races, and singing and dancing at festivals. Cattle were the basis of their diet and economy, even serving as money. Wealth was measured in cattle, and so the Aryans raided each other's herds. They were often at war.

The fertile Indus Valley was ideal for farming, and the Aryans soon settled down into an agricultural way of life. Dozens of Aryan words describe cattle, indicating their continued prominence in Aryan life. Cattle provided meat, fresh milk, and ghee, or liquid butter. The Aryans also hunted game and butchered sheep and goats from their herds. Later, their herds would be considered so sacred that a ban was placed on eating meat. The

Aryans also ate cucumbers, bananas, and barley cakes.

Men dominated the Aryan world. Although a woman had some say in choosing a husband, the man she married expected no challenge to his authority. Even so, women took part in religious ceremonies and social affairs, and they were allowed to remarry if they were widowed—freedoms they would lose in the centuries to come. Both girls and boys from families of high rank attended school, where they learned Aryan traditions.

Language and Traditions

As a nomadic people, the Aryans had no written language. Sanskrit, their spoken language, evolved slowly and became one of the major languages of India. As part of the great Indo-European language family, Sanskrit has many of the same root words as English, Spanish, French, and German. It also includes many words from the languages of the peoples living in India before the Aryan invasions.

The Aryan warrior-herders sang rousing hymns and recited epics, long poems celebrating their heroes. For centuries these hymns and poems were passed by word of mouth from generation to generation. Families of warriors and priests were responsible for preserving this oral heritage. Over and over they repeated the legends, striving for complete accuracy.

Eventually, the Aryans developed a written form of Sanskrit. Priests collected the hymns, poems, legends, and religious rituals into holy books known as Vedas (VAY•duhz), or "Books of Knowledge," which formed the basis of Aryan religious practices.

Indeed, the Vedas are extremely valuable sources of knowledge, for without them historians would know little about the Aryans. Unlike the Indus River valley people, the Aryans left no artifacts or structures. Whatever we know of their life and culture we know from the Vedas. Indeed, Indian history from 1200 B.C. to 500 B.C. is known as the Vedic Age. The oldest of the four Vedas, the *Rig-Veda*, dates from around 1000 B.C. It records legends that tell us about Aryan life. The *Rig-Veda* is one of the world's oldest religious texts still in use.

Social Structure

The Vedas reveal the complex social system of ancient India. The invading Aryans brought a system of four main social classes, or *varnas*. At first the warriors, called Kshatriyas (KSHA•tree•uhz), were the most honored *varna*. They were followed by the priests, or Brahmans; merchants, artisans, and farmers, called Vaisyas (VYSH•yuhz); and

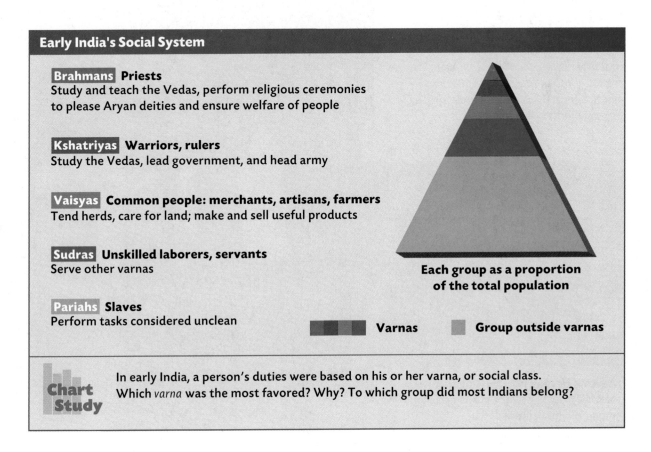

Early India's Social System

Brahmans Priests
Study and teach the Vedas, perform religious ceremonies to please Aryan deities and ensure welfare of people

Kshatriyas Warriors, rulers
Study the Vedas, lead government, and head army

Vaisyas Common people: merchants, artisans, farmers
Tend herds, care for land; make and sell useful products

Sudras Unskilled laborers, servants
Serve other varnas

Pariahs Slaves
Perform tasks considered unclean

Each group as a proportion of the total population

■ Varnas   ■ Group outside varnas

Chart Study In early India, a person's duties were based on his or her varna, or social class. Which *varna* was the most favored? Why? To which group did most Indians belong?

unskilled laborers and servants, known as Sudras (SHOO•druhz).

Only priests and warrior families were allowed to hear and recite the Vedas. Over the years, rituals grew more secret and complex, and priests replaced warriors as the most honored members of society. The priests alone knew how to make sacrifices properly and to repeat the appropriate hymns. The social system changed to reflect the importance of priests.

Each *varna* had its own duties and took pride in doing them well. The Brahmans performed the elaborate rituals and studied the Vedas; only they could teach the Vedas. As warriors, Kshatriyas took charge of the army and the government. They led the councils of elders who ran small villages. Kshatriyas could study the Vedas but were not allowed to teach them. Vaisyas had the important tasks of tending the cattle, lending money, trading goods, and caring for the land. The Sudras' job was to serve the other varnas. They worked in the fields and acted as servants.

By 500 B.C. the division among the four *varnas* had become more rigid. Varnas were divided into smaller groups known as *jati*. *Jati* were formed according to occupations: shoemakers, potters, farmers, and so on. Priests were higher than cultivators, and cultivators were higher than carpenters, for example. *Jati* had their own rules for diet, marriage, and social customs. Groups lived in separate neighborhoods and did not mix socially with others.

Centuries later, Europeans named the Indian system of *varnas* and *jati* the caste system. The word *caste* has no one definition, but how it worked is clear. Within the system people were always ranked. They were born into a group, and that group could not be changed. People married within their own group. Moreover, that group determined a great deal about people's everyday lives. Members of the group lived in the same neighborhoods and did not mix socially with those outside.

Outside the system of *varnas* and *jati* were a group later called the pariahs. They did work that

Images of the Times

Hindu Beliefs

The three main gods of Hinduism are Brahma, Vishnu, and Siva. Brahma is creator of the world, Vishnu is preserver, and Siva is destroyer. These three are part of the same universal spirit.

Meeting to read holy writings such as the *Mahabharata* is a long-standing custom among Hindus in India.

was considered unclean, such as skinning animals and tanning their hides for leather. Sometimes called "outcastes" or "untouchables," the pariahs lived outside the villages and were shunned by most other people.

Concept of Duty

The Vedas outlined the dharma, or duties, of the males who belonged to each *varna*. Members of each *varna* were urged to do their duty. The epic poem called the *Mahabharata* (muh•HAH•BAH•ruh•tuh) makes the concept clear. One eloquent section, called the *Bhagavad Gita* (BAH•guh•VAHD GEE•tuh), or "Song of the Lord," includes the story you read at the beginning of this chapter. Arjuna's decision—to fight no matter what the personal cost—illustrates the importance of dharma in Indian life. As a warrior, Arjuna had to do his duty, even if it meant fighting against family.

The concept of dharma included doing what was proper for one's age. For instance, a male student would follow an occupation that was appropriate for his class. He then took a wife, and assumed responsibility for a family. In old age, he retired. As he neared death, he withdrew from his friends and family to pray. A woman was educated in household tasks. She married and served her husband and family until he died or retired, at which time she was expected to retire from active life and be taken care of by her sons and daughters-in-law. This concept of duty affected every member of society.

India's Two Epics

Two epics addressed the concepts of good and evil and became the spiritual forebears of India's main religions. The tale of Arjuna is a small part of the *Mahabharata*, which is 100,000 verses in length—as long as the first five books of the Bible. The epic—like the Bible—is a collection of writings by several authors. Some characters are historical, while others represent human ideals and various deities. Woven into the story of two families' struggle for power are discussions of religion and philosophy.

Much of India's fine art is related to its religions. Hindus built elaborate temples, such as this Mehsana Sun Temple (interior shown).

This sculpture of Ganesha, god of good fortune and auspicious beginnings, was done in the A.D. 1700s.

REFLECTING ON THE TIMES

1. How did Hinduism contribute to the development of fine art in India?
2. What epic describes the concept of duty that affects every member of Hindu society?

205

One passage tells of how the need for a king arose when dharma no longer guided people in everyday life:

> 66 Bhishma said: … Neither kingship nor king was there in the beginning, neither scepter nor the bearer of the scepter. All people protected one another by means of righteous conduct (dharma). Thus, while protecting one another by means of righteous conduct, O Bharata, men eventually fell into a state of spiritual lassitude [weariness]. Then delusion overcame them … their sense of righteous conduct was lost. When understanding was lost, all men … became victims of greed. 99

Later, the God Vishnu chooses "… that one person among mortals who alone is worthy of high eminence." A man named Virajas is brought forth, and he becomes the first king.

A second epic, the well-loved *Ramayana*, grew to 24,000 verses before it was written down. It presents the moving tale of Rama and Sita (SEE•tuh). Rama was the ideal king; Sita, his faithful wife. Vividly describing the struggle between good and evil, the *Ramayana* tells how the demon Ravana captures Sita. When Rama finds that she is missing, he cries:

> 66 Sita! Gentle Sita! If you have wanted to prove my love, if you are hiding from us, let the agony of my fear suffice. Come to me, my love, come to me!"
>
> He stood there, both his arms held wide, as though half hoping she might run forward to his embrace. The country lay very still around him. Only the old tree shivered in every leafy spray and seemed to wring its hands for pity.
>
> Slowly that gleam of hope quite faded, and his arms fell to his sides. 99

Rama at first doubts Sita; but later she is saved, and they reunite. Like other Indian epics, the *Ramayana* ends with good winning over evil.

Hinduism

The Aryan conquerors believed in many deities and thought their gods and goddesses had power over the forces of nature. They worshiped Agni, the god of fire; Indra, the god of thunder and war; and Usha, the goddess of dawn. Aryan priests created

elaborate rituals and offered sacrifices to appease the gods and win their favor.

Over the centuries, as political and social organizations evolved, the Aryan religion slowly changed into Hinduism and became the national religion of India.

Universal Spirit

Hinduism was not founded on the teachings of one person, nor did it have one holy book. Instead it was based on different beliefs and practices, many of which had their roots in the Vedas and the Indian epics. As a result, Hinduism became a complex religion of many deities. Three gods, however, eventually emerged as the most important: Brahma, the Creator; Vishnu, the Preserver; and Siva, the Destroyer.

Other ideas that became part of Hinduism came from religious thinkers who looked for a single religious truth behind the many Hindu deities and rituals. Between 800 B.C. and 400 B.C., their personal searches and philosophies were reflected in the religious writings known as the *Upanishads* (oo•PAH•nih•SHAHDZ).

The *Upanishads* tell of a universal spirit present within all life, "a light that shines beyond all things on earth." According to these writings, all living things—including gods, humans, and animals—have souls. All souls, say the *Upanishads*, are part of the one eternal spirit, sometimes called Brahman Nerguna. Their bodies tie them to the material world, but only for a short time. To know true freedom, a soul must be separated from the material world and united with Brahman Nerguna: "As a lump of salt thrown in water dissolves, and cannot be taken out again as salt, though wherever we taste the water it is salt."

The authors of the *Upanishads* taught that forms of self-denial such as fasting helped people achieve union with the universal spirit. They encouraged the practice of yoga, a discipline that combines physical and mental exercises designed to help one achieve a state of tranquility.

Cycle of Rebirth

Another idea that came from the *Upanishads* was that of reincarnation, or the rebirth of the soul. Hindus believe the soul passes through many lifetimes before it finally achieves union with the universal spirit. The *Upanishads* offer this picture of rebirth:

> 66 As a caterpillar, having reached the end of a blade of grass, takes hold of another blade, then draws its body from the first,

so the Self, having reached the end of his body, takes hold of another body, then draws itself from the first. **99**

The cycle of rebirth is determined by a principle called karma. According to this principle, how a person lives his or her life determines what form the person will take in the next life. To move toward the universal spirit, one must live a good life and fulfill one's dharma. For example, a conscientious diplomat, a Kshatriya, might be reborn as a Brahman. The souls of those who fail to fulfill their dharma, however, might be reborn in a lower *varna*, or perhaps even as snakes or insects.

The concept of karma creates the desire to live a good life, for "By good deeds a man becomes what is good, by evil deeds what is bad." Out of that desire arose the practice of nonviolence toward all living things—still important to Hindus today. Called ahimsa (uh•HIHM•SAH), this practice requires the believer to protect humans, animals, and even insects and plants.

The cycle of reincarnation continues until a person reaches spiritual perfection. The ultimate aim of life is *moksha*, or release from the pain and suffering of rebirth after rebirth. In *moksha* a person finds freedom from reincarnation in a state of complete oneness with Brahman Nerguna. Hindus teach that a life committed to prayer, religious rituals, strict self-denial, and rejection of all worldly possessions will help a person to achieve the final goal of *moksha*.

Jainism

As Hinduism evolved, many holy people stressed different aspects of Hindu belief and practice. The teacher Mahavira (muh•hah•VEE•ruh) placed a special emphasis on the practice of ahimsa. Born a noble in northern India, Mahavira gave up his wealthy lifestyle and traveled for many years throughout the country. About 500 B.C. Mahavira founded Jainism, a new religion that rejected sacrifices and rigid Hindu social divisions. Believing in

History & Art Siva, ringed by a circle of flames, dances on the back of the dwarf Apasmara. *Why do Hindus regard animals as sacred?*

the sacredness of all life, the Jains, as Mahavira's followers were called, used brooms to sweep aside insects so they would not step on them. They refused to farm for fear of plowing under living things. Instead, they turned to commerce and gained great wealth and influence.

SECTION I REVIEW

Recall
1. **Define** rajah, epic, *varna, jati*, dharma, reincarnation, karma, ahimsa.
2. **Identify** the Aryans, Sanskrit, Vedas, *Mahabharata, Bhagavad Gita, Ramayana*, Hinduism,

Upanishads.
3. **Explain** how geography affected the life of the Aryan groups that invaded India.

Critical Thinking
4. **Applying Information** Illustrate the Hindu concept of

dharma by telling the story of the warrior-prince Arjuna.

Understanding Themes
5. **Movement** How did the Aryan invasion beginning about 1500 B.C. affect the development of Indian culture?

600 B.C.	550 B.C.	500 B.C.

c. 566 B.C.
Siddhartha
Gautama is born.

c. 540 B.C.
Gautama begins
spiritual search.

c. 500 B.C. Gautama
(the Buddha) dies.

Section 2

Rise of Buddhism

Setting the Scene

▶ **Terms to Define**
  nirvana, stupa

▶ **People to Meet**
  Siddhartha Gautama

Find Out Why did Buddhism appeal to many people in India, Southeast Asia, and East Asia?

The Storyteller

Siddhartha stood still, as if a snake lay in his path. Suddenly the icy thought stole over him: he must begin his life completely afresh. "I am no longer what I was, … I am no longer a hermit, no longer a priest, no longer a Brahmin. How can I return home? What would I do at home with my father? Study? Offer sacrifices? Practice meditation? All this is over for me now." He realized how alone he was. Now he was Siddhartha, the awakened. He must begin his life afresh. He began to walk quickly, no longer homewards, no longer looking back.

—from *Siddhartha,* Herman Hesse, translated by Hilda Rosner, 1957

Gautama, the Buddha

During the 500s B.C., changes occurred in Indian religious life. Many devout Hindus became dissatisfied with external rituals and wanted a more spiritual faith. They left the towns and villages and looked for solitude in the hills and forests. Through meditation, many of these religious seekers developed new insights and became religious teachers. Their ideas and practices often led to the rise of new religions. The most influential of the new religions was Buddhism.

The Buddha

Siddhartha Gautama (sih•DAHR•tuh GOW•tuh•muh), the founder of Buddhism, began his life as a Kshatriya prince. Born around 566 B.C., Gautama was raised in luxury. As a young man he continued to live a sheltered life, shielded from sickness and poverty. Tradition states that one day Gautama's charioteer drove him around his estates, and for the first time Gautama saw sickness, old age, and death. Shocked at these scenes of misery, Gautama decided to find out why people suffered and how suffering could be ended. Around the age of 29, he left his wife and newborn son and wandered throughout India.

For seven years Gautama lived as a hermit, seeking the truth through fasting and self-denial. This did not lead him to the truth, however. One day, while meditating under a tree, Gautama gained a flash of insight that he felt gave him an answer to the problem of suffering. He began to share with others the meaning of his "enlightenment." Dressed in a yellow robe, he preached his message to people and began to gather followers. His closest friends began calling him the Buddha, or "Enlightened One."

Rajesh Bedi

The Buddha's First Sermon

From this stupa, or domed shrine, in Isipatana, a village in northern India, the Buddha is said to have delivered his first sermon. Once a small village, Isipatana is now Sarnath, a suburb of the city of Varanasi. Here, Buddhists believe, in the 500s B.C. the Buddha delivered his first sermon to five followers. A large monastery, which once housed 1,500 monks, was founded on this sacred spot. Today the shrine stands empty.

The Buddha began India's second religion, after the far older Hindu religion had become entrenched. He lived in a unique moment of history. The 500s B.C. gave birth not only to Buddhism in India but also to Confucianism in China and to new rationalist philosophies in Greece. Buddhism became one of the world's major religions and the Buddha one of the most notable spiritual leaders in the history of the world. ⊕

Four Noble Truths

The Buddha developed a new religious philosophy. He outlined his main ideas in the Four Noble Truths. First, as he had discovered, all people suffer and know sorrow. Next, said the Buddha, people suffer because their desires bind them to the cycle of rebirth. He told his followers:

“ The thirst for existence leads from rebirth to rebirth; lust and pleasure follow. Power alone can satisfy lust. The thirst for power, the thirst for pleasure, the thirst for existence; there, O monks, is the origin of suffering. ”

The third truth, said the Buddha, was that people could end their suffering by eliminating their desires. And according to the fourth truth, one could eliminate desire by following the Eightfold Path.

The Eightfold Path

The Buddha urged his disciples to do eight things: know the truth, resist evil, say nothing to hurt others, respect life, work for the good of others, free their minds of evil, control their thoughts, and practice meditation. By avoiding extremes and following the Eightfold Path, a person could attain nirvana, a state of freedom from the cycle of rebirth. Nirvana is not a place, like heaven, but a state of extinction. In fact, the root meaning of the word *nirvana* is a "blowing out," as of a candle. In nirvana, a person would be in a state of oneness with the universe.

The Buddha rejected the *varna* system. He taught that a person's place in life depended on the person, not on the person's birth. He taught that anyone, regardless of caste, could attain enlightenment. He did not believe in the Hindu deities. He believed in reincarnation but taught that one could escape the cycle of suffering and reach nirvana by following the Eightfold Path.

POINT

Spread of Buddhism

The Buddha spent 40 years teaching the Four Noble Truths and the Eightfold Path. He gathered thousands of disciples around him. After their master's death, traveling monks carried the new religion beyond India to other parts of Asia, especially to China, Japan, Korea, and the Middle East.

Architecture and the Arts

The rise of Buddhism led to a flowering of architecture and the arts. Buddhist architects built stupas, or large stone mounds, over the bones of Buddhist holy people. Stupas were known for their elaborately carved stone gateways. Paintings and statues of the Buddha, carved of polished stone or wood covered with gilt, adorned stupas and cave temples. Exquisite smaller statues were made from fine porcelain. Books about the Buddha's life and teachings were often beautifully illustrated.

Divisions

As Buddhism spread, disagreements developed among the Buddha's followers. Two distinct branches of Buddhism soon arose. One branch, known as Theravada, was established in South Asia and Southeast Asia. It remained fairly close in practice to the original teachings of the Buddha, regarding him as simply a teacher.

The other branch of Buddhism was known as Mahayana. It became dominant in China, Korea, and Japan. Mahayana encouraged the worship of the Buddha as a divine being and savior.

Today, only a few Indians are Buddhists. Most are Hindus. Muslims, Jains, Christians, and others make up the rest of the population. Recently, however, Buddhism has gained new followers in India, as well as in the West. ▬

SECTION 2 REVIEW

Recall
1. **Define** nirvana, stupa.
2. **Identify** Siddhartha Gautama, Four Noble Truths.
3. **Locate** on a map in the Atlas the Asian countries to which monks and merchants carried the teachings of the Buddha: China, Japan, Korea, Myanmar, Malaysia, Indonesia. How did monks and merchants help to assure the survival of Buddhism as a worldwide religion?

Critical Thinking
4. **Synthesizing Information** Compare the religions of Hinduism and Buddhism, explaining which Hindu beliefs and practices the Buddha accepted and which he rejected in his teaching.

Understanding Themes
5. **Innovation** Decide how your own life and goals would be different if you tried to live by the Four Noble Truths and the Eightfold Path.

Section 3

Indian Empires

Setting the Scene

▶ **Terms to Define**
"Arabic numerals"

▶ **People to Meet**
Chandragupta Maurya, Asoka, Chandragupta I, Chandragupta II

▶ **Places to Locate**
Magadha

Find Out ▶ What were the cultural achievements of the Mauryan and Gupta Empires?

The Storyteller

It troubled King Asoka that criminals continued their wrongdoing within his empire. Therefore he was proud of his latest merciful decree, carved on stone monuments: "Thus speaks the Beloved of the Gods.... This is my instruction from now on: Men who are imprisoned or sentenced to death are to be given three days respite. Thus their relations [relatives] may plead for their lives, or, if there is no one to plead for them, they may make their donations or undertake a fast for a better rebirth in the next life. For it is my wish that they should gain the next world."

—from *Asoka and the Decline of the Mauryas*, Romila Thapar, 1961

Lion-headed capital atop a Rock Edict pillar of Asoka

Despite the high mountain barriers in the north, India has never been completely cut off from other lands. The Aryans marched through the mountain passes to invade the Indus River valley; later, others followed. In the 500s B.C., Persian ruler Darius I conquered lands in the Indus River valley. Alexander the Great invaded the same area in 327 B.C., and Indian merchants carried on a busy trade with the Roman Empire. In all that time, however, no Indian king or foreign conqueror had ever succeeded in uniting the separate kingdoms into one Indian nation.

At the time of Darius's invasion, one Indian kingdom, **Magadha**, was expanding in the north. King Bimbisara, who ruled Magadha from 542 B.C. to 495 B.C., added to its territory by conquest and marriage. Although Magadha declined after Bimbisara's death, it was to become the center of India's first empire.

The Mauryan Empire

At the time of Alexander's invasion, Magadha was only one of many small warring states in northern India. Then, in 321 B.C., a military officer named **Chandragupta Maurya** (CHUHN•druh•GUP•tuh MAH•oor•yuh) overthrew the Magadhan king and proclaimed himself ruler.

Chandragupta Maurya was a skilled administrator whose achievements included the development of an efficient postal system. He kept control of his empire by maintaining a strong army and by using an extensive spy network. He founded a Mauryan kingdom that included most of northern and central India and lasted until 184 B.C.

Asoka's Enlightened Rule

Indian civilization blossomed during the reign of Chandragupta's grandson, **Asoka** (uh•SHOH•kuh). Asoka's rule began in 274 B.C. with fierce wars of conquest. His merciless armies swept

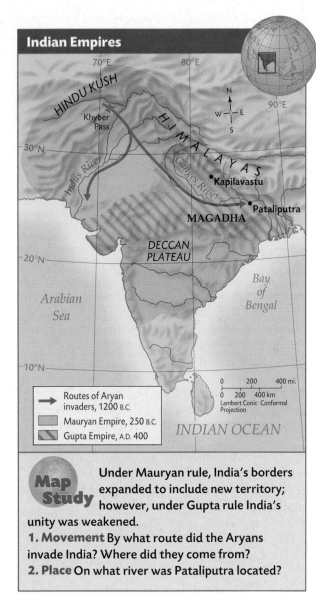

Indian Empires

HINDU KUSH
Khyber Pass
Indus River
HIMALAYAS
Ganges River
•Kapilavastu
•Pataliputra
MAGADHA
DECCAN PLATEAU
Arabian Sea
Bay of Bengal
INDIAN OCEAN

Routes of Aryan invaders, 1200 B.C.
Mauryan Empire, 250 B.C.
Gupta Empire, A.D. 400

0   200   400 mi.
0 200 400 km
Lambert Conic Conformal Projection

Map Study Under Mauryan rule, India's borders expanded to include new territory; however, under Gupta rule India's unity was weakened.
1. Movement By what route did the Aryans invade India? Where did they come from?
2. Place On what river was Pataliputra located?

today as the Rock Edicts, were carved on rocks and on tall stone pillars throughout the vast empire.

Asoka's public projects reflected the same care for people. He provided free hospitals and veterinary clinics. He built fine roads, with rest houses and shade trees for the travelers' comfort.

Although he promoted Buddhism, Asoka permitted his non-Buddhist subjects to continue to practice Hinduism if they wished. The Hindu caste system continued.

Collapse of Mauryan Empire

The Mauryan Empire declined after Asoka's death in 232 B.C. because his successors were not as enlightened as he was. They levied heavy taxes on the goods sold by merchants and seized large portions of the crops grown by peasants. Such harsh policies caused the people to turn against the Mauryas. When the last Mauryan ruler was murdered in 184 B.C., northern India again split into many small warring kingdoms.

The Gupta Empire

After the Mauryan Empire, 500 years passed before much of India was again united. About A.D. 310, **Chandragupta I** began to build an empire. He was not related to Chandragupta Maurya, but like that earlier ruler he made Magadha the base of his kingdom.

Chandragupta I introduced the Gupta dynasty, which ruled northern India for more than 200 years. The arts and sciences flourished, and the Gupta period would later be called India's Golden Age.

The Guptas governed a much smaller empire than the Mauryas. They never gained control of the Indus Valley or of the Deccan, the broad plateau that forms most of India's southern peninsula. The Guptas did manage to build a strong state, however, and worked to maintain unquestioned authority. They trained soldiers and used spies and political assassins. In short, they did whatever they felt had to be done to maintain power.

Gupta Religion

The Gupta rulers encouraged learning based on the ideas found in the *Upanishads*. They made Hinduism the religion of their empire. Hindu temples were built—elaborate structures with brightly painted sculptures depicting tales in the *Mahabharata* and the *Ramayana*. Although each temple had its presiding god or goddess, the Hindus viewed the many deities as different ways of worshiping Brahman Nerguna, the eternal spirit.

across the plains and into the forests and cities, hunting down and killing their enemies. He built an empire that covered two-thirds of the Indian subcontinent.

After one particularly brutal battle, Asoka rode out to view the battlefield. The experience changed his life. As he looked on the bloodied bodies of the dead and maimed, the Indian ruler was horrified. Determined never again to rule by force and terror, Asoka renounced war. Henceforth, he announced, he would follow the teachings of the Buddha and become a man of peace. Asoka kept his word. During his reign, missionaries spread Buddhism throughout India and other parts of Asia.

Asoka issued laws stressing concern for other human beings. To make sure these laws became widely known, Asoka wrote them in the local languages rather than in Sanskrit. The laws, known

Indian Music

Like the other arts of India, Indian music has a long and rich history. It began in Hindu temples and the courts of Indian rulers centuries ago. Traditionally, Indian musicians play instruments and sing without using chords or other harmonies. A group of musicians starts out with a basic melody called a

Ravi Shankar

raga, which each player then develops with his or her own spontaneous arrangements. The musicians perform on a number of different instruments, including drums, flutes, and a stringed instrument known as a sitar. Their performances often go on for several hours at a time.

Probably the best-known modern Indian musician is Ravi Shankar, often called India's "sitar king" and the "godfather of world music." Shankar, almost as well known in the West as in India, has brought an appreciation of Indian music to Western audiences. He has worked with George Harrison of the Beatles and other musicians, such as violinist Yehudi Menuhin, flutist Jean-Pierre Rampal, and composer Philip Glass.

Linking Past and Present   ACTIVITY

Discuss the origins of Indian music and its major characteristics. What contribution has Ravi Shankar made to world music?

Gupta Life

The Gupta Empire reached its height under **Chandragupta II**, who ruled from A.D. 375 to A.D. 415. Faxian (FAH•SYEN), a Buddhist monk from China, traveled to India and recorded in his diary:

❝ In the Gupta Empire, people are numerous and happy; only those who cultivate the royal land have to pay [in] grain.… If they want to go, they go; if they want to stay, they stay. The king governs without decapitation [cutting off heads] or corporal [bodily] punishment.… The leaders of Vaisya families have houses in the cities for dispensing charity and medicine. ❞

Faxian may have exaggerated the benefits of Gupta rule, but he provided a useful glimpse into Indian life. By easing tax burdens, Chandragupta II gave people more freedom. Of all the Gupta monarchs, he was the most chivalrous and heroic. Though he expanded the empire, he is remembered for more than conquest. Gupta rulers believed they had reached a high level of civilization. They began to write down rules for everything, from grammar to drama to politics. The Sanskrit of the Gupta court became the major language in the north.

In one respect, though, daily life did not improve during the Gupta period. The status of Indian women had declined since Aryan times. Aryan women at first often had a say about whom they would marry. By Gupta times, parents were choosing mates for their children, and child marriages were common. Women and mothers were

Footnotes to History

Highway Rest Stops
Asoka's highway rest stops were marked by stone pillars engraved with Buddhist teachings. On one of these pillars, Asoka explained:

I have ordered banyan trees to be planted along the roads to give shade to men and animals. I have ordered mango groves to be planted. I have ordered wells to be dug every [half-mile], and I have ordered rest houses built.

—The Edicts of Asoka

Buddhist monks carved this 24-foot-long reclining Buddha on the wall of the Chai-tya-griha cave in the first century B.C. *What do the Ajanta carvings reveal about life in Gupta India?*

advances in developing the principles of algebra. They also explained the concept of infinity and invented the concept of zero. The symbols they devised for the numbers 1 to 9 were adopted by traders from the Middle East and so came to be called "Arabic numerals" in the West.

Gupta astronomers used these mathematical discoveries to advance their understanding of the universe. They realized that the earth is round, and they had some knowledge of gravity. In medicine, Gupta doctors set bones, performed operations, and invented hundreds of medical instruments.

Many countries benefited from Gupta achievements, as both ideas and products traveled the land and sea trade routes that connected India to the rest of the world. Indian exporters traded such items as gems, spices, cotton, teak, and ebony for horses from Arabia and central Asia, silk from China, and gold from Rome.

highly respected, but they had little power or independence.

Gupta Achievements

Learning flourished under the Guptas. The court welcomed poets, playwrights, philosophers, and scientists. Much of the writing was concentrated on religion, but folktales were also popular. A collection of tales called the *Panchatantra* presented moral lessons through animals who acted like humans. Many of these stories eventually spread to the Middle East and the West, where they were retold by other authors. Drama was also important during Gupta times. Kalidasa, the most famous playwright, wrote *Shakuntala*, a play about romantic love between a king and a forest maiden.

Gupta mathematicians contributed significantly to mathematics as it is today, making major

The Golden Age Ends

After Chandragupta II's death in A.D. 415, the Gupta Empire began to fail. As the government weakened, the Guptas faced invasions along India's northwestern border. By A.D. 600, the Gupta Empire had dissolved into a collection of small states.

However, much of the culture that was uniquely Indian survived. Many aspects of India's life today grew out of the social structures and religions, the arts and sciences, that were born during the 2,000 years that followed the Aryan invasions.

SECTION 3 REVIEW

Recall
1. **Define** "Arabic numerals."
2. **Identify** Chandragupta Maurya, Asoka, Chandragupta I, Chandragupta II, *Panchatantra*, *Shakuntala*.
3. **Locate** the map on page 212,

and find the Mauryan Empire and the Gupta Empire. Compare and contrast their sizes and features.

Critical Thinking
4. **Analyzing Information** How did the rulers of India's empires

have an effect on the religious life of the Indian people?

Understanding Themes
5. **Cultural Diffusion** What aspects of early Indian empires have had a lasting impact on India and the rest of the world?

Determining Cause and Effect

As you read a mystery novel, you may try to figure out which events or actions caused the main character to act in specific ways. Understanding history is a similar process. We try to find reasons behind people's actions. Looking for cause-effect relationships unlocks the mystery of history.

Learning the Skill

To identify cause-effect relationships in history, first select an event. Then examine the situation before this event. How was it different? Look for related problems and actions. These are likely causes of the event. Suppose you select the following event: Asoka's renunciation of war. What events preceded Asoka's decision? In earlier years, Asoka had led many brutal wars of conquest. Eventually, he was horrified by the bloody results of war. This combination of underlying and specific events caused him to renounce war altogether.

Now examine what happened after Asoka renounced war. He became a Buddhist, promoted Buddhist ideas of compassion, and passed laws based on this philosophy. He also built hospitals and roads and worked to improve conditions for his people. These were direct and indirect effects of Asoka's change of direction.

Certain words and phrases often indicate cause-effect relationships; these include *because, due to, therefore, as a result of, led to, and brought about*. It can be hard to determine causes and effects of historical events. Facts may be missing. Moreover, we can't test our ideas as we can in science experiments. Instead, we must rely on logic and common sense.

Practicing the Skill

Read the paragraph below. Then answer the questions that follow.

“Cattle were the basis of the Aryan diet and economy, even serving as money. Wealth was measured in cattle, and so the Aryans raided each other's herds. They were often at war…. Dozens of Aryan words describe cattle, indicating their continued prominence in Aryan life. Later, their herds would be considered so sacred that a ban was placed on eating meat. **”**

1. What were causes of conflict among Aryans?
2. How did the importance of cattle affect the culture and language of Aryans?

Applying the Skill

Reread Section 2, "Rise of Buddhism." Then describe causes of Buddhism's rise in India and its effects on India and other parts of the world.

For More Practice

Turn to the Skill Practice in the Chapter Review on page 217 for more practice in determining cause and effect.

Buddha with halo, Gupta period

Connections Across Time

Historical Significance The civilization that developed in India between 1500 B.C. and A.D. 500 produced two of the world's great religions: Hinduism and Buddhism. Hinduism became not only India's major faith but also its way of life. Buddhism rejected many Hindu social practices and affirmed a disciplined life to achieve peace and deliverance from suffering. The belief in nonviolence has influenced modern leaders in their struggle for peace and human rights. Over the centuries, the two religions have inspired magnificent achievements in architecture and the arts. Especially since the A.D. 1800s, Hindu and Buddhist ideas and art forms have influenced the West.

Using Key Terms

Write the key term that completes each sentence. Then write a sentence for each term not chosen.

a. ahimsa	f. nirvana
b. dharma	g. rajah
c. epics	h. reincarnation
d. *jati*	i. stupas
e. karma	j. *varnas*

1. The invading Aryans brought to the Indian subcontinent a system of four main social classes, or _____.
2. Hindus believe in _____, a process of rebirth in which the soul resides in many bodies before it finally unites with Brahman Nerguna, or the universal spirit.
3. A person's _____ determines whether he or she will be closer to the universal spirit in the next life.
4. For purposes of prayer, Buddhist architects built large elaborate ____ over the remains of holy people.
5. Each *varna* was made up of social groups called _____ that were defined and ranked by different occupations.

Technology Activity

Using a Word Processor Search the Internet or your local library to locate information about the following religions of India: Buddhism, Hinduism, Jainism, Sikhism, Christianity, and Islam. Use a word processor to organize your research into a fact sheet. Include headings such as religion, number of followers, basic beliefs, and major figures. Illustrate your chart with symbols of the different regions.

Using Your History Journal

Refer to a world almanac to determine how many Buddhists and how many Hindus live in each region of the world today. Build a graph or create a world map that illustrates this information.

Reviewing Facts

1. **History** Identify Chandragupta Maurya and his role in developing early Indian civilization.
2. **Culture** Explain in your own words the Four Noble Truths of Buddhism.
3. **Culture** Define *ahimsa* and describe how it is practiced in Indian society.
4. **Culture** Identify the *Bhagavad Gita*.
5. **Culture** Discuss the concept of dharma and how it affected Indian family life. What were the duties of husbands? Of wives?
6. **Science** List some of the achievements of Indian mathematicians during the Gupta Empire.
7. **History** Describe the achievements of Asoka's reign and their impact on Indian society.

Critical Thinking

1. **Apply** How could a person use the principle of nonviolence, or ahimsa, as a force for social change?
2. **Making Comparisons** In what ways are Buddhism and Christianity different? In what ways are they similar?
3. **Synthesize** What might have happened if Asoka had not been horrified while viewing the carnage after a fierce battle?

4. Analyze Here, two Brahman cattle stand in a street of Mumbai, India. Why do Hindus abstain from eating meat?

Understanding Themes

1. **Movement** How was India affected by the Aryan invasions?
2. **Innovation** What might make Buddhism attractive to people from different cultures?
3. **Cultural Diffusion** Why did Gupta achievements in science and the arts spread quickly to other parts of the world, both Eastern and Western?

Linking Past and Present

1. The *varna* system created a huge underclass that Europeans called "the untouchables." How do you think this system created problems for modern India?
2. Religion has always had a major part in Indian society. How have religious differences hindered Indian unity in modern times?
3. Early in the 1900s, India applied the Hindu principle of nonviolence to help win its independence from Great Britain. Do you think people can still use nonviolence effectively to win freedom and human rights?

Geography in History

1. **Location** What mountain range forms India's northern border?
2. **Movement** What routes did the Aryan invaders take to the interior of India?
3. **Region** What effect did the invasion of the Aryans have on the developing culture of India?
4. **Human/Environment Interaction** What physical features made it difficult for one empire to unify all of northern and southern India?

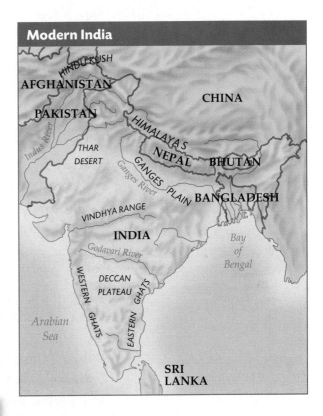

Skill Practice

Reread the discussion of "The Gupta Empire" in Section 3. Then answer the following questions.

1. What caused the Gupta rulers to use spies and assassins?
2. The Guptas adopted Hinduism as India's religion. What effects did this have on art and architecture?
3. What were the effects of Gupta science and mathematics on world civilization?
4. What caused the breakup of the Gupta Empire?

Chapter

9

1100 B.C.–A.D. 200

China's Flourishing Civilization

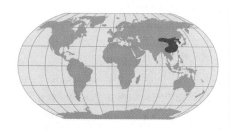

Chapter Themes

▶ **Uniformity** The Qin and Han dynasties establish and maintain a strong central government. *Section 1*

▶ **Innovation** The Chinese formulate ethical philosophies and make scientific and technological advances. *Section 2*

▶ **Cultural Diffusion** Traders carry ideas and products along the Silk Road. *Section 3*

Storyteller

Whom do you agree with in the following conversation, dating from the 500s B.C.? What is right, or "straightness," in this case?

The Governor of She said to Confucius: "In our village there is a man nicknamed Straight Body. When his father stole a sheep, he gave evidence against him." Confucius answered, "In our village those who are straight are quite different. Fathers cover up for their sons, and sons cover up for their fathers...."

This conversation involves a conflict between law and family. Confucius's view—that family should always take precedence—reflects an attitude toward families that was dominant in Chinese culture for a long time.

Historical Significance

How did the ideas of Confucius and other Chinese thinkers affect behavior in Chinese society for centuries? How have their ideas influenced China's development and its relationship with other parts of the world?

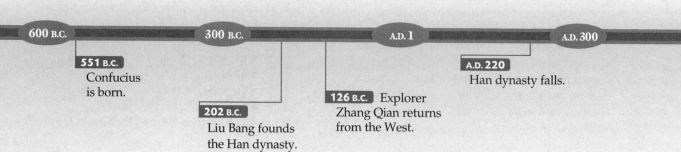

600 B.C.	300 B.C.	A.D. 1	A.D. 300

551 B.C. Confucius is born.

202 B.C. Liu Bang founds the Han dynasty.

126 B.C. Explorer Zhang Qian returns from the West.

A.D. 220 Han dynasty falls.

The Great Wall of China at Huang Ya Guan, a view of a section of the 4,000-mile-long wall

Your History Journal

Chinese inventions and discoveries include many "firsts" such as printed books, the compass, and gunpowder. Choose one Chinese invention or discovery reported in this chapter and write a short research report on its early history.

Section 1

Three Great Dynasties

Setting the Scene

▶ **Terms to Define**
  cavalry, civil service, mandarin

▶ **People to Meet**
  Qin Shihuangdi, Liu Bang, Wudi, Zhang Qian

▶ **Places to Locate**
  Great Wall of China, Silk Road

Find Out ▶ What major advances did China make under the Zhou, Qin, and Han dynasties?

The Storyteller

Seeing the Marquis Chao of Han asleep on the cold floor, the keeper of the royal hat covered him with a robe. Upon awakening, the marquis demanded to know who had covered him. Learning the keeper of the hat was responsible, the marquis punished the keeper of the robe for failing to perform his duty. Then he punished the keeper of the hat for undertaking tasks not his to perform. The trespass of one official upon the duties of another was considered a great danger.

—adapted from Basic Writing of Mo Tzu, Hsün Tzu, and Han Fei Tzu, *reprinted in* The Global Experience: Readings in World History to 1500, *1987*

Late Zhou jade dragon

Around 1100 B.C., the Chinese people were fashioning ideas that would result in a unique civilization. From then until the A.D. 200s, the Chinese lived under three dynasties, or ruling families—the Zhou (JOH), the Qin (CHIN), and the Han (HAHN). The first of these, the Zhou, ruled the nation for more than 800 years, longer than any other Chinese dynasty.

The Enduring Zhou

The Zhou conquered the last Shang dynasty king around 1028 B.C., claiming the Mandate of Heaven, or heaven's approval. They called their king the Son of Heaven, saying that the Shang had lost the mandate by ruling poorly.

Eventually, the Zhou held a vast realm. To control their holdings, Zhou kings set up an agricultural system in which nobles owned the land and peasants worked it. They appointed their relatives to govern, giving each one a city-state.

Each local lord had total authority on his own lands and built his own army. At first all the lords pledged allegiance to the Son of Heaven. In time, though, some grew strong enough to challenge the king's authority.

In 771 B.C. the Zhou suffered a severe defeat in a conflict with their enemies. After that, political power fell increasingly to local nobles. In the next centuries, the nobles fought small wars until by the 200s B.C., several city-states were locked in a struggle that ended the Zhou era.

Even though Zhou rulers lost their power, the Zhou are remembered for many technological advances. During the Zhou period the Chinese built roads and expanded foreign trade. They obtained horses from western nomads, forming a

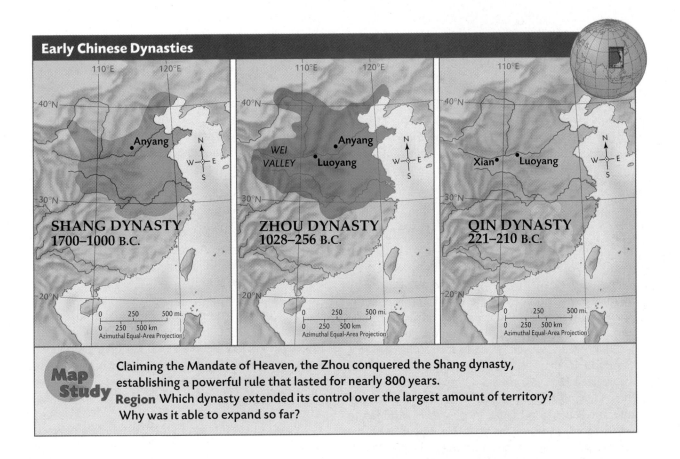

SHANG DYNASTY
1700–1000 B.C.

ZHOU DYNASTY
1028–256 B.C.

QIN DYNASTY
221–210 B.C.

Map Study

Claiming the Mandate of Heaven, the Zhou conquered the Shang dynasty, establishing a powerful rule that lasted for nearly 800 years. **Region** Which dynasty extended its control over the largest amount of territory? Why was it able to expand so far?

cavalry, or group of mounted warriors, along with horse-drawn chariots. The Zhou also added a deadly weapon: the crossbow. They further elaborated the system of picture writing begun by the Shang, a system that is the ancestor of modern Chinese writing. Under the Zhou, iron plows were invented, irrigation systems were developed, and flood-control systems were initiated. These and other advances led to population growth, and Zhou China became the world's most densely populated country.

The Mighty Qin

Meanwhile, several small states were struggling for control in China. Among them was a state on the western border ruled by the Qin. By 221 B.C., the Qin had wiped out the Zhou and conquered the rest of northern China, uniting much of the nation under a strong central authority for the first time. Westerners would later call the nation *China* after the Qin, whose first ruler added the title Shihuangdi (SHUR•HWONG•DEE), or First Emperor, to his name.

A tireless ruler, **Qin Shihuangdi** set out to create a government directly under his control. He reorganized the empire into military districts, appointing officials to govern them. This system prevented local lords from becoming strong enough to challenge the power of the central government—the problem that had led to the downfall of the Zhou.

The First Emperor made other changes to further centralize his control. He devised a system of weights and measures to replace the various systems used in different regions. He standardized coins, instituted a uniform writing system, and set up a law code throughout China.

Qin had grandiose plans for his empire, and he used forced labor to accomplish them. Gangs of Chinese peasants dug canals and built roads.

Footnotes to History

Court Magic

A court magician made a potion for Wudi, claiming that it would give immortality. Before the emperor got the potion, a scholar drank it. The scholar was immediately sentenced to death but told Wudi that, if the potion was genuine, Wudi would not be able to kill him. If the potion was a fake, he had done no harm. Wudi had to agree. Needless to say, the scholar had exposed a fraud.

The Great Wall

To Qin, one building project seemed especially urgent—shoring up China's defenses to the north. Earlier rulers had built walls to prevent attacks by nomadic invaders. Qin ordered those walls connected. Over several years some 300,000 peasants toiled—and thousands died—before the work was done. Eventually the wall stretched more than 4,000 miles (6,437 km). Rebuilt by later rulers, the **Great Wall of China** stands today as a monument to Qin's ambition and to the peasants who carried out their emperor's will.

Qin's Strict Rule

Qin Shihuangdi imposed a new order on China. He ended the power of the local lords by taking land from many of them and imposing a tax on landowners. He appointed educated men instead of nobles as officials to run his government.

Qin even imposed an early form of censorship, clamping down on scholars who discussed books and ideas. In 213 B.C. he ordered all books burned except those dealing with "practical" subjects like agriculture, medicine, and magic. In this way he hoped to break people's ties to the past. He agreed with his adviser, who said, "anyone referring to the past to criticize the present … should be put to death." About 460 scholars resisted and were executed.

Qin's subjects saw him as a cruel tyrant who had lost the Mandate of Heaven. Nobles were angry because he had destroyed the aristocracy; scholars detested him for the burning of books; and peasants hated his forced-labor gangs. In 210 B.C. Qin died, and soon the dynasty itself came to an end. Even so, the rule of the Qin brought lasting changes. The most influential changes were new ways of organizing the nation, establishing foundations for the Chinese state that would last 2,000 years.

The Glorious Han

In 207 B.C. **Liu Bang** (LYOH BONG) overthrew the Qin government. A military official from a peasant background, Liu defeated his most powerful rival in 202 B.C. and declared himself the emperor of a new dynasty, the Han.

The Han governed China until A.D. 220, more than 400 years. The Han emperors used the same forms of centralized power that the Qin had set up, but without the harshness of Qin rule. Han China rivaled the Roman Empire in its power and achievement.

Advances Under Wudi

The Han dynasty reached its peak during the reign of **Wudi** (WOO•DEE), who ruled from 141 B.C. to 87 B.C. Wudi, one of the most talented and dynamic rulers in Chinese history, personally supervised all aspects of his government.

An ambitious ruler, Wudi extended his empire. He sent huge armies against the nomadic invaders and other non-Chinese peoples. He conquered lands to the north, including Korea and Manchuria, south into Southeast Asia, and west as far as northern India.

In 139 B.C. Wudi sent out an expedition led by **Zhang Qian** (JAHNG CHYEN), a general and explorer. Thirteen years later, Zhang staggered back. His troops had been nearly wiped out by barbarian attacks, and the general had endured more than 10 years of captivity.

Although he had made no conquests, Zhang brought back amazing tales he had heard on his travels. He told of a great empire to the west, with huge cities full of people "who cut their hair short, wear embroidered garments, and ride in very small chariots." Zhang, who was describing Rome, gave Han rulers their first hint of another civilization as advanced as their own.

Wudi's new interest in the West, fed by news of Zhang Qian's explorations, led to the expansion of trade routes later known as the **Silk Road**. Winding past deserts and through mountain passes, the Silk Road linked East and West. It allowed traders to exchange China's fine silk for Middle Eastern and European products, such as gold, glassware, and wool and linen fabrics.

Pax Sinica

Under the Han, China enjoyed a 400-year period of prosperity and stability, later referred to as the *Pax Sinica* (PAHKS SIH•nuh•kuh), the Chinese Peace. The *Pax Sinica* coincided with the *Pax Romana* in the West.

During the *Pax Sinica*, Wudi adopted an economic policy designed to prevent food shortages and high prices. Government agents stored surplus food during years of plenty and sold it when harvests were poor. Under this system, China was able to feed its growing population.

Before Wudi, emperors had chosen as their officials members of their families or of the aristocracy, a practice that led easily to corruption in government. Wudi wanted talented people to govern, and so he initiated changes. First, he asked people to recommend candidates for public posts. These candidates took long, difficult written examinations. After an official "graded" the tests, the emperor evaluated the results and appointed those with the highest scores.

Thomas J. Abercrombie

Silk Road

The Silk Route

A caravan of men and mules walk a trail that once formed part of the old Silk Road, a network of paths cutting across Asia from the Pacific coast of China to the Mediterranean Sea. The route, first traveled many years before the Christian era, was the passageway not only for Chinese silk but for a great range of products including jade and fruit, ideas and paintings. Today it is still possible to see how poles and rocks created the actual highway over which goods moved throughout many centuries—before ships, trains, buses, and airplanes replaced mules and packs.

You can trace the length of the trip on the accompanying map. A trader setting forth from the Chinese city of Nanjing would soon leave Chinese territory and enter a world of Muslim ethnic groups and treacherous terrain. The trail loops south and north of the scorching Takla Makan Desert and rises high through mountain passes across the Pamir Mountains. The whole trip was far too long for a single caravan to undertake. Instead, Chinese or Persian merchants dealt with central Asian middlemen from lands such as Afghanistan and Turkestan. ⊕

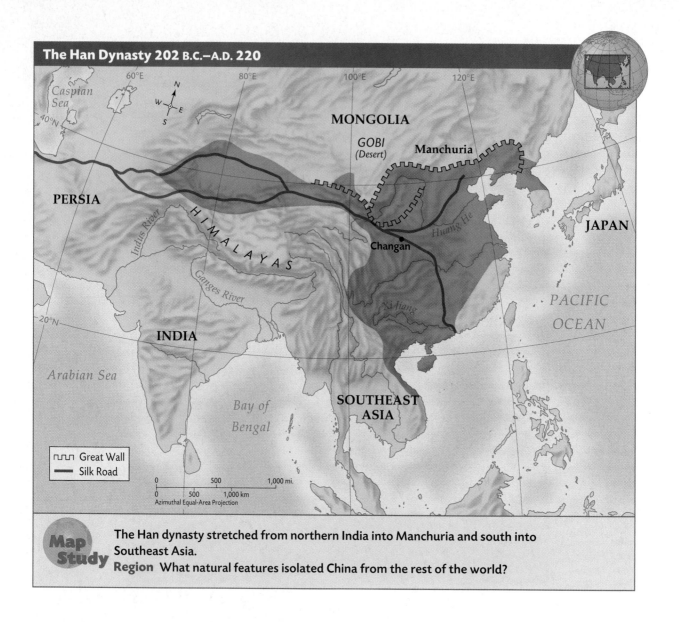

The Han Dynasty 202 B.C.–A.D. 220

MONGOLIA

GOBI (Desert)   Manchuria

PERSIA

Caspian Sea

HIMALAYAS

Indus River

Ganges River

Huang He

Changan

Xi Jiang

JAPAN

PACIFIC OCEAN

INDIA

Arabian Sea

Bay of Bengal

SOUTHEAST ASIA

Great Wall
Silk Road

0   500   1,000 mi.
0   500   1,000 km
Azimuthal Equal-Area Projection

Map Study The Han dynasty stretched from northern India into Manchuria and south into Southeast Asia.
Region What natural features isolated China from the rest of the world?

Wudi's examinations evolved into the civil service, a system that allowed anyone with ability to attain public office. At least, that was the theory. In practice, the system favored the wealthy, for education was expensive, and usually only the wealthy could afford to obtain enough education to pass the exams.

The civil service system made scholars the most respected members of Chinese society. A new class of well-educated civil servants, called mandarins, controlled the government, and they would continue to do so until the early 1900s.

After Wudi's reign, Han power declined until the dynasty eventually fell in A.D. 220. However, Han achievements in government, technology, science, and the arts were lasting.

SECTION 1 REVIEW

Recall
1. **Define** cavalry, civil service, mandarin.
2. **Identify** Qin Shihuangdi, Liu Bang, Wudi, Zhang Qian.
3. **List** two of the major

achievements the Chinese people made under each dynasty—the Zhou, the Qin, and the Han.
Critical Thinking
4. **Analyzing Information** Did

Wudi's civil service system offer equal opportunity to all Chinese? Explain.
Understanding Themes
5. **Uniformity** How did Qin Shihuangdi unify China?

c. 522 B.C. Confucius begins to teach.

c. 500 B.C. Daoism emerges as a major Chinese philosophy.

c. A.D. 400 Buddhism becomes a popular religion in China.

Section 2

Three Ways of Life

Setting the Scene

▶ **Terms to Define**
ethics, filial piety, yin and yang

▶ **People to Meet**
Confucius (Kongfuzi), Laozi

Find Out What philosophic ideals shaped China's government, and how did they shape it?

The Storyteller

One of the duties of Prince Wei-hui's cook was to slaughter cattle for the royal table. When he performed this task, all his movements were harmonious, like a dance. The prince was amazed and asked his servant how he was able to do such heavy work so effortlessly. The cook explained, "What your servant loves is the Tao, which I have applied to the skill of carving. I work with my mind, and not with my eyes." In this way, the toughest cuts yielded easily before his skill. He had learned how to nurture his spirit while maintaining his livelihood.

—adapted from A Source Book in Chinese Philosophy, reprinted in Lives and Times: A World History Reader, James P. Holoka and Jiu-Hwa L. Upshur, 1994

Confucius

During the late Zhou era, scholars sought solutions to the problems of political breakdown and social disorder that were paralyzing China. Their efforts led to the rise of major philosophies, such as Confucianism, Legalism, and Daoism. These philosophies dealt very little with the supernatural or with eternal life; instead, they focused on life in this world and how it should be lived. By the latter part of the Han dynasty, between A.D. 50 and A.D. 100, Buddhism had reached China, and the Chinese blended its insights with those of Confucianism and Daoism.

TURNING POINT

Confucianism

China's most influential scholar was **Kongfuzi** (KOONG•FOO•DZUH), known in the West as **Confucius**. Born about 551 B.C. to a peasant family, Confucius at first sought a political post but later became a teacher. In his teachings, Confucius stated that social harmony and good government would return to China if people lived according to principles of ethics—good conduct and moral judgment. When a student asked Confucius for a single word that could serve as a principle for conduct, he responded: "Perhaps the word *reciprocity* will do. Do not do unto others what you would not want others to do unto you." This rule is similar to a familiar teaching of Judaism and Christianity, sometimes called the Golden Rule: "Do unto others as you would have others do unto you."

The Five Relationships

Confucius stressed the importance of moral behavior in five basic relationships: ruler and subject, parent and child, husband and wife, old and young, and friend and friend. A code of proper conduct governed each of these relationships. For example, rulers had a duty to rule justly and to set an example of right living. In return, subjects should be loyal and obey the law.

The most basic relationships, however, concerned the family. Confucius cared especially about filial piety, or children's respect for their parents and elders. For Confucius, the family represented society in miniature. He said:

> ❝ The superior man spreads his culture to the entire nation by remaining at home…. The teaching of filial piety is a preparation for serving the ruler of the state; the teaching of respect for one's elder brothers is a preparation for serving all the elders of the community; and the teaching of kindness in parents is a training for ruling over people….When individual families have learned kindness, then the whole nation has learned kindness. ❞

After Confucius died in 479 B.C., his teachings were collected in a work called the *Analects*. During the Han dynasty, Confucian ethics provided the basis for the civil service system. They would continue to shape Chinese society and government until the early 1900s.

Legalism

Opposition to Confucian ideas, however, came from scholars known as Legalists. Legalism, as their philosophy was called, rejected the Confucian idea of learning by example. Instead, it emphasized the importance of strict laws and harsh punishments.

Legalism developed from the teachings of Hanfeizi (HAHN•FAY•DZEE), a scholar who lived during the 200s B.C. According to Hanfeizi, humans were by nature evil and required a strong, forceful government to make them attend to their duties. Because of its justification of force and power, Legalism was favored by many nobles and became the official policy of the Qin dynasty that unified China during the 200s B.C. Legalism later gave way to Confucianism. However, Legalism's influence was reflected in the harsh laws and punishments often inflicted on China's peasant population.

Daoism

In spite of their differences, Confucianism and Legalism both stressed the importance of an orderly society. Another philosophy called Daoism, however,

---

CONNECTIONS

Science and Technology

Measuring Earthquakes

People in Han China believed that earthquakes were caused by angry spirits expressing their displeasure with society. Scholars studied quakes closely in hope of finding a divine message.

In A.D. 132 Zhang Heng invented the world's first seismograph, an instrument for detecting and measuring earthquakes. Zhang's device resembled a domed, cylindrical urn. Each of eight dragons around the top held a ball in its jaws. At the base of the urn sat eight toads with upturned heads and open mouths, each directly under a dragon.

Zhang Heng's seismograph

When a tremor occurred, a mechanism caused one of the balls to fall into a toad's mouth. This action showed that somewhere an earthquake was taking place. The side of the seismograph where that toad was sitting indicated the quake's direction. As the ball popped into the toad's mouth, the loudness indicated the tremor's strength.

Today we know that shifting in the earth's crust causes earthquakes. This movement sends seismic waves across the earth's surface much as dropping a pebble in a pond sends ripples across water. Modern seismographs have sensors that can detect ground motions caused by seismic waves from both near and distant earthquakes. The sensors produce wavy lines that reflect the size of seismic waves passing beneath them. Impressions of the waves are registered on paper, film, or recording tape, or are stored and displayed by computers.

Linking Past and Present ACTIVITY

Contrast the workings of ancient and modern seismographs. Then, examine the differences in ancient Chinese and modern views about the causes of earthquakes.

---

emphasized living in harmony with nature. Daoism rejected formal social structures and the idea that people must fill specific roles in society.

Daoist Ideas

Daoism traced its origins to the teachings of a scholar named **Laozi** (LOW•DZUH), who is thought to have lived sometime around the 500s B.C. Laozi's ideas were recorded in the *Dao De Jing*, a Chinese classic. His followers, known as Daoists, believed that people should renounce worldly ambitions and turn to nature and the Dao, the universal force that guides all things. They used examples from nature to describe how one follows the Dao:

> **❝** The highest good is like water.
>   Water gives life to the ten thousand things
>   and does not strive.
>   It flows in places men reject and so is like
>   the Dao.
>   In dwelling, be close to the land.
>   In meditation, go deep in the heart.
>   In dealing with others, be gentle and kind.
>   In speech, be true.
>   In ruling, be just. **❞**

By emphasizing harmony with nature, Daoists deeply influenced Chinese arts, particularly painting and poetry.

Daoist simplicity seems to oppose Confucian formalism, but a person could be both a Confucianist and a Daoist. Confucianism provided the pattern for government and one's place in the social order, and Daoism emphasized harmony within the individual attuned to nature. Because the emphasis of each was different, a person could easily be both.

Yin and Yang

A Chinese theory related to Daoist ideas was the concept of **yin and yang,** the two opposing forces believed to be present in all nature. Yin was cool, dark, female, and submissive, while yang was warm, light, male, and aggressive. Everything had both elements. For harmony the two elements had

History & Art Laozi on his buffalo. Guimet Museum, Paris, France. *How did the teaching of Laozi as recorded in the* Dao De Jing *influence Chinese arts and poetry?*

to be in balance. Human life and natural events resulted from the interplay between yin and yang.

The concept of yin and yang helped the Chinese reconcile seeming opposites—like Dao simplicity and Confucian formalism. It also helped them accept Buddhist ideas brought to China by monks and traders from India.

Buddhism

Buddhism reached China just as the Han Empire was collapsing, and its emphasis on personal salvation in nirvana appealed to many people seeking an escape from suffering. Confucianists could follow its Eightfold Path, and Daoists admired its use of meditation. By the A.D. 400s, Buddhism was widely embraced in China.

SECTION 2 REVIEW

Recall
1. **Define** ethics, filial piety, yin and yang.
2. **Identify** Confucius, Laozi.
3. **Explain** why Confucius believed the five relationships were important to Chinese

society. What was the goal of his philosophy?

Critical Thinking
4. **Making Comparisons**
   How would you compare Confucianists and Daoists in their ideas and also in their ways of life?

Understanding Themes
5. **Innovation** How did the concept of yin and yang help the Chinese people reconcile ideas in the thought of Daoism that seemed opposed to Confucianism?

1000 B.C.   500 B.C.   A.D. 1

1000 B.C. Chinese begin poems in the *Book of Songs*.

240 B.C. Chinese astronomers record appearance of Halley's comet.

c. 100 B.C. Chinese invent paper.

Section 3

Society and Culture

Setting the Scene

▶ **Terms to Define**
hierarchy, extended family, nuclear family, acupuncture

▶ **People to Meet**
Sima Qian

Find Out How was early Chinese society organized, and what scientific and technological breakthroughs took place in early China?

The Storyteller

Wu Phu was a physician, trained by Hua Tho, an outstanding medical theorist. Hua Tho impressed upon his pupils the importance of physical exercise as a means of obtaining good health. He compared an exercised body to running water, which never became stale. "When the body feels ill," he counseled, "one should do one of these exercises. After perspiring, one will sense the body grow light and the stomach will manifest hunger." There was merit in those recommendations. Wu Phu had carefully followed his master's regimen, and although he was past ninety years of age, his hearing, vision, and even his teeth were all still excellent.

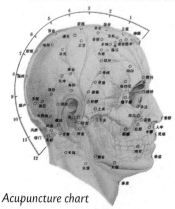

Acupuncture chart

—adapted from "Hygiene and Preventive Medicine in Ancient China," reprinted in *Reflections on World Civilization*, edited by Ronald H. Fritze, James S. Olson, and Randy W. Roberts, 1994

Confucian values governed all aspects of personal and social life in Han China. "With harmony at home, there will be order in the nation," Confucius had said. "With order in the nation, there will be peace in the world." And indeed, the family was supreme in Chinese society. It was the focus of life, bound together strongly by mutual love, loyalty, and dependence.

Family Life

The members of a Chinese family of the Han era lived and worked together. In an ideal family every member knew his or her role and the duties that went with it.

Relationships

Family members did not relate to each other as equals; instead, the family was a strict hierarchy, organized into different levels of importance. The oldest male in the home, usually the father, was dominant. Next in rank was the oldest son, followed by all the younger sons and all the females. The mother came before the daughters, and finally—at the bottom—the youngest daughter or childless daughter-in-law. Each family member expected obedience from those who were further down in the hierarchy, and each obeyed and respected those who were above.

Family Rules

Strict rules governed the relationships between husbands and wives, parents and grandparents, uncles and aunts, brothers and sisters, and other relatives. Each family member knew his or her place and understood its duties, and each was careful not to bring dishonor on the family by failing in those duties. Moreover, the duty to family members did not stop at death; all were expected to pay respect to departed ancestors.

Typical homes in Han China did not have the extended families, or families of many generations living together, that would later be typical. Rather, they had what we call today nuclear families, each consisting of parents and their children. The father assigned his children's careers, determined their education, arranged their marriages, meted out rewards or punishments, and controlled the family finances. The family also provided support for members who themselves could not contribute—the aged, the young, the sick, and even the lazy.

No doubt the system offered many opportunities for exploiting those further down in the hierarchy. Nevertheless, few fathers were tyrants. Like other family members, they practiced ethical principles of kindness and compassion, either from genuine love or from fear of the disapproval of others and the scorn of their ancestors.

Status of Women

Under the Confucian social system, women were subordinate to men. Confucius himself had little regard for women, saying, "Women and uneducated people are the most difficult to deal with."

Girls began life subservient to their fathers and brothers. Later their husbands and in-laws were their superiors, and eventually even a mother came under the authority of her own sons. Parents valued baby girls far less than baby boys. A poor family had to work hard to raise and support a child, and if that child was a daughter, she left home to become part of her husband's family as soon as she married.

Some women were able to gain respect in Chinese homes. With marriage and motherhood, they became revered. Other opportunities for women, such as education, were limited. In spite of Confucianism's predominance, women fared far better under the Han than they would in later centuries. They could inherit property, even own it after they married, and they could remarry after a husband's death.

Society and Economy

Chinese society consisted of three main classes: landowners, peasants, and merchants. Landowning families were wealthy. They lived in tile-roofed mansions with courtyards and gardens. They surrounded their homes with walls to protect them from bandits. They filled their rooms with fine furniture and adorned them with silk wall hangings and carpets. Wealthy families feasted on a rich variety of foods.

The landholders' wealth was generally limited, however, and families rarely kept their holdings for

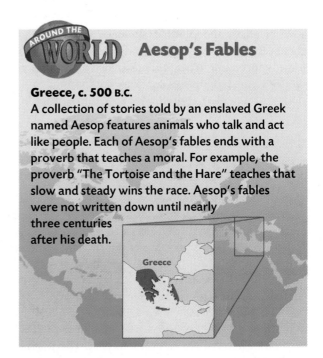

AROUND THE WORLD

Aesop's Fables

Greece, c. 500 B.C.
A collection of stories told by an enslaved Greek named Aesop features animals who talk and act like people. Each of Aesop's fables ends with a proverb that teaches a moral. For example, the proverb "The Tortoise and the Hare" teaches that slow and steady wins the race. Aesop's fables were not written down until nearly three centuries after his death.

Greece

more than a few generations. When a family's land was divided, it went to all the sons, not just the oldest, with the result that in time individual landowners had less and less property.

Probably 90 percent of the Chinese people were peasants. The wealth that supported the lifestyles of the rich was gained from the hard labor of the peasants who cultivated the land. Unlike Western farmers, who usually lived on the land they farmed, most Chinese peasants lived in rural villages and worked fields outside their mud walls. Their homes were simple, and they ate a plain diet that featured millet, rice, beans, turnips, and fish.

The peasants raised livestock and toiled long hours in the grain fields. They faced constant threats from floods and from famines. As rent for the land, peasants turned over part of their produce to the landowner. The government required them to pay taxes and to work one month each year on public works projects such as road building. In times of conflict, peasants were drafted into the army as soldiers.

At the bottom of the social hierarchy were merchants—a group that included shopkeepers, traders, service workers, and even bankers. The merchants lived in towns and provided goods and services for the wealthy. In spite of the great wealth that many merchants accumulated, Chinese society generally held them in contempt. Confucianism taught that the pursuit of profit was an unworthy pastime for the "superior" individual. Merchants were not allowed to take the civil service examinations and enter government service.

For all the people in Han society except merchants, the civil service system provided opportunities for advancement, though the expense of education blocked most of the poor from competing. Still, poor but talented individuals sometimes rose to positions of power and influence.

Literature

Although the Qin burned thousands of books, many survived in royal libraries and secret private collections. Particularly prized was a collection of books called the Five Classics, some of which were written before Confucius. All candidates for the civil service were required to master them. No better example is recorded of the Chinese reverence for history.

The oldest of the Five Classics, the *Book of Songs*, preserves 305 of the earliest Chinese poems, written between 1000 B.C. and 600 B.C. The poems deal with political themes, ritual, and romance. Many seem modern, with their everyday topics and simple, concrete imagery—this one, for example:

❝ Near the East Gate
Young women go
Like so many clouds all day.
Like drifting clouds
A thought of them
Soon blows away.

There. White robe
and a blue scarf—
she makes my day.

Near the Great Tower and Wall
Go slender girls
Like reeds by river's edge:
Like bending reeds
A thought of them
Soon passes by. ❞

The *Book of Documents* records political speeches

Images of the Times

Han China

The Han dynasty was a golden age of Chinese history. Important political, economic, and cultural changes took place.

Wudi's examinations developed into a civil service system, leading to a wealthy class of mandarins who controlled the government.

and documents from early in the Zhou dynasty, including the earliest statement of the Mandate of Heaven. The *Book of Changes* presents a complex system for foretelling the future and choosing a course of action. In *Spring and Autumn Annals* Confucius reported major events that occurred in the state of Lu between 722 B.C. and 481 B.C.

The Five Classics were thought to carry solutions to most problems. Officials studied them closely to find support for their positions, such as the conduct of political leaders. Accounts of solar eclipses, meteor showers, and droughts were used to show what terrifying events and disasters could befall poor political leaders.

Another great collection of books, the Thirteen Classics, included the *Analects*—Confucius's sayings compiled by his students after his death. Many appeared as answers to questions. For example, Confucius was asked about the gentleman, or the "superior man." Among other replies he gave this one: "What the gentleman seeks, he seeks within himself; what the small man seeks, he seeks in others."

The Han Chinese encouraged literary pursuits and made literature available to everyone. An especially valuable work produced during the Han dynasty period was the *Historical Record*. Written by **Sima Qian** during the reign of Wudi, it is the first true history of ancient China.

Science and Technology

Besides literature and philosophy, China made major contributions in science and technology. By the 300s B.C., Chinese astronomers had calculated the length of the solar year as $365\frac{1}{4}$ days. They gazed through bronze tubes equipped with a device that divided the sky into measured segments, allowing them to make accurate measurements. They kept valuable records of solar and lunar eclipses and comet sightings. In 240 B.C. Chinese astronomers recorded the appearance of the object that would later be called Halley's comet—many centuries before Halley's birth.

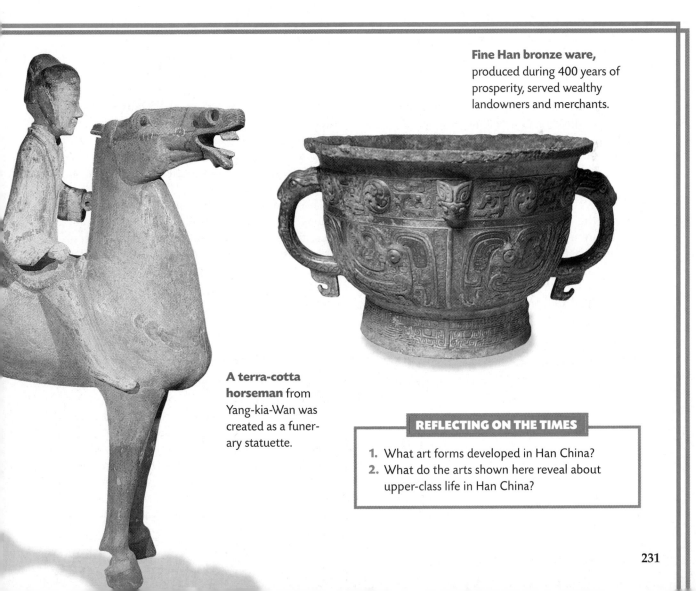

Fine Han bronze ware, produced during 400 years of prosperity, served wealthy landowners and merchants.

A terra-cotta horseman from Yang-kia-Wan was created as a funerary statuette.

REFLECTING ON THE TIMES

1. What art forms developed in Han China?
2. What do the arts shown here reveal about upper-class life in Han China?

Women prepare newly woven silk. Han weavers created beautiful damasks of many colors. *How did Chinese arts and inventions spread to other civilizations?*

save many farm animals. New canals and improved roadways reduced the cost of distributing food and permitted ideas to spread more rapidly.

Inventions

Many inventions in ancient China were especially vital to Chinese life and the economy. Made by the Chinese since prehistoric times, silk was in great demand as a trade item; its worth was attested to by the name of one of history's greatest trade routes—the Silk Road. Caravans carried the precious cargo as far as Rome.

Paper was probably invented by 100 B.C., although it was officially credited to an inventor of about 200 years later. Artisans pounded tree bark, hemp, or rags into a pulp. By treating it with gelatin, they discovered that they could then make paper. Used first for wrapping and clothing, paper was soon recognized as an ideal writing material.

The invention of paper benefited the bureaucratic Han government. Its centralized structure resulted in an explosion in the number of documents. Most were written on strips of wood, which were fragile and cumbersome to work with. The use of paper had many obvious advantages.

Other inventions improved mining and construction. Miners, using iron drill bits driven by workers on seesaw-like levers, drilled boreholes to obtain salt from the earth. Another invention was the wheelbarrow, which was first used on building sites around 100 B.C.

These are only a few examples from a list of Chinese "firsts," which also includes the first printed books, the earliest technologies for casting bronze and iron, the suspension bridge, the compass, and gunpowder. Such achievements caused China to remain far ahead of Europe in science and technology until the A.D. 1300s.

Medicine

Chinese physicians recognized nutrition as vital and realized that some diseases resulted from vitamin deficiencies. Although they did not identify vitamins as such, they discovered and prescribed foods that would correct some problems. They also understood that many herbs had medicinal value.

Chinese doctors treated ailments and relieved pain with acupuncture, a technique in which the skin is pierced with thin needles at vital points. They believed acupuncture restored the balance between yin and yang in a person's body.

Farming and Transport

Under the Han, many improvements occurred in agriculture and transportation. Complex irrigation systems drained swamps and diverted rivers to quench parched fields. Advances in fertilizing crops helped farmers produce enough to feed China's growing population. Veterinary medicine helped

---

Recall
1. **Define** hierarchy, extended family, nuclear family, acupuncture.
2. **Identify** the Five Classics, *Spring and Autumn Annals*, the *Analects*, Sima Qian.
3. **Explain** how families and

government during the Han era reflected the Confucian idea of order.

Critical Thinking
4. **Making Comparisons** Compare a typical Han Chinese family with families you consider typical of America today.

Understanding Themes
5. **Cultural Diffusion** What ideas and products from ancient China have become popular in the West in recent years? What factors account for their popularity among Western thinkers and consumers?

Critical Thinking SKILLS

Identifying Central Issues

The saying "He can't see the forest for the trees" refers to someone so focused on separate details that he cannot see the entire situation. Sometimes we face this problem when studying history. It is easy to focus on details such as names, dates, and places, thus losing sight of the bigger picture. To avoid this, it is important to identify the central issues. Central issues are the main ideas of historical material.

Learning the Skill

First, skim the material to identify its general subject. Look for headings and subheadings; often they highlight central issues. A central issue may also appear in the topic sentence of a paragraph. The other sentences in the paragraph usually explain and support the central issue.

When looking for central issues, ask yourself these questions: What is the general topic of this material? What ideas have the greatest emphasis? What main idea holds the details together? If I had to summarize this material in one sentence, what would it be? If you can answer one or more of these questions, you can identify central issues.

Practicing the Skill

Read the passage about the *Book of Changes* and answer the questions that follow.

❝ The *Book of Changes*—*I Ching* in Chinese—is unquestionably one of the most important books in the world's literature…. Nearly all that is greatest and most significant in the three thousand years of Chinese cultural history has either taken its inspiration from this book, or has exerted an influence on the interpretation of its text…. Indeed, not only the philosophy of China but its science and statecraft as well have never ceased to draw from the spring of wisdom in the *I Ching*…. Even the

commonplaces of everyday life in China are saturated with its influence. In going through the streets of a Chinese city, one will find, here and there at a street corner, a fortune teller sitting behind a neatly covered table, brush and tablet at hand, ready to draw from the ancient book of wisdom pertinent counsel and information on life's minor perplexities…. ❞

1. What is the general subject of the passage?
2. Which idea has the greatest emphasis?
3. What are some details that support this idea?
4. Which sentence states the central issue of the passage?

Applying the Skill

Find a newspaper or magazine article that interests you. Identify the central issues in this article and summarize them in your own words.

For More Practice

Turn to the Skill Practice in the Chapter Review on page 235 for more practice in identifying central issues.

Connections Across Time

Historical Significance Confucian ideas have had a major impact on China's development. On the negative side, some historians point to the Confucian denial of women's rights and its stress on total obedience to authority. On the positive side, others state that the Confucian emphasis on stability helped early China build a strong government and that Confucius's ideas about relationships resulted in a more compassionate society. Confucius also left a revolutionary legacy. He considered it a society's duty to overthrow an unjust ruler and to ensure a fair distribution of wealth.

Using Key Terms

Write the key term that completes each sentence. Then write a sentence for each term not chosen.

a. acupuncture
b. civil service
c. extended family
d. hierarchy
e. ethics
f. mandarin
g. yin and yang
h. filial piety
i. cavalry
j. nuclear family

1. An _____ consists of parents, children, grandparents, and other relatives living together in one household.
2. Chinese doctors treated ailments and relieved pain with _____, a technique in which the skin is pierced with thin needles at vital points.
3. A Chinese theory related to Daoism was the concept of _____, the two opposing forces believed to be present in all of nature.
4. Confucius taught that individuals should live according to principles of _____.
5. The Chinese cared especially about _____, or children's respect for their parents.

Technology Activity

Building a Database The teachings of the ancient Chinese teacher Confucius date back to 479 B.C. Many of his teachings are still practiced in China today. Search the Internet or your local library for additional information about Confucius. Build a database of collected Confucian sayings, or analects. Organize analects by headings reflecting different categories according to Confucius's principles or ethics. Examples of categories would be a person's conduct or filial piety.

Using Your History Journal

Many of Confucius's sayings compiled after his death are similar to proverbs. Write a set of your own proverbs about everyday decisions and situations.

Reviewing Facts

1. **Culture** Identify Confucius and his ideas.
2. **Government** Explain how Mandarins came to shape China's government.
3. **Culture** List the five relationships in Chinese society that were identified by Confucius.
4. **Culture** Describe the *Book of Songs*, the *Spring and Autumn Annals*, and the *Historical Record*.
5. **History** Explain why Qin Shihuangdi ordered the construction of the Great Wall of China.
6. **Culture** Identify three groups in Han China.
7. **Government** List the characteristics of China's government and politics under the Zhou, Qin, and Han dynasties.
8. **Government** Analyze how Confucius applied the idea of filial piety to governments.
9. **Culture** Explain why Qin rulers strongly opposed the teachings of Confucius, though Han rulers like Wudi promoted Confucianism.
10. **Technology** List three Chinese inventions and state how they changed Chinese life.

Critical Thinking

1. **Synthesize** Create a time line showing major events in China from the Zhou to the Han dynasties.

2. Evaluate Was a strong family structure a positive or a negative influence on Chinese society?

3. Apply How does your society make use of the Han concept of appointing officials by ability?

4. Synthesize How would you respond if your government adopted the social policies of the Qin dynasty?

5. Compare How is Confucianism different from Christianity and Judaism? How is it similar?

6. Synthesize Think about how merchants were viewed in Han society and why. How might the United States be different if we felt that way about merchants?

Geography in History

1. Movement Refer to the map below. Buddhism came to China from which area of the world?

2. Location What cities became major Buddhist sites in China?

3. Region What large area was a major stronghold of Daoism?

4. Region What Daoist concepts made it possible for much of China to accept the teachings of Confucius, Laozi, and the Buddha into a unified belief system?

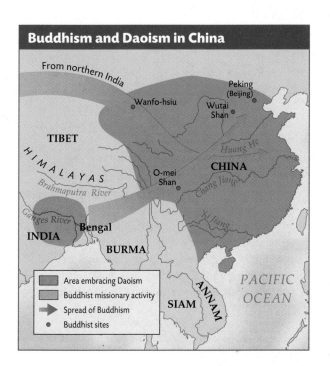

Buddhism and Daoism in China

From northern India

- Peking (Beijing)
- Wanfo-hsiu
- Wutai Shan
- Huang He
- TIBET
- HIMALAYAS
- Brahmaputra River
- O-mei Shan
- CHINA
- Chang Jiang
- Ganges River
- Bengal
- Xi Jiang
- INDIA
- BURMA
- SIAM
- ANNAM
- PACIFIC OCEAN

- Area embracing Daoism
- Buddhist missionary activity
- Spread of Buddhism
- Buddhist sites

Understanding Themes

1. Uniformity What methods did Qin Shihuangdi use to unify China? What was their impact?

2. Innovation How did the ethical philosophy of Confucius influence Chinese society?

3. Cultural Diffusion How did Buddhism reach China?

Linking Past and Present

1. The Qin tried to control people's ideas by limiting the books they could read. Provide an example of a modern government that limits the information its people receive.

2. All candidates for China's civil service were required to master the Five Classics. Can you think of literature from our own culture that everyone should know? Why would it be difficult for Americans to agree on five classics?

Skill Practice

Read the passage below and answer the questions that follow.

❝ Females should be strictly grave and sober, and yet adapted to the occasion. Whether in waiting on her parents, receiving or reverencing her husband, rising up or sitting down, when pregnant, in times of mourning, or when fleeing in war, she should be perfectly decorous. Rearing the silkworm and working cloth are the most important employments of the female; preparing food for the household and setting in order sacrifices follow next, each of which must be attended to. After that, study and learning can fill up the time. ❞

Book of Changes (I Ching)

1. What is the general topic of this passage?
2. What details are offered on this topic?
3. Which sentence, if any, states the central issue of this passage?
4. State the central issue in your own words.

ABCNEWS INTERACTIVE™

Turning Points in World History

Democracy in Greece

Setting up the Video

Work with a group of your classmates to view "Democracy in Greece" on the videodisc *Turning Points in World History*. The foundation of present-day democracy can be traced almost 2,500 years ago to ancient Greece. Athenians developed the idea of a democratic government in which the majority rules but the minority still has rights. This program takes a look at the origins of democracy and how it has influenced modern governments and cultures.

Side One, Chapter 5

View the video by scanning the bar code or by entering the chapter number on your keypad and pressing Search. (Also available in VHS format.)

Hands-On Activity

Organize into cooperative groups. Write and perform five-minute skits about the importance of voting in a democratic society. Videotape skits to share with other classes.

Surfing the "Net"

African Artifacts

The African continent is rich with precious artifacts ranging from tools to jewelry. To find out more about African artifacts, look on the Internet.

Getting There

Follow these steps below to gather information about African artifacts on the Internet.

1. Go to a search engine. Type in the phrase *African artifacts*.
2. After typing in the phrase, enter words like those below to focus your search:
   - *jewelry*
   - *tools*
   - *pottery*
   - *countries*

3. The search engine should provide you with a number of links to follow. Links are "pointers" to different sites on the Internet and commonly appear as blue underlined words.

What to Do When You Are There

Click on the links to navigate through the pages of information and gather your findings. Design a bulletin board by printing images of African artifacts that you have located on the Internet. Use a word processor to create captions explaining what the artifacts are and where they are from. Include a map of Africa and label the countries where the various artifacts were found.

Unit 2 Digest

Chalices from the court of a wealthy Mycenaean king. *Besides the Mycenaeans, what other people influenced the development of early Greek civilization?*

From about 2000 B.C. to A.D. 500, major civilizations arose throughout the world. Although each civilization had unique traits, they all had common features, such as a stable political system, one or more major religions, and an interest in the arts and sciences. These civilizations produced many achievements that still influence the world today.

Chapter 4
The Rise of Ancient Greece

Although Greece's mountains protected against invaders, they also limited travel and communication among the Greeks and prevented them from uniting politically. Numerous harbors and closeness to the sea, however, encouraged the Greeks to become traders, and eventually they founded colonies around the Mediterranean Sea.

Greek civilization had its origins in the Minoan civilization on the Mediterranean island of Crete and the Mycenaean civilization on the European mainland. The Greeks provided a record of their legends and early history in two epic poems, the *Iliad* and the *Odyssey*. These epics taught such values as courage, dignity, and love of beauty. The Greeks worshiped gods and goddesses—who were both humanlike and superpowerful—and imitated their deities by themselves striving for excellence.

The polis—the Greek city-state—served as the center of Greek life. The two major Greek city-states were Sparta and Athens. Sparta was a military society that emphasized physical strength and service in the army. Athens built a much freer society that stressed education and public service. It also introduced the Western concept of democracy.

During the 400s B.C., the Greeks defeated the Persians in a series of wars. A golden age of cultural achievement in Athens followed the Persian conflicts. Later, resentment against Athenian power led to the Peloponnesian War between a Sparta-led alliance of city-states and Athens. The war brought defeat for Athens and a decline for the Greek city-state system.

Chapter 5
The Height of Greek Civilization

During the 400s B.C., Athens became the center of Greek civilization. Its classical style of art, architecture, and literature have endured in Western civilization. The Athenians expressed their love of beauty and harmony in such buildings as the Parthenon. They decorated their pottery with paintings and created masterpieces of sculpture. The Greeks were the first to write and perform plays—comedies and tragedies.

Greek thinkers believed in the power of reason to explain all things, a belief that became a basic principle of science. Socrates constructed a way of teaching known as the Socratic method. His student Plato studied human behavior and wrote the first book on political science. Aristotle wrote on logic and poetry, among other topics. The Greeks also produced the first true historians, Herodotus and Thucydides, and the father of medicine, Hippocrates.

By 330 B.C., a new political leader named Alexander of Macedonia had defeated the Persians and conquered an area from Egypt to India. His goal was to combine the best of Greek and Persian cultures into one civilization. After Alexander's death, his empire was divided among three of his generals.

Although Greek political unity had vanished, Greek culture spread and mixed with Middle Eastern cultures to form the Hellenistic civilization. This new civilization, which excelled in the sciences, developed in newly built cities, such as Alexandria, Egypt.

Chapter 6
Ancient Rome and Early Christianity

In the 500s B.C. the Romans set up a republic ruled by the upper classes but increasingly influenced by the common people. To protect their republic, the Romans formed a powerful army and began to expand their territory. By 264 B.C., Rome had conquered the entire Italian Peninsula. It then fought the Punic Wars against Carthage, finally defeating the North African city-state in 146 B.C

Rome's military conquests brought the Roman Republic wealth but also substituted slave labor on large estates for small, independent citizen-farmers. Mounting social tensions led to civil war and an increased political role for the army. In 45 B.C, the general Julius Caesar came to power and set up a dictatorship. In 27 B.C. his grandnephew Octavian, or Augustus, became the first Roman emperor.

About this time, the Roman Empire entered a long period of peace and prosperity known as the *Pax Romana*. The Romans of this era developed their system of laws and built roads, aqueducts, and public buildings. Great literary figures included the poets Horace and Virgil and the historians Livy and Tacitus.

During the *Pax Romana*, Christianity—based on the life and teachings of Jesus—began as a part of Judaism but quickly spread through the Roman world as a new religion. At the heart of early Christian preaching was the belief that Jesus was the Son of God and the way of salvation. After periodic persecutions, Christianity became the official religion of the empire in A.D. 392.

By the A.D 300s, political chaos, economic crisis, and Germanic invasions had led to the decline of the Roman Empire. Reform efforts by Emperors Diocletian and Constantine helped preserve the eastern part of the empire but only delayed the downfall of the western part of the empire until the late A.D 400s.

Visualizing History

Octavian, known as Augustus, preferred to be called "first citizen." *What was the period that began with his reign called?*

Chapter 7
Flowering of African Civilizations

Africa's diverse geography influenced the development of its civilizations. In areas of scarce rainfall, settlements arose near lakes or rivers, such as the Nile. Trading civilizations, such as Kush and Axum in eastern Africa, exchanged ideas and goods with places as far away as Rome and India. Movement of peoples, such as the Bantu migrations, spread culture to other parts of Africa.

In West Africa, a series of kingdoms arose and prospered between A.D. 300 and A.D. 1500. Ghana, the first of these territories, traded salt for gold brought by Arab traders. Mali, a nation that broke away from Ghana, also became powerful. Its king, Mansa Musa, created a rich trading empire through his contacts with the Middle East. Islamic culture spread throughout Africa. Songhai, the last of the great West African kingdoms, expanded its territory and developed a strong legal system based on the religion of Islam.

Trade contacts also brought power and wealth to city-states along the coast of East Africa. There Arab traders brought cotton, silk, and Chinese porcelain from India and Southeast Asia to exchange for ivory and metals from Africa's interior. Meanwhile, powerful kingdoms thrived in Southern Africa. These inland areas mined rich deposits of copper and gold. Traders from the East African coast made their way to the southern African kingdoms and began an active trade there.

Chapter 8
India's Great Civilization

About 1500 B.C. Aryan invaders conquered northern India and created a new society. Early Indian religious writings—the *Rig-Veda*, the *Mahabharata*, and the *Upanishads*—taught the principles of Hinduism, India's major religion. Hinduism includes belief in many deities and the concept of an eternal spirit, reincarnation, and the obligation to perform the duties of one's social group.

During the 500s B.C., Siddhartha Gautama founded Buddhism, which later spread from India to East Asia and Southeast Asia. Known as the Buddha, or Enlightened One, Gautama taught that people can free themselves from suffering by eliminating desire and by following rules of behavior, the Eightfold Path. Buddhism, as well as Hinduism, had a profound influence on the literature, arts, and architecture of Asia.

The Mauryas, who ruled from 321 B.C. to 184 B.C., founded an empire in northern India, and the Mauryan ruler Asoka helped spread Buddhism. About 500 years later, the Guptas reunited India, and their empire lasted from A.D. 320 to A.D. 600. Under the Guptas, scholars made numerous advances—including the development of algebra, the numbers 1 to 9, and the concept of zero.

Chapter 9
China's Flourishing Civilization

Under the Zhou dynasty, which ruled from about 1000 B.C. to 256 B.C., China made many technological advances and grew in population. Later the Qin and Han dynasties set up powerful central governments that brought stability, expanded Chinese territory, and increased foreign trade. Two notable achievements were the building of the Great Wall to protect against invaders and the creation of a civil service system in which officials were appointed on the basis of examinations.

Visualizing History A treasure of 6,000 terra-cotta soldiers from the Qin dynasty was uncovered in Shensi Province. *What other large structure was built during this time?*

Two major philosophies—Confucianism and Daoism—developed in early China. Founded by Confucius (Kongfuzi), Confucianism stressed basic moral rules in human relationships and the ideal of a courteous, well-educated individual. Daoism emphasized living in harmony with nature.

Chinese society consisted of landowners, peasants, and merchants. The Chinese family, dominated by the oldest male, played an important role. It functioned as an economic unit to which all members gave their earnings and which supported the old, the young, and the sick.

In addition to many literary works, the Chinese made great contributions in science and technology. These include the first printed book and the development of paper and gunpowder.

SURVEYING UNIT 2

1. **Chapter 4** How did the people of Athens and Sparta differ in their general attitudes toward life?
2. **Chapter 5** In what ways did the ancient Greeks lay the foundation of the arts and sciences of the West?
3. **Chapter 6** How did Christianity begin and later develop?
4. **Chapter 7** Why was trade so important to early African kingdoms and city-states?
5. **Chapter 8** What mathematical advances did early India pass on to other parts of the world?
6. **Chapter 9** How did the people of early India compare with the people of early China in their religious beliefs?

Regional Civilizations

Then & Now

As this period opened, advanced civilizations began to develop in many regions of the world. Although some cultures were cut off from other regions, trade and migrations spread ideas across continents and among several different peoples. Emerging centers of trade and commerce brought more highly organized social structures and governments. These regional civilizations contributed many ideas that influenced the development of the modern world. Christianity, Islam, Confucianism, and Buddhism spread over wide areas. Scientific discoveries crossed cultures. Some contact between cultures caused conflict that lasted for decades or centuries.

A Global Chronology

	A.D. 500	A.D. 700	A.D. 900
Political	A.D. 527 Justinian becomes Byzantine emperor.	A.D. 638 Arabs conquer Jerusalem.	
Scientific/ Technological		A.D. 850 Arabs perfect the astrolabe.	A.D. 1000 Chinese invent gunpowder.
Social/Cultural		A.D. 622 Muhammad flees Makkah (Islamic Year 1).	

Mayan clay figurine of a man and a woman wrapped in a blanket, c. A.D. 700–1000. Campeche, Mexico

Portfolio Project

Americans share the benefits of foods, inventions, discoveries, and ideas from all over the world. Often we do not think about the cultures that contributed these things. Create a map on which you show some products or ideas that originated in each of the following areas: the Middle East, Asia, Africa, South America, or Europe.

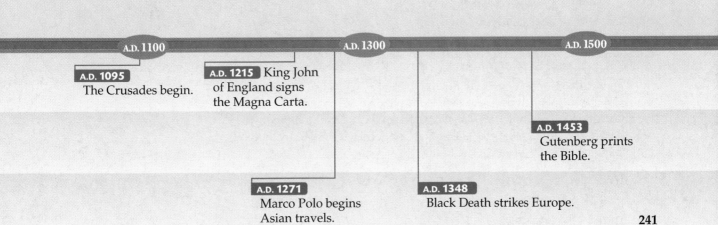

A.D. 1100

A.D. 1095
The Crusades begin.

A.D. 1215 King John of England signs the Magna Carta.

A.D. 1300

A.D. 1500

A.D. 1453
Gutenberg prints the Bible.

A.D. 1271
Marco Polo begins Asian travels.

A.D. 1348
Black Death strikes Europe.

The Spread of Ideas

Mathematics

The invention of mathematics changed the course of civilization. Astronomers used mathematics to account for the movements of the sun and moon so they could mark the seasons. Geometry enabled people to calculate the volume of a cylindrical granary. Mathematics supported travel, from the earliest sea travel to the development of the space program. It all began with the Sumerians.

Sumerian cuneiform tablet

Indus Valley
The Use of Numerals

The Sumerians devised one of the world's earliest numbering systems. They used two wedge-like symbols for counting. One symbol stood for 1, the other for 10. But these symbols—and others to follow—basically came from the Sumerian cuneiform. The wedges served double-duty for symbolizing words and figures.

Other early peoples who invented numbering systems used letters from their alphabets. Then, around A.D. 500, Hindu people in the Indus River valley abandoned the use of letters. They created instead special number symbols to stand for the figures 1 to 9. Although modernized over time, these 9 Hindu symbols are the ones we use today.

The Middle East
The Rise of Algebra

Trade introduced people in the Middle East to the Hindu number system. About A.D. 825 an Arab mathematician, al-Khowarizmi of Baghdad, wrote a book recommending the new system to everyone. In a second book, al-Khowarizmi showed how the system could be used. He called the book *al-jabr w'al-muqabalah*, which roughly means "the art of bringing together unknowns to match a known quantity." The word *algebra* comes from the key word in the title—*al-jabr*, or "bringing together."

The wonder of the system caught Arab imaginations. Arabs especially liked the concept of zero—developed by the Hindus after they created the symbols for 1-9. In explaining this concept, one Arab mathematician wrote: "When [in subtraction] nothing is left over, then write the little circle so that the place does not remain empty." With the use of zero, mathematicians could build numbers of astronomical size using just 10 symbols.

Persian astronomer

The astrolabe was used by Muslim astronomers and navigators to observe and calculate the position of stars and other heavenly bodies.

Europe
The Triumph of Arabic Numerals

Muslims ruled in Spain from the A.D. 700s to the A.D. 1400s. Their presence opened the door for European use of the new Hindu-Arabic number system. At first, many Europeans rejected it. They clung instead to Roman numerals. The Italian city-state of Florence even passed a law banning the use of the Hindu-Arabic system.

Later, however, "Arabic numerals," as they were called, proved a more powerful conqueror than Arab soldiers. European merchants found knowledge of the symbols necessary for dealings with merchants in Muslim ports. Europeans who learned the new arithmetic also found it easier to do their tallies. By the A.D. 1400s, the numbers could even be found in popular art.

As you will read in this unit, Europeans began to adopt other practices from the Middle East as well. The pace of change quickened as wars and trade brought more people in contact with each other.

Book of Hours with Arabic numerals

LINKING THE IDEAS

1. How did the Hindu system of numbers differ from earlier systems?
2. What was the importance of the invention of zero?

Critical Thinking

3. **Cause and Effect** What was the role of conquest and trade in spreading the use of the Hindu-Arabic number system?

Byzantines and Slavs

Chapter Themes

▶ **Conflict** Byzantines fight off invaders and struggle over use of icons. *Section 1*
▶ **Innovation** Byzantines develop Eastern Orthodox theology and distinctive art forms. *Section 2*
▶ **Cultural Diffusion** Trade routes and invasions spread beliefs and ideas. *Section 3*

$\mathcal{S}$toryteller

The awestruck visitor arriving in A.D. 600 in the city of Constantinople in southeastern Europe scarcely knew where to turn. Splendid public buildings as well as simple private homes lined the streets; the scent of rare spices perfumed the air; people dressed in fine silk thronged the church of Hagia Sophia. "One might imagine that one has chanced upon a meadow in full bloom," the Greek historian Procopius wrote about the newly built church. "For one would surely marvel at the purple hue of some [columns], the green of others, at those on which the crimson blooms, at those that flash with white, at those, too, which nature, like a painter, has varied with the most contrasting colors." The church's grandeur reflected that of Constantinople, "city of the world's desire," capital of a prosperous empire that controlled east-west trade and laid the basis for the Greek and Slavic cultures of modern Europe.

Historical Significance

What cultural achievements did the Byzantines pass on to western Europe? How did their civilization affect the development of the peoples of eastern Europe?

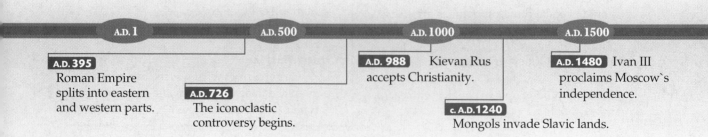

A.D. 1

A.D. 500

A.D. 1000

A.D. 1500

A.D. 395
Roman Empire splits into eastern and western parts.

A.D. 726
The iconoclastic controversy begins.

A.D. 988 Kievan Rus accepts Christianity.

c. A.D. 1240
Mongols invade Slavic lands.

A.D. 1480 Ivan III proclaims Moscow's independence.

History & Art The archangel Gabriel, an icon on wood, from the Russian State Museum, St. Petersburg, Russia

Your History Journal

Find out about a specific law in Justinian's Code in an encyclopedia or a book on the history of legal systems. Write the law as an illuminated manuscript, an art form described in this chapter.

| A.D. 300 | A.D. 600 | A.D. 900 | A.D. 1200 |

A.D. 330 Constantine builds city of Constantinople.

A.D. 527 Justinian becomes eastern Roman emperor.

A.D. 787 Church council at Nicaea approves use of icons.

A.D. 1054 Eastern and Western Churches split.

Section 1

The New Rome

Setting the Scene

▶ **Terms to Define**
clergy, laity, icon, iconoclast, schism

▶ **People to Meet**
Constantine, Justinian, Theodora, Leo III

▶ **Places to Locate**
Byzantine Empire, Constantinople

Find Out What made the Byzantine Empire rich and powerful?

The Storyteller

Byzantium [Constantinople] was in flames. A mob was screaming insults at Emperor Justinian and Empress Theodora. The emperor swiftly ordered the imperial treasury loaded onto ships to prepare for escape. Half crazed and without hope, Justinian held a final council of a few loyal friends; Theodora was present. After the military generals expressed their fears, Theodora suddenly rose and broke the silence. "I do not choose to flee," she said. "Never shall I see the day when

I am not saluted as the empress.... You have the money, the ships are ready, the sea is open. As for me, I shall stay." Hearing her, the others took heart. That day, Theodora saved Justinian's throne.

—adapted from *Theodora, Empress of Byzantium,* Charles Diehl, 1972

Theodora, detail of mosaic

After the Roman Empire was divided in A.D. 395, the eastern half became known as the **Byzantine Empire**. At its height in the A.D. 500s, the Byzantine Empire included most of the Balkan Peninsula, Italy, southern Spain, Asia Minor, Syria and North Africa. Its major population group, the Greeks, lived mainly in the central part of the empire. Also included in the empire were Egyptians, Syrians, Arabs, Armenians, Jews, Persians, Slavs, and Turks. These varied peoples and cultures gave Byzantine civilization an international character.

Byzantine Foundations

The location of **Constantinople**, the Byzantine capital, reinforced this multicultural character. The city was located near the centers of early Christianity as well as on major trade routes.

A Strategic City

In A.D. 330 the Roman emperor **Constantine** built Constantinople at a strategic place where Europe and Asia meet. Located on a peninsula, Constantinople overlooked the Bosporus, the narrow strait between the Sea of Marmara and the Black Sea. A second strait, the Dardanelles, connects the Sea of Marmara and the Aegean Sea, which leads to the Mediterranean. These straits gave the occupiers of the peninsula control over movement between the Mediterranean and the Black Seas and, as a result, over the routes leading east to Asia and north to northern Europe. The site of Constantinople itself offered natural protection from attack at a time when Germanic invaders were assaulting Rome to the west. Water protected the city on three sides, and triple walls fortified the side open to attack by land. Eventually a huge chain was strung across the narrow mouth of the deep harbor on Constantinople's north side for still greater protection.

The straits also made the peninsula a natural crossroads for trade. By A.D. 400 the Byzantine capital had become the wealthiest part of the Roman Empire, handling rich cargoes from Asia, Europe, and Africa.

Cultural Blend

After Rome's fall, the Byzantine Empire was regarded as heir to Roman power and traditions. Constantinople was known as the New Rome because its emperors were Romans who spoke Latin and many of its wealthy families came from Rome. Despite these ties, the Byzantine Empire was more than a continuation of the old Roman Empire.

Lands once part of the Greek world formed the heart of the Byzantine Empire. The Byzantine people not only spoke Greek but also stressed their Greek heritage. Eventually Byzantine emperors and officials also used Greek rather than Latin. Religious scholars expressed their ideas in Greek and developed a distinct form of Christianity known today as Eastern Orthodoxy. In addition to the Byzantine Empire's classical Greek heritage and Christian religion came cultural influences from eastern civilizations such as Persia. This mixture of cultures created a distinct Byzantine civilization. Between A.D. 500 and A.D. 1200, this civilization was one of the most advanced in the world and had a higher standard of living than western Europe.

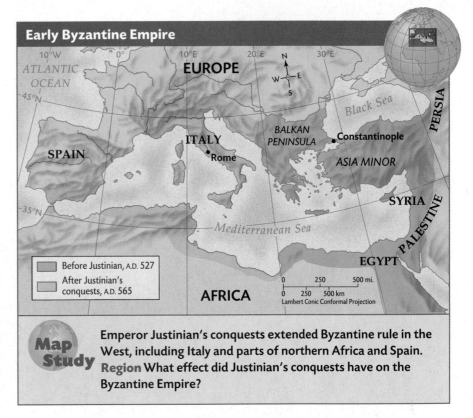

Early Byzantine Empire

Map Study

Emperor Justinian's conquests extended Byzantine rule in the West, including Italy and parts of northern Africa and Spain. **Region** What effect did Justinian's conquests have on the Byzantine Empire?

Before Justinian, A.D. 527
After Justinian's conquests, A.D. 565

POINT
Justinian's Rule

At its height the Byzantine Empire was ruled by **Justinian**, the son of prosperous peasants from Macedonia in the western part of the empire. While a young man in the court of his uncle, Emperor Justin I, he worked late into the night at his studies. Justinian's enthusiasm for knowledge and hard work continued after he became emperor in A.D. 527, at age 44.

Theodora's Support

Justinian's wife, **Theodora**, was beautiful, intelligent, and ambitious. Justinian had married her in spite of court objections to her occupation as an actress—a profession held in low esteem in the empire. A capable empress, Theodora participated actively in government, rewarding friends with positions and using dismissals to punish enemies.

Theodora was especially concerned with improving the social standing of women. She persuaded Justinian to issue a decree giving a wife the right to own land equal in value to the wealth she brought with her at marriage. This land gave a widow the income she needed to support her children without the assistance of the government.

In A.D. 532 Theodora's political talents helped save Justinian's throne. When a revolt of taxpayers in Constantinople threatened the government, Justinian's advisers urged him to leave the city. As flames roared through Constantinople and the rebels battered at the palace gates, Justinian prepared to flee. Theodora, however, persuaded him to remain in control.

Inspired by his wife's determination, Justinian reasserted his power. His army crushed the rebels, killing 30,000 people. From that time until his death in A.D. 565, Justinian ruled without challenge.

The Emperor Justinian, a mosaic from the A.D. 500s from Ravenna, Italy. *What architectural landmark did Justinian build?*

Military Campaigns

During Justinian's reign, the Byzantines faced a serious military threat from the East. The Sassanian Empire of Persia, under Chosroes (kaz•ROH•eez) I, grew in strength and threatened to conquer the eastern provinces of the Byzantine Empire. The Byzantines rallied their forces and threw back the Persians. Justinian gained a brief period of security for the eastern borders by agreeing to pay tribute in return for peace.

Justinian dreamed of restoring the Roman Empire. In A.D. 533 he began the reconquest of Italy, North Africa, and Spain—Roman lands that had fallen to Germanic invaders. Under the general Belisarius, the Byzantine armies were strengthened and reorganized. Between A.D. 533 and A.D. 555, they fought a series of wars against the Vandals in North Africa, the Ostrogoths in Italy, and the Visigoths in southern Spain. The Byzantines conquered these Germanic groups and extended Byzantine rule in the west.

The successful reconquest, however, proved costly for the empire. The wars exhausted most of the Byzantine resources. Funds were low for defending the eastern borders, which faced attack by an expanding Persian Empire. Justinian's conquests did not last. Within a generation of his death, the empire lost many of its outlying territories.

Code of Laws

Justinian's legal reforms did last, affecting Western law even today. Shortly after becoming emperor, Justinian appointed a commission to codify, or classify, the empire's Roman laws. For centuries, these laws had accumulated without organization or classification.

The commission was made up of 10 scholars headed by a legal expert named Tribonian. For more than 6 years, the commission collected and organized vast numbers of laws. It threw out the ones that were outdated, simplified many, and put the remainder into categories. The commission's work was recorded in a collection of books known as the *Corpus of Civil Law,* or the Justinian Code. This massive work preserved Rome's legal heritage and later became the basis for most European legal systems.

The Arts

Under Justinian, Byzantine art and architecture

thrived and achieved their distinct character. The emperor ordered the construction of new roads, fortresses, aqueducts, monasteries, and other buildings. His most famous project was the church of Hagia Sophia, "Holy Wisdom," in Constantinople. The largest and most beautiful church in the empire, Hagia Sophia still stands today as one of the world's great architectural landmarks.

Byzantine Religion

Strong ties linked Byzantine emperors and the Church. The emperors were regarded as God's representatives on earth. Starting in the A.D. 400s, Byzantine emperors and empresses were crowned by the patriarch of Constantinople and took an oath to defend the Christian faith.

Church and State

Byzantine emperors frequently played a major role in church affairs. They appointed church officials, defined the style of worship, and used the wealth of the Church for government purposes.

Justinian strengthened this control over the Church by intervening in disputes over church beliefs. He also tried to unify the empire under one Christian faith, a practice that sometimes led to persecution of Jews and non-Greek Christians.

Religious Controversy

Both Byzantine clergy—church officials such as priests and bishops—and laity—church members who were not clergy—were intensely interested in religious matters. In their homes, markets, and shops, Byzantines often engaged in heated religious discussions. Visitors to Constantinople saw shoppers in the marketplaces having lively discussions about such topics as the exact relationship of Jesus the Son to God the Father. Such arguments often became political issues and led to fights and riots.

In the A.D. 700s, a dispute broke out over the use of icons (EYE•KAHNZ), or religious images, in worship. Although Christians had disagreed about this practice since the A.D. 400s, the use of icons in churches became a political issue by the A.D. 700s.

Those who objected to the use of icons in Christian worship argued that the Bible, in the Ten Commandments, prohibited such images. Defenders stressed that icons were symbols of

Byzantine Architecture

Hagia Sophia, completed in A.D. 537, was built to symbolize both Christianity's importance in the Byzantine Empire and the Byzantine emperor's authority. It also represented the beginning of what became known as the Byzantine style of architecture.

Early Byzantine churches featured a central dome on a flat roof supported by four arches springing from columns or piers. Often the dome was pierced by windows and covered with glittering mosaics. Light streamed into the church from all directions and reflected off the decorated surfaces.

The Byzantine style eventually spread to other lands, such as Ukraine and Russia, that accepted Eastern Christianity. Architects in these lands modified the original Byzantine model to suit their own needs. For example, the Russians, who lived in a cold climate with a lot of snow, replaced the flat roof and large central dome with sloping roofs and onion-shaped domes.

Today, Eastern Christians throughout the world still use some form of the Byzantine style. In cities and towns of North America, the descendants of Eastern Christian immigrants who came during the late 1800s and early 1900s have sometimes combined traditional Byzantine architectural principles with modern ones in their churches.

Hagia Sophia

Linking Past and Present ACTIVITY

Examine a church or other building in your community that is built in the Byzantine style. What elements of its architecture do you think reflect the basic Byzantine model? What elements do you think are modern or come from other cultural traditions?

Simplified Alphabet Becomes Popular

Japan, A.D. 860

The Japanese alphabet, hiragana, became popular around A.D. 860. It consisted of characters developed by simplifying the Chinese alphabet. Hiragana was popularized by women of the Heian court, who used the system in writing poetry, diaries, and novels. It was called "letters of women" because men continued to use kanji, or the Chinese system.

Japan

God's presence in human affairs. The leading champion of icons was the Byzantine theologian John of Damascus. Although a resident of the Islamic Empire, he wrote many religious articles defending the use of icons.

Believing that icons encouraged superstition and the worship of idols, in A.D. 726 Emperor **Leo III** ordered all icons removed from the churches. The emperor's supporters—mostly military leaders, government officials, and many of the people in Asia Minor—became known as iconoclasts, or image breakers.

Church leaders and other Byzantines resisted the order, and were supported by the Church in Rome, which was as important a center of Christianity as Constantinople. The Roman pope's involvement in the controversy strained relations between the Eastern and Western Churches.

Feeling his authority was being challenged, Leo asserted his power and suppressed demonstrations in favor of icons. Although several later emperors followed Leo's lead, they were not supported by

the people. In A.D. 787 a church council at Nicaea approved the use of icons. Soon after, the Empress Irene—the first woman to hold the Byzantine throne in her own right—allowed the use of icons as long as they were not given the worship due to God. The Eastern Church further settled the issue in A.D. 843, allowing the use of pictures, but not statues, in worship.

Conflict With Rome

Since the A.D. 300s, the Eastern and Western Churches had disagreed on a number of religious and political issues. As centuries passed, the disagreements intensified.

The iconoclastic controversy was but one of many reasons that divided the two churches. The most serious issue concerned the source of religious authority. The pope in Rome and the patriarch of Constantinople did not agree on their roles in the Christian Church. The pope stated that he was supreme leader of the Church; the patriarch of Constantinople opposed this claim. The two church leaders also disagreed over points of doctrine. They challenged each other for control of new churches in the Balkan Peninsula.

Relations between Eastern and Western Churches worsened in the A.D. 700s when the Germanic Lombards invaded central Italy. When the Byzantine emperor refused to give the pope in Rome military protection, the pope turned to the Franks, a Germanic Catholic people in western Europe. After the Franks defeated the Lombards, the pope gave the Frankish leader, Charlemagne, the title of emperor—a title which only the Byzantine ruler could legally grant. This action made the Byzantines even more bitter toward the pope and the Western Church.

By A.D. 1054 doctrinal, political, and geographical differences finally led to a schism (SIH•zuhm), or separation, of the Church into the Roman Catholic Church in the West and the Eastern Orthodox Church in the East. The split further weakened the Byzantine Empire, which had faced attacks from numerous peoples since its founding.

SECTION 1 REVIEW

Recall
1. **Define** clergy, laity, icon, iconoclast, schism.
2. **Identify** Constantine, Justinian, Theodora, Leo III.
3. **Locate** Constantinople on the

map on page 247. Why was Constantinople's location significant?

Critical Thinking
4. **Analyzing Information** How were Byzantine emperors and

the Christian Church linked?

Understanding Themes
5. **Conflict** How did religious disputes, such as the iconoclastic controversy, affect Byzantine political affairs?

A.D. 500

A.D. 550 Byzantines send expedition to China.

A.D. 1000

A.D. 863 Cyril develops alphabet for the Slavs.

A.D. 1184 Queen Tamara begins her reign in Georgia.

A.D. 1500

A.D. 1453 Constantinople falls to Ottoman Turks.

Section 2

Byzantine Civilization

Setting the Scene

▶ **Terms to Define**

theology, regent, mosaic, illuminated manuscript, monastery, missionary

▶ **People to Meet**

Cyril, Methodius, the Seljuk Turks, the Ottoman Turks, Tiridates III, Tamara

▶ **Places to Locate**

Venice, Armenia, Georgia, Bulgaria, Serbia

 **ind Out** What role did Christianity play in Byzantine and neighboring societies?

The Storyteller

A bishop from Italy wrote home describing the Byzantine court: "In the audience-hall sat the Emperor on a throne before which stood an artificial tree, all gilded, on whose branches mechanical birds perched, singing. To either side of the throne stood a mighty lion, which, as the visitor approached, lashed the ground with its tail and from whose open jaws … there came a terrifying roar." The visitor threw himself to the ground three times, and looking up beheld the Emperor raised by an invisible mechanism to the roof of the hall, where he sat glittering among his jewels.

—adapted from *Istanbul*, Martin Heurlimann, 1958

Emperor Constantine IX

From A.D. 500 to A.D. 800, when western Europe was in decline, the Byzantine Empire was a brilliant center of civilization. Its scholars preserved Greek philosophy and literature, Roman political and legal ideas, and Christian theology, or religious teachings. The Byzantines also created new art forms and spread the religion of the Eastern Orthodox Church into eastern Europe.

Byzantine Life

Byzantine society was divided into a hierarchy of social groups. Yet, there were few barriers to prevent a person from moving from one group to another. This flexibility brought variety and change to Byzantine life.

Family Life

The family was the center of social life for most Byzantines. Both the Church and the government supported marriage as a sacred institution. Divorce was difficult to obtain, and the Church generally forbade more than one remarriage.

Byzantine women were expected to live partly in seclusion, and so rooms in homes and churches were set aside for their sole use. Nevertheless, women had gained some rights through Theodora's efforts. Like the empress herself, some women became well educated and influential in the government. Several governed as regents, or temporary rulers, and a few ruled in their own right as empresses.

The Economy

Most Byzantines made a living through farming, herding, or working as laborers. Farmers paid heavy taxes that supported the government.

Although the base of the Byzantine economy was agricultural, commerce thrived in cities such as Constantinople, which was the site of a natural crossroads for trade. Byzantine ships loaded with cargo sailed between the Mediterranean and Black Seas by way of the Bosporus and Dardanelles. At the eastern shore of the Black Sea, goods could be shipped overland through Asia. Rivers such as the Dnieper, which flows from the Baltic region south to the Black Sea, provided access to northern Europe.

Merchants traded Byzantine agricultural goods and furs and enslaved people from northern Europe for luxury goods from the East. To Constantinople's busy harbor, called the Golden Horn, ships brought cloves and sandalwood from the East Indies; pepper, copper, and gems from India and Ceylon (present-day Sri Lanka); and silk from China.

The major Byzantine industry was weaving silk. It developed after A.D. 550, when Justinian sent two monks to China, the center of the silk industry.

On a visit to a silk factory the monks stole some silkworm eggs, hid them in hollow bamboo canes, and smuggled their precious cargo out of China. Brought to Constantinople, the silkworms fed on mulberry leaves and spun the silk that made the empire wealthy.

Byzantine Art and Learning

Among the products of Byzantine culture were beautiful icons, jewel-encrusted crosses, and carved ivory boxes for sacred items. These art forms were adopted by eastern Europe and also influenced western Europe and the Middle East.

Art

Religious subjects were the sources of most Byzantine art. Icons, the most popular art form, portrayed saints and other religious figures. Icons were displayed on the walls of churches, homes, and shrines. Magnificent churches were

Images *of the* Times

Byzantine Art

Byzantine art reflected the strong influence of Christianity.

The Byzantine church of St. Kosmas at Loukas, Greece, displays a colorful mosaic.

The crucifix was a familiar Byzantine icon both in churches and in homes.

embellished with gold and silver, polished and carved marble, ivory, and jewels, as well as icons and other religious images.

The Byzantines also excelled in the art of mosaic, or pictures made of many tiny pieces of colored glass or flat stone set in plaster. The most masterly mosaics captured the finest gradations of skin tones and textures of clothing—a skill even painters found difficult to master. Byzantine emperor Constantine VII, historian, painter, and author, described one mosaic:

> ❝ As you move, the figures seem to move, too. You could swear that their eyes are turning and shining and that their garments are rustling … the Byzantine mosaicist has succeeded in creating the illusion that his jig-saw puzzle has come to life. ❞

Religious scholars of the Byzantine Empire created another art form, the illuminated manuscript. These were books decorated with elaborate designs, beautiful lettering, and miniature paintings. The brilliantly colored paintings portrayed religious themes as well as scenes of Byzantine daily life. Adopted in western Europe, the art of illuminating manuscripts provided a vivid record of daily life between A.D. 300 and A.D. 1200.

Education

Schools and learning also played an important role in Byzantine culture. The government-supported University of Constantinople, established in A.D. 850, trained scholars and lawyers for government jobs; the Eastern Orthodox Church provided religious schools to train priests and theological scholars. Beyond the religious subjects that reflected the primary role of the Church, areas of study included medicine, law, philosophy, arithmetic, geometry, astronomy, grammar, and music. Wealthy people sometimes hired tutors to instruct their children, particularly their daughters, who were usually not admitted to schools and universities.

Beautiful illuminated manuscripts, such as this from St. Catherine's Monastery at Sinai, were the work of religious scholars. Monasteries were financed by the emperor and by wealthy citizens.

REFLECTING ON THE TIMES

1. How do these images reveal the prosperity of the Byzantine Empire?
2. Who paid to have much of the religious art at churches and monasteries created?

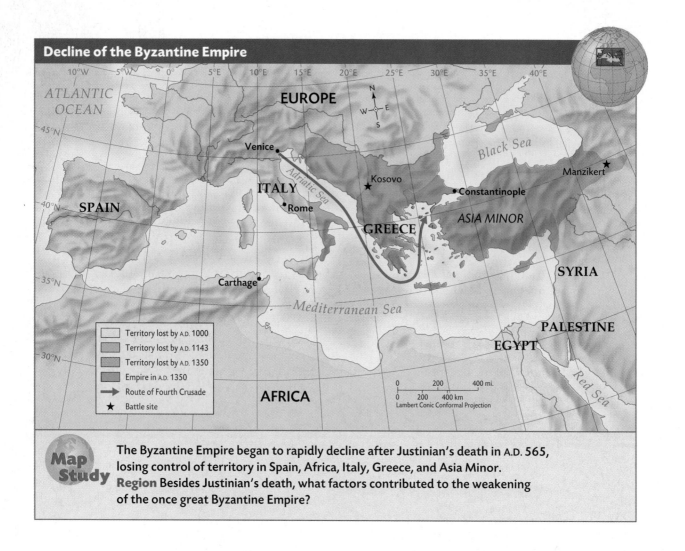

Decline of the Byzantine Empire

Map Study

The Byzantine Empire began to rapidly decline after Justinian's death in A.D. 565, losing control of territory in Spain, Africa, Italy, Greece, and Asia Minor. **Region** Besides Justinian's death, what factors contributed to the weakening of the once great Byzantine Empire?

Map legend:
- Territory lost by A.D. 1000
- Territory lost by A.D. 1143
- Territory lost by A.D. 1350
- Empire in A.D. 1350
- Route of Fourth Crusade
- ★ Battle site

Byzantine literature focused on salvation of the soul and obedience to God's will. Writers composed hymns and poems in praise of Christ and his mother, Mary. Instead of popular fiction, Byzantine authors wrote books about the lives of the saints, which provided readers with moral lessons as well as accounts of the saints' miracles and adventures.

The foremost occupation of Byzantine scholars, however, was copying the writings of the ancient Greeks and Romans. By preserving ancient works on science, medicine, and mathematics, the Byzantines helped spread classical knowledge to the Western world.

Spread of Christianity

Near the end of the A.D. 300s, devout Christians throughout the Byzantine Empire formed religious communities called monasteries. In the monasteries, men called monks sought to develop a spiritual way of life apart from the temptations of the world. At the same time, they could help other people by doing good deeds and by setting an example of Christian living. Christian women who did the same were called nuns and lived in quarters of their own known as convents.

Monasteries and convents soon played an important role in Byzantine life. They helped the poor and ran hospitals and schools for needy children. They also spread Byzantine arts and learning. Monasteries also sent missionaries—people who carry a religious message—to neighboring peoples to convert them to the Christian faith.

Footnotes to History

Greek Fire

In fighting their enemies, the Byzantines used a terrifying weapon known as Greek fire, one of the earliest uses of chemicals in warfare. This chemical mixture exploded when it came into contact with fire or water. The formula remains a mystery; it probably included highly flammable oil, pitch, quicklime, sulfur, and resin.

Among the most successful missionaries were the brothers **Cyril** and **Methodius**. They reasoned that Christianity would be more acceptable to the Slavic peoples who lived north of the empire if it were presented in their own language. About A.D. 863 Cyril devised an alphabet for the Slavic languages. Known today as the Cyrillic (suh•RIH•lihk) alphabet in honor of its inventor, this script is still used by Russians, Ukrainians, Bulgarians, and Serbs. When Cyril and Methodius presented the Slavs with Cyrillic translations of the Bible and church ceremonies, they won many converts.

Decline and Fall

From its founding, the Byzantine Empire suffered frequent attacks by invading armies. Among them were Germanic Lombards, Slavs, Avars, Bulgars, Persians, and Arabs.

Unending Attacks

After Justinian died in A.D. 565, the Germanic Lombards took over most of Italy, the Avars attacked the northern frontier, Slavic peoples moved into the Balkans, and the Persians resumed their attacks in the east. By A.D. 626 the Slavs were at the walls of Constantinople. Although a brilliant counterattack stopped their advance, a new enemy—the Arabs from the Middle East—entered the scene. Followers of the new religion of Islam, the Arabs sought to spread their faith and acquire wealth. By the A.D. 630s, they occupied Syria and Palestine and had expanded into Persia and across North Africa. The Byzantines stopped the Arabs at Constantinople, but could not regain the lost territories in the Middle East and North Africa.

By A.D. 700 the Byzantine Empire was reduced to the territories that were primarily Greek. The loss of the non-Greek lands actually helped strengthen the empire because it now had one religion, one language, and one culture.

Christian Conquest

In A.D. 1071 northern European people called Normans seized the Byzantine lands in southern Italy. **Venice**, an Italian trading city on the Adriatic Sea, agreed to help the Byzantines' effort to regain the lands in return for trading privileges in Constantinople. The attempt failed, however, and the Byzantines soon lost control of trade, badly weakening an economy already strained by war.

In the same year, **the Seljuk** (SEHL•JOOK) **Turks**, who had come from central Asia and converted to Islam, defeated the Byzantines at the town

Visualizing History St. Jacob holding script in the Cyrillic alphabet, a modified form of the Greek alphabet. *What peoples use the Cyrillic alphabet today?*

of Manzikert. As the invaders advanced, the Byzantine emperor asked the pope's help in defending Christianity. Expeditions sent by the pope against the Islamic forces were more interested in taking over Palestine.

In A.D. 1204 Christian soldiers from western Europe agreed to help the Venetians attack Constantinople. For three days the attackers burned and looted the city, stealing and destroying priceless manuscripts and works of art. Their actions were so brutal that Pope Innocent III publicly condemned them:

❝ These defenders of Christ, who should have turned their swords only against the infidels [followers of Islam], have bathed in Christian blood. They have respected neither religion, nor age, nor sex.... It was not enough for them to squander the treasures of the Empire and to rob private individuals, whether great or small.... They have dared to lay their hands on the wealth of the churches. They have been seen tearing from the altars the silver adornments, breaking them in fragments, over which they quarreled, violating the sanctuaries, carrying away the icons, crosses, and relics. **99**

The western Christians established "a Latin empire" in Constantinople. The Byzantine people resisted this rule successfully and reestablished their own culture in A.D. 1261.

Fall of Constantinople

The years of fighting had severely weakened the Byzantine Empire. Soon Serbs and Bulgars took over Balkan territory. New invaders from central Asia, **the Ottoman Turks**, attacked the eastern provinces. By the late A.D. 1300s, the Byzantine Empire consisted of only Constantinople and part of Greece.

About 100,000 people still lived in the capital; food was scarce, and wealth was gone. In A.D. 1453 the Ottomans laid siege to Constantinople. For six weeks their huge cannon blasted away at the city's walls. The Byzantines fought fiercely until their last emperor was killed.

For a thousand years, the Byzantine Empire had protected the Christian lands to its north. With the fall of Constantinople, central Europe lay open to attack by Islamic forces. Despite the empire's fall, the Byzantine heritage lived on in the civilization developed by the Eastern Slavs.

Neighboring Kingdoms

During the time of the Byzantine Empire, four neighboring kingdoms went through periods of prosperity and decline. Northeast of the empire, and south of the Caucasus Mountains between the Black and Caspian Seas, lay the kingdoms of **Armenia** and **Georgia**. Northwest of Byzantine territory, in Europe's Balkan Peninsula, arose two other realms— **Bulgaria** and **Serbia**.

Armenia

Located at a crossroads between Europe and Asia, Armenia struggled against foreign invasions. Settling the area in the 700s B.C., the Armenians within 300 years had become part of the Persian Empire. When Alexander the Great conquered Persia in the 330s B.C., his armies acquired Armenia but allowed it some freedoms. King Tigran II, who came to power about 95 B.C., built an independent Armenian kingdom stretching from the Caspian Sea to the Mediterranean Sea. The Romans, however, defeated Tigran in 69 B.C., and Armenia became part of the Roman Empire.

In the early A.D. 300s, the Armenians, under King **Tiridates** (TEER•uh•DAH •teez) **III**, accepted Christianity. This decision made Armenia the first officially Christian country in the world. Christianity gave Armenians a sense of national identity. Mesrob (MEH•zrohb), an Armenian scholar-monk, developed the Armenian alphabet in the early A.D. 400s. In A.D. 451, the Armenians successfully

Visualizing History **Portrait of Sultan Mahmet II, who conquered Constantinople and renamed it Istanbul.** *How long did the Byzantine city hold out against the sultan's siege?*

defended their Christian state against the Persians in the Battle of Avarair (ah•vah•RAHR).

Arab armies invaded Armenia in the A.D. 600s, but they failed to conquer the entire country. An independent Armenian kingdom eventually arose in the northern region. In the A.D. 1000s the Seljuk Turks swept into Armenia, followed by the Ottoman Turks in the A.D. 1400s. Within 300 years, Armenia had became a battlefield among the Ottomans, Persians, and Russians. During the A.D. 1800s, it was divided between the Russian and Ottoman empires.

Georgia

Like Armenia, Georgia continually faced waves of foreign invasions. Ancient Georgia consisted of two kingdoms known as Colchis and Iberia. Both realms came under Roman rule in 65 B.C. The Roman conquerors built new roads and introduced their laws and customs to the region. The Silk Road, which passed through the Caucasus Mountains, allowed the Georgians to prosper from trade between Europe and Asia. Caravans of silk cloth, spices, and other goods reached ports on Georgia's Black Sea coast and continued on to the Middle East and Europe.

Georgia accepted Christianity in the A.D. 300s. Georgian tradition states that a Christian woman named Nino was responsible for converting the Georgians. Meanwhile, newly Christianized Georgia was attacked by rival Persian and Byzantine armies.

During the A.D. 1100s and early A.D. 1200s, Georgia enjoyed a golden age of freedom and culture under Queen **Tamara** (tah•MAH•rah). However, from the late A.D. 1200s to the A.D. 1700s, the Georgians again faced a series of conquerors, including the Mongols, the Persians, and the Ottomans. Turning northward to the Russians for military aid, Georgia by the early A.D. 1800s had become part of the Russian Empire.

Bulgaria

The Balkan Peninsula also underwent upheavals. Conquered by Roman armies, the region that is present-day Bulgaria became part of the Roman Empire in the A.D. 40s. When Rome fell about 400 years later, Slavs from east central Europe and Bulgars from central Asia settled Bulgaria, where they eventually intermarried to become the Bulgarians.

Influenced by Byzantine culture and religion, the first Bulgarian state arose in the A.D. 600s. It reached its peak 300 years later under King Simeon I, and finally fell prey to Byzantine conquest in A.D. 1018. Byzantine decline, however, enabled the Bulgarians to regain their freedom. This second Bulgarian kingdom survived from the late A.D. 1100s to the late A.D. 1300s, when Ottoman invaders from central Asia conquered the territory. Ottoman rule of Bulgaria lasted more than 500 years.

Serbia

Northwest of Bulgaria was the Slavic kingdom of Serbia. During the A.D. 500s and 600s, groups of Slavs settled in the Balkan Peninsula. By the 1100s, the Serbs, one of the most powerful of these groups, had accepted Eastern Orthodox Christianity and the Cyrillic alphabet. They also formed a state. The Serbian kingdom enjoyed its greatest period of prosperity in the A.D. 1300s under Stefan Dusán (STEH•fahn•doo•SHAHN), who assumed the title of emperor of the Serbs. Dusán's armies successfully fought the Byzantines, expanding Serbian rule throughout much of the Balkans.

After Dusán's death in 1355, his heirs lacked the skills to keep the Serbian kingdom united. The Serbs valiantly fought the Ottomans but were eventually defeated in 1389 in the Battle of Kosovo. Almost 500 years of Ottoman rule followed, but the desire to reverse the shame of Kosovo helped keep alive Serbian national pride.

SECTION 2 REVIEW

Recall
1. **Define** theology, regent, mosaic, illuminated manuscript, monastery, missionary.
2. **Identify** Cyril, Methodius, the Seljuk Turks, Manzikert, the Ottoman Turks, Tiridates III, Tamara.

3. **Explain** why the Bosporus and the Dardanelles are strategic waterways.

Critical Thinking
4. **Analyzing Information** Examine how the doctrinal and cultural split between the Roman Catholic Church and the Eastern Orthodox Church contributed to the Byzantine Empire's decline.

Understanding Themes
5. **Innovation** How did Christianity affect culture in the Byzantine Empire and in neighboring kingdoms? What was the role of art and religion in these lands?

A.D. 980 Vladimir becomes Grand Prince of Kiev.

A.D. 1240 Alexander Nevsky defeats the Swedes.

A.D. 1380 Moscow defeats Mongols at the Battle of Kulikovo.

A.D. 1472 Ivan III of Moscow takes title of czar.

Section 3

The Eastern Slavs

Setting the Scene

▶ **Terms to Define**
steppe, principality, boyar, czar

▶ **People to Meet**
the Slavs, Rurik, Olga, Vladimir, Yaroslav, the Mongols, Alexander Nevsky, Ivan III

▶ **Places to Locate**
Dnieper River, Kiev, Novgorod, Moscow

Find Out How did the Eastern Slavs develop separate cultures from those of western Europe?

The Storyteller

As a pagan prince, Vladimir behaved kindly; once he became a Christian, his generosity became unlimited. Beggars assembled in his courtyard every

day for food, drink, clothing, and money. For the sick and weak, supply wagons were loaded up and driven around the city of Kiev. Once, when his friends showed disgust at having to eat with plain wooden spoons, Vladimir laughed and had silver ones cast for them. He was also the first Kiev prince to mint gold and silver coins. The first of these, made by inexperienced Russian crafts work-

Eastern Orthodox church

ers, were slightly lumpy and uneven, but bore Vladimir's picture and the inscription, "Here is Vladimir on his throne. And this is his gold."

—from *Vladimir the Russian Viking,* Vladimir Volkoff, 1985

After the fall of Constantinople in A.D. 1453, the leadership of the Eastern Orthodox world passed from the Byzantines to **the Slavs**. The Slavs were among the largest groups living in eastern Europe. Because of their location, the Slavs had been in close contact with the Byzantines since the A.D. 900s.

This relationship made a lasting mark on the development of Slavic history. The Slavs, especially those living in the areas that are today the Balkan Peninsula, Ukraine, Belarus, and Russia, borrowed much from the Byzantines. On the basis of Byzantine religion, law, and culture, the Slavs built a new civilization. They also borrowed heavily from western European and Asian cultures. As a result of these different influences, Russia—the farthest north and east of the Slavic lands—never became a completely European or completely Asian country.

The Setting

One of the Byzantine trade routes ran north across the Black Sea and up the **Dnieper River**, then overland to the Baltic Sea. From trading posts along the river grew the roots of early Slavic civilization.

The Steppe

North of the Black Sea are vast plains, thick forests, and mighty rivers. Much of the land is an immense plain called the steppe. Ukrainian author Nikolay Gogol vividly captures its spirit in his *Cossack Tales*:

❝ The farther the steppe went the grander it became … one green uninhabited waste. No plow ever furrowed its immense wavy plains of wild plants; the wild horses, which herded there, alone trampled them down. The whole extent of the steppe was nothing but a green-gold ocean, whose surface seemed besprinkled with millions of different colored flowers. ❞

Although the steppe has rich black soil, the harsh climate makes farming difficult and crop failures common. Too far inland to be reached by moist ocean breezes, the steppe often has scanty rainfall. In addition, most of the land lies in the same latitudes as Canada and has the same short growing season. During the long, hard winter, blasts of Arctic air roar across the land and bury it deep in snow.

Forests and Rivers

North of the steppe stretch seemingly endless forests of evergreens, birch, oak, and other hardwoods. North–south flowing rivers such as the Dnieper, Dniester, and Volga cross the steppe and penetrate the forests, providing the easiest means of transportation. Yet travel is difficult for much of the year. In winter, deep drifts of snow cover the ground, and in the spring thaw the land turns to knee-deep mud.

The People

Historians know little about the origin of the first Slavic peoples. Some believe the Slavs came from present-day eastern Poland. Others think they may have been farmers in the Black Sea region. It is known that by about A.D. 500 the Slavs had formed into three distinct groups and had settled in different parts of eastern Europe.

Slavic Groups

One group, known as the West Slavs, lived in the marshlands, plains, and mountains of east-central Europe. They successfully fought the Germans to the west and the Scandinavians to the north for control of territory. Today the descendants of the West Slavs are the peoples of Poland, the Czech Republic, and Slovakia. Their religious ties came to be with the Roman Catholic Church, and their cultural ties were with western Europe.

Another group, known as the South Slavs, settled in the Balkan Peninsula, and had frequent contacts with the Byzantines. Today, their descendants are the Serbs, Croats, and Slovenes, whose languages and cultures were shaped by both the Roman Catholic West and the Orthodox East. One group of South Slavs—the Bosnians—were influenced by the religion of Islam from the Middle East.

The third and largest Slavic group, the Eastern Slavs, includes those now known as Ukrainians, Russians, and Belarussians. They lived north of the Black Sea between the Dnieper and Dniester Rivers and traded with the Byzantine Empire and northern Europe. From A.D. 500 to A.D. 800, some Eastern Slavs moved eastward toward the Volga River.

East Slavic Lands A.D. 1100s

Map Study Trade with the Byzantine Empire helped build Kiev into a major city. **Movement** In what direction would traders have traveled from Kiev to Sweden?

Early Ways of Life

The early Eastern Slavs lived in villages made up of related families. They were farmers who hunted wild game and birds to supplement the wheat, rye, and oats they grew. In the forests they cleared land by cutting and burning trees and scattering the ash to enrich the soil. On the steppes they ignited a "sea of flame" to burn off the grass for planting.

Most farm homes were sturdy log houses. With knife, chisel, and ax the peasants skillfully shaped the logs, notching them so that they would fit together without nails. Many log houses had wooden gables and window frames decorated with painted carvings of flowers and animals. Skilled artisans also used wood to make furniture, cooking utensils, musical instruments, boats, and images of favorite deities.

The Eastern Slavs used the many rivers in their region for transportation and trade. They set up trading towns along the riverbanks. By the A.D. 800s, a trade route ran from the Baltic Sea in the north to the Black Sea in the south.

Kievan Rus

The early Eastern Slavs were not warlike. During the late A.D. 800s, they relied on Vikings, a group of warriors and traders from Scandinavia, to protect their trade routes. The Vikings not only provided military aid, they also helped to lay the foundations of Slavic government.

The arrival of the Vikings is recorded in the *Primary Chronicle*, a collection of Eastern Slavic history, tales, and legends written around A.D. 1100. According to the *Chronicle*, in about A.D. 860 the Slavic people from the northern forest village of Novgorod asked Vikings from Scandinavia for aid: "Our land is great and rich, but there is no order in it. Come to rule and reign over us." The Viking leader **Rurik** accepted the invitation. The Slavs called the Vikings and the area they controlled *Rus*; the word *Russia* is probably derived from this name.

Rise of Kiev

In about A.D. 880, Rurik's successor, Prince Oleg, conquered the fortress-village of **Kiev** (Kyiv in Ukrainian) to the south. Built high on a bluff where the forest meets the steppe, Kiev prospered because it lay on the Dnieper River trade route. Some still call it the mother of Eastern Slavic cities.

Control of Kiev enabled Oleg to dominate the water trade route. Towns along the route were brought together under his leadership. Kiev soon became the major city of a region of Slavic territories known as Kievan Rus. The rulers of Kiev, known as Grand Princes, conducted raids against Constantinople. They were attracted by the wealth and

civilization of the Byzantine capital. In A.D. 911 a treaty ended these raids and established trade between the Byzantines and the Eastern Slavs. During the summer months, Slavic merchants carried furs, honey, and other forest products by boat to Constantinople. There they traded their goods for cloth, wine, weapons, and jewelry.

Kievan Government

By A.D. 900, Kievan Rus had organized into a collection of city-states and principalities, or territories ruled by princes. Each region enjoyed local self-government; however, they all paid special respect to the Grand Prince of Kiev. The Grand Prince collected tribute from the local princes to support his court and army. The major duties of these princes were to administer justice and to defend the frontiers. The princes were assisted by councils of wealthy merchants and landed nobles, who were known as boyars. Assemblies represented all free adult male citizens. They handled daily affairs and had the power to accept or remove princes.

These three institutions—the princely office, the council, and the assembly—varied in power from region to region. In the northeastern territories, the prince wielded a great deal of political power. In the southeastern areas, the boyars had the greatest political influence. In Novgorod and a few northern trading towns and cities, the assemblies overshadowed both princes and boyars. In these areas, the assemblies came close to establishing a tradition of representative government in the Eastern Slavic lands. However, later princes limited the powers of the assemblies.

Jim Brandenburg

Rurik the Rus

This 19th-century statue of Kievan Rus's ruler Rurik stands in the center of the Russian city of Novgorod. The bronze Rurik, a mighty Prince, holds symbols of military might and political power: a shield and sword. His fur cape sweeps proudly over his shoulders. Founder of nations, the Viking warrior proclaims a glorious past.

Rurik and his Viking warriors came from Scandinavia to what is now Russia and Ukraine in the A.D. 800s, perhaps invited there by native Slavic tribes constantly warring with each other. The Eastern Slavs during the A.D. 800s had little political stability, which made farming and commerce difficult. The Vikings changed that. Trading with the strong, plundering the weak, they moved south from Novgorod to Kiev, where they founded a political state, and from there they moved on to Odessa on the shores of the Black Sea. It took them two centuries to complete their expansion. By then the Vikings had lost their Scandinavian ways and had become assimilated into the local cultures. ⊕

Arrival of Christianity

Before the late A.D. 900s, the Eastern Slavs honored nature spirits and ancestors, and worshiped many deities. The most popular gods were Perun, god of thunder and lightning, and the Great Mother, goddess of the land and harvest. Images of the deities were built on the highest ground outside the villages.

Vladimir's Conversion

Because of contact with the Byzantine Empire, many Eastern Slavs were influenced by Eastern Orthodoxy. **Olga**, a princess of Kiev, became the first member of the Kievan nobility to accept the faith. Her grandson, Prince **Vladimir** of Kiev, decided to abandon the old beliefs and to adopt a new religion that he thought would help the Eastern Slavs become a more powerful civilization. An old Slavic legend states that Vladimir sent observers abroad to examine Judaism, Roman Catholicism, Eastern Orthodoxy, and Islam. Only the beautiful ceremony in the splendid Byzantine church of Hagia Sophia impressed the observers. In A.D. 988, after his own conversion to Eastern Orthodoxy, Vladimir ordered a mass baptism in the Dnieper River for his people.

Visualizing History This ancient monastery stands as a symbol of the influence of Byzantine Christianity. *How was Eastern Orthodoxy introduced in Kievan Rus?*

Effects of Conversion

The conversion to Eastern Orthodoxy brought Byzantine culture to Kievan Rus. Byzantine priests and bishops introduced the Eastern Slavs to colorful rituals and taught them the art of painting icons. The Eastern Slavs also learned to write their language in the Cyrillic alphabet. Schools were established in the towns for the sons of boyars, priests, and merchants. Byzantine architects arrived in Kiev to build stone churches with magnificent domes. Monasteries also were founded in the towns and countryside, and attracted many new converts.

Acceptance of Eastern Orthodoxy, however, tended to isolate the Eastern Slavs from the outside world. Following the split between the Eastern and Western Churches, Kievan Rus was separated from western Europe. Its people lost contact with developments that took place in that area after A.D. 1200. At the same time, the Byzantine practice of translating the Bible and Orthodox church services into local languages had an important impact. Because Kievan scholars had translations of some classical and Christian writings in their own language, they did not learn Greek or Latin. As a result, they did not deepen their knowledge of the heritage of western European civilization. Instead, they turned for inspiration to the traditions of their own local culture.

Kiev's Golden Age

Vladimir, who ruled from A.D. 980 to A.D. 1015, was one of the most important grand princes of Kiev. Known for his skills as a warrior, he successfully defended Kievan Rus's eastern frontiers against nomadic invaders. He also expanded its western borders by capturing lands in Poland and near the Baltic Sea.

Yaroslav's Reign

After a time of dynastic conflict, Vladimir's son **Yaroslav** became Grand Prince in A.D. 1019. Under Yaroslav's rule, Kievan culture reached its height. Yaroslav encouraged the spread of learning by establishing the first library in Kiev. Yaroslav also organized the Kievan legal system, drawing from Justinian's Code. Written primarily for the princes and merchants, the code treated crimes against property as well as against persons.

A skilled diplomat, Yaroslav arranged for his daughters and sisters to marry kings in Norway, Hungary, France, and Poland. To the Europeans, who were just arising from the isolation and disorder of the early Middle Ages, Kiev was a glittering capital whose culture outshone that of any in western Europe.

Kiev's Decline

After Yaroslav's death, Kiev declined in power and wealth for several reasons. First, Yaroslav began the practice of dividing up his lands among all his sons instead of willing them to one heir. Since no law established a clear line of succession, the heirs battled one another over control of Kiev. Second, the Latin Christian state created in Constantinople disrupted trade with the Byzantines and weakened Kiev's economy. Finally, in A.D. 1240 Mongol invaders from central Asia captured Kiev and completely destroyed it.

Mongol Rule

The Mongols, or Tatars, as the Slavs called them, defeated the armies of the Eastern Slavic princes and conquered most of the country except for Novgorod. They sacked towns and villages and killed thousands. Mongols sought to tax the peoples they conquered, rather than impose their culture. The Slavs were allowed to practice their Christian faith, but the Mongols required allegiance to the Mongol ruler and service in the Mongol army.

For two centuries, Mongol rule isolated most of the Eastern Slavs from European civilization. Although the occupation helped unify the Eastern Slavs, it also further distanced them from ideas and trends of the Western world.

Rise of Moscow

As city life in the south declined after the fall of Kiev, many Eastern Slavs—led by monks, farmers, and artisans—moved into the remote northern forests to escape Mongol rule. By the late A.D. 1200s, Vladimir–Suzdal and **Novgorod** were the strongest Eastern Slavic principalities.

Alexander Nevsky

The Mongols had never advanced as far north as Novgorod because the spring thaw turned the land into a swamp they could not cross. Instead, the city faced attacks in the Baltic Sea area from Swedes and Germans who wanted to convert the Eastern Slavs to Roman Catholicism. In a ferocious battle on the Neva River in A.D. 1240, Alexander,

Visualizing History Alexander Nevsky, ruler of Novgorod, fought the German Teutonic Knights in A.D. 1242. *Why did the Germans and Swedes attack the Eastern Slavs?*

prince of Novgorod, defeated the invading Swedes. This victory earned him the nickname **Alexander Nevsky**, Alexander "of the Neva," and his victory established Novgorod as a strong, independent principality.

Moscow's Beginnings

Daniel, the youngest son of Alexander Nevsky, became ruler of **Moscow**, a small but prosperous town located near vital land and water routes. Using war and diplomatic marriages, the princes of Moscow gradually expanded their state's territory. Moscow's importance grew in A.D. 1325 when the metropolitan, or leader of the Orthodox Church in the Eastern Slavic lands, was transferred there. By about A.D. 1350, Moscow had become the most powerful city. Cooperation with Mongol policies had kept it free from outside interference. Daniel's son, Prince Ivan I, became known as Money Bag because the Mongols even trusted him to collect taxes for them.

Muscovite forces defeated the Mongols at the Battle of Kulikovo in A.D. 1380. The tide had turned in favor of Moscow. Over the next hundred years, the Eastern Slavs steadily drove out the Mongols. In A.D. 1480 during the rule of **Ivan III**, Moscow

Visualizing History Gold-domed spires of the Church of the Annunciation reach toward the sky behind the Kremlin's walls. *What was the original purpose of the Kremlin?*

1472 when Ivan III married Sophia, niece of the last Byzantine emperor, he took the title czar, or "caesar," the title used by the Roman and Byzantine emperors. Ivan also made the two-headed Byzantine eagle the symbol of his rule.

In A.D. 1493 Ivan added the title Sovereign of All Russia. The lands he ruled, eventually known as Russia, were a hundred times as large as the original Muscovite state. The people spoke one language, and the princes served one czar. The Russian Orthodox Church, which identified its interests with those of the Muscovite ruler, proclaimed that Moscow was the Third Rome. The Church regarded Ivan as both the successor of the Byzantine emperor and protector of the Eastern Orthodox Church, a claim all succeeding Russian czars would also make.

Moscow's Culture

Eastern Orthodoxy shaped the development of Moscow's culture. Its leaders stressed the importance of obedience to the czar and the government. The Church taught the people that submission to authority was a Christian duty. Joseph Sanin, an influential church leader during Ivan III's reign, wrote that "although the [ruler] was like other men in his physical characteristics, in his power he was similar to God in heaven."

Although western European influences reached Russia, they were transformed by local Russian styles and tastes. Instead of using Greek, Latin, or other classical languages, the Church used an early Slavic language in its worship and writings. Russia's religious leaders and political rulers also encouraged the development of a unique national style of icon painting and building construction. Ivan III had western European and Russian architects rebuild the Moscow Kremlin, or fortress. In spite of Western influences on its construction, the Kremlin became known for the typically Russian splendor of its beautiful onion-domed churches and ornately decorated palaces. Today the Kremlin in Moscow is still a center of government, religion, and culture for Russia.

finally refused to pay taxes to the Mongols. The long submission to the Asian rulers was over. Today, Ivan is known as Ivan the Great because he was able to bring many of the Eastern Slavic principalities under his rule. His major gain was Novgorod, which controlled territory all the way east to the Ural Mountains, the traditional division between Europe and Asia.

The Third Rome

Other factors helped to strengthen the power of Moscow's rulers. After Constantinople fell to the Ottoman Turks in A.D. 1453, Moscow stood alone as the center of the Eastern Orthodox Church. In A.D.

SECTION 3 REVIEW

Recall
1. **Define** steppe, principality, boyar, czar.
2. **Identify** the Slavs, Rurik, Olga, Vladimir, Yaroslav, the Mongols, Alexander Nevsky, Ivan III.
3. **Locate** Kiev on the map on page

259. Why did Kiev prosper?

Critical Thinking
4. **Making Comparisons** Compare Kievan Rus with Moscow. How was each dependent on geography? What role did the Orthodox Church play in each?

Understanding Themes
5. **Cultural Diffusion** What traditions that had originated with Rome became part of Russian culture? How did Russian culture differ from the civilization of western Europe? Why?

Distinguishing Between Fact and Opinion

Imagine that you are watching two candidates for President debate the merits of the college loan program. One candidate says, "In my view, the college loan program must be reformed. Sixty percent of students do not repay their loans on time."

The other candidate replies, "College costs are skyrocketing, but only 30% of students default on their loans for more than one year. I believe we should spend more money on this worthy program."

How can you tell who or what to believe? First, you must learn to distinguish between fact and opinion.

Learning the Skill

A fact is a statement that can be proved to be true or false. In the example above, the statement "Sixty percent of students do not repay their loans on time" is a fact. By reviewing statistics on the number of student loan recipients who repay their loans, we can determine whether it is true or false. To identify facts, look for words and phrases indicating specific people, places, events, dates, times.

An opinion, on the other hand, expresses a personal belief, viewpoint, or emotion. Because opinions are subjective, we cannot prove or disprove them. In the opening example, most statements by the candidates are opinions.

Opinions often include qualifying words and phrases such as *I think, I believe, probably, seems to me, may, might, could, ought, in my judgment*, or *in my view*. Also, look for expressions of approval or disapproval such as *good, bad, poor*, and *satisfactory*. Be aware of superlatives such as *greatest, worst, finest*, and *best*. Notice words with negative meanings and implications such as *squander, contemptible*, and *disgrace*. Also, identify generalizations such as *none, every, always*, and *never*.

Practicing the Skill

For each pair of statements below, determine which is fact and which is opinion. Give a reason for each choice.

1. (a) The Byzantine Empire came to a pitiful end at the hands of the savage Turks.
   (b) The Byzantine Empire ended when Constantine XI died while defending Constantinople from invading Turks in A.D. 1453.
2. (a) The alliance with the Byzantine Empire made Kiev a major trading link between Europe and Asia and between Scandinavia and the Middle East.
   (b) In the A.D. 900s Kiev was the most isolated, uncivilized place and possessed little in the way of culture.

3. (a) The Byzantine culture was more advanced than any other of its day.
   (b) Vladimir's conversion to Eastern Orthodoxy brought Byzantine culture to Kievan Rus.

Applying the Skill

In a newspaper, find a news article and an editorial on the same topic or issue. Identify five facts and five opinions from these sources.

For More Practice

Turn to the Skill Practice in the Chapter Review on page 267 for more practice in distinguishing between fact and opinion.

Connections Across Time

Historical Significance As a crossroads of trade, the Byzantine Empire was a center for cultural diffusion. Its scholars transmitted Roman law and classical and Christian learning to western Europe. The Byzantine Church spread Christianity by sending missionaries to convert the Slavs and other neighboring peoples.

In addition, the Byzantines were cultural innovators who made a lasting impact. Their icons and mosaics became part of the Christian artistic heritage of Europe, and their architecture inspired building styles in eastern Europe and the Middle East.

Using Key Terms

Write the key term that completes each sentence. Then write a sentence for each term not chosen.

a. boyars
b. clergy
c. mosaic
d. iconoclasts
e. monasteries
f. illuminated manuscripts
g. missionary
h. regent
i. schism
j. laity
k. czar
l. steppe

1. Wanting to prevent superstition and idol worship, _____, or image breakers, supported the removal of all images from churches.
2. North of the Black Sea are thick forests, mighty rivers, and a vast plain known as the _____.
3. In A.D. 1054 doctrinal, political, and geographic differences led to a _____ between the Roman Catholic Church in the West and the Eastern Orthodox Church in the East.
4. In Kievan Rus, wealthy nobles and landowners who assisted the princes were called _____.
5. In A.D. 1472 the Muscovite ruler Ivan III took the title _____, the title used by the Roman and Byzantine emperors.

Using Your History Journal

Write a short story describing a fictional case that may have come before an official of Justinian's court. Base the story on the law you described in Your History Journal at the beginning of this chapter.

Reviewing Facts

1. **Government** Explain the significance of Justinian's Code to later generations.
2. **Culture** Describe three major art forms that developed in the Byzantine Empire. What are the leading themes in Byzantine arts?
3. **Culture** Analyze how the Byzantine Empire promoted Christianity.
4. **Culture** Discuss the role of women in Byzantine society, especially in family life.
5. **Culture** Explain the contribution that Nino made to the development of Georgia.
6. **Geography** State the ways the early Eastern Slavs made use of their environment.
7. **History** Explain why the reign of Yaroslav is considered a golden age for Kievan Rus.
8. **History** Explain the effects of the Mongol invasions on Kievan Rus.
9. **History** Describe how Moscow's rise affected the Eastern Slavs.

Critical Thinking

1. **Analyze** Was the title of New Rome suitable or unsuitable for the city of Constantinople? Explain.

Technology Activity

Using the Internet Locate a Web site dealing with the history of the Cyrillic written language. Focus your search by using phrases such as *Cyrillic language* and *Slavic languages*. Create a bulletin board showing examples of Cyrillic words with their English translations. When possible, include illustrations.

2. Evaluate Why was the preservation of Greek and Roman learning a significant contribution of Byzantine civilization?

3. Analyze What do these Byzantine coins reveal about the level of development of Byzantine civilization?

4. Analyze What were the causes of the schism in the Christian Church? Could the split have been prevented? Explain.

5. Evaluate Would Justinian have been an effective ruler if he had not married Theodora? Explain.

6. Analyze How did trade affect the Byzantine Empire?

7. Synthesize What were the three parts of Kievan government? Why did representative government not develop in the East Slavic lands?

8. Synthesize Imagine you are a Russian boyar under Ivan III. Would you resist calling him Czar? Explain.

Understanding Themes

1. Conflict How does conflict—such as the iconoclastic controversy in the Byzantine Empire—weaken a government?

2. Innovation Using Byzantine civilization as an example, explain how one civilization's ideas can be adapted to other societies.

3. Cultural Diffusion How can two societies be enriched by sharing cultural aspects? Give examples from the cases of Kievan Rus and Moscow.

Linking Past and Present

1. Investigate the role the Bosporus played in World War I and World War II.
2. Explain the historical reasons why Russia has a continuing interest in the affairs of eastern European nations.
3. Investigate the historical roots of religious controversies in modern societies, such as Bosnia and Northern Ireland.

Skill Practice

Read the following statements. Determine which are facts and which are opinions. Give a reason for each choice.

1. The *Primary Chronicle* states that in A.D. 911 Grand Prince Oleg agreed on a peace treaty with the Byzantine emperors Leo and Alexander.
2. The Volga River is longer than the Danube River.
3. The Russian Orthodox Church is the most spiritually uplifting faith in the world.
4. Nomads wandered aimlessly throughout the steppes and lived in flimsy shelters.

Geography in History

1. Location Refer to the map below. By what year had the area around the Volga River been added to Moscow's holdings?

2. Place What geographic factors enabled the princes of Moscow to expand their territory?

3. Region By A.D. 1493 Moscow's ruler claimed to be "Sovereign of All Russia." About how far did Moscow's territory stretch from north to south in A.D. 1462?

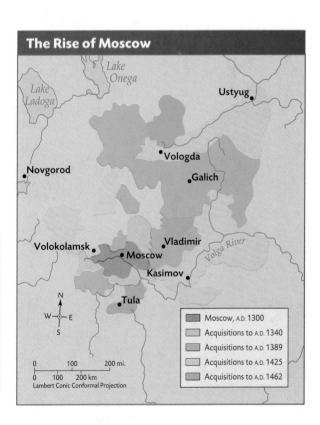

The Rise of Moscow

Lake Onega
Lake Ladoga
Ustyug
Vologda
Novgorod
Galich
Volokolamsk
Vladimir
Volga River
Moscow
Kasimov
Tula

N
W—E
S

0   100   200 mi.
0   100   200 km
Lambert Conic Conformal Projection

Moscow, A.D. 1300
Acquisitions to A.D. 1340
Acquisitions to A.D. 1389
Acquisitions to A.D. 1425
Acquisitions to A.D. 1462

Chapter
11
A.D. 600–1300
Islamic Civilization

Chapter Themes

▶ **Innovation** The faith and principles of Islam become the basis of a new civilization. *Section 1*
▶ **Movement** Armies and merchants spread Islam through the Middle East and North Africa, and into Spain and Asia. *Section 2*
▶ **Cultural Diffusion** Contributions from many cultures and peoples enrich the Islamic state. *Section 3*

The Storyteller

"I was in Makkah at last," writes a devout Muslim woman about her pilgrimage to Makkah, the holiest city of the religion of Islam. She continues, "Before me was the Kaaba, a great black cube partly submerged in a torrent of white-robed pilgrims circling round and round. Around us, like a great dam containing the torrent, stood the massive walls and the seven slim minarets of the Sacred Mosque. High above, the muezzin began the evening call to prayer: 'Allahu Akbar! … God is Most Great!'…

"Around the Kaaba … repeating the customary prayers, swirled men and women of every race and nation, from every corner of the earth.…"

All believers of Islam hope to share in this event at least once in their lives. Since the A.D. 600s, it has been one of the unifying celebrations for all Muslims.

Historical Significance

What are the basic beliefs and principles of Islam? What contributions has Islamic civilization made to world knowledge and culture?

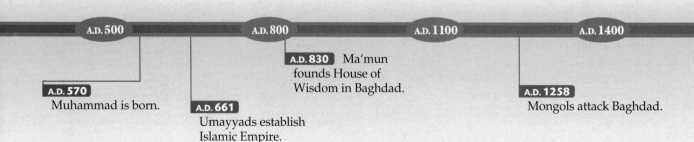

A.D. 500

A.D. 800

A.D. 1100

A.D. 1400

A.D. 830 Ma'mun founds House of Wisdom in Baghdad.

A.D. 570 Muhammad is born.

A.D. 661 Umayyads establish Islamic Empire.

A.D. 1258 Mongols attack Baghdad.

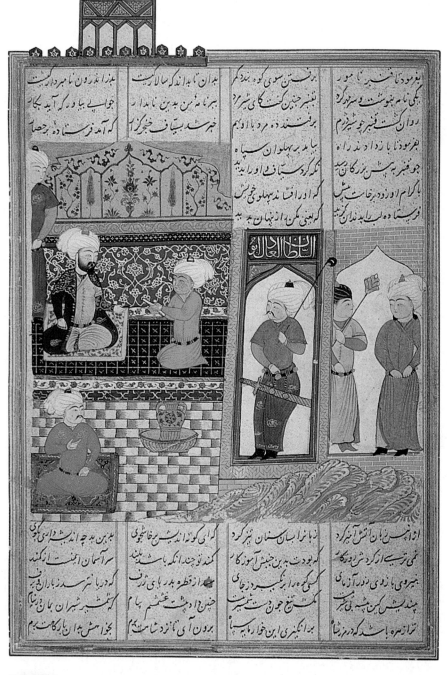

Apocryphal Life of Ali, from the
Kharar-nama, late A.D. 1400s

Your History Journal

Choose a topic from the text headings on astronomy and geography, chemistry and medicine, or art and architecture in the Muslim world. Research the subject in a library and write a short report.

A.D. 600   A.D. 625   A.D. 650

A.D. 610
Muhammad has
his first revelation.

A.D. 622
Muhammad and
followers depart
on the *Hijrah*.

A.D. 630
The people
of Makkah
accept Islam.

A.D. 632
Muhammad dies
at Madinah.

Section 1

A New Faith

Setting the Scene

▶ **Terms to Define**
sheikh, revelation, *shari'ah*, mosque, imam, hajj

▶ **People to Meet**
Muhammad

▶ **Places to Locate**
Arabian Peninsula, Makkah

 **ind Out**   What are the basic beliefs and
practices of Islam?

The Storyteller

(Allah) Most Gracious!
It is He Who has taught the Qur'an.
He has created man:
He has taught him speech (and Intelligence)
The sun and the moon follow courses (exactly)
computed; And the herbs and the trees-both
(alike) bow in adoration.
And the Firmament has He
raised high and He has set
up the balance (of Justice)
In order that you may not
transgress (due) balance.
So establish weight with
justice and fall not short in
the balance. It is He Who
has spread out the earth
for (His) creatures:
Therein is fruit and date-
palms producing spathes
(enclosing dates):
Also corn with (its) leaves
and stalk for fodder and
sweet-smelling plants.

—from *The Quran*,
Chapter 55

*Abu-Zayd preaching in the
Mosque of Samarkand*

South of Asia Minor lies the **Arabian Peninsula**, home of the Arabs. This location placed the Arabs at the margins of the great Middle Eastern civilizations. Like the ancient Israelites, Phoenicians, and Chaldeans, the Arabs were descended from Semitic tribes. Archaeologists have traced Arab civilizations in the Arabian Peninsula to at least 3000 B.C.

Arab Life

The relative geographic remoteness of the Arabian Peninsula kept the empires in the northern part of the region from invading Arab lands. Their isolation allowed the Arabs to create their own civilization.

The Setting

The Arabian Peninsula is a wedge of land of about 1 million square miles (2.6 million sq. km) between the Red Sea and the Persian Gulf. It is made up of two distinct regions. The southwestern area, across from the northeast coast of Africa, has well-watered valleys nestled between mountains. The rest of the peninsula, however, consists of arid plains and deserts.

Yet the peninsula is not entirely forbidding. Grass grows quickly during the showers of the rainy season, and oases, the fertile areas around springs and water holes, provide a permanent source of water for farmers, herders, and travelers. For centuries, nomadic herders and caravans have crisscrossed the desert, traveling from oasis to oasis.

Lives of the Bedouin

In ancient times many of the Arabs were bedouin (BEH•duh•wuhn), nomads who herded sheep, camels, and goats and lived in tents made of felt from camel or goat hair. They ate mainly fresh or dried dates, and they drank milk from their herds; on special occasions they also ate mutton.

The bedouin lived in tribes, each made up of related families. Arabs valued family ties because they ensured protection and survival in the harsh desert environment. Leading each tribe was a **sheikh** (SHAYK), or chief, appointed by the heads of the families. A council of elders advised the sheikh, who ruled as long as he had the tribe's consent. Warfare was part of bedouin life. The Arab tribes went on raids to gain camels and horses and battled one another over pastures and water holes, the most precious resources in the desert. To protect their honor and their possessions, the bedouin believed in retaliation—"an eye for an eye, and a tooth for a tooth."

For entertainment the bedouin enjoyed many activities. Camel and horse races and other games sharpened the men's abilities as warriors, and then everyone enjoyed an evening of storytelling around the campfires. Poets composed and recited poems about battles, deserts, camels and horses, and love. In these lines an Arab sheikh states his view of war:

> **❝** From the cup of peace
> drink your fill;
> but from the cup of war
> a sip will suffice. **❞**

Growth of Towns

By the A.D. 500s, many tribes had settled around oases or in fertile valleys to pursue either farming or trade. Groups of merchants soon founded prosperous market towns. The most important of these towns was **Makkah**, a crossroads of commerce about 50 miles (80 km) inland from the Red Sea.

People from all over the Arabian Peninsula traveled to Makkah to trade animal products for weapons, dates, grain, spices, jewels, ivory, silk, and perfumes. Enormous caravans from the fertile southwest passed through Makkah en route to Syria, Iraq, and as far away as China. Arabs also visited Makkah to worship at the peninsula's holiest shrine, the Kaaba, which contained statues of the many Arab deities. The business the pilgrims brought to Makkah made its merchants wealthy.

Signs of Change

As business ties replaced tribal ties in the trading towns, the old tribal rules were no longer adequate. At the same time, the Byzantine and Persian Empires were threatening to take over Arab lands. The Arabs had a common language, but they lacked a sense of unity and had no central government to solve these new problems.

Religious ideas were also changing. Contacts with the Byzantines, the Persians, and the

Heraclius Recaptures the True Cross

Jerusalem, A.D. 630

In A.D. 622 the Emperor Heraclius set out from Constantinople to recapture what was believed to be the "True Cross" on which Christ died. The cross had been taken by the Persians when they conquered Jerusalem. Heraclius advanced on the Persian capital of Ctesiphon, demanding the return of the cross. In A.D. 630, a triumphant Heraclius restored the True Cross to the Church of the Holy Sepulchre in Jerusalem.

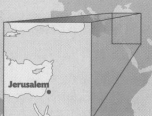

Ethiopians introduced the teachings of the monotheistic religions of Judaism and Christianity. Moreover, a number of Christian and Jewish Arabs lived in the peninsula. Dissatisfied with their old beliefs, many idol-worshiping Arabs searched for a new religion. Holy men known as hanifs (hah•NEEFS) denounced the worship of idols and believed in one god. They rejected Judaism and Christianity, however, preferring to find a uniquely Arab form of monotheism.

This ferment in Arab religious life contributed to the emergence of the religion known as Islam, which means "submission to the will of Allah (God)." This faith would bring the Arabs into contact with other civilizations and change Arab history.

Muhammad and His Message

The prophet of Islam, **Muhammad**, was born in the bustling city of Makkah around A.D. 570. Muslim traditions state that Muhammad was orphaned at an early age and raised by an uncle.

Life of Muhammad

During his teens, Muhammad worked as a caravan leader on a trade route. His reputation as an exceptionally honest and able person prompted his employer, a wealthy widow of 40 named Khadija (kuh•DEE•juh), to put him in charge of her business affairs. When Muhammad was about 25 years old, Khadija proposed marriage to him.

Muhammad's marriage to Khadija relieved

him of financial worries and gave him time to reflect on the meaning of life. Muhammad was troubled by the greed of Makkah's wealthy citizens, the worship of idols, and the mistreatment of the poor. Seeking guidance, Muhammad spent time alone praying and fasting in a cave outside the city.

Revelation

Islamic tradition holds that, in A.D. 610, Muhammad experienced a revelation, or vision. He heard a voice calling him to be the apostle of the one true deity—Allah, the Arabic word for God. Three times the voice proclaimed, "Recite!" When Muhammad asked what he should recite, the voice replied:

> **"** Recite in the name of your Lord,
>   the Creator,
> Who created man from clots of blood.
> Recite! Your Lord is the most bountiful
>   One
> Who by the pen has taught mankind
>   things they did not know. **"**

A second revelation commanded Muhammad to "rise and warn" the people about divine judgment. Although Muhammad had doubts about the revelations, he finally accepted his mission and returned to Makkah to preach.

In A.D. 613 Muhammad began sharing his revelations with his family and friends. He preached to the people of Makkah that there was only one God and that people everywhere must worship and obey him. He also declared that all who believed in God were equal. Therefore the rich should share their wealth with the poor. Muhammad also preached that God measured the worth of people by their devotion and good deeds. He told the people of Makkah to live their lives in preparation for the day of judgment, when God would punish evildoers and reward the just.

Muhammad made slow progress in winning converts. Khadija and members of Muhammad's family became the first Muslims, or followers of Islam. Many of the other converts came from Makkah's poor, who were attracted by Muhammad's call for social justice.

Opposition to Islam

Most Makkans rejected Muhammad's message. Wealthy merchants and religious leaders were upset by the prophet's attacks on the images at the Kaaba. They feared that monotheistic worship would end the pilgrimages to Makkah. Wealthy Makkans believed that this development would ruin the city's economy and lead to the loss of their prestige and wealth. Driven by these fears, the merchants persecuted Muhammad and the Muslims.

Muhammad persisted in his preaching until threats against his life forced him to seek help outside the city. He found it in Yathrib, a small town north of Makkah. In A.D. 622 Muhammad sent about 60 Muslim families from Makkah to Yathrib; soon after, he followed them in secret. His departure to Yathrib is known in Muslim history as the *Hijrah* (HIH•jruh), or emigration. The year in which the *Hijrah*

Visualizing History Nineteenth-century Turkish decorative tile with inscription "Allah is Great." The Ottoman Turks built an Islamic state that lasted until 1918. *What was the command Muhammad received in the second revelation?*

took place, A.D. 622, marks the beginning of the Islamic era and is recognized as the first year of the Muslim calendar.

The Islamic Community

Yathrib accepted Muhammad as God's prophet and their ruler. As the center of Islam, it became known as Madinat al-Nabi, "the city of the prophet," or Madinah (muh•DEE•nuh).

Origin of the Islamic State

Muhammad was a skilled political as well as religious leader. In the Madinah Compact of A.D. 624, Muhammad laid the foundation of an Islamic state. He decreed that all Muslims were to place loyalty to the Islamic community above loyalty to their tribe. Disputes were to be settled by Muhammad, who was declared the community's judge and commander in chief. All areas of life were placed under the divine law given to Muhammad and recorded in the Quran (kuh•RAHN), the holy scriptures of Islam. Muhammad also extended protection to Jews and Christians who accepted Islam's political authority.

Acceptance of Islam

Eventually the Makkans invaded Yathrib, forcing the Muslims to retaliate in self-defense. In the resulting battles, the Muslims defeated the Makkans, and the Muslims won the support of many Arab groups outside Madinah.

When Muhammad and his followers entered Makkah in A.D. 630, they faced little resistance. The Makkans accepted Islam and acknowledged Muhammad as God's prophet. The Muslims destroyed the idols in the Kaaba and turned the shrine into a place of worship believed to have been built by the prophet Abraham. Makkah became the spiritual capital of Islam, and Madinah remained its political capital.

The Muslims also expanded into new areas. By A.D. 631 their state included the entire Arabian Peninsula and was supported by a strong army representing each of the Arab tribes.

After a brief illness, Muhammad died at Madinah in A.D. 632. He left behind two major achievements. The first achievement was the formation of a religious community based on carefully preserved sacred writings. The second was the example of his life as an interpretive guide for Muslims to follow. ◣━━

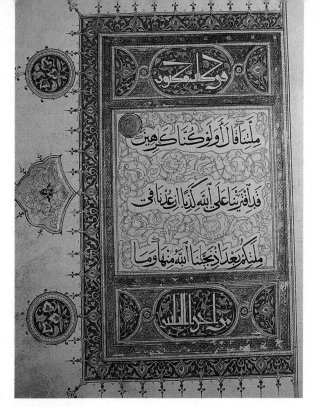

Visualizing History Because the Quran was written in Arabic, Muslims of many cultures adopted Arabic as a universal language. *What does the name "Quran" mean?*

Beliefs and Practices of Islam

Muhammad established beliefs and practices for his followers based on his revelations. In spite of social and political changes, these Islamic beliefs and practices have remained remarkably stable through the centuries.

The Quran

According to Muslim tradition, the angel Gabriel revealed divine messages to Muhammad over a 22-year period. Faithful Muslims wrote down or memorized these messages, but they were not compiled into one written collection until after Muhammad died. Then his successor, Abu Bakr, ordered Muslims to retrieve these messages from wherever they could be found, from the "ribs of palm-leaves and tablets of white stone and from the breasts of men." It took 20 years before the messages were compiled into the Quran, whose name means "recital." For all Muslims, the Quran is the final authority in matters of faith and lifestyle.

Written in Arabic, the Quran is believed to contain God's message as revealed to Muhammad. This message is expressed in stories, teachings, and exhortations. Some of the stories—such as Noah's

Lynn Abercrombie

Tower Mosque

In Samarra, Iraq, modern Muslim worshippers make their way up the spiral of a mosque built in the A.D. 800s. Some of the women, clothed from head to foot in black, are in purdah, or fully veiled from the public eye.

After Muhammad's death in A.D. 632, Islam spread through the Middle East, into Africa and Europe, and to the borders of India and China. This mosque was built during Islam's golden age, after the Abbasid caliphs assumed power over the Muslim Empire in A.D. 750. The new rulers shifted the capital of the still expanding Muslim Empire to the brand-new city of Baghdad and ended the legal distinctions between Arab Muslims and non-Arab Muslims, a division that had long deprived the non-Arabs of many legal rights. The peoples of the empire were now given greater freedom, and the Abbasids ruled over a period of great cultural flowering, peace, and order. ⊕

ark and Jonah in the belly of the whale—are variations of those found in the Bible.

Values

The Quran presents the basic moral values of Islam, which are similar to those of Judaism and Christianity. Muslims are commanded to honor their parents, show kindness to their neighbors, protect orphans and widows, and give generously to the poor. Murder, stealing, lying, and adultery are condemned.

The Quran also lays down specific rules to guide Muslims in their daily activities. It forbids gambling, eating pork, or drinking alcoholic beverages. It also contains rules governing marriage, divorce, family life, property inheritance, and business practices.

Law

Law cannot be separated from religion in Islamic society. Islam has no ranked order of clergy. Instead, generations of legal scholars have organized Islamic moral principles into a body of law known as the *shari'ah* (shuh•REE•uh). Based on the Quran and the Hadith (huh •DEETH), or sayings of Muhammad, the *shari'ah* covers all aspects of Muslim private and public life.

Five Pillars of Islam

The Quran presents the Five Pillars of Islam, or the five essential duties that all Muslims are to fulfill. They are the confession of faith, prayer, almsgiving, fasting, and the pilgrimage to Makkah.

Faith

The first pillar is the confession of faith: "There is no god but God, Muhammad is the messenger of God." It affirms the oneness of an all-powerful, just, and merciful God. All Muslims are required to submit to God's will as given in the Quran.

The confession stresses Muhammad's role as a prophet; he is not considered divine. Believing that at no time are humans without knowledge of God's will, Muslims view Muhammad as the last and greatest of several prophets whom God has sent to different peoples. Taking their lead from Muhammad, devout Muslims see their lives as a preparation for the Day of Judgement, when people will rise from death and be judged according to their actions. If they were faithful, they will be rewarded with eternal happiness in paradise. If they were not faithful, they will be condemned forever in hell.

To Muslims, Allah is the same god as the God of the Jews and the Christians. Adam, Abraham, Moses, and Jesus are considered prophets in the divine chain of messengers ending with Muhammad. As a result, Muslims have a great respect for the Bible, Judaism, and Christianity. They call Jews and Christians "People of the Book." Muslims believe the Arabs are descendants of Abraham through his son Ishmael and the Jews are descendants of Abraham through his son Isaac. The Quran also states that Jesus transmitted God's message and performed miracles.

Prayer

Muslims express their devotion in prayers offered five times each day—sunrise, noon, afternoon, sunset, and evening. Worshipers pray while facing Makkah, always using the same set of words and motions—kneeling, bowing, and

Visualizing History A Turkish pulpit tile from the A.D. 1600s depicts the plan of the Kaaba at Makkah. *What is the fifth pillar of Islam?*

Alms

The third pillar of Islam is the giving of alms, or charity. It reflects the Islamic view that the wealthy should assist the poor and weak. Almsgiving is practiced privately through contributions to the needy and publicly through a state tax that supports schools and aids the poor.

Fasting

The fourth pillar of Islam, fasting, occurs in the month of Ramadan (RAH•muh•DAHN), the ninth month in the Muslim calendar. During Ramadan, Muhammad received the first revelation. From sunrise to sunset Muslims neither eat nor drink, although they work as usual. Children, pregnant women, travelers, and the sick are exempt from fasting. At sunset the call for prayer—and in large cities the sound of a cannon—announces the end of the fast. Muslims then sit down to eat their "evening breakfast." In the cool evening hours, people stream out into the streets to greet their friends. At the end of Ramadan, there is a three-day celebration for the end of the fast.

Pilgrimage

The fifth pillar of Islam is the annual pilgrimage, or hajj, to Makkah. Every able-bodied Muslim who can afford the trip is expected to make the pilgrimage at least once in his or her lifetime. Those who perform the hajj are especially honored in the community.

The hajj takes place two months and ten days after the Ramadan fast and involves three days of ceremony, prayer, and sacrifice. Today, hundreds of thousands of Muslims come together to worship at the Kaaba and other shrines of Islam in Makkah and Madinah. The hajj is more than a religious pilgrimage. A visible expression of Muslim unity, the hajj allows a continuing exchange of ideas among the peoples of Africa, Europe, Asia, and the Americas who follow Islam.

Visualizing History Islamic mosque lamp from the Sulmaniyeh Mosque in Istanbul, **Turkey** *What are the various uses that a mosque may serve in an Islamic community?*

touching one's forehead to the ground as a sign of submission to God.

Muslims can offer their daily prayers outside or inside, at work or at home. At noon on Fridays, many Muslims pray together in a mosque, a building that may serve as a place of worship, a school, a court of law, and a shelter.

An imam (ih•MAHM), or prayer leader, guides believers in prayer, and a sermon sometimes follows. Any male Muslim with the proper religious education can serve as an imam.

SECTION 1 REVIEW

Recall

1. **Define** sheikh, revelation, *shari'ah*, mosque, imam, hajj.
2. **Identify** Arabian Peninsula, Makkah, Muhammad, Muslims, *Hijrah*, Madinah Compact, Quran.
3. **Explain** What made life possible in the harsh environment of the Arabian Peninsula?

Critical Thinking

4. **Analyzing Information** In what ways was Islam a unique religion? In what ways was it similar to other religions that were also founded in this region—Judaism and Christianity?

Understanding Themes

5. **Innovation** Describe the Five Pillars of Islam and the Madinah Compact, and tell how they changed life in the Arabian Peninsula.

A.D. 600	A.D. 800	A.D. 1000	A.D. 1200

A.D. 632
Abu Bakr becomes
the first caliph.

A.D. 732
Muslims and Christians
fight the Battle of Tours.

A.D. 750
The Abbasid dynasty
comes to power.

c. A.D. 1050 The Abbasids
enter period of decline.

Section 2

Spread of Islam

Setting the Scene

▶ **Terms to Define**
   caliph, jihad

▶ **People to Meet**
   Abu Bakr, Ali, Mu'awiyah, Husayn,
   the Sunni, the Shiite, Harun al-Rashid

▶ **Places to Locate**
   Damascus, Baghdad

Find Out How did the Islamic state expand,
and how did it affect a variety of cultures?

The Storyteller

*From the far reaches of the Mediterranean to
the Indus River valley, the faithful approached the
holy city. All had the same objective—to worship
together at the holiest shrine of Islam, the Kaaba in
Makkah. One such traveler was Mansa Musa, king
of Mali in western Africa. Musa had prepared carefully for the long journey he and his attendants
would take. He was determined to go, not only for
his own religious fulfillment, but also for recruiting
teachers and leaders, so that his land could learn
more of the Prophet's
teachings.*

—adapted from *The
Chronicle of the Seeker*,
Mahmud Kati, reprint-
ed in *The Human
Record*, Alfred J.
Andrea and James H.
Overfield, 1990

*Pilgrimage to
Makkah*

When Muhammad died in A.D. 632, he
had left no clear instructions about
who was to succeed him as the
leader of Islam. Muslims knew that no one could
take Muhammad's place as the messenger of God.
They realized, however, that the Islamic community needed a strong leader who could preserve its
unity and guide its daily affairs. A group of prominent Muslims met and chose a new type of leader,
whom they called *khalifah* (kuh•LEE•fuh) or caliph
(KAY•luhf), meaning "successor."

"The Rightly Guided Caliphs"

The first four caliphs were chosen for life. All
were close friends or relatives of Muhammad. The
first caliph was Muhammad's father-in-law and
close friend, **Abu Bakr** (uh•BOO BA•kuhr). The last,
his son-in-law Ali, was married to Muhammad's
daughter Fatimah (FAH•tuh•muh). The first four
caliphs followed Muhammad's example, kept in
close touch with the people, and asked the advice
of other Muslim leaders. For these reasons,
Muslims have called them "the Rightly Guided
Caliphs."

Early Conquests

The Rightly Guided Caliphs sought to protect
and spread Islam. Their military forces carried
Islam beyond the Arabian Peninsula. In addition to
religious motives, the Arabs were eager to acquire
the agricultural wealth of the Byzantine and
Persian Empires to meet the needs of their growing
population.

Arab armies swept forth against the weakened
Byzantine and Persian Empires. By A.D. 650, these
armies had acquired Palestine, Syria, Iraq, Persia,
and Egypt. The conquests reduced the Asian part of
the Byzantine Empire to Asia Minor and the
Constantinople area and brought the Persian
Empire completely under Muslim control.

The Arab armies were successful for several reasons. First, they were united in the belief that they had a religious duty to spread Islam. The Islamic state, therefore, saw the conquests as a **jihad** (jih•HAHD), or holy struggle to bring Islam to other lands. In addition, continual warfare between the Byzantines and the Persians had weakened both of their empires and made them open to Arab attacks. Still another factor was the attempt of Byzantine and Persian rulers to impose religious unity on their peoples. Because of persecution, members of unofficial religions in both empires readily accepted Muslim rule.

Divisions Within Islam

While Muslim armies were achieving military success, rival groups fought for the caliphate, or the office of caliph. The struggle began when **Ali**, Muhammad's son-in-law, became the fourth caliph in A.D. 656. One of Ali's powerful rivals was **Mu'awiyah** (moo•UH•wee•uh), the governor of Syria. Mu'awiyah carried out conquests in Egypt and Iraq, steadily weakening Ali's hold on the caliphate. In A.D. 661, Ali was murdered by a disillusioned follower, and Mu'awiyah became the first caliph of the powerful Umayyad (oo•MY•uhd) dynasty. Ali's son **Husayn** (hoo•SAYN), however, refused to accept Umayyad rule and continued the struggle. In A.D. 680, Husayn and many of his followers were massacred by Umayyad troops in a battle at Karbala in present-day Iraq.

The murders of Ali and Husayn led to a significant division in the Islamic world. The majority of Muslims, known as **the Sunni** (SU•nee), or "followers of the way," believed that the caliph was primarily a leader, not a religious authority. They also claimed that any devout Muslim could serve in the office with the acceptance of the people. However, **the Shiite**, the smaller group of Muslims who followed Ali and Husayn, believed that the caliphate should be held only by descendants of Muhammad through his daughter Fatimah and her husband Ali. Shiite Muslims stressed the spiritual, rather than political, aspects of Islamic leadership. Because of

Images *of the* Times

Islamic Art and Architecture

Inspired by their faith, artists and architects of Islam created unequaled geometric designs, floral patterns, and calligraphy.

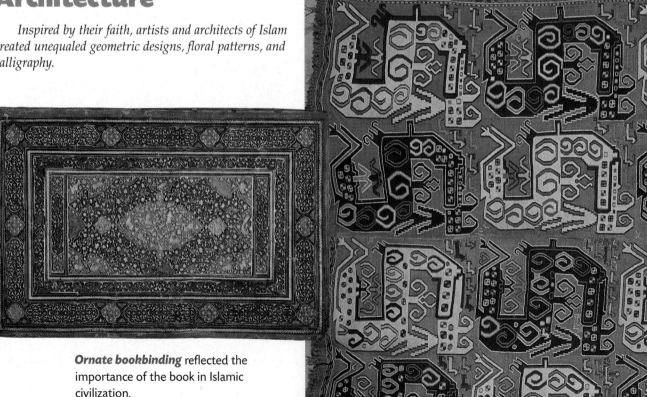

Carpets and other textiles were turned into fine art pieces by the skilled hands of Islamic weavers.

Ornate bookbinding reflected the importance of the book in Islamic civilization.

their conflicts with Sunni leaders, the Shiite also came to regard suffering and martyrdom as signs of their devotion to Islam.

The split between Sunni and Shiite Muslims had a profound impact on Islam and has lasted into modern times. Today, about 90 percent of Muslims are Sunnis; the minority Shiites live primarily in Iran, Iraq, and Lebanon. The Shiite movement itself has divided into several groups. In spite of differences, all Sunni and Shiite Muslims believe in the oneness of God, regard the Quran as sacred scripture, and make the hajj, or the yearly sacred pilgrimage to Makkah.

During the struggle for the caliphate, other Muslims, dissatisfied with the worldliness of the Umayyads, developed a mystical form of Islam known as Sufism. The Sufis, as the followers of this movement were called, sought direct contact with God through prayer, meditation, fasting, and spiritual writing. In addition to their devotional activities, many Sufis carried out missionary work that helped in spreading Islam to remote areas of India, Central Asia, Turkey, and North Africa.

The Islamic State

The Umayyad dynasty, which was founded by Mu'awiyah, ruled from A.D. 661 to A.D. 750. The Umayyads moved the capital from Madinah to **Damascus**, Syria, which was more centrally located in the expanding state.

Umayyad Conquests

In the next century, Umayyad warriors carried Islam east, to the borders of India and China. In the west, they swept across North Africa and into Spain, the southernmost area of Christian western Europe.

By A.D. 716 the Muslims ruled almost all of Spain. They advanced halfway into France before the Frankish leader Charles Martel stopped them at the Battle of Tours in A.D. 732. This battle halted the spread of Islam into western Europe.

Life in the Umayyad State

The Umayyads built a powerful Islamic state that stressed the political, rather than the religious,

Court of the Myrtles, Alhambra, Granada, Spain, remains as a striking example of intricate Islamic architectural design.

REFLECTING ON THE TIMES

1. What details characterize the interior walls of the Court of the Myrtles?
2. Why do you think the decorative arts flourished in the Islamic world during this period?

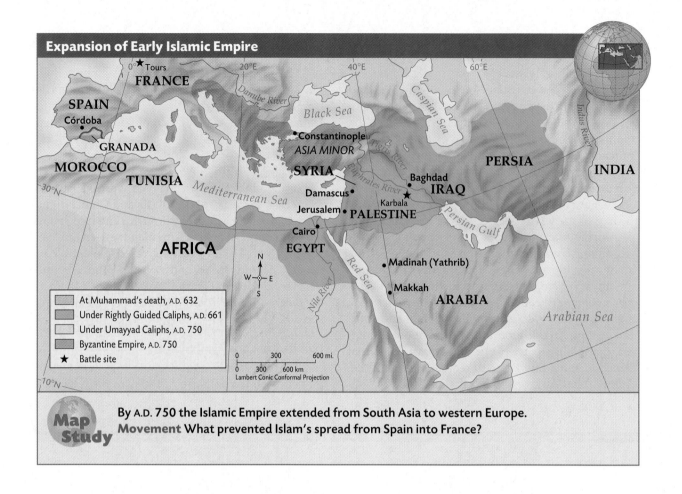

Expansion of Early Islamic Empire

Legend:
- At Muhammad's death, A.D. 632
- Under Rightly Guided Caliphs, A.D. 661
- Under Umayyad Caliphs, A.D. 750
- Byzantine Empire, A.D. 750
- ★ Battle site

0   300   600 mi.
0 300 600 km
Lambert Conic Conformal Projection

Map Study By A.D. 750 the Islamic Empire extended from South Asia to western Europe.
Movement What prevented Islam's spread from Spain into France?

aspect of their office. As time went by, they ruled more like kings and less like the earlier caliphs.

The Umayyads did, however, help to unite the lands they ruled. They made Arabic the official language, minted the first Arabic currency, built roads, and established postal routes. Their administration depended on a civil service made up of well-trained bureaucrats who had served as officials in the Byzantine and Persian Empires.

Umayyad rule also improved conditions for many, particularly Jews and non-Greek Christians, who had often suffered under Byzantine rule. They had to pay a special tax, but they were tolerated because they believed in one God. The great Arab commander Khalid ibn al-Walid, who had led the conquest of Syria and Persia, described Muslim policy:

❝ In the name of Allah, the compassionate, the merciful, this is what Khalid ibn al-Walid would grant to the inhabitants of Damascus.... He promises to give them security for their lives, property and churches. Their city wall shall not be demolished, neither shall any Muslim be quartered in their houses. Thereunto we give to them the pact of Allah and the protection of His Prophet, the Caliphs and the believers. So long as they pay the tax, nothing but good shall befall them. ❞

Opposition to Umayyad Rule

Despite this enlightened outlook, Umayyad rule caused dissatisfaction among non-Arab Muslims. They paid higher taxes, received lower wages in the army and government, and were discriminated against socially. Discontent was particularly strong in Iraq and Persia, the center of the Shiite opposition to Umayyad rule.

The Abbasids

In the year A.D. 747, the anti-Umayyad Arabs and the non-Arab Muslims in Iraq and Persia joined forces, built an army, and, in three years of fighting, overwhelmed the Umayyads. The new caliph, Abu'l-'Abbas, was a descendant of one of Muhammad's uncles. He established the Abbasid (uh•BA•suhd) dynasty, and his successor, al-Mansur, had a new city, **Baghdad**, built on the banks of the Tigris River. By the A.D. 900s, about 1.5 million people lived in Baghdad.

Baghdad lay at the crossroads of the land and

water trade routes that stretched from the Mediterranean Sea to East Asia. The city was shaped like a circle and surrounded by walls. Highways led from Baghdad's center to different parts of the empire and divided the city into districts. At Baghdad's heart stood the great mosque and the caliph's magnificent palace, where he ruled in splendor like the Persian rulers. Surrounding areas contained the luxurious homes of court members and army officials. Outer districts of the city were made up of the homes of the common people.

Abbasid Diversity

The Abbasid Empire reached its height under Caliph **Harun al-Rashid** (ha•ROON ahl•rah•SHEED), who ruled from A.D. 786 to A.D. 809. During this time, the Abbasids developed a sophisticated urban civilization based on the diversity of the empire's peoples. Harun and his successors worked to ensure equality among all Muslims, Arab and non-Arab. They set up a new ruling group that included Muslims of many nationalities. Persians became the dominant group in the government bureaucracy, while the Turks became the leading group in the army. Arabs, however, continued to control religious life and administration of law.

Breakup of the Islamic State

The Abbasids ruled the Islamic state from A.D. 750 to A.D. 1258; during this time, however, many of the lands that had been won by the Umayyads broke free from Baghdad. In central Asia, during the A.D. 800s, Persian Muslims set up the Samanid dynasty in the city of Bukhara (boo•KAHR•uh). Under Samanid rule, Bukhara and other central Asian cities, such as Samarkand and Tashkent, became major commercial, religious, and educational centers. Their wealth was based on caravans that traveled through the region, bringing silk, spices, and animal products from East Asia to European areas as far north as the Baltic Sea.

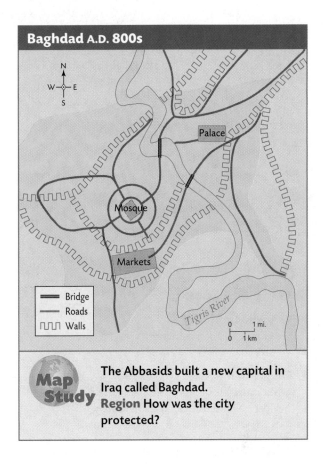

Baghdad A.D. 800s

Bridge
Roads
Walls

Map Study The Abbasids built a new capital in Iraq called Baghdad. **Region** How was the city protected?

Independent states also emerged in other parts of the crumbling Abbasid Empire. One of the last Umayyad princes fled to Spain and continued Umayyad rule there. The Egyptian dynasty, the Fatimids, gained control over areas in North Africa and the Middle East, rivaling Baghdad for power. Much of Persia also came under the control of rival rulers. By the A.D. 1000s, the Abbasids ruled little more than the area around Baghdad.

During the next 200 years, Baghdad and its Abbasid rulers came under the control of the Seljuk Turks and later, the Mongols. In their ferocious assault on the city in A.D. 1258, the Mongols burned buildings and slaughtered 50,000 inhabitants, among them the last Abbasid caliph.

SECTION 2 REVIEW

Recall
1. **Define** caliph, jihad.
2. **Identify** Abu Bakr, Ali, Mu'awiyah, Husayn, the Sunni, the Shiite, the Umayyads, the Abbasids, Harun al-Rashid.
3. **Locate** the cities of Damascus and Baghdad on the map on page 280. Why did the caliphs move the capital of the Islamic state to each of these cities?

Critical Thinking
4. **Evaluating Information** What were the strengths and weaknesses of Umayyad rule?

Understanding Themes
5. **Movement** How did expansion affect the ethnic diversity of the Islamic Empire? How did expansion affect the empire's stability?

A.D. 600	A.D. 800	A.D. 1000	A.D. 1200

c. A.D. 635
The Quran is compiled.

c. A.D. 830 Baghdad reaches its height as a major center of learning.

c. A.D. 910
Arab chronicler al Tabari writes a history of the world.

A.D. 1135
The Jewish philosopher Maimonides is born.

Section 3

Daily Life and Culture

Setting the Scene

▶ **Terms to Define**
madrasa, bazaar, calligraphy, arabesque, chronicle

▶ **People to Meet**
Ma'mun, al-Razi, Ibn Sina, Omar Khayyám, Moses Maimonides, Ibn-Khaldun

Find Out What were the achievements of Islamic civilization, and how did they spread to other parts of the world?

The Storyteller

One hundred and twenty camels were required to transport Ismail's books as he prepared to move from Baghdad to Cairo. It was not that he would be unable to obtain books in Cairo. That city, like Baghdad, was lavishly supplied with both public and private libraries whose collections numbered in the tens of thousands. Like many scholars in the Muslim world, Ismail had amassed a collection of works on topics from poetry, history, and law to medicine, mathematics, and astronomy. Now it would take a major effort to move them.

—adapted from *The Mind of the Middle Ages*, Frederick B. Artz, 1990

An astrolabe

In the Abbasid state, the arts and learning flourished despite political disunity. The time of conquest had ended, and the people had enough leisure to enjoy cultural activities. Because Arabic was the language of the Quran, it became the common language. Its widespread use enabled scientists, rulers, and writers from different lands to communicate with one another. This blend of people and ideas gave the Islamic state a new multicultural character and created a golden age.

Family Life

Islam set the guidelines for the way people lived. It laid down rules for family life and business as well as for religious practices.

Role of Women

Early Islam stressed the equality of all believers before God; however, as in the case of contemporary Christian and Jewish communities, in Islamic communities men and women had distinct roles and rights. The Quran told Muslims that "men are responsible for women." A woman's social position was therefore largely defined by her relationship as wife, mother, daughter, or sister to the male members of her family.

Islam did, however, improve the position of women. It forbade the tribal custom of killing female infants and also limited polygamy (puh•LIH•guh •mee), or the practice that allowed a man to have more than one wife. A Muslim could have as many as four wives, but all were to be treated as equals and with kindness. Also, a woman had complete control over her own property. If she were divorced, she could keep the property she had brought with her when she married. A woman could also inherit property from her father and remarry.

Most women's lives revolved around family and household. Other roles, however, were available to Muslim women, especially among the upper classes. Scholarship was a prominent way for women to win recognition, and many important teachers of Islamic knowledge were women. Women often used their control over property for investment in trade and in financing charitable institutions. The lists of Muslim rulers include a number of prominent women, both as members of the court and as leaders in their own right.

Many Muslim women made contributions in the arts, and several women in the caliph's court were renowned for their poetry. Some of them were not always happy with their lives, though, as indicated by this poem written by Maisuna, the bedouin wife of Mu'awiyah. Her comments made Mu'awiyah so furious that he sent her back to the desert:

> ❝The coarse cloth worn in the serenity
> of the desert
> Is more precious to me than the luxurious
> robes of a queen;
> I love the bedouin's tent, caressed by the
> murmuring breeze, and standing amid
> boundless horizons,
> More than the gilded halls of marble in
> all their royal splendor.
> I feel more at ease with my simple crust,
> Than with the delicacies of the court;
> I prefer to rise early with the caravan,
> Rather than be in the golden glare of
> the sumptuous escort.
> The barking of a watchdog keeping away
> strangers
> Pleases me more than the sounds of the
> tambourine played by the court singers;
> I prefer a desert cavalier, generous and
> poor,
> To a fat lout in purple living behind closed
> doors. ❞
>
> —Najib Ullah, *Islamic Literature*

Role of Men

In addition to politics and the army, Muslim men worked at a variety of businesses or in the fields. For leisure they visited public baths and meeting places where they relaxed and talked. Men also played chess and practiced gymnastics.

When Muslim boys reached age seven, they entered mosque schools, which cost little and were open to all boys. Wealthier families paid tuition, but many poor children were admitted without charge.

Being able to speak Arabic fluently and to write with grace and ease were skills that Muslims valued. For all but the sons of the wealthy, however, schooling ended with learning to read and write. Some young men continued their studies at *madrasas*, or theological schools. Those who were to become leaders in Muslim society studied the classical literature of Islam, memorized poetry, and learned to compose original verses.

City and Country

Most Arabs lived in rural or desert places. The leadership of the Islamic state, however, came from the cities.

Many cities, such as Damascus, in Syria, developed as trading centers even before the rise of Islam. Others, such as Kufa, in Iraq, developed from military towns set up during the early conquests. Muslim cities were divided into distinct business and residential districts. A maze of narrow streets, often covered to protect pedestrians from the scorching sun, separated the closely packed buildings.

Urban Centers

City homes were designed to provide maximum privacy and to keep the occupants cool in the blazing heat. Houses were centered around courtyards; in wealthy homes, these courtyards had fountains and gardens. Thick walls of dried mud or brick and few windows kept the interior dim and cool.

The interiors of most Muslim homes were plain with few pieces of furniture. They were decorated with beautiful carpets and small art objects. Most people sat on carpets or leaned on cushions or pillows. At mealtime, household members sat in a circle and ate from large trays of breads, meats, and fruits.

Footnotes to History

Magic Carpets
The magic carpet gliding through the air is a familiar form of transportation in *The Arabian Nights*. The real magic of Islamic carpets, however, is their glowing colors and intricate designs. During the Islamic Empire, carpets adorned both caliphs' palaces and shepherds' tents. Today, carpets from the Islamic world still give their magic to modern walls and floors.

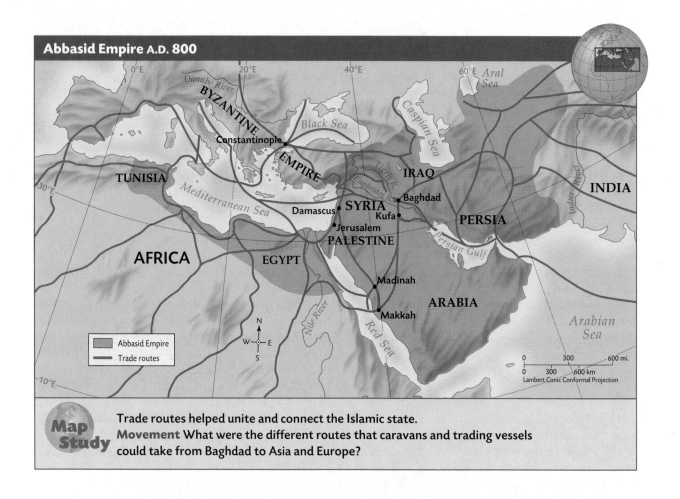

Trade routes helped unite and connect the Islamic state.
Movement What were the different routes that caravans and trading vessels could take from Baghdad to Asia and Europe?

The main religious, government, and business buildings were at the center of the city. Dominating the skyline were graceful mosques and their slender minarets, or towers from which people were called to prayer. Mosques usually included a prayer hall where worshipers gathered on Fridays. At one end of this hall a mihrab, or niche, marked the direction of Makkah. Often mosques included schools and shelters for travelers.

Trade and the Bazaar

Muslim merchants dominated trade throughout the Middle East and North Africa until the A.D. 1400s. Caravans traveled overland from Baghdad to China. Muslim traders crossed the Indian Ocean gathering cargoes of rubies from India, silk from China, and spices from Southeast Asia. Gold, ivory, and enslaved people were brought from Africa, Asia, and Europe. From the Islamic world came spices, textiles, glass, and carpets.

The destination of these goods were the city bazaars, or marketplaces. In major cities, such as Baghdad, Damascus, and Cairo, the bazaars consisted of mazes of shops and stalls, often enclosed to shut out the glare of the sun. Buyers at the major bazaars included Europeans who purchased Asian goods,

shipped them across the Mediterranean Sea to Italy and then on to other parts of Europe. Men also met at the bazaars for conversation as well as business. Nearby were large warehouses and lodging houses that served traveling merchants.

Rural Areas

Because of the dry climate and the scarcity of water, growing food was difficult in many areas of the Islamic state. Farmers, however, made efficient use of the few arable areas. They produced good yields by irrigating their fields, rotating crops, and fertilizing the land. Most productive land was held by large landowners who received grants from the government. They had large estates and employed farmers from nearby villages to work the land. Muslim farms produced wheat, rice, beans, cucumbers, celery, and mint. Orchards provided almonds, blackberries, melons, apricots, figs, and olives. Farmers also cultivated flowers for perfume.

After Arab irrigation methods were introduced into Spain, Muslims there could cultivate valuable new crops, including cherries, apples, pears, and bananas. Seville, Córdoba, and other Spanish Islamic cities grew rich from the produce they sold in international trade.

Islamic Achievements

The use of Arabic not only promoted trade but also encouraged communication among the different peoples in the Islamic state. From these peoples the Islamic state built a rich storehouse of knowledge and scientific discovery.

Between the A.D. 800s and A.D. 1300s, Islamic scientists made important contributions in several scientific areas, such as mathematics, astronomy, chemistry, and medicine. They based their work on two main intellectual traditions. The first, and most important, was that of Greece. The second was that of India, which came to the Arabs by way of Persia.

The House of Wisdom

The Islamic world experienced a scientific awakening under the Abbasids. During the A.D. 800s, Baghdad became a leading intellectual center.

According to Muslim tradition, the Abbasid caliph **Ma'mun** (mah•MOON) founded the House of Wisdom at Baghdad in A.D. 830. This research center specialized in the translation into Arabic of Greek, Persian, and Indian scientific texts. Ma'mun staffed the institute with Christian, Jewish, and Muslim scholars who shared ideas from different intellectual traditions. They performed scientific experiments, made mathematical calculations, and built upon the ideas of the ancients. The House of Wisdom, therefore, sparked many of the mathematical and scientific achievements in the Islamic world.

Muslim science involved more than just theory; it was put to practical use. For example, mathematics was used to solve daily problems in business and agriculture. Astronomy was used to determine the hours of prayer and the time period of celebrations.

Mathematics

As you read in Chapter 8, Gupta mathematicians in India devised the numerals we know as Arabic numerals and the concept of zero. Muslim mathematicians adopted these numerals and used them in a place-value system. In this system, today used worldwide, a number's value is determined by the position of its digits. The place-value system made possible great achievements in mathematics.

Muslim mathematicians invented algebra and expressed equations to define curves and lines. Their work in geometry led to the development of trigonometry, which was used to calculate the distance to a star and the speed of a falling object. Mathematicians also were interested in practical applications, such as devising pumps and fountains and applying their skills to building and surveying.

Astronomy and Geography

At Ma'mun's observatory in Baghdad, astronomers checked the findings of the ancient Greeks, made observations of the skies, and produced physical and mathematical models of the universe. They accurately described solar eclipses and proved that the moon affects the oceans.

Muslim astronomers improved on a Greek device called the astrolabe, with which they determined the positions of stars, the movements of planets, and the time. The astrolabe made navigation easier and safer. It was also useful in religious practices, enabling Muslims to ascertain the direction of Makkah, the beginning of Ramadan, and the hours of prayer.

Using the astrolabe, Muslim geographers measured the size and circumference of the earth with accuracy unmatched until the 1900s. From such studies, geographers concluded that the earth was round, although most continued to accept the Greek theory that heavenly bodies revolve around the earth.

By the A.D. 1100s, Muslim geographers had determined the basic outlines of Asia, Europe, and North Africa and had produced the first accurate maps of the Eastern Hemisphere. They also traveled widely to gain firsthand knowledge of the earth's surface, its climates, and its peoples.

Chemistry and Medicine

Muslims developed alchemy, the branch of chemistry that attempted to change lead into gold. Although alchemists never succeeded in their goal, they did develop the equipment and methods that are still used in modern chemistry.

The renowned chemist and physician **al-Razi** (ahl•RAH•zee), who lived from A.D. 865 to A.D. 925, classified chemical substances as animal, mineral, or vegetable, a classification system that remains in use today. Al-Razi also made invaluable contributions to medicine. Among his nearly 200 works are a medical encyclopedia that describes the origin of disease and a handbook identifying the differences between smallpox and measles.

In the A.D. 900s, the doctor **Ibn Sina** (IH•buhn SEE•nuh) produced the *Canon of Medicine*, a monumental volume that attempted to summarize all the medical knowledge of that time. It described the circulation of the blood and the functions of the kidneys and the heart. It also offered diagnosis and treatment for many diseases.

Muslim physicians founded the science of optics, or the study of light and its effect on sight. Ibn al-Haytham, the founder of optics, discovered that the eye sees because it receives light from the object seen. Earlier physicians had believed the opposite: that the eye sees because it produces rays that give light to the object seen. Muslim medicine, in fact, was centuries ahead of the medicine practiced in the West.

Art and Architecture

Like mathematics and science, Islamic art and architecture benefited from the cultural diversity of the Islamic Empire. Opposed to idol worship, Muslim scholars discouraged artists from making images or pictures of living creatures. Instead, artists used **calligraphy** (kuh•LIH•gruh•fee), or the art of elegant handwriting, to decorate the walls of mosques and other public buildings with passages from the Quran. Often the beautiful script of written Arabic was accompanied by geometric designs entwined with plant stems, leaves, flowers, and stars. These **arabesques** (AR•uh•BEHSKS) decorated books, carpets, swords, and entire walls.

Islamic architects and artists did their best work in architecture, particularly in building and decorating mosques. Gardens and water, both precious in the arid Islamic lands, became artistic objects. Sun-drenched courtyards in mosques, palaces, and wealthy homes had trees to provide cool shade and flowers to delight the eye and nose; splashing fountains and running water refreshed both eye and ear.

Literature

Until the A.D. 600s, Arabic literature consisted mostly of poetry passed orally from one generation to the next. After the rise of Islam, religion had much influence in the creation of Arabic literature. The Quran, the first and greatest work in Arabic prose, was familiar to every Muslim, and its style influenced Islamic writing.

During the A.D. 700s, nonreligious prose appeared that both taught and entertained. The most famous of these writings was *Kalila and Dimna*, a collection of animal fables that presented moral lessons.

During the Abbasid period, Islamic literature blossomed as a result of contact with Greek thought, Hindu legends, and Persian court epics.

CONNECTIONS
Science and Technology

At the Doctor's

Today we take it for granted that the doctor can make us better when we get sick. In A.D. 765, however, the caliph al-Mansur was not so fortunate. His personal physicians—the best in Baghdad—could find no remedy for his chronic indigestion.

Medicinal herb from an Islamic manuscript

The caliph had heard that physicians in a Persian medical school based their practices on rational Greek methods of treatment. Traditional Arab medicine was based mainly on magic or superstition.

When the caliph asked the medical school for help, the chief physician, a Christian named Jurjis ibn Bakhtishu, cured al-Mansur. This encouraged other Muslim doctors to practice medicine based on the methods of the Greeks and Persians. Muslim doctors were the first to discover the functions of internal organs and to diagnose illnesses such as meningitis. They also advanced surgery, carrying out head and stomach operations with the aid of anesthetics such as opium.

Believing that medicine required long training, Muslim doctors studied in hospitals and medical schools. Doctors based their treatments upon careful observation of their patients rather than superstition. They also diagnosed diseases such as measles and smallpox, prescribed treatments, and performed surgery. Such practices were unknown in the West until the A.D. 1100s and A.D. 1200s, when Islamic knowledge reached western Europe.

Linking Past and Present ACTIVITY

Explain why Islamic medicine was far ahead of Western medicine during the Middle Ages. Then, research sources and list five new methods of treatment developed by doctors in the past 50 years.

The upper classes valued elegant speech and the ability to handle words cleverly. Reading and appreciating literature became the sign of a good upbringing; every wealthy person took pride in having a well-stocked library. Córdoba, the Umayyad capital in Spain, had 70 libraries and more than half a million books. In contrast, the largest library in the Christian monasteries, at that time the center of European learning, held only a few hundred volumes.

In the A.D. 1000s, Persian became a second literary language in the Muslim world. Persian authors wrote epics about warrior-heroes, religious poetry, and verses about love. One of the best known works of this period is the *Rubaiyat* of **Omar Khayyám** (OH•MAHR KY•YAHM), a Persian mathematician and poet. You may also have heard some of the stories found in *A Thousand and One Nights*, also known as *The Arabian Nights*—stories such as "Sinbad the Sailor," "Aladdin and His Lamp," and "Ali Baba and the Forty Thieves." Originating in Arabia, India, Persia, Egypt, and other lands, the tales reflect the multinational character of the Islamic state.

Philosophy and History

Muslim philosophers tried to reconcile the Quran with Greek philosophy. They believed that religious truths could be analyzed and defended using logic. Many of their works were translated into Latin and later brought a new understanding of philosophy to western Europe. Ibn Sina, known in Europe as Avicenna, wrote numerous books on logic and theology as well as medicine. Ibn-Rushd, a judge in Córdoba, was the most noted Islamic philosopher. Christian schol-

ars in western Europe called him Averroës and used his commentaries on Aristotle.

Moses Maimonides (my•MAH•nuh•DEEZ), a Spanish Jew born in A.D. 1135, fled to North Africa to escape persecution from Spanish Christians. Maimonides became a leader in the Jewish community and a doctor to the Egyptian ruler. Like several Muslim scholars, Maimonides attempted to reconcile his faith with the teachings of Aristotle.

One of Maimonides' major contributions was the *Mishne Torah*, a 14-volume work on Jewish law

History & Art Turkish miniature depicting angels, from the *Ajac, ib Mahlukat* by Sururi, A.D. 1500s. British Museum, London, England *What cultural influences shaped the development of Islamic arts?*

Visualizing History A modern Islamic mosque in Isfahan, Iran, one of the most magnificent cities in the early Muslim world. *What kind of writings traced the early historical events of Islam?*

and tradition, written in Hebrew. His other major religious work, *The Guide of the Perplexed,* was written in Arabic and later translated into Hebrew and Latin. After his death in A.D. 1204, Maimonides was recognized as one of the world's great philosophers.

Like Judaism and Christianity, Islam traces its origins to historical events. Therefore, Islamic scholars were interested in writing history. At first they wrote chronicles, or accounts in which events are arranged in the order in which they occurred. The most famous of the Islamic chroniclers were al Tabari (al tah•BAH•ree), who in the early A.D. 900s wrote a multivolume history of the world, and Ibn

al-Athir (IH•buhn ahl•ah•THEER), who wrote an extensive history during the early A.D. 1200s.

Later, historians began to organize their accounts around events in the lives of rulers and others. The first Muslim historian to examine history scientifically was a North African diplomat named **Ibn-Khaldun** (IH•buhn KAL•DOON). He looked for laws and cause-and-effect relationships to explain historical events. Ibn-Khaldun believed that history was a process in which human affairs were shaped by geography, climate, and economics, as well as by moral and spiritual forces. His work later influenced European historical writing.

SECTION 3 REVIEW

Recall
1. **Define** *madrasa,* bazaar, calligraphy, arabesque, chronicle.
2. **Identify** Ma'mun, House of Wisdom, al-Razi, Ibn Sina, Omar Khayyám, Moses Maimonides, Ibn-Khaldun.
3. **Locate** on the map on page

284 the major trade routes used by Muslim merchants. What features gave the Islamic state its multicultural character?

Critical Thinking
4. **Evaluating Information** Most Muslim scholars objected to the portrayal of living beings, but some Islamic art—such as

the painting on page 287—does show figures. Why is this so?

Understanding Themes
5. **Cultural Diffusion** What examples of cultural diffusion in the Islamic state can you find in these areas: (a) art, (b) mathematics, (c) commerce, and (d) literature?

Interpreting Demographic Data

Demographic data are statistics about a population, or group of people. Demographic data can tell us a great deal about where and how people live.

Learning the Skill

Demographers measure populations in different ways. Sometimes they simply count the number of people living in a country or region. By comparing these numbers, we can determine which countries have more people than others.

Suppose, however, that country A and country B each has five million people, but country A has five times more land area than country B. Country B would be more crowded, or more densely populated, than country A. Population density measures the number of people living within a certain area. Demographers also measure the population distribution, or the pattern of settlement within a country. For example, in Egypt most people live in the fertile Nile River valley and few people live in the desert.

Demographic data also describe population growth. Zero population growth occurs when births equal deaths. If births exceed deaths, the population is growing; if deaths exceed births, the population is shrinking. Population growth is expressed as a percentage rate. Demographers use growth rates to predict the future size of a population. A population pyramid is a graph showing the age distribution of a population. If the pyramid is wider at the bottom than at the top, the population is growing. If a pyramid is smaller at the bottom, the population is shrinking.

Practicing the Skill

The graphs on this page show demographic data for seven countries in the modern Islamic world. Use the graphs to answer these questions.

1. What kind of demographic data appears in each graph?
2. Which three countries have the largest total populations?
3. Which four countries are growing fastest?
4. How is population size related to growth rates in the graphs of these countries?

Applying the Skill

At the library, find demographic data about your city or county and illustrate it in a table, graph, or map. You could show population increase or decrease, population distribution, population growth rates, or age distribution. Write a short paragraph or pose questions that can help in interpreting your data.

For More Practice

Turn to the Skill Practice in the Chapter Review on page 291 for more practice in interpreting demographic data.

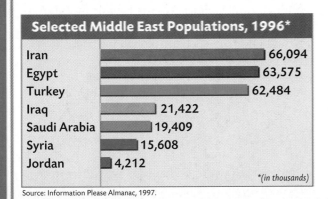

Selected Middle East Populations, 1996*

Iran	66,094
Egypt	63,575
Turkey	62,484
Iraq	21,422
Saudi Arabia	19,409
Syria	15,608
Jordan	4,212

*(in thousands)

Source: Information Please Almanac, 1997.

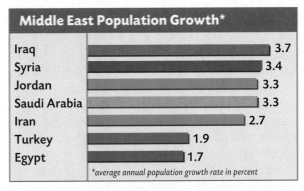

Middle East Population Growth*

Iraq	3.7
Syria	3.4
Jordan	3.3
Saudi Arabia	3.3
Iran	2.7
Turkey	1.9
Egypt	1.7

*average annual population growth rate in percent

Connections Across Time

Historical Significance From Muhammad's revelations in the A.D. 600s grew the religion of Islam, which now includes more than a billion worshipers and ranks as one of the world's leading faiths. Today, Muslims predominate in the Middle East, Central Asia, Southeast Asia, and parts of Africa. Other areas of the world have significant numbers of Muslims.

During the Islamic Empire, Muslims preserved much ancient knowledge and made advances in the arts and sciences. Their achievements have enriched the cultures of the world.

Using Key Terms

Write the key term that completes each sentence. Then write a sentence for each term not chosen.

a. arabesques
b. caliph
c. chronicle
d. hajj
e. imam
f. jihad
g. *madrasa*
h. bazaars
i. revelations
j. calligraphy
k. *shari'ah*
l. sheikh
m. mosque

Using Your History Journal

Calligraphy, an elegant form of handwriting, is still used as an art form. Look at samples of calligraphy in an encyclopedia. Then, in calligraphy, reproduce the beginning page of your short report on Muslim life.

1. Islamic scholars and theologians organized Islamic moral rules into the _____, or code of law.
2. Islamic artists used the beautiful script of Arabic in _____ , or the art of elegant handwriting.
3. After Muhammad's death in A.D. 632, a group of prominent Muslims chose a _____ to head the Muslim community.
4. Muslims believed they had a religious duty to struggle for their faith through conquests known as _____.
5. Islamic geometric designs entwined with plant stems, leaves, flowers, and stars that decorate walls, books, and various objects are known as _____.

Technology Activity

Building a Database Search a library or the Internet to find information about different modern Islamic countries. Build a database collecting information about all Islamic countries of the world. Include information about beliefs, practices, and demographics of each country. Include a world map and label all countries that have a large Muslim population.

Reviewing Facts

1. **History** Identify the changes in the Arabian Peninsula during the A.D. 600s.
2. **Government** Explain how the Madinah Compact formed the basis for the Islamic state.
3. **Government** Discuss how disputes were resolved in the early Islamic community.
4. **Citizenship** Explain why some Muslims revolted against the Umayyads.
5. **Culture** Describe the role of women in the Islamic Empire.
6. **Science** Discuss some Islamic achievements in science and the changes they produced.
7. **Culture** Describe the career of Moses Maimonides. In what ways did he reflect the multicultural character of the Islamic Empire?
8. **Culture** Name the work in which a person would find tales such as "Sinbad the Sailor" and "Ali Baba and the Forty Thieves."
9. **History** Describe the change in writing history that was introduced by Ibn-Khaldun.

Critical Thinking

1. **Contrast** How did bedouin society differ from the society that formed under Islam?

2. Apply Would there have been a struggle for the caliphate if Muhammad had named a successor before his death?

3. Analyze Why do you think Abu Bakr wanted to compile Muhammad's revelations into one written collection?

4. Synthesize If the hajj was not among the Five Pillars of Islam, how might its omission have affected the Islamic state?

5. Evaluate How did Muslim scholars contribute to the world's knowledge?

6. Contrast How did the Islamic Empire under the Abbasids differ from the early Islamic community under Muhammad?

Geography in History

1. Movement Refer to the map below. Identify how far the Abbasid Empire had spread by A.D. 800 by naming the areas that it encompassed.

2. Place What was the capital city of the Abbasid Empire, and where was it located?

3. Location How did the city of Baghdad fortify itself against invasion?

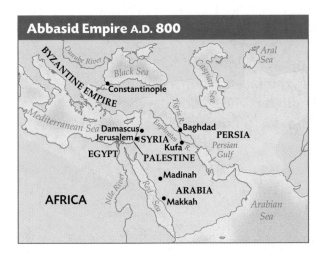

Abbasid Empire A.D. 800

Understanding Themes

1. Innovation What changes did the religion of Islam bring to the peoples of the Arabian Peninsula and the rest of the Middle East?

2. Movement How was the Umayyads' decision to move the nation's capital from Madinah to Damascus a result of Islamic expansion?

3. Cultural Diffusion How did the failure of the Umayyad government to embrace non-Arab Muslims destroy Umayyad rule?

Linking Past and Present

1. What evidence can you find in today's world of the split between the Sunni and the Shiite?

2. How have students today benefited from the work done at the House of Wisdom?

3. What words in the English language have their origins in the Arabic language?

Skill Practice

Study the population pyramid below and then answer these questions.

1. What is the general shape of the graph?

2. What percentage of the female population is between 10 and 19 years old?

3. Are there equal numbers of males and females in this population? How can you tell?

4. What conclusion can you draw about the growth rate in this population? On what data do you base this conclusion?

Age Distribution in Jordan

Age	% of Pop'n	Male	Female	% of Pop'n	Age
70+	0.8%			0.8%	70+
60-69	1.2%			1.1%	60-69
50-59	2.4%			2.2%	50-59
40-49	3.8%			3.4%	40-49
30-39	4.5%			4.2%	30-39
20-29	8.1%			7.3%	20-29
10-19	13.9%			12.4%	10-19
0-9	17.6%			16.3%	0-9

640   320   0   320   640

Total Population: 4,212,000
Total Male Population: 2,161,000
Total Female Population: 2,051,000
Life Expectancy (Male): 71 years
Life Expectancy (Female): 74 years
Sources: Broderbund Software, Inc., CIA World Factbook 1996.

A.D. 500–1300

The Rise of Medieval Europe

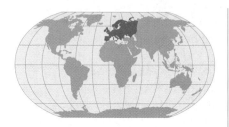

Chapter Themes

▶ **Movement** Invasions by Vikings, Magyars, and Muslims influence medieval Europe. *Section 1*

▶ **Cooperation** Nobles, church officials, and peasants develop ties of loyalty and service to one another. *Section 2*

▶ **Uniformity** The Catholic Church affects every aspect of medieval life. *Section 3*

▶ **Conflict** European kings, feudal lords, and popes struggle for political dominance. *Section 4*

The Storyteller

It was tournament day. As trumpets flourished, the marshal shouted, "In the name of God and St. Michael, do your battle!" Knights on horseback thundered toward each other and met with a deafening clash. Lords and ladies cheered as their favorite unhorsed his opponents. The victor was awarded a prize from the lady whose colors he wore.

Such tournaments provided more than just entertainment. They also trained soldiers for combat. After the fall of Rome, wars were frequent. A professional warrior class—the knights—led the new, vigorous, competitive society that would reshape western Europe.

Historical Significance

How did Christianity, the classical heritage, and Germanic practices combine to form a new European civilization? How did this civilization develop and lay the foundation for modern European life?

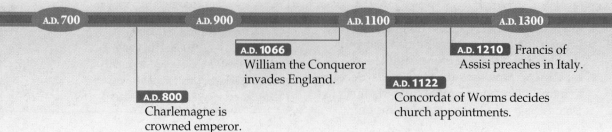

A.D. 700	A.D. 900	A.D. 1100	A.D. 1300

A.D. 1066 William the Conqueror invades England.

A.D. 1210 Francis of Assisi preaches in Italy.

A.D. 800 Charlemagne is crowned emperor.

A.D. 1122 Concordat of Worms decides church appointments.

Apparition Before the Chapter of Arles by Giotto di Bondone. San Francesco, Assisi, Italy

Your History Journal

Monarchies and representative assemblies arose in medieval Europe. Draw a time line of key events in the development of these institutions.

Section 1

Frankish Rulers

Setting the Scene

▶ **Terms to Define**
   mayor of the palace, count

▶ **People to Meet**
   Clovis, Charles Martel, Pepin the Short, Charlemagne, the Vikings

▶ **Places to Locate**
   Frankish Empire, Scandinavia

 **Find Out** What made Frankish rulers, such as Charlemagne, exceptional rulers for their time?

The Storyteller

The men of medieval times, including Charlemagne, loved hunting. It was a cruel sport, but at least it provided meat for the royal tables.

When Charlemagne sat down to dinner, the main course was usually a roast of game from the morning hunt. During the meal, one of the poets of the royal court might rise to read aloud a poem—to the dismay of the king's soldiers, who sometimes clapped their hands over their ears and glared at the poet until Charlemagne scolded them. With dinner, the king enjoyed "the wine of learning."

—freely adapted from *Charlemagne,* Richard Winston, 1968

Charlemagne

By A.D. 500, Germanic invasions had all but destroyed the urban world of the Roman Empire. Trade declined. Cities, bridges, and roads fell into disrepair and disuse. Law and order vanished, and education almost disappeared. Money was no longer used. For most people, life did not extend beyond the tiny villages where they were born, lived, and died.

Western Europe was so backward because of this decline that the early part of this period was once called "the Dark Ages." Scholars later combined the Latin terms *medium* (middle) and *aevum* (age) to form the term *medieval,* recognizing that this period was an era of transition between ancient and modern times. Out of this violent medieval period, or Middle Ages, a dynamic civilization arose. It combined elements of classical and Germanic cultures with Christian beliefs.

Merovingian Rulers

During the A.D. 400s the Franks, who settled in what is now France and western Germany, emerged as the strongest Germanic group. Their early rulers, known as Merovingian (MEHR•uh•VIHN•jee•uhn) kings for the ruler Merowig, held power until the early A.D. 700s.

Clovis

In A.D. 481 a brutal and wily warrior named **Clovis** became king of the Franks. Fifteen years later, Clovis became the first Germanic ruler to accept Catholicism. Clovis's military victories and his religious conversion gave his throne stability.

A century later the Frankish kingdom began to decline. Frankish kings had followed the custom of dividing the kingdom among their heirs. Heirs became rivals and fought each other for land. By A.D. 700 political power had passed from kings to government officials known as mayors of the palace.

Charles Martel

In A.D. 714 **Charles Martel**, or "Charles the Hammer," became mayor of the palace. When Muslim forces threatened Europe in A.D. 732, Charles led the successful defense of Tours, in France. This victory won him great prestige. As you read in Chapter 11, the victory ensured that Christianity would remain the dominant religion of Europe.

Pepin the Short

In A.D. 752, with the backing of nobles and church officials, **Pepin the Short**, the son of Charles Martel, became king of the Franks. The pope anointed, or put holy oil on, Pepin, making him a divinely chosen ruler in the eyes of the people.

In return for the Church's blessing, Pepin was expected to help the pope against his enemies. In A.D. 754 Pepin forced the Lombards, a Germanic people, to withdraw from Rome. He then gave the pope a large strip of Lombard land in central Italy. In appreciation, the pope cut his political ties to the Byzantine Empire and looked to the Franks as his protector. As a result, the fortunes of western Europe and Catholicism were bound more closely together.

Charlemagne's Empire

In A.D. 768 Pepin's son, **Charlemagne**, became the Frankish king. Charlemagne, or Charles the Great, was one of Europe's great monarchs. In Latin his name is written *Carolus Magnus*, which gave the name Carolingian to his dynasty. The king cut an imposing figure. His biographer, a monk named Einhard, described him this way:

> 66 Charles was large and strong, and of lofty stature, though not disproportionally tall … nose a little long, hair fair, and face laughing and merry…. He used to wear the national, that is to say, the Frankish, dress—next his skin a linen shirt and linen breeches, and above these a tunic fringed with silk; white hose fastened by bands covered his lower limbs and shoes his feet, and he protected his shoulders and chest in winter by a close-fitting coat of otter or marten skins. Over all he flung a blue cloak, and he always had a sword girt about him. 99

Charlemagne nearly doubled the borders of his kingdom to include Germany, France, northern Spain, and most of Italy. His enlarged domain became known as the **Frankish Empire**. For the

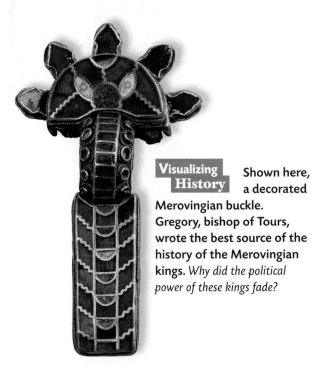

Visualizing History Shown here, a decorated Merovingian buckle. Gregory, bishop of Tours, wrote the best source of the history of the Merovingian kings. *Why did the political power of these kings fade?*

first time since the fall of Rome, most western Europeans were ruled by one government.

Because few western Europeans could read and write, Charlemagne wanted to revive learning. He set up a palace school at Aachen, his capital, to educate his officials. Alcuin (AL•kwihn), a scholar from England, ran the school and developed a program of study based on the Bible and Latin writings. Under Alcuin's direction, scholars preserved classical learning by copying ancient manuscripts. Charlemagne's school helped provide western Europeans with a common set of ideas.

A Christian Realm

One of the ideas that united western Europeans was the creation of a Christian Roman Empire. Church leaders believed that Charlemagne could turn this idea into reality. In A.D. 800 Charlemagne came to Rome to militarily defend Pope Leo III against the Roman nobles. To show his gratitude, Leo crowned Charlemagne the new Roman emperor. As protector of the Church and ruler of much of western Europe, Charlemagne wanted the title, but he had misgivings about receiving it from the pope. By crowning a monarch, the pope seemed to be saying that church officials were superior to rulers.

In spite of his concern, Charlemagne accepted his duties as emperor and worked to strengthen the empire. Because the central bureaucracy was small, he relied on local officials called counts to assist him. Each count was carefully instructed in the duties of office. The counts solved local problems, stopped feuds, protected the weak, and raised

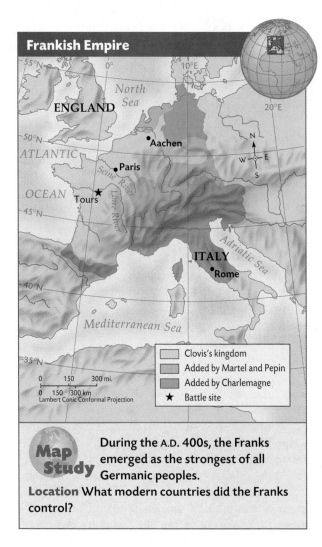

North Sea

ENGLAND

ATLANTIC

OCEAN

Aachen

Paris

Tours ★

Seine River

Loire River

ITALY

Rome

Adriatic Sea

Mediterranean Sea

0   150   300 mi.
0   150   300 km
Lambert Conic Conformal Projection

Clovis's kingdom
Added by Martel and Pepin
Added by Charlemagne
★   Battle site

Map Study   During the A.D. 400s, the Franks emerged as the strongest of all Germanic peoples.

Location What modern countries did the Franks control?

armies for the emperor. Each year royal messengers, the *missi dominici*, went on inspections in which they informed Charlemagne about the performance of the counts and other local administrators. The emperor also traveled throughout the empire observing the work of his officials firsthand.

Collapse of Charlemagne's Empire

More than anything else, Charlemagne's forceful personality held his empire together. His death in A.D. 814 left a void that his only surviving son, Louis the Pious, could not fill. After Louis's death, Charlemagne's three grandsons fought one another for control of the empire.

In A.D. 843 the three brothers agreed in the Treaty of Verdun to divide the Carolingian lands. Charles the Bald took the western part, which covered most of present-day France. Louis the German acquired the eastern portion, which today is Germany. Lothair, who became the Roman emperor, took a strip of land in the middle of the empire stretching from the North Sea southward to Italy.

Invasions Increase Disunity

While internal feuding weakened the Carolingian kingdoms, outside invasions nearly destroyed them. Muslims from North Africa seized parts of southern Italy and gained control of the western Mediterranean. The Slavs marched out of the east to invade central Europe. From Asia a new group of fierce nomads called Magyars galloped west, leaving a trail of destruction. The most threatening attacks, however, came from **the Vikings**, raiders from **Scandinavia** to the north.

Viking Invasions

In medieval Scandinavian, to go *a-viking* means to fight as a warrior. Viking warriors traveled in long, deckless ships with one sail that were designed to slide swiftly through the water propelled by long oars. These boats were sturdy enough to cross the Atlantic Ocean, shallow enough to navigate Europe's rivers, and light enough to be carried past fortified bridges. The Vikings became known for surprise attacks and speedy retreats. What they could not steal they burned. No place in Europe was safe from attack.

Boasting names like Eric Bloodax and Harald Bluetooth, the Vikings sought riches and adventure. In the A.D. 800s they left their overpopulated homeland, which later became the kingdoms of Norway, Denmark, and Sweden. Viking warriors fought ferociously and showed their victims no mercy.

Viking Trade

The Vikings, however, were more than just raiders. They were also explorers and settlers. Skilled in sailing and trading, they moved along the Atlantic and Mediterranean coasts of Europe. The Norwegians settled the North Atlantic islands of Greenland and Iceland, and even reached North America. The Danes temporarily held England and established the Viking state of Normandy in northwestern France. The Swedes settled in present-day Ukraine and Russia.

Viking Culture

In Scandinavia and their new homelands, the Vikings worshiped many deities. They were proud of their gods and told stories of the gods' great deeds. These stories became written poems called *Eddas*. The Vikings also made up sagas, or long tales. At first, storytellers recited them at special feasts. After A.D. 1100 the Vikings wrote down their sagas. By this time they had converted to Christianity. With their acceptance of the new religion, the Vikings began to write their languages with Roman letters.

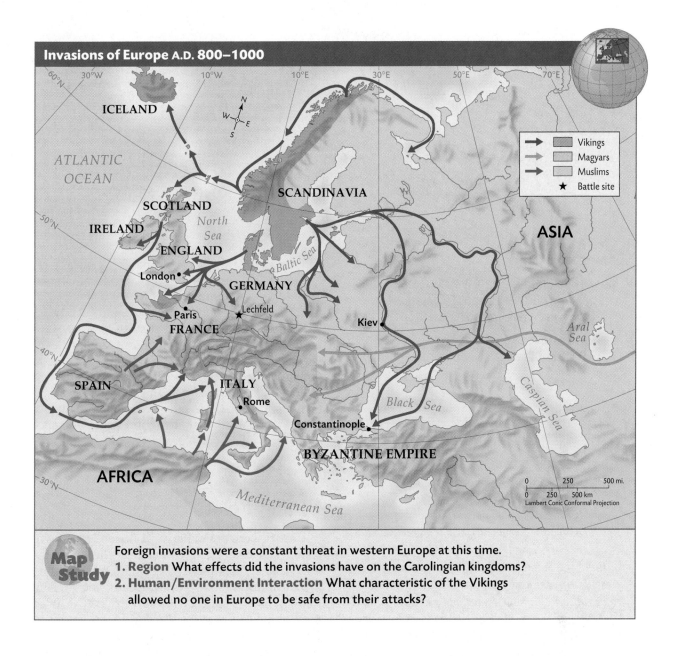

Invasions of Europe A.D. 800–1000

	Vikings
	Magyars
	Muslims
★	Battle site

Map Study

Foreign invasions were a constant threat in western Europe at this time.

1. **Region** What effects did the invasions have on the Carolingian kingdoms?
2. **Human/Environment Interaction** What characteristic of the Vikings allowed no one in Europe to be safe from their attacks?

A New Europe

The people of western Europe suffered at the hands of Vikings and other invaders. These raids isolated communities and severely weakened the central authority of monarchs. Trade declined, and many areas faced economic collapse. As a result of royal weakness, nobles and local officials took over the local defense. Beginning in the A.D. 900s, a new political and social system brought more stability to western Europe.

SECTION I REVIEW

Recall

1. **Define** mayor of the palace, count.
2. **Identify** Clovis, Charles Martel, Pepin the Short, Charlemagne, Treaty of Verdun, the Vikings.
3. **Explain** what problem resulted when Charlemagne was crowned by the pope.

Critical Thinking

4. **Making Comparisons** How did Charlemagne work to achieve European unity? How are European leaders trying to achieve the same goal in Europe today?

Understanding Themes

5. **Movement** Why did the Vikings, the Magyars, and the Slavs leave their homelands and invade western Europe?

A.D. 700	A.D. 900	A.D. 1100

c. A.D. 750 Charles Martel grants warriors landed estates with peasants.

c. A.D. 900 Feudalism takes hold in northern France.

c. A.D. 1000 Peasants begin to use three-field system in farming.

Section 2

Medieval Life

Setting the Scene

▶ **Terms to Define**
  feudalism, fief, vassal, homage, tournament, chivalry, manorialism, serf

▶ **People to Meet**
  knights, lords, ladies, peasants

ind Out How were loyalties maintained in a divided and often violent Europe?

The Storyteller

  Medieval law laid down rules for marriage. When a young woman arrived at marriageable age, one of her brothers or male relatives had to find her a suitable husband. If he did not, she could register a complaint, and her relative could be called to the king's court and given a year and a day to find her one. The husband had to be suited to her social status and property. If the relative did not do this, the king would step in and assign the woman a part of the family inheritance. Then she could marry whomever she wished.

  —from *Women's Lives in Medieval Europe, A Sourcebook*, edited by Emile Amt, 1993

Medieval tournament

With the weakening of central government, a new political system known as feudalism developed in western Europe. Feudalism was a highly decentralized form of government that stressed alliances of mutual protection between monarchs and nobles of varying degrees of power. The system was based on giving land to nobles in exchange for loyalty and military aid. With the land came peasants to farm it and many powers usually reserved for governments. Feudalism took hold in northern France around A.D. 900 and spread through the rest of western Europe by the A.D. mid-1000s.

Feudal Relationships

The tie between military service and land ownership that characterized feudalism began in the A.D. 700s. At that time, Charles Martel was fighting the Muslims. Unlike the Europeans, the Muslim soldiers used saddles with stirrups that enabled them to fight on horseback, using a sword or lance. Charles wanted to adopt the stirrup and develop a cavalry. However, the cost of keeping such a force required a new type of military system. To support the cavalry, Martel began granting warriors fiefs, or estates with peasants. From these fiefs, warriors got the income to buy horses and battle equipment.

Frankish kings later enlarged this system by giving fiefs to counts and local officials. In time, such nobles assumed many of the powers usually held by government: raising armies, dispensing justice, and in some cases even minting coins. In return, the nobles swore an oath of loyalty and pledged military support to the king.

By the A.D. 900s, such arrangements among nobles and monarchs emerged as feudalism. Lords who had been granted fiefs were allowed to pass their lands on to their heirs. In return, these nobles were to provide **knights**, or mounted warriors, for the royal army.

In theory, feudal relationships were like a pyramid. The king was at the top. In the middle were various ranks of lords. Each lord was a vassal—a noble who served a lord of the next higher rank. At the bottom were the knights. In practice, however, a noble might be both a lord and a vassal, since a noble could pledge his allegiance to more than one lord. In fact, one German warrior, Siboto of Falkenstein, was vassal to 20 different lords. Of course, conflicts of loyalty arose if one of a vassal's lords went to war with another.

Feudal Obligations

Ties between a lord and a vassal were made official in a solemn ceremony known as homage. In return for a fief, the vassal pledged to perform certain duties. The most important obligation was military service. The vassal agreed to provide his lord with a certain number of knights for battle during a period of 40 to 60 days each year. In addition, the vassal agreed to serve in the lord's court, to provide food and lodging when the lord came visiting, and to contribute funds when the lord's son became a knight or when his oldest daughter married. Vassals also pledged to pay ransom in the event of the lord's capture in battle.

Castles for Defense

Because of the lack of a strong central government, warfare occurred frequently in feudal society. As a result, every noble built a castle, or fortified manor house, for defense against enemies. The first castles were wooden buildings with high fences of logs or mounds of hard-packed earth around them. By the A.D. 1100s castles were built of stone, with thick walls and turrets, or small towers. Each castle was built on a hill or mound surrounded by a deep moat. Castles had a square tower called a keep. The keep, located in the strongest part of the castle, contained many rooms, a hall, and a dungeon. Surrounding the keep was a large open area called a bailey. Within the bailey were various buildings, including barracks, storerooms, workshops, and a chapel.

Life of the Nobility

Lords, ladies, and knights made up the nobility of the Middle Ages. Although the nobles lived much easier lives than the peasants who worked for them, their lives can hardly be called luxurious or glamorous. Castles were built for security, not comfort, and were largely cold, dingy, and damp places.

Within his fief, a **lord**, or nobleman, had almost total authority. He collected rents in goods from

Visualizing History An illustration from the *Trés Riches Heures du Duc de Berry* shows peasants at work outside a castle. *Why did feudal lords need castles?*

peasants and settled disputes between his vassals. Any outside attempt to seize the land or control the inhabitants of his fief was met with violent resistance.

In contrast, a **lady**, or noblewoman, had few, if any, rights. A noblewoman could be wed as early as her twelfth birthday to a man her father selected. Her primary duties lay in bringing up children and taking care of the household. Noblewomen took pride in their needlework, turning out cloth and fine embroidery. They also learned to make effective medicines from plants and herbs. Some women shared the supervision of the estate with the lord and took over their husband's duties while the men were away at war.

Entertainment

Nobles looked forward to tournaments—mock battles between knights—as a show of military

1–Moat; 2–Drawbridge; 3–Guardroom; 4–Latrine; 5–Armory; 6–Soldiers' quarters; 7–Kitchen garden;
8–Storerooms and servants' quarters; 9–Kitchen; 10–Great hall; 11–Chapel; 12–Lord and lady's quarters; 13–Inner ward

Harry Bliss

Life in the Castle

The medieval castle was both fortress and home. The first castles, raised in the A.D. 900s, were square towers encircled by wooden ramparts. By the A.D. 1100s, castles had become mighty stone fortresses. From the towers and walls archers took aim and soldiers dumped boiling liquids on attackers. The castle was surrounded by a moat—a body of water encircling the castle—that could be crossed when a drawbridge was let down.

Inside it was crowded, smelly, dirty, and damp. The animals ate and slept with the people, and the smell of animal and human waste was everywhere. The occupants of the castle had to contend with cold earthen or stone floors, drafty halls, smoky rooms, and windows without glass that let in cold and heat along with light. Not even the lord and lady had their own private room. Grand but never comfortable, the castle's main purpose was military security. ⊕

skills. They also loved to hunt, and both men and women learned the art of falconry and archery. A dinner featuring several dishes of game and fish might follow. In a castle's great hall, nobles and their guests ate while being entertained by minstrels, or singers.

Becoming a Knight

A nobleman's son began training for knighthood at age 7. Beginning as a page, or assistant, in the house of a lord, he learned manners and the use of weapons. At 15, the page became a squire who assisted a knight and practiced using weapons. Once he proved himself in battle, the squire was knighted in an elaborate ceremony.

The behavior of knights was governed by a code of chivalry. This code called for knights to be brave in battle, fight fairly, keep promises, defend the Church, and treat women of noble birth in a courteous manner. Chivalry eventually became the basis for the development of good manners in Western society.

The Manorial System

The wealth of a feudal lord came from the labor of the **peasants** who lived on and worked the lord's land. Since the last years of the Roman Empire, many peasants had worked for large landowners, in part because they could not afford their own land and in part for protection. By the Middle Ages, economic life across Europe centered around a system of agricultural production called manorialism. It provided lords and peasants with food, shelter, and protection.

Manors, or estates, varied in size from several hundred to several hundred thousand acres. Each manor included the lord's manor house, pastures for livestock, fields for crops, forest areas, and a

Visualizing History A suit of armor made of steel, brass, and leather belonging to an English knight, Master Jacobe. *What knightly code became the basis of good manners in Western society?*

village where the peasants lived. While feudalism describes the political relationships between nobles, manorialism concerns economic ties between nobles and peasants.

Work on a Manor

In return for the lord's protection, the peasants provided various services for the lord. Chief among the obligations were to farm the lord's land and to make various payments of goods. For example, each time a peasant ground grain at the lord's mill, he was obligated to leave a portion for the lord. If he baked in the lord's oven, he left a loaf behind for the lord. In addition, peasants were obligated to set aside a number of days each year to provide various types of labor, such as road or bridge repair.

Warfare and invasions made trade almost impossible, so the manor had to produce nearly everything its residents needed. Most of the peasants farmed or herded sheep. A few worked as skilled artisans, for each manor needed a blacksmith to make tools, a carpenter for building, a

Footnotes to History

Identifying a Knight
To identify themselves, knights had individual designs painted on their shields and tunics. His particular design became known as the knight's coat of arms. In noble families, coats of arms were passed down from one generation to the next. The flags of some modern countries are based on the system of designs that were developed by the knights.

shoemaker, a miller to grind grain, a vintner to make wine, and a brewer to make beer. Peasant women made candles, sheared sheep, spun wool, and sewed clothing.

Peasants rarely left the manor. Most were serfs, people who were bound to the manor and could not leave it without permission. But the serfs were not slaves—they could not be "sold" apart from the land they lived on.

Increased Production

The manorial system normally produced only enough food to support the peasants and the lord's household. However, a number of improvements gradually boosted productivity and eased the threat of famine.

The first improvement was the development of a new, heavier type of plow. The new plow made deeper cuts in the ground and had a device called a mould-board that pushed the soil sideways. The heavier plow meant less time in the fields for peasant farmers. As a result, farmers developed a better method of planting.

Instead of dividing plots of land into two fields, one of which lay fallow, or unsown, each year, farmers in the A.D. 1000s began to use a three-field system. One field might be planted with winter wheat, a second with spring wheat and vegetables, and a third left fallow. The next year, different crops were planted in the fallow field. One of the two remaining fields was planted, and the other one was left fallow until the next year. This system produced more crops than the old system and helped to preserve the soil.

Peasant Life

Poverty and hardship characterized peasant life, and few serfs lived beyond the age of 40. Famine and disease were constant dangers. In times of war, the peasants were the first and hardest hit. Invading knights trampled crops and burned villages, causing famine and loss of life. To support the war, their lord might require additional payments of crops or labor. A monk of Canterbury described an English serf's account of his day:

> I work very hard. I go out at dawn, driving the oxen to the field, and I yoke them to the plough; however hard the winter I dare not stay home for fear of my master; but, having yoked the oxen and made the ploughshare and coulter fast to the plough, every day I have to plough a whole acre or more.
>
> —Aelfric, *Colloquy*, A.D. 1005

Serfs like this man lived in tiny, one-room houses with dirt floors, no chimney, and one or two crude pieces of furniture—perhaps a table and stools. People slept huddled together for warmth. Coarse bread, a few vegetables from their gardens, and grain for porridge made up their usual diet. Meat was a rarity.

In spite of hardships, peasants were able to relax on Sundays and holy days. They enjoyed dancing, singing, and such sports as wrestling and archery. In addition, there were other amusements, such as religious plays, pageants, and shows by minstrels.

Despite the obvious differences between serfs and nobles, the two groups did share a common interest in the land. Medieval Europeans believed that every person was equal in the "eyes of God." In practice, however, society was viewed as a hierarchy with ranked leaders from top to bottom. Each person—no matter what his or her place might be in the hierarchy—had certain duties that were attached to his or her position in life. In general, people did not question their standing or obligations. Although the manorial system seemed to lack freedom and opportunity for most of the people involved in it, it did create a very stable and secure way of life during a time that was generally violent and uncertain.

SECTION 2 REVIEW

Recall
1. **Define** feudalism, fief, vassal, homage, tournament, chivalry, manorialism, serf.
2. **Identify** knight, lord, lady, peasant.
3. **Describe** the role of women in medieval Europe and male attitudes toward women.

Critical Thinking
4. **Making Comparisons** Compare and contrast the feudal class structure in medieval Europe with the *varna* system in early India discussed in Chapter 8.

Understanding Themes
5. **Cooperation** Diagram the ways nobles, knights, and peasants cooperated during the medieval period.

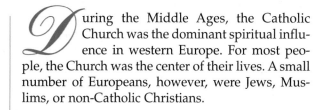

A.D. 529 Benedict introduces rule for monasteries.

c. A.D. 650 Irish missionaries win converts in western Europe.

A.D. 1073 The monk Hildebrand becomes Pope Gregory VII.

A.D. 1232 The Inquisition begins.

Section 3

The Medieval Church

Setting the Scene

▶ **Terms to Define**
sacrament, abbot, abbess, cardinal, lay investiture, heresy, excommunication, friar

▶ **People to Meet**
Benedict, Gregory I, Gregory VII, Innocent III, Francis of Assisi, Dominic

▶ **Places to Locate**
Monte Cassino, Cluny

 How did the Catholic Church shape the development of medieval Europe?

The Storyteller

Alcuin, a Benedictine monk, arose to begin his day. The day's work in a monastery depended on sunlight hours, for candles were expensive and no one in medieval times had access to cheap artificial light. Because it was winter, Alcuin had to get up at 2:30 A.M., and go to bed at 6:30 P.M.

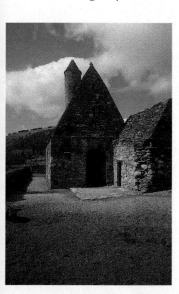

after sunset. Sometimes he was already tired by noon! His workday included reading, choir practice, bookbinding, sewing, gardening, and worship services—which were the only times during the day that he was permitted to break his vow of silence and speak.

—from *Monastic Life in Medieval England*, J.C. Dickinson, 1962

Ancient monastery in Glendalough, Ireland

During the Middle Ages, the Catholic Church was the dominant spiritual influence in western Europe. For most people, the Church was the center of their lives. A small number of Europeans, however, were Jews, Muslims, or non-Catholic Christians.

The Medieval Church

Although the Church's primary mission was spiritual, the decline of Rome in the A.D. 400s led the Church to assume many political and social tasks. During this time, the bishop of Rome, now called the pope, became the strongest political leader in western Europe. The pope claimed spiritual authority over all Christians, basing this claim on the belief that Peter the Apostle, Rome's first bishop, had been chosen by Jesus to lead the Church.

Religious Role

The Catholic Church taught that all people were sinners and dependent on God's grace, or favor. The only way to receive grace was by taking part in the sacraments, or church rituals: baptism, penance, eucharist, confirmation, matrimony, anointing of the sick, and holy orders. One of the most important sacraments was the eucharist, or holy communion, which commemorated Christ's death. People shared in the eucharist at a mass, or worship service. At each mass, the priest blessed wheat wafers and a cup of wine that stood on an altar. According to Catholic teaching, the priests and the worshippers received Jesus' invisible presence in the forms of the bread and the wine.

During the Middle Ages, people generally had a limited understanding of church rituals. Masses were said in Latin, a language few people understood. Also, many priests were poorly educated

Chapter 12 *The Rise of Medieval Europe* **303**

and did not preach effectively. Moreover, few worshippers could read or write. What the average person learned about the Christian faith came from the statues, paintings, and later the stained glass windows that adorned most medieval churches.

Church Organization

The church hierarchy, which was described in Chapter 6, remained largely the same during the Middle Ages. The contact most people had with the Church was through parish priests, who conducted services and oversaw the spiritual life of the community. Occasionally bishops visited a parish to supervise the priests.

The pope, bishops, and priests formed what is called the secular clergy because they lived *in saeculo*, a Latin phrase that means "in the world." Other clergy, known as regular clergy, lived by a *regula*, or rule. Regular clergy included monks and nuns who lived apart from society. These Christians played an important role in strengthening the medieval Church.

Benedict's Rule

In A.D. 529 a Roman official named **Benedict** founded a monastery at **Monte Cassino** in Italy. His monastery became a model for monks in other communities. Benedict drew up a list of rules that provided for manual work, meditation, and prayer. According to the Benedictine rule, monks could not own goods, must never marry, and were bound to obey monastic laws. Their life was one of poverty, chastity, and obedience to the directives of an abbot, or monastery head.

Monastic Life

Monks dressed in simple, long robes made of coarse material and tied at the waist by a cord. They ate one or two plain meals each day. Most monasteries had a rule of silence; monks could not converse with one another except for a short time each day. In some monasteries total silence was the rule. During meals, one monk might read passages from

Images of the Times

Monastic Life

Although monasteries were closed religious communities, they profoundly influenced European culture during the Middle Ages.

An illustrated page from a book copied by monks shows the careful, artistic writing that became the manuscript before printing was developed.

St. Benedict and his monks, like all those who lived at the monasteries, ate together in a refectory.

Mont St. Michel presents a view of the beautiful old monastery's lower ramparts.

the Bible while the others meditated.

Women took part in monastic life by living in a convent under the direction of an abbess. Known as nuns, they wore simple clothes and wrapped a white cloth called a wimple around their face and neck. They alternated prayer with spinning, weaving, and embroidering items such as tapestries and banners. They also taught needlework and the medicinal use of herbs to the daughters of nobles.

Influence of Monastics

Although monks and nuns lived apart from society, they were not completely isolated. Indeed, they played a crucial role in medieval intellectual and social life. Since few people could read or write, the regular clergy preserved ancient religious works and the classical writings. Scribes laboriously copied books by hand, working in a small drafty room with only a candle or small window for light. Illuminated manuscripts decorated with rich colors and intricate pictures indicate that, although the task was tedious, it was lovingly done.

Monasteries and convents provided schools for young people, hospitals for the sick, food for the needy, and guest houses for weary travelers. They taught peasants carpentry and weaving and made improvements in agriculture that they passed on to others. Some monks and nuns became missionaries who spread Christian teachings to non-Christians.

Missionary Efforts

Pope **Gregory I** was so impressed with the Benedictine Rule that he adopted it to spread Christianity in Europe. In A.D. 597 he sent monks to England, where they converted the Anglo-Saxons to Catholicism. From England, missionaries carried Christianity to northern Germany. During the A.D. 600s, monasteries in Ireland sent missionaries throughout the North Atlantic and western Europe. Although the Irish were isolated from the pope in Rome, their missionaries won many converts. By the A.D. mid-1000s, most western Europeans had become Catholics.

A father who has bought a place for his son in a monastery presents the youngster to an abbot.

REFLECTING ON THE TIMES

1. Where did monks normally have their meals?
2. Why do you think all monks dressed alike?

Power of the Church

The medieval Catholic Church helped to govern western Europe. It had its own laws and courts that dealt with cases related to the clergy, doctrine, and marriage and morals. Disobedience to church laws resulted in severe penalties for a common person and ruler alike. For example, a lord or king who violated Church law could face an interdict, which banned an entire region or country from receiving the sacraments necessary to salvation.

The Church also had feudal ties that boosted its wealth and political power but often undermined its spiritual vitality. Many high church officials were nobles and held land from kings in return for military service. Because their religious duties prevented them from fighting, these church leaders gave some of their land to knights who would fight for them. The Church also received donations of land and money from nobles wanting to ensure their salvation. Nobles, however, began to influence church policies, especially by having relatives appointed to church positions. Many of these appointees had little devotion to their spiritual calling.

A young boy, having obtained the office of bishop, carries sacred church relics. *How did Pope Gregory try to stop the selection of church officials by secular rulers?*

Church Reform

By the A.D. 900s, many devout Christians were calling for reform. The reform movement began in the monasteries and spread throughout much of western Europe. Most famous was the monastery at **Cluny** in eastern France, whose monks won respect for leading lives of pious simplicity. The abbots of Cluny sent representatives to other monasteries to help them undertake similar reforms.

Other church leaders tried to free the Church from the control of feudal lords. They wanted the Church, not the state, to be the final authority in Western society. In A.D. 1059 a church council declared that political leaders could no longer choose the pope. Instead, the pope would be elected by a gathering of cardinals—high church officials in Rome ranking directly below the pope. In addition, the reformers insisted that the pope, not secular rulers such as lords and kings, should be the one to appoint bishops and other officials to church offices.

In A.D. 1073 the cardinals elected a reform-minded monk named Hildebrand as Pope **Gregory VII**. Gregory believed that the pope should have complete jurisdiction over all church officials. He especially criticized the practice of lay investiture, in which secular rulers gave the symbols of office, such as a ring and a staff, to the bishops they had appointed.

Fighting Heresy

Innocent III, one of the most powerful popes, also tried to reform the Catholic Church. In A.D. 1215 he convened a council that condemned drunkenness, feasting, and dancing among the clergy. The council also laid down strict rules for stopping the spread of heresy, or the denial of basic church teachings. Heresy had increased as corruption and scandal had rocked the Church. In the Middle Ages, heresy was regarded as seriously as the crime of treason is viewed today.

At first, the Catholic Church tried to convert heretics, or those who challenged its teachings. When that failed, however, heretics were threatened with excommunication, or expulsion from the Church. An excommunicated person was not allowed to take part in the sacraments and was also outlawed from any contact with Christian society. Since receiving the sacraments was considered to be essential for salvation, banishment was an especially severe penalty.

Early in the A.D. 1200s, for example, the Church became concerned about a group of heretics in France known as Albigensians (AL•buh•JEHN •shuhnz). The Albigensians believed that the material world was evil and rejected church sacraments. To end this heresy, Pope Innocent III sent French knights to crush the group.

The Inquisition

In order to seek out and punish people suspected of heresy, the Church set up a court in A.D. 1232 known as the Inquisition. Those brought before the court were urged to confess their heresy and to ask forgiveness. Often, however, Inquisition officials accused people without sufficient proof; sometimes they even used torture to obtain confessions. The Church welcomed back those who repented, but those who did not repent were punished. Punishment ranged from imprisonment to loss of property and even execution. According to church officials, these punishments were needed to save the souls of the heretics.

Friars Inspire Reform

Other reformers of the Church during the early A.D. 1200s were friars, or wandering preachers. At a time when church leaders were criticized for their love of wealth and power, the friars lived simply, owned no possessions, and depended on gifts of food and shelter to survive.

The friars followed monastic rules but did not isolate themselves from the rest of the Christian community. Instead, they lived in towns and preached Christianity to the people. The best-known friars were the Franciscans and the Dominicans. Because they were well known and liked, the friars kept many people loyal to the Catholic Church.

Francis of Assisi, the son of a wealthy Italian cloth merchant, founded the Franciscan friars about A.D. 1210. Francis and his followers sought to follow the simple life of Jesus and his disciples. They became known for their cheerful trust in God and their respect for nature as a divine gift.

A Spanish priest named **Dominic** organized the Dominican friars in A.D. 1215. Like the Franciscans, the Dominicans lived a life of poverty, simplicity, and service. In addition, they were well-educated, persuasive preachers who could reply to the arguments of heretics.

The Jews

As the Church's power increased in medieval Europe, the position of the Jews worsened. In the early Middle Ages, Jews and Christians had lived peacefully together in most of Europe. Many Jews had become merchants, artisans, or landowners, and their contributions to society were valued by their Christian neighbors.

By the 1000s, however, many Christians increasingly saw the Jews as outsiders and a threat to society. They unfairly blamed the Jews for plagues, famines, and other social problems. Such false accusations gave mobs the excuse to attack and kill thousands of Jews.

The most powerful source of anti-Semitism, or hatred of the Jews, came from interpretations of Christian doctrine. Many church leaders and laity blamed the Jews for Jesus' death and resented the Jews' refusal to become Christians. With church approval, political leaders required Jews in certain areas to wear badges or special clothes that identified them as Jews. Jews were also forced to live in separate communities that became known as ghettos. They also lost the right to own land and to practice certain trades. To earn a living, many Jews became peddlers or money-lenders, jobs despised by medieval Christians.

Beginning in the late 1200s, rulers in England, France, and certain parts of central Europe even expelled their Jewish subjects. Many of the expelled Jews settled in eastern Europe, especially Poland, where they received protection. Over the centuries, the Jews of eastern Europe developed thriving communities based on their religious traditions.

SECTION 3 REVIEW

Recall
1. **Define** sacrament, abbot, abbess, cardinal, lay investiture, heresy, excommunication, friar.
2. **Identify** Benedict, Gregory I, Gregory VII, Innocent III, Francis of Assisi, Dominic.
3. **Explain** how the Catholic Church provided the link between the ancient world and the medieval world.

Critical Thinking
4. **Synthesizing Information** Imagine that you are a religious, but superstitious, peasant living during the Middle Ages. Invent an explanation for the famine that has struck your village.

Understanding Themes
5. **Uniformity** How effective were the actions of the Catholic Church in trying to make all western Europeans believe and practice one faith?

A.D. 700	A.D. 900	A.D. 1100	A.D. 1300

A.D. 871 Alfred the Great begins rule in England.

A.D. 955 German King Otto defeats the Magyars at Lechfeld.

A.D. 1180 Philip Augustus becomes king of France.

A.D. 1215 English King John and his barons sign the Magna Carta.

Section 4

Rise of European Monarchy

Setting the Scene

▶ **Terms to Define**
common law, grand jury, petit jury, middle class

▶ **People to Meet**
Alfred the Great, William the Conqueror, Henry II, Thomas à Becket, Eleanor of Aquitaine, Philip Augustus, Henry IV

▶ **Places to Locate**
England, France, Germany

 **ind Out** What were the achievements of medieval European monarchs?

The Storyteller

The English throne was at stake as the Battle of Hastings approached. William decided to provoke Harold to fight in single combat and called on him to spare the blood of his followers. Under Norman law, personal combat decided difficult cases, looking for the judgment of God to settle the matter. Harold refused because he knew the cause was not personal, but national. It would take a full-scale invasion to decide who would wear the English crown.

—adapted from *William the Conqueror*, Edward A. Freeman, 1927

William the Conqueror

After the decline of Rome, central authority in western Europe disappeared. Except for Charlemagne's reign in the late A.D. 700s, kings were rulers in name only, their lands and power gradually lost to nobles. However, in the A.D. 1100s, many European monarchs began to build strong states.

England

After the Romans abandoned Britain in the A.D. 400s, the island was invaded by Germanic Angles, Saxons, and Jutes. These groups took over much of Britain from the native Celts (KEHLTZ) and set up several kingdoms. In the late A.D. 800s, the Danish Vikings from Scandinavia posed another threat. King Alfred of Wessex, known as **Alfred the Great**, united the Anglo-Saxon kingdoms and defeated the Danes in A.D. 886. His united kingdom eventually became known as "Angleland," or **England**.

The Anglo-Saxons

Alfred ruled Anglo-Saxon England from A.D. 871 to A.D. 899. Like Charlemagne, he was interested in the revival of learning. The English king founded schools and hired scholars to translate many books from Latin to Anglo-Saxon. He also had the scholars write a history of England, known as the *Anglo-Saxon Chronicle*.

The kings who followed Alfred were weak rulers. When the last Anglo-Saxon king, Edward the Confessor, died in A.D. 1066, three rivals claimed the throne.

The Norman Conquest

One of the claimants to the throne was William, the Duke of Normandy. A cousin of the late English king and vassal of the French king, William had a feudal stronghold in northwestern France. Gathering a force of several hundred boats and some 6,000 soldiers, he invaded England in A.D. 1066. At the Battle of Hastings, William defeated Harold Godwinson, the king chosen by the Anglo-Saxon nobles. The victory won William the English crown and the name **William the Conqueror**.

As king, William kept tight control over the government. He took Anglo-Saxon lands, kept some of the land for himself, and gave the rest to his Norman vassals in return for military service. He later made all landowners swear direct loyalty to him. William also set up a council of nobles to advise him and named local officials called sheriffs to collect taxes. To determine taxable wealth, William carried out the first census in western Europe since Roman times. Every person, manor, and farm animal became an entry in the *Domesday Book*.

Royal Power

Although William's court and nobles were French-speaking, England's population remained largely Anglo-Saxon. Over the next 300 years, however, Norman French and Anglo-Saxon ways blended to form a new English culture. During this time, William's successors further strengthened the monarchy. Henry I, William's son who ruled from A.D. 1100 to A.D. 1135, created a royal exchequer, or treasury, to collect taxes and gave royal courts greater authority. Henry's grandson, **Henry II**, set up a system of common law, using traveling judges to apply the law equally throughout the land. In each community, the judges met with a grand jury that submitted the names of suspects. A petit jury soon developed to establish the guilt or innocence of the accused.

Henry's plan to try clergy in the royal courts brought him into conflict with **Thomas à Becket**, the archbishop of Canterbury. In A.D. 1170 four of Henry's knights, who believed they were acting on the king's command, murdered Becket in his cathedral.

At the height of his power, Henry ruled western France as well as England. His wife, **Eleanor of Aquitaine**, once married to the French king, owned vast lands in southwestern France. Although Henry's relations with Eleanor soured, Eleanor continued to influence royal policies through their sons, Richard I (the Lionhearted) and John.

CONNECTIONS

The Arts

Tapestries

The Bayeux Tapestry, made between A.D. 1073 and A.D. 1083, is a remarkable example of medieval art. It is a work of embroidery, a band of linen upon which pictures and patterns are stitched in colored wool. Twenty inches high and 230 feet long, it probably once decorated the walls of an entire room.

The 72 scenes on the tapestry illustrate William the Conqueror's invasion of England in A.D. 1066. Probably the work of William's wife, Matilda, and the ladies of her court, the tapestry tells the story of the invasion in a series of individual scenes, much as a story is told in a comic book today. The images are lively and simple and give a sense of movement and vitality. The tapestry even includes words to reveal what is happening in each scene.

The popularity of tapestries among the European nobility continued into the A.D. 800s and then declined. However, since World War II, interest in this art form has revived. Artists today experiment with materials and weaving to create many new kinds of wall tapestry. One of the most famous modern tapestries, "Christ in Glory," was done in 1962 by the English artist Graham Sutherland and hangs above the high altar in England's new Coventry Cathedral.

Bayeux Tapestry (detail)

Linking Past and Present ACTIVITY

Visit an art museum in your community that has medieval and modern tapestries. Compare and contrast the tapestries of both time periods in terms of their themes, techniques, and the materials used to make them.

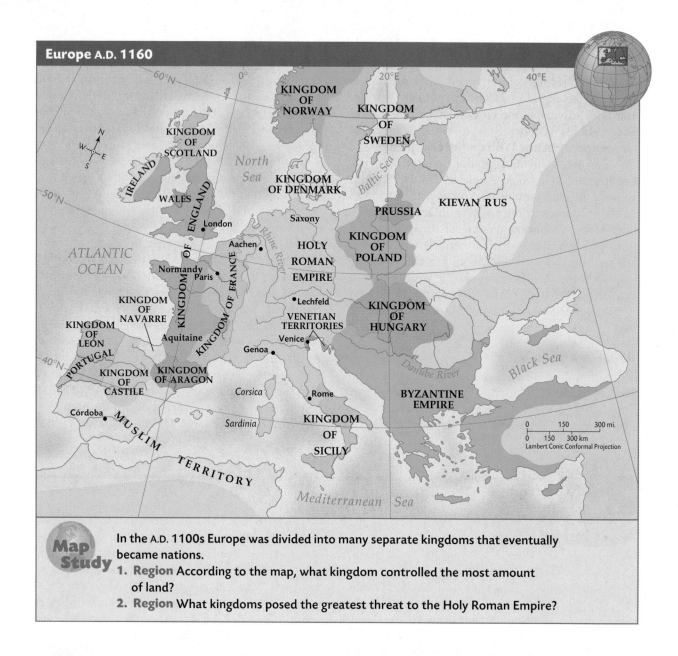

KINGDOM
OF
NORWAY

KINGDOM
OF
SWEDEN

KINGDOM
OF
SCOTLAND

*North
Sea*

KINGDOM
OF DENMARK

Baltic Sea

PRUSSIA

KIEVAN RUS

IRELAND

WALES

Saxony

London

Aachen

Rhine River

HOLY
ROMAN
EMPIRE

KINGDOM
OF
POLAND

*ATLANTIC
OCEAN*

Normandy
Paris

Lechfeld

KINGDOM
OF
NAVARRE

Aquitaine

VENETIAN
TERRITORIES
Venice

KINGDOM
OF
HUNGARY

KINGDOM
OF
LEÓN

Genoa

Danube River

Black Sea

PORTUGAL

KINGDOM
OF
CASTILE

KINGDOM
OF ARAGON

Corsica

Sardinia

Rome

BYZANTINE
EMPIRE

Córdoba

MUSLIM

Mediterranean Sea

KINGDOM
OF
SICILY

TERRITORY

| 0 | 150 | 300 mi. |
| 0 | 150 | 300 km |

Lambert Conic Conformal Projection

**Map
Study**

In the A.D. 1100s Europe was divided into many separate kingdoms that eventually
became nations.
1. **Region** According to the map, what kingdom controlled the most amount
of land?
2. **Region** What kingdoms posed the greatest threat to the Holy Roman Empire?

The Magna Carta

During his reign, John lost some English land to
France and became unpopular when he increased
taxes and punished his enemies without trial.
Alarmed at the loss of their feudal rights, a group of
nobles met at Runnymede in A.D. 1215. They forced
John to sign the Magna Carta, or Great Charter, one
of the most important documents in the history of
representative government.

The Magna Carta placed clear limits on royal
power. The charter prevented the king from collecting taxes without the consent of the Great Council.
It also assured freemen the right of trial by jury.
Article 39 stated:

❝No freeman shall be taken, or imprisoned,
or disseized [dispossessed], or outlawed,
or exiled, or in any way harmed—nor will
we go upon or send upon him—save by
the lawful judgment of his peers [equals]
or by the law of the land. ❞

The nobles intended the Magna Carta to protect their feudal rights. Over time, however, it guaranteed the rights of all English people.

Rise of Parliament

During the reign of John's son, Henry III, an
increase in population encouraged the growth of
towns. A new social class—the middle class—was
emerging. The middle class did not fit in
the medieval social order of nobles, clergy, and

peasants. Its income came from business and trade, not from the land. This group played an increasingly important role in government.

Recognizing the towns' growing power, Henry III added knights and burgesses, or important townspeople, to the Great Council that advised the king. By that time the Great Council was called Parliament, the name by which it is still known.

In A.D. 1295 Henry's son, Edward I, called into session the Model Parliament, which included representatives from the clergy, nobility, and burgesses. As England's government became more representative, Edward encouraged members of Parliament to advise him on business matters, submit petitions to him, and meet frequently.

By A.D. 1400 Parliament had divided into two chambers. Nobles and clergy met as the House of Lords, while knights and burgesses met as the House of Commons.

France

Like England, **France** developed a strong monarchy in the Middle Ages. The type of government that emerged in France, however, differed considerably from the increasingly representative government in England.

Beginnings of Central Government

After Charlemagne's death, the Frankish lands disintegrated into separate territories governed by feudal lords. These lords defended their own lands and were virtually independent rulers.

In A.D. 987 a noble named Hugh Capet seized the French throne from the weak Carolingian king. Capet controlled only the city of Paris and a strip of land between the Seine and Loire Rivers in northern France. The Capetian (kuh•PEE•shuhn) dynasty he established, however, lasted for more than three centuries. By the A.D. 1100s Capetian kings had established the principle of the eldest son inheriting the throne. The Capetians strengthened the power of the monarchy and brought French feudal lords under royal control.

As in England, the number of towns in France increased during the A.D. 1100s. Louis VI, who became king in A.D. 1108, used the townspeople to strengthen the royal government at the expense of the nobles. Louis awarded both the townspeople and the clergy positions on his court of advisers and also granted self-government to towns, freeing them from obligations to feudal lords. These measures led local officials to be loyal to the monarch rather than to feudal lords.

Strengthening the Monarchy

Philip II, known as **Philip Augustus**, ruled France from A.D. 1180 to A.D. 1223. Barely 15 when he succeeded to the throne, Philip was determined to strengthen the monarchy. During his 43-year reign Philip doubled the area of his domain, acquiring some territory through marriage and recapturing French land from England. By appointing local officials who were loyal to the king and forming a semipermanent royal army, Philip further weakened the power of feudal lords.

A Saintly Ruler

Philip's grandson became King Louis IX in A.D. 1226. Louis made royal courts dominant over feudal courts and decreed that only the king had the right to mint coins. Bans on private warfare and the bearing of arms further promoted the French monarch.

A very religious man, Louis was regarded as the ideal for his chivalry and high moral character. His advice to his son reveals these characteristics:

“ [Have] a tender pitiful heart for the poor … [and] hold yourself steadfast and loyal toward your subjects and your vassals, without turning either to the right or to the left, but always straight, whatever may happen. And if a poor man have a quarrel with a rich man, sustain the poor rather than the rich, until the truth is made clear, and when you know the truth, do justice to them. ”

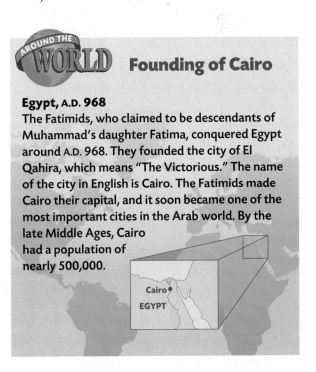

AROUND THE WORLD **Founding of Cairo**

Egypt, A.D. 968
The Fatimids, who claimed to be descendants of Muhammad's daughter Fatima, conquered Egypt around A.D. 968. They founded the city of El Qahira, which means "The Victorious." The name of the city in English is Cairo. The Fatimids made Cairo their capital, and it soon became one of the most important cities in the Arab world. By the late Middle Ages, Cairo had a population of nearly 500,000.

Cairo
EGYPT

Signs of a Strong Monarchy

Louis IX's grandson, Philip IV, was so handsome he was nicknamed Philip the Fair. The blond, blue-eyed Philip increased France's territory and trade by defeating both England and Flanders in war. To pay for the wars, he raised taxes and taxed new groups, such as the clergy. Although Pope Boniface VIII opposed taxing the clergy, he could not force Philip to back down.

Before he died in A.D. 1314, Philip summoned the Estates-General, an assembly of nobles, clergy, and townspeople. He wanted to use the assembly to raise taxes on a national level rather than locally. The assembly, however, never became as powerful as Parliament in England. French kings kept a firm hand on government affairs.

The Holy Roman Empire

While monarchs in England and France were building strong central governments, rulers in **Germany** remained weak and often powerless. Among the major reasons were their disputes with the pope and with powerful German nobles.

"Emperor of the Romans"

During the A.D. 1000s and A.D. 1100s, German kings posed the biggest threat to the pope's authority. King Otto I, or Otto the Great, of Germany tried to restore Charlemagne's empire. After defeating the Magyars at the Battle of Lechfeld in A.D. 955, King Otto set his sights on Italy. In A.D. 962 Pope John XII sought Otto's help against Roman nobles who opposed the pope. In return for the German king's help, the pope in Rome crowned Otto Holy Roman emperor.

Problems of the Holy Roman Empire

Otto and his successors claimed the right to intervene in the election of popes, and Otto himself appointed and deposed several popes. The pope, as you have read, claimed the right to anoint and depose kings. These two conflicting claims led to centuries of dispute between the Holy Roman emperors and the Roman Catholic popes.

Powerful German lords also prevented the Holy Roman emperors from building a strong, unified state. Their challenges to imperial power caused several civil wars. Numerous wars with the Slavic states—Poland and Bohemia—and with Hungary also weakened the Holy Roman emperor's power.

Emperor and Pope Collide

During the rule of **Henry IV**, a major quarrel broke out with Pope Gregory VII. In A.D. 1073 the pope condemned lay investiture, hoping to free the Church from secular control. Since the bishops supported Henry in his struggle with feudal lords, the emperor refused to halt the practice.

The pope promptly proclaimed Henry deposed and urged the German nobles to elect another ruler. Henry gave in. In A.D. 1077 he made his way southward in bitter January weather across the snowy mountains to Canossa, Italy. There he sought forgiveness from the pope. He showed his repentance by standing before the gate of the castle begging for mercy for three days.

Gregory pardoned Henry, but the struggle between the Holy Roman emperor and the pope resumed later. Finally, in A.D. 1122, church officials and representatives of the Holy Roman emperor reached a compromise at the German city of Worms. This agreement, known as the Concordat of Worms, allowed the emperor to name bishops and grant them land. It also gave the pope the right to reject unworthy candidates.

Popes and monarchs would continue to struggle over power and territory in the coming years. The increasing strength of Europe's monarchies not only threatened the authority of the Church, but it also paved the way toward other changes on the European scene.

SECTION 4 REVIEW

Recall
1. **Define** common law, grand jury, petit jury, middle class.
2. **Identify** Alfred the Great, William the Conqueror, Henry II, Thomas à Becket, Eleanor of Aquitaine, Magna Carta, Philip Augustus, Henry IV.

3. **Explain** what factors account for the differences in the way French and English monarchs built strong states.

Critical Thinking
4. **Evaluating Information** Judge the importance of the Magna Carta and the English

Parliament in the development of representative government.

Understanding Themes
5. **Conflict** Why did conflicts develop between popes and monarchs? Could their disputes have been resolved peacefully?

Critical Thinking SKILLS

Making Inferences

Just as you leave home to catch your school bus, you hear a news flash. Firefighters are battling a blaze near the bus garage. Your bus arrives 45 minutes late. Though no one told you directly, you know that the fire disrupted the bus schedule.

Learning the Skill

In the situation above, you made an *inference*. That is, from the limited facts at hand, you formed a conclusion. You knew that the fire was near the garage. From past experience, you knew that fire trucks often create traffic jams. By combining immediate facts and general knowledge, you inferred that the fire trucks delayed your bus.

To make accurate inferences, follow these steps:

- Read or listen carefully for stated facts and ideas.
- Then review what you already know about the same topic or situation.
- Use logic and common sense to form a conclusion about the topic.
- If possible, find specific information that proves or disproves your inference. In the example above, you could determine whether your inference was correct by asking the bus driver why she was late. Or you could read news reports describing the fire and its consequences.

Practicing the Skill

Read the passage about Pepin the Short and then answer the questions that follow.

❝ Charles's son, Pepin the Short, succeeded his father and became mayor of the palace in A.D. 741. Pepin … wished to be named king of the Franks. Since he had no blood claim to the throne, Pepin used his influence with the Frankish bishops and the pope to bring about a change in dynasties. In a show of support, the pope journeyed to France and anointed King Pepin I with holy oil.

In return for the Church's blessing, Pepin was to defend the pope against his enemies. In A.D. 754 the new king forced the Lombards, a Germanic people, to withdraw from Rome. Pepin seized a large tract of Lombard territory around Rome and gave it to the pope. ❞

1. What facts are stated about Pepin the Short's acquisition of the title King of the Franks?
2. Using these facts, what inference can you make about the pope's power in Europe at this time?
3. What facts are stated about Pepin's actions on behalf of the pope?
4. Using these facts, what inference can you make about the Lombards' relations with the pope and with the Franks?

Applying the Skill

Review the sections on "Monastic Life" and the "Influence of Monastics" on pages 304-305. Many men and women adopted the monastic lifestyle during the Middle Ages. What inferences can you make about their motivations? Also, do you think motivations were the same for men and women? How might you prove or disprove these inferences?

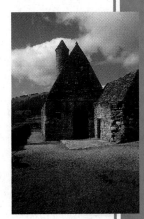

Ancient monastery

For More Practice

Turn to the Skill Practice in the Chapter Review on page 315 for more practice in making inferences.

Connections Across Time

Historical Significance Many of today's European nations, such as Great Britain and France, as well as many of the Western world's legal procedures and forms of government, trace their origins to the political struggles of medieval times.

The medieval Catholic Church wove Christianity into the fabric of Western culture and laid the basis for modern scholarship by preserving and transmitting the learning of the ancient world. Debates today concerning the relationship of Church and state have their echoes in the contest of medieval popes and monarchs for political supremacy.

Using Key Terms

Write the key term that completes each sentence. Then write a sentence for each term not chosen.

a. counts
b. cardinals
c. chivalry
d. fief
e. feudalism
f. friars
g. heresy
h. manorialism
i. abbess
j. common law
k. excommunication
l. sacraments
m. serfs
n. vassal

1. _____ are formal church rituals, such as baptism, eucharist, confirmation, marriage, anointing of the sick, and holy orders.
2. During the Middle Ages, economic life in Europe centered around a system of agricultural production called _____.
3. Peasants in medieval Europe often were _____, people who were bound to the manor.
4. In place of old feudal rules, Henry II of England established a _____ that applied throughout his kingdom.
5. The code of _____ called for knights to be brave in battle, fight fairly, keep promises, defend the Church, and treat noblewomen courteously.

Using Your History Journal

The Church had a significant role in medieval life. Imagine living as a monk or a nun. Write a short diary entry called "Today at the Monastery" or "Today at the Convent," describing the life of a monk or a nun.

Technology Activity

Using a Word Processor Use the draw program on your word processor, or software, to illustrate the layout of a typical medieval manor and surrounding fields. Include the lord's manor house, pastures for livestock, fields for crops, forest areas, and a village where peasants lived. Use a word processor to create a short story from a peasant's point of view, describing a typical day on a medieval manor.

Reviewing Facts

1. **History** List the invading groups that attacked the Carolingian Empire.
2. **History** Describe the major characteristics of feudalism and manorialism.
3. **History** Describe how medieval and ancient Roman life were similar and different.
4. **Culture** Outline briefly how missionaries carried Christianity across Europe.
5. **History/Culture** Describe the organization of the medieval Catholic Church.
6. **Culture** List the factors that helped maintain religious uniformity during medieval times.
7. **Culture** List several services that monasteries and convents provided for the community in medieval times.
8. **History** Explain why historians consider A.D. 1066 an important date.
9. **Culture** Describe the role of Eleanor of Aquitaine in medieval English history.

Critical Thinking

1. **Apply** Until the 1970s, "good manners" required a man to help a woman with her coat,

and push in her chair. How do these customs relate to chivalry?

2. **Evaluate** Every society has to develop ways to deal with ignorance, ill health, hunger, and homelessness. How did feudal society handle these problems compared to the way modern society handles them?

3. **Compare** How did medieval Europe treat its Jewish population? How have Europe's Jews fared in modern times?

Geography in History

1. **Place** Refer to the map below. Where did Leif Eriksson's journey lead him?

2. **Movement** What reasons did Vikings have for leaving Scandinavia and venturing out into the Atlantic?

3. **Human/Environment Interaction** Why did the Vikings sail across the far northern part of the Atlantic rather than through the warmer waters to the south?

4. **Location** After leaving Scandinavia, which landmasses did the Vikings explore?

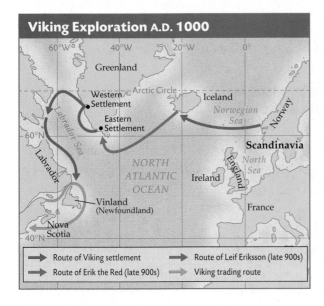

Understanding Themes

1. **Movement** How can the movement of people both have created and crippled Frankish society?

2. **Cooperation** How were lords and peasants mutually dependent?

3. **Uniformity** How is uniformity implied in the term *regular clergy*?

4. **Conflict** How did the conflict between King John and the nobles, resolved in the Magna Carta, eventually have positive results for all English people?

1. Common law, developed in England during the A.D. 1100s, later crossed the Atlantic Ocean and shaped the legal system of the United States. How does the American legal system today reveal the influence of English common law?

2. People often cherish a romantic view of medieval life: for example, medieval Europeans lived in elegant castles, wore beautiful clothes, and enjoyed festivals. Is such a view justified by historical evidence?

3. Improvements changed farming in Europe around A.D. 1000. What improvements today will increase farm productivity? What far-reaching effects will they have?

Skill Practice

Read the passage about knights. Use stated facts and your knowledge to answer the questions that follow.

" A knight cannot distinguish himself in [war] if he has not trained for it in tourneys. He must have seen his blood flow, heard his teeth crack under fist blows, felt his opponent's weight bear down upon him as he lay on the ground and, after being twenty times unhorsed, have risen twenty times to fight. **"**

1. From this passage, what can you infer about the physical appearance of many European knights?

2. What fact(s) or observations helped you make this inference?

3. What can you infer about the average length of a knight's career?

Chapter

13

A.D. 1050–1500

Medieval Europe at Its Height

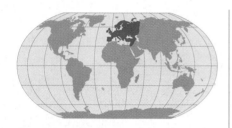

Chapter Themes

▶ **Cultural Diffusion** The Crusades increase European contact with other areas. *Section 1*
▶ **Innovation** Advances in commerce, learning, and the arts change Europe. *Section 2*
▶ **Conflict** England and France battle while their monarchs gain power. *Section 3*
▶ **Conflict** The Church faces a split from within and opposition from without. *Section 4*

$\mathcal{S}$toryteller

"*Well-beloved father*," wrote a medieval student, "*I have not a penny, nor can I get any save through you, for all things at the University are so dear: nor can I study in my [law books], for they are all tattered. Moreover, I owe ten crowns in dues to the [university administrator], and can find no man to lend them to me.*

"*Well-beloved father, to ease my debts ... at the baker's, with the doctor ... and to pay ... the laundress and the barber, I send you word of greetings and of money.*"

This letter from a medieval student sounds very much like something a modern student might write. At that time, however, the university was something new. It was part of the cultural awakening that took place in the High Middle Ages.

Historical Significance

What features of modern Western civilization had their beginnings during the height of the Middle Ages in western Europe? What new developments changed European society during the High Middle Ages?

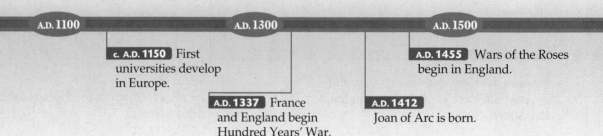

A.D. 1100

c. A.D. 1150 First universities develop in Europe.

A.D. 1300

A.D. 1337 France and England begin Hundred Years' War.

A.D. 1412 Joan of Arc is born.

A.D. 1500

A.D. 1455 Wars of the Roses begin in England.

The Church Militant and Triumphant, a fresco from the A.D. 1300s by Andrea de Bonaiuto. The Spanish Chapel in Santa Maria Novella, Florence, Italy

Your History Journal

Medieval literature contains epics that were put into writing for the first time. Read an excerpt from Beowulf, *the* Song of Roland, *or* The Canterbury Tales *and take notes about life in Europe at the time.*

Section 1

The Crusades

Setting the Scene

▶ **Terms to Define**
the Crusades

▶ **People to Meet**
the Seljuk Turks, Pope Urban II, Saladin, Richard I

▶ **Places to Locate**
Jerusalem, Constantinople

 **Find Out** How did the Crusades begin, and what were their results?

The Storyteller

Geoffrey de Renneville was footsore, thirsty, and covered with dust. He had joined the Crusade as an adventure. The Crusaders had traveled for weeks and were beset by flies, bandits, disease, poor food, and limited drink. The cavalcade stopped and the weary men dropped into an uneasy slumber. Suddenly, they were startled awake by the cry "Help for the Holy Sepulchre!" One by one the knights took up the cry. Shouting with the others, Geoffrey was reminded of the Crusade's purpose.

—adapted from *The Dream and the Tomb*, Robert Payne, 1984

Leaving for the Crusades

Life in the Early Middle Ages was characterized by decentralized government, warfare, cultural isolation, famine, and wretched living conditions. Trade was sparse, and agricultural production—the mainstay of the European economy—was inefficient.

By A.D. 1100, however, conditions in Europe had begun to improve. Some European monarchs succeeded in building strong central governments. Better farming methods led to larger crop yields and a growth in population. Towns and trade began to reappear. The Church held a powerful sway over the emotions and energies of the people. Changes in religion, society, politics, and economics made the High Middle Ages—the period between A.D. 1050 and A.D. 1270—a springboard for a new and brilliant civilization in western Europe.

The transformation of medieval society began with a holy war over the city of **Jerusalem**. European Christians undertook a series of military expeditions—nine in all—to recover the Holy Land from the Muslims. These expeditions were called the Crusades, from the Latin word *crux*, meaning "cross." Those who fought were called Crusaders because they vowed to "take up the cross."

Call for a Crusade

Jerusalem was a holy city for people of three faiths. Jews treasured it as Zion, God's own city, and as the site of Solomon's temple. To Christians, the city was holy because it was the place where Jesus was crucified and resurrected. Muslims regarded Jerusalem as their third holiest city, after Makkah and Madinah. According to Muslim tradition, Muhammad ascended to heaven from Jerusalem.

Jerusalem and the entire region of Palestine fell to Arab invaders in the A.D. 600s. Mostly Muslims, the Arabs tolerated other religions. Christians and

Jews were allowed to live in Jerusalem as long as they paid their taxes and followed certain regulations. European traders and religious pilgrims traveled to Palestine without interference.

In the late A.D. 1000s, **the Seljuk Turks**—a Muslim people from central Asia—took Jerusalem. Their conquest left Palestine in chaos, and the hazards of pilgrimage increased. Meanwhile, the Seljuks threatened the Byzantine Empire, especially **Constantinople**. The Byzantine emperor wrote to the pope in A.D. 1095 requesting military aid from the West. Concerns about the safety of Christian pilgrims gave added urgency to the emperor's request.

First Crusade

On a cold November day in A.D. 1095, **Pope Urban II** mounted a platform outside the church at Clermont, France. His voice shaking with emotion, he addressed the assembled throng, asking for a volunteer army to take Jerusalem and Palestine from the Seljuks:

> 66 I exhort you … to strive to expel that wicked race from our Christian lands…. Christ commands it. Remission of sins will be granted for those going thither…. Let those who are accustomed to wage private war wastefully even against believers go forth against the infidels…. Let those who have lived by plundering be soldiers of Christ; let those who formerly contended against brothers and relations rightly fight barbarians; let those who were recently hired for a few pieces of silver win their eternal reward. 99

"Deus vult!" (God wills it!) shouted the crowd in response to the pope's plea. Knights and peasants alike vowed to join the expedition to the Holy Land. For knights, the Crusade was a welcome chance to employ their fighting skills. For peasants, the Crusade meant freedom from feudal bonds while on the Crusade. All were promised immediate salvation in heaven if they were killed freeing the Holy Land from non-Christians. Adventure and the possibility of wealth were other reasons to join the Crusade. In preparation for the holy war, red crosses of cloth were stitched on clothing as a symbol of service to God.

This First Crusade heightened already existing hatred of non-Christians and marked the onset of a long period of Christian persecution of the Jews. During the First Crusade, which began in A.D. 1096, three armies of Crusader knights and volunteers

Pope Urban II arrives at the Council of Clermont. *What did the pope ask the people to do?*

traveled separately from western Europe to the eastern Mediterranean. On the way, many of them killed Jews and sometimes massacred entire Jewish communities.

Led by French nobles, the three armies finally met in Constantinople in A.D. 1097. From there the Crusaders made their way to Jerusalem, enduring the hardships of desert travel as well as quarrels among their leaders. In June A.D. 1099, the Crusaders finally reached the city. After a siege of almost two months Jerusalem fell. Crusaders swarmed into the city and massacred most of its Muslim and Jewish inhabitants.

The success of the First Crusade reinforced the authority of the Church and strengthened the self-confidence of western Europeans. The religious zeal of the Crusaders soon cooled, however, and many knights returned home. Those who stayed set up feudal states in Syria and Palestine. Contact between the Crusaders and the relatively more sophisticated civilizations of the Byzantines and the Muslims would continue for the next 100 years and become a major factor in ending the cultural isolation of western Europe.

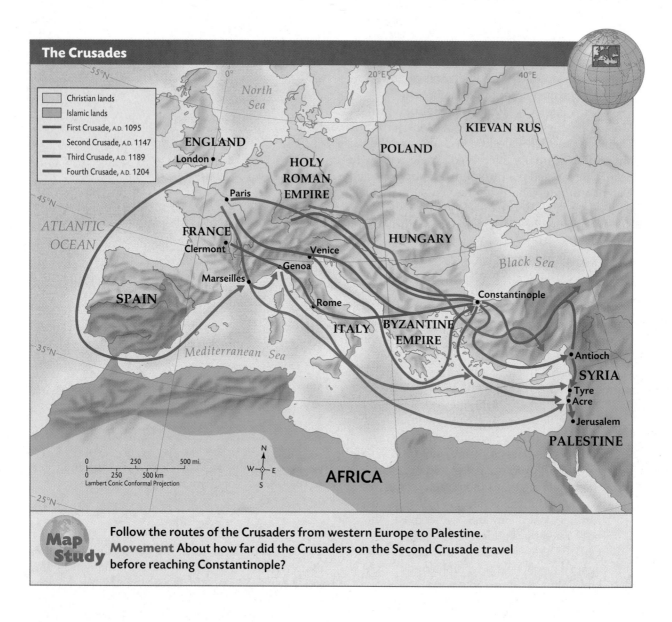

The Crusades

Legend:
- Christian lands
- Islamic lands
- First Crusade, A.D. 1095
- Second Crusade, A.D. 1147
- Third Crusade, A.D. 1189
- Fourth Crusade, A.D. 1204

North Sea
ENGLAND
London
HOLY ROMAN EMPIRE
Paris
ATLANTIC OCEAN
FRANCE
Clermont
POLAND
KIEVAN RUS
HUNGARY
Venice
Genoa
Marseilles
SPAIN
Rome
ITALY
Black Sea
BYZANTINE EMPIRE
Constantinople
Antioch
SYRIA
Tyre
Acre
Jerusalem
PALESTINE
Mediterranean Sea
AFRICA

0   250   500 mi.
0   250   500 km
Lambert Conic Conformal Projection

Map Study Follow the routes of the Crusaders from western Europe to Palestine. **Movement** About how far did the Crusaders on the Second Crusade travel before reaching Constantinople?

Second Crusade

Less than 50 years after the First Crusade, the Seljuks conquered part of the Crusader states in Palestine. Pope Eugenius IV called for a Second Crusade to regain the territory. Eloquent sermons by the monk Bernard of Clairvaux (KLAR•VOH) persuaded King Louis VII of France and Holy Roman Emperor Conrad III to lead armies to Palestine. The Second Crusade, which lasted from A.D. 1147 to A.D. 1149, was unsuccessful. Louis VII and Conrad III quarreled constantly and were ineffective militarily. They were easily defeated by the Seljuks.

Third Crusade

A diplomatic and forceful leader named **Saladin** (SA•luh•DEEN) united the Muslim forces and then captured Jerusalem in A.D. 1187. The people of western Europe were stunned and horrified. Holy Roman Emperor Frederick Barbarossa of

Germany, King Philip Augustus of France, and King **Richard I** of England assembled warriors for the Third Crusade. This "Crusade of Kings" lasted from A.D. 1189 to A.D. 1192 and was no more successful than the Second Crusade. Frederick Barbarossa died on the way to Palestine, and his army returned home. Philip Augustus returned to France before the army reached Jerusalem. Richard continued the struggle alone.

Although his army defeated the Muslims in several battles, Richard could not win a decisive victory over Saladin's well-trained and dedicated forces. After three years of fighting, Richard signed a truce with the Muslims and tried to persuade Saladin to return Jerusalem to the Christians. "Jerusalem," he wrote to the Muslim leader, "we are resolved not to renounce as long as we have a single man left." Saladin's reply to Richard showed his equal determination to keep the city:

> **"** To us Jerusalem is as precious, aye and more precious, than it is to you, in that it was the place whence our Prophet made his journey by night to heaven and is destined to be the gathering place of our nation at the last day. Do not dream that we shall give it up to you…. It belonged to us originally, and it is you who are the real aggressors. **"**

Although Saladin refused to turn over Jerusalem, he allowed Christian pilgrims access.

Other Crusades

Other Crusades followed in the A.D. 1200s, but none succeeded in winning permanent Christian control of Palestine. By this time, western Europeans had lost sight of the religious goal of the Crusades. They were now more concerned about political and economic gain.

In the Fourth Crusade of A.D. 1204, Crusaders put aside their goal of marching to Jerusalem and instead attacked the Christian city of Constantinople. They burned libraries, destroyed churches, and stole valuable treasures. Their actions left a lasting bitterness between the Eastern Orthodox world and western Europe. The Fourth Crusade seriously weakened the Byzantine Empire, making possible a later Muslim advance into eastern Europe.

Effects of the Crusades

Although Western Europeans failed to gain control of Palestine, the Crusades helped to speed the pace of changes already underway in western Europe. They helped break down feudalism and increase the authority of kings. European monarchs levied taxes, raised armies, and cooperated on a large scale. Some nobles died in battle without leaving heirs, and their lands passed to kings. To raise money for weapons and supplies, many lesser nobles sold their estates or allowed their serfs to

History & Art *Return from the Crusade* by Karl Friedrich Lessing. Rheinland Museum, Bonn, Germany *How did the Crusades help to break down feudalism?*

buy their freedom to become freeholders on the land or artisans in the towns.

During the Crusades contact with the more advanced Byzantine and Muslim civilizations broadened European views of the world. The European presence in the East heightened demand at home for Eastern luxury goods: spices, sugar, melons, tapestries, silk, and other items. Commerce increased in the eastern Mediterranean area and especially benefited Italian trading cities, such as Venice and Genoa.

From the Muslims the Crusaders learned how to build better ships, make more accurate maps, use the magnetic compass to tell direction, and improve their weaponry. Religious military orders of knights primarily aided pilgrims, but they were also bankers for both princes and merchants.

The Crusades had less impact on the Muslims. Crusader states were relatively weak in an area divided among powerful Muslim rivals. The arrival of the Crusaders, however, helped unite the Muslims against a common enemy.

SECTION 1 REVIEW

Recall
1. **Define** the Crusades.
2. **Identify** the Seljuk Turks, Pope Urban II, Saladin, Richard I.
3. **Explain** why both Christians and Muslims of the A.D. 1000s and A.D. 1100s felt that

Jerusalem should belong to them.

Critical Thinking
4. **Analyzing Information** In what ways were the Crusades a success? In what ways were they a failure? Could Christians

and Muslims have resolved their differences peacefully? Explain.

Understanding Themes
5. **Cultural Diffusion** Describe how the Crusades contributed to cultural diffusion.

c. A.D. 1000 Europe's economy begins to revive.

c. A.D. 1150 French architects begin to build in the Gothic style.

c. A.D. 1348 The Black Death spreads throughout Europe.

c. A.D. 1386 Geoffrey Chaucer begins writing *The Canterbury Tales*.

Section 2

Economic and Cultural Revival

Setting the Scene

▶ **Terms to Define**
money economy, guild, master, apprentice, journeyman, charter, scholasticism, troubadour, vernacular

▶ **People to Meet**
Thomas Aquinas, Dante Alighieri, Geoffrey Chaucer

▶ **Places to Locate**
Venice, Flanders, Champagne, Bologna

ind Out How did the growth of towns affect the society of medieval Europe?

Storyteller

To help rebuild the cathedral, people for miles around brought their goods. So that the church might rise swiftly, larger and more beautiful than any they had seen, peasants, skilled workers, and even nobles pulled heavy carts filled with wood and stone. Religious fervor motivated the people, and the reward was a renewed spirit in the community. Perfect harmony reigned. During the night, the workers formed a camp with their wagons, and by the light of candles, they sang canticles and psalms. Everyone was doing penance and forgiving their enemies.

—adapted from *Chronique*, Robert de Torigni, in *Chartres*, Emil Mâle, translated by Sarah Wilson, 1983

Cathedral at Reims, France

The Crusades accelerated the transformation of western Europe from a society that was crude, backward, and violent—showing little cultural and technological advancement—to a civilization that exhibited some early features of modern Western civilization. Towns grew, trade expanded, and learning and the arts thrived.

Economic Expansion

The economy of western Europe had begun to show vigor around A.D. 1000. Agricultural production increased. Expanding opportunities in trade encouraged the growth of towns, and the lively atmosphere of the towns in turn stimulated creative thought and innovations in art.

Agricultural Advances

Plows during the Early Middle Ages were light and did not cut much below the surface of the soil. The invention of a new, heavier plow made it possible to cut through the rich, damp soils of northwestern Europe. This plow enabled farmers to produce more and to cultivate new lands, increasing food production. Nobles and freeholders—peasants not bound to the land—migrated to new areas, clearing forests, draining swamps, and building villages. In one of the largest migrations of the time, the Germans moved to areas of eastern Europe, doubling the territory they controlled.

About the same time, the collar harness replaced the ox yoke. Horses were choked by the ox yoke, but the new harness shifted weight off the neck and onto the shoulders, allowing farmers to replace oxen with horses. Horses pulled the plow faster than oxen, allowing farmers to plant and plow more crops.

As you read in Chapter 12, the three-field system of planting also made the land more productive. As the land began to feed more people, the population naturally increased.

Expansion of Trade

The revival of towns caused a rapid expansion of trade. Soon the sea-lanes and roads were filled with traders carrying goods to market. Important sea and river routes connected western Europe with the Mediterranean, eastern Europe, and Scandinavia. The repaired and rebuilt Roman road system carried international traders to and from Europe.

Italian towns, such as **Venice**, Pisa, and Genoa controlled the Mediterranean trade after A.D. 1200, bringing silks and spices from Asia to Europe. **Flanders,** a region including present-day northern France and southwestern Belgium, became the center of trade on Europe's northern coast. Textiles produced there were sent by way of an eastern route to the Black Sea and then traded at Middle Eastern markets for porcelain, silk, and silver. Towns along the Baltic coast formed the Hanseatic League, which controlled trade between eastern Europe and the North Atlantic.

The merchandise for sale in a town was varied and seemingly endless. This was especially true during trade fairs. Each year hundreds of traders met at large trade fairs in places convenient to land and water routes. Feudal lords charged the merchants fees, charged taxes on goods, and offered protection to the merchants. The most famous fair was at **Champagne** in eastern France, located in almost the exact center of western Europe. For four to six weeks each year, Champagne was a distribution point for goods from around the world.

Banking

Early merchants used the barter system, trading goods without using money. Before long, however, merchants found this system impractical. Moreover, some of the merchants who supplied luxury goods such as silk would only accept money in payment. European merchants therefore needed a common medium of exchange.

The rise of a money economy, or an economy based on money, had far-reaching consequences. Initially, it led to the growth of banking. Since traders came from many countries, they carried different currencies with different values. Moneychangers—often Jews or Italians—determined the value of the various currencies and exchanged one currency for another. They also developed procedures for transferring funds from one place to another, received deposits, and arranged loans, thus becoming the first bankers

Visualizing History **Italian bankers, from** *Treatise on the Seven Vices: Avarice.* **The Church viewed lending with the intent to charge interest as evil.** *What is the origin of the term "bank"?*

in Europe. Indeed, the word *bank* comes from the *banca*, or bench, that the moneychangers set up at fairs.

As the money economy grew, it put the feudal classes in an economic squeeze. Kings, clergy, and nobles became dependent on money from banks to pay their expenses. To pay off their loans, they had to raise taxes, sell their lands, or demand money in place of traditional feudal services. As serfs became able to buy their freedom, the feudal system declined.

Growth of Towns

The number of towns in western Europe grew tremendously in the A.D. 1000s and A.D. 1100s. Many grew up beside well-traveled roads or near waterways. Although warfare had declined, settlements still faced bandits. To protect themselves, townspeople built walls around their towns. At first these enclosures were simple wooden fences. As the population grew, stone walls were built, with guard towers at the gates.

Inside the walls narrow, winding streets bustled with people, carts drawn by horses and oxen, and farm animals on the way to market. A din of noise and overpowering smells attacked the senses. Church bells chimed the hours; carts piled high with goods creaked and rumbled through streets that were little more than alleys. Shops lined the streets at ground level, and the shop owners often lived in quarters above. Most buildings were of wood and had thatch roofs, making fire a constant hazard.

Medieval towns had almost no sanitation, and a constant stench assailed the people from the garbage and sewage tossed into the streets. These conditions caused the rapid spread of diseases such as diphtheria, typhoid, influenza, and malaria. In crowded towns such diseases often turned into epidemics and took many lives. The worst of these epidemics—the bubonic plague—ravaged Europe between A.D. 1348 and 1350, killing one-third of the population and earning the name the Black Death.

Guilds

During the A.D. 1100s, merchants and artisans organized themselves into business associations called guilds. The primary function of the merchant guild was to maintain a monopoly of the local market for its members. To accomplish this end, merchant guilds severely restricted trading by foreigners in their city and enforced uniform pricing. The following regulations from Southampton, England, indicate the power of the merchant guilds:

> **❝** And no one shall buy honey, fat, salt herrings, or any kind of oil, or millstones, or fresh hides, or any kind of fresh skins, unless he is a guildsman; nor keep a tavern for wine, nor sell cloth at retail, except in market or fair days … **❞**

Images *of the* Times

Medieval Life

The recovery of commerce and the beginnings of industries stimulated the growth of European towns.

Market scene in a medieval town is the subject of this fresco from Castello de Issogne, Val d' Aosta, Italy.

Craft guilds, by contrast, regulated the work of artisans: carpenters, shoemakers, blacksmiths, masons, tailors, and weavers. Women working as laundresses, seamstresses and embroiderers, and maidservants had their own trade associations.

Craft guilds established strict rules concerning prices, wages, and employment. A member of the shoemakers' guild could not charge more (or less) for a pair of shoes than other shoemakers, nor could he advertise or in any way induce people to buy his wares. Although the guilds prohibited competition, they set standards of quality to protect the public from shoddy goods.

Craft guilds were controlled by masters, or artisans who owned their own shops and tools and employed less-skilled artisans as helpers. To become a master at a particular craft, an artisan served an apprenticeship, the length of which varied according to the difficulty of the craft. Apprentices worked for a master without pay. An apprentice then became a journeyman and received pay. However, a journeyman could only work under a master. To become a master, a journeyman submitted a special sample of his work—a masterpiece—to the guild for approval. If the sample was approved, the journeyman became a master and could set up his own shop.

Aside from business activities, guilds provided benefits for their members such as medical help and unemployment relief. Guilds also organized social and religious life by sponsoring banquets, holy day processions, and outdoor plays.

Rise of the Middle Class

The medieval town, or burg, created the name for a new class of people. In Germany they were called *burghers*; in France, the *bourgeoisie* (BURZH•WAH•ZEE); and in England, *burgesses*. The name originally referred to anyone living in a town. Gradually it came to mean the people who made money through the developing money economy. They were a middle class made up of merchants, bankers, and artisans who no longer had to rely on the land to make a living.

Heraldic arms of the blacksmith's guild, in stained glass, adorns Freiburg Cathedral in Germany.

Troubadours appear in scenes of romance, a novel idea in medieval times.

REFLECTING ON THE TIMES

1. Is this scene a realistic or typical example of a medieval town? Why or why not?
2. What was the purpose of a craft guild?

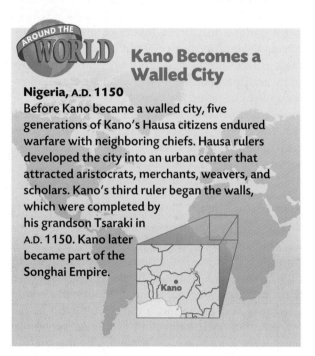

Kano Becomes a Walled City

Nigeria, A.D. 1150
Before Kano became a walled city, five generations of Kano's Hausa citizens endured warfare with neighboring chiefs. Hausa rulers developed the city into an urban center that attracted aristocrats, merchants, weavers, and scholars. Kano's third ruler began the walls, which were completed by his grandson Tsaraki in A.D. 1150. Kano later became part of the Songhai Empire.

Kano

The middle class helped turn towns into organized municipalities. Businessmen created councils to administer town affairs and gained political power for themselves. As the money economy spread, kings began to depend on the middle class for loans and for income from the taxes they paid. The leading merchants and bankers became advisers to lords and kings.

Town Government

Conflict gradually developed between the feudal classes and the burghers. City dwellers did not fit into the feudal system; they resented owing taxes and services to lords. They wanted to run their own affairs and have their own courts and laws. At the same time, feudal lords feared the growing wealth and power of the middle class. To try to keep the burghers in line, the lords began to strictly enforce feudal laws.

The money economy gave the towns the income and power they needed to win the struggle against the lords. In the A.D. 1000s Italian towns formed groups called communes. Using the political power they gained from the growing money economy, the communes ended the power of feudal lords and made the Italian towns into independent city-states. In other areas of Europe, kings and nobles granted townspeople charters, documents that gave them the right to control their own affairs. At the same time, many towns remained a part of a kingdom or feudal territory.

Education

During the Early Middle Ages, most people were illiterate. Education was controlled by the clergy. In monastery and cathedral schools, students prepared for monastery life or for work as church officials. In addition to religious subjects, students learned grammar, rhetoric, logic, arithmetic, geometry, astronomy, and music.

As towns grew, the need for educated officials stimulated a new interest in learning. The growth of courts and other legal institutions created a need for lawyers. As a result, around A.D. 1150, students and teachers began meeting away from monastery and cathedral schools. They formed organizations that became known as universities.

Universities

At first the university was not so much a place as it was a guild of scholars organized for learning. Classes were held in rented rooms, churches, or outdoors. Because books were scarce, a teacher read the text and discussed it, while students took notes on slates. Classes did, however, meet regularly, and university rules set down the obligations of students and teachers toward each other. To qualify as a teacher, students had to pass an examination leading to a degree, or certificate of completion.

By the end of the A.D. 1200s, universities had spread throughout Europe. Most southern European universities were modeled after the law school at **Bologna** (buh•LOH•nyuh), Italy, and specialized in law and medicine. Universities in northern Europe, on the other hand, specialized in liberal arts and theology. These were generally modeled after the University of Paris.

New Learning

Medieval scholars studied Roman law, the works of Aristotle, and Muslim writings. Much of this knowledge reached Europe by way of Muslim and Jewish scholars in European Muslim strongholds, such as Spain and Sicily. European contact with Muslim scientific thought sparked an interest in the physical world that eventually led to the rise of Western science.

Many church leaders opposed the study of Aristotle's works, fearing that his ideas threatened Christian teachings. In contrast, some scholars thought the new knowledge could be used to support Christian ideas. They applied Aristotle's philosophy to theological questions and developed a system of thought called scholasticism. This new type of learning emphasized reason as well as faith in the interpretation of Christian doctrine. Scholastics sought to reconcile classical philosophy with the Church's teachings. They believed all knowledge could be integrated into a coherent whole.

One early scholastic teacher, Peter Abelard, taught theology in Paris during the early A.D. 1100s. In his book *Sic et Non* (Yes and No), he collected statements from the Bible and the writings of early Christian leaders that showed both sides of controversial questions. Abelard then had his students reconcile the differences through logic.

In the A.D. 1200s the most important scholastic thinker was **Thomas Aquinas** (uh•KWY•nuhs). In his work *Summa Theologica*, Aquinas claimed that reason was God's gift that could provide answers to basic philosophical questions. Reason, he said, existed in harmony with faith, both pointing to God and the orderliness of creation. The Catholic Church later accepted and promoted Aquinas's way of thinking.

Medieval Literature and Art

The spread of universities and the revival of intellectual endeavor stimulated advances in literature and the arts. Songs and epics of the Early Middle Ages were put in writing for the first time.

Epics and Romances

One of the earliest surviving literary works of the feudal world was the Anglo-Saxon epic *Beowulf*. A tale of grim battle and gloomy scenery, *Beowulf* reveals the harshness of life in northern Europe. Handed down by oral tradition for two centuries, it was finally written down in Old English (Anglo-Saxon) by an unknown poet in about A.D. 700. In colorful verses and exciting narrative, the epic describes how the Anglo-Saxon warrior Beowulf defeats a horrible monster named Grendel.

French epics called *chansons de geste*, or songs of high deeds, celebrated the courage of feudal warriors. The *Song of Roland*, written around A.D. 1100, gives an account of the chivalrous defense of Christianity by Charlemagne's knights.

Romances about knights and ladies were also popular. In southern France in the A.D. 1100s and A.D. 1200s, traveling poet-musicians called troubadours composed lyric poems and songs about love and the feats of knights. They helped define the ideal knight celebrated in the code of chivalry.

The Plague

The Black Death—known today as the bubonic plague—was the worst medieval epidemic. It began in China and spread across Asia. Trading ships carried the disease west to the Mediterranean and to Europe. During the worst phase of the plague—between A.D. 1348 and A.D. 1350—nearly 25 million Europeans died. Not until the early 1900s were rats carrying bacteria-infected fleas identified as the carriers of the plague.

The plague brought terror to many medieval Europeans, who saw it as God's punishment. As deaths increased, production declined, and prices and wages rose. To cut costs, many landowners switched from farming to sheep raising (which required less labor) and drove villagers off the land. Merchants in towns laid off workers and demanded laws to limit wages. These setbacks, as well as the fear of plague, sparked peasant and worker uprisings. It would take at least a century for western Europe to recover.

Today, plague occasionally occurs in developing areas of Asia, Africa, and South America. Knowledge of disease prevention and the development of vaccines, however, have largely isolated plague outbreaks and reduced their devastating impact on societies.

The Black Death

Linking Past and Present ACTIVITY

Examine the effects of disease on medieval and modern societies. How is the spread of disease related to human movement?

Vernacular Literature

Late medieval literature was increasingly written in the vernacular, or the language of everyday speech. Instead of using the Latin, people spoke the language of their own country—English, French, German, Italian, or Spanish. These languages gave each kingdom a separate identity. Use of vernacular languages in writing made literature accessible to more people.

Major literary works in the vernacular appeared during the A.D. 1300s. **Dante Alighieri** (DAHN•tay A•luh•GYEHR•ee) wrote *The Divine Comedy*, an epic poem in Italian that describes an imaginary journey from hell to heaven. In England, **Geoffrey Chaucer** produced *The Canterbury Tales* from about A.D. 1386 to A.D. 1400. These narrative poems describe a varied group of pilgrims who tell stories to amuse one another on on their way to Thomas à Becket's shrine at Canterbury.

Medieval Art

Early medieval churches were built in a style called Romanesque, which combined features of Roman and Byzantine structures. Romanesque churches had thick walls, columns set close together, heavy curved arches, and small windows. About A.D. 1150, French architects began to build in a new style called Gothic. They replaced the Romanesque heavy walls and low arches with flying buttresses. These stone beams, extending out from the walls, took the weight of the building off the walls. This allowed the walls to be thinner, with space for stained-glass windows. The ceiling inside was supported by pointed arches made of narrow stone ribs reaching out from tall pillars. These supports allowed architects to build higher ceilings and more open interiors.

Medieval painters, by contrast, turned their attention to a much smaller art form, the illuminated manuscript. Adorned with brilliantly colored illustrations and often highlighted with gold leaf, these works were miniature masterpieces whose beauty has endured to the present day.

Visualizing History Interior of a Gothic cathedral at Reims, France. *How did the Gothic style differ from the Romanesque?*

Talented writers were also found among women in convents and at royal courts. The German abbess Hildegard of Bingen, known for her spiritual wisdom, wrote about religion, science, and medicine. She was also a noted composer of music. Another abbess, Herrad of Landsberg, assisted by her nuns, compiled the *Garden of Delights*, an encyclopedia of world history. Christine de Pisan, who grew up at the French royal court, authored numerous love poems.

SECTION 2 REVIEW

Recall

1. **Define** money economy, guild, master, apprentice, journeyman, charter, scholasticism, troubadour, vernacular.

2. **Identify** Peter Abelard, Thomas Aquinas, *Beowulf*, Dante Alighieri, Geoffrey Chaucer.

3. **Explain** why membership in a guild was advantageous for a medieval artisan. Why was it disadvantageous?

Critical Thinking

4. **Synthesizing Information** Create an imaginary medieval town. Briefly explain its physical characteristics. Then describe what a typical day for an artisan working there would be like.

Understanding Themes

5. **Innovation** Choose one of the following and trace its effect on medieval society: three-field system, money economy, guilds.

Section 3

Strengthening of Monarchy

Setting the Scene

▶ **Terms to Define**
  cortes

▶ **People to Meet**
  Joan of Arc, Louis XI, Richard III, Henry VII, Ferdinand of Aragon, Isabella of Castile

▶ **Places to Locate**
  Crécy, Agincourt, Burgundy, Castile, Aragon

 **ind Out** How did European monarchs strengthen their powers during the Middle Ages?

The Storyteller

A popular legend in English history is the story of the first Prince of Wales. Edward, King of England, desired to make the proud chieftains of Wales acknowledge his power. He campaigned against them, soon controlling their lands. The Welsh chiefs refused to accept Edward as their prince. They agreed, however, to serve a prince whom Edward would choose— provided he was noble and spoke neither English nor French. Edward accepted these terms and showed them their prince, his newborn son, who was indeed of noble birth and could speak neither language. The chiefs accepted the baby as their lawful lord, the Prince of Wales.

—adapted from *The Three Edwards*, Thomas Costain, 1964

The Tower of London

During the late Middle Ages, Europe's monarchs set up stronger central governments. They won the loyalty of their people and began to limit the powers of clergy and nobles. Gradually educated common people and laymen became royal advisers. At the outset, however, violent warfare engulfed western Europe.

The Hundred Years' War

Between A.D. 1337 and A.D. 1453, England and France fought a series of conflicts, known as the Hundred Years' War. For centuries, England's rulers had fought hard to keep the French lands inherited from the Normans. France's kings, however, wanted to unite these lands to their kingdom. In 1337 warfare began anew when England's Edward III laid claim to the French crown.

Major Battles

At first, the English were victorious—at **Crécy** in 1346 and **Agincourt** in 1415. Their success was primarily due to their weapons: a firearm that was the forerunner of the cannon and the longbow. About as tall as a man, the longbow could shoot arrows capable of piercing heavy armor at 300 yards (274 km). French historian Jean Froissart described the impact of the longbow at Crécy:

❝ Then the English archers stept forth one pace and let fly their arrows so wholly [together] and so thick, that is seemed snow. When the [French soldiers] felt the [arrows piercing through heads, arms, and breasts, many of them cast down their cross-bows and did cut their strings and [retreated]… ❞

"La Pucelle!" Jeanne d' Arc Leads Her Army by Franck Craig, 1907. Musée d' Orsay, Paris, France *What did the "Maid of Orléans" accomplish for the French?*

Joan of Arc

Just as French fortunes had sunk to their lowest, a young woman helped bring about a dramatic reversal. In A.D. 1429, 17-year-old **Joan of Arc** appeared at the court of France's King Charles VII. She told the king that heavenly voices had called her to save France. With Charles's support, she inspired a French army to victory at Orléans, a town that had been placed under siege by the English. Soon after her triumph, Joan fell into English hands, was tried for witchcraft, and burned at the stake. Her courage, however, led the French to rally around their king and to gradually drive the English out of France. When the war ended in A.D. 1453, the port of Calais was the only French territory still in English hands.

Effects of the War

The Hundred Years' War deeply affected the peoples of France and England. France had suffered more severely than England, since the fighting had occurred on French soil. Yet victory gave the French a new sense of unity. England had been spared destruction, but its defeat led to bitterness among the nobles who had lost French lands. For the rest of the A.D. 1400s, England was divided by social conflict. In the long run, however, England's departure from France contributed to its unity and enabled the English to focus on problems at home.

The Hundred Years' War also hastened the decline of feudalism. The use of the longbow and firearms made feudal warfare based on castles and mounted knights outdated. Monarchs replaced feudal soldiers with national armies made up of hired soldiers. Maintaining these armies, however, was expensive. Monarchs turned to townspeople and the lower nobility for new sources of revenue. These groups willingly paid taxes and made loans in return for security and good government.

France

During the late 1400s, France's monarchy won much power and prestige. **Louis XI**, son of Charles VII, strengthened the bureaucracy, kept the nobles under royal control, and promoted trade and agriculture. Above all, he worked to unite all French feudal lands under his crown. Louis especially desired **Burgundy**, one of Europe's most prosperous areas. Burgundy's ruler, Charles the Bold, however, wanted to make his territory independent. Rather than fight Charles openly, Louis encouraged quarrels between Burgundy and the neighboring Swiss. After Charles's death in battle with the Swiss in A.D. 1477, Burgundy was divided between his daughter Mary and the French king.

Adam Woolfitt

Cathedral of Chartres

The cathedral stands out against a lowering sky. The old town of Chartres, France, crowds the foreground, where artisans, merchants, bakers, and stonemasons once lived, clustered near the great church. At the center of the photograph, the rose window provides a perfect example of medieval stained glass. The two towers, one ornate, the other plain, were finished in different periods. They pierce the sky—giving form to the faith and spirit of Europe's Middle Ages.

The cathedral reflects the technology of the High Middle Ages. Built before A.D. 1300, Chartres Cathedral, located about 50 miles southwest of Paris, is one of many works of Gothic architecture expressing both the fervor of the medieval era and the revival of the European economy, beginning around A.D. 1000. The growth of towns such as Chartres was a result of such changes. The combination of new building techniques, financial resources, and professional skills enabled the construction of the great cathedrals of Europe. ⊕

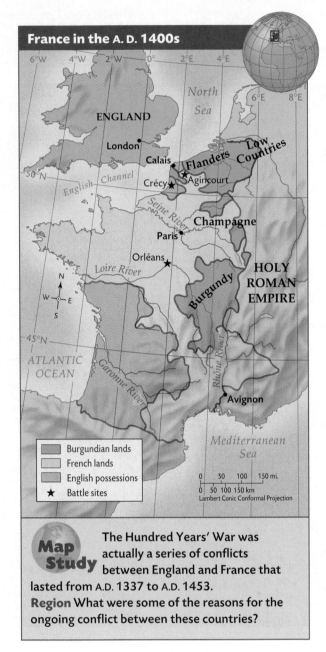

France in the A.D. 1400s

Burgundian lands
French lands
English possessions
★ Battle sites

0   50   100   150 mi.
0 50 100 150 km
Lambert Conic Conformal Projection

Map Study The Hundred Years' War was actually a series of conflicts between England and France that lasted from A.D. 1337 to A.D. 1453.
Region What were some of the reasons for the ongoing conflict between these countries?

England

During the Hundred Years' War, the English monarchy's power was limited by Parliament, which had won the right to levy taxes, approve laws, and provide advice. Royal authority further eroded as a result of a struggle among the nobility for control of the throne. Begun in A.D. 1455, this conflict became known as the Wars of the Roses because of the symbols of the rival families involved. The royal house of Lancaster bore the red rose; its rival, the house of York, a white rose.

During the Wars of the Roses, Edward, duke of York, overthrew the weak Lancaster dynasty and became King Edward IV. As king, Edward worked to strengthen royal government and to promote trade. His death in A.D. 1483 brought uncertainty to England. The heirs to the throne were the late king's two sons. Edward's brother, Richard, however, had himself proclaimed king and locked his young nephews in the Tower of London, where they were probably murdered. **Richard III** tried to rule well but lacked widespread support. He finally fell to the forces of Henry Tudor, a Lancaster noble, on Bosworth Field in A.D. 1485.

Henry became **King Henry VII**, the first Tudor king. Henry eliminated royal claimants to the throne, avoided costly foreign wars, and increased royal power over the nobles. As a result, the English monarchy emerged from the Wars of the Roses strengthened and with few challengers.

Spain

During the late A.D. 1400s, Spain emerged as a leading European power. Even before Pope Urban's call for the Crusades, the Christian rulers of northern Spain had been fighting the *Reconquista* (RAY•kohn•KEES•tuh), or "reconquest," of Muslim areas in Spain. By A.D. 1250, the Iberian Peninsula consisted of three Christian realms: Portugal in the west, **Castile** in the center, and **Aragon** on the Mediterranean coast. Only Granada in the south remained in the hands of the Moors, or Spanish Muslims.

In A.D. 1469 **Ferdinand of Aragon** and **Isabella of Castile** were married. Their two kingdoms, however, maintained separate governments, and royal power was limited by local interests. Christians settling in formerly Muslim areas, as well as large Jewish and Muslim communities in Castile and Aragon, had their own laws and officials. Special royal charters allowed many towns to keep their courts and local customs. Finally, assemblies known as cortes, in which nobles were powerful, had the right to review royal policies.

In Castile, however, the two monarchs worked to strengthen royal power. They sent out officials to govern the towns and set up special courts in the countryside to enforce royal laws. In A.D. 1492 their armies forced the surrender of the last Moorish stronghold at Granada. Shortly afterward, Ferdinand and Isabella ended religious toleration. To unite Spain, they wanted all Spaniards to be Catholic. Spanish Jews and Moors were ordered to convert or to leave Spain. The persecution and departure of many Jews and Moors, known for their banking, business, and intellectual skills, weakened Spain's economy and culture.

The Spanish monarchy also set up the Spanish Inquisition to enforce Catholic teaching. The Inquisition believed that Jews and Moors who had converted to Catholicism were still practicing their old religions in secret. It tortured, tried, and punished anyone suspected of heresy. The fear created by the Inquisition further strengthened the power of Spanish monarchs over their people.

The Holy Roman Empire

During the Middle Ages, the Holy Roman Empire, made up largely of German, Italian, and Slavic lands, was Europe's largest political unit. Despite its size, the Empire was far from achieving unity under a strong monarch. While most European rulers came to power through family ties, the Holy Roman emperor was elected by a diet, or assembly of mostly German princes who governed their local territories as independent rulers. The princes had the right to reject or accept the emperor's requests for taxes and soldiers.

In A.D. 1356 the number of princes taking part in imperial elections was limited to seven. Whenever an emperor died, these seven electors chose as his successor a politically weak noble with small landholdings. In the early 1400s, they began choosing emperors from the Hapsburgs, a family of nobles based in Austria. Once in power, Hapsburg emperors could not control the princes and unify the empire. Yet they were able to increase their prestige by securing other areas of Europe.

One of the most ambitious Hapsburg emperors was Maximilian I. Elected emperor in A.D. 1493, Maximilian married Mary of Burgundy and acquired the Low Countries (present-day Belgium, the Netherlands, and Luxembourg) as part of the Hapsburg inheritance. His grandson, Charles, born in A.D. 1500, eventually became king of Spain. German princes elected him Holy Roman emperor as Charles V. Under Charles, the Hapsburgs became the most powerful European royal family, ruling Spain, Austria, Germany, the Low Countries, and much of Italy.

Eastern Europe

The Middle Ages also saw the rise of kingdoms in the area of eastern Europe between present-day Germany and Russia. The largest and most powerful of these lands were Poland and Hungary.

Poland

Formed in the A.D. 900s by West Slavs, Poland had accepted Roman Catholicism and close ties with western Europe. About A.D. 1000, the Poles began fighting groups of German warriors known as the Teutonic Knights for control of areas of Poland near the Baltic Sea.

During the A.D. 1300s, Poland enjoyed a golden age under King Casimir III, who reduced the power of local nobles and formed a strong central government. In A.D. 1386, one of Casimir's successors, Queen Jadwiga (yahd•VEE•gah) married Wladyslaw Jagiello (vwah•DIHS•wahv yahg•YEH•loh), duke of neighboring Lithuania. Their marriage led to a union of Poland and Lithuania, creating one of the largest states in medieval Europe. With the added strength of the Lithuanians, Polish forces were finally able to defeat the Teutonic Knights at the Battle of Tannenburg in A.D. 1410.

Hungary

South of Poland, the kingdom of Hungary was made up of Magyars, Germans, and Slavs. In A.D. 1000 King Stephen I became a Roman Catholic and introduced his people to western European ways. His reign marked the beginning of a strong Hungarian monarchy.

In A.D. 1241 Mongols from central Asia invaded Hungary and caused widespread destruction. They soon withdrew, however, and the kingdom was able to rebuild. During the A.D. 1400s and A.D. 1500s, Hungary faced periodic attacks from the Ottoman Turks. In A.D. 1526 Hungary's King Louis II was defeated by the Ottoman ruler Suleiman I at the Battle of Mohacs (MOH•hahch). Most of Hungary came under the Ottomans; the rest was ruled by the Hapsburg emperors.

SECTION 3 REVIEW

Recall
1. **Define** cortes.
2. **Identify** Joan of Arc, Louis XI, Richard III, Henry VII, Ferdinand of Aragon, Isabella of Castile.

3. **Explain** the causes and effects of the Hundred Years' War.

Critical Thinking
4. **Applying Information** Relate how one European monarchy

changed during the Middle Ages.

Understanding Themes
5. **Conflict** Explain the reasons for the struggles between the various European monarchies.

A.D. 1300	A.D. 1400	A.D. 1500

A.D. 1309 Pope's court moves to Avignon, France.

A.D. 1378 Great Schism in the Church occurs.

A.D. 1415 Church authorities burn Jan Hus as a heretic.

A.D. 1436 Compromise reached between the Church and Hussites.

Section 4

The Troubled Church

Setting the Scene

▶ **Terms to Define**
pilgrimage, simony

▶ **People to Meet**
Pope Clement V, John Wycliffe, the Lollards, Jan Hus

▶ **Places to Locate**
Avignon, Bohemia

 **ind Out** Why was the Church under pressure to reform?

The Storyteller

The situation was intolerable, Nicholas of Clèmanges thought angrily. The Church was increasingly corrupt. Greed, pride, and love of luxury prevailed in place of humility and charity. Comparing the current priests and bishops with the holy leaders of antiquity, he reflected, was like comparing mud to gold. What would come of such ills? "So great a flood of evils must assuredly be crushed and utterly destroyed by God's most righteous judgment. It does not seem possible in any other way to chasten it." Nicholas prayed that the Church might be spared from complete destruction—that a little seed might remain in the world.

—adapted from *On the Ruin and the Repair of the Church*, Nicholas Clèmanges, reprinted in *Readings in Western Civilization*, 1986

The Church besieged by evil forces

During the upheavals of the Late Middle Ages—caused by warfare, the plague, and religious controversy—many people turned to the Church for comfort and reassurance. Religious ceremonies multiplied, and thousands of people went on religious pilgrimages, or journeys to holy places. In spite of this increase in religious devotion, the temporal authority of the Church was weakening due to the influence of strong monarchs and national governments. A growing middle class of educated townspeople and a general questioning of the Church's teachings also contributed to this decline.

Babylonian Captivity

During the early A.D. 1300s, the papacy came under the influence of the French monarchy. In A.D. 1305 a French archbishop was elected **Pope Clement V.** A few years later, Clement decided to move his court from Rome to **Avignon** (A•veen•YOHN), a small city in southern France, to escape the civil wars that were disrupting Italy. While in France, the pope appointed only French cardinals. Pope Clement V and his successors—all French—remained in Avignon until A.D. 1377.

This long period of the exile of the popes at Avignon came to be known as the Babylonian Captivity, after the period of the exile of the Jews in Babylon in the 500s B.C. For centuries, Rome had been the center of the western Church. With the pope in France, people feared that the papacy would be dominated by French monarchs. Others disliked the concern the Avignon popes showed for increasing church taxes and making church administration more efficient. They believed the popes had become corrupted by worldly power and were neglecting their spiritual duties. The Italian poet Petrarch complained:

❝ Here reign the successors of the poor fishermen of Galilee; they have strangely

forgotten their origin. I am astounded …
to see these men loaded with gold and
clad in purple, boasting of the spoils of
princes and nations. **”**

The Great Schism

Finally, in A.D. 1377, Pope Gregory XI left
Avignon and returned to Rome. After his death,
Roman mobs forced the College of Cardinals to
elect an Italian as pope. The cardinals later declared
the election invalid, insisting they had voted under
pressure. The cardinals then elected a second pope,
who settled in Avignon. When the Italian pope
refused to resign, the Church faced the dilemma of
being led by two popes.

This controversy became known as the Great
Schism because it caused serious divisions in the
Church. The Great Schism lasted from A.D. 1378 until
A.D. 1417 and seriously undermined the pope's
authority. People wondered how they could regard
the pope as the divinely chosen leader of Christianity
when there was more than one person claiming to be
the single, unquestioned head of the Church.

Calls for a Council

Many kings, princes, and church scholars
called for a reform of church government. The most
popular remedy was a general church council.
However, this solution posed many problems. First,
such councils were traditionally called by popes.
No pope was willing to call a council that would
limit his authority. However, the legality of a council would be questionable if it did not receive papal
approval. Second, different rulers in Europe supported particular popes for political reasons. Such
political divisions made it almost impossible to
reach agreement on even the site of a council, let
alone to reach agreement on the deeper and more
important issues involved.

By A.D. 1400 many western Europeans were
committed to the idea of a church council. In A.D.
1409 a council met at Pisa, Italy, to unite the Church
behind one pope. It resulted in the election of a
third pope, since neither the pope at Rome nor the
pope at Avignon would resign. Finally, in A.D. 1414,
another council met at Constance, Germany. It
forced the resignation of all three popes and then
elected Pope Martin V, ending the Great Schism.
The long period of disunity, however, had seriously weakened the political influence of the Church.
Moreover, many Europeans had come to feel a
greater sense of loyalty to their monarchs than to
the pope.

Calls for Reform

Church authority was also weakened by people's dislike of abuses within the Church. The clergy used many unpopular means to raise money.
Fees were charged for almost every type of service
the Church performed. Common people especially
disliked simony—the selling of church positions—
because the cost of buying these positions was
passed on to them. The princely lifestyles of the
clergy further eroded regard for the Church. Many
Europeans called for reform. Two of the clearest
voices belonged to an English scholar and a
Bohemian preacher.

John Wycliffe

John Wycliffe (WIH•KLIHF), a scholar at
England's Oxford University, criticized the
Church's wealth, corruption among the clergy, and
the pope's claim to absolute authority. He wanted
secular rulers to remove church officials who were
immoral or corrupt.

Wycliffe claimed that the Bible was the sole
authority for religious truth. He began to translate
the Bible from Latin into English so people could
read it themselves. Since church doctrine held that
only the clergy could interpret God's word in the
Bible, this act was regarded as revolutionary. Some
of Wycliffe's followers, known as **the Lollards**,
angrily criticized the Church. They destroyed
images of saints, ridiculed the Mass, and ate communion bread with onions to show that it was no
different from ordinary bread.

Widespread antipapal feelings made it difficult
for the English government to suppress Lollards.
Wycliffe was persuaded to moderate his views and
received only a mild punishment. He died peacefully in A.D. 1384, but his ideas spread.

Among those who supported the Lollards was
Bohemian-born Queen Anne, the wife of King

Footnotes to History

Silver Spoons
During the Middle Ages,
pewter spoons became
common utensils for eating. In the A.D. 1400s silver "apostle spoons," bearing the image of a
child's patron saint, were favored gifts for new-
borns in Italy. Only the wealthy could afford such
a luxury. From these apostle spoons came the saying that a privileged child is "born with a silver
spoon in his or her mouth."

John Wycliffe Reading His Translation of the Bible to John of Gaunt by Ford Madox Brown. *Why was Wycliffe's translation of the Bible revolutionary?*

Richard II. Anne sent copies of Wycliffe's writings to her homeland in the Holy Roman Empire, where they influenced another great religious reformer.

Jan Hus

During the late A.D. 1300s and A.D. 1400s, the Slavs of **Bohemia**, known as Czechs, became more aware of their own national identity. They wanted to end German control of their country and backed sweeping reforms in the Catholic Church in Bohemia, which had many German clergy. Their religious and political grievances combined to produce an explosive situation.

The Czechs produced religious pamphlets and copies of the Bible in Czech and criticized the corruption of leading church officials, many of whom were German. The leader of the Czech religious reform movement was **Jan Hus**, a popular preacher and professor at the University of Prague. When Hus and his works were condemned by the Church and political leaders, a violent wave of riots swept across Bohemia.

Faced with a possible full-scale rebellion against the Church, in A.D. 1415 the council at Constance demanded that Hus appear before them to defend his views. The Holy Roman emperor promised Hus safe conduct to Constance, Germany, but this guarantee was ignored. Hus was burned at the stake as a heretic, but his heroic death caused many Czechs to rally around their new martyr.

From A.D. 1420 to A.D. 1436, Hus's supporters, called Hussites, resisted the Church and the Holy Roman emperor, and the Church launched five crusades against the Hussites. All five failed. Using firearms and the tactic of forming movable walls with farm wagons, the Hussites defeated the crusading knights.

In A.D. 1436 representatives of the pope and the Holy Roman emperor reached a compromise with the Hussite leaders. They gave the Hussites certain religious liberties in return for their allegiance to the Church. The ideas of Jan Hus, however, continued to spread throughout Europe to influence later and more radical reformers. While this agreement gave the appearance that the Church had successfully met the challenges to its authority, the basic spiritual questions raised by Hus and others did not go away.

SECTION 4 REVIEW

Recall
1. **Define** pilgrimage, simony.
2. **Identify** Pope Clement V, Babylonian Captivity, Great Schism, John Wycliffe, the Lollards, Jan Hus, the Hussites.
3. **Explain** the effects of the Babylonian Captivity and the Great Schism on the Church.

Critical Thinking
4. **Synthesizing Information** Imagine you are a follower of Jan Hus just after his execution. How would you feel about carrying on his work?

Understanding Themes
5. **Conflict** Explain the rise of dissent among many devout Europeans. Why were they against the Church and its leadership?

SKILLS

Analyzing Historical Maps

When you walk through your town, you may see changes in progress. Perhaps a new restaurant has opened, or an old factory has been torn down. Change also takes place on a larger scale across nations and continents. Historical maps illustrate political, social, and cultural changes over time.

Learning the Skill

To analyze a historical map, first read the title to identify its theme. Then identify the chronology of events on the map. Many historical maps show changes in political boundaries over time. For example, the map below of the Frankish Empire uses colors to show land acquisitions under three different rulers. On the other map, however, colors represent areas controlled by different rulers at the same time. Read the map key, labels, and captions to determine what time periods and changes appear on the map.

To compare historical maps of the same region in different time periods, first identify the geographic location and time period of each map. Then look for similarities and differences. Which features have remained the same and which have changed? What groups control the area in each map? Has the country grown larger or smaller

over time? Have other features changed?

After analyzing the information on historical maps, try to draw conclusions about the causes and effects of these changes.

Practicing the Skill

The two maps on this page show the same region in different time periods. Study both maps and answer these questions.
1. What is the time period of each map?
2. How did the Frankish Empire change from A.D. 500 to A.D. 800?
3. Did France grow larger or smaller between A.D. 800 and A.D. 1400?
4. What other changes appear on these maps?

Applying the Skill

Compare a map of Europe today with a map of Europe in 1985 or earlier. Identify at least five changes that have occurred since the early 1980s.

For More Practice

Turn to the Skill Practice in the Chapter Review on page 339 for more practice in analyzing historical maps.

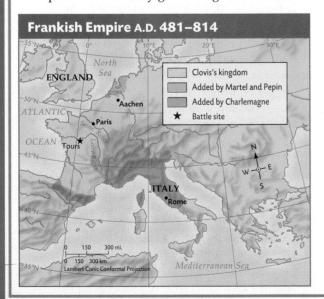

Frankish Empire A.D. 481–814

- Clovis's kingdom
- Added by Martel and Pepin
- Added by Charlemagne
- ★ Battle site

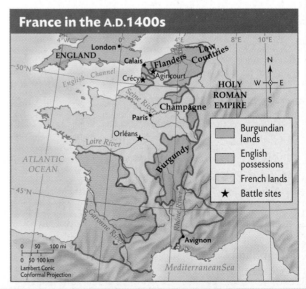

France in the A.D. 1400s

- Burgundian lands
- English possessions
- French lands
- ★ Battle sites

Connections Across Time

Historical Significance Many features of modern Western civilization arose during the Middle Ages. The medieval history of Europe can still be seen in great cathedrals and in the rituals of the Roman Catholic Church. Modern labor unions and institutions of higher learning are related to medieval guilds and universities. Today's national languages in Europe first appeared during the Middle Ages. Finally, the middle class, which plays an important role in the world today, also had its beginnings during this period.

Using Key Terms

Write the key term that completes each sentence. Then write a sentence for each term not chosen.

a. apprentice
b. *cortes*
c. charter
d. scholasticism
e. Crusade
f. guilds
g. vernacular
h. simony
i. money economy
j. pilgrimages
k. master
l. troubadours

1. Church scholars developed a system of thought known as _____ that sought to reconcile faith and reason.
2. The rise of a _____ led to the growth of banking and put the feudal classes in an economic squeeze.
3. In Spain, assemblies known as _____ at first had the right to review the policies of Spanish monarchs.
4. In medieval France, traveling poet-musicians called _____ composed lyric poems and songs about love and the feats of knights.
5. During the Middle Ages, the rise of _____ languages gave each kingdom of Europe a separate identity.

Technology Activity

Using E-mail Locate an E-mail address for your local historical society or chamber of commerce. Write a letter requesting information about various styles and influences of medieval architecture found in your area. Using your response, create an illustrated tourist pamphlet of information about area structures. Include a map.

Using Your History Journal

From your notes on Beowulf, *the* Song of Roland, *or* The Canterbury Tales, *write a short description of the manners, customs, and values of the Europeans described in the work.*

Reviewing Facts

1. **History** List the various medieval Crusades and their results.
2. **Technology** Describe several agricultural improvements in the Middle Ages.
3. **Culture** Discuss the contributions made by women to the society of the Middle Ages.
4. **History** List the key events in the Hundred Years' War.
5. **Culture** Identify two church reformers and a major event in the life of each.
6. **Culture** Describe a typical medieval town.
7. **Economics** Identify the bourgeoisie and state their role in late medieval Europe.
8. **History** Discuss the impact of the Black Death.
9. **Government** Explain why townspeople and the lower nobility supported the rise of strong monarchies in western Europe.
10. **Culture** List the problems that the Catholic Church faced at the end of the Middle Ages.
11. **Government** State how Louis XI strengthened the French monarchy.
12. **History** Discuss the major result of the Wars of the Roses.
13. **History** Identify the *Reconquista*. How did it contribute to the unity of Spain?
14. **Economics** List new business methods that developed in Europe by the A.D. 1400s. How did they change European life?

Critical Thinking

1. **Apply** How did the medieval middle class change European society?
2. **Analyze** What various forces led to Europe's economic growth during the Middle Ages?
3. **Evaluate** How would Europe be different today if there had been no Crusades?
4. **Apply** How did European monarchies change during the Middle Ages? What were the effects of this change on culture, religion, and politics in Europe?

Geography in History

1. **Place** Refer to the map "Trade Routes A.D. 1400s." Name the major trading cities in western Europe during the 1400s.
2. **Human/Environment Interaction** Why did most European traders avoid overland routes whenever possible?
3. **Location** With which two areas to the east did the cities of Europe most want to trade?
4. **Movement** How did the desire for luxuries from the East lead to changes in transportation in the West?

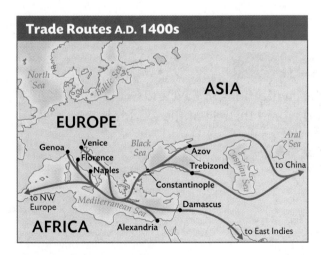

Understanding Themes

1. **Cultural Diffusion** How did a mix of cultures affect medieval Europe?
2. **Innovation** Choose one medieval innovation and describe its influence on medieval society. Do the same for a modern innovation and modern society.
3. **Conflict** How did continual conflict between England and France strengthen the monarchies of those countries?
4. **Conflict** Why was there religious dissent in the Catholic Church of the Late Middle Ages?

1. The Crusades were a series of "holy wars" conducted by Christians against Muslims. Can you find examples of holy wars in modern times?
2. Compare the rise of towns in medieval Europe with the rise of towns in America.
3. How do medieval European universities compare to today's higher educational institutions?

Skill Practice

Study the map "Spread of the Black Death" and answer the questions below.

1. What is the topic and time period of this map?
2. What does color represent?
3. When and where did the Black Death begin?
4. In which direction did the Black Death spread? How does the map show this?
5. What factor do you think caused this pattern of the epidemic?`

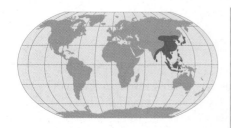

Chapter Themes

▶ **Movement** The Mongols of central Asia conquer China and parts of Europe. *Section 1*
▶ **Uniformity** A centralized government, a state religion, and a common language maintain China's cultural continuity. *Section 2*
▶ **Cultural Diffusion** The civilizations of Southeast Asia reflect the influences of India and China. *Section 3*
▶ **Innovation** Japan and Korea produce innovations from a blend of Chinese and local traditions. *Section 4*

The Storyteller

In China, in the year A.D. 1200, a lone student sat behind a desk in a room furnished only with a lamp, some paper, a writing brush, and an inkstone. He labored over a grueling government exam designed to test his knowledge of Confucian texts. He worried because examiners could fail a person for even a single misquotation. If he passed, he would be one of the Song emperor's officials. If he failed, he would have to hawk cheap goods in the streets.

Civil service examinations helped ancient China to maintain a consistent government no matter which dynasty was in power. Later, the neighboring countries of Korea and Japan adopted these civil service examinations as well as other aspects of Chinese culture.

Historical Significance

How did the civilizations of East and South Asia influence each other and the rest of the world?

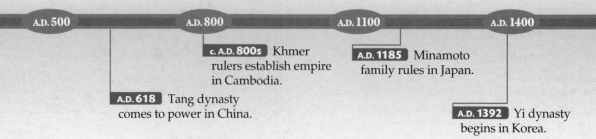

A.D. 500   A.D. 800   A.D. 1100   A.D. 1400

c. A.D. 800s Khmer rulers establish empire in Cambodia.

A.D. 618 Tang dynasty comes to power in China.

A.D. 1185 Minamoto family rules in Japan.

A.D. 1392 Yi dynasty begins in Korea.

Visualizing History A partial view of the summer palace constructed under Emperor Ch'ien Lung. Bibliothèque Nationale, Paris, France

Your History Journal

Consult an atlas and create a map of East Asia. As you read the chapter, place 10 to 20 key events on your map in the countries or areas where they occurred. Include the dates of these events.

A.D. 1200		A.D. 1300		A.D. 1400	

c. A.D. 1206 Genghis Khan becomes ruler of all Mongol tribes.

c. A.D. 1279 The Mongols establish rule in China.

A.D. 1398 Timur Lenk (Tamerlane) sacks Delhi in central Asia.

Section 1

Central Asia

Setting the Scene

▶ **Terms to Define**
clan, yurt, *yasa*, khan

▶ **People to Meet**
the Seljuk Turks, the Mongols, Genghis Khan, Timur Lenk (Tamerlane)

▶ **Places to Locate**
Mongolia

Find Out How did the Mongols acquire the world's largest land empire?

The Storyteller

The caravan halted for the night. Chaghatai, the leader, before retiring posted a sign and fastened bells around the animals' necks. Maffeo, a young foreigner, wondered at these precautions. Chaghatai explained that strange things may happen in the Desert of Lop. "When a man is riding by night through this desert and something happens to make him … lose touch with his companions ... he hears spirits talking.… Often these voices make him stray from the path.… For this reason bands of travellers make a point of keeping very close together.… And round the necks of all their beasts they fasten little bells, so that by listening to the sound they may prevent them from straying from the path."

—adapted from *The Travels of Marco Polo*, Marco Polo, translated by Ronald Latham, 1958

Porcelain figure on camel

From the A.D. 1000s to the A.D. 1400s, invaders from the steppe of central Asia conquered territories in eastern Asia, the Middle East, and eastern Europe. Originally nomads, the invaders settled in many of the conquered areas. They adapted to the local cultures, advanced trade, and encouraged the exchange of goods and ideas.

The Steppe Peoples

At the beginning of the A.D. 1000s, large numbers of nomadic groups roamed the steppe of central Asia. Loosely organized into **clans**, or groups based on family ties, they depended for their livelihood on the grazing of animals. To protect their pastures and provide for a growing population, they organized under powerful chiefs. The chiefs formed cavalry units of warriors armed with bows and arrows. The nomadic peoples became a military threat to neighboring territories that were more culturally developed. They carried out a series of invasions that transformed the cultures of eastern Asia, the Middle East, and eastern Europe.

The Seljuk Turks

The first people of the steppes to engage in conquest were the Turks. Around A.D. 800, weak Abbasid rulers centered in Baghdad hired Turkish warriors to fight in their armies. As a result, the Turks became powerful and soon controlled the Abbasid government. Later, about A.D. 1000, a group of Muslim Turks called **the Seljuk Turks** moved from central Asia into the Middle East. There they formed settlements and restored the Sunni caliphate. The Seljuks also gained control of the main trade routes between eastern Asia, the Middle East, and Europe. They benefited from this trade and used their wealth to build an empire.

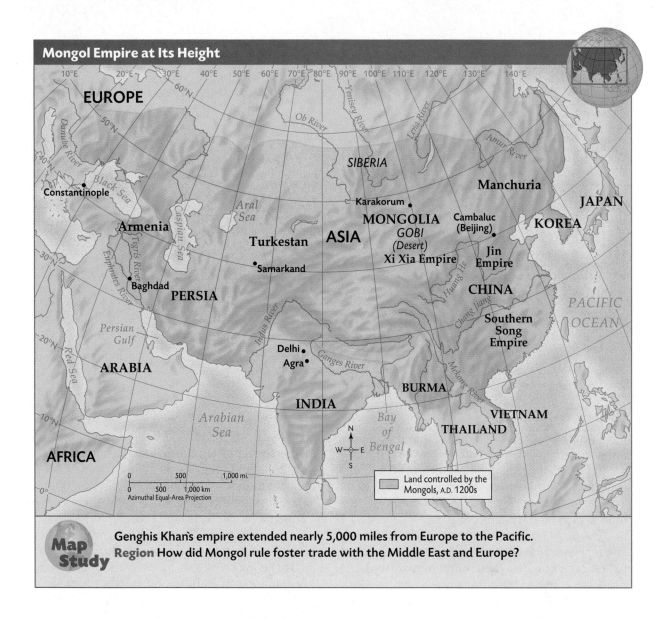

Mongol Empire at Its Height

SIBERIA

EUROPE

Constantinople

Armenia

PERSIA

Baghdad

ARABIA

AFRICA

Karakorum

MONGOLIA

GOBI (Desert)

Xi Xia Empire

Turkestan

Samarkand

ASIA

Cambaluc (Beijing)

Manchuria

JAPAN

KOREA

Jin Empire

CHINA

Southern Song Empire

PACIFIC OCEAN

Delhi

Agra

INDIA

Ganges River

BURMA

VIETNAM

THAILAND

Bay of Bengal

Arabian Sea

Persian Gulf

Aral Sea

Black Sea

Caspian Sea

0   500   1,000 mi.
0   500   1,000 km
Azimuthal Equal-Area Projection

Land controlled by the Mongols, A.D. 1200s

Map Study Genghis Khan's empire extended nearly 5,000 miles from Europe to the Pacific.
Region How did Mongol rule foster trade with the Middle East and Europe?

Seljuk warriors also invaded the plains and highlands of Asia Minor. There they defeated the Byzantines at the Battle of Manzikert in A.D. 1071. The Byzantine emperor Alexius I Comnenus feared the loss of Byzantine territory to the Seljuks and appealed to the pope and the monarchs of western Europe for aid. About 20 years later, the Seljuk conquest of Palestine led to Pope Urban II's calling of the First Crusade.

Though the Seljuks were skilled warriors, they were unable to develop a well-organized government to rule their territories. Seljuk rulers lacked strong traditions of government administration and had difficulties holding the empire together. Local officials ignored the central government and acted like independent rulers. They began to fight each other for control of land. Weakened by internal upheavals, the Seljuks became prey to new nomadic invaders from central Asia.

The Mongols

During the late A.D. 1100s, **the Mongols** became the dominant nomadic group in central Asia. Their homeland was **Mongolia**, a region of forests and steppe northwest of China. In this wild and isolated area, they wandered from pasture to pasture with their herds of sheep, horses, and yaks, or long-haired oxen. Because of their nomadic life, the Mongols lived in movable tents called **yurts**. Their principal foods were meat and mare's milk. In a few fertile areas, Mongol farmers established small communities. There women raised grains while men herded animals.

Genghis Khan

Like other nomads, the Mongols at first were divided into clans. They were expert fighters on horseback, using bow and arrow. About A.D. 1206

Some people in Mongolia still live in yurts, circular domed tents of skins or felt stretched over a lattice frame. *Why did ancient Mongols choose this kind of housing?*

a Mongol leader named Temujin (teh•MOO•juhn) organized the scattered clans under one government. He brought together Mongol laws in a new code known as the *yasa*. Under Temujin's guidance, an assembly of tribal chiefs met for the first time to plan military campaigns.

Temujin's greatest achievement was in military affairs. He organized the Mongol armies into disciplined cavalry units. These units were then placed under the command of officers chosen for their abilities and not for their family ties. These changes made the Mongols the most skilled fighting force in the world at that time. As a result of his efforts, Temujin was recognized as khan, or absolute ruler. Now called **Genghis Khan** (JEHN•guhs KAHN), or "universal ruler," Temujin set out to create a large empire.

Mongol Conquests

The Mongol armies under Genghis Khan first conquered the other steppe peoples, most of whom were Turks. These victories brought tribute money to the Mongol state as well as new recruits for the Mongol armies. By A.D. 1211 the Mongols were strong enough to attack major civilizations. In that year, 100,000 Mongol horsemen invaded China. While fighting against the Chinese, the Mongols learned Chinese techniques of siege warfare. Using gunpowder, storming ladders, and battering rams, they won significant victories against their opponents. In spite of Genghis Khan's death in A.D. 1227, the Mongols continued their advance. By A.D. 1279 all of China's territory was in their hands, and a Mongol dynasty ruled the entire country.

Under Ogadai (OH•guh•DY) Khan, the other Mongol forces moved westward. During the A.D. 1230s and A.D. 1240s, a Mongol army led by the commander Batu (bah•TOO) conquered East Slavic lands and then crossed the Carpathian Mountains into eastern and central Europe. Upon hearing of Ogadai's death, Batu's army returned to Russia. There they awaited the selection of a new khan. Meanwhile, Ogadai's widow ruled the Mongols.

During the same period, other Mongols invaded the Middle East. Using terror to subdue the region, the Mongols destroyed cities and killed many people. In A.D. 1258 the commander Helagu (heh•lah•GOO) captured Baghdad, the old Abbasid capital, and enslaved its inhabitants. The destruction of Baghdad represented a major setback to Islamic civilization. However, the Mongol advance was finally halted by the Mamluks, a Muslim military group that ruled Egypt.

The Mongol Empire

The Mongols created the largest land empire in history. Their territories extended from China to the frontiers of western Europe. Many of the great trade routes between Europe and Asia passed through Mongol lands. During the A.D. 1200s Mongol rule brought peace to the region. This advanced the growth of trade and encouraged closer cultural contacts between East and West.

The Mongols respected the highly advanced culture of conquered groups and learned from them. In China, Mongol rulers gradually adopted Chinese ideas and practices. In Persia and central Asia, Mongol settlers converted to Islam and intermarried with the local Turkish population. Turkish became the principal language of the region. The Mongols of Russia, however, kept their traditional customs and lived apart from the Slavs. They settled in the empty steppe region north of the Caspian Sea. From there, they controlled the Slavic principalities located in the northern forests.

The unity of the Mongol Empire did not last long. All Mongols gave allegiance to the khan in Mongolia. However, local rulers became increasingly independent. By the end of the A.D. 1200s, Mongol territories in Russia, central Asia, Persia, and China had developed into separate and independent domains.

Timur Lenk

About 100 years later, another powerful nomadic force emerged from central Asia. In the A.D. 1390s a Turkish-Mongol chief named **Timur Lenk** (in English, Tamerlane) rose to power in the region. As a youth, Timur was known for his athletic abilities, especially in horse riding. He began his rise as leader of a small nomadic tribe and extended his rule through numerous wars with neighboring tribes.

A devout Muslim, Timur hoped to spread Islam to new areas. His religious zeal also made him oppose Muslims who differed with his understanding of Islam. Claiming descent from Genghis Khan, Timur united the Turkish-Mongols by conquest and eventually extended their rule over much of the Middle East.

Although Timur was ruthless, the people under

Visualizing History Timur Lenk, or Tamerlane, devoted much of his life to conquest, from India to Russia to the Mediterranean. *What city was the center of his empire?*

his rule created important centers of civilization in central Asia. The most influential city in the region was Samarkand. A wealthy trading and craft center, it became known for its beautifully decorated mosques and tombs.

In A.D. 1402 Timur and his armies swept into Asia Minor, defeating another Turkish group—the Ottomans—at Ankara. However, Timur's effort to gain territory in Asia Minor never succeeded. In A.D. 1405 Timur died and was buried at Samarkand. The huge empire that he had created soon collapsed. The Ottomans were then able to regain their lost lands and began the building of their state.

SECTION 1 REVIEW

Recall
1. **Define** clan, yurt, *yasa*, khan.
2. **Identify** the Seljuk Turks, the Mongols, Genghis Khan, Batu, Helagu, Timur Lenk.
3. **Explain** why the empire of the Seljuk Turks declined quickly.

Critical Thinking
4. **Synthesizing Information** What factors led the steppe peoples to expand their territories and to create empires?

Understanding Themes
5. **Movement** How did the Mongol conquests contribute to the spread of culture and ideas throughout Asia and parts of Europe?

A.D. 600   A.D. 1000   A.D. 1400

c. A.D. 649 Empress Wu begins
to control the Chinese Empire.

A.D. 907 Tang
dynasty ends.

A.D. 1260 Kublai
Khan begins reign.

A.D. 1368 Yuan
dynasty collapses.

Section 2

China

Setting the Scene

▶ **Terms to Define**
meritocracy, mandarin

▶ **People to Meet**
Tai Cong, Empress Wu, Xuanzang, Duo Fu, Li Bo, Zhao Kuangyin, Kublai Khan, Marco Polo

▶ **Places to Locate**
Changan, Hangzhou

 What were the significant achievements of the Tang, Song, and Yuan dynasties?

Storyteller

Thoughtfully, Gui Xi considered the civil service examination. He was to select a single line of poetry and, using his finest calligraphy, write it on a silk scroll. Then he must create a painting linked to the chosen text, filling the scroll. To pass this vital test a man needed to be able to read, drawing conclusions and inferences. He also needed to demonstrate proficiency in the brush arts, a discipline requiring many years to master. Gui Xi recollected the steps essential to writing and painting. One must first find the spirit, rhythm, and thought, then one could seek to control the scenery, brush, and ink. For good work to result, mental and physical aspects must balance.

—adapted from *Record of Brush Methods: Essay on Landscape Painting*, Ching Hao, reprinted in *Varieties of Visual Experience*, 1991

Chinese calligraphy

For more than 350 years after the collapse of the Han dynasty in A.D. 220, Chinese kingdoms and invaders from the north rivaled each other for control of China. Then in A.D. 589, a northern official named Yang Jian (YAHNG JYEN) united China by conquering both the north and the south. Yang Jian took the title Emperor Wen and founded the Sui (SWAY) dynasty. Emperor Wen renewed many of the goals and traditions that had been accepted during the reign of the Han dynasty. He organized public works projects such as the rebuilding of the former Han capital city at **Changan** (CHONG•ON), the repair of the Great Wall, and the construction of a Grand Canal to link northern and southern China. However, to accomplish these projects Emperor Wen used crews of forced laborers, which made him quite unpopular with the peasants.

The Tang Dynasty

In A.D. 618 peasant uprisings against the Sui dynasty enabled a rebellious lord named Li Yuan (LEE YOO•AHN) to take control of the country and proclaim himself emperor. He established the Tang (TONG) dynasty, which lasted from A.D. 618 to A.D. 907. Under the Tang, the Chinese Empire expanded its borders to include new territories.

Government and Society

The military genius behind the early Tang expansion was a son of Li Yuan who took the name **Tai Cong** (TIE TSOONG). Not only was Tai Cong a warrior, but he was also a shrewd administrator. By restoring a strong central government in China, he maintained control of his enormous empire while continuing to expand it.

To obtain a position in the Tang government, candidates had to pass civil service examinations. Under Tang rule, these tests measured the degree to which candidates had mastered Confucian principles. According to Confucianism, an individual was expected to obey the emperor just as a son was expected to obey his father.

Because almost any male could take these examinations, the Chinese government claimed that it was a meritocracy—a system in which people are chosen and promoted for their talents and performance. But in practice it did not meet that ideal. Few boys from poor families could afford to pay tutors to help them prepare for the exams. Most could not spare the time away from their labor to study on their own.

Nevertheless, some peasants benefited from the Tang dynasty's rule. The Tang government gave land to farmers and enforced the peace that enabled them to till their land. In the Chang Jiang (Yangtze River) region, farmers were able to experiment with new strains of rice and better methods for growing it—both of which led to greater crop yields. With more food available, the Chinese population increased as well.

Foreign Influences

Tang rulers also devoted resources to the construction of roads and waterways. These routes made travel within China and to neighboring countries much easier. New and improved routes helped government officials to perform their duties. They also enabled Chinese merchants to increase trade with people from Japan, India, and the Middle East.

Chinese luxury goods, such as silk and pottery, passed through central Asia along the Silk Road. Beginning in central China, traders' camel caravans traveled north to the Great Wall and then headed west, crossing into central Asia just north of the Tibetan plateau. Some traveled as far west as Syria. These caravans brought Chinese goods and ideas to other cultures and returned with foreign products and new ideas as well. The Buddhist, Christian, and Islamic religions came to China by way of the Silk Road. During the Tang dynasty, Buddhism especially became very popular in China.

As trade increased the wealth of the empire, the Tang capital at Changan grew into the largest city in the world. Dazzling tales attracted merchants and scholars from countries throughout Asia to this city of 2 million people. Visitors to Changan spoke of wide, tree-shaded avenues and two vast market squares where merchants sold goods from Asia and the Middle East. They said that acrobats, jugglers, and dancers performed in the streets and that wealthy Chinese—including women—played the Persian games of chess and polo.

The Arts

In A.D. 649 Gaozong (GOW•DZOONG) succeeded Tai Cong as emperor of China. But Gaozong's wife, **Empress Wu**, actually ruled the empire. She expanded the bureaucracy and strengthened China's military forces.

History & Art *Four Travelers on Horseback,* porcelain figures from the Tang dynasty **Chinese potters discovered how to make porcelain in the A.D. 800s by firing pieces at very high temperatures.** *What constructions helped merchants trade fine Chinese wares with other countries?*

In A.D. 712 Empress Wu's grandson, **Xuanzang** (SEE•WAHN•DZONG), became emperor of China. Because Xuanzang welcomed artists to his splendid court, the arts flourished during his reign. Tang artisans made porcelain, a fine translucent pottery that became a prized commodity known in the West as "china."

Two of China's greatest poets, **Duo Fu** (DWA FOO) and **Li Bo** (LEE BWAW), produced their works in Xuanzang's court. Scholars compiled encyclopedias, dictionaries, and official histories of China. Writers popularized stories about ghosts, crime, and love. And while European monks were still slowly and laboriously copying texts by hand, Chinese Buddhist monks invented the more efficient technique of block printing. They carved the text of a page into a block of wood. Then they reproduced the page by inking the wood and pressing a piece of paper onto it.

Tang Decline

For a time the cultural splendor of Xuanzang's court masked its military weakness. However, the Tang ruler's vulnerability to attack was revealed in A.D. 755, when Turkish armies in central Asia successfully revolted against China. They cut off China's trade routes to the Middle East, and they put an end to the thriving exchange of goods and ideas along the Silk Road. Border wars with the Tibetans and rebellions in famine-stricken provinces plagued the Tang from A.D. 766 on. In A.D. 907 this turmoil finally caused the fall of the Tang dynasty.

The Song Dynasty

From A.D. 907 to 960, China was ruled by military dynasties. Then a military general named **Zhao Kuangyin** (JOW KWONG•YIN) seized the throne and established the Song (SOONG) dynasty.

Footnotes to History

Pasta

Almost everyone associates noodles, or pasta, with Italy. But, according to tradition, the Chinese were the first to make noodles, and their recipes were brought to Italy in the A.D. 1200s by the Polos. Some recent historians, however, claim that pasta actually originated in Persia and from there spread east and west.

Song emperors kept peace with a group of Mongols in the north, the Khitan, by paying them generously in silver. But in A.D. 1127 the Jurchen, a nomadic people, captured the Song capital of Kaifeng (KIE•FUHNG). The Song rulers set up their royal court in the southern city of **Hangzhou** (HONG•JOH).

Cultural Contributions

Song scholars, resentful of foreign influences, produced an official state philosophy called neo-Confucianism. This philosophy combined Confucian values with elements of Buddhism and Daoism.

Song rulers also more firmly entrenched the civil service system that the Tang had resurrected. They made determining one's knowledge of Confucian curriculum the main focus of these tests. The scholars who had passed the tests eventually formed a wealthy elite group, called mandarins by Westerners.

Rich and Poor

During the Song dynasty, China experienced unprecedented economic growth, partly because Song rulers used tax revenues to fund several public-works projects that benefited the economy. For example, they used these revenues to fund the digging of irrigation ditches and canals, which in turn helped farmers increase their crop yields.

The introduction of new crops from Southeast Asia, such as tea and a faster-growing rice plant, further boosted China's farming economy. The new crops also led to an increase in China's trade with India and Southeast Asia. With farming, trade, and commerce all thriving, urban centers prospered.

The urban wealthy lived in spacious homes and enjoyed going to teahouses, restaurants, and luxurious bathhouses. The capital of the dynasty, Hangzhou, grew to nearly 1 million residents.

Of course, the country still had many urban poor. The urban poor lived in flimsy houses. To survive they hawked cheap goods in the streets, worked as manual laborers, begged, or stole.

Song Arts and Sciences

Song achievements in the arts and sciences were many. The cuisine which people recognize today as distinctively Chinese originated during the Song dynasty. Experts regard Song porcelain as the best ever made. Landscape painting reached its peak during Song rule. Song inventors perfected the compass, a tool that enabled Chinese sailors to navigate on journeys far offshore. They also produced gunpowder that was first used in fireworks. Bamboo-tube rocket launchers charged with gunpowder made the Song army a powerful fighting force.

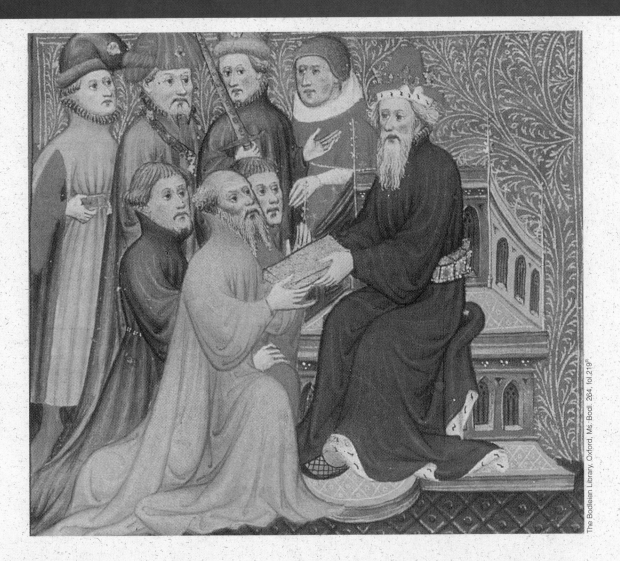

The Bodleian Library, Oxford, Ms. Bodl. 264, fol.219ª

Kublai Khan and Marco Polo

This medieval English manuscript shows the Chinese emperor Kublai Khan presenting golden tablets to Marco Polo and his family to ensure their safe passage back to the West. In A.D. 1297 Marco Polo wrote an account of a trip he claimed to have made to China, and his book eventually became popular with the small literate class in Europe. The painter who embellished this manuscript had never met Marco Polo nor had he ever seen a picture of an Asian. Maybe that's why the emperor looks European rather than Asian.

The Mongol rulers of China put the country in closer touch with the Middle East and Europe. The Mongolian khans were outsiders who distrusted, and were distrusted by, their Chinese subjects. The khans turned to outsiders to help them rule, especially after Kublai Khan moved the Chinese capital to Beijing. The Polos (Marco Polo's father and uncle accompanied him to China) were but three of hundreds of European and Muslim merchants and artisans who moved in and out of China. But Marco Polo became famous, both in his time and in ours, because he wrote a book about his adventures. The Polos may have brought Chinese noodles back to Europe, and other European and Muslim travelers brought Chinese inventions such as gunpowder and the compass back to the West. This transfer of technology had a major impact on the history of Europe. ⊕

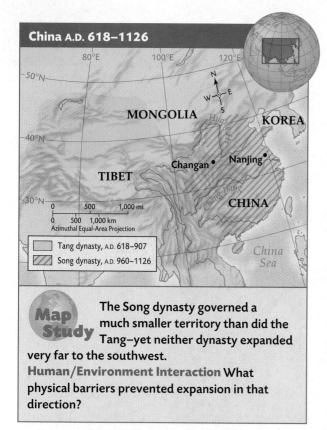

China A.D. 618–1126

Tang dynasty, A.D. 618–907

Song dynasty, A.D. 960–1126

Map Study The Song dynasty governed a much smaller territory than did the Tang—yet neither dynasty expanded very far to the southwest. **Human/Environment Interaction** What physical barriers prevented expansion in that direction?

Kublai Khan

The first great Mongol emperor of China was **Kublai Khan** (KOO•BLUH KAHN). A grandson of Genghis Khan, Kublai ruled from A.D. 1260 to A.D. 1294. Kublai Khan extended Mongol rule beyond China's borders. He conquered Korea in the north and part of Southeast Asia. He made two attempts to invade Japan, using Chinese and Korean ships. Both efforts failed because the Mongols were not skilled in naval warfare.

Although Kublai complied with some Chinese traditions to better control the Chinese, he tried to maintain Mongol culture. Government documents were written first in Mongolian, then translated into Chinese. Moreover, the highest positions in the emperor's court were given to Mongols or foreigners.

The most famous of these foreigners may have been a Venetian named **Marco Polo**. Polo claimed to have arrived in China about A.D. 1271 and to have stayed 17 years, traveling through Mongol territory on the Khan's missions. Whether true or not, Polo's tales of the splendor of Chinese civilization astounded Europeans.

Mongol Peace and Decline

Travel throughout China greatly improved because the Mongols enforced a relatively stable order. Merchants could safely travel the roads built by the Mongols. Mongol rule thus fostered trade and connections with Europe.

Through contact with the Middle East, Russia, and Europe, the Chinese obtained enslaved people as well as products such as glass, hides, clothes, silver, cotton, and carpets. In return, Europeans got exotic products such as silk, porcelain, and tea.

After Kublai Khan died in A.D. 1294, a series of weak successors took over the throne. The Chinese, still resentful of foreign rule, began to stage rebellions against these rulers. Finally, in A.D. 1368, a young Buddhist monk named Zhu Yuanzhang (JOO YOO•AHN•JAHNG) led an army against the capital and overthrew the Yuan dynasty.

China's enemies, however, were eventually able to obtain the secrets of Song military technology. Thus, using the Song Empire's own technology against it, the Mongols were able to completely capture northern China in A.D. 1234 and bring about the fall of the Song dynasty in southern China in A.D. 1279.

The Yuan Dynasty

During the A.D. 1200s, the Mongols invaded China and overthrew the Jurchen and Song rulers. They established the Yuan (YOO•AHN), or Mongol, dynasty. They became the first conquerors to rule most of the country.

SECTION 2 REVIEW

Recall
1. **Define** meritocracy, mandarin.
2. **Identify** Tai Cong, Empress Wu, Xuanzang, Duo Fu, Li Bo, Zhao Kuangyin, Kublai Khan, Marco Polo.
3. **Locate** the city of Changan in central China on the map above. Describe the capital city's human and physical characteristics.

Critical Thinking
4. **Evaluating Information** Do you think the Tang and Song systems of government were true meritocracies? Explain.

Understanding Themes
5. **Uniformity** What methods did the rulers of the Tang, Song, and Yuan dynasties use to unite China?

A.D. 802 The Khmer people establish capital at Angkor.

A.D. 938 The Vietnamese defeat the Chinese in the Battle of Bach Dang River.

c. A.D. 1200s The Mongols destroy Burman city of Pagan.

A.D. 1350 The Thai establish kingdom of Ayutthaya.

Section 3

Southeast Asia

Setting the Scene

▶ **Terms to Define**
archipelago, animism

▶ **People to Meet**
the Khmer, Suryavarman II, Trung Trak, Trung Nhi, Ngo Quyen, Ramkhamhaeng

▶ **Places to Locate**
Angkor Wat, Pagan, Sukhothai, Ayutthaya, Melaka

Find Out How were Southeast Asians influenced by the cultures of China and India?

The Storyteller

The situation was a general's nightmare, T'u Sui thought despairingly. His lord, the Chinese emperor, was determined to subjugate the land of Yueh [Vietnam]. T'u Sui had gladly accepted the command of five hundred thousand men of ability to complete the task. However, when he attacked the Yueh fled into the mountains and forests where it was impossible to fight them or even to find them. Gradually, the troops grew weary of their duties. The Yueh would then attack, inflicting great losses upon the powerful Chinese army.

—from *Huai Nan Tzu*, reprinted in *Ancient Vietnam*, Keith W. Taylor

Mountains of Vietnam

Although China was the most culturally diverse and influential society in Asia from about A.D. 220 until A.D. 1400, other Asian civilizations were creating distinct and influential cultures of their own at the same time. Southeast Asian cultures were among these new societies.

Crossroads of Asia

South of China and east of India is the region known as Southeast Asia. Southeast Asia includes the present-day countries of Myanmar (Burma), Thailand, Vietnam, Laos, Cambodia, Malaysia, Singapore, Brunei, Indonesia, and the Philippines. Located in the tropics, many of these countries have fertile soils, warm climates, and abundant rainfall. Geographically, Southeast Asia is divided into mainland and maritime Southeast Asia. The latter includes more than 10,000 islands of the Philippine and Indonesian **archipelagos**, or chains of islands.

During the A.D. 100s, an exchange of goods and ideas began between India and Southeast Asia. This exchange led Southeast Asia to adopt many elements of Indian culture. For instance, at that time, traveling Indian traders and scholars introduced to Southeast Asia the Sanskrit language and the religions of Hinduism and Buddhism. Indian epics such as the *Ramayana* were interwoven with Southeast Asian stories and legends. Indian architecture, law codes, and political ideas also deeply influenced the cultures of the region. As contact with India increased, Indian culture gradually spread throughout Southeast Asia.

Southeast Asians nevertheless retained many of their own traditions. They continued to perform the art of shadow puppetry, to make intricately patterned cloth called batik, and to play their own unique instruments and music. They also believed in **animism**, the idea that spirits inhabit living and nonliving things.

The Khmer

In A.D. 802 **the Khmer** (kuh•MEHR) people of the mainland Southeast Asian country of Cambodia established a great Hindu-Buddhist empire with its capital at Angkor. The Khmer Empire reached its height during the A.D. 1100s, when it conquered much of the land that now includes Laos, Thailand, and Vietnam.

The empire's wealth came primarily from its rice production. Elaborate hydraulic engineering projects enabled the Khmer to irrigate and produce three crops of rice a year. With the wealth from this bountiful harvest, Khmer rulers subsidized mammoth construction projects. Adapting Indian building techniques to create their own distinctive architecture, the Khmer built hundreds of temples that glorified Hindu and Buddhist religious figures. They also constructed roads, reservoirs, irrigation canals, harbors, and hospitals. Khmer rulers were known for the splendor of their court. Borrowing from the Indian idea of kingship, Khmer rulers presented themselves as incarnations of the Hindu gods or as future Buddhas, which served to enhance their power. They bedecked themselves in elaborate finery and filled their palaces with ornate thrones and beautiful furnishings. A Chinese traveler named Zhou Dakuan (JOH DAH•KWON) described the splendor of a Khmer king in dress and manner:

❝ His crown of gold is high and pointed like those on the heads of the mighty gods. When he does not wear his crown, he wreathes his chignon [hair gathered in a bun] in garlands of sweet-scented jasmine. His neck is hung with ropes of huge pearls (they weigh almost three pounds); his wrists and ankles are loaded with bracelets and on his fingers are rings of gold set with cats' eyes. He goes barefoot—the soles of his feet, like the palms of his hands, are rouged with a red stuff. When he appears in public he carries the Golden Sword. ❞

Images *of the* Times

Angkor Wat

Angkor Wat (meaning "temple of the capital") was built in the A.D. 1100s by the Khmer ruler Suryavarman II. Suryavarman believed he was the incarnation of the Hindu god Vishnu.

The temple complex at Angkor Wat is encircled by a three-mile moat. The temples and monuments within the complex honored the god-king Suryavarman II and impressed visitors with their size and detailed ornamentation.

A bas–relief of the Bayon depicts a battle between the Khmer and the Chams.

Seen through a doorway the pavilion and the central sanctuary reveal a five-headed Naga serpent.

During the A.D. 1100s, under the rule of King **Suryavarman** (soor•yah•VAHR•mahn) **II**, the Khmer kingdom reached the height of its power. Having expanded Cambodia by conquest to include parts of areas known today as Laos, Vietnam, and Thailand, the king decided to glorify both the Hindu god Vishnu and himself. He ordered the construction of **Angkor Wat**, a temple complex covering nearly a square mile. Carvings depicting the Hindu gods cover the walls of Angkor Wat, and, at the center of the complex, the sanctuary stands 130 feet (40 m) high. Angkor Wat also was used as an astronomical observatory.

The Khmer king poured so much of the empire's wealth into building Angkor Wat, however, that he severely weakened the kingdom. This excess, along with rebellions against Khmer rule and infighting between members of the royal family, further crippled the empire. In A.D. 1431 the Thai, a neighboring Southeast Asian people, captured the capital city of Angkor, bringing an end to Khmer rule there.

Vietnam

East of Cambodia and south of China lies the area of present-day Vietnam. Because of Vietnam's proximity to China and because the Chinese dominated Vietnam for more than 1,000 years, Vietnam's culture in some ways came to resemble that of China.

The Vietnamese absorbed elements of Chinese belief systems such as Confucianism, Daoism, and Buddhism. The Vietnamese also adopted Chinese forms of writing and government. Just as in China, Vietnamese officials were selected through civil service exams based on Confucian principles.

The Vietnamese retained many of their own traditions, however. They adopted Chinese religions and beliefs, but they continued to believe in animism. The Vietnamese built a *dinh*, or spirit house, in each village. This tiny house served as the home for the guardian spirit of a village. The Vietnamese wore their hair long and tattooed their skin. They wrote and spoke their own Vietnamese

A stone bas–relief of elephant and gods helps tell the story of the ancient Khmer civilization.

REFLECTING ON THE TIMES

1. What values of the Khmer are reflected in these images?
2. How did Suryavarman attempt to impress upon visitors that he was an incarnation of Vishnu?

100°E 120°E 140°E

50°N

N
W—E
S

Hokkaido

Honshu

Silla JAPAN
•Nara
KOREA Shikoku
Kyushu

CHINA

30°N

INDIA

PACIFIC
OCEAN

INDOCHINA
PENINSULA

(PHILIPPINES)

10°N
Strait of
Malacca

MALAY
PENINSULA

SUMATRA

0°

INDIAN
OCEAN

0   300   600 mi.

0 300 600 km
Azimuthal Equal-Area Projection

Borobudur

JAVA

Map Study Much of Southeast Asia (shown in purple on the map) lies in the tropics. **Region** What conditions in this region have made farming an important part of the economy?

language, although in writing it they used Chinese characters. Even though the Chinese controlled Vietnam almost continuously from about 200 B.C. to A.D. 939, the Vietnamese fought hard to retain—and then to regain—their independence.

> The Viets [Vietnamese] were very difficult to defeat. They did not come out to fight, but hid in their familiar mountains and used the jungle like a weapon. As a result, neither side could win.... The Viets would raid suddenly, rob and get away fast, so that just as our army obtained its supplies from the home base, the Viets obtained theirs from our army.
>
> —Chinese general, c. 200 B.C.

In A.D. 39 two Vietnamese sisters, **Trung Trak** and **Trung Nhi**, clad in armor and riding atop elephants, led a successful revolt against the Chinese. For two years Vietnam was independent of China. Then the Chinese returned in greater numbers and defeated the Vietnamese. Rather than surrender to the Chinese, the Trung sisters are said to have drowned themselves in a river.

During the confusion after the overthrow of the Tang dynasty, the Vietnamese took advantage of China's disunity to revolt again. The Chinese sent a fleet of warships to Vietnam to try to subdue the rebels. In A.D. 938, however, under the leadership of **Ngo Quyen** (noo chu•YEHN), the Vietnamese defeated the warships in the Battle of the Bach Dang River. Although Emperor Tai Cong countered this defeat by launching an invasion of Vietnam, the Vietnamese date their independence from the battle, because Tai Cong's invasion failed.

After the Song dynasty gained control of China, the Song emperor threatened the Vietnamese with invasion. To keep peace with China, the Vietnamese agreed to send tribute—gifts—to the Chinese emperor. In return, China agreed not to invade Vietnam. From then on, the Vietnamese ruler called himself emperor at home, but in his messages to the Chinese court he referred to himself merely as a king.

Myanmar

The westernmost area of mainland Southeast Asia today includes the country of Myanmar (Burma). The first peoples to extensively settle most of present-day Myanmar were the Mons and the Tibeto-Burmans. From 200 B.C. to A.D. 100, these two groups gradually occupied different parts of the country. The Mons established villages in southern Burma, while the Tibeto-Burmans lived along the Irrawaddy (IHR•uh•WAH•dee) River in the northern part of the country. Although they developed their own traditions, the Mons and the Tibeto-Burmans accepted Buddhism and other aspects of Indian culture from visiting South Asian sailors and traders.

During the A.D. 500s, the Tibeto-Burmans became the dominant group and pushed the Mons southward. In A.D. 849 they set up a capital city called **Pagan** (pah•GAHN), which eventually became a center of Buddhist learning and culture. By the A.D. 1200s, skilled architects had transformed Pagan from a small settlement into a city of elaborate Buddhist temples and monasteries.

During the A.D. 1200s, the Mongol armies of Kublai Khan captured Pagan and ended its glory. To escape Mongol rule, many Burmans moved into the southern part of Myanmar. There they founded fortified towns along the rivers between their ruined capital and the Andaman Sea. Although Burman culture was preserved, a united kingdom did not arise again in Myanmar until the A.D. 1500s.

The Thai

More than four out of every five people who live in the Southeast Asian country of Thailand today belong to the ethnic group called Thai. They are descendants of people who began migrating south from China about A.D. 700. About A.D. 1238 the Thai established their first kingdom at **Sukhothai** (SOO•kah•TY) in the north-central part of the country.

Sukhothai

The Sukhothai kingdom lasted only about 100 years, but it was known for its wise leaders. The kingdom's greatest monarch, King **Ramkhamhaeng** (rahm•KAHM•hong), ruled from A.D. 1275 to A.D. 1317. He made Sukhothai into a center of learning and the arts. During Ramkhamhaeng's reign, the Thai developed an alphabet and writing system based on the Khmer script. Artisans from China taught the making of porcelain, and Buddhist monks from South Asia won most of the Thai people to Buddhism. Beautiful Buddhist temples, with many levels of roofs, rose gracefully above the skyline of Sukhothai. Even during Ramkhamhaeng's lifetime, the Thai saw his reign as a golden age. A stone pillar erected in A.D. 1292 and still standing has the following words engraved on it:

❝ This Sukhothai is good. In the water there are fish. In the fields there is rice. The king does not levy a [tax] on his people.… Who wants to trade in elephants, trades. Who wants to trade in horses, trades. Who wants to trade in gold and silver, trades.… **❞**

Ayutthaya

In A.D. 1350 a prince named Ramathibodi (rah•MAH•thee•BOH•dee) overthrew the last Sukhothai ruler and founded a new kingdom known as **Ayutthaya** (ah•YOO•thy•yuh). He set up his capital south of Sukhothai and up the Chao Phraya River (chow PRY•uh) from where Bangkok, the present Thai capital, is today.

Visualizing History Wat Mahathat, an ancient Buddhist temple now restored, is in Sukhothai Historic Park, which was opened to the public in 1980. *What was accomplished in Sukhothai's golden age?*

The Ayutthaya kingdom lasted for about 400 years, with a succession of 33 kings. At its height, it held control over large areas of Southeast Asia, including parts of Myanmar and the Malay Peninsula. Like Sukhothai, Ayutthaya was an important center of Buddhist learning and culture. Economically prosperous, Ayutthaya carried on trade in teakwood, salt, spices, and hides with China and neighboring Asian kingdoms.

Seafaring Kingdoms

Many kingdoms in early Southeast Asia developed around strategic ports. The Indonesian islands became a crossroads in the expanding international trade that stretched from the Arabian Peninsula to China. Merchants of many lands—Arabs, Chinese, Indians, and Persians—traded such products as porcelain, textiles, and silk for Southeast Asian spices and valuable woods.

The Srivijaya (SHREE•vih•JAY•uh) Empire arose on the islands of Java and Sumatra in present-day Indonesia. Lasting from about A.D. 600 to A.D. 1100, the Srivijaya Empire was one of the region's

Visualizing History The Hindu temple of Pura Ulun Danau on Lake Bratan in the Central Mountains of Bali has a typical thatched roof. *How is Bali's religious heritage different from that of the rest of Indonesia?*

great seafaring powers. It controlled shipping along the Strait of Malacca that separates Sumatra from the Malay Peninsula. By the end of the A.D. 1100s, Srivijaya was reduced to a small kingdom, and the Majapahit (mah•jah•PAH•heet) kingdom began to dominate the Indonesian islands.

From the A.D. 400s to the A.D. 1400s, Buddhism and Hinduism were the dominant religious influences that affected maritime Southeast Asian life. During the early A.D. 1200s Muslim traders from the Arabian Peninsula and India brought Islam to the peoples of the Malay Peninsula and Indonesia.

The first major center of Islam in Southeast Asia was **Melaka**, a port kingdom on the southwestern coast of the Malay Peninsula.

From Melaka, Islam spread throughout the Indonesian islands. The only island to remain outside of Muslim influence was Bali, which has kept its Hindu religion and culture to the present day.

During the A.D. 1500s, a number of Muslim trading kingdoms competed for control of the Indonesian islands. European explorers, beginning with the Portuguese in A.D. 1511, gradually won control by setting local rulers against each other.

SECTION 3 REVIEW

Recall
1. **Define** archipelago, animism.
2. **Identify** the Khmer, Suryavarman II, Trung Trak, Trung Nhi, Ngo Quyen, Ramkhamhaeng.
3. **Locate** mainland Southeast Asia on the map on page 354.

Why would the mainland, and not the Indonesian and Philippine archipelagos, be more likely to come under the influence of India and China?

Critical Thinking
4. **Synthesizing Information** How might Buddhism or

Confucianism complement a belief in animism?

Understanding Themes
5. **Cultural Diffusion** What were some of the ways in which the cultures of China and India influenced the peoples of Southeast Asia?

Critical Thinking SKILLS

Making Generalizations

Have you heard statements such as "Only tall people play basketball well" or "Dogs make better pets than cats"? Do you consider the validity of such statements? Or do you accept them at face value?

Learning the Skill

These statements, called generalizations, are broad statements about a topic. To be valid, a generalization must be based on accurate information. Let's examine the generalization "Only tall people play basketball well." Is this accurate? We can find many examples of tall basketball players. However, there are also many shorter players who excel at this sport.

In this case, we began with a generalization and looked for facts to support or disprove it. In other cases, you will make a generalization from a group of facts about a topic. To make a valid generalization, first collect information relevant to the topic. This information must be accurate facts, not opinions.

Suppose that you want to make a generalization about the relative danger of air and automobile travel. First, you would collect accident statistics involving airplanes and cars. Then classify the information into categories. Look for relationships between these categories. For example, you might put the airplane and automobile statistics in separate categories. You might also categorize the number of accidents and the number of fatalities. Finally, make a generalization that is consistent with most of the information.

Practicing the Skill

Read the passage about literature in the Tang dynasty and answer the questions that follow.

“Xuanzang welcomed artists to his splendid court.... Two of China's greatest poets, Duo Fu and Li Bo, produced their works in Xuanzang's court. Scholars compiled encyclopedias, dictionaries, and official histories of China. Writers popularized stories about ghosts, crime, and love. And while European monks were still slowly and laboriously copying texts by hand, Chinese Buddhist monks invented the more efficient technique of block printing. ”

1. What facts about literature in the Tang dynasty are presented?
2. Organize these facts into categories.
3. How does the invention of block printing relate to the other facts?
4. What generalization can you make about literature during the Tang dynasty?

Chinese pouring vessel

Applying the Skill

Review the information in the chapter about religion in China, Cambodia, Vietnam, Korea, and Japan. Write a generalization about religion in East and Southeast Asia. Then support your generalization with at least five facts.

For More Practice

Turn to the Skill Practice in the Chapter Review on page 371 for more practice in making generalizations.

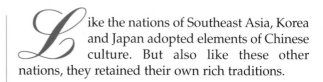

A.D. 400	A.D. 1000	A.D. 1600

c. A.D. 400 Yamato clan founds Japanese imperial dynasty.

A.D. 668 The Silla kingdom conquers all of Korea.

A.D. 1274 Mongols make first attempt to invade Japan.

A.D. 1336 The Ashikaga family rules in Japan.

Section 4

Korea and Japan

Setting the Scene

▶ **Terms to Define**
shamanism, shogun, shogunate, samurai, daimyo

▶ **People to Meet**
Sejong, Yi-Sun-shin, Prince Shotoku, Lady Shikibu Murasaki, Yoritomo Minamoto

▶ **Places to Locate**
Heian (Kyoto)

Find Out How did the Koreans and the Japanese accept China's culture?

The Storyteller

Zeami Motokiyo was adamant as he lectured his students. "Actors are not thoughtless mimics incapable of intellectualism or philosophy. We seek excellence, as do courtiers and men of letters." Motokiyo had been developing a new form of drama, the Noh play, that had uplifting stories and moral lessons, aspects that appealed to the educated upper classes. "Actors must always bear in mind the correct balance between mental and physical actions. An actor, using his intelligence, will make his presentation seem beautiful." Motokiyo wanted his actors to think as well as to rehearse.

—adapted from *Sources of Japanese Tradition,* Ryusaku Tsunoda, reprinted in *Sources of World History,* Volume 1, edited by Mark A. Kishlansky, 1994

Noh theater mask

---

*L*ike the nations of Southeast Asia, Korea and Japan adopted elements of Chinese culture. But also like these other nations, they retained their own rich traditions.

Korea

A glance at Korea on the map on page 354 will reveal why a Korean proverb describes the country as "a shrimp between whales." Korea forms a peninsula on the east coast of Asia, extending south toward the western tip of Japan. Thus, it acts as a bridge between its two neighbors, China and Japan.

Early History

By legend, the Koreans claim descent from Tangun, the son of a bear and a god who supposedly founded the first Korean kingdom 5,000 years ago. Historians believe that the first Korean people were immigrants from northern Asia. These settlers lived in villages, grew rice, and made tools and other implements of bronze. They were animists who practiced shamanism, a belief that good and evil spirits inhabit both living and nonliving things. Shamans, or priests, interceded between the spirit world and humans.

In 109 B.C. China first invaded Korea, putting Korea under the control of the Han dynasty. From 109 B.C. until the fall of the Han dynasty in A.D. 220, Korea was dominated by China. But after the fall of the Han dynasty, Koreans regained control of their peninsula and, by A.D. 313, eventually formed three kingdoms—Silla, Paekche (pah•EHK•chee), and Koguryo. During the Three Kingdoms period, from A.D. 313 to A.D. 668, the Koreans adopted many elements of Chinese culture. Among these were Confucianism, Buddhism, calligraphy, and ideas about government.

Koreans also used Chinese knowledge of arts and sciences to make their own unique creations. For example, in the A.D. 300s, Koguryo artists produced mammoth cave art murals. In Silla, Queen Sondok built an astronomical observatory that still stands today and is the oldest observatory in Asia.

In A.D. 668 the kingdom of Silla conquered all of Korea, ushering in a period of peace, prosperity, and creativity. Korean potters produced superb porcelain decorated with flower designs. Koreans also created a unique mask dance that expressed sentiments of shamanism and Buddhism, which had been adopted as the state religion in A.D. 528. Over a 16-year period, Korean scholars compiled the *Tripitaka Koreana*, the largest collection of Buddhist scriptures in the world today. The *Tripitaka* has 81,258 large wooden printing plates.

The Yi Dynasty

In A.D. 1392 a dynasty called the Yi came to power in Korea. The Yi called their kingdom Choson and built Hanyang—today the city of Seoul—as their capital. They opened schools to teach Chinese classics to civil service candidates and made neo-Confucianism the state doctrine.

The adoption of Korean neo-Confucianism deeply affected people's roles and relationships. According to Korean Confucian doctrine, the eldest son in each family was bound by duty to serve his parents until their death. Korean women—who had been accorded high status under shamanism and Buddhism—were given much lower standing under Korean Confucianism. In fact, women from the higher ranks of society had to stay indoors until nightfall, when a great bell signaled the closing of the city gates. Even then, to go out they had to obtain permission from their husbands.

One of the greatest Yi rulers, King **Sejong**, had two significant accomplishments. He ordered bronze instruments to be used in measuring rain. As a result, Korea now has the oldest record of rainfall in the world. He and his advisers made a greater contribution by creating simplified writing to spread literacy. Together they devised *hangul*, an alphabet that uses 14 consonants and 10 vowels to represent Korean sounds. Although scholars continued to write with Chinese characters after the invention of *hangul*, writers began using *hangul* to transcribe folk tales and popular literature.

Although the Japanese tried to capture Korea in A.D. 1592, the Yi dynasty managed to successfully rebuff the Japanese invaders, mainly because of an invention created by Korea's Admiral **Yi-Sun-shin**. The admiral's ironclad warships, or "turtle ships," devastated the Japanese fleet. The Koreans won the war. However, in the years that followed, they increasingly avoided contact with the outside world and isolated themselves so totally that Korea became known as the Hermit Kingdom.

Japan

Just 110 miles (177 km) east of Korea lies the Japanese archipelago. As the map on page 354 shows, Japan consists of four large islands—Honshu, Shikoku, Kyushu, and Hokkaido—and many smaller ones.

Visualizing History Shown here is the world's oldest astronomical observatory in Asia. It was built at Silla, Korea, from 365 stones. *How much territory did the kingdom of Silla hold by A.D. 668?*

Mount Fuji and Lake Ashi at Hakone, Japan. *How did the physical beauty of the land affect Japanese art?*

Island Geography

Because of its island geography, Japanese culture formed mostly in isolation from mainland Asian cultures, except for that of China. Although the Japanese borrowed from Chinese civilization, their customs and traditions were different from those of most other Asian peoples.

The geography of these islands influenced the formation of Japanese culture in other ways as well. Because much of the land is mountainous—less than 20 percent of it is suitable for farming—the Japanese learned to get most of their food from the sea. They also learned to rely on the sea for protection from invaders—being a natural barrier to invasion from the mainland—and yet to regard it as a route of transport between the islands. The physical beauty of the land inspired deep reverence for nature in works by many Japanese painters and poets. Because these islands are located in an area where earthquakes, typhoons, floods, and volcanic eruptions are frequent, the Japanese long ago created a myth that helped to explain the stormy weather there.

Creation Myth

An ancient Japanese creation myth is the oldest explanation for the origins of Japan, its turbulent weather, and its first emperor. According to the myth, brother and sister gods Izanagi and Izanami dipped a spear into the churning sea. When they pulled it out, the drops of brine that fell upon the water's surface became the islands of Japan. The two gods then created the sun goddess Amaterasu, and because they loved her best of all their children, they sent her to heaven to rule over the world. Next they created Tsuki-yumi, the moon god, and Susanowo, the storm god, to be her companions.

Amaterasu gave life to everything around her. But Susanowo, who had a fierce temper, ruined his sister's rice crop and so frightened her that she hid in a cave. Without her in heaven, the world became dark. The other gods placed a jewel and a mirror on a tree outside the cave to coax Amaterasu back outside. When she came out and told them why she had hidden, the other gods banished Susanowo to the earth.

According to the myth, Susanowo's descendants were the first inhabitants of Japan. Amaterasu sent her grandson, Ninigi, to govern these descendants on the island of Honshu. So that all would acknowledge his divine power, she sent with him her mirror, her jewel, and a great sword. According to legend, Ninigi's grandson, Jimmu, conquered the rest of Susanowo's descendants in 660 B.C., becoming the first emperor of Japan.

By tradition, each successive emperor has received Amaterasu's three gifts: a mirror, a jewel, and a sword. Also by tradition, each emperor—until Hirohito—has claimed to be Amaterasu's descendant. In 1945, after the Japanese defeat in

World War II, Emperor Hirohito announced that he did not possess divine status.

Early Inhabitants

Among the first people to inhabit the Japanese islands were hunter-gatherers who came there from the mainland more than 10,000 years ago. These people had developed the technology to make pottery but not to make bronze or iron. When Koreans and others from mainland Asia invaded Japan during the 200s B.C. and 100s B.C., they were easily able to defeat the early inhabitants by using iron and bronze weapons.

The invaders introduced the islanders to agricultural methods, such as how to grow rice in flooded paddies. Heavy summer rains in Japan made it the ideal place to grow rice, which soon became Japan's most important crop.

Between A.D. 200 and A.D. 300, another influx of mainlanders came to Japan. According to scholars, these armor-clad warriors who fought on horseback were probably the ancestors of the aristocratic warriors and imperial family of Japan referred to in the creation myth.

In early Japan, though, even before there was an emperor or an imperial family, separate clans ruled their own regions. Clan members practiced a form of animism called Shinto, meaning "the way of the gods." Each clan included a group of families descended from a common ancestor, often said to have been an animal or a god. The clan worshiped this ancestor as its special *kami*, or spirit. Practitioners of Shinto believed that *kami* dwelled within people, animals, and even nonliving objects such as rocks and streams. To honor this *kami*—and the *kami* of their ancestors—they held festivals and rituals. Often these ceremonies were conducted by the chief of the clan, who acted as both military leader and priest.

The Yamato Clan

By about A.D. 400, the military skill and prestige of the Yamato clan, which claimed descent from Amaterasu, enabled it to extend a loose rule over most of Japan. Although other clans continued to rule their own lands, they owed their loyalty to the Yamato chief. In effect, he became the emperor.

Initially, the emperor had a great deal of political power. By the A.D. mid-500s, however, the emperor had become more of a ceremonial figure who carried out religious rituals. The real political power was held by the members of the Soga

Samurai Arts

Kiyomatsu, a samurai hero

In the A.D. 1100s the rise of military rule in Japan brought in a new style of art. Supported by daimyo and samurai, artists created paintings highlighting the skill and bravery of soldiers. These works show warriors in richly patterned clothing, riding magnificent horses and wielding long swords. The expressions of the riders and their horses often convey wild—but controlled—emotions.

Today in Japan the samurai artistic tradition is most prominent in movies and television. Many popular Japanese films are samurai tales set in feudal times and filled with action and adventure. Akira Kurosawa, one of the world's renowned directors, has made a number of samurai movies. His film *The Hidden Fortress*—about a brave general who leads an endangered princess to safety—helped inspire American director George Lucas to create the epic film *Star Wars*.

Linking Past and Present | **ACTIVITY**

Study a painting with a samurai theme. What values are expressed in the painting? You might want to view the films *The Hidden Fortress* and *Star Wars*. In what ways do you think these films reflect samurai values? In what ways do you think they do not?

family. The emperors kept their position as heads of Japan because people believed that only they could intercede with the gods. But the Soga family controlled the country.

Chinese Influences

In A.D. 552 a Korean king sent a statue of the Buddha and some Buddhist texts to the Japanese court. The king wrote, "This religion is the most excellent of all teachings" and suggested that the emperor make Buddhism the national religion. Buddhism had come to Korea from China, and its introduction to Japan made the Japanese open to Chinese culture. This curiosity about China was especially strong among Japan's nobles and scholars.

Through a kind of cultural exchange program that lasted four centuries, the Japanese learned much from the Chinese. Not only did they learn about the teachings of the Buddha, they also learned a great deal about Chinese art, medicine, astronomy, and philosophy. They incorporated much of this knowledge into Japanese culture. For instance, the Japanese adopted the Chinese characters for writing to create their own writing system.

Prince Shotoku was responsible for much of this cultural exchange. When he became the leading court official in A.D. 593, he instituted programs that encouraged further learning from Chinese civilization. He ordered the construction of Buddhist monasteries and temples and sent officials and students to China to study. When Shotoku heard about the Chinese Confucian ideas of government, he wrote a constitution for Japan in which he set forth general principles that explained how government officials should act.

After Shotoku's death, the Fujiwara family seized power in the name of the emperor and began to urge him to pattern the government more closely on that of China. China had a strong central government at that time.

In A.D. 646 government officials instituted the Taika reforms, or "Great Change." These reforms proclaimed that all the land was the property of the emperor rather than clan leaders. Clan leaders could oversee the peasants working the land, but they could no longer assign them land or collect taxes from them. Instead, government officials were to allocate plots to peasants and collect part of their harvest in taxes for the emperor.

In modeling their government on China, however, the Japanese did not always adopt Chinese ways. For example, civil service examinations were never accepted; instead officials gained their posts through family ties. Also, even after the Taika reforms, much of Japan remained under the control of regional clan leaders.

The Nara Period

Greater government centralization did not take place until A.D. 710, when Japan built its first permanent capital at Nara. A smaller version of China's Changan, Nara had an imperial palace, broad streets, large public squares, rows of Chinese-style homes, and Buddhist temples.

With the completion of the colossal Todaiji Temple at Nara in A.D. 752, Buddhist fervor in Japan reached its peak. Buddhism, however, did not replace Shinto, for each religion met different needs. Shinto linked the Japanese to nature and their homeland. Buddhism promised spiritual rewards to the good. Therefore, people practiced both.

During the Nara period, the Japanese also produced their first written literature. Scribes wrote histories of ancient Japan that combined the creation myths with actual events. Other writers compiled collections of Japanese poems.

The Heian Period

In A.D. 794 the Japanese established a new capital in **Heian,** later called **Kyoto.** For more than 1,000 years, this city remained the capital of Japan.

A century after the city was founded, Japan stopped sending cultural missions to China. In the period that followed, a small group of about 3,000 Japanese aristocrats, calling themselves "dwellers among the clouds," created Heian culture.

The focus of Heian court life was the pursuit of

AROUND THE WORLD Temple of Kailasa

India, A.D. 760
Emperor Krishna of the Rashtrakuta dynasty ordered construction of the Kailasa Temple at Ellora. The temple, completed in A.D. 760, was cut from a single outcropping of rock. It was 165 feet (50 m) long and 96 feet (29 m) high. Kailasa was dedicated to the Hindu god Siva. Its elaborate carvings featured Hindu gods and mythological figures in various poses.

INDIA
• Ellora

History & Art *The Lady Fujitsubo Watching Prince Genji Departing in the Moonlight* by A. Hiroshige and U. Toyokuni, A.D. 1853. *What was a major theme of the Heian novel,* The Tale of Genji?

beauty. It pervaded all of life's activities, from wrapping presents to mixing perfumes and colors. People devoted hours each day to writing letters in the form of poems. Calligraphy was as important as the poem itself, for a person's handwriting was taken to be an indication of his or her character. People were even said to fall in love upon seeing each other's handwriting.

During the Heian period, women were the creators of Japan's first great prose literature. About A.D. 1010 **Lady Shikibu Murasaki** wrote *The Tale of Genji*, which some believe to be the world's first novel. The novelist chronicles the life and loves of a fictional prince named Genji. Filled with poems about the beauty of nature, *The Tale of Genji* quickly became very popular.

The Heian aristocrats were so deeply involved in their search for beauty, however, that they neglected tasks of government. Order began breaking down in the provinces. Warlike provincial leaders started running their estates as independent territories, ignoring the emperor's officials and refusing to pay taxes. Thus the Heian aristocrats eventually lost control of the empire completely.

The Way of the Warrior

As Heian power faded, two powerful court families, the Taira and the Minamoto, struggled for control. The families fought a decisive battle in A.D. 1185 in which the Taira were defeated. To **Yoritomo Minamoto**, head of the Minamoto family, the emperor then gave the title shogun, or "general," and delegated to him most of the real political and military power. While the emperor remained with his court in the capital of Kyoto carrying on ritual tasks, Yoritomo and his soldiers ran a shogunate, or military government, from Kamakura near present-day Tokyo.

The shogunate proved to be quite strong. Even though Kublai Khan tried twice to invade Japan— once in A.D. 1274 and again in A.D. 1281—he did not succeed. On the first occasion, Japanese warriors and the threat of a storm forced the Mongols to withdraw. On the second occasion, 150,000 Mongol warriors came by ship, but a typhoon arose and destroyed the fleet. The Japanese thought of the storm as the *kamikaze*, or "divine wind," and took it to be confirmation that their islands were indeed sacred.

In A.D. 1336 the Ashikaga family gained control of the shogunate. But the family failed to get control of regional warriors. Japan soon broke into individual warring states, leaving the shogun and the emperor as mere figureheads.

The powerful landowner-warriors in the countryside were called samurai. The most powerful samurai became daimyo (DY•mee•OH), or lords. Like the medieval knights of feudal Europe who pledged their loyalty to lords, samurai pledged their loyalty and military service to their daimyo. There were many samurai and many daimyo. Poor

Friends mourn the death of the Buddha in this Japanese painting. *How was Buddhism introduced to Japan?*

rice farmers paid high taxes for the right to farm a daimyo's lands. In return, that daimyo provided the farmers with protection. The system in which large landholders give protection to people in exchange for their services is called feudalism. Japanese feudalism was similar to European feudalism as described in Chapter 12.

The samurai fought on horseback with bows, arrows, and steel swords. They dressed in loose-fitting armor. The samurai followed a strict code of honor called Bushido, meaning "the way of the warrior." Bushido stressed bravery, self-discipline, and loyalty. It demanded that the samurai endure suffering and defend his honor at all costs. If a samurai was dishonored or defeated, he was expected to commit suicide.

Japanese women too could be warriors. This passage from *The Tale of the Heike* describes a female Minamoto samurai:

❝ Tomoe had long black hair and a fair complexion, and her face was very lovely; moreover she was a fearless rider whom neither the fiercest horse nor the roughest ground could dismay, and so dexterously did she handle sword and bow that she was a match for a thousand warriors and fit to meet either god or devil. Many times

had she … won matchless renown in encounters with the bravest captains, and so in this last fight, when all the others had been slain or had fled, among the last seven there rode Tomoe. ❞
—*The Tale of the Heike*, A.D. 1200s

Growth of a Merchant Class

Despite the political turmoil during its feudal period, Japan developed economically at this time. Workshops on daimyo estates produced arms, armor, and iron tools. Each region began to specialize in goods such as pottery, paper, textiles, and lacquerware. Trade increased between regions.

The increasing trade led to the growth of towns around the castles of the daimyos. Merchants and artisans formed guilds to promote their interests— just as they did in medieval Europe. These guilds, called *za* in Japan, benefited their members in many ways. A *za* might pay a fee to exempt its members from paying tolls for shipping their goods. Over a long period of time, this exemption would save the members quite a bit of money.

Japanese merchants began to trade with Chinese and Korean merchants. Chinese copper coins became the chief means of exchange. The Japanese exported raw materials such as lumber, pearls, and gold, as well as finished goods such as swords and painted fans. The Japanese imported items such as medicines, books, and pictures.

Religion and the Arts

By the A.D. 1200s Buddhism had spread from the nobles to the common people. The opening words of *The Tale of the Heike* describe the Buddhist sentiments that were prevalent in Japan during its feudal period:

❝ In the sound of the bell of the Gion Temple echoes the impermanence of all things. The pale hue of the flowers of the teak tree show the truth that they who prosper must fall. The proud do not last long, but vanish like a spring-night's dream. And the mighty ones too will perish in the end, like dust before the wind. ❞

During Japan's feudal age, Buddhist teachings were simplified and gave rise to many religious groups. The new varieties of Buddhism all taught about a personal afterlife in paradise. The way to paradise, they stated, was through simple trust in the Buddha. With salvation so easily available, the influence of priests, monks, and nuns declined. For

Zen Buddhist monks sit in a meditation garden at Ryoanji Temple in Kyoto, Japan. *To a Zen Buddhist, what is the purpose of meditation?*

the first time, the common people began to play an important role in Buddhist life. With widespread support, Japanese Buddhist groups linked religion with patriotism. Some believed that Japanese Buddhism was the only true Buddhism and that Japan was the center of the universe.

While the common people turned to new forms of Buddhism, the samurai followed a form of Buddhism called Zen. The Japanese scholar Eisai had brought Zen to Japan from China late in the A.D. 1100s. Zen taught that the individual had to live in harmony with nature and that this harmony could be achieved through a deep religious understanding called enlightenment. The followers of Zen rejected book learning and logical thought, embracing instead bodily discipline and meditation. They believed that by meditation a student could free his mind and arrive at enlightenment.

Zen was particularly useful for warriors because it taught them to act instinctively, and thinking was a hindrance to action. Samurai could improve skills such as archery by freeing their minds from distractions to better concentrate on the object or target.

Zen also perfected art forms and rituals such as ikebana, or flower arranging, meditation gardens, and the tea ceremony. Ikebana grew out of the religious custom of placing flowers before images of the Buddha. The Zen practice of meditation gave rise to meditation gardens, consisting of carefully placed rocks surrounded by neatly raked sand.

Meditation also sparked the tea ceremony, an elegant, studied ritual for serving tea. One tea master said of the ceremony that it was intended to "cleanse the senses … so that the mind itself is cleansed from defilements." These and other arts and rituals derived from Buddhism are still popular in Japan today.

SECTION 4 REVIEW

Recall
1. **Define** shamanism, shogun, shogunate, samurai, daimyo.
2. **Identify** Sejong, Yi-Sun-shin, Amaterasu, Jimmu, Shinto, Prince Shotoku, Taika reforms, Lady Shikibu Murasaki, Yoritomo Minamoto, Bushido.

3. **Explain** What is traditionally given to each new emperor of Japan? Why?

Critical Thinking
4. **Evaluating Information** Which would you prefer to follow, the ideals of the Heian court or the samurai code of Bushido? Why? What effects

do you think each viewpoint might have had on the people of Japan?

Understanding Themes
5. **Innovation** Identify one Chinese innovation that the Koreans or Japanese borrowed, and describe how they made it their own.

from

Four Poems
by Li Bo

Li Bo was born in A.D. 701 in western China. People began praising his beautiful poems even before he reached adulthood. Throughout his life he traveled extensively in China, amazing people with his ability to compose insightful, touching poems. He usually wrote about the world around him, the people he met, and the emotions he felt. By the time of his death in A.D. 762, he was regarded as one of China's greatest poets, a distinction he still holds today.

In the following poem, Li Bo comments on an experience everyone faces at some time: parting with a close companion.

Taking Leave of a Friend

Blue mountains to the north of the walls,
White river winding about them;
Here we must make separation
And go out through a thousand miles
    of dead grass.

Mind like a floating wide cloud,
Sunset like the parting of old acquaintances
Who bow over their clasped hands at a distance.
Our horses neigh to each other
    as we are departing.

The following poem is a favorite of many Chinese citizens who have left their homeland and settled in the United States or elsewhere.

On a Quiet Night

I saw the moonlight before my couch,
And wondered if it were not the frost
    on the ground.
I raised my head and looked out on the
    mountain moon;
I bowed my head and thought of my
    far-off home.

*L*i Bo used extensive symbolism in his writing. In the following poem, he compares life to a traveler on a journey.

Hard Is the Journey

Gold vessels of fine wines,
    thousands a gallon,
Jade dishes of rare meats,
    costing more thousands,

I lay my chopsticks down,
    no more can banquet,
And draw my sword and stare
    wildly about me:

Ice bars my way to cross
    the Yellow River,
Snows from dark skies to climb
    the T'ai-hang Mountains!

At peace I drop a hook
    into a brooklet,
At once I'm in a boat
    but sailing sunward …

    (Hard is the Journey,
    Hard is the Journey,
    So many turnings,
    And now where am I?)

So when a breeze breaks waves,
    bringing fair weather,
I set a cloud for sails,
    cross the blue oceans!

Visualizing History *Dawn Over Elixir Terrace* depicts a tranquil river scene. *How do the river and mountains present obstacles to the traveler in the poem?*

*S*ince Li Bo spent much of his time traveling, he was often separated from his family. He wrote and sent the following poem to his children.

Letter to His Two Small Children Staying in Eastern Lu at Wen Yang Village Under Turtle Mountain

Here in Wu Land mulberry leaves are green,
Silkworms in Wu have now had three sleeps:

My family, left in Eastern Lu,
Oh, to sow now Turtle-shaded fields,
Do the Spring things I can never join,
Sailing Yangtse always on my own—

Let the South Wind blow you back my heart,
Fly and land it in the Tavern court
Where, to the East, there are sprays and leaves
Of one peach-tree, sweeping the blue mist;

History & Art *Landscape of the Four Seasons* by **Shen Shih-Ch'ung.** *In what season did Li Bo write the above poem?*

Visualizing History This winter scene is a detail from the Ming dynasty painting *Landscape of the Four Seasons. How many winters have passed since the author was at home?*

This is the tree I myself put in
When I left you, nearly three years past;
A peach-tree now, level with the eaves,
And I sailing cannot yet turn home!

Pretty daughter, P'ing-yang is your name,
Breaking blossom, there beside my tree,
Breaking blossom, you cannot see me
And your tears flow like the running stream;

And little son, Po-ch'in you are called,
Your big sister's shoulder you must reach
When you come there underneath my peach,
Oh, to pat and pet you too, my child!

I dreamt like this till my wits went wild,
By such yearning daily burned within;
So tore some silk, wrote this distant pang
From me to you living at Wen Yang....

RESPONDING TO LITERATURE

1. In "On a Quiet Night," why is the person unhappy?

2. In "Hard Is the Journey," what do the gold vessels and jade dishes symbolize?

3. What types of images did Li Bo use in each of his poems included here?

4. Supporting an Opinion Which poem do you like best? Explain why.

Connections Across Time

Historical Significance Contacts among the civilizations of Asia led to an exchange of ideas and practices. The Chinese acquired tea and faster-growing rice plants from the Southeast Asians. The Mongols became an even more powerful fighting force once they learned to use Chinese gunpowder. The Khmer people of Cambodia acquired architectural skills from India and built huge temples. Japan and Korea adopted features of China's system of government.

Today, because of technological advances, cultural diffusion occurs on a global scale. Thus, Westerners learn a great deal from the peoples of Asia, and Asians, likewise, benefit from their encounters with Westerners.

Using Key Terms

Write the key term that completes each sentence. Then write a sentence for each term not chosen.

a. yurts
b. *yasa*
c. daimyo
d. meritocracy
e. samurai
f. shamanism
g. shogun
h. shogunate
i. archipelago
j. mandarins
k. clans

1. The Mongol warrior Temujin, later known as Genghis Khan, developed a code of law known as the _____.
2. The early Koreans practiced _____, a belief that priests could intercede between humans and spirits.
3. The Japanese _____ consists of four large islands and many smaller ones.
4. Because of its examination system, the Chinese government claimed that it was a _____, or a system in which people are chosen and promoted for their talents and performance.
5. In return for protection, Japanese farmers farmed the lands of powerful landowner-warriors known as _____.

Technology Activity

Creating a Multimedia Presentation Search a computerized card catalog or the Internet to locate information about Genghis Khan. Using multimedia tools, create a presentation about the reign of Genghis Khan. Incorporate images from the Internet in your presentation. Cite all electronic resources used.

Using Your History Journal

Choose one country from your map of East Asia. Draw that country on a separate sheet of paper. From the section of Chapter 14 that provides information on your chosen country, list 5 to 10 important facts or events beside your map.

Reviewing Facts

1. **History** Identify Tai Cong and name his important political achievements.
2. **Science/Culture** List the scientific and artistic accomplishments of the Song dynasty.
3. **History** Explain the significance of the Battle of the Bach Dang River to the Vietnamese.
4. **History** Discuss the importance of the *kamikaze*, the "divine wind," in early Japanese history.
5. **Culture** Describe examples of female leadership in early East and South Asia.

Critical Thinking

1. **Apply** How did civil service examinations aid in the development of a strong central government in China?
2. **Analyze** Why did China's economy expand during Song rule?
3. **Synthesize** Do you think the strengths of Mongol society would benefit a nation today? Why or why not?
4. **Evaluate** In what ways did Chinese innovations change the cultures of Korea and Japan?

5. Analyze Japanese gardens show a love for nature and order. How did the geography of the islands influence Japanese arts and gardening?

Japanese garden

Linking Past and Present

1. How has Japan's possession of Heian and samurai values helped it to become a world leader in industry today?
2. Confucianism spread to many East and South Asian countries. How do Confucian values benefit these countries today?

Skill Practice

Read the passage below and answer the questions that follow.

❝ Indian traders and scholars introduced to Southeast Asia the Sanskrit language and the religions of Hinduism and Buddhism. Indian epics such as the *Ramayana* were interwoven with Southeast Asian stories and legends. Indian architecture, law codes, and political ideas also deeply influenced the cultures of the region.... In A.D. 802 the Khmer people of Cambodia established a great Hindu-Buddhist empire.... Borrowing the Indian idea of kingship, Khmer rulers presented themselves as incarnations of the Hindu gods or as future Buddhas.... ❞

1. What facts are presented about India's influence on Southeast Asia in general?
2. What generalization can you make based on these facts?

Understanding Themes

1. **Movement** The Mongols were able to conquer a vast territory, but their empire survived for a relatively short time. Provide a hypothesis that might explain this situation.
2. **Uniformity** What elements of Chinese society remained the same during the Tang, Song, and Yuan dynasties? What effect did this stability have on China's culture?
3. **Cultural Diffusion** What are some of the similarities between Southeast Asian cultures and Chinese culture?
4. **Innovation** Identify one Chinese discovery and explain some of the ways in which it has been used by the Chinese and others. Name things in our culture that derive from this innovation.

Geography in History

1. **Place** Refer to the map below. What river formed a natural border between China and the kingdom of Koguryo?
2. **Region** How did geography contribute to Korea's becoming known as the Hermit Kingdom?

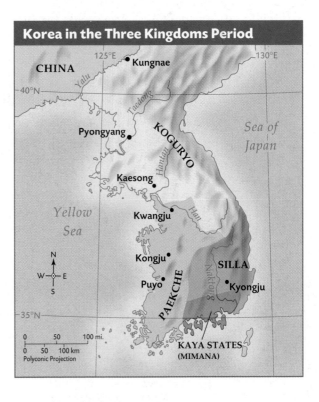

Korea in the Three Kingdoms Period

The Americas

Chapter Themes

▶ **Relation to Environment** Native Americans in North America adapt to a variety of environments. *Section 1*

▶ **Innovation** The Mesoamerican civilizations develop an understanding of astronomy and mathematics. *Section 2*

▶ **Change** The Aztec and the Inca conquer neighboring territories and establish powerful empires in Mexico and South America. *Section 3*

The Storyteller

In the Andes Mountains of South America, an Inca boy begs to hear how the Inca came to be. "The sun was unhappy with the world," the storyteller begins, "for he saw people living like wild beasts among the mountains and cliffs. He decided to send his son and daughter to teach them to adore the sun as their god. He gave special instructions: 'Each day that passes I go around all the world ... to satisfy [men's] needs. Follow my example: Do unto all of them as a merciful father would do unto his well-beloved children; for I have sent you on earth for the good of men, that they might cease to live like wild animals.'"

This legend describes what the Inca people believed about the beginnings of their empire. Close to nature and deeply religious, the Inca were only one of a number of Native American groups who built powerful civilizations in the Americas.

Historical Significance

What were the achievements of Native Americans? How did Native American traditions shape the development of the Americas?

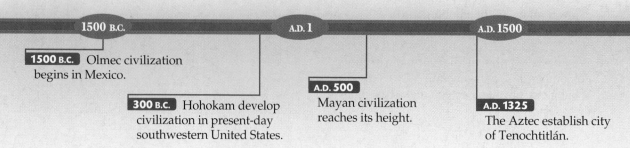

1500 B.C.	A.D. 1	A.D. 1500

1500 B.C. Olmec civilization begins in Mexico.

300 B.C. Hohokam develop civilization in present-day southwestern United States.

A.D. 500 Mayan civilization reaches its height.

A.D. 1325 The Aztec establish city of Tenochtitlán.

History & Art Aztec turquoise mosaic of double-headed serpent, Mexico

Your History Journal

Using dates from section time lines and each section narrative, build a time line of important dates in Native American civilizations between 1500 B.C. and A.D. 1500.

5000 B.C.	2500 B.C.	A.D. 1	A.D. 2500

c. 5000 B.C. Hunter-gatherers first plant maize in the highlands of Mexico.

c. 3000 B.C. Native Americans make use of stone axes and digging sticks for farming.

c. A.D. 1500 Eastern Woodland peoples form the Iroquois League.

Section 1

The Early Americas

Setting the Scene

▶ **Terms to Define**
   maize, weir, potlatch, confederation

▶ **People to Meet**
   the Kwakiutl, the Hohokam, the Pueblo, the Apache, the Navajo, the Plains peoples, Mound Builders

▶ **Places to Locate**
   Mexico, Great Plains

Find Out How did early Native Americans make use of their environment?

The Storyteller

A Navajo tale describes the origin of the twelve months of the year: First Man and First Woman built a hogan in which to live. Turquoise Boy and White Shell Girl came from the underworld to live with them. "It is not unwise that we plan for the time to come, how we shall live," said First Man. First Woman and First Man whispered together during many nights. They planned that there should be a sun, and day and night. Whenever Coyote, called First Angry, came to make trouble and asked them what they were doing, they told him: "Nothing whatsoever." He said, "So I see," and

went away. After he had gone, they planned the twelve months of the year.

—adapted from *The Portable North American Indian Reader*, edited by Frederick W. Turner III, 1974

Navajo rug

When did the earliest humans come to the Americas? Until recently, archaeologists believed that humans arrived in the Western Hemisphere about 12,000 years ago. The theory was that tribes migrated from Asia to North America, following herds of bison and other game across the then-exposed land bridge that today is the Bering Strait.

New evidence, however, challenges this old theory. Archaeologists working in North America and South America have found sites that indicate the presence of humans as early as 40,000 years ago. New theories argue that humans arrived in more than one migratory wave. Some early humans may also have traveled by boat along the Pacific coast from Siberia to Alaska, then to South America.

Once in the Western Hemisphere, the peoples dispersed throughout North America and South America. As they adapted to particular environments, they developed distinct ways of life. Some remained nomadic, while others settled and developed complex civilizations.

The First Americans

Hunter-gatherers in the Americas used the resources of their environments for food, clothing, and shelter. People living along seacoasts collected mussels and snails. Those inland hunted game or fished in rivers and streams. Archaeologists have unearthed evidence of these ways of life in artifacts, such as rounded stones for grinding seeds, bone hooks for fishing, and heaps of shells at campsites.

By about 5000 B.C., a group of hunter-gatherers in a highland area of present-day **Mexico** had discovered that the seeds of **maize**, or corn, and other native plants could be planted and harvested, providing a reliable source of food. As this discovery spread from Mexico into the southwestern United States, groups of early people began to settle in permanent villages. About 3000 B.C. farmers made use of stone axes to clear their fields and pointed digging sticks to plant improved varieties of maize, beans, and squash.

As the food supply improved, the population of the Americas grew. By the time Europeans arrived in North America around A.D. 1500, about 30 million to 100 million Native Americans belonging to more than 2,000 different groups were inhabiting the two continents. About 15 to 20 million of these early inhabitants lived in the present-day United States and various parts of Canada.

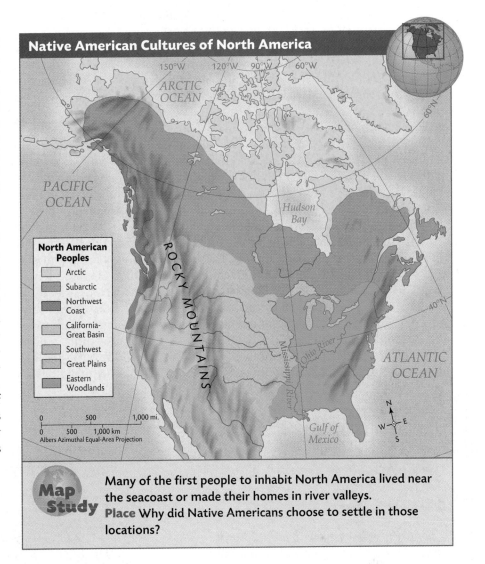

Native American Cultures of North America

North American Peoples
- Arctic
- Subarctic
- Northwest Coast
- California-Great Basin
- Southwest
- Great Plains
- Eastern Woodlands

0   500   1,000 mi.
0   500   1,000 km
Albers Azimuthal Equal-Area Projection

Map Study Many of the first people to inhabit North America lived near the seacoast or made their homes in river valleys.
Place Why did Native Americans choose to settle in those locations?

North Americans

Much of what we know about the early people of northern North America comes from the work of archaeologists. Archaeological digs have uncovered homes, burial mounds, pottery, baskets, stone tools, and the bones of people and animals in the Arctic and Northwest, California and the Great Basin, the Southwest, the Great Plains, and the Eastern Woodlands. By studying these artifacts, archaeologists discovered that there were distinct regional differences. People who settled in a particular region developed a common culture. Gradually the arts and crafts and religious customs of each region grew to be distinct from those of other regions, a pattern historians call cultural differentiation. In each region, culture reflected the local geography and natural resources.

The Arctic and Northwest

The early people of the Arctic lived in the cold northern regions of present-day Canada and Alaska. The severe climate of this region prohibited

farming. Thus, small bands of extended families moved about, hunting and fishing. By 6500 B.C. some Arctic people were living in small villages of pit houses, covered with dome-shaped roofs of whalebone and driftwood. Villagers hunted whales, sea lions, seals, and water birds. They ate the meat and used the skins to make warm, protective clothing.

In contrast to the cold and snow of the Arctic, the thickly forested seacoast of the Pacific Northwest had a milder climate. Rainfall was plentiful, and mild winters and warm ocean currents kept rivers and bays free of ice. Like the people of the Arctic, those who settled along the Pacific Coast—**the Kwakiutl,** for example—hunted whales, fish, and other sea animals as their main source of food. Forests of the Northwest provided additional sources of food—small forest animals and acorns. After about A.D. 500 the people of the Northwest used other resources from the surrounding forests and rivers. With stone and copper woodworking tools they split cedar, fir, and redwood trees into planks to make houses and large canoes. They also developed ways to harvest salmon with fiber nets, stone-tipped spears, and elaborate wooden traps called **weirs**.

Society among the Kwakiutl and other Northwest peoples was organized into lineages, each of which claimed to be descended from a mythical ancestor. A lineage group lived together in a single large house and owned the right to use or display special designs, songs, ceremonies, or prized possessions, such as patterned sheets of copper. A lineage maintained exclusive use of its own fishing area and berry-picking grounds. The wealth of each lineage was displayed and given away as gifts at festive gatherings called **potlatches**. At a potlatch a chief might give away canoes, blankets, and other goods. In turn, guests might bring the chief deerskins and food.

To obtain items they themselves could not make, some people of the Northwest developed trading networks with people living farther south. Traders paddled redwood canoes along the coast, stopping at villages along the shore to exchange goods. Trade networks stretched from southern Alaska to northern California.

California–Great Basin

Native Americans living along the California coast enjoyed a warm climate and an abundance of food resources. Many communities lived on diets of abalone and mussels. Near San Francisco Bay, archaeologists have found evidence of this diet in heaps of discarded shells that date from 2000 B.C. In addition to shellfish, the first Californians fished for sea bass, hunted seals, and gathered berries and nuts. Having such abundant resources made food gathering easier for the people living in this region.

Like other Native Americans, they developed elaborate religious ceremonies designed to worship nature spirits believed to inhabit all of the natural world, but especially those spirits related to animals or plants used for food. The Chumash, who

Images *of the* Times

Native Americans

A variety of peoples have inhabited North America for thousands of years. Some mysteries of the earliest cultures have yet to be revealed.

Georgia's Etowa Mounds sheltered these two-foot high marble images of a man and a woman more than 500 years ago.

lived in the area of present-day southern California, would gather together at harvest festivals to celebrate the goodness of the earth. Villagers participated in dances and games.

Compared with those living along the coast, people living farther inland scratched their living from a harsh desert and mountain environment. Great Basin people moved about in small bands, living in windbreak shelters and eating seeds, grasshoppers, and small animals.

Southwest

People who settled in the high desert regions of present-day Arizona, New Mexico, southern Colorado and Utah, and northern Mexico had fewer resources than those who settled along the Pacific Coast. Nevertheless, the people of the Southwest adapted to their harsh environment by inventing techniques of irrigation to farm the land. For example, around 300 B.C., **the Hohokam** living in the area of present-day Arizona dug an irrigation canal 3 miles (4.8 km) long to draw the waters of the Gila and Salt Rivers onto fields planted with maize, kidney beans, and squash.

Farther north the Anasazi and their descendants, **the Pueblo,** grew maize on flat-topped hills or on the plains. They built two- or three-story dwellings of adobe, a sun-dried brick. Some of these peoples constructed their villages under ledges on the sides of cliffs to shade residents from the desert sun and to make the villages easier to defend.

Religious leaders governed these villages. In underground chambers called kivas, they held ceremonies to ensure harmony with the spiritual world. They believed that, if harmony existed, the spirits would provide rain for crops.

Another Southwest group known as **the Apache** lived in areas that were unsuitable for farming. They hunted wild birds and rabbits and gathered plants. Sometimes they raided Pueblo fields; other times they traded meat and hides with Pueblo villagers for maize and other food supplies. A neighboring people, **the Navajo,** did manage to

The Great Serpent Mound of the Adena culture (about 1000 B.C.), unlike other mounds, contains no graves or artifacts. The enormous serpent is about to swallow a huge oval. What does this mean? The builders left no clue.

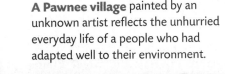

A Pawnee village painted by an unknown artist reflects the unhurried everyday life of a people who had adapted well to their environment.

An Iroquois condolence cane was carved to record the attendance of chiefs at a memorial ceremony for a deceased Iroquois chief.

REFLECTING ON THE TIMES

1. How do researchers today try to discover information about early Native American cultures?
2. Why was the lifestyle of the Pawnee much different from that of the Iroquois?

In the Northwest a totem represented a bond of unity and was the symbol and protector of the group. *What does this totem reveal about Northwest Native Americans?*

raise a breed of sheep that could live on the sparse desert vegetation.

Great Plains

In contrast to the sparse Southwestern environment, vast grasslands covered the **Great Plains**, stretching from the Rocky Mountains to the Mississippi River. This environment provided a different challenge for the early people who inhabited the region. Native Americans adapting to life on the plains needed a reliable source of food. Farming in the region was difficult, as the thick plains sod was hard to plow. Moreover, maize needs more water than is naturally available on most parts of the Great Plains.

Although some farming was done along streams, most of **the Plains peoples** depended on one abundant resource—the great herds of bison, or buffalo, that roamed the plains. From earliest times, the Kiowa, Crow, Blackfoot, and other peoples of the plains followed the herds from one grazing ground to another. They used every part of the bison for their food, clothing, shelter, and tools.

Eastern Woodlands

Unlike the Plains peoples who depended on the bison, Native Americans of the woodlands east of the Mississippi River hunted deer, turkey, and other small game for food and clothing. Like the Plains peoples, Eastern Woodlands peoples made use of every part of the animals they killed. They ate deer meat, wore deerskin clothing, and made tools out of animal bones and antlers. Because of the warm summers, abundant rainfall, and fertile soil, the Woodlands peoples lived in farming villages and grew corn, squash, beans, and tobacco.

In the Ohio and Mississippi Valleys, groups of Native Americans known as **Mound Builders** erected large earthen mounds. Archaeologists today believe the mounds were ceremonial centers or tombs for leaders. A number of mounds were made in the shape of animals. The largest ceremonial center was Cahokia, in present-day Illinois. It had about 40,000 people and was probably a political and commercial as well as a religious settlement.

Native Americans living in the northeastern forests cleared the land and built fenced-in villages of long houses, made of poles covered with tree bark. While the women farmed, the men hunted, warred, and governed. During the A.D. 1500s, five groups allied to form the Iroquois League—a confederation, or loose union. A council of male representatives from each group discussed and resolved disputes, but every clan had an elderly female known as a "clan mother," who named and deposed chiefs and council members. When Europeans entered Native American land, they met strong resistance from the Iroquois League.

SECTION 1 REVIEW

Recall
1. **Define** maize, weir, potlatch, confederation.
2. **Identify** the Kwakiutl, the Hohokam, the Pueblo, the Apache, the Navajo, the Plains peoples, Mound Builders, Iroquois League.

3. **Describe** farming methods developed by early Native Americans of Mexico and the Southwest.

Critical Thinking
4. **Analyzing Information** Compare the structure of the Iroquois League with that of

the United States government.
Understanding Themes
5. **Relation to Environment** How did Native American peoples within the seven regions of North America depend on their environment and natural resources?

c. 400 B.C. Olmec civilization declines.

c. A.D. 300 The Maya begin to expand their territory.

c. A.D. 800 Mayan civilization begins to decline.

Section 2

Early Mesoamerican Cultures

Setting the Scene

▶ **Terms to Define**
  jaguar, slash-and-burn farming, obsidian

▶ **People to Meet**
  the Olmec, the Maya, the Teotihuacános, the Toltec

▶ **Places to Locate**
  San Lorenzo, La Venta, Yucatán Peninsula, Teotihuacán, Tula

Find Out ▶ How did trade encourage the growth of city-states and kingdoms in the areas of present-day Mexico and Central America?

The Storyteller

How did the world begin? According to Mayan myth, "All was in suspense, all calm, in silence; all motionless, still.... There was nothing standing; only the calm water, the placid sea, alone and tranquil. Nothing existed. There was only silence in the darkness, in the night. Only the Creator[s] were there. By nature they were great thinkers. They decided: when day dawned for the first time, the human being must appear. Thus they spoke. "Let there be light, let there be dawn in the sky and on the earth."

—adapted from *Sources of World History*, edited by Mark A. Kishlansky, 1995

Chichén Itzá temple figure

Between 1500 B.C. and A.D. 1200, a series of sophisticated civilizations emerged in the areas of present-day Mexico, Guatemala, Honduras, El Salvador, and Belize. Amid volcanic mountains, cool valleys, dense rain forests, and dry forested plains, early farmers developed methods that produced plentiful harvests and supported large populations. Maize was their basic crop.

Ruins of ancient cities reveal an astonishing way of life. Ideas from earlier civilizations were adopted and modified by later ones. Although each culture had unique features, they shared common elements. Archaeologists have labeled them together as Mesoamerican civilizations. The prefix *meso-* means "middle" and refers to the fact that these people lived in the middle land area that joins North America and South America. Descendants of the early Mesoamericans continue to live in this region and maintain many of their early traditions.

The Olmec

About 150 years before Tutankhamen ruled Egypt, **the Olmec** emerged as one of the earliest Mesoamerican civilizations. Between 1500 B.C. and 400 B.C., the Olmec flourished in the swampy, lowland river valleys near the Gulf of Mexico. Our knowledge of the Olmec way of life and Olmec beliefs has come primarily from excavations of two principal Olmec sites, **San Lorenzo** and **La Venta**, discovered in the late 1930s. Until then, Olmec culture had been buried by centuries of accumulated layers of earth and rain forest.

Among the objects unearthed at San Lorenzo and La Venta were enormous stone heads carved from basalt, a volcanic rock. Some were more than 9 feet (2.7 m) tall and weighed as much as 40 tons.

This jade ceremonial ax in the form of a feline monster is from the pre-Columbian Olmec culture. *Why do archaeologists believe that religion played an important role in Olmec life?*

These heads are believed to be portraits of rulers, and may have been part of larger monuments. Without the aid of wheels or beasts of burden, but perhaps using river rafts, the Olmec had moved the heads some 60 miles (97 km) from the mountains to the sites where they were discovered.

Evidence suggests that San Lorenzo and La Venta each had populations of only about 1,000 at their peak. Yet there was clearly organization, planning, and a division of labor. A hilltop at San Lorenzo was sheared off to create a central plaza for market and ceremonial purposes. Stone drains were built to direct water during the rainy season. Early forms of hieroglyphic writings were developed as well as an early calendar.

From jade carvings, figurines, and carved stone murals, archaeologists infer that religion played an important role in the lives of the Olmec. Many carvings show the Olmec god, a being with a human body and the catlike face of a jaguar, the large spot-ted wild cat that roamed the region. The Olmec believed the jaguar-god controlled their harvests.

Early Olmec farmers practiced what is known as slash-and-burn farming. To clear land, farmers cut down trees, let them dry, and then burned them. They planted maize among the fertile ashes. Since the soil became exhausted after a few years, farmers shifted fields and repeated the cycle on other lands.

Trade with other parts of Mesoamerica was common. Olmec artifacts have been found throughout the region, and Olmec ideas were echoed in later Mesoamerican civilizations.

The Maya

As early as 900 B.C., **the Maya** began to settle the **Yucatán Peninsula** of present-day Mexico. Mayan civilization reached its peak between A.D. 300 and A.D. 900. Mayan ruins can be found throughout the region in diverse terrains: highlands, lowlands, and coastal plains. The Maya adapted to their various environments, developing different farming practices, languages, and governments. The Maya were not unified in one empire. Instead, the patchwork of city-states and kingdoms were linked by culture, political ties, and trade.

Religion

Religion was at the center of Mayan life. The Maya believed in two levels of existence. One level was the daily physical life they lived. The second level was the Otherworld, a spiritual world peopled with gods, the souls of ancestors, and other supernatural creatures. The two levels were closely intertwined. Actions on each level could influence the other. Mayan myths explained the workings of this world and the Otherworld.

Mayan kings were spiritual leaders as well as political leaders. They were responsible for their people's understanding of the Otherworld and for their behaving in ways that would keep the gods pleased. Rulers performed rituals and ceremonies to satisfy the gods. In their great cities, the Maya constructed plazas, temples, and huge pyramids—symbolically sacred mountains—where thousands of people could gather for special religious ceremonies and festivals.

Images on Mayan temples, sacred objects, and pottery provide clues about Mayan beliefs and practices. The rain god, Chac, appears frequently. Images depict other gods in the form of trees, jaguars, birds, monkeys, serpents, reptiles, fish, and shells. Mythical creatures that combine parts of several animals are also shown.

Blood symbols also appear. Human sacrifices and bloodletting rituals were part of Mayan practice. These ceremonies were considered important to appease the gods and to maintain and renew life.

Some festivals also included a ceremonial ball game called *pok-a-tok*. For this game, the Maya invented the use of solid rubber balls about the size of basketballs. Players wearing protective padding batted the balls back and forth across a walled court. These games recalled games played by mythical Mayan heroes.

Sciences

Like the ancient Greeks, the Maya believed that the movements of the sun, moon, and planets were journeys of gods across the sky. Since the gods controlled nature—including harvests—charting the movements of the celestial bodies was essential.

To do this charting, Mayan priests became excellent mathematicians and astronomers. The Maya built on the earlier work of the Olmec. The Maya developed a system of mathematics using the base 20. They used three symbols to represent numbers. A dot stood for the number one; a bar was five; and a shell figure symbolized zero. Rather than expressing place value with the highest place to the left, the Maya expressed their numbers vertically with the largest place at the top. The Maya also developed accurate calendars, a 260-day sacred calendar and another 365-day calendar. The calendars were used to predict eclipses, schedule religious ceremonies, and determine times to plant and harvest.

Economy

The Mayan economy was based on agriculture and trade. In addition to maize, farmers grew beans, squash, pumpkins, chili peppers, and tomatoes. Slash-and-burn farming continued in some areas. Elsewhere the Maya produced larger harvests by intensively farming raised plots surrounded by canals.

Perhaps as often as every five days, farmers brought surplus crops to the open-air markets of the major cities. Maize and other produce were traded for cotton cloth, jade ornaments, pottery, fish, deer meat, and salt.

Mayan merchants participated in long-distance trade throughout Mexico and Central America. Traders transported their cargoes by canoes on rivers and coastal waterways. Overland, goods were carried by humans, for wheeled vehicles and beasts of burden to haul them were unknown.

CONNECTIONS — The Arts

Mayan Architecture

Temple-pyramid at Chichén Itzá

Mayan temple-pyramids were the religious and political centers of Mayan cities. Built of stone, these vast stepped structures were mainly platforms for religious ceremonies. Stone temples at the summit of the pyramids were erected to memorialize dead rulers by associating them with the gods. Religious sacrifices conducted by priests took place outside the temple on top of the pyramid platform.

Archaeologists believe the stepped levels of the pyramids may have represented the harmonious layers of the universe. Mayan astronomers and priests held high administrative positions. Much of a priest's power was in his ability to predict the movements of stars and planets. Thus, a priest would consult with astronomers before projects were undertaken to see when the heavens would favor such actions.

Since the mid-1900s, Mexican architects have combined Mayan and other Native American designs with modern construction methods. Their work includes the buildings of the University of Mexico and the National Museum of Anthropology in Mexico City, as well as many resorts along Mexico's Caribbean and Pacific coasts.

Linking Past and Present **ACTIVITY**

What purpose did the Mayan temple-pyramids serve? How might you compare Mayan temple-pyramids with public buildings today?

Louis S. Glanzman

Serious Sport

In this illustration of an ancient Mayan game a rubber ball bounces off the leather pad on the player's chest. The object was to drive the ball through a stone ring, but players could not throw or bat the ball. They had to hit it off a leather pad on their elbow, wrist, torso, or hip. Making a goal was so rare that when a player scored, crowds rewarded the hero with all their clothing and jewelry—unless they could first flee.

Scholars believe that these games were played not only for sport but also on special holidays as ritual reenactments of Mayan raids. Large cities contained numerous walled courts lined with images of warfare and sacrificial victims. According to Mayan religious beliefs, ordinary humans could never outwit death, and so the Mayan ball court became a symbolic meeting ground—a kind of threshold between earth and the underworld. ⊕

Writings

The Maya were one of the first Native American peoples to develop a writing system. They wrote in accordion-folded books made of flattened bark covered with a thin layer of plaster. Four of these books have survived. They also carved inscriptions in clay, and on jade, bone, shells, and large stone monuments. Only within the past 25 years have linguists made major breakthroughs in translating Mayan writing. Linguists discovered that some inscriptions are phonetic syllables, while others represent full words. The Maya recorded the genealogy of their kings and royal families, mythology, history, ritual practices, and trade.

Collapse

By A.D. 900 the Maya in the lowlands showed signs of collapse. They stopped building and moved elsewhere. Why this happened is unclear. There is evidence of increasing conflict and warfare among Mayan royal and nonroyal families. Outsiders were also attacking. Agricultural breakdown, perhaps caused by warfare or by erosion and over-farming, may have produced rising malnutrition, sickness, and death rates.

Visualizing History The Teotihuacáno rain god Tlaloc is shown in an *incensario* (container for burning incense) from A.D. 400–700. *Where was the Teotihuacáno civilization located?*

Other Mesoamericans

In a high fertile valley 30 miles (48 km) northeast of present-day Mexico City, **the Teotihuacános** (TAY•oh•TEE•wuh•KAHN•ohs) flourished for about 750 years. By A.D. 100, they dominated the centrally located Mexican Plateau. At its height their main city, **Teotihuacán**, had an estimated 120,000 to 200,000 inhabitants.

Teotihuacán was laid out on a grid. The most important buildings were built along the north-south axis. Excavations of the ruins have revealed 600 pyramids, 2,000 apartment compounds, 500 workshop areas, and a huge marketplace. A valuable source of obsidian was found near Teotihuacán. Obsidian, a volcanic glass, was used for sharp-edged tools, arrow points, and other objects. It was easily traded, because Teotihuacán lay on the trade routes east to the Gulf of Mexico.

Teotihuacán declined about A.D. 750. Historians still are uncertain about the reasons for its decline. Drought may have been the cause, or invasion by **the Toltec**, a people from the north.

With a powerful army, the Toltec conquered land as far south as the Yucatán Peninsula. The Toltec capital of **Tula** was the center of a powerful mining and trading empire. Their gods Quetzalcoatl (ket•suhl•KWAH•tuhl), the "plumed serpent" god of the air, and Tezcatlipoca (tehz•KAHT•lee•POH•kuh), the god of war, would be adopted by the Aztec, a later Mesoamerican group. When invaders destroyed Tula in A.D. 1170, the Toltec Empire collapsed.

SECTION 2 REVIEW

Recall
1. **Define** jaguar, slash-and-burn farming, obsidian.
2. **Identify** the Olmec, the Maya, the Teotihuacános, the Toltec, Quetzalcoatl.
3. **Use** the map on page 390 to locate the area settled by the Maya. What large city did the Maya establish? On what landform was it located?

Critical Thinking
4. **Synthesizing Information** What common features linked the Mesoamerican civilizations?

Understanding Themes
5. **Innovation** What were some of the major achievements of the Mesoamerican civilizations?

The Maya

Some 2,000 years ago, the lowland Mayan civilization of what is now Central America flourished. A society dating to 1200 B.C., the Maya developed the most complex writing system in the Americas, built majestic temple-pyramids and palaces, and mastered astronomy and mathematics. Then suddenly, in the A.D. 800s, the record of life in the region fell silent: The people stopped erecting monuments, carving hieroglyphic texts, and making pottery. Their cities lay in ruins, their fields and villages were abandoned to the jungle, and the great civilization of the Maya vanished.

What happened to end the golden age of the Maya more than a thousand years ago? To answer that question, in 1989 an international team of archaeologists, sponsored in part by the National Geographic Society and Vanderbilt University, went to the Petexbatún rain forest of northern Guatemala. Amid the ruins of the ancient city of Dos Pilas, the team set to work on one of archaeology's greatest mysteries.

Enrico Ferorelli

Enrico Ferorelli

NGS Cartographic Division

After setting up a fully functioning camp complete with a computer lab and drafting workstations, scientists began their task. They studied thousands of potsherds, scores of monuments, bone fragments, spearheads, trash heaps, and miles of fortifications of Dos Pilas—built by renegades from the great Mayan center of Tikal—and nearby cities.

One spectacular find that told the fate of the Maya was a hieroglyphic stairway. Five limestone steps, about 20 feet wide, each with two rows of glyphs carved on the risers, climb to the base of the royal palace near the main plaza at Dos Pilas. Experts at deciphering glyphs were on hand to translate each glyph as it was uncovered. The story on the steps gives an account of the battles of the first ruler of the Petexbatún (referred to as Ruler 1) against his brother at Tikal, some 65 miles northeast of Dos Pilas.

One of the epigraphists summed up the inscription: "It begins by talking about the 60th birthday of

A Mayan warrior-king is portrayed on a stela carved in A.D. 731. Discoveries at Dos Pilas have led to new theories on the collapse of the Mayan civilization along the border of Guatemala and Mexico.

A stairway of five long steps (top) came to light during excavations at the Dos Pilas site.

Enrico Ferorelli

  As Vanderbilt graduate student Stacy Symonds excavated a defensive wall, she discovered the hieroglyphic stairway beneath it. Here she records information about the glyphs.

Ruler 1, that he danced a ritual dance. As you read down the steps, the glyphs give a historical sequence to his reign. We think Ruler 1 left Tikal and started a splinter kingdom at Dos Pilas. There's an emblem glyph—which is like a political title —for Tikal, and both brothers claimed it. Ruler 1 was defeated, but then there was another war. This time Dos Pilas won."

Although the glyphs told archaeologists about the origin of a dynasty, what was even more intriguing was a stone wall built on top of the stairs during the kingdom's fall. Less than a hundred years after memorializing their founder, the people of Dos Pilas threw a wall up over his monument in what must have been a desperate attempt to protect themselves. Why did the people of Dos Pilas build defensive walls, which are rarely found at Mayan sites?

The second and third rulers of Dos Pilas changed traditional warfare when they set forth on campaigns of expansion. Digging a 30-foot shaft into the burial temple of Ruler 2, archaeologists discovered hieroglyphs on fine pottery that offered more clues. These glyphs suggest that Ruler 2, who reigned from A.D. 698 to A.D. 726, expanded the influence of Dos Pilas and gained control of other cities through marriage and political alliances.

Ruler 3 went on to wed a royal lady from the city of Cancuén and to dominate the entire region. He traveled to the cities of Tamarindito, Aguateca, Seibal, and others to perform ceremonies and quell unrest. After Ruler 3 died in A.D. 741, Ruler 4 took control, living mostly at Aguateca—by then a twin capital— which rests on a limestone bluff high above Lake Petexbatún.

In A.D. 761 something went wrong. According to hieroglyphs, the kings of the Petexbatún had overextended their domain. There had been hints of trouble for more than a decade: Ruler 4 had spent much of his 20-year reign racing from one end of the realm to the other, performing bloodletting rituals, leading battles, and contracting alliances. He used every technique to sustain the kingdom, but to no avail.

Then the city of Tamarindito threw off the yoke of Dos Pilas. Hieroglyphs at Tamarindito tell us that its warriors attacked the capital and killed Ruler 4.

About that time the citizens of Dos Pilas made a valiant last stand. In desperation they ripped stones from temples and monuments, including the tomb of Ruler 2 and the hieroglyphic stairway. They tore down much of the royal palace to build two walls around the central palaces and temples.

The surviving nobles deserted their citizens and fled to Aguateca, proclaiming themselves the new rulers of the kingdom. They chose Aguateca as its final capital because of its defensive location. The people of Aguateca held out for about 50 years, but disappeared in the early A.D. 800s

❧

IN A SPAN of only a few hundred years the kingdom rose, expanded, and collapsed as a succession of kings moved from limited conflict to widespread warfare. Scholars have argued that the Mayan civilization simply outgrew its environment, exhausting the soil and creating environmental and economic stress. But another possibility is that intensive warfare forced the Maya, at least in the Petexbatún area, to move close to fortresses such as Aguateca, where they would have soon run out of fertile land. Perhaps farmers were limited to fortified areas near cities that could provide protection, forcing them to forsake traditional agricultural practices that had sustained them for hundreds of years. The wars must have disrupted trade, upset population distribution, destroyed crops, and killed young farmer-warriors, exacting a huge price.

Scholars have added greatly to our view of Mayan society. Once regarded as a network of ceremonial centers ruled by peaceful priest-kings, Mayan civilization is no longer seen that way. Battle and human sacrifice were aspects of life. Perhaps siege warfare was ultimately too costly for the Maya. For years to come, scientists will study the ruins in the Petexbatún rain forest researching changes that may have contributed to the collapse of the lowland Mayan civilization.

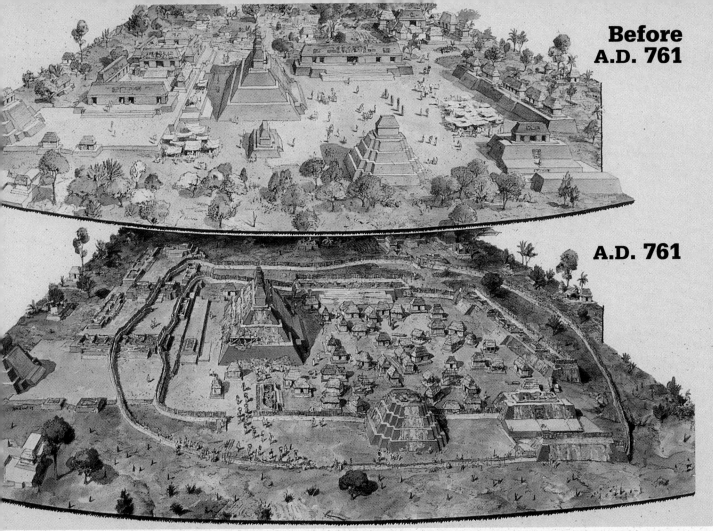

Enrico Ferorelli

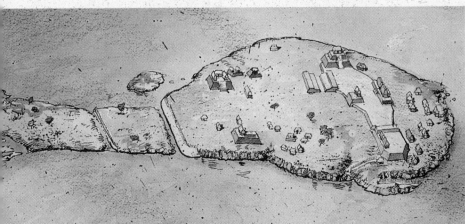

Enrico Ferorelli

◈ *In proper Mayan style Dos Pilas's ceremonial precinct (above, top) featured palaces for rulers and temples to the gods. But an apparent golden age came to an abrupt end in A.D. 761 (above, bottom). After the killing of Ruler 4, warfare consumed the region. Residents tore down facades of temples and palaces to raise two walls. A cleared area between the walls likely served as a killing alley. Seeking refuge, farmers moved into the plaza and erected huts. Soon the city was abandoned.*

◈ *A peninsula became an island (left, top and bottom) as defenders of the Lake Petexbatún port dug three moats across the neck of land. At the tip of the island, a walled wharf protected a canoe landing. Perhaps the enemy proved too strong or conditions too harsh, for the outpost was abandoned.*

Chapter 15 *The Americas* 387

A.D. 1300   A.D. 1400   A.D. 1500

A.D. 1325 The Aztec found their capital, Tenochtitlán.

A.D. 1438 The Inca emperor Pachacuti comes to power.

c. A.D. 1500 The Aztec control all of central and southern Mexico.

Section 3

The Aztec and Inca Empires

Setting the Scene

▶ **Terms to Define**
chinampas, hierarchy, quinoa

▶ **People to Meet**
the Aztec, the Inca, the Moche, Pachacuti

▶ **Places to Locate**
Tenochtitlán, Cuzco

Find Out   What factors led to the rise and decline of the Aztec and the Inca Empires?

The Storyteller

Cortés captured many Aztec cities. This Aztec song remembers how it was:
"Broken spears lie in the roads;
we have torn our hair in our grief.
The houses are roofless now, and their walls
are red with blood....
We have pounded our hands in despair against
the adobe walls, for our inheritance, our
city, is lost and dead.
The shields of our warriors
were its defense, but they
could not save it.
We have chewed dry twigs
and salt grasses;
We have filled our mouths
with dust and bits of
adobe; we have eaten
lizards, rats and
worms...."

—from *Sources of World History,* edited by Mark A. Kishlansky, 1995

Aztec Stone of the Sun calendar

Like other Native American groups, **the Aztec** of Mexico and Central America and **the Inca** of South America lacked metal tools, large work animals, and a practical use of the wheel. Yet they were able to develop centralized governments, raise armies and conquer empires. Both civilizations, however, came to sudden ends in the early A.D. 1500s, when they were overwhelmed and destroyed by Spanish invaders from Europe.

The Aztec Empire

The early Aztec were hunters and warriors who moved from the north into central Mexico during the A.D. 1200s. In A.D. 1325 they founded a city in central Mexico named **Tenochtitlán** (tay•NAWCH•teet•LAHN), today the site of Mexico City. According to Aztec legend, Aztec priests told their people to settle in the area where they would find an eagle sitting on a cactus and holding a snake in its beak. After much wandering, the Aztecs finally saw on an island in Lake Texcoco what the priests had described. There, they established Tenochtitlán.

Tenochtitlán

The Aztec turned Tenochtitlán into an agricultural center and marketplace. Since land for farming was scarce on the island, they built *chinampas,* or artificial islands, by piling mud from the bottom of the lake onto rafts secured by stakes. These became floating gardens where farmers grew a variety of crops, including corn and beans. With a plentiful food supply, the population grew and people moved outside the city to the mainland. A network of canals, bridges, and causeways was built to connect the mainland with the capital city.

Empire

Strengthened by early alliances with neighboring city-states, the Aztec then conquered more distant rivals. By A.D. 1500 their empire stretched from north-central Mexico to the border of Guatemala, and from the Atlantic Ocean to the Pacific Ocean. Conquered peoples had to pay heavy tribute in the form of food, clothing, raw materials, and prisoners for sacrifice.

As the Aztec Empire expanded, Tenochtitlán prospered. Estimates of the city's population by A.D. 1500 range from 120,000 to 200,000. Goods and tribute came to the city from all parts of the empire.

Government and Society

The Aztec civilization was organized as a hierarchy—divided into levels of authority, each level more powerful than the level below it. At the top was the emperor. His power came from his control of the army and was reinforced by religious beliefs.

The Aztec social order had four classes: nobility, commoners, serfs, and slaves. Land could be owned by noble families and commoners. Commoners included priests, merchants, artisans, and farmers. Serfs were farmworkers tied to noble lands. The lowest class included criminals and debtors, as well as female and children prisoners of war. Male prisoners of war were sacrificed to the Aztec gods.

Religion and the Arts

Religion motivated the Aztecs to engage in war and sacrifice. Borrowing ideas from the Maya and the Toltec, the Aztecs believed that live human sacrifices were needed to keep the gods pleased and to prevent drought, floods and other natural disasters. The chief deity was the sun god Huitzilopochtli (wee•tsee•loh•POHKT•lee), whose giant pyramid-temple arose in the center of Tenochtitlán.

Priests used a 360-day religious calendar to determine appropriate days for activities, such as planting crops or going to war. The Aztec also had a 365-day solar calendar that consisted of 18 months of 20 days plus 5 extra days. One of the most famous surviving pieces of Aztec sculpture is a large, circular calendar stone that represents the Aztec universe, with carvings that stand for the days of the Aztec month.

Aztec artists decorated temple-pyramids with scenes of deities or battles. Writers glorified Aztec victories in their works. The empire, however, proved to be fragile. Revolts in outlying areas weakened Aztec control. In A.D. 1521 the rebels joined the Spaniards in destroying the Aztec heritage.

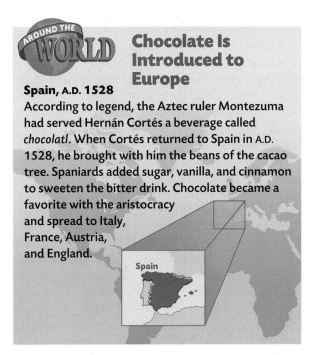

AROUND THE WORLD
Chocolate Is Introduced to Europe

Spain, A.D. 1528
According to legend, the Aztec ruler Montezuma had served Hernán Cortés a beverage called *chocolatl*. When Cortés returned to Spain in A.D. 1528, he brought with him the beans of the cacao tree. Spaniards added sugar, vanilla, and cinnamon to sweeten the bitter drink. Chocolate became a favorite with the aristocracy and spread to Italy, France, Austria, and England.

Spain

The Inca Empire

Other Native American civilizations arose in western South America. One of the earliest was **the Moche**, who lived on the north coast of present-day Peru between A.D. 100 and A.D. 600. In A.D. 1987 archaeologists discovered a noble's tomb that revealed the Moche had a social order based on ranks, skilled artisans who made metal ornaments, and rituals that included sacrifices.

Rise of the Inca

The Inca began as one of many small tribes competing for scarce fertile land in the valleys of the Andes mountain ranges. Around A.D. 1200 the Inca settled in **Cuzco** (KOOS•koh), which became their capital. They raided other tribes and slowly established a powerful empire.

The decisive period of Inca expansion began in A.D. 1438, when **Pachacuti**, the ninth Inca ruler, came to power. He and his son, Topa Inca Yupanqui, have been compared to Philip and Alexander the Great of Macedonia. By persuasion, threats, and force, they extended Inca boundaries far to the north and south.

The Inca Empire eventually included all of present-day Peru, much of Chile, and parts of Ecuador, Bolivia, and Argentina. It stretched more than 2,500 miles (4,020 km) through coastal deserts, dry highlands, fertile river valleys, and rain forests. Most of the Inca lived in the Andes highlands and adjusted to high altitudes. Cuzco was 11,600 feet (3,560 m) above sea level.

Government and Society

Pachacuti created a strong central government to control the vast realm. He permitted local rulers to continue governing conquered territories as long as they were loyal. Rebellious peoples were resettled elsewhere where they could pose less of a threat. Pachacuti instituted a complex system of tribute collections, courts, military posts, trade inspections, and local work regulations to bind outlying territories to the center. To further unite the diverse peoples, the Inca established a common imperial language—Quechua (KEH•chuh•wuh).

The Inca emperor and his officials closely regulated the lives of the common people. As a divine ruler, the emperor owned all land and carefully regulated the growing and distribution of foods, such as potatoes and quinoa (keen•wah), a protein-rich grain. To make good use of the limited arable land, Inca farmers cut step terraces into hillsides and built irrigation systems in the dry coastal plain. After harvest, part of their crops went to the government as taxes. Under the emperor's direction, work crews built roads and woven fiber suspension bridges that linked the regions of the empire.

The Inca believed in many deities, including the creator god Viracocha and the sun god Inti. Priests offered food, animals, and sometimes humans as sacrifices to please the deities. In A.D. 1995 archaeologists discovered in the Andes the frozen, preserved body of a teenage Inca girl. Food and pottery remains seemed to indicate that she was a sacrificial victim. Priests also served as doctors, using herbs to treat illnesses and performing an early form of brain surgery.

Instead of developing a writing system, the Inca kept records by using *quipu*, a rope with knotted cords of different lengths and colors. Each knot represented a different item or number. They also observed the heavens to predict seasonal changes. They were able to perform certain mathematical calculations that they used to design their buildings and roads.

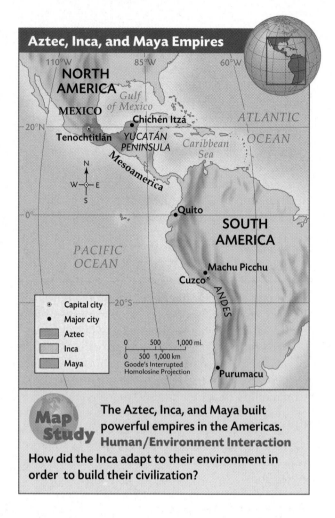

Aztec, Inca, and Maya Empires

Legend:
- ⊙ Capital city
- • Major city
- Aztec
- Inca
- Maya

0   500   1,000 mi.
0   500 1,000 km
Goode's Interrupted
Homolosine Projection

Map Study The Aztec, Inca, and Maya built powerful empires in the Americas.
Human/Environment Interaction
How did the Inca adapt to their environment in order to build their civilization?

Inca Decline

The obedient, well-disciplined Inca would prove to be no match for the Spanish conquerors who arrived in South America in A.D. 1531. In spite of fierce resistance, the Inca Empire declined and eventually disappeared. Spanish forces slew those Inca who threatened their authority—an action that would be repeated in many parts of the Americas. Aspects of Inca culture, however, have survived among the Inca descendants living today in western areas of South America.

SECTION 3 REVIEW

Recall

1. **Define** *chinampas*, hierarchy, quinoa.
2. **Identify** the Aztec, the Inca, the Moche, Pachacuti.
3. **Use** the maps in the Atlas to describe the physical geography of Mexico and western South America. How did geography affect the early civilizations that arose in each of these two areas?

Critical Thinking

4. **Synthesizing Information** What do modern nations take as tribute after a war? How is this the same as or different from the tribute paid by Aztec people?

Understanding Themes

5. **Change** Contrast the methods used by the Aztec and the Inca to expand and administer their vast empires.

Analyzing Primary and Secondary Sources

You see a television interview with an eyewitness to a tornado. Later you read a newspaper account. Is one account more accurate than the other?

Learning the Skill

To determine the accuracy of an account, you must analyze its source. There are two main kinds of sources—primary and secondary. Primary sources are accounts or artifacts produced by eyewitnesses to events. Diaries, letters, autobiographies, interviews, artifacts, and paintings are primary sources. Secondary sources use information gathered from others. Textbooks and biographies are secondary sources. Because primary sources convey personal experiences, they often communicate the emotions and opinions of participants in an event. Secondary sources, written at a later time, often help us to understand events in a larger context.

Determine the reliability of the source. For a primary source, find out who wrote it and when. An account written during or immediately after an event is more reliable than one written years later. For a secondary source, look for good documentation. In a reliable account, researchers cite their sources of information in footnotes and bibliographies.

For both types of sources evaluate the author. Is this author biased? What background and authority does he or she have? Finally, compare two accounts of the same event. If they disagree, you should question their reliability.

Practicing the Skill

Read the sources and answer the questions.

“Finally the two groups met...When all was ready Moctezuma placed his feet, shod in gold-soled, gem-studded sandals, on the carpeted pavement and... advanced to an encounter that would shape both his own destiny and that of his nation....Moctezuma had servants bring forward two necklaces of red shells hung with life-size shrimps made of gold. These he placed around Cortés's neck.”
—from *Cortés* by William Weber Johnson, 1975

“When we had arrived at a place not far from the town, where several small towers rose together, the monarch raised himself in his sedan...Montezuma himself, according to his custom, was sumptuously attired, had on a species of half boot, richly set with jewels, and whose soles were made of solid gold....Montezuma came up to Cortés, and taking him by the hand, conducted him himself into the apartments where he was to lodge, which had been beautifully decorated...He then hung about his neck a chaste necklace of gold, most curiously worked with figures all representing crabs.”
—from an account by Conquistador Bernal Díaz del Castillo, 1519

1. What is the general topic of the two sources?
2. Which is a primary source and which is a secondary source? How can you tell?
3. Though each quote deals with the same topic, what is a different technique each uses to approach that topic?

Applying the Skill

Find two accounts of a recent event or a historical event. Analyze the reliability of each. When were the accounts written? Is the author qualified to write on this topic? Is the account well-documented? Do the two accounts agree?

For More Practice

Turn to the Skill Practice in the Chapter Review on page 393.

Connections Across Time

Historical Significance Throughout the early history of the Americas, Native Americans established a variety of cultures and civilizations. The environment gave these peoples spiritual strength and economic support. Regarding the earth as sacred, they used the land's natural resources to develop agriculture, build ceremonial centers, and advance trade. Several Native American groups in Mesoamerica and South America formed vast empires that linked diverse peoples and spread new ideas and products.

The cultural aspects of these empires are still held by Native Americans living today in Mexico, Central America, and South America. In recent years, Native Americans in North America have reclaimed much of their heritage that had been suppressed with the advance of European civilization in the Americas.

Using Key Terms

Write the key term that completes each sentence. Then write a sentence for each term not chosen.

a. *chinampas*   f. maize
b. weirs   g. obsidian
c. quinoa   h. potlatches
d. confederation   i. hierarchy
e. jaguar   j. slash-and-burn farming

1. Around A.D. 1500 the Cayuga, Mohawk, Oneida, Onondaga, and Seneca formed a _____, or loose union.
2. Because of the scarcity of land to farm, the Aztec devised a way of making _____, or artificial islands.
3. Among Native Americans of the Pacific Northwest, the wealth of each lineage group was given away at _____.
4. The early Olmec practiced a form of agriculture known as _____.
5. By about 5000 B.C., hunter-gatherers in the highland area of present-day Mexico had discovered that the seeds of _____ could be planted.

Technology Activity

Using the Internet Access the Internet to locate a Web site about the Inca Empire. Use a search engine to help focus your search by using phrases such as *inca empire, mesoamerican civilizations,* or *native americans.* Create a bulletin board using the information found, and incorporate illustrations of Inca culture and artifacts.

Using Your History Journal

Parallel to your time line of important dates in Native American civilizations, add a time line of significant civilizations and achievements in Africa, Asia, and Europe. Use dates from the Unit 3 Digest on pages 395–397.

Reviewing Facts

1. **Geography** Explain how the food resources of Native Americans along the California coast differed from those of Native Americans living in the Great Basin.
2. **Geography** Discuss how the people of southwestern North America adapted to the desert.
3. **Culture** Identify the purposes of the mounds left by the Mound Builders.
4. **History** Name the two principal sites where excavations have revealed an ancient Olmec culture.
5. **Culture** Describe the four books that have survived from the Mayan civilization.
6. **History** Identify the events in the early A.D. 1500s that were responsible for the sudden end to the Inca and the Aztec civilizations.
7. **Science/Technology** Explain how mathematical, technical, and scientific innovations affected Native Americans.
8. **Geography** State what was unique about the location of the Aztec city of Tenochtitlán.
9. **Citizenship** Discuss the ways in which the Inca served their emperor and the empire.

Critical Thinking

1. **Analyze** How did the rise and decline of the Aztec and Inca Empires differ?
2. **Analyze** High in the Andes mountain ranges, the city of Machu Picchu was the last refuge of the Inca. Why did Inca rulers retreat to a city in such a remote location?

Ruins of Machu Picchu

Understanding Themes

1. **Relation to the Environment** How did Native Americans in the Eastern Woodlands differ from the Native Americans of the Great Plains? How were they similar?
2. **Innovation** What were some of the cultural achievements of the Mayan civilization?
3. **Change** How did Spaniards affect the Aztec and Inca civilizations?

Linking Past and Present

1. What impact do Native American traditions have on life in the Americas today? In what ways has modern civilization been affected by the early Native Americans?
2. Religion played an important role in early American and other ancient civilizations. What role does religion have in modern societies?

Skill Practice

Read the following excerpt and answer the questions.

❝ The things the Incas built were copied from the older civilizations that they conquered. In their cities, fortresses, roads, terraces, temples, they did only what had been done before by the people around them, but a great deal more of it. The ornamentation, the woven fabrics, the work in gold they pursued so avidly as a symbol of the Sun, all were adopted by their predecessors. ❞

— From *The Last Americans: The Indian in American Culture* by the American historian, William Brandon, 1974

1. What is the topic of the source?
2. Is this a primary or a secondary source? Explain your answer.
3. What authority does the author have?

Geography in History

1. **Movement** Refer to the map below. In the A.D. 1500s and A.D. 1600s Native American civilizations declined as the whole region came under the rule of powerful European nation-states. The triangular trade linked four continents between A.D. 1600 and A.D. 1760. How did trade change the population of the Caribbean Islands?
2. **Human/Environment Interaction** How did farming change when crops such as sugarcane began to be raised for trade?
3. **Movement** What positive and negative changes resulted from the cultural contact of peoples from four different continents?

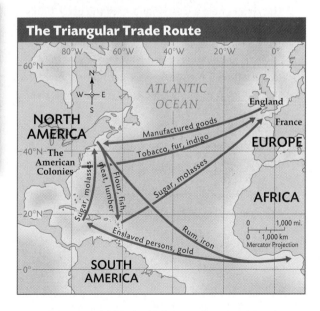

The Triangular Trade Route

Turning Points in World History

The Crusades

Setting up the Video

Work with a group of your classmates to view "The Crusades" on the videodisc *Turning Points in World History*. The Crusades left lasting effects on the economic and political development of western Europe. Improvements abounded in the areas of new knowledge, trade, and technology. This program introduces the Crusades and the changes that occurred in European culture, art, and architecture.

Hands-On Activity

Create an oral history by interviewing a person about his or her experiences during a modern-day "crusade" (such as the civil rights or women's rights movements) that has left a lasting effect on our society. Create questions to ask this individual during a recorded interview. Share the results of your interview with the class.

Side One, Chapter 7

View the video by scanning the bar code or by entering the chapter number on your keypad and pressing Search. (Also available in VHS format.)

Surfing the "Net"

The Aztecs

The Aztecs held a vast empire until the early 1500s, when they were ultimately defeated by Spanish invaders from Europe. Their civilization was very advanced in areas such as building, agriculture and the creation of a highly centralized government. To learn more about the Aztecs, access the Internet.

Getting There

1. Go to a search engine. Type in the phrase *aztec culture*.
2. After typing in the phrase, enter words such as those below to focus your search:
   - *government*
   - *religion*
   - *innovations*
   - *contributions*

3. The search engine should provide you with a number of links to follow. Links are "pointers" to different sites on the Internet and commonly appear as blue underlined words.

What to Do When You Are There

Click on the links to navigate through the pages of information and gather your findings. Create a fact sheet of information about all aspects of Aztec culture. Include information such as type of government, agriculture, religion, and innovations. Include an accompanying map showing the Aztec Empire sphere of influence.

Unit 3 Digest

A Turkish pulpit tile from the A.D. 1600s depicts the plan of the Kaaba at Makkah. *What is the fifth pillar of Islam?*

The period from A.D. 500 to A.D. 1500 was one of growth in many areas of the world. Expanded trade routes and missionaries' journeys spread intellectual, cultural, and religious beliefs from one people to another. Such contact between cultures caused conflict that lasted for decades, even centuries; yet at other times, ideas and ideals were peacefully adopted.

Chapter 10
Byzantines and Slavs

After the Roman Empire split in A.D. 395, the eastern half—at the crossroads of trade linking Europe, Asia, and Africa—developed into the Byzantine Empire. Primarily Greek, but populated by a diversity of peoples, the Byzantine Empire blended Greek and Roman thought, Christian belief, and cultural influences from Persia and other areas of the Middle East. The Byzantines continued the Roman tradition of rule by emperors and practiced their own form of Christianity. In A.D. 1054 most of Christianity split into two separate bodies: the Roman Catholic Church in western Europe and the Eastern Orthodox Church in the Byzantine Empire. This religious division heightened hostility between the Byzantines and the Christian kingdoms that had emerged in western Europe after the fall of the western Roman Empire. Throughout their history, the Byzantines held out against a series of invaders, including Persians, Arabs, and western European Christian Crusaders. In A.D. 1453 the Byzantine Empire finally came to an end when its capital, Constantinople, fell to the Ottoman Turks.

Byzantine culture, however, had a lasting effect on neighboring peoples, especially the Slavs of eastern Europe. Byzantine missionaries had converted many of the Slavic peoples to Christianity. Kiev, a Slavic fortress-town on the Dnieper River in present-day Ukraine, traded with Constantinople and became the first major center of Eastern Slavic civilization. Although Kiev declined after the A.D. 1200s, its cultural achievements became the foundation of the civilizations of Ukraine, Belarus, and Russia. The Russian city of Moscow became a leading center of Eastern Orthodox Christianity after the fall of Constantinople.

Chapter 11
Islamic Civilization

While the Byzantines were building a Christian empire in the Mediterranean world, the Arabs of the Arabian Peninsula were spreading the religion of Islam. In A.D. 610 Muhammad, a merchant in the city of Makkah (Mecca), preached a message he claimed came from Allah (the Arabic name for God). Muhammad called for devotion to one God and for moral reform. From his revelations came the Quran, the holy book of Islam, and the Five Pillars: faith, prayer, almsgiving, fasting, and pilgrimage to Makkah.

Initially suffering persecution, Muhammad and other Muslims, or followers of Islam, finally created an Islamic state that placed divine law above local, tribal laws. After Muhammad's death, Islam divided into two separate groups, the Sunnis and the Shiites. However, the caliphs, or successors of Muhammad, spread Islam through a series of military victories over the Byzantine and Persian Empires. The Umayyad caliphs (A.D. 661-750) carried Islam eastward to India and China, as well as to North Africa and parts of southern Europe. They based their rule in Syria and created an Islamic empire that embraced many different peoples. Later, in the A.D. 800s, the Abbasid caliphs shifted the empire's center of power eastward to Iraq, where they set up Baghdad as the capital.

During the period of the Islamic empire, Muslim scholars preserved Greek philosophy and made advances in mathematics, astronomy, geometry, and medicine. Muslim artists, architects, and writers also made many contributions. In later centuries, western Europe, Africa, and parts of Asia would benefit from Islamic scientific and cultural achievements.

Chapter 12
The Rise of Medieval Europe

Historians today label the period from A.D. 500 to A.D. 1500 in western Europe as the Middle Ages, an age of transition between ancient and modern times. Compared with the Byzantine and Islamic societies of this period, western European culture was relatively backward. However, during the Middle Ages, Christianity, the Greek and Roman heritage, and the culture of Germanic invaders combined to create a new western European civilization.

Charlemagne, a Germanic king, became Holy Roman emperor in A.D. 800 and united western Europe for the first time since the fall of Rome. He also strengthened ties between his throne and the pope, the leading western European Christian leader based in Rome.

During the Middle Ages, the Roman Catholic Church exercised strong religious and political influence over western Europe. Devoutly religious men and women lived apart from society in communities known as monasteries. By preserving religious writings, establishing schools, and providing models of Christian living, they helped spread and strengthen Christianity in western Europe.

After Charlemagne's death, his empire divided, and western Europe entered a period of internal strife and external invasions. Feudalism, a new type of social organization, emerged to provide order and protection. It joined loyalty between higher and lesser nobles to ownership of land and military service. With the decline of central government and trade, estates owned by individual feudal nobles provided for most local needs. Most Europeans, however, were not warriors, but peasant farmers bound to the nobles' lands on which they worked.

European kings at this time were generally weak rulers, but they gradually created government bureaucracies and laid the foundations of Europe's modern nation-states. This strengthening of monarchy was especially advanced in England and France. In England, however, Parliament, an assembly that advised the king, placed limits on royal power and played a key role in passing laws. Meanwhile, the

Holy Roman Empire based in Germany saw its monarchy weakened by conflict between its emperors and various popes.

Chapter 13
Medieval Europe at Its Height

In the late A.D. 1000s, the Christians of western Europe began the first of a series of Crusades, or military expeditions, to win Palestine from Muslim rulers. The goal of making "the Holy Land" Christian did not succeed in the long run, but the Crusades did open Europe to Islamic and other ways of life and stimulated trade between European and Islamic peoples.

Around A.D. 1000, improvements in farming increased food production, and Europe's economy began to revive. As trade and the use of money expanded, towns grew up along trade routes. A new wealthy middle class emerged that sought political power and challenged the feudal system. Increased prosperity influenced the growth of art, literature, and learning based in universities.

During the A.D. 1300s and 1400s, French and English monarchs fought each other for control of French territory. Although England was eventually driven out of France, the conflict strengthened loyalty to royal authority in both countries. Meanwhile, Christian monarchs in Spain reconquered Muslim-ruled Spanish areas, and the Holy Roman emperor in Germany struggled for power with the pope. The increasing wealth of the clergy and the involvement of popes in political affairs damaged the Church's prestige.

Chapter 14
East and South Asia

Between A.D. 1000 and A.D. 1400, a series of steppe peoples from central Asia conquered vast areas of territory in Europe and Asia. The most important of these peoples were the Mongols, who ruled the world's largest land empire stretching from eastern Europe to China. Internal weaknesses, however, led to the breakup of the Mongol Empire into smaller units.

In China, the Tang dynasty, which ruled from A.D. 618 to A.D. 907, expanded Chinese borders and created a stable government. Trade with Japan and India increased, as well as overland trade to the Middle East along the Silk Road. The Tang capital,

Visualizing History This illuminated manuscript depicts Charlemagne's coronation as emperor in A.D. 800. *How did Charlemagne affect the history of medieval Europe?*

Changan, became the largest city in the world. Later weakened by rebellion and invasion, the Tang dynasty declined.

The Song dynasty then came to power, and with it a golden age of achievement in the arts, literature, science, and technology. Confucianism continued to exert an influence on the culture, resulting in social reforms. Great strides were made in economic growth, as well as science and technology, before China fell to the Mongols about A.D. 1270.

The Mongols became the first conquerors to control most of the country. They established a dynasty in China and enforced their peace. Under Mongol rule, China's trade increased with Europe, the Middle East, and Russia. By A.D. 1300, however, Mongol society in China had declined.

Meanwhile China's influence had extended to Korea and Japan and to parts of Southeast Asia. The Koreans were influenced by Chinese religion, government, and science. Japan, isolated from mainland Asia because of its island geography, had developed traditions different from those of other Asian countries. Yet, it too adopted certain Chinese ideas and practices. The Japanese later developed a feudal society of warrior landowners. Trade, however, increased and towns were established.

Chapter 15
The Americas

The earliest inhabitants on the North American continent came from Asia by way of the Beringia land bridge. They eventually settled as far as the southern tip of South America. As in other parts of the world, geography and climate influenced their ways of life.

A variety of Native American groups flourished in North America. Native Americans in the northeastern part of the continent had a high level of political organization. By the late A.D. 1500s, several groups had formed the Iroquois League to maintain peace among the Iroquois. The Iroquois League's representative structure provided a flexible but stable system of government.

Powerful Native American empires emerged in the Americas, especially the Maya and Aztec in Mexico and Central America, and the Inca in South America. They built large ceremonial centers that included temple-pyramids, marketplaces, and palaces. Religion played a large role in daily life and in public ceremonies. These civilizations also developed an understanding of science, mathematics, and engineering.

SURVEYING UNIT 3

1. **Chapter 10** What cultural influences shaped the development of the Byzantine Empire?
2. **Chapter 11** How did Islamic civilization benefit western Europe, Africa, and parts of Asia?
3. **Chapter 12** Why did feudalism develop in western Europe during the Middle Ages?
4. **Chapter 13** How did Europe's economy change during the Middle Ages?
5. **Chapter 14** What areas of Asia were influenced by the spread of Chinese civilization?
6. **Chapter 15** What were the major achievements of the Native American empires?

Unit
4
1400–1800

Emergence of the Modern World

Then & Now

The Renaissance and Reformation changed European culture and created powerful political alliances. Europeans set out on uncharted seas to explore the world as powerful European monarchs competed for trade, influence, and territory. While the peoples of the Americas struggled against European invaders, civilizations in Asia reached pinnacles of cultural achievement.

Every time you use paper money or write a check, you are trusting in a system based on banking that originated during this period. As European trade and commerce increased, merchants turned to bankers for the capital to finance their ventures. Wealthy banking families even made loans to European monarchs. By the 1600s government-chartered banks began to replace family-owned banks. These banks issued banknotes and checks that made trading in heavy coins obsolete.

A Global Chronology

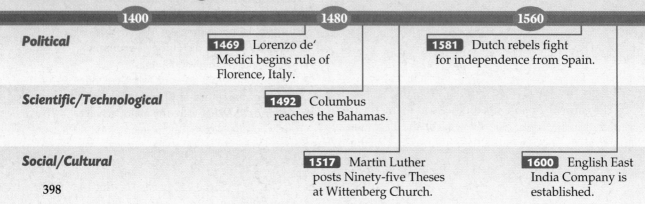

	1400	1480	1560
Political		**1469** Lorenzo de' Medici begins rule of Florence, Italy.	**1581** Dutch rebels fight for independence from Spain.
Scientific/Technological		**1492** Columbus reaches the Bahamas.	
Social/Cultural		**1517** Martin Luther posts Ninety-five Theses at Wittenberg Church.	**1600** English East India Company is established.

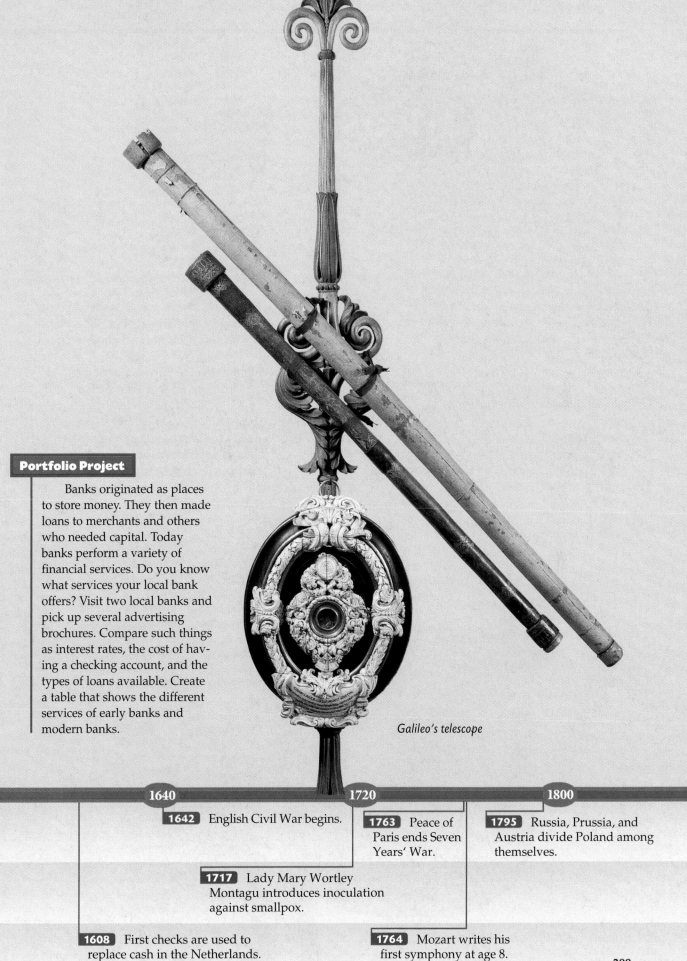

Galileo's telescope

Portfolio Project

Banks originated as places to store money. They then made loans to merchants and others who needed capital. Today banks perform a variety of financial services. Do you know what services your local bank offers? Visit two local banks and pick up several advertising brochures. Compare such things as interest rates, the cost of having a checking account, and the types of loans available. Create a table that shows the different services of early banks and modern banks.

1640

1642 English Civil War begins.

1717 Lady Mary Wortley Montagu introduces inoculation against smallpox.

1608 First checks are used to replace cash in the Netherlands.

1720

1763 Peace of Paris ends Seven Years' War.

1764 Mozart writes his first symphony at age 8.

1800

1795 Russia, Prussia, and Austria divide Poland among themselves.

399

The Spread of Ideas

Music

In the 1400s and 1500s, European ships edged into uncharted waters. These voyages set the stage for one of the greatest cultural exchanges in history, as people from Europe, Africa, and the Americas came face-to-face for the first time. One of the products of this exchange was the birth of "America music," a collection of styles deeply rooted in West Africa.

West Africa
Traditional Rhythms

"We are almost a nation of dancers, musicians, and poets," recalled a West African named Olaudah Equiano. "Every great event ... is celebrated ... with songs and music suited to the occasion."

Equiano's words highlighted the importance of music to everyday life among the varied peoples of West Africa. Here musicians won fame for the skill with which they played complicated rhythms on drums, flutes, whistles, and stringed instruments. People added the sounds of their voices to a rhythm known as a call-and-response pattern. A leader would sing out a short piece of music, and people would sing it back to the beat of a drum.

African-style drum

North America
New Musical Forms

The musical heritage of West Africa traveled to the Americas aboard European slave ships. To endure the pains of slavery, West Africans kept alive musical patterns that reminded them of their ancestral homelands. Because most West Africans came as laborers, work songs took root first. The rhythmic patterns of these songs set the pace for repetitive tasks. West African laborers added field hollers—long calls by a worker in which other workers answered back. Outside the fields, enslaved Africans cried out for freedom in religious folk songs known as spirituals.

Over hundreds of years, these musical forms came together to create new styles. The blues grew out of the field songs and spirituals of slavery. Ragtime echoed the complicated rhythms of West African music. On these foundations grew yet other styles—jazz, rock 'n' roll, and rap.

Steel drums of the Caribbean

The Caribbean
Afro-Caribbean Beats

The sounds of West Africa could be heard wherever large enslaved African populations lived in the Americas. On islands in the Caribbean, the beat of bongos, the conga, the tambour, and other West African drums became the soul of Afro-Caribbean music. Added to the drums were European instruments such as the Spanish guitar and a variety of Native American instruments such as the marimba (xylophone), maraca, and wooden rhythm sticks called claves. Out of this blend of influences emerged a range of styles as diverse as the Caribbean islands themselves—reggae, calypso, salsa, and more.

Chicago 1955 by Ben Shahn

LINKING THE IDEAS

1. What are some of the features of West African music?
2. How did West African music influence musical styles in North America and the Caribbean?

Critical Thinking

3. **Evaluating Information** Which styles of music that you listen to at least once a week are influenced by West African musical patterns?

Renaissance and Reformation

Chapter Themes

- ▶ **Innovation** The Renaissance leads to an artistic and intellectual awakening in Europe. *Section 1*
- ▶ **Cultural Diffusion** Renaissance ideas and artistic styles spread from Italy to northern Europe. *Section 2*
- ▶ **Conflict** Martin Luther's protests against the Catholic Church result in Protestantism. *Section 3*
- ▶ **Cultural Diffusion** Protestant religious groups spread reform through northern Europe. *Section 4*
- ▶ **Reaction** The Catholic Church enacts its own reform, the Catholic Reformation. *Section 5*

S*toryteller*

Isabella d'Este, married in 1490 at the age of 16 to the Marquis of Mantua, played a vital role in ruling the Italian city-state of Mantua. A brilliant and well-educated young woman who loved Latin literature, Isabella gathered a fashionable assemblage of artists and statesmen in her sparkling court. In a room decorated with ornately carved woodwork and paintings that illustrated Greek myths, Isabella entertained her guests to her own lute recitals and poetry readings. Isabella was one of the many Italians of her time who rediscovered and repopularized Greek and Roman classics, educating their contemporaries to the glories of their classical past after a thousand years of neglect. The word **Renaissance**, *coming from the French word meaning "rebirth," was coined to refer to this rebirth of interest in classical ideas and culture.*

Historical Significance

What happened during the Renaissance that changed Europeans' outlook on the world? How did the Reformation shape the religious and political life of Europe?

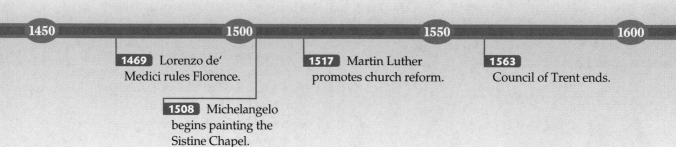

1450	1500	1550	1600

1469 Lorenzo de' Medici rules Florence.

1508 Michelangelo begins painting the Sistine Chapel.

1517 Martin Luther promotes church reform.

1563 Council of Trent ends.

Detail of *The Court* by Andrea Mantegna.
Palazzo Ducale, Mantua, Italy

Your History Journal

Choose a Renaissance sculptor, architect, or painter mentioned in this chapter. Research and write a short report on the work and influence of this person.

1400	1450	1500

1436 Filippo Brunelleschi completes dome for Florence Cathedral.

c. 1490 Florence enjoys economic prosperity.

c. 1500 Rome becomes a major center of Renaissance culture.

Section 1

The Italian Renaissance

Setting the Scene

▶ **Terms to Define**

humanism, secular, individualism, sonnet, doge

▶ **People to Meet**

Niccolò Machiavelli, Lorenzo de' Medici, Michelangelo Buonarroti, Leonardo da Vinci

▶ **Places to Locate**

Florence, Rome, Venice

Find Out ▶ What factors inspired the Renaissance?

The Storyteller

Michelangelo finished the Sistine Chapel in September 1512. Pope Julius came to see the completed work. One man had covered ten thousand square feet with the greatest wall painting in Italy. Michelangelo wrote to his father, "I have finished the chapel which I have been painting. The Pope is very satisfied.... Your Michelangelo, sculptor, in Rome." The artist, tired and in poor health, went home to Florence, hoping for rest and relaxation.

—adapted from *Michelangelo The Man*, Donald Lord Finlayson, 1935

Ancestors of Christ, detail from the Sistine Chapel

The Renaissance—the period from about 1350 until 1600 during which western Europeans experienced a profound cultural awakening—was in many ways a continuation of the Middle Ages, but it also signaled the beginning of modern times. The Renaissance caused educated Europeans to develop new attitudes about themselves and the world around them.

The Renaissance began first in the city-states of Italy. Unlike other areas of Europe, Italy had largely avoided the economic crisis of the late Middle Ages. Italian towns remained important centers of Mediterranean trade and boosted their production of textiles and luxury goods.

More than other Europeans, Italians were attached to classical traditions. The ruins of ancient Roman buildings, arches, and amphitheaters constantly reminded them of their heritage. Moreover, through trade Italian towns remained in close contact with the Byzantine Empire, where scholars preserved the learning of ancient Greece.

Humanism

Through renewed contact with the classics, Italian scholars improved their understanding of Greek and Latin, studied old manuscripts, and copied the classical writing style. This interest in classical learning, however, was more than just a fascination with ancient times. It led to a new intellectual movement known as **humanism** that focused on **secular**, or worldly, themes rather than on the religious ideas that had concerned medieval thinkers. Humanists—the scholars who promoted humanism—accepted classical beliefs and wanted to use them to renew their own society. Among the most important beliefs was **individualism**, an emphasis on the dignity and worth of the individual person.

Another was the idea of human improvement, that people should develop their talents through many activities: politics, sports, and the arts.

Education and Literature

Humanists believed that education could help people improve themselves. They opened schools that taught the *studia humanitas*, or humanities—Greek, Latin, history and philosophy, the subjects taught in ancient times. These schools became so popular that humanists began to replace the clergy as teachers of the sons of the wealthy.

Humanism also inspired new forms of literature written in the vernacular and focusing on personal feelings. During the 1300s, Francesco Petrarca, or Petrarch (PEE•TRAHRK), wrote sonnets, or short poems, that expressed his love for Laura, a woman who had died during the Black Death. His friend, Giovanni Boccaccio, in the work *Decameron*, described young people who tell stories to divert their attention from the plague's horrors.

As the Renaissance developed, writers also focused on the topics of individual ambition and success. During the 1500s, Benvenuto Cellini, a goldsmith and sculptor, glorified his achievements in one of the first modern autobiographies. In a popular manual, *The Book of the Courtier*, Baldassare Castiglione (bahl•dahs•SAHR•ray kahs•steel•YOHN•ay) gave advice to men and women on the Renaissance ideal of good behavior. Men were to be skilled in many activities; women were to be graceful, attractive, and courteous. The diplomat Niccolò Machiavelli (mak•ee•uh•VEHL•ee) wrote *The Prince*, a book that realistically analyzed the politics of Renaissance Italy. Rulers, Machiavelli said, should be ready to use force and deceit to hold power. Critics charged that *The Prince* justified immoral behavior in politics, but Machiavelli's book appealed to power-hungry Renaissance rulers. It also influenced the thought and actions of later political leaders.

Scholarship

Humanist scholars influenced more than just literature. With their independent thinking, they began to challenge long-accepted traditions, assumptions, and institutions. As they made all sorts of unsettling discoveries, it further validated their desire to challenge and question nearly everything—even long-standing church traditions. For example, in an exciting piece of Renaissance detective work, the scholar Lorenzo Valla determined that a document that supposedly provided the legal basis for the pope's supremacy over kings was actually a forgery.

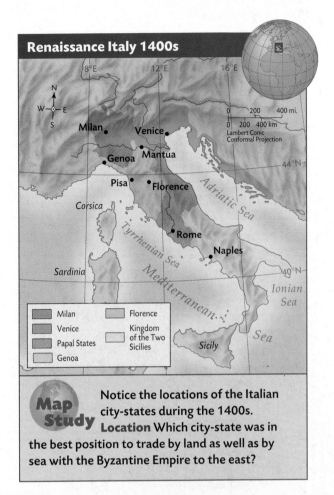

Renaissance Italy 1400s

Milan · Venice · Papal States · Genoa · Florence · Kingdom of the Two Sicilies

Map Study Notice the locations of the Italian city-states during the 1400s. **Location** Which city-state was in the best position to trade by land as well as by sea with the Byzantine Empire to the east?

Through their teaching and writing, humanists reawakened the educated public to classical values. They also encouraged a ferment of new ideas that eventually spread from Italy throughout Europe and reshaped European civilization.

City Life

Town life was stronger in Italy than in other parts of Europe. As a result, Italians could easily discard feudalism and other medieval institutions that had their origins in the rural north. Italy did not become unified as did France and England. Wealthy and successful, most Italian communes, or communities, resisted the efforts of emperors, kings, and nobles to control them. They became independent city-states, each of which included a walled urban center and the surrounding countryside.

Social Groups

The Italian city-states fashioned a new social order in which wealth and ability mattered more than aristocratic titles and ownership of land. Wealthy merchants and bankers replaced the landed nobility as the most powerful social and political group—the upper class. Shopkeepers and artisans ranked below the wealthy merchants, forming a moderately prosperous middle class that employed large numbers of poor workers. Most of these workers—who were the majority of town dwellers—came to urban areas from the countryside. At the bottom of the social order were the peasants who worked on the country estates of the wealthy classes.

Government

During the Renaissance, Italy was not under one government, but instead consisted of individual city-states, each ruled by wealthy families whose fortunes came from commercial trading or banking. Workers often rebelled against the upper classes. Their demands for equal rights and lower taxes, however, were suppressed.

During the 1400s, social conflicts created upheaval so often that certain city-states felt it necessary to turn over all political authority to a single powerful leader to restore peace. These powerful political leaders were called signori (seen•YOHR•ee). Some signori ruled as dictators, using violence to maintain control. Others successfully ensured popular loyalty by improving city services, supporting the arts, and providing festivals and parades for the lower classes.

While dealing with internal unrest, city-states also fought with each other in territorial disputes. But the prosperous merchants and bankers, unlike the nobility they had supplanted, did not want to fight in these battles. Since military service would interfere with conducting business and trade, the signori chose to replace citizen-soldiers with hired soldiers known as condottieri (KAHN•duh•TYEHR•ee).

Hiring condottieri made wars very costly. To avoid this expense, signori began to seek territorial gain through negotiated agreements. To carry out this policy, they assembled the first modern diplomatic services. Permanent ambassadors were appointed to represent their city-states at foreign

Images
of the Times

Art of the Italian Renaissance

The Italian Renaissance produced a host of great Italian artists and sculptors. Among the most notable of these were Michelangelo, Raphael, and Leonardo da Vinci.

Michelangelo created *David*, a gigantic marble sculpture, while at home in Florence between 1501 and 1504. A painter, architect, sculptor, and poet, he has had an unparalleled influence on Western art.

courts. The city-states also worked out an agreement among all the city-states that no one city-state would be allowed enough power to threaten the others. During the 1500s other European states adopted similar agreements with one another and also began to practice diplomacy.

Although the Italian city-states had much in common, each developed its own characteristic life. Three cities in particular played leading roles in the Renaissance: **Florence**, **Rome**, and **Venice**.

Florence

Originally a republic, Florence in the 1400s came under the control of a prominent banking family known as the Medici (MEH•duh•chee). Medici rulers helped to foster the spirit of humanism among the city-state's scholars and artists. With this spirit alive throughout the city, Florence became the birthplace of the Italian Renaissance.

Cosimo de' Medici gained control of Florence in 1434. He worked to end worker uprisings by introducing an income tax that placed a heavier burden on wealthier citizens. He used the tax revenues to make city improvements, such as sewers and paved streets, that benefited everyone. Cosimo also worked to establish peaceful relations between the city and its neighbors.

Cosimo's grandson **Lorenzo de' Medici** ruled Florence from 1469 to 1492, and he continued policies like those of his grandfather. He used his wealth to support artists, philosophers, and writers and to sponsor public festivals. As a result of the city's prosperity and fame, Lorenzo was known as "the Magnificent."

During the 1490s Florence's economic prosperity, based mostly on the banking and textile industries, began to decline with increasing competition from English and Flemish cloth makers. Tired of the Medici rule, discontented citizens rallied in support of a Dominican friar named Girolamo Savonarola (SA•vuh•nuh•ROH•luh). In fiery sermons before hundreds of people, Savonarola attacked the Medici for promoting ideas that he claimed were causing the downfall of Florence:

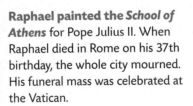

Leonardo da Vinci painted the *Mona Lisa* during a period of intensive study in Florence in 1503. His talent was also expressed in sculpture, architecture, and engineering.

Raphael painted the *School of Athens* for Pope Julius II. When Raphael died in Rome on his 37th birthday, the whole city mourned. His funeral mass was celebrated at the Vatican.

REFLECTING ON THE TIMES

1. What Renaissance values are reflected in the paintings and sculpture shown in this feature?
2. Why are there many similarities in style and subject matter among works of the Italian Renaissance?

Brunelleschi's sculpture of the sacrifice of Isaac was a contest entry for the east doors of the Baptistry in Florence. *Brunelleschi lost but is remembered for what architectural feat?*

> ❝ In the mansions of the great prelates and great lords there is no concern save for poetry and the oratorical art. Go … and see; [you] shall find them all with books of the humanities in their hands…. Arise and come to deliver [your] Church from the hands of the devils! ❞

So many people were won over by Savonarola that the Medici family was forced to turn over the rule of Florence to his supporters. On Savonarola's advice, the city's new leaders imposed strict regulations on public behavior. Gambling, swearing, and horse racing were banned. Savonarola urged his listeners to repent of their "worldly" ways. He had crowds make bonfires to burn books, paintings, fancy clothes, and musical instruments.

Savonarola soon aroused a great deal of opposition to his preaching. His criticism of church officials angered the pope. Many people in Florence disliked his strict ways. In 1498 Savonarola was hanged for heresy, and the Medici family returned to power. By this time, however, Florence's greatness had passed.

Rome

During the 1500s Rome emerged as a leading Renaissance city. In Rome, the pope and the cardinals living in the Vatican made up the wealthiest and most powerful class.

Eager to increase their prestige, Renaissance popes rebuilt the ancient city. Architects constructed large churches and palaces, and artists created magnificent paintings and sculptures to decorate these buildings. Scholars came from all over Europe to study manuscripts and books in the Vatican Library.

Renaissance popes often placed political goals ahead of religious duties. In ruling Rome and its surroundings, they sent ambassadors to other lands, collected taxes, and fought wars. The most politically minded pope was Alexander VI. Elected pope in 1492, Alexander had bribed the College of Cardinals to vote for him. Once in office, he used the wealth of the Church to support his family, the Borgias. He especially encouraged his son Cesare, who raised an army and conquered much of central Italy.

After Alexander's death in 1503, his successors, Julius II and later Leo X, promoted artistic projects to beautify Rome. Their most notable effort was the rebuilding of St. Peter's Basilica, the largest church in the Christian world.

Venice

Another Renaissance center was Venice, the port city on the Adriatic Sea. Venice's economic power, enjoyed since the Crusades, was fading because of changing trade routes and Muslim invasions in the east. However, the city's role as a link between Asia and western Europe still drew traders from all over the world. Venetian shipyards also turned out huge galleys, and Venetian workshops produced high quality glass.

One benefit of Venice's prosperity was political stability. Venice's republican government was headed by an elected **doge**, (DOHJ), or leader. The doge officially ran the city, but the wealthiest merchants meeting in committee as the Council of Ten held the real power. This council passed laws, elected the doge, and even had to be consulted should the doge's son want to marry.

Influenced by Byzantine as well as western European culture, Venice was known for its artistic achievements. Painters, such as Titian, Tintoretto, and Giorgione, used brilliant oil colors to portray rural landscapes and classical and religious themes. Venetian architects, such as Sansovino and Palladio, erected buildings in the classical style.

Renaissance Arts

What were the unique characteristics of Renaissance art? The humanists' emphasis on cultivating individual talent inspired Italian artists to express their own values, emotions, and attitudes. No longer content with creating symbolic representations of their subjects, artists made their subjects as lifelike and captivating as possible. Although much of the art was still devoted to religious subjects, it had more secular, or worldly, overtones. Interest in ancient Greece and Rome moved artists to include classical mythology as well as biblical themes in their works.

To make their creations lifelike and captivating, artists experimented with new techniques. For example, they learned to create a sense of perspective, which gave their paintings depth. They studied anatomy so they could portray human figures more accurately and naturally. Artists also learned to depict subtleties of gesture and expression to convey human emotions. Much of their work consisted of frescoes, or paintings done on damp plaster.

The public in Renaissance Italy appreciated works of art and hailed great artists as geniuses. Nobles and townspeople used art to decorate homes as well as churches. They lavishly rewarded artists and gave them a prominent place in society.

Architecture

During the Middle Ages, cathedral architects had pointed soaring arches and spires heavenward for the glory of God. During the Renaissance, however, Italian architects returned to the classical style. On churches, palaces, and villas they substituted domes and columns from classical Greek and Roman architecture for the medieval arches and spires. They sought both comfort and beauty in their buildings, adorning them with tapestries, paintings, statues, finely made furniture, and glass windows. Unlike the anonymous architects of the Middle Ages, Renaissance architects took credit for their fine buildings.

The most famous Italian Renaissance architect was Filippo Brunelleschi (BROO•nuhl•EHS•kee), best known for the dome he designed and completed in 1436 for the Cathedral of Florence. Until Brunelleschi submitted his design, no one had been able to come up with a way to construct a dome large or strong enough to cover the cathedral without the dome collapsing from its own weight. Brunelleschi's design—based on his own study of the domes, columns, and arches of ancient Rome—was considered to be the greatest engineering feat of the time.

Sculpture

Renaissance sculpture reflected a return to classical ideals. The free-standing statues of nude figures sculpted in bronze or marble during the Renaissance resembled ancient Greek and Roman sculptures of nude figures much more than they did medieval sculptures. Human figures in medieval sculptures had usually been portrayed in a stiff, stylized manner.

Some of the best-known Renaissance sculptors—Donatello, Michelangelo, and Ghiberti (gee•BEHR•tee)—came from Florence. There the Medicis opened a school for sculptors. Donatello was the first sculptor since ancient times to cast a large, free-standing nude statue. Although the sculptor **Michelangelo Buonarroti** later went to Rome to sculpt works for the pope, he learned his craft in Florence. Florentine sculptor Lorenzo Ghiberti took 21 years to create 10 biblical scenes on bronze doors for Florence's cathedral baptistry.

Painting

Italian Renaissance painters departed from the flat, symbolic style of medieval painting to begin a more realistic style. This change first appeared in the early 1300s when the Florentine artist-sculptor-architect Giotto (jee•AH•toh) effectively captured human emotions in a series of frescoes portraying the life of Francis of Assisi. In the 1400s Florentine

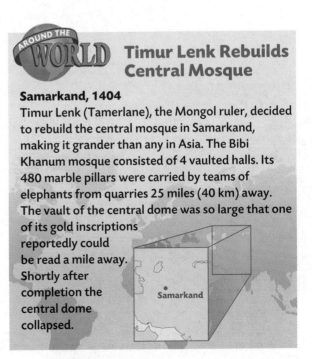

Timur Lenk Rebuilds Central Mosque

Samarkand, 1404

Timur Lenk (Tamerlane), the Mongol ruler, decided to rebuild the central mosque in Samarkand, making it grander than any in Asia. The Bibi Khanum mosque consisted of 4 vaulted halls. Its 480 marble pillars were carried by teams of elephants from quarries 25 miles (40 km) away. The vault of the central dome was so large that one of its gold inscriptions reportedly could be read a mile away. Shortly after completion the central dome collapsed.

Samarkand

Victor R. Boswell, Jr.

"The Last Supper"

Victor R. Boswell, Jr.

"One of you shall betray me," said Jesus, sitting amid the disciples gathered around in a flurry of worry, gossip, and fear. Between 1495 and 1497 Leonardo da Vinci painted *The Last Supper* on the walls of a monastery in Milan, Italy. Unstable paint and centuries of wear slowly destroyed the mural. In 1977 restoration of the painting began, as shown in the detail (above) depicting the apostles Matthew, Thaddeus, and Simon. The larger view of the master-piece (left) shows visitors clustered around while restorers continue their work.

Da Vinci was one of the most famous painters of the Italian Renaissance. During the Renaissance the peoples of Europe began to see themselves as Europeans rather than as members of the kingdom of Christendom whose single passport was belief. The Renaissance was a period of upheaval and change in religion, politics, and economy. The arts flourished. Writers began using the language of their own nations instead of Latin. Painters, architects, and sculptors experimented with new techniques. Expressing his belief in the newfound power of paintings, da Vinci boasted that the painter could "even induce men to fall in love with a picture that does not portray any living woman." Indeed, people throughout the ages have fallen in love with *The Last Supper*. ◍

artist Masaccio (muh•ZAH•chee•oh) employed lighting and perspective in his paintings to give depth to the human body and to set off his figures from the background. He thus created an even greater sense of realism than Giotto had.

One of the greatest Renaissance artists was **Leonardo da Vinci** (VIHN•chee). A citizen of Florence, he did much of his work in Milan and Rome. Da Vinci is best known for the *Mona Lisa*, a portrait of a strangely smiling young woman of Florence, and *The Last Supper*, a wall painting of Jesus' last meal with his disciples. In both works, da Vinci skillfully portrayed the subjects' personalities, thoughts, and feelings. He also made designs in notebooks on astronomy, mathematics, and anatomy. These drawings often pictured parachutes, flying machines, and other mechanical inventions far ahead of his time.

Another outstanding Renaissance artist—Michelangelo Buonarroti—began his career as a sculptor in Florence. There he did a famous marble statue of David, after the heroic biblical king. Later in Rome he sculpted *La Pietà* (PEE•ay•TAH), which shows the dead Jesus in the arms of his mother, Mary. Most of Michelangelo's sculptures were awesome in size and suggested controlled but intense emotions.

In 1508 Pope Julius II hired Michelangelo to work at the Vatican, painting the ceiling of the Sistine Chapel with scenes from the Bible. All of Michelangelo's painted figures resembled sculptures. They had well-formed muscular bodies that expressed vitality and power. Michelangelo ended his career by designing the dome of the new St. Peter's Basilica.

Like Michelangelo, the artist Raphael Santi worked at the Vatican. He completed a series of paintings on classical and religious themes for the pope's apartment. Raphael is most noted for his paintings of Mary, the mother of Jesus. These works were done in bright colors and reflected the Renaissance ideals of grace, harmony, and beauty.

History & Art *La Pietà* by Michelangelo Buonarroti. St. Peter's Basilica, The Vatican, Rome, Italy
What is the subject of La Pietà?

Women and the Arts

Although Renaissance women had few roles independent of men, some of them did contribute to the arts. These women were either daughters of artists who trained in their fathers' workshops or children of noblemen, who were expected to have literary, musical, and artistic skills. Among the most celebrated female artists were the portrait painters Lavinia Fontana and Sofonisba Anguissola (soh•foh•NIHZ•bah ahn•gwee•SOH•lah). An Italian noblewoman, Anguissola became a painter at the Spanish royal court of King Philip II.

SECTION 1 REVIEW

Recall
1. **Define** humanism, secular, individualism, sonnet, doge.
2. **Identify** Niccolò Machiavelli, Lorenzo de' Medici, Savonarola, Michelangelo Buonarroti, Leonardo da Vinci.
3. **Discuss** the meaning of the term "Renaissance." To what does it refer? What were its major characteristics?

Critical Thinking
4. **Making Comparisons** How does the role of female artists today compare with that of female artists in Renaissance times?

Understanding Themes
5. **Innovation** Identify one masterpiece in Renaissance literature or the arts. Explain how it reflects Renaissance ideals. Also state what subject is represented.

1400	1450	1500	1550

c. 1456 Johannes Gutenberg uses movable metal type in printing.

1494 Francis I of France invades Italy.

1509 Desiderius Erasmus writes *The Praise of Folly*.

Section 2

The Northern Renaissance

Setting the Scene

▶ **Terms to Define**
châteaux

▶ **People to Meet**
Johannes Gutenberg, François Rabelais, Desiderius Erasmus, Pieter Brueghel, Thomas More, William Shakespeare

▶ **Places to Locate**
the Low Countries

 **Find Out** How did the Renaissance reach northern Europe?

The Storyteller

When Shakespeare's play Hamlet *opened in London, about 2,000 people crowded in to see the performance. Admission was one penny. Down in front of the stage, where it was standing room only, the crowd could be noisy. One writer complained: "Such heaving, and shoving, such pushing and shouldering— especially by the women! Such care for their clothes, that no one step on their dress;.... Such smiling and winking.... Never mind the stage—it is a comedy to watch them!"*

—freely adapted from *Shakespeare: Of an Age For All Time*, The Yale University Festival Lectures, edited by Charles Tyler Prouty, 1954

William Shakespeare

During the late 1400s, Renaissance art and humanist ideas—characterized by a revival of interest in classical antiquity— began to filter northward from Italy to France, England, the Netherlands, and other European countries. War, trade, travel, and a newly invented method of printing helped to promote this cultural diffusion. The people of the Northern Renaissance adapted ideas of the Italian Renaissance to their own individual tastes, values, and needs.

Spreading Ideas

War, as usual, helped spread ideas by furthering contact between people of different cultures. After France invaded Italy in 1494, French kings and their warrior-nobles became fascinated by Italian Renaissance art and fashions. In 1517 King Francis I brought Leonardo da Vinci to his court in France, thus helping to promote the entry of Renaissance ideas into northern Europe. Other European monarchs also developed an enthusiasm for the Renaissance. Kings and queens so eagerly supported scholars and artists that the number of humanists in the north grew rapidly along with the popularity of humanist ideas.

At the same time, Italian traders living in the north set an example for northern European merchants, who began to appreciate wealth, beauty, personal improvement, and other Renaissance values. These northern merchants—having only recently become successful enough to afford lifestyles based upon such values—began to spend their wealth on education, fine houses, and material goods. Some northern Europeans began to travel to Italy to study with Italian masters. Thus began the emergence of a newly educated middle class.

This spread of knowledge among the middle class was aided by the invention of the printing press. By the 1400s, German engravers had developed movable type, in which the type was set into adjustable molds, inked, and then pressed onto a sheet of paper. In 1456 **Johannes Gutenberg** printed a complete edition of the Bible using movable metal type. As a result of this invention, books were published more quickly and less expensively. Production of humanist texts could now begin to match the newfound desire for such works.

Although Italian Renaissance ideas became quite popular in the north, they were not merely transplanted there. Rather, northern scholars interpreted them according to their own individual ways of thinking. Furthermore, the people of each northern culture adapted these ideas to suit their own needs and traditions.

The French Renaissance

The French Renaissance had a character all its own. French architects blended medieval Gothic towers and windows with the classical arches used by Italian architects to create **châteaux** (sha•TOHZ), or castles, for Francis I and his nobles. These large country estates were erected primarily in the Loire River valley. The château of Chambord is a fine example.

Many French Renaissance writers borrowed extensively from the new literary forms of the Italian Renaissance. Inspired by Petrarch's sonnets, Pierre Ronsard (rohn•SAHR) wrote his own sonnets with common humanist themes such as love, the passing of youth, and the poet's immortality. Michel de Montaigne (mahn•TAYN) may have based his informal and direct style on Italian literary models. He cultivated the literary form called the personal essay, a short prose composition written to express clearly the personal view of a writer on a subject. In his essay "Of the Disadvantages of Greatness," Montaigne analyzed the authority of royalty:

❝ The most difficult occupation in the world, in my opinion, is to play the part of a king worthily. I excuse more of their faults than people commonly do, in consideration of the dreadful weight of their burden, which dazes me. It is difficult for a power so immoderate to observe moderation.... **❞**

Physician-monk **François Rabelais** (RA•buh •LAY), France's most popular Renaissance author, wrote comic tales, satires, and parodies on a broad spectrum of contemporary life. He rejected the

Erasmus by Quentin Metsys. The "Prince of the Humanists" joined a love for the classics with respect for Christian values. *What reforms did Christian humanists promote?*

Middle Ages' focus on the afterlife and believed that people should enjoy life to the fullest. Exceptionally knowledgeable and gifted as a writer, he also wrote on such subjects as law, medicine, politics, theology, botany, and navigation.

Northern Europe

The Italian Renaissance was enthusiastically accepted by the wealthy towns of Germany and **the Low Countries** (present-day Belgium, Luxembourg, and the Netherlands). Universities and schools promoted humanist learning, and printers produced a large quantity of books. Latin was still the main scholarly language, but writers increased their use of German and Dutch.

Christian Humanism

Unlike in Italy, the Renaissance in northern Europe had a more religious tone. Groups of scholars, known as Christian humanists, wanted reforms in Catholicism that would eliminate abuses and restore the simple piety of the early Church. They believed that humanist learning and Bible study were the best ways to promote these goals.

The most famous Christian humanist, **Desiderius Erasmus** (dehz•ih•DEER•ee•uhs ih•RAZ•muhs), inspired his colleagues to study

Peasant's Dance by Pieter Brueghel the Elder. **The painting emphasizes the enjoyments of common people.** *What four subjects did northern European realistic artists paint?*

Greek and Hebrew so that they could understand older versions of the Bible written in these languages. Erasmus also used biting humor to make people take a more critical view of society. He specifically attacked the wealth of Renaissance popes. In his noted work, *The Praise of Folly*, he describes these popes, claiming that they were so corrupt they no longer practiced Christianity:

> 66 Scarce any kind of men live more [devoted to pleasure] or with less trouble.... To work miracles is ... not in fashion now; to instruct the people, troublesome; to interpret the Scripture, [too bookish]; to pray, a sign one has little else to do ... and lastly, to die, uncouth; and to be stretched on a cross, infamous. 99

Northern European Painters

Artists in northern Europe developed a style of painting that relied more on medieval than classical models. In the early 1400s, a group of Flemish painters, led by the brothers Jan and Hubert van Eyck (EYEK), painted scenes from the Bible and daily life in sharp, realistic detail. They developed the technique of painting in oils. Oils provided artists with richer colors and allowed them to make changes on the painted canvas. Painting in oils soon spread to Italy. Meanwhile, Italian Renaissance art reached northern Europe. Artists such as Albrecht Dürer and **Pieter Brueghel** (BROY•guhl) combined Italian technique with the artistic traditions of their homelands. They painted realistic portraits, religious themes, landscapes, and scenes of daily life.

The English Renaissance

Renaissance ideas did not spread to England until 1485, when the Wars of the Roses—bloody conflicts over who was the rightful heir to the throne—ended. Ultimately, the Tudor family defeated the York family, bringing the Tudor king Henry VII to power. Henry invited Italian Renaissance scholars to England, where they taught humanist ideas and encouraged the study of classical texts.

English humanists expressed deep interest in social issues. **Thomas More**, a statesman and a friend of Erasmus, wrote a book that criticized the society of his day by comparing it with an ideal society in which all citizens are equal and prosperous. The book, written in Latin, was called *Utopia*.

The English Renaissance was especially known for drama. The best-known English playwrights were **William Shakespeare** and Christopher Marlowe. They drew ideas for their works from medieval legends, classical mythology, and the histories of England, Denmark, and ancient Rome. Shakespeare dealt with universal human qualities such as jealousy, ambition, love, and despair so effectively that his plays are still relevant to audiences today.

SECTION 2 REVIEW

Recall
1. **Define** châteaux.
2. **Identify** Johannes Gutenberg, Michel de Montaigne, François Rabelais, Desiderius Erasmus, Jan and Hubert van Eyck, Pieter Brueghel, Thomas More, William Shakespeare.

3. **Describe** some elements of Italian Renaissance architecture used by French architects. How did they transform French architecture?

Critical Thinking
4. **Applying Information** Choose one writer or artist from the Northern Renaissance and explain how the works of this writer or artist reflected Renaissance ideas.

Understanding Themes
5. **Cultural Diffusion** How did Italian Renaissance ideas spread to northern Europe?

1517 Martin Luther preaches against indulgences.

1520 The Church condemns Luther's works.

c. 1550 Lutheranism spreads through northern Europe.

Section 3

The Protestant Reformation

Setting the Scene

▶ **Terms to Define**
justification by faith, indulgences, vocation

▶ **People to Meet**
Martin Luther, Pope Leo X

▶ **Places to Locate**
Wittenberg, Worms

 How did Luther's religious reforms lead to Protestantism, a new branch of Christianity?

The Storyteller

In later years, Martin Luther remembered the fateful day he entered the monastery: "Afterwards I regretted my vow, and many of my friends tried to persuade me not to enter the monastery. I, however, was determined to go through with it.... I invited certain of my best men friends to a farewell party.... In tears they led me away; and my father was very angry ... yet I persisted in my determination. It never occurred to me to leave the monastery." Luther's break with the Church was an even bigger decision than the one to enter monastic life.

—adapted from Luther and His Times, E.G. Schweibert, 1950

Martin Luther

The Renaissance values of humanism and secularism stimulated widespread criticism of the Catholic Church's extravagance. By about 1500, educated Europeans began calling for a reformation—a change in the Church's ways of teaching and practicing Christianity. In Germany the movement for church reform eventually led to a split in the Church that produced a new form of Christianity known as Protestantism. The series of events that gave birth to Protestantism is known as the Protestant Reformation.

Martin Luther

The Protestant Reformation was begun by a German monk named **Martin Luther**, born in 1483, the son of middle-class townspeople. His father wanted him to become a lawyer, but Luther was interested in religion. In 1505 he was nearly struck by lightning in a thunderstorm. Terrified that the storm was God's way of punishing him, the law student knelt and prayed to Saint Anne. In return for protection, he promised to become a monk. Shortly thereafter, Luther entered a monastery.

As a young monk, Luther struggled to ensure his soul's salvation. He would confess his sins for hours at a time. Yet still he worried that God might not find him acceptable.

Then he read Saint Paul's Epistle to the Romans: "He who through faith is righteous shall live"—and Luther's worries dissolved. He interpreted this to mean that a person could be made just, or good, simply by faith in God's mercy and love. Luther's idea became known as justification by faith. Luther later stated that because of this discovery he felt as if he "had been born again and had entered Paradise through wide open gates."

Luther's Protest

Luther's ideas gradually matured and eventually brought him into conflict with the Church. At this time **Pope Leo X** was trying to raise money to rebuild St. Peter's Basilica in Rome. To this end, the pope sold church positions to his friends and also authorized sales of indulgences.

Indulgences were certificates issued by the Church that were said to reduce or even cancel punishment for a person's sins—as long as one also truly repented. People purchased indulgences believing that the document would assure them admission to heaven. John Tetzel, the Church's agent for selling indulgences in northern Germany, even went so far as to promise peasants that indulgences would relieve them of guilt for *future* sins. He also encouraged people to buy indulgences for the salvation of their dead relatives. Tetzel's sale of indulgences inspired a popular jingle: "Once you

hear the money's ring, the soul from purgatory is free to spring." (According to church teaching, purgatory is a place in the afterlife where people are made fit for heaven.)

Luther, a professor and priest in the town of **Wittenberg**, preached against the sale of indulgences. He also lectured against other church practices he believed were corrupt. Then, on October 31, 1517, Luther nailed on the door of the Wittenberg Church a placard with 95 theses, or statements, criticizing indulgences and other church policies.

Breaking With Rome

Printed copies of the Ninety-five Theses spread quickly all over Germany. Sales of indulgences declined sharply. Encouraged by this reaction, Luther published hundreds of essays advocating justification by faith and attacking church abuses.

Pope Leo X responded to the decline in indulgence sales by sending envoys to Germany to persuade Luther to withdraw his criticisms. But Luther refused. In 1520 the pope formally condemned Luther and banned his works. In 1521 Pope Leo X excommunicated Luther from the Church.

Printing

Before the 1400s books had to be copied by hand—a time-consuming method. Consequently, books were rare, owned and read only by scholars and the wealthy. Gutenberg's invention of movable type changed all that: books could be produced faster at lower cost; more people were able to buy books and expand their knowledge; and traditional ideas were questioned. German printers quickly adopted Gutenberg's invention and set up similar printing presses in other European countries.

Martin Luther was one of the first authors to benefit from the new technology. Since his books could be reproduced inexpensively and in large quantities, they could be easily obtained throughout Europe short-

Gutenberg's press

ly after Luther completed them. Thus, Luther was able to spread his ideas and gain widespread support before the Catholic Church could respond.

In the past few decades, more advances have been made in printing than in all the years since Gutenberg. Today high-speed machines and computer technology together have revolutionized the printing industry. Images are now transferred onto paper directly from computer files. The development of copy machines and laser printers has also made smaller printing jobs easier.

 **ACTIVITY**

Describe how Gutenberg's printing press transformed European society during the 1400s and 1500s. How did Luther benefit from Gutenberg's invention? Explain how computer technology and other innovations have transformed printing and other means of communication today.

History & Art *Luther Preaching to the Faithful,* (artist unknown). National Museum, Copenhagen, Denmark *What was Luther's view of vocations?* **(below) Indulgence box—an item that Luther opposed.**

Shortly after Luther's excommunication, a diet, or council, of German princes met in **Worms**, Germany, to try to bring Luther back into the Church. They decided that Luther should take back his criticisms of the papacy. Meanwhile, Luther traveled to Worms as crowds of cheering people lined the road. Luther strode into the assembly hall and, when asked to take back his teachings, gave this reply: "I am bound by the Sacred Scriptures I have cited … and my conscience is captive to the Word of God. I cannot and will not recant [take back] anything.… God help me." Luther, condemned as a heretic and outlaw, was rushed out of Worms and hidden at a castle in Wartburg by a friend, Prince Frederick of Saxony.

While in hiding, Luther translated the New Testament into German. Earlier German translations of the Bible were so rare and costly that few people had them. With Luther's more affordable translation, most people could now read the Bible.

Lutheranism

After Worms, Luther laid the foundation of the first Protestant faith: Lutheranism. While Catholicism stressed faith and good works in salvation and the importance of church teaching as a spiritual guide, Lutheranism emphasized salvation by faith alone and the Bible's role as the only source of religious truth. Lutheran services centered on biblical preaching rather than ritual and were held in the language of the people instead of Latin. In this way people could understand and participate in the services. Luther and his followers also held that the Church was not a hierarchy of clergy, but a community of believers. All useful occupations, not just the priesthood, were vocations, or callings, in which people could serve God and neighbor.

Lutheranism brought a new religious message to Germany, but it also stirred social unrest among peasants wanting to end serfdom. When a major peasant revolt erupted in 1525, Luther, fearing social chaos, backed the princes against the peasants. The princes cruelly put down the uprising, killing thousands of people. Lutheranism became a more conservative movement as a result; however, it had already sown the seeds of more radical Protestant movements that would transform Europe's religious landscape.

SECTION 3 REVIEW

Recall
1. **Define** justification by faith, indulgences, vocation.
2. **Identify** Protestant Reformation, Martin Luther, Pope Leo X.
3. **Discuss** the religious changes brought by Luther's protest against the Catholic Church.

Critical Thinking
4. **Synthesizing Information** If you wanted to protest against something today, what medium would you use to communicate your cause? Why?

Understanding Themes
5. **Conflict** Why did the pope ask Luther to recant his beliefs and then excommunicate him when Luther would not do so?

1509 John Calvin is born.

1525 Huldrych Zwingli establishes theocracy in Zurich.

1536 John Calvin publishes *The Institutes of the Christian Religion*.

1558 Queen Elizabeth I establishes Anglicanism in England.

Section 4

The Spread of Protestantism

Setting the Scene

▶ **Terms to Define**
   theocracy, predestination

▶ **People to Meet**
   Huldrych Zwingli, John Calvin, the Anabaptists, Henry VIII, Catherine of Aragon, Anne Boleyn, Mary, Elizabeth I

▶ **Places to Locate**
   Zurich, Geneva

Find Out What different forms of Protestantism emerged in Europe as the Reformation spread?

The Storyteller

Mary Queen of Scots was a prisoner for seventeen long years. What was she to do, as she and her keeper's wife sat together all that time? She could sew. Over the years, she and her attendant ladies embroidered seas of fabric: tablecloths, cushions, and hangings, every piece scattered with coats of arms and emblems, every piece sprinkled with gold and silver spangles to catch the light. Some became gifts; but occasionally her presents were rudely refused. Her own son, King James VI, returned a vest his mother had embroidered for him because she had addressed it to "The Prince of Scotland."

—adapted from *Mary Queen of Scots*, Roy Strong and Julia Trevelyan Oman, 1972

Mary Queen of Scots

Although the Protestant Reformation spread throughout Europe in the 1500s, divisions began to appear within the movement soon after it had started. Not only did the Protestant reformers not believe in the same methods; they did not even agree on the same goals.

Swiss Reformers

After the rise of Lutheranism in Germany, many preachers and merchants in neighboring Switzerland separated from Rome and set up churches known as Reformed. **Huldrych Zwingli**, a Swiss priest who lived from 1484 to 1531, led the Protestant movement in Switzerland. Like Luther, Zwingli stressed salvation by faith alone and denounced many Catholic beliefs and practices, such as purgatory and the sale of indulgences. Unlike Luther, though, Zwingli wanted to break completely from Catholic tradition. He wanted to establish a theocracy, or church-run state, in the Swiss city of **Zurich**. By 1525 Zwingli had achieved this goal. But in 1531 war broke out over Protestant missionary activity in the Catholic areas of Switzerland. Zwingli and his force of followers were defeated by an army of Catholics.

In the mid-1500s **John Calvin**, another reformer, established the most powerful and influential Reformed group in the Swiss city of **Geneva**. Here Calvin set up a theocracy similar to Zwingli's rule in Zurich.

Born in 1509, Calvin grew up in Catholic France at the start of the Reformation. He received an education in theology, law, and humanism that prompted him to study the Bible very carefully and to formulate his own Protestant theology. In 1536 Calvin published his theology in *The Institutes of the Christian Religion*, soon one of the most popular books of its day, influencing religious reformers in Europe and later in North America.

The cornerstone of Calvin's theology was the belief that God possessed all-encompassing power and knowledge. Calvin contended that God alone directed everything that has happened in the past, that happens in the present, and that will happen in the future. Thus, he argued, God determines the fate of every person—a doctrine he called predestination.

To advance his views, Calvin tried to turn the city of Geneva into a model religious community. He began this project in 1541 by establishing the Consistory, a church council of 12 elders that was given the power to control almost every aspect of people's daily lives. All citizens were required to attend Reformed church services several times each week. The Consistory inspected homes annually to make sure that no one was disobeying the laws that forbade fighting, swearing, drunkenness, gambling, card playing, and dancing. It dispensed harsh punishments to people who disobeyed any of these laws. This strict atmosphere earned Geneva the title "City of God" and attracted reformers from all parts of Europe.

Visitors to Geneva helped to spread Calvinism, or John Calvin's teaching, throughout Europe. Because the Calvinist church was led by local councils of ministers and elected church members, it was easy to establish in most countries. Furthermore, the somewhat democratic structure of this organization gave its participants a stake in its welfare and inspired their intense loyalty.

The people of the Netherlands and Scotland became some of Calvin's most ardent supporters. John Knox, a leader of the Reformation in Scotland, and other reformers used Calvin's teachings to encourage moral people to overthrow "ungodly" rulers. They preached, as Calvin had, "We must obey princes and others who are in authority, but only insofar as they do not deny to God, the supreme King, Father, and Lord, what is due Him." Calvinism thus became a dynamic social force in western Europe in the 1500s and contributed to the rise of revolutionary movements later in the 1600s and 1700s.

Radical Reformers

Several new Protestant groups in western Europe, called **the Anabaptists**, initiated the practice of baptizing, or admitting into their groups, only adult members. They based this practice on the belief that only people who could make a free and informed choice to become Christians should be allowed to do so. Catholic and established Protestant churches, in contrast, baptized infants, making them church members.

Many Anabaptists denied the authority of local governments to direct their lives. They refused to hold office, bear arms, or swear oaths, and many lived separate from a society they saw as sinful. Consequently, they were often persecuted by government officials, forcing many Anabaptists to wander from country to country seeking refuge.

Although most Anabaptists were peaceful, others were fanatical in their beliefs. These zealots brought about the downfall of the rest. When in 1534 radical Anabaptists seized power in the German city of Münster and proceeded to burn books, seize private property, and practice polygamy, Lutherans and Catholics united to crush them. Together they killed the Anabaptist leaders and persecuted any surviving Anabaptist believers.

As a result, many Anabaptist groups left Europe for North America during the 1600s. In the Americas, the Anabaptists promoted two ideas that would become crucial in forming the United States of America: religious liberty and separation of church and state. Today, Protestant groups such as the Baptists, Mennonites, and Amish all trace their ancestry to the Anabaptists.

England's Church

Reformation ideas filtered into England during the 1500s. A serious quarrel between King **Henry VIII** and the pope, however, brought these ideas to the forefront.

The quarrel arose over succession to the throne. Although Henry's wife **Catherine of Aragon** had borne six children, only one child, Mary, survived. Henry wanted to leave a male heir to the throne so that England might not be plunged into another civil war like the Wars of the Roses. Believing that Catherine was too old to have more children, the king decided to marry **Anne Boleyn**. In 1527 Henry

King Henry VIII
Henry VIII was a typical Renaissance ruler who tried to excel in many areas. He enjoyed tennis, jousting, music, and discussions about religion and the sciences. He wrote a book of theology and composed several pieces of music, one of which may have been the song "Greensleeves."

English Church instead of the pope. Despite this break with Rome, Henry was not a Protestant reformer. The new Church of England kept Catholic doctrines and forms of worship. Devout Catholics, however, opposed the king's rule of the Church. The most noted Catholic, the humanist scholar Thomas More, was beheaded for treason in 1535. Henry took other measures against supporters of the old religion. Between 1536 and 1540, he closed monasteries and convents, seized their land, and shared the gains with nobles and other high officials. In this way, the king filled his treasury and ensured influential support for his religious policies.

Henry also worked to strengthen the succession to the throne. He had the Church of England end his marriage to Catherine and then wed Anne Boleyn. Anne bore him a daughter, Elizabeth. In the years that followed, Henry married four more times but had only one son, Edward. When Henry died in 1547, 9-year-old Edward succeeded him to the throne. The young king was dominated by devout Protestant officials who introduced Protestant doctrines into the Church of England.

When Edward VI died in his teens, his Catholic half sister **Mary** became queen. Mary tried to restore Catholicism in England and ended up burning hundreds of Protestants at the stake. This persecution earned her the nickname of "Bloody Mary" and only served to strengthen her people's support for Protestantism.

After Mary's death in 1558, her Protestant half sister, **Elizabeth I**, became queen. To unite her people, Elizabeth followed a moderate course in religion. She made the English Church Protestant with some Catholic features. Anglicanism, as this blend of Protestant belief and Catholic practice was called, pleased most English people. However, radical Protestants known as Puritans wanted to "purify" the English Church of Catholic rituals. Although at first small in numbers, the Puritans gradually became influential both in the Church of England and the English Parliament.

History & Art *Henry VIII, a portrait by Hans Holbein, shows the king's splendid royal attire, reflecting his authority. Why did Henry seek Parliament's support in breaking with the Catholic Church?*

asked the pope to agree to a divorce between himself and Catherine. But Catherine's nephew was the powerful Holy Roman Emperor Charles V, upon whom the pope depended for protection. Charles wanted Catherine to remain as queen of England in order to influence the country's policies in favor of his own interests. The pope refused Henry's request.

Henry would not be thwarted. With Parliament's support, he had a series of laws passed that separated the English Church from the pope. The most important law, the Act of Supremacy passed in 1534, made Henry head of the

---

SECTION 4 REVIEW

Recall

1. **Define** theocracy, predestination.
2. **Identify** Huldrych Zwingli, John Calvin, the Anabaptists, Henry VIII, Catherine of Aragon, Anne Boleyn, Edward VI, Mary, Elizabeth I.

3. **Explain** why divisions appeared among the different reformers within the Protestant movement.

Critical Thinking

4. **Making Comparisons** How did the Calvinists and Anabaptists differ in their attitudes

toward church members participating in government activities?

Understanding Themes

5. **Cultural Diffusion** Why did the Catholic Church want to stop the spread of Protestant ideas?

Critical Thinking SKILLS

Identifying Evidence

In a geography trivia game, you picked the following question: What is the longest river in the world? The game card says it is the Amazon River, but you think it is the Nile River. Your friends insist that you are wrong. How can you prove you are right?

You must identify evidence that will establish your claim. In the example above, you could consult an atlas, almanac, or encyclopedia to find the lengths of both rivers. In fact, you are correct! The Nile River is 4,160 miles long, while the Amazon is 4,000 miles long.

Learning the Skill

There are four basic kinds of evidence: 1) oral accounts (eyewitness testimony); 2) written documents (diaries, letters, books, articles); 3) objects (artifacts); and 4) visual items (photographs, videotapes, paintings). These kinds of evidence fall into one of two categories—primary evidence and secondary evidence.

Primary evidence is produced by participants or eyewitnesses to events. Eyewitness accounts or photographs of a fire are examples of primary evidence. Secondary evidence is produced later, by those who have not experienced the events directly. Textbooks and encyclopedias are examples of secondary evidence.

To identify evidence that proves a claim, first clearly define the claim. Search available information to find the kind of evidence that can prove or disprove the claim. Compare the pieces of evidence to see if they agree. Also, rate the objectivity of your evidence. In the example above, the sources you consulted— atlas, almanac, or encyclopedia—are all reliable sources of information.

However, if you are using primary sources such as letters, diaries, and news accounts, carefully assess which evidence is most reliable.

Practicing the Skill

Read the claim below. Then read each piece of evidence that follows. Decide which pieces of evidence prove the claim to be true and explain why.

Claim: *Humanism's emphasis on the value of the individual led to artistic flowering in the Renaissance.*

1. In Renaissance Italy humanist scholars opened schools to promote the study of history, philosophy, Latin, and Greek.
2. Renaissance artists used painting and sculpture to convey human emotions and values.
3. In Rome, the pope and cardinals made up the wealthiest and most powerful class of people.
4. In England, William Shakespeare wrote plays that dealt with universal human qualities such as jealousy, ambition, love, and despair.
5. The invention of the printing press spread knowledge of humanism throughout the newly emerging middle class.

Applying the Skill

Think about this claim: The humanist values of the Renaissance still dominate modern American culture. Find at least five pieces of evidence from newspapers, magazines, and other sources to prove or disprove this claim.

For More Practice

Turn to the Skill Practice in the Chapter Review on page 431 for more practice in identifying evidence.

Section 5

The Catholic Reformation

Setting the Scene

▸ **Terms to Define**
　　seminary, baroque

▸ **People to Meet**
　　Pope Paul III, the Jesuits, Ignatius of Loyola

▸ **Places to Locate**
　　Trent

Find Out　How did the Catholic Church try to halt the spread of Protestantism?

The Storyteller

The Inquisition sometimes used "ordeals" to determine guilt or innocence, confident that God would give victory to an innocent person and punish the guilty. In the "Trial of the Cross," both parties, accuser and accused, stood before a cross with arms outstretched. The first to drop his arms was judged guilty. In the "Trial by Hot Water," the accused lifted a stone from the bottom of a boiling cauldron. If, after three days, his wound had healed, he was innocent. In the "Trial by Cold Water," the accused was tied up and lowered into water. If he sank, he was innocent. If he floated, he was guilty.

—from The Medieval Inquisition, Albert Clement Shannon, 1983

Trial of Books *(detail)*

Most of the people in Spain, France, Italy, Portugal, Hungary, Poland, and southern Germany remained Catholic during the Protestant Reformation. Nevertheless, Catholicism's power was threatened by Protestantism's increasing popularity in northern Europe. To counter the Protestant challenge, Catholics decided to enact reforms. The Catholic Church had had a history of periodic reform since the Middle Ages. Thus, in the movement that came to be known as the Counter-Reformation, or Catholic Reformation, the Church eliminated many abuses, clarified its theology, and reestablished the pope's authority over church members.

TURNING POINT

Reaffirming Catholicism

During the 1530s and 1540s, **Pope Paul III** set out to reform the Church and stem the Protestant advance. To establish the goals of the Catholic Reformation, he called a council of bishops at **Trent**, Italy, in 1545.

The Council of Trent

The Council of Trent, which met in several sessions until 1563, reaffirmed Catholic teachings that had been challenged by the Protestants. Salvation, it declared, comes through faith and good works, and church tradition is equal to the Bible as a source of religious truth. The Latin Vulgate translation of the Bible was made the only acceptable version of scripture.

The Council also put an end to many church abuses. It forbade the selling of indulgences. Clergy were ordered to follow strict rules of behavior. The

The Council of Trent by **Titian**. **Held off and on for about 20 years, this church council reaffirmed Catholic doctrine and introduced reforms.** *What Bible was made the only acceptable version?*

Council decided that each diocese had to establish a seminary, or theological school, to ensure a better-educated clergy.

The Inquisition

To deal with the Protestant threat, Pope Paul also strengthened the Inquisition. As you read in Chapter 12, the Inquisition was a church court set up to stamp out heresy. In addition to carrying out its traditional functions, the Inquisition in the 1500s introduced censorship to curtail humanist and Protestant thinking. In 1543 it published the Index of Forbidden Books, a list of works considered too immoral or irreligious for Catholics to read.

The Arts

The Church also used the arts to further the Catholic Reformation. The Council of Trent maintained the Church's elaborate art and ritual, and it declared that the Mass should be said only in Latin.

Church art and Latin ritual were to serve as sources of inspiration for educated and less educated Catholics alike. Many artists were influenced by the intensely emotional devotion of the Catholic Reformation. One of these was the Greek painter Domenikos Theotokopoulos, known in Spain as El Greco, or "The Greek." Residing in Spain, El Greco painted the saints in distorted figures that showed strong religious feelings.

As the Catholic Reformation spread through Europe, it helped spark a new style of art and architecture called baroque (buh•ROHK). The Renaissance arts had shown restraint, simplicity, and order, but the baroque arts stressed emotion, complexity, and exaggeration for dramatic effect. In painting, Peter Paul Rubens of Flanders was a master of the baroque style. He painted large altarpieces of emotional religious scenes as well as mythological subjects. Another master was the Spaniard Diego Velázquez, who painted portraits at the Spanish royal court. Among the most famous

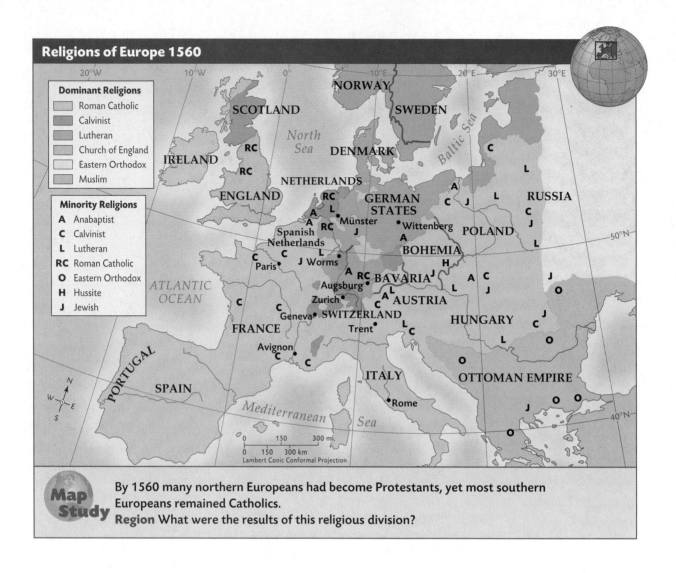

Religions of Europe 1560

Dominant Religions
- Roman Catholic
- Calvinist
- Lutheran
- Church of England
- Eastern Orthodox
- Muslim

Minority Religions
- **A** Anabaptist
- **C** Calvinist
- **L** Lutheran
- **RC** Roman Catholic
- **O** Eastern Orthodox
- **H** Hussite
- **J** Jewish

Map Study

By 1560 many northern Europeans had become Protestants, yet most southern Europeans remained Catholics.
Region What were the results of this religious division?

baroque architects was the Italian artist Gian Lorenzo Bernini. His best known work is the public square of St. Peter's Basilica in Rome, which is enclosed by two great semicircles of columns.

Spreading Catholicism

The Church also set out to win converts and to strengthen the spiritual life of Catholics. Many religious orders and individuals in the Church became involved in these efforts.

Ignatius of Loyola

In 1540 the pope recognized a new religious order, the Society of Jesus, or **Jesuits**. Founded by **Ignatius of Loyola**, the Jesuits worked to spread Catholicism and combat heresy.

Ignatius was a Spanish noble whose military career had ended abruptly when he was wounded in battle. During a long recovery, he found comfort in the lives of the saints and vowed to serve God.

The outcome of his vow was the founding of the Jesuits, who followed a strict spiritual discipline and pledged absolute obedience to the pope.

The Jesuits wore the black robes of monks, lived simple lives, but did not withdraw from the world. They preached to the people, helped the poor, and set up schools. They also served as advisers in royal courts and founded universities. Jesuit centers of learning taught not only theology but also physics, astronomy, mathematics, archaeology, and other subjects.

As missionaries, the Jesuits helped strengthen Catholicism in southern Germany, Bohemia, Poland, and Hungary. They also carried their message to the Americas, Africa, and Asia. The Jesuit priest Matteo Ricci, for example, traveled to China and preached Christianity at the court of the Ming emperor. To make his message relevant to Chinese needs, Ricci learned to speak Chinese and dressed in Chinese clothing. Although he had little success in spreading his religious beliefs, Ricci shared with Chinese scholars his knowledge of European arts and sciences.

Teresa of Avila

Another supporter of Catholic renewal was the Spanish nun Teresa of Avila. Born to a noble family in 1515, Teresa entered a Carmelite convent. Daily life there, however, was not strict enough for the deeply religious Teresa, so she set up her order of Carmelite nuns. With the pope's approval, Teresa later opened many new convents throughout Spain. Made a saint after her death, Teresa became known for her spiritual writings that rank among the devotional classics of Christianity.

A Divided Europe

While Catholicism carried out reforms, the Catholic Holy Roman Emperor Charles V tried, but failed, to stem the spread of Protestantism in his domains. Finally, in 1555, Charles and the German princes signed the Peace of Augsburg, which allowed each prince—whether Catholic or Lutheran—to choose the religion of his subjects.

This treaty set the stage for the division of Europe into a Protestant north and a Catholic south, a division that remains to this day. Northern Germany and Scandinavia were Lutheran as a result of the efforts of monarchs and princes. Areas of southern Germany, Switzerland, the Netherlands, and Scotland—with their economic wealth based in towns—held to Calvinism. England set up its own Anglican Church, a blend of Protestantism and Catholicism under royal control.

There were many reasons why Europeans in large numbers supported Protestantism. One reason was undoubtedly religious conviction. However, nonreligious factors were also involved. German princes often favored Protestantism in order to increase their power. They made Protestantism the official religion of their territories, placing it under their control. They also seized lands and wealth owned by the Catholic Church. Townspeople also rallied to the new faith, which supported their business practices. Above all, northern Europeans saw Protestantism as a way to

Visualizing History Jesuit missionaries in Japan are depicted by a Japanese painter. *Who founded the Society of Jesus?*

defy an Italian-controlled Catholic Church that drew so much money from their homelands.

During the 1500s and early 1600s, religious wars engulfed Europe, bringing widespread killing and destruction. In France, a struggle for the monarchy heightened bitter fighting between French Protestants, or Huguenots, and the Catholic majority. Both sides carried out terrible atrocities. The most infamous event was the Saint Bartholomew's Day Massacre. On that day—August 24, 1572—violence erupted that led to the killing of 3,000 Huguenots.

Religious bigotry also brought hard times to European Jews caught in the middle of the Christian feuding. One exception to this pattern of intolerance was the Netherlands, which took in Jews driven out of other areas of Europe.

SECTION 5 REVIEW

Recall
1. **Define** seminary, baroque.
2. **Identify** Pope Paul III, the Jesuits, Ignatius of Loyola.
3. **List** the educational opportunities provided by the Jesuits.

Critical Thinking
4. **Analyzing Information** List any three of the reforms proposed by the Council of Trent. Beside each, give the Protestant viewpoint to which it responded.

Understanding Themes
5. **Reaction** Evaluate the actions the Church took to halt the spread of Protestantism and their effects. Which were successful, and which were not?

from

The Prince

by Niccolò Machiavelli

Like many other Renaissance thinkers, Niccolò Machiavelli (1469–1527) analyzed human actions rather than spiritual issues. Unlike many of his contemporaries, however, he focused on the selfish side of human nature more than on humanity's potential for progress. Machiavelli observed how successful politicians won and secured power. He sent his thoughts to an Italian prince, hoping to win a position as an adviser. His ruthlessly honest look at how politicians act both confirms and challenges the views we have toward our leaders.

It is the custom of those who are anxious to find favor in the eyes of a prince to present him with such things as they value most highly or in which they see him take delight. Hence offerings are made of horses, arms, golden cloth, precious stones and such ornaments, worthy of the greatness of the Prince. Since therefore I am desirous of presenting myself to Your Magnificence with some token of my eagerness to serve you, I have been able to find nothing in what I possess which I hold more dear or in greater esteem than the knowledge of the actions of great men which has come to me through a long experience of present-day affairs and continual study of ancient times. And having pondered long and diligently on this knowledge and tested it well, I have reduced it to a little volume which I now send to Your Magnificence. Though I consider this work unworthy of your presence, nonetheless I have much hope that your kindness may find it acceptable, if it be considered that I could offer you no better gift than to give you occasion to learn in a very short space of time all that I have come to have knowledge and understanding of over many years and through many hardships and dangers. I have not adorned the work nor inflated it with lengthy clauses nor pompous or magnificent words, nor added any other refinement or extrinsic ornament wherewith many are wont to advertise or embellish their work, for it has been my wish either that no honor should be given it or that simply the truth of the material and the gravity of the subject should make it acceptable....

As for the exercise of the mind, the prince should read the histories of all peoples and ponder on the actions of the wise men therein recorded, note how they governed themselves in time of war, examine the reasons for their victories or defeats in order to imitate the former and avoid the latter, and above all conduct himself in accordance with the example of some great man of the past....

We now have left to consider what should be the manners and attitudes of a prince toward his subjects and his friends. As I know that many have written on this subject I feel that I may be held presumptuous in what I have to say, if in my comments I do not follow the lines laid down by others. Since, however, it has been my intention to write something which may be of use to the understanding reader, it has seemed wiser to me to follow the real truth of the matter rather than what we imagine it to be. For imagination has created many principalities and republics that have never been seen or known to have any real existence, for how we live is so different from how we ought to live that he who studies what ought to be done rather than what is done will learn the way to his downfall rather than to his preservation. A man striving in every way to be good will meet his ruin among the great number who are not good. Hence it is necessary for a prince, if he wishes to remain in power, to learn how not to be good and to use his knowledge or refrain from using it as he may need....

Here the question arises; whether it is better to be loved than feared or feared than loved. The answer is that it would be desirable to be both

Visualizing History Machiavelli advised Lorenzo de' Medici, who became the ruler of Florence in 1513, to be as cunning as his grandfather, Lorenzo the Magnificent, shown here. *Why did Machiavelli believe it is better to be feared than loved?*

CAES · BORGIA · VALENTINV

Visualizing History This portrait of Cesare Borgia embodies the pride and confidence of the prince about whom Machiavelli wrote his political commentary. Borgia, the son of the controversial Pope Alexander VI, used his position as duke of Romagna to enhance papal political power. *When should a leader not keep his word, according to Machiavelli?*

but, since that is difficult, it is much safer to be feared than to be loved, if one must choose. For on men in general this observation may be made: they are ungrateful, fickle, and deceitful, eager to avoid dangers, and avid for gain, and while you are useful to them they are all with you, offering you their blood, their property, their lives, and their sons so long as danger is remote, as we noted above, but when it approaches they turn on you. Any prince, trusting only in their words and having no other preparations made, will fall to his ruin, for friendships that are bought at a price and not by greatness and nobility of soul are paid for indeed, but they are not owned and cannot be called upon in time of need. Men have less hesitation in offending a man who is loved than one who is feared, for love is held by a bond of

obligation which, as men are wicked, is broken whenever personal advantage suggests it, but fear is accompanied by the dread of punishment which never relaxes.…

Hence a wise leader cannot and should not keep his word when keeping it is not to his advantage or when the reasons that made him give it are no longer valid. If men were good, this would not be a good precept, but since they are wicked and will not keep faith with you, you are not bound to keep faith with them.…

So a prince need not have all the aforementioned good qualities, but it is most essential that he appear to have them. Indeed, I should go so far as to say that having them and always practicing them is harmful, while seeming to have them is useful. It is good to appear clement [merciful], trustworthy, humane, religious, and honest, and also to be so, but always with the mind so disposed that, when the occasion arises not to be so, you can become the opposite. It must be understood that a prince and particularly a new prince cannot practice all the virtues for which men are accounted good, for the necessity of preserving the state often compels him to take actions which are opposed to loyalty, charity, humanity, and religion. Hence he must have a spirit ready to adapt itself as the varying winds of fortune command him. As I have said, so far as he is able, a prince should stick to the path of good but, if the necessity arises, he should know how to follow evil.

A prince must take great care that no word ever passes his lips that is not full of the above mentioned five good qualities, and he must seem to all who see and hear him a model of piety, loyalty, integrity, humanity, and religion. Nothing is more necessary than to seem to possess this last quality, for men in general judge more by the eye than the hand; as all can see but few can feel. Everyone sees what you seem to be, few experience what you really are and these few do not dare to set themselves up against the opinion of the majority supported by the majesty of the state. In the actions of all men and especially princes, where there is no court of appeal, the end is all that counts. Let a prince then concern himself with the acquisition or the maintenance of a state; the means employed will always be considered honorable and praised by all, for the mass of mankind is always swayed by the appearances and by the outcome of an enterprise.…

I am not ignorant of the fact that many have

Visualizing History *The Pier and the Ducal Palace* **(detail) by Luca Carlevaris.**
According to the principles of Machiavelli, why should a ruler carefully maintain the exterior of the palace?

held and hold the opinion that the things of this world are so ordered by fortune and God that the prudence of mankind may effect little change in them, indeed is of no avail at all. On this basis it could be argued that there is no point in making any effort, but we should rather abandon ourselves to destiny. This opinion has been the more widely held in our day on account of the great variations in things that we have seen and are still witnessing and which are entirely beyond human conjecture. Sometimes indeed, thinking on such matters, I am minded to share that opinion myself. Nevertheless I believe, if we are to keep our free will, that it may be true that fortune controls half of our actions indeed but allows us the direction of the other half, or almost half.…

RESPONDING TO LITERATURE

1. Describe in your own words Machiavelli's view of human nature.
2. Write a brief essay giving an example that explains whether today's politicians follow Machiavelli's advice.
3. Propose an alternative principle to Machiavelli's

view that "where there is no court of appeal, the end is all that counts."

4. **Making Judgments** Do you think individuals should follow Machiavelli's advice in dealing with their family, friends, and classmates? Why or why not?

Connections Across Time

Historical Significance During the Renaissance, Europeans focused less on religion and the afterlife and more on individual achievement and on worldly concerns. Like the ancient Greeks and Romans whom they admired, Europe's educated classes stressed human achievement and supported the arts—especially architecture, painting, and sculpture.

With a renewed interest in learning, Europeans began to question age-old traditions and called for church reforms. When changes did not take place, some Europeans broke away from Catholicism and formed Protestant churches. Protestantism—emphasizing individual salvation and the worthiness of ordinary occupations—profoundly influenced the lands and cultures of northern Europe.

Using Key Terms

Write the key term that completes each sentence. Then write a sentence for each term not chosen.

a. baroque	h. theocracy
b. humanism	i. doge
c. seminary	j. sonnet
d. vocations	k. châteaux
e. indulgences	l. secular
f. predestination	m. individualism
g. justification by faith	

1. The Catholic Reformation made use of a new style of art known as _____.
2. _____, or the Renaissance interest in the ancient classical writings, sparked an interest in human creativity and fulfillment.
3. A _____ was a Renaissance form of writing that dealt with the theme of love.
4. _____ is the belief that a person could be made good simply by faith in God's mercy and love.
5. The Italian city of Venice had a republican style of government headed by an elected official called a _____.

Technology Activity

Using a Computerized Card Catalog Make use of a library's computerized card catalog to choose a Renaissance artist to research. Find information about the person's life and achievements. Using your research, create an oral history about that person by role-playing him or her. Have the class ask you questions about your life and your contributions to the Renaissance. Your responses should reflect your researched information.

Using Your History Journal

One effect of the Reformation was the migration of thousands of people to colonial America. Research and write a brief history of one religious group's migration. Create a map that shows the origin and destination(s) of that group.

Reviewing Facts

1. **Government/Culture** Explain how the city-states of Renaissance Italy were governed. What social classes were present in the typical city-state?
2. **Culture** Describe how the art and architecture of the Renaissance differed from the art and architecture of the Middle Ages.
3. **History** Discuss why the Protestant and Catholic Reformations were important turning points in the history of Europe.
4. **Culture** Explain why Henry VIII separated from the Catholic Church and created the Church of England.
5. **Culture** State how Ignatius of Loyola and Teresa of Avila helped to reform Catholicism.

Critical Thinking

1. **Apply** Why did the Medici rulers use tax revenues to fund public works projects that benefited all the citizens of Florence?
2. **Analyze** What were the causes of the Protestant Reformation? Could the Reformation have occurred without a reformer such as Luther?

3. **Evaluate** How did the religious reformations of the 1500s affect Europe? How might Europe's religious heritage affect efforts toward unity today?

4. **Analyze** Apollonio Giovanni, an Italian artist, painted the entry of a group of cavaliers into a town in the 1300s, shown below. In what ways does this painting show how Renaissance artists broke away from traditional forms?

Understanding Themes

1. **Innovation** Why did the Renaissance begin in Italy? How did the movement change European thought and culture?

2. **Cultural Diffusion** How did the people of northern Europe adapt Italian Renaissance ideas to their society?

3. **Conflict** Could the conflict between Luther and the pope have been resolved if either had reacted differently? Explain.

4. **Cultural Diffusion** What factors helped Protestant ideas to spread so rapidly?

5. **Reaction** In what ways could the Catholic Reformation be called the Counter-Reformation?

Skill Practice

Use the information in Chapter 16 to find evidence for each claim below. Then decide which claim you support.

1. Martin Luther was a sincere believer who only wanted to reform the Catholic Church.

2. Martin Luther was a rebel intent on splitting the Catholic Church.

Linking Past and Present

1. Do you think ancient Greek and Roman culture influences artists, architects, and writers as much today as it did during the Renaissance? Why or why not?

2. What ideas of the Protestant Reformation do you think affect the United States today?

Geography in History

1. **Location** What is the approximate location of the first Spanish bishopric in South America?

2. **Region** In what geographic region were most Spanish missions established during the 1500s?

3. **Human/Environment Interaction** Large areas of South America were unreached by missionaries in the first 200 years of Spanish, Portuguese, and French mission activity. What geographic feature contributed to this?

4. **Place** What river did Jesuit missionaries use as a means of gaining access to the interior of South America?

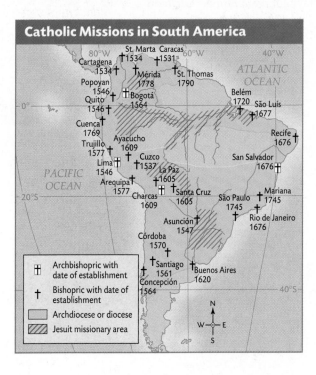

Catholic Missions in South America

St. Marta 1534
Caracas 1531
Cartagena 1534
Mérida 1778
St. Thomas 1790
Popoyan 1546
Bogotá 1564
Quito 1546
Belém 1720
São Luís 1677
Cuenca 1769
Trujillo 1577
Ayacucho 1609
Cuzco 1537
Recife 1676
Lima 1546
La Paz 1605
San Salvador 1676
Arequipa 1577
Santa Cruz 1605
Charcas 1609
São Paulo 1745
Mariana 1745
Asunción 1547
Rio de Janeiro 1676
Córdoba 1570
Santiago 1561
Buenos Aires 1620
Concepción 1564

ATLANTIC OCEAN
PACIFIC OCEAN

✛ Archbishopric with date of establishment
✝ Bishopric with date of establishment
▨ Archdiocese or diocese
▨ Jesuit missionary area

Chapter 16 *Renaissance and Reformation* **431**

1400–1750

Expanding Horizons

Chapter Themes

▶ **Innovation** European sailors borrow technological and navigational ideas from Asia. *Section 1*

▶ **Movement** European nations establish colonies in the lands they explore in Asia, Africa, and the Americas. *Section 2*

▶ **Change** The wealth of overseas colonies sparks the Commercial Revolution in Europe. *Section 3*

The Storyteller

On the night of October 11, 1492, Christopher Columbus scanned the horizon, praying that landfall was near. "About 10 o'clock at night, while standing on the sterncastle, I thought I saw a light to the west. It looked like a little wax candle bobbing up and down. It had the same appearance as a light or torch belonging to fishermen or travellers...."

The light flickered out, though, and the ship sailed on. The moon rose, but no land appeared. Two hours later, the boom of a cannon roared across the water. A sailor aboard the Pinta, the fastest of the expedition's three ships, had sighted land. For Spain and other nations of Europe, the land that appeared in the darkness was part of a far greater treasure. As a result of Columbus's voyage, contacts increased among Europeans, Native Americans, Africans, and Asians.

Historical Significance

How were Europe, Asia, Africa, and the Americas changed as the result of cross-cultural contacts from the 1400s to the 1700s?

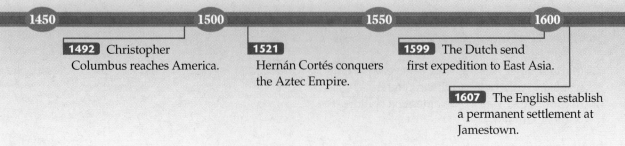

1450	1500	1550	1600

1492 Christopher Columbus reaches America.

1521 Hernán Cortés conquers the Aztec Empire.

1599 The Dutch send first expedition to East Asia.

1607 The English establish a permanent settlement at Jamestown.

This busy English port of the 1700s reveals England's position
as one of Europe's major seafaring nations.

Your History Journal

Imagine crossing the Atlantic, the Pacific, or the Indian Ocean in the early 1600s. Compared to today, ships were small, and the journey was neither safe nor pleasant. Write a diary of a few days on such a voyage.

1400	1450	1500

1432 Prince Henry the Navigator's explorers reach the Azores.

1488 Bartholomeu Dias of Portugal sails to the tip of Africa.

1519 Magellan expedition sets sail from Seville, Spain.

Section 1

Early Explorations

Setting the Scene

▶ **Terms to Define**
cartographer, line of demarcation, circumnavigation

▶ **People to Meet**
Prince Henry the Navigator, Bartholomeu Dias, Vasco da Gama, Christopher Columbus, Ferdinand Magellan

▶ **Places to Locate**
Cape of Good Hope, Strait of Magellan

ind Out Why did Europeans risk dangerous ocean voyages to discover sea routes to other parts of the world?

The Storyteller

Wealth was on everyone's mind when they thought about the New World. Ferdinand and Isabella wrote, "We have commanded [Columbus]

Spanish treasure

to return … because thereby our Lord God is served, His Holy Faith extended and our own realms increased." The King and Queen offered financial incentives for accompanying Columbus: "Whatever persons wish to … dwell in … Hispaniola … shall pay no tax whatsoever and shall have for their own … the houses which they build and the lands which they work…." As a final enticement, Columbus insisted, "The Indians are the wealth of Hispaniola—for they perform all labor of men and beasts."

—adapted from *Ferdinand and Isabella,* Felipe Fernández-Armesto, 1975

$\mathcal{I}$n the 1400s European explorers tested uncharted oceans in search of a better trade route to Asia. They left their homelands filled with a desire for gold, glory, and for spreading Christianity. In just over 250 years, their ventures had destroyed and built empires at a great cost in human life. Their efforts, however, linked people of different cultures and ended forever the isolation of the world's major civilizations.

Age of Exploration

Europe in the 1300s had depended on spices from Asia. Such spices as pepper, cinnamon, and nutmeg were in great demand. Used chiefly to flavor and preserve meat, spices were also used for perfumes, cosmetics, and medicine.

The spice trade was controlled by Arab and Venetian merchants. Chinese and Indian traders sold spices to Arab merchants, who then shipped the cargoes overland to Europe and reaped huge profits in the sale of the spices to the Venetians. Europeans, eager to amass quick fortunes through direct trade with Asians, began to look for quicker routes eastward. Because the Mongols by the mid-1300s could no longer guarantee safe passage for traders on overland routes, Europeans were forced to consider the sea as a possible route to Asia.

Several motivations led Europeans into an era of exploration. Not only did merchants seek a profitable trade with Asia, but also church leaders sought to halt the expansion of Islam and to spread Christian teachings. Learning and imagination also played a part. Renaissance thinkers had expanded the European world view to include new possibilities for exploration and discovery.

Overseas voyages would end Europe's isolation and set it on the path of worldwide expansion.

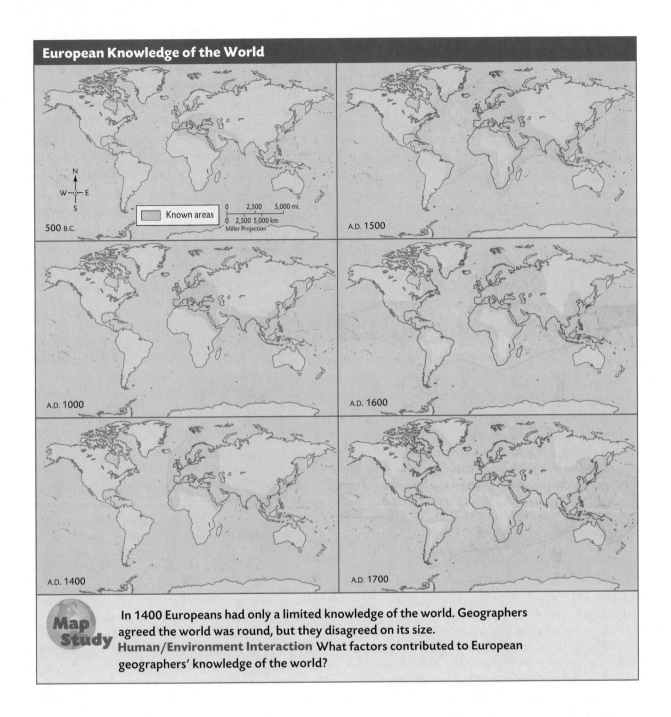

European Knowledge of the World

Known areas

0   2,500   5,000 mi.
0 2,500 5,000 km
Miller Projection

500 B.C.

A.D. 1500

A.D. 1000

A.D. 1600

A.D. 1400

A.D. 1700

Map Study In 1400 Europeans had only a limited knowledge of the world. Geographers agreed the world was round, but they disagreed on its size.
Human/Environment Interaction What factors contributed to European geographers' knowledge of the world?

They would also prepare the way for the rise of the world's first global age.

Technology of Exploration

Open-water ocean sailing—necessary to find a water route to Asia—required sailors trained in navigation, accurate maps, and oceangoing ships. For exploration to succeed, ships had to be able both to leave the coastal waters and sight of land and to return home. Ancient navigators stayed close to the coast, using landmarks to determine their position. Later, sailors who traveled beyond sight of land used the positions of stars and the sun to determine in which direction they were traveling. Hourglasses told them how long they had traveled. Keeping track of speed, direction, and time theoretically enabled a captain to tell where the ship was. However, these calculations were very inaccurate.

The compass, of Chinese origin, enabled sailors to determine geographical direction. By 1100, sailors used the astrolabe—perfected by the Arabs—to determine the altitude of the sun or other heavenly bodies. But in practice, standing on the deck of a heaving ship, few ship captains had the skill and patience that the astrolabe required.

An astrolabe

Maps were another problem for early navigators. Most maps were wildly inaccurate, drawn from scattered impressions of travelers and traders. Cartographers, or mapmakers, filled their parchments with lands found only in rumor or legend.

Cartographers' skills gradually improved. By about 1300, coastal charts showed the Mediterranean coastline with a great degree of accuracy. During the Renaissance, works by the Hellenistic astronomer Ptolemy reappeared in Europe. His maps, improved over the centuries by Byzantine and Arab scholars, gave Europeans a new picture of the world. Ptolemy also introduced the grid system of map references based on the coordinates of latitude and longitude still in use today all over the world.

Innovations were also made in the construction of ships. Late in the 1400s, shipwrights began to outfit ships with triangle-shaped lateen sails perfected by Arab traders. These sails made it possible for ships to sail against the wind, not simply with it. Shipwrights also abandoned using a single mast with one large sail. Multiple masts, with several smaller sails hoisted one above the other, made ships travel much faster. In addition, moving the rudder from the ship's side to the stern made ships more maneuverable.

In the 1400s a European ship called a caravel incorporated all these improvements. The caravel was up to 65 feet (20 m) in length with the capability of carrying about 130 tons (118 metric tons) of cargo. Because a caravel drew little water, it allowed explorers to venture up shallow inlets and to beach the ship to make repairs. A Venetian mariner called the caravels "the best ships that sailed the seas." The caravels also carried new types of weapons—rifles and cannons.

Portugal Leads the Way

Portugal was the first European country to venture out on the Atlantic Ocean in search of spices and gold. Between 1420 and 1580, Portuguese captains pushed farther and farther down the west coast of Africa in search of a sea route to Asia.

Although **Prince Henry the Navigator**, son of King John I of Portugal, was not a sailor—never making an ocean voyage—he brought together mapmakers, mathematicians, and astronomers to study navigation. He also sponsored many Portuguese exploratory voyages westward into the Atlantic and southward down Africa's west coast. In the early 1400s Henry's explorers discovered the Azores, the Madeira Islands, and the Cape Verde Islands. These discoveries were the foundation of what in the 1500s became the Portuguese Empire.

In August 1487 **Bartholomeu Dias** left Portugal, intent upon finding the southern tip of Africa. In 1488 his expedition discovered the southern tip of Africa, which was later named the **Cape of Good Hope**. Dias's voyage proved that ships could reach East Asia by sailing around Africa.

In 1497 four ships led by **Vasco da Gama** sailed from Portugal for India. The expedition rounded the Cape of Good Hope, made stops at trading centers along the east coast of Africa, and landed at Calicut on the southwest coast of India in 10 months. There da Gama found Hindus and

Richard Schlecht

"Little Girl"

The *Niña*—"Little Girl"—was Christopher Columbus's favorite ship, a small, fast, seaworthy vessel about 67 feet long. Descriptions of the *Niña* discovered in a Spanish document from the period have enabled historians to draw pictures of what the craft actually looked like. In this drawing the lines in red show the *Niña*'s sails and riggings. The document also revealed that the *Niña* had four masts, not two or three, as previously believed. Columbus's beloved "Little Girl," the most technically advanced craft of her day, probably made three of his four voyages to the Americas.

The Europe of 1500 was on the brink of the modern era. Monarchs Isabella and Ferdinand of Spain could command Columbus and other explorers, who combined knowledge of sophisticated naval technologies with bravery and determination. In quick succession Columbus (1492), Vasco da Gama (1498), and Magellan (1519–21), among others, linked Europe with the rest of the world. The sea-sheltered Americas were invaded. The slave trade expanded and brought much of Africa into the shadow of the Americas. The Muslim peoples of Africa and Asia lost their central position as guardians of trade between Europe, Asia, and Africa. Within a few centuries, the whole world came within European explorers' reach. ⊕

Muslims trading fine silk, porcelain, and spices that made the glass beads and trinkets of the Portuguese appear shoddy.

Da Gama tried to persuade the ruler of Calicut and Muslim merchants in India to trade with the Portuguese. He had little success and returned home. In Portugal, however, da Gama was regarded as a national hero. He had pioneered a water route to India, and he had provided a glimpse of the riches that could come from direct trade with the East.

Spain's Quest for Riches

In the late 1400s Spain ended a long period of internal turmoil and wars against the Moors. Under King Ferdinand and Queen Isabella, Spain entered the race for Asian riches by backing the expeditions of an Italian navigator named **Christopher Columbus**.

Columbus Crosses the Atlantic

In 1492 Christopher Columbus approached Queen Isabella with an intriguing plan—to reach India by sailing west across the Atlantic. For years

History & Art *Columbus Before the Queen* by Peter Rothermel, 1842. National Museum of American Art, Washington, D.C. **Seven years of persistent pleading earned Spain's support.** *How many voyages did Columbus make seeking proof that he had discovered a new route to India?*

Columbus had tried unsuccessfully to persuade other European rulers to finance his voyage. With Queen Isabella his persistence paid off.

In August 1492 Columbus sailed from Spain with three small ships. He calculated the distance to India to be 700 leagues, about 2,200 nautical miles; he knew that the actual distance might be greater. To calm the crews' fears, he showed them a log that understated the distance they had sailed from home.

The days out of sight of land wore on and on, however, and the terrified sailors begged Columbus to turn back. After a false sighting of land, the crews began to talk of mutiny. Columbus reluctantly agreed to turn back if they did not reach land within three days.

After midnight on the second day, the expedition sighted land. In the morning Columbus and his men went ashore, becoming the first Europeans to set foot on one of the islands of the Bahamas. Columbus wrote of the inhabitants:

  ❝ The islanders came to the ships' boats, swimming and bringing us parrots and balls of cotton thread … which they exchanged for … glass beads and hawk bells … they took and gave of what they had very willingly, but it seemed to me that they were poor in every way. They bore no weapons, nor were they acquainted with them, because when I showed them swords they seized them by the edge and so cut themselves from ignorance. ❞

Believing he was off the coast of India, Columbus called the islanders "Indians." Columbus spent the next three months exploring the islands Hispaniola (present-day Haiti and the Dominican Republic) and Cuba in search of gold. Although he found enough gold to raise Spanish hopes, he saw no evidence of the great civilizations of Asia.

When Columbus returned to Spain, Ferdinand and Isabella gave him the title "Admiral of the Ocean Sea, Viceroy and Governor of the Islands he hath discovered in the Indies." Before he died in 1506, Columbus made three more voyages to the Caribbean islands and South America seeking proof that he had discovered a new route to Asia. He died certain that he had.

Even without sure proof, it was difficult for anyone to dispute Columbus's claim. Maps of the time did not show any landmass between Europe and Asia. It was not until 1507 that another Italian explorer, Amerigo Vespucci (veh•SPOO•chee), suggested that Columbus had discovered a "New World." In honor of Vespucci, the name *America* began to appear on maps that included the newly discovered lands.

Dividing the World

Both Spain and Portugal wanted to protect their claims in the Americas and turned to the pope for help. In 1493 the pope drew a line of demarcation, an imaginary line running down the middle of the Atlantic from the North Pole to the South Pole. Spain was to have control of all lands to the west of the line, while Portugal was to have control of all lands to the east of the line.

The Portuguese, however, feared that their line was so far to the east that Spain might take over their Asian trade. As a result, in 1494 Spain and Portugal signed the Treaty of Tordesillas (TAWR•duh•SEE•yuhs), an agreement to move the line of demarcation farther west. The treaty divided the entire unexplored world between just two powers, Spain and Portugal.

History & Art *Discovery of Magellan Strait* (artist unknown). **By this point in Magellan's voyage, one ship foundered on the rocks and another turned back.** *What did the journey prove?*

Voyage of Magellan

In 1519 an expedition led by **Ferdinand Magellan**, a Portuguese soldier of fortune, set sail from Seville under the Spanish flag to find a western route to Asia. The five ships and 260-man crew sailed across the Atlantic and made their way along the eastern coast of South America, searching every bay and inlet for this route.

Along the coast of Argentina, crews of three of the ships attempted a mutiny because Magellan had decided to halt the expedition until spring. Magellan executed the captain who had instigated the mutiny, regained control of the fleet, and resumed the expedition. Finally, near the southern tip of South America, the ships reached a narrow water passageway now called the **Strait of Magellan**. The ships threaded their way through the maze of rocky islands in the 350-mile- (504-km-) long strait. Strong currents and unpredictable gales separated one ship from the others, and its crew forced its return to Spain. Another was shipwrecked.

Magellan's ship and the two other remaining ships finally passed through the strait into the South Sea, which had been discovered and named seven years earlier by Vasco Núñez de Balboa. Because the water was so calm, Magellan renamed it the Pacific Ocean. The fleet then sailed nearly four months before reaching land. Water and food ran out, and some sailors died. One of the crew wrote in his journal, "We ate biscuit, which was no longer biscuit, but powder of biscuits swarming with worms, for they had eaten the good."

At last the ships reached the present-day Philippines. Caught in a skirmish between a local chief and his enemy, Magellan was killed. The surviving crew escaped and sailed for Spain.

In 1522, after three years at sea, the last ship with its 18 survivors arrived at Seville, completing the first circumnavigation, or circling of the globe. The spices they brought back barely covered the cost of the voyage, but the expedition had a value far beyond money. It proved that the world was round and much larger than anyone had believed, that the oceans of the world were connected, and that the lands discovered by Columbus were not part of Asia.

SECTION I REVIEW

Recall

1. **Define** cartographer, line of demarcation, circumnavigation.
2. **Identify** Prince Henry the Navigator, Bartholomeu Dias, Vasco da Gama, Christopher Columbus, Ferdinand Magellan.

3. **Explain** why Portugal and Spain wanted to find a sea route to Asia.

Critical Thinking

4. **Synthesizing Information** Using the text as a resource, write a journal entry describing your experiences as a sailor on an expedition of Dias, Columbus, Magellan, or da Gama.

Understanding Themes

5. **Innovation** What sciences and new technologies led to voyages of exploration?

1500 Pedro Alvares Cabral claims Brazil for Portugal.

1532 Francisco Pizarro of Spain invades the Inca Empire.

1608 France's Samuel de Champlain founds Quebec.

1640 English planters introduce sugarcane in the West Indies.

Section 2

Overseas Empires

Setting the Scene

▶ **Terms to Define**
conquistador, triangular trade, the Middle Passage

▶ **People to Meet**
Pedro Alvares Cabral, Hernán Cortés, Montezuma II, Francisco Pizarro, Atahualpa, Henry Hudson, Jacques Cartier, Samuel de Champlain, John Cabot

▶ **Places to Locate**
Brazil, Peru, West Indies, Quebec, Jamestown

 **Find Out** How did the Europeans exploit the lands and the peoples they found in Africa, Asia, and the Americas?

The Storyteller

John Sparke, who traveled with English admiral John Hawkins, wrote an account of the

Native Americans digging gold

inhabitants of the Florida coast in 1589: "They have for apothecary [medicine] herbs, trees, roots, and gum, myrrh, and frankincense, with many others, whereof I know not the names.... Gold and silver they want [lack] not, for when the Frenchmen came, they offered it for little or nothing. They received for a hatchet two pounds of gold. The soldiers, being greedy, took it from them, giving them nothing for it. When the Floridians perceived that, they stopped wearing their gold ornaments, for fear that they would be taken away."

—from *The Hawkins Voyages*, edited by Clements R. Markham, reprinted in *The Annals of America*, 1968

The Treaty of Tordesillas claimed to divide the world between Spain and Portugal. Only Spain and Portugal, however, recognized the treaty. The Netherlands, France, and England soon joined them in a race to exploit wealth from the lands beyond Europe.

Portugal and Spain

Portugal's main interest lay in Africa and Asia, and in trade rather than colonization. When the Portuguese became the first Europeans to reach the Indian Ocean, they found themselves in waters already thoroughly explored by seafarers from Asian lands. Eager to seize control of the spice trade, the Portuguese reacted quickly to Vasco da Gama's voyage to India. In 1500, less than six months after da Gama's return, 13 ships were dispatched to Calicut. Led by **Pedro Alvares Cabral**, the Portuguese won a bloody trade war with Muslim merchants and defeated a large Arab fleet to establish Portuguese control of the Indian Ocean.

The Portuguese then built naval bases along the Indian Ocean—along the Persian Gulf and in Southeast Asia. They soon controlled shipping in the Indian Ocean. Next, they expanded eastward toward the Moluccas, or the Spice Islands. From the Spice Islands, the Portuguese established trading ports in China and Japan.

Portugal also colonized the area of present-day **Brazil**. Cabral claimed this territory as he swung west across the Atlantic to India in 1500. Because this area of South America juts east of the line of demarcation, it became Portuguese. The rest of South America had been claimed by Spain.

Settlers in Brazil grew income-producing crops such as sugarcane, tobacco, coffee, and cotton. Because the local population did not supply enough labor, enslaved people were brought from Africa. By the late 1500s, Brazil was one of Portugal's most important colonies.

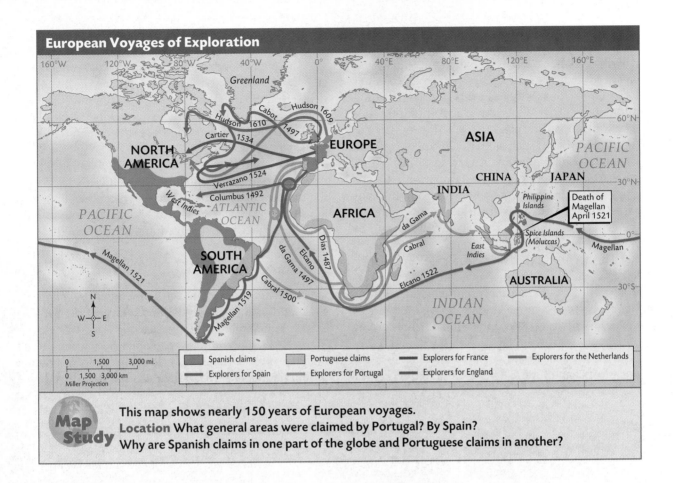

European Voyages of Exploration

This map shows nearly 150 years of European voyages.
Location What general areas were claimed by Portugal? By Spain?
Why are Spanish claims in one part of the globe and Portuguese claims in another?

Map Study

Spain

Spanish **conquistadors**, or conquerors, came to the Americas "to serve God and his Majesty, to give light to those who were in darkness and to grow rich as all men desire to do."

One conquistador, **Hernán Cortés**, landed in Mexico in 1519 with about 600 men, 16 horses, and a few cannons. Guided by Malinche (mah•LIHN •chay), a Native American woman who learned Spanish, Cortés allied with local enemies of the Aztecs and journeyed inland to Tenochtitlán. Meanwhile, in the Aztec capital, messengers told the Aztec ruler **Montezuma II** that the approaching soldiers were "supernatural creatures riding on hornless deer, preceded by wild animals on leashes, dressed in iron." Thinking that Cortés might be the long-awaited god-king Quetzalcoatl returning from the east, Montezuma offered gifts of gold.

Tenochtitlán's riches were beyond anything the Spaniards had ever seen. Soon fighting broke out. With the advantage of horses and guns, the Spanish force ultimately slaughtered thousands of Aztec people. Within three years, Aztec resistance had ended and Cortés ruled Mexico.

In 1532 another conquistador, **Francisco Pizarro**, invaded the Inca Empire in present-day Peru. The Spaniards' arrival followed a conflict in which the Incan ruler **Atahualpa** (AH•tuh•WAHL •puh) won the throne from a brother. Aided by Native American allies, Pizarro captured Atahualpa and had thousands of Inca massacred. Although a ransom was paid for Atahualpa's release, the Spaniards killed him anyway. Inca resistance continued, but Spanish forces eventually conquered vast stretches of Inca territory in South America.

Building an Empire

By the 1600s, Spain's empire in the Americas included much of North America and South America as well as islands in the **West Indies**. Keeping close watch over their empire, Spanish monarchs named viceroys, or royal representatives, to rule local provinces with the advice of councils of Spanish settlers.

Spain had two goals for its American empire— to acquire its wealth and to convert Native Americans to Christianity. Farmers set up plantations, or large estates, for the growing of sugarcane; landowners drew gold and silver from mines. At the same time priests founded missions—settlements where many Native Americans lived, worked, and adopted European ways.

Under the encomienda system, Spanish monarchs granted landowners the right to use Native American labor. Some Native Americans were enslaved and mistreated. Disease also took its toll. Exposed to diseases from Europe for the first time, millions of Native Americans died during the first 50 years of Spanish rule.

A few priests, such as Bartolomé de Las Casas, tried to protect the Native Americans. The Spanish government responded with laws meant to end abuses, but the laws were never enforced. In many cases, Native Americans resisted Spanish rule on their own by preserving their local cultures and by staging periodic revolts.

The decline in the Native American population led the Spaniards to bring over enslaved workers from Africa. As sugarcane production and profits soared, more and more Africans arrived to work in the fields and in various trades. In time, the coming together of African, Native American, and European peoples in Spain's American colonies gave rise to a new culture.

Colonies of the Netherlands

The Netherlands was also interested in expansion. In the late 1500s the Dutch won their independence from Spain. This small country on the North Sea had few natural resources and limited farmland. A large Dutch middle class saw commerce as the key to survival.

The period of the 1600s was the golden age of the Netherlands. Dutch ships were efficient, carrying more cargo and smaller crews than other ships. Amsterdam became the world's largest commercial city, and the Dutch enjoyed the world's highest standard of living.

The first Dutch expedition to East Asia returned in 1599. Three years later the Dutch chartered the Dutch East India Company to expand trade and ensure close relations between the government and enterprises in Asia.

In 1619 the company set up headquarters at Batavia on the island of Java in present-day Indonesia. Soon the Dutch controlled island trade

Images of the Times

The Dutch Republic

With no monarchy or aristocracy, the tastes and ideals of society as reflected in Dutch art were determined largely by the middle class.

The Flower Vendor and the Vegetable Vendor by Arnout de Muysor focuses on two important themes in Dutch painting of this period—middle-class life and trade.

The World Upside-down by Jan Steen, the son of a brewer, is representative of his earthy, humorous scenes of ordinary people.

in sugar, spices, coffee, and tea. Using Batavia as a base, the Dutch pushed the Portuguese and English out of Asian outposts. After taking Malacca from the Portuguese in 1641, the Netherlands controlled all trade with the Spice Islands. The Dutch also used force against local Muslim rulers to win lands and ports in the region.

At the same time, the Dutch set out for North America. An English navigator, **Henry Hudson**, claimed land for the Dutch along the Atlantic coast of North America, and in 1621 the government chartered the Dutch West India Company to establish colonies in the Americas. The company founded New Amsterdam on Manhattan Island at the mouth of the Hudson River. This settlement was soon a center for European and colonial trade.

The Dutch established a colony in Africa as well. In 1652 Dutch farmers known as Boers settled at the Cape of Good Hope to provide fresh food and water for sailing ships. By the 1700s, however, Dutch power was declining, and England had emerged as Europe's leading maritime nation.

French and English Colonies

The French and the English played only a small part in the early voyages of exploration. Religious conflicts and civil wars kept their interests focused at home. During the 1500s, however, France and England searched for overseas trading colonies.

Thwarted by the Portuguese and later the Dutch control of Asian markets, England and France turned toward North America and the Caribbean. In general, the French companies sought quick profits from trade rather than the long-term investment of farming. For the English, colonies could provide the raw materials—lumber, fish, sugarcane, rice, and wheat—they would otherwise have to purchase from other countries.

France

In 1524 the French hired an Italian captain, Giovanni da Verrazano, to find a Northwest Passage through America to Asia. Da Verrazano explored the North American coast from North

Rembrandt van Rijn, the celebrated Dutch painter, earned fame with his portraits of himself and of his family. Although he died poor and forgotten, his paintings were of more spiritual depth than those of his contemporaries.

REFLECTING ON THE TIMES

1. How does Dutch art compare with art from a nation like France that had a monarch and nobility?
2. Why did Rembrandt's work receive greater acclaim after he died?

443

Carolina to Maine without success. About ten years later the French navigator **Jacques Cartier** continued the search and sailed up the St. Lawrence River to the site of the present-day city of Montreal. He claimed much of eastern Canada for France.

In 1608 **Samuel de Champlain**, a French mapmaker, founded **Quebec**, the first permanent French settlement in the Americas. In 1673 missionaries Jacques Marquette and Louis Joliet explored the Mississippi Valley. Later, Robert Cavelier, known as Sieur de La Salle, claimed the entire inland region surrounding the Mississippi River for France.

Like the Spanish, the French sent Jesuit missionaries to convert Native Americans to Christianity. French explorers traded the Native Americans blankets, guns, and wine for animal skins. Trapping, fishing, and lumbering were also profitable.

Some French settlers went to the West Indies, where they claimed the islands of St. Kitts, Martinique, and Guadeloupe. The French brought enslaved Africans to work on sugar and tobacco plantations on the islands. Although most of their interests were in North America, the French also established trading posts in India.

England

England also showed an interest in overseas trade. In 1497 the Italian-born navigator **John Cabot** explored the coast of present-day Newfoundland. During the 1500s, English sea captains, such as Francis Drake, raided Spanish ships for gold and silver. English overseas expansion, however, did not begin until the founding of the English East India Company in 1600. This trading enterprise set up posts in India and Southeast Asia.

During the 1600s, the English also founded settlements in the Americas. On West Indian islands, such as Jamaica, they introduced sugarcane, worked by enslaved African labor. **Jamestown**, the earliest English settlement in North America, was founded in 1607 in present-day Virginia. In 1620 devout Protestants, calling themselves Pilgrims, sought religious freedom by establishing Plymouth in present-day Massachusetts. Before landing, the Pilgrims set down rules for governing Plymouth in the Mayflower Compact:

❝ We, whose names are underwritten… having undertaken for the glory of God, and advancement of the Christian faith…a voyage to plant [a] colony…do…enact, constitute, and frame …just and equal Laws…as shall be

thought most [appropriate] and convenient for the general good of the colony. ❞

In the 1600s and 1700s, English settlements arose and thrived along the eastern coast of North America. In northern areas, family-operated farms emerged, while in southern areas, plantation farming based on African enslaved labor was established. Although English monarchs supervised these settlements by sending out governors, the English in North America enjoyed a large degree of self-government in their representative assemblies modeled on the English Parliament.

English settlement, however, pushed out the earlier inhabitants, the Native Americans. Concerned about land, the English had little desire to Christianize Native Americans, although they adopted Native American farming methods and foods, such as corn and beans. On the other side, Native Americans fought back to save their lands, but disease and food shortages had reduced their numbers. As the settlers expanded inland, they also came into conflict with the Dutch and the French. By 1765, after a series of wars, the English had emerged as the leading European power in much of North America.

Slave Trade

In the 1600s European territories in the Americas based their economies on agricultural products that required intensive labor. Enslaved Africans planted and harvested sugar, tobacco, and coffee crops. They also worked silver mines.

The Triangular Trade

The slave trade was part of what was called the triangular trade. Ships sailed the legs of a triangle formed by Europe, Africa, and the Americas. Typically, European ships left their home ports carrying manufactured goods—knives, swords, guns, cloth, and rum. In West Africa the ship captains traded their goods with local rulers for enslaved people, most of whom were war captives. During the second leg of the journey, the ships brought enslaved Africans across the Atlantic to various Caribbean islands or to mainland areas in North America and South America. The enslaved Africans were sold, and the money was used to buy sugar, molasses, cotton, and tobacco. Finally, the ships returned to Europe to sell the goods purchased in America.

The Middle Passage

An enslaved person's journey from the west coast of Africa to the lands of the Americas was a ghastly ordeal called the Middle Passage. This middle leg of the triangular trade originated from ports along a 3,000-mile (4,800-km) stretch on the west coast of Africa. Captured by other Africans, enslaved Africans were sold to European slave traders along the coast for transport to American plantations.

Because large cargoes brought large profits, the slave traders packed the captives as tightly as possible. Below deck, each African occupied a space only 4 or 5 feet (122 cm to 153 cm) long and 2 or 3 feet (60 cm to 92 cm) high. Chained together, they could neither stand nor lie at full length. In the darkness and stifling heat, many Africans suffocated or died of disease.

Estimates of the number of enslaved Africans brought to America range from 10 to 24 million. One in five who began the trip did not survive it. Because of the enormous value of their "cargo," however, slave traders made some effort to keep the enslaved people alive. Psychological torment may have been worse than physical conditions. Some Africans committed suicide by jumping overboard. Others simply lost the will to live and refused to eat. Enslaved people on hunger strikes were fed forcibly.

An Enslaved Person's Life

Africans who survived the long Middle Passage faced another terror when they arrived in American ports: the slave auction. Examined and prodded by plantation owners, most Africans were sold to work as laborers—clearing land, hoeing, planting, weeding, and harvesting. The work was hard, the hours long, and life expectancy short. Because many

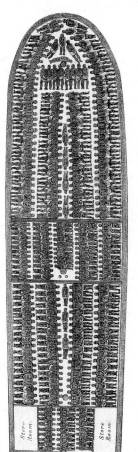

Visualizing History A deck plan shows tightly packed ranks of enslaved people on a ship bound from Africa to the Americas. *What did enslaved people experience on the Middle Passage?*

Europeans believed that Africans were physically suited to hard labor, especially in hot, humid climates, the enslaved people were viewed as nothing more than a unit of labor to exploit for profit.

Resistance

In addition to its inhumanity, the slave trade wrenched untold numbers of young, productive Africans from their homelands. This population loss at least temporarily weakened many African societies. As a result, many Africans tried to resist the slave trade. One of them was Affonso I, ruler of Kongo in central Africa. As a Christian, Affonso favored contact with Europeans but spoke out against the trade in human lives. The slave trading network, however, was too powerful for Affonso and other African opponents to end it.

Enslaved people also acted to obtain freedom. Despite heavy odds, a few escaped their masters and got far enough away to set up their own free communities. The ultimate weapon, however, was mass rebellion. In many areas of the Americas, enslaved people outnumbered free populations, who constantly feared uprisings. The most successful uprising occurred in the French-ruled West Indian island of Saint Domingue. There, a prolonged rebellion in the 1790s led to the creation of the republic of Haiti in 1804. By the early 1800s, humanitarian concerns and fear of uprisings both had fueled an anti-slavery movement that saw slavery as an evil bringing only violence, oppression, and suffering.

SECTION 2 REVIEW

Recall
1. **Define** conquistador, triangular trade, the Middle Passage.
2. **Identify** Pedro Alvares Cabral, Hernán Cortés, Montezuma II, Francisco Pizarro, Atahualpa, Henry Hudson, Jacques Cartier, Samuel de Champlain, Jacques Marquette, Louis Joliet, John Cabot.
3. **State** the goals that Spain had for its American empire.

Critical Thinking
4. **Making Comparisons** How did treatment of Native Americans differ in the colonies of Spain, France, and England?

Understanding Themes
5. **Movement** What motivated Europeans to move from their countries to the Americas?

1400 **c. 1400s** Increased trade leads to advanced banking methods.

1500 **c. 1500s** The nation replaces the city and the village as Europe's primary economic unit.

1600 **c. 1600** Europe's population reaches 100 million.

Section 3

Changing Ways of Life

Setting the Scene

▶ **Terms to Define**
joint-stock company, entrepreneur, mercantilism, bullion, balance of trade

▶ **Places to Locate**
Florence, Augsburg

 How did increased trade and colonial expansion set the stage for a global economy?

The Storyteller

The English and French considered piracy against Spain practically a religious crusade. Pirates sometimes held Holy Communion before starting a raid on a Spanish ship! The strangest pirate fleet of all, based in England, attacked Spaniards passing anywhere near, and openly sold their stolen cargo in the market. Even their Spanish prisoners were publicly auctioned for prices set by the ransom money each one might bring. Public opinion finally forced Elizabeth I to put a stop to all this: She declared the pirates public outlaws—"Rascals of the Sea."

—adapted from *The Pirate Picture*, Rayner Thrower, 1980

Pirate ship

The age of exploration brought far-reaching changes to global cultures. Overseas trade and the conquest of empires expanded Europe's economy. This search for wealth led to the rise of free enterprise, or modern capitalism, an economic system in which money is invested in business to make profits.

The Commercial Revolution

By the 1600s the nation had replaced the city and village as the basic economic unit in Europe. Nations competed for markets and trade goods. New business methods were instituted for investing money, speeding the flow of wealth, and reducing risks in commercial ventures. These changes, which came to be known as the Commercial Revolution, formed the roots of modern financial and business life.

New Business Methods

Launching an overseas trading venture was a major undertaking. The financial backer of the voyage had to raise money for supplies and to hire a crew. Often several years passed before a fleet finished trading overseas and returned home. Only then could the initial investment be recovered. Governments and rich merchants alone had enough money to back such trading voyages, and even they needed financial assistance.

At first merchants turned to bankers for the money to finance their ventures. Families like the Medici of **Florence**, Italy, and the Fuggers of **Augsburg**, Germany, loaned money as part of their operations. By the 1500s these families were so wealthy that they accepted deposits, made loans, and transferred funds over long distances. Both banking families had branches in several European cities and also made loans to European monarchs.

Visualizing History This European port scene by Jan Griffier the Elder shows the mix of cultures that resulted from the increased trade between Europeans and the rest of the world. *How did merchants protect themselves against losses?*

By the 1600s, however, these banking families were beginning to be replaced by government-chartered banks. The banks accepted deposits of money and charged interest on loans. Before long the banks began to provide other services. They issued banknotes and checks, making large payments in heavy coins a thing of the past. They acted as money changers, exchanging currencies from other countries. The banks even provided official exchange rates for foreign currency.

Individual merchants who wanted to invest in exploration often raised money by combining their resources in joint-stock companies, organizations that sold stock, or shares, in the venture, enabling large and small investors to share the profits and risks of a trading voyage. If a loss occurred, investors would lose only the amount they had invested in shares. This sharing of risk provided a stable way of raising funds for voyages.

A few joint-stock companies became rich and powerful through government support. For example, the Dutch government gave the Dutch East India Company a monopoly in trade with Africa and the East Indies. It also gave the company the power to make war, to seize foreign ships, to coin money, and to establish colonies and forts. In return

the government received customs duties, or taxes on imported goods, from the company's trade.

Increase in Money

As gold and silver flowed into Europe from abroad, the supply of coined money increased. This, in turn, led to inflation, or a dramatic rise in prices. Money, however, became more widely available for large enterprises, and ideas changed about the nature and goals of business. Gradually, a sys-

Spanish Doubloons and Pieces of Eight

During the 1500s, Spanish ships called galleons sailed the seas loaded with gold doubloons and silver pieces of eight. Minted from the plunder of Central and South American mines, the coins were a favorite target for pirates of other nations. Today, marine archaeologists have explored a number of sunken galleons and recovered hundreds of doubloons and pieces of eight—still worth a fortune.

tem based on the belief that the goal of business was to make profits took shape. Individuals known as **entrepreneurs** combined money, ideas, raw materials, and labor to make goods and profits. Profits were then used to expand the business and develop new ventures.

An entrepreneur in the cloth industry, for example, would buy wool and employ spinners to make the wool into yarn. Weavers and dyers would also be hired to turn the yarn into cloth. The entrepreneur would then sell the cloth on the open market for a price that brought a profit. Of course, entrepreneurs took risks when they put up capital for businesses. They could lose their investment if prices fell or workers could not produce goods at a specified time or for a specific market.

In the 1600s the greatest increase in trade took place in the countries bordering the Atlantic Ocean—Portugal, Spain, England, and the Netherlands—in large part because they had the largest colonial empires. Italian cities such as Venice and Genoa, formerly the leading trade centers in Europe, found themselves cut out of overseas trade as trade routes and fortunes gradually moved westward toward the Atlantic Ocean and the Americas.

Mercantilism

A new theory of national economic policy called **mercantilism** also appeared. This theory held that a state's power depended on its wealth. Accordingly, the goal of every nation was to become as wealthy as possible.

Europeans believed that the measure of a nation's wealth was the amount of **bullion**, or gold and silver, it owned. One Venetian summed up the general feeling about bullion: "[It is] the sinews of all government, it gives it its pulse, its movement, its mind, soul, and it is its essence and its very life. It overcomes all impossibilities, for it is the master …without it all is weak and without movement."

Under mercantilism, nations could gain wealth by mining gold and silver at home or overseas. Thus, Spain sent conquistadors to the Americas to seize the silver and gold mines of the Aztec and Inca Empires. Governments could also gain wealth through trade. Nations sought to create a favorable **balance of trade** by exporting more goods than they imported. The gold and silver received for exports would exceed that paid for imports. This greater wealth meant greater national power and influence in the world.

CONNECTIONS

Economics

The Commercial Revolution

Queen Elizabeth opens the Royal Exchange

Europe's economic prosperity during the 1500s and 1600s made European merchants eager to increase their fortunes. Overseas trade, however, was costly and dangerous. Individual merchants found it impossible to take the entire burden on themselves. If a voyage failed, the merchant would lose everything.

This uncertainty led to the rise of joint-stock companies, which shared expenses, risks, and profits by selling stock to many investors. Joint-stock companies became so popular that stock exchanges, where investors could buy and sell stock, developed in western Europe.

Setting up a joint-stock company involved getting a charter from the monarch, who controlled merchant trade. Charters became important in the founding of settlements and trading ventures in the Americas. Also, with their emphasis on shared risk and gain, joint-stock companies were the forerunners of modern corporations. Today, the Hudson's Bay Company, chartered in 1670 to operate the fur trade in Canada, exists as a large retail corporation with many business interests.

Linking Past and Present ACTIVITY

Explain why joint-stock companies were popular among merchants. Compare and contrast the joint-stock company of the 1600s with the modern corporation.

Coffeehouses, such as this one depicted in London in 1668, were places to converse about the news of the day—fires, feasts, riots, weddings, plays, and scandals. *Besides coffee, what other foods and drinks were introduced to Europe in this period?*

To increase national wealth, governments often aided businesses producing export goods. They sold monopolies, or the right to operate free of local competition, to producers in certain key industries. They also set tariffs, or taxes on imported goods, to protect local industries from foreign competitors.

Colonies, or overseas territories ruled by a parent country, were highly valued in the mercantilist system. They were both the sources of raw materials as well as vital markets for finished goods provided by the parent country. The primary reason for having colonies was to help make the parent country self-sufficient.

European Daily Life

The Commercial Revolution had a noticeable impact on European society. Merchants prospered most from the expansion of trade and empire. They began to surpass the nobility in both wealth and power. Hereditary nobles had to rely on rents from their lands for wealth, but rents did not rise as fast as prices.

The newly rich entrepreneurs set trends in lifestyles. Coffeehouses became their favorite gathering places where business and gossip were exchanged. A Spaniard described a coffeehouse in Amsterdam in 1688:

❝ [They] are of great usefulness in winter, with their welcoming stoves and tempting pastimes; some offer books to read, others gaming-tables and all have people ready to converse with one; one man drinks chocolate, another coffee, one milk, another tea

and practically all of them smoke tobacco …In this way they can keep warm, be refreshed and entertained for little expense, listening to the news. ❞

Joseph de la Vega, *The Wheels of Commerce*, 1817

In the countryside, however, peasants lived as meagerly as they ever had. The French writer Jean de La Bruyère (LAH•broo•YEHR) remarked that European peasants worked like animals, lived in hovels, and survived on a diet of water, black bread, and roots.

A Global Exchange

During the Commercial Revolution, Europe's population grew rapidly. In 1450 Europe had about 55 million people; by 1650, Europeans numbered about 100 million. They also had become more mobile. Towns expanded outside their walls as more and more people left rural areas to be closer to centers of trade.

Europe's growing population demanded more goods and services. This demand was met by Europe's increasing contacts with the rest of the world. As Europe's trade expanded, it contributed to a worldwide exchange of people, goods, technologies, ideas, and even diseases that had profound consequences for the entire globe.

Known as the Columbian Exchange, after Christopher Columbus, the transfer of products from continent to continent brought changes in

History & Art *Man-o'-War Firing a Salute* by Jan Porcellis. **Building an empire called for military strength in this period of intense European rivalry.** *What caused many Europeans to venture to America?*

ways of life throughout the world. Europeans brought wheat, grapes, and livestock to the Americas. From Native Americans, Europeans acquired food items such as corn, potatoes, tomatoes, beans, and chocolate, which they brought back to Europe. Easy-to-grow food crops, such as the potato, fed Europe's growing population. Some foods, such as corn, also spread to Asia and Africa, boosting population growth there. From Asia and Africa, Europeans brought to Europe and the Americas tropical products—bananas, coffee, tea, and sugarcane—and luxury goods, such as ivory, perfumes, silk, and gems.

New global trading links increased the movement of people and cultures from continent to continent. Europeans, seeking wealth or fleeing economic distress and religious persecution, moved to the Americas and other parts of the world. They exchanged food, ideas, and practices with the peoples living in these areas. European influences profoundly affected local cultures. European traders spread European languages, and European missionaries taught Christianity and European values. Wealthy Europeans, in turn, developed an interest in the arts, styles, and foods of Asia, especially Chinese porcelain, Indian textiles, and Southeast Asian spices. At the same time, the drastic decline of the Native American populations and the forcible removal of Africans to the Americas revealed that European expansion often had a disruptive effect on cultures in other parts of the world.

SECTION 3 REVIEW

Recall
1. **Define** joint-stock company, entrepreneur, mercantilism, bullion, balance of trade.
2. **Identify** capitalism and discuss the changes of the Commercial Revolution that led to its rise.
3. **Discuss** the changes brought by European expansion to other parts of the globe.

Critical Thinking
4. **Synthesizing Information** Imagine that you are an entrepreneur of the 1700s. Invent a way for making profits by using your capital and talents.

Appraise the potential risks and profits in your venture.

Understanding Themes
5. **Change** Decide which class of European society benefited most from the Commercial Revolution. Why?

Using a Computerized Card Catalog

By now you probably have been assigned several research reports. Skill in using a computerized card catalog will help you find the information you need to complete your assignment.

Learning the Skill

Go to the card-catalog computer in your school or local library. What information do you need? Type in the name of an author or performer (for tapes, cassettes, and CDs); the title of a book, videotape, audiocassette, or CD; or a subject heading. You will access the on-line, or computerized card catalog that lists all the library's resources for that topic. The computer will list on screen the title's author, or the information you requested.

The "card" that appears on screen will provide other information as well, including the year the work was published, who published it, what media type it is, and the language in which it is written or recorded. Use this information to determine if the material meets your needs. Then check to see if the item is available. In addition, find the classification (biography, travel, and so on) and call number under which it is shelved.

Practicing the Skill

This chapter discusses explorers. The following steps will help you use the computerized card catalog to find additional information on the subject "explorers":

1. Type "s/explorers."
2. From the list of subjects that appears on the screen, determine which might apply to European explorers from the 1400s to the 1700s.
3. Follow the instructions on the computer screen to display all the titles under each subject you selected. For example, the

instructions might be to type the line number next to the subject and press RETURN.
4. Determine which of the books, videos, audiocassettes, and CDs now on the screen you want to learn more about.
5. What do the instructions on the screen tell you to do to find more details?
6. What do the instructions on the screen tell you to do if you want to find out how many copies of the title the library owns and if and where a copy is available?

Applying the Skill

Use the computerized card catalog in your school or local library to identify four resources—books, videotapes, CDs, or audiocassettes—you can use to write two reports. Write one report on French explorer Jacques Cartier, and the other report on technological advances in exploration from 1400 to 1700.

For More Practice

Turn to the Skill Practice in the Chapter Review on page 453 for more practice in using a computerized card catalog.

Connections Across Time

Historical Significance The period from the 1400s to the 1700s is often called the first global age. During this time, the peoples of Europe, Asia, Africa, and the Americas came into direct contact. Through exploration, the size and dimensions of the world and its oceans became known. Europeans established overseas empires, bringing prosperity to their homelands. However, the European process of establishing colonies often left a negative impact on the cultures that Europeans encountered. In the long run, the meeting of civilizations throughout the world laid the foundation of the global community that we know today, with its exchange of ideas and practices among different peoples.

Using Key Terms

Write the key term that completes each sentence. Then write a sentence for each term not chosen.

a. cartographers
b. circumnavigation
c. conquistadors
d. entrepreneurs
e. joint-stock companies
f. line of demarcation
g. Middle Passage
h. mercantilism
i. balance of trade
j. bullion
k. triangular trade

1. An enslaved person's journey from Africa to the Americas was known as the _____.
2. As a result of discoveries made by early European explorers, _____ were able to draw maps with greater accuracy.
3. In 1522 Ferdinand Magellan's crew arrived at Seville, Spain, completing the first _____, or circling of the globe.
4. _____, or organizations that sold stock in ventures, enabled large and small investors to share the risks and profits of a trading voyage.
5. The theory of _____ held that a nation's power rested on its accumulated wealth.

Technology Activity

Using a Spreadsheet Search the Internet or your local library for additional information about early European explorers and their achievements. Organize your information by creating a spreadsheet. Include headings such as name, regions of exploration, types of technology used, and contributions. Provide a map of the world labeling oceans, continents and the routes that European explorers took in discovering the world.

Using Your History Journal

Exploration brought people from Europe into contact with the cultures of Asia, Africa, and the Americas for the first time in this period. Imagine and describe such a meeting. Remember that these people did not, when meeting, understand each other's language or culture.

Reviewing Facts

1. **History** Identify the causes and effects of European expansion in the 1500s.
2. **Technology** Describe the improvements that shipbuilders incorporated in the caravel.
3. **Economics** Explain why the Dutch turned to commerce instead of agriculture in the late 1500s.
4. **Government** Identify the Mayflower Compact and discuss politics in England's colonies.
5. **Citizenship** Describe what the Middle Passage was like for enslaved Africans.
6. **History** Explain in what ways the French and the English differed in their aims for their colonies.
7. **Economics** State how a joint-stock company enabled small investors to profit from a major voyage.

Critical Thinking

1. **Apply** Why did Columbus's plan to reach Asia by a western route appeal to Spain?
2. **Analyze** Were the English and the Spanish justified in colonizing the Americas? Why or why not?

3. Evaluate How would the colonies have been different if Europeans had not used slave labor?

4. Synthesize Why is the era from the 1400s to the 1700s called the Age of Exploration? What are its major features? What was its impact?

5. Evaluate How did the influx of wealth from the colonies help bring about the Commercial Revolution in Europe?

6. Analyze What were the results of Ferdinand Magellan's circumnavigation?

7. Apply Why were the Dutch eager to establish overseas colonies?

Geography in History

1. Place What European city was the first to have potatoes for consumption?

2. Movement Why were potatoes introduced into Sweden and Finland so much later than they were in other nations?

3. Human/Environment Interaction How would new crops such as the potato affect agriculture?

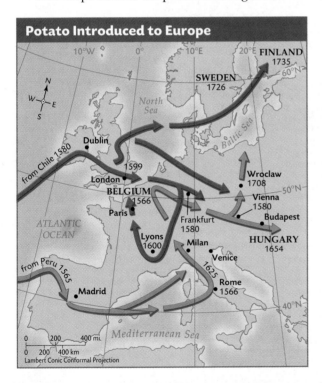

Potato Introduced to Europe

Understanding Themes

1. Innovation How did Chinese and Arab discoveries aid European voyages of exploration?

2. Movement How did the Columbian Exchange affect changes in world populations?

3. Change How did the Commercial Revolution encourage more European voyages of exploration and colonization?

Linking Past and Present

1. History books used to say that Columbus "discovered" America. What did they mean, and why do we no longer see his voyage in this way?

2. Making profits motivated early entrepreneurs. Is this still the goal of entrepreneurs today?

3. Compare and contrast modern space explorations with European voyages of exploration. Consider the technologies used, the ways explorations were funded, and the impact of these ventures on human knowledge.

Skill Practice

Use the card catalog computer in your school library to find out more about Spain's empire from the 1500s to the 1700s.

1. Type "s/Spain."
2. From the list of subjects that appears on screen determine which might apply to Spain's empire from the 1500s to the 1700s.
3. Follow the instructions on the computer screen to display all the titles under each subject you selected. Which book on the screen do you want to learn more about?
4. Who is the author and publisher of the book and in what year was the book published?
5. What is the call number of the book?
6. Is the book available?
7. Go back to the screen that displays all the titles under the subject you selected. Are there any videotapes, audiocassettes, or CDs listed? If so, which resource do you want to learn more about? What is the call number? Is the resource available?

Empires of Asia

Chapter Themes

▶ **Movement** Muslim rulers govern empires that cover vast regions of Asia, North Africa, and Europe. *Section 1*

▶ **Cultural Diffusion** China is directly challenged by its contacts with western European cultures. *Section 2*

▶ **Reaction** Japan enforces isolationist policy to keep out Western influences. *Section 3*

▶ **Change** Southeast Asian lands face the growth of European trade and commerce in their region. *Section 4*

The Storyteller

Within the city walls of Vienna, Austria, people quaked as thundering cannonballs signaled the beginning of the Turkish siege of the city on September 27, 1529. Occupying the surrounding hills were 100,000 Turkish soldiers led by their skilled commander Suleiman.

By mid-October, Turkish troops twice had broken through part of Vienna's walls, but failed to capture the city as the Austrians and their allies rushed to plug the breaches. This clash between European and Asian armies was one of many encounters between different civilizations during the early modern period.

Historical Significance

What kinds of empires arose in Asia during the early modern period? How did they respond to the arrival of Europeans in their areas?

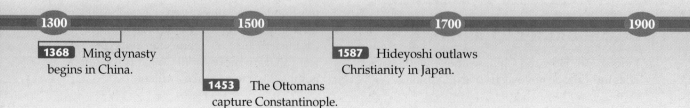

1300	1500	1700	1900

1368 Ming dynasty begins in China.

1453 The Ottomans capture Constantinople.

1587 Hideyoshi outlaws Christianity in Japan.

History & Art *Voyage of the Emperor Qianlong* (detail of a scroll), Qing dynasty. Musée Guimet, Paris, France

Your History Journal

Research one of the following topics, make notes, and write an outline for a short paper: the Imam Mosque of Isfahan, the Taj Mahal, the Forbidden City, and the Imperial Palace of Tokyo.

1526 Babur founds the Mogul dynasty in India.

c. 1740 Nader Shah expands the empire of Safavid Persia.

1856 The Hatt-I Humayun decree sets out reforms for the Ottoman Empire.

Section 1

Muslim Empires

Setting the Scene

▶ **Terms to Define**
  sultan, grand vizier, janissary, *millet*

▶ **People to Meet**
  Suleiman I, Shah Abbas, Babur, Akbar

▶ **Places to Locate**
  Istanbul, Isfahan, Delhi

Find Out How did Muslim rulers control and govern much of the Middle East, North Africa, and India between the 1500s and 1800s?

The Storyteller

On the day that Jahangir was crowned emperor of the Moghuls [Moguls], favorable omens abounded. His coronation was a scene of splendor, illuminated by nearly three thousand wax lights in branches of gold and silver. By his command, the imperial crown was brought to him. On each of the twelve points of this crown was a single diamond.... At the point in the center was a single pearl ... and on different parts of the same were set two hundred rubies. The Emirs of his empire, waiting for Jahangir's commands, were covered from head to foot in gold and jewels.

—adapted from *Memoirs of the Emperor Jahangir Written by Himself*, translated by David Price, reprinted in *The Human Record*, Alfred J. Andrea and James H. Overfield, 1990

Mogul warriors

etween the 1400s and the 1800s, three Muslim empires—the Ottoman Empire, the Persian Empire, and the Mogul Empire—conquered and controlled much of eastern Europe, central Asia, and India respectively. Strong leaders used powerful armies to amass territory that gave them economic control over major trade routes. As these empires spread into new areas, the religion and culture of Islam also expanded.

The Ottoman Empire

During the late 1200s, Turkish clans—calling themselves Ottoman Turks after their first leader, Osman—settled part of Asia Minor and began conquests to build an empire. They conquered much of Byzantine territory, making Constantinople their capital in 1453. Extending their Muslim empire even farther, by the 1500s the Ottomans controlled the Balkan Peninsula and parts of eastern Europe. By the end of their rule in the early 1900s, they had acquired much of the Middle East, North Africa, and the Caucasus region between the Black and Caspian Seas.

The Ottoman Empire maintained a strong navy in the Mediterranean to protect the lucrative trade they controlled there. Alarmed by the threat to their trade and to Christianity, Europeans under Philip II of Spain fought and defeated the Ottoman fleet at the Battle of Lepanto in 1571. But the Ottomans rebuilt their navy and remained a significant seapower until the 1700s.

Suleiman I

Suleiman I was one of the early Ottoman rulers who strengthened Muslim forces prior to the Battle of Lepanto. He was a multitalented man—a heroic military commander, a skillful administrator, and a patron of the arts. Ruling from 1520 to 1566, Suleiman received the name "The Lawgiver" for his work in organizing Ottoman laws.

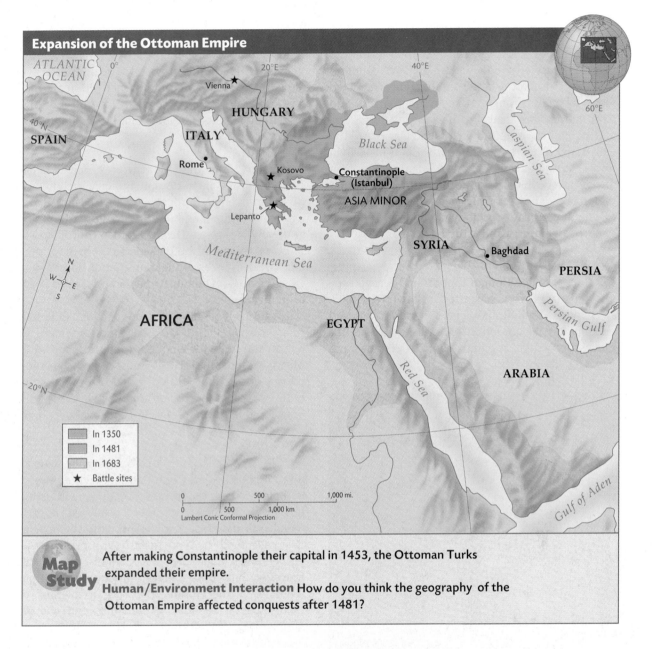

Expansion of the Ottoman Empire

ATLANTIC OCEAN

Vienna ★

HUNGARY

SPAIN

ITALY

Rome •

Kosovo ★

Constantinople (İstanbul) •

Black Sea

Caspian Sea

ASIA MINOR

Lepanto ★

Mediterranean Sea

SYRIA

Baghdad •

PERSIA

Persian Gulf

AFRICA

EGYPT

Red Sea

ARABIA

Gulf of Aden

In 1350
In 1481
In 1683
★ Battle sites

0   500   1,000 mi.
0   500   1,000 km
Lambert Conic Conformal Projection

Map Study After making Constantinople their capital in 1453, the Ottoman Turks expanded their empire.
Human/Environment Interaction How do you think the geography of the Ottoman Empire affected conquests after 1481?

Suleiman acted as both the **sultan**, or political ruler, and the caliph, or religious leader; he enjoyed absolute authority. To rule effectively, however, Suleiman needed support from his personal advisers, the bureaucracy, a group of religious advisers known as the Ulema, and a well-trained army. A **grand vizier**, or prime minister, headed the bureaucracy that enforced the sultan's decisions throughout the empire. The Ulema made rulings on questions of Islamic law, and the army held much control within the empire by conquering and controlling new territories.

The Ottomans recruited officers from among the conquered peoples of their empire. An elite corps of officers called **janissaries** came from the Balkans, where Christian families were required by the Ottomans to turn over young boys to the govern-

ment. Converted to Islam, the boys received rigorous training that made them a loyal fighting force.

Ottoman Law

Because the empire was so large, Ottoman Muslims ruled diverse peoples, including Arabs, Greeks, Albanians, Slavs, Armenians, and Jews. The population was divided into several classes: a ruling class made up of the sultan's family and high government officials; the nobility, which administered agricultural estates; and the largest class, the peasants who worked on those estates.

To accommodate these diverse populations, the government made special laws affecting those who did not practice Islam, the empire's official religion. Non-Muslims were allowed to practice their faith. Ottoman law also permitted the empire's diverse religious groups to run affairs in their own *millets*, or communities, and choose their own leaders to present their views to the Ottoman government.

The Ottoman Islamic civilization borrowed many elements from the Byzantine, Persian, and Arab cultures they had absorbed. Mosques, bridges, and aqueducts reflected this blend of styles. The Christian city of Constantinople was transformed into a Muslim one and renamed **Istanbul**. Ottoman architects renovated Hagia Sophia into a mosque and then planned new mosques and palaces that added to Istanbul's beauty. Ottoman painters produced detailed miniatures and illuminated manuscripts.

Decline of the Ottomans

By 1600 the Ottoman Empire had reached the peak of its power; thereafter it slowly declined. Even at its height, however, the empire faced enemies on its borders. Conquests ended as the Ottomans tried to fight both Persians and Europeans. In 1683 Polish King John III Sobieski led European forces in ending an Ottoman siege of Vienna. This European victory dealt a decisive blow to the Ottoman Empire. When Ottoman military conquests ceased, massive poverty and civil discontent afflicted Ottoman lands.

Reform

By the 1700s, the Ottoman Empire had fallen behind Europe in trade and military technology. Russia and other European nations began taking Ottoman territory, and local rulers in North Africa gradually broke away from Ottoman control. In the 1800s uprisings in the Balkans led to freedom for the Greeks, Serbs, Bulgarians, and Romanians. Unsuccessful revolts in Armenia and Arabia were brutally crushed.

Wanting to halt Ottoman decline, Ottoman rulers during the 1800s used European ideas to reform and unify the empire. In 1856 Sultan Abdul-Mejid I issued the Hatt-I Humayun, a sweeping reform decree that created a national citizenship, reduced the authority of religious leaders, and opened government service to all peoples.

Reaction

Powerful resistance to change grew among the religious leaders, who had lost civil authority in their own communities. Although many Muslim, Jewish, and Christian leaders protested reform, merchants and artisans in the individual communities welcomed it. Non-Turkish groups, such as Armenians, Bulgarians, Macedonians, and Serbs, however, had little interest in any reform that would save the empire. They began to think of themselves as separate nationalities and wanted nation-states of their own.

After Abdul-Mejid's death in 1861, the reform movement lacked the strong leadership needed to guarantee its success. To gain public support, reformers known as the Young Ottomans overthrew the weak sultan Abdul-Aziz and replaced him with Abdul-Hamid II.

At first the new sultan went along with the reformers. In 1876 he proclaimed a new constitution. He affirmed the unity of the empire and promised individual liberties for his subjects. In 1877 the first Ottoman parliament met in Istanbul. But later that same year Abdul-Hamid II decided to resist reform. He suddenly dissolved the parliament and ended constitutional rule. The sultan believed that moving the Ottoman government toward liberalism would lead to ruin. To further protect the empire from change, he drove many of the Young Ottomans into exile. Then he imposed absolute rule.

Visualizing History **Portrait of Suleiman, "The Lawgiver," from the late 1600s.** *What provision did the Ottoman law make for peoples of diverse religions?*

Safavid Persia

To the east of the Ottoman Empire lay Persia, a land that had once been part of the Islamic Empire, but which had broken away because of religious differences. In the 1500s Shiite Muslims, bitter enemies of the Ottoman Turks, conquered the land of present-day Iran. The Shiite leader, Ismail (ihs•MAH•EEL), conquered and unified the numerous people living there, declaring himself to be the founder of the Safavid (sah•FAH•weed) dynasty.

Safavid rulers required all of their Persian subjects to accept the Shiite form of Islam. Belief in the Shia branch of Islam distinguished people living in Persia from neighboring Sunni Muslim peoples—the Arabs and Turks.

Shah Abbas

The Safavid leader **Shah Abbas** came to the throne in 1587. His army regained some western territory lost to the Ottomans in previous years. Then the shah sought allies against the Ottomans even among such Christian states as England. The English used their alliance with Persia to seize the strategic Persian Gulf port of Hormuz in 1622, gaining control of the Persian silk and East Indian spice trade.

With his empire secure against the Ottoman forces, Shah Abbas set up his court in **Isfahan**, which became one of the most magnificent cities in the entire Muslim world. Towering above the city was the blue dome of the Imam Mosque, which was covered with lacy white decorations. Near the mosque, Abbas had a three-story palace built for his personal use. He also ordered beautiful streets and parks constructed throughout the city.

During the reign of Abbas, Persian spread as the language of culture, diplomacy, and trade in most of the Muslim world. Later the language spread to India. Urdu, spoken in Pakistan today, is partly based on Persian.

Nader Shah

After the death of Shah Abbas in 1629, inept Safavid rulers weakened the empire, bringing on its decline. In 1736, after the Safavid decline, Nader Shah came to power. He expanded the Persian Empire to its greatest height since Darius. But after his assassination in 1747, territory was lost and the country was divided.

In the late 1700s another Turkic group, the Qajar dynasty, seized the Persian throne and established a new dynasty in Tehran. The Qajars ruled Persia until 1925.

Visualizing History The Imam Mosque in Isfahan (in present-day Iran) was built by Shah Abbas during the early 1600s. *What cultural impact did Safavid Persia have on the Muslim world?*

The Mogul Empire

Even before the Ottomans and the Safavids built their empires, Islamic invaders from central Asia had conquered much of northern India by the 1100s. The invaders set up a sultanate, or Muslim kingdom, in **Delhi** in 1206. Once order was restored, northern India prospered economically and culturally. Traditional Hindu culture survived the invasions and blended with Islamic civilization.

Timur Lenk in India

By the late 1300s the Muslim Mongol ruler, Timur Lenk (Tamerlane), had conquered much of central Asia and made Samarkand the capital of his empire. Although a devout Muslim, Timur Lenk was also a ruthless leader. His forces sacked the city of Delhi in 1398, killing thousands and leaving the city in rubble. After Timur Lenk's death, his Islamic

Otis Imboden

Taj Mahal

The beauty of the Taj Mahal has awed visitors for centuries. A pear-shaped dome crowns the square central building, complete with a reflecting pool. The marble surface glitters with semiprecious stones: jade from China; turquoise from Tibet; lapis lazuli from Afghanistan; chrysolite from Egypt; and mother-of-pearl from the Indian Ocean. Inside all this wealth and beauty lies Mumtaz Mahal, wife of the Mogul emperor of India, Shah Jahan, who ruled from 1628 to 1658. He fell in love with Mumtaz at 16 and adored his queen throughout her life. In 1629, shortly after Shah Jahan's reign began, Mumtaz died in childbirth, after giving birth to their 14th child. Her death left him in black despair, and in his grief he decided to build the world's greatest tomb.

Or so goes the legend. Contemporary scholars argue that Shah Jahan built the Taj Mahal not only as a resting place for his well-loved wife—and later for himself—but also as a symbol of his power and wealth. The Moguls were Muslims—outsiders and conquerors who ruled India in an absolute monarchy. Their administration left India weak and, by the 1800s, vulnerable to British conquest. In their art and architecture they gave India a more lasting legacy. "The Taj Mahal," wrote Indian poet Rabindranath Tagore, is "like a solitary tear suspended on the cheek of time." ⊕

empire disintegrated; yet northern India would face other Muslim invasions.

Akbar the Great

In the early 1500s **Babur**, who was a descendant of Timur Lenk, led another attack on northern India. Using artillery and with cavalry riding elephants and horses, Babur conquered Delhi at the Battle of Panipat in 1526. Then he set up the Mogul dynasty, the Persian name for Mongol, which lasted three centuries in India. Unlike Timur Lenk, the Moguls encouraged orderly government, and they expanded the arts.

Babur's grandson, **Akbar**, was a benevolent ruler who brought peace and order to northern India. Recognizing that most of the people he ruled were Hindus, Akbar encouraged religious tolerance to end quarrels between Hindus and Muslims. Whereas Muslims believed in one God, Hindus worshiped many deities. Hindus and Muslims differed about sacred foods, social organization, and religious customs. To reduce tension among his people, Akbar repealed a tax on Hindus.

Extremely curious about all religions, Akbar invited religious scholars of other faiths to his court to learn about other religions. He concluded that all religions revealed the same divine truth, whatever their external practices were. He tried to set up a new religion that he called Divine Faith. The new religion included features of many of the world's religions such as Islam, Hinduism, and Christianity.

Mogul Civilization

Under Akbar's rule music, painting, and literature flourished in Mogul India. Mogul rulers made their lavish courts centers of art and learning. Although Akbar could not read, he understood the value of education and set up a large library, employing more than 100 court painters to illustrate the elegantly bound books.

Another Mogul ruler, Shah Jahan, created one of the world's most beautiful buildings—the Taj

History & Art *Akbar Hunting Tigers Near Gwalior* by Husain Haqqash, c. 1580, from the *Akbar-Nama*. Victoria and Albert Museum, London, England *How did Akbar encourage religious tolerance?*

Mahal at Agra—a magnificent example of Muslim architecture. Muslim architects introduced the arch and dome to India, and in trading contacts with China, Muslim merchants brought gunpowder, paper, and Chinese porcelain to Mogul India.

Mogul Decline

During the late 1600s, Mogul rulers, such as Shah Aurangzeb, abandoned religious toleration. They persecuted India's Hindu majority as well as the Sikhs, followers of Sikhism (SEE•KIH•zuhm), a new religion founded by the teacher Nanak in the 1500s. Sikhism holds to a belief in one God and teaches that good deeds and meditation bring release from the cycle of reincarnation. Today there are about 14 million Sikhs, most of whom live in the northern Indian state of Punjab. During the late 1600s, both Sikhs and Hindus rebelled against the Moguls and helped weaken Mogul authority. As Mogul central government declined, local rulers became more independent.

SECTION I REVIEW

Recall
1. **Define** sultan, grand vizier, janissary, *millet*.
2. **Identify** Suleiman I, Hatt-I Humayun, Shah Abbas, Babur, Akbar.
3. **Use** the map on page 457 to compare the Ottoman Empire's boundaries in 1481 to those in 1683. How did the growth of the Ottoman Empire lead to decline?

Critical Thinking
4. **Making Comparisons** How did Shah Abbas's patronage of the arts compare to that of a contemporary European monarch?

Understanding Themes
5. **Movement** How do you think the movement of Muslims into northern India affected the people already living there?

1405 China begins first seagoing expedition.

1644 The Manchus establish the Qing dynasty.

1800 China's population reaches 350 million.

Section 2

Chinese Dynasties

Setting the Scene

▶ **Terms to Define**
junk, queue, labor-intensive farming

▶ **People to Meet**
Hong Wu, Yong Le, Zheng He

▶ **Places to Locate**
Beijing, the Forbidden City

Find Out ▶ Why did China flourish and then decline during the Ming and Qing dynasties?

The Storyteller

The examination process for civil servants was riddled with corruption. "There are too many men who claim to be pure scholars and yet are stupid and arrogant," K'ang-hsi [Kangxi] fumed. Incompetent examiners were set on memorization instead of independent thinking. Candidate lists were manipulated to favor specific provinces.

Some candidates even hired people to take the exams for them. As an active ruler K'ang-hsi was determined to have officials who were able and efficient. He addressed the problems by holding the exams under armed supervision and reading the exam papers himself.

—adapted from *Emperor of China: Self-Portrait of K'ang-hsi*, translated by Johnathan D. Spence, reprinted in *The Human Record*, Alfred J. Andrea and James H. Overfield, 1990

Han civil service exam

In 1368, after the Yuan dynasty fell, a new era of reform began. The Ming and the Qing dynasties built strong central governments that implemented agricultural and public works projects. As food production and trade increased, so did China's population. At the same time, China looked to earlier achievements to invigorate its culture. After years of prosperity, Chinese emperors isolated themselves from their people and the outside, resulting in government corruption, rebellions, and decline.

The Ming Dynasty

After 89 years of Mongol rule, a military officer named Zhu Yuanzhang (JOO YOO•AHN•JAHNG) led a rebellion that overthrew the Yuan dynasty. Born into a poor peasant family, Zhu had been a Buddhist monk before entering the army. In 1368 he became emperor, taking the name **Hong Wu** and establishing his capital at Nanjing. For the first time in more than 1,000 years, the Son of Heaven was of peasant origin. Hong Wu gave the name *Ming* ("brilliant") to his dynasty, which would rule China for nearly 300 years.

Peace and Stability

The Ming dynasty brought peace and stability to China. Hong Wu and the early Ming rulers imposed new law codes, reorganized the tax system, and reformed local government.

The new law codes were harsher than those of previous Chinese dynasties. Scholars, traditionally exempt from corporal punishment, had to endure public whippings if they displeased the emperor and his officials. Formerly, the saying was that "a gentleman could be ordered to die but should never be humiliated."

The Forbidden City in the heart of the city of Beijing contains hundreds of buildings. Many of these buildings housed the emperors of China and their imperial court from 1421 to 1911. *How did the Ming Emperor Yong Le contribute to Chinese scholarship?*

Chinese persons replaced Mongols in all civil service posts, and Confucianism again became the empire's official doctrine. The Ming dynasty restored the old examination system, making the tests even stricter than in earlier dynasties.

Strong rulers at the beginning of the dynasty enforced peace throughout the land. With peace and additional revenues from a reformed tax system, economic prosperity came to China. But northern China had been devastated by nomadic invaders. To encourage farmers to move there, the government offered free land, tools, seeds, and farm animals. Farmers reclaimed and restored much of the land in the north, and the policy helped secure the northern frontier from invaders.

With more land under cultivation, farmers could sell their surplus produce at local markets. Government workers repaired and maintained the canal system that connected local markets. Increased agricultural productivity also freed workers for nonfarming tasks. Artisans in larger numbers expanded the production of silk, textiles, tea, and porcelain to meet the demands of growing urban populations. Thus, trade within China increased, enriching merchants in cities such as Shanghai and Guangzhou (GWONG•JOH).

As city merchants and artisans grew wealthier, they demanded more popular entertainments and learning. The third Ming emperor, **Yong Le**, ordered 2,000 scholars to compile a treasury of Chinese histories and literature. This massive library included neo-Confucian writings from the Song dynasty and also many Buddhist scriptures.

Ming writers preferred the novel to other forms of fiction. Their works were based largely on tales told over the centuries by storytellers. One of the most popular novels, *The Romance of the Three Kingdoms*, describes military rivalries at the end of the Han era.

Chinese Exploration

The early Ming emperors spent government money on a navy that could sail to foreign ports and collect tribute for the emperor. The ships, known as **junks**, usually traveled along the coastline, but they could also venture into open water.

From 1405 to 1433, emperors sent out seven seagoing expeditions. Their purpose was "glorifying Chinese arms in the remote regions and showing off the wealth and power of the [Middle] Kingdom." The leader of the voyages was a Chinese Muslim named **Zheng He** (JUNG HUH).

Zheng He took his first fleet to the nations of Southeast Asia. In later voyages he reached India, sailed up the Persian Gulf to Arabia, and even visited eastern Africa. Everywhere he went, he demanded that the people submit to the emperor's authority. If they refused, he applied force; rulers who accepted were rewarded with gold or silk.

Zheng He brought back trade goods and tribute from many lands. From Africa he returned home with animals for the emperor's zoo. As a result of Zheng He's voyages, Chinese merchants settled in Southeast Asia and India and spread Chinese culture.

Later Ming emperors, however, did not follow through: ocean voyages were costly, and in the early 1400s China concentrated its funds on military forces to combat threats from nomadic tribes to the north. The emperor's officials saw no great benefit in exploring expeditions and halted them. The government discouraged trade with foreign countries partly because Confucian philosophy regarded trade as the lowest of occupations. The emperor even forbade construction of seagoing vessels. ◣

Inside the Forbidden City

To help defend the northern border, Yong Le shifted his capital from Nanjing to Cambaluc, renaming it **Beijing** (BAY•JING), which means "northern capital." He ordered the city completely rebuilt, modeled after the great Tang capital of Changan. For 16 years, from 1404 to 1420, workers labored on its construction. On the Chinese New Year's Day in 1421, the government moved to Beijing.

A visitor entering Beijing walked through the great gate in the 30-foot-(9-meter-) high southern wall. Government workers passed through the Gate of Heavenly Peace to the offices of the Imperial City.

Chinese Life

Under the stable, centralized rule of the Ming and Qing dynasties, crafts, industry, and agriculture flourished.

Breeding the silkworm required patience, but the reward was income from trade.

The Gate of Supreme Harmony at Beijing's Forbidden City is guarded well by a centuries-old lion.

Farther north, across a moat and through the Meridian Gate, stood **the Forbidden City**, where the emperor and his family lived. The Forbidden City had two main sections: one for the emperor's personal use and another for state occasions. The main courtyard outside the gate held 90,000 people. The emperor sometimes appeared before guests here, but ordinary people stayed out or faced a penalty of death.

The residential section of the Forbidden City consisted of many palaces with thousands of rooms. Pavilions and gardens gave comfort to the imperial family, who spent their days in fabulous splendor. Later Ming emperors devoted much of their time to pleasure. In the last 30 years of one emperor's reign, he met with his closest officials only five times.

Corrupt officials, eager to enrich themselves, took over the country. As law and order collapsed, Manchu invaders from Manchuria attacked the northern frontier settlements. Revenues for military spending were limited by the expenses of the lavish court. The Manchus managed to conquer a weakened China.

The Qing Dynasty

In 1644 the Manchus set up a new dynasty, called the Qing (CHING), or "pure." For only the second time in history, foreigners controlled all of China. The Manchus slowly extended their empire to the north and west, taking in Manchuria, Mongolia, Xinjiang (SHIN•JEE•ONG), and Tibet. The offshore island of Taiwan became part of the empire in 1683. For almost 300 years the Qing dynasty ruled over the largest Chinese empire that ever existed.

Adapting Chinese Culture

The Manchus had already accepted Confucian values before invading China. Their leaders understood that these precepts benefited the ruling class. Ruling over an empire in which Chinese outnumbered Manchus by at least 30 to 1, the Manchu rulers controlled their empire by making every effort to adopt many of the native Chinese customs and traditions.

A Ming porcelain bowl painted in underglaze displays the familiar blue willow pattern.

Iron workers decorate this Chinese vase preserved in the Golestan Palace, Tehran, Iran.

REFLECTING ON THE TIMES

1. What artistic creation was done under the emperor's patronage?
2. How do these objects and scenes reflect life under the Ming and Qing dynasties?

Economics

Feeding China

During the Ming and Qing eras, China expanded its agricultural production. Rapid population growth, particularly in eastern China, made it necessary for farmers to grow more food. Terracing—the steplike areas that farmers dug out of hillsides—helped them make full use of their lands. To help farmers water their crops and transport them to market, the government continued building canal and irrigation systems.

Chinese irrigation

Meanwhile, new crops from the Americas arrived in China on Chinese ships that traveled regularly to Southeast Asia. During the 1500s, Spanish ships brought sweet potatoes, maize, and peanuts as well as silver and gold from the Americas to the Philippines. There Chinese merchants exchanged silk or porcelain for the precious metals and exotic foods. All these factors helped make China's population the largest in the world.

Today, China is still the world's most populous country, despite government efforts to limit population growth. Farm production also has significantly risen because of better opportunities for farmers to make profits on the open market. Electricity reaches many villages, and a few rural households now operate small factories and businesses. Dam construction, bridge building, and other public works have transformed rural China, while new products have come to China through increased trade with other parts of the world.

Linking Past and Present ACTIVITY

Discuss past and present ways used by the Chinese to expand food production. In doing so, how have they changed their environment? How have modern farming practices affected the environment in various parts of the world?

Manchus kept control by naming Manchus to the officer corps and by ensuring that most of the soldiers were Manchus. To control the Chinese civil service, Manchus reserved the top jobs in the government hierarchy for their people. Even Chinese officials in lower positions had a Manchu supervisor monitoring their work. Critical military and government positions thus remained loyal to the Manchu leadership.

In 1645 the Manchu emperor ordered all Chinese men to shave their heads leaving a single queue, or braid, at the back of their heads—or be executed. Among the people this order was known as "Keep your hair and lose your head" or "Lose your hair and keep your head." The upper classes had to adopt the Manchu tight, high-collared jacket and abandon their customary loose robes. But in spite of the many-layered controls, the Manchu rulers took on more elements of Chinese culture.

The Qing were fortunate in having able emperors in the first years of their rule. Emperor Kangxi, who ruled from 1661 to 1722, reduced taxes and undertook public works projects, such as flood control. Kangxi, himself a poet, also sponsored Chinese art. Other emperors secured new territory, extending the Qing Empire.

Daily Life

The Manchus made few changes in China's economy. The government-sponsored work projects and internal peace contributed to economic prosperity in the 1700s. Agricultural improvements increased food production, whereupon China's population exploded, from about 150 million in 1600 to 350 million in 1800. China was the most populous country in the world.

More than three-fourths of the Chinese people lived in rural areas. In the south where Chinese farmers worked as tenants, each family farmed its plot and paid rent to a landlord. In the north, more families owned their land. But because a family divided its land among its sons, over the generations the average peasant's share of land shrank.

As population increased, every inch of land had to be made productive. Although the Chinese had invented such simple machines as the wheelbarrow and paddle-wheel pumps, farmers depended on human labor for most farm tasks. In hill country, farm workers dug flat terraces into the hillsides where rice and other crops could be grown. Workers carried pails of water to fill the rice paddies. This labor-intensive farming, in which work is performed by human effort, contrasts with agriculture in which the hard work is done by animals or machinery.

Subsistence farming was not a year-round occupation during the Qing dynasty. Many farmers grew cash crops such as cotton, rather than just their own food. A writer in the 1700s described the life of farm families in one district:

❝ The country folk only live off their fields for the three winter months.... During the spring months, they ... spin or weave, eating by exchanging their cloth for rice.... The autumn is somewhat rainy, and the noise of the looms' shuttles is once again to be heard everywhere in the villages.... Thus, even if there is a bad harvest ... our country people are not in distress so long as the other counties have a crop of cotton [for them to weave]. ❞

Silk production provided extra income for farm families. They grew mulberry trees, whose leaves provided food for silkworms. From the leaves women and girls plucked the cocoons and carefully unwound them. Then the silk was ready for those who spun it into thread and others who wove it into silk cloth.

Internal trade flourished during the Qing period. There was a lively exchange of goods within and between the various regions of China. Great merchant families made fortunes trading rice, silk, fish, timber, cloth, and luxury goods. The growth of trade prompted specialization. Some regions were famous for textiles; others for cotton, porcelain, tea, or silk. At Jingdezhen, the emperor's porcelain factory employed thousands of workers. Artists painted delicate patterns or scenes on vases, bowls, and plates. Others made chemical glazes that formed a hard, shiny surface on the pottery after it was fired in a hot kiln.

Contacts With Europeans

European demand for Chinese goods such as silk and porcelain was high, attracting European ships to China's coast. The first Europeans arrived in China during the Ming dynasty. In 1514 Portuguese caravels landed near Guangzhou. The Chinese called Portuguese sailors ocean devils, and local officials refused to deal with them. Nonetheless, by 1557 the Portuguese had built a trading base at Macao.

Jesuit missionaries followed the Portuguese traders with the dream of converting China's huge population to Christianity. Although most Chinese officials were not interested in Christianity, the Jesuits' scientific knowledge impressed them. In 1611 the emperor placed a Jesuit astronomer in charge of the Imperial Calendar, and in years to come Jesuits gained other government positions. They also converted some court officials to Christianity. By the 1700s, however, Qing rulers worried that Jesuits were too involved in government affairs and forced the missionaries to leave. The Jesuits had failed to make China a Christian nation.

Qing Decline

During the 1700s corruption and internal rebellions forced the Qing dynasty into a slow decline. As the population grew, the government raised taxes to support public services. High-ranking officials, however, kept much of the revenue. Peasant rebellions followed.

By 1850 the Qing faced the Taiping Rebellion. The leader of this revolt came in contact with Christian missionaries and developed his version of Christianity. He organized many Chinese into a political movement to replace the Qing dynasty with a "Heavenly Kingdom of Great Peace." Lasting 14 years, the rebellion left much of southern China destroyed and the central government weakened. Thus undermined, the Qing faced new threats from foreign imperialistic powers.

SECTION 2 REVIEW

Recall
1. **Define** junk, queue, labor-intensive farming.
2. **Identify** Hong Wu, Yong Le, Zheng He, the Forbidden City, the Manchus.
3. **Use** the world map on pages A4 and A5 in the Atlas to determine the distance Chinese explorers traveled to reach the east coast of Africa. How does this record compare to Prince Henry's expeditions?

Critical Thinking
4. **Evaluating Information** How did the achievements of the Ming and Qing dynasties differ? Did the Qing build on the successes of the Ming, or did they create a completely new civilization?

Understanding Themes
5. **Cultural Diffusion** What might have happened if the Chinese had continued moving westward? Would China have colonized as Europeans did?

1600	1700	1800

1600 Tokugawa Ieyasu wins the Battle of Sekigahara.   **1636** Act of Seclusion forbids Japanese to leave the country.   **c. 1700s** Japanese cities grow in size and population.

Section 3

The Japanese Empire

Setting the Scene

▶ **Terms to Define**
   sankin-kotai, *metsuke*, *geisha*, *haiku*

▶ **People to Meet**
   Oda Nobunaga, Toyotomi Hideyoshi, Tokugawa Ieyasu, Francis Xavier, Matsuo Basho

▶ **Places to Locate**
   Edo, Nagasaki

Find Out Why was Japan more adaptable to changes than China before the 1800s?

The Storyteller

Yamaga Soko bowed deeply. The shogun, Tokugawa Ieyasu, would determine if Yamaga was prepared to assume a samurai's responsibilities. "In peacetime, we should not be oblivious to the danger of war. Should we not then prepare ourselves for it?" asked Tokugawa. Yamaga understood that many considered the use of arms evil. "Beyond these military duties, we have other functions. We are examples for all society, leading simple and frugal lives," Yamaga responded. Not only would the samurai excel at death; they should also cultivate all aspects of life. Tokugawa spoke again, "A samurai's life calls for constant discipline. Are you, Yamaga Soko, prepared to devote yourself to this?"

—adapted from *Sources of Japanese Tradition*, reprinted in *The Human Record*, Alfred J. Andrea and James H. Overfield, 1990

Samurai in combat

While China enjoyed stability in the 1400s and 1500s, Japan experienced a period of turmoil. The shogun was a mere figurehead, and the emperor performed only religious functions. Daimyos, who controlled their own lands, waged war against their neighbors as feudal lords had done in Europe in the 1400s. "The strongest eat and the weak become the meat" was a Japanese expression of the time. Warriors showed no chivalry or loyalty. This time of local wars left Japan with a political system known as the Tokugawa shogunate that combined a central government with a system of feudalism.

Tokugawa Shogunate

Oda Nobunaga (oh•DAH noh•boo•NAH•gah) was the first military leader to begin uniting the warring daimyos. He announced his ambition on his personal seal: "to bring the nation under one sword." After winning control of a large part of central Japan, Nobunaga led his army against the capital city of Kyoto in 1568. Five years later, amid the chaos caused by the weak Ashikaga (ah•shee•KAH•gah) family, Nobunaga deposed the Ashikaga shogun. Meanwhile, his forces had moved against Buddhist military strongholds around Kyoto. After a 10-year siege, he won and so became the most powerful man in the country. In 1582, however, a treacherous soldier murdered him.

Toyotomi Hideyoshi

Power then shifted to Nobunaga's best general, **Toyotomi Hideyoshi** (toh•yoh•TOH•mee HEE•day•YOH•shee), who rose from a peasant family to his high position in the military. By 1590 Hideyoshi had forced Japan's daimyos to pledge their loyalty to him. Acting as a military dictator, Hideyoshi furthered his goal of unity by disarming the peasants to prevent them from becoming warriors. In 1588 he ordered the "great sword hunt," demanding that all peasants turn in their weapons. To stabilize the daimyo realms he controlled, he imposed laws that prevented warriors from leaving their daimyo's service to become merchants or farmers. The laws also prevented farmers and merchants from becoming warriors.

Hideyoshi, planning to expand Japan's power abroad, invaded Korea as a step toward conquering China. The invasion had another purpose—to rid the country of warriors who could start rebellions at home. However, as you learned in Chapter 14, Admiral Yi's Korean turtle ships thwarted Hideyoshi's conquest.

Tokugawa Ieyasu

After Hideyoshi's death in 1598, a third leader, **Tokugawa Ieyasu** (toh•kuh•GAH•wah ee•YAH•soo), completed the work of unification. At the Battle of Sekigahara (seh•kee•gah•HAR•ah) in 1600, Ieyasu defeated the last of his opponents. Three years later, Ieyasu asked the emperor to make him shogun. The Tokugawa family retained the shogunate for 265 years.

Tokugawa Rule

Ieyasu established his government headquarters at the fishing village of **Edo**, present-day Tokyo. There he built a stone fortress protected by high walls and moats. Today, the fortress is the Imperial Palace, but during the Tokugawa shogunate, the Japanese emperor continued to live in Kyoto. Although the emperor remained the official leader of Japan, the shogun exercised the real power.

After taking control, Ieyasu reassigned the daimyos' lands. He divided the daimyos into three groups: Tokugawa relatives, longtime supporters of the Tokugawa family, and those who came to the Tokugawa side only after the Battle of Sekigahara. He issued the most productive lands near Edo to the Tokugawa relatives. The others—potential enemies—received less desirable lands in outlying areas of Japan.

To ensure daimyo loyalty, Ieyasu set up a system called *sankin-kotai*, or attendance by turn. Each daimyo had to travel to Edo every other year, bringing tribute and remaining in the shogun's service for a full year. Thus, half the daimyos were directly under the shogun's control at any one time. Even when the daimyos returned to their estates, they had to leave their families at Edo as hostages.

The daimyos spent much of their income traveling to and from Edo and maintaining several households. They also had to get the shogun's permission to marry and to repair or build their castles. *Sankin-kotai* kept them weak, obedient to the

shogun, and less able to rebel against the government. Much like Louis XIV of France, the shogun turned his aristocracy into courtiers who were carefully watched and controlled.

Political System

The Tokugawa family and a select group of daimyos controlled the government. Together they made up the Council of Elders, the leading administrative body. Assisting the Council, as the "eyes and ears" of the state, was a group of officials known as the *metsuke*. The *metsuke* toured the country and reported on possible uprisings or plots against the shogun. A genuine bureaucracy began to develop, working on the principles of joint decision making and promotion based on talent and success.

Social Classes

Before 1600 there had been some social mobility between classes in Japan. Hideyoshi and Ieyasu

Visualizing History As a member of a professional class of women, a geisha might serve a samurai in song or dance, by playing a musical instrument, or engaging in stimulating conversation. *What were the symbols of authority permitted only to a samurai?*

had both risen to the top from lowly backgrounds. To maintain social stability and limit future rivals, they introduced measures that froze the Japanese social structure.

Under Tokugawa rule, the Japanese were divided into four social classes. At the top were the samurai, including the daimyos, who held all political power. They alone could wear symbols of authority: a sword and a distinctive topknot in their hair. The farmers, as major food producers, were the second-highest class. They were followed by artisans who made goods. Merchants were at the bottom of society, because they only exchanged goods and thus were not productive.

No one could change his social class or perform tasks that belonged to another class. One samurai recalled that his father took him out of school because he was taught arithmetic—a subject fit only for merchants. A character in a popular puppet play, written by the author Chikamatsu, described the proper order of society:

> **❝** A samurai's child is reared by samurai parents and becomes a samurai himself because they teach him the warrior's code. A merchant's child is reared by merchant parents and becomes a merchant because they teach him the way of commerce. A samurai seeks a fair name in disregard for profit, but a merchant, with no thought to

his reputation, gathers profit and amasses a fortune. This is the way of life proper to each. This strict social order helped maintain peace and stability throughout Japan. **❞**

Tokugawa Ethics

Tokugawa ethics placed loyalty to the shogun above the family. Duty and honor became the central values. Individuals had to develop strict inner discipline to live up to the requirements of their assigned place in life. These values gradually spread from the samurai through all social classes in Japan.

Over the course of time, Tokugawa rules for personal conduct evolved into complex rituals and etiquette. Minute details came to have heavy symbolic meaning. They became a way to maintain conformity and control. This was important for a society that had a large population and only a small area of productive land.

Contacts With the West

The peace and order of the Tokugawa shogunate were interrupted when the first Europeans—the Portuguese—arrived in Japan in 1543. Although the Japanese looked upon Europeans as barbarians, the warrior society saw that European weapons meant power. They purchased muskets and cannon to defeat their opponents.

Roman Catholic missionaries soon followed the Portuguese merchants. **Francis Xavier**, the earliest of the Jesuit priests who came to Japan, admired the Japanese people. To convert them, the Jesuits adopted their customs. Jesuit missionaries learned the subtleties of conversing in polite Japanese and set up a tea room in their houses so that they could receive their visitors properly.

After Xavier won the support of some local daimyos, Christianity spread rapidly. Oda Nobunaga himself lent support to the Christians, for during this time he was moving against the Buddhist monasteries that were serving as military strongholds. Jesuits trained Japanese priests to create a strong Japanese Christian church. By 1614 the Jesuits had converted 300,000 Japanese.

Many Japanese welcomed the first contact with Westerners, whose customs and styles became widespread in Japanese society. Even for Japanese who had not converted to Christianity, Christian symbols became fashionable. A missionary described non-Christian daimyos who would wear "rosaries of driftwood on their breasts, hang a

Visualizing History In Tokugawa Japan, cities became leading centers of Japanese culture. Artisans began to produce goods for a growing urban market. *What social classes made up Tokugawa Japan?*

Merchants from the West arrive in Japan accompanied by Jesuit missionaries. *How did Christian missionary activity end under Tokugawa rule?*

crucifix from their shoulder or waist … they think it good and effective in bringing success in daily life."

Hideyoshi began to suspect that Christian influence could be harmful to Japan. He had heard of Spanish missionaries in the Philippines who had helped establish Spain's control over the islands. In 1587 Hideyoshi outlawed Christianity. Although some priests were crucified, Hideyoshi generally did not enforce his ban on the religion.

Tokugawa Ieyasu and his successors also feared that Christianity threatened their power and so continued to persecute Christians, killing them or forcing them to leave Japan. When Japanese Christians in the port city of **Nagasaki** defied authorities and refused to disband, the government attacked their community in 1637 and finally wiped them out in 1638.

Japan barred all Europeans except the Dutch. Unlike the Spanish and the Portuguese, the Dutch were interested only in trade, not conquest or religious conversion of the Japanese. For this reason, after 1641 the Tokugawa government confined the Dutch to a tiny island in Nagasaki harbor where they and a few Chinese carried on a tightly regulated trade. Through the Dutch traders, a trickle of information about the West continued to flow into Japan.

Despite Japan's geographic isolation and the Tokugawa policy of isolation, Japan's society and economy continued to change internally. During the early Tokugawa period, agriculture brought wealth to daimyos and samurai, who profited from the rice produced on their lands. Merchants, in turn, grew wealthy by lending money to daimyos and samurai.

Japan's Policy of Isolation

The Tokugawa rulers, deciding that contact with outsiders posed too many dangers, laid down edicts. Their seclusion policy lasted 200 years. The Act of Seclusion of 1636 forbade any Japanese to leave the country and added, "All Japanese residing abroad shall be put to death when they return home." The government banned construction of ships large enough for ocean voyages.

Footnotes to History

Karate

Karate is unarmed combat in which a person uses primarily the hands or feet to strike a blow at an opponent. This martial art began on the island of Okinawa near Japan. During the 1600s, Okinawa's Japanese conquerors forbade the local people to own weapons. In response, many Okinawans learned to turn their hands and feet into fighting instruments.

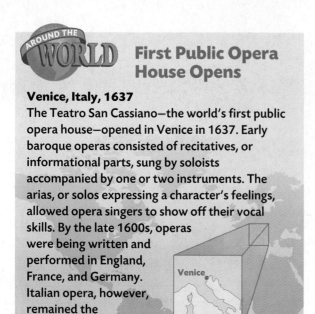

First Public Opera House Opens

Venice, Italy, 1637

The Teatro San Cassiano—the world's first public opera house—opened in Venice in 1637. Early baroque operas consisted of recitatives, or informational parts, sung by soloists accompanied by one or two instruments. The arias, or solos expressing a character's feelings, allowed opera singers to show off their vocal skills. By the late 1600s, operas were being written and performed in England, France, and Germany. Italian opera, however, remained the accepted style.

Venice

As the daimyos became a debtor class, the merchant class became more powerful.

The system of *sankin-kotai* also helped merchants to prosper and trade to increase, because merchants provided the goods and services that the daimyos needed on their twice-yearly trips to Edo. To smooth the daimyos' journey, the government built roads, which also made it easier for traders to take their goods to distant regions. Rest stations along the roads often grew into trading or administrative towns of considerable size.

At the same time, the demands for increased taxes led the daimyos to increase agricultural yields. As agriculture became more efficient, farming required fewer people. Unemployed farmworkers moved to prosperous towns and cities, seeking work as artisans. In urban centers such as Edo, Kyoto, and Osaka, social order began to break down and class distinctions became less rigid.

Social life in the cities converged on bathhouses, restaurants, and theaters. Japanese merchants and samurai could relax in the company of geishas, women who were professional entertainers. Geishas were trained in the arts of singing, dancing, and conversation. Urban amusement centers also provided employment for playwrights, artists, and poets. At this time a new form of theater known as Kabuki developed. Kabuki became popular for its portrayal of historical events and emotion-filled domestic scenes. Another form of drama that arose during this period was the elaborate Japanese puppet theater called Bunraku, in which three-man teams manipulated each puppet as a backstage chorus sang a story.

A popular form of art called ukiyo-e developed from the demand for prints of famous actors and their plays. At first, ukiyo-e prints were black-and-white, but soon ornate, brightly colored prints appeared in street stalls. Printed on delicate rice paper, they are highly prized collectors' items today.

A new form of poetry called haiku (HY•koo) also became popular among city people. In only 17 syllables, the haiku was to express a thought that would surprise the reader. **Matsuo Basho**, one of the great haiku masters, wrote this haiku:

> 66 In my new clothing
> I feel so different
> I must
> Look like someone else. 99

As cities grew in size and population during the 1700s and 1800s, the ban on foreign contacts was gradually relaxed. Some Japanese began to study Western medicine in books that the Dutch brought to Nagasaki. Their interest in the so-called Dutch learning spread to Western science and technology. However, it would not be until the other Europeans arrived in the 1800s that Japan would begin to absorb other Western ideas.

SECTION 3 REVIEW

Recall

1. **Define** *sankin-kotai, metsuke,* geisha, haiku.
2. **Identify** Oda Nobunaga, Toyotomi Hideyoshi, Tokugawa Ieyasu, Francis Xavier, Matsuo Basho.
3. **Describe** how the *sankin-kotai* system affected the daimyos.

How did shoguns benefit from the system? How was the emperor affected?

Critical Thinking

4. **Synthesizing Information** Imagine that you lived in Japan during the Tokugawa shogunate. Which social class would you have wanted to

belong to? Explain.

Understanding Themes

5. **Reaction** Explain why Japan reacted to Western ideas by adopting a policy of isolation. How did this reaction to outside influences affect Japan's development over the next few centuries?

Using a Word Processor

There are several ways to create a professional looking printed document. You may use a word processor or a computer word processing software program. A word processor is a keyboard-operated terminal with a video display.

Learning the Skill

When you open most word processors, you are initially presented with a blank document. To create a new document, simply begin typing. Use the following tips to help you format the document to make it look the way you want:

1. Text fonts, or size and style of type, can be chosen. To choose font or size and style of type, click **Font** on your Standard toolbar.
2. Text can be made to appear **bold**, *italicized*, or underlined. To do this, first highlight the text (drag the cursor, or pointer, over the text with the left mouse button depressed). Then choose the modification mentioned above (the way you do this depends on the word processor you are using).
3. Press **Tab** to indent a paragraph. Press **Enter** to start a new paragraph.
4. To insert new text in a line, move the cursor to the point where you want the line to go and type. The word processing program moves the existing text to the right to make room for the new text.
5. When you finish typing, click the **Spell Check** button on the Standard toolbar to check the spelling of your document.

Practicing the Skill

This chapter focuses on the empires of Asia from 1350 through 1850. Create a newspaper article about an important event during one of these empires. Be sure to include a headline in your article. To use a word processor to create this document, complete the following steps.
1. Choose a font and the text size from the stan-dard toolbar. Use a different text and size for your headline than you use for the rest of the text.
2. Type two or three paragraphs of copy about the event you chose for your article. As you type, make modifications to the text, such as bold, italics, or underlining.
3. Press **Tab** to indent a paragraph. Press **Enter** to start a new paragraph.
4. Insert new text in a line.
5. Use **Spell check** to check the spelling of your document.

Applying the Skill

Using a word processor, create an official-looking document that explains the Ottoman Laws described on pages 457–458 of this textbook.

For More Practice

Turn to the Skill Practice in the Chapter Review on page 479 for more practice in using a word processor.

1500		1700		1900

1511 Portuguese seize port of Melaka on the Malay Peninsula.

1565 Spaniards found a colony in the Philippines.

1767 Troops from Burma seize Ayutthaya.

1868 Chulalongkorn becomes king of Siam.

Section **4**

Southeast Asia

Setting the Scene

▶ **Terms to Define**
colony, *datus*, animism

▶ **People to Meet**
Trailok, Phraya Chakkri, Mongkut, Chulalongkorn

▶ **Places to Locate**
Manila, Java, Indochina, Bangkok

Find Out How was the Thai kingdom able to keep its independence while other parts of Southeast Asia gradually came under European control?

The Storyteller

The century-old Bayon Temple of Angkor swarmed with workers. Huge stone faces with faint, haunting smiles gazed in all directions. A European merchant stepped closer to examine the temple and nearly collided with a monk. When asked about the faces, the monk replied, "This old Hindu shrine will become a Buddhist temple. Jayavarman, our king, has adopted the Buddhist religion and wishes to introduce its teaching throughout our land. Sculptors have been commissioned to create new images on the temple. Most important is the image of boddhisattva, a compassionate being who looks everywhere for souls to save."

—freely adapted from *World History*, Volume 1, William Duiker and Jackson Spielvogel, 1994

Relief from Bayon Temple of Angkor

By the mid-1400s, Southeast Asia was carrying on extensive trade with other regions. This was partly because of its location on the water route between India and China. In addition, Southeast Asia produced valuable spices and woods that people in other parts of the world wanted to buy.

European Influences

In the early 1500s the first European explorers reached Southeast Asia in search of new trade routes and products. With the coming of the Europeans, Southeast Asian kingdoms faced a growing challenge to their independence and traditional ways of life.

The Portuguese Spice Trade

Coming from India, the Portuguese were the first Europeans to reach Southeast Asia in the early 1500s. They set out to control the region's lucrative spice trade which, for many years, had been controlled by Muslim traders. In 1511 Portuguese soldiers captured the most important of the Muslim ports—Melaka, on the west side of the Malay Peninsula.

During the next 25 years, the Portuguese built a number of new trading posts in Southeast Asia. They patrolled the seas near the islands of present-day Indonesia to keep out the ships of other countries. The Portuguese also tried to spread Catholicism in maritime Southeast Asia. They had little success, however, because most Southeast Asian islanders resented Portuguese disregard for their traditional cultures.

Spanish Rule in the Philippines

The Spaniards were eager to find their own route to the spices of Southeast Asia. In 1521 Ferdinand Magellan, exploring for Spain, reached Southeast Asia by sailing westward around the

Visualizing History During the 1600s, the Netherlands reached its height as a sea-faring power. Dutch merchant ships sailed the seas from the Caribbean region to the East Indies (Indonesia). *How did the Dutch win control of the Indonesian island of Java?*

southern tip of South America. Magellan and his crew landed in the Philippines, becoming the first Europeans to visit these islands.

In 1565 the Spanish founded a colony, or overseas territory ruled by a parent country, in the Philippines. Although the Spanish did not find spices in the Philippines, they did find fertile land and an excellent location for trade. Spanish soldiers and officials established a fortified settlement at **Manila** on the island of Luzon. Manila's magnificent harbor made the Philippines a valuable link in Spain's trade with Asia and the Americas.

The Spaniards gradually expanded their control to other parts of the islands. They persuaded many of the *datus*, or local rulers, to pledge loyalty to Spain in return for keeping their regional powers. Under Spanish rule, most of the people of the Philippines—largely of Malay and Chinese descent—accepted many Spanish customs as well as the Roman Catholic faith. Spanish Roman Catholic clergy established missions, learned the local languages, taught the people European agricultural methods, and introduced new crops—such as maize (corn) and cocoa—from the Americas. Spain's control of the Philippines would last well into the late 1800s.

Dutch Traders in Indonesia

By the end of the 1500s, English and Dutch traders were also wanting a share in the Southeast Asian spice trade. After breaking Portuguese control of the trade, they began to fight each other. During the 1620s, the Dutch finally succeeded in forcing the English to leave the islands that now make up present-day Indonesia. A further step toward Dutch control of the islands came in 1677 when the ruler of Mataram, a kingdom on the island of **Java**, asked the Dutch to help him defeat a rebel uprising. In return for their assistance, the Dutch received important trading rights and

Javanese lands. Through similar agreements and by force, the Dutch had gained control of most of the other Indonesian islands by the late 1700s.

The French in Vietnam

The French were latecomers in the European pursuit of trade and colonies in Southeast Asia. Beginning in the 1600s, French traders based in India carried out only limited trade with the Vietnamese and other peoples in the Southeast Asian region of **Indochina**. Because of the weakness of this trade link, the Vietnamese and their Indochinese neighbors were able to keep the French from taking control of their area. Roman Catholic missionaries from France, however, converted many Vietnamese to Christianity.

By the early 1800s most of Indochina was ruled by local emperors who came from the region of Annam in present-day Vietnam. At this time, Indochina was predominantly Chinese in culture. Devoted to Confucian ideas, the Annamese emperors persecuted their Christian subjects and tried to keep Indochina closed to Europeans. Angered at the policies of the Annamese court, the French in 1858 returned to Southeast Asia in force. Their stated purpose was to protect local Christians from persecution. However, they also wanted Indochina's rubber, coal, and rice. In the 1860s the French began to colonize the region.

The Thai Kingdom

While European influence grew throughout Southeast Asia, the independent kingdom of Ayutthaya (ah•YU•tuh•yuh) continued to flourish in the area that is present-day Thailand. Under a series of powerful kings, the Thai people of Ayutthaya developed a rich culture based on Buddhism, Hinduism, and animism, the idea

This bronze bas-relief of the Buddha reveals the important role that Buddhism has played in unifying the Thai people and in supporting their rulers. *What other religious influences shaped the development of Thai culture?*

that both living and nonliving things have spirits or souls.

Trailok's Rule

One of the most powerful Ayutthaya monarchs was King **Trailok**, who ruled from 1448 to 1488. Trailok set up a strong central government with separate civil and military branches directly responsible to him. He also brought local leaders to Ayutthaya and put them in charge of new governmental offices. These officials were required to live in the capital where the king could easily oversee their work.

Trailok set up a rigid class system based on loyalty to the Thai monarchy. All male Thai were given the use of varying amounts of land according to their rank. Nobles and merchants were given as much as 4,000 acres (1,620 ha), while enslaved people, artisans, and other subjects with little status received 10 acres (4 ha) or less. Women were not included in this distribution of land.

Expansion

While the Ayutthaya kingdom set its internal affairs in order, Thai soldiers fought battles with neighboring peoples, such as the Khmer, Burmans, and Malays. Through conquests, the Ayutthaya kingdom grew to almost the size of present-day Thailand. In 1431 Thai soldiers from Ayutthaya captured Angkor Wat and destroyed it. They also overcame the Malays in the south as well as smaller Thai kingdoms in the north.

During the mid-1500s a border dispute led to war between the Ayutthaya kingdom and Burma (Myanmar). Soldiers from Burma briefly captured the city of Ayutthaya in 1569, but the Thai king Naresuan defeated Burma's ruler in the Battle of Nong Sarai in 1593.

European Contacts

The 1500s also saw the beginning of European contacts with Ayutthaya. The Portuguese and later the Dutch and the English sent delegations to the kingdom to encourage trade. For much of the 1600s, Thai rulers allowed Europeans the right to carry out trade in their territory. In 1612

British traders took a letter from King James I to the Thai monarch. They reported back that the city of Ayutthaya, with its palaces and Buddhist temples, was as large and awesome as London.

The Thai, however, became concerned that Europeans wanted to colonize as well as trade. In 1688 a Thai group that opposed European influences took over the kingdom. The new rulers expelled most of the Europeans except for a few Dutch and Portuguese traders. The kingdom closed its ports to the West until 1826.

The Bangkok Era

Free of European influence, Thai rulers hoped for a period of calm. Burma, however, wanted to resume the conflict with Ayutthaya that it had lost in the late 1500s. In 1767 an army from Burma defeated the Thai and sacked and burned the city of Ayutthaya. The Thai, however, soon rallied after the disaster. Phraya Taksin (PRY•uh tahk•SEEN), a Thai general, led his troops against Burma's army and drove it out of the region.

After proclaiming himself king, Taksin forced rival Thai groups to accept his rule. He reigned until 1782, when rebel leaders overthrew him. The rebels called on General **Phraya Chakkri** (PRY•uh SHAH•kree) to be the new Thai monarch. Chakkri founded the royal dynasty that still rules Thailand today. Chakkri built a new capital called **Bangkok** on the Chao Phraya River. Under Chakkri's rule, the reborn Thai kingdom became known as Siam.

Reforming Monarchs

By the mid-1800s Europeans were pressuring Thai rulers to widen trade opportunities in Siam. King **Mongkut** recognized the threat that Western colonial nations posed to the independence of his kingdom. He moved quickly to protect Siam by setting foreign nations against one another through competition.

Mongkut achieved this goal by allowing many Western nations to have commercial opportunities

Visualizing History King Mongkut ruled Siam from 1851 to 1868. He increased the powers of the monarchy while supporting social reforms to improve the conditions of his subjects. *How did Mongkut work to preserve Siam's independence?*

in the kingdom. The Thai king welcomed what he judged to be the positive influences of Western commerce on his country. He encouraged his people to study science and European languages with the Christian missionaries who had accompanied European traders to the kingdom.

After Mongkut's death in 1868, his son **Chulalongkorn** (choo•lah•LAHNG•kohrn) came to the throne. Like Mongkut, Chulalongkorn worked to modernize Siam while protecting the kingdom from European controls. He ended slavery, founded schools, encouraged his people to study abroad, and built railways and roads.

Connections Across Time

Historical Significance From 1350 to 1850 many social and political changes came to Asia. Islam continued to expand and reached South Asia as a result of the Mogul invasions. Despite efforts at toleration, conflicts developed between Muslims and Hindus that still divide South Asia today.

During the early modern period, China turned inward instead of meeting the challenge of the West. Japan and Siam at first took the same route; however, they eventually introduced reforms that preserved their freedom. In Japan's case, reforms also enabled it to compete successfully with Western countries.

Using Key Terms

Write the key term that completes each sentence. Then write a sentence for each term not chosen.

a. geisha
b. grand vizier
c. haiku
d. janissaries
e. *sankin-kotai*
f. colony
g. labor-intensive farming
h. sultan
i. queue
j. *datus*
k. *millets*

1. The Ottoman leader Suleiman I acted as both the _____, or political ruler, and the caliph, or religious leader.
2. During the Manchu dynasty, the Chinese practiced _____ in which workers dug flat terraces into hillsides to grow rice.
3. Ottoman sultans maintained a special corps of soldiers known as _____ who were noted as a fierce and loyal fighting force.
4. Japanese writers developed _____, a form of poetry made up of 17 syllables, that became popular among city people.
5. Ottoman law allowed religious groups to run affairs in their own _____, or communities.

Technology Activity

Using a Computerized Card Catalog Use a computerized card catalog to locate sources about traditional Japanese customs that are practiced in Japan today. Write an essay discussing how political power, leadership, and loyalty in traditional Japan compare to how these characteristics are viewed in modern democracies. Share your opinions with the rest of the class.

Using Your History Journal

From your notes and outline write a three-page paper on one of the four sites listed on page 455. Discuss what that place reveals about the civilization that built it.

Reviewing Facts

1. **History** Name the three great Muslim empires in eastern Europe, central Asia, and India.
2. **Culture** Define the relationship between Sunni Muslims and Shiite Muslims living in the Ottoman Empire and the Persian Empire.
3. **Culture** Explain how the Moguls' religion brought them into conflict with the majority of India's people. Describe how Mogul rulers reacted.
4. **History** Explain the purpose of the voyages of Zheng He.
5. **History** List the steps taken by the Manchus to maintain their control over China.
6. **Culture** Describe the role of geishas in Japan.
7. **Culture** Discuss the effects of the shogunate's policies on Japan's Christian population.

Critical Thinking

1. **Apply** How did religious differences cause strife between Muslim empires?
2. **Evaluate** Would you consider Suleiman I a successful ruler? Why was he called "The Lawgiver" by the Ottomans?
3. **Analyze** How did Akbar's religious tolerance in India differ from that of the Manchus in China?

4. Evaluate Which government described in this chapter was most successful in meeting its people's needs? Why?

5. Evaluate How did the movement of Islamic peoples affect northern India? What impact did Islam have on religion in this part of India?

6. Analyze What factors led to China's growth in both land and population during the Qing dynasty? How did government policies contribute to this growth?

7. Evaluate Was the Ming dynasty's policy of isolationism beneficial to China? Explain.

8. Analyze How did new urban centers in Japan influence growth in the arts and entertainment?

Geography in History

1. Region Refer to the map below that shows the political divisions of Japan about 1560. For more than a century, feudal lords fought for control of territory. How many daimyo clans ruled in Japan during this period?

2. Location What is the relative location of the Takeda domains?

3. Human/ Environment Interaction What geographic conditions helped make it possible for Japan to enforce a policy of isolation from the rest of the world in the 1600s?

Civil War in Japan

Colors indicate most powerful daimyo clans
— boundaries of daimyo domains

Sea of Japan

Uesugi
Takeda Hojo
Oda
Mori   Imagawa
Sogabe
Otomo
Shimazu

0   100   200 mi.
0 100 200 km
Conic Projection

Understanding Themes

1. Movement What areas of Asia came under the rule of the Muslim empires?

2. Cultural Diffusion How did Christianity spread to China? To Japan?

3. Reaction What good and bad effects resulted from Japan's policy of isolation?

4. Change What development was crucial in advancing Dutch control of the islands of Indonesia?

Linking Past and Present

1. Do you think it is possible for today's nations to follow a policy of isolation like Japan's in the early modern period? Have any tried to?

2. From the 1300s to the 1800s powerful Asian rulers took drastic measures to implement changes that they supported. Is a powerful ruler or a strong central government necessary today for technological advancement and economic prosperity? Give reasons to support your position.

Skill Practice

Using a word processor or a computer word processing software program, create a one-page professional-looking document using the subject of Japan's isolationist policy—The Act of Seclusion of 1636. For example, you might wish to create a letter written by the Tokugawa rulers to European rulers or create a handbill that was given out to European traders to warn them about the isolation policy. Be sure to complete the following steps while creating your document:

1. use more than one font and text size
2. use bold, italics, and underlining
3. include paragraph indents
4. run spell check
5. try other word processing techniques that help create a professional-looking document

Chapter

19

1500–1750

Royal Power and Conflict

Chapter Themes

▶ **Conflict** Spanish and English monarchs engage in a dynastic struggle. *Section 1*

▶ **Change** Tudor monarchs bring stability and prosperity to England. *Section 2*

▶ **Uniformity** France's Louis XIV strengthens absolute monarchy in France and limits rights of religious dissenters. *Section 3*

▶ **Conflict** Dynastic and religious conflicts divide the German states. *Section 4*

▶ **Innovation** Peter the Great attempts to modernize Russian society. *Section 5*

The Storyteller

"We hunted all morning, got back around 3 o'clock in the afternoon, changed, went up to gamble until 7 o'clock, then to the play, which never ended before 10:30, then on to the ball until 3 o'clock in the morning.... So you see how much time I had for writing."

Princess Elizabeth-Charlotte, sister-in-law of France's King Louis XIV, described court life at the Palace of Versailles in a letter to a friend as an endless round of social activities. A man of tremendous energy and drive, Louis routinely devoted eight or nine hours daily to matters of state, regularly rode and hunted, ate with great enthusiasm, and expected courtiers, or members of his court, to do the same as well.

Historical Significance

How did monarchs build strong nation-states in early modern Europe? How did their efforts in national expansion contribute to Europe's legacy of territorial disputes and wars?

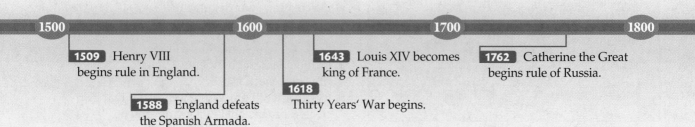

1500	1600	1700	1800

1509 Henry VIII begins rule in England.

1588 England defeats the Spanish Armada.

1618 Thirty Years' War begins.

1643 Louis XIV becomes king of France.

1762 Catherine the Great begins rule of Russia.

The vast palace and grounds of Versailles lie outside of Paris, France. Versailles was home to France's monarchs and the royal court during the late 1600s and most of the 1700s.

Your History Journal

Choose a country from this chapter. As you read the section, create a time line of important events between 1500 and 1750. Include the reigning monarchs, expansions of territory, laws, and conflicts.

Section 1

Spain

Setting the Scene

▶ **Terms to Define**
absolutism, divine right, armada, inflation

▶ **People to Meet**
Philip II, the Marranos, the Moriscos, Charles II

▶ **Places to Locate**
Madrid

Find Out ▶ Why did Philip II and other Spanish monarchs have difficulty ruling the Spanish Empire?

The Storyteller

The Duke of Alva's son, ten-year-old Alejandro, was ecstatic. He had been appointed as a page to King Philip—an excellent beginning to a career with the Spanish court. Alejandro would learn to fence and to perform feats of horsemanship, as well as the rudiments of reading and writing. In five or six years, when he completed his education, Alejandro would become a member of His Majesty's court and would be expected to serve at arms. That position was the fulfillment of most young men's desires. If he proved himself truly outstanding, he might become one of Philip's personal attendants, a position usually reserved for the sons of princes.

Philip II

—from *Charles V and Philip His Son*, Marino Cavalli, reprinted in *The Portable Renaissance Reader*, Mary Martin McLaughlin, 1977

In the 1500s and 1600s, European monarchs sought to create powerful kingdoms in which they could command the complete loyalty of all their subjects. This form of government, known as **absolutism**, placed absolute, or unlimited, power in the monarch and his or her advisers. The strength of absolutism rested on **divine right**—the political idea that monarchs receive their power directly from God and are responsible to God alone for their actions. An absolute monarchy, it was reasoned, would unify diverse peoples and bring greater efficiency and control.

During the age of absolutism, the Hapsburgs remained Europe's most powerful royal family. But their lands were too scattered for any one person to rule effectively. To remedy this problem, Charles V retired in 1556 and divided the empire, leaving the Hapsburg lands in central Europe to his brother, Ferdinand, who became Holy Roman emperor. He gave Spain, the Netherlands, southern Italy, and Spain's overseas empire to his son, **Philip II**.

Philip II

Philip II, who ruled from 1556 to 1598, was the most powerful monarch in Spanish history. A devout Catholic, Philip saw himself as the leading defender of the faith. His efforts to end Protestantism in his domains made him the enemy of all Protestants. Son of the Holy Roman Emperor Charles V and Isabella of Portugal, Philip worked to increase the Hapsburg family's power throughout Europe. This effort led Philip to involve Spain in a number of costly European wars.

Known as the Prudent King, Philip II was cautious, hardworking, and suspicious of others. He built a granite palace called El Escorial, which served as royal court, art gallery, monastery, and tomb for Spanish royalty. There Philip spent most of his time at his desk, carefully reading and responding to hundreds of documents from all over the empire. Bureaucrats advised him and handled routine matters, but he made all decisions and signed all papers that he received.

Unrest

Philip II faced many difficulties in ruling Spain. The Spanish kingdoms had united when Ferdinand of Aragon married Isabella of Castile in 1469. A uniform system of government for the entire country, however, had not been set up. Separate laws and local authorities remained in place, but the ways of Castile eventually came to dominate Spanish life. In the 1500s Castile had more territory, people, and wealth than any other part of Spain.

Philip II made Castile the center of Spain and the empire. **Madrid**, located in Castile, became the capital. The Castilian, or literary, form of Spanish was spoken at the royal court. Most of Philip's advisers came from Castile. Trade from the overseas empire was controlled by the Castilian city of Seville, and Castilian merchants benefited most from trade. Leaders in Aragon and other Spanish provinces resented the dominance of Castile, and in the 1590s Aragon revolted. The revolt was put down, but discontent continued into the 1600s.

Religious Policy

Philip had to deal with a number of troubling religious issues in his European domains. He was concerned about the loyalty of large religious minorities in Spain. These minorities included Protestants, **the Marranos** (Jews who had converted to Christianity), and **the Moriscos** (Muslims who had become Christians). Philip supported the Inquisition's efforts to uproot the heresies believed to exist among these groups. He personally attended several *autos da fé*, the elaborate public rituals of sentencing usually followed by executions. The Inquisition was so thorough that Protestantism never took hold in Spain. Its actions, however, led to a revolt by the Moriscos in 1569. The revolt was brutally crushed, and finally in 1609 the Moriscos were expelled from the country.

In 1567, when Philip had sought to impose Catholicism on the Netherlands, Dutch Protestants rebelled against his rule. This conflict proved to be long, bloody, and complex. The Dutch declared their independence in 1581, but the fighting continued. England gave support to the Dutch and to the English "sea dogs" who raided Spanish ships in their ports. Meanwhile, Philip extended his crusading zeal into the eastern Mediterranean, where in 1571 he defeated the Ottoman Turks in a naval battle at Lepanto off the coast of Greece.

Visualizing History The Spanish Armada entered the English Channel in late July, 1588. *What advantages did the English fleet have over the Spanish Armada?*

POINT

Spanish Armada

Catholic Spain faced a growing challenge from Protestant England. Philip at first had supported Elizabeth I as England's queen against the pope's wishes. When Elizabeth aided the Dutch, Philip decided to act against her.

In 1586 Philip laid plans to invade England. In May 1588 a force of 130 ships and 33,000 men, known as the Spanish Armada, sailed for the English coast. (An armada is a fleet of warships organized to carry out a mission.) Two months later, the Armada entered the English Channel in crescent formation. The English had faster, more maneuverable ships and longer-range cannons than did the Spaniards. Yet they were unable at first to block the Spanish formation. English fire ships, however, were able to separate the Spanish vessels. Running out of shot and short of water, the Spanish fleet retreated to the stormy North Sea. After circling the northern tip of Great Britain, a number of Spanish ships later sank near the rocky coasts of Scotland and Ireland.

The defeat of the Armada not only ended Philip's plan to invade England, it also marked the beginning of Spain's decline as a sea power. During the next two centuries, the Dutch Netherlands, England, and France would gradually reduce Spanish might in Europe and around the world.

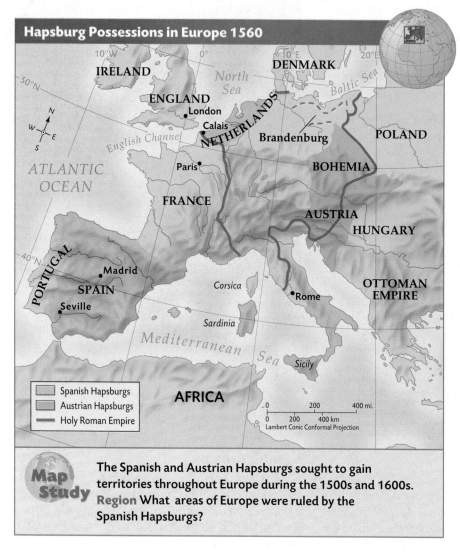

Hapsburg Possessions in Europe 1560

Legend:
- Spanish Hapsburgs
- Austrian Hapsburgs
- Holy Roman Empire

0 200 400 mi.
0 200 400 km
Lambert Conic Conformal Projection

Map Study The Spanish and Austrian Hapsburgs sought to gain territories throughout Europe during the 1500s and 1600s. **Region** What areas of Europe were ruled by the Spanish Hapsburgs?

presented a new kind of hero who did not conform to commonly accepted beliefs and practices.

Cervantes's novel also symbolized the steady decline of Spain as a European power. Despite Spain's resource-rich overseas empire, costly wars drained the national treasury, forcing the government to borrow money from foreign bankers. This, along with the flow of gold and silver from the Americas, led to inflation, an abnormal increase in currency resulting in sharp price rises. In addition, Spain's industry and agriculture declined. The government excessively taxed and weakened the industrious middle class. It also expelled the Muslims and Jews, many of whom were skilled artisans and merchants.

Philip II's successors lacked his political skills and turned the government over to corrupt and incompetent nobles. Spain became involved in a series of European wars, and overtaxed citizens in various parts of the empire rebelled. **Charles II**, who became king in 1665, was the last of the Spanish Hapsburgs. No one expected him to rule long, since he was physically and mentally weak. Although Charles later married, he did not have any children. With no heirs to the throne of Spain, European monarchs plotted to control the succession to the Spanish throne.

Last of the Spanish Hapsburgs

The period from 1550 to 1650 is called Spain's cultural *siglo de oro*, or "golden century." Midway through this era, the Spanish author Miguel de Cervantes (suhr•VAN•teez) wrote *Don Quixote*, a novel about a landowner who imagines himself a knight called to perform heroic deeds. In making fun of medieval romances of chivalry, *Don Quixote*

SECTION 1 REVIEW

Recall
1. **Define** absolutism, divine right, armada, inflation.
2. **Identify** Philip II, El Escorial, the Marranos, the Moriscos, Spanish Armada, Charles II.
3. **Use** the map of the Hapsburg domains above to locate Spain, Portugal, and the Netherlands. Why was the Netherlands opposed to Hapsburg rule?

Critical Thinking
4. **Analyzing Information** Why did Philip II send the Spanish Armada against England? What was the outcome of this effort?

Understanding Themes
5. **Conflict** What were the reasons for internal unrest in the Spanish Empire under Philip II's rule? How did Philip respond?

1500   1550   1600

1547 Henry VIII dies.   **1558** Elizabeth I becomes queen of England.   **1597** Poor Law makes local areas responsible for care of the unemployed.

Section 2

England

Setting the Scene

▶ **Terms to Define**
  gentry, yeomen, balance of power

▶ **People to Meet**
  Henry VII, Henry VIII, Elizabeth I, William Shakespeare

▶ **Places to Locate**
  Scotland, Ireland

Find Out How did Tudor monarchs influence English and European affairs?

The Storyteller

On this day, Elizabeth would be crowned Queen of England. London was arrayed with pavilions and bright banners, and the city's fountains offered wine, not the usual brackish water. Alison Crisp eagerly awaited the royal procession to Westminster Abbey. Although only six years of age, she would present a costly gift to Elizabeth from the Orphans Home board of directors. When the procession neared, the queen commanded her coachmen to stop. Alison flawlessly presented the gift. As the queen prepared to move on, Alison surprised her with another gift, a bouquet of flowers she had picked. With Elizabeth's acceptance of the child's humble offering, the rapport between the queen and her people strengthened.

—from *Description of Elizabeth I's Coronation Procession in 1559*, John Hayward, in *The Past Speaks*, L.B. Smith and J.R. Smith, 1993

Elizabeth I

England, like Spain, developed a strong monarchy. Its Tudor dynasty, which ruled from 1485 to 1603, brought unity to the country after a long period of decline and disorder. Tudor monarchs were hardworking, able, and popular. They greatly expanded the power and authority of the Crown. They were not, however, as absolute in their rule as other European monarchs. Instead, institutions such as Parliament and the courts of law set bounds to the authority that Tudor monarchs could exercise.

Early Tudors

Henry VII, the first Tudor monarch, became king in 1485 after the Wars of the Roses. He used shrewd maneuvering to disarm his rivals and to increase the prestige of his family. Most of Henry's close advisers came from the gentry and merchant classes. Titles were given to these officials, who formed a new aristocracy dependent on the king.

Henry VII helped rebuild England's commercial prosperity. He encouraged the expansion of foreign trade, especially the export of finished woolens to the Netherlands, Germany, and Venice. He promoted the improved collection of taxes as well as careful government spending. In foreign policy Henry avoided war, using diplomacy and the arrangement of suitable royal marriages to strengthen England's interests abroad.

Henry VIII

The second Tudor to rule was **Henry VIII**, son of Henry VII and the most powerful of all Tudor monarchs. Unlike his father, Henry VIII fought wars on the European continent and began to make England a great naval power. His personal life, however, would have a lasting effect on English history. In his pursuit of a male heir, Henry married six times. He worked with Parliament to obtain his personal goals and to break with the Catholic

Church. As a result of this cooperation, the House of Commons increased its power during Henry VIII's reign. Henry, however, furthered support for his policies by seizing monastery lands and selling them to wealthy landowners.

Edward VI and Mary I

After Henry VIII's death in 1547, England entered a brief period of turmoil. Edward VI, Henry's son and successor, was only 9 years old when he became king. He died in 1553 after a short reign. Protestant nobles then plotted to prevent Edward's Catholic half sister, Mary, from becoming queen. The English people, however, supported Mary's claim to the Tudor throne.

Mary's Catholic policies soon offended the English. Despite strong opposition, Mary married Philip II of Spain in 1554. The next year, she restored Catholicism and had about 300 Protestants burned at the stake for heresy. At Philip's urging, Mary involved England in a war with France. As a result, England lost the port of Calais, its final foothold on the European continent. Many English people feared that England would be controlled by Spain. Before this fear could be realized, Mary died childless, and the throne then passed to her Protestant half sister, Elizabeth.

Elizabeth I

Elizabeth I became queen in 1558, when she was 25 years old. She was shrewd, highly educated, and had a forceful personality. With a sharp tongue she asserted her iron will, causing sparks to fly in exchanges with Parliament. Elizabeth, however, used her authority for the common good of her people. On frequent journeys throughout the kingdom Elizabeth earned the loyalty and confidence of her subjects. During her travels, Elizabeth stayed at the homes of nobles who entertained her with banquets, parades, and dances.

Elizabeth's reign was one of England's great cultural periods. Poets and writers praised

Images *of the* Times

Tudor England

Under Tudor monarchs, England enjoyed a period of stability and relative prosperity.

Mary I married Philip II of Spain in 1554, against the wishes of her Protestant subjects. This coat of arms represents the marital union of the two monarchs.

Elizabeth in their works. The theater flourished under playwrights such as **William Shakespeare**. During Elizabeth's reign, English was transformed into a language of beauty, grace, vigor, and clarity.

Marriage

People fully expected that Elizabeth would marry and that her husband would rule. The common attitude of the time was that only men were fit to rule and that government matters were beyond a woman's ability. Elizabeth, however, was slow in seeking a husband. She had learned from the lesson of her sister Mary: to marry a foreign prince would endanger England. At the same time, marrying an Englishman would cause jealousies among the English nobility. In the end, Elizabeth refused to give up her powers as monarch for the sake of marriage. To one of her suitors she stormed, "God's death! My lord, I will have but one mistress [England] and no master." Elizabeth's refusal to marry caused a great deal of speculation as to who would succeed her.

Court and Government

In matters of government, Elizabeth was assisted by a council of nobles. With her approval they drafted proclamations, handled foreign relations, and supervised such matters as the administration of justice and the regulation of prices and wages. These advisers were assisted by small staffs of professional but poorly paid bureaucrats.

Although Parliament did not have the power to initiate legislation, it could plead, urge, advise, and withhold approval. These powers gave Parliament some influence, especially when it was asked to consider tax laws.

The task of enforcing the queen's law was performed by unpaid respected community members known as justices of the peace. Most justices belonged to the rural landowning classes. They knew both the law and local conditions. They maintained peace, collected taxes, and kept the government informed of local problems. Their voluntary participation in support of the government was a key to its success.

The Court of Elizabeth I was known for its love of fashions and style. Noble men and women who served the queen wore elegant clothes and enjoyed music and the arts.

The Globe Theater in London was the site where many of William Shakespeare's plays—tragedies, comedies, and histories—were performed.

REFLECTING ON THE TIMES

1. Why is Elizabeth's reign considered one of England's great cultural eras?
2. Why was Mary I an unpopular ruler?

Social and Economic Policy

Elizabeth believed in the importance of social rank. During the late 1500s, English society was led by the queen and her court. Next were prominent nobles from the great landed families and a middle group of gentry, or lesser nobles, merchants, lawyers, and clergy. This group provided the source of Tudor strength and stability. The lowest social rank was comprised of yeomen, or farmers with small landholdings, and laborers.

Government laws and policies closely regulated the lives of the common people. The Statute of Apprentices of 1563 declared work to be a social and moral duty. It required people to live and work where they were born, controlled the movement of labor, fixed wages, and regulated apprenticeships. The Poor Laws of 1597 and 1601 made local areas responsible for their own homeless and unemployed. These laws included means to raise money for charity and to provide work for vagabonds.

Elizabeth inherited a monarchy that was badly in debt. Royal revenues, which came from rents of royal land, fines in court cases, and duties on imports, barely covered annual expenses. The queen, however, spent lavishly on court ceremonies to show the power and dignity of the monarchy. In other matters, she showed the greatest financial restraint, leading many to call her a "pinchpenny."

To raise funds without relying on Parliament, Elizabeth sold off royal lands, offices, licenses, monopolies, and the right to collect customs. These measures helped but could not solve the problem. England faced the costs of war and mounting inflation. Elizabeth was therefore forced to turn to Parliament for funds. When she ended her reign, England remained badly in debt.

Foreign Policy

By Elizabeth's time, England had lost all of its possessions on the European continent. France was too powerful for England to defeat in order to regain territories. Although England could not completely withdraw from continental affairs, it developed a foreign policy suitable for a small island nation with limited resources.

For security, the English relied on the English Channel to protect their island from European invaders. Building and maintaining a strong navy was therefore important in defending the nation. For that reason, Elizabeth continued the efforts begun by her Tudor predecessors to build such a navy.

History & Art *Elizabeth I* by George Glower, 1596. National Portrait Gallery, London, England **A woman of keen intellect, Elizabeth I was gifted in music, languages, and the arts. In addition, she was an excellent public speaker.** *What foreign policy strategy did England develop under Elizabeth I's reign?*

Spain and France posed the greatest naval threats to England. The attack of the Spanish Armada made England realize the dangers of an alliance between Spain and France. England might be able to defeat one power, but certainly not both. As a result, the English relied on diplomacy as well as sea power to protect their interests.

During Elizabeth's reign, England worked to balance the power of European nations. In international affairs, balance of power refers to the system in which each nation helps to keep peace and order by maintaining power that is equal to, or in balance with, rival nations. One nation cannot overpower another. If one nation becomes more powerful than the other, a third nation can reestablish the balance by supporting the second nation.

Under Elizabeth's rule, England operated as the third balancing nation. In the early part of Elizabeth's reign, England and Spain feared the power of the French. England cooperated with Spain in order to keep France out of the Netherlands. Later, when the Netherlands revolted against Philip II, the English supported the rebels and allied with the weaker power against the stronger one.

Scotland was largely Catholic and hostile toward England during the 1550s. Although part of **Ireland** was under English rule, the rest of the country resisted English armies. To protect English interests, Elizabeth sought to solidify her ties with Scotland and Ireland so they could not be used as bases for Spanish and French attacks on England.

In the 1560s, with Elizabeth's help, Scotland became Protestant and an ally of England. Mary Stuart, later known as Mary, Queen of Scots, was Elizabeth's cousin. She was forced to abdicate her position as queen of Scotland in 1567. She later fled to England, where her presence caused controversy. Mary was a Catholic and heir to the English throne. Many English Protestants feared she would try to replace Elizabeth. In 1586 Mary was accused of plotting with English and foreign Catholics against Elizabeth. Public fears of a Catholic monarchy were strong. In 1587 Elizabeth finally agreed to Mary's

Visualizing History Sir Francis Drake was one of England's most famous explorers and military leaders. After sailing around the world, Drake was knighted in 1581 by Queen Elizabeth I. His naval warfare later helped make England a major sea power. *What European nation was England's primary enemy during the time of Elizabeth I and Francis Drake?*

execution, although she was hesitant to sentence to death another monarch.

In the 1590s, England carried out military campaigns in Ireland to conquer the Irish. With Scotland and Ireland allied with England, a period of temporary peace came to the British Isles.

Elizabeth died in 1603 at the age of 69. With her death came the end of the Tudor dynasty. King James VI of Scotland, the Protestant son of Mary, Queen of Scots, became the new monarch of England. As James I, he founded the Stuart dynasty and united Scotland and England under a common ruler.

SECTION 2 REVIEW

Recall
1. **Define** gentry, yeomen, balance of power.
2. **Identify** Henry VII, Henry VIII, Edward VI, Mary I, Elizabeth I, William Shakespeare, Poor Laws, James I.

3. **Explain** England's foreign policy under Elizabeth I.

Critical Thinking
4. **Evaluating Information** Contrast the effect on English history of Henry's many marriages with the effect of

Elizabeth I's refusal to marry.

Understanding Themes
5. **Change** How did the rule of the Tudor monarchs, especially the rule of Elizabeth I, affect the development of England?

1550   1600   1650   1700

1598 Henry IV issues the Edict of Nantes. **1648** Fronde uprising grips Paris. **1661** Louis XIV takes sole charge of the government. **1701** War of the Spanish Succession begins.

Section 3

France

Setting the Scene

▶ **Terms to Define**
   intendant

▶ **People to Meet**
   Henry IV, Cardinal Richelieu, Louis XIV

▶ **Places to Locate**
   Versailles

Find Out What kind of monarchy developed in France under the Bourbon monarchs?

The Storyteller

A flourish of trumpets sounded. The crowd of courtiers bowed as King Louis entered the Grand Salon at Versailles, accompanied by his attendants. The Duke of Saint-Simon, one of many noblemen whose power Louis was systematically eclipsing, was nonetheless required to be present. He observed that the king "liked splendor, magnificence, and profusion in everything: you pleased him if you shone through the brilliancy of your houses, clothes, tables, equipages." Because everyone tried to emulate the king, a taste for extravagance and luxury was spreading through all classes of society.

—adapted from *The Memoires of the Duke of Saint-Simon,* reprinted in *Aspects of Western Civilization, Volume II,* Perry M. Rogers, 1988

Louis XIV's lavish court life

After a period of religious conflict, peace was restored to most of France when Henry of Navarre became King **Henry IV** in 1589. He founded the Bourbon dynasty, which ruled France with some interruptions until the early 1800s. During most of that time, Bourbon kings maintained an absolute monarchy that was imitated by monarchs throughout Europe.

Henry IV

Henry IV was a Protestant, but he converted to Catholicism to quiet his Catholic opponents. Believing that people's religious beliefs need not interfere with their loyalty to the government, Henry issued the Edict of Nantes in 1598 to reassure the Huguenots, the name given to France's Protestants. The edict allowed Protestant worship to continue in areas where the Protestants were a majority, but barred Protestant worship in Paris and other Catholic strongholds. The edict granted Huguenots the same civil rights as Catholics.

These actions ended religious strife and enabled France to rebuild itself. With the help of his minister of finance, Henry restored the Crown's treasury, repaired roads and bridges, and supported trade and industry. He also tried to restore discipline in the army and bring order to the government bureaucracy. All of these royal policies were put into effect without the approval of the Estates-General and thus laid the foundation for the absolute rule of later Bourbon monarchs.

Cardinal Richelieu

When Henry IV was assassinated in 1610, his 9-year-old son, Louis XIII, became king. Louis's mother, Marie de Medici, was regent for the next 7 years. In 1617 Louis gained the throne by force and exiled his mother from court. A few years later, he gave power to one of her advisers, **Cardinal Richelieu**.

Gradually Louis gave complete control of the government to the cardinal, who set out to build an absolute monarchy in France. To realize this goal, Richelieu had to reduce the power of the nobles and the Huguenots.

When Louis XIII came to the throne, the nobility was in control of the provinces. Nobles collected taxes, administered justice, appointed local officials, and even made alliances with foreign governments. To end the nobles' power, Richelieu destroyed their fortified castles and stripped them of their local administrative functions. The nobility retained social prestige, while authority in local government affairs was given to special agents of the Crown known as intendants. Non-nobles, Richelieu believed, would not assert themselves and challenge the king's authority.

Richelieu also sought to take away the military and territorial rights given to the Huguenots by the Edict of Nantes. The Huguenots were seen as a threat to the French state. In 1625 radical Huguenots revolted against Louis XIII. After the defeat of Protestant forces at the seaport of La Rochelle in 1628, Richelieu took away the Huguenots' right to independent fortified towns. The Huguenots were, however, allowed to keep their religious freedom.

Having weakened the monarchy's internal enemies, Richelieu sought to make France the supreme power in Europe. He strengthened the French army and took steps to build up the economy. In order to strengthen national unity, he supported French culture. Under Richelieu's direction, France's leading writers in 1635 organized the French Academy. The Academy received a royal charter to establish "fixed rules for the language ... and render the French language not only elegant but also capable of treating all arts and sciences." In the following century, French became the preferred language of European diplomacy and culture.

Louis XIV

Louis XIV is recognized as the most powerful Bourbon monarch. He became king in 1643 at the age of 5. At first, France was ruled by his two regents—his mother, Anne of Austria, and Cardinal Mazarin, Richelieu's successor. When Mazarin died in 1661, Louis announced that he would run his own government. He was then 23 years old.

The 72-year reign of Louis XIV was the longest in European history. It set the style for European

Visualizing History Cardinal Richelieu strengthened France's economy by promoting the manufacture of luxury goods. He also gave charters to commercial companies for overseas trade. *How did Richelieu encourage the growth of French culture?*

monarchies during the 1600s and 1700s. During his own lifetime, Louis was known as the Sun King, around whom the royalty and nobility of Europe revolved. He set up a lavish court and surrounded himself with pomp and pageantry. Louis's monarchy had power as well as style. Although Louis relied on a bureaucracy, he was the source of all political authority in France. In one of his audiences, he is said to have boasted, *"L'état, c'est moi!"* ("I am the state!").

Absolute Rule

Louis emphasized a strong monarchy because of his fear of disorder without it. As a child, he had lived through the Fronde, a series of uprisings by nobles and peasants that occurred between 1648 and 1653. During the Fronde, royal troops lost control of Paris and mobs rioted in the streets. The young Louis and his regents were called to give an account of their actions before the *Parlement*, or supreme court of law, in Paris. The Fronde was crushed, but Louis never forgot this attempt to limit royal power. As king, he intended never to let it happen again.

Louis XIV's feelings about absolute monarchy were later supported by Jacques Bossuet (ZHAHK baw•SWAY), the leading church official of France during the 1600s. Bossuet's defense of the divine

Chapter 19 *Royal Power and Conflict* **491**

origins of monarchy became one of the most famous justifications of absolute rule. He wrote:

> ❝ What grandeur that a single man should embody so much! … Behold this holy power, paternal and absolute, contained in a single head: you see the image of God in the king, and you have the idea of royal majesty. ❞

According to Bossuet, subjects had no right to revolt even if the king was unjust. Kings need account to no one except God, but they should act with humility and restraint because "God's judgment is heaviest for those who command."

Court Life

After the Fronde, Louis made plans to live outside of Paris. He moved his court and government to a new palace that he built at **Versailles**. The Palace of Versailles was a large, splendid structure. No expense was spared, for Versailles was to demonstrate the wealth, power, and glory of France.

The palace had elegant royal apartments, sweeping staircases, mirrored halls, priceless tapestries, and lavish formal salons and dining rooms. There were offices for government bureaucrats as well as tiny, cramped rooms where officials lived. As many as 10,000 people lived at Versailles. Outside the palace were acres of formal gardens, filled with marble sculptures and fountains.

In this setting Louis felt secure from the danger of Parisian mobs. Here he had the nobility attend his court so that he could control them. Instead of using the nobles in government service, Louis had them wait on him in a round of daily court rituals. The nobility depended on the king's favor for pensions, court posts, and protection from creditors.

In exchange for ending the nobles' power, Louis freed them from taxation. To nobles and non-nobles alike, he sold many offices with salaries. The sale of offices provided needed royal income but became a long-term drain on the treasury.

Government Policies

Louis continued the efforts of Henry IV and Richelieu to strengthen the power of the monarch and the state. He followed the tradition of Richelieu and chose his top advisers not from the nobility, but from middle-class families. Sons often succeeded their fathers in government service.

Although Louis was an absolute monarch, he was not able simply to change the traditions of his country's feudal past. Legal systems varied throughout France. Private tolls and customs were levied on

History & Art *Louis XIV of France* by Hyacinthe Rigaud, c. 1701, The Louvre, Paris, France **Louis XIV worked six to eight hours a day at what he called "the business of being king."** *How does this painting reflect the monarchy of Louis XIV?*

goods moving from one province to another. Weights and measures were not uniform. There were separate authorities and districts for financial, judicial, religious, and administrative affairs.

If Louis had tried to change these practices, it would have disrupted the kingdom and endangered his throne. Instead, the king kept the traditional ways, but added to them new administrative offices and practices. Two key people aided Louis XIV in his efforts—Jean-Baptiste Colbert (kohl •BEHR) and François Michel Le Tellier, the Marquis de Louvois (loov•WAH). As economic and financial minister, Colbert followed mercantilist policies to promote trade and industry. Louvois served as minister of war and helped make France's army the strongest in Europe.

Taxation

While reforming some aspects of government practice, Louis failed to adjust the complicated and unjust tax system. The poor carried most of the tax burden, while nobles, clergy, and government officials were exempt from many payments. Independent tax collectors often made large profits from their work, but they were allowed to continue this practice since the money they provided was needed to support the army.

The unreformed tax system heightened the economic differences between the regions of France. Since any visible improvement in one's farm or household might lead to higher tax payments, there was little desire to improve one's output. The tax system encouraged people to move from heavily taxed regions to regions with lower taxes. As a result, heavily taxed regions became poorer.

Religious Policy

Louis regarded the Huguenots as a threat to his absolute monarchy. Many Huguenots were military leaders and prosperous merchants. They often controlled local commerce. In spite of their high social standing, the Huguenots faced mounting persecution from Louis's government. The king wanted the Huguenots to accept Catholicism. He believed that, in this way, they would prove their loyalty to the throne. In 1685 the Edict of Nantes was repealed. Huguenots could no longer practice their religion, and their children had to become Catholics.

The result of the king's policy was the emigration of about 200,000 Huguenots to such places as the Netherlands, England, and England's American colonies. Many of these talented people contributed to the economic growth and prosperity of the lands where they settled.

Expansion

Louis XIV pursued a bold and active foreign policy. His goal was to expand the glory and power of France. Other European rulers were fearful of Louis's desire for expansion, and as a result, allied in opposition to France.

At the end of Louis XIV's reign, Europe was concerned about the succession to the Spanish throne. It was expected that Charles II of Spain would die without an heir. Both France and Austria had claims to the throne. The rest of Europe was alarmed that the balance of power would be disrupted if France inherited Spain's vast empire. Prior to Spanish king Charles II's death, the European powers worked out a plan to divide the Spanish Empire. The will of Charles II upset this plan by stating that the entire empire should remain intact and pass to Louis XIV's grandson, Philip of Anjou. Louis XIV accepted the provisions of the will. When Charles II died in 1700, Philip of Anjou became King Philip V of Spain. As a result, Europe was plunged into a conflict known as the War of the Spanish Succession.

Conflict

The War of the Spanish Succession lasted from 1701 to 1713. During the conflict England, the Dutch Netherlands, and Austria led a Grand Alliance of European nations against France and Spain.

Peace was finally restored with the Treaty of Utrecht in 1713. England and the Dutch Netherlands recognized Philip V as king of Spain, on the condition that France and Spain never be united under one crown. England gained trade advantages with the Spanish colonial empire. France, however, was forced to surrender the North American territories of Acadia (Nova Scotia) and Newfoundland to England. The War of the Spanish Succession drained the French treasury, brought increased poverty, and created opposition to Louis's rule.

Louis XIV's Legacy

France enjoyed one of its most brilliant cultural periods under Louis XIV. Builders and artisans designed and decorated palaces and churches. Artists and playwrights portrayed the daily life of the king's court, the nobility, and the lower classes. Louis's building projects and his wars, however, had left the country near financial ruin. The ways in which Louis weakened the French nobility also had their costs. The nobles lost their ability to govern, but not the desire for power. The peasants and the middle class resented the privileges and wealth of the nobles. After Louis XIV's death in 1715, the nobility sought to expand its power under Louis's great-grandson, Louis XV. Conflicts between the nobles and the middle and lower classes would bring France to the brink of revolution.

SECTION 3 REVIEW

Recall
1. **Define** intendant.
2. **Identify** Henry IV, Edict of Nantes, Cardinal Richelieu, Louis XIV, Treaty of Utrecht.
3. **Explain** how Henry IV tried to bring religious peace to France.

Critical Thinking
4. **Evaluating Information** What do you think were the successes and failures of Louis XIV's reign?

Understanding Themes
5. **Uniformity** What were Cardinal Richelieu's political goals? How did Richelieu reduce the power of the nobility? Of the Huguenots?

Section 4

The German States

Setting the Scene

▶ **Terms to Define**
    pragmatic sanction

▶ **People to Meet**
    Maria Theresa, Frederick II

▶ **Places to Locate**
    Austria, Prussia

Find Out   How was the Thirty Years' War different from prior European wars?

The Storyteller

Thomas Taylor traveled slowly and cautiously from Dresden to Prague. He was overwhelmed by a harshness he had never witnessed in his native England. Life all around him was insecure and uncomfortable. Violent outlaws roamed the highways, torture was part of the judicial process, executions were horrible, famine and disease were evident in every town. Taylor detoured around public refuse heaps, swarming with rats and carrion crows. He dodged the bodies of executed criminals dangling from the gallows. Taylor had heard rumors of war. If the rumors were true, he judged it would be long, brutal and terrible.

—freely adapted from *The Thirty Years' War,* C.V. Wedgwood, 1961

The Thirty Years' War

While the Bourbons were building the strongest monarchy in Europe, the Hapsburgs of Austria were trying to set up their own absolute monarchy in central and eastern Europe. Their efforts renewed tensions between Europe's Catholics and Protestants. This eventually led to yet another conflict—the Thirty Years' War. Though most of the fighting took place in Germany, all the major European powers except England became involved.

The Thirty Years' War

Conflicts between Catholics and Protestants had continued in Germany after the Peace of Augsburg in 1555. These disputes were complicated by the spread of Calvinism, a religion that had not been recognized by the peace settlement. Furthermore, the Protestant princes of Germany resisted the rule of Catholic Hapsburg monarchs.

In 1618 the Thirty Years' War began in Bohemia, where Ferdinand of Styria had become king a year earlier. Ferdinand was also the Hapsburg heir to the throne of the Holy Roman Empire. An enemy of Protestantism who wanted to strengthen Hapsburg authority, Ferdinand began his rule by curtailing the freedom of Bohemian Protestants, most of whom were Czechs. In 1618 the Czechs rebelled and took over Prague. Soon the rebellion developed into a full-scale civil war—Ferdinand and the Catholic princes against the German Protestant princes. Philip III of Spain, a Hapsburg, sent aid to Ferdinand.

The Czech revolt was crushed by 1620 and, over the next 10 years, the Czechs were forcefully reconverted to Catholicism. Instead of ending, however, the war continued. Protestant Denmark now fought against the Hapsburgs, hoping to gain German territory. The Danes were soon defeated and forced to withdraw. Then Sweden entered the war to defend the Protestant cause. By this time the war had been going on for 12 years, and religious issues were taking second place to political ones. In 1635, under Cardinal Richelieu, Roman Catholic France took up arms against the Roman Catholic Hapsburgs to keep them from becoming too powerful.

For 13 more years the war dragged on—rival armies plundering the German countryside and destroying entire towns. Historians estimate that Germany lost about one-third of its people.

When the conflict finally ended in 1648, the outcome was the further weakening of Germany and the rise of France as Europe's leading power. The Peace of Westphalia ending the war recognized Calvinism among the official religions and divided the Holy Roman Empire into more than 300 separate states. The Hapsburgs still ruled Austria and Bohemia, but their control of the other German states was in name only, thus ending their hope of establishing an absolute monarchy over all of Germany.

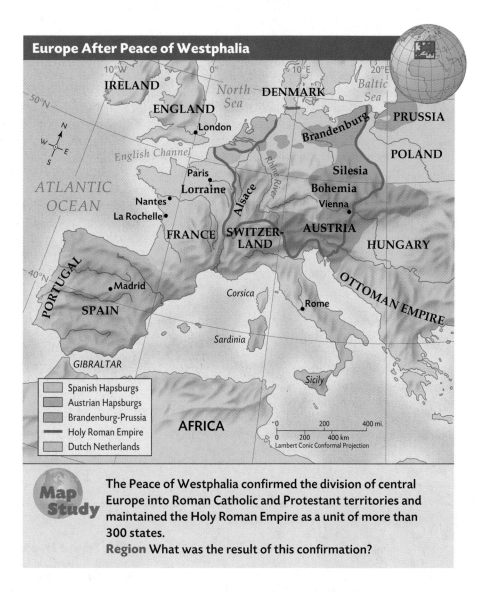

Europe After Peace of Westphalia

Spanish Hapsburgs
Austrian Hapsburgs
Brandenburg-Prussia
Holy Roman Empire
Dutch Netherlands

Map Study The Peace of Westphalia confirmed the division of central Europe into Roman Catholic and Protestant territories and maintained the Holy Roman Empire as a unit of more than 300 states.
Region What was the result of this confirmation?

Austria

After the Thirty Years' War, the Austrian Hapsburgs concentrated on building a strong monarchy in **Austria**, Hungary, and Bohemia. Austria was still the most powerful of the German states. In 1683 the Austrians, with the aid of the Poles, lifted an Ottoman siege of Vienna. By 1718, Austrian armies had regained territory in the Balkan Peninsula from the Ottomans. As a result of the War of the Spanish Succession, the Austrians received the Spanish Netherlands and acquired lands in Italy.

In 1740, 23-year-old **Maria Theresa** inherited the throne of Austria from her father, Holy Roman

Emperor Charles VI. According to law and custom, women were not permitted to rule Austria. In 1718 Charles had convinced the monarchs of Europe to accept a pragmatic sanction, or royal decree having the force of law, by which Europe's rulers promised not to divide the Hapsburg lands and to accept

Footnotes to History

Tulip Mania
During the Thirty Years' War, western Europeans fell in love with tulips. Dutch traders brought tulip bulbs into Europe from Ottoman Turkey beginning in the 1500s, and gardeners in the Netherlands and other parts of Europe took a liking to the blossoms. This led to a public craze for tulips that reached a peak in the 1630s.

female succession to the Austrian throne.

Maria Theresa had not received any training in political matters, yet she proved to be a clever and resourceful leader. Overcoming the opposition of the nobility and most of her ministers, Maria Theresa greatly strengthened the Austrian central government. She reorganized the bureaucracy, improved tax collection, and furthered the building of roads. Understanding that the unity of her empire depended on a strong economy, Maria Theresa ended trade barriers between Austria and Bohemia and encouraged exports. She also used government funds to boost the production of textiles and glass.

Prussia

Maria Theresa faced a number of enemies in Europe. One of these was France, the traditional rival of the Hapsburgs. In the 1700s a new European rival rose to prominence in northeastern Germany. Brandenburg-Prussia was ruled by the Hohenzollern family, which had governed the territory of Brandenburg since the 1400s. During the Thirty Years' War, they gained control of **Prussia** and other widely scattered lands in Germany.

Great Elector

One of the greatest of the Hohenzollern monarchs was Frederick William. He held the title "Great Elector." After the Thirty Years' War, Frederick William increased the strength of Brandenburg-Prussia by creating a permanent standing army. To meet the cost of his army, he proposed raising taxes. The Junkers, or nobles, opposed this plan. Frederick William then worked out a compromise with them. He permitted only Junkers to be landowners, freed them from taxes, and gave them full power over the peasants. In return, the Junkers agreed that Frederick William could tax townspeople and peasants. These two groups were too weak to organize and oppose this increased burden. In 1663 the Junkers further strengthened their ties to the Hohenzollerns. They pledged allegiance to Frederick William. As a result of this alliance with the Junkers, Frederick William was able to become an absolute ruler.

Frederick William was succeeded by his son Frederick I. Frederick aided the Austrian Hapsburgs against Louis XIV in the War of the Spanish Succession. As a reward, Frederick was given the title of king. He was, however, a weak ruler who did little to strengthen his country.

CONNECTIONS

The Arts

The Sounds of Bach

Johann Sebastian Bach

Born in Eisenach, Germany, in 1685, Johann Sebastian Bach was one of the world's most talented composers. He wrote music for the Lutheran Church, wealthy nobles, and other musicians. Bach's work reflects the baroque style of music, which reached its height during the early 1700s. Baroque music was characterized by lively, complex dramatic compositions that appealed to the listener's mind and emotions.

Bach is especially known for two types of baroque music—counterpoint and fugue. In counterpoint, two or more melodies are combined. In the fugue, several instruments or voices play together, each playing the same melodies but with variations.

For about 50 years after Bach's death in 1750, his work was neglected. Today Bach is esteemed as a brilliant musician, and his influence has touched even modern popular music and film. Walt Disney had Mickey Mouse conducting Bach's *Toccata and Fugue in D Minor* in the 1940 movie classic *Fantasia*. Bach's style is at least hinted at in the rock song *A Whiter Shade of Pale* and in rock musician Jethro Tull's jazz-like arrangement of the *Bourrée* from the *E Minor Lute Suite*.

Linking Past and Present ACTIVITY

Explain why Johann Sebastian Bach's work is called "baroque." How was he regarded after his death? How is he regarded today? What impact has Bach had on modern music?

Frederick William I

Frederick William I, who ruled from 1713 to 1740, was a powerful leader. He centralized the Prussian government, uniting all functions into one bureaucracy under his direct control. He supported production and trade and brought more revenue into the government treasury. Known as the Royal Drill Sergeant, Frederick William devoted his life to the Prussian army and made it the most efficient fighting force in Europe. Royal agents recruited men from rural areas of Germany. Frederick William I especially delighted in recruiting tall soldiers. He formed a special "regiment of giants" that he drilled himself.

Frederick II

In 1740 **Frederick II**, Frederick William I's son, became king of Prussia. As a boy, Frederick preferred music and art to horseback riding and military drills. However, when he became king, Frederick adopted his father's military ways and set out to expand Prussian territory. Frederick the Great, as he became known, rejected Austria's pragmatic sanction and seized the Austrian province of Silesia.

Frederick's attack on Silesia began a conflict called the War of the Austrian Succession. Prussia's forces were stronger than those of Austria. In spite of Austria's disadvantage, the Austrian empress, Maria Theresa, decided to send her forces into battle. Spain and France backed Prussia, while Great Britain (formed in 1707 as the result of a union between England and Scotland) and the Dutch Netherlands supported Austria.

After seven years of fighting, in 1748 the European powers signed the Treaty of Aix-la-Chapelle, which officially recognized Prussia's rise as an important nation. Frederick was allowed to keep Silesia; Maria Theresa was able to hold the rest of her domain: Austria, Hungary, and Bohemia.

The Austrian ruler, however, was not satisfied with the treaty and was determined to recover Silesia. To this end, Maria Theresa changed her alliance from Great Britain to France. She also gained the support of Russia since Prussia's Frederick II was

The War of Jenkins' Ear

Caribbean Sea, 1739

The War of Jenkins' Ear was part of a series of conflicts among European nations in the 1700s. In the waters off Florida, an English smuggler named Robert Jenkins lost his ear in a fight with Spaniards in 1731. Jenkins' appearance in Parliament in 1738 further incited public opinion against Spain. The result was war, declared in June 1739, over possession of Georgia and commercial rivalry at sea. Within a year, the War of Jenkins' Ear had become part of the more serious War of Austrian Succession.

an archenemy of Empress Elizabeth of Russia. These alliances set the stage for further conflict.

The Seven Years' War—from 1756 to 1763—was a worldwide conflict in which Great Britain and France competed for overseas territory, and Prussia opposed Austria, Russia, France, and other nations. The war between Austria and Prussia erupted in 1756. After victories in Saxony—a German state and an ally of Austria—and after a later victory over the Austrians in Silesia, Frederick II signed a peace agreement that enabled him to retain most of Silesia.

The struggle between Great Britain and France in North America was known as the French and Indian War. The British and French also fought in India. At the Treaty of Paris in 1763, France gave up most of French Canada and its lands east of the Mississippi River to Great Britain. Great Britain also replaced France as the leading power in India. As a result of the Seven Years' War, Great Britain emerged as the strongest colonial empire and Prussia retained the province of Silesia.

SECTION 4 REVIEW

Recall
1. **Define** pragmatic sanction.
2. **Identify** Ferdinand of Styria, Peace of Westphalia, Maria Theresa, Frederick II, Silesia.
3. **State** what primary factor

caused the Thirty Years' War. What were the war's results?

Critical Thinking
4. **Analyzing Information** How did Maria Theresa strengthen the central government in Austria

and in her other domains?

Understanding Themes
5. **Conflict** How did the many conflicts among the German states affect the balance of power?

Section 5

Russia

Setting the Scene

▶ **Terms to Define**
boyar, *dvorianie*, serf

▶ **People to Meet**
Ivan IV, Peter I, Catherine II

▶ **Places to Locate**
Poland, Siberia, St. Petersburg

Find Out ▶ How did the power of Russian czars differ from that of other European monarchs?

The Storyteller

When first posted, no one could believe the decree. Czar Peter had ordered all children from the nobility and clerical classes [clergy] to study mathematics and geometry. Those who refused were forbidden to marry until they mastered the material. Such commands seemed absurd and many scoffed at the czar's ability to enforce his demands. However, teachers arrived in each district and local taxes were increased for support. Priests likewise received notification and no priest dared solemnize a marriage without proper certification. Father Konstantin looked sadly at the couple before him and explained, "You do not have the proper certification. I cannot marry you."

Russian Orthodox Bishop

—adapted from *Decree on Compulsory Education of the Russian Nobility*, reprinted in *The Human Record, Volume 2*, Alfred J. Andrea and James H. Overfield, 1990

Between 1500 and 1800, Russia made tremendous territorial gains and became a major European power. Slavs elsewhere lost ground and were taken over by other powers.

In southeastern Europe, the Ottoman Turks ruled most of the Balkan Peninsula and the Serbs, Bosnians, and Macedonians who lived there. Under the Ottomans, some of these Slavs converted to Islam, while the rest remained Eastern Orthodox. Hungary ruled the Croats (KROH•ATZ), and Austria controlled the Slovenes (SLOH•VEENZ). Both these Slavic peoples remained Roman Catholic and oriented to western Europe.

In central Europe, Austria ruled the Slovaks and Czechs. Neighboring **Poland** had been an important European power from the late 1300s. Polish monarchs created one of the larger states of Europe, but by the 1600s Poland had gradually weakened. Ukrainian subjects rebelled against Polish rule in the mid-1600s and allied with Russia. By 1764 almost all of Ukraine was under Russian control. In the late 1700s Prussia, Austria, and Russia divided Poland among themselves. The Belarus region and its people, the Belarussians, passed from Polish to Russian control at this time.

Rise of Russia

From the 1200s to the early 1700s, Russia was isolated from western European developments, such as the Crusades, the Renaissance, and the Reformation. Russia developed its own civilization based on the values of the Eastern Orthodox Church and the Byzantine Empire. The Russian monarchy became all-powerful and easily crushed its opponents. The nobility, the established church, and the towns—all of whom had posed repeated opposition to royal power elsewhere in Europe—never posed the same challenge in Russia.

Ivan IV

The most powerful of the early czars was **Ivan IV**, who ruled from 1533 to 1584. Known as Ivan "the Terrible" or "the Awesome," he was at once learned, religious, and cruel. Ivan became czar at the age of three. While growing up, he was caught between rival groups of nobles who sought to rule the country. He witnessed much cruelty and was never able to rid himself of his early memories. As an adult, Ivan saw treason everywhere and arrested, exiled, or executed many of his closest advisers. In a fit of rage, he even killed his own son.

Ivan took many steps against the boyars (boh•YAHRZ), or nobles, to reduce their potential threat to his throne. He seized their scattered lands and placed them under his direct control. The former owners were uprooted and dispersed. On the seized land, which made up about one-half of the country, Ivan placed his own loyal people. They became a secret police force, the *oprichniki*, (aw•PREECH•nee•kee) and terrorized the rest of the country.

Ivan IV also increased Russia's trade with western Europe and worked to expand his borders. Despite Russia's vast size, it had few seaports free of ice throughout the year. Gaining more access to the sea for trade and security became a major goal of Russian rulers. During the late 1500s, Ivan conquered Mongol lands east and south of Moscow but waged unsuccessful war against Poland, Lithuania, and Sweden for territory near the Baltic Sea.

The Time of Troubles

After Ivan's death in 1584, Russia drifted toward chaos. During the "Time of Troubles," from 1598 to 1613, noble feuds over the throne, peasant revolts, and foreign invasions plagued the country. Finally in 1613, an assembly of clergy, nobles, and townsmen named 17-year-old Michael Romanov as czar. Michael began the Romanov dynasty that ruled Russia until 1917.

During the 1500s and 1600s, Russian society experienced many changes. Boyars became more closely tied to the czar's service, townspeople lost what little influence they had on government, and peasants were bound to the land as a virtually enslaved workforce. To escape, many peasants moved to borderlands south of Moscow. In Ukraine, some formed self-governing villages of warrior pioneers and their families and became known as Cossacks. Peasants, traders, and adventurers also moved into **Siberia**, the vast stretch of land east of European Russia.

Visualizing History Peter the Great, a man of restless energy and sometimes hasty decisions, attempted many reforms. *What reforms did he introduce to make Russia more like western European nations?*

Peter the Great

In 1689 **Peter I**, known as Peter the Great, came to the throne. He was a towering figure, nearly 7 feet (2 m) tall. Peter had boundless energy and volcanic emotions. During his reign, he sought to bring Russia into the mainstream of European civilization.

Encounter With the West

As a young man, Peter enjoyed practical subjects, such as mechanics, geography, and military strategy. He sought out tutors among the foreign community in Moscow to learn the basic skills of navigation and shipbuilding. He discovered that Russian knowledge of the outside world was quite limited. Most Russians were illiterate peasants; only a few nobles were well educated.

After becoming czar, Peter took an 18-month study tour of England and the Netherlands. He visited shipyards, factories, mills, and laboratories. He learned carpentry and developed enough skill in surgery and dentistry to want to practice on others.

Steve Raymer

Peter's Great City

G.D. Talbot

Where he first set foot on the Baltic coast, legend has it, Peter the Great proclaimed: "Here there shall be a town." On May 16, 1703, Russian workers laid the foundations for a fortress on the Baltic coast. The city of St. Petersburg soon spread out, and in 1712 Peter made it the new capital of Russia. A traveler in his youth, he was determined that his new capital would imitate the imposing European cities he had visited. St. Petersburg did not remain the capital of Russia, but the new city offered Peter the Great a chance to consolidate the power of the Russian central government and to drag Russia into the modern world. Many changes were inaugurated: He forbade men to wear beards or to dress in the traditional long robes called caftans. He simplified the Cyrillic alphabet. He was relentless. At times he even resorted to terror. But he transformed Russia and made his new city on the Baltic Sea a window to the West.

Today Peter's legacy is everywhere: in the shipyards, the research centers, and the architecture of ornate palaces such as the Winter Palace (center), completed during the reign of Catherine the Great in 1762. "I have a whole labyrinth of rooms ... and all of them are filled with luxuries," she wrote of the Winter Palace and the adjoining Hermitage, where Pavilion Hall (top) fills one small corner. ⊕

When he returned home, Peter forced the Russian nobility to adopt the ways of western Europe. He ordered members of the court to wear western European clothing. Men entering Moscow were forced to shave their beards or pay a fine. Women, who had always been excluded from social gatherings, were ordered to attend parties.

Peter sent Russians abroad to study shipbuilding, naval warfare, mathematics, and foreign languages. He invited foreign experts to train Russians. His greatest effort to open Russia to Europe was the building of a new capital, which he named **St. Petersburg**. Located at the mouth of the Neva River near the Baltic Sea, St. Petersburg became Russia's "window to the West."

Foreign Policy

Peter's goal was to make Russia a European power. He expanded Russia's borders in the south, east, and northwest. In 1689 Russia forced China to accept Russian control of Siberia. In the early 1700s, the Danish navigator Vitus Bering claimed for Russia what became known as the Bering Strait between Siberia and Alaska. Russian settlements eventually started in Alaska and even California.

During much of Peter's reign, Russia fought Poland, Sweden, or the Ottoman Empire. Russian failures to win warm-water ports on either the Baltic or Black Seas convinced Peter to modernize the military. His reforms paid off in 1721, when Russia defeated Sweden and won control of the eastern end of the Baltic region.

Government Administration

Peter made sweeping changes in the Russian government. Borrowing ideas from France, he introduced a central bureaucracy and placed local governments under its control. Peter brought the Eastern Orthodox Church under his direct authority. In place of a single independent church leader, Peter created the Holy Synod, a council of bishops responsible to the government.

Peter also created a new class of nobles called *dvorianie* (DVOH•ree•YAH•nee•YUH), who, in return for government service, were allowed to own hereditary, landed estates. A noble's duty to the czar started at age 15 and continued until death.

Peter used privileges and force to make the established nobility accept government service. Nobles were given full control over the serfs, or peasant laborers who worked the estates and were bound to the land. While freedom for peasants had gradually increased in western Europe, the opposite was true in Russia.

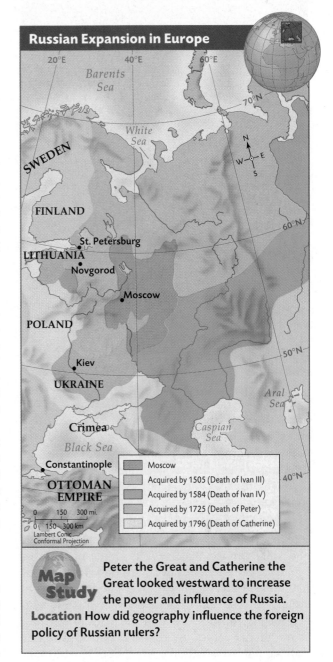

Russian Expansion in Europe

	Moscow
	Acquired by 1505 (Death of Ivan III)
	Acquired by 1584 (Death of Ivan IV)
	Acquired by 1725 (Death of Peter)
	Acquired by 1796 (Death of Catherine)

Map Study Peter the Great and Catherine the Great looked westward to increase the power and influence of Russia.
Location How did geography influence the foreign policy of Russian rulers?

Finally, Peter changed the tax laws to increase government income and efficiency. Under the plan, nobles paid no taxes. As in France, the tax burden fell on the poorest classes.

Economic Changes

To stimulate economic growth, Peter brought agriculture and craft production under strict government control. He gave incentives to increase production in favored areas such as mining and metalworking. New production centers were provided with land, money, and workers. Most of the workers were tied to their trades as the serfs were to the land.

Portrait of Catherine the Great by Alexandre Roslin. Musée des Beaux Arts, La Rochelle, France *What changed Catherine's mind about the equality of all people?*

Catherine the Great

After Peter's death in 1725, Russia was ruled by a series of weak or ordinary monarchs. The next notable ruler was **Catherine II**. In 1762, Catherine seized the throne from her weak husband, Peter III, and ruled as empress of Russia until 1796. Although born a German princess, Catherine easily adopted Russian ways and earned the respect of her people.

As monarch, Catherine was greatly influenced by leading western European thinkers. She studied their works and corresponded with a number of them. For a time, she believed that all people were born equal and that it was "contrary to the Christian faith and to justice to make slaves of them."

Early in her reign, Catherine considered freeing the serfs. A peasant rebellion that threatened her rule, however, made Catherine change her mind. To ensure the continued support of the nobles, she released them from the government service required by Peter I. Catherine also allowed the nobles to treat their serfs as they pleased. During Catherine's reign, more peasants were forced into serfdom than ever before, and their conditions worsened. The common people of Russia had fewer rights than those in any other part of Europe. When groups of them revolted, Catherine brutally crushed the uprisings.

A successful foreign policy earned her the name Catherine the Great. She significantly expanded Russia's borders to the south and achieved the goal of securing a warm-water port on the Black Sea. In making this gain, Russian armies defeated the Ottoman Turks. In the west, Catherine acquired territory from Poland. Prussia and Austria took the rest of Poland, which then ceased to exist until 1919.

Catherine was the last of the great absolute monarchs of the 1700s. By the time of her death in 1796, new ideas of liberty and equality had spread throughout western Europe. These new ideas directly challenged and questioned the age-old institution of monarchy.

Effects

Peter's reforms strengthened Russia's role in foreign affairs. In his own country, however, Peter had only limited success. His domestic policies broke the traditional Eastern Orthodox culture that had united nobles and peasants. With Peter's reign, a dangerous split developed between the few who accepted European ways and the many who clung to traditional values. An observer noted: "The tsar pulls uphill alone with the strength of ten, but millions push downhill." Many of Peter's reforms were incomplete and hasty. Yet his measures brought Russia into the mainstream of western European civilization.

SECTION 5 REVIEW

Recall

1. **Define** boyar, *dvorianie*, serf.
2. **Identify** Ivan IV, the Romanovs, Peter I, Catherine II.
3. **Locate** the cities of Moscow and St. Petersburg on the map on page 501. Why did Czar Peter the Great move the Russian capital from Moscow to St. Petersburg?

Critical Thinking

4. **Synthesizing Information** How did the reigns of Peter the Great and Catherine the Great affect the Russian nobility and the common people?

Understanding Themes

5. **Innovation** How did Peter the Great try to make Russia accept western European ideas and practices?

Recognizing a Stereotype

Emanuella asks her friend Ashley if she would date a football player. Ashley says, "No way. Football players are all muscle and no brains." Ashley has expressed a stereotype—an oversimplified description of a group. Because stereotypes may be both inaccurate and harmful, we must learn to recognize them in speaking, writing, and thinking.

Learning the Skill

A stereotype can describe any group—a gender, race, religion, country, region, city, neighborhood, school, or profession. Stereotypes blur or ignore the characteristics of individuals within the group. In the example above, Ashley may reject the friendship of a very considerate and intelligent person just because he plays football. While this is a negative stereotype, other stereotypes may have positive or neutral connotations. "Blondes have more fun," for example, is a positive stereotype. Negative stereotypes, however, are the least accurate and most harmful.

Stereotypes can influence not only our attitude about a group's members, but also can affect our behavior toward them. History is full of examples of oppression and persecution directed at particular groups of people. Negative stereotypes usually accompany and support these destructive acts.

Because stereotypes are so common, it is easy to ignore or accept them. Instead, learn how to recognize and evaluate them. Certain words, phrases, and thoughts signal the presence of stereotypes. In any kind of material, written or oral, first notice characteristics attributed to a particular group. Look for exaggerations, often indicated by words such as *all*, *none*, *every*, *always*, and *never*. Identify strong negative adjectives such as *lazy*, *sneaky*, *cruel*, and *corrupt*. Note a consistently positive or negative tone to the description.

Once you recognize a stereotype, then evaluate its accuracy. Think about whether the stereotype puts a positive or negative slant on the information concerning a specific group. Ask yourself: Does this stereotype agree or disagree with what I know about individual members of this group?

Practicing the Skill

Each statement below contains a stereotype held by people from the 1500s to the 1700s. Identify the stereotype in each statement. Identify any words or phrases that helped you recognize the stereotype, and tell whether it has a negative, positive, or neutral connotation.

1. England is an isle fouled by heretics and barbarians. *(Spain, 1554)*
2. It is against the law, human and divine, that a woman should reign and have empire above men. *(England, 1560)*
3. The Italians are so jovial and addicted to music that nearly every countryman plays on the guitar, and will commonly go into the field with a fiddle. *(England, 1600)*
4. Do not put such unlimited power into the hands of husbands. Remember all men would be tyrants if they could. [We ladies] will not hold ourselves bound by any laws in which we have no voice, or representation. *(United States, 1776)*

Applying the Skill

Identify three stereotypes about groups within your community. For each stereotype, write a paragraph evaluating its accuracy by recalling your own experiences with individual members of the group.

For More Practice

Turn to the Skill Practice in the Chapter Review on page 505 for more practice in recognizing a stereotype.

Connections Across Time

Historical Significance One of the results of the Age of Monarchy was the emergence of strong national states in Europe. Absolute monarchs centralized their governments and established powerful military forces to protect and to expand their countries' natural borders.

Monarchs plunged Europe into wars over territorial, religious, and economic issues. By forcefully asserting their power, monarchs created the national boundaries that would form the basis of modern Europe. Later wars would modify the boundaries but not change them completely. Today, monarchs reign but do not rule in several European democracies.

Using Key Terms

Write the key term that completes each sentence. Then write a sentence for each term not chosen.

a. absolutism
b. balance of power
c. intendants
d. serfs
e. divine right
f. boyars
g. armada
h. inflation
i. yeomen
j. pragmatic sanction
k. *dvorianie*

1. Ivan IV of Russia took steps against the _____ to reduce their potential threat to his throne.
2. In 1718 the Holy Roman emperor Charles VI convinced Europe's monarchs to accept a _____ in which they promised to accept Maria Theresa as the future Hapsburg monarch.
3. During Spain's decline as a European power, its economy suffered from _____, an abnormal increase in currency resulting in sharp price increases.
4. During the 1600s and the 1700s, European monarchs claimed to rule by _____, the theory that monarchs derive their power from God.
5. During Elizabeth I's reign, England worked for a _____ on the Continent to prevent one European power from becoming too strong.

Technology Activity

Building a Database Search the Internet or your library for additional information about European monarchies since the early 1500s. Build a database collecting biographical information about European monarchies from the 1500s to present day. Include information such as name of monarchy, country, date of coronation, achievements, and names of heirs.

Using Your History Journal

Choose an event from the country time line you created. Write a short opinion paper on why you believe that this was the most significant development, person, or decision in that nation during the period 1500 to 1750.

Reviewing Facts

1. **History** List at least four European royal families and their countries during the period from about 1500 to about 1800.
2. **History** Identify major characteristics of Europe's age of absolutism.
3. **Government** Explain how England's Henry VIII strengthened support for his policies.
4. **Citizenship** State why Henry IV's issuing of the Edict of Nantes was a significant event.
5. **History** Identify the changes that Peter the Great brought to Russia.

Critical Thinking

1. **Analyze** How were the Hapsburg and Tudor monarchies of the 1500s similar? How were they different? Which one do you think was more successful?
2. **Synthesize** Imagine you are a soldier during the Thirty Years' War. Describe how you joined the army and what conditions were like during the war. What hopes do you have for the future?
3. **Evaluate** Consider the leadership style of Maria Theresa of Austria, who had no training in political matters. Can a person today be a successful political leader with no prior training or experience?

4. **Evaluate** Which of the monarchs described in this chapter do you most admire? Which one do you least admire? Explain your reasons.
5. **Evaluate** What does the portrait of Frederick the Great below reveal about the values and characteristics of the Prussian monarchy?

Understanding Themes

1. **Conflict** How did Spain's rivalry with England develop during the period from about 1500 to about 1750?
2. **Change** How did Tudor monarchs bring stability to England?
3. **Uniformity** How did Louis XIV try to strengthen French loyalty to his monarchy?
4. **Conflict** What dynastic and religious issues divided the German states?
5. **Innovation** Why did Peter the Great want to make innovations in government and society?

Skill Practice

The following lines from William Shakespeare's plays include stereotypes that were common in 16th-century England. Identify each stereotype and any words or phrases that helped you recognize it.

1. "Frailty, thy name is woman!"
2. "These Moors are changeable in their moods."
3. "This Hebrew will turn Christian; he grows kind."
4. "Today the French … all in gold, like heathen gods, shone down the English."

Linking Past and Present

1. European monarchs in the 1600s and 1700s resolved their territorial disputes and ambitions through war. How do present-day leaders resolve disputes? Explore the similarities and the differences between contemporary world leaders and monarchs in early modern Europe.
2. European monarchs in the 1600s and 1700s were powerful leaders who claimed to rule by divine right. What is the position of monarchs in Europe today? How is power exercised in modern European governments?

Geography in History

1. **Location** Refer to the map below. Along what body of water did Pomerania lie? What was the population loss over much of its area?
2. **Place** Of Bohemia, Saxony, and Silesia, which area had suffered the least population loss?
3. **Region** In general, what parts of the Holy Roman Empire retained the most population? Why do you think this was so?

ABCNEWS INTERACTIVE™ Turning Points in World History

Age of Exploration

Setting up the Video

Work with a group of your classmates to view "Age of Exploration" on the videodisc *Turning Points in World History*. The voyages of the age of exploration opened new doors for European explorers to gain new contacts for trade, expansion, and innovation that profoundly changed European culture. This program highlights the history of European exploration and speculates about future trends for modern explorers.

Side One, Chapter 9

View the video by scanning the bar code or by entering the chapter number on your keypad and pressing Search. <u>*(Also available in VHS format.)*</u>

Hands-On Activity

Research information about current discoveries that are taking place in space explorations. Using a word processor, write a minireport about the latest findings. Share your results with the rest of the class.

Surfing the "Net"

Sunken Treasures

During the 1500s, Spanish galleons were constantly searching for treasure to take back to Spain. Typically, the loot included precious stones, gold doubloons, and silver pieces of eight. Many treasure-laden vessels were sunk due to bad weather or pirates trying to steal the fortune in the midst of a battle. To find out more about recent discoveries of sunken treasures, access the Internet.

Getting There

Follow these steps to gather information about sunken treasure.

1. Go to a search engine. Type in the phrase *sunken treasure*.
2. After typing in the phrase, enter words such as the

following to focus your search:
- *spanish history*   • *florida keys*   • *location*

3. The search engine should provide you with a number of links to follow. Links are "pointers" to different sites on the Internet and commonly appear as blue underlined words.

What to Do When You Are There

Click on the links to navigate through the pages of information and gather your findings. Using a word processor, create a chart to organize your information. Include headings such as location of a sunken galleon, date of sinking, date of discovery, and treasure recovered from the galleon. Include a map labeling the location of discovered sunken ships.

Unit 4 Digest

The Marriage of Giovanni Arnolfini and Giovanna Cenami by Jan van Eyck, 1434. National Gallery, London, England *What values were popular throughout Renaissance Europe?*

From 1400 to the mid 1700s, rulers in various parts of the world increased the power and prestige of their territories. In Europe two major movements—the Renaissance and the Reformation—encouraged Europeans to gain new knowledge, explore lands overseas, acquire new resources, and spread Christianity.

Religion, politics, and economic needs also spurred new developments in Asia. There, Muslim empires ruled over vast areas between the Mediterranean Sea and South Asia. Other parts of Asia—China, Japan, and Southeast Asia—developed their traditional cultures while facing growing challenges from European explorations. A new age dawned in which the world's different civilizations for the first time came into close contact with each other.

Chapter 16
Renaissance and Reformation

In the 1300s scholars in Italy revived the ancient Greek ideal of individual achievement. Their interest in the classics sparked a new era of European thought and art known as the Renaissance. For the first time since the fall of Rome, European artists and writers emphasized the value of human activities and feelings in their works. This represented a departure from the medieval concern with religion and spiritual values. During the Italian Renaissance, highly talented people—such as Michelangelo Buonarroti and Leonardo da Vinci—also created works of art that have been admired throughout the centuries for their technical skill and beauty.

From Italy the Renaissance spread to northern Europe, where it became more religious in its emphasis. Scholars such as Erasmus and Thomas More called for simpler forms of worship and other church reforms. Johannes Gutenberg's use of movable type in printing made an increasing number of books at cheaper prices available to more people. As a result, Renaissance ideas spread rapidly and challenged traditional religious and cultural beliefs.

Protests against church abuses soon led to a split in Western Christianity. Reformers such as Martin Luther and John Calvin criticized the pope's authority and many Catholic teachings and practices. Their two major ideas—that the Bible, rather than church tradition, was the source of authority and that salvation was by faith alone—won support throughout northern Europe and led to a new form of Christianity known as Protestantism. In England, the monarch replaced the pope as head of the Church in England. Later the English Church became Protestant with Catholic features.

To counter Protestantism, the Roman Catholic Church began its own reform movement to correct church abuses and to more clearly define its teachings. As part of this effort, the pope sent the Jesuits, a new religious order, as missionaries to Protestant areas in Europe and non-Christian areas in Asia.

Chapter 17
Expanding Horizons

During the 1400s, Muslims and Italians controlled the rich overland spice trade from Asia. Wanting to share in this wealth, European countries bordering the Atlantic Ocean sought a direct sea route to the spice-producing islands of Southeast Asia. Advances in navigation by Chinese and Muslim inventors made their oceangoing voyages possible. By the 1500s, Portugal had discovered a route to South Asia around the southern tip of Africa. Its traders followed the route and founded trading centers in India and Southeast Asia.

Portugal's rival, Spain, joined in the effort to reach Asia. By 1522, Columbus, Magellan, and other explorers under Spain's flag had reached the Americas or had circled the globe. The Spaniards later set up a large overseas empire that included Mexico, Central America, most of South America, and the Philippines.

France, England, and the Netherlands led the search for shorter routes to Asia, and they eventually surpassed Spain in overseas exploration. The Dutch acquired Portugal's spice trade in Southeast Asia. France traded with Native Americans in North America's interior lands. England set up colonies or trading posts in the Americas and South Asia.

European overseas expansion brought riches to European countries. However, the same expansion often had both a positive and negative impact on the cultures that Europeans encountered. Europeans brought new skills, beliefs, and goods to overseas areas. Peoples in Asia, Africa, and the Americas, however, saw their traditional cultures undermined by European expansion, and millions died of mistreatment or diseases brought by Europeans. Portugal, Spain, and England relied on enslaved people from Africa to work their plantations and mines in the Americas.

The slave trade became part of the larger trading network that was beginning to link Europe, Asia, Africa, and America. Gold and silver from the Americas to Europe increased trade between Europe and Asia, where demand for the precious metals was high. European manufactured goods flowed around the world, while agricultural products, such as corn, chocolate, yams, potatoes, coffee, and tea, came to Europe from Asia, Africa, and the Americas. All of these exchanges, both positive and negative, contributed to the rise of the global community that we know today.

Chapter 18
Empires of Asia

From the late 1400s to the 1700s, three Muslim empires—the Ottoman, the Safavid Persian, and the Mogul—ruled parts of Asia, Europe, and Africa. The Ottomans controlled the Middle East and much of North Africa and Europe's Balkan Peninsula. Suleiman I, who ruled from 1520 to 1566, strengthened government administration, but later military defeats at Lepanto (1571) and Vienna

Visualizing History During the 1500s and 1600s, European explorers, traders, and missionaries traveled the seas to Africa, the Americas, and Asia. *What earlier developments in European finance and business encouraged voyages of exploration?*

(1683) halted the Ottoman advance into Europe. To the east, the Safavid dynasty ruled Persia, or present-day Iran. Under Safavid leadership, Persia enjoyed a flowering of culture, and the Persian language became the language of culture, diplomacy, and trade in most of the Muslim world. Muslims from central Asia conquered northern India and set up the Mogul dynasty. Akbar, a Muslim ruler of the 1500s, fostered religious tolerance among Muslims and Hindus. Mogul rulers encouraged the arts—music, painting, and literature.

In China the Ming dynasty, which ruled from 1368 to 1644, encouraged the development of agriculture and sponsored overseas explorations that sailed as far as Africa and Arabia. Although the expeditions brought back rich tribute, the Chinese did not continue their voyages of discovery. In 1644 Manchu invaders conquered China and set up the Qing dynasty. Internal peace and government-sponsored improvements brought prosperity and increased population. During the 1700s, government corruption and internal revolts weakened the dynasty. Meanwhile, the Chinese faced new challenges from European explorations in their part of the world.

In the 1500s Japan's warrior classes came under the rule of a military leader known as a shogun. During this period, Portuguese traders reached Japan, and European Catholic missionaries made many converts among the Japanese. Fearing this foreign influence, Japan's military leaders closed Japan's borders to all except a few Dutch traders.

Visualizing History The Ottoman ruler Selim I, who was crowned in 1512, fought wars of expansion against the neighboring Persians and Egyptians. *What areas eventually made up the territory of the Ottoman Empire?*

From the 1400s to the 1800s, large areas of Southeast Asia came under European influence. The Thai kingdom (Siam) was the only Southeast Asian area to remain free of European control. Thai kings built a strong central government and employed reforms that preserved their country's independence.

Chapter 19
Royal Power and Conflict

During the 1500s and 1600s, European monarchs strengthened their thrones and created powerful central governments. Their efforts paved the way for the rise of modern nation-states in Europe.

In Spain, Philip II sought national unity by using the Spanish Inquisition to force Protestants, Jews, and Muslims to accept Catholicism. His religious policy sparked revolts, especially among the Protestant Dutch in the Spanish-ruled Netherlands.

Protestant England supported the Dutch and challenged Spanish sea power. After the defeat of the Spanish Armada by the English in 1588, Spain began to lose much of its power. During the 1600s, the Spanish monarchy and economy declined, although Spain still held on to its overseas empire.

English Tudor monarchs, such as Henry VIII and Elizabeth I, brought England peace and stability. They increased royal power while allowing Parliament and other non-royal institutions to flourish. As the English economy prospered, the first steps were taken toward building an overseas empire based on trade.

Elsewhere in Europe, wars of religion between Protestants and Catholics shaped political boundaries and brought much hardship to Europe's people. When the Hapsburg monarchs of Austria tried to advance Catholicism and curtail Protestant liberties, war erupted among central Europe's Protestant and Catholic rulers. Other European nations, including Catholic France and Protestant Sweden, entered this conflict known as the Thirty Years' War. The Peace of Westphalia finally ended the war in 1648. By this time, the concerns of Europe's rulers had shifted from enforcing religious uniformity to extending their own political powers.

From 1600 to 1789, European monarchs wielded great power. They believed in the theory of absolute monarchy, which held that kings and queens ruled as representatives of God and were responsible to God alone, not to parliaments or citizens. In France, monarchs such as Louis XIV created a strong royal government that became the model for other European royal houses. Louis also sought to expand French territory in a series of wars that cost France thousands of lives and much wealth. During the 1700s, major wars between France and Great Britain (formed by a union in 1707 between England and Scotland) spread overseas to Europe's colonies. By the 1760s, France had lost much of its overseas empire to Great Britain.

Meanwhile, Russia, once largely isolated from European affairs, began to take on an international role under the rule of Peter the Great. Peter rebuilt the Russian state, enhanced its military power, and increased contacts with western Europe. His reforms, however, created a large gap between the Europeanized upper classes and the traditionally Russian lower classes.

SURVEYING UNIT 4

1. **Chapter 16** How did the use of movable type in printing affect developments in Europe during the 1500s?
2. **Chapter 17** What effect did European expansion have on Europeans? On peoples living in Asia, Africa, and the Americas?
3. **Chapter 18** Would the world be different if China had continued its voyages of exploration? Explain.
4. **Chapter 19** How did Ottoman, Mogul, or Ming rulers in Asia compare with monarchs in Europe during the period from the 1500s to the 1700s?

Unit

5

1500–1830

Age of Revolution

Then & Now The discoveries and writings of the Age of Revolution ignited a fuse of knowledge that exploded in a scientific revolution so complete and far-reaching that the years from 1500 to 1830 are often called "the beginning of the modern age."

Every time you have your temperature taken with a mercury thermometer, receive medication through a fine-needled syringe, let a doctor listen to your heartbeat through a stethoscope, or have your tooth drilled by a dentist, you are seeing instruments invented during the Age of Revolution. When you study a cell through a microscope or a star through a telescope, you are using equipment developed to fill the needs of sixteenth- and seventeenth-century scientists for precise, accurate scientific instruments. Even the simple multiplication symbol × was proposed during this age of scientific revolution.

A Global Chronology

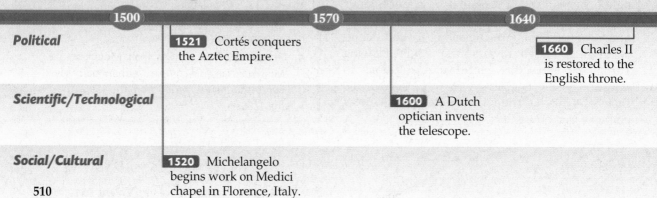

	1500	1570	1640
Political	**1521** Cortés conquers the Aztec Empire.		**1660** Charles II is restored to the English throne.
Scientific/Technological		**1600** A Dutch optician invents the telescope.	
Social/Cultural	**1520** Michelangelo begins work on Medici chapel in Florence, Italy.		

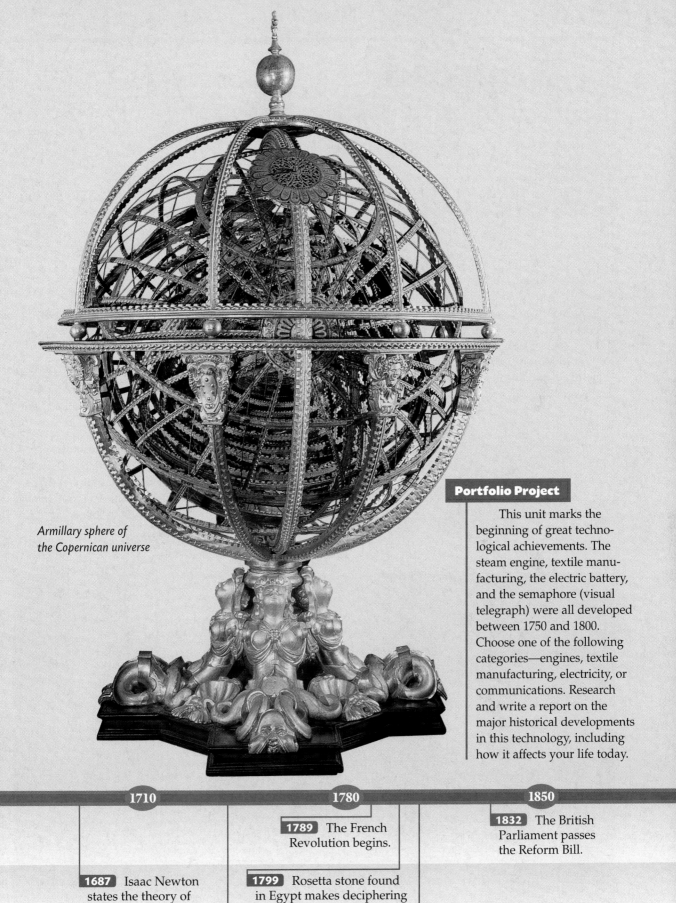

Armillary sphere of the Copernican universe

Portfolio Project

This unit marks the beginning of great technological achievements. The steam engine, textile manufacturing, the electric battery, and the semaphore (visual telegraph) were all developed between 1750 and 1800. Choose one of the following categories—engines, textile manufacturing, electricity, or communications. Research and write a report on the major historical developments in this technology, including how it affects your life today.

1710

1780

1850

1789 The French Revolution begins.

1832 The British Parliament passes the Reform Bill.

1687 Isaac Newton states the theory of gravity.

1799 Rosetta stone found in Egypt makes deciphering hieroglyphics possible.

1740 Frederick the Great introduces freedom of the press and of worship in Prussia.

1804 Ludwig van Beethoven composes his Third Symphony, the *Eroica*.

511

The Spread of Ideas

Revolution

In the 1600s and 1700s, revolution bounced back and forth across the Atlantic. The pattern started with the arrival of the first English colonists in North America. They carried with them ideals born of the English Revolution. They believed that governments existed to protect the rights and freedoms of citizens.

The United States
Revolutionary Ideas

In 1776 the colonists fought a revolution, making clear the principles of freedom and rights in the Declaration of Independence:

> We hold these truths to be self-evident, that all men are created equal, that they are endowed by their Creator with certain unalienable rights, that among these are life, liberty, and the pursuit of happiness.

These ideas bounced back across the Atlantic to influence the French Revolution. French rebels in 1789 fought in defense of *Liberté, Egalité, Fraternité* (Liberty, Equality, Fraternity). In drafting their declaration of freedom, French revolutionaries repeated the principles of the American Declaration of Independence: "Men are born and remain free and equal in rights."

Signing of the Declaration of Independence

Italy
The Age of Revolution

The spread of ideas—specifically, revolutionary ideas—forms the subject of Unit 5. The spark that sent the spirit of revolution flashing across Europe and the Americas began in the minds of sixteenth-century European scientists. These thinkers challenged established ideas defended by the Roman Catholic Church. Church officials tried to stop the spread of new scientific ideas. But once unleashed, the ideas respected neither authority nor geographic boundary. Defiance of one authority, in this case, the Church, soon led people to question other authorities as well. The result was the intellectual and political upheavals that historians call the Age of Revolution.

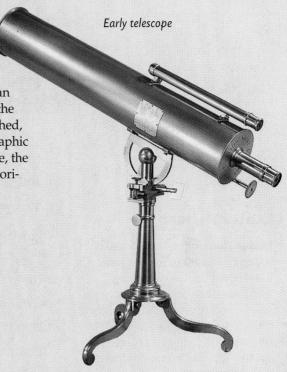

Early telescope

Haiti
Exporting Revolution

In 1791 the ideals of the American and French Revolutions traveled across the Caribbean and the Atlantic to the French-held island colony of Saint Domingue. Inspired by talk of freedom, enslaved Africans took up arms. Led by Toussaint-Louverture, they shook off French rule. In 1804 Saint Domingue, present-day Haiti, became the second nation in the Americas to achieve independence from colonial rule. "We have asserted our rights," declared the revolutionaries. "We swear never to yield them to any power on earth."

Toussaint-Louverture

LINKING THE IDEAS

1. What was the role of government according to the American colonists?
2. What ideals did the Americans and the French share?

Critical Thinking

3. **Cause and Effect** Why do you think revolutionary ideas respect neither authority nor geographic boundaries?

Scientific Revolution

Chapter Themes

▶ **Innovation** European interest in science leads to discoveries and ideas based on reason. *Section 1*
▶ **Conflict** Changing views based on science and reason conflict with traditional beliefs. *Section 2*
▶ **Reaction** Reason and order are applied to many human endeavors. *Section 3*

The Storyteller

Antonie van Leeuwenhoek, a Dutch cloth merchant in the late 1600s, found that his unusual hobby unlocked the door to an unknown world. By carefully grinding very small lenses out of clear glass, van Leeuwenhoek discovered that he could make things look much bigger than they appeared to the naked eye.

Soon the Dutch merchant turned his lenses to everything he could find—from the cloth he had just bought to the scales of his own skin. His most remarkable find was tiny microorganisms, which he described as "wretched beasties" with "incredibly thin feet" swimming through a tiny universe.

New technology such as van Leeuwenhoek's microscope and scientific study in general captured the imagination of many European people in the 1600s. A scientific revolution would lead to a new era in Western thought.

Historical Significance

How did the scientific revolution of the 1600s and 1700s transform European society? What impact has the growth of science had on the world today?

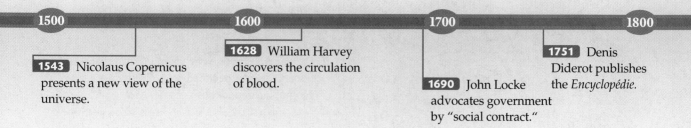

1500	1600	1700	1800

1543 Nicolaus Copernicus presents a new view of the universe.

1628 William Harvey discovers the circulation of blood.

1690 John Locke advocates government by "social contract."

1751 Denis Diderot publishes the *Encyclopédie*.

The Establishment of the Academy of Science and the Foundation of the Observatory by Louis XIV by Henri Testelin. Musée National du Chateau de Versailles, Versailles, France

Your History Journal

Research a scientific discovery or invention from the 1600s. Write the story of the discovery or invention as it might have appeared in a publication at the time.

Section 1

New Scientific Ideas

Setting the Scene

▶ **Terms to Define**

hypothesis, ellipses, scientific method, calculus, alchemist

▶ **People to Meet**

Nicolaus Copernicus, Johannes Kepler, Galileo Galilei, Francis Bacon, René Descartes, Isaac Newton, Andreas Vesalius, William Harvey, Robert Hooke, Robert Boyle, Joseph Priestley, Antoine and Marie Lavoisier

▶ **Places to Locate**

Poland

 **Find Out** How did scientific thought change during the 1600s?

Storyteller

Christina, Grand Duchess of Tuscany, was intrigued. She had asked the renowned Galileo to describe his studies to her. "Nature," he explained in his letter, "never transgresses the laws imposed upon her, or cares whether her reasons and methods of operation are understandable to men." But Christina knew that others might find Galileo's opinions dangerous, for he also claimed that one could learn truth from these studies as much as from religion. "I do not feel obliged to believe that the same God who has endowed us with senses, reason, and intellect has intended us to forgo their use."

—adapted from *Letter to Christina of Tuscany*, reprinted in *Western Civilization: Sources, Images, and Interpretations*, Dennis Sherman, 1995

Galileo Galilei

*M*agic, mysticism, and ancient writings ruled scientific thought in Europe throughout the Middle Ages. Scholars based their ideas on theories proposed almost a thousand years before by ancient Greek thinkers such as Aristotle, Ptolemy, and Galen. During the Middle Ages, most Europeans believed that the earth was flat, and they accepted the Catholic Church's view that the earth was the center of the universe. According to church doctrine, God created the universe to serve people. Therefore, the Church reasoned, the people's home—the earth—must be at the center of the universe.

In the 1600s, however, such ideas would topple as a scientific revolution spread throughout Europe. New technology, combined with innovative approaches to seeking knowledge, led to a breakthrough in Western thought. At the forefront of this scientific revolution was a Polish astronomer named **Nicolaus Copernicus.**

A Scientific Revolution

Copernicus started his scientific career at the University of Kraków in **Poland** in 1492—the same year in which Christopher Columbus reached the Americas. Like Columbus, Copernicus began his questioning in a time when few people dared to question age-old beliefs and superstitions.

As Copernicus delved into his studies, he became convinced that ideas commonly accepted about the universe were wrong. Copernicus believed that the earth was round and that it rotated on its axis as it revolved around the sun. The sun stayed still at the center of the universe.

Copernicus realized, however, that his ideas were revolutionary and even dangerous. Disputing or even questioning traditional views about the universe could mean persecution, excommunication, or even imprisonment. To avoid this risk, Copernicus worked in privacy, without publishing

Visualizing History In 1633, the Inquisition in Rome found Galileo guilty of heresy and sentenced him to life imprisonment. Recanting many of his views, Galileo was allowed to serve his sentence at home. *Why was Galileo charged with heresy?*

his ideas. The Polish scientist spent more than 30 years writing his treatise. Friends who realized the significance of Copernicus's ideas helped publish his work just before his death.

New Theories About the Universe

Other scientists took Copernicus's ideas and ventured even further into a scientific understanding of the universe. Copernicus had based his hypotheses, or theories that attempt to explain a set of facts, on study and observations. He could not provide proof, however, because the necessary mathematics was not available to him at the time. In the late 1500s, the Danish astronomer Tycho Brahe (TEE•koh BRAH•uh) set up an observatory to study heavenly bodies and accumulated much data on planetary movements. After Brahe's death, the German astronomer and mathematician **Johannes Kepler** used Brahe's data with the goal of providing mathematical proof for Copernicus's hypotheses.

Using mathematical formulas, Kepler did show that the planets revolve around the sun. His findings, however, also refuted some of Copernicus's views. For example, Kepler proved that the planets move in oval paths called ellipses—not in circles as Copernicus had believed. He also found that planets do not always travel at the same speed, but

move faster as they approach the sun and slower as they move away from it.

Challenging the Church

Kepler challenged the teachings of many academic and religious leaders. Because Kepler was a Protestant, however, he did not have to fear the Catholic Church. His Catholic contemporary, the Italian mathematician **Galileo Galilei**, did face considerable opposition from church leaders.

In 1609 Galileo built his own telescope and observed the night skies. His discovery of moons circling a planet convinced him that the Copernican theory about the earth revolving around the sun was correct. Because these moons revolved around Jupiter, Galileo reasoned, not all heavenly bodies revolved around the earth. It was possible that some planets did move around the sun.

In 1632 Galileo published his ideas. Soon afterward, the Catholic Church banned the book. The Church would not tolerate Galileo's spreading of ideas that contradicted its own position. An outraged Pope Urban VIII demanded that Galileo come to Rome and stand trial.

Urban's threats of torture and possible death forced Galileo to recant many of his statements and publicly state that he had gone too far in some of his writing:

“ I, Galileo Galilei, ... swear that with honest heart and in good faith I curse ... the said heresies and errors as to the movement of the earth around the sun and all other heresies and ideas opposed to the Holy Church; and I swear that I will never assert or say anything either orally or in writing, that could put me under such suspicion. **”**

Galileo continued his work after the trial. As he experimented with the motion of objects on the earth, he helped to establish the universal laws of physics. Among these discoveries was the law of inertia, which specifies that an object remains at rest or in straight-line motion unless acted upon by an external force. Other investigations into the workings of the pendulum helped to advance its application as a time controller in clocks.

New Ways of Thinking

As European scientists revolutionized the world of astronomy, philosophers such as **Francis Bacon** and **René Descartes** incorporated scientific thought into philosophy. Bacon, an English philosopher, claimed that ideas based solely on tradition or unproven facts should be discarded completely.

To Bacon, truth resulted only from a thorough investigation of evidence. He helped develop what is known today as the scientific method. The scientific method is made up of several steps. The scientist begins with careful observations of facts or things. Then the scientist tries to find a hypothesis to explain the observations. By experimenting, the scientist then tests the hypothesis under all possible conditions and in every possible way to see whether it is true. Finally, if careful and repeated experiments show that the hypothesis does prove true under all conditions, it is considered a scientific law. In other words, a scientific truth is not assumed—it is deduced from observations and a series of thorough experiments.

Like Bacon, French philosopher and mathematician René Descartes believed that truth must be reached through reason. The inventor of analytic geometry, Descartes saw mathematics as the perfect model for clear and certain knowledge. In 1637 he published *Discourse on Method* to explain his philosophy. In the book, Descartes began his search for knowledge by doubting everything except his own existence. He believed he had found one unshakable and self-evident truth in the statement "I think, therefore I am."

Newton's Universe

In 1642, after Bacon and Descartes had transformed European thinking, one of the most influential figures in modern science was born in England. His name was **Isaac Newton**. Newton used the scientific method as he studied science and mathematics. He once commented, "Asking the correct question is half the problem. Once the question is formulated there remains to be found only proof.... "

At Cambridge University, Newton was a below-average student with few friends. He almost left school without realizing his mathematical genius. But one of his teachers recognized his ability and began tutoring him. With this help Newton quickly became an eager and successful student. He explored the most complicated mathematics of his day, reading the writings of Copernicus and Galileo.

In 1665 an outbreak of the plague closed the university and forced Newton to return to his family's farm. There, he began his ground-breaking studies in mathematics and physics. The legend of Newton's apple originated during these years. It was claimed that while sitting in his garden one day, Newton watched an apple fall to the ground. The apple's fall led him to the idea of gravity.

Nearly 20 years later, in 1687, Newton published his theories about gravity and other scientific concepts in his book *Mathematical Principles of Natural Philosophy*, often called *Principia*. Newton offered in the *Principia* a new understanding of the universe, explaining and expanding the work of Copernicus, Galileo, and Kepler.

The book stated Newton's theory of universal gravitation, explaining why the planets move as they do. According to this theory, the force of gravity not only prevents objects from flying off the

The Circus

Identified by Newton, centripetal force pulls an object traveling in a circular path toward the center of the circle. In 1768 the English performer Philip Astley relied on centripetal force to perform stunts on horseback while the horse ran in a circle at full gallop. He took his horse show to Paris in 1774, beginning the first circus. *Circus* is the Latin word for "circle."

Bubbling Waters

Have you ever sipped a fizzy soft drink to settle an upset stomach? People have long believed that bubbling waters contain healing properties. For centuries royalty and wealthy Europeans sought the health benefits of the mineral-rich, bubbling springs scattered throughout Europe.

Scientists in Europe and the United States attempted to reproduce these effervescent waters. In 1775 the French chemist Antoine Lavoisier identified the gaseous compound as carbon dioxide. In 1782 the English chemist Thomas Henry described how to make artificial carbonated waters commercially. Factories and bottling

plants soon began operating in London, Paris, Dublin, and Geneva.

"Soft drinks" were originally sold in drugstores in the United States as syrupy tonics used for medicinal purposes. In the early 1800s it became popular to combine these tonics with carbonated water. Bottled colas appeared on the market in the late 1800s.

Today mineral waters and carbonated beverages are popular throughout the world. People like the tangy, sparkling taste provided by carbonation, which also prevents spoilage.

Soft drink advertisement

Linking Past and Present ACTIVITY

Determine whether or not carbonated soda has a positive or negative effect on your health. Can you think of any inventions or technologies that have been produced by the soft-drink industry?

---

revolving earth, but it also holds the entire solar system together by keeping the sun and the planets in proper orbits. To prove his theory, Newton developed calculus, a system of mathematics that calculates changing forces or quantities.

Newton's work greatly influenced the thinking of his own age and all later scientific thought. It suggested that precise mathematical formulas could be used to describe an orderly universe. ●—

Studying the Natural World

As astronomy, philosophy, and mathematics advanced at an incredible pace, so too did the sciences of anatomy and chemistry. Like astronomy and physics, anatomy had been based on ancient works. Most knowledge of anatomy had come from the work of Galen, an ancient Greek.

Because Roman law forbade the dissection of human corpses, Galen formulated his theories of human anatomy by dissecting dogs and apes. Galen did make many anatomical discoveries, such as the existence of blood within the arteries, but he also held many mistaken views. Galen believed, for example, that the liver digested food and processed it into blood. A thousand years would pass before anyone began to question his findings.

Investigating the Human Body

French lawmakers in the 1500s also considered dissecting human bodies illegal. This limitation, however, did not stop a young medical student from making great advances in anatomy. Self-assured and outspoken, **Andreas Vesalius** made it clear to his professors that because Galen's views were based on dissected apes and dogs, his beliefs about human anatomy could not be accepted as truth. By dissecting human bodies, Vesalius made groundbreaking discoveries in anatomy. In 1543 he published his work in *On the Structure of the Human Body*.

Almost 100 years later, English physician **William Harvey** made a discovery that also disproved many of Galen's hypotheses. From his direct observations of humans, Harvey concluded that blood circulates throughout the body, pumped by the heart and returning through the veins. His findings astounded a medical world that had based its beliefs about circulation on Galen.

As Vesalius and Harvey explained the workings of the human body, English scientist **Robert Hooke** made a more fundamental biological discovery—the cell. Using the newly invented microscope, Hooke recognized cells in vegetable tissue. He called them "cells" because they reminded him of the cells in a honeycomb.

Franklin Experiments With Electricity

Philadelphia, Pennsylvania, 1752
American scientist and inventor Benjamin Franklin performed an experiment to prove his theory that lightning is electricity. During a thunderstorm, Franklin flew a homemade kite with a wire attached to it. A bolt of lightning struck the wire and traveled down the wet kite string to a key fastened at the end, where it caused an electric spark. Franklin reported the results in his pamphlet *Experiments and Observations in Electricity*.

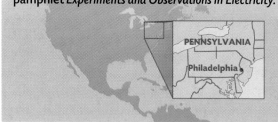

Experimenting With Chemistry

European scientists working in the field of chemistry joined their peers in astronomy, mathematics, and medicine in challenging traditional ideas. By careful scientific experimentation, **Robert Boyle** was primarily responsible for taking chemistry from its mystical and unscientific origins and establishing it as a pure science.

When Boyle was born into an Irish noble family in 1627, the chemistry of the day was alchemy. People who practiced alchemy, called alchemists, spent much of their time trying to transform base metals, such as lead and copper, into precious metals, such as silver and gold. They also held to the age-old belief that all matter was made up of four elements: earth, fire, water, and air.

Boyle criticized alchemists and attacked the theory of the four elements in his book *The Skeptical Chymist*, published in 1661. Boyle proved that air could not be a basic element because it was a mixture of several gases. He also defined an element as a material that cannot be broken down into simpler parts by chemical means.

A century later, in 1774, an English chemist and clergyman named **Joseph Priestley** conducted further experiments into the properties of air and discovered the existence of oxygen. His study of the properties of carbon dioxide resulted in his invention of carbonated drinks. Toward the end of his career, Priestley wrote, "Every year of the last twenty or thirty has been of more importance to science … than any ten in the preceding century."

In France, **Antoine Lavoisier** contributed still more to knowledge about oxygen. Lavoisier conducted scientific experiments that probed the nature of air and discovered that materials do not throw off a substance called phlogiston when burned, as commonly believed, but rather they consume oxygen. Lavoisier discovered the nature of combustion, which results from the chemical union of a flammable material with oxygen.

Marie Lavoisier contributed significantly to her husband's work. She learned English and Latin so that she could translate scientific essays and books for him. She also read numerous articles and condensed them so that he could be informed on many scientific subjects. Madame Lavoisier also made illustrations for her husband's writing.

Perhaps more significant than any single discovery in the 1700s was the application of the scientific view to an understanding of the world. Influenced by the discoveries in science, European philosophers in the 1700s began to apply the scientific method to all human ideas and practices. Most people, caught up in the daily struggle for survival, at first took little notice. In the years to come, however, science would profoundly alter humanity's view of the world.

SECTION 1 REVIEW

Recall
1. **Define** hypothesis, ellipses, scientific method, calculus, alchemist.
2. **Identify** Nicolaus Copernicus, Johannes Kepler, Galileo Galilei, Francis Bacon, René Descartes, Isaac Newton, Andreas Vesalius, William Harvey, Robert Hooke, Robert Boyle, Joseph Priestley, Antoine and Marie Lavoisier.
3. **List** three scientific discoveries that were made during the period from 1500 to 1800.

Critical Thinking
4. **Analyzing Information** What was the scientific revolution? How did it change the way Europeans viewed the universe and the workings of the human body?

Understanding Themes
5. **Innovation** How did Robert Boyle revolutionize chemistry by applying the scientific method?

1651 Thomas Hobbes publishes *Leviathan*.

1662 Charles II establishes the Royal Society of London.

1700s Deism becomes popular in Europe and America.

Section 2

Impact of Science

Setting the Scene

▶ **Terms to Define**
natural law, natural rights, pacifism, deism

▶ **People to Meet**
Thomas Hobbes, John Locke, Thomas Jefferson, Hugo Grotius, William Penn

▶ **Places to Locate**
Pennsylvania

Find Out What effects did changes in scientific thought have on thinking in other fields?

The Storyteller

Donald MacAdam bent forward to hear better. The lecturer was about to read from a new poem from the pen of Nicolas Boileau-Despreaux.

*"What-e'er you write of Pleasant or Sublime,
Always let sense accompany your Rhyme:
Falsely they seem each other to oppose;
Rhyme must be made with Reason's Laws to close:
And when to conquer her you bend your force,
The Mind will Triumph in the Noble Course."*

Donald wondered, how would poetry survive if it must always be so rational?

—adapted from *The Reasonableness of Poetry*, reprinted in *From Absolutism to Revolution*, edited by Herbert H. Rowen, 1964

European salon conversation

*A*s scientists made revolutionary discoveries about people, nature, and the universe, popular interest in science spread throughout Europe. Using new technology such as the microscope, scientists and amateurs alike looked with wonder at the world inside a drop of pond water. Others tinkered and prodded in their home laboratories, studying gases and other substances. At social gatherings across Europe, people discussed the latest findings with lively interest.

Monarchs helped the new sciences by supporting scientific academies, observatories, and museums. In England Charles II established the Royal Society of London in 1662. The group included Isaac Newton and Robert Boyle among its members. In 1666 Louis XIV of France supported the founding of the French Academy of Science. These societies provided financial support to scientists and published scientific books and journals.

Exploring Political Ideas

The advances in science led philosophers and other thinkers to believe that if systematic laws governed the workings of nature and the universe, it followed that political, economic, and social relationships could also be understood through reasoned analysis. Scientific thought and method profoundly influenced political theory. Political philosophers believed in the idea of **natural law**, or a universal moral law that, like physical laws, could be understood by applying reason.

Two English philosophers, **Thomas Hobbes** and **John Locke**, grappled with their ideas of natural law and government during the 1600s, as England struggled with the political tensions of a civil war. The country was torn between people who wanted the king to have absolute power and those who thought the people have the right to govern themselves.

Luis Marden

Jean-Leon Huens

Tower Physics

In a modern re-creation (left) of Galileo's famous experiment from the Leaning Tower of Pisa, two lighted plastic balls, one heavier than the other, plummet to the ground at once—a result the scientific community of Galileo's day refused to acknowledge. In 1591 Italian scientist Galileo Galilei (right) wanted to test the Aristotelian theory of motion—the idea that when two bodies of unequal weight are dropped simultaneously, the heavier object will hit the ground first. So he dropped a ten-pound weight and a one-pound weight from the top of the bell tower.

Galileo's experiment demonstrated that objects of different weights fell at the same rate—hit the ground at the same time—if one allowed for the impact of air resistance. Galileo proved Greek philosopher Aristotle's theory of motion wrong. In investigating the science of the motion of bodies, Galileo was part of the scientific revolution, a reformulation of ideas that overturned those held by medieval thinkers and the Catholic Church. Scientists began carefully testing old theories of how the material world worked; they used careful measurements, exact observations, and precise experiments. The conflict between these new ideas and the power of the older theories forced the new scientists to develop techniques to prove their claims. Today we call this the scientific method—and admire men like Galileo, who sought to understand motion by dropping things from the tallest building in Pisa. ⊕

Hobbes Explores Government

Thomas Hobbes used the idea of natural law to argue that absolute monarchy was the best form of government. He believed that violence and disorder came naturally to human beings and that without an absolute government, chaos would occur. In his book *Leviathan*, published in 1651, Hobbes wrote about a state in which people lived without government. The book showed how "nasty, brutish, and short" life in such a world would be.

Hobbes believed that people should form a social contract, an agreement to give up their freedom and live obediently under a ruler. In this way, they would be governed by a monarch who would protect them and keep their world peaceful and orderly. According to Hobbes, people generally do not have the right to rebel against their government, no matter how unjust it might be.

Locke Offers a Different View

Another English philosopher, John Locke, also based his theories on the idea of natural law. He came to a different conclusion, however. Like Hobbes, Locke held that government was based on a social contract and that it was necessary to establish order. Unlike Hobbes, he believed that people in a state of nature are reasonable and moral, and that they have natural rights, or rights belonging to all humans from birth. These included the right to life, liberty, and property.

In *Two Treatises of Government*, Locke stated that people created government to protect natural rights. A government functioned best when its powers were limited and it was acceptable to all citizens. However, if a government failed in its basic duty of protecting natural rights, people had the right to overthrow the government.

Locke's writings were widely read throughout Europe and the Americas. Ironically, many of the ideas that the American colonists later used to justify their independence from Britain came from Locke and other British thinkers. For example, **Thomas Jefferson** based much of the Declaration of Independence on Locke's ideas about the social contract and the right of people to overthrow an unjust government.

Reason Influences Law

As Europeans searched for new principles that would meet the standards of reason, great changes were made in the practice of law. Incorporating scientific or reasoned thought in applying the law helped to end unjust trials. Lawmakers placed less value on hearsay and on confessions made under torture in determining the guilt or innocence of suspected criminals.

In the 1600s several people made the first attempts to create a body of international law. A Dutch jurist named **Hugo Grotius** called for an international code based on natural law. He believed that one body of rules could reduce the dealings of governments to a system of reason and order.

In the American colonies, **William Penn**, founder of the Quaker colony of **Pennsylvania**, believed in pacifism, or opposition to war or violence as a means of settling disputes. Penn advocated an assembly of nations committed to world peace.

Examining Religion

Many Europeans also applied reason to religious beliefs. Members of the upper and middle classes increasingly turned away from traditional religious views, and Europe became a more secular society. In the 1700s a new religious philosophy called deism swept through Europe and America. Although believing in God, Deists often denounced organized religion, declaring that it exploited people's ignorance and superstitions. Deism was intended to construct a simpler and more natural religion based on reason and natural law. Its followers asserted the rightness of humanity's place in an orderly universe.

SECTION 2 REVIEW

Recall
1. **Define** natural law, natural rights, pacifism, deism.
2. **Identify** Thomas Hobbes, John Locke, Thomas Jefferson, Hugo Grotius, William Penn.

3. **Explain** Locke's social contract theory. What was its impact?

Critical Thinking
4. **Making Comparisons** Contrast Hobbes's views with Locke's views.

Understanding Themes
5. **Conflict** What was the purpose of the new religious philosophy known as deism, and how did deism conflict with traditional religion?

1700	1750	1800

c. 1736 John Wesley promotes religious revival in Great Britain.

1748 Baron de Montesquieu publishes *The Spirit of Laws.*

1780s Joseph II of Austria introduces Enlightenment reforms.

Section 3

Triumph of Reason

Setting the Scene

▶ **Terms to Define**
philosophe, salon, enlightened despot, classicism, metaphysics, romanticism

▶ **People to Meet**
Madame de Pompadour, Denis Diderot, Baron de Montesquieu, Voltaire, Jean-Jacques Rousseau, Immanuel Kant, John Wesley

▶ **Places to Locate**
Paris

 ind Out What factors helped Enlightenment ideas to spread throughout Europe?

The Storyteller

The notorious criminal Jean Chatel had just been executed. Moments before his death, the priests announced that the murderer had confessed all his sins and received absolution. Therefore, he had died in a state of grace and his soul would eventually reach Paradise. The proclamation greatly disturbed Joseph Leveque and his friends. They had just read Voltaire's comments about universal toleration. How could good and bad be defined in such absolute terms? They asked them-

Voltaire *selves and each other, would the Creator condemn Confucius and Socrates to lim-*

itless torment, while blessing a villain simply because he died according to a prescribed formula?

—adapted from *Treatise on Toleration,* Voltaire, reprinted in *The Human Record,* Alfred J. Andrea and James H. Overfield, 1990

Compared to their ancestors, who lived in a world that seemed to be run by inexplicable forces and filled with magic, Europe's new thinkers believed that their scientific approach helped illuminate and clarify both the natural world and the study of human behavior. As a result, the period in Europe from the late 1600s through the 1700s came to be called the Age of Enlightenment.

Men and women of the Enlightenment studied the world as though they were looking at it for the first time. No longer held back by tradition, they defined the world in their own way, using science as their base. Natural scientists analyzed and classified thousands of animals, insects, and plants. Geologists drew maps of the earth's surface. Astronomers continued to make discoveries about the universe.

Largely due to reading Newton's *Principia,* Enlightenment thinkers perceived the universe as a machine governed by fixed laws. They saw God as the master mechanic of the universe—the builder of a machine who provided laws and then allowed it to run on its own, according to these orderly principles. They also believed in progress, or the idea that the world and its people could be improved.

Such radically new perceptions and ideas started a philosophical revolution. Jean Le Rond d'Alembert, a French mathematician, claimed that the new method of thinking and the enthusiasm that accompanied it had "brought about a lively fermentation of minds, spreading through nature in all directions like a river which has burst at its dams."

Spreading Ideas

The thinkers of the Enlightenment who spread these exciting new ideas came to be called **philosophes** (FEE•luh•ZAWFS), the French word for "philosopher." Most philosophes passionately believed in Locke's political philosophy and

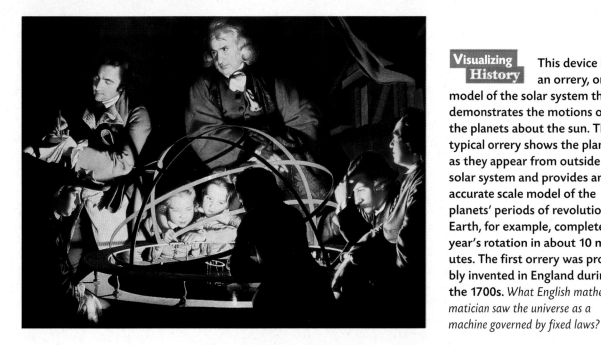

This device is an orrery, or model of the solar system that demonstrates the motions of the planets about the sun. The typical orrery shows the planets as they appear from outside the solar system and provides an accurate scale model of the planets' periods of revolution. Earth, for example, completes a year's rotation in about 10 minutes. The first orrery was probably invented in England during the 1700s. *What English mathematician saw the universe as a machine governed by fixed laws?*

Newton's scientific theories. Most disapproved of superstition and religious opposition to new scientific endeavors. They believed in both freedom of speech and the individual's right to liberty. Many philosophes were talented writers whose essays and books helped to spread and popularize ideas and beliefs of the Enlightenment.

Activity in Paris

France was the most active center of ideas. In **Paris** especially, the new intellectuals delighted in gatherings called salons held in the homes of wealthy patrons. In a salon, writers, artists, and educated people of the growing middle class mingled with men and women of the nobility. Besides discussing the philosophies of the day, salon guests prized the art of conversation and often engaged in contests to see who had the sharpest wit.

Wealthy and influential women ran many of the popular salons. **Madame de Pompadour** was perhaps the most celebrated. A mistress to Louis XV, Pompadour's intelligence and courtly charm won the admiration of many philosophes.

A remarkable achievement compiled by some of the most prominent philosophes of the Enlightenment was the *Encyclopédie*. First published in 1751, these 28 volumes covered everything then known about the sciences, technology, and history in more than 3,000 pages crammed with illustrations.

The *Encyclopédie* was initially conceived to be simply a French translation of a two-volume English encyclopedia, but its editor, **Denis Diderot** (dee•DROH), had a work of much greater scope in mind. Diderot devoted much of his life to this project. Among other things, the *Encyclopédie* criticized the Church and government and praised religious tolerance.

The Catholic Church banned the *Encyclopédie*. When Diderot discovered that the printer, frightened by the controversial material in the volumes, had omitted passages that might offend the Church's leaders, he became enraged and screamed at the printer:

> ❝ You have massacred … the work of twenty good men who have devoted to you their time, their vigils, their talents, from a love of truth and justice, with the simple hope of seeing their ideas given to the public…. ❞

For their writings, Diderot and several others went to prison. Still, the *Encyclopédie* was widely read and its ideas spread all through Europe.

Montesquieu

A contributor to the *Encyclopédie* and one of the most learned of the philosophes in political matters was Charles-Louis de Secondat, the **Baron de Montesquieu** (MAHN•tuhs•KYOO). His masterwork, *The Spirit of Laws*, appeared in two volumes in 1748.

After studying various existing governments, Montesquieu wrote about his admiration for the English government and promoted the idea of separating governmental powers. Montesquieu believed that power should be equally divided among the branches of government: the legislative branch, which made the laws; the executive branch, which enforced them; and the judicial branch, which interpreted the laws and judged when they were violated.

Montesquieu strongly believed in the rights of individuals. His work powerfully influenced the writing of the constitutions in many countries, including the United States.

Voltaire

Perhaps the most celebrated of the philosophes was François-Marie Arouet, known to the world by his pen name, **Voltaire**. A French author and Deist, Voltaire wrote poetry, plays, essays, and books in a style that was entertaining and often satirical. *Candide*, his most celebrated satire, challenged the notion that everything that happens is for the best in "the best of all possible worlds."

In his youth, Voltaire twice served time in the Bastille, the notorious prison in Paris. His satirical works that mocked the Church and the royal court of France earned him one prison term; he received the other term when he was accused of insulting a nobleman. After his second offense, Voltaire was given a choice between further imprisonment and exile from France. He chose the latter. When Voltaire moved to England, he felt unfettered in an atmosphere of political and religious freedom.

During the three years he spent in England, Voltaire wrote books promoting Bacon's philosophy and Newton's science. Voltaire deeply admired the English ideal of religious liberty and its relative freedom of the press. Voltaire is credited with the famous statement in defense of free speech, "I disapprove of what you say, but I will defend to the death your right to say it."

Women and the Enlightenment

Enlightenment ideas about equality and freedom spread throughout Europe, but they were not

Images
of the Times

Salon Society

During the Enlightenment, Europe's high society gathered in the salons of wealthy patrons to discuss the ideas and events of the day.

Upper-class society of the 1700s enjoyed card games as well as intellectual discussions.

applied to women. Although some upper- and middle-class women hosted salons, women generally did not participate in public life on an equal basis with men. Their rights were limited to the home and family. By the mid-1700s, a small but vocal number of women began to affirm women's equality with men. In *A Vindication of the Rights of Women*, the British author Mary Wollstonecraft favored equal education for women and men so that both sexes could contribute equally to society.

Some Leaders Initiate Reform

The Enlightenment attracted the support of European monarchs eager to bring political and social change to their countries. These leaders became enlightened despots, or rulers who sought to govern by Enlightenment principles while maintaining their royal powers.

Prussia's Frederick II, the most famous of the enlightened despots, ruled as an absolute monarch.

Yet he believed that as king, he was the "first servant of the state," dedicated to the welfare of his realm. Frederick's reforms included abolishing the use of torture except for treason and murder, establishing elementary schools, and promoting industry and agriculture. Frederick corresponded with Voltaire, and it was the French philosophe who first honored Frederick with the title "the Great." In one letter Frederick wrote to Voltaire:

> **"** My chief occupation is to fight the ignorances and the prejudices in this country.... I must enlighten my people, cultivate their manners and morals, and make them as happy as human beings can be; as happy as the means at my disposal permit me to make them. **"**

Catherine II of Russia also exchanged letters with Voltaire and other philosophes. She made reforms in law and government but was inclined to praise Enlightenment values more than practice

Parisian aristocratic women often posed for their portraits dressed as classical mythological figures.

Madame de Geoffrin's Salon **by Jean-Baptiste Lemoyner** shows one of the Paris salons that influenced art, literature, and politics.

REFLECTING ON THE TIMES

1. How did salon gatherings in Europe during the 1700s reflect Enlightenment ideals?
2. What role do you think women played in the salon society of the 1700s?

The Grand Théâtre was built by the French architect Victor Louis in the mid-1700s. Located in the French city of Bordeaux, this magnificent theater reflects the dominant classical style of the time. *What were two major characteristics of the classical style?*

them. For example, Catherine spoke out against serfdom but forced more peasants into serfdom than ever before. When groups of serfs revolted, she brutally crushed the uprisings.

The most far-reaching measures of enlightened despotism occurred in Austria. As a Catholic, Empress Maria Theresa disagreed with the secularism of the Enlightenment. However, she introduced humanitarian reforms, including setting up elementary schools and freeing all serfs who worked on her estates. Her son, Joseph II, carried reforms even further. He abolished serfdom completely, made land taxes equal for peasants and nobles, and named middle-class officials instead of nobles to government posts. He gave freedom to the press and took property from the Catholic Church, using the money to support hospitals. The Austrian monarch also granted religious freedom to the empire's Protestants and Jews.

Most of Joseph's reforms failed, however. His abrupt changes antagonized too many people. Rebellion by the nobles forced him to repeal many reforms. Joseph's brother and successor, Leopold II, revoked most of Joseph's remaining laws.

Throughout Europe, nobles and church leaders, afraid of losing too much political power to the common people, frustrated many reform efforts made by enlightened despots. In addition, many monarchs backed away from Enlightenment ideals when they realized that their own positions would be threatened by giving too much power to their subjects. In doing so, they struck down many of the political reforms that might have prevented the violent revolutions that were to come.

Classical Movements

The worlds of art, music, and literature also shared in the Enlightenment beliefs. Writers, artists, and architects strove to achieve the ideals of Greek and Roman classicism, which to them represented ultimate order and reason. Using classical titles and imitating classical themes and styles, artists of the Enlightenment attempted to capture the refined and simplified spirit of the ancients.

Architects built palaces, opera houses, and museums based on the architecture of ancient Rome. They used simple forms, such as squares and circles, rather than the elaborate swirls of the baroque style.

Sculptors and painters also emulated the ideals and forms of antiquity. Whereas artists following the baroque style tended to appeal to their viewers with elegant, swirling forms, these artists sought a return to a calm, rational style of art that would appeal to the mind through the logic and geometry of its forms.

Sculptors such as Antonio Canova created works based on subjects from classical mythology. Jean-Antoine Houdon carved sculptures of contemporary figures, such as Voltaire, in poses that recall portraits of ancient philosophers.

In painting, Jacques-Louis David (dah•VEED) also drew from classical subjects and forms. *The Oath of the Horatii*—showing Roman soldiers vowing to fight for Rome—and other David works' reveal a balance and simplicity that results in monumental images. David used uncomplicated primary colors—reds, yellows, and blues—to create powerful contrasts and accent the clarity of his forms.

Writers worked to achieve the classical ideal while maintaining their devotion to the concept of reason. Often, imitation of a classical model resulted in an ornate and affected style that was focused more on form than on content. French dramatists Molière, Jean Racine, and Pierre Corneille as well as English poets John Dryden, Alexander Pope, and John Milton mastered the classical tradition.

Musical composers of the Enlightenment also stressed classical elements such as balance, contrast, and refined expression of emotion. At the same time, they witnessed a great evolution in music. Music made the transition from merely supporting religious services and dance and opera companies, to being an "art" in its own right. For the first time, people began going to concerts for the pleasure of listening to the music itself.

The piano, evolving in the 1700s, allowed musicians to produce much greater ranges of loudness and softness. The violin was perfected at the same time, changing the sound of music. As composers grouped similar instruments, they laid the foundations for chamber music and the modern orchestra. Germany's Johann Sebastian Bach, Great Britain's German-born George Frideric Handel, and Austria's Joseph Haydn and Wolfgang Amadeus Mozart were among the musicians of this era.

Enlightenment Opponents

Not everyone agreed with the ideas of the Enlightenment. Some saw the structured and ordered view of the universe as overly rational and devoid of emotion and feeling. English poet William Blake exclaimed, "God is not a mathematical diagram!"

Jean-Jacques Rousseau

During the 1700s the French philosopher **Jean-Jacques Rousseau** criticized what he saw as his era's excessive reliance on reason and claimed that people should rely more on instinct and emotion. Born in Geneva, Switzerland, to French Huguenot parents, Rousseau became a leading thinker and writer of his day. He believed that human beings were naturally good but that civilization and institutions were corrupting. He urged people to throw off civilization and return to nature, as far as that was possible. In 1760 he published *La Nouvelle Héloise*, a novel that described the beauties of nature and the pleasures of simple country life. The book influenced people from every level of society. Even the queen of France, Marie Antoinette, had a cottage built for herself at Versailles, where she enjoyed pretending to be a milkmaid.

A second book, *Émile* (1762), used the novel form to emphasize the importance of education in the development of human personality. In *Émile*, Rousseau called for a type of education that would preserve what he believed was a child's natural goodness.

In 1762 Rousseau also published his most famous work, *The Social Contract*. It began, "Man is born free, and everywhere he is in chains." According to Rousseau, sovereignty, or the right to rule, rested in the people. Therefore, the people had the right to remove the "chains" of an oppressive society and to create a government devoted to the common good. The basis of government, Rousseau held, is a social contract through which people give

Visualizing History The Austrian composer Wolfgang Amadeus Mozart died before the age of 36, but he still left the world more than 600 musical works. *Who were three other noted classical musicians?*

John Wesley, a clergyman of the Church of England, founded the Protestant movement known as Methodism. His outdoor preaching drew large crowds. *What value did Methodism stress?*

up their individual rights to the "general will," the will of the majority. Those opposing the "general will," however, must accept it or "be forced to be free." By opposing injustice and supporting government by the people, *The Social Contract* has shaped democratic thought from the 1700s to the present. However, dictators have used its ideas about the "general will" to justify their policies.

Immanuel Kant

Another critic of the Enlightenment was the German thinker **Immanuel Kant**. He believed that reason could not answer the problems of metaphysics—the branch of philosophy that deals with spiritual issues such as the existence of God. In his work *Critique of Pure Reason* (1781), Kant asserted that reality consisted of separate physical and spiritual worlds and that the methods for knowing

varied greatly in these two realms. In the physical world, knowledge came through the senses and reason; in the spiritual world, it was acquired through faith and intuition. Thus, ideas and feelings about religion, morality, and beauty were true even though reason and science could not explain them.

Religious Movements

Not only philosophers, but ordinary men and women found something lacking in the Enlightenment's emphasis on reason. Many rejected deism, the religion of reason, and searched for a religion that was more emotionally satisfying.

In Germany, Count von Zinzendorf established the Moravian Brethren, which emphasized the emotional and mystical side of Christianity. In England, a movement called Methodism, led by **John Wesley**, also stressed the value of personal religious experience. Methodism was a reaction to the cold formality of the Church of England.

The need for a religion with more feeling also led to a Catholic revival in France. In eastern Europe, Hasidism, which promoted mysticism and religious zeal—as opposed to an emphasis on external ritual—spread among Jews. All of these religious movements rejected reason in favor of an enthusiastic faith.

As people questioned the philosophies of the Enlightenment, classicism in the arts gave way to romanticism, which was a cultural movement that celebrated emotion and the individual. These developments marked the ending of the Age of Enlightenment. Tired of the privileged ruling classes and inspired by new ideas such as the writings of Rousseau, the lower classes began to demand more rights. The sun set on the tranquil world of the Enlightenment as history moved on to a period of tumult and revolution.

SECTION 3 REVIEW

Recall
1. **Define** philosophe, salon, enlightened despot, classicism, metaphysics, romanticism.
2. **Identify** the Enlightenment, Madame de Pompadour, Denis Diderot, Baron de Montesquieu, Voltaire,

Jean-Jacques Rousseau, Immanuel Kant, John Wesley.
3. **Describe** some of the main ideas of the Enlightenment thinkers.

Critical Thinking
4. **Making Comparisons** How do John Locke's ideas about

government compare with those of Jean-Jacques Rousseau?

Understanding Themes
5. **Reaction** In what ways did Europeans of the 1700s react to Enlightenment ideas and values?

Developing Multimedia Presentations

You have been assigned a research report to present to your class. You want to really hold the attention of your classmates. How can you do this? One way is to use a variety of media.

Learning the Skill

At its most basic, a multimedia presentation involves using several types of media. To discuss the Age of Enlightenment, for example, you might show photographs or slides of the art, play and listen to recordings of the music or literature, or present a video of a play written during this time period.

You can also develop a multimedia presentation on a computer. Multimedia as it relates to computer technology is the combination of text, video, audio, and animation in an interactive program.

In order to create multimedia productions or presentations on a computer, you need to have certain tools. These may include traditional com-

puter graphic tools and draw programs, animation programs that make still images move, and authoring systems that tie everything together. Your computer manual will tell you which tools your computer can support.

Practicing the Skill

This chapter focuses on the Age of Revolution from 1500 to 1830. Ask yourself questions such as the following to develop a multimedia presentation on the politics of that era:

- Which forms of media do I want to include? Video? Sound? Animation? Photographs? Graphics? Other?

- Which of these media forms does my computer support?

- What kind of software programs or systems do I need? A paint program? A draw program? An animation program? A program to create interactive, or two-way, communication? An authoring system that will allow me to change images, sound, and motion?

- Is there a "do-it-all " program I can use to develop the kind of presentation I want?

Applying the Skill

Keeping in mind the four guidelines given above, write a plan describing a multimedia presentation you would like to develop. Indicate what tools you will need and what steps you must take to make the presentation an exciting reality.

For More Practice

Turn to the Skill Practice in the Chapter Review on page 533 for more practice in developing multimedia presentations.

Connections Across Time

Historical Significance The scientific revolution and the Enlightenment marked a turning point in the history of human thought. Scientists and thinkers constructed a new understanding of knowledge that stressed observation, experimentation, and reasoning rather than reliance on faith and tradition. Thinkers analyzed the existing political systems and focused on the rights of individuals. Their views challenged the concept of absolute monarchy and paved the way for the rise of democracy.

The Age of Enlightenment continues to shape our lives. The United States Constitution incorporates many Enlightenment beliefs, and scientists employ approaches in research today that are based on the scientific method.

Using Key Terms

Write the key term that completes each sentence. Then write a sentence for each term not chosen.

a. philosophes	g. pacifism
b. classicism	h. enlightened despots
c. salons	i. scientific method
d. hypotheses	j. deism
e. natural law	k. metaphysics
f. romanticism	l. natural rights

1. _____, with its emphasis on emotion and the individual, opposed the values of the Enlightenment.
2. Political philosophers of the Enlightenment believed in the idea of _____, or a universal moral law that, like physical laws, could be understood by applying reason.
3. William Penn believed in _____ and favored the creation of an assembly of nations committed to world peace.
4. Enlightenment writers, artists, and architects strove to achieve the ideals of _____, which to them represented ultimate order and reason.
5. The philosophy of _____ favored a simpler religion based on reason.

Technology Activity

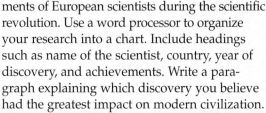

Using a Word Processor Search the Internet or a library for information about the achievements of European scientists during the scientific revolution. Use a word processor to organize your research into a chart. Include headings such as name of the scientist, country, year of discovery, and achievements. Write a paragraph explaining which discovery you believe had the greatest impact on modern civilization.

Using Your History Journal

Rewrite the story of a scientific discovery or invention from the 1600s as a television news story. Include an interview with the inventor or discoverer.

Reviewing Facts

1. **Science** Explain how Copernicus, Galileo, Kepler, and Newton each added something new to an understanding of the solar system.
2. **Culture** Describe the ways in which European thinking about the universe, philosophy, and law changed during the Enlightenment.
3. **History** Explain how the study of history was influenced by the Enlightenment.
4. **Government** State the political idea advocated by Montesquieu that can be found in the United States Constitution.
5. **Culture** Identify two philosophers in the 1700s who disagreed with Enlightenment ideas. What were their views?

Critical Thinking

1. **Apply** How did classical art reflect the values of the Enlightenment? Give examples to support your answer.
2. **Synthesize** Why do you suppose a belief in witches and ghosts largely became a thing of the past in Europe after the period of the Enlightenment?
3. **Evaluate** Were the 1700s an era of optimism or pessimism? Explain.

4. **Synthesize** Do scientific laws apply to human society in the way that they apply to the physical universe? Why or why not?
5. **Analyze** Why were the enlightened despots unable to carry out thorough reforms?
6. **Evaluate** Has science fulfilled the promise of progress that it seemed to hold in the 1700s? Why or why not? Give examples.

Geography in History

1. **Region** Refer to the map below. What conclusion can you draw about European interest in science and learning during the period of the 1500s and 1600s?
2. **Place** In what two nations were organizations founded for people interested in sharing scientific information?
3. **Movement** How do you think scientific ideas and theories spread from one nation of Europe into other nations?

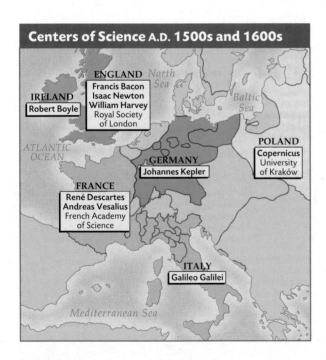

Centers of Science A.D. **1500s and 1600s**

IRELAND
Robert Boyle

ENGLAND *North Sea*
Francis Bacon
Isaac Newton
William Harvey
Royal Society of London

Baltic Sea

ATLANTIC OCEAN

GERMANY
Johannes Kepler

POLAND
Copernicus
University of Kraków

FRANCE
René Descartes
Andreas Vesalius
French Academy of Science

ITALY
Galileo Galilei

Mediterranean Sea

Understanding Themes

1. **Innovation** How did the scientific revolution change the ways in which Europeans investigated the natural world?

2. **Conflict** Catholic Bishop Bossuet said that the skepticism of the philosophes was an "unending error, a risk-all boldness, a deliberate dizziness, in a word, a pride that cannot accept its proper cure, which is legitimate authority." Explain the bishop's view in your own words. What does he mean by "legitimate authority"?
3. **Reaction** What religious movements formed as a reaction to the ideas of the Enlightenment thinkers? Why?

Linking Past and Present

1. William Penn envisioned an assembly of nations working for world peace. What modern organization reflects Penn's idea?
2. Classical movements in music, art, and literature reflected the spirit of the Enlightenment. Does popular music, art, and literature reflect how people feel about society today? Why or why not? Give examples.
3. Do you agree or disagree with Jean-Jacques Rousseau's view that people are naturally good but that civilization and institutions make them evil? Give examples from modern life to support your viewpoint.

Skill Practice

Study the list of topics below. Choose one of the topics and explain how you would use at least three types of media in a presentation to best teach the topic to a class.

1. Michelangelo's work
2. The causes of the French Revolution
3. The American Revolution
4. The Scientific Revolution of the 1600s and 1700s
5. The Salon Society of the 1700s
6. Religious movements of the 1700s

Chapter 21

1600–1800

English and American Revolutions

Chapter Themes

▶ **Conflict** Disputes over the monarchy plunge England into civil war. *Section 1*

▶ **Change** The English Parliament limits the monarchy's powers. *Section 2*

▶ **Conflict** The American colonies resist British control. *Section 3*

▶ **Revolution** The American colonies revolt against Great Britain and form the United States of America. *Section 4*

S The toryteller

In 1649 a crowd gathered around a public platform near Whitehall Palace in London. There they watched Charles I, the king of England, prepare to die. The king made a short speech, prayed silently, and then knelt with his head on the block.

With just one blow, the executioner severed the king's head from his body. At that moment, the crowd uttered "such a [groan] by the thousands then present as I never heard before and desire I may never hear again," said a seventeen-year-old boy present at the execution.

By the late 1600s, England would undergo two revolutions limiting the power of the monarch. A new political age was dawning in England and throughout the world.

Historical Significance

How did the English and American Revolutions change government and society in the English-speaking world? What impact did the two revolutions have on the development of democracy?

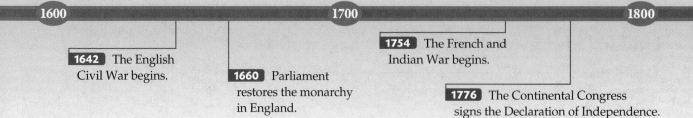

1600	1700	1800

1642 The English Civil War begins.

1660 Parliament restores the monarchy in England.

1754 The French and Indian War begins.

1776 The Continental Congress signs the Declaration of Independence.

534

After Naseby, 1645 by Edgar Bundy, c. 1850. John Noott Galleries, Worcester, England

Your History Journal

In this chapter English and American people make major changes to their governments. What should be the basic ideas upon which government is built? List the ideas you believe to be basic.

1600	1620	1640	1660

1603 Queen Elizabeth I dies.　**1625** Charles I becomes king of England.　**1640** The Long Parliament meets in London.　**1653** Oliver Cromwell is named Lord Protector.

Section 1

Civil War

Setting the Scene

▶ **Terms to Define**
   divine right, martial law, royalist, commonwealth

▶ **People to Meet**
   James I, the Puritans, Charles I, the Cavaliers, the Roundheads, Oliver Cromwell

▶ **Places to Locate**
   Scotland, Ireland

Find Out ▶ What factors led to the outbreak of civil war in England?

The Storyteller

"I say you are no Parliament; I will put an end to your sitting; call them in, call them in." Oliver Cromwell brought in two lines of men armed with muskets, adjourned the session, and locked the doors. That afternoon he intruded upon the Council of State and tried the same. But the chairman, Bradshaw, who had faced worse from King Charles, faced Cromwell. "Sir, we have heard what you did in the morning, and before many hours all England will hear it; but sir, you are mistaken to think that the Parliament is dissolved; for no power under heaven can dissolve them but themselves; therefore take you notice of that."

—from *Oliver Cromwell*, John Morley, M.P., 1901

Oliver Cromwell

Elizabeth I, daughter of Henry VIII and Anne Boleyn, ruled England from 1558 to 1603. She was a strong monarch, but she did not have absolute power. Elizabeth took into consideration the views of Parliament, which grew more politically involved during her reign.

An able leader, Queen Elizabeth recognized the importance of the goodwill of the people—and of Parliament. She once said, "Though God has raised me high, yet this I account the glory of the crown, that I have reigned with your loves." For its part, Parliament was willing to defer to the popular queen. After Elizabeth died in 1603, Parliament, especially the House of Commons, was determined to increase its control over national policy. This move by Parliament resulted in a conflict with the Crown that tore the nation apart.

Opposition to the Crown

Because Elizabeth died childless, **James I**, the son of Elizabeth's cousin, Mary, Queen of Scots, became king in 1603. James, a member of the Stuart family, was the king of **Scotland** when he assumed the English throne.

King and Parliament

Soon after James became king of England, problems arose with the English Parliament. James professed his belief in **divine right**—that monarchs derive their power directly from God and that such power is absolute. He lectured the Parliament:

❝ Kings are not only God's lieutenants upon earth and sit upon God's throne, but even by God himself they are called Gods.… I will not be content that my power be disputed on. **❞**

Such statements aroused the resentment among the members of Parliament.

James I's greatest political weakness was his constant need to ask Parliament for money. He spent huge sums of money on the government as well as on himself and his advisers. After one of James's parties, a member of Parliament remarked that James had "given away more plate [money] than Queen Elizabeth did in her whole reign." When Parliament refused to vote him enough funds, James resorted to other means of raising money, such as selling titles of nobility.

Parliament also criticized the king's foreign policy. James's decision to end a war with Spain created outrage in Parliament. The war repayments that were part of the peace treaty put England deep into debt. Opposition to James's policies grew even stronger when James tried to arrange the marriage of his son, Charles, to a Spanish Catholic princess. Fearing the return of Catholics to power, the people celebrated when James's marriage plans for his son failed.

Religion and the Monarchy

England's unsettled religious issues only added to the tension between Parliament and the Crown. In the 1600s most English people belonged to the Church of England, but they had differences of opinion about the doctrine and rituals of the Church. One powerful group of dissenters, or opponents, within the Church was **the Puritans**. They wanted the Church to be "purified" of remaining Catholic rituals and symbols. Many Puritans in Parliament called for these reforms.

James I, as head of both church and government in England, thought that anyone who criticized the Church of England was not a loyal subject. When James had become king, the Puritans presented him with a petition asking for reforms to be made in the Church of England. Not only did James reject the suggested changes, he warned the Puritans that if they did not conform to the Church of England, he would "harry [force] them out of the land." When the king refused to support the Puritan cause, the Puritans turned against him. Because of James's policies, many Puritans left England and settled in North America.

Despite his controversial ways, James I made a lasting and important contribution to the religion and literature of the English-speaking world. In 1604 he had a group of scholars prepare a new translation of the Bible from Greek and Hebrew into English. The new version appeared in 1611 and became known as the "King James" Bible. Written in the eloquent prose and poetry of Shakespeare's time, it became the best-known English version of the Bible.

History & Art *Portrait of Charles I Hunting* by Anthony Van Dyck, c. 1636. The Louvre, Paris, France *Why were the English Parliament and people unhappy with Charles by 1628?*

Charles Inherits the Throne

When James I died in 1625, his son Charles became king. **Charles I** inherited the country's religious conflicts and political divisions. Like his father, Charles opposed the Puritans and believed in the divine right of kings. Adding to the tension, Charles eventually married a Catholic woman— Henrietta Maria, sister of France's King Louis XIII.

Early in his reign, Charles asked Parliament for money to fight a war against Spain and France. When it gave him only a fraction of the sum he had requested, the king dissolved Parliament immediately and tried to raise money without its consent. Charles then forced landowners to give "loans" to the government. When they refused, he put them in jail. People were outraged by the king's behavior.

People were also angered by Charles's demand to billet, or board and lodge, his troops in private homes. The king also placed some areas under martial law, or temporary military rule with limitations on individual rights. Thus, discontent ran high when Charles again called Parliament into session in 1628.

Pilgrims Signing the Mayflower Compact by Percy Moran, c. 1900. The Pilgrim Hall Museum, Plymouth, Massachusetts Why did groups like the Pilgrims and the Puritans leave England?

By this time England was at war with both France and Spain. Parliament, however, was now ready to press changes on the king. In return for its approval of additional taxes to support the war, Parliament forced Charles to sign the Petition of Right. The Petition severely limited Charles's power in four ways. First, the king was forbidden to collect taxes or force loans without Parliament's consent. Second, the king could not imprison anyone without just cause. Third, troops could not be housed in a private home against the will of the owner. Fourth, the king could not declare martial law unless the country was at war.

Charles's desire to maintain his power, however, was not checked by the Petition of Right. Nearly a year after Parliament had authorized funds in return for his signature on the document, Charles dissolved Parliament and vowed never to call it again. For the next 11 years, Charles ruled without the advice or consent of the Parliament. He continued to collect taxes and imprison opponents—ignoring the Petition of Right he had signed.

At the same time, Charles deepened the religious divisions within England. He named William Laud to be Archbishop of Canterbury, the leading official of the Church of England. Laud and Charles persecuted the Puritans. They denied Puritans the right to preach or to publish. They burned Puritan

writings, and punished outspoken Puritans with public whippings.

As a result, thousands of Puritans sought religious freedom in the English colonies in America. Their exodus from England from 1630 through 1643 is known as the Great Migration. Most Puritans, however, remained in their homeland, determined to fight Charles and others who opposed them.

Charles and Archbishop Laud then turned their attention to Scotland. In an effort to establish the Church of England in Scotland, the king and the archbishop tried to force the Calvinist Church of Scotland to accept the Church of England's prayer book. The Scots rejected the new prayer book and formed a National Covenant, or agreement, in which they pledged to preserve their religious freedom. Outraged by the king's actions, they were prepared to go to war to do so.

Beginnings of the Civil War

By 1640 the Scots had invaded England. In dire need of money, Charles was forced to recall a Parliament that he had ignored for 11 years. The members of Parliament, however, refused to discuss anything without first voicing their complaints about Charles's handling of religious and political issues. As a result, Charles dissolved this Parliament, known as the Short Parliament, after only 3 weeks.

Charles became so desperate for money that he had no choice but to summon Parliament once again. By this time members of Parliament were seething with anger and demanded to voice their complaints to the king. Controlled by Puritans, this session of Parliament, called the Long Parliament, would meet for almost 20 years.

The Long Parliament was determined to decrease Charles's power. The members abolished the special courts used to imprison Charles's opponents and passed a law requiring Parliament to be called every 3 years. They ended all forms of illegal taxation and jailed and later executed the hated Archbishop Laud.

While Parliament convened, trouble erupted in **Ireland**. Relations between England and Ireland had been strained since the 1100s. The Irish people remained Roman Catholic and refused to accept the Church of England. What angered the Irish most was the continuing English practice of seizing land from Irish owners and giving it to English and Scottish settlers. In 1641 the Irish rebelled. Faced with rebellion in both Scotland and Ireland, Charles was at the mercy of the Puritan-controlled Parliament.

As the Puritans grew stronger, a royalist, or pro-monarchy, group formed in Parliament. It was made up of people who supported the king and opposed Puritan control of the Church of England. As time went on, debates between Puritans and royalists became more heated.

Despite resistance by the royalists, Parliament in June 1642 sent Charles "Nineteen Propositions" that made Parliament the supreme power in England. Charles, however, refused to agree to its demands. With a dramatic personal appearance, Charles led troops into the House of Commons and attempted to arrest five of its leaders. The five were hidden and protected from capture. The king's use of force meant there could be no compromise. Both Charles and Parliament prepared for war.

The English Civil War

Charles gathered an army that included nobles and landowners in the north and west of the country. They were called **the Cavaliers** because many belonged to the king's cavalry, or armed horsemen. Supporters of Parliament and Puritans drew their strength from the south and east of England. They were called **the Roundheads** because many of them had close-cropped hair.

Parliament organized its military forces under the leadership of **Oliver Cromwell**. Cromwell was a very religious man and a brilliant military commander. His rigorous training and firm discipline of the parliamentary forces led to several decisive victories. After nearly four years of conflict, the royalist armies surrendered in May 1646. Parliament had won complete control of the English government. The Puritans removed their remaining opponents from Parliament, leaving behind what was known as the Rump Parliament.

After a failed attempt to escape from his enemies, Charles surrendered in 1647. The army then tried, sentenced, and executed the king in 1649. It was a shocking moment for many English people, no matter how they felt about Charles.

A New Government

After the execution, the Rump Parliament ended the monarchy and set up a republic known as a commonwealth, a state ruled by elected representatives. From the outset, the new government faced much opposition. It relied on Cromwell's army to crush royalist uprisings in Scotland and Ireland. Severe measures were placed on Ireland's Catholic majority, many of whom were killed or lost lands to Protestant landlords. In England, Cromwell and his officers later suppressed the Levellers, a group wanting the vote for all men.

Overseas, the republic's mercantilist policies advanced English trade. The Navigation Act (1651) required that imports be brought to England in English ships or in ships of the country producing the goods. This law angered the Dutch, who had grown rich from carrying goods to England on their ships. A strengthened English navy, however, met the Dutch threat. During the 1650s, English military victories over the Dutch and later the Spanish heightened England's position as a European power.

At home, Cromwell dismissed the ineffectual Rump Parliament and placed England under military rule, with himself as Lord Protector. Cromwell's government granted religious freedom to all non-Anglican Protestants, but enforced Puritan rules requiring people to attend church and to avoid drinking, swearing, and gambling. When Cromwell died in 1658, his son Richard was unable to maintain the government. Most English people were tired of military rule and unhappy with Puritan restrictions. In 1660 a newly elected Parliament restored the monarchy under Charles I's son, Charles II. Representative government and individual rights would survive, however. No English monarch would ever be able to claim absolute power again.

SECTION I REVIEW

Recall
1. **Define** divine right, martial law, royalist, commonwealth.
2. **Identify** James I, the Puritans, Charles I, Petition of Right, William Laud, the Cavaliers, the Roundheads, Oliver Cromwell.
3. **Discuss** how the Puritans shaped English religion and politics in the 1600s.

Critical Thinking
4. **Analyzing Information** How did Elizabeth I and the Stuart monarchs James I and Charles I differ in getting what they wanted from Parliament?

Whose methods were more effective? Why?

Understanding Themes
5. **Conflict** What problems did Parliament face before the English Civil War? After the war? Did Parliament achieve its political goals?

1650   1700   1750

1688 The Glorious Revolution brings William III and Mary II to the English throne.

1707 The Act of Union unites England and Scotland.

1714 George I becomes king of Great Britain.

Section 2

A King Returns to the Throne

Setting the Scene

▶ **Terms to Define**
   constitutional monarchy, habeas corpus, cabinet, prime minister

▶ **People to Meet**
   Charles II, the Whigs, the Tories, William III, Mary II, George I, Sir Robert Walpole

▶ **Places to Locate**
   London

Find Out How did England establish a constitutional monarchy?

The Storyteller

"What pillars and arches to be pulled down! What new ones to be erected! What scaffold and engines to lay the foundation of an endless and incalculable future expenditure." The authorities in charge of restoring St. Paul's Cathedral believed Christopher Wren's designs went too far and would cost too much. Just when it seemed as though the great architect would have to change his plans, disaster changed everything. In the Great Fire of London, buildings were demolished overnight. At St. Paul's Cathedral, heated stones flew like grenades and lead ran in rivers down the streets. Wren would design a new cathedral.

—adapted from *The Architecture of Wren*, Kerry Downes, 1982

Christopher Wren

As the son of Charles I, **Charles II** had faced danger throughout the English Civil War and Cromwell's rule. He risked death on the battlefield as he joined the royalist forces in their fight and in their defeat. He saw his father imprisoned and put to death. He narrowly escaped his own capture and execution by disguising himself as a servant and fleeing to the European continent.

In Europe, Charles wandered from country to country. While some European rulers received him as royalty, others threatened him with arrest as a fugitive. In his own country, the Puritans kept a close watch on Charles. Since he was the direct heir to the English throne, Charles posed a threat to their political power. By the time Parliament had restored the monarchy, Charles had learned a good deal about pleasing people he needed for support and safety. Charles willingly accepted a change from the absolute power of his ancestors.

The Merry Monarch

When Charles II returned to **London**, on May 29, 1660, the English people celebrated wildly. They felt released from a violent, unstable period followed by harsh Puritan rule. A court member described the happiness of the English people as they rejoiced in a lavish parade marking the king's return:

“ A triumph of above 20,000 horse and foot soldiers, brandishing their swords and shouting with inexpressible joy; the ways strewed with flowers, the bells ringing, the streets hung with tapestry, fountains running with wine.... I stood and beheld it, and blessed God. ”

This period, in which the House of Stuart was returned to the throne, is called the Restoration. In contrast to the severe and religious rule of Cromwell, Charles II was known as the Merry Monarch. He loved parties, games, and witty conversation. He supported the arts, science, and entertainment. People once again danced and enjoyed sports and theater. Charles married a Portuguese princess; and though they had no children, he fathered illegitimate children by his mistresses.

Dealing With Religious Questions

Outwardly, Charles was a member of the Church of England; secretly, however, he favored Catholicism. Although hoping for religious toleration, the king recognized that the settlement of England's religious divisions rested on Parliament. During the 1660s, the largely royalist Cavalier Parliament passed the Clarendon Code, a series of laws that made the Church of England once again the state religion. Only Church of England members could attend the universities, serve in Parliament, or hold religious services. Hundreds of Puritan clergy were driven from their churches.

During this time of troubles for the Puritans, the Puritan writer John Milton wrote *Paradise Lost* (1667), generally considered to be the greatest epic poem in the English language. *Paradise Lost* retells the biblical story of creation, the devil's revolt against God, and the fall of Adam and Eve.

Limiting Royal Power

In addition to its anti-Puritan policies, Parliament kept limits on royal power. All laws that Charles I had accepted, such as the Petition of Right, were still in effect. The Restoration thus gave England a constitutional monarchy, a form of government in which the monarch's powers are limited by a constitution. Rather than being a single document, however, England's constitution was made up of many documents—such as the Magna Carta and the Petition of Right—plus other laws and customs. Although Charles II disagreed with some of the reforms he never fought Parliament forcefully. Charles was determined to avoid his father's fate.

The French ambassador to England was astonished at the mood of the country. In France, the king had absolute power. The ambassador commented

Rebuilding London

In 1666 a major fire destroyed much of London. Over the next decades, it was rebuilt as a beautiful capital. One of the men chosen to work on the commission rebuilding the city was Christopher Wren, a noted mathematician and astronomer at Oxford University. He is best known, however, as the architect of St. Paul's Cathedral, a London landmark begun in 1675.

The new St. Paul's Cathedral was the first major church built for Anglican worship, and Wren designed it to be an impressive, monumental structure. He used classical and baroque styles to produce a cathedral that combined orderliness with dramatic visual effects. Wren also designed other architecturally attractive churches for the city.

During World War II, the area around

St. Paul's Cathedral

St. Paul's Cathedral was heavily bombed by the German air force. St. Paul's was spared extensive damage, but other Wren churches were among the many buildings destroyed. Since then, heavily bombed areas, including some of these churches, have been rebuilt.

Today, skyscrapers rather than churches dominate the landscape of central London. As the city has built upward, it has also spread outward. A number of new towns have arisen in outlying areas, separated from central London by a greenbelt, a wide band of open country.

Linking Past and Present ACTIVITY

Discuss how Christopher Wren contributed to the architecture of London in the 1600s. How has the city's appearance changed since World War II? In what ways is London like, or unlike, other modern cities?

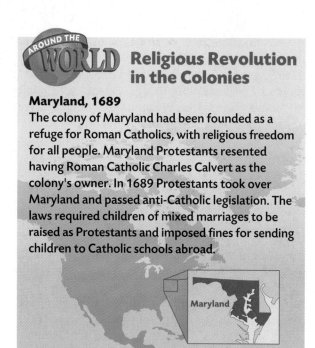
on the changes in England in a letter to the French king, Louis XIV:

> ❝ This government has a monarchical appearance because there is a King, but at bottom it is far from being a monarchy.... The members of Parliament are ... allowed to speak their mind freely.... ❞

While the English celebrated the end of Puritan rule, they were struck by two disasters. In 1665 the plague returned to London for the last time, killing as many as 100,000 people. Later, a terrible raging fire destroyed much of London. Some people falsely blamed Catholics for setting the fire as part of a plan to gain control of the country.

Establishing Political Parties

Opposition to Catholicism helped to spark the growth of England's first political parties. The parties grew out of a debate over who would succeed Charles as the king of England. Because Charles had no legitimate children, James II, Charles's brother, was next in line to be king. James, who was a practicing Catholic, ignited the fears of a revival of Catholic power in England.

In 1679 Parliament tried to pass the Exclusion Bill, which would have kept James from becoming king. During this conflict, those members of Parliament who wanted to exclude James from the throne were known as **the Whigs**. Those who defended the hereditary monarchy were referred to as **the Tories**.

In a compromise, the Tories agreed to defeat the Exclusion Bill by accepting another bill supported by the Whigs. The Whig-proposed bill established the principle of habeas corpus as law. According to habeas corpus, a person could not be held in prison by the king (or anyone else) without just cause or without a trial. It was another step that increased individual rights and reduced those of the Crown.

A Bloodless Revolt

When Charles II died in 1685, his Catholic brother, James II, became king, effectively ending the peaceful relations between Parliament and the Crown. James wanted absolute power and claimed he had the right to suspend the law. Ignoring Parliament's religious laws, James appointed Catholics to government and university positions. He also allowed people of all Christian faiths to worship freely.

The Glorious Revolution

These actions alarmed many of the members of Parliament, but they tried to be patient. They were waiting for James to die and for the English throne to pass to his Protestant daughter Mary, who was married to William of Orange, the ruler of the Netherlands.

In 1688, however, a royal birth prompted Parliament to take action. James's second wife bore a son, who would be raised a Catholic. He would inherit the throne, rather than the Protestant Mary. Both Whig and Tory leaders united against James and invited Mary's husband William to invade England and take over the Crown. James fled to France when he realized he had little support in England. **William III** and **Mary II** gained the English throne without battles or bloodshed. This peaceful transfer of power was so welcome and so different from previous struggles that the English called it the Glorious Revolution.

New Limits on Royal Power

At previous coronations, English kings and queens had sworn to observe the laws and customs established by their royal ancestors. In 1689, however, William and Mary swore an oath that they would govern the people of England "according to the statutes in Parliament agreed upon, and the laws and customs of the same."

In that same year, Parliament further strengthened its power by passing the Bill of Rights. According to the Bill of Rights, the king could not raise taxes or maintain an army without the consent of Parliament and could not suspend laws. Further, it declared that Parliament should be held often and that there should be freedom of debate in sessions of Parliament.

The Bill of Rights also guaranteed certain individual rights. It guaranteed the right to a trial by jury, outlawed cruel and unusual punishment for a crime, and limited the amount of bail money that could be required for a person to be temporarily released while awaiting trial. Citizens were given the right to appeal to the monarch and to speak freely in Parliament.

In 1689 the exiled James II landed in Ireland and led Irish Catholics in a revolt to recapture the Crown. Although the uprising failed a year later, English Protestants controlling Irish affairs began to exclude the Catholic majority in Ireland from government and business. This action only deepened the hatred Irish Catholics had for English policies.

Anti-Catholic feelings throughout the country also led the English Parliament in London to pass more legislation limiting the Crown's power. In the Act of Settlement (1701), Parliament excluded any Catholic from inheriting the English throne.

Parliament and the Crown

The Bill of Rights and the Act of Settlement made it clear that Parliament had won the long battle with the Crown. England was still a monarchy, but a king or queen could not rule without Parliament's consent.

England was not yet a true democracy, however. Although members of the House of Commons were elected, only male property owners—250,000 people out of 6 million, or 4 percent of the population—had the right to vote. Members of the House of Commons were not paid, so only the wealthy could afford to run for office. Parliament was controlled by people of property—nobles, gentry, wealthy merchants, and clergy.

Succession and Union

The power of Parliament further increased when Mary's sister Anne succeeded William in 1702. (Mary had died in 1694.) At the same time, Parliament had to establish a new order of succession to the throne. Since Anne had no living children to succeed her, she would be succeeded by the children of Sophia, a Protestant granddaughter of James I. Sophia was married to the German elector, or ruler, of Hanover. In short, the English throne would pass to the heirs or heiresses from the German House of Hanover.

Yet there still remained a danger that the Scots might prefer a Stuart monarch to a member of the House of Hanover. Parliament also feared that the Scots would form an alliance with France against England. After negotiations with the Scots, who were militarily and economically weak, the two governments signed the Act of Union in 1707. It united the two countries into a new nation called Great Britain. Both the English and the Scots would now be "British." Although the Scots gave up their own parliament, they were given representation in the English Parliament. Scotland also retained its own Calvinist religion, and its own laws, courts, and educational system as well.

Visualizing History In 1688 Parliament presented the Crown of England to William and **Mary.** *Why did Parliament decide to give the Crown to the royal couple?*

Sir Robert Walpole became a close friend of King George II and Queen Caroline. He directed policy as the leading cabinet official. *What title did the main cabinet official earn?*

Political Parties and the Cabinet

During Anne's reign (1702-1714), Parliament's political powers continued to increase. Anne was unskilled in British politics and sought guidance from a cabinet, a small group of advisers selected from the House of Commons. Because a cabinet made up of both Whigs and Tories often quarreled, it became the custom to choose cabinet members only from the party holding a majority of the seats in Parliament.

Anne died in 1714, and Sophia's son **George I** took the throne according to the Act of Settlement. George had been raised in Germany, and did not speak English very well.

George I relied on the cabinet even more than Anne had. Eventually, **Sir Robert Walpole**, the leader of the Whigs, gained control of the cabinet. Although he spoke no German, Walpole advised the king. Walpole's position as head of the cabinet was later called prime minister, the chief executive of a parliamentary government. Walpole remained prime minister when a new king, George II, took the throne in 1727. With the king's encouragement, Walpole gradually took over many political responsibilities: managing finances, appointing government officials, and requesting the passage of laws. He helped avoid wars and allowed the North American colonies to grow without interference from the British government.

In 1760 George III, grandson of George II, became king at the age of 22. George III greatly expanded the British Empire through victory in a war against France. Great Britain gained Canada and all of France's territory east of the Mississippi River. The cost of waging the war—and the ways in which George III and his ministers tried to deal with that cost—would eventually lead to rebellion in Great Britain's American colonies.

SECTION 2 REVIEW

Recall

1. **Define** constitutional monarchy, habeas corpus, cabinet, prime minister.

2. **Identify** Charles II, the Restoration, the Whigs, the Tories, William III, Mary II, Bill of Rights, George I, Sir Robert Walpole.

3. **Explain** why Charles II was called the Merry Monarch. How was his reign different from that of his father, Charles I?

Critical Thinking

4. **Analyzing Information** How did the royal power of William and Mary compare with that of Charles II? How had Parliament's powers expanded by the time William and Mary came to the throne?

Understanding Themes

5. **Change** Briefly describe how England evolved into a constitutional monarchy. What rights did individual citizens gain as a result of this change?

c. 1730 Colonial assemblies win the right to limit royal governors' salaries.

1754 The French and Indian War begins.

1763 British proclamation bans colonial settlement west of the Appalachians.

1774 First Continental Congress meets in Philadelphia.

Section 3

Road to Revolt

Setting the Scene

▶ **Terms to Define**
duty, direct tax, boycott

▶ **People to Meet**
George Grenville, George III, John Adams, Patrick Henry, George Washington, Samuel Adams

▶ **Places to Locate**
New York City, Boston, Philadelphia

Find Out What factors led to disagreement and eventual conflict between the British and the American colonies?

The Storyteller

Boston's newspapers announced that a ship bearing tea would arrive soon. All over town, this handbill appeared: "Friends! Brethren! Country–men! That worst of plagues, the detested tea, shipped for this port by the East India Company, is now arrived in this harbor; the hour of destruction or manly opposition to the machinations [schemes] of tyranny stares you in the face; every friend … is now called upon … to make a united and successful resistance. Boston, November 29, 1773."

—adapted from *Tea Leaves, Being a Collection of Letters and Documents Relating to the Shipment of Tea to the American Colonies …*, 1970

Boston Tea Party

While Great Britain struggled through civil war and a changing government, its colonies in America changed as well. By the mid-1700s, 13 colonies thrived on the eastern coast of North America. As more people migrated to North America to escape religious persecution or to gain a new start in life, the population of the colonies grew to more than 1.5 million by 1763.

Since most of the colonists were British, they shared a common language and political background. Although many radical political ideas—ideas about republicanism, universal suffrage, liberty, and equality—had died out in Great Britain, many political radicals had fled to the colonies. Here the old ideas stayed alive. In the colonies, there was no aristocracy. The hardships of life on the frontier and the easy availability of land tended to blur class divisions. Each American colony had a representative assembly, much like Parliament in Great Britain, and the colonists were used to governing themselves.

The British Empire in America

Except for regulating trade, the British government generally left the colonies alone. In the British mercantilist view, the American colonies were valuable to Great Britain only to the extent that they benefited British trade. The role of the colonies was to produce goods—mostly raw materials—that could not be produced in Great Britain, and to provide markets for British manufactured goods.

By the early 1700s, the colonies pulsated with economic activity. In the South, plantations produced tobacco, rice, and indigo with the labor of thousands of enslaved Africans. Settlers in the rich farming land of the Middle Colonies grew enough food to feed their families and trade throughout the year. New England colonists turned to the sea because of their poor soil and harsh climate. In 1673 a sea captain described busy Boston Harbor, reporting that "ships arrive dayly from Spain, France, Holland & Canarys bringing all sorts of wine, linens, silks, and fruits, which they transport to all the other plantations...."

To protect this profitable trade with its colonies, Parliament passed a series of Navigation Acts in the 1600s. According to these laws, the colonists were required to export certain products only to Great Britain or to other British colonies. In addition, all goods going to the colonies had to first pass through Great Britain, where a **duty**, or tax, had to be paid before shipment to the colonies. Finally, all goods going to or coming from the colonies were to be carried by ships built in British or colonial ports.

The colonists did not suffer as much as one might imagine from the effects these laws had on trade. Actually, the Navigation Acts had some benefits. Some colonies were able to develop a strong shipping industry, and some businesses grew prosperous in the absence of foreign competition. Moreover, the British government was never able to

adequately enforce these laws. Smuggling goods in and out of ports along the coast became a major part of colonial trade.

Colonial Political Power

As people in the colonies grew more settled and economically secure, they also became more involved in their government. Most of the colonies were managed by a governor appointed by the king. The royal governor then appointed judges and other officials, but each colony also had an elected assembly. Voting in the colonies was restricted to men who owned property or paid taxes, as it was in Great Britain. In the colonies, however, it was much easier to acquire land. A much greater percentage of the population therefore could vote for their government.

The assemblies often struggled with the royal governors for power in the same way that Parliament and the Crown struggled in Great

Images of the Times

Colonial America

The colonies became prosperous and began to drift away from Great Britain. When the British Parliament tried to take control, Americans revolted.

A New England dame school fulfilled the Massachusetts General Court's requirement for public school financed by taxes.

A creche doll with a wooden face and glass inset eyes looked much like an adult. Colonists treated their children as miniature adults.

Britain. These power struggles were often over money. In the early 1700s assemblies won the right to limit the salaries of governors and judges. If a governor would not do as colonists desired, the assembly would reduce or withhold his salary for the next year. In 1731 the New Hampshire assembly refused to pay the governor's salary for five years.

The assemblies also held fast to their right to approve any taxes requested by the Crown or governors. This issue would become a central point of conflict between the colonies and Great Britain. Just as the British Parliament had fought hard for its right to approve or refuse any taxes, so too would the American colonists.

Tightening Colonial Controls

A bitter rivalry between Great Britain and France for territory in North America would eventually lead the British government to interfere more actively in the colonial economy. A dispute over French and British land claims in North America as well as rights to the rich North American fur trade led France and Great Britain to war in 1754. The conflict, called the French and Indian War, brought French troops and French Canadian colonists against British forces and the American colonists. Some Native Americans fought on behalf of the British, while others supported the French.

After six years of war, the British-led forces finally defeated the French in 1760. Three years later, a treaty was signed in Paris. Under the treaty's terms, Great Britain acquired nearly all of France's possessions in North America, including Canada and lands in the area that lay west of the Appalachian Mountains.

Great Britain's empire had grown both in size and in power, but at a considerable cost. The war strained the British economy, and defending the huge new lands they had gained would cost the British even more.

George Grenville, whom **George III** appointed First Lord of the Treasury in 1763, took the first

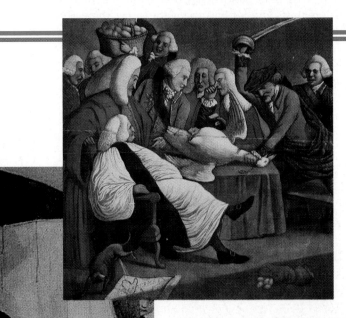

"The Wise Men of Gotham," a political cartoon, appeared in a colonial paper in 1776. It shows the British killing the American goose that laid the golden egg (trade) for the British.

The Stamp Act required stamps such as this on all legal documents. Colonists protested vigorously.

REFLECTING ON THE TIMES

1. Why did colonial legislatures instead of Parliament exercise authority in matters such as education?
2. Why did colonists object to Parliament's authority in the Stamp Act?
3. What attitude toward British policies is reflected in the cartoon "The Wise Men of Gotham"?

Bitter feelings erupted in bloodshed on March 5, 1770, in Boston, when British soldiers fired into a crowd and killed five people. This incident became known to the colonists as the Boston Massacre. *What happened as a result of the unrest in Boston?*

steps to solve these problems. Grenville issued a proclamation that said the colonists could not, for the time being, settle in the lands west of the Appalachians. This move, he hoped, would avoid wars with Native Americans until Great Britain had the area under control and could gradually open the land to settlers. The colonists, however, were eager to build new settlements in the west, and they were outraged by this attempt to stop them.

Grenville also believed that colonists should help pay the costs of their own defense. He began raising money by enforcing the Navigation Acts with the British navy. British warships hunted down smugglers, who were then tried in British military courts rather than in colonial courts. Another new law allowed British troops to be housed in colonists' homes.

It was the Stamp Act, however, that most infuriated the colonists. Passed in 1765, the Stamp Act was different from previous tax measures because it was a direct tax—a tax paid directly to the government rather than being included in the price of goods. It required that all printed materials, from newspapers and shipping documents to playing cards, bear a stamp to show that a tax had been paid to Great Britain. Colonial lawyers, tavern owners, merchants, and printers were most affected by the Stamp Act.

Colonial Protests

Colonists reacted to these measures quickly. They protested with a boycott—a refusal to buy British goods. They attacked stamp agents and burned stamps in the streets. In 1765 nine colonies sent 28 representatives to a Stamp Act Congress in

New York City. The Congress resolved that Parliament could not tax the colonies because the colonies did not have representatives in Parliament. They rallied under the cry "No taxation without representation!" and insisted that only their own colonial assemblies had the right to tax them. The British Parliament repealed the Stamp Act in 1766. The struggle for control of the colonies, however, had begun in earnest. **John Adams**, a colonial leader from Massachusetts, wrote in his diary:

❝ The people have become more attentive to their liberties, … and more determined to defend them.… Our presses have groaned, our pulpits have thundered, our legislatures have resolved, our towns have voted; the crown officers have everywhere trembled, and all their little tools and creatures been afraid to speak and ashamed to be seen. **❞**

Unrest in Boston

The British Parliament reasserted its right to pass laws governing the colonies in the Declaratory Act of 1766. The next year Great Britain placed new taxes on glass, lead, paper, and tea coming into the colonies. Royal agents trying to enforce these laws pleaded for British soldiers to protect them from the angry colonists.

In 1770 the first clash between the Americans and British troops took place. Two regiments of British troops had been sent to **Boston** to support the governor. One evening a squad of soldiers was harassed by a Boston crowd throwing snowballs and rotten eggs. Gunfire erupted, and five people died in what became known as the Boston Massacre.

Because of the unrest in Boston, Parliament repealed most of the taxes but kept the tax on tea.

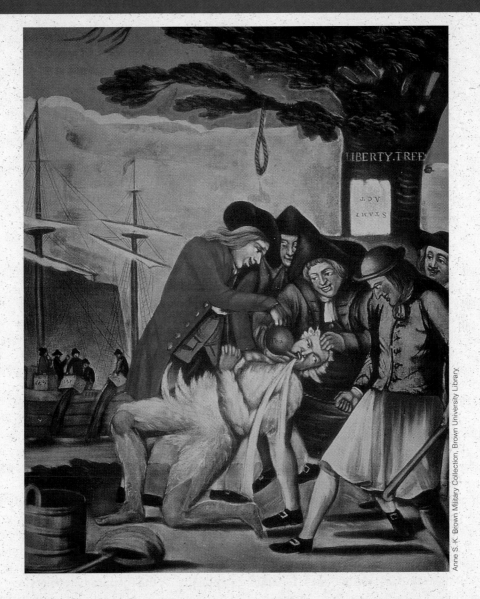

Anne S. K. Brown Military Collection, Brown University Library

Tarred and Feathered

This 1774 British cartoon depicting the tarring and feathering of a British customs officer made a simple point: The American rebels were not men of goodwill simply petitioning for parliamentary representation. The American upstarts, the cartoon implied, were revolutionaries determined to upset the prevailing order in both the Americas and Europe.

In January 1774 a mob took a customs officer named John Malcolm, tarred and feathered him, and then beat him with clubs and ropes until he agreed to speak against His Majesty's government. Even then the mob did not let him go but led him half-naked through the snow for four hours. By then the skin hung off his back in strips and his body was frozen solid—or so the British governor of Massachusetts wrote in his report to the British secretary of state. The men of Massachusetts thus earned a reputation for violence and disorder. The cartoon of Malcolm's ordeal made good anticolonial propaganda in Great Britain, and the idea of hot tar on human flesh still sears our imaginations with the violence of the Revolutionary period. ⊕

The Rattlesnake Flag with 13 alternating red and white stripes warns: "Don't Tread on Me." *What was the significance of most colonies sending delegates to the First Continental Congress?*

The First Continental Congress

The latest repressive measures of the British convinced the thirteen colonies to form a union of resistance. On September 5, 1774, 56 colonial delegates met at **Philadelphia** at the First Continental Congress. The Congress marked an important event in colonial affairs in which leaders from different colonies met face to face. Usually, most colonies considered their differences with Great Britain individually. Now they were united as a group. **Patrick Henry**, a leading statesman from Virginia, commented: "There are no differences between Virginians, Pennsylvanians, New Yorkers, and New Englanders. I am not a Virginian but an American." **George Washington** of Virginia and **Samuel Adams** of Massachusetts were among the leading members of the Congress.

The Congress, which met for more than 7 weeks, resolved that the "English colonists … are entitled to a free and exclusive power of legislation in their several provincial legislatures." In other words, only the colonial assemblies should have the right to make laws in the colonies. Although the Congress recognized Parliament's right to regulate trade, the Congress agreed that the colonies would not import goods from Great Britain after December 1774. After September 1775, they resolved not to send colonial goods to Great Britain.

Many colonists, however, were determined to take more radical steps to end British rule. In every colony a volunteer army was organized and weapons collected. In New England, minutemen (so named because they could be ready for battle on a minute's notice) drilled on village greens, while the town officials stored ammunition, weapons, and food. In the Southern Colonies, planters recruited soldiers at their own expense. It began to appear that the dispute between Great Britain and the colonies would be settled only by force.

In 1772 the law was changed to permit the British East India Company to export tea directly to America and sell it in wholesale markets. Although this law meant much cheaper prices for tea, colonists reacted against the 3-cents-per-pound tax. Some American ports turned tea ships away. At Boston, colonists disguised as Native Americans boarded the ships and dumped the chests of tea into the harbor.

The British quickly punished the Massachusetts colonists for the Boston Tea Party by passing what the colonists called the Intolerable Acts. These laws closed Boston Harbor until the tea had been paid for and required colonists to feed and house British soldiers in their homes. The acts also greatly reduced the colonists' right of self-government. Town meetings, for example, could not be held more than once a year without special permission from the royal governor. Parliament also passed the Quebec Act, placing Canada and territories north of the Ohio River under a separate government, thus closing the area to colonists.

SECTION 3 REVIEW

Recall

1. **Define** duty, direct tax, boycott.
2. **Identify** Navigation Acts, French and Indian War, George Grenville, George III, Stamp Act, John Adams, First Continental Congress, Patrick Henry, George Washington, Samuel Adams.
3. **Explain** why relations between Great Britain and the colonies worsened after the French and Indian War.

Critical Thinking

4. **Evaluating Information** Do you think that the British monarch and his ministers were right in expecting the colonists to shoulder the burden of defending the American colonies? What other approaches might Grenville have taken?

Understanding Themes

5. **Conflict** Compare and contrast Parliament's struggles for power with the king with the American colonists' later struggle for control of their own affairs. What were the key issues for Parliament? For the colonists?

Outlining

To sketch a scene, first you would draw the rough shape, or outline, of the picture. Then you would fill in this rough shape with details. Outlining written material is a similar process. You begin with the rough shape of the material and gradually fill in the details.

Learning the Skill

Outlining has two important functions. When studying written material, it helps you identify main ideas and group together related facts. In writing, it helps you put information in a logical order.

There are two kinds of outlines–formal and informal. An informal outline is similar to taking notes. You write only words and phrases needed to remember ideas. Under the main ideas, jot down related but less important details. This kind of outline is useful for reviewing material before a test.

A formal outline has a standard format. In a formal outline, label main heads with Roman numerals, subheads with capital letters, and details with Arabic numerals. Each level would have at least two entries and should be indented from the level above. All entries use the same grammatical form. If one entry is a complete sentence, all other entries at that level must also be complete sentences.

When outlining written material, first read the material to identify the main ideas. In textbooks, section heads provide clues to main topics. Then identify the subheads. Place details supporting or explaining subheads under the appropriate head.

Practicing the Skill

Study the outline below of Chapter 21, Section 1 and then answer these questions.

1. Is this an example of a formal or an informal outline?
2. What are the three main headings?

3. How do subheads under the heading "Commonwealth" relate to this main idea?
4. Give two examples of grammatical consistency in this outline.

    I. Monarchy
        A. James I
            1. Believed in the divine right of kings
            2. Fought with Parliament over money and religion
        B. Charles I
            1. Continued to believe in divine right
            2. Tried to rule without Parliament
            3. Lost the Civil War and was beheaded
    II. Commonwealth
        A. England ruled by Parliament
        B. Army led by Cromwell
    III. Military dictatorship
        A. Headed by Oliver Cromwell
        B. Enforced Puritan rules

Applying the Skill

Write a formal outline for Section 2 of this chapter.

For More Practice

Turn to the Skill Practice in the Chapter Review on page 557 for more practice in outlining.

Oliver Cromwell

1775	1780	1785	1790

1775 British and American forces exchange fire at Lexington and Concord.

1781 British General Cornwallis surrenders at Yorktown.

1783 Great Britain recognizes American independence.

1787 Delegates in Philadelphia write the United States Constitution.

Section 4

A War for Independence

Setting the Scene

▶ **Terms to Define**
revolution, confederation, federal system

▶ **People to Meet**
Paul Revere, George Washington, Thomas Paine, Thomas Jefferson

▶ **Places to Locate**
Yorktown

Find Out What kind of government did the Americans establish after the American Revolution?

The Storyteller

Mercy Warren lived through the American Revolution and wrote about its horrors. "The roads [were] filled with frighted women and children; some in carts with their tattered furniture, others on foot fleeing into the woods. But what added greatly to the horrors of the scene, was our passing through the bloody field at Monotong, which was strewed with mangled bodies. We met one affectionate father with a cart, looking for his murdered son...." She concluded one of her letters, *"Be it known unto Britain, even American daughters are politicians and patriots, and will aid the good work with their female efforts."*

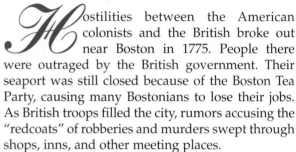

Powder horn

—adapted from *The Women of the American Revolution*, Elizabeth F. Ellet, 1850

ostilities between the American colonists and the British broke out near Boston in 1775. People there were outraged by the British government. Their seaport was still closed because of the Boston Tea Party, causing many Bostonians to lose their jobs. As British troops filled the city, rumors accusing the "redcoats" of robberies and murders swept through shops, inns, and other meeting places.

Sensing the tension in the city, the British Parliament ordered the governor of Massachusetts, General Thomas Gage, to seize the colonists' military supplies. Before dawn on April 19, 1775, Gage sent a troop of 700 British soldiers to destroy weapons collected in the town of Concord, about 18 miles (29 km) from Boston.

Colonists **Paul Revere** and William Dawes learned of the British plan and rode to warn the colonial minutemen. As the British marched into Lexington on their way to Concord, they found about 70 farmers and villagers blocking their path. When the colonists refused to put down their guns, a shot was fired, though no one knows which side fired first. In the skirmish, British soldiers killed 8 colonists; later at Concord, the "redcoats" held off a sharp attack by more minutemen.

As the British troops marched back toward Boston, colonists fired at them from behind buildings, trees, and stone walls. The next day, almost 300 British soldiers and nearly 100 colonists lay dead. The British were humiliated. No one expected the colonists to be any match for the professional British soldiers.

Moving Toward Separation

News of the colonial attack on the British troops spread throughout the American colonies.

Signing of the Declaration of Independence by John Trumbull, c. 1825. The Yale University Art Gallery, New Haven, Connecticut **To the British, those who signed the Declaration of Independence committed an act of treason.** *How did the document justify revolution?*

When the Second Continental Congress gathered in Philadelphia one month after the battles at Lexington and Concord, it immediately organized an army and named **George Washington** as military commander.

Many colonists, however, still resisted the idea of declaring war on Great Britain. The Congress tried one last time to arrange a peaceful compromise with Parliament and the king. They sent a proposal, called the Olive Branch Petition, to King George III. When the British government refused the petition, chances of a peaceful settlement between Great Britain and the American colonies grew dimmer. To more and more colonists, independence seemed the only answer.

A Call to Part

The most stirring arguments in favor of independence came from the pen of colonist **Thomas Paine**. Paine, who recently had come to the American colonies from Great Britain, wrote a pamphlet called *Common Sense* in January 1776. In it he called upon the colonists to break away from Great Britain. Paine promoted independence for economic, social, and moral reasons:

❝ Every thing that is right begs for separation from [Great] Britain. The Americans who have been killed seem to say, 'TIS TIME TO PART. England and America are located a great distance apart. That is itself strong and natural proof that God never expected one to rule over the other. ❞

—Thomas Paine, *Common Sense*, 1776

Common Sense circulated widely and helped to convince thousands of American colonists that it was "time to part." The delegates to the Congress sensed the changing mood in the colonies and assigned five of their best thinkers and writers to prepare a declaration of independence that would clearly state their resolve.

The Declaration of Independence

Thomas Jefferson, a young Virginian, was the principal author of the colonists' declaration of independence. The document set forth the colonists' reasons for separation from Great Britain. Jefferson, like many other colonial leaders, knew and valued the works of John Locke and other Enlightenment thinkers. He incorporated many of their ideas into the Declaration of Independence.

The Declaration stated that individuals have certain basic rights that cannot be taken away by any government. Focusing on John Locke's concept of the "social contract," the Declaration announced that governments are created by an agreement, or contract, between the rulers and those ruled. If a ruler loses the support of the people by taking away basic rights, the people have a right to change the government through rebellion. The beginning of the Declaration reads:

❝ We hold these truths to be self-evident, that all men are created equal, that they are endowed by their Creator with certain unalienable Rights, that among these are Life, Liberty, and the pursuit of Happiness. That to secure these rights, Governments are instituted among Men, deriving their just powers from the consent of the governed; that whenever any Form of Government becomes destructive of those ends, it is the Right of the People to alter or to abolish it.... ❞

The Declaration continued with a long list of the ways in which Great Britain and George III had abused their power and concludes that "these United Colonies are and of Right ought to be Free and Independent States."

On July 4, 1776, the Congress adopted the Declaration of Independence. A few days later, George Washington had the Declaration read to his troops to inspire them and give them hope as war loomed ahead. Cheers went up from the ranks when the reading was done. That night some of the troops joined a crowd of townspeople who pulled down a statue of George III.

The War for Independence

The Declaration of Independence made a reconciliation with the British impossible. The only course open to the colonists was revolution, the violent overthrow of a government. For the revolutionary leaders, now seen as traitors to the British king, failure would mean death. As Benjamin Franklin said, "Yes, we must, indeed, all hang together, or, most assuredly, we shall all hang separately."

The War of Independence was long and bitter. The Americans did not have an army that could face the British in the open field, but they did have a skillful general in Washington. They also had military help from the French, who wanted to revenge the losses of the Seven Years' War. France, however, did not enter the conflict until American victory seemed certain.

The British had the disadvantage of trying to fight a long-distance war. Also, they had to conquer the whole country to win. The Americans had only to hold out until the British admitted defeat.

The turning point came in October 1777 with a British defeat at Saratoga, New York. The

American victory persuaded France to come in on the American side. Spain followed in 1779. Faced with a naval war against France and Spain, Great Britain became less interested in defeating its rebellious colonies. In October 1781 the Americans forced the British army to surrender at **Yorktown**, Virginia.

United States Government

In 1783 Great Britain recognized American independence. At first, the United States was a confederation, or a loose union of independent states, under the Articles of Confederation. Its central government, however, was too weak to deal effectively with national problems. In 1787 the nation's leaders meeting in Philadelphia wrote the Constitution of the United States, a strong, but flexible, framework for a new national government.

The Constitution

The Constitution set up a federal system, in which political authority was divided between the national government and state governments. It also provided for a separation of powers among the national government's executive, legislative, and judicial branches, an idea that came directly from Montesquieu's *The Spirit of Laws*. A system of checks and balances enabled each branch to limit the power of the other branches.

Under the Constitution, the United States was a republic with an elected president instead of a hereditary monarch. Elections held in 1789 made George Washington the first President of the United States. Yet, at the time, only white males who met certain property qualifications could vote in elections. Among the groups excluded were women, African Americans, and Native Americans. Not until this century would the right to vote—and other civil rights—be extended to all adult Americans.

In 1789, however, the United States was closer to democratic rule than any other country in the world. By 1791, a Bill of Rights was added to the Constitution in the form of ten amendments. It affirmed the principle that people had basic liberties that government must protect. These liberties included freedom of religion, speech, and the press, as well as the right to private property and to trial by jury. As in the case of the vote, not all Americans at first had equal protection under the law but would later be included.

Footnotes *to* History

"Yankee Doodle"

The song "Yankee Doodle" was first sung by the British to mock the American colonists:

"Yankee Doodle came to town,

Riding on a pony;

He stuck a feather in his cap

And called it macaroni."

"Macaroni" was a term used for British men who thought they dressed in style but actually looked ridiculous. The colonists loved the tune and added verses of their own to make it a song of defiance.

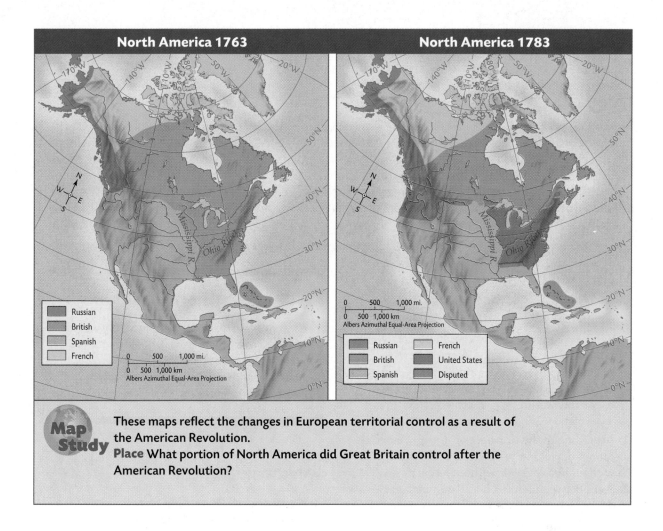

| North America 1763 | North America 1783 |

Russian **British** **Spanish** **French**

0   500   1,000 mi.
0   500 1,000 km
Albers Azimuthal Equal-Area Projection

0   500   1,000 mi.
0   500 1,000 km
Albers Azimuthal Equal-Area Projection

Russian **French**
British **United States**
Spanish **Disputed**

Map Study These maps reflect the changes in European territorial control as a result of the American Revolution.
Place What portion of North America did Great Britain control after the American Revolution?

The Republic's Significance

The creation of the American republic proved that Enlightenment values could work in practice. Based on the ideas of Locke, Montesquieu, and Rousseau, the Constitution of the United States was an example of a social contract based on the sovereignty of the people, with separation of powers among government branches and guarantees for protecting natural rights. Since their writing, the Constitution and the Declaration of Independence both have inspired peoples throughout the world seeking freedom from oppression. In the 1700s and 1800s, many Europeans and Latin Americans appealed to these American documents of liberty in ending absolute monarchy and creating new forms of government. In the 1900s people in many lands throughout the world did the same in their struggles against empires and dictators.

SECTION 4 REVIEW

Recall
1. **Define** revolution, confederation, federal system.
2. **Identify** Paul Revere, George Washington, Thomas Paine, Thomas Jefferson, the Declaration of Independence.
3. **Explain** the basic message of the Declaration of Independence. Why did the American colonists believe the Declaration was necessary?

Critical Thinking
4. **Evaluating Information** Do you think that if Great Britain had treated the colonists differently, they would have been content to remain under British rule? Support your answer.

Understanding Themes
5. **Revolution** Compare the Americans' attempts to organize a new form of government with those of the English after executing King Charles I. Did both governments ensure representation and individual rights?

Connections Across Time

Historical Significance The English and American Revolutions helped to establish the rights of citizens within a representative government. In England, and later Great Britain, the monarchy steadily lost power, Parliament became supreme, and legal documents guaranteed certain individual rights.

In the United States, the colonists established a republic with a written constitution, separation of powers, and an elected president. The Bill of Rights spelled out the rights of individual citizens that government could not violate. The American Revolution would become a source of inspiration to people seeking freedom throughout the world.

Using Key Terms

Write the key term that completes each sentence. Then write a sentence for each term not chosen.

a. habeas corpus
b. divine right
c. duty
d. prime minister
e. commonwealth
f. revolution

g. constitutional monarchy
h. federal system
i. royalists
j. direct tax
k. confederation
l. martial law

1. According to the principle of _____, a person cannot be held in prison by the government without just cause or without a trial.
2. A rift between James I and Parliament grew deeper when the king publicly professed his belief in _____.
3. During times of _____, military authorities are given temporary rule and individual rights are limited.
4. In the English Civil War, supporters of the monarchy were known as _____.
5. When the monarchy was abolished in 1649, England became a _____, a state governed by elected representatives.

Technology Activity

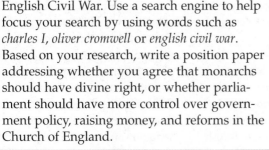

Using the Internet Access the Internet to locate a Web site about the history of the English Civil War. Use a search engine to help focus your search by using words such as *charles I, oliver cromwell* or *english civil war*. Based on your research, write a position paper addressing whether you agree that monarchs should have divine right, or whether parliament should have more control over government policy, raising money, and reforms in the Church of England.

Using Your History Journal

From your list of key ideas that should be the basis of government, write a short constitution or structure for governing a small group—a club, voluntary organization, or a community.

Reviewing Facts

1. **Government/Citizenship** State the changes brought by the English Bill of Rights.
2. **Government** Discuss how the military rule of Oliver Cromwell helped set the stage for the Restoration in 1660.
3. **Government** Describe the Glorious Revolution.
4. **History** Identify the causes and effects of the English Civil War. How did it change England? How did it later affect America?
5. **History** State the causes and effects of the American Revolution. What was its impact?

Critical Thinking

1. **Apply** What political ideas transformed England and America during the 1600s and 1700s? Are these ideas relevant today? Explain.
2. **Contrast** How has American voting changed since the 1700s? What factors do you think have brought about this change?
3. **Evaluate** How were the ideas of separation of powers and checks and balances applied to the government of the United States? Why were these ideas adopted by the framers of the Constitution? How do they affect you today?

4. Synthesize How did the Enlightenment influence the American Revolution?

Geography in History

1. Region Refer to the map below. One of Great Britain's major challenges in the American Revolution was to control rebellion over a wide area. How far is it from the Battle of Saratoga to the Battle of Camden, South Carolina?

2. Movement Why did most British troop movement from one location to another occur by sea?

3. Region The dates and stars identify major Revolutionary battles. How do these battles indicate a shift in the region of the most significant battles from the earliest to the latest period?

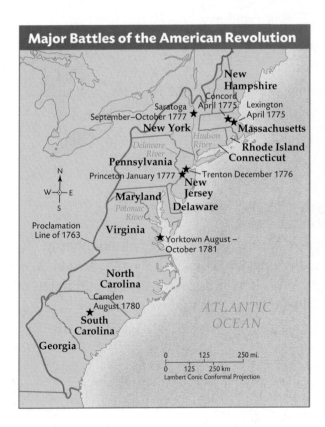

Major Battles of the American Revolution

Understanding Themes

1. Conflict What factors caused the conflict between Parliament and the Stuart monarchs?

2. Change Why do you think the English restored the monarchy after the Commonwealth? What changes came to the monarchy after 1660?

3. Conflict How did the British punish Massachusetts colonists after the Boston Tea Party?

4. Revolution Why did the American Revolution lead to a stable republic in the colonies, while the English Civil War did not do so in England?

Linking Past and Present

1. Some of the Revolutionary quarrels concerned taxes. In what ways does the United States today struggle with the issue of fair taxation?

2. After 1945, many peoples won their freedom from Great Britain. Compare their struggles with that of Americans in the 1700s.

3. The United States and Great Britain today are both democracies. How are their governments similar? How are they different? To what extent do they base their political principles on the events of the 1600s and 1700s?

Skill Practice

Complete the following formal outline for Section 3, "Road to Revolt."

I. Great Britain's American Empire
   A. Economic relationship between Great Britain and colonies
   B. _____
      1. Some colonial products exported only to Great Britain
      2. _____
      3. No foreign-made ships in colonies

II. _____
   A. Structure of colonial governments
      1. _____
      2. Elected assemblies
   B. Early power struggles
      1. Limited salaries of officials
      2. _____

III. Tightening British Control
   A. Effects of French and Indian War
      1. _____
      2. _____
   B. Stamp Acts

IV. _____
   A. Boston Massacre
   B. _____
   C. First Continental Congress

The French Revolution

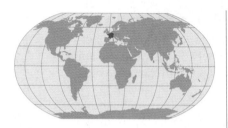

Chapter Themes

▶ **Revolution** The French overthrow their absolute monarchy. *Section 1*

▶ **Change** The National Assembly establishes a constitutional government. *Section 2*

▶ **Conflict** The new French Republic faces enemies at home and abroad. *Section 3*

▶ **Movement** Napoleon becomes France's emperor and conquers much of Europe. *Section 4*

▶ **Reaction** European leaders try to reestablish the old order. *Section 5*

The Storyteller

In 1792 the violence of the French Revolution filled the streets of Paris, where a young seamstress named Marie-Victoire Monnard lived and worked. Walking back to her workshop one afternoon, Marie-Victoire saw six large carts coming toward her. The 13-year-old girl later wrote in her diary, "The carts were full of men and women who had just been slaughtered … legs and arms and heads nodded and dangled on either side of the carts."

The next year she wrote again about the carts, "People just went on working in the shops when they passed by, often not even bothering to raise their heads to watch or to turn their backs to avoid the grisly sight."

Historical Significance

What happened during the French Revolution that allowed people to become accustomed to the bloodied bodies? How did the French Revolution alter society in Europe? What lasting effects did it have on the rest of the world?

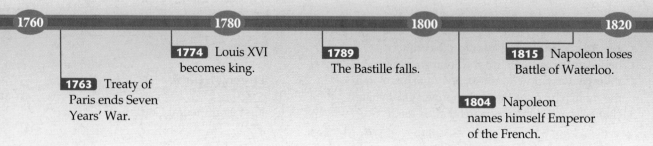

1760   **1780**   **1800**   **1820**

1774 Louis XVI becomes king.

1789 The Bastille falls.

1815 Napoleon loses Battle of Waterloo.

1763 Treaty of Paris ends Seven Years' War.

1804 Napoleon names himself Emperor of the French.

Assault on the Bastille, (artist unknown)
Musée National du Chateau de Versailles, Versailles, France

Your History Journal

Imagine living through the tumultuous events of the French Revolution. Choose a point of view represented by one of the following: a Catholic bishop, a landed aristocrat, a wealthy merchant, a poor artisan, or a peasant. From your chosen viewpoint, describe your reactions to three major events of the times as you read the chapter.

Section 1

The Old Order

Setting the Scene

▸ **Terms to Define**
estate, tithe, bourgeoisie

▸ **People to Meet**
Louis XVI, Marie Antoinette

▸ **Places to Locate**
Versailles, Paris, the Bastille

Find Out Why was France's class system a cause of the French Revolution?

The Storyteller

Fear tightened young Claudette Leroux's throat as she waited for the questioning. She could not deny that she was smuggling salt. She could only explain that the gabelle—the tax on salt—made the cost ten times what it should be. French peasants simply could not afford the Farmers General's prices. She wondered who gave these corrupt officials the power to store, inspect, tax, register, and force people to buy their salt. Did anyone understand the peasants' plight?

—adapted from *Citizens: A Chronicle of the French Revolution*, Simon Schama, 1989

Peasant woman's burden

At its height, the absolute monarchy in France controlled the richest and possibly the most powerful state in Europe. The French aristocracy set European trends in literature, clothing, art, and ideas for change. Yet the majority of the people did not share the wealth or privileges of the aristocracy. Working men and women who had few rights yearned for a better way of life. The success of the American Revolution fueled their desire for change.

French Society Divided

The source of the unhappiness lay within France's class system, which fostered great inequalities among the French people. All French people belonged to one of three estates, or orders of society. The estates determined a person's legal rights and status. The Catholic clergy formed the First Estate. The nobility formed the Second Estate. Everyone else, 97 percent of the French people, made up the Third Estate.

Members of the Third Estate deeply resented the privileges that members of the First and Second Estates enjoyed. For example, neither the First Estate nor the Second Estate was required to pay taxes. The nobility received high positions in the Church, in the government, and in the army, and they could also hunt and carry swords. Third Estate members enjoyed none of these social and political privileges. No matter how successful and well-educated Third Estate members became, they were always excluded from the First and Second Estates—simply because of the families into which they were born.

The First Estate

The First Estate consisted of Roman Catholic clergy and made up about 1 percent of the population. The First Estate comprised two groups: the higher clergy and the lower clergy.

Bishops and abbots, noblemen by birth, made up the higher clergy. These powerful men controlled between 5 and 10 percent of the land in France and enjoyed many privileges. At their disposal were the revenues from their land as well as a tithe, or a 10 percent tax on income, from each church member. Although this money was used to support schools, aid poor people, and maintain church property, it also paid for the grand lifestyles the higher clergy enjoyed, often at the expense of their religious duties.

The lower clergy, made up of parish priests, came from poorer backgrounds and were socially more a part of the Third Estate. Many lower clergy members who carried out religious duties, ran schools, and cared for the poor resented the luxurious lifestyles of the higher clergy.

The Second Estate

The nobility, the Second Estate, formed about 2 percent of the population and owned about 25 percent of the land in France. Like the upper clergy, the members of the Second Estate enjoyed many privileges and lived in great style.

The nobility held high posts in the government and the military. Some resided in the palace at **Versailles**. Others lived in lavish homes on inherited land, some of which they rented to peasants to farm. The Second Estate's main income came from the feudal dues they collected from the peasants who lived on and worked their land.

The Third Estate

The Third Estate made up the largest social group in France during the late 1700s. Peasants and artisans, as well as members of the bourgeoisie (BURZH•WAH•ZEE), or middle class, belonged to the Third Estate. Yet they had very few political rights or privileges.

The doctors, lawyers, merchants, and business managers of the bourgeoisie generally lived in the towns and cities. Educated and well-to-do, they had read Enlightenment works and believed in freedom and social justice.

Other members of the Third Estate, such as thousands of poor artisans and their families, also lived in the cities. Artisans worked for low wages and in poor working conditions. Many lived in the slums of **Paris**.

The peasants, the Third Estate's largest group, lived in rural areas. Although they owned 40 percent of the land, they were very poor because of the payments they had to make to the other estates. These payments included a tithe to the clergy; feudal dues and fines to the nobles; and a land tax to the king. Although members of the Third Estate worked hard, they had no effective voice in the government.

Growing Unrest

Unhappy with this unfair social structure, the people of the Third Estate began to call for change. An Englishman traveling in France saw this growing unrest reflected in a conversation he had with a peasant woman:

66 Walking up a long hill … I was joined by a poor woman who complained of the times, and that it was a sad country; … she said her husband had but a morsel of land, one cow, and a poor little horse, yet they had [42 lbs.] of wheat and three chickens to pay as rent to one [lord], and [4 lbs.] of oats, one chicken and 1s. [shilling] to pay to another, besides very heavy tailles and other taxes. 99

—Arthur Young, from *Travels*, 1789

As a growing population put increasing demands on resources, and the cost of living in France increased, the peasants' anger rose. Nobles also charged the peasants higher fees for the use of such equipment as mills and wine presses.

At the same time, artisans in the cities faced higher prices while their wages stayed the same. Members of the bourgeoisie also wanted change. Although they were prosperous, they wanted more political power. Nobles, too, were unhappy. They resented the king's absolute power and wanted to increase their political influence in the government.

A growing financial crisis in government only added to the country's problems. The 1700s had begun with debts from the wars waged by Louis XIV. The extravagant court of Louis XV had further enlarged this debt.

In 1774 Louis XV's 19-year-old grandson followed his grandfather to the throne as **Louis XVI**. His wife, **Marie Antoinette**, was a year younger. In spite of his inexperience, the young king recognized the growing financial crisis. Supporting the American Revolution had only increased his debt. After initiating government cost-cutting measures, Louis decided that he had no choice but to begin taxing the nobility and the clergy. Both groups, however, refused to be taxed.

By 1786 banks began to refuse to lend money to the ailing government. The economy suffered a further blow when crop failures caused bread shortages in 1788 and 1789. When the privileged classes refused to aid the government, Louis made a bold choice. He summoned the Estates-General to meet in May 1789 in Versailles. Only in this way could he get additional taxes.

Calling the Estates Together

The Estates-General, which had not met since 1614, was made up of delegates representing each estate. The king hoped that the gathering would agree to new taxes on the First and Second Estates. The nobles, however, intended to use the Estates-General to protect their privileges, weaken royal power, and gain control of the government. Because each estate in the Estates-General had a single vote, the nobles hoped that the First and Second Estates together could easily dominate the Third Estate.

Members of the Third Estate refused this plan. Claiming that they had more right to represent the nation than either the clergy or the nobles, Third Estate delegates called for a joint meeting of the three estates, with each delegate voting as an individual. The Third Estate was as large as the other

two combined, and many reform-minded nobles and clergymen supported their views. A mass meeting would give the Third Estate a majority vote. A clergy member who supported the Third Estate, the Abbé Sieyès (see•AY•YEHS), wrote:

> **66** Therefore, what is the Third Estate? Everything; but an everything shackled and oppressed. What would it be without the privileged order? Everything, but an everything free and flourishing. Nothing can succeed without it, everything would be infinitely better without the others. **99**

The king, however, insisted that the estates meet separately. Refusing the king's demands, the representatives of the Third Estate, most of whom were members of the bourgeoisie, were eventually locked out of the Estates-General. They named themselves the National Assembly and gathered at a nearby indoor tennis court with deputies from the other estates who supported their cause. Here the representatives took an oath, known as the Tennis Court Oath, promising not to disband until they had written a constitution for France.

The king recognized the danger of letting the Third Estate alone draw up a constitution. He ordered the first two estates to join the Third Estate in the National Assembly. Fearing trouble, he also called for troops to concentrate in areas around Paris.

A Call to Revolt

In the National Assembly, delegates loudly voiced their unhappiness with the rigid French social order and the government. While the upper clergy and nobility fought to keep their privileges, some members of the Third Estate called for complete social equality. The spirit of rebellion against the government also spread throughout Paris. Debates raged on streets and in cafes. Some members of the Third Estate even physically attacked people who would not support their cause.

The king only added to the anxiety by gathering more troops at his palace in Versailles. Fearing that he planned to dissolve the National Assembly and halt reforms, the citizens reacted. They focused their action on a Paris prison called **the Bastille** (ba•STEEL).

The Fall of the Bastille

To many French people, the Bastille symbolized the injustices of the monarchy. On July 14, 1789, a huge mob surrounded the Bastille in an attempt to

History & Art *The Oath of the Tennis Court,* detail from a painting by L.C.A. Couder
The National Assembly, locked out of the meeting hall for three days, resumed their meeting at an indoor tennis court. *What caused members to fear that the National Assembly would be dissolved by force?*

steal weapons needed to defend the National Assembly. Tensions grew as the angry crowd tried to force its way into the fortress.

Hoping to calm the crowd, the prison commander finally lowered a drawbridge. The mob, however, angrily pressed forward into the main courtyard. Armed with axes, they freed the 7 prisoners held in the Bastille. The soldiers opened fire, and 98 rioters were killed. The prison commander and several soldiers were also killed as the rioters took over the prison. This outbreak led to the formation of a revolutionary government in Paris.

Violence in the Countryside

The storming of the Bastille released a wave of violence throughout France called the Great Fear. When rumors spread wildly that nobles had hired robbers to kill peasants and seize their property, the peasants armed themselves. No robbers came, but fear fanned the peasants' anxiety into violence. Swearing never again to pay feudal dues, they drove some landlords off their property. Peasants broke into manor houses, robbed granaries, and destroyed feudal records. The first wave of the French Revolution had struck.

SECTION 1 REVIEW

Recall
1. **Define** estate, tithe, bourgeoisie.
2. **Identify** Louis XVI, Marie Antoinette, National Assembly, Tennis Court Oath.
3. **Use** a chart to describe France's class system under the rule of

King Louis XVI. What conflicts set the nobility against the members of the Third Estate?

Critical Thinking
4. **Analyzing Information** July 14, Bastille Day, is celebrated in France like an independence

day. Why is it an important national event?

Understanding Themes
5. **Revolution** When did events in France become a revolution? Give specific evidence to support your reasoning.

1789 National Assembly adopts Declaration of the Rights of Man and of the Citizen.

1791 New French constitution is presented to the people.

1792 France declares war on Austria.

Section 2

Constitutional Government

Setting the Scene

▶ **Terms to Define**
unicameral legislature, émigré

▶ **People to Meet**
Pope Pius VI

Find Out What political reforms did the National Assembly adopt for France?

The Storyteller

Sharp differences of political opinion disrupted the Paris opera. At a performance of Iphigenia *the chorus sang "Let us honor our Queen." Royalists applauded, but the opposing party booed. Lainez, an actor who remarked that "every good Frenchman should love the king and queen," was thrown a laurel wreath. Two days later, the revolutionaries would not let Lainez act until he had trampled that wreath underfoot.*

—adapted from *Blood Sisters, The French Revolution in Women's Memory,* Marilyn Yalom, 1993

French social groups

As violence swept the countryside, the National Assembly worked to form a new government. This task was complicated by power struggles among royalists, moderates, and radicals. Most royalists still favored absolute monarchy, but a growing number of moderates wanted the king to share power with a new legislature. Their leader was the Marquis de Lafayette, who had aided the colonists in the American Revolution. A radical group, the Paris Commune, won control of Paris's city government and pushed for an end to the monarchy.

End of the Old Order

Peasant unrest and urban violence finally forced the National Assembly to make reforms. On August 4, 1789, the nobles in that body voted to end their privileges. In a session lasting until 2 A.M., deputies wept and cheered as the last remains of feudalism in France were destroyed. The nobles gave up feudal dues as well as their exemption from taxation. They also agreed that all male citizens could hold government, army, or church office.

The Declaration of Rights

With the old order abolished, the deputies turned to ensuring the equality of all citizens before the law. Inspired by the American Declaration of Independence and Constitution, as well as the English Bill of Rights, the National Assembly composed the Declaration of the Rights of Man and of the Citizen in late August 1789. It is in the French Constitution today.

The Declaration of Rights, which incorporated the ideas of Enlightenment writers Locke, Montesquieu, and Rousseau, stated that all people are equal before the law. It also guaranteed freedom of speech, press, and religion, and protected against arbitrary arrest and punishment.

The Declaration, however, did not grant equal rights to women. When the journalist Olympe de Gouges and other women called for equality, revolutionary leaders rejected their demands. Women did, however, benefit from reforms that made divorce easier and allowed them to inherit property.

March to Versailles

The king refused to accept the new reforms and the Declaration of Rights. This rejection raised the fears of the citizens of Paris that he would take action against the National Assembly. The people wanted Louis to move to Paris from his countryside palace in the town of Versailles to show his support for the Assembly.

In October 1789 thousands of women demanding bread marched in the rain to the king's palace in Versailles. Wielding sticks and pitchforks, the angry mob surrounded the palace, shouting for the king and queen. As the cries grew louder and armed guards were not able to hold back the surging crowd, the king declared at last, "My friends, I will go to Paris with my wife and children."

That afternoon, women waving banners and loaves of bread on bayonets surrounded the king's carriage as it drove from Versailles to Paris. In Paris, fervent anti-royalists watched the king, Marie Antoinette, and their two children. A few days later the National Assembly moved to Paris.

A New France

With the king and the National Assembly settled in Paris, government affairs began to move forward again. The delegates could turn their attention to political reforms.

Political Reforms

One problem faced by the National Assembly was government financing. With the backing of a liberal bishop, Maurice de Talleyrand, the Assembly in 1790 voted to take and sell church lands to pay off the huge government debt. To weaken the power of the Catholic Church, it also passed the Civil Constitution of the Clergy, a measure that placed the French Church under government control and turned the clergy into elected, salaried officials. The Civil Constitution created a deep rift between the Church and the Revolution. **Pope Pius VI** condemned the legislation, and many clergy refused to accept it. Other opponents of the Civil Constitution were many conservative peasants in the provinces.

The Constitution of 1791

In 1791 the National Assembly presented a new constitution to the people. The constitution kept the monarchy but limited royal powers. It set up a unicameral legislature, or one-house assembly, whose members were to be chosen by voters. Although equal rights were declared for all, the suffrage, or

Visualizing History *Louis XVI Arrested at Varennes* (engraving) **After an attempted escape in June 1791, the royal family was watched closely in Paris.** *Why did revolutionary leaders declare war on Austria?*

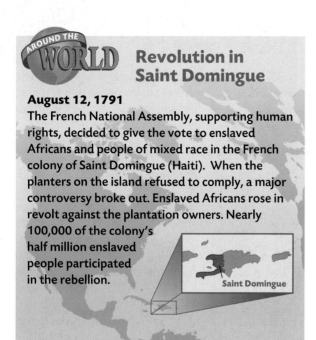

Revolution in Saint Domingue

August 12, 1791

The French National Assembly, supporting human rights, decided to give the vote to enslaved Africans and people of mixed race in the French colony of Saint Domingue (Haiti). When the planters on the island refused to comply, a major controversy broke out. Enslaved Africans rose in revolt against the plantation owners. Nearly 100,000 of the colony's half million enslaved people participated in the rebellion.

Saint Domingue

the right to vote, was limited to only males who paid a minimum tax.

To the moderates, the Constitution of 1791 had achieved their goals. It guaranteed basic rights and created a limited monarchy largely controlled by the wealthy middle class and freed from the power of the Church and the nobles. However, many French people were not happy with the Constitution. For some, the reforms had gone too far; for others, not far enough. Delegates in the newly elected Legislative Assembly were seated according to their political beliefs: the reactionary royalists on the right; the moderates in the center; and the radicals, who wanted a republic, on the left. Today political scientists use the terms *right*, *center*, and *left* to describe similar political positions.

As political groups became more divided, France entered one of the most tumultuous periods in its history. Disagreements led to unrest and violence throughout the country. Many upper-class people feared the breakdown of law and order.

Decline of the Monarchy

Living in Paris, Louis XVI and Marie Antoinette were aware of the unrest. In June 1791 they decided to flee to Austria, where the queen's brother was emperor. Disguised as ordinary people, the royal family left Paris in a carriage late at night.

A bystander recognized the king at a road stop in Varennes, a town east of Paris. Soldiers immediately arrested the royal family, returning them to Paris. A virtual prisoner, Louis reluctantly accepted the limited monarchy established by the National Assembly. The limited monarchy, though, had little chance of success, for the people distrusted the king and were leaning toward a republic.

As news of the revolt against the French monarchy spread to neighboring countries, monarchs in the German states and the Austrian Empire began to worry about the stability of their own governments. French émigrés (EH•mih•GRAY), nobles who had fled France, hoped to restore Louis XVI to full power. The émigrés tried to convince the leaders of these governments that their own rule would be threatened unless they smashed the revolution before it spread.

Meanwhile French revolutionary leaders, fearing that Austria would try to reinstate Louis, declared war on Austria in 1792. Austria was soon supported by other monarchies, including Prussia and Sardinia.

War threw France into total upheaval. In August 1792, Paris crowds attacked the king's palace and killed many royal guards. Seeking protection, the king and his family fled to the Legislative Assembly. There they were given no safety; instead the radicals voted for their imprisonment. A month later, Paris mobs carried out the "September massacres," killing imprisoned nobles and priests accused of political crimes. Meanwhile, the radicals, backed by Paris crowds, took over the Assembly and called for a National Convention to create a new constitution. They also extended the vote to all males, whether or not they owned property.

SECTION 2 REVIEW

Recall
1. **Define** unicameral legislature, émigré.
2. **Identify** the Declaration of the Rights of Man and of the Citizen, Civil Constitution of

the Clergy, Pope Pius VI.
3. **Discuss** the Legislative Assembly's impact on modern politics.

Critical Thinking
4. **Analyzing Information** Contrast the views of French

moderates and radicals. What type of government did each want?

Understanding Themes
5. **Change** How did the Civil Constitution of the Clergy affect church-government relations?

1792   **1794**   **1796**   **1798**   **1800**

1793 King Louis XVI is beheaded on the guillotine.

1795 The Directory comes to power in France.

1799 Napoleon helps to overthrow the Directory.

Section 3

Dawn of a New Era

Setting the Scene

▶ **Terms to Define**
   conscription, coup d'état

▶ **People to Meet**
   Jacobins, Girondists, Napoleon Bonaparte

▶ **Places to Locate**
   Prussia, Valmy

 Why did the French Revolution lead to war between France and its neighbors?

The Storyteller

Paul Lemieux was both excited and anxious. At age 16 he had just received a notice that he would be one of the 3,000 young citizens to attend the new School of Mars. The Committee of Public Safety created the new school for learning and public military instruction. He read the Committee's report, "Loyalty to your own families must end when the great family calls you. The Republic leaves to parents the guidance of your first years, but as soon as your intelligence develops, it loudly proclaims the right it has over you. You are born for the Republic and not to be the pride of family despotism or its victims...." Paul wondered how this choice would affect his life.

—from *The Era of the French Revolution, 1789-1799*, Leo Gershoy, 1957

A sans-culotte

In September 1792 the French revolutionary leaders faced the result of their declaration of war on Austria and **Prussia**. Prussian troops had taken the major French fort of Verdun, and the road to Paris was now open for them. As fear gripped the country, Georges-Jacques Danton, a revolutionary orator, exclaimed: "All are burning with a desire to fight! We need boldness ... and France will be saved."

In response to Danton's words, thousands of volunteers came forward to defend the revolution. A week later, thoughts of defeat vanished when the French army won an astonishing victory at **Valmy**, less than 100 miles (161 km) from Paris. The French commander later wrote in his diary:

   Our soldiers were badly clothed, they had no straw to sleep on, no blankets, they sometimes went two days without bread. I never once saw them complain.... The tiredness and hardship they have suffered have been rewarded. The enemy has [yielded] to the season, misery, and illness. Its formidable army is in flight, its numbers halved....

—Commander Dumouriez, 1792

The victory at Valmy boosted the spirits of the revolutionaries. French forces had halted the powerful armies of Europe's monarchs and had saved the revolution for the time being.

TURNING POINT

The French Republic

As cannons thundered at Valmy, the National Convention met in Paris to create a new government for France. Shouts of "Long live the Nation!" echoed through the chamber as the delegates ended the monarchy and made France a republic.

The National Convention met from 1792 to 1795. Its members—who were all male and mostly lawyers, doctors, and other middle-class professionals—passed into law a number of democratic reforms. The Convention wrote France's first democratic constitution. The constitution placed political power in a single national legislature based on universal male suffrage, meaning that every man could vote, whether or not he owned property. Convention members also replaced the monarchy's confusing system of weights and measures with the metric system still used throughout the world today.

The National Convention also adopted a new calendar, naming September 22, 1792—the date of the republic's creation—as the first day of the Year I of Liberty. The year was divided into months with such names as *Nivôse* ("the snowy month"), *Germinal* ("seed time"), and *Thermidor* ("the warm month"). Although this calendar did not last, it and the other democratic reforms expressed the French people's hope that the republic would be the dawn of a new era of freedom.

Death of a King

Before it could enter the republican era, the Convention had to deal with the legacy of the past. Its first task was to decide Louis XVI's fate. In November 1792 a large iron box holding Louis's secret correspondence with foreign monarchs was found in the royal palace. Although the letters provided little evidence against Louis, the radicals successfully used them to discredit the royal family.

In December 1792 Louis was tried before the Convention and convicted of having "conspired against the liberty of the nation." In January 1793 he was beheaded on the guillotine—a killing machine the revolutionaries had adopted as a humane means of execution. As he faced execution, the king reportedly said:

> **"** I forgive my enemies; I trust that my death will be for the happiness of my people, but I grieve for France and I fear that she may suffer the anger of the Lord. **"**

History & Art *Marie Antoinette in the Park of Trianon* by Antoine Vestier **Because of her extravagance, the people referred to the queen as "Madame Deficit."** *How did Parisians show their feelings about elaborate clothes?*

Parisian crowds joyously celebrated the king's death. For them, it meant that there was no turning back; the republic would remain.

Toward the Future

In the days that followed, republican enthusiasm swept the country. Parisians were the most fervent. The *sans-culottes*—Paris's shopkeepers, artisans, and workers—saw themselves as heroes and heroines and demanded respect from the upper classes.

Soon even wealthy Parisians addressed each other as "citizen" or "citizeness" rather than "mister" or "madame." They rejected elaborate clothes and powdered wigs in favor of simple styles. Men wore long trousers instead of knee-length breeches (hence the name *sans-culottes*, meaning "without breeches"); women wore long dresses in the style of ancient Rome.

While the nation celebrated the republic, debate over the revolution's future erupted in the Convention. There, supporters of the *sans-culottes* and extreme radicals called the **Jacobins** (JA•kuh•buhns) formed the Mountain, so called because its members sat on high benches at the rear of the hall. Under leaders such as Maximilien Robespierre, Georges-Jacques Danton, and Jean-Paul Marat, the Mountain saw itself as the defender of the revolution and as the voice of the people.

Across the aisle was a group of moderates known as **Girondists** (juh•RAHN•dihsts), because many of them came from the Gironde, a region in southwestern France. The Girondists felt that the revolution had gone far enough and wanted to

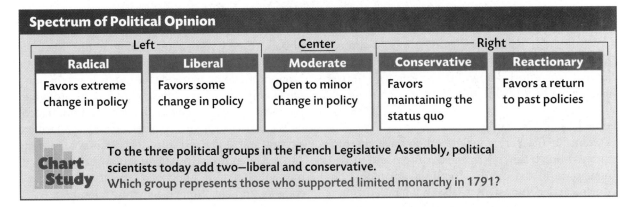

Spectrum of Political Opinion

Left		Center	Right	
Radical	**Liberal**	**Moderate**	**Conservative**	**Reactionary**
Favors extreme change in policy	Favors some change in policy	Open to minor change in policy	Favors maintaining the status quo	Favors a return to past policies

Chart Study To the three political groups in the French Legislative Assembly, political scientists today add two—liberal and conservative. Which group represents those who supported limited monarchy in 1791?

protect the wealthy middle class from radical attacks. They organized support to resist the growing strength of the Mountain in Paris.

Seated between these two rivals on the main floor was a group called the Plain. It was made up of undecided deputies who were a majority of the Convention. As the influence of the *sans-culottes* increased during 1793, members of the Plain came to support the Mountain. Together, they helped make the revolution more radical, more open to extreme and violent change.

Spreading the Revolution

Meanwhile, Europe's monarchs viewed events in France with horror. After Louis's execution, they feared democratic revolutions could spread from France and endanger their thrones and their lives. In January 1793 the monarchs of Great Britain, the Netherlands, Spain, and Sardinia joined those of Austria and Prussia in an alliance against the revolutionary government of France.

French Expansion

At the same time, France's leaders were determined to overthrow royalty everywhere. Early in 1793 Danton declared that "the kings in alliance try to frighten us, [but] we hurl at their feet, as a gage of battle, the French king's head." He then called upon French forces to expand France's territories to their natural frontiers: the Alps, the Pyrenees, the Rhine River, and the Mediterranean Sea.

In response to this call, an army made up of volunteers poured outward from France, eager to seize the natural frontiers and to bring "liberty, equality, and fraternity" to Europe's peoples. Although poorly trained, the French forces often caught the enemy off guard and won many battles. The enemy's professional soldiers, however, soon inflicted on the French a string of defeats. In despair, the French commander in chief abandoned his troops and surrendered.

As French forces retreated, the National Convention took steps to repel the foreign invasion. It formed the Committee of Public Safety to direct the entire war effort. In the summer of 1793 the Committee adopted conscription, or the draft, calling up all men between the ages of 18 and 45 for military service. It also called upon the skills and resources of all civilians, both men and women. The Committee turned the conflict into what has been called the world's first "people's war."

The Revolution in Crisis

While waging war, France's revolutionaries had to struggle with problems at home. A fierce civil war raged in western France as royalist peasants revolted against the revolutionaries. They were angered by the drafting of their sons to fight a war they opposed. Mobs in French cities rioted to protest rising food prices and food shortages.

Meanwhile, the government itself was embroiled in a political crisis. The Girondists accused the Jacobins of seeking the favor of the mob. The Jacobins responded by charging that the Girondists were secretly royalists. The Jacobins in the Mountain won control of the Convention and arrested Girondist delegates.

In retaliation Girondist supporters rebelled against the Jacobins in the Convention. During the uprising Charlotte Corday, a loyal Girondist supporter, killed the Jacobin leader Marat and was sent to the guillotine.

The Wax Museum
A young Swiss woman living in Paris immortalized the revolution's leaders by making wax models of them. She escaped to London, where she opened a museum—Madame Tussaud's Exhibition—that is open today.

The Reign of Terror

Overwhelmed by enemies at home and abroad, the Jacobins set out to crush all opposition within France. This effort, known as the Reign of Terror, lasted from July 1793 to July 1794.

Crushing Opposition

During the Terror, neighborhood watch committees hunted down suspected traitors and turned them over to the courts. Pressured by mobs, the courts carried out swift trials and handed down harsh sentences. Innocent people often suffered—many of them sentenced because of false statements made by hostile neighbors. Among the victims of the Terror was Marie Antoinette, Louis XVI's wife. Royalty and aristocrats, however, were only a few of those killed. Historians estimate that about 85 percent of the 40,000 people who died were probably commoners—merchants, laborers, and peasants. The Committee of Public Safety ruled France, and Robespierre ruled the committee.

Republic of Virtue

Meanwhile, the Jacobin-controlled Committee of Public Safety went about setting up the "Republic of Virtue." By this the Jacobins meant a democratic republic made up of good citizens. Toward this end, the Committee opened new schools and promoted the idea of universal elementary education. In economic matters, it issued pamphlets to teach farmers agricultural skills and introduced temporary wage and price controls to halt inflation. In the area of human rights, it abolished slavery in France's colonies and encouraged religious toleration.

Radical revolutionaries, however, bitterly opposed Catholicism because of its traditional links with monarchy and its claim to be the sole source of religious truth. They closed churches or turned them into "temples of reason." Fearing a further loss of support for the revolution among believers, the Committee opposed these actions. Robespierre himself sponsored the worship of a Supreme Being in an effort to unite Catholics, deists, and nonbelievers.

Images of the Times

Revolutionary Life

Although the causes of the French Revolution had existed for years, the events of 1789 sparked the beginning of the revolution.

After a failed harvest caused bread prices to increase, about 6,000 Parisian women marched on Versailles.

Tri-color badge

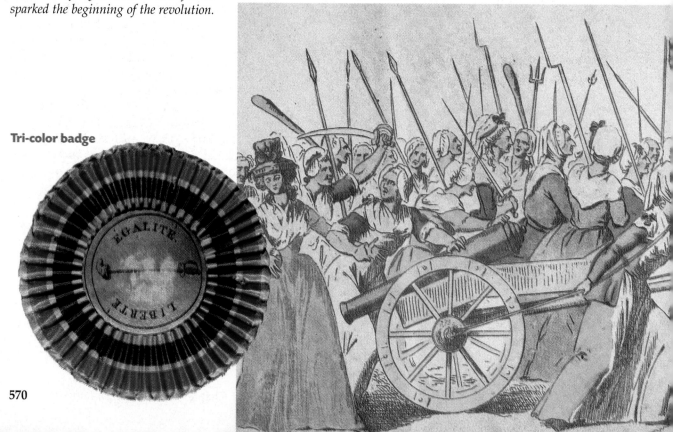

End of the Terror

By the spring of 1794, the French had taken the offensive in the war. With the republic out of danger, Danton and his supporters called for an end to the Terror. Robespierre, however, accused them of treason and had them sent to the guillotine. Fearing for their own safety, other leaders then turned against Robespierre and had him executed. The day after the execution, a Paris newspaper expressed the relief that everyone felt: "We are all throwing ourselves into each other's arms."

After Robespierre's death, the Jacobins lost power and the Terror came to an end. A reaction against Jacobin ideas began, and the wealthier middle class took control of the Convention. Fashions changed as people rebelled against the "Republic of Virtue." Once again, people wore knee breeches, luxurious dresses, and wigs. Price controls were relaxed, and prices rose sharply, causing hardship for the poor. Riots broke out, but the leaderless lower classes were easily put down by the army. By mid-1794, many people even favored a restoration of the monarchy.

The Directory

After Robespierre's fall the Convention briefly carried on as France's government. In 1795 it wrote a new constitution. Universal male suffrage was ended; only citizens who owned property could vote. This constitution, in effect, brought the government under the control of the wealthy middle class. The constitution also set up an executive council of five men called directors. The Directory, as the council was called, ruled with a two-house legislature.

Once in power the Directory faced many enemies. Despite the Terror, enough royalists remained to threaten a takeover. Even more alarming was the growing discontent of the radical *sans-culottes*, angered by food shortages and rising prices. During its rule from 1795 to 1799, the Directory used the army to put down uprisings by both groups.

Meanwhile, the Directory made little effort to resolve a growing gap between the rich and the poor people of France. It was having its own problems: the revolutionary government was on the

Symbols of the revolution carried the message of liberty, equality, and fraternity—or death.

REFLECTING ON THE TIMES

1. Why would these images cause European monarchs to react in horror?
2. How might peasants in neighboring European countries react?

James L. Stanfield

Guillotine

This dreaded machine, pictured here in eerie stillness, embodies the violence and upheaval of the French Revolution. Yet this device used to chop off heads represents not only the terror of the revolution but also its reforms. The guillotine was adopted as a more humane form of capital punishment, a civilized advance over hanging or the executioner's ax. The swift, sharp blade was, according to its French inventor, Dr. Joseph-Ignace Guillotin, "a cool breath on the back of the neck."

A saga of social and political upheaval, the French Revolution transformed the people of France from subjects of an absolute monarch to citizens of a nation. The revolution marked the beginning of the modern age in Europe. "It roused passions," said 19th-century French writer Alexis de Tocqueville, that "revolutions had never before excited." In France people still argue over its importance and meaning. ◉

brink of bankruptcy, and the directors were beset by financial and moral scandals in their personal lives. As the Directory appeared more and more inept, French people of all classes looked to the power of the army to save France from ruin.

Napoleon Takes Over

As the Directory faced growing unpopularity at home, the French army won victories in the continuing war with the European monarchies. One of the many able French military leaders who attracted public attention was a young general named **Napoleon Bonaparte**.

Napoleon's Early Fame

During the French Revolution, Napoleon's great military skills won him quick promotion to the rank of general. In 1795, at age 26, he crushed an uprising against the Directory. Napoleon placed his artillery so that he cleared the streets of Paris "with a whiff of grapeshot."

A year later Napoleon married Josephine de Beauharnais, a leader of Paris society. Using Josephine's connections, he won command of the French army that was fighting the Austrians in Italy. Upon arriving, Napoleon improved the soldiers' conditions and mustered their support.

Rapidly moving and massing French forces at weak points on the enemy's line, Napoleon defeated the Austrians. He forced them to sign a peace treaty giving France control over most of northern Italy. Napoleon, France's leading general, was now ready to influence events at home.

Napoleon's Bold Move

In 1799 Napoleon seized his opportunity. For more than a year, he had been fighting the British in Egypt, hoping to cut off Britain's trade with the Middle East and India. Napoleon won victories on land against Egyptian forces. However, the British

History & Art *Napoleon Crossing the Great St. Bernard* by Jacques-Louis David. Chateau de Malmaison, Ruiel-Malmaison, France **Known for his classical style, David was the leading artist of the French Revolution.** *How does David portray Napoleon?*

navy under Admiral Horatio Nelson destroyed the French fleet that was located at a harbor east of Alexandria. French forces were left stranded among the Pyramids. Hearing of the troubled political situation back home, Napoleon abandoned his army in Egypt and returned to France.

Napoleon landed unannounced on the French Mediterranean coast in October 1799. When he entered Paris, he was greeted by cheering crowds. Quickly, Napoleon joined leaders in a coup d'état, or a quick seizure of power, against the Directory.

Section 4

Napoleon's Empire

Setting the Scene

▶ **Terms to Define**

dictatorship, plebiscite, nationalism

▶ **People to Meet**

Duke of Wellington, Alexander I, Louis XVIII

▶ **Places to Locate**

Trafalgar, Moscow, Waterloo

Find Out How did Napoleon build and then lose an empire?

The Storyteller

Carl von Clausewitz, a military theoretician, analyzed the French disaster in Russia: "[Napoleon] had hoped from that centre [Moscow], to influence by opinion [St.]Petersburg and the whole of Russia.... He reached Moscow with 90,000 men, he should have reached it with 200,000. This would have been possible if he had handled his army with more care and forbearance. But these were qualities unknown to him.... It is, moreover, to be considered as a great neglect ... to have made so little preparation as he did for retreat."

—translated from *Campaign of 1812 in Russia,* Carl von Clausewitz, 1835

Napoleon Bonaparte

In 1804 Napoleon named himself Emperor of the French. At the brilliant coronation ceremony in Paris, the people witnessed an astonishing act. Napoleon took the crown from the pope's hands and placed it on his own head. Napoleon's action spoke loudly of his intention to be a strong ruler. How had the French government been transformed from a democracy to an empire in five short years?

The Consulate

After his successful overthrow of the Directory in 1799, Napoleon had proclaimed a new constitution, which theoretically established a republic. The constitution actually set up a dictatorship, a government headed by an absolute ruler. The executive branch was a committee of three members, called consuls, who took their title from ancient Rome. Napoleon, however, became First Consul and quickly concentrated power in his own hands.

Restoring Order

Napoleon wanted to bring order to the country. One of his first goals was to restructure the government. Although he tried to keep many of the revolutionary reforms, Napoleon replaced elected local officials with men he appointed himself. He also placed education under the control of the national government, creating technical schools, universities, and secondary schools. The secondary schools, called lycées (lee•SAY), were designed to provide well-educated, patriotic government workers. Although students who attended the lycées came mostly from wealthy families, some poorer students received scholarships. In this way the French schools were a step toward a public school system open to all children.

Napoleon also changed the country's financial system. He created the Bank of France and required that every citizen pay taxes. The collected taxes

The Consecration of Emperor Napoleon I and the Coronation of the Empress Josephine (detail) by Jacques-Louis David. The Louvre, Paris, France

In imitation of Pepin and Charlemagne, Napoleon seized the crown from Pope Pius VII and placed it on his own head in 1804. A virtual dictator, Napoleon had the support of most people in France. *How had Napoleon earlier made peace with the Catholic Church?*

were deposited in the bank and used by the government to make loans to businesses. These changes gradually brought inflation and high prices under control.

Napoleon's many supporters welcomed his strong government and the peace and order it brought. In 1802 Napoleon named himself Consul for life. This move was overwhelmingly approved by a plebiscite, or popular vote.

The Napoleonic Code

Many historians say that Napoleon made his greatest impact on French law. Old feudal and royal laws were often contradictory and confusing. To make French law clear and consistent, Napoleon had a new law code written. Commonly known as the Napoleonic Code, it was based on Enlightenment ideas, such as the equality of all citizens before the law, religious toleration, and advancement based on merit. However, the Code placed the state above the individual. For example, it limited freedom of speech and press by allowing the censorship of books, plays, and pamphlets. Women also lost

many of the rights they had gained during the revolution. Male heads of households were given extensive authority over wives and minor children.

The Church

Napoleon also made peace with the Catholic Church. Realizing that French Catholics had objected to the Civil Constitution of the Clergy, he negotiated an agreement called the Concordat of 1801 with Pope Pius VII. In this agreement Napoleon acknowledged that Catholicism was the religion of the majority of French people but affirmed religious toleration for all. Napoleon did, however, retain the right to name all bishops, who had to swear allegiance to the state. The pope agreed to accept the loss of church lands; in return the state agreed to pay salaries to the Catholic clergy.

Building an Empire

Although Napoleon proved that he was an able administrator, he was more interested in building an empire. Soon after becoming First Consul, Napoleon commanded the French forces that defeated both Italy and Austria. He also persuaded Russia to withdraw from the war. Though Napoleon was not able to defeat the British navy, the British were ready for peace because their commerce had suffered during the war. The two powers signed the Treaty of Amiens in March 1802.

Over the next few years Napoleon combined his talents as a masterful military leader and brilliant diplomat to build an empire. In 1804 he named himself Emperor of the French and soon set his armies on the road to conquest.

The Battle of Trafalgar

Despite his successes on the continent of Europe, Great Britain remained Napoleon's most tenacious enemy. By 1805 Napoleon felt he was ready to invade Great Britain from the English Channel; his fleet never made it that far, however. In October 1805 at the Battle of **Trafalgar**, off the southern coast of Spain, the British admiral Lord Nelson soundly defeated the French navy, removing once and for all the possibility of a French invasion of Great Britain.

Economic Blockades

After Trafalgar, Napoleon decided to use economic warfare against the British. He believed he could defeat Great Britain by destroying its economic lifeline—trade. In a plan called the Continental System, Napoleon ordered all European nations he had conquered to stop trade with the British. In another decree he forbade British imports entry to the European ports that he controlled. Napoleon also required Russia and Prussia to go along with the blockade of British goods.

Meanwhile, Great Britain responded to the trade blockade with a counterthreat: Any ship on its way to a European port had to stop first at a British port. Napoleon responded that he would seize any ship that did so.

This conflict put the United States and other neutral nations in a difficult position. The United States relied heavily on its trade with both Great Britain and France. If the United States ignored the British threat, American ships would be seized by the British navy. If the United States obeyed the British, the French navy would seize its ships. This conflict on the seas was one of the causes that eventually led to the War of 1812 between the United States and Great Britain.

Despite the blockades, the aggressive British navy did maintain control of the seas, and Napoleon's Continental System failed. French trade

suffered, and the French economy worsened. Yet Napoleon's empire kept growing as he continued to win battles on land.

Napoleonic Europe

By 1812 Napoleon controlled most of Europe. France's boundaries now extended to the Russian border. Through successful French military conquests, Napoleon became king of Italy, his brother Joseph became king of Naples and later Spain, and his other brother, Louis, became king of Holland. Napoleon then abolished the Holy Roman Empire and created the Confederation of the Rhine, a loose organization of the German states. This move led Prussia to declare war on France, but the French easily crushed the weak Prussian army.

The people who lived in the countries under Napoleon's rule resented paying taxes to France and sending soldiers to serve in Napoleon's armies. This resentment ignited in the conquered people a feeling of nationalism, the yearning for self-rule and restoration of their customs and traditions. Nationalism helped stir revolts against French rule throughout Europe.

The first signs of trouble appeared in Spain, where Spanish forces carried out guerrilla warfare, or hit-and-run attacks, on French forces. In 1812, aided by British troops under the command of Arthur Wellesley (later named **Duke of Wellington**), the Spaniards overthrew their French occupiers. They reinstated their old king under a system of limited monarchy. Prussia also joined in the revolt against Napoleon, as nationalist leaders rebuilt its army and amassed political support in the hope of ridding themselves of French rule.

Downfall of the Empire

When Russia joined the movement against Napoleon, it signaled the end of the empire. Czar **Alexander I** of Russia viewed Napoleon's control of Europe as a threat to Russia. Additionally, Napoleon's Continental System had hurt the Russian economy. In 1811 Alexander withdrew from the Continental System and resumed trade with Great Britain.

The Invasion of Russia

Alexander's withdrawal outraged Napoleon, leading him to invade Russia. Napoleon assembled a massive army of 600,000 soldiers from countries

Europe at Height of Napoleon's Power 1812

Legend:
- Napoleon's empire
- Under Napoleon's control
- Napoleon's allies
- → Napoleon's campaign in Russia

0 150 300 mi.
0 150 300 km
Lambert Conic Conformal Projection

Map Study

Before he invaded Russia, Napoleon dominated most of Europe.

1. **Location** What geographic factors helped to protect Great Britain and Russia from conquest by Napoleon's armies?
2. **Movement** How far would a foot soldier have traveled walking from Paris to Moscow?

throughout Europe. The long French march toward **Moscow** began in May 1812. The Russians, however, refused to yield to Napoleon's threat. They retreated to central Russia, adopting a "scorched-earth policy" in which they burned everything as they went. On September 14, one of Napoleon's men finally saw the city of Moscow from a nearby hill. But the day after the French entered Moscow, a giant fire, probably started by Russian patriots, destroyed most of the city.

Shortly afterward the harsh Russian winter began to set in, and the French army could not remain in Russia without shelter. Despite the difficult conditions, Napoleon delayed before ordering a retreat. When the French troops finally did withdraw, the Russians relentlessly attacked them. Amid the extreme conditions the retreat became a rout. Of the 600,000 soldiers who entered Russia, about 400,000 died of battle wounds, starvation, and exposure.

Defeat

The Russian blow to Napoleon's power ruined him. From all directions his enemies—Russians, Prussians, Spaniards, English, Austrians, Italians—sent armies against Napoleon's forces. Russia and Prussia announced a War of Liberation. Joined by Austria, they defeated Napoleon at Leipzig in Saxony, part of present-day Germany, in October 1813.

By March 1814 the allies were in Paris, forcing Napoleon to surrender and abdicate as emperor. The victors restored the French throne to **Louis XVIII**, a member of the Bourbon family and the brother of Louis XVI. Napoleon was exiled to Elba, an island off the coast of Italy. The boundaries of France were reduced to those of 1792.

Still determined to rule, Napoleon returned to France on March 1, 1815, and easily won widespread popular support. The troops of the restored Bourbon king, Louis XVIII, deserted to their former

Music of Revolutions

Rouget de Lisle Singing "The Marseillaise" at Dietrich's *by Isidore Pils*

The French Revolution found its voice in a rousing military march written in 1792 by Joseph Rouget de Lisle, a young captain in the army engineers. The march, later known as "The Marseillaise," rallied French citizens by sounding the call to battle:

> *To arms, citizens!*
> *Form your battalions,*
> *Let us march, let us march!*

"The Marseillaise" became the French national anthem in 1795. Because of its revolutionary character, it was banned under the reigns of Napoleon, Louis XVIII, and Napoleon III. It once again became the national anthem in 1879.

The best-known and most enduring song of the American Revolution was "Yankee Doodle." The British had originally used the term "yankee" as an insult. Singing "Yankee Doodle" as they marched, the British showed scorn for the American soldiers. The American colonists, however, turned the insult into a battle cry for freedom.

Revolutionary and protest groups today use music to gain public support. For example, since the 1960s, "We Shall Overcome" has been a unifying force in movements for freedom throughout the world.

Linking Past and Present ACTIVITY

Examine ways in which revolutionary music can be used to motivate people. Can you think of cases today where music is used to unite people around a cause?

---

commander when Napoleon announced, "Your general, summoned to the throne by the prayer of the people and raised upon your shields, is now restored to you; come and join him." In a period known as the Hundred Days, Napoleon again reigned as emperor. To avoid war he announced that France wanted no more territory.

The European governments, however, feared that Napoleon might regain his former strength. Determined to stop him, the armies of Prussia, Great Britain, and the Netherlands advanced toward France under the command of the Duke of Wellington. Napoleon met them at **Waterloo** in the Austrian Netherlands in June 1815; the French troops were decisively defeated. Napoleon was then placed under house arrest on the island of Saint Helena in the South Atlantic. He died there in 1821.

Napoleon's Legacy

Napoleon did not allow true representative government. He did, however, secure the revolution in France and spread throughout Europe ideas such as equality before the law, religious toleration, and advancement by merit rather than by birth. Napoleon's rule also set uniform standards of government, reformed tax systems, promoted education, and improved agriculture and industry. After the collapse of Napoleon's empire, many Europeans still wanted to keep these benefits from the French Revolution. They especially did not forget their taste of freedom from absolute monarchy.

SECTION 4 REVIEW

Recall
1. **Define** dictatorship, plebiscite, nationalism.
2. **Identify** the Napoleonic Code, the Continental System, Duke of Wellington, Alexander I, Louis XVIII, Waterloo.
3. **Discuss** the changes brought by the Napoleonic Code.

Critical Thinking
4. **Making Comparisons** Compare Napoleon's rule after the French Revolution to Cromwell's rule after the English Civil War.

Understanding Themes
5. **Movement** How did the principles of the French Revolution spread throughout Europe and contribute to the rise of nationalism?

Interpreting Graphs

When you divide a pizza among four people, it is easy to estimate where the circle should be sliced. A circle graph is similar to a round pizza. Circle graphs are useful for showing percentages, such as 25 percent of a pizza. A line or bar graph, however, can be used to show changes over a period of time.

Most graphs also use words to identify or label information. These steps will help you interpret graphs.

- Read the title.
- Read the captions and text.
- Determine the relationships among all sections of the graph.

Learning the Skill

The circle on the right is like a clock. It visually compares the time periods from the following information about revolution and empire in France between 1789 and 1815.

1. **Estates-General and National Assembly**
   May 1789–September 1791
   Limited constitutional monarchy
2. **Legislative Assembly**
   October 1791–September 1792
   New constitution; delegates seated according to political beliefs
3. **National Convention**
   September 1792–October 1795
   King executed; Reign of Terror
4. **Directory**
   October 1795–November 1799
   New constitution with bicameral legislature, five executive directors; Napoleon seizes control
5. **Consulate**
   December 1799–May 1804
   New constitution sets up three consuls; Napoleon rules
6. **Empire**
   May 1804–June 1815
   Napoleon I, emperor until overthrown

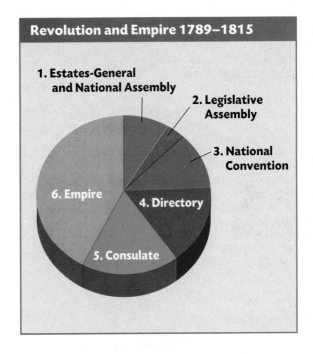

Revolution and Empire 1789–1815

1. Estates-General and National Assembly
2. Legislative Assembly
3. National Convention
4. Directory
5. Consulate
6. Empire

Practicing the Skill

Study the graph and answer the following questions.
1. What was the longest of the six periods of the French Revolution?
2. What was the shortest of the six periods?
3. About what percentage of the total time did Napoleon rule France (during the Consulate and Empire)?
4. About what percentage of the time did the Directory rule?

Applying the Skill

Draw a circle graph showing the major divisions of your day.

For More Practice

Turn to the Skill Practice in the Chapter Review on page 589 for more practice in interpreting graphs.

1814 Congress of Vienna meets.

1819 Carlsbad Decrees impose censorship in Prussia.

1821 Greek nationalists revolt against Turkish rule.

Section 5

Peace in Europe

Setting the Scene

▶ **Terms to Define**
buffer state, reactionary, liberalism

▶ **People to Meet**
Prince Klemens von Metternich

▶ **Places to Locate**
Vienna

Find Out ▶ How successful were the plans of the reactionaries to thwart the spread of liberalism in Europe?

The Storyteller

Vienna, native city of Haydn, home of Brahms, and host to Europe's greatest musicians, was known for its opera and its pageantry. The medieval streets of the old city, dominated by the tall Gothic tower of St. Stephen's Cathedral, were once occupied by Napoleon's troops. Now Vienna would host the victorious assembled aristocracies. The czar of Russia, the kings of Prussia, Denmark, Bavaria, and Saxony, and the nobility dined at forty lavish tables in the Hofburg. Colorful military parades, fireworks, balls in the Grand Hall, and Beethoven's concerts all served to disguise the serious discussions that would establish Europe's "balance of power."

—adapted from *Western Civilization, an Urban Perspective,* F. Roy Willis, 1973

The Old University in Vienna

Walking along the streets of **Vienna**, Austria, in the autumn of 1814 were the kings, princes, and diplomats who had gathered for a peace conference known as the Congress of Vienna. With Napoleon in exile, the delegates had come to Vienna to restore order and stability in Europe after nearly 25 years of war.

The Congress met from September 1814 to June 1815. Nearly every European nation sent delegates, but the Congress's main work was done by Austria's **Prince Klemens von Metternich** of Austria, Russia's Czar Alexander I, and Great Britain's Lord Robert Castlereagh (KAS•uhl•ray). Prince Maurice de Talleyrand, once a bishop, represented defeated France.

The Congress of Vienna

Austria's chief minister, Prince Klemens von Metternich, served as host to the Congress and presided over it. Metternich believed that in order to establish European stability, Europe should be restored to the way it was before the French Revolution. To achieve his goal, Metternich maintained that settlements reached at Vienna would be guided by three principles: compensation, legitimacy, and balance of power. Compensation meant that all countries should be repaid for the expenses they incurred while fighting the French. By legitimacy, Metternich meant restoring to power the royal families who had ruled before Napoleon. Finally, balance of power meant that no country should ever again dominate continental Europe.

Redrawing the Map

As the victors of the war claimed their rewards, they redrew the map of Europe. France was forced to give up its recently gained territory and to pay a large indemnity, or compensation, to other countries for war damages. Although Great Britain did not gain land in continental Europe, it took from France most of its remaining islands in the West

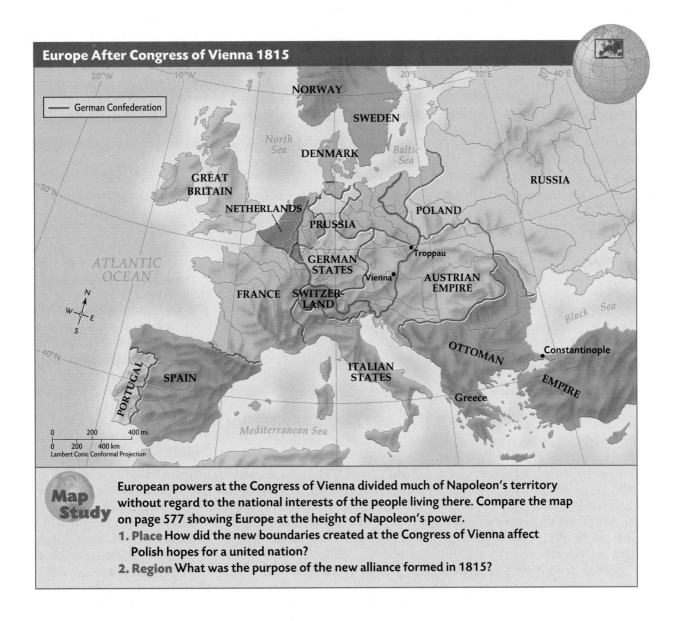

— German Confederation

NORWAY
SWEDEN
DENMARK
GREAT BRITAIN
NETHERLANDS
PRUSSIA
POLAND
RUSSIA
North Sea
Baltic Sea
ATLANTIC OCEAN
GERMAN STATES
Troppau
Vienna
FRANCE
SWITZER-LAND
AUSTRIAN EMPIRE
Black Sea
PORTUGAL
SPAIN
ITALIAN STATES
OTTOMAN EMPIRE
Constantinople
Greece
Mediterranean Sea

0   200   400 mi.
0   200   400 km
Lambert Conic Conformal Projection

Map Study

European powers at the Congress of Vienna divided much of Napoleon's territory without regard to the national interests of the people living there. Compare the map on page 577 showing Europe at the height of Napoleon's power.

1. **Place** How did the new boundaries created at the Congress of Vienna affect Polish hopes for a united nation?

2. **Region** What was the purpose of the new alliance formed in 1815?

Indies. Austria gained the Italian provinces of Lombardy and Venetia as well as territory on the eastern coast of the Adriatic Sea.

At the conference Prussia and Russia also made it known that they wanted to expand their borders by seizing formerly French-held lands. Yet Great Britain and Austria feared that increased Prussian and Russian influence in central Europe would lead to an imbalance of power on the continent. To put pressure on Prussia and Russia, Great Britain and Austria made an agreement with France. The agreement bound the three powers—Great Britain, Austria, and France—to resist any further Prussian or Russian territorial expansion in Europe by armed force if it was necessary.

In the end a compromise was reached. Prussia received extensive territories along the Rhine River and almost half the kingdom of Saxony for its compensation. Russia received most of the Polish

territory formerly held by Prussia and Austria. This increased the Polish territory held by Russia. A new kingdom of Poland was then formed under the czar.

Restoring the Monarchies

Once the territorial compensation was settled, delegates at the Congress of Vienna turned to stabilizing European governments. Believing that divine-right monarchy was necessary for proper order, the delegates made settlements based on legitimate claims to the throne and restored the absolute monarchs who ruled Europe before Napoleon. The Congress reestablished royal dynasties in France, Spain, Portugal, Naples, Sardinia, and Sicily. In France the Congress officially recognized the Bourbon heir Louis XVIII as the legitimate, or legal, ruler.

To safeguard other ruling dynasties, the Congress placed further controls on France. It reduced French borders to those of 1790 and established buffer states, or neutral territories, around French territory. To the north of France, the Austrian Netherlands and the Dutch Netherlands became one country under the Dutch ruler. Thirty-nine independent German states formed the German Confederation, headed by Austria. Switzerland regained its neutrality and independence as a federal league of states. The Italian kingdom of Piedmont united with the Mediterranean island of Sardinia.

Forces Changing Europe

The diplomats responsible for most of the agreements made at the Congress of Vienna were reactionaries, people who opposed change and wanted to return things to the way they had been in earlier times. They strongly felt that Europe could maintain peace only by returning to the tradition of strong absolute monarchies in effect before the French Revolution.

The reactionaries hoped that their plans would thwart the spread of liberalism, a political philosophy influencing European peoples in the 1800s. The liberals accepted the ideas of the Enlightenment and the democratic reforms of the French Revolution. Believing in individual freedom, liberals supported ideas such as freedom of speech, freedom of the press, and religious freedom—which had led to revolution.

The reactionaries also hoped to crush the rise of nationalism throughout Europe. When they redrew national boundaries, the delegates reflected the wishes of the rulers rather than those of the people they governed. The new boundaries thwarted the nationalistic hopes of many European groups. For example, the boundaries crushed the Polish people's hopes for a united nation of their own. Instead, their land was parceled out among their neighbors: Austria, Prussia, and Russia.

Alliances

The diplomats knew that nationalistic desires for independence, democratic rule, and national unity could well lead to revolution, and revolution threatened everything they believed in. To prevent democratic revolutions, they agreed to form new alliances. Great Britain, Austria, Prussia, and Russia joined in the Quadruple Alliance to maintain the settlements of Vienna. The four powers concluded the alliance in November 1815. France was admitted three years later, when the members of the alliance met for the first time at Aix-la-Chapelle.

According to the alliance agreement, representatives of the great powers were to meet periodically to discuss the security of Europe. Their goals included preservation of territorial boundaries set at the Congress of Vienna, exclusion of Napoleon Bonaparte and his heirs from French rule, and prevention of any revolutionary movements from taking hold in Europe.

With the goals of securing international order based on "Justice, Christian Charity, and Peace," Czar Alexander I of Russia created the Holy Alliance. Issued in the name of the czar, the Prussian king, and the Austrian emperor, the Holy Alliance called for Christian rulers in Europe to cooperate as a union of monarchs. Metternich dismissed the idea as "a loud-sounding nothing." Nevertheless, all the invited rulers joined the Holy Alliance except Pope Pius VII and the British government. The pope had said that "from time immemorial the papacy had been in possession of Christian truth and needed no new interpretation of it." The British government

Visualizing History The serious work of the Congress of Vienna was nearly overshadowed by lavish entertainment—plays, musicals, and balls. *What did Metternich want to achieve by a balance of power?*

excused itself on the grounds that, without approval by Parliament, such an alliance would violate the British constitution.

The Concert of Europe

The two alliances encouraged European nations to work together to preserve the peace. The members decided to have regular meetings to settle international problems. These meetings became known as the Concert of Europe. This system helped to avoid major European conflicts by resolving local problems peaceably.

For nearly 30 years, Metternich used the system set up by the Congress of Vienna to achieve his own political goals: to oppose liberalism and nationalism and to defend absolute monarchies in Europe. His system of beliefs came to be known as the Metternich system.

Metternich's political goals and the Concert of Europe did not go unchallenged, however. In Germany university students demonstrated for liberal reforms and national unity. Alarmed by this revolutionary activity, Metternich persuaded King Frederick William III of Prussia to pass a series of repressive measures in 1819. These so-called Carlsbad Decrees imposed strict censorship on all publications and suppressed freedom of speech. Metternich, with the support of the Prussian king, managed to end student agitation in Germany, but new challenges to the status quo arose in other areas.

Liberal reformers in Spain, for example, forced their monarch to agree to constitutional government in 1820. Metternich pressured members of the Quadruple Alliance to intervene in European countries and their territories to prevent the spread of liberalism. Great Britain, with a tradition of liberalism in government, opposed the action and broke from the alliance. Metternich's system did prevail, however, as French troops restored the Spanish king to full power. But the spirit of revolt did not die, for

Visualizing History **Metternich pushed for the creation of the Quadruple Alliance.** *What was the alliance's major role?*

Spanish colonies in Latin America successfully revolted against Spanish control during the 1820s.

The Greeks also fought for their independence in 1821 when Greek nationalists revolted against Turkish rule. Metternich intervened by attempting to stop other countries from aiding the rebellion. The British and the French provided assistance to the Greek nationalists despite Metternich's threats. Greece finally won independence from the Ottoman Empire in 1829.

The stable political system Metternich envisioned throughout Europe would soon be under attack. The nationalistic spirit fostered by the French Revolution would not die in Europe.

SECTION 5 REVIEW

Recall
1. **Define** buffer state, reactionary, liberalism.
2. **Identify** the Congress of Vienna, Prince Klemens von Metternich, Quadruple Alliance.
3. **List** the three guiding principles Metternich used at the Congress of Vienna.

Critical Thinking
4. **Making Comparisons** Compare and contrast the political philosophies of a liberal and a reactionary in the 1800s.

Understanding Themes
5. **Reaction** Why were the countries at the Congress of Vienna mostly represented by reactionaries? What effect did their views and policies have on the spread of liberalism and nationalism throughout Europe?

from
Les Misérables
by Victor Hugo

*As we have seen, litera-
ture can be a bridge to
the past, transporting
us to a world that may seem strange or
obscure at first, but that has much in
common with our own. Across the gap
between then and now we can see faces
that we recognize, situations that are
familiar, hopes that we share. The selection that follows was written by one of
France's most celebrated writers, Victor
Hugo. Hugo lived from 1802 to 1885, a
time of dramatic and violent change for
France. In this scene, Monsieur
Gillenormand snoops through the
belongings of his grandson, Marius.
Assisting the grandfather is Marius's
aunt. Marius's father has recently died.*

M. Gillenormand, who had risen early
like all the elderly who are in good
health, had heard [Marius] come in, and hurried
as fast as he could with his old legs, to climb to
the top of the stairs where Marius's room was,
to give him a kiss, question him while embracing him, and find out something about where
he had come from.

But the youth had taken less time to go
down than the old man to go up, and when
Grandfather Gillenormand went into the garret
room, Marius was no longer there.

The bed had not been disturbed, and on it
were trustingly laid the coat and the black
ribbon.

"I like that better," said M. Gillenormand.

And a moment later he entered the drawing
room [room for receiving guests] where Mlle.
Gillenormand the elder was already seated,
embroidering her carriage wheels.

The entrance was triumphant.

In one hand M. Gillenormand held the coat
and in the other the neck ribbon, and cried out,
"Victory! We are about to penetrate the mystery!
We shall know the end of the mystery, unravel
the wanton ways of our rascal! Here we are
right to the core of the romance. I have the portrait!"

In fact, a black shagreen box, rather like a
medallion, was fastened to the ribbon.

The old man took this box and looked at it
for some time without opening it, with that air
of desire, delight, and anger, with which a poor,

hungry devil sees an excellent dinner pass right under his nose, when it is not for him.

"For it is clearly a portrait. I know all about these things. They are worn tenderly against the heart. What fools they are! Some abominable floozy, probably enough to bring on the shudders! Young people have such bad taste nowadays!"

"Let's see, father," said the old maid.

The box opened by pressing a spring. They found nothing in it but a piece of paper carefully folded.

"More and more predictable," said M. Gillenormand, bursting with laughter. "I know what that is. A love letter!"

"Ah! Then let's read it!" said the aunt.

And she put on her spectacles. They unfolded the paper and read this:

"*For my Son.*—The emperor made me a baron on the battlefield of Waterloo. Since the Restoration contests this title I have bought with my blood, my son will take it and bear it. I need not say that he will be worthy of it."

The feelings of the father and daughter are beyond description. They felt chilled as by the breath of a death's head [skull]. They did not exchange a word. M. Gillenormand, however, said in a low voice, and as if talking to himself, "It is the handwriting of that bandit."

The aunt examined the paper, turned it over every which way, then put it back in the box.

At that very moment, a little rectangular package wrapped in blue paper fell out of the coat pocket. Mademoiselle Gillenormand picked it up and unwrapped the blue paper. It was Marius's hundred

[calling] cards. She passed one of them to M. Gillenormand, who read: *Baron Marius Pontmercy.*

The old man rang. Nicolette [the chambermaid] came. M. Gillenormand took the ribbon, the box, and the coat, threw them all on the floor in the middle of the drawing room, and said:

"Take those things away."

A full hour passed in complete silence. The old man and the old maid sat with their backs turned to one another, and were probably each individually thinking over the same things. At the end of that hour, Aunt Gillenormand said, "Pretty!"

A few minutes later, Marius appeared. He was just coming home. Even before crossing the

Visualizing History A French salon displays the wealth of the bourgeoisie. With the end of the revolution, the return of social class distinctions accompanied the restoration of the monarchy. *Why was Monsieur Gillenormand angry about Marius's calling cards?*

A republican club meets in Paris in 1848. Victor Hugo's concern for the common people underlies much of his writing. Social commentary and support for democratic movements mark his works in the 1850s and 1860s. *How does the character of Monsieur Gillenormand portray aristocracy?*

threshold of the drawing room, he saw his grandfather holding one of his cards in his hand; the old man, on seeing him, exclaimed with his crushing air of sneering bourgeois superiority, "Well! Well! Well! Well! Well! So you are a baron now. My compliments. What does this mean?"

Marius blushed slightly, and answered, "It means I am my father's son."

M. Gillenormand stopped laughing, and said harshly, "Your father; I am your father."

"My father," resumed Marius with downcast eyes and stern manner, "was a humble and

heroic man, who served the Republic and France gloriously, who was great in the greatest history that men have ever made, who lived a quarter of a century in the camps, under fire by day, and by night in the snow, in the mud, and the rain, who captured colors [flags], who was twenty times wounded, who died forgotten and abandoned, and who had but one fault; that was to have too dearly loved two ingrates [ungrateful persons], his country and me."

This was more than M. Gillenormand could bear. At the word, "Republic," he rose, or rather, sprang to his feet. Every one of the words

Marius had just spoken, produced on the old royalist's face the effect of a blast from a bellows on a burning coal. From dark he had turned red, from red to purple, and from purple to flaming.

"Marius!" he exclaimed, "abominable child! I don't know what your father was! I don't want to know! I know nothing about him and I don't know him! But what I do know is that there was never anything but miserable wretches among them! That they were all beggars, assassins, thieves, rabble in their red bonnets! I say all of them! I say all of them! I don't know anybody! I say all of them! Do you hear, Marius? Look here, you are as much a baron as my slipper! They were all bandits, those who served Robespierre! All brigands who served Bu-o-na-parté! All traitors who betrayed, betrayed, betrayed! Their legitimate king! All cowards who ran from the Prussians and English at Waterloo! That's what I know. If your father is among them I don't know him, I'm sorry, so much the worse. Your humble servant, sir!"

In turn, it was Marius who now became the coal, and M. Gillenormand the bellows. Marius shuddered in every limb, he had no idea what to do, his head was burning. He was the priest who sees all his wafers thrown to the winds, the fakir [member of a Muslim religious order] seeing a passerby spit on his idol. He could not allow such things to be said before him. But what could he do? His father had just been trodden underfoot and stamped on in his presence, but by whom? By his grandfather. How could he avenge the one without outraging the other? It

was impossible for him to insult his grandfather, and it was equally impossible for him not to avenge his father. On one hand a sacred tomb, on the other a white head. For a few moments he felt dizzy and staggering with all this whirlwind in his head; then he raised his eyes, looked straight at his grandfather, and cried in a thundering voice: "Down with the Bourbons, and that great hog Louis XVIII!"

Louis XVIII had been dead for four years; but that made no difference to him.

Scarlet as he was, the old man suddenly turned whiter than his hair. He turned toward a bust of the Duc de Berry that stood on the mantel and bowed to it profoundly with a sort of peculiar majesty. Then he walked twice, slowly and in silence, from the fireplace to the window and from the window to the fireplace, covering the whole length of the room and making the parquet creak as if an image of stone were walking over it. The second time, he bent toward his daughter, who was enduring the shock with the stupor of an aged sheep, and said to her with a smile that was almost calm, "A baron like Monsieur and a bourgeois like myself cannot remain under the same roof."

And all at once straightening up, pallid, trembling, terrible, his forehead swelling with the fearful radiance of anger, he stretched his arm towards Marius and cried out, "Be off!"

Marius left the house.

The next day, M. Gillenormand said to his daughter, "You will send sixty pistoles [old gold coins] every six months to that blood drinker, and never speak of him to me again."

RESPONDING TO LITERATURE

1. What political conflict of the period does the heated clash between Marius and his grandfather represent?
2. What sort of person is Monsieur Gillenormand?
3. If Marius's father had not been a hero at the Battle of Waterloo, do you think Marius still would have become a revolutionary? Explain your answer.
4. **Supporting an Opinion** Was the era of the French Revolution and Napoleon "the greatest history that men have ever made," as Marius claims? Support your answer with evidence.

Connections Across Time

Historical Significance The French Revolution's ideals of "liberty, equality, and fraternity" continue to inspire people around the world. In parts of Africa, China, the Middle East, and Latin America, people of diverse backgrounds struggle for political freedom.

Many of these struggles have been ignited by feelings of nationalism, as people yearn for self-rule and the return of their traditions. As Napoleon learned in the collapse of his empire, even the strictest military control cannot suppress the power of nationalism.

Using Key Terms

Write the key term that completes each sentence. Then write a sentence for each term not chosen.

a. bourgeoisie
b. buffer states
c. conscription
d. coup d'état
e. émigrés
f. estate
g. dictatorship
h. liberalism
i. nationalism
j. plebiscite
k. reactionaries
l. tithe
m. unicameral legislature

1. Napoleon Bonaparte's move to become Consul for life was supported by a _____ , or popular vote.
2. Intense feelings of _____ caused people to fight for self-rule and a return to their traditional customs.
3. French revolutionaries resorted to _____ , or drafting civilians, in their fight against European powers.
4. _____ wanted to return absolute monarchs to Europe after the collapse of Napoleon's empire in 1814.
5. Before the revolution the Catholic Church in France was supported by a _____ , or a 10 percent tax on income.

Technology Activity

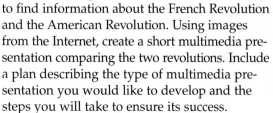

Developing a Multimedia Presentation Use a computerized card catalog or the Internet to find information about the French Revolution and the American Revolution. Using images from the Internet, create a short multimedia presentation comparing the two revolutions. Include a plan describing the type of multimedia presentation you would like to develop and the steps you will take to ensure its success.

Using Your History Journal

Napoleon's army lost 400,000 soldiers in the retreat from Russia. Many more died in other battles. Were the reforms of the French Revolution worth its cost? Answer this question from the viewpoint of the character you chose at the beginning of the chapter in an opinion article for a French newspaper to be published upon the death of Napoleon in 1821.

Reviewing Facts

1. **History** Identify the causes and effects of the French Revolution.
2. **History** Explain why Louis XVI was executed.
3. **Government** List three accomplishments of the French National Assembly.
4. **Citizenship** Describe the role of women, peasants, and urban workers in the French Revolution.
5. **History** Describe the Concert of Europe.

Critical Thinking

1. **Apply** Why was the creation of a French republic a significant turning point in history?
2. **Apply** What Enlightenment ideas affected the French Revolution?
3. **Synthesize** What circumstances, if any, justify a violent revolution? What other means could be used to change an unfair or tyrannical system of government?
4. **Evaluate** In your opinion, did Napoleon's thirst for power help or hurt France? Europe?

Geography in History

1. **Location** Refer to the map below. What is the global address of Paris?
2. **Place** What role did agriculture play in starting the French Revolution?
3. **Movement** Why did Napoleon want to prevent British ships from trading at various European ports?

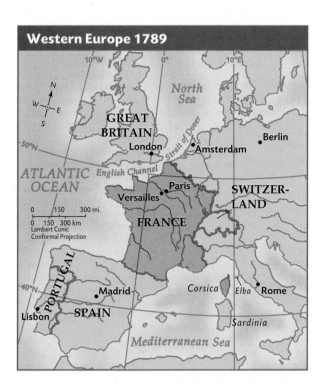

Western Europe 1789

Understanding Themes

1. **Revolution** What similarities and differences do you see between the American and the French Revolutions?
2. **Change** What specific rights did the Declaration of Rights apply to French citizens? How did the Declaration and other revolutionary events affect the position of French women?
3. **Conflict** How did violence and fear among the French people contribute to Napoleon's seizure of power?
4. **Movement** How did the desire to expand his European empire help to bring about the downfall of Napoleon?
5. **Reaction** How did the Congress of Vienna show itself to be a strong reaction to revolutionary ideals?

Linking Past and Present

1. Napoleon tried to use military force to unite Europe under his rule. What attempts have been made in this century to forcibly bring Europe or large areas of Europe under one form of government?
2. Unity remains a goal of many Europeans. What recent efforts are peacefully uniting the countries of Europe?

Skill Practice

The diagram below shows the growth of the French army in the early years of the French Revolution. The graph is divided into sizes relative to the additions made to the army between 1791 and 1793. Study the diagram and answer the following questions.

1. How large was the French army in the summer of 1792?
2. How many troops were added to France's army in 1793?
3. What was the total number of French troops called into service during this period?
4. If this information were on a bar graph, the horizontal axis (line) would list the dates. The vertical axis would have labels in units of 100,000 each. What would each bar represent?

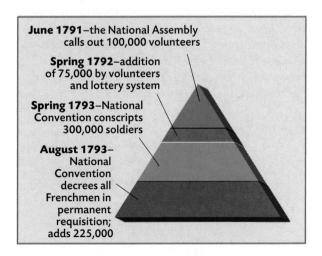

June 1791–the National Assembly calls out 100,000 volunteers

Spring 1792–addition of 75,000 by volunteers and lottery system

Spring 1793–National Convention conscripts 300,000 soldiers

August 1793– National Convention decrees all Frenchmen in permanent requisition; adds 225,000

ABCNEWS iNTERACTIVE™

Turning Points in World History

The Scientific Revolution

Setting up the Video

Work with a group of your classmates to view "The Scientific Revolution" on the videodisc *Turning Points in World History*. The scientific revolution played a large role in shaping the world as we know it today. The seventeenth century changed dramatically from a reliance on faith and mysticism to include scientific thinking that led to many new inventions. This program examines the scientific revolution and its effects on civilization.

Hands-On Activity

Collect the following items for an invention you will create: two plastic spoons, one rubber band, two paper clips, a sheet of paper measuring 8x11, and a roll of scotch tape. Use all of the items to invent a gadget for practical use. Demonstrate your invention to the class.

Side One, Chapter 10

View the video by scanning the bar code or by entering the chapter number on your keypad and pressing Search. (Also available in VHS format.)

Surfing the "Net"

Napoleonic Code

One of Napoleon's greatest gifts to France was his contribution to French civil law. In the Napoleonic Code, he changed old feudal laws to laws that were consistent and included some revolutionary reforms. The Napoleonic Code was a compromise between the ideas of the French Revolution and older ideas. It gave new freedoms to the people, for example, but maintained the system of inheritance. To learn about the Napoleonic Code look on the Internet.

Getting There

Follow these steps to gather information about the Napoleonic Code.
1. Go to a search engine. Type in the phrase *napoleonic code*.

2. After typing in the phrase, enter words such as the following to focus your search:
   • *principles*   • *government*   • *law*
3. The search engine should provide you with a number of links to follow. Links are "pointers" to different sites on the Internet and commonly appear as blue underlined words.

What to Do When You Are There

Click on the links to navigate through the pages of information and gather your findings. Using a word processor, create a chart comparing the American Bill of Rights to the Napoleonic Code. Share your findings with the class.

Unit 5 Digest

From about 1600 to the early 1800s, people in the Western world lived through a time of revolution, or swift and far-reaching change. During this period, Western thinkers laid the foundation of modern science and developed new ideas about society and politics. The two most important ideas were democracy—the right of the people to take an active part in government—and nationalism—the right of people who share a common culture to have their own nation. In some areas, people influenced by the new ideas rebelled against monarchs in the hope of creating better and more democratic societies.

During the 1700s Europeans boasted they had entered an Age of Enlightenment, when the light of reason would free all people from the darkness of ignorance and superstition. They looked to France as the leading center of Enlightenment thought. Through the printed word and at public gatherings, French thinkers called philosophes claimed that science and reason could be used to promote progress in all areas of human life.

Chapter 20
Scientific Revolution

During the 1500s and 1600s, European thinkers began relying on their own reasoning rather than automatically accepting traditional beliefs. In their investigation of nature, they gradually developed the scientific method, a way of finding scientific truth through observation and experimentation. They also developed new instruments, such as the telescope and microscope, to help them in their work. Over time, each discovery or invention led to others, creating an explosion of knowledge known as the scientific revolution.

The advance of science transformed the European understanding of the natural world. The work of scientists such as Galileo and Isaac Newton enabled Europeans to view the universe as a huge, orderly machine that worked according to definite laws that could be stated mathematically. Many European thinkers also came to believe that people could also use reason to discover the natural laws governing human behavior. They claimed that once these laws were known, people could use the laws to improve their society. English philosophers Thomas Hobbes and John Locke applied scientific reasoning to the study of government. Locke's basic conclusions—that government's authority rested on popular consent, and that the people had a right to overthrow an unjust government—were later important in the development of democracy in Europe and North America.

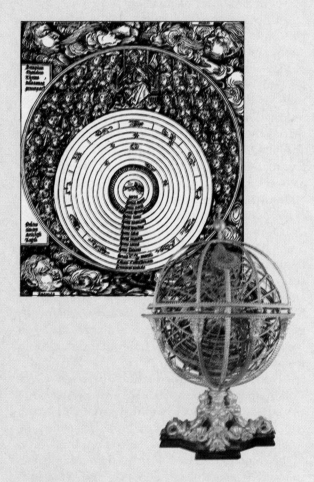

Visualizing History **The Copernican model of the universe placed the sun at the center.** Ptolemy's second-century model had the sun and the planets revolving around Earth. *The work of what two scientists enabled Europeans to view the universe as a huge, orderly machine?*

Chapter 21
English and American Revolutions

While Europe experienced a revolution in science and ideas, its monarchs faced growing opposition to royal authority. The first successful challenge to the power of monarchy came in England. There, during the 1640s, a violent civil war between supporters of the Crown and the supporters of Parliament ended with the monarchy's defeat. A republic under the leading parliamentary general Oliver Cromwell brought reforms and efficient government, but most English people grew to resent its Puritan rules. In 1660 the monarchy was restored, with the king and Parliament sharing power in an uneasy relationship.

In 1685 James II, a Roman Catholic, angered the English with his desire to restore Catholicism and a strong monarchy. In 1688 Protestant nobles in Parliament invited Mary, James's Protestant daughter, and William of Orange, her husband and the ruler of the Netherlands, to take the throne. In return, William and Mary agreed to a Bill of Rights that assured the English people basic civil liberties and made the monarch subject to Parliament. During the next 100 years, England developed into a constitutional monarchy, in which the monarch's authority was limited and Parliament became the major political institution.

During the mid-1700s, Great Britain (formed by a union of England and Scotland in 1707) tried to tighten its control over its recently acquired overseas empire, especially in North America. Already enjoying a large measure of self-government, the North American colonies opposed Parliament's efforts to enforce trade laws and impose taxes on them. They began to press for even more freedom from the home country.

During the 1700s, relations between Great Britain and the North American colonies steadily worsened. The arrival of British troops in North America to put down colonial protests signaled the beginning of the American Revolution. In 1776, 13 of the colonies declared their freedom from British rule and became a new nation—the United States of America. Five years later, the American victory at

Visualizing History Mocking British Rule, *Horse Throwing His Master* represented American colonists in revolt against the British monarchy. *How did colonial economic interests help to ignite the American Revolution?*

Yorktown ended the war, and in 1783 the British officially recognized the independence of their former colonies. Following the Revolutionary War, the 13 newly independent states in 1788 ratified the Constitution of the United States. This document established the framework for a federal republic and later provided a Bill of Rights that protected personal liberties. From the 1700s to the present century, the democratic ideals of the American Revolution have inspired colonial peoples struggling to escape from the hold of empires.

History & Art *The Spirit of '76 by* Archibald Willard. Abbot Hall, Marblehead, Massachusetts
Revolution was romanticized in the art of the 1800s. *Why did the American colonies rebel?*

Chapter 22
The French Revolution

The American Revolution influenced the French people, who became increasingly critical of their monarchy. Under the rule of King Louis XVI, France's nobles and clergy enjoyed power and privileges, while the majority of people paid most taxes and had little say in the government. In 1789, social injustice, economic distress, and Enlightenment ideas combined to spark the French Revolution.

The early period of the Revolution saw the creation of a constitutional monarchy with a representative form of government. Delegates in the new National Assembly ended class privileges and guaranteed rights for all citizens. The king's refusal to accept the Revolution and the threat of foreign invasion, however, led to the monarchy's overthrow and the formation of a democratic republic. The revolutionaries then raised a large army to push back the foreign invaders and carried out a Reign of Terror at home to crush opposition to the Revolution.

Instability eventually brought the general Napoleon Bonaparte to power in 1799. Although Napoleon professed revolutionary ideals, he made himself emperor. With a powerful army, he brought much of Europe under French control. By 1814, the combined might of France's enemies and the growth of anti-French nationalism in conquered lands led to Napoleon's defeat. European leaders at the Congress of Vienna sought to limit French power and restore monarchies in Europe. Democracy and nationalism, however, emerged as powerful forces in the 1800s.

SURVEYING UNIT 5

1. **Chapter 20** Why did European political thinkers during the Enlightenment stress the importance of natural laws?
2. **Chapter 21** How was Enlightenment thought reflected in the political events and the political changes that took place in North America during the 1700s?
3. **Chapter 22** Compare the political revolutions in England, North America, and France. Which revolution was the most conservative? Which was the most radical? Explain your answers.

Industry and Nationalism

Then & Now

For centuries wealthy landowners in Europe controlled a static agricultural economy. Peasant families farmed strips of land, and small industries and trades met local needs. Then, in England in the late 1700s, innovations in farming made agriculture a profitable business. An agricultural revolution helped start a revolution in industry, beginning in textiles. The factory system expanded the power and wealth of the middle class. While scientific and medical advances improved life for many, in much of Europe the poor remained powerless.

How long would it take you to walk to school? The railroad began the revolution in transportation. When a German engineer redesigned the internal combustion engine to run on gasoline, the automobile took center stage. Within a few decades the automobile would transform society in every industrial country.

A Global Chronology

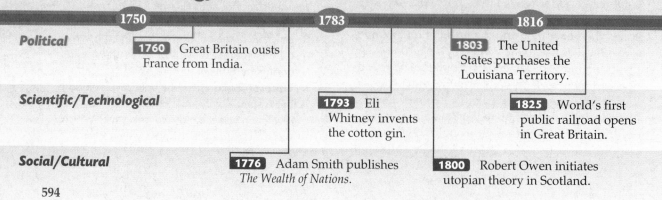

1750 **1783** **1816**

Political
   1760 Great Britain ousts France from India.
   1803 The United States purchases the Louisiana Territory.

Scientific/Technological
   1793 Eli Whitney invents the cotton gin.
   1825 World's first public railroad opens in Great Britain.

Social/Cultural
   1776 Adam Smith publishes *The Wealth of Nations.*
   1800 Robert Owen initiates utopian theory in Scotland.

Steam locomotive and wood car

Portfolio Project

Graphs can show the dramatic changes caused by the Industrial Revolution. Create several graphs that illustrate these changes from the early 1800s to the 1900s. Subjects of your graphs for any industrializing nation or group of nations may include: population growth; spread of railroads; and production of goods such as cotton, steel, coal, and oil. Libraries and the Internet have good historical references for these statistics. After completing the graphs, write a list of questions that can be answered from the data shown in each graph.

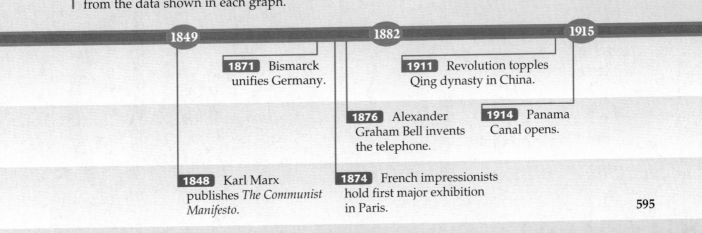

1849

1882

1915

1871 Bismarck unifies Germany.

1911 Revolution topples Qing dynasty in China.

1876 Alexander Graham Bell invents the telephone.

1914 Panama Canal opens.

1848 Karl Marx publishes *The Communist Manifesto*.

1874 French impressionists hold first major exhibition in Paris.

595

The Spread of Ideas

Industrialization

*T*he rise of industry changed the world forever. So dramatic were the changes that historians have labeled the period the Industrial Revolution. Although the revolution began in Britain, it respected neither time nor place. The revolution traveled beyond Britain to touch every nation on earth.

Great Britain
Workshop of the World

The birth of industry needed certain preconditions: the science, incentive, and money capital to build machines; a labor force to run them; raw materials and markets to make the system profitable; and efficient farms to feed a new group of workers. At the start of the 1700s, Great Britain possessed all these conditions. Here industrialism first took root.

As with the development of agriculture, no one person can be credited with the invention of industry. Instead, it grew from the innovations of individuals who developed machines to do work formerly done by humans and animals. One inventor built on the ideas of another. In 1705, for example, Thomas Newcomen devised a crude steam engine to pump water out of coal mines. In 1769 James Watt improved upon Newcomen's work and built a more efficient steam engine. Other inventors adapted Watt's engine to run cloth-making machines. Business owners soon brought machines and workers together in a single place called a factory.

By the 1800s, industry had catapulted Great Britain into a position of world leadership. "[Britain has] triumphantly established herself as the workshop of the world," boasted one leader. It was impossible to monopolize this idea. Workshops began to hum in America.

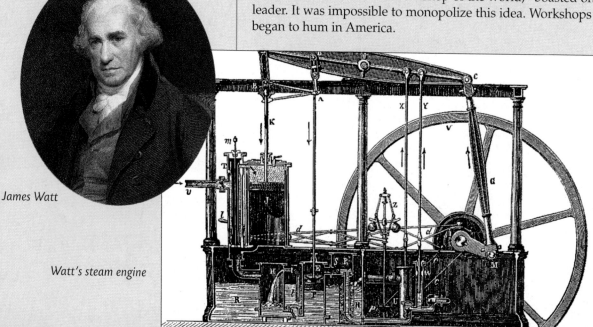

James Watt

Watt's steam engine

The United States
The Revolution Spreads

Great Britain tried to keep the secrets of industry locked up. It forbade the export of industrial machines. It also barred the people who built and operated the machines from leaving the country. In 1789, however, a young factory supervisor named Samuel Slater found a way to escape. He disguised himself as a farmhand and boarded a ship for New York.

Working entirely from memory, Slater built a mill in Pawtucket, Rhode Island. On December 20, 1790, the mill turned out the first machine-made cotton yarn produced in America.

Within two years, Slater had sales offices in Salem, New York City, Baltimore, and Philadelphia. As Slater's mills turned out cotton, the United States began churning out its own brilliant industrial inventors. They produced more than just machines. They came up with new industrial principles such as Eli Whitney's use of standardized parts and Henry Ford's use of the assembly line. Together these two ideas gave the world mass production—a concept that would revolutionize people's lives around the globe.

Samuel Slater's mill

Japan
The Search for Markets

In 1853, the Industrial Revolution traveled to Japan in the form of a fleet of United States steamships sent to open the island to trade. "What we had taken as a fire at sea," recalled one Japanese observer, "was really smoke coming out of their smokestacks."

The military power produced by United States industry shook the Japanese. Recalled the same observer, "What a joke, the steaming teapot fixed by America—Just four cups [ships], and we cannot sleep at night."

The Japanese temporarily gave in to American demands. But they also vowed that they too would possess industry. By the start of the 1900s, Japan had joined other industrial nations in the search for markets. By 1914 Japan's merchant fleet was the sixth largest in the world and their foreign trade had increased one hundred-fold in value in fifty years.

Matthew Perry's steamboat in Tokyo Bay

LINKING THE IDEAS

1. How was the idea for a cotton mill brought from Great Britain to the United States?
2. What feature of the American fleet most impressed the Japanese in 1853?

Critical Thinking

3. **Drawing Conclusions** Why did the British want to control the spread of an idea that made production of goods easier?

Age of Industry

Chapter Themes

▶ **Relation to Environment** Before the Industrial Revolution of the 1700s and 1800s, most Europeans live in isolated rural villages and depend on the land. *Section 1*

▶ **Innovation** A series of inventions and new procedures in agriculture and industry transform economies in Europe and North America. *Section 2*

▶ **Change** Throughout the Western world, new urban centers based on industry develop along with the rise of new social classes. *Section 3*

▶ **Conflict** Workers in Europe and North America organize to gain better wages and improved working conditions. *Section 4*

The Storyteller

Change swept through Europe and North America as new coal mines and iron works began to dominate rural landscapes. Susan Pitchforth, an 11-year-old British girl, was just one of the millions of men, women, and children who left farming villages to find work in these growing industries.

Like countless others, Susan suffered difficult and dangerous industrial working conditions. When the British Parliament investigated horrible conditions in coal mines, young Susan told them her story:

"I have worked at this pit going on two years ... I walk a mile and a half to my work, both in winter and summer. I run 24 [loads] a day; I cannot come up till I have done them all."

Historical Significance

What changes took place in Europe and North America during the Industrial Revolution? How does the Industrial Revolution affect life throughout the world today?

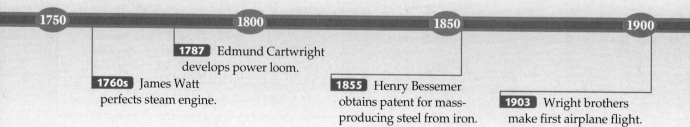

| 1750 | 1800 | 1850 | 1900 |

1787 Edmund Cartwright develops power loom.

1760s James Watt perfects steam engine.

1855 Henry Bessemer obtains patent for mass-producing steel from iron.

1903 Wright brothers make first airplane flight.

Coalbrookdale by Night by Philip de Loutherberg.
Science Museum, London, England

Your History Journal

Build a time line of inventions of the Industrial Revolution beginning with John Kay's improved loom and ending with the first airplane.

c. 1700s Domestic system is widespread in European towns and villages.

c. 1750 About 75 percent of Europeans live in rural areas.

Section 1

Living From the Land

Setting the Scene

▶ **Terms to Define**
  domestic system

▶ **People to Meet**
  Charles Dickens

▶ **Places to Locate**
  London

Find Out What was daily life like before the rise of modern industry?

The Storyteller

Landlords increased their income by removing common farmers from their rented fields. An anonymous poem passed judgment on the enclosure of Thornborough landlords in 1798:

Ye Thornbro' youths bewail with me;
Ye shepherds lay your pipes aside,
  No longer tune the merry glee,
  For we are rob'd of all our pride.
  The time alas will soon approach,
  When we must all our pasture yield;
  The wealthy on our rights encroach
  And will enclose our common field.

Haymaking in rural England

—adapted from *English Parliamentary Enclosure*, Michael Turner, 1980

During the 1700s and 1800s, a series of innovations in agriculture and industry led to profound economic and social change throughout Europe and the United States. Urban industrial economies emerged in these areas and eventually spread around the world. This transformation, which became known as the Industrial Revolution, began when power-driven machinery in factories replaced work done in homes—altering the way people had lived and worked for hundreds of years.

Cloth making provides a dramatic example of the far-reaching effects of the Industrial Revolution. In the 1700s a home weaver worked many hours to produce a yard of cloth. A century later, a worker operating machines in a textile mill could make 50 times more cloth.

As adventurous businesspeople brought machines and workers together in factories, industries produced mass quantities of goods. Millions of people in search of new opportunities to make a living left rural villages to find factory work in growing towns and cities. A new era of mechanization had arrived.

A Harsh Way of Life

Before the dawn of the Industrial Revolution in the 1700s, people lived in much the same way their ancestors had lived for hundreds of years. Nature's seasons and religious traditions measured time, and social change was rare. Relying almost solely on farming to make a living, people planted and harvested fields, hoped for good weather, and lived always under the threat of disease.

Families, both rich and poor, remained relatively small because of a very high infant death rate. One baby in three died in his or her first year of life, and only one in two people reached age 21. Life expectancy hovered around age 40. People expected life to be short and harsh. As one mother in the 1770s said after her baby's death, "One cannot grieve after her much, and I have just now other things to think of."

Only 25 percent of Europeans lived in towns or cities in the 1700s. **London** was the largest city in Europe in 1750 with about 700,000 people. Yet it too had a rural character. The famous British novelist **Charles Dickens** described the sights of a London morning in the early 1800s:

History & Art *Harvest Scene* by George Vicat Cole. Christie's, London, England *What were the village commons?*

> 66 By degrees, other shops began to be unclosed, and a few scattered people were met with. Then, came straggling groups of labourers going to their work; then men and women with fish baskets on their heads; donkey carts laden with vegetables; chaise carts filled with live-stock or whole carcasses of meat, milk women with pails; an unbroken concourse of people.... 99
> —Charles Dickens, *Oliver Twist*, 1837

Most people in preindustrial times lived in small country villages consisting of a few hundred people. Many never ventured beyond the village borders. When braver people traveled to other cities and towns, their tales delighted their less worldly neighbors.

Village Life

Virtually all rural villagers were farmers. Wealthy landowners controlled the majority of the village land, renting most of it to small farming families. Families owned or rented small strips of land in several areas of the village. This practice ensured both fair land distribution and economic protection should disaster strike any one field. Farmers worked the land cooperatively, jointly deciding what crops to grow and when to plant and harvest.

In most of the villages, private and public lands were not separated or fenced off. The public lands, called the village commons, consisted of woodlands, pastures, and less fertile land near the village. For centuries, farmers could gather wood and

graze their livestock on the commons. Poorer farmers even used these public lands for raising crops.

Village economies were limited largely to the local area because transporting goods to other areas was difficult and unprofitable. Rain turned the few roads into muddy rivers. For this reason, villages had to be nearly self-sufficient. People grew enough food for their families and perhaps a small amount to sell to nearby towns. They made their own homes, clothes, and tools from products raised in the fields or gathered from the land.

The richest rural landowners lived on sprawling country estates with a huge main house, cottages, several barns, and extensive fields. Landowners and their families lived lavishly. Servants ran the households and catered to the families' needs.

People who rented land from the landowners lived quite differently. Most lived in small, smoky, poorly lighted cottages with dirt floors. Since the poorest farming families often did not have barns, they sometimes shared their cramped living quarters with farm animals.

All daily activities revolved around farming, an occupation dominated by tradition. Farmers used the same simple methods and tools their ancestors had used and relied on nature to provide good growing seasons. Nature, however, was never predictable, and harvests ranged from plentiful to disastrously small.

Everyone in the farming family worked hard. From morning to night, husband, wife, and children worked together. Boys helped their fathers in the fields or at the workbench. Girls helped their mothers with chores such as milking cows and household duties such as churning butter and preparing meals.

Early Industries

In addition to farming, many people worked in small industries or in coal mines. These industries met local needs for goods such as coal, glass, iron, and clothing and employed a small number of workers. Since many workers were also farm workers, work schedules were coordinated with the agricultural cycle.

During harvest time nail makers, glassblowers, ironworkers, and miners helped farmers with the crops; likewise, in the winter farmworkers worked in the mines and in the workshops. This close relationship between farming and industry provided a steadier income to workers than either farming or industry alone.

Making Wool

In Great Britain, the woolen industry had for centuries been second only to farming in the numbers of people it employed and in the volume of trade it created. In the 1700s the demand for wool grew so great that merchants hired workers to produce woolens in their own homes. This system of labor, called the **domestic system**, spread to other industries such as leather working and lace making and was a widespread method used throughout Europe in the 1700s.

The domestic system depended on a network of workers. In the case of wool, a merchant first bought the raw fiber and divided it among several families. Women and children usually cleaned, sorted, and spun the fiber into thread or yarn. Men usually did the actual weaving. Then the merchant collected the yarn, paid the spinner a fee, and took the yarn to a weaver. The material next went to a fuller, who shaped and cleaned the material, and at last to the dyer for coloring. Finally, the merchant took the finished products to market and sold them for the highest possible price.

The domestic system had many benefits. Workers set their own hours and could tend to duties at home during work breaks. Women cared for children, tended vegetable gardens, and cooked meals while they earned money at home. Men carried on farming tasks, such as plowing and planting fields. Children also helped their parents. In one British region, children attended special schools to learn the art of lace making. With this skill they contributed to the family income. The domestic system provided work and income during hard times, saving many families from starvation. Its simple rural domestic practices later became the basis on which the technology and skills of the Industrial Revolution were built.

Mining Coal

The domestic system also had its place in coal mining. Coal fields often lay under farmland. The people who worked the mines often became farm laborers during the harvest, and farm horses pulled coal wagons from the pits. In some coal fields, women and children even hauled baskets of coal from the pits. One observer described these loaded baskets, saying it was "frequently more than one man could do to lift the burden."

With the money earned from mining or farmwork, country people might buy in nearby towns the few things they could not manufacture for themselves. Craftspeople sold handmade guns, furniture, and clothing in their small shops. Some craftspeople sent their goods to foreign markets in exchange for imported goods and traded the rest for food from nearby farmers and products from other local craftspeople.

Yet changes to this way of life were on the horizon. The development of new machinery and sources of power would soon upset the domestic system, transforming forever the way people lived and worked.

Section 2

The Beginnings of Change

Setting the Scene

▶ **Terms to Define**

enclosure movement, capital, entrepreneur, factory system

▶ **People to Meet**

James Hargreaves, Richard Arkwright, Edmund Cartwright, Eli Whitney, James Watt, Henry Bessemer, Robert Fulton

Find Out   Why did the Industrial Revolution begin in Great Britain?

The Storyteller

About 210,000 men built the first railroads in Britain. They called themselves "navvies." Mostly the men worked in silence. The only British navvies whose singing was noticed were the Welsh, whose songs were mainly hymns. Most other songs that navvies sang while they worked have disappeared. One tune, however, heard on the railway in 1859 gives some insight into the navvies' lives:

> *…I'm a navvy on the line.*
> *I get me five-and-twenty bob a week,*
> *Besides me overtime.*
> *Roast Beef and boiled beef*
> *An' puddin' made of eggs….*

—adapted from *The Victorian Railway*, Jack Simmons, 1991

For hundreds of years, British farmers had planted crops and kept livestock on unfenced private and public lands. Village society depended on this age-old system of farming and grazing. By the late 1700s, however, wealthy British landowners would end this open-field system, which had been slowly giving way to private ownership since the 1100s.

The landowners felt that larger farms with enclosed fields would increase farming efficiency and productivity. Parliament supported this enclosure movement, passing laws that allowed landowners to take over and fence off private and common lands. In the 1700s the enclosure movement transformed rural Great Britain. Many small farmers dependent on village lands were forced to move to towns and cities to find work. At the same time, landowners practiced new, more efficient farming methods.

To raise crop yields, landowners mixed different kinds of soils and used new crop rotation systems. One landowner, Lord Charles Townshend, urged the growing of turnips to enrich exhausted soil. Another reformer, Robert Bakewell, bred stronger horses for farm work and fatter sheep and cattle for meat. The inventor Jethro Tull developed a seed drill that enabled farmers to plant seeds in orderly rows instead of scattering them over the fields. As innovation and competition replaced traditional methods, agriculture underwent a revolution that improved the quality, quantity, and profitability of farm goods.

Great Britain Leads the Way

This agricultural revolution helped Great Britain to lead the Industrial Revolution. Successful farming businesses provided landowners with money to invest in growing industries. Many

Early train

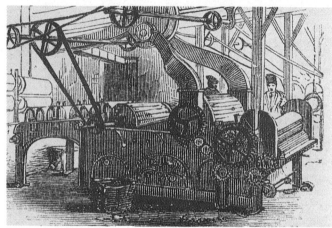

The task of beating cotton by hand was replaced by a beating and lapping machine in the 1700s. *How did Parliament encourage investment in industry?*

displaced farmers became industrial workers. These factors added to the key elements for industrial success that Great Britain already possessed—capital, natural resources, and labor supply.

Money and Industry

Capital, or money to invest in labor, machines, and raw materials, is essential for the growth of industry. Many British people became very wealthy during the 1700s. Landowners and other members of the aristocracy profited not only from new large-scale farming but also from overseas commerce and the slave trade, as you learned in Chapter 17. At the same time, an emerging middle class of British merchants and shopkeepers had grown more prosperous from trade.

Industry provided the aristocracy and the middle class with new opportunities to invest their money. By investing in growing industries, they stood a good chance of making a profit. Parliament encouraged investment by passing laws that helped the growing businesses.

Natural Resources

Great Britain's wealth also included its rich supply of natural resources. The country had fine harbors and a large network of rivers that flowed year-round. Water provided power for developing industries and transported raw materials and finished goods.

Great Britain also had huge supplies of iron and coal, the principal raw materials of the Industrial Revolution. Iron and the steel made from it proved to be the ideal materials for building industrial machinery. An abundance of coal also helped to fuel industry.

Large Labor Supply

Perhaps the country's greatest natural resource was its growing population of workers. Improvements in farming led to an increased availability of food. Better, more nutritious food allowed people to enjoy longer, healthier lives. In just one century, England's population nearly doubled, growing from about 5 million in 1700 to about 9 million in 1800.

The changes in farming also helped to increase the supply of industrial workers. With the introduction of machinery such as the steel plow, farms needed fewer workers. Former farmworkers left their homes to find jobs in more populated and industrialized areas.

Ambitious British people in the middle and upper classes organized and managed the country's growing industries. These risk-taking entrepreneurs (AHN•truh•pruh•NUHRS), or businesspeople, set up industries by bringing together capital, labor, and new industrial inventions.

By the mid-1700s, the British domestic system was ready for change. The textile industry led the way.

Growing Textile Industries

In the 1700s people in Great Britain and overseas were eager to buy cool, colorful cotton cloth. Since the domestic system could not meet the demand, cotton merchants looked for new ways to expand production. A series of technological advances would revolutionize cloth production.

Advances in Machinery

One of the first innovations in cloth making occurred at the dawn of the Industrial Revolution. Weaving cloth was difficult and time-consuming work. Weavers had to push a shuttle back and forth across a loom by hand. Then they had to beat the woof—the threads that run crosswise—down tightly against the previous row. The width of the fabric was limited by the distance a weaver could "throw" the shuttle.

In 1733 British clock maker John Kay improved the loom with his "flying shuttle." Instead of pushing the shuttle by hand, the weaver simply pulled sharply on a cord, and the shuttle "flew" across the loom. Wider fabrics could be woven at a faster pace.

Using the flying shuttle, weavers could produce two to three times more material; thus they needed more yarn than ever from the spinners. To answer this need, **James Hargreaves**, a weaver-carpenter, in the 1760s invented a more efficient spinning machine that he called the spinning jenny. Early models of the spinning jenny enabled one person to spin 6 to 7 threads at a time; later refinements increased this number to 80 threads.

While the spinning jenny revolutionized spinning in the home, another invention revolutionized spinning in factories and industrial settings. In 1768 **Richard Arkwright**, a struggling barber with a great interest in machines, developed the water frame, a huge spinning machine that ran continually on waterpower.

By 1779 spinner Samuel Crompton combined the best features of the spinning jenny and the water frame into a new machine called the "spinning mule." It produced strong thread that could be woven into high-quality muslin cloth. Until this time, such fine cloth had to be imported from Asia.

Producing More Cloth

The new spinning machines produced more yarn or thread than there were weavers to use it. In 1787 **Edmund Cartwright**, a British poet and minister, answered this shortage of weavers with the development of a power loom. Running on horse, water, or steam power, the mechanical loom made it possible for weavers to keep up with the amount of yarn produced.

These new inventions created a growing need for raw cotton. Yet raw cotton was expensive because cleaning the seeds out of it was a slow and tedious job. In 1793 **Eli Whitney**, an American inventor, developed a machine that cleaned cotton 50 times more quickly than a person could. The cotton gin helped the booming British textile industry to overcome its last major hurdle on its journey toward full mechanization.

Geography

An Industrial City

The growth of industrial cities depended on geographic factors such as the availability of raw materials and accessible routes. The city of Manchester in northern England has had many geographic advantages. It lies close to coal fields and the Irwell and Mersey rivers. A canal connects the city to the Irish Sea, making Manchester an inland port.

Despite being a wool trade center, Manchester retained a rural atmosphere in the 1700s. Merchants lived in city townhouses, and people enjoyed sailing on the Irwell River. During the 1800s, Manchester grew into a textile-manufacturing city with world markets. Mills and warehouses replaced private homes in many areas, and

Manchester, England

the Irwell became so polluted it was described as "a flood of liquid manure." Some Britons at the time saw Manchester's transformation as evidence of the evils of industrialization. Others, however, saw the change as a symbol of progress.

During the first half of the 1900s, Manchester's production of textiles declined steadily. The growth of other businesses, however, helped the city and its surrounding communities to retain their economic importance in the British economy. Today, Manchester is England's third largest urban area, after London and Birmingham, and is still a major center of trade and finance.

Linking Past and Present **ACTIVITY**

Discuss how Manchester became an industrial city. Do you think that what happened to Manchester can be called "progress"? How do cities today compare/contrast with cities of the 1800s?

Eli Whitney's original cotton gin was a simple device that one person could turn by hand. *What task did the cotton gin perform?*

The Factory System

Since the new textile machinery was too large and costly for most workers to use in their homes, industrialists gradually moved cloth production out of workers' cottages and into the large buildings they built near major waterways. This marked the beginning of the factory system, an organized method of production that brought workers and machines together under the control of managers. The waterways powered the machines and provided transportation for raw materials and finished cloth.

As the factory system spread, manufacturers required more power than horses and water could provide. Steam power answered these growing needs. In the 1760s a Scottish mathematician named

James Watt designed an efficient steam engine. Watt's steam engine helped to set the Industrial Revolution in full motion. Factories that had once closed down when the river froze or flowed too low could now run continuously on steam power. The steam engine also enabled industrialists to build factories far from waterways.

Industrial Developments

The use of factory machinery increased demand for iron and steel. In response, the iron industry developed new technologies. In the mid-1800s William Kelly, an American ironworker, and **Henry Bessemer**, a British engineer, developed methods to inexpensively produce steel from iron. Steel answered industry's need for a sturdy, workable metal.

At the same time, people worked to advance transportation systems throughout Europe and the United States. Improvements to the slow, often impassable roadways began when private companies began building and paving roads. Two Scottish engineers, Thomas Telford and John McAdam, further advanced road making with better drainage systems and the use of layers of crushed rock.

Water transportation also improved. In 1761 British workers dug one of the first modern canals to link coal fields with the industrial city of Manchester. Soon, a canal building craze began both in Europe and the United States.

A combination of steam power and steel would soon revolutionize both land and water transportation. In 1801 British engineer Richard Trevithick first brought steam-powered travel to land. He devised a steam-powered carriage that ran on wheels, and three years later, a steam locomotive that ran on rails. Later, in 1807 **Robert Fulton**, an American inventor, designed the first practical steamboat. Railroads and steamboats laid the foundations for a global economy and opened up new forms of investment.

SECTION 2 REVIEW

Recall
1. **Define** enclosure movement, capital, entrepreneur, factory system.
2. **Identify** James Hargreaves, Richard Arkwright, Edmund Cartwright, Eli Whitney, James Watt, Henry Bessemer, Robert Fulton.

3. **List** the factors that favored the early growth of industry in Great Britain.

Critical Thinking
4. **Synthesizing Information** Write a diary entry describing the thoughts of a British farmer who has lost land because of the enclosure movement.

Understanding Themes
5. **Innovation** Is an Industrial Revolution still happening today? If so, name some of today's revolutionary inventions or technological developments. How have these inventions and technological developments changed modern life?

1800		1850		1900

1839 Germany builds its first major railway.

1870 The Standard Oil Company is formed in the United States.

1895 Guglielmo Marconi develops wireless telegraph.

Section 3

The Growth of Industry

Setting the Scene

▶ **Terms to Define**
industrial capitalism, interchangeable parts, division of labor, partnership, corporation, depression

▶ **People to Meet**
Eli Whitney, Frederick Taylor, Henry Ford, Samuel Morse, Guglielmo Marconi, Alexander Graham Bell, Thomas Edison, Rudolf Diesel, Wilbur and Orville Wright

Find Out How did new technology advance the growth of industry?

The Storyteller

The people on the street in Paris waited impatiently for word from inside the store. "It works!" cried a spectator suddenly. Someone held up a hand. "Not so much noise. The people in Brantford [Canada] are talking ... and singing. It can be heard as plain as day." Now everyone wanted a turn at the receiver. Finally, at eleven o'clock the crowd went home. Mr. Bell's telephone was a success.

—adapted from *The Chord of Steel, The Story of the Invention of the Telephone*, Thomas B. Costain, 1960

Alexander Graham Bell's telephone

In 1789 a tall, ruddy young British worker boarded a ship bound for New York, listing his occupation in the ship's record as farmer. Although he looked like the farmer he claimed to be, Samuel Slater was actually a smuggler. Slater was stealing a valuable British commodity—industrial know-how. The 21-year-old spinner headed for the United States with the knowledge of how to build an industrial spinning wheel. When he arrived two months later, Slater introduced spinning technology to the United States.

By keeping spinning and other technologies secret, Great Britain had become the most productive country in the world. To maintain its position, Parliament passed laws restricting the flow of machines and skilled workers to other countries. Until 1824 the law that Samuel Slater had ignored prohibited craftspeople from moving to other countries. Another law made it illegal to export machinery. Nonetheless, by the late 1820s many mechanics and technicians had left Great Britain, carrying industrial knowledge with them.

Spread of Industry

As British workers left the country, Great Britain gave up trying to guard its industrial monopoly. Wealthy British industrialists saw that they could make money by spreading the Industrial Revolution to other countries.

In the mid-1800s, financiers funded railroad construction in India, Latin America, and North America. In Europe, British industrialists set up factories, supplying capital, equipment, and technical staff. The industrialists earned Great Britain the nickname "the workshop of the world." In other lands, however, large-scale manufacturing based on the factory system did not really take hold

Chapter 23 *Age of Industry* **607**

until 1870 or later. The major exceptions were France, Germany, and the United States.

Because the French government encouraged industrialization, France developed a large pool of outstanding scientists. In spite of this, France's industrialization was slow-paced. The Napoleonic Wars had strained the economy and depleted the workforce. For a long time the French economy depended more on farming and small businesses than on new industries. Yet with the growth of mining and railway construction, railway lines radiated in every direction from Paris by 1870.

Germany's efforts to industrialize proved more successful. Before 1830 Germans brought in some machinery from Britain and set up a few factories. In 1839 they used British capital to build the country's first major railway. In the following decade, strong coal, iron, and textile industries emerged. Even before the German states united in 1871, government funding had helped industry to grow.

At the same time, industrialization increased in the United States, especially in the Northeast. British capital and machinery, combined with American mechanical skills, promoted new indus-try. In time, shoe and textile factories flourished in New England. Coal mines and ironworks expanded in Pennsylvania. By 1870 the United States ranked with Great Britain and Germany as one of the world's three most industrialized countries.

Growth of Big Business

A major factor in spurring industrial growth was free enterprise, or capitalism, the economic system in which individuals and private firms, not the government, own the means of production—including land, machinery, and the workplace. In a capitalist system, individuals decide how they can make a profit and determine business practices accordingly.

Industrialists practiced industrial capitalism, which involved continually expanding factories or investing in new businesses. After investing in a factory, industrial capitalists used profits to hire more workers and buy materials and machines.

History & Art *Beirmeister and Wain Steel Forge* by P. S. Kroyer. Statens Museum, Copenhagen, Denmark **Industrialization spread throughout Europe.** *What were the three most industrialized nations in 1870?*

Mass Production

Looking to increase their profits, manufacturers invested in machines to replace more costly human labor. Fast-working, precise machines enabled industrialists to mass-produce, or to produce huge quantities of identical goods.

In the early 1800s **Eli Whitney**, inventor of the cotton gin, contributed the concept of interchangeable parts that increased factory production. Whitney's system involved machine-made parts that were exactly alike and easily assembled or exchanged. In the past, handmade parts were not uniform—each differed from the next to some degree.

By the 1890s industrial efficiency had become a science. **Frederick Taylor** encouraged manufacturers to divide tasks into detailed and specific segments of a step-by-step procedure.

Using Taylor's plan, industrialists devised a division of labor in their factories. Each worker performed a specialized task on a product as it moved by on a conveyor belt. The worker then returned the product to the belt where it continued down the line to the next worker. Because products were assembled in a moving line, this method was called the assembly line.

American automobile manufacturer **Henry Ford** used assembly-line methods in 1913 to mass-produce his Model T automobiles. Ford described the assembly line this way:

> ❝ The man who places a part does not fasten it. The man who puts in a bolt does not put in a nut; the man who puts on the nut does not tighten it. Every piece of work in the shop moves; it may move on hooks, on overhead chains…. No workman has anything to do with moving or lifting anything. Save ten steps a day for each of the 12,000 employees, and you will have saved fifty miles of wasted motion and misspent energy. ❞
>
> —Henry Ford, *Ford*, 1913

As Ford produced greater quantities of his cars, the cost of producing each car fell, allowing him to drop the price. Millions of people could then buy what earlier only a few could afford.

Organizing Business

As production increased, industrial leaders developed various ways to manage the growing business world and to ensure a continual flow of capital for business expansion. In addition to individual and family businesses, many people formed partnerships. A partnership is a business organization involving two or more entrepreneurs who can raise more capital and take on more business than if each had gone into business alone. Partners share management responsibility and debt liability.

Corporations take the idea of partnership many steps further. Corporations are business organizations owned by stockholders who buy shares in a company. Stockholders vote on major decisions concerning the corporations. Each vote carries weight according to the number of shares owned. Shares decrease or increase in value depending on the profits earned by the company. In the late 1800s, as industries grew larger, corporations became one of the best ways to manage new businesses.

Business Cycles

As market needs grew more complex, individual businesses concentrated on producing a particular kind of product. This increase in specialization made growing industries dependent on each other. When one industry did well, other related industries also flourished. A great demand for cars, for example, led to expansion in the petroleum industry. Likewise, bad conditions in one industry often spread rapidly to other related industries.

The economic fate of an entire country came to rest on business cycles, or alternating periods of business expansion and decline. Business cycles follow a certain sequence, beginning with expansion. In this "boom" phase, buying, selling, production, and employment rates are high. When expansion ends, a "bust" period of decreased business activity follows. The lowest point in the business cycle is a depression, which is characterized by bank failures and widespread unemployment. As industry increasingly dominated the economy, more people suffered during "bust" periods.

Science and Industry

Amateur inventors relying heavily on trial and error produced most industrial advances at the beginning of the Industrial Revolution. By the late 1800s, manufacturers began to apply more scientific findings to their businesses.

Communications

Science played an important role in the development of communications. In the 1830s **Samuel Morse**, an American inventor, assembled a working model of the telegraph. Using a system of dots and dashes, the telegraph carried information at high speeds. Soon telegraph lines linked most European and North American cities.

Detail from "Steel", mural by Thomas Hart Benton, The New School for Social Research, NY

Steel

Coal, iron, and steel; railroads, steamships, and airplanes; factories, skyscrapers, and steel forges: This was the new world of the age of industry depicted by artist Thomas Hart Benton in this mural painted in 1930. This section, called "Steel," was taken from a drawing Benton had sketched of a Maryland steel plant. The workers in the mural are skilled and strong, the kind of American citizens who will make the American democracy, originally designed for an agricultural world, thrive in the industrial environment.

The Industrial Revolution began in Great Britain in the late 1700s. By applying steam power to iron machinery the British profoundly transformed how things were made. These new industries began to change how people worked, where they lived, how they ate, and what they needed to know in order to survive. After 1870 the United States and Germany began to take the lead in industrialization, and steel became the most important metal used in industry. In this mural Benton welded a new industrial image to an older republican ideal. ⊕

Other communications advances occurred. In 1864 British physicist James Clerk Maxwell theorized that electromagnetic waves travel through space at the speed of light. In 1895 Italian inventor **Guglielmo Marconi** devised the wireless telegraph, later modified into the radio. The invention of the telephone in 1876 is credited to **Alexander Graham Bell**, a Scottish-born American teacher of the deaf. Tiny electrical wires carrying sound allowed people to speak to each other over long distances.

Electricity

By the early 1900s, scientists were able to harness electrical power. As a result, electricity replaced coal as the major source of industrial fuel. In 1831 British physicist Michael Faraday had discovered that a magnet moving through a coil of copper wire produced an electric current. In the 1870s, this principle led to the development of an electric generator. During the same decade, American inventor **Thomas Edison** developed the phonograph, which reproduced sound. He also invented incandescent lightbulbs, making electric lighting cheap and accessible.

Energy and Engines

Advances also occurred in the making of engines. In the late 1880s, Gottlieb Daimler, a German engineer, redesigned the internal-combustion engine to run on gasoline. The small portable engine produced enough power to run vehicles and boats. Another German engineer, **Rudolf Diesel**, developed an oil-burning internal-combustion engine that could run factories, ships, and locomotives. These inventions ushered in the age of the motor car.

Gasoline engines influenced aviation technology. In the 1890s Germany's Ferdinand von Zeppelin streamlined the dirigible, a balloonlike invention that could carry passengers. Other scientists experimented with flying heavier aircraft. In 1903, the American inventors **Wilbur and Orville Wright** car-

Milestones of Free Enterprise

Modern free enterprise, or capitalism, which has its roots in medieval Europe, has increased the production of goods, raised standards of living, and advanced trade throughout the world. Below are some milestones of capitalist development in world history.

- **1200s–1500s** European merchants use currency instead of barter and develop banking procedures.

- **1500s–1700s** European joint-stock companies finance large ventures for overseas exploration, colonization, and trade.

- **1700s–1800s** Beginning in Great Britain, entrepreneurs bring together energy sources, machines, and workers to form factories that allow for efficient and increased production.

- **1800s–1900s** Large corporations in North America and Europe unify management, limit individual investment risk, and rely on banks for large amounts of capital.

- **1900s** Multinational corporations link activities in an emerging global economy. North America, Europe, and Asia's Pacific Rim are leading centers of free enterprise.

ried out the first successful flight of a motorized airplane. The flight covered a distance of only 120 feet (37 m), but five years later, the brothers flew their wooden airplane a distance of 100 miles (161 km).

Airplanes and other vehicles needed a steady supply of fuel for power and rubber for tires. As a result, petroleum and rubber industries skyrocketed. Advances in transportation, communications, and electricity sped the world forward into an era of ever-increasing mechanization.

SECTION 3 REVIEW

Recall
1. **Define** industrial capitalism, interchangeable parts, division of labor, partnership, corporation, depression.
2. **Identify** Eli Whitney, Frederick Taylor, Henry Ford, Samuel Morse, James Clerk Maxwell, Guglielmo Marconi, Alexander Graham Bell, Michael Faraday, Thomas Edison, Rudolf Diesel, Wilbur and Orville Wright.
3. **List** factors that aided the growth of industrial capitalism.

Critical Thinking
4. **Synthesizing Information** Imagine you are a teenager living in the early 1900s. Choose one invention mentioned in this section and describe how it has changed your life.

Understanding Themes
5. **Change** What effects do you think that industrial advancements, such as mass production and the assembly line, have had on workers' lives?

c. 1800 Combination Acts passed by British Parliament ban labor unions.

1845 Massachusetts mill workers petition state for better working conditions.

1870 British Parliament legalizes labor's right to strike.

c. 1900 Labor union membership grows steadily in Europe and North America.

Section 4

A New Society

Setting the Scene

▶ **Terms to Define**
labor union, collective bargaining

▶ **Places to Locate**
Massachusetts

Find Out ▶ How did the Industrial Revolution affect people's lives?

The Storyteller

Factory inspectors interviewed a little boy who worked carrying coal early in the Industrial Revolution:

I don't know how old I am; father is dead; mother is dead also. I began to work when I was about 9. I first worked for a man who used to hit me with the belt or with tools and fling coals at me. I left him and went to see if I could get another job. I used to sleep in the old pits that had no more coal in them; I laid upon the shale all night. I used to eat whatever I could get; I ate for a long time the candles that I found in the pits. I work now for a man who serves me well; he pays me with food and drink.

—freely adapted from Hard Times, Human Documents of the Industrial Revolution, E. Royston Pike, 1966

Child at work

Before the Industrial Age, a person's position in life was determined at birth, and most people had little chance of rising beyond that level. Few managed to rise above their inherited place in the rigid European society.

As the Industrial Revolution progressed throughout the 1700s and 1800s, however, new opportunities made the existing social structure more flexible. Many people, such as inventor Richard Arkwright, used their talents and the opportunities presented by the Industrial Age to rise from humble beginnings to material success.

The youngest of 13 children of poor parents, Arkwright trained to become a barber. Yet machines, not his barbershop, occupied his time and energy. Spurred by the developments in the textile industry, Arkwright developed the huge water-frame spinning wheel that was powered by water and spun continuously. Arkwright persuaded investors to join him in establishing textile mills throughout Great Britain.

Soon Arkwright's mills employed more than 5,000 people. He amassed a great fortune, became active in politics, and was eventually knighted by Great Britain's King George III.

The Rise of the Middle Class

Although few businesspeople in Europe and America prospered as Arkwright had, industrialization did expand the size, power, and wealth of the middle class. Once made up of a small number of bankers, lawyers, doctors, and merchants, the middle class now also included successful owners of factories, mines, and railroads. Professional workers such as clerks, managers, and teachers added to the growing numbers.

Many wealthy manufacturers and other members of the middle class strongly believed in education as the key to business success. Politically active, they became involved in many reform efforts, including education, health care, prison improvements, and sanitation.

Middle-Class Lifestyles

As European and American middle-class men rose in society and assumed the role of sole provider for families, family life began to change. By the end of the late 1800s, stereotypes emerged from the middle class that created and reinforced the idea that men and women occupied different roles based on differences in their characters. Men centered their energy on the workplace, while women concentrated their efforts on maintaining the home and bringing up children.

Visualizing History During the late 1800s, the middle classes in North America and Great Britain stressed the importance of leisure activities shared by the entire family. *How did middle-class male and female roles differ?*

As soon as the family could afford it, a middle-class woman would hire domestic help. The number of her servants increased with her wealth. In 1870 an English guidebook listed the sequence in which women hired new help. First she "hires a washerwoman occasionally, then a charwoman, then a cook and housemaid, a nurse or two, a governess, a lady's maid, a housekeeper...." Servants, usually women, did the more difficult and unpleasant household chores, such as carrying loads of wood and coal, washing laundry, and cleaning house.

As middle-class women freed themselves from more tedious labor, they devoted their time to other occupations, such as educating their children, hand-sewing and embroidering, and planning meals. Magazines for women proliferated at this time, instructing housewives in everything from cooking and housekeeping to geography and natural science.

A typical day for one American middle-class woman in the early 1800s began at 6:00 A.M. and lasted until after 10:00 P.M. After waking up the family, the woman fed her infant son and then sat down to breakfast with her family. She read the Bible to her other three children, prayed with the servants, and then ordered the meals for the day. During the day she wrote letters, took one child to the park, and supervised the older daughters in feeding the younger children and folding up the laundry. The woman's schedule continued after nightfall. "After tea," she wrote, "read to [the children] till bedtime...."

Middle-class parents sent their boys to school to receive training for employment or preparation for higher education. Sons often inherited their fathers' positions or worked in the family business. Most daughters were expected to learn to cook, sew, and attend to all the workings of the household so that they would be well prepared for marriage.

Lives of the Working Class

As the middle class in Europe and America grew, so too did the working class in even greater numbers. The members of this class enjoyed few of the new luxuries that the upper and middle classes could now afford. Most people in the working classes had once labored on rural farms and now made up the majority of workers in new industries. Workers depended solely on the money they earned to buy what they needed. Unlike in earlier days, they did not grow or make what their families needed.

Footnotes to History

Shampoo
In the early 1900s, 25-year-old Joseph Breck tried in vain to find a cure for premature baldness. His efforts, however, led to a full line of hair care products that replaced the harsh soaps used at that time. Breck's businesses soon led the United States in shampoo production.

At the Mercy of Machinery

When British and American industrialists first established mill towns such as Lowell, Manchester, Sheffield, and Fall River, work conditions were tolerable. As industrial competition increased, however, work became harder and increasingly more dangerous. Managers assigned workers more machines to operate and insisted that workers perform their tasks as fast as possible throughout the day.

Under the system of division of labor, workers did the same tasks over and over again, and did not have the satisfaction of seeing the completed work. The combination of monotonous work and heavy, noisy, repetitive machinery made the slightest interruption in the work potentially dangerous. Many workers—often children—lost fingers and limbs, and even their lives, to factory machinery.

Time ruled the lives of the industry workers down to the second. On the farms, workers' days had followed the sun and the weather. Now rigid schedules clocked by ringing bells commanded their every minute. One woman who worked in a Lowell, **Massachusetts**, textile mill wrote about her frustration in 1841:

> ❝ I am going home, where I shall not be obliged to rise so early in the morning, nor be dragged about by the factory bell, nor confined in a close noisy room from morning to night. I shall not stay here…. Up before day, at the clang of the bell—and out of the mill by the clang of the bell—into the mill, and at work in obedience to that ding-dong of a bell—just as though we were so many living machines. ❞
> —anonymous worker, *The Lowell Offering*

In the textile mills, workers spent 10 to 14 hours a day in unventilated rooms filled with lint and dust. Diseases such as pneumonia and tuberculosis spread throughout the factories, killing many workers. In coal mines, workers faced the danger of working with heavy machinery and of breathing in coal dust in the mines.

Images *of the* Times

The Industrial Age

Industrialization brought new products and leisure activities to many people. It also produced terrible working conditions that gave rise to labor unions.

A badge of an early labor union represents the cooperative efforts of workers to seek fair wages and a more humane workplace.

For these long hours at dangerous work, employees earned little to support themselves and their families. Factory owners kept workers' wages low so that their businesses could make profits. Women often made half the wages as men for the same job. Children were paid even less.

Workers' Lives

To earn enough money, whole families worked in the factories and mines, including small children as young as 6 years old. Children often worked 12-hour shifts, sometimes longer and through the night, with only a short break to eat a small meal.

Working-class children did not usually go to school, spending most of the day working instead. Many became crippled or ill from working under unhealthful and dangerous conditions. In 1843 an observer wrote that a child worker in the brickfields "works from 6 in the morning till 8 or 9 at night … Finds her legs swell sometimes … and [suffers] pains and aches between the shoulders, and her hands swell."

For many women, the industries offered new opportunities for independence. For centuries, women's choices were limited almost entirely either to marriage or to life in a convent. Now they could earn a living. Textile mills in New England, for example, provided young single women an opportunity to make money while making new friends. These "mill girls" lived together in mill boardinghouses where they often gathered in study groups devoted to reading and discussing literature.

Yet for the majority of working-class women and their families, life consisted of a difficult working life and an uncomfortable home life. Workers often lived in crowded, cold apartments in poorly constructed tenement housing near factories. Sometimes whole families lived in one or two rooms.

Because the mill owners often owned the workers' housing, they controlled the rent and decided when and whether to improve living conditions. New urban problems complicated life. Human and industrial waste contaminated water supplies and spread diseases such as cholera and typhoid. In the

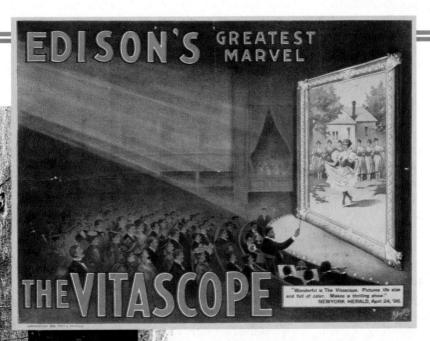

Edison's Vitascope, an early type of motion picture projector, fascinated large audiences.

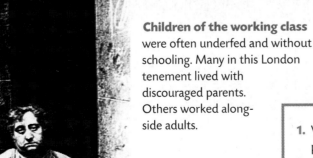

Children of the working class were often underfed and without schooling. Many in this London tenement lived with discouraged parents. Others worked alongside adults.

REFLECTING ON THE TIMES

1. Why did labor unions organize in the industrial period?
2. How did the Industrial Revolution tend to divide people into separate classes?

Visualizing History Through posters, early labor unions called for unity, realizing that the individual worker was powerless. *How did factory owners try to prevent unionization?*

late 1800s, Holyoke, a Massachusetts mill town, had the highest infant mortality rate in the United States.

POINT

Workers Unite

Although governments in western Europe began to recognize the workers' complaints and initiate reforms, workers still labored under harsh conditions. Only through forming organized labor groups were workers able to begin to improve their working conditions in the late 1800s and early 1900s.

Workers knew that they could not fight successfully as individuals against the factory owners. They had to join together into groups to make their problems heard. In Great Britain, many workers joined to form worker associations, which were groups dedicated to representing the interests of workers in a specific industry. The associations hoped to improve the wages and working conditions of their members. Eventually these worker associations developed into labor unions both in Europe and in the United States in the 1800s.

Union Tactics

Workers in labor unions protested in many ways. They organized strikes, in which every worker refused to work. Other times, in sit-down strikes, workers stopped working but refused to leave their work area.

Despite these efforts, unions faced great opposition. Manufacturers complained that the shorter hours and higher wages would add to production costs, increase the price of goods, and hurt business. To discourage workers from joining unions, factory owners added the names of suspected union members to a blacklist to prevent them from getting jobs throughout the industry. The British Parliament even banned unions in the Combination Acts of 1799 and 1800.

Yet British workers kept their cause alive. They finally won their cause in the 1820s when Parliament agreed that workers could meet to discuss working hours and wages. In the following years, skilled British workers formed unions based on a specific trade or craft. Because they had valuable skills, these trade union members were able to bargain with employers. When union leaders and an employer meet together to discuss problems and reach an agreement, they practice collective bargaining. The British unions' power increased in the 1870s after Parliament legalized strikes.

Following the skilled trade unions' success, unskilled workers formed unions in the late 1880s. By the beginning of the 1900s, union membership grew steadily in Europe and the United States.

<table>
<tr><td colspan="3">SECTION 4 REVIEW</td></tr>
<tr>
<td valign="top">

Recall
1. **Define** labor unions, collective bargaining.
2. **Identify** Combination Acts.
3. **Discuss** what effect the separation of home and work had on

</td>
<td valign="top">

middle-class and working-class people in America and Europe.
Critical Thinking
4. **Analyzing Information** Why were industrialists often able to subject workers to poor work-

</td>
<td valign="top">

ing conditions?
Understanding Themes
5. **Conflict** What were some of the problems that factory workers faced? Why did they form labor unions to solve them?

</td>
</tr>
</table>

Critical Thinking SKILLS

Detecting Bias

Suppose you see a billboard showing two happy customers shaking hands with "Honest Harry," the owner of a used-car sales business. The ad says, " Visit Honest Harry for the best deal on wheels." That evening you see a television program that investigates used-car sales businesses. The report says that many of these businesses cheat their customers.

Each message expresses a strong bias. A bias is an inclination or prejudice that inhibits impartiality. Most people have preconceived feelings, opinions, and attitudes that affect their judgment on many topics. For this reason, ideas that profess to be facts may turn out to be opinions. Detecting bias enables us to evaluate the accuracy of information.

Learning the Skill

In detecting bias, first identify the writer's or speaker's purpose. For example, the billboard ad is a marketing tool for selling cars. We would expect that it has a strong bias. The television report may also have a bias, because bad news attracts more viewers.

Another clue to identify bias is emotionally charged language such as *exploit*, *terrorize*, and *cheat*. Also look for visual images that provoke an emotional response. For example, in the television report an interview with a person who bought a "lemon" automobile may elicit a strong response.

Look for overgeneralizations such as *unique*, *honest*, and *everybody*. Notice italics, underlining, and punctuation that highlights particular ideas. Watch for opinions stated as facts without substantiating evidence. Finally, examine the material to determine whether it presents equal coverage of differing views.

Practicing the Skill

Industrialization produced widespread changes in society and widespread disagreement on its effects. While many people hailed the abundance of manufactured goods, others criticized its impact on working people. Karl Marx and Friedrich Engels presented their viewpoint on industrialization in the *Communist Manifesto* in 1848. Read the following excerpt and then answer these questions.

1. What is the purpose of this manifesto?
2. What are three examples of emotionally charged language?
3. According to Marx and Engels, which is more inhumane—the exploitation by feudal lords or by the bourgeoisie? Why?
4. What bias about industrialization is expressed in this excerpt?

> ❝ The bourgeoisie *[the class of factory owners and employers]* … has put an end to all feudal, patriarchal, idyllic relations. It has pitilessly torn asunder the motley feudal ties that bound man to his "natural superiors," and has left remaining no other nexus *[link]* between man and man than naked self-interest, than callous "cash payment." It has drowned the most heavenly of ecstasies of religious fervor, of chivalrous enthusiasm … in the icy water of egotistical calculation.… In one word, for exploitation, veiled by religious and political illusions, it has substituted naked, shameless, direct, brutal exploitation. ❞

Applying the Skill

Find written material about a topic of interest in your community. Possible sources include editorials, letters to the editor, and pamphlets from political candidates and interest groups. Write a short report analyzing the material for evidence of bias.

For More Practice

Turn to the Skill Practice in the Chapter Review on page 619 for more practice in detecting bias.

Connections Across Time

Historical Significance The Industrial Revolution has led to seemingly limitless possibilities. Many of the cities created by the early factories have grown and prospered. International business today is carried on with the aid of computer technology.

The Industrial Age has carried with it many social problems as well as a depletion of natural resources. Today, people face the challenge of combining economic development with preservation of the environment.

Using Key Terms

Write the key term that completes each sentence. Then write a sentence for each term not chosen.

a. factory system
b. partnership
c. division of labor
d. corporation
e. enclosure movement
f. collective bargaining
g. industrial capitalism
h. entrepreneurs
i. labor unions
j. domestic system
k. capital
l. depression

1. The lowest point in the business cycle is a _____, which is characterized by bank failures and widespread unemployment.
2. A _____ is a business organization owned by stockholders who buy shares in the company and vote on major decisions concerning the future of the business.
3. When union leaders and an employer meet together to discuss problems and reach an agreement, they practice _____.
4. Under a _____, workers perform a particular task on a product as it is moved by on a conveyor belt.
5. Money invested in labor, machines, and raw materials is known as _____.

Technology Activity

Using E-mail Locate an E-mail address for your chamber of commerce. Compose a letter requesting information about various industries in your area. Create an illustrated pamphlet of information about area industries. Include advancement of technology within these industries, and their impact on the community. Provide a circle graph illustrating the percentage of people employed by specific industries within your community.

Using Your History Journal

From your time line of inventions choose one invention that you believe affects your life every day. How would people live today without this invention? Write a paragraph describing life without it.

Reviewing Facts

1. **Technology/Society** Identify the Industrial Revolution, and list its causes and effects.
2. **Technology** Explain the role of steam engine in the development of the factory system.
3. **Technology/Society** Discuss the impact of industrialization on working-class women and children.
4. **Science** Identify three inventors in industry, transportation, and communication, and list their individual contributions.
5. **Technology/Society** Track the spread of industry. How did industrialization differ from country to country?

Critical Thinking

1. **Apply** How did the Industrial Revolution affect Great Britain's social structure?
2. **Analyze** In what ways did the life of a farm laborer differ from the life of a factory worker?
3. **Synthesize** Great Britain had an early lead in industrialization. Which factor was the most critical in this development? Why?
4. **Evaluate** What do you see as the positive and negative effects of the Industrial Revolution?

5. Evaluate How can consumer demand influence technological development?

Geography in History

1. Region Refer to the map below. Why did England have an advantage in developing heavy industry?

2. Place What industrial center is closest to several iron ore and coal fields?

3. Movement Railways in northern Scotland and Ireland were not built for transporting iron and coal. How can you tell this from the map? What may have been transported on these railways?

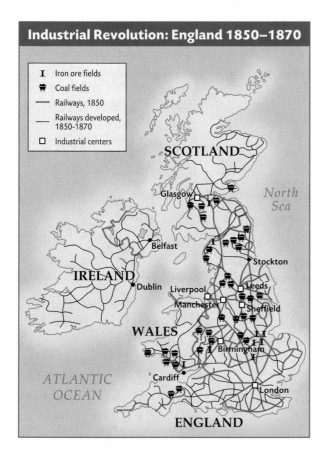

Industrial Revolution: England 1850–1870

- I   Iron ore fields
- 🛒   Coal fields
- —   Railways, 1850
- —   Railways developed, 1850-1870
- ☐   Industrial centers

SCOTLAND
Glasgow
North Sea
Belfast
Stockton
IRELAND
Dublin
Liverpool
Leeds
Manchester
Sheffield
WALES
Birmingham
ATLANTIC OCEAN
Cardiff
London
ENGLAND

Understanding Themes

1. Relation to Environment How were industry and farming related during the period before the Industrial Revolution?

2. Innovation It is often said that "necessity is the mother of invention." Using one invention in this chapter, illustrate this statement.

3. Change Do you think that progress is a necessary result of change? Give examples.

4. Conflict How have differences between employers and workers produced positive effects for workers in the modern world?

Linking Past and Present

1. What effects do you see from the Industrial Revolution in your everyday life?

2. What changes and challenges has industry presented society in recent years?

3. The Industrial Revolution replaced many handcrafted items with mass-produced ones. What things that we use today are made mostly by hand?

Skill Practice

Read the following excerpt from "The Gospel of Wealth," an 1889 essay by Andrew Carnegie. Then answer the questions that follow.

“ The contrast between the palace of the millionaire and the cottage of the laborer with us today measures the changes which had come with civilization. The change, however, is not to be deplored, but welcomed as highly beneficial. It is well, nay, essential for the progress of the race that the houses of some should be homes for all that is highest and best in literature and the arts, and for all the refinements of civilization, rather than that none should be so. Much better this great irregularity than universal squalor. ”

1. Does the term *cottage* coincide with the description of how workers lived that is found on page 615?

2. How does Carnegie's use of this term indicate bias?

3. How does Carnegie justify large differences in lifestyle between rich and poor?

4. How does Carnegie describe the condition of most of humanity, except the wealthy?

Cultural Revolution

Chapter Themes

▶ **Change** Political and economic philosophies attempt to make sense of a changing industrial world. *Section 1*

▶ **Innovation** Scientific discoveries lead to improved health and revolutionary views about the natural world and human society. *Section 2*

▶ **Movement** People move from rural to urban areas and from continent to continent in search of better lives. *Section 3*

▶ **Innovation** Artists and writers in the Western world reflect the changes in urban industrial society. *Section 4*

The Storyteller

A new world was in the making. Factories boomed. Cities grew. By the late 1800s, steamships and trains allowed people to move in search of better lives. American novelist Theodore Dreiser described the excitement that drew people to Chicago:

"Its many and growing commercial opportunities gave it widespread fame, which made of it a giant magnet, drawing to itself, from all quarters, the hopeful and the hopeless.... It was a city of over 500,000 with the ambition, the daring, the activity of a metropolis of a million."

The Industrial Revolution also brought challenges to Europeans and North Americans. Cities became overcrowded, and the gap between rich and poor widened. People struggled to make sense of an increasingly complex society.

Historical Significance

What changes occurred in the economics, the sciences, and the arts of the West between 1750 and 1914? How did these changes alter people's values and daily lives?

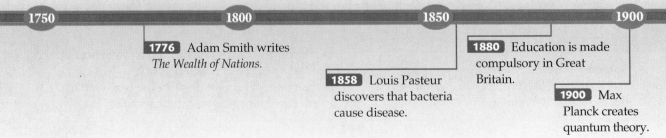

1750	1800	1850	1900

1776 Adam Smith writes *The Wealth of Nations.*

1858 Louis Pasteur discovers that bacteria cause disease.

1880 Education is made compulsory in Great Britain.

1900 Max Planck creates quantum theory.

History & Art *Boulevard Des Capuchines and Théâtre de Vaudeville, 1889,* by Jean Beraud. Musée Carnavalet, Paris, France

Your History Journal

This chapter introduces thinkers and reformers who wanted to create a better society. Write an essay suggesting ways to improve the society in which we live today.

1817 David Ricardo writes about the "iron law of wages."

1847 British Parliament passes the Ten Hours Act.

1867 Karl Marx publishes *Das Kapital*.

Section 1

New Ideas

Setting the Scene

▶ **Terms to Define**

laissez-faire, utilitarianism, socialism, proletariat, bourgeoisie, communism

▶ **People to Meet**

Adam Smith, David Ricardo, Jeremy Bentham, John Stuart Mill, Robert Owen, Karl Marx, Friedrich Engels

 **Find Out** Why did Karl Marx advocate doing away with the capitalist system?

The Storyteller

Karl Marx, the chief architect of communism, was always and everywhere a student. At an early age his withdrawal from all university activities except the intellectual brought stern advice from his father:

"My clever and gifted son Karl passes wretched and sleepless nights, wearying body and mind with cheerless study.... But what he builds today he destroys again tomorrow.... At last the body begins to ail and the mind gets confused, whilst ordinary folk ... attain their goal if not better at least more comfortably than those who condemn youthful pleasures and undermine their health...."

—from *The Life and Teaching of Karl Marx*, M. Beer, 1921

Karl Marx

English essayist William Hazlitt, writing in the early 1800s, described Europe in the critical years after the French Revolution:

❝ There was a mighty ferment in the heads of statesmen and poets, kings and people. According to the prevailing notions, all was to be natural and new. Nothing that was established was to be tolerated.... The world was to be turned topsy-turvy. ❞

The Western world did appear to be turning upside down, as society underwent a transformation. In little more than 100 years, the Industrial Revolution converted Europe from a farming economy centered in the country to an industrial economy based in urban areas.

Industry in the short term brought great wealth to a few and imposed hardships on the many. In the long run, however, it provided material benefits to all people. Still, the gap between "haves" and "have nots" remained to create unrest in many societies.

TURNING POINT

Capitalist Ideas

During the Industrial Revolution, European thinkers for the first time studied and explained how capitalism worked. Rejecting mercantilism with its government controls, many supported **laissez-faire** (LEH•SAY•FAHR), a policy allowing business to operate without government interference. Laissez-faire, from a French term meaning "let them alone," was developed in France during the 1700s by the Physiocrats. These thinkers valued land as the primary source of national wealth. They held that fewer taxes and regulations would enable farmers to grow more produce. In the early 1800s, the middle-class owners of railroads, factories, and mines began supporting laissez-faire. They believed that freedom from government controls would mean a growing economy with material progress for all people.

Adam Smith

Industrial leaders relied on the ideas of **Adam Smith**, a Scottish economist who set down the workings of a laissez-faire economy. In *The Wealth of Nations* (1776), Smith stated that an economy works best when the natural forces of supply and demand operate without government interference. In such a free market, individual sellers and buyers act on self-interest. Smith did not think this was necessarily bad, believing that a natural order in the universe made all individual striving for self-interest add up to the common good. Businesses compete to produce goods as inexpensively as possible, and consumers buy the best goods at the lowest prices. Efficient producers make more profit, hire more workers, and continue to expand, to everyone's benefit.

As the Industrial Revolution gathered momentum and spread throughout the world, Smith's ideas profoundly influenced economic thought and practice. By the 1850s, Great Britain, the world's leading industrial power, had adopted free trade and other laissez-faire policies.

Malthus and Ricardo

Not all thinkers, however, held Smith's optimism about the future. Thomas Malthus, an Anglican clergyman, wrote in *An Essay on the Principle of Population* (1798) that poverty, famine, and misery were unavoidable because population was increasing faster than the food supply. Influenced by Malthus, the British economist **David Ricardo** stated in his "iron law of wages" that rapid population growth would lead only to fierce competition for jobs, lower wages, and higher unemployment. Continual poverty was all that was in store for the working class. As strong believers in laissez-faire, both Malthus and Ricardo opposed government aid to the poor. Instead, they believed that the poor could help themselves by working hard, saving their earnings, and having fewer children.

Because of these gloomy theories, people in the 1800s called economics "the dismal science." However, the forecasts of Malthus and Ricardo were not fulfilled. Population continued to rise, but as a result of the agricultural revolution, the food supply grew even faster. By the 1900s, higher living standards and lower birthrates prevailed in many

Visualizing History **Grim-faced young coal mine workers in Kingston, Pennsylvania, pose for the camera.** *How would photographs such as this support criticism of laissez-faire economics?*

Western countries such as Great Britain, the United States, and Germany. Yet, industrialization benefited some more than others and fueled demands for reforms that would create a more just society.

A Better Society

During the 1800s, reformers set out to improve the lives of the disadvantaged, especially enslaved people and the urban poor. At the same time, a new generation of thinkers questioned laissez-faire and urged government to work for a better society.

Evangelicals and Reform

During the late 1700s and early 1800s, a series of religious awakenings swept through the Protestant churches. The outcome of these revivals was Evangelicalism, a movement that joined personal faith with social improvement. Some Evangelicals supported strict laissez-faire; others, however, believed that government needed to involve itself in the lives of the disadvantaged. One of the most noted participants in the Evangelical cause was William Wilberforce, a member of Parliament. Opposed to slavery, Wilberforce had Parliament pass a bill in 1807 that ended the British slave trade. Later, in 1833—the year of Wilberforce's death—Parliament abolished slavery throughout the British Empire.

Many socialist groups used posters and cartoons to win support for the overthrow of Europe's monarchies as well as the capitalist system. *What were two other goals of the socialist movement?*

Another Evangelical leader, Lord Shaftesbury, promoted laws to limit working hours for women and children. Aiding Shaftesbury's efforts were parliamentary commissions investigating factories and mines. Commission reports detailing miserable working conditions raised a public outcry. Parliament responded with the first factory laws of the industrial era. Passed during the 1830s and 1840s, these measures regulated child employment in factories, prohibited women and children from working in underground mines, and established a 10-hour day in textile factories for children under 18 and women.

Utilitarian Reformers

Many secular social reformers also believed that laissez-faire policies should be changed to allow for some government involvement in economic and social affairs. British philosopher **Jeremy Bentham** promoted utilitarianism, the idea that society should work for "the greatest happiness for the greatest number" of citizens. To Bentham, laws should be judged by their usefulness, whether they advanced human happiness and reduced human misery. To this end, Bentham called for a better code of law, education for all, a public health service, and improved prisons.

Bentham's follower, **John Stuart Mill**, challenged strict views of laissez-faire economics, calling on government to distribute national wealth more justly by taxing income. However, he also held a firm belief in individual freedom. In works such as *On Liberty*

(1859), Mill stated that freedom of thought and discussion promoted social progress and supported extending the vote to all adults. A believer in full democracy, Mill advocated equal rights for women.

TURNING POINT
Rise of Socialism

Not everyone in Europe agreed with the capitalist way of thinking in the early 1800s. Some people believed that ending the misery of workers required eliminating capitalism completely. They advocated socialism—the belief that the means of production—capital, land, raw materials, and factories—should be owned and controlled by society, either directly or through the government. In this way, wealth could be distributed equally among all citizens.

Early Socialism

Some early advocates of socialism planned and built communities where everyone was supposed to share equally in the benefits of the industrial age. Among the first to establish such a community was **Robert Owen**, a wealthy Welsh manufacturer. Owen believed that competition caused society's problems. Thus, he reasoned that if cooperation replaced competition, life would improve.

In 1800 Owen set out to prove his point in New Lanark, a dreary Scottish mill town. In time he reconstructed it into a model industrial community. Although he did not turn the textile mill completely over to the workers, he greatly improved their living and working conditions. In 1825 Owen stopped managing New Lanark and bought New Harmony, Indiana, where he tried to set up a cooperative community. New Harmony, however, did not meet with the same success as New Lanark. Feuding among Owen and the residents led Owen to return to Great Britain.

Marx and Engels

German philosopher **Karl Marx** dismissed the ideas of the early socialists as impractical and set out to provide a scientific basis for socialism. The son of a prosperous German lawyer, Marx received a doctorate in history and philosophy. When his radical views got him into trouble with the Prussian government, he fled to Paris. There in 1844 he met **Friedrich Engels**. Engels was on his way home from one of his father's factories in Manchester, England. Horrified by what he saw there, Engels wrote a classic book called *The Condition of the Working Class in England*.

Marx later settled in London, and he and Engels became lifelong friends and collaborators. Engels, a successful businessman, supported Marx, who devoted his life to writing about economics.

Marx's Theories

Marx based his ideas in part on the teachings of the German philosopher G.W.F. Hegel. Hegel taught that changing ideas were the major force in history. As ideas clashed, new ideas emerged. This produced new changes, conflicts, and ideas.

Like Hegel, Marx believed that history advanced through conflict. In Marx's view, however, economics was the major force for change. Production was at the base of every social order. Laws, social systems, customs, religion, and art all developed in accord with a society's economic base.

The most important aspect of the economic base was the division of society into classes. The class that controlled production became the ruling class. The only way to make the ruling class give up control was through revolution. Therefore, conflict between classes was inevitable. Marx stated "class struggle," was what pushed history forward.

Marx argued that Europe had moved through four stages of economic life—primitive, slave, feudal, and capitalist. During the primitive stage, people produced only what they needed to live. There was no exploitation, or unfair use of a person for one's own advantage. Once tools were developed, however, and people could produce a surplus, they became exploitable. From then on, history was a class struggle. It was the "haves" against the "have–nots."

Marx believed that capitalism was only a temporary phase. As the makers of goods, the proletariat, or the working class, was the true productive class. An economic crisis in one of the advanced industrial countries would give the proletariat the chance to seize control from the bourgeoisie (BURZH•WAH•ZEE), or middle class. The proletariat would then build a society in which the people owned everything. Without private property, classes would vanish, and the government would wither away. In this last stage, known as communism, the governing principle would be "from each according to his ability, to each according to his need."

Marx and Engels published their views in *The Communist Manifesto* in 1848. In it they appealed to the world's workers:

> 66 Let the ruling classes tremble at a Communist revolution. The proletarians have nothing to lose but their chains. They have a world to win. Working men of all countries, unite! 99

In 1867 Marx developed his ideas further in the work *Das Kapital*.

The Socialist Legacy

History did not proceed by Marx's plan. When Marx was writing, workers' poverty contrasted sharply with industrialists' wealth. By 1900 conditions had changed in western Europe. Workers could buy more with their wages than they could 50 years earlier. Rather than overthrow their governments, workers gained the right to vote and used it to correct the worst social ills. They also remained loyal to their individual nations rather than ally with workers in other countries to promote revolution.

In time, democratic socialism developed in western Europe. Democratic Socialists urged public control of some means of production, but they respected individual values and favored democratic means to implement Socialist policies.

In the early 1900s, however, revolution swept Russia, a largely agricultural society. There a small group of Marxist revolutionaries had developed a radical form of socialism that became known as "communism." Rising to power in the revolution, the Russian communists imposed their beliefs on the country and shunned democratic values.

SECTION 1 REVIEW

Recall

1. **Define** laissez-faire, utilitarianism, socialism, proletariat, bourgeoisie, communism.

2. **Identify** Adam Smith, David Ricardo, Jeremy Bentham, John Stuart Mill, Robert Owen, Karl Marx, Friedrich Engels.

3. **Explain** why, according to Adam Smith, a laissez-faire policy would promote economic progress and social harmony.

Critical Thinking

4. **Making Comparisons** How are the viewpoints of the Evangelicals and the Utilitarians similar? How are they different?

Understanding Themes

5. **Change** Why did industrialization make people think about the causes and cures of poverty? Can poverty be totally eliminated? Which thinkers of the period would agree with your views?

1796 Edward Jenner invents smallpox vaccine.

1803 John Dalton develops atomic theory.

1859 Charles Darwin publishes *On the Origin of Species*.

1898 Marie Sklodowska Curie and Pierre Curie discover radium.

Section 2

The New Science

Setting the Scene

▶ **Terms to Define**
cell theory, evolution, genetics, atomic theory, sociology, psychology

▶ **People to Meet**
Charles Darwin, Gregor Mendel, Edward Jenner, Louis Pasteur, John Dalton, Marie Sklodowska Curie, Pierre Curie, Ivan Pavlov, Sigmund Freud

Find Out What advances made in science between 1750 and 1914 have improved life today?

The Storyteller

Dr. Hugh Barrett's hands shook with anger as he met with the industrial board of directors. They had requested his presence because many workers were falling ill and dying, costing them loss of labor. They hoped that modern medicine could offer a cure. Dr. Barrett tried to explain. "Cholera and typhoid will continue to rage as long as elementary hygiene is impossible. The congested, unsanitary housing—all your workers can afford on the wages you give them—is a breeding ground for disease." His persuasive words fell on deaf ears. What good is it, he wondered, to explain how disease is transmitted, if his recommendations were not to be followed?

Family in London slum

—freely adapted from *History of Private Life, Volume 4, From the French Revolution to the Great War*, edited by Michelle Perrot, 1987

During the 1800s and early 1900s, scientific discoveries were beginning to unravel some intriguing mysteries. Not only did discoveries help our understanding of life and the universe, they also led to medical advances, longer life spans, and cures for deadly diseases.

New Look at Living Things

In the 1600s scientists had observed under a microscope the cells that make up living things, but they did not understand what they saw. It was not until 1838 that German botanist Mathias Schleiden and biologist Theodor Schwann formulated the **cell theory**: All living things are made up of tiny units of matter called cells. They also discovered that all cells divide and multiply, causing organisms to grow and mature.

The Diversity of Life

Cell theory could not explain why the world has so many kinds of plants and animals. In the 1800s scientists proposed the theory that all plants and animals descended from a common ancestor by **evolution** over millions of years. During that time, they said, plants and animals had evolved from simple to complex forms.

In France, the scientist Jean-Baptiste de Lamarck observed similarities between fossils and living organisms. He found that an animal's parts—its legs, for example—might grow larger or smaller depending on how much it used them. He suggested that living things adapt to their environment and then pass the changes on to the next generation. Lamarck's theory, though later disproved, influenced **Charles Darwin**, a British naturalist who would build his own theory of evolution.

In December 1831 Charles Darwin set off on a world voyage on HMS *Beagle*, a British naval ship. While traveling he became curious about the great variety of plants and animals. He also wondered why some kinds had become extinct while others lived on.

Influenced by the theories of Malthus, Darwin developed a theory of evolution based on natural selection. In his book *On the Origin of Species*, Darwin stated that most animal groups increase faster than the food supply and are constantly struggling for survival. The plants and animals that survive are better adapted to their environment, so that they alone live on, producing offspring having the same characteristics. In another book, *The Descent of Man*, Darwin traced human evolution from animal species. Darwin's writings created controversy because many religious leaders believed that his views contradicted the biblical account of creation and ignored divine purpose in the universe.

Development of Genetics

In the 1860s **Gregor Mendel** wondered how plants and animals pass characteristics from one generation to another. Mendel, an Austrian monk, experimented with pea plants. He concluded that characteristics are passed from one generation to the next by tiny particles. The particles were later called genes, and Mendel's work became the basis for genetics, the science of heredity.

Medical Advances

Through most of history, diseases have killed more people than famines, natural disasters, and wars. In the 1800s knowledge of living organisms brought medical advances that would give people longer, healthier lives.

Fighting Disease

Smallpox, which killed millions of people over the centuries, was one of the most dreaded diseases. In 1796 **Edward Jenner**, an English doctor, noticed that dairy workers who had contracted cowpox, a mild disease, never caught smallpox. Jenner hypothesized that he could prevent smallpox by injecting people with cowpox. To prove his theory, Jenner injected a boy with cowpox serum and later with smallpox serum. As Jenner expected, the boy contracted cowpox but not smallpox. Jenner had given the world's first vaccination.

About 50 years later, **Louis Pasteur**, a French chemist, learned why Jenner's vaccination worked. In the 1850s Pasteur discovered bacteria, or germs, and proved that they cause infectious diseases. He also discovered that bacteria do not appear spontaneously, but instead reproduce like other living

Science and Technology

Triumph Over an Ancient Enemy

Louis Pasteur

When a wine maker asked his friend French scientist Louis Pasteur to find out why some wines turned sour as they fermented, science and medicine vaulted into a new era. Pasteur discovered that the wines would not sour if they were heated to a specific temperature and bottled without contact with the air.

With his microscope, Pasteur saw that tiny microbes were destroyed in this heating, later called pasteurization. He had proved that the germs that caused contamination came from an outside source. Pasteur worked to show that bacteria were carried in the air, on hands or clothes, and in other ways. He developed the theory that bacteria can cause disease, and he argued that bacteria could be killed only by heat or other means.

Pasteur applied his knowledge of bacteria to fighting diseases. In the 1880s he developed a successful vaccine against rabies. That same decade, the Pasteur Institute was founded in Paris, with Pasteur as director. Today, as one of the world's leading research centers, the Institute has been involved in medical breakthroughs to control many deadly diseases. In 1983 Institute researchers were the first to isolate the AIDS virus.

Linking Past and Present ACTIVITY

Discuss how Pasteur developed the germ theory of disease and changed people's thinking about illness. How does his work influence the world today?

things. Pasteur knew then that they could be killed and that many diseases could be prevented.

New Approaches to Surgery

Surgery benefited from advances in chemistry. Until the mid-1800s, surgeons could operate only when their patients were forcibly held down. The experience was gruesome and often fatal. In the 1840s a Boston dentist demonstrated surgery using ether. When ether was administered, patients slept through their operations, feeling no pain. Sir James Simpson, a professor at the University of Edinburgh, investigated the use of another sleep-producing chemical, chloroform. Using the anesthetics ether and chloroform led to painless surgery.

Still, many people died after surgery because of infection introduced during the procedure. Joseph Lister, an English surgeon, searched for a way to destroy bacteria and make surgery safe. He found that carbolic acid could be used to sterilize medical instruments. Lister's use of an antiseptic moved surgery into a new era.

Breakthroughs in Physics

The explosion of ideas also advanced the physical sciences. Expanding the ideas of Galileo and Newton, scientists created our modern ideas about atomic energy. Atomic theory is the idea that all matter is made up of tiny particles called atoms.

John Dalton, an English chemist, provided proof of this theory. He discovered that elements are composed of atoms, and that all atoms of an element are identical and unlike the atoms of any other element. Dalton then determined chemical formulas showing which atoms make up specific elements.

Until the 1890s scientists believed that atoms were solid and indivisible; then in 1895 German physicist Wilhelm K. Roentgen discovered X rays, or high-energy electromagnetic waves that could penetrate solid matter. Later scientists showed that X rays are made up of particles of electricity called electrons, which are part of every atom.

These beginnings led scientists to frame modern physics. In 1898 the physicists **Marie Sklodowska** (skluh•DAWF•skuh) **Curie** and **Pierre Curie** discovered the highly radioactive element of radium and proved that it emits energy. In 1900 German physicist Max Planck theorized that energy is not continuous, but is released in separate units called quanta. Another German scientist, Albert Einstein, developed his theory of relativity, changing ideas about time, space, mass, and motion.

Social Sciences

Meanwhile, other scientists used the scientific method to study human behavior. This led to the development of two new social sciences— sociology, the study of human behavior in groups, and psychology, the science of human behavior in individuals. The French thinker Auguste Comte (KOHNT) was one of the founders of sociology. Comte believed that society, like nature, operated by certain laws. He stated that once these laws were discovered, people could apply scientific methods to the study of human social groups.

In the 1890s **Ivan Pavlov**, a Russian researcher, experimented with animals to see what effects outside stimuli had on their behavior. His findings suggested that human actions were unconscious reactions to stimuli and could be changed by training. Another researcher who held that an unconscious part of the mind governs human behavior was the Austrian physician **Sigmund Freud** (FROYD). Freud's theories led to psychoanalysis, a method of treatment to discover people's motives.

SECTION 2 REVIEW

Recall
1. **Define** cell theory, evolution, genetics, atomic theory, sociology, psychology.
2. **Identify** Charles Darwin, Gregor Mendel, Edward Jenner, Louis Pasteur, John Dalton, Marie Sklodowska Curie, Pierre Curie, Ivan Pavlov, Sigmund Freud.
3. **Describe** Charles Darwin's theory of natural selection and how it changed thinking about the development of life.

Critical Thinking
4. **Applying Information** Explain in writing how a scientist discussed in Section 2 helped to change the ideas of the day.

Understanding Themes
5. **Innovation** How are the scientific understandings of the 1800s and early 1900s being expanded today? What impact are scientific discoveries having on your life?

1837 Mary Lyon opens the first women's college in the United States.

1858 Frederick Law Olmsted designs New York City's Central Park.

c. 1890s Many Russian Jews flee persecution and settle in the United States.

Section 3

Popular Culture

Setting the Scene

▶ **Terms to Define**
emigration, immigration, urbanization

▶ **People to Meet**
Frederick Law Olmsted, Mary Lyon

▶ **Places to Locate**
London, New York City, Paris

Find Out Why did population grow dramatically in Europe and North America during the 1800s?

The Storyteller

A book titled Host and Guest *described dining for wealthy Europeans in the late 1800s:* "The first course consists of soups and fish, followed by boiled poultry, ham or tongue, roasts, stew, etc.; with vegetables ... curries, hashes, cutlets, patties, etc. For the second course, roasted poultry or game at the top and bottom, with dressed vegetables, omelets, macaroni, jellies, creams, salads, preserved fruit, and all sorts of sweet things and pastry are employed.... The third course consists of game, confectionary, the more delicate vegetables dressed in the French way...." Dessert, of course, followed.

—adapted from *Manners and Morals in the Age of Optimism, 1848-1914,* James Laver, 1966

Dining scene in Victorian England

As the 1900s began, the new science and technology were making a difference throughout Europe and North America. Most people could now expect a longer and healthier life. The rate of infant mortality dropped in the late 1800s, and life expectancy climbed. In 1850 the average person lived about 40 years; by 1900 most people could expect to live beyond 50.

Thus, as industrialization grew, so did world population. At the beginning of the Industrial Revolution, 140 million people lived in Europe. By 1850, about 100 years later, Europe's population had soared to 266 million. In Europe and the United States, the first industrialized areas, the rate of population growth was highest.

Improved Living Conditions

The medical advances of the 1800s were partly responsible for this dramatic growth in population. So too was the availability of more and better food. Before 1740 many people died of starvation and of diseases caused by vitamin deficiency such as rickets. At that time a person's entire daily diet might have consisted of three pounds of bread.

In the 1800s, however, bread ceased to be the staple it had been for centuries. With new machinery and scientific methods, farmers could produce many kinds of foods. Potatoes, nutritious and easy to grow, became popular. Methods for preserving foods, including canning and eventually refrigeration, enabled people to take advantage of the greater variety of food that was available.

One observer of working-class life in London during the late 1890s wrote: "A good deal of bread is eaten and tea is drunk especially by the women and children, but ... bacon, eggs and fish appear regularly in the budgets. A piece of meat cooked on Sundays serves also for dinner on Monday and Tuesday." Some Europeans imported corn from the

Chapter 24 *Cultural Revolution* **629**

United States and fruit and frozen meat from Australia and New Zealand.

Seeking a Better Life

As the population grew, people became more mobile. Railroads revolutionized not only the food people ate, but also the way they lived. In 1860 London's Victoria Station opened, making it easier for Londoners to leave their crowded city. Steamships carried people to other countries and continents in search of a better life. Between 1870 and 1900, more than 25 million people left Europe for the United States; others moved to South America, South Africa, and Australia.

For a number of reasons, some Europeans chose emigration, leaving their homelands to settle elsewhere. Some looked for higher-paying jobs and better working conditions. Others sought to escape discrimination and persecution by oppressive governments. Still others hoped to escape famine.

Advertisements of steamship companies, along with low fares, lured many immigrants to the United States. Industries looking for cheap labor offered additional encouragement. Some American industrialists sent recruiters whose task was to urge people to leave Europe and obtain permanent jobs and homes in the United States.

Twelve-year-old Mary Antin joined thousands of Russian Jews fleeing persecution in 1894. Many years earlier Mary's father had decided on immigration, or coming to settle permanently in a foreign land. His new homeland was the United States. Mary, her mother, and her brothers and sisters endured a harrowing journey across Europe and the Atlantic Ocean to join him in Boston, Massachusetts. Mary wrote of her experiences: "And so suffering, fearing, brooding, and rejoicing, we crept nearer and nearer to the coveted shore until on a glorious May morning … our eyes beheld the Promised Land and my father received us in his arms."

Most people left their homelands knowing that they would never see their parents or their birthplace again. The ocean voyage often proved a frightening experience. One youngster

Leisure Time

An urban environment offered many people new opportunities for leisure activities.

A Bicycle was a fashionable new means of getting around, for those who could afford it.

Perth Station, Going South by George Earl captures the happy confusion of a London holiday.

remembered "the howling darkness, the white rims of the mountain-high waves speeding like maddened dragons toward the tumbling ship."

When the immigrants reached their new homes, many learned that their troubles had only begun. Now they had to find housing and jobs in strange surroundings where they did not know the culture or the language. Some people took advantage of the European immigrants, who seemed to them strange "foreigners."

From Country to City

During the 1800s and early 1900s, many people moved within their own country. Cities around the world were absorbing newcomers who were moving from rural villages to find new opportunities. As farms grew larger and more mechanized, they needed fewer workers. The growing industries in or near the cities offered new and challenging ways to make a living.

Although the new city dwellers faced no language barriers, some of their problems were similar to those of the European immigrants. Their old life was gone, with its known boundaries, familiar people, and established routines. Although work was plentiful, living quarters in the cities were often cramped, and neighbors might be less friendly than people they had known. British poet Lord Byron summed up the feelings of many newcomers to the city:

> ❝ I live not in myself, but I become a
> Portion of that around me: and to me
> High mountains are a feeling, but the hum
> Of human cities torture. ❞

Growth of Cities

The movement of people into the cities resulted in the urbanization, or the spread of city life, of the industrialized countries. A country is urbanized when more people live in cities than in rural areas. Great Britain is a prime example. In 1800 **London**

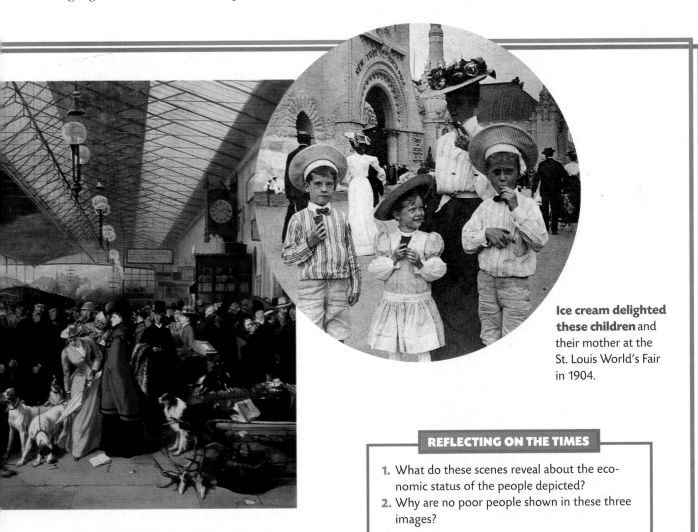

Ice cream delighted these children and their mother at the St. Louis World's Fair in 1904.

REFLECTING ON THE TIMES

1. What do these scenes reveal about the economic status of the people depicted?
2. Why are no poor people shown in these three images?

was its only city with a population of more than 100,000. By 1851 Britain had 9 such cities. In the same year, and for the first time, slightly more than half of the British people lived in cities. By 1914 that figure had reached 80 percent.

Urbanization was taking place elsewhere as well. In 1914, 60 percent of the Germans, 50 percent of the Americans, and 45 percent of the French were city dwellers.

As people moved to cities, they began to marry earlier. Children could increase a family's income by working in factories. As a result, people had more children, adding to the population.

The cities' growth soon outpaced their ability to provide needed housing and sanitation. Few cities had building codes that mandated adequate housing. Houses were built close together in long rows, one against another. The workers crowded together in damp, cold, unsanitary rooms, with fire a constant danger.

The factories added to the unpleasant city environment. Here is a report on the working conditions of British miners in 1843: "Sheffield is one of the dirtiest and most smoky towns I ever saw. The town is also very hilly, and the smoke ascends the streets, instead of leaving them…. One cannot be long in the town without experiencing the necessary inhalation of soot."

City Services

City governments in Europe and the United States began to look for solutions to the overwhelming troubles. They saw that one of the most pressing problems was sanitation. An observer in the British city of Leeds reported, "The ashes, garbage, and filth of all kinds are thrown from the doors and windows of the houses upon the surface of the streets and courts." Ditches and open sewers carried waste from public toilets. Polluted water

encouraged epidemics of cholera and other diseases, especially in the crowded slums.

In the late 1800s, the germ theory and the newly invented iron pipe spurred city leaders to clean up their cities. They installed closed sewer lines and improved garbage collection. Police and fire protection created safer cities.

As city planning progressed, a number of city governments set aside areas as parks. In **New York City**, landscape architect **Frederick Law Olmsted** saw the need for "a simple, broad, open space of clean greensward [grassy turf]" enclosed by a large enough green space to "completely shut out the city." With the architect and landscape designer Calvert Vaux, Olmsted designed Central Park in 1858.

Leisure Time

Leisure time activities expanded for the middle classes and for the working classes. Men and women took more outings and enjoyed more cultural activities. Newspapers helped to make people interested in places and events outside of their own neighborhoods and communities.

In the 1700s the fine arts were available only to the wealthy upper classes. Concerts were performed in palaces and grand homes, or they were performed in churches. Wealthy aristocrats, prosperous merchants, and religious leaders commissioned cultural events and artworks, such as concerts and paintings, to commemorate special events or to honor special people.

In the 1800s, however, fine art and music became available to middle- and working-class people in the city. City governments in Europe and North America built concert halls and opera houses, such as London's vast Royal Albert Hall, erected in 1871. Cities sponsored the opening of art museums, such as the great Louvre (LOOV) Museum in **Paris**.

When people were not visiting libraries and museums, they went to amusement parks, which provided shows, rides, games, and food. Sports such as soccer and rugby began to be organized between cities and around the nation. Many people also enjoyed archery, lawn tennis, and cricket.

New Interest in Education

In the early 1800s, when governments began to support public schools, their reasons were political. For example, the Prussian government established public schools to train its people in citizenship and in devotion to the monarchy and the army. In the

Footnotes to History

Moving to the Suburbs
During the late 1800s, suburbs, or small communities next to large cities, grew in Europe and the United States along with the development of streetcar lines and railroads. Middle-class people could afford to live in less urban areas and ride the trolley or train to their jobs in the city. In the United States, suburban growth greatly increased in the 1950s as more and more families were able to buy one or two automobiles.

United States, government support for public schools grew out of a desire to foster national unity after the Revolutionary War.

By the late 1800s, as people grew more and more interested in improving their lives, they became more actively involved in promoting education. Both in Europe and the United States, they supported education that was funded by the government and available to everyone. Believing education would improve their children's chances for a better life, they voted for increased educational opportunities. Schools and colleges were also established to provide better training for teachers.

The new kind of society—urbanized and industrialized—also benefited from the cause of public education. Industrialists needed employees who could read and write. Advanced technologies based on science depended on workers who had scientific training. Many people came to see that an ever more complex society would demand a well-educated populace. People were needed who could participate intelligently in public affairs.

Education for Women

Education for women was a hotly debated topic in the 1800s. Some felt that women's roles as wives and homemakers did not require education. Others believed women should be given the same educational opportunities as men. Girls were included in the laws providing education to all. Still, they could usually attend only elementary schools. Access to secondary education was limited only to the wealthy few.

Determined to offer higher education to women, some people began to open secondary schools and colleges especially for them. In 1837 American educator **Mary Lyon** opened the first women's college, the Mount Holyoke Female Seminary, which later became Mount Holyoke College in Massachusetts. In 1874 the London School of Medicine was opened, and after two years of bitter debate, the British Parliament finally allowed women to be registered as doctors.

History & Art *Piccadilly Circus, 1912* by Charles Ginner. Tate Gallery, London, England **The circular street of Piccadilly Circus was built near the shopping district of London.** *By 1914, what percent of the British lived in cities?*

Results of Education

The advances in education created a growing demand for accessible reading materials. Magazines and books became popular. Libraries with large collections opened as early as the 1840s in major cities such as Paris and London. Lending libraries loaned books for small fees.

Mass-circulation newspapers were first printed at this time, and by 1860, more than 3,000 newspapers were published in the United States. Newspaper publishers benefited from the combination of rapid communication provided by the telegraph, cheaper printing methods, and improved distribution by railroad and steamship.

SECTION 3 REVIEW

Recall
1. **Define** emigration, immigration, urbanization.
2. **Identify** Frederick Law Olmsted, Mary Lyon.
3. **List** three improvements in city life that were made in the 1800s and the early 1900s.

Critical Thinking
4. **Making Comparisons** How do attitudes about women's education today differ from attitudes in the late 1800s? Explain reasons for the differences.

Understanding Themes
5. **Movement** Why did many people in Europe and North America move in the late 1800s and early 1900s? Do the same reasons apply today?

Using E-Mail

Sharing information, thoughts, and feelings with others is communication. *Telecommunication* refers to communicating at a distance through the use of a telephone, video, or computer. How can you communicate using your computer?

Learning the Skill

In order to use your computer to telecommunicate, you must add two parts to it. The first part is a piece of hardware called a *modem*. A modem is a device that enables computers to communicate with each other through telephone lines.

The second part is *communications software* which lets your computer prepare and send information to the modem. It also lets your computer receive and understand the information it receives from the modem.

Electronic mail, or *E-mail*, for short, is one way of sending and receiving messages electronically. Anyone who is part of an E-mail network can send and receive private messages.

Before you can send or receive E-mail, you must obtain an E-mail address. This address identifies the location of your electronic "mailbox"—the place where you receive your E-mail. To send an E-mail message to another person you must include that person's E-mail address, just as you might address an envelope. There is no central listing of E-mail addresses. The best way to find out an address is to ask the person for their address.

Many corporations are using E-mail communications, which makes some environmentalists happier. More electronic communication means less use of paper and more saved trees.

Practicing the Skill

To send a message to a friend on an E-mail network, complete the following steps.

1. Select the "message" function from your communications software.
2. Type in the E-mail address.
3. Type in your message. Proofread it for errors.
4. Select the "send" function.

The E-mail system places the message in the receiver's "mailbox." He or she can read the message at any time—and then send you a reply.

Applying the Skill

Many scientific discoveries took place in the mid-1700s to the early 1900s. Use E-mail to contact a librarian. Ask for recommendations of young adult books related to scientific discoveries from 1750–1914.

For More Practice

Turn to the Skill Practice in the Chapter Review on page 645 for more practice in using E-mail.

Section 4

Revolution in the Arts

Setting the Scene

▶ **Terms to Define**

romanticism, realism, symbolism, impressionism, Postimpressionism

▶ **People to Meet**

Peter Tchaikovsky, Johann Wolfgang von Goethe, George Sand, Honoré de Balzac, Charles Dickens, Leo Tolstoy, Claude Monet, Vincent van Gogh

▶ **Places to Locate**

Paris

Find Out How did writers and artists in Europe and North America reflect changes in society between 1750 and 1914?

The Storyteller

Gustave frowned as he read his mother's letter. "I am tired of seeing your talent receive no recognition. You must acknowledge what people want. You need to cater to the popular taste ... paint imaginary scenes of Roman or medieval heroes. Then your paintings might win prizes or be purchased by influential collectors." Gustave Courbet would not follow the crowd or popular tastes, just because others were doing it. He would paint images of his own time.

—freely adapted from *Realism*, Linda Nochlin, 1971

Landscape
by Gustave Courbet

European and American artists in the 1800s mirrored society's mixed feelings about the rapid disappearance of the old order and the uncertainty of the new. A growing middle class created a larger audience for music, literature, and poetry. Formerly, artists had depended on patronage by the wealthy. Now, although some artists sought support in the new industrial society, others rebelled against middle-class values and shunned patronage of any kind, preferring to work independently. Those who rebelled would dominate the arts in the late 1700s and early 1800s.

The Romantic Movement

By the late 1700s, artists had begun to react to the Enlightenment's emphasis on order and reason. The French philosopher Jean-Jacques Rousseau taught that people were naturally good and needed only to be free. In rejecting society's formal structures and rules, Rousseau anticipated romanticism, a movement in which artists would emphasize human emotion and imagination over reason.

Romantic artists tried to free themselves from the rigid forms and structures of neoclassical art. Rejecting the mechanization and ugliness of industrialized society, many turned to nature, glorifying its awesome power and quiet beauty.

Many romantic artists looked to the past, admiring the mythical heroes of old. They felt compassion for the weak and oppressed, and they celebrated the lives of "simple peasants." The struggle for personal freedom and heroic rebellion against society's established rules are frequent themes in their works. The French poet Charles Baudelaire described the movement: "Romanticism is precisely situated neither in choice of subject nor in exact truth, but in a way of feeling."

Chapter 24 *Cultural Revolution* **635**

Romantic Music

The composers of the Enlightenment had emphasized form and order, but romantic composers departed from traditional forms and styles. They often fused music with imaginative literature, creating operas—dramas set to music—and *lieder* (LEED•uhr)—art songs, or poems set to music.

Romantic music was meant to stir the emotions—whether in large works, such as symphonies by German composer Ludwig van Beethoven (BAY•TOH•vuhn) or Russian composer **Peter Tchaikovsky** (chy•KAWF•skee), or in smaller, more intimate works, such as piano pieces by Poland's Frédéric Chopin (SHOH•PAN) or the *lieder* of Austria's Franz Schubert. Melodies from folk music added emotional power to romantic music, as in works by Czech composer Antonín Dvořák (DVAWR•ZHANK), whose *Symphony From the New World* echoes American spirituals.

Romantic Literature

Like romantic composers, romantic writers created emotion-filled, imaginative works. Early leaders of the romantic movement in literature include German writers Friedrich von Schiller and **Johann Wolfgang von Goethe** (GUHR•tuh). Schiller glorified freedom fighters, such as the legendary hero William Tell. His drama with that title is about the medieval Swiss struggle for freedom. Goethe is best known for *Faust*, a drama about human striving and the need for redemption.

France produced some of the most popular romantic writers. Alexandre Dumas's novel *The Three Musketeers* recounts the exploits of three dashing adventurers in the 1600s. Aurore Dupin, better known as **George Sand**, made peasants and workers heroes in her fiction. The novels of Victor Hugo, the foremost French romanticist, include *The Hunchback of Notre Dame* and *Les Misérables*, tales portraying human suffering with compassion and power.

Romanticism also influenced Great Britain. Scots writer Sir Walter Scott won a huge following with his historical novels *Ivanhoe*, *Quentin Durward*, and *The Talisman*. Another Scot, Robert Burns, showed deep feeling for nature and romantic love in his poetry. English poet and painter William Blake attacked the growing results of industrialization in *Songs of Innocence* and *Songs of Experience*. Similar themes fill the works of English poets Samuel Taylor Coleridge, William Wordsworth, John Keats, Percy Bysshe Shelley, and Lord Byron.

Romantic Painting

Painters, like writers, reflected romantic ideals. Turning from the order, clarity, and balance of the neoclassical style, painters began to portray exotic, powerful subjects in a dramatic and colorful way. For example, the painting *Liberty Leading the People*, by Eugène Delacroix (DEH•luh•KWAH), shows the figure of Liberty as a brave woman carrying a flag and leading patriots through the streets of **Paris**. Like many other romantic works, the painting was meant to stir the emotions, not appeal to the intellect.

The Turn Toward Realism

In the mid-1800s, some artists began to reject the sentimentality of romanticism. They sought to portray life in a realistic manner. In France, painter Gustave Courbet (kur•BAY) expressed the idea behind this style, known as **realism**: "Painting … does not consist of anything but the presentation of real and concrete things." Realist painters and writers wished to portray life as it was, not to escape from it.

Courbet's own large, somber canvases called attention to the less fortunate members of society and their difficult circumstances. *Burial at Ornans*

History & Art *Girl With Goats by a Fiord* by Hans Dahl. Christie's, London, England **This painting exemplifies romantic ideals.** *What characteristics of romanticism does the painting show?*

National Gallery of Art

French Impressionists

Purest of the impressionists, Claude Monet captured the essence of light and air. A stiff breeze swirls through *Woman With a Parasol—Madame Monet and Her Son*, painted between 1875 and 1878. "His pictures always were too draughty for me!" commented fellow impressionist Edgar Degas. "If it had been any worse, I should have had to turn up my coat collar." Unlike Monet and other French impressionists who insisted on painting from life, Degas was the master of the fleeting moment. He relied on quick sketches and his memory of posture, light, and color, and painted later at his studio.

One of Monet's paintings entitled *Impression—Sunrise*, exhibited in a Paris art show gave impressionism its name. An art critic reviewing the show ridiculed the painting and invented the term "impressionism." French impressionists such as Monet, Degas, and others rebelled against the strict traditions and rules of the art world of the late 1800s to capture the natural appearances of objects. Using dabs and strokes of primary colors, they tried to give the impression of actual reflected light. They often painted outdoors, trying to capture natural light, shadow, and color on canvas. ⊕

Futabatei Publishes *The Drifting Clouds*

Japan, 1889

Beginning in the 1880s, Western ideas began to influence Japanese writing. A group of Japanese authors, who had been educated in Western languages, broke from traditional forms of literature. These writers believed that Japan's technological development should be accompanied by the development of modern European-style literary works. In 1889 Futabatei Shimei produced a novel titled *The Drifting Clouds* which helped establish the novel as a respected form of Japanese literature.

portrayed peasants from his hometown standing around the grave of a loved one. By the end of the 1850s, other French artists had joined Courbet in painting realistically. Among the most notable were Honoré Daumier (doh•MYAY) and Jean-François Millet (mee•YAY).

Realism in Literature

Realism also flourished in literature. French writer **Honoré de Balzac** grouped about 90 of his novels and short stories of French life in the 1800s into a collection he called *The Human Comedy*. Many described frankly the greed and stupidity that Balzac saw in the growing middle class. Gustave Flaubert (floh•BEHR), another French writer, portrayed the conflict between dreary realities and romantic dreams in *Madame Bovary*, the story of a young woman married to a dull provincial doctor.

The English novelist, Mary Ann Evans wrote under the pen name George Eliot. Her novels portrayed the rigidity and senselessness of the British social order. **Charles Dickens**, the foremost English realistic writer, spoke out on behalf of the poor. Dickens focused on the deplorable conditions in the prisons, hospitals, and poorhouses of London. In his novel *Hard Times*, he attacked the materialism of Coketown, a fictional city.

Russian writers came to be known for their penetrating novels about the human spirit. The novels of Russian writer **Leo Tolstoy** also reflected his compassion for the peasants and gave his analysis of social customs. *War and Peace* is a family novel in which Tolstoy takes five families through the stages of life. It is also a historical novel about Napoleon's invasion of Russia in 1812.

The works of American novelist Theodore Dreiser belong to a pessimistic style of realism called naturalism, in which writers tried to apply scientific methods to imaginative writing. In Dreiser's novel *An American Tragedy*, a young man is executed for killing his pregnant girlfriend. To Dreiser, the man is a victim whose tragedy results from circumstances over which he has no control.

Symbolism

Some writers became disgusted with what they viewed as the ugly and brutal realities of European industrial civilization. To escape, they created a world of shadowy images evoked by symbols. This movement, called symbolism, began in France and was led by the poet Stéphane Mallarmé (MA•LAHR•MAY), who believed that "to name an object is to destroy three-quarters of the enjoyment of a poem, which is made up of the pleasure of guessing little by little." He and his followers, Paul Verlaine (vehr•LAYN) and Arthur Rimbaud (ram•BOH), gave impressions by suggestion rather than by direct statement.

Symbolism spread to the other arts and to other countries. The symbolists focused on the exotic, using imagery to suggest the world of the spirit. Intellectuals applauded this effort, but the average person found symbolism difficult to understand.

New Trends in Painting

Intense competition and rigid, traditional standards characterized the artistic world in the 1800s. An artist's works had to be considered "correct" and the subject matter "proper" by judges at London's Royal Academy of Art or Paris's École des Beaux-Arts (School of Fine Arts). Acceptance by those schools and a place in their yearly exhibitions were crucial to a beginning artist's success.

In 1863 the École turned down more than 3,000 of the 5,000 works that were submitted for its approval—the highest proportion of rejections that anyone could remember. Napoleon III, the French emperor at the time, decided to hold an exhibit to let the public see the paintings that had been rejected by the École. Those paintings delighted many people and gave the painters renewed hope that their works would win recognition.

Impressionism

During the 1870s, a group of French artists developed a style called impressionism. The impressionist painters abandoned many of the rules on which earlier painters had based their art—rules about proper subject matter and traditional techniques of line, perspective, and studio lighting. Fascinated by color and light, the impressionists sought to capture the momentary impression a subject made on their senses. They moved out of the studio and into the real world, choosing to work outdoors, in theaters, and in cafes.

Pierre-Auguste Renoir (REHN•WAHR) painted idealized portraits of women and children and outdoor scenes. **Claude Monet** (moh•NAY), one of the most famous impressionists, painted series of paintings on the same subject to show variations in light and color during various times of the day and seasons of the year.

Postimpressionism

In the late 1880s some artists turned away from impressionism. Known as Postimpressionists, they formed their styles independently to express in different ways the chaos and complexity around them. One of their leaders was Paul Cézanne (say•ZAN). Earlier, he had identified with romanticism and impressionism. By the 1880s he had laid the foundation for Postimpressionism when he declared, "I do not want to reproduce nature, I want to re-create it."

Georges Seurat (suh•RAH), another Postimpressionist, applied science to his paintings. He developed a method called pointillism, placing small dabs of color close together to produce a three-dimensional effect. His painting *A Sunday Afternoon on the Island of La Grande Jatte* consists of thousands of different-colored dots.

Paul Gauguin (goh•GAN) moved to the Pacific island of Tahiti, where he painted *Where do we come from? What are we? Where are we going?* It was an attempt to find universal truths in the symbols of a nonindustrial culture.

The son of a Dutch minister, **Vincent van Gogh** (van GOH) led an unhappy life. After failing at the ministry, he turned to painting. Within two years,

History & Art *The Swing* by Pierre-Auguste Renoir, 1876. Musée d'Orsay, Paris, France *What did France's impressionist painters, such as Renoir and Monet, seek to capture in their works?*

he produced most of the paintings for which he is known, using brilliant colors and distorted forms to make intense statements.

Henri de Toulouse-Lautrec (tu•LOOZ loh •TREHK) used Paris nightlife as a major subject. He painted with vivid detail, using bright colors to catch the reality of lives he portrayed. His use of line and color in posters of Paris's Moulin Rouge nightclub attracted worldwide attention.

SECTION 4 REVIEW

Recall
1. **Define** romanticism, realism, symbolism, impressionism, Postimpressionism.
2. **Identify** Peter Tchaikovsky, Johann Wolfgang von Goethe, George Sand, Honoré de Balzac, Charles Dickens, Leo Tolstoy, Claude Monet, Vincent van Gogh.
3. **Explain** what factors led to the rise of realism.

Critical Thinking
4. **Analyzing Information**
How might the painting *Liberty Leading the People* have influenced French attitudes about revolution?

Understanding Themes
5. **Innovation** How was nature significant in romantic art?

from

The Beggar

by Anton Chekhov

*A*nton Chekhov, who died in 1904 at age 44, wrote several plays and short stories that became classics of Russian literature. The issue he confronts in the following excerpt—how to help those in need—remains a vital issue today. A wealthy lawyer, Skvortsoff, is angered by the lies a beggar tells to win sympathy and money from passersby. Skvortsoff complains to the beggar that "you could always find work if you only wanted to, but you're lazy and spoiled and drunken!"

*B*y God, you judge harshly!" cried the beggar with a bitter laugh. "Where can I find manual labor? It's too late for me to be a clerk because in trade one has to begin as a boy; no one would ever take me for a porter because they couldn't order me about; no factory would have me because for that one has to know a trade, and I know none."

"Nonsense! You always find some excuse! How would you like to chop wood for me?"

"I wouldn't refuse to do that, but in these days even skilled wood-cutters find themselves sitting without bread."

"Huh! You loafers all talk that way. As soon as an offer is made you, you refuse it. Will you come and chop wood for me?"

"Yes, sir; I will."

"Very well; we'll soon find out. Splendid—we'll see—"

Skvortsoff hastened along, rubbing his hands, not without a feeling of malice, and called his cook out of the kitchen.

"Here, Olga," he said, "take this gentleman into the wood-shed and let him chop wood."

The tatterdemalion [clothed in ragged garments] scarecrow shrugged his shoulders, as if in perplexity, and went irresolutely after the cook. It was obvious from his gait that he had not consented to go and chop wood because he was hungry and wanted work, but simply from pride and shame, because he had been trapped by his own words. It was obvious, too, that his strength had been undermined by vodka and that he was unhealthy and did not feel the slightest inclination for toil.

Skvortsoff hurried into the dining room. From its windows one could see the wood-shed and everything that went on in the yard. Standing at the window, Skvortsoff saw the cook and the beggar come out into the yard by the back door and make their way across the dirty snow to the shed. Olga glared wrathfully at her companion, shoved him aside with her elbow, unlocked the shed, and angrily banged the door.

"We probably interrupted the woman over her coffee," thought Skvortsoff. "What an ill-tempered creature!"

Next he saw the pseudo-teacher, pseudo-student seat himself on a log and become lost in thought with his red cheeks resting on his fists. The woman flung down an ax at his feet, spat angrily, and, judging from the expression of her lips, began to scold him. The beggar irresolutely pulled a billet [log] of wood toward him, set it up between his feet, and tapped it feebly with the ax. The billet wavered and fell down. The beggar again pulled it to him, blew on his freezing hands, and tapped it with his ax cautiously, as if afraid of hitting his overshoe or of cutting off his finger. The stick of wood again fell to the ground.

Skvortsoff's anger had vanished and he now began to feel a little sorry and ashamed of himself for having set a spoiled, drunken, perchance sick man to work at menial labor in the cold.

"Well, never mind," he thought, going into his study from the dining room. "I did it for his own good."

An hour later Olga came in and announced

Religious Procession in the Province of Kursk by Ilya Repin. Tretyakov Gallery, Moscow, Russia **Ilya Repin painted realistic scenes of everyday Russian life.** *How does Chekhov portray Russian life in his story "The Beggar"?*

History & Art **Female Farmers** by Kazimir Malevich. Russian State Museum, St. Petersburg, Russia **Malevich used modern painting techniques to portray the life of peasant women in rural Russia.** *What role does Olga play in Chekhov's story?*

that the wood had all been chopped.

"Good! Give him half a ruble [the Russian unit of currency]," said Skvortsoff. "If he wants to he can come back and cut wood on the first day of each month. We can always find work for him."

On the first day of the month the waif made his appearance and again earned half a ruble, although he could barely stand on his legs. From that day on he often appeared in the yard and every time work was found for him. Now he would shovel snow, now put the wood-shed in order, now beat the dust out of rugs and mattresses. Every time he received from twenty to forty kopecks [one kopeck equals one-hundredth of a ruble], and once, even a pair of old trousers were sent out to him.

When Skvortsoff moved into another house he hired him to help in the packing and hauling of the furniture. This time the waif was sober, gloomy, and silent. He hardly touched the furniture, and walked behind the wagons hanging his head, not even making a pretense of appearing busy. He only shivered in the cold and became embarrassed when the carters jeered at him for his idleness, his feebleness, and his tattered, fancy overcoat. After the moving was over Skvortsoff sent for him.

"Well, I see that my words have taken effect," he said, handing him a ruble. "Here's for your pains. I see you are sober and have no objection to work. What is your name?"

"Lushkoff."

"Well, Lushkoff, I can now offer you some

other, cleaner employment. Can you write?"

"I can."

"Then take this letter to a friend of mine tomorrow and you will be given some copying to do. Work hard, don't drink, and remember what I have said to you. Good-bye!"

Pleased at having put a man on the right path, Skvortsoff tapped Lushkoff kindly on the shoulder and even gave him his hand at parting. Lushkoff took the letter, and from that day forth came no more to the yard for work.

Two years went by. Then one evening, as Skvortsoff was standing at the ticket window of a theater paying for his seat, he noticed a little man beside him with a coat collar of curly fur and a worn sealskin cap. This little individual timidly asked the ticket seller for a seat in the gallery and paid for it in copper coins.

"Lushkoff, is that you?" cried Skvortsoff, recognizing in the little man his former wood-chopper. "How are you? What are you doing? How is everything with you?"

"All right. I am a notary [a clerk who certifies legal documents] now and get thirty-five rubles a month."

"Thank Heaven! That's fine! I am delighted for your sake. I am very, very glad, Lushkoff. You see, you are my godson, in a sense. I gave you a push along the right path, you know. Do you remember what a roasting I gave you, eh? I nearly had you sinking into the ground at my feet that day. Thank you, old man, for not forgetting my words."

"Thank you, too," said Lushkoff. "If I hadn't come to you then I might still have been calling myself a teacher or a student to this day. Yes, by flying to your protection I dragged myself out of a pit."

"I am very glad, indeed."

"Thank you for your kind words and deeds. You talked splendidly to me then. I am very grateful to you and to your cook. God bless that good and noble woman! You spoke finely then, and I shall be indebted to you to my dying day; but, strictly speaking, it was your cook, Olga, who saved me."

"How is that?"

"Like this. When I used to come to your house to chop wood she used to begin: 'Oh, you sot [drunkard], you! Oh, you miserable creature! There's nothing for you but ruin.' And then she would sit down opposite me and grow sad, look into my face and weep. 'Oh you unlucky man! There is no pleasure for you in this world and there will be none in the world to come. You drunkard! You will burn in hell. Oh, you unhappy one!' And so she would carry on, you know, in that strain. I can't tell you how much misery she suffered, how many tears she shed for my sake. But the chief thing was—she used to chop the wood for me. Do you know, sir, that I did not chop one single stick of wood for you? She did it all. Why this saved me, why I changed, why I stopped drinking at the sight of her I cannot explain. I only know that, owing to her words and noble deeds a change took place in my heart; she set me right and I shall never forget it. However, it is time to go now; there goes the bell."

Lushkoff bowed and departed to the gallery.

RESPONDING TO LITERATURE

1. Explain how the beggar Lushkoff's character and behavior change between the beginning of Chekhov's story and the conclusion of the story.

2. Contrast Skvortsoff's plan for helping Lushkoff improve his life and what actually helped Lushkoff.

3. What advice do you think Chekhov would give to people today who want to help the poor?

4. **Predicting an Outcome** What might have happened if Skvortsoff had found out immediately that Olga was chopping the wood for Lushkoff?

Connections Across Time

Historical Significance The Industrial Revolution created new businesses and social classes. Living standards improved although a wide gap separated rich and poor.

Today Communist ideas have been discredited and capitalism is the world's dominant economic system. Since the 1930s, democratic societies have combined capitalism with social welfare policies. The role of government in social affairs, however, currently provokes much debate, and there are calls for greater personal responsibility and less government involvement.

Using Key Terms

Write the key term that completes each sentence. Then write a sentence for each term not chosen.

a. atomic theory	g. socialism
b. evolution	h. sociology
c. laissez-faire	i. genetics
d. immigration	j. emigration
e. impressionism	k. urbanization
f. realism	l. psychology

1. In the mid-1800s artists and writers in Europe and North America developed a style called _____ that often called attention to the less fortunate members of society.
2. Supporters of _____ believe that society, directly or through the government, should own the means of production.
3. The research of Gregor Mendel laid the foundation for the development of _____, the science of heredity.
4. Freud's theory that human actions grew out of subconscious motives led to the development of the science of _____.
5. Supporters of _____ believed that people should be able to buy and sell, hire and fire, free from government interference.

Technology Activity

Using the Internet Search the Internet for a Web site that provides additional information about the history of Marxism. Use a search engine to help focus your search by using words such as *karl marx*, *history*, and *socialism*. Write a research report based on your findings. Explain Marx's stages toward true communism, and provide examples of governments that were influenced by Karl Marx's ideas.

Using Your History Journal

After reading the literature selection from "The Beggar" by Anton Chekhov, write a review of the piece. Do you agree or disagree with Chekhov's assumptions about the poor? Why?

Reviewing Facts

1. **Economics** Explain why business leaders during the 1800s promoted laissez-faire economics.
2. **Economics** Discuss the impact of the ideas of Adam Smith and Karl Marx on world history.
3. **Science** List the contributions of Marie Curie and other physicists and state their impact.
4. **Economics** Identify the factors that led to the rise and spread of socialism in the 1800s.
5. **Culture** Describe one work by each of these writers: Hugo, Tolstoy, Dreiser.

Critical Thinking

1. **Apply** What are three examples of the romantics' emphasis on emotion?
2. **Analyze** How did Charles Darwin's theories answer his question about the great variety of living things?
3. **Synthesize** A frame of reference is a set of ideas that determines how something will be understood. Explain how the Industrial Revolution would be viewed from a capitalistic frame of reference and a Marxist frame of reference.
4. **Evaluate** Write a letter to the editor of an 1800s newspaper, expressing your views on secondary-school education for women.

5. **Analyze** The painting *Dinner at Haddo House* shows the lifestyle of the wealthy. How did this show of wealth further separate social classes?

Understanding Themes

1. **Change** According to Karl Marx, what steps would societies follow in moving toward the goal of communism?
2. **Innovation** Describe one innovation of the 1800s and early 1900s in each of these sciences: biology, physics, psychology. How did each innovation affect people's lives?
3. **Movement** How did improved methods of transportation affect the movement of people and products?
4. **Innovation** Select a cultural movement such as romanticism, realism, symbolism, impressionism, or Postimpressionism, and explain how the movement reflected the way people felt about changes in the 1800s.

Linking Past and Present

Explain why modern Russia has turned to capitalism from the radical Socialism born during the Industrial Revolution.

Skill Practice

Using your communications software, type a message to another student naming your favorite writer or artist from one of the following artistic movements. Explain why this artist is your favorite.

- Romanticism
- Realism
- Symbolism
- Impressionism
- Postimpressionism

Geography in History

1. **Place** Refer to the map "Population Growth in the United Kingdom." What were the major industrial cities of the United Kingdom by 1900?
2. **Place** How much did the population per square mile in the London and Bristol areas grow during this period?

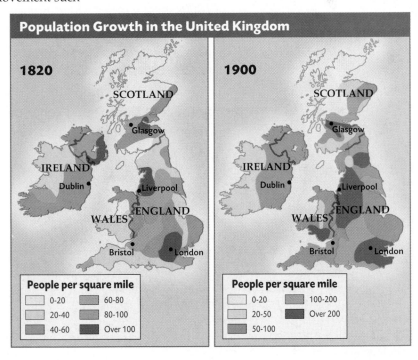

Population Growth in the United Kingdom

1820 — SCOTLAND, Glasgow, IRELAND, Dublin, Liverpool, ENGLAND, WALES, Bristol, London

People per square mile
- 0–20
- 20–40
- 40–60
- 60–80
- 80–100
- Over 100

1900 — SCOTLAND, Glasgow, IRELAND, Dublin, Liverpool, ENGLAND, WALES, Bristol, London

People per square mile
- 0–20
- 20–50
- 50–100
- 100–200
- Over 200

1800–1914

Democracy and Reform

Chapter Themes

▶ **Change** Great Britain carries out democratic reforms. *Section 1*

▶ **Movement** Immigrants from Great Britain and other countries settle Canada, Australia, and New Zealand. *Section 2*

▶ **Revolution** France undergoes political upheaval during the 1800s. *Section 3*

▶ **Change** The United States extends its borders and develops its economy. *Section 4*

▶ **Nationalism** Latin American nations achieve self-government. *Section 5*

The Storyteller

British politician Richard Cobden stood before the House of Commons in 1845. In a loud voice, he demanded that the middle and working classes be given more representation in a government that unfairly favored the landed aristocracy. Cobden declared:

"I say without being revolutionary ... that the sooner the power of this country is transferred from the landed ruling class, which has so misused it, and is placed absolutely ... in the hands of the intelligent middle and industrious classes, the better for the condition and destinies of this country."

While Cobden worked for change within the British political system, people in Europe and Latin America faced fiercer and often bloody struggles for democratic reform. By the end of the 1800s, democracy had triumphed in many parts of the world.

Historical Significance

Why did democratic reform movements develop and flourish in Europe and other parts of the world? How did independence change the lives of people in Latin America?

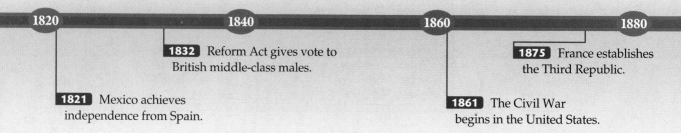

1820	1840	1860	1880

1832 Reform Act gives vote to British middle-class males.

1875 France establishes the Third Republic.

1821 Mexico achieves independence from Spain.

1861 The Civil War begins in the United States.

History & Art

Celebration of the Concorde of May 21, 1848 by Jean Jacques Champin. Musée de la Ville de Paris, Musée Carnavalet, Paris, France

Your History Journal

On an outline map of the world, draw and label all the territories once held by Great Britain and the dates when they became self-governing, or independent.

1837 Victoria becomes queen of Great Britain.

1867 Reform Act extends vote to all male homeowners and renters.

1886 Gladstone introduces Irish home rule legislation.

1900 Trade unionists and Socialists begin to form the Labour party.

Section 1

Reform in Great Britain

Setting the Scene

▶ **Terms to Define**

apportion, disenfranchised, suffragette, home rule

▶ **People to Meet**

the Chartists, Queen Victoria, William Gladstone, Benjamin Disraeli, the Fabians, Emmeline Pankhurst, Charles Stewart Parnell

▶ **Places to Locate**

Ireland

Find Out How did political change come to Great Britain during the 1800s?

The Storyteller

When women first lobbied for voting rights, some critics feared that if they won the vote, men would become women's servants. Political cartoons and works of art appeared that showed sour-faced men caring for babies and wringing out dirty laundry, while women happily rode around in carriages or talked excitedly around the ballot box. Other opponents claimed that if women won the vote, they would spend all their time at the polls. One poster nicknamed a woman who ran for office "Susan Sharp-Tongue, the Celebrated Man Tamer."

—adapted from *On To Victory, Propaganda Plays of the Woman Suffrage Movement*, edited by Bettina Friedl, 1987

Woman suffrage rally

Political change in Great Britain took place gradually and peacefully. The British government moved toward greater democracy through evolution rather than revolution. By the 1800s Great Britain was a limited constitutional monarchy. The monarch's authority consisted only of the rights to encourage, to warn, and to be consulted by those who really governed Great Britain. Actual executive power belonged to the Cabinet led by the prime minister, while Parliament maintained legislative control.

Although all British people in theory were represented in the House of Commons, the British government was not a true democracy in the early 1800s. Political power remained with the landed aristocracy, while the middle and working classes had no voting rights.

Electoral Reforms

In the early 1800s some rural districts were well represented in the House of Commons, while growing industrial areas had little representation. Factory workers, farm laborers, and the middle class began to demand that they receive a greater political voice. The liberal minority party, the Whigs, continually introduced bills to give voting rights to more people and to **apportion**, or divide and share, electoral districts more fairly. The Whigs' efforts were repeatedly defeated by the Tory party, which opposed such bills.

When the Whigs came to political power in 1830, however, their demands could no longer be ignored. In 1832 the Whigs forced the king to announce that he would create as many new lords as necessary to give the reform bill a majority in the House of Lords. To avoid this action, the lords gave in and passed the bill.

The Reform Act of 1832

The Reform Act of 1832 lowered the property qualifications for voting and gave more middle-class males the right to vote. The proportion of voters increased from 1 in 100 to 1 in 32 men. The act also took representation rights away from areas that had declined in population. With 143 seats freed in the House of Commons, the heavily populated cities finally increased their representation. One observer recalled the moments after the passing of the reform bill:

> ❝ We shook hands and clapped each other on the back, and went out laughing, crying … into the lobby. And no sooner were the outer doors opened than another shout answered that within the House. All the passages … were thronged by people who had waited till four in the morning to know the issue [outcome]. ❞

Reform Movements

While the Reform Act gave middle-class men the right to vote, it only frustrated the industrial and farm workers, who remained **disenfranchised**, or deprived of the right to vote. These disenfranchised citizens banded together to demand further reforms. In a document called *A People's Charter*, **the Chartists**, an important reform group of the working class, proposed political changes. The Chartists' demands included voting rights for all adult men, no property qualifications for voting, a secret ballot, salaries for members of Parliament so that the middle and lower classes could take seats, and equal electoral districts.

The Chartists submitted two petitions to Parliament, one with more than a million signatures and the other with more than 3 million. Parliament rejected both petitions. After the defeat, the Chartists had little success and their movement faded by the 1850s. Parliament did, however, eventually pass many of their reforms.

Another reform movement, the Anti-Corn Law League, was supported by the middle class. The aim of the League was to repeal the Corn Law, which since 1815 had severely limited and taxed the importation of foreign grain. Wealthy landowners benefited from the law, as it ensured them a profitable hold on the grain market. Middle-class industrialists fought the Corn Law because it forced them to pay higher wages to workers to enable them to buy bread.

The League—the first major political pressure group in Great Britain—captured public attention with lectures, pamphlets, books, and meetings.

Visualizing History In this British cartoon, Prime Minister Benjamin Disraeli presents the crown of India to Queen Victoria. *What other noted prime minister served during Victoria's reign?*

When an Irish crop failure forced Great Britain to import much grain, Parliament responded to the pressure and repealed the Corn Law.

Political Parties

One result of electoral reform was more elaborate organization of political parties. Before 1800 both parties—the Tories and the Whigs—represented wealthy landowners. They had no formal organization. They were actually loose groups of politicians with common interests. As more middle-class men gained voting rights, the old parties reorganized to win support from the new voters. After 1832 the Tory and Whig parties began to change into the modern Conservative and Liberal parties.

Support for the Conservative party came largely from the aristocracy and members of the old Tory party. The industrial and commercial classes and members of the old Whig party supported the Liberal party. Both parties eventually competed for middle-class and working-class votes.

Political Leadership

This era of political reform took place during the reign of **Queen Victoria**. She came to the throne in 1837 at age 18 and reigned for 64 years. Two brilliant prime ministers—**William Gladstone** and **Benjamin Disraeli**—served during Victoria's reign. Both men offered dynamic leadership for the emerging Liberal and Conservative parties. Through their efforts Great Britain continued toward full democracy.

William Gladstone

William Gladstone of the Liberal party served 4 times as prime minister between 1868 and 1894. His first term, from 1868 to 1874, became known as the Great Ministry because of his many social reforms. Deeply religious, Gladstone always sought to apply morality to politics.

Gladstone directed reforms in such areas as government administration, education, and elections. A civil service reform of 1870 made appointments to most civil service positions dependent on competitive examinations. The Education Act of 1870 divided the country into school districts, which were maintained by local control. With the Ballot Act of 1872, Gladstone satisfied the old Chartist demand for the secret ballot. He also changed election districts. The Redistribution Act of 1885 divided Britain into electoral districts almost equal in population.

Benjamin Disraeli

Benjamin Disraeli of the Conservative party first gained fame in Great Britain as a novelist and later as a politician. He served two terms as prime minister—his first term briefly in 1868 and his second term from 1874 to 1880.

Disraeli believed that the Conservative party could save aristocratic traditions while cautiously adopting democratic reforms. He realized that blocking change would be damaging to the Conservative party, which began to base its primary support among the upper middle class.

In 1867 Disraeli had introduced a Conservative-backed reform bill. By lowering property qualifications for voters, the Reform Bill of 1867 extended the vote to all male homeowners and most men who rented property. The bill increased the electorate by about 1 million men, adding to it many working-class voters.

Growth of Democracy

The British government changed in the last quarter of the 1800s. As steps were taken toward democracy, the working class, women, and Irish Catholics began to influence political life.

Rise of Labor

Political reforms inspired many groups to fight for increased rights. Labor unions had been steadily growing and gaining political strength since the mid-1700s. By the time of Gladstone's Great Ministry, unions had become a way of life among the working classes. Laborers from nearly every trade organized into unions, which achieved great gains by staging strikes and demonstrations.

At the same time that labor unions were growing stronger, socialism was also gaining followers. In 1884 a group of middle-class intellectuals formed the Fabian Society, an organization whose aim was to peacefully and gradually prepare the way for a Socialist government. Through education, its members promoted social justice such as improved conditions and fair wages for workers. Unlike labor unions, **the Fabians** favored parliamentary action over strikes and demonstrations.

In 1900 trade unionists and Socialists laid the foundation for a new political party—the Labour party—to speak for the working class. Labour party supporters backed the reform-minded Liberal government elected in 1906. Together the Liberal and Labour members of Parliament promoted government reform to improve workers' lives. Between 1906 and 1914, new legislation provided the working classes with old-age pensions, a minimum wage, unemployment assistance, and health and unemployment insurance.

A Constitutional Crisis

To finance these measures, the Liberal government called for higher taxes in the budget of 1909. The largely Conservative House of Lords vehemently opposed the proposed taxation, because it directly threatened the wealth of the aristocracy.

The contest ended in victory for the House of Commons when the 1911 Parliament Act narrowed the powers of the House of Lords by removing money bills from their control. This action symbolized the aristocracy's political decline.

Women Demand Greater Rights

Women also sought to benefit from Great Britain's move toward more representative democracy. British women, mostly from the middle class, spoke out for political and social equality in the mid-1800s. In the 1850s women's rights activists fought to win property rights for married women. Their efforts led to the passage of the Married Women's Property Acts of 1870 and 1882, which gave women increased legal control over a family's earnings and property.

Achieving women's voting rights came more slowly. Although women had gained the right to vote in local elections in 1869, they still could not vote on a national level. In 1903 **Emmeline**

Pankhurst and her two daughters, Christabel and Sylvia, founded the Women's Social and Political Union (WSPU). They led a voting rights campaign on behalf of all British women and became known as **suffragettes**. The WSPU attracted attention to its cause through street demonstrations and hunger strikes. The violence cost the movement much support. Nevertheless, the movement grew. In 1918 Parliament finally granted women over 30—along with all men—the right to vote. Ten years later, it gave the vote to all women over 21.

Ireland

Like others in the British Isles, Irish Catholics sought greater participation in the government. Their ultimate goal, however, was to govern themselves. For centuries, English and Scottish Protestants who had settled in **Ireland** enjoyed almost total political and economic control of the island. This privileged minority owned large amounts of land. They rented it at high prices to Irish Catholic peasants, who were prohibited from purchasing land. Most Irish people lived in poverty. Ireland was predominantly Catholic, and a law requiring Catholics to pay taxes to the Anglican Church of Ireland only intensified anti-British feeling.

In 1801 Parliament had passed the Act of Union, joining Ireland and Great Britain. This union entitled Ireland to representation in Parliament, but it was not until 1829 that Catholics in the British Isles won the right to vote and hold office. Although these acts increased their rights, most Irish people still demanded to rule themselves.

Irish hatred of British rule heightened when a disastrous potato famine known as the "Great Hunger" hit the country in the 1840s. Because peasants were forced to export the grain they grew in order to pay their high rents, they came to rely on the potato as their main source of food. In 1845 a deadly fungus destroyed much of the potato crop,

Visualizing History **Irish activists seeking home rule riot in Belfast in 1872.** *What minority group controlled most of the land in Ireland for centuries?*

and the British government sent inadequate aid to Ireland during the famine. In four years, at least one million Irish died of starvation and disease. Millions more emigrated to the United States, Canada, and Australia.

Various groups fought for Irish rights. **Charles Stewart Parnell**—Irish-born member of a Protestant family—led Irish nationalists who sought to have the question of **home rule**, or self-government, heard in Parliament. Liberal Prime Minister Gladstone tried to pass legislation granting Irish home rule. His action split the Liberal party, and the measure was defeated. In 1914 Parliament finally passed a home rule bill, but it never went into effect. Irish Protestants threatened to fight British troops if Parliament enforced it.

SECTION 1 REVIEW

Recall
1. **Define** apportion, disenfranchised, suffragette, home rule.
2. **Identify** the Chartists, Anti-Corn Law League, Queen Victoria, William Gladstone, Benjamin Disraeli, the Fabians,

Emmeline Pankhurst, Charles Stewart Parnell.
3. **List** three democratic reforms that occurred in Great Britain during the 1800s.

Critical Thinking
4. **Synthesizing Information** Imagine that you are an Irish

Catholic farmworker living in Ireland in the 1800s. Express your feelings and attitudes about the British government.

Understanding Themes
5. **Change** What might have happened if Parliament had opposed democratic reform?

1850	1875	1900	1925

1840 Treaty of Waitangi guarantees Maori rights in New Zealand.

1867 British North America Act forms the Dominion of Canada.

1885 Canadian Pacific Railway links eastern and western parts of Canada.

1901 Australia becomes a dominion in the British Empire.

Section 2

The Dominions

Setting the Scene

▶ **Terms to Define**
dominion

▶ **People to Meet**
the Loyalists, Lord Durham, John A. Macdonald, the Aborigines, the Maori

▶ **Places to Locate**
Canada, Australia, New Zealand

Find Out How did new societies emerge in Canada, Australia, and New Zealand?

The Storyteller

On the long sea voyage to Australia, first-class passengers could go anywhere on board; other passengers, traveling more cheaply, were more restricted. Seamen were most restricted of all, and after three months on board, got their revenge for staying below-deck in curious ways. Sometimes the crew would protest their rights by tossing a pig or sheep down among the cabins at night, to invade the passengers' space and keep them awake. One emigrant wrote in her diary: "From every quarter of the cabin you could hear the 'Ma, Ma' during the greater part of the night."

—adapted from *Sailing to Australia*, Andrew Hassam, 1994

Immigrant mother and children

As Great Britain moved toward greater democracy, the British Empire reached its height. With its colonies making up one-fourth of the world's land and people, Great Britain became the richest and most powerful country in the world. Political changes also took place in the empire, especially in territories largely inhabited by British settlers. Colonies such as **Canada**, **Australia**, and **New Zealand** sought self-government.

Canada

By the mid-1800s, Canada consisted of a number of British colonies dependent on the British government. The colonial population was ethnically divided. One part was French, another immigrant British, and a third part descendants of **the Loyalists**—Americans loyal to Great Britain during the American Revolution. Most Britons and Loyalists lived in Nova Scotia, New Brunswick, and near the Great Lakes. The French were concentrated in the Saint Lawrence River valley.

In 1763, as a prize for their victory in the French and Indian War, the British gained control of Quebec, which included most of French Canada. From that time, the French in Quebec firmly resisted British colonial rule. The predominantly Catholic French population were irritated by the influx of British immigrants, English-speaking and Protestant, that began about 1760.

To solve the growing English and French problem, the British government passed the Constitutional Act of 1791. This law divided Quebec into two colonies: Lower Canada and Upper Canada. Lower Canada remained French-speaking, but Upper Canada became English. Each colony had an assembly whose laws were subject to veto by a governor appointed by the British government. This arrangement worked until political differences brought rebellion in each colony.

Quebec City, founded in 1608, is Canada's oldest city. Located on the St. Lawrence River, Quebec City was a major lumber and ship-building center during the 1800s. *What three groups contributed to the founding of Canada?*

By the late 1830s the French began to feel threatened by the growing English-speaking minority. Meanwhile, the British-Loyalist community was divided by disagreements between the conservative upper-class leadership and a group of liberal reformers who wanted a share in government. In 1837 unrest triggered rebellions in both colonies.

Canadian Self-Government

Uprisings in both Upper Canada and Lower Canada convinced the British that they had a serious problem in North America. In 1838 the British Parliament ordered **Lord Durham** to Canada to investigate. In a report to Parliament, Durham urged granting virtual self-government to Canada. Durham insisted that the real authority should be an elected assembly, not a British-appointed governor-general or the British government in London. With acceptance of the Durham report by the British Parliament, self-government developed in Canada. This pattern was later adopted by other territories of the British Empire.

In 1867 the British Parliament passed the British North America Act. This law established Canada as a dominion, or a self-governing territory owing allegiance to the British king or queen. The British North America Act joined Upper Canada (Ontario), Lower Canada (Quebec), Nova Scotia, and New Brunswick in a confederation called the Dominion of Canada. This act became the basis of the modern nation of Canada. In that same year, Canadian voters elected their first parliament. The first Canadian prime minister was **John A. Macdonald**, a Scottish-born lawyer.

Expanding Canadian Territory

At first the Dominion of Canada consisted of four provinces in the southeast, extending from the Great Lakes to the Atlantic Ocean. Then, in 1869 the dominion acquired the Northwest Territory, which extended west across vast prairies and forestlands and north to the Arctic wilderness. Most of this area was populated by Native Americans and European and American fur traders. Following sporadic violence between traders and Native Americans, the Canadian government set up and sent westward a special law-keeping force known as the Northwest Mounted Police. The police largely won the respect and loyalty of the Native Americans before the arrival of large numbers of Canadian settlers.

Canada further expanded its territory during the late 1800s. From the eastern part of the Northwest Territory, the province of Manitoba was formed in 1870. In 1871 British Columbia, a separate British colony on the Pacific coast, became a province. In 1873 tiny Prince Edward Island near the Atlantic Ocean joined Canada. To link the eastern provinces with the western provinces, the Canadian Pacific Railway was completed in 1885. This made possible the development of the Canadian prairies. In 1905 the prairie provinces of Saskatchewan and Alberta were added to the dominion.

Australia and New Zealand

On the other side of the world—in the south and southwest Pacific—the British colonies of Australia and New Zealand also sought self-government.

Australia

Initially, Great Britain established Australia as a prisoners' colony to relieve overcrowded British jails. By 1860, after a gold rush lured new immigrants, the population reached 1 million, and the practice of transporting prisoners to Australia was abolished.

In settling the land, Europeans came into contact with **the Aborigines**, the original people of Australia. Many early European settlers treated the Aborigines badly, occupied their land, and killed many of them. Large numbers of Aborigines died from diseases introduced by the Europeans.

The increase in European settlement called for a better administration of colonial Australia. By the late 1800s Australia was made up of six British colonies—New South Wales, Victoria, Queensland, Tasmania, Western Australia, and South Australia. In 1901 Parliament made Australia a dominion that included the colonies plus a region known as the Northern Territory.

New Zealand

The first Europeans to settle in New Zealand were from James Cook's expedition in 1770. Hunters from Great Britain and the United States set up whaling stations during the 1790s. New Zealand also attracted timber traders.

Foreigners brought many problems to the original inhabitants, known as **the Maori**. Firearms, for example, increased warfare among the Maori tribes. Foreigners also brought diseases to which the Maori had no immunity, causing an almost 50 percent reduction in the Maori population in 20 years.

In an effort to provide law for the Maori and the settlers, British naval officers and Maori chiefs concluded the Treaty of Waitangi in 1840. The treaty protected Maori rights, including property rights, while the Maori gave the British sovereignty over New Zealand. In 1840 the first permanent British settlements were founded at Wellington and Wanganui. Their economies were based on wool exports to British markets.

As with Australia, New Zealand's British population was small until the discovery of gold. The gold discovery also brought conflict between the newcomers and the Maori.

Prospectors unsuccessful in finding gold in New Zealand remained to farm. To gain more land, they violated those Maori land rights guaranteed by the treaty with the British. During the Maori Wars in the mid-1800s, the New Zealand government sided with the newcomers and seized some Maori land for public use.

New Zealand received a constitution from Great Britain in 1852 and became a largely self-governing colony. In the 1890s, the New Zealand government carried out an extensive program of social reforms, such as pensions for the elderly and protection of workers' rights. At this time Great Britain itself had not yet introduced many of these reforms. In 1907 New Zealand finally became a dominion within the British Empire.

SECTION 2 REVIEW

Recall
1. **Define** dominion.
2. **Identify** the Loyalists, Lord Durham, John A. Macdonald, British North America Act, Northwest Mounted Police, the Aborigines, the Maori, Treaty of Waitangi.
3. **State** the terms of the Treaty of Waitangi. Were its terms carried out?

Critical Thinking
4. **Evaluating Information** The Canadians at first wanted to call their confederation "the Kingdom of Canada." The British government, however, suggested the term *dominion* because they felt *kingdom* would be offensive to the United States. Why might Americans find *kingdom* an offensive title?

Understanding Themes
5. **Movement** What was the original purpose for British settlement of Australia?

1830 Revolution overthrows Bourbon dynasty.

1848 Voters elect Louis-Napoleon president.

1870 Revolutionaries establish Commune of Paris.

1890s The Dreyfus affair divides French society.

Section 3

Political Struggles in France

Setting the Scene

▶ **Terms to Define**
ultraroyalist, coup d'état, plebiscite

▶ **People to Meet**
Charles X, Louis Philippe, Louis-Napoleon, General Georges Boulanger, Alfred Dreyfus

▶ **Places to Locate**
Paris

Find Out What changes in government did France undergo during the 1800s?

The Storyteller

Louis-Napoleon Bonaparte (Emperor Napoleon III) had grand ideas for the government of France—including a grand role for himself. Of course, he would not revive the excesses of royalty that France had groaned under before. Still, Frenchmen could not help but notice that his plans for the new constitution of France included the following ideas: "The executive power vests in the Emperor alone. The Emperor is the supreme head of the state; he commands the national forces both on land and sea; declares war, makes treaties of peace, of alliance, and of commerce...."

—adapted from *The Political and Historical Works of Louis Napoleon Bonaparte*, Volume 1, 1852

Louis-Napoleon Bonaparte

The Congress of Vienna sought to reduce France's might and restore traditional monarchs to their thrones. Although the European balance of power was restored, Congress delegates found their plans for monarchy frustrated as liberal and nationalist ideas spread among the peoples of Europe. The clash between old and new ideologies, or systems of thought and belief, sparked revolutions throughout Europe from the 1820s to the 1840s.

TURNING POINT

Revolt in France

Because of its revolutionary traditions, France was the center point of these upheavals. In 1815 the Congress of Vienna restored the Bourbon monarchy under Louis XVIII. Many French republicans accepted Louis because he was willing to rule as a constitutional monarch.

After Louis's death in 1824, his brother and successor **Charles X** set out to restore absolute monarchy—with help from the ultraroyalists—nobles favoring a return to the old order. When Charles tried to repay nobles for lands lost during the revolution, liberals in the legislative assembly opposed him. The king then dissolved the assembly and held new elections; but voters only elected more liberals to reject Charles's policies. Finally the king issued the July Ordinances, measures designed to dissolve the assembly, end press freedom, and restrict voting rights.

On July 27, 1830, angry Parisian workers and students rose up against the king. By July 29, after *Les Trois Glorieuses* (three glorious days) they forced

Visualizing History The Revolution of 1848 that began in France triggered revolts throughout Europe. *What happened to the Second Republic within four years of its constitution?*

Charles X to give up his right as monarch and abdicate the throne. The fallen king fled to Great Britain.

The "Citizen-King"

After the chaos had subsided, revolutionary leaders set up a new constitutional monarchy that did not have close ties to the old aristocracy. **Louis Philippe**, a cousin of Charles, accepted the throne. Because he dressed and behaved like a middle-class person, Louis Philippe became known as the "Citizen-King" and won the support of the growing middle class.

From 1830 to 1848, however, many French people became discontented with Louis Philippe's government. At heart, the "Citizen-King" favored the wealthy, and many working-class citizens began to demand political reforms, especially voting rights.

Louis Philippe refused their demands. When they appealed to Prime Minister François Guizot (gee•ZOH), he too refused. Frustrated, leaders organized political banquets, where they called for an extended vote and Guizot's resignation.

The Revolution of 1848

In 1848 Guizot canceled a banquet, fearing a demonstration. This order, however, came too late. On February 22, crowds flooded the streets, singing "The Marseillaise" and shouting protests against Guizot. Louis Philippe called in troops, but the soldiers sympathized with the rebels and joined them. Over the next days, at least 52 civilians were killed or wounded. The disturbances forced Louis Philippe to abdicate and flee to Great Britain. The Revolution of 1848 ended with the rebels proclaiming France a republic.

Inspired by events in France, revolutionaries in other European countries also fought for greater political rights. Political discontent in Austria, Italy, and Prussia was particularly significant. In these areas, however, the political status quo was more or less maintained despite the uprisings.

The Second Empire

When the political turmoil in France had finally subsided, the revolutionary leaders proclaimed the Second Republic of France and set out to create a new constitution. The French constitution featured many democratic reforms, including a legislative branch called the National Assembly, the election of a president, and an extension of voting rights to all adult men. Nine million men eagerly set off to the polls to elect a new National Assembly in the spring of 1848. Only briefly, however, would the French enjoy the freedoms brought by the Second Republic.

The Rise of Louis-Napoleon

In presidential elections held in December 1848, French voters gave **Louis-Napoleon** Bonaparte, the nephew of Napoleon Bonaparte, an overwhelming victory. Louis-Napoleon's popularity came more from his name than from his political skills. The name "Napoleon" reminded the French people of the greatness their nation had once enjoyed under Napoleon I.

Although Louis-Napoleon presented himself as a democratic reformer, the president hoped to use his popularity to make himself an emperor. To guarantee victory, Louis-Napoleon worked to win the support of powerful groups in France—the army, the Church, the middle class, and the peasants. For example, in 1849 he won the confidence of French Catholics by ordering French troops to help the pope suppress an attempt by Italian nationalists to set up a republic in Rome. He also gave the Church more control over French education.

This support for the Catholics, however, created an uproar in **Paris**. Demonstrators opposing support for the pope filled the streets. Alarmed by the mob action, the National Assembly restricted people's rights in order to keep law and order. They also revoked voting rights for about a third of the voters.

Louis-Napoleon used this uproar to his advantage by convincing the French people that the republic was a failure. Deciding to take control of the French government, Louis-Napoleon directed a coup d'état, or a quick seizure of power, on December 2, 1851. He dissolved the National Assembly and arrested many of his opponents. With shrewd planning, he won popular support by reestablishing voting rights for all French men.

Louis-Napoleon then called for a plebiscite, or national vote, asking the people to give him the power to create a new French constitution. The people enthusiastically gave him their support. Now Louis-Napoleon had complete legislative and executive control, and the people appeared happy with the order and stability he provided. In a second plebiscite, a large percentage of the people approved the transformation of the French republic into a hereditary empire. In 1852 Louis-Napoleon became Napoleon III, Emperor of France.

Although Napoleon III restricted the press and limited civil liberties, he had a successful economic program. During the 1850s French industrial growth doubled and foreign trade tripled. France built new railroads and roads, including Paris's famous wide boulevards.

The Crimean War

In 1854 Napoleon III led France into the Crimean War. The war pitted France and Great Britain against Russia and arose from the interests that all three countries had in the Ottoman Empire. The immediate cause of the conflict was a dispute between France and Russia over which of them had the right to protect Christians in the empire or those visiting the Holy Land. In this dispute the Ottoman emperor sided with France.

Angered by the decision, Russia's Czar Nicholas I in July 1853 seized Ottoman territory in the Balkans. This Russian invasion upset both Great Britain and France, who wanted to protect their trade and financial interests in the Middle East. After the Ottoman Empire declared war on Russia in October 1853, Great Britain, France, and the tiny Italian kingdom of Sardinia eventually joined the conflict.

In the fall of 1854, French and British armies invaded the Russian-ruled Crimean Peninsula on the north shore of the Black Sea. At first, little fighting occurred as the armies battled cold, violent storms, and disease. By war's end, disease would cause more deaths on both sides than war injuries. Among British forces, however, a nurse, Florence Nightingale, improved hospital care and saved many lives. In the fall of 1855, French and British forces finally defeated the Russians, who lacked supplies, reinforcements, and railroads. The 1856 Treaty of Paris ending the war made Russia return some of the Ottoman territory it had seized and banned warships and forts around the Black Sea.

End of the Empire

In 1870 conflict with Prussia ended Napoleon III's empire. Alarmed by Prussia's growing power, Napoleon made his most costly error in judgment: he declared war on the Prussians on July 19, 1870.

Few French or foreign observers anticipated the quick and relatively easy defeat of France in the Franco-Prussian War. The French armies were slow to mobilize, and German forces crossed into France with little armed resistance. The Prussians defeated the French in just over six weeks. On September 2, after winning a decisive victory at Sedan, the Prussians took Napoleon III as prisoner.

History & Art *The Siege of Paris* by **Ernest Meissonier.** **The Louvre, Paris, France** *What impact did the Franco-Prussian conflict of 1870–1871 have on France and the government of Napoleon III?*

When the news of the emperor's capture reached Paris on September 4, crowds filled the streets and forced the collapse of the Second Empire. The people of Paris endured a Prussian siege for four months before a truce was signed.

Making Peace With Prussia

The French people elected a new National Assembly, dominated by royalists, to make peace with Prussia. The Assembly surrendered the provinces of Alsace and Lorraine and agreed to pay 5 billion francs—the equivalent of 1 billion dollars—to Prussia. Prussian forces further humiliated France by staging a victory march through Paris. The people of Paris, strong republicans who wanted a renewal of the war with Prussia instead of peace, were angered by the peace terms. They sank into despair after their loss.

In March the National Assembly set about restoring order in France, particularly in Paris. The provisional government inspired an angry outcry when it demanded that Parisians pay the rents and the debts that had been suspended during the siege. At the same time, the Assembly stopped payments to the National Guard, which many Parisian workers had joined during the Prussian

siege. These drastic measures led to unrest and to an uprising in Paris.

The Commune of Paris

During the revolt, the workers established a Socialist government known as the Commune of Paris. The leaders of the Commune refused to recognize the National Assembly and called for the conversion of France into a decentralized federation of independent cities. The Commune declared war on the propertied classes and the Church. It advocated an end to government support for religion, the adoption of a new revolutionary calendar, and the introduction of a 10-hour workday.

In a bitter civil war, the National Assembly took the offensive and reasserted its control over Paris. Armies pushed past the Commune's barricades throughout the strife-ridden city. In defiance, the supporters of the Commune burned public buildings, including the Tuileries Palace and the City Hall. During the "Bloody Week" in May 1871, the Assembly's powerful military forces arrested nearly 40,000 people and killed more than 20,000. The horror of rebellion set back the political and social advances made by workers and caused distrust between France's middle and working classes.

CONNECTIONS

Science and Technology

The Development of Photography

For centuries scientists tried to record lasting images, but it was not until 1826 that the world's first camera was made. Its inventor, the Frenchman Joseph Niépce, produced a blurry image of a farmyard by coating a metal plate with a light-sensitive chemical. In 1837 Louis Daguerre perfected Niépce's methods and fixed an image on silver-coated copper. Daguerreotypes, as these images were called, produced detailed pictures.

Photography progressed rapidly throughout the 1800s. Some photographers took portraits of wealthy families. Others risked their lives

Early Camera

photographing the horrors of war. Gradually scientific and technical discoveries made cameras more efficient and easier to operate. In 1888 George Eastman developed the small, lightweight, and relatively inexpensive box camera. Mass-produced, the box camera put photography into the hands of millions.

Today, a picture can be taken simply by aiming the camera and pressing a button. In sophistication, cameras range from simple fixed-focus models to ones that have many lenses and built-in features.

Linking Past and Present ACTIVITY

Discuss how photography helped people record their lives in the 1800s. In what ways does photography affect events today? Consider the power of the media.

The Third Republic

After the fall of the Commune, the dispirited French again tried to rebuild their government. This proved to be a difficult task, as royalists and republicans alike fought bitterly over the form the government should take.

Finally, in 1875 a new constitution made France once again a republic. The Third Republic's constitution provided for a two-house legislature. The two houses elected a president, who served for four years and who had little real power. Every official act required the full support of both houses of the legislature to be signed into law. A cabinet of ministers was responsible for government policy, and the post of premier was created to handle all executive business.

Threats to the Republic

Although France had finally established itself as a republic, the new government was particularly vulnerable to attack. One of its greatest threats came from **General Georges Boulanger** (BOO•lahn•ZHAY), who was a popular war hero. Boulanger urged the French people to seek revenge against Prussia. He launched a campaign to demand the election of a new legislature in 1888.

Boulanger won great support from royalists and others who opposed the republic. In 1889 his supporters urged him to overthrow the Third Republic with a coup d'état. When the government ordered him arrested for treason, Boulanger fled the country to Belgium. Without the direction of its popular leader, the Boulanger movement collapsed.

A second threat to the republic in the early 1890s centered around the construction of a canal through Panama. The canal would provide France with a waterway connecting the Atlantic and Pacific Oceans.

When the Panama Company collapsed and the Panama project failed, thousands of French stockholders lost all of the money they had invested. Charges of dishonesty and poor managerial practices erupted. The scandal spread to the highest government offices, as members of both houses were accused of accepting bribes to get more funding for the troubled project. The Panama scandal partly benefited France's growing Socialist movement. In 1893 nearly 50 Socialists won seats in the national legislature.

The Dreyfus Affair

The 1890s saw the Third Republic's greatest crisis—the Dreyfus affair. In 1894 **Alfred Dreyfus**, a French army officer, was convicted by a military court of selling military secrets to the Germans and sentenced to a life term on Devil's Island, a prison colony off the coast of French Guiana in South America. The French army was, at the time, influenced by anti-Semitic views, and its suspicion had fallen on Dreyfus, who was Jewish.

Dreyfus, however, protested his innocence and it soon became known that another officer was the real traitor and that the official evidence used in Dreyfus's trial had been forged. In an article, "J'accuse (I Accuse)", the novelist Émile Zola took a strong stand in support of Dreyfus. In 1899 a new trial was ordered, but the military court, unable to admit error, found Dreyfus guilty once again. This time, Dreyfus won a presidential pardon, and a civilian court later declared him innocent.

While it lasted, the Dreyfus affair deeply divided France. Republicans, Socialists, and anti-Catholics united to defend Dreyfus and to discredit the military. Wanting to uphold the army's honor, royalists, nationalists, and many Catholics joined anti-Semites—those hostile to Jews—in regarding Dreyfus as guilty.

Despite its divisiveness, the Dreyfus affair proved that republican government was able to survive in France. The immediate effect of the affair was to bring to power radical republicans and Socialists, who carried out changes such as the separation of church and state in 1905.

SECTION 3 REVIEW

Recall
1. **Define** ultraroyalist, coup d'état, plebiscite.
2. **Identify** Charles X, Louis Philippe, Louis-Napoleon, Commune of Paris, General Georges Boulanger, Alfred Dreyfus.

3. **Explain** how the French government changed under the rule of Louis-Napoleon.

Critical Thinking
4. **Analyzing Information** Why was the government of the Third Republic especially vulnerable to political opposition?

Understanding Themes
5. **Revolution** Trace France's political history during the 1800s. What factors sparked revolutions in 1830 and 1848? What impact did these revolutions have on the rest of Europe?

1800   1850   1900

1803 The United States gains the Louisiana Purchase.

1846 War begins between the United States and Mexico.

1865 The Civil War ends.

c. 1890s Immigrants arrive in the United States from eastern and southern Europe.

Section 4

Expansion of the United States

Setting the Scene

▶ **Terms to Define**
sectionalism, secede, ratify

▶ **People to Meet**
Thomas Jefferson, Abraham Lincoln, Susan B. Anthony, Woodrow Wilson

▶ **Places to Locate**
Louisiana Purchase, Gadsden Purchase

Find Out ➤ How did the United States change during the 1800s?

The Storyteller

During the Civil War when Confederate casualties returned in large numbers from the front, buildings quickly became makeshift hospitals. Miss Sally Tomkins was one of the most tireless workers among the many brave women who served in the overcrowded places of mercy. As a "soldier without a gun," she received a commission in the Confederate Army as well as a commendation—the only such commission ever issued to a woman, and a unique "first" for any American army. In a note to the War Department, she said: "I accepted the commission ... but would not allow my name to be placed on the payroll of the army."

—adapted from *A Pictorial History of the Confederacy*, Lamont Buchanan, 1951

Civil War nurse and patient

While many political upheavals shook Europe during the 1800s, the United States grew in size, wealth, and power. The vast area of forests and plains west of the original colonies lured American settlers by the thousands, and no European powers with colonial interests blocked their westward drive. The conflicts between European countries during the early years of the nation had created opportunities for the United States to acquire more territory.

The Young Nation Grows

The United States gained its biggest territorial prize as a result of Napoleon I's desire to conquer his most hated enemy, Great Britain. In 1803 Napoleon was preparing to go to war against Great Britain and needed money to finance it. Desperate for money, Napoleon offered to sell the French-owned Louisiana territory to the United States. With a quick stroke of the pen and a payment of $15 million, President **Thomas Jefferson** acquired the **Louisiana Purchase**—all the land between the Mississippi River and the Rocky Mountains. The area eventually formed 13 states.

The United States also gained land as a result of Spain's internal conflicts. Weakened by political and financial problems, Spain ceded, or gave up, Florida in 1819.

Later acquisitions of new land from other nations proved to be not so easy or peaceful. In 1845 the Republic of Texas was annexed to the United States. By 1846 this territorial gain resulted in a conflict between the United States and Mexico that escalated into war. The United States defeated the Mexicans in 1848, and in the resulting treaty Mexico gave up a vast area that later formed all of California, Utah, and Nevada and parts of

Denver Public Library, Western History Department

Pioneers

Y ou can see the fatigue in the faces of these pioneers, moving West in Conestoga wagons. Prairie stretched behind them, mountains ahead—and an unbearable distance to go. From the settlement of Jamestown in 1607 to the settlement of the West two centuries later, Americans explored, moved, and endured unspeakable hardships. Their journeys stretched their endurance, as they battled hunger, Native Americans, and the difficulties of the terrain itself. The West was dry: Wood shrank; wheels fell off wagons; and the hooves of oxen split. "Dust is two or three inches in depth and as fine as flour," one pioneer wrote. "We cannot see the wagons next to us...." Settled into new homes, the pioneers' hardships did not end. Families lived through winters so harsh that cows, sheathed in ice, had to be brought inside. Summers brought plagues of grasshoppers and prairie fires. And always there was isolation and loneliness.

By 1860 the United States stretched from the Atlantic to the Pacific. But expansion brought problems for the nation as well as benefits. The territory won in the Mexican-American War (1846–1848) shifted the issue of slavery into the political mainstream with such force that it took the Civil War to resolve the conflict between North and South. ⊕

Colorado, Arizona, Wyoming, and New Mexico. This large acquisition of territory added a sizable Hispanic population to the United States.

Farther north, the United States argued with Great Britain over the borders of the Oregon Country. In a treaty with Great Britain, the United States gained part of this area. Oregon, Washington, and Idaho, as well as parts of Wyoming and Montana, were later created from this territory.

By the mid-1800s, only one step remained in the country's move across the continent. In 1853 James Gadsden, the American ambassador to Mexico, gave Mexico $10 million for 45,000 square miles (116,550 sq. km) of land in southern New Mexico and Arizona, south of the Rio Grande.

With the **Gadsden Purchase**, the United States finally stretched from "sea to shining sea." This westward expansion brought new opportunities to settlers, who forged communities and built states in the new lands. The expansion also brought suffering—loss of land, culture, and often life—to Native Americans who had inhabited lands in the West for centuries.

TURNING POINT
Rise of the United States

As Americans moved westward, democratic rights in the United States expanded. When the nation was first founded, the right to vote and hold public office was generally restricted to white male property owners.

The people of the West sought to extend these voting rights. All of the new states adopted constitutions that granted the right to vote to all men. These new states gradually gained power in Congress, and, over time, their liberal policies influenced the country. By 1856 every state had granted all white men the vote.

An Expanding Economy

Many factors contributed to the rapid growth of the American economy. The Industrial Revolution, which began in Great Britain, spread to

Images *of the* Times

The Civil War

There had always been economic and cultural differences between the North and the South. In 1861 these differences led to the American Civil War, or the War Between the States.

Union naval forces took New Orleans in May 1862. In the Civil War, both North and South suffered heavy losses, but the North's industrial strength gave it an advantage over the agricultural South.

135,000 SETS, 270,000 VOLUMES SOLD.

UNCLE TOM'S CABIN

FOR SALE HERE.

AN EDITION FOR THE MILLION, COMPLETE IN 1 Vol. PRICE 37 1-2 CENTS.
"   IN GERMAN, IN 1 Vol. PRICE 50 CENTS.
"   IN 2 Vols. CLOTH, 6 PLATES, PRICE $1.50.
SUPERB ILLUSTRATED EDITION, IN 1 Vol. WITH 153 ENGRAVINGS,
PRICES FROM $2.50 TO $5.00.

The Greatest Book of the Age.

Antislavery feeling in the North was stimulated by Harriet Beecher Stowe's *Uncle Tom's Cabin*, a novel portraying slavery at its worst. The book sold 300,000 copies in 1852, its first year of publication.

the United States. Busy commercial regions filled with factories and heavily populated cities characterized the North. Irish, German, and Scandinavian immigrants joined the Northern workforce, settling in cities and farmlands. Northern workers received pay for their labor, as well as the right to leave their jobs for better ones. This system of work was called free labor.

In contrast, the South became the chief producer of raw cotton for the booming British textile industry. The South's economy remained primarily agricultural and depended on the labor of enslaved African Americans. Most white Southerners, even those who held no enslaved people, believed in slave labor. As the United States expanded, it was clear that the different economic interests of the two regions would cause conflict.

A Nation Divided

The differences in their economies led the two regions, the North and the South, to take widely different positions on many political and economic issues. The result was sectionalism, the devotion to the political and economic interest of a region or a section of the country. The most divisive issue, however, was slave labor. The South wanted to expand slavery into the territories gained during the Mexican War. The North wanted these new western areas to remain territories employing free labor.

By 1860 the United States consisted of 18 free states and 15 slave states. In the presidential election of 1860, proslavery and antislavery forces vied for power. When **Abraham Lincoln** won the presidency, the South feared he would abolish slavery.

To protest the election, South Carolina decided to secede, or withdraw, from the Union. Other Southern states followed suit. By February 8, 1861, seven states had joined to form their own nation, the Confederate States of America. In Washington, D.C., Congress worked on a compromise, but to no avail. When Lincoln was sworn in as President in March, he declared that "no state, upon its own mere motion, can lawfully get out of the Union." By April the divided nation was at war. The Civil

Union and Confederate caps reveal the war's colors: blue for the North (shown right), and gray for the South (shown left). More Americans died in the Civil War than in any other conflict in American history.

REFLECTING ON THE TIMES

1. What major issue helped spark conflict between the North and the South?
2. Why was the Civil War unique in American history?

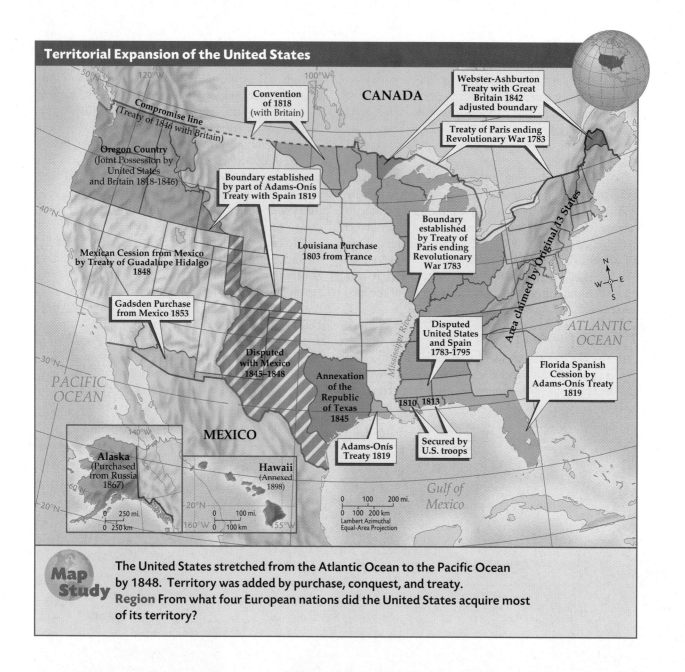

Territorial Expansion of the United States

Convention of 1818 (with Britain)

CANADA

Webster-Ashburton Treaty with Great Britain 1842 adjusted boundary

Treaty of Paris ending Revolutionary War 1783

Compromise line (Treaty of 1846 with Britain)

Oregon Country (Joint Possession by United States and Britain 1818-1846)

Boundary established by part of Adams-Onís Treaty with Spain 1819

Mexican Cession from Mexico by Treaty of Guadalupe Hidalgo 1848

Louisiana Purchase 1803 from France

Boundary established by Treaty of Paris ending Revolutionary War 1783

Area claimed by Original 13 States

Gadsden Purchase from Mexico 1853

Disputed with Mexico 1845–1848

Disputed United States and Spain 1783-1795

PACIFIC OCEAN

ATLANTIC OCEAN

Mississippi River

Annexation of the Republic of Texas 1845

Florida Spanish Cession by Adams-Onís Treaty 1819

1810 1813

MEXICO

Alaska (Purchased from Russia 1867)

0 250 mi.
0 250 km

Hawaii (Annexed 1898)

0 100 mi.
0 100 km

Adams-Onís Treaty 1819

Secured by U.S. troops

Gulf of Mexico

0 100 200 mi.
0 100 200 km
Lambert Azimuthal Equal-Area Projection

Map Study

The United States stretched from the Atlantic Ocean to the Pacific Ocean by 1848. Territory was added by purchase, conquest, and treaty.
Region From what four European nations did the United States acquire most of its territory?

War, pitting North against South and lasting from 1861 to 1865, was one of the bloodiest struggles of the 1800s.

Although the North had 22 million people and the South only 9 million, of which nearly a third were enslaved, Southern forces won many early victories under skilled military leaders such as Robert E. Lee. Later, however, the North threw the full weight of its massive resources against the South.

After four years of war that claimed the lives of more than 600,000 Americans, the Northern forces defeated the Confederate forces. After the war, Congress passed three amendments to the Constitution of the United States. These amendments abolished slavery and gave formerly enslaved African Americans citizenship and equal protection under the law, as well as the right to vote. The nation set about to rebuild itself.

A New Society

After the Civil War, the growth of industries and cities in the United States continued with new vigor. Across the country textile mills, lumberyards, mines, and factories increased their output. In 1900 oil fields provided about 130 times more oil than they had in 1860, ironworks 10 times more iron, and steelworks almost 60 times more steel. The "captains of industry" who developed and invested in these thriving industries amassed great fortunes and gained widespread admiration.

Immigration

As industry grew, so did the nation's population. Between 1870 and 1900, the number of Americans doubled from approximately 38 million to 76 million. Immigrants contributed significantly to this growth. Before the Civil War, most immigrants had come from northern Europe, mainly the British Isles, Germany, and Scandinavia. The Irish potato famine of the 1840s brought nearly 1 million Irish people to the United States. The failed German revolution of 1848 had prompted many disappointed liberals and intellectuals to leave their homeland.

After the Civil War, immigration from northern Europe decreased, while immigration from southern and eastern Europe increased. By 1900, immigrants from Italy, Russia, and Austria-Hungary made up more than three-fourths of the United States's foreign-born population. After landing at Ellis Island in New York, most of these immigrants headed for urban areas to work.

Along the West coast by the late 1800s, communities of Asian immigrants thrived. Chinese immigrants first came to California in the late 1840s to find gold and stayed to work in the mines and build railroads. By 1900, immigrants from Japan had also arrived in the country. Anti-Asian feelings, however, led to legal limits or bans on further Asian immigration. Also, Asian Americans faced widespread discrimination, much of which lasted well into the 1900s.

Women's Rights

As women gained economic opportunities, they also demanded political equality. A women's rights movement had flourished in the 1850s under leaders such as Lucretia Mott and Sojourner Truth. During the late 1800s, women known as suffragists fought hard for women's right to vote. Forming organizations such as the National Woman Suffrage Association (NWSA), suffragists such as Elizabeth Cady Stanton and **Susan B. Anthony** wrote books,

Visualizing History During the late 1800s and early 1900s, suffragists pushed for an amendment to the Constitution granting women the right to vote. *By 1918, in which of the states could women vote?*

testified before state legislatures, and spoke at public meetings to urge votes for women.

Slowly women achieved the right to vote at the state level, beginning with Wyoming, Colorado, and Utah. By 1918 women had gained full suffrage in many Western states, Michigan, Illinois and New York. Finally, because of women's contribution in World War I, it became impossible for politicians to ignore women's demands. In September 1918 President **Woodrow Wilson** asked Congress to pass a constitutional amendment guaranteeing the vote to all United States citizens 21 years of age and older regardless of their sex. In 1920, the constitutionally-required number of states acted to ratify, or approve, the Nineteenth Amendment.

SECTION 4 REVIEW

Recall
1. **Define** sectionalism, secede, ratify.
2. **Identify** Thomas Jefferson, Louisiana Purchase, Abraham Lincoln, the Civil War, Susan B. Anthony, Woodrow Wilson.
3. **Explain** how the United States acquired territory to achieve its present-day continental borders.

Critical Thinking
4. **Analyzing Information** How did the Industrial Revolution in the North contribute to the outbreak of the Civil War?

Understanding Themes
5. **Change** Describe the changes to the economy of the United States in the late 1800s. What caused these changes?

1800	1820	1840

1804 Haiti proclaims its independence.

1819 Simón Bolívar defeats Spaniards at the Battle of Boyacá.

1825 Portugal recognizes Brazil's independence.

Section 5

Latin American Independence

Setting the Scene

▶ **Terms to Define**

peninsulares, creoles, mestizos

▶ **People to Meet**

François Toussaint-Louverture, Miguel Hidalgo, Simón Bolívar, José de San Martín, Pedro I

▶ **Places to Locate**

Haiti, Mexico, Central America, Venezuela, Argentina, Chile, Peru, Brazil

 **Find Out** How did the countries of Latin America win independence?

The Storyteller

Simón Bolívar sent a joyous letter to a fellow general on January 8, 1822, displaying his belief in a unified America. He wrote, "America's greatest day has not yet dawned. We have indeed driven out our oppressors, smashed the tablets of their

tyrannical laws, and established legitimate institutions; but we have yet to lay the foundation ... that will make of this part of the world a nation of republics." Bolívar was confident that this unified America would impress Europe: "Who shall oppose an America united in heart, subject to one law, and guided by the torch of liberty?"

—adapted from *Selected Writings of Bolívar*, compiled by Vicente Lecuna and edited by Harold A. Bierck, Jr., 1951

Simón Bolívar

For 300 years Spain and Portugal held colonies in the Americas without facing serious threats to their rule. In the early 1800s, however, the situation changed. Inspired by the American and French Revolutions, Latin Americans sought an end to colonial rule and joined independence movements.

Ruling the Colonies

Like other European nations, Spain and Portugal regarded their Latin American colonies with a mercantilist view—the idea that colonies existed chiefly to increase the home countries' wealth. Mexico, Peru, and Brazil contained large deposits of gold and silver as well as forests that yielded valuable exotic woods such as mahogany and ebony.

Farming provided another major source of colonial income. Spanish and Portuguese monarchs granted huge tracts of fertile land to explorers and nobles for the growing of cash crops, such as corn, sugar, and cocoa. The landowners then forced the Native Americans to work the farms. When they died from forced labor and diseases that the Europeans had introduced to the Americas, the Spanish and the Portuguese imported large numbers of enslaved Africans.

The Catholic Church also played a critical role in the colonial economies, strengthening Spanish and Portuguese rule in Latin America. Both the Spaniards and the Portuguese brought the Catholic religion with them to the Americas. Priests and monks converted the Native Americans who worked on the farms to Catholicism and taught them loyalty to the Crown.

The colonial governments and the clergy worked very closely together. Clergymen held high government offices. The government, in turn, supported the Church. By 1800 the Catholic Church controlled almost half the wealth of Latin America.

Over the years, colonists became increasingly unhappy with colonial rule. They resented the trade restrictions and high taxes Spain and Portugal imposed upon them. Most of all, they resented the rigid colonial social structure.

A Rigid Social Order

Social classes based on privilege divided colonial Latin America. Colonial leaders, called *peninsulares*, were born in Spain or Portugal and stood at the top level of the social order. Appointed by the Spanish and Portuguese governments, the *peninsulares* held all important military and political positions. Below them were the colonial-born white aristocrats, called creoles. Although they controlled most of the land and business in the colonies, the creoles were regarded as second-class citizens by the *peninsulares*. The creoles envied the privileged leadership positions that were held exclusively by the *peninsulares*.

At the bottom of the colonial social pyramid were the majority of Latin Americans. Some were Native Americans. Others were of African or African and European ancestry. The largest of this group, however, were mestizos (meh•STEE•zohz), Latin Americans of mixed Native American and European ancestry. Spurned by the ruling white classes, these Latin Americans faced social and racial barriers in colonial society. They worked as servants for *peninsulares* and creoles, and as unskilled laborers and carpenters. Some worked as plantation overseers and farmhands.

Growing Discontent

In the 1800s Latin Americans began to challenge the rigid social order and its controls with revolts throughout Latin America. The creoles played the largest leadership roles in these conflicts. Wealthy and well educated, many were well versed in the liberal political philosophies of the Enlightenment, but their colonial birth prevented them from holding the highest government positions. The creoles were eager to take control of Latin American affairs.

Uprising in Haiti

Although the Spanish and Portuguese colonies were ripe for revolt, the first successful uprising in the Latin American colonies took place in the French colony of **Haiti** (Saint Domingue), on the island of

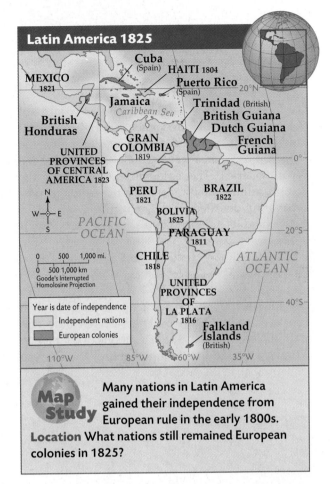

Latin America 1825

Map Study
Many nations in Latin America gained their independence from European rule in the early 1800s.
Location What nations still remained European colonies in 1825?

Hispaniola in the Caribbean Sea. Huge plantations of sugar, cotton, and coffee spread across the mountains and valleys of the lush tropical land. France and many other countries depended on the tiny colony for their supply of sugar and coffee.

The plantations were owned by French planters and worked by the colony's enslaved African population. More than 500,000 of the 560,000 people living in Haiti in the late 1700s were enslaved or had been. The few French planters who controlled the French colony often went to severe and brutal extremes to control the African majority.

Unrest erupted in the early 1790s when enslaved Africans led by a formerly enslaved man named **François Toussaint-Louverture** (TOO•SAN LOO•vuhr•TYUR) revolted, setting fire to plantation homes and fields of sugarcane. One observer described the horrifying scene:

❝ Picture to yourself the whole horizon a wall of fire, from which continually rose thick vortices [whirling columns] of smoke, whose huge black volumes could be likened only to those frightful storm-clouds ... for nearly three weeks we could barely distinguish between day and night, for so long as the rebels found anything to feed the flames, they never ceased to burn…. **"**

In 1802 Napoleon sent forces to take control of the colony. Captured by French officers, Toussaint-Louverture was imprisoned in France, where he died in 1803. Then a wave of yellow fever aided the revolutionaries. The epidemic swept across the colony, killing thousands of French soldiers. The rebel army defeated the French, and in 1804 Haiti proclaimed its independence.

Mexico Struggles for Freedom

One of the earliest uprisings against Spanish rule occurred in **Mexico**, which at that time was part of New Spain. In 1810 a Catholic priest named **Miguel Hidalgo** led the fight against the Spanish government in Mexico. Hidalgo cared deeply for the poverty-stricken Native Americans and mestizos in his parish of Dolores. In addition to political freedom, he also wanted to end slavery and to improve living conditions for Mexico's poor. To Hidalgo, revolt was the only way to bring change to Mexico.

On September 16, 1810, Hidalgo gave a stirring address that became known as "el Grito de Dolores" —the cry of Dolores. In the speech, he called on Mexicans to fight for "Independence and Liberty." Hidalgo then led Native Americans and mestizos on a freedom march to Mexico City that eventually turned into an armed movement. In spite of early advances, Hidalgo and his forces faced mounting opposition from the Spaniards and their Mexican creole allies. In 1811 the well-trained Spanish army finally overwhelmed the rebels, and Hidalgo was captured and executed.

Another priest, José María Morelos, took charge of the revolution after Hidalgo died. Morelos captured a large portion of southern Mexico. In 1813 he called a conference that declared Mexico's independence from Spain. Morelos's forces fought the Spaniards but were defeated in 1815. Like Hidalgo, Morelos was executed.

Despite many battles, Mexico did not gain full independence until 1821. That year, a liberal revolt in Spain threatened to overthrow the monarchy and establish a constitution. This reform frightened wealthy Mexican creoles, who feared such a change might infringe on their own privileges. To make sure this did not happen, they declared independence from Spain in 1821.

Ironically, their leader was Agustín de Iturbide (EE•TUR•BEE•thay), the army officer who had crushed Morelos's movement. Iturbide made himself emperor in 1822, but opposition to his oppressive rule developed. The Mexican people soon deposed Iturbide and declared their country a republic in 1823.

When Mexico became a republic, the Central American provinces in New Spain declared their independence. In Guatemala, representatives established the United Provinces of **Central America**. In the 1830s leaders divided the region into the countries of Costa Rica, El Salvador, Guatemala, Honduras, and Nicaragua.

History & Art *Father Miguel Hidalgo,* a fresco by José Clemente Orozco, 1937. Governor's Mansion, Guadalajara, Mexico *What two groups made up the rebel force that Hidalgo led against the Spanish army?*

Spanish South America

Creoles in the Spanish colonies of South America gained an opportunity for independence in 1808 when Napoleon seized control of the Spanish government. The refusal of the Spanish

American colonists to acknowledge Napoleon's government resulted in revolts throughout the empire. In addition, Spain's fight against France, together with the colonies' isolation from their home country, left the Spanish weak and vulnerable to attack. Three outstanding leaders—Simón Bolívar, José de San Martín, and Bernardo O'Higgins—led South American colonies in their fight against Spanish rule.

Simón Bolívar, a creole from **Venezuela**, led many colonies to independence. Bolívar believed in equality and saw liberty as "the only object worth a man's life." Bolívar had witnessed the reforms of the French Revolution. Called "the Liberator," Bolívar devoted his life to freedom for Latin Americans.

In 1810 Bolívar started a revolt against the Spaniards in Caracas. After nearly 9 years of fighting, Bolívar crushed Spain's power in northern South America at the Battle of Boyacá in 1819. During the next 20 years, Bolívar and his forces won freedom for the present-day countries of Venezuela, Colombia, Panama, Bolivia, and Ecuador.

While Bolívar fought in Venezuela, another revolutionary leader, **José de San Martín** of **Argentina**, led Latin American armies over the Andes Mountains and into **Chile**. In Chile, San Martín joined Bernardo O'Higgins. Together, their forces successfully achieved independence for Chile in 1818. San Martín then set off to free **Peru** in 1820. Within a year he captured Lima and declared Peru independent.

In July 1822 San Martín and Bolívar met in the Ecuadorian port of Guayaquil (GWY•uh•KEEL) to discuss the future of Latin America. Though they shared a common goal, they could not agree on strategy and policy. San Martín finally decided to withdraw from the revolt and allowed Bolívar to take command. By 1826 Bolívar and his armies had liberated all of South America.

Brazil Gains Independence

Brazil achieved its independence without the bloodshed that accompanied the liberation of Spanish America. In 1808 Napoleon's French army had invaded Portugal, causing the Portuguese royal family to flee to Brazil.

King João transferred his monarchy to Brazil, declaring Rio de Janeiro capital of the Portuguese Empire. João immediately introduced governmental reforms in Brazil. He reinstated more favorable trade laws by opening Brazil's ports to the world. João also worked to make the agriculture and

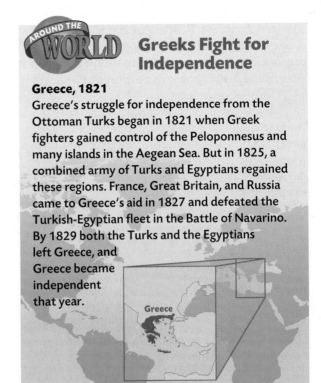

Around the World

Greeks Fight for Independence

Greece, 1821

Greece's struggle for independence from the Ottoman Turks began in 1821 when Greek fighters gained control of the Peloponnesus and many islands in the Aegean Sea. But in 1825, a combined army of Turks and Egyptians regained these regions. France, Great Britain, and Russia came to Greece's aid in 1827 and defeated the Turkish-Egyptian fleet in the Battle of Navarino. By 1829 both the Turks and the Egyptians left Greece, and Greece became independent that year.

Greece

mining industries more profitable. Soon both industry and commerce were flourishing.

The liberal ruler brought Brazilians increasing opportunities by funding public education, including military academies, an art school, and medical schools. With these reforms Brazil moved quickly toward independence, and in 1815 João made Brazil a self-governing kingdom within the Portuguese Empire.

King João came to love the semitropical land of mountains and endless forests; he chose to remain there after Napoleon was defeated in 1815. In 1820, however, liberals took over the Portuguese government. Determined to save his throne, he returned to Portugal. He left Brazil in the hands of his 23-year-old son, Dom Pedro.

The new Portuguese government fought to make Brazil a colonial possession again. Leaders ended free trade and many of the other advantages Brazil had enjoyed under João's monarchy. They also demanded that Dom Pedro abandon his rule and immediately return to Portugal. Supported by his father, Dom Pedro declared that he would remain in Brazil. Dom Pedro defied Portuguese leaders by calling a constitutional convention and answered their angry response with a cry of "Independence or death!"

In September 1822 Brazil won full independence from Portugal. Three months later Dom Pedro was crowned Emperor **Pedro I** of Brazil. With Pedro ruling the empire under a constitution, Brazil became the only independent country in South America to freely choose a constitutional monarchy as its form of government.

Meanwhile, João maintained his support of his beloved Brazil by refusing to allow the Portuguese government to send new military forces to fight the rebels. Great Britain also pressured Portugal to end its battle. In 1825 Portugal finally recognized Brazil's independence.

Challenges to Growth

By the mid-1820s most Latin American countries had won their independence. Their next task was to achieve national unity and a stable government. These goals, however, were difficult to reach. Simón Bolívar, who had dreamed of uniting all of northern South America into one large and powerful state, became so disappointed and disillusioned that he wrote, "Those who have toiled for liberty in South America have plowed the sea."

Common Problems

In trying to build stable and prosperous nations, Latin Americans faced a number of challenges. One obstacle was the geography of Central and South America. High mountains and thick jungles made transportation and communication difficult, hindering trade and economic growth. Vast areas of fertile land remained undeveloped. Population centers, separated by physical barriers, became rivals instead of allies.

Other problems were part of Latin America's colonial heritage. Spanish and Portuguese rule had given the Latin Americans little practice in governing themselves. Instead, they were used to authoritarian government, which was not responsible to the people and demanded obedience from them.

In the colonial system, political power was in the hands of the executive branch of government.

The judicial branch was weak and limited, and the legislative branch was practically nonexistent. Latin Americans had strong, well-educated leaders, but they had no experience in the legislative process. Simón Bolívar complained that the colonial system had kept his people in a state of "permanent childhood" with regard to knowledge of running a government. "If we could have at least managed our domestic affairs and our internal administration, we could have acquainted ourselves with the process and machinery of government," he wrote.

Independence did not bring about much change in social conditions in Latin America. Catholicism remained the official religion, and Church and government continued to be closely tied. The new countries also continued to maintain a separation between upper and lower classes. The dominant group was now the creoles instead of the *peninsulares*. Creoles owned the best land and controlled business and government. Their privileged position was resented, especially by the mestizos.

Continuing Political Conflicts

Soon after independence, political conflicts increased. Liberals called for separation of Church and state, the breakup of large estates, higher taxes on land, public social services, and civilian control of the government. Most of the liberals were mestizos, intellectuals, or merchants who wanted free trade. Opposed to this group were the creoles, most of whom were rich landowners, church leaders, and military officers. These conservatives favored strong central government and a powerful Church and army.

The decades that followed the wars for independence saw an ongoing struggle for economic strength and social justice. Although many South American governments were republics in appearance, many actually were military dictatorships. Today, there still remains in many Latin American countries a vast gap between the ruling rich and the underprivileged poor.

SECTION 5 REVIEW

Recall
1. **Define** *peninsulares*, creoles, mestizos.
2. **Identify** François Toussaint-Louverture, Miguel Hidalgo, Simón Bolívar, José de San Martín, Pedro I.

3. **Explain** why creoles were strong supporters of independence movements in Latin America.

Critical Thinking
4. **Making Comparisons** How did the independence move-

ment in Mexico differ from that in Brazil?

Understanding Themes
5. **Nationalism** Did independence bring social advances in Latin American countries? Why or why not?

Reading a Cartogram

On most maps, land areas are drawn in proportion to the actual surface areas on the earth. On some maps, however, a small country may appear much larger than usual, and a large country may look much smaller. Even the shapes of the countries may look different. If maps are supposed to outline the earth's features, why are these maps so distorted?

Learning the Skill

Maps that distort country size and shape are called **cartograms**. In a cartogram, country size reflects some value *other* than a land area, such as population or gross national product. For example, on a conventional map Canada appears much larger than India. In a cartogram showing world population, however, India would appear larger than Canada because it has a much larger population. The cartogram is a tool for making visual comparisons. At a glance, you can see how each country or region compares with another in a particular value.

To use a cartogram, first read the title and key to identify what value the cartogram illustrates. Then examine the cartogram to see which countries or regions appear. Find the largest and smallest countries. Compare the cartogram with a conventional land-area map to determine the degree of distortion of particular countries. Finally, draw conclusions about the topic.

Practicing the Skill

Study the cartogram shown at the top right and answer these questions.
1. What is the subject of the cartogram?
2. Which country appears largest on the cartogram? Which appears smallest?
3. Compare the cartogram to the map of Europe found in the Atlas. Which countries are most distorted in size compared to a land-area map?

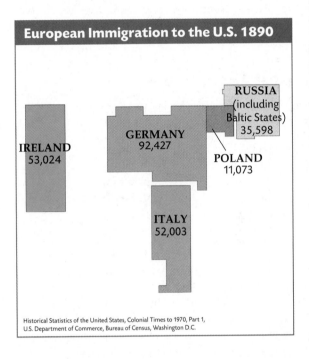

European Immigration to the U.S. 1890

RUSSIA (including Baltic States) 35,598

GERMANY 92,427

IRELAND 53,024

POLAND 11,073

ITALY 52,003

Historical Statistics of the United States, Colonial Times to 1970, Part 1, U.S. Department of Commerce, Bureau of Census, Washington D.C.

4. What accounts for these distortions?

Applying the Skill

At the library, find statistics that compare some value for different states or countries. For example, you might compare the number of farms in each state, or annual oil consumption of countries in North America. Be creative in your choice of value.

Convert these statistics into a simple cartogram. Determine the relative size of each country or state according to the chosen value. If the United States consumes five times more oil than does Mexico, then the United States should appear five times larger.

For More Practice

Turn to the Skill Practice in the Chapter Review on page 673 for more practice in reading a cartogram.

Connections Across Time

Historical Significance The 1800s saw the growth of democracy and nationalism in Europe and the Americas. In Great Britain, the British dominions, and the United States, democracy came peacefully. In France and Latin America, violent upheavals led to democracy or independence.

Although some revolts of the 1800s were unsuccessful, they planted the seeds of self-government in some Central and Eastern European countries. Today, many of the nations of the world are democracies with guarantees of protection for citizens' rights.

Using Key Terms

Write the key term that completes each sentence. Then write a sentence for each term not chosen.

a. creoles
b. disenfranchised
c. dominion
d. home rule
e. seceded
f. ratify
g. *peninsulares*
h. sectionalism
i. ultraroyalists
j. suffragettes
k. plebiscite
l. mestizos

1. A self-governing country other than Great Britain that recognizes the British monarch as its head of state is called a _____.
2. _____ are Latin Americans of mixed Native American and European ancestry.
3. Women in Great Britain who led a voting rights campaign for women became known as _____.
4. In 1851 Louis-Napoleon called for a _____, or national vote, asking the French people to give him support to create a new constitution.
5. While the Reform Act of 1832 gave middle-class men the right to vote, agricultural laborers, factory workers, and women remained _____.

Technology Activity

Using a Computerized Card Catalog Use the computerized card catalog in your school or local library to locate sources about Latin American countries. Research current information about a country from that region. Organize your research into a fact sheet. Include headings such as history, culture, religion, demographics, economics, and government. Provide a map of your country illustrating features such as mountain ranges, bodies of water, natural resources and major cities.

Using Your History Journal

Write a short report on a political issue in one of Great Britain's former territories, such as Hong Kong's return to Chinese rule in 1997, or the movement for an independent Quebec.

Reviewing Facts

1. **Citizenship** List the groups in Great Britain that gained the right to vote under the Reform Act of 1832. What groups were still excluded from voting?
2. **Government** Explain why many French people came to oppose the constitutional monarchy of Louis Philippe. How did this opposition affect Louis Philippe's rule?
3. **History** Explain why France went to war in 1870. What was the result of the conflict?
4. **Geography** Identify three land acquisitions that significantly expanded the territorial borders of the United States in the 1800s.
5. **Government** Name three leaders who helped win freedom for Latin American countries.

Critical Thinking

1. **Apply** Compare the movement toward democratic reform in Great Britain with similar movements in France under Louis Philippe. How were they alike? How did they differ?
2. **Synthesize** How did expansion and the Civil War affect the growth of democracy and civil rights in the United States?

3. Evaluate How did conflict in Europe in the 1800s contribute to the development of the United States?

Geography in History

1. Movement Refer to the map below. Which European nation lost the most emigrants in this period?

2. Movement To which nation did most Europeans migrate during this period?

3. Human/Environment Interaction What caused many Irish people to migrate to the United States in the 1840s?

4. Region What circumstances in Europe caused millions of people to migrate during this period?

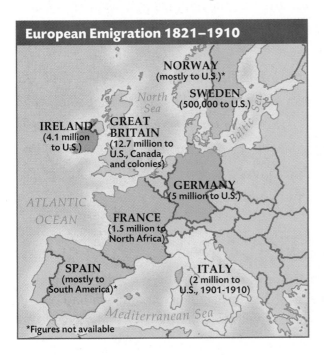

European Emigration 1821–1910

NORWAY
(mostly to U.S.)*

SWEDEN
(500,000 to U.S.)

IRELAND
(4.1 million
to U.S.)

GREAT
BRITAIN
(12.7 million to
U.S., Canada,
and colonies)

North
Sea

Baltic Sea

GERMANY
(5 million to U.S.)

ATLANTIC
OCEAN

FRANCE
(1.5 million to
North Africa)

SPAIN
(mostly to
South America)*

ITALY
(2 million to
U.S., 1901-1910)

Mediterranean Sea

*Figures not available

Understanding Themes

1. Change From your reading, would you say that the method of gradual reform was the best way that the British could have taken to change their government and society in the 1800s?

2. Movement How did British settlement of the dominions affect the original inhabitants?

3. Revolution Why do you think revolutions are often followed by governments led by dictators?

4. Change How did immigration affect the economic growth of the United States?

5. Nationalism How did the American Revolution affect Latin America in the early 1800s?

Linking Past and Present

1. British and American women fought to win the right to vote. What rights do women seek today? Are their methods today similar to or different from past methods?

2. After slavery was abolished in the United States, African Americans and other groups still had to struggle for equality. What educational and employment opportunities do some Americans seek today?

3. The Irish were granted home rule in 1914, but it never went into effect. How does this relate to the politics in Ireland today?

Skill Practice

Study the cartogram below and then answer these questions.

1. What is the subject of the cartogram?

2. Which country appears largest on the cartogram? Which appears smallest?

3. Compare the cartogram to a world map or globe. Which countries are most distorted in size compared to a land-area map?

4. What accounts for these distortions?

Value of U.S. Merchandise Exports 1870

CANADA
25

MEXICO
CUBA
6   14

UNITED
KINGDOM
248

GERMANY
42

FRANCE
46

BRAZIL
6

(Value of exports in millions of dollars)

Reaction and Nationalism

Chapter Themes

▶ **Nationalism** The rise of nationalism contributes to the unification of Italy. *Section 1*

▶ **Conflict** Bismarck uses war and diplomacy to bring unity to Germany. *Section 2*

▶ **Change** Bismarck's German Empire allows for economic growth but limits political freedoms. *Section 3*

▶ **Reaction** Russian czars oppose the forces of liberalism and nationalism in the Russian Empire. *Section 4*

▶ **Diversity** The large empire of Austria-Hungary contains many different nationalities seeking self-rule. *Section 5*

S*toryteller*

One Sunday in 1821, 16-year-old Giuseppe Mazzini walked along a street in Genoa, Italy. Suddenly a tall, black-bearded stranger approached him. With a piercing look, the stranger held out his hand for money and said, "for the refugees of Italy." Everyone knew that the refugees were those who had recently rebelled against the Austrians to win independence for Italy.

Forty years later, Mazzini—now a leader of the Italian nationalist movement—wrote of this incident: "That day was the first in which … [I realized that] … we Italians could and therefore ought to struggle for the liberty of our country." During the early 1800s feelings of nationalism similar to Mazzini's began to stir all across Europe.

Historical Significance

How has the force of nationalism repeatedly changed the map of Europe? What impact has nationalism had on European and world developments in the twentieth century?

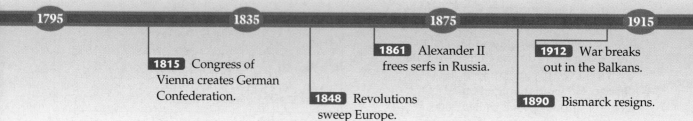

1795   1835   1875   1915

1861 Alexander II frees serfs in Russia.

1815 Congress of Vienna creates German Confederation.

1912 War breaks out in the Balkans.

1848 Revolutions sweep Europe.

1890 Bismarck resigns.

History & Art

<u>Meeting at Teano</u> by Cesare Maccari. Palazzo Pubblico, Siena, Italy
A desire to unite Italy brought together Sardinia's King Victor Emmanuel II
(left) and the revolutionary leader Giuseppe Garibaldi (right).

Your History Journal

Write a report on a subtopic from "Powder Keg in the Balkans" in Section 5 of this chapter. Suggested titles: Decline of the Ottoman Empire, The Crimean War, Russo-Turkish War, The Congress of Berlin, Russian Objectives in the Balkans, British Objectives in the Balkans.

1831 Giuseppe Mazzini founds Young Italy.

1861 Italians establish a united kingdom.

1871 Victor Emmanuel II moves the capital from Florence to Rome.

Section 1

The Unification of Italy

Setting the Scene

▶ **Terms to Define**

nationalism, nation-state, guerrilla warfare

▶ **People to Meet**

Giuseppe Mazzini, Charles Albert, Victor Emmanuel II, Count Camillo di Cavour, Giuseppe Garibaldi

▶ **Places to Locate**

Florence, Genoa, Sicily, Sardinia, Rome

Find Out How did nationalism lead to a united Italy in the 1860s?

The **Storyteller**

As the crowd shouted "Viva Verdi!", Giuseppe Verdi smiled. He understood the phrase's double meaning. Although the throng appreciated his operas, they were actually demonstrating for a unified Italy. The Risorgimento, *those wishing for a unified Italy, adopted Verdi's music as a rally-cry supporting Victor Emmanuel, the king of Sardinia. When people cheered "Viva Verdi," the occupying Austrians thought they were praising the musician. But the words meant* Viva Vittorio Emanuele, Re D'Italia—*long live Victor Emmanuel, king of Italy.*

—adapted from *A History of Western Music*, Donald J. Grout and Claude V. Palisca, 1988

The Musician Giuseppe Verdi *by Boldini*

From about the 1100s to the 1800s, central Europe was made up of numerous kingdoms, principalities, and free cities. Stimulated by the desire for economic growth, by the success of the American Revolution, and by the experience of the Napoleonic Wars, a small but dedicated group of Italians and Germans worked to unify these territories into nations in the 1800s. The desire for national independence that inspired them, known as nationalism, became one of the most powerful forces at work in Europe during the 1800s.

In 1815 the modern nation of Italy did not yet exist. At that time the Italian Peninsula was divided into a number of independent states, many of which had foreign rulers. A French Bourbon monarch ruled the Kingdom of the Two Sicilies, while Austria controlled Lombardy and Venetia and the pope controlled the Papal States.

In addition to political divisions, cultural and economic differences divided the regions of the Italian Peninsula. Not only did people speak different dialects of the Italian language, but trade barriers and poor transportation discouraged the flow of goods and people. To move goods the 200 miles (322 km) from **Florence** to Milan often took 8 weeks.

While cultural and economic divisions continued into the 1900s, a growing unification movement eventually swept aside the political divisions on the Italian Peninsula. By the 1860s, Italy had become a single country.

Early Attempts

The name given to the movement for Italian unity was *Risorgimento* (ree•ZAWR•jih•MEHN •toh), meaning the "resurgence" or "revival."

Giuseppe Mazzini was its most effective speaker. A native of Genoa and a bold and active leader in the fight for Italian independence, Mazzini founded in 1831 a secret society called Young Italy. The goal of this society was to transform Italy into an independent sovereign nation. According to Mazzini, the nation-state, a political organization consisting of one nationality rather than several nationalities, was very important. Through it, people in one unified country with common ideals could best contribute their efforts to the well-being of all its citizens.

In January 1848, Mazzini-inspired nationalists led a republican revolution in **Sicily**. Some weeks later, news of larger revolutions in France and Austria sparked uprisings throughout the Italian Peninsula. When fighting began against Austrian forces in Lombardy and Venetia, King **Charles Albert** of the Kingdom of **Sardinia** joined the war to expel the foreigners. Nationalists pressured the rulers of Naples, Tuscany, and the Papal States to send troops against the Austrians.

By April 1848 the united Italian forces had almost succeeded in driving the Austrians from the peninsula. Then, saying that he opposed a war with another Catholic country, Pope Pius IX suddenly withdrew his troops. Naples followed suit. Their withdrawal enabled Austria to defeat the army of Charles Albert and reestablish its control over Lombardy and Venetia.

The pope's decision infuriated Italian nationalists. In November 1848 angry mobs forced the pope to flee the city. Nationalists proclaimed **Rome** a republic and summoned Mazzini to the capital to head the government. The expulsion of the pope, however, aroused the Catholic governments of Naples, Spain, and France. As a result, Louis-Napoleon sent a French army to Rome. His troops occupied the city and restored the pope to power.

The events of 1848 caused many Italians to lose faith in Mazzini's revolutionary methods. They became more conservative and turned to Charles Albert, who had earned their respect with his brave stand against the Austrians. Nationalists now looked to Sardinia to lead the struggle for Italian unification.

Count Cavour's Diplomacy

In 1849 **Victor Emmanuel II**, Charles Albert's son, became king of Sardinia. During the next few years Victor Emmanuel II toiled to keep popular support for the unity movement alive. He was greatly helped in his efforts by a shrewd and determined adviser named **Count Camillo di Cavour**.

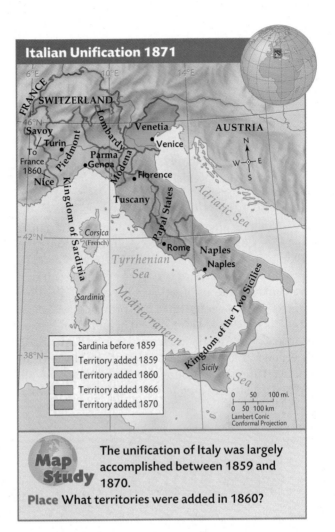

Italian Unification 1871

Sardinia before 1859
Territory added 1859
Territory added 1860
Territory added 1866
Territory added 1870

0   50   100 mi.
0 50 100 km
Lambert Conic Conformal Projection

Map Study The unification of Italy was largely accomplished between 1859 and 1870.

Place What territories were added in 1860?

Physically, Cavour was not impressive, as this description by a contemporary illustrates:

❝ The squat … pot-bellied form; the small, stumpy legs; the short, round arms, with the hands stuck constantly in the trousers' pockets … and the sharp grey eyes, covered by the goggle spectacles … The dress itself seemed a part and property of the man. ❞

Cavour's looks were deceptive, however. Hidden behind the rumpled clothes and strange appearance was a bold, intelligent man of great personal charm. By the time of the Crimean War in 1854, Cavour dominated Sardinia's council of ministers. His major goals were the promotion of rapid industrial growth, the reduction of the Catholic Church's influence, and the advancement of Sardinia's national interests in foreign affairs.

The defeat of Sardinia in 1848 convinced Cavour that the kingdom needed the aid of a foreign power to expel Austria and achieve Italian unity. To win such aid, Cavour decided to support France and Britain in the Crimean War. One historian later called this action "one of the most brilliant strokes of statecraft in the nineteenth century."

By sending an army to the Crimea in 1854, Sardinia established a claim to equality with the other warring nations. Participating in the war also won Sardinia admittance to the Congress of Paris, which settled treaty matters after the war.

War With Austria

Not long after the Crimean War, in the summer of 1858, Cavour met secretly with Napoleon III at Plombiéres-les-Bains in France. There Napoleon III promised to aid Sardinia in expelling Austria if Sardinia found itself at war. In return, Sardinia agreed that it would give the provinces of Savoy and Nice to France in the event of an Italian-French victory over Austria. Cavour next forced Austria to declare war against Sardinia. He did this by encouraging nationalist groups in Lombardy to revolt. When Austria demanded that Sardinia withdraw

its support of the rebels, Sardinia refused. Austria declared war in April 1859. As he had promised, Napoleon III led a force of 120,000 French soldiers to aid Sardinia.

The combined forces of France and Sardinia defeated the Austrians at Magenta and Solferino in June 1859. Austria was on the run. The French suffered heavy losses, however, and Napoleon III feared the loss of public support at home if the fighting in Italy continued.

Without consulting Cavour, Napoleon III withdrew from the fighting in July and signed a treaty with Emperor Francis Joseph of Austria. By the terms of the treaty, Austria gave Lombardy to Sardinia but retained control of Venetia. When Cavour read these terms, he became furious. He insisted that Victor Emmanuel II continue to fight. Believing that victory was impossible without France, the king refused.

The fighting, however, did not stop. People in Tuscany, Parma, Modena, and the papal province of Romagna overthrew their rulers in late 1859 and

Images of the Times

Uniting Italy

Before 1860 Italy was made up of many separate states. After 1860 it became a united kingdom but remained culturally and economically divided. The deepest division was between northern and southern parts of the country.

Southern Italy remained a leading rural and agricultural area. Traditional customs were strong, and artisans excelled in various crafts.

early 1860. Their new governments demanded the right to unite with Sardinia. To gain Napoleon III's consent for this unification, Cavour gave Savoy and Nice to France. In April 1860 Victor Emmanuel II accepted the territories into his kingdom.

Garibaldi Seizes the South

Southern Italy remained isolated from the revolutionary fever sweeping the rest of the peninsula, but at the death of Ferdinand II, ruler of the Kingdom of the Two Sicilies, Italian nationalists prepared for a revolution. Their leader was a charismatic military commander and adventurer named **Giuseppe Garibaldi**.

As a young man, Garibaldi had joined Young Italy. Forced into exile after taking part in the 1830 uprisings, he went to South America, where he fought in several revolutionary wars. As a result of this experience, Garibaldi became an expert in guerrilla warfare, a method of warfare using hit-and-run tactics. Garibaldi returned to Italy in 1848 and took part in Mazzini's short-lived Roman Republic. When the Roman Republic fell in 1849, Garibaldi again fled his homeland, this time to the United States.

Sensing that the people of the Kingdom of the Two Sicilies were ready to revolt, Garibaldi returned to Italy in 1860. After collecting a thousand volunteers in Genoa, he set out for Sicily. When his troops faltered in the midst of the first battle of the Sicilian campaign, Garibaldi rallied them to victory. In a few weeks, he gained total control of the island.

He then crossed to the mainland and advanced toward Naples. The army of the Kingdom of the Two Sicilies proved no match for the guerrilla tactics of Garibaldi's Red Shirts, so called because of the color of their uniforms. Naples fell, and the king of the Two Sicilies fled.

Garibaldi's successes in the south made Cavour nervous. He worried about his fellow countryman's political ambitions. To prevent Garibaldi

Northern Italy became a highly urbanized and industrialized region. The city of Milan was known both for its economic prosperity and its festive outdoor celebrations.

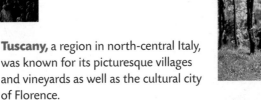

Tuscany, a region in north-central Italy, was known for its picturesque villages and vineyards as well as the cultural city of Florence.

REFLECTING ON THE TIMES

1. How was Italy organized politically before 1860?
2. What economic and social differences distinguished northern Italy from southern Italy?

After gaining control of Sicily in 1860, Giuseppe Garibaldi and his forces left the island for the Italian mainland. *What type of warfare did Garibaldi carry out on behalf of Italian national unity?*

from further victories, Cavour sent an army into the Papal States. On September 18 the forces of Sardinia defeated the papal army at Castelfidaro. The victory kept Cavour in control of the campaign for national unity.

When voters in southern Italy supported union with Sardinia in October 1860, Garibaldi surrendered his conquests to Victor Emmanuel II. By February 1861 the whole peninsula, with the exception of Rome and Venetia, was united under one government. Victor Emmanuel II was now king of the newly created constitutional monarchy of Italy.

Building a New Nation

Three months after the unification of Italy, Count Cavour died. His last words were "Italy is made. All is safe." Despite Cavour's optimism, many difficult problems faced the new nation. For example, national unification had not erased the profound cultural and economic divisions that separated the south and north of Italy. The south was poor and agricultural, while the north had begun to industrialize. The gap in the standards of living between the two regions fueled discontent and hampered unification efforts.

In the name of national unity, Sardinia often tried to force its laws and customs onto the other Italian states. This tactic only fanned resentment. Former rulers also encouraged discontent. When some of these rulers tried to regain their thrones, bloody civil wars erupted.

Gradually the Italian government developed a unified military force and a national educational system. It built railroads, linking not only the south with the north but also Italy with the rest of Europe. While these developments were important steps in the process of unification, cultural and economic barriers remained.

Another problem concerned the location of the nation's capital. Most Italians thought that **Rome** should be the capital of the new nation. During the 1860s, however, the pope still ruled the city. In addition, the Austrians continued to control Venetia.

Italy again sought foreign help to solve a political problem. In 1866 Italy allied itself with Prussia in a war against Austria. In return, Prussia promised to give Venetia to Italy. Although Austria defeated Italian forces in the conflict, the Prussian victory was so overwhelming that Prussia gave Venetia to Italy anyway.

Foreign intervention also played a role in helping Italy win Rome. When war broke out between France and Prussia in 1870, Napoleon III withdrew French troops that had been protecting the pope. Italian troops then entered Rome and conquered the pope's territory. In 1871 Victor Emmanuel II moved the national capital from Florence to Rome. The political unification of Italy was finally complete.

SECTION 1 REVIEW

Recall
1. **Define** nationalism, nation-state, guerrilla warfare.
2. **Identify** Giuseppe Mazzini, Charles Albert, Victor Emmanuel II, Count Camillo di Cavour, Giuseppe Garibaldi.

3. **List** three problems Italy faced after unification.

Critical Thinking
4. **Applying Information** Select a leader in the movement for Italian unification and show how that leader furthered the aims of the movement.

Understanding Themes
5. **Nationalism** Explain how the papacy and the Catholic Church responded to the rise of nationalism in the Italian Peninsula.

Section 2

The Unification of Germany

Setting the Scene

▶ **Terms to Define**
realpolitik, kaiser, chancellor

▶ **People to Meet**
William I, Otto von Bismarck

▶ **Places to Locate**
Frankfurt, Austria, Prussia, Schleswig, Holstein

 **Find Out** What methods did Bismarck use to unite the German states?

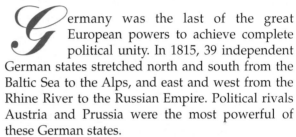 **Storyteller**

Klaus von Erlach was impressed by Otto von Bismarck's message, although many of Klaus's fellow aristocrats disliked the Iron Chancellor, considering him a traitor to his class. Who other than a great leader, Klaus wondered, would be able to defend a change of political opinion? As Bismarck stated, "The man who does not learn also fails to progress and cannot keep abreast of his time. People are falling behind when they remain rooted in the position they occupied two years ago." If Germany was to progress, the old systems would have to adapt.

—adapted from "Professorial Politics," Otto von Bismarck, reprinted in *Sources of World History*, Mark A. Kishlansky, 1995

Otto von Bismarck

Germany was the last of the great European powers to achieve complete political unity. In 1815, 39 independent German states stretched north and south from the Baltic Sea to the Alps, and east and west from the Rhine River to the Russian Empire. Political rivals Austria and Prussia were the most powerful of these German states.

While Great Britain and France were developing as strong industrial nations, Germany remained divided and economically disadvantaged. The Reformation and the Thirty Years' War contributed to Germany's social and political divisions. Antagonisms between Protestant and Catholic states ran deep. By 1871, however, the German states—excluding Austria and Switzerland—had united into a single nation.

Steps Toward Unity

The Congress of Vienna had created the German Confederation in 1815 as a buffer against possible future French expansion. This first major step toward German unity established closer economic ties between the German states and helped pave the way for greater political union.

The German Confederation loosely tied together the numerous German states with a diet, or assembly, sitting at **Frankfurt**. **Austria** dominated the confederation. Its position as head of the diet eventually brought it into conflict with **Prussia**. Neither Austria nor the smaller German states wanted to see a united Germany. Austria feared the economic competition, while the smaller states feared domination by Prussia.

The largest of the German states, Prussia had a well-organized government and a strong economy. Political power in Prussia lay in the hands of influential aristocratic landowners called Junkers (YUN•kuhrs), but members of the rising business class demanded a share of political power. To reduce trade barriers, German states in 1834 formed a *Zollverein*, or economic union. This step toward unity strengthened the influence of Prussia, while weakening that of Austria, in German affairs.

In 1848, as revolutions swept Europe, power in the German states shifted to the liberals. From all parts of Germany, delegates met in the Frankfurt Assembly to unite the country under a liberal constitution. Internal feuding, however, weakened this effort, allowing the conservatives to regain control. In 1849 the Prussian military forced the Assembly's closure and later put down street revolts. Many liberal and radical Germans fled abroad, especially to the United States. During the 1850s, in Germany as in other parts of Europe, conservatives in many cases came to control nationalist causes.

Rise of Bismarck

German conservatives looked to Prussia for help in uniting Germany. In 1861 **William I** became king of Prussia. Opposed to liberal ideas, William believed in a strong military and took steps to expand the Prussian army. Liberal German nationalists, however, saw no use for a strong military except to control the Prussian people. They wanted the king to adopt democratic policies to gain support from the other German states. As a result, liberal deputies in the Prussian assembly overwhelmingly defeated new taxes to support a larger army.

Frustrated by the defeat, the king appointed as his new prime minister a man who shared his views on army reconstruction. That man was **Otto von Bismarck**. A Junker himself, Bismarck had served in the Prussian assembly and as ambassador to Russia and France. He shared the king's view that Prussia needed a strong government and army to achieve German unity. A brilliant negotiator, Bismarck embraced the policy of realpolitik, the right of the nation-state to pursue its own advantage by any means, including war and the repudiation of treaties.

In September 1862 Bismarck defied the finance committee of the Prussian assembly. He declared that the great issues of the times would not be decided "by speeches and majority decisions ... but by blood and iron." When the lower house again refused to approve the new army budget, Bismarck pushed the program through by simply collecting the necessary taxes without authorization.

German Confederation 1815

Map Study

The German Confederation consisted of many small independent states in 1815.
1. Location Which was the largest and most important of these states?
2. Place What characteristics of the largest state in the German Confederation made it so important?

Three Wars

Bismarck once said, "Show me an objective worthy of war and I will go along with you." As prime minister, he found several worthy objectives. His initial goal was to raise money for army expansion. Then he wanted Prussia to use its military and economic power to reduce Austrian influence among the German states. Finally, he planned to arrange the unification of all German states except Austria and Switzerland under Prussian domination. To accomplish these objectives, Bismarck went to war three times.

War Against Denmark

By inheritance, the king of Denmark ruled the territories of **Schleswig** and **Holstein**. Schleswig's population was part German and part Danish; Holstein's population was entirely German. When King Christian IX proclaimed Schleswig a Danish province in 1863, Germans in both territories appealed to the larger German states for support.

To prevent Danish annexation of Schleswig, Bismarck persuaded Austria to join Prussia in declaring war against Denmark in 1864. Prussia and Austria soon won this war and forced Denmark out of the disputed provinces. By mutual agreement, Prussia took control of Schleswig, and Austria took over the administration of Holstein. This arrangement strained the relationship between these rival powers.

The war accomplished two of Bismarck's objectives. First, it made Europe aware of Prussia's military might and influence. Second, the tension resulting from the war settlement gave Bismarck the excuse he wanted for going to war with Austria.

Seven Weeks' War

One month before the invasion of Schleswig, Bismarck wrote to his envoy in Paris:

> ❝ You do not trust Austria. Neither do I. But I consider it the correct policy at present to have Austria with us. Whether the moment of parting will come, and on whose initiative, we shall see.… I am not in the least afraid of war, on the contrary … you may very soon be able to convince yourself that war also is included in my program. ❞

Bismarck prepared for war by stripping Austria of possible allies. He gained Russia's goodwill by offering the czar aid against Polish rebels in 1863. He offered France possible "compensations" for its neutrality in case of an Austro-Prussian war. He also forged an alliance with Italy by supporting its claim to Venetia in return for military support against Austria.

Bismarck gained public support for his actions when Austria sided with the duke of Augustenburg, who claimed title to Schleswig and Holstein. To prevent an alliance between Austria and the duke, Bismarck ordered Prussian troops into Austrian-occupied Holstein. When Austria then asked the German Confederation to take military action against Prussia for this invasion, Bismarck responded by declaring war against Austria.

The war between Austria and Prussia began on June 15, 1866, and ended in a Prussian victory just seven weeks later. For Bismarck, the conflict had been a limited war with limited objectives. Its purpose was to separate Austria from Germany and

---

CONNECTIONS
Geography

A Divided Land

Germany's geography has made it a country of distinct regions. Throughout German history, rivers have drawn people in different directions. The north-flowing Rhine, Weser, and Oder Rivers have linked the peoples of these river valleys to the northern plains. In southern Germany, the Danube River has oriented people of that region to the southeast.

Mountains and highland areas—especially the Alps and the Central Highlands—have isolated populations

A divided Berlin

and strengthened local dialects and traditions.

In the past, political and religious conflict heightened divisions; Swabians considered Westphalians as foreigners, and Bavarians regarded Prussians as archrivals. This regionalism led Germans to resist political unity until the late 1800s. In the 1900s, the German defeat in World War II and the rivalry between the United States and the Soviet Union caused Germany's division into eastern and western parts. With communism's fall, Germany finally reunited in 1990.

Linking Past and Present   ACTIVITY

Discuss the geographical and historical factors contributing to German regionalism. What has been the relationship between regionalism and national unity in the United States?

end the chance for a united Germany under Austrian control. In the end, Bismarck did not want to destroy Austria with a harsh peace settlement. He knew that he would probably need an alliance with Austria in the future.

The treaty ending the war was negotiated in the city of Prague. The settlement dissolved the German Confederation and gave Holstein to Prussia and Venetia to Italy. The treaty also called for "a new organization of Germany without the participation of Austria."

This "new organization" became the North German Confederation in 1867. It embraced all the German states north of the Main (MYN) River. The Confederation's constitution gave each state the right to manage its domestic affairs, but put foreign policy and national defense in the hands of Prussia. Legislative authority was vested in a federal council composed of representatives from the various governments and a diet, or assembly, elected by universal male suffrage.

The establishment of a strong confederation by Prussia made Bismarck a hero among German nationalists. Bismarck's work of uniting Germany, however, was not finished.

The Franco-Prussian War

The southern German states, which were largely Catholic, remained outside the new German confederation. Most of them feared Protestant Prussia's military strength and its control of Germany. The kingdoms of Bavaria and Württenberg (WUHR•tehm•BUHRG), in particular, steadfastly opposed German unification under Prussian rule. They would accept German unification only if Prussia gave up some of its authority in a united government. Prussia would not agree to this, however.

France posed the most serious obstacle to a united Germany. Napoleon III would not accept German unification unless France received some territory—its compensation for not joining Austria in the Seven Weeks' War. To resolve the situation, Bismarck again chose war.

Some historians believe that Bismarck was responsible for the Franco-Prussian War. In his memoirs, Bismarck had written that "a Franco-German [Prussian] war must take place before the construction of a united Germany could be realized." If Napoleon III had not wanted war as much as Bismarck, however, the war may never have taken place. Bismarck knew that he could not invade France without public support. Instead, he had to lure France into war, taking advantage of Napoleon III's weakness in foreign policy and of the French public's current anti-Prussian feeling.

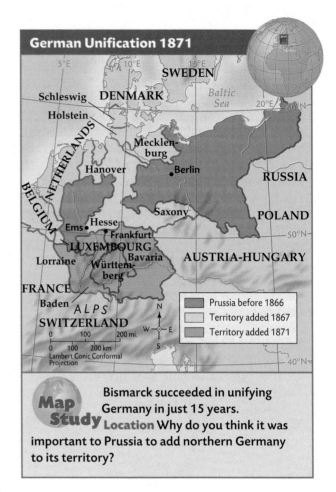

German Unification 1871

Prussia before 1866
Territory added 1867
Territory added 1871

Map Study Bismarck succeeded in unifying Germany in just 15 years.
Location Why do you think it was important to Prussia to add northern Germany to its territory?

Bismarck's chance came in 1870 in connection with the Hohenzollern candidacy for the Spanish throne.

A revolution in 1868 had deposed Queen Isabella of Spain. The Spanish government offered the throne to Prince Leopold of Hohenzollern, a Catholic cousin of William I of Prussia. Fearing a Spanish-German alliance against France, Napoleon III protested the offer. William brushed aside this protest, but Leopold later voluntarily declined the throne.

In July 1870, France demanded a promise from William that a Hohenzollern would never sit on the Spanish throne. William, who was vacationing at the German resort of Ems, refused. In a telegram to Bismarck, he described the details of his meeting with the French ambassador. To make it appear that William had deliberately insulted the French envoy, Bismarck altered the Ems telegram and released it to the press. Newspaper coverage of the supposed insult enraged the French, leading Napoleon to declare war on Prussia.

The fighting began on July 19, 1870. More anti-French than anti-Prussian, the southern German states allied with Prussia. With highly efficient military forces, the Prussians easily defeated the French.

Otto von Bismarck by Franz von Lenbach, Art History Museum, Vienna, Austria **Otto von Bismarck poses in military uniform with a Prussian helmet. He came from the Junker class of Prussia and supported a strong monarchy.** *What does Bismarck's style of dress reveal about the German Empire formed in 1871?*

Bismarck then gained support from all the German states for the unification of Germany under Prussia.

Formation of an Empire

On January 18, 1871, William I assumed the title of kaiser, or emperor, of a united Germany. He ruled over a domain that stretched from the Baltic Sea in the north to the Alps in the south. Bismarck became the German chancellor, or chief minister.

The new empire united 25 German states into one federal union. Although each state had its own ruler, and some had their own armies and diplomatic staffs, the kaiser headed the national government. He had authority to make appointments, command the military in time of war, and determine foreign policy. Prussian Junkers now shared power with wealthy industrialists. Unification did not make Germany a model democratic state.

William's son, Crown Prince Frederick of Prussia, was a liberal and a supporter of reform. He deplored the means Bismarck used to bring about the unification of Germany. In his diary, he wrote of his despair: "We are no longer looked upon as the innocent victims of wrong, but rather as arrogant victors." While he foresaw many of the consequences of Bismarck's policies, Frederick did nothing to change them.

SECTION 2 REVIEW

Recall
1. **Define** realpolitik, kaiser, chancellor.
2. **Identify** William I, Otto von Bismarck.
3. **Locate** Schleswig and Holstein on the map on page 684. Why do you think the Danish king claimed Schleswig and not Holstein as a Danish province?

Critical Thinking
4. **Synthesizing Information** Imagine that you are a member of the Prussian assembly opposed to Bismarck's policy for German unification. What alternative policy would you have suggested to William I?

Understanding Themes
5. **Conflict** Compare Bismarck's methods for achieving the unification of Germany with Cavour's methods for bringing about the unification of Italy.

1870   1885   1900   1915

1872 Bismarck expels Jesuits from Germany.

1883 German government provides health insurance to workers.

1888 William II becomes emperor of Germany.

1913 Germany's standing army numbers more than 800,000 soldiers.

Section 3

Bismarck's Realm

Setting the Scene

▶ **Terms to Define**
papal infallibility, militarism

▶ **People to Meet**
Pope Pius IX, Ferdinand Lassalle, William II

Find Out ▶ How did Bismarck's policies affect the German Empire?

The Storyteller

Erich Klein's Uncle Karl enjoyed talking politics and was eager to explain the German political system to his American nephew. "Germany consists of twenty-six different states that were once independent but now are united. Each state has its own governmental officials and hereditary princes, but they are all subject to Kaiser [William] I." Erich remarked, "This government sounds similar to the United States." Uncle Karl agreed, but mentioned an important difference: "The Kaiser was not elected. He was acclaimed by the various princes who were willing to concede their power so that aristocracy by birth would remain within the German government."

Kaiser William I

—adapted from *Im Vaterland [In the Fatherland]*, Paul V. Bacon, 1910

Victory on the battlefield brought about Germany's political unity, but the Germans were not united as a people. Religious, economic, social, and political divisions remained. German leaders now had to encourage a sense of common purpose in the population.

Bismarck became the key figure in early German nation building. With the support of Kaiser William I, Bismarck took charge of policy in the German Empire. Over the years, he faced several direct challenges to the German nation-state and his own political authority.

Bismarck and the Church

One of the first challenges Bismarck faced was with the Catholic Church in the so-called Kulturkampf (kul•TUR•KAHMF), or cultural struggle, between Church and state. After German unification, Catholics in Germany organized the Center party to represent their interests in opposition to the predominantly Protestant Prussians.

Bismarck viewed Catholicism as an antinationalist force and consequently supported the Protestants in political affairs. In part, he was annoyed at the popularity of the Center party. He was also worried about an 1870 proclamation by Catholic bishops in Rome declaring papal infallibility—the doctrine that the pope, when speaking on matters of faith and morals, is infallible, or free from error.

Since the Jesuits, in Bismarck's eyes, were papal agents working to destroy the German Empire, the chancellor launched his campaign against the Church by expelling the Jesuits from Germany in 1872. One year later, the German legislature began passing a series of laws aimed at destroying Catholic influence in Germany. These so-called May Laws deprived Catholic bishops of much of their authority and even required that weddings be performed by secular officials. In response,

Pope Pius IX declared the laws invalid and broke diplomatic ties with Germany.

Bismarck soon realized that he was fighting a losing battle. Instead of weakening the Center party, Bismarck's repressive measures strengthened it. In the legislative elections of 1877, the Center party gained even more seats. Even the Junker-controlled Conservative party began to oppose Bismarck's policies. Knowing that he needed the support of the Center party to defeat a serious challenge from the Socialists, Bismarck sought to make peace with the Catholics.

When Pope Pius IX died in 1878, his successor, Leo XIII, made an effort to heal the rift with Germany. Eventually, the German legislature repealed most laws directed against Catholics. By 1881 the Kulturkampf was over.

Germany's Industrial Growth

Prior to unification, Germany was not a great industrial nation. Primarily agricultural, the German states lagged far behind Great Britain in the production of textiles, coal, iron, and steel. Knowing that Germany's position as a major political and military power depended on a strong economy, German political and business leaders worked to expand the nation's industry. By the mid-1800s, advances in many areas began to transform Germany's economy. The establishment of the *Zollverein* had already encouraged economic growth and spurred efforts to improve transportation. After unification, investment capital from Great Britain, France, and Belgium helped to modernize industrial production and establish a mechanized factory system.

The development of deep-pit coal mining in the provinces along the Rhine and the opening of new coal mines in the Saar made available large reserves of cheap fuel for the new plants. Cities grew rapidly. Many young men and women streamed in from the villages to work in the new factories. As a result, at the end of the 1800s, Germany finally became a major industrial power.

The economic changes sweeping Germany conferred on at least some of its people the highest standard of living in Europe. The middle class and the business leaders benefited enormously from the rapid industrialization of the country. Every improvement in factory machinery, however, resulted in lower wages and higher unemployment for many German workers. They lived in crowded, filthy tenements and toiled long hours under dangerous working conditions.

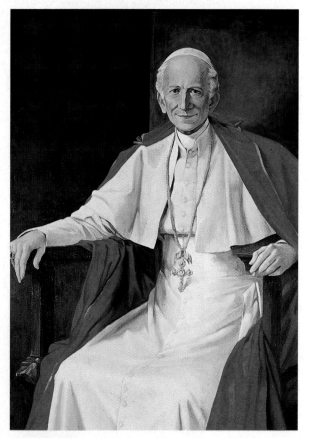

Visualizing History **Pope Leo XIII took a more conciliatory approach to new forms of secular government than did earlier popes.** *What effect did Leo's papacy have on church relations with Bismarck's Germany?*

Workers and Socialism

Poor wages, long workdays, and job uncertainty made German workers receptive to a more hopeful vision of the future. They looked forward to a democratic social order in which they would no longer be exploited. To help bring about this new order in Germany, **Ferdinand Lassalle**, a writer and labor leader, founded the Universal German Workingmen's Association in 1863. Although he called himself a Socialist and a disciple of Karl Marx, Lassalle did not preach revolution. Whereas Marx called for the workers of the world to revolt against capitalism, Lassalle advocated mass political action to change the system.

Lassalle was a national celebrity who knew Bismarck and lectured him on the workers' plight. He did not live long enough, however, to finish the fight, for he was killed in a duel in 1864. The party he founded grew slowly until it merged with the Social Democratic party in 1875 and became a major political force.

Richmond Crawford, Jr.

Mad Ludwig's Castle

Ludwig II, King of Bavaria, ruled the independent German kingdom of Bavaria until 1871 and built for himself the storybook Neuschwanstein castle. He came to the throne unprepared to rule but enthusiastic about indulging his two passions: opera and palaces. Ludwig's castles were based on his romantic vision of the past. In each new mansion, rooms were decorated to look like scenes from the famous operas of nineteenth-century composer Richard Wagner. Ludwig's dreamy castles glorified and enshrined a bygone Germany. Ludwig's ministers, who had to find the cash to pay for his follies, finally had him declared insane and removed from power. Today his castle is one of Germany's leading tourist attractions.

While Ludwig dreamed and listened to romantic operas, Count Otto von Bismarck set about uniting the German Confederation and creating a modern German nation through military strength. "The great questions of the age," Bismarck once remarked, "are not settled by speeches and majority votes ... but by iron and blood." ⊕

Bismarck and the Socialists

Despite his association with Lassalle, Bismarck believed that any Socialist party was out to change the government and that it therefore posed a serious threat to the German Empire. To destroy the Socialist movement in Germany, he set out to crush its organization. In 1878 the German legislature passed an anti-Socialist bill introduced by Bismarck. Although the bill did not outlaw the party itself, it banned all Socialist meetings and publications.

Bismarck's efforts to suppress the Socialists met with only temporary success. Consequently, Bismarck changed his tactics. He tried to show the workers that the government, and not the Socialists, had their true interests at heart. He directed the passage of several bills that gave workers some measure of comfort and security. In 1883, for example, the Sickness Insurance Law gave limited compensation to those who missed work because of illness. In 1889 the Old Age Insurance Law protected industrial workers in retirement.

Bismarck's reform efforts, however, did not go far enough to end the popularity of the Socialists. In 1890 the Social Democratic party won 35 seats in the legislature. With strong Socialist backing, the legislature refused to renew Bismarck's anti-Socialist law.

The Fall of Bismarck

In 1888 Kaiser William I died at the age of 91. Crown Prince Frederick, his liberal-minded son, succeeded him. Frederick III, however, died about 100 days after his coronation. **William II**, his son, succeeded him as emperor in 1888.

Only 29 years old at the time of his coronation, William II was a man of great energy and strong conservative opinions. Like his grandfather, William I, he favored militarism, or support for a powerful military prepared for war. His belief in the absolute authority of the emperor immediately

Visualizing History After governing the German Empire for almost thirty years, Bismarck resigned in 1890. This cartoon was published upon Bismarck's departure from office. *What is the cartoon saying about Bismarck's relationship with Kaiser William II?*

brought him into conflict with Bismarck. Bismarck wanted the kaiser to leave political affairs to him.

Under William I, Bismarck often got his way by threatening to resign. When Bismarck offered his resignation in 1890, the kaiser accepted it. Much to Bismarck's surprise, William II "sent the veteran pilot over the side," as a popular cartoon of the time illustrated Bismarck's dismissal.

Bismarck's policies had left Germany strong, but they frustrated the German people. His strict rule prevented the development of a parliamentary democracy. With Bismarck gone, William II was free to pursue his own policies. During his reign Germany became one of the world's major industrial and military powers.

SECTION 3 REVIEW

Recall
1. **Define** papal infallibility, militarism.
2. **Identify** Kulturkampf, Pope Pius IX, Ferdinand Lassalle, William II.
3. **List** the economic and technological advances that contributed to the growth of industry in Germany.

Critical Thinking
4. **Evaluating Information** Predict what might have happened if Frederick III had not died so soon after becoming kaiser.

Understanding Themes
5. **Change** What tactics did Bismarck use in his attempt to block challenges from Catholicism and the Socialist movement?

1815	1845	1875	1905

1825 The Decembrist uprising fails. **1855** Nicholas I dies. **c. 1870** Populist movement reaches out to peasants. **1905** Nicholas II issues the October Manifesto.

Section 4

Empire of the Czars

Setting the Scene

▶ **Terms to Define**
autocracy, emancipation, zemstvo, anarchy, nihilist, Russification, pogrom, soviet, duma

▶ **People to Meet**
Alexander I, Nicholas I, Alexander II, Nicholas II, Empress Alexandra, Mensheviks, Bolsheviks, Lenin

▶ **Places to Locate**
Poland, St. Petersburg

 **ind Out** Why did revolutionary movements develop in Russia?

The Storyteller

Prince Peter Kropotkin, a student in the Corps of Pages for the sons of the aristocracy, went to the opera with his friends the evening after Czar Alexander proclaimed an end to serfdom. The students planned to sing the hymn "God Save the Czar," and expected that everyone would join them. When they arrived they found the band of the opera was already playing the hymn, which was drowned immediately in enthusiastic cheers from all parts of the hall. This night, Prince Kropotkin thought, was undoubtedly the czar's finest hour.

—adapted from A Source Book for Russian History from Early Times to 1917, reprinted in Sources of World History, Mark A. Kishlansky, 1995

Czar Alexander II

In the early 1800s the Russian Empire stretched from Europe to the Pacific Ocean. More than 60 nationalities, speaking over 100 different languages, populated this vast territory. Although Slavs, including Russians, comprised nearly two-thirds of the population, many other European, Middle Eastern, and Asiatic peoples lived within the empire.

The agricultural economy of the Russian Empire was more oppressive but not much more effective than it had been during the Middle Ages. Serfdom, long in decline in western Europe, still bound the peasants living and working in rural areas. As a result of this entrenched agricultural system, Russia's level of industrialization remained lower than that of western Europe.

As an **autocracy**, a government in which one person rules with unlimited authority, the political structure of the Russian Empire had also remained much as it was in the days of Peter the Great. The forces of reform, already at work in western Europe in the early 1800s, soon threatened this traditional economic and political order of the Russian Empire.

Autocracy on the Defensive

Alexander I, who ruled from 1801 to 1825, dreamed of improving Russia's system of government and even granted a constitution to Russian-ruled **Poland** for a brief period of time. Convinced by the Napoleonic Wars that he was the savior of Europe, Alexander soon lost his desire to improve social, political, and economic conditions within his country.

The Russian officers who fought in the Napoleonic Wars were impressed by the reforms they saw in western Europe. Many of these officers joined secret societies to discuss the need in their country for economic reform, for a constitutional government, and for freeing the serfs. In December

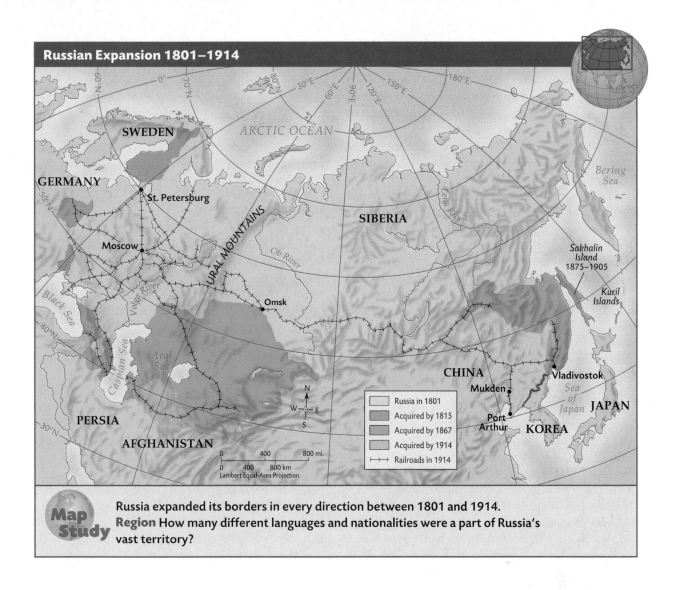

SWEDEN

ARCTIC OCEAN

GERMANY

St. Petersburg

SIBERIA

Bering
Sea

Moscow

URAL MOUNTAINS

Ob River

Lena River

Sakhalin
Island
1875–1905

Omsk

Volga River

Kuril
Islands

Black
Sea

Caspian Sea

Aral
Sea

CHINA

Mukden

Vladivostok

Sea
of
Japan

JAPAN

PERSIA

Port
Arthur

KOREA

AFGHANISTAN

	Russia in 1801
	Acquired by 1815
	Acquired by 1867
	Acquired by 1914
+++	Railroads in 1914

0   400   800 mi.
0   400   800 km
Lambert Equal-Area Projection

Map Study

Russia expanded its borders in every direction between 1801 and 1914.
Region How many different languages and nationalities were a part of Russia's vast territory?

1825, some of these officers took advantage of the uncertainty about the transfer of power after Alexander I's death and staged a military revolt.

Although the government quickly crushed the so-called Decembrist Revolt, the uprising had two very different effects. Its leaders were seen as martyrs and inspired later generations of revolutionaries. In the short term, however, the uprising hardened the determination of Alexander I's successor, **Nicholas I**, to strengthen the autocracy and suppress all opposition.

Under Nicholas I, the secret police had unlimited power to arrest and imprison people without trial and to censor the press. Despite Nicholas I's efforts to resist change, demands for reform persisted during the 1830s and 1840s. Russian losses in the Crimean War underscored the fact that the Russian Empire was in serious trouble. Nicholas, however, was too ill to begin any reforms. Following Nicholas I's death in 1855, his son **Alexander II** undertook the task of saving the autocracy and preventing a revolution.

Alexander II and Reforms

Russia's humiliating defeat in the Crimean War revealed the extent to which the nation lagged behind the other European powers militarily and economically. One major reason for Russia's backwardness was its system of serf labor. To progress, Russia needed to industrialize, but to industrialize, the factories needed a steady source of cheap labor. Only the serfs could provide this labor force, but they were not free to leave the land.

On March 3, 1861, Alexander II decreed the emancipation, or freeing, of the serfs. Although the serfs attained legal freedom, they received no land individually. Their village communities, called mirs, were granted varying amounts of the landlords' holdings, for which they had to undertake a 50-year mortgage. Peasants could not leave the mirs without paying their share, so they were still bound to the worst land and had an additional tax to pay. The landlords kept the best land and received compensation from the government for their losses.

Many peasants gave up farming rather than return to bondage. Landless peasants moved from the farms to the cities, adding to the growing numbers of unskilled urban workers. Their discontent revealed itself in occasional minor uprisings and produced new stirrings of revolutionary activity in the Russian Empire.

Because the emancipation decree took control of the provinces away from the landowners, it also created the need for a new system of local government. An 1864 law created this new system. Locally elected assemblies called zemstvos took charge of provincial matters such as schools and health care. Three groups could vote in zemstvo elections: the nobility, the wealthy townspeople, and the peasants. The vote was weighted, however, so that noblemen and rich taxpayers dominated the local assemblies.

Czar Alexander II became known as the Czar Liberator for freeing the serfs and for his many reforms. In addition to those already mentioned, he limited the use and authority of the secret police, eased restrictions on the press, modernized the judicial system, and expanded the educational system. Alexander also reorganized the Russian army, reducing the period of active military service from 25 years to 6 years.

Unfortunately, the reforms of Alexander II satisfied few Russians. The landowners had lost both land and power. The peasantry had made few economic gains. Conservatives feared weakening of the autocracy, while reformers pushed for even greater changes. Designed to stem discontent, the reforms failed to halt the growth of revolutionary movements.

Footnotes to History

A Sickly Prince

In 1904 Czar Nicholas II and Empress Alexandra finally had a son—an heir to the throne— after four girls. Tragically, Alexis suffered from hemophilia, an inherited disease preventing the normal clotting of blood. To ease her son's agonies, Alexandra relied on a mystic healer named Grigori Rasputin (ra•SPYOO•tuhn). Rasputin's apparent success in helping Alexis gave him great political influence over the czar. This in turn increased Nicholas's isolation from his people and the forces of change sweeping his empire.

Terror and Reaction

Among the most vocal critics of the Russian government during Alexander II's reign were intellectuals and students from the upper and middle classes. Although these reformers had strong ideals, they had little practical political experience and almost no direct contact with the Russian people, especially the peasants.

Radical Movements

Some radical reformers, such as Michael Bakunin, advocated anarchy, or the absence of government, and called for the complete destruction of the state, the family, law, property, and other institutions. Nihilists (from the Latin *nihil*, meaning "nothing") also rejected all traditions, believing that Russia would have to destroy the czarist autocracy and build a completely new society.

Beginning in the early 1870s, many reformers became active in a new movement known as populism. The populists believed that the peasants would eventually lead a revolution, overthrow the czar, and establish a socialist society. To further their cause, groups of students and intellectuals went to the villages to prepare the peasants for revolution. The peasants, however, often grew suspicious of the young revolutionaries and sometimes even turned them over to the police. Frustrated by their lack of success, many populists turned to violent tactics.

The most radical faction of the revolutionaries plotted the assassinations of key officials in order to frighten the government into making radical reforms. Beginning in 1866, revolutionaries made several attempts to assassinate Alexander II. Although Alexander insisted that these radicals be crushed, he eventually responded to popular pressure by drafting a plan to establish a national assembly. Before the plan could be enacted, however, a young revolutionary killed the czar with a bomb in 1881.

Alexander III

Alexander III, who succeeded his father, vowed to maintain the old order and crush revolutionaries. He warned that he would not tolerate a constitution and reduced the powers of the zemstvos. Reversing his father's reforms, he abolished autonomy in the schools, restored censorship of the press, and extended the powers of the secret police.

To protect the autocracy, Alexander III used a resurgence of nationalism to promote a policy of Russification. Designed as an attempt to unite the empire's many peoples, Russification instead

 **Moscow workers, students, and intellectuals fought czarist troops during the 1905 Revolution.** *How did the czarist government under Alexander III and Nicholas II deal with its opponents?*

became an official policy of intolerance and persecution of non-Russian peoples. Anyone who questioned the czar's authority, who spoke a language other than Russian, or who followed a religion other than Eastern Orthodoxy risked prosecution.

Russification singled out the Jews in particular for persecution. Government decrees deprived Jews of the right to own land and forced them to live in a certain area of the empire called the Pale. The government also encouraged bloody pogroms, or organized massacres of a minority group, in Jewish communities.

TURNING POINT

The Revolution of 1905

After Alexander III's death in 1894, many Russians were disappointed when his son **Nicholas II** stated he would also rule as an autocrat. The new czar, however, lacked the strong will to make absolute rule effective. He was easily influenced by those around him, particularly his wife, **Empress Alexandra**, who wanted their son to inherit an autocracy.

During the reign of Nicholas II, a revolutionary mood swept over Russia. Peasants grew increasingly dissatisfied; national minorities called for an end to persecution; and middle-class reformers pushed for a constitutional monarchy. At the same time, the emancipation of the serfs and rapid industrialization had resulted in a marked increase in the size of the urban working class. Russian factories at the turn of the century lacked proper lighting, ventilation, and sanitation. Workers toiled long hours for little pay and lived in terrible, overcrowded housing. Not surprisingly, then, urban workers joined the ranks of the dissatisfied.

Russian Marxists

By the early 1900s several revolutionary groups in Russia followed the teachings of Karl Marx. Their members believed that the working class, not the peasants, would lead the revolution. The **Mensheviks** believed that Russia needed to develop into an industrial state with a sizable working class before a socialist revolution could occur. The more radical **Bolsheviks**, led by Vladimir Ilyich Ulyanov—commonly known as **Lenin**—believed that a small party of professional revolutionaries could use force to bring about a socialist society in the near future.

Upheavals

War between Russia and Japan in 1904 over control of Manchuria furthered the Socialists' cause. Russian land forces suffered major setbacks, and a Russian fleet attempting to deliver supplies lost many ships in a Japanese attack. With the mediation of the United States, the war-exhausted empires finally concluded a peace agreement in 1905.

Russia's humiliating military performance heightened already mounting opposition to the czar's government by urban workers, middle-class thinkers, and peasants. The war had strained the Russian economy, raising food prices while keeping wages low.

Spontaneous strikes began to break out in many cities throughout the empire. On Sunday, January 22, 1905, about 200,000 workers marched in a peaceful procession to the czar's palace in **St. Petersburg** to present a petition for reform. Palace soldiers opened fire on the crowd, killing hundreds of workers. Bloody Sunday, as the demonstration was called, sparked riots and strikes in most industrial centers and set off a wave of political protests.

Middle-class organizations drew up programs for political reform. The zemstvos issued lists of demands. In the spring of 1905, the first soviets, or workers' councils, formed to voice workers' grievances. From all reformist and revolutionary groups came the cry for the establishment of a representative government elected by universal suffrage.

In October 1905, angry workers seized control of the major cities in a general strike. As disorder and violence in the cities and rural areas continued, Nicholas II announced a law providing for the election of a national duma, or legislature. The czar, however, proposed that the Duma serve as an advisory council rather than a genuine legislative body. Instead of appeasing the Russian people, the measure set off more nationwide strikes.

Slavery Is on Its Way Out

Washington, D.C., 1863
During the American Civil War, President Abraham Lincoln issued the Emancipation Proclamation that eventually led to the end of slavery in the United States. This historic document declared freedom for all enslaved people in the Confederacy—the states that were in rebellion against the Union. The Emancipation Proclamation strengthened the Union's war effort and made the war a fight against slavery. It also weakened the Confederacy by discouraging France and England from entering the war.

The events of October forced Nicholas to yield reluctantly to the demands of his people. The czar issued the October Manifesto, granting civil rights to citizens and allowing the Duma to make laws. In theory, Russia had become a constitutional monarchy; however, in practice, Nicholas continued to keep his powers. Stern measures to restore order, including pogroms against the Jews and the arrest of peasant and labor leaders, remained in place. When the Duma tried to act independently of the czar, Nicholas quickly dissolved it.

Nicholas II's ability to silence opposition was only temporary. Russia's many serious troubles had not been resolved. On the eve of World War I, growing numbers of peasants, workers, national minorities, and middle-class reformers supported an immediate end to the autocracy. Their demands and the stress of war would soon bring revolution to Russia.

SECTION 4 REVIEW

Recall
1. **Define** autocracy, emancipation, zemstvo, anarchy, nihilist, Russification, pogrom, soviet, duma.
2. **Identify** Alexander I, Nicholas I, Alexander II, Nicholas II, Empress Alexandra, Mensheviks, Bolsheviks, Lenin.
3. **Name** the two major Russian revolutionary groups that followed the teachings of Karl Marx, and explain the differences between the two.

Critical Thinking
4. **Applying Information** Select one of the Russian czars and tell how his policies affected the Russian Empire.

Understanding Themes
5. **Reaction** Why was effective reform difficult to achieve in Russia during the reign of Nicholas II?

1867 Austria and Hungary form a dual monarchy.

1878 Congress of Berlin settles Russo-Turkish War.

1913 Treaty of Bucharest ends Balkan conflict.

Section 5

Austria-Hungary's Decline

Setting the Scene

▶ **Terms to Define**
   dual monarchy, jingoism

▶ **People to Meet**
   Francis Joseph, Francis Deak

▶ **Places to Locate**
   Austria, Vienna, Hungary, Bohemia, Moravia, Serbia, Bulgaria, Romania, Montenegro, Bosnia and Herzegovina

 **ind Out** How did the growth of nationalistic feelings affect the empire of Austria-Hungary?

The Storyteller

Josef Heismann knew that the army was edgy. Once a powerful force, Austria was now regarded as second-rate. Inflammatory newspaper articles called for Austria to annex Bosnia, Serbia, and other Slav republics. Josef read an army newspaper article calling for an immediate invasion: "On us depends the future of our Empire. If we return victorious, we shall not only have conquered a foreign land: we shall have won back Austrian self-respect, given new life to the Imperial idea and vanquished ... the enemy in our midst."

—adapted from *The Origins of World War I*, Roger Parkinson, 1970

Austrian soldiers of the 1860s

In the early 1800s, in addition to Russia and the Ottoman Empire, there was a third dominant power in eastern Europe: **Austria**. The Austrian Empire at this time contained more than 11 different national groups, including the Germans of Austria and the Magyars of Hungary.

Like Russia, Austria lacked national and geographical unity. Also as in Russia, life in Austria remained almost feudal at the beginning of the 1800s. A powerful landed nobility controlled a large peasant population and resisted any change in the old agricultural system. Through strict censorship and the arrest and intimidation of protesters, the government sought to stem the forces of nationalism and revolution sweeping through Europe.

The Revolution of 1848

As you learned in Chapter 22, the principal political figure in Austria during the early 1800s was Prince Klemens von Metternich, who held the office of minister of foreign affairs from 1809 to 1848. Metternich believed that democratic and nationalist movements would destroy the Austrian Empire and threaten peace in Europe. As a result, Metternich worked to crush all revolutionary activity, both within and outside the empire.

Despite Metternich's conservative policies, however, the revolutionary movement that had begun in France in 1848 spread to Austria the same year. Throughout the empire, nationalist groups demanded freedom of speech and press, peasant relief from feudal dues, and a representative government. The Austrian Empire seemed on the verge of collapse.

The tide of revolutionary activity was to turn once more, however. Infighting among nationalist groups and within radical factions with different

Chapter 26 *Reaction and Nationalism* **695**

political ideas enabled conservative forces to strike back. In **Vienna**, for example, conflict between middle-class moderates who wanted to reform the political system and radical workers who wanted to overthrow it weakened the revolutionary movement. By October 1848, the government once more occupied the capital. When Emperor Francis Ferdinand resigned his throne, his nephew, **Francis Joseph**, became emperor at the age of 18.

Francis Joseph moved quickly to restore the conservative order. He dissolved the revolutionary assembly and rejected the new constitution. Although threatened, the old regime had managed to withstand revolutionary change by playing one nationalist faction against another.

Throughout his 68-year reign, Francis Joseph struggled to maintain a unified empire. Neither repressive measures nor reforms, however, helped ease the nationalist tensions that threatened Austria. At the same time, a series of foreign crises further weakened the empire. In 1859 Austria was forced to give up the Italian province of Lombardy. Then in 1866, during the Seven Weeks' War with Prussia, Austria lost its influence over its German states as well.

The Dual Monarchy

Francis Joseph's efforts to strengthen his authority were most effectively challenged by the Magyars of **Hungary**. In 1848 Hungarian nationalists led by Louis Kossuth declared Hungary an independent republic, but this achievement was short-lived. With Russian help, Austrian forces defeated the Hungarian nationalists, and Hungary was restored to the Austrian Empire. After Austria's defeat in the Seven Weeks' War (1866), however, Francis Joseph realized that his empire's stability depended on better relations with the Hungarians. He met with Hungarian leader **Francis Deak** to see if a compromise could be worked out.

After months of negotiations, Austria and Hungary finally reached an agreement in 1867. The *Ausgleich* (OWS•glyk), or Compromise, restored Hungary's independence and divided the Austrian Empire into a dual monarchy: the empire of Austria and the kingdom of Hungary. Francis Joseph remained ruler of both areas. He kept his title as emperor of Austria, and the Hungarians crowned him king of Hungary.

In addition to sharing a monarch, the two states had common ministries of foreign affairs, war, and finance. A system of committees handled other matters of mutual concern. In internal affairs, however, Austria and Hungary were completely independent of each other. Each had its own constitution, prime minister, and parliament.

While Austria and Hungary were independent politically, they were dependent on each other economically. Industrialized Austria supplied manufactured goods for the peoples of the dual

Visualizing History Francis Joseph ruled the Austrian Empire for 68 years. When he came to the throne in 1848, Europe was in the midst of revolutions. When he died in 1916, Europe was in the midst of World War I. *What change did Francis Joseph agree to in 1867 in order to save his empire?*

monarchy. Agricultural Hungary supplied food products. Their cooperation, however, was not without conflict. Disputes inevitably developed between Austria and Hungary over foreign trade, tariffs, and currency.

During the mid-1800s, Austrian industrial growth had been slow. After the creation of the dual monarchy, however, the empire's production of coal, iron, steel, and manufactured goods grew rapidly. The territories of **Bohemia** and **Moravia** became the empire's leading industrial centers, producing machine tools, textiles, armaments, shoes, and chemicals. The concentration of industry in Bohemia and Moravia caused a more rapid urbanization in those areas.

The dual monarchy was satisfactory to both the Austrian-Germans, who maintained power in Austria, and the Magyars, who controlled Hungary. Other nationalities remained discontented. Three-fifths of the population of Austria-Hungary were Slavs—Poles, Czechs, Slovaks, Serbs, and Bosnians— who had no voice in the government. Many Slavic nationalist groups dreamed of breaking free from the Austro-Hungarian Empire and forming a large Slav kingdom. Their discontent became a threat to the empire's unity.

Powder Keg in the Balkans

By the mid-1800s, the Ottoman Empire had declined to a weakened and diminished state. In 1829 Greece won its independence. By 1850 the Ottomans had lost the provinces of Moldavia and Wallachia to Russia and Algeria to France. In addition, Egypt, Arabia, and several Balkan territories had gained their autonomy.

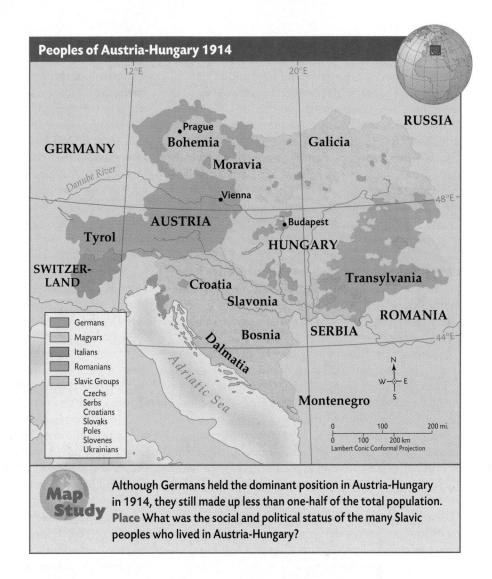

Peoples of Austria-Hungary 1914

Germans
Magyars
Italians
Romanians
Slavic Groups
  Czechs
  Serbs
  Croatians
  Slovaks
  Poles
  Slovenes
  Ukrainians

0   100   200 mi.
0   100   200 km
Lambert Conic Conformal Projection

Map Study Although Germans held the dominant position in Austria-Hungary in 1914, they still made up less than one-half of the total population. **Place** What was the social and political status of the many Slavic peoples who lived in Austria-Hungary?

Foreign powers watched the decline of the Ottoman Empire closely. Austria hoped to expand into the Balkan region. France sought to protect persecuted Catholics within the empire. Great Britain feared disruption of its Mediterranean trade. The primary objective of these foreign powers, though, was to prevent Russian expansion into the region. "We have a sick man on our hands," declared Czar Nicholas I, referring to Turkey, and Russia stood ready to contribute to its final collapse.

During the Crimean War, from 1854 to 1856, France, Great Britain, and Sardinia helped defend the Ottoman Empire against Russia's advances. Although the Ottoman allies defeated Russia in this war, the empire continued to lose power and territory. In 1875 nationalists in the Balkan states of **Serbia**, **Bulgaria**, and **Romania** rose up in revolt, demanding immediate independence from Turkey. The Turks brutally suppressed these revolts with widespread massacres.

The Congress of Berlin

In 1877 Russia went to war on behalf of the Slavic people in the Balkan Peninsula. Publicly embracing the Slavic nationalist movement because it suited the government's imperial ambitions, Russia used the conflict known as the Russo-Turkish War to justify its expansion into Balkan territory. The Treaty of San Stefano (1878), which ended the war, created a large Russian-controlled Bulgarian state.

As news of Russian victories reached Great Britain, the public cried out for war. A popular slogan in Great Britain at the time captured the heightened public sentiment: "We don't want to fight, but by jingo, if we do, we've got the men, we've got the ships, we've got the money, too." From this slogan came the term jingoism, used to describe extreme patriotism, usually provoked by a perceived foreign threat.

The great European powers protested the Treaty of San Stefano. In the end a congress of European leaders met in Berlin, Germany, to revise it. At the meeting, which began in June 1878, representatives of the European powers divided Bulgaria into three parts, one of which remained under Ottoman rule. Neighboring Serbia, **Montenegro**, and Romania, on the other hand, won their complete independence. Britain gained control of Cyprus, and Austria-Hungary won the Balkan provinces of **Bosnia and Herzegovina**.

The Congress of Berlin satisfied few. Russia lost its war gains, and the Ottoman Empire lost much of its European territory. In addition, the congress dealt with the Balkan states inequitably, granting independence for some, but not all, of the people of any given nationality.

Balkan Conflict

By 1912 the Balkan states had joined forces and moved to free members of their respective nationalities from Ottoman rule. Encouraged by Italy's easy victory over the Turks in North Africa, the Balkan League—consisting of Bulgaria, Greece, Montenegro, and Serbia—declared war on Turkey in 1912. As a result of the war, the Ottomans lost all of their European territory with the exception of Istanbul and a small surrounding area.

Unity among members of the Balkan League was short-lived. No sooner had the Balkan states won the war than they began to fight among themselves over the lands they had gained. Before the war, Serbia and Bulgaria had secretly arranged for land distribution in case of victory. After the war, Bulgaria refused to go along with the plan. The Bulgarians did not want to give up territory won directly in battle.

To keep their land, the Bulgarians in June 1913 attacked Greek and Serb forces in the disputed area. In this second Balkan War, Montenegro and Greece sided with Serbia against Bulgaria. Romania joined the fighting when it saw the opportunity to win land from Bulgaria. The Balkan conflict brought new hope to the Ottomans. Seeing the chance to recover its own lost European territory, the Ottoman Empire attacked Bulgaria.

The fighting ended in 1913 with the Treaty of Bucharest, and the disputed land was redistributed. Bulgaria, which lost the war, surrendered much of the land it had won from the Ottomans in the previous Balkan conflict.

The Treaty of Bucharest did not bring lasting peace to the Balkans. Serbia's increased power encouraged nationalism among Slavs and threatened Austria-Hungary. Russia, in supporting the pan-Slavic movement, sought to extend its own influence in the Balkans. The French, British, and German governments tried to preserve the existing balance of power to prevent either Austria-Hungary or Russia from gaining greater influence in the area. It is not difficult to see why writers of the time called the Balkans "the powder keg of Europe." It seemed inevitable that events in the Balkans would sooner or later explode into a major European war.

SECTION 5 REVIEW

Recall
1. **Define** dual monarchy, jingoism.
2. **Identify** Francis Joseph, Francis Deak, the Congress of Berlin.
3. **List** two ways in which Austria and Hungary were dependent upon each other in the dual monarchy. List two ways they were independent of each other.

Critical Thinking
4. **Analyzing Information** How did Austria-Hungary and Russia differ from the Balkan countries in their reasons for intervening in the Ottoman Empire's problems?

Understanding Themes
5. **Diversity** Explain how ethnic diversity contributed to the decline of Austria-Hungary. Could this decline have been avoided? Why or why not?

Selecting and Using Research Sources

You have to write a report, so you head off to the library. There you are surrounded by bookshelves filled with books. Where do you begin?

Learning the Skill

Libraries contain many kinds of research sources. Understanding the content and purpose of each type will help you find relevant information more efficiently. Here are brief descriptions of important sources:

Reference Books Reference books include encyclopedias, biographical dictionaries, atlases, and almanacs.

An encyclopedia is a set of books with short articles on many subjects arranged alphabetically. General encyclopedias present a wide range of topics, while specialized encyclopedias have articles on a theme—e.g., an encyclopedia of music.

A biographical dictionary provides brief biographies listed alphabetically by last names. Each biography gives data such as the person's place and date of birth, occupation, and achievements.

An atlas is a collection of maps and charts for locating geographical features and places. An atlas can be general or thematic. An atlas contains an alphabetical index of place names that directs you to the map(s) where that place appears.

An almanac is an annually updated reference that provides current statistics together with historical information on a wide range of subjects.

Card Catalog The library's catalog, on computer or cards, lists every book in the library. Search for books by author, title, or subject. Each listing gives the book's call number and location. Computer catalogs also show whether the book is currently available.

Many libraries have joined networks. A library network usually has a single computer catalog listing all the books in the network. A patron can borrow any book in the system. Find out whether your library is part of a network.

Periodical Guides A periodical guide is a set of books listing topics covered in magazine and newspaper articles.

Computer Databases Computer databases provide collections of information organized for rapid search and retrieval.

If you have trouble finding the needed information, ask the librarian for help.

Practicing the Skill

Suppose you are going to Germany and want to learn more about the country before you go. Read the research questions below. Then decide which of the following sources you would use to answer each question and why.

a. encyclopedia
b. atlas
c. historical atlas
d. almanac
e. biographical dictionary
f. catalog entry: Germany—travel
g. catalog entry: Germany—modern history
h. periodical guide

1. Where is each city on the trip itinerary located?
2. What are the places of interest in each city?
3. What have been the major events in German history since 1800?
4. What political issues face Germany today?

Applying the Skill

Use research resources from your school or local library to research the following topic:

What medical treatment was given to Czarevitch Alexis, son of Nicholas II and Alexandra? How has medical care of hemophiliacs improved since 1910? List your sources.

For More Practice

Turn to the Skill Practice in the Chapter Review on page 701 for more practice in selecting and using research sources.

Connections Across Time

Historical Significance The forces of nationalism changed the map of Europe dramatically in the 1800s. In the 1860s, the independent states on the Italian Peninsula united into the nation of Italy.

About 10 years later, a loose confederation of states in the heart of Europe became the modern nation of Germany.

Nationalism, however, weakened the Austrian Empire, where various ethnic groups wanted independence. Nationalist tensions increased throughout Europe during the late 1800s and early 1900s. They pushed European nations closer to an all-out war.

Using Key Terms

Write the key term that completes each sentence. Then write a sentence for each term not chosen.

a. anarchy
b. duma
c. jingoism
d. nationalism
e. Russification
f. autocracy
g. dual monarchy
h. nihilists
i. kaiser
j. pogroms
k. emancipation
l. zemstvo

1. In the 1800s some radical reformers in Russia called for _____, the complete destruction of the government, the family, law, property, and other institutions.
2. In 1867 Austria and Hungary reached an agreement to transform the Austrian Empire into a _____, consisting of two separate but interrelated kingdoms.
3. During the 1800s the Russian Empire was an _____, a government in which one person rules with unlimited authority.
4. Among Russian revolutionaries, the _____ rejected all traditions, believing that Russia would have to completely build a new society.
5. The Russian government encouraged bloody _____, or organized massacres, in Jewish communities of the Russian Empire.

Technology Activity

Using a Word Processor Search the Internet or your local library for sources about the history of Russian czars. Using a word processor or software, create a genealogy chart of the Romanov dynasty. Include a short report explaining why the empire of the czars ended and how it impacted Russian culture.

Using Your History Journal

Read two or three recent news magazine reports on Bosnia and Herzegovina. Write an essay about how to achieve lasting peace in the Balkans.

Reviewing Facts

1. **Government** Explain how Sardinia gained control of the Italian struggle for unification.
2. **Government** Identify the leaders of Italy's unification movement.
3. **Economics** Describe the *Zollverein*. How did it help Prussia lead the German Confederation?
4. **Government** List the challenges that faced the new German state.
5. **Government** Explain why the reforms of Alexander II satisfied few Russians.
6. **History** State the effects of the 1905 Revolution on Russian government and society.

Critical Thinking

1. **Apply** How did foreign powers help Italians achieve independence?
2. **Contrast** How did the problems that Italy faced after unification differ from the problems that Germany faced?
3. **Synthesize** Why do you think Austria agreed to the compromise with Hungary that established the dual monarchy?
4. **Evaluate** What do you think might have happened if Russia's Czar Nicholas II had given the Duma full legislative power?

Geography in History

1. **Place** Refer to the map below. In what two areas was most of the fighting during the Russo-Japanese War?
2. **Movement** Across what two bodies of water were Japanese troops transported to the war zone?
3. **Movement** What railway helped in moving Japanese forces north?
4. **Region** What effect did Russia's setback in this region have on the czar's government?

Russo–Japanese War

Harbin
Manchuria
Chinese Eastern Railway
RUSSIA
Kirin
Changchun
Vladivostok
Kirin
(occupied by Russia 1897 to 1905)
South Manchurian Railway
Liaoyang
Anshan
CHINA
Shanhaikuan
Antung
Sea of Japan
Wonsan
Port Arthur
Dairen
Pyongyang
Seoul
KOREA
Yellow Sea
Kiaochow
Tsingtao
Pusan
Mokpo
Masampo
Shimonoseki
Sasebo
JAPAN

← Movement of Japanese forces, 1904–1905
⊢⊢⊢ Railways in 1918

Understanding Themes

1. **Nationalism** How did the rise of nationalism spur the unification movement in Italy?
2. **Conflict** How did Bismarck promote his goal of German unification?
3. **Change** What changes came to Germany's economy after unification?
4. **Reaction** How did the policies of Alexander III affect the Jews and other non-Russian groups within the Russian Empire?
5. **Diversity** How did the great diversity of nationalities in the Austrian Empire lead to the establishment of the dual monarchy in the mid-1800s?

Linking Past and Present

1. Bismarck had the difficult task of forging a strong, united German nation. What problems did he face? What problems have confronted German leaders since the early 1990s in reuniting Germany today after nearly 50 years of division into Communist and democratic areas?
2. Alexander III carried out a policy of Russification that led to intolerance and persecution of non-Russian groups in the Russian Empire. Are similar policies carried out today in Russia and the other countries of the former Soviet Union? Explain your answer.

Skill Practice

For each research question below, decide which of these sources would provide relevant information.

a. encyclopedia
b. atlas
c. historical atlas
d. almanac
e. biographical dictionary
f. catalog entry: European history 19th century
g. catalog entry: nationalism
h. periodical guide

1. How have the borders of the countries discussed in Chapter 26 changed since World War I?
2. What are the latest population statistics for Germany, Italy, Austria, Hungary, and Russia?
3. What were Otto von Bismarck's greatest accomplishments?
4. What nationalist struggles have occurred in Europe in the last decade?

Chapter 27

1800–1914

The Age of Imperialism

Chapter Themes

▶ **Movement** Political, economic, and social factors lead to a new period of expansion known as the Age of Imperialism. *Section 1*

▶ **Change** European powers divide most of Africa into colonies, and Africans resist European intervention and colonialism. *Section 2*

▶ **Reaction** India and China come under European control or influence, while Japan adopts reforms to meet the Western challenge. *Section 3*

▶ **Nationalism** Nationalism intensifies in Latin America as United States involvement in the region increases. *Section 4*

The Storyteller

No one knows how the rumor started, but it spread quickly. The bullets for the new rifles, the story went, were greased with the fat of cows and pigs. The sepoys, Indian soldiers in the British army, were outraged. Because Hindus regarded the cow as sacred and Muslims could not touch pork, using these bullets would violate the beliefs of both groups. As a result, the sepoys started a rebellion in May 1857 that soon engulfed much of India.

The Indian Revolt of 1857 was not an isolated incident. As European powers acquired new territories in the 1800s, conflicts between colonial rulers and colonial peoples developed. By the early 1900s European nations ruled large parts of Asia and Africa, while the United States was expanding its interests in Latin America.

Historical Significance

How did the spread of empires affect peoples in Asia, Africa, and Latin America? How did colonial peoples respond to Western rule?

1850	1875	1900	1925

1869 Suez Canal opens.

1911 China becomes a republic.

1853 Commodore Perry lands in Japan.

1885 European powers meet in Berlin to divide Africa into colonies.

An Indian prince hosts a British officer at a nauch (a form of entertainment by professional dancers).

Your History Journal

Draw or copy the map "Imperialism in Africa 1914" on page 710 of this chapter. Then, using the map of modern Africa in the Atlas as a guide, write in the new national names and draw in present boundaries.

1800   1850   1900

c. 1800 Age of Imperialism begins.

c. 1840s French citizens settle in Algeria.

1899 British author Rudyard Kipling writes the poem "The White Man's Burden."

Section 1

Pressures for Expansion

Setting the Scene

▶ **Terms to Define**

imperialism, colony, protectorate, sphere of influence

▶ **People to Meet**

Cecil Rhodes, Rudyard Kipling

▶ **Places to Locate**

Algeria, Australia, New Zealand, Rhodesia (Zimbabwe)

 **Find Out** What were the political, economic, and social causes of imperialism?

The Storyteller

In India, British schools taught English and required students to adopt Christianity. The wife of a British official described attending a graduation ceremony in the year 1886. "The proceedings began with a hymn. The children sang pretty well, though in a harsh voice…. Then a boy stood up, put his hands together, and repeated the Lord's Prayer. Others followed him, and then Mr. Summers [the teacher] read a chapter from the Old Testament about Adam and Eve…. We could just tell he was speaking of the various nations—English, Parsee, [Muslim], Hindu, all came from Adam and Eve, we were all one family here."

—adapted from An Indian Journal, Nora Scott, 1994

Indians and British

The term imperialism is a Latin word from the days of the Roman Empire. Imperialism means one country's domination of the political, economic, and social life of another country. About 2,000 years ago, imperial Rome controlled most of the Mediterranean world. By the end of the 1800s, a handful of European countries, together with the United States, controlled nearly the entire world. Not surprisingly, the era between 1800 and 1914 has come to be known as the Age of Imperialism.

The imperialism of the 1800s resulted from three key factors. First, nationalism prompted rival European nations to build empires in their competitive quests for power. Second, the Industrial Revolution created a tremendous demand for raw materials and expanded markets, which prompted industrialized nations to seek new territories. Finally, both religious fervor and feelings of racial and cultural superiority inspired Europeans to impose their cultures on distant lands.

Political Rivalries

In the mid-1800s European countries saw themselves as actors on the world stage, and each country wanted to play a starring role. If Great Britain started a small colony in distant Asia or Africa, France had to start one too—and so did Belgium, Germany, Italy, Holland, Spain, Portugal, and Russia.

Once begun, the quest for colonies became a continuing enterprise that seemed to have no limits. Slow and difficult communication between remote territories and European capitals often enabled colonial governors and generals to take matters into their own hands. If a colony's borders did not provide military security, for instance, military officials

Visualizing History In this cartoon Bismarck (representing Germany), John Bull (representing Great Britain), and Uncle Sam (representing the United States) decide the fate of Samoa. *What phrase described Great Britain's vast overseas holdings?*

based in the colony used their armies to expand the colony's borders. This strategy worked well enough until colonial governments started claiming the same territories. Then new conflicts arose, and European troops found themselves facing off on remote battlefields in Africa and Asia.

Desire for New Markets

The Industrial Revolution of the 1800s knew no borders. Factories in Europe and the United States consumed tons of raw materials and churned out thousands of manufactured goods. The owners and operators of these factories searched constantly for new sources of raw materials and new markets for their products. They hoped to find both in foreign lands.

Rubber, copper, and gold came from Africa, cotton and jute from India, and tin from Southeast Asia. These raw materials spurred the growth of European and American industries and financial markets, but they represented only the tip of the iceberg. Bananas, oranges, melons, and other exotic fruits made their way to European markets. People in Paris, London, and Berlin drank colonial tea, coffee, and cocoa with their meals and washed themselves with soap made from African palm oil.

The colonies also provided new markets for the finished products of the Industrial Revolution. Tools, weapons, and clothing flowed out of the factories and back to the colonies whose raw materials had made them possible.

Seeking New Opportunities

Imperialism involved more than just guns, battles, raw materials, and manufactured goods. Colonies needed people who were loyal to the imperialist country. Great Britain, France, and Germany needed British, French, and German citizens to run their newly acquired territories and keep them productive.

Throughout the 1800s European leaders urged their citizens to move to far-off colonies. Many of them responded. In the 1840s, for example, thousands of French citizens sailed across the Mediterranean Sea to **Algeria**, where they started farms and estates on lands seized from local Algerian farmers.

The British, meanwhile, emigrated to the far corners of the globe, hoping to find opportunities not available at home. Many rushed to **Australia** and **New Zealand** in the 1850s in search of gold. As the British government continued to acquire vast tracts of land in Africa, Asia, and the Pacific, the phrase "the sun never sets on the British Empire" became a popular way of describing Great Britain's vast holdings.

Strong-minded individuals saw emigration as a chance to strike it rich or make a name for themselves. Perhaps the most spectacular success story of the era belonged to **Cecil Rhodes**, a British adventurer who made a fortune from gold and diamond mining in southern Africa. Rhodes went on to found a colony that bore his name: **Rhodesia** (now **Zimbabwe**).

"Civilizing" Mission

Some emigrants had motives that went beyond mere personal glory and profit. Religious and humanitarian impulses inspired many individuals to leave their secure lives at home and head for the distant colonies. The desire to spread Western technology, religion, customs and traditions also fueled colonial expansion.

During the Age of Imperialism, growing numbers of Catholic and Protestant missionaries decided to bring the Christian message to the most remote corners of Africa and Asia. Over the decades they set up hundreds of Christian missions and preached to thousands of Africans and Asians throughout these two continents. Like many other Europeans and Americans of this period, these missionaries believed that Christianity and Western civilization together could benefit and transform the world.

The missionaries were not military conquerors, but they did try to change people's beliefs and practices. They believed that, in order to become "civilized," the people of Africa and Asia would have to reject their old religions and convert to Christianity. To achieve this goal, missionaries built churches and taught Christian doctrine. Missionaries often set up schools and hospitals as well.

Other Europeans also believed that Western civilization was superior to the civilizations of colonial peoples. As a result, some colonial officials tried to impose Western customs and traditions on the people they conquered. These officials insisted that their colonial subjects learn European languages, and they encouraged Western lifestyles as well. They also discouraged colonial peoples from practicing traditional customs and rituals.

Some Europeans seized on the theory of social Darwinism as proof of their cultural superiority. This theory adapted Darwin's ideas about the evolution of animals—particularly his notion of "the survival of the fittest"—to explain differences among human beings. Social Darwinists believed that white Europeans were the "fittest" people in the world and that Western nations had a duty to spread Western ideas and traditions to "backward" peoples living overseas.

In 1899 the British writer **Rudyard Kipling** captured the essence of the imperialist attitude in his famous poem "The White Man's Burden." Kipling addressed the poem to the United States, which at this time had just begun to acquire and govern colonies of its own:

> **66** Take up the White Man's burden—
> Send forth the best ye breed—
> Go bind your sons to exile
> To serve your captives' need;
> To wait in heavy harness
> On fluttered folk and wild—
> Your new-caught, sullen peoples,
> Half-devil and half-child. **99**

Forms of Imperialism

Imperial nations gained new lands through treaties, purchases, and military conquest. Once in power, they used several forms of territorial control. The first of these, a colony, was a territory that an imperial power ruled directly through colonial officials. A protectorate had its own government, but its policies were guided by a foreign power. A sphere of influence was a region of a country in which the imperial power had exclusive investment or trading rights.

Within these general forms of control, each imperial nation exercised its power differently. For example, the French used their colonial officials not only to govern but to spread French culture and to make territories overseas extensions of France. The British, by contrast, focused strictly on administration and were less inclined to convert colonial peoples to British ways. In many cases, the British allowed local rulers to govern territories as their representatives.

SECTION I REVIEW

Recall

1. **Define** imperialism, colony, protectorate, sphere of influence.
2. **Identify** Cecil Rhodes, Rudyard Kipling.
3. **List** five raw materials that imperial powers took from their colonies. What did they send to these colonies?

Critical Thinking

4. **Evaluate** What does the Kipling poem reveal about his attitude toward Africans and Asians?

Understanding Themes

5. **Movement** Explain why the period from 1800 to 1914 is the Age of Imperialism.

1870   1890   1910

c. 1870 David Livingstone explores Africa.

1896 The Ethiopians defeat the Italians in the battle of Adowa.

1904 The French win special rights in Morocco.

1910 The British form the Union of South Africa.

Section 2

The Partition of Africa

Setting the Scene

▶ **Terms to Define**
partition

▶ **People to Meet**
David Livingstone, Abd al-Qadir, Muhammad Ali, Samory Touré, Menelik II, the Afrikaners, Shaka

▶ **Places to Locate**
Morocco, Egypt, the Sudan, Liberia, Ethiopia, Union of South Africa

ind Out What effects did imperialism have on the continent of Africa?

The Storyteller

An eyewitness to the opening ceremonies for the Suez Canal reported: "Fireworks in front of the Viceroy's Palace. Open house everywhere.... Luxurious dinners, vintage wines, exquisite fish, partridges, wild duck. Seven or eight thousand people sitting down to dinner in the middle of the desert. It was like something out of the Arabian Nights.... *At last I got back to my houseboat....*

All through the night I could hear the noise of the fair—the sound of music, the banging of fireworks, and the shouting of happy revelers."

—adapted from *World Ditch, The Making of the Suez Canal,* John Marlowe, 1964

Opening of Suez Canal

Until the 1800s Europeans knew little of Africa beyond its northern, western, and southern coasts. Then, in the mid-1800s, a few brave explorers began to venture into the African interior. The most famous of these was Scottish doctor and missionary **David Livingstone**, who first went to Africa in 1840. For the next 30 years, Livingstone explored wide tracts of central and eastern Africa, setting up Christian missions and sending back to Great Britain detailed reports of his discoveries, such as Victoria Falls.

When Europeans temporarily lost touch with Livingstone late in the 1860s, the *New York Herald* hired a British journalist and explorer named Henry M. Stanley to track him down. Their famous meeting in 1871 is best remembered for Stanley's understated greeting, "Dr. Livingstone, I presume?" With help from European financial backers, Stanley went on to lead several major expeditions through central Africa himself.

The publicity surrounding the explorations of Livingstone and Stanley generated new interest in Africa throughout Europe. This interest swelled when subsequent explorers sent back excited reports about the continent's abundance of resources. Reports such as these helped set off a mad European scramble for Africa between 1880 and 1914. One European country after another laid claim to parts of Africa. In 1885, 14 nations met in Berlin, Germany, and agreed to partition, or divide, the prize King Leopold II of Belgium called "this magnificent African cake." By 1914 European nations controlled 90 percent of the continent.

North Africa

The world's largest desert—the Sahara—stretches across North Africa from the Atlantic

Ocean to the Red Sea. Most of the people in North Africa live on a thin strip of land located north of the Sahara along the Mediterranean coast. Here the land is fertile and the climate mild. In the early 1800s Muslim Arabs under the authority of the Ottoman ruler in Istanbul governed the large territories west of Egypt, which at that time were called Tripoli, Tunis, and Algiers. Today Tripoli, Tunis, and Algiers are the independent North African countries of Libya, Tunisia, and Algeria.

The French in North Africa

In 1830 King Charles X of France ordered an invasion of Algiers with the aim of colonizing that country. French troops encountered stiff resistance from the Algerians, whose leader was **Abd al-Qadir** (AB•duhl KAH•duhr). About 10 years passed before 100,000 French soldiers finally subdued the determined Algerians. After conquering Algiers, the French seized neighboring Tunis in 1881 and secured special rights in **Morocco** in 1904. About 1 million French people settled in North Africa during these years of struggle.

Britain and Egypt

During the early 1800s, Ottoman **Egypt** was virtually independent under its governor, **Muhammad Ali**. Muhammad Ali's armies conquered neighboring lands, making Egypt a power in the eastern Mediterranean. To modernize Egypt, Ali reformed tax and land systems, encouraged industry, and supported irrigation projects to boost cotton production. Under Ali's successors, however, Egypt's debts rose along with European influence.

In 1859 a French entrepreneur, Ferdinand de Lesseps, set up a company to build the Suez Canal. Joining the Mediterranean and Red Seas, this waterway became a vital shortcut between Europe and Asia and was especially valued by the British as an important link to India. In 1875 Great Britain gained effective control of the canal when Egypt sold its canal shares to the British to pay off its debts. During the next few years, British influence increased over Egypt. In 1882 British forces put down a revolt led by nationalist leader Ahmed Arabi, and Egypt became a British protectorate.

Meanwhile, in **the Sudan**, south of Egypt, a Muslim revival stirred nationalist feelings. Since the 1880s, the Sudanese, under their leader the Mahdi, had challenged British expansion. In 1898, however, British forces, using Maxim machine guns, defeated the more simply armed Sudanese army at the Battle of Omdurman. Soon after the battle, the British also confronted a French force at Fashoda, bringing Great Britain and France to the brink of war. In the end, the French withdrew their army and their claim to the Sudan when the British recognized French control of Morocco.

Italy Seizes Libya

Libya lies between Egypt on the east and Algeria and Tunisia on the west. Known as Tripoli in the 1800s, the country had almost no economic value, but it was coveted by Italy, the nearest European nation. Entering the imperialist race late, Italy was eager to establish an African empire. After seeking guarantees of neutrality from other European nations, Italy in 1911 declared war on the Ottoman Empire, which ruled Tripoli. Italy easily defeated the Ottoman Turks and took Tripoli as a colony, renaming it Libya. Libya was the last country in North Africa to be conquered by European nations.

West, Central, and East Africa

West, Central, and East Africa have varied landscapes: mountains, plains, deserts, and rain forests. During the 1800s, these regions consisted of many territories, each with its own history and traditions. Europeans, however, exploited the Africans' lack of political unity and swallowed up most of these lands in the late 1800s.

West Africa

In the 1500s and 1600s Europeans traded along the coasts of Africa. From West African coastal trading posts, they carried out the transatlantic slave trade that provided labor for plantations and mines in the Americas. West African states traded salt, gold, and iron wares with the Europeans, but some local rulers also supplied prisoners of war to the slave trade.

During the early 1800s, many Western nations declared an end to the slave trade and abolished slavery. Slave trading, however, continued as Arab and African traders sent people from Central and East Africa to perform slave labor in the Middle East and Asia. Meanwhile, West African states, weakened by the population losses of the slave trade, traded natural products, such as palm oil, ivory, rubber, cotton, and cacao beans, for European manufactured goods.

To control this trade and to expand their coastal holdings, European nations began to push inland in the 1870s. Before this time, Europeans had avoided inland Africa because of the difficult terrain and deadly diseases, such as malaria. In the late 1800s, the discovery of the natural ingredient, quinine, to fight malaria and the use of steamships for river transportation made European exploration of inland Africa easier. By 1900, European powers, especially Great Britain and France, had acquired vast new territories in West Africa.

European expansion, however, did not go unchallenged. In the 1890s West African rulers, such as **Samory Touré** (sah•MOHR•ree too•RAY) and Behanzin, led armies against the French. In the Gold Coast, the Ashanti queen Yaa Asantewaa rallied her people against British expansion. All of these efforts were defeated by well-armed European forces. By 1900, **Liberia** was the only remaining independent state in West Africa. Established in 1822 by free African Americans, Liberia became a republic in 1847. Its ties to the United States made it off limits to European expansion.

Central and East Africa

In 1877 the explorer Henry M. Stanley reached the mouth of the Congo River. He later described the river as a "grand highway of commerce to … Central Africa." As a result of Stanley's exploration, Belgium's King Leopold II claimed the Congo region as his own private plantation. He enslaved the Congolese people and had them cut down forests for rubber trees and kill elephant herds for ivory tusks. In pursuing his ambitions, Leopold stripped the Congo of many people and resources.

Leopold's brutal control of the Congo lasted about 20 years, despite the world's outrage. In 1908 he finally agreed to give his plantation to the Belgian government in return for a large loan. Thus, in that year, the Congo region owned by Leopold became the Belgian Congo.

Visualizing History This wood carving of a man reading a book is a Yoruba artist's depiction of a Swedish missionary. *Besides establishing missions, what were other European objectives in Africa?*

While the Belgians were claiming the Congo Basin, the British, the Germans, and the Italians were doing the same in East Africa. The only country in East Africa to remain independent during this period was **Ethiopia**, located in a remote region known as the Horn of Africa. Beginning in the 1880s, Italy tried to conquer this country, but the Italians underestimated the determination of their opponent, Ethiopia's Emperor **Menelik II**. As emperor, Menelik had conquered many small kingdoms and reunified the Ethiopian Empire.

When the Italians attacked Ethiopia in 1896, Menelik's well-trained forces crushed the invaders at the battle of Adowa. His victory was so devastating

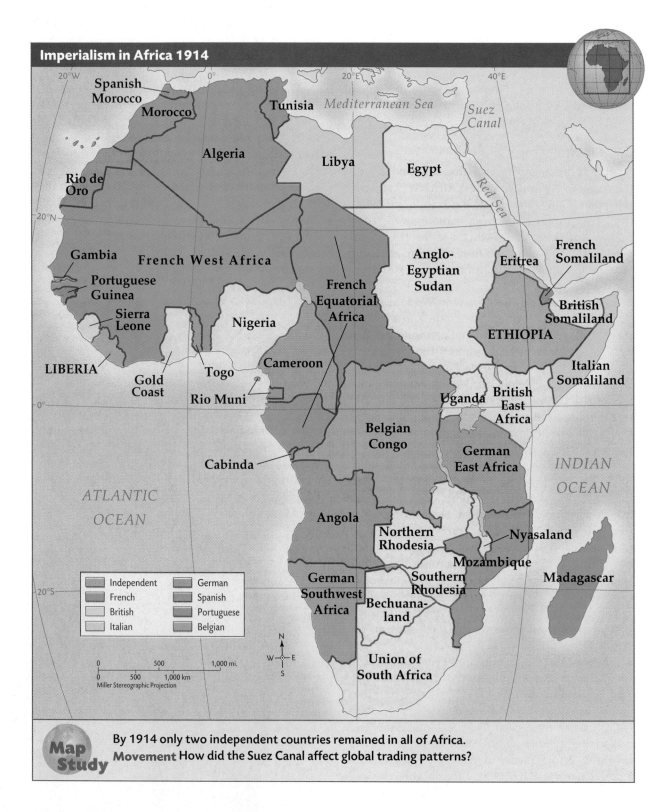

Imperialism in Africa 1914

Independent | **German** | **French** | **Spanish** | **British** | **Portuguese** | **Italian** | **Belgian**

Map Study By 1914 only two independent countries remained in all of Africa.
Movement How did the Suez Canal affect global trading patterns?

that no Europeans dared invade his country again during his lifetime. Ethiopia and Liberia were the only two African nations to escape European domination completely during the Age of Imperialism.

Southern Africa

Dutch settlers came to southern Africa in 1652 and established the port of Cape Town. For the next 150 years, **the Afrikaners**, as these settlers came to be called, conquered the lands around the port. The lands they eventually acquired became known as Cape Colony.

Before construction of the Suez Canal, the quickest sea route to Asia from Europe was around the Cape of Good Hope at the southern tip of Africa. Sensing the strategic value of Cape Colony, the British seized it during the Napoleonic Wars in the early 1800s. The Afrikaners resented British rule, particularly laws that forbade the enslaving of black Africans. The white Afrikaners believed that they were superior to black Africans and that God had ordained slavery.

In the 1830s about 10,000 Afrikaners, whom the British called *Boers* (the Dutch word for "farmers"), decided to leave Cape Colony rather than live under British rule. In a move known as the Great Trek, the Afrikaners migrated northeast into the interior. Here they established two independent republics, the Transvaal and the Orange Free State. The constitution of the Transvaal stated, "There shall be no equality in State or Church between white and black."

The Afrikaners fought constantly with their neighbors. First they battled the powerful Zulu nation for control of the land. Under their king **Shaka**, the Zulu in the early 1800s had conquered a large empire in southern Africa. The Zulu and

Boers were unable to win a decisive victory. Finally, in 1879, the British became involved in battles with the Zulu. Under their king, Cetywayo, the Zulu at first defeated British forces. With guns and greater numbers, however, the British eventually destroyed the Zulu Empire.

Conflict also developed between the British and the Boers. During the 1880s, British settlers moved into the Boer-ruled Transvaal in search of gold and diamonds. Eager to acquire this mineral wealth for Great Britain, Cecil Rhodes—now prime minister of Cape Colony—and some other British leaders wanted all of South Africa to come under British rule. They began pressuring the Boers to grant civil rights to the British settlers in the Transvaal. Growing hostility between the British and the Boers finally erupted in 1899 into the Anglo-Boer War, which the British won three years later.

In 1910 Great Britain united the Transvaal, the Orange Free State, Cape Colony, and Natal into the **Union of South Africa**. The constitution of this British dominion made it nearly impossible for nonwhites to win the right to vote. As one black African writer of the time said, "The Union is to be a Union of two races, namely the British and the Afrikaners—the African is to be excluded."

Racial equality became a dominant issue in South African affairs after the formation of the Union. Several nonwhite South African groups tried to advance their civil rights against the white minority government. Mohandas K. Gandhi, a lawyer from India, worked for equality for Indians in South Africa. He urged the Indians to disobey laws that discriminated against them. Gandhi's efforts brought some additional rights for the Indian community.

South Africa's black majority also was stirred into action against racial injustices. In 1912 black South Africans founded the South African Native

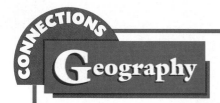

Geography

Coastal Trading Centers

"The king of the white people wishes to find out a way by which we may bring our own merchandise to you and sell everything at a much cheaper rate," said British explorer Mungo Park to a West African king in 1805.

Dakar, Senegal

Park was interested in the possibilities of trade on the Niger River.

Like the other great rivers of Africa—the Congo, the Nile, and the Zambezi—the Niger flows to the sea. To the European traders of the 1800s, few places were more important than the mouth of a river. These were the only places where the large trading ships could unload European manufactured goods in exchange for African raw materials.

At the mouth of the Niger in the late 1800s, trade centered on palm oil. The British used the oil for making soap. Barrels of the precious oil were floated down the Niger and collected at depots, or ports, with names like Calabar and Port Harcourt.

Today these ports are growing cities that draw people from all parts of Nigeria. Port Harcourt now has a population of 400,000 inhabitants, while Calabar has about 160,000. Both ports still provide oil to the world, but today it is crude oil, the lifeblood of the world's industries and transportation.

Linking Past and Present ACTIVITY

Explain why Mungo Park was interested in Africa. Why did the mouths of African rivers become centers of trade with Europeans? Describe African port cities today.

National Congress (SANNC). The SANNC's goal was to work for black rights in South Africa. In 1923 the SANNC shortened its name to the African National Congress (ANC).

Effects of Imperialism

Imperialism had profound effects on Africa. These effects varied from colony to colony, but they centered mainly on economic and social life. The imperialists profited from the colonies by digging mines, starting plantations, and building factories and ports. They hired Africans at low wages and imposed taxes that had to be paid in cash. Men were often housed in dormitories away from their families and subjected to brutal discipline.

Schools set up by Europeans taught Africans that European ways were best. In some cases, African traditions declined, although most Africans held on to their cultures while accepting some European ways. For example, many Africans came to accept some form of Christianity.

By the early 1900s, a western-educated elite had emerged in many European colonies in Africa. These Africans condemned imperialism as contrary to western ideals of liberty and equality. They founded nationalist groups to push for self-rule. By the end of the twentieth century, Africa's peoples had won their political independence from European rule.

SECTION 2 REVIEW

Recall

1. **Define** partition.
2. **Identify** David Livingstone, Abd al-Qadir, Muhammad Ali, Samory Touré, Menelik II, the Afrikaners, Shaka.
3. **Locate** the countries of North Africa on the map on page 710. What geographical feature separates these countries from the rest of Africa?

Critical Thinking

4. **Analyzing Information** How did European rule affect civil rights in South Africa? What steps did Africans and Asians take to bring about change?

Understanding Themes

5. **Change** What were the main causes and effects of the European partition of Africa?

Section 3

The Division of Asia

Setting the Scene

▶ **Terms to Define**
sepoy, viceroy, sphere of influence, culture system, westernization

▶ **People to Meet**
Ci Xi, Sun Yat-sen, Matthew C. Perry, Mutsuhito, Diponegoro, Emilio Aguinaldo

▶ **Places to Locate**
Beijing, the East Indies, the Philippines, Indochina

ind Out How did the countries of Asia respond to imperialism?

The Storyteller

"Until the year 1924 I was the only foreigner privileged to witness and to participate in the great ceremonies...." So wrote Reginald Johnston, Professor of Chinese at the University of London, and witness to the end of an empire in the "Palace of Cloudless Heaven" within the Forbidden City. "It was not without difficulty that even the emperor was able to ... invite a few 'ocean-men' to witness the New Year ceremonial which took place on February 5, 1924. It turned out to be the last occasion on which the ceremony was performed. Before another year had passed, the life of the Manchu court had come to an end."

—adapted from *Twilight in the Forbidden City,* Reginald F. Johnston, 1934

China's Forbidden City

In his book *Description of the World,* written in 1298, Italian explorer Marco Polo relates the many stories he heard about Zipangu, an East Asian island with a supposedly inexhaustible supply of gold. Polo never did visit Zipangu, now called Japan, but his description of its imagined treasures, and of the Asian riches he did see, inspired generations of Europeans. They looked eastward to Asia, dreaming of wealth.

The British in India

European trade with Asia opened up in the 1500s as sea routes replaced difficult overland routes. British involvement in India dates back to this period, when English traders first sailed along India's coast. In 1600 some of these traders formed the East India Company, which later became one of the richest and most powerful trading companies the world had ever known.

After its founding, the East India Company built trading posts and forts in strategic locations throughout India. The French East India Company did the same and challenged the British for control of the India trade. In 1757 Robert Clive, a British East India Company agent, used an army of British and Indian troops to defeat the French at the Battle of Plassey. During the next hundred years, the British expanded their territory in India through wars and commercial activity.

The Sepoy Rebellion

As a result of steady expansion, the East India Company came to control most of India by 1857. Their power was tested that year, however, when the **sepoys**, or Indian soldiers, rebelled against their British commanders. Long before the greased bullet rumor discussed at this chapter's beginning triggered the Indian Revolt of 1857, sepoy resentment had been growing over British attempts to impose Christianity and European customs on them.

Chapter 27 *The Age of Imperialism* **713**

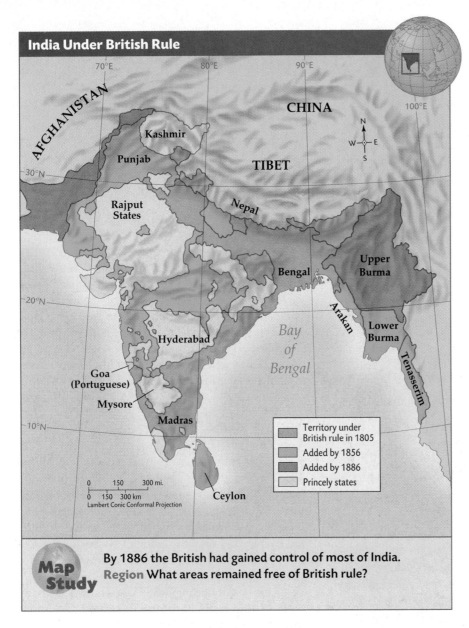

AFGHANISTAN

CHINA

Kashmir

Punjab

TIBET

Rajput States

Nepal

Upper Burma

Bengal

Arakan

Lower Burma

Hyderabad

Bay of Bengal

Tenasserim

Goa (Portuguese)

Mysore

Madras

0   150   300 mi.
0   150   300 km
Lambert Conic Conformal Projection

Ceylon

Territory under British rule in 1805
Added by 1856
Added by 1886
Princely states

Map Study   By 1886 the British had gained control of most of India.
Region What areas remained free of British rule?

telegraph lines and dug irrigation canals; and it established schools and universities.

At the same time, British colonial officials discriminated against Indians and forced them to change their ancient ways, often with tragic results. Indian farmers, for example, were told to grow cotton instead of wheat, because British textile mills needed cotton. The lack of wheat then led to severe food shortages that killed millions of Indians during the 1800s.

Outraged by the food shortages and other problems, many Indians wanted to move toward self-rule. In 1885 a group of Indian business and professional leaders formed the Indian National Congress. Accepting western ideas such as democracy and equality, the Congress at first used peaceful protest to urge the British to grant more power to Indians. Later, as the Congress party, it led the long struggle for complete independence.

The sepoy rebellion spread across northern and central India, in some places resulting in the massacre of British men, women, and children. Within a year, British forces put down the uprising. In revenge for the massacres, they killed thousands of unarmed Indians. The revolt left bitterness on both sides and forced the British to tighten their control of India. In 1858 Parliament ended the East India Company and sent a viceroy to rule as the monarch's representative. Treaties secured the loyalty of the remaining independent Indian states.

Indian Nationalism

The British government tried to quell further unrest in India by spending vast amounts of money on India's economic development. It built paved roads and an extensive railway system; it installed

China Faces the West

While the British increased their hold on India, they and other Europeans developed trade with China. During the 1500s, Chinese civilization had been highly advanced, and the Chinese at that time had little interest in European products. There was only limited trade between China and Europe during the next 300 years. During this period, while technological changes transformed Europe, China's political, economic, and military position weakened under the Qing dynasty. Qing emperors ruled China from 1644 to 1912.

The Unequal Treaties

In the early 1800s, British merchants found a way to break China's trade barriers and earn huge profits. In exchange for Chinese tea, silk, and porcelain—and to avoid paying cash—the merchants smuggled a drug called opium, which they obtained from India and Turkey, into China. In 1839 Chinese troops tried to stop the smuggling. When the British resisted, war broke out. The British used gunboats to bombard Chinese ports and easily defeated the Chinese, who lacked modern weapons.

British victory in the Opium War in 1842 led to the Treaty of Nanking, the first of many "unequal treaties" that forced China to yield many of its rights to Western powers. The Nanking treaty granted the British payment for war losses as well as the island of Hong Kong. British citizens in China also gained extraterritoriality, the right to live under their own laws and courts. Over the next 60 years, the "unequal treaties" increased foreign influence in China and weakened the Qing dynasty. Civil wars, such as the Taiping Rebellion (1850-1864), also eroded the dynasty's control.

By the 1890s, European powers as well as Japan claimed large sections of China as spheres of influence—areas where they had exclusive trading rights. Coming late to the imperialist scramble, the United States did not claim a sphere of influence. Instead, it tried to open China to the trade of all nations through the Open Door Policy. Deadlocked by their own rivalries, the other powers reluctantly agreed to this policy in 1899.

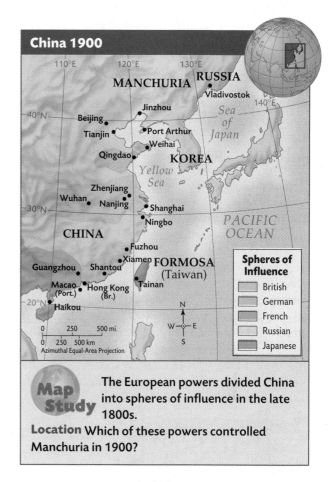

China 1900

Spheres of Influence
- British
- German
- French
- Russian
- Japanese

Map Study The European powers divided China into spheres of influence in the late 1800s.

Location Which of these powers controlled Manchuria in 1900?

Chinese Responses

To modernize China, some reformers during the late 1800s began a "self-strengthening" movement. This program involved importing both Western technology and educational methods. They also worked to improve agriculture, strengthen the armed forces, and end the European practice of extraterritoriality.

Lack of government support stalled these efforts. Chinese weakness was only further exposed in an 1894 war against a modernizing Japan that ended in China's defeat and loss of territory. From China, Japan gained the island of Taiwan and the Liaodong Peninsula as well as trading benefits in Chinese territory. The Japanese also ended China's influence in Korea.

After this setback, reformers regained influence with the support of the young emperor Guang Xu (gwawng SHYOO). They launched the Hundred Days of Reform to modernize the government and encourage new industries. However, conservatives led by the emperor's mother, **Ci Xi** (TSUH•SEE), returned to power, arrested the emperor, and halted the reforms.

By the late 1890s, anti-foreign feelings in China had led to the formation of secret societies dedicated to removing diplomats, entrepreneurs, missionaries, and other foreigners from the country. One group, the Righteous and Harmonious Fists, practiced a Chinese form of boxing, and Westerners named its members Boxers. In 1900 the Boxers carried out attacks against foreigners and Chinese Christians, besieging foreign communities in **Beijing**, the Chinese capital. In response, the Western powers and Japan sent a multinational force that ended the uprising. The empress, who had supported the Boxers, reversed her policy.

The Revolution of 1911

After the Boxer Uprising, Ci Xi struggled to hold on to power. She agreed to allow foreign troops to remain in China and gave in to some of her people's demands for change. For example, she established schools and reorganized the government. But it was too little, too late. Many Chinese believed that a modern republic should replace the Qing dynasty. In their view, the only way to achieve this goal was through revolution.

The revolutionaries wanted China to regain its former power and influence. One of them, a doctor named **Sun Yat-sen**, wrote in the early 1900s: "Today we are the poorest and weakest nation in the world and occupy the lowest position in international affairs. Other men are the carving knife and serving dish; we are the fish and the meat."

In 1905 Sun and other revolutionaries formed the United League (later known as the *Guomindang*, or Nationalist party). Their goal was to modernize China on the basis of the "Three Principles of the People": nationalism (freedom from foreign control), democracy (representative government), and livelihood (economic well-being for all Chinese). The revolutionary cause was strengthened in 1908 when Ci Xi died, and two-year-old Prince Pu Yi became emperor. Three years later, revolution swept China as peasants, workers, soldiers, and court officials turned against the weak dynasty. Sun Yat-sen hurried home from a fund-raising tour of the United States. In January 1912, he became the first president of the new Chinese republic.

Modernization of Japan

Japan's dealings with the European powers began in much the same way as China's, but they ended differently. European traders first came to the island country in the 1500s. Like the Chinese, the Japanese were uninterested in European products, and they cut off almost all trade with Europe in the early 1600s. At the time a military commander called a shogun ruled Japan. Although the country also had an emperor, he had no real power.

Japan did not trade again with the outside world until 1853, when four American warships commanded by Commodore **Matthew C. Perry** sailed into the bay at Edo (present-day Tokyo). Perry wanted Japan to begin trading with the United States. The shogun, knowing what had happened to China in the recent Opium War, decided early in 1854 to sign a treaty with Perry.

Images *of the* Times

The British Empire

From the late 1700s to the early 1900s, Great Britain ruled the world's largest overseas empire. British territories were found in every continent.

British naval forces demonstrated British power in countries that were not directly under Queen Victoria's crown. Here a British ship attacks Chinese warships off the coast of China.

The Meiji Leaders

In the first five years after Perry's arrival, the shogun signed trade treaties with Britain, France, Holland, Russia, and the United States. Since the treaties favored the imperialist powers, the Japanese people called them unequal treaties, just as the Chinese had. Unhappiness with the treaties led to the overthrow of the shogun in 1868. A group of samurai gave its allegiance to the new emperor, **Mutsuhito**, but kept the real power to themselves. Because Mutsuhito was known as the Meiji (MAY•jee), or "Enlightened" emperor, Japan's new rulers were called the Meiji leaders.

The Meiji leaders tried to make Japan a great power capable of competing with Western nations. Adopting the slogan "Rich country, strong military" they brought the forms of parliamentary government to Japan, strengthened the military, and worked to transform the nation into an industrial society. The Meiji leaders established a system of universal education designed to produce loyal, skilled citizens who would work for Japan's mod-ernization. In this way, the Japanese hoped to create a new ruling class based on talent rather than birth.

Industrialization

In the 1870s Japan began to industrialize in an effort to strengthen its economy. The Japanese did this with little outside assistance. They were reluctant to borrow money from the West, fearing foreign takeovers if loans could not be repaid. In any case, most Western banks were not interested in making loans to Japan, because they considered the country a poor financial risk.

The Japanese government laid the groundwork for industrial expansion. It revised the tax structure to raise money for investment. It also developed a modern currency system and supported the building of postal and telegraph networks, railroads, and port facilities.

Beginning in the late 1880s, Japan's economy grew rapidly. A growing population provided a continuing supply of cheap labor. The combination of new technological methods and cheap labor

India was the most important British possession. This painting shows a British military officer traveling by elephant through northern India with his cavalry and foot soldiers.

Australia drew many British settlers, who made their homes in the harsh outback, or semi-dry interior, as well as in coastal areas.

REFLECTING ON THE TIMES

1. What types of people were found throughout Great Britain's empire?
2. In the 1800s, people often said that "the sun never sets on the British Empire." What do you think this phrase meant?

allowed Japan to produce low-priced goods. Wars at the turn of the century further stimulated Japan's economy and helped it enter new world markets. By 1914 Japan had become one of the world's leading industrial nations.

Japan as a World Power

By the 1890s the Meiji leaders had taken great strides toward creating a modern nation. Japan had acquired an efficient government, a vigorous economy, and a strong military. Needing more natural resources, the Japanese government began to establish its own overseas empire. The first prize it attempted to take was Korea.

When the people of Korea revolted against their Chinese rulers in 1894, Japan decided to intervene. Japanese troops easily defeated the Chinese army in the Sino-Japanese War. Although Korea officially became independent, Japan gained partial control of its trade. Over the next few years, thousands of Japanese settled in Korea.

Korea also figured in Japan's next war. The Russian Empire had interests in Korea as well, and its interests began to clash with Japan's. Even more important was neighboring Manchuria, where the Russians kept troops and had a naval base at Port Arthur. In 1904 the Japanese navy launched a surprise attack on Port Arthur. Few people expected Japan to win the Russo-Japanese War, but the Japanese piled up victory after victory. The conflict ended in 1905, when Russia signed a treaty granting the country of Japan control over Korea and other nearby areas.

Japan's victory over Russia inspired non-Western nationalist leaders throughout the world. It proved that the European empires could be defeated if one had the will and determination. On the other hand, Japan had now become an imperialist country itself. It annexed Korea as a colony in 1910 and continued to expand its empire for the next 35 years. ◼▬

Footnotes to History

A Teenage Emperor
Mutsuhito was only 15 when he became Japan's emperor in 1867. During his 44-year reign, he often led the way in adopting Western customs. He cut his traditional topknot, a tuft of hair on the top of the head, and wore European-style clothes. While previous emperors lived apart from the people, Mutsuhito rode around Tokyo in an open carriage and toured the countryside.

Southeast Asia

Southeast Asia consists of two distinct geographic areas. Island Southeast Asia is made of two archipelagos, or groups of islands: **the East Indies** and **the Philippines**. To the north and west lies mainland Southeast Asia. It includes all of the territories that occupy the Indochinese and Malay Peninsulas.

The growth of imperialism in these areas followed a familiar pattern. Beginning in the 1500s, imperialist powers came, saw, and conquered. Over the next 400 years Portugal, Spain, the Netherlands, Great Britain, France, and the United States all set up colonies in that region. They ranged in size from the huge Dutch East Indies that included thousands of islands to the tiny British settlements on the island of Singapore.

The Islands of Southeast Asia

For centuries, the island region of Southeast Asia had attracted foreign traders and colonizers. At the beginning of the 1800s, the Dutch controlled most of the East Indies and Spain controlled the Philippines.

The Dutch East Indies, present-day Indonesia, had many natural resources, including rich soil. Farmers grew coffee, pepper, cinnamon, sugar, indigo, and tea; miners dug for tin and copper; loggers cut down ebony, teak, and other hardwood trees. The Dutch government used a method of forced labor called the culture system to gather all these raw materials. The Dutch also discouraged westernization, or the spread of European civilization. The enormous profits the Dutch received from the East Indies made the colony the envy of the imperialist powers.

Diponegoro, a native prince from the East Indian island of Java, started a revolt against the Dutch in 1825. Although it lasted 10 years, this revolt eventually ended in failure, and the Dutch encountered little real opposition for the next 80 years. One of the Dutch governors put it this way: "We have ruled here for 300 years with the whip and the club and we shall still be doing it in another 300 years." In the early 1900s, the Dutch won control of the entire archipelago, extending their rule into northern Sumatra and the Celebes. But within a generation, nationalist forces would bring the Dutch East Indian empire to its knees.

The Spanish rule of the Philippines resembled the Dutch rule of the Dutch East Indies. Native Filipinos worked for very low wages, if any, on tobacco and sugar plantations owned by wealthy Spaniard landowners. During the 1800s the

This view of Whampoa Reach in China (about 1860) shows an English barque and an American ship. *How did Western trade and commerce affect Southeast Asia?*

Filipinos' resentment grew until it finally exploded into revolution in 1896.

When the United States declared war on Spain in 1898, the American government promised to free the Philippines in return for the rebels' help against the Spanish. After winning the Spanish-American War, the United States broke its promise and ruled the Philippines as a colony. The Filipinos led by **Emilio Aguinaldo** (ah•gee•NAHL•doh) then arose against American rule, but United States troops defeated them two years later.

Mainland Southeast Asia

The mainland region of Southeast Asia consisted of several large territories in the early 1800s, including Burma (present-day Myanmar) and Malaya in the west, Vietnam in the east, and Siam (Thailand), Cambodia, and Laos in the middle. All through the 1800s, Great Britain and France struggled for domination of the area—more for military gain than for economic reasons.

The British swept into Burma from India in the 1820s. Over the next 60 years, they took full control of Burma and neighboring Malaya. Meanwhile, the French were slowly conquering **Indochina**, the region that includes present-day Vietnam, Cambodia, and Laos. They, too, established complete control in the 1880s.

Squeezed between the two growing blocks of British and French territory lay the kingdom of Siam. In 1893 the French invaded Siam, sending forces into Bangkok, the capital city. Great Britain and France avoided armed conflict, however, when they agreed to define their spheres of influence in Southeast Asia. As a result of the agreement, Siam remained independent.

European rivalries for control of resources brought much disturbance to mainland Southeast Asia. Western influences changed traditional ways of life. Colonial landowners and trading companies forced local farmers and workers to grow cash crops, mine coal, and cut teak trees.

SECTION 3 REVIEW

Recall
1. **Define** sepoy, viceroy, sphere of influence, culture system, westernization.
2. **Identify** Ci Xi, Sun Yat-sen, Matthew C. Perry, Mutsuhito, Diponegoro, Emilio Aguinaldo.

3. **Explain** why the British government dissolved the East India Company.

Critical Thinking
4. **Synthesizing Information** How did European imperialism differ in India, China, and Southeast Asia?

Understanding Themes
5. **Reaction** How did the Japanese succeed in avoiding extensive Western interference in its affairs, while China could not?

Using the Internet

Have you heard the expression, "surfing the Net"? This means you can search through the Internet to find information on many subjects. You won't get wet, but you sure can learn a lot and have fun!

Learning the Skill

The Internet is a global computer network that offers many features, including the latest news and weather, stored information, E-mail, and on-line shopping. Before you can connect to the Internet and use the services it offers, however, you must have three things: a computer, a modem, and a service provider. A service provider is a company that, for a fee, gives you entry to the Internet.

Once you are connected, the easiest and fastest way to access sites and information is to use a "Web browser," a program that lets you view and explore information on the World Wide Web. The Web consists of many documents called "Web pages," each of which has its own address, or Uniform Resource Locator (URL). Many URLs start with the keystrokes *http://*

Practicing the Skill

This chapter focuses on the Age of Imperialism, when the Panama Canal and the Suez Canal were completed. Surf the Internet to learn about the history of these canals.

1. Log on the Internet and access one of the World Wide Web search tools, such as Yahoo at website http://www.yahoo.com *or* Lycos at http://www.lycos.com *or* WebCrawler at http:/www.webcrawler.com

2. Search by category or by name. If you search by category in Yahoo, for example, click on *Social* Science. To search by name, type in *Panama Canal and Suez Canal.*

3. Scroll the list of Web pages that appears when the search is complete. Select a page to bring up and read or print it. Repeat the process until you have enough information you can use to develop a short report on the two major canals completed during the Age of Imperialism.

Applying the Skill

Go through the steps just described to search the Internet for information on the Sepoy Rebellion in India. Based on the information, write an article for your school newspaper or magazine about your topic.

For More Practice

Turn to the Skill Practice in the Chapter Review on page 727 for more practice in using the Internet.

1823 The United States proclaims the Monroe Doctrine.

1898 The United States declares war on Spain.

1914 The Panama Canal opens.

Section 4

Imperialism in the Americas

Setting the Scene

▶ **Terms to Define**
   arbitration

▶ **People to Meet**
   James Monroe, José Martí, William McKinley, Theodore Roosevelt, Benito Juárez, Porfirio Díaz, Emiliano Zapata, Francisco "Pancho" Villa, Venustiano Carranza, Woodrow Wilson

▶ **Places to Locate**
   Cuba, Puerto Rico, the Virgin Islands, Isthmus of Panama, Mexico

 How did Latin Americans respond to the growth of American influence in their region?

Frederic Remington was one of the first "foreign correspondents"—a journalist in Cuba during the Spanish-American War. He wrote: "At night I lay up beside the road outside of Siboney, and cooked my supper by a soldier fire, and lay down under a mango-tree on my raincoat, with my haversack for a pillow. I could hear the shuffling of the marching troops, and see by the light of the fire near the road the ... sweaty men."

—adapted from *Frederic Remington and the Spanish-American War*, Douglas Allen, 1971

Teddy Roosevelt and the Rough Riders

On the floor of the Senate in 1898, United States Senator Albert J. Beveridge delivered a stirring speech on America's growing role as a world power:

❝ Fate has written our policy for us; the trade of the world must and shall be ours. We will establish trading-posts throughout the world as distributing-points for American products…. Great colonies governing themselves, flying our flag and trading with us, will grow about our posts of trade. ❞

Senator Beveridge's grand ambition capped a half-century of growing American influence in world affairs. The imperialist powers of Europe had already laid claim to much of the world. Now that the United States had grown considerably in size, wealth, and power, it was determined to use the Monroe Doctrine to block the spread of European imperialism in neighboring Latin America, an area that includes Mexico, the Caribbean islands, Central America, and South America. In doing so, the United States was also promoting its own brand of imperialism that involved the penetration of new economic markets and the acquisition of overseas territories.

TURNING POINT

The Monroe Doctrine

Even before the independence of all the Latin American countries was well established, Spain had sought the support of other European powers in reconquering its former colonies. Both the United States and Great Britain opposed Spain's

United States Marines hoist the American flag in Cuba. *What was Spain's economic interest in Cuba?*

plan. The United States did not want a strong European power so close to its borders. Great Britain had developed good trade relations with the Latin Americans and did not feel that its commercial interests would be served by the return of Spanish control to the Americas.

Great Britain suggested to the United States that a joint warning be issued to the various European powers. However, President **James Monroe** and Secretary of State John Quincy Adams decided to act alone. In 1823 Monroe warned the European powers not to interfere in the countries of the Western Hemisphere. The Monroe Doctrine, as it was later called, contained two major points:

❝ 1. The American continents, by the free and independent condition which they have assured and maintain, are henceforth not to be considered as subjects for future colonization by any European powers.

2. We should consider any attempt on their part to extend their system to any portion of this hemisphere as dangerous to our peace and safety. ❞

At the time the Monroe Doctrine was declared, it was not clear what the United States would do if European powers tried to conquer any part of Latin America. The support of the British Royal Navy, however, ensured that the infant states of Latin America would remain free to determine their own political destinies.

As the United States grew in strength during the late 1800s and early 1900s, it began to make its power felt in Latin America. In 1895, when Great Britain was in conflict with Venezuela over the boundaries of British Guiana, the United States urged that the dispute be submitted to arbitration, or settlement by a third party that is agreeable to both sides. Appealing to the Monroe Doctrine, the United States Department of State issued a strong warning to the British to pressure them into accepting arbitration. Aware of the power of the United States and involved with problems in its empire, Great Britain agreed to a peaceful settlement. ➖

The Spanish-American War

Soon after the Guiana border dispute was settled, the United States turned its attention to **Cuba**. Cuba and the neighboring island of **Puerto Rico** were still Spanish colonies in the late 1800s. Cuba was particularly important to Spain, which reaped huge profits from the island's many sugar and tobacco plantations.

In 1895 **José Martí**, a writer and political activist, led Cubans in a revolution against Spanish rule. Cuba's Spanish leaders embarked on a bloody attack on the rebel forces. Martí was killed in a battle against the Spaniards, and Spanish troops rounded up thousands of Cubans and sent them to prison camps where conditions were brutal. Disease and starvation soon claimed more than 400,000 Cuban lives.

Remember the *Maine*!

The struggle of the Cubans for freedom attracted much sympathy in the United States. American newspapers printed vivid stories describing the cruelty and killings in Cuba. Soon, prominent American politicians began clamoring for war with Spain. Businesspeople who had invested in Cuba also joined in. Finally, in January 1898, President **William McKinley** ordered the battleship *Maine* to Havana, the capital of Cuba, to demonstrate growing American interest in Cuban affairs. A few weeks later, an explosion ripped through the *Maine* while it was still anchored in Havana harbor, sinking the ship and killing 260 American sailors.

The cry "Remember the *Maine!*" swept across the United States. American newspapers left little doubt that Spain was responsible for the disaster. In April 1898, under pressure from all sides, McKinley asked Congress to declare war on Spain. The Spanish-American War lasted four months and ended with a victory for the United States.

Bettmann

George F. Mobley

Panama Canal

Harvard College Library

The Panama Canal was a testament to the skill of American engineers. The enormous lock gates (under construction, left) were made of steel plates attached to a skeleton of steel girders. (Note the size of the men working around these gates.) Each gate weighed 700 tons (784 short tons) but was hollow and could float. Because they were buoyant, the gates exerted less stress on their hinges as the gates were opened and closed. Without the significant advances made in technology during the 1800s, this canal could not have been built.

Without President Theodore Roosevelt (center) the Panama Canal would not have been built. During his presidency he decided that the United States would build a canal across the Isthmus of Panama—and he made it happen. Roosevelt wanted to boost American power and to compete more effectively with the imperial powers of Europe and Japan. The Panama Canal helped accomplish this goal by strengthening the military posture of the United States. The canal eliminated 7,800 miles (12,550 km) from the sea voyage between New York and San Francisco. It cost $380 million and tens of thousands of lives, and took ten years to complete. ⊕

American Territorial Gains

During the late 1800s, the United States made many significant territorial gains. In 1867 it purchased Alaska from Russia, and in 1898 annexed Hawaii, shortly after American entrepreneurs on the islands had overthrown the Hawaiian queen Liliuokalani (lee•lee•oo•oh•kah•LAH•nee). As a result of the Spanish-American War, the United States gained from Spain territories in the Pacific Ocean (the Philippines and Guam) and in the Caribbean Sea (Puerto Rico). Although independent, Cuba was under American protection. In 1917 the United States purchased **the Virgin Islands** (St. Thomas, St. John, and St. Croix) from Denmark.

The Panama Canal

Victory in the Spanish-American War made the United States a world power. It became important for the United States to be able to move its fleet quickly between the Pacific and Atlantic Oceans. What was needed was a canal across the **Isthmus of Panama**, a narrow neck of land that linked Central America and South America.

For centuries, Europeans and Americans had dreamed of building a canal across Central America. In the 1880s the Frenchman Ferdinand de Lesseps, who had built the Suez Canal, tried—and failed—to build a canal in Panama. Thirteen years after the bankruptcy of de Lesseps's company, United States President **Theodore Roosevelt** received the backing of Congress to acquire the Panama canal rights and property.

In 1902 Panama was part of Colombia. Roosevelt tried to negotiate a treaty with Colombia that year that would give the United States land to build the canal in Panama. When Colombia refused to sign the treaty, Roosevelt and the American public were outraged.

Roosevelt soon developed a plan, however. With his approval, American agents encouraged the people of Panama to revolt against the government of Colombia. They did so on the night of November 3, 1903, with the help of the United States Navy, which prevented Colombian troops from landing. The rebellion was over by the next day, and the new Republic of Panama quickly signed a treaty granting the United States the land to build the Panama Canal.

Construction of the canal began in 1904 and took 10 years to complete. More than 40,000 workers cut through hills, built dams, and drained swamps until the two mighty oceans were connected. Many of the workers, however, died of malaria and yellow fever. This problem eventually was solved by implementing a sanitation program to control disease-carrying mosquitoes. When the first ship finally steamed through the canal in August 1914, the canal was hailed as one of the world's great engineering feats.

Possession of the Panama Canal gave the United States even more of a stake in Latin America. Thus, the United States continued to exert its power in the region throughout the early 1900s. In 1904 President Theodore Roosevelt extended the Monroe Doctrine in what became known as the Roosevelt Corollary. Under this addition, the United States would actively intervene to force Latin American countries to honor their foreign debts. During the next two decades, United States forces intervened in such countries as the Dominican Republic, Haiti, and Nicaragua. The United States hoped its interventions would provide stability and prepare the way for democracy. Most Latin Americans, however, viewed American actions as moves to turn their countries into "colonies" of the United States and to protect foreign businesses that were exploiting their resources.

Mexico

During the 1800s and early 1900s, the United States became deeply involved in the affairs of its southern neighbor, **Mexico**. During the 1830s, opposition to the dictatorial rule of General Antonio López de Santa Anna grew in the Mexican state of Texas, where many Americans had settled. In 1835 the Americans and some Mexicans in Texas revolted and the next year set up an independent republic. Ignoring Mexican opposition, Texas in 1845 joined the American republic as a state, and conflict soon developed between Mexico and the United States. Despite the bravery of its soldiers, Mexico lost the Mexican War. In the Treaty of Guadalupe Hidalgo (1848), nearly half of Mexico's territory went to the United States.

Reform and Conflict

After the Mexican War, Mexico entered an era of change known as La Reforma. In 1855 Mexican voters chose **Benito Juárez**, a lawyer of Native American background, as president. Juárez reduced the power of the military, separated church and state, and improved the lot of impoverished farmers. In 1863, when Mexico could not pay its foreign debts, French troops occupied Mexico City. Juárez fled the capital to organize a guerrilla movement in the countryside. In 1864 Mexican conservatives, supported by the French, named Austrian Archduke

Maximilian emperor of Mexico. In 1867 the French, under American pressure, withdrew their troops from Mexico, and Juárez returned to power after his forces had ousted and executed Maximilian.

Four years after Juárez's death in 1872, General **Porfirio Díaz** seized power. To ensure "Order and Progress," Díaz strengthened the army and limited individual freedoms. Under Díaz's harsh rule, however, Mexico made economic advances, building railroads, developing industries, expanding farmlands, and opening new mines. Unfortunately, for the Mexican people, most profits went to foreign investors and wealthy landowners. While the rich prospered, most Mexicans remained poor farmers, working on large estates for low wages.

The Mexican Revolution

Discontent with Díaz eventually led to revolution. From 1910 to 1920, Mexico was engulfed by the first major social upheaval in modern Latin America. During this time, armies of farmers, workers, ranchers, and even *soldaderas*, or women soldiers, fought the authorities and each other across Mexico. The unrest also sparked a wave of Mexican immigration to the United States.

The revolution began when Francisco Madero, a liberal reformer, and his supporters overthrew Díaz in 1911. Once in power, Madero was murdered by one of his generals, Victoriano Huerta. A year later, Huerta himself was toppled from power by Mexican revolts and American intervention.

No strong leader emerged to take Huerta's place. Instead, three revolutionary leaders—**Emiliano Zapata**, **Francisco "Pancho" Villa**, and **Venustiano Carranza**—competed for power. Using the battle cry, *"Tierra y Liberdad!"* (Land and Liberty!), Zapata and his followers fought for the rights of impoverished farmers. Like Zapata, Villa proposed radical reforms. The more conservative

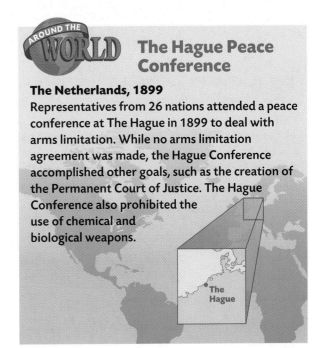

The Hague Peace Conference

The Netherlands, 1899

Representatives from 26 nations attended a peace conference at The Hague in 1899 to deal with arms limitation. While no arms limitation agreement was made, the Hague Conference accomplished other goals, such as the creation of the Permanent Court of Justice. The Hague Conference also prohibited the use of chemical and biological weapons.

The Hague

Carranza, however, was able to become president in 1915 with American support. In retaliation, Villa crossed the border into New Mexico and killed 18 Americans. United States President **Woodrow Wilson** then sent American troops into Mexico to capture Villa. American entry into World War I in 1917 led to the withdrawal of these troops.

That same year, Carranza reluctantly introduced a liberal constitution but was slow in carrying out reforms. Force was often used against Carranza's opponents. For example, in 1919 a pro-Carranza military officer murdered Zapata, who had protested Carranza's disregard of land reform. A year later, Carranza himself was killed during a revolt that brought General Álvaro Obregón to power. As the revolutionary violence began to subside in the early 1920s, relations between Mexico and the United States were less tense. The memory of American intervention, however, lingered in the minds of Mexicans for years to come.

SECTION 4 REVIEW

Recall
1. **Define** arbitration.
2. **Identify** James Monroe, Monroe Doctrine, José Martí, William McKinley, Theodore Roosevelt, Benito Juárez, Porfirio Díaz, Emiliano Zapata, Francisco "Pancho" Villa,

Venustiano Carranza, Woodrow Wilson.
3. **Explain** the impact of the Monroe Doctrine and the Roosevelt Corollary.

Critical Thinking
4. **Analyzing Information** Why do you think the United States

government was so concerned about maintaining its influence in Latin America during the late 1800s and early 1900s?

Understanding Themes
5. **Nationalism** What factors led to the Mexican Revolution that began in 1910?

Connections Across Time

Historical Significance The Age of Imperialism brought much of the globe under Western control. An unparalleled exchange of ideas and products resulted. European ways, however, often challenged many cultures.

By the mid-1900s, after two world wars and many smaller conflicts, Europe saw its world leadership pass to the United States. Meanwhile, nationalist movements in Africa, Asia, and Latin America challenged the West's control of global events.

Using Key Terms

Write the key term that completes each sentence. Then write a sentence for each term not chosen.

a. sepoys
b. protectorate
c. partition
d. arbitration
e. westernization
f. imperialism
g. spheres of influence
h. viceroy
i. culture system
j. colony

1. Before revolting in 1857, _____ had resented British attempts to impose Christianity and European customs on them.
2. _____ means one country's control of the political, economic, and social life of another country.
3. The acquisition of colonies by Europeans led to _____, or the spread of European civilization to other parts of the world.
4. In the East Indies, the Dutch used a method of forced labor called the _____ to gather raw materials and harvest crops.
5. In 1885, 14 nations met in Berlin, Germany, and agreed to _____ the continent of Africa among themselves.

Using Your History Journal

Choose one nation in Africa and research its history from the colonial era to the present. Write a short paper about your chosen country's independence and its prospects for the future.

Technology Activity

Using the Internet Search the Internet for a Web site that provides a map of the world around 1900 that includes political boundaries and a distance scale. Color code all countries that the British Empire controlled. Describe the relative location of the countries that were part of the British Empire in terms of the approximate distance from each country to Great Britain. Use the distance scale on the map. Then organize your findings in a chart. In addition, find out which countries remain under British control today.

Reviewing Facts

1. **History** Explain how imperial nations acquired and ruled overseas lands. In what ways did the British and the French differ in ruling their empires?
2. **Geography** Identify the locations and state the significance of the Suez and Panama Canals.
3. **Culture** Describe the role of religion in the spread of Western values during the 1800s.
4. **History** Identify how Asians, Africans, and Latin Americans reacted to Western imperialism after the mid-1800s.

Critical Thinking

1. **Apply** How did science, industry, and technology aid the growth of imperialism?
2. **Evaluate** Why was Japan able to establish itself as an imperial and military power?
3. **Synthesize** How did imperialism affect peoples in Africa, Asia, and Latin America? What impact did imperialism have on the peoples of Europe and North America?
4. **Analyze** Contrast the ways in which the Age of Imperialism contributed to the growth of unity in the world with the ways in which it contributed to disunity.

Geography in History

1. **Place** Refer to the map below. What two large bodies of water does the Panama Canal connect?
2. **Human/Environment Interaction** Why do you think engineers chose this particular location in which to build the canal?
3. **Location** Why is the Pacific Ocean located on the southeast side of this map?
4. **Region** What geographic features of this region made building the canal difficult?

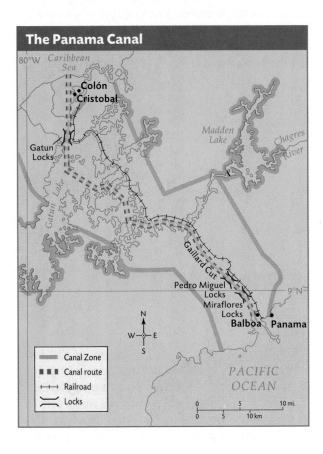

The Panama Canal

Understanding Themes

1. **Movement** What factors stimulated outward expansion by the European powers in the Age of Imperialism?
2. **Change** How did Africans react to the changes brought by the spread of imperialism in Africa?
3. **Reaction** In what two ways did Indian nationalists respond to British rule in India?

4. **Nationalism** Trace the events of the Mexican Revolution. Why was the Revolution an important development in modern Latin America?

Linking Past and Present

1. Historical context refers to the setting in which an event occurs. Throughout the 1900s the United States continued to intervene in Latin America. Investigate three recent interventions, and explain how the historical context surrounding American interventions has changed from 1900 to the present.
2. Have attitudes about imperialism changed from the 1800s to the present time? Explain. What factors do you think account for any changes?
3. Does imperialism exist in some form today? What factors do you think account for any changes? If imperialism exists today, does it differ from the imperialism of the 1800s?
4. Examine the role of the South African Native Congress (SANNC) in South Africa after its founding in 1912. As the African National Congress (ANC) after 1923, how did the organization's involvement change under independent white-dominated South African governments from the 1920s to the early 1990s? How does the ANC influence developments in South Africa today?

Skill Practice

Using the steps described on page 720, search the Internet for information about one of the following topics from the Age of Imperialism. Write an article for the school newspaper or magazine based on the information you retrieved about your topic.

- writings of Rudyard Kipling
- establishment of Liberia
- African Imperialism 1914
- Cecil Rhodes
- Russo-Japanese War
- Spanish-American War

ABCNEWS iNTERACTIVE™ Turning Points in World History

The Industrial Revolution

Setting up the Video

Work with a group of your classmates to view "The Industrial Revolution" on the videodisc *Turning Points in World History*. The Industrial Revolution started in the late 1700s and changed the way people lived. The introduction of modern machines and the building of factories brought both technical advancement and its own set of problems. This program examines the social issues of the Industrial Revolution and where we are today within our own technological revolution.

Side Two, Chapter 3

View the video by scanning the bar code or by entering the chapter number on your keypad and pressing Search. (*Also available in VHS format.*)

Hands-On Activity

Using multimedia tools, create a presentation about present technology innovations and how these advancements are changing people's lives. Be sure to include some innovations that affect how most people live their daily lives.

Surfing the "Net"

Imperialism

During the Age of Imperialism, world powers lay claim to different parts of the world. Spheres of influence included the region of Latin America. Access the Internet to find out about the effects of imperialism on Latin American countries.

Getting There

Follow these steps to gather more information about the history of various Latin American countries.
1. Find a search engine. Type in the name of a *Latin American country*.
2. After typing in the name of a Latin American country, enter words such as these to focus your search:

- *history*
- *colonialism*
- *imperialism*
- *independence*

3. The search engine should provide you with a number of links to follow. Links are "pointers" to different sites on the Internet and commonly appear as blue underlined words.

What to Do When You Are There

Click on the links to navigate through the pages of information and gather your findings. Create a news report researching the specific country's history of colonialism, and how the country attained its independence. Videotape all news reports and show to other classes.

Unit 6 Digest

From the late 1700s to the early 1900s, the primarily rural, agricultural economies of Europe and North America developed into industrial economies based on cities, factories, and manufactured goods. This sweeping transformation became known as the Industrial Revolution, and its effects would eventually impact the rest of the world.

During the 1800s, the rise of industry in the Western world—Europe and North America—inspired people living in these areas to push for social and political reforms. At the same time, Western nations, seeking new markets and resources, expanded overseas trade and strengthened their control of foreign areas. The peoples of Asia, Africa, and Latin America faced enormous challenges as their cultures were threatened by forceful Western takeovers.

History & Art *The Gas Factory at Courcelles* by Ernest Jean Delahae. Musée du Petit Palais, Paris, France *How did increasing industrialization affect the social order?*

Chapter 23
Age of Industry

The Industrial Revolution began in Great Britain during the late 1700s. Wealthy British landowners at this time took over more agricultural land and used new farming methods to increase crop yields. With more food available, people were able to live healthier, longer lives. As these changes spread throughout Great Britain and the rest of Europe, the population increased dramatically.

Meanwhile, farmers displaced by rural changes moved to the cities to find work. This growing urban population, combined with skilled inventors who provided new technology and business people who had money and organizational skills, helped to ignite the Industrial Revolution. The availability of natural resources—coal, iron, and water power—led to the use of power-driven machinery in factories. This new kind of manufacturing replaced the handwork done in the home.

From Great Britain, industrialization spread to the rest of Europe and to North America, creating a new social order in the Western world. A growing middle class of prosperous factory owners and managers began to exert political power, while an even larger working class pressed for reforms to end poor working conditions and improve their lives.

Chapter 24
Cultural Revolution

Western Europeans and North Americans sought solutions to the social divisions arising in the new industrial society. Some thinkers, such as the British philosopher Adam Smith, held that capitalism, or private ownership of industry, benefited society as a whole and should operate without government controls. Others, including British philosophers Jeremy Bentham and John Stuart Mill, accepted capitalism, but held that it needed some government regulation to ensure a just society for all classes. Still others, such as the German thinker Karl Marx, believed that capitalism promoted sharp inequalities and that it would be replaced by socialism, a system in which the workers by themselves or through government would control industry for the public good.

The Age of Industry also saw many exciting advances in science, from new ideas about human origins to new methods for fighting diseases. In addition, improved means of transportation enabled people to leave their native lands to seek new opportunities in other parts of the world. Increased interest in education led to the spread of literacy as public schools and libraries were established throughout Europe and North America. Instead of following one approach, artists and writers responded to the industrial age in a variety of ways.

Chapter 25
Democracy and Reform

Economic and social changes inspired new political movements in Europe and the Americas during the 1800s. In some countries, political change was gradual and relatively peaceful; in other countries, it was sudden and often violent.

Great Britain was the world's strongest economic and political power during most of the 1800s. The British government moved slowly toward democracy as political parties came to control Parliament and more people gained voting rights. Social reforms somewhat improved the lives of workers, women, and other groups traditionally outside of the political system. Overseas colonies such as Canada, Australia, and New Zealand won increasing self-rule within the British Empire.

France's political development was more violent and uncertain than that of Britain, with the French government changing in form several times—from empire to monarchy to republic to empire to republic—during the course of the 1800s. France developed industrially during this period, but agriculture still remained an important part of its economy. The most enduring achievements of France's Third Republic, created in 1875, were its safeguards of civil liberties and educational reforms.

The United States was the world's most advanced democracy during the 1800s. Although Native Americans, African Americans, women, and other groups often faced rejection, discrimination, or second-class status, an increasing number of Americans were able to participate in the political process and fulfill their dreams of a better life. The country also steadily expanded westward toward the Pacific Ocean. A growing debate over slavery, however, led to territorial division and a bloody civil war in the early 1860s during the administration of President Abraham Lincoln. After the Civil War, the United States, once more united, became increasingly industrialized, attracted large numbers of immigrants, and emerged as a world power.

In Latin America, the Enlightenment and the American and French Revolutions influenced the growth of independence movements. During the late 1700s and early 1800s, Latin Americans, under the leadership of Touissant L'Ouverture, Simón Bolívar, José de San Martín, and others, won their freedom from Spanish, Portuguese, or French rule. The newly independent Latin American countries, however, lacked experience in self-rule, and military dictators frequently came to power during the 1800s. National unity was often hindered by a huge social gap that divided wealthy landowners from impoverished farmers.

Chapter 26
Reaction and Nationalism

Nationalism, or the desire of people sharing the same culture to have their own nation, became one of the most powerful forces in Europe during the 1800s. In some cases, people struggled to unify small, individual states into one nation. In others people fought to break free from large empires.

In Italy, Austrian rule, territorial divisions, and the pope's opposition had long hindered the growth of a united nation. During the 1800s, leaders such as Giuseppe Garibaldi and Count Camilo di Cavour rallied Italian and international support to expel Austria, end the pope's political power, and join individual territories into a united Italy. In 1861 Italy became a constitutional monarchy, but national unity was hindered by differences between its industrial north and its agricultural south.

A similar quest for unity took place in Germany, which was divided into numerous independent territories. There, Otto von Bismarck, the prime minister of the largest territory, Prussia, used diplomacy and the Prussian army to create a German Empire by 1871. While in office, Bismarck discouraged the growth of democracy, although he enacted social reforms for German workers. Conflict between Bismarck and the kaiser, or emperor, William II, led to Bismarck's resignation in 1890. By this time, Germany had become a prosperous industrial nation with claims to world power.

To the east, the Russian Empire generally resisted nationalism and democracy. Czar Alexander II, however, recognized that some changes were necessary if the empire was to survive. In the 1860s he freed the serfs and reformed aspects of the empire's government. Radicals wanting a revolution assassinated Alexander II in 1881, and political repression returned under his successors, Alexander III and Nicholas II. Meanwhile, the advance of industry in the empire created a small, urban working class that became a major political force after 1900. Strikes and protests after the Russian Empire's setbacks in a war with Japan forced limited political reforms from the czar.

The Austrian Empire also tried to resist political change, but faced growing demands for independence and reform from its diverse nationalities. In 1867, after Austria's defeat in a war with Prussia, Austrian Emperor Francis Joseph agreed to give Hungary equal standing with Austria in the empire. Meanwhile, the Slavic peoples of the empire continued to push for greater political rights.

Chapter 27
The Age of Imperialism

Between 1800 and 1914, various Western nations carried out policies of imperialism, in which they sought to control the political, economic, and social life of countries in Asia, Africa, and Latin America. Three key factors led to the rise of imperialism: competition among Western countries for more territory, their demand for raw materials and new markets, and feelings of cultural and racial superiority that influenced Western peoples to impose their cultures on distant lands.

Beginning in the 1870s, European nations expanded their control over Africa, dividing the continent among themselves and exploiting its rich variety of natural resources. In spite of African resistance, only two African nations—Ethiopia and Liberia—had managed to escape European control by 1914.

Visualizing History The Boxers in China launched a series of attacks against foreigners in 1900. *What were "spheres of influence"?*

In India, an uprising in 1857 brought direct British control over Indian affairs. To prevent further unrest, the British took steps to develop India economically, but many Indians failed to benefit from the growth of railroads and industries. In 1885 nationalists formed the Indian National Congress, beginning a long struggle for independence.

Also, during the 1800s, European powers intervened in China. Using military power or the threat of it, they claimed large areas of China as spheres of influence—areas where they had exclusive trading rights. When the Chinese fought back in the Boxer Uprising of 1900, the Europeans quickly crushed the revolt. In 1912 Chinese revolutionaries overthrew the weakened Qing dynasty and set up a republic.

The United States in 1853 forced the Japanese to open their doors to trade, sending shock waves through Japanese society. The Meiji leaders who came to power in Japan during the 1860s decided to make Japan a great power capable of competing with the West. They reformed Japan's government and began to industrialize the nation. By 1914 Japan had emerged as a modern industrial nation.

During the era of imperialism, the United States used the Monroe Doctrine to oppose European involvement in Latin America. At the same time, the United States government and American businesses were becoming increasingly involved in Latin American affairs. In the early 1900s, American military forces often intervened in Latin American countries when either government policies or social unrest threatened American interests. This involvement heightened tensions between the United States and Latin America. Anti-American feelings were often a factor in the upsurge of nationalism that swept through the region during this period. The Mexican Revolution, which lasted from 1910 to about 1920, was the first major social upheaval in modern Latin America.

SURVEYING UNIT 6

1. **Chapter 23** What factors led to the Industrial Revolution in Great Britain?
2. **Chapter 24** How did Adam Smith and Karl Marx differ in their view about economics and society?
3. **Chapter 25** How did Great Britain differ from France in the advance toward democracy?
4. **Chapter 26** What effect did nationalism have on Italy? On the Austrian Empire?
5. **Chapter 27** Why did imperialism become a significant force in world affairs during the 1800s?

Unit 7

1914–1945

World in Conflict

Then & Now Nationalism and imperialism had dire consequences for Europe and the world. When national pride and the scramble for overseas territories dictated foreign relations among industrial states, conflict was inevitable. Two world wars resulted. Never before in the history of civilization had the world endured devastation on such a massive scale.

When you climb aboard a jetliner, you may reflect on the technology of air travel developed in this period. After World War II, many people hoped that the refined instruments of war could be turned to peaceful purposes. The power of the atom could be used to produce energy rather than bombs. Airplanes, developed in World War I and refined in World War II, could become a major means of transportation.

A Global Chronology

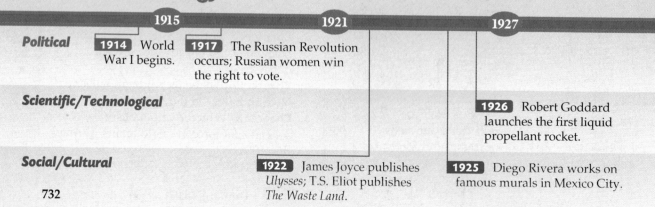

	1915	1921	1927
Political	**1914** World War I begins.	**1917** The Russian Revolution occurs; Russian women win the right to vote.	
Scientific/Technological			**1926** Robert Goddard launches the first liquid propellant rocket.
Social/Cultural		**1922** James Joyce publishes *Ulysses*; T.S. Eliot publishes *The Waste Land*.	**1925** Diego Rivera works on famous murals in Mexico City.

A 1938 Zenith console radio

Portfolio Project

In the 1930s and 1940s radio reported dramatic news to anxious listeners. At first radio news was simply newspaper-style writing that was read on the air. Soon radio news developed a style of its own. Listen to a few radio news stories. How do they lead in? How much detail is given? How long is the typical report? From the dramatic developments of 1930–1945, compose several radio news reports and read them as an announcer on audiotape.

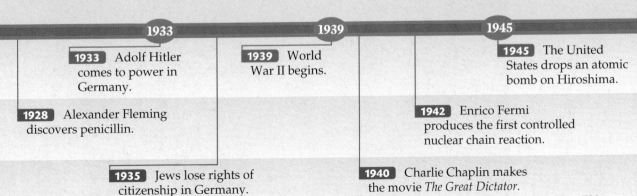

1933

1933 Adolf Hitler comes to power in Germany.

1928 Alexander Fleming discovers penicillin.

1935 Jews lose rights of citizenship in Germany.

1939

1939 World War II begins.

1940 Charlie Chaplin makes the movie *The Great Dictator*.

1945

1945 The United States drops an atomic bomb on Hiroshima.

1942 Enrico Fermi produces the first controlled nuclear chain reaction.

The Spread of Ideas

International Peacekeeping

*T*he 1900s taught people the meaning of world war. No previous century in history had ever seen conflicts that literally spanned the globe. In addition to numerous regional conflicts, the 20th century witnessed two world wars. As the scope of war grew, so did the commitment to collective security—the principle in which a group of nations join together to promote peace.

Europe
The League of Nations

As early as 1828, an American named William Ladd sought to establish a Congress of Nations to settle international disputes and avoid war. Nearly a century later, at the end of World War I, the victorious nations set up a "general association of nations" called the League of Nations.

By 1920 42 nations had sent delegates to the League's headquarters in Geneva, Switzerland. Another 21 nations eventually joined, but conspicuously absent was the United States. Opponents in the United States Senate had argued that membership in the League went against George Washington's advice against "entangling alliances."

When the League failed to halt warlike acts in the 1930s, these same opponents pointed to the failure of collective security. The League was a peacekeeper without a sword—it possessed neither a standing army nor members willing to stop nations that used war as a method of diplomacy.

UN distribution center in the Gaza Strip

Rwandan child at a refugee camp

South Africa
The Power of World Opinion

Like the League of Nations, the UN could be only as strong as its members were prepared to make it. The development of atomic weapons, however, was a powerful incentive for members to cooperate. By 1995, the UN had taken part in 35 peacekeeping missions—some successful, some failures. It also had provided protection for more than 30 million refugees.

The UN's ability to use world opinion to promote justice was perhaps best tested in South Africa. In 1977 the UN urged nations to use an arms embargo and economic sanctions against South Africa until apartheid was lifted. In 1994 South Africa held its first all-race elections. Many believed this was a major triumph for collective international action.

The United States
The United Nations

Non-membership in the League did not protect the United States from the horrors of war. The Japanese air attack on Pearl Harbor, Hawaii, ended the notion that the United States could isolate itself from the rest of the world.

As World War II drew to a close, the United States hosted a meeting in San Francisco to create a new global peacekeeping organization. Here delegates from 50 nations hammered out the Charter of the United Nations. The document's Preamble sets forth a formula for international peace:

> *We the peoples of the United Nations, determined to save succeeding generations from the scourge of war, which twice in our lifetime has brought untold sorrow to mankind and to reaffirm faith in fundamental human rights … and to promote social progress and to better standards of life and to promote our strength to maintain international peace and security, and to ensure … that armed force shall not be used, save in the common interest … have resolved to combine our efforts to accomplish these aims.*

UN troops in Beirut, Lebanon

In the years following, the United Nations (UN) attempted to eliminate the root causes of war. In 1946 it founded the UN Educational, Scientific, and Cultural Organization (UNESCO) and the UN Children's Fund (UNICEF). These agencies promoted global education and the well-being of children. Two years later, in 1948, United States delegate Eleanor Roosevelt convinced the UN to adopt The Universal Declaration of Human Rights. This committed the UN to the elimination of oppression wherever it existed.

LINKING THE IDEAS

1. What factors made it difficult for the League of Nations to promote world peace?
2. What methods has the United Nations used to encourage peace?

Critical Thinking

3. **Forming Opinions** The United Nations Declaration of Human Rights sees injustice in one part of the world as a threat to peace in all parts of the world. Do you agree? Why or why not?

Chapter

28

1914–1920
World War I

Chapter Themes

▶ **Cooperation** European powers form a series of alliances before World War I. *Section 1*

▶ **Conflict** Tensions between the two European alliances erupt into a European-wide conflict. *Section 2*

▶ **Conflict** The European war is transformed into a war that engulfs much of the world; the global conflict directly affects many civilians as well as soldiers. *Section 3*

▶ **Revolution** Revolution in Russia overthrows the czar and brings Lenin and the Bolsheviks to power. *Section 4*

▶ **Internationalism** The Treaty of Versailles provides for the creation of a League of Nations to mediate international disputes. *Section 5*

⎰Storyteller

To survive days of bombardment on the Western Front during World War I, men crouched down in deep ditches. During these times there was nothing to do but wait and watch. Finally, they would receive orders to attack:

"Suddenly the nearer explosions cease. The shelling continues but it has lifted and falls behind us, our trench is free. We seize the hand-grenades, pitch them out in front of the dug-out and jump after them. The bombardment has stopped and a heavy barrage now falls behind us. The attack has come."

In this passage from All Quiet on the Western Front, *Erich Maria Remarque captures the chaos and horror of what is now called World War I. When this war broke out in the summer of 1914, most Europeans thought it would be over by Christmas. Instead, it lasted four long years and changed Europe and the world forever.*

Historical Significance

In what ways was World War I different from previous wars? How did it affect the countries and peoples involved? What impact did it have on the future course of the 1900s?

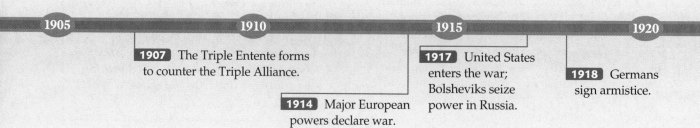

1905   1910   1915   1920

1907 The Triple Entente forms to counter the Triple Alliance.

1914 Major European powers declare war.

1917 United States enters the war; Bolsheviks seize power in Russia.

1918 Germans sign armistice.

 American Troops Arriving in Paris July 14, 1918 by J. F. Foucher.
West Point Museum, West Point, New York

Your History Journal

Write a letter home as a first-person account of one of the following events: Poison gas at Ypres, the Sinking of the Lusitania, the Battle of Verdun.

1882 Italy joins Germany and Austria-Hungary to form the Triple Alliance.

1894 France and Russia become allies to counter the Triple Alliance.

c. 1900 Germany has the most powerful weapons and the best army in Europe.

1905 France and Germany come close to war over Morocco.

Section 1

The Seeds of War

Setting the Scene

▶ **Terms to Define**

militarism, conscription, alliance system, *entente*

▶ **People to Meet**

Otto von Bismarck

▶ **Places to Locate**

Morocco, Alsace-Lorraine, Bosnia-Herzegovina

 **Find Out** What were the underlying causes of World War I?

The Storyteller

Herbert Marlow, foreign editor for a large United States newspaper, was amazed. His correspondents in Paris, Vienna, and Berlin had all wired similar reports concerning European nationalism and attitudes favoring war. Roland Doregelès wrote, "No more poor or rich ... there were only Frenchmen." Stefan Zweig in Vienna

German military parade

observed, "As never before, thousands and hundreds of thousands felt what they should have felt in peacetime, that they belonged together." Marlow reread Philipp Scheidermann's dispatch from Berlin, resolving to use it as his headline. Scheidermann had noted Germans proclaiming "It is the hour we yearned for."

—adapted from articles reprinted in *Sources of the Western Tradition*, edited by Marvin Perry, 1991

In the summer of 1914, an assassination took place in the Austro-Hungarian province of Bosnia in the Balkans. Although some people mourned, there was no broad sense of outrage or alarm. There had been other assassinations in the recent past with no major consequences.

Within weeks, it became apparent that this assassination was different. By August, the major European powers were at war with each other. The war was to last from 1914 to 1918; it led to the development of new weapons that changed warfare forever. By the time it was over, the war had involved most nations of the world and was the largest that the world had ever seen.

It was known as the Great War, the "war to end all wars." The name by which it was called was not important. The changes it brought about were. The way of life that had existed before the war was destroyed. Empires were swept away, and governments toppled. European dominance of the world was shaken. The war marked the close of a long era of international peace.

European Rivalries

Since the mid-1800s, rivalries had been building up and intensifying among some of the countries of Europe. As Western nations industrialized, each sought the most favorable conditions for economic growth. This led to intense competition. As industrialization spread, the competition grew keener. One by one, Great Britain, France, Germany, Austria-Hungary, Russia, and Italy sought to acquire new markets and to establish and expand global empires.

Great Britain wanted to maintain the lifelines of its empire and keep open the sea-lanes it needed for trade. It also wanted to make sure no other nation became strong enough to attack it. France was intent on adding mineral-rich **Morocco** to its gains.

Race to the South Pole

Antarctica, 1911

Two European explorers–Roald Amundsen of Norway and Robert Scott of Great Britain–became engaged in a dramatic race to reach the South Pole. Amundsen and his companions began crossing the Ross Ice Shelf on October 19, 1911. They traveled on skis and used dogsleds to carry their supplies. They arrived at the South Pole on December 14. Scott and his party reached the Pole in January to find a Norwegian flag and a message from Amundsen. Then tragically, Scott and all his companions died on the return trip.

South Pole

ANTARCTICA

Germany hoped to gain economic control of the declining Ottoman Empire. Austria-Hungary set out to gain territorial access through the Balkans to the Aegean Sea. Russia aspired to take control of the Bosporus and the Dardanelles near the Black Sea and to extend the influence it already had over Manchuria in East Asia.

Competition turned to hostility as one power crossed another in its efforts to accomplish its goals. In 1898, for example, Great Britain and France confronted one another over rival claims in Egypt and the Sudan. The following year, Germany started to build the Berlin-Baghdad railway, which created resentment among both the British and the Russians. The British feared that the railroad would interfere with their interests in India and reduce traffic through the Suez Canal. The Russians thought the railroad interfered in their traditional areas of interest. In 1905, 1908, and 1911, Germany and France came close to war over control of Morocco.

Nationalism

Contributing to the tension was a growing spirit of nationalism. Nationalism had unified Germany and was rapidly becoming popular in France. There, French nationalists sought revenge against Germany for depriving France of the border provinces of **Alsace-Lorraine** in the 1870–1871 Franco-Prussian War.

The French novelist Victor Hugo urged France to "have but one thought: to reconstitute her forces, gather her energy, nourish her sacred anger.... Then one day she will be irresistible. Then she will take back Alsace-Lorraine." This put the Germans on their guard. They were well aware that the issue of Alsace-Lorraine was not settled permanently.

Slavic Nationalism

In Austria-Hungary, nationalism was creating the most violent tensions in Europe. The empire's Slavs were attracted to Pan-Slavism, the idea that the Slavs had a historic mission to develop their culture and unite into an empire. Slavic nationalists in neighboring Serbia supported the Slavs of Austria-Hungary. They wanted their own country to be the center of a South Slav, or Yugoslav, nation. This new Slavic state would be formed out of Slavic territories in Austria-Hungary.

Austria-Hungary was alarmed by Serbian activities in the Balkans. It feared that the idea of a Yugoslav state would attract restless Slavic groups in Austria-Hungary. Such a development would harm the security of the empire and lead to its eventual breakup.

In 1908 Austria-Hungary annexed the Slavic territories of **Bosnia-Herzegovina**, once the provinces of the Ottoman Empire. Angered at the Austro-Hungarian move, Serbia called on Russia, its traditional protector, for help. Russia, however, was still weak from the Russo-Japanese War and was not ready to fight again. In addition, Russia had made a secret deal with the Austro-Hungarians. The Russians had agreed to let Austria-Hungary have Bosnia-Herzegovina in exchange for the right for Russian warships to go through the Dardanelles. So, Russia persuaded the Serbs to restrain themselves. Then, Russia discovered that Austria-Hungary had made its move before Russia could get its part of the deal. As a result, the Russians were bitter.

Balkan Wars

The first Balkan war in 1912 further inflamed the Serbs. One of Serbia's war aims had been to acquire Albania, a small territory along the coast of the Adriatic Sea, an arm of the Mediterranean Sea. This would give Serbia the water outlet it desired. When, after winning the war, Serbia did not get Albania, Serb resentment grew even stronger.

In 1913 a second Balkan war broke out. Albania was made independent, frustrating once again Serbian ambitions. In this war, as in the last one, the Russians had not been able to support Serbia. This upset the Serbs and humiliated the Russians. Austria-Hungary, meanwhile, became increasingly worried about its future role in European affairs.

Militarism

As tensions began to rise, so did militarism, the glorification of war and the military. The European powers assessed each other's military strength. They compared military training programs and levels of spending. They also looked at levels of industrialization and tried to estimate how fast a nation could ready its troops for battle.

Diplomats maneuvered to win new allies. Military leaders argued for increased military spending and more arms. After 1870, all the powers except Great Britain adopted conscription, the compulsory call-up of civilians for military service, and universal military training. They were sure that their national security depended almost entirely on the technology, skill, and readiness of their military forces.

Each nation's actions caused a reaction in the other nations. For example, when Germany decided in 1898 to expand its navy, Great Britain felt threatened. The Germans argued that they needed a larger navy to protect colonial and merchant shipping and "for the general purpose of greatness." Great Britain claimed that as an island nation that depended on trade for many vital supplies, it had to be able to control the seas. To do this, said the British, they had to maintain a navy as large as the combined fleet of their two nearest rivals.

Alliances

Along with militarism came a hardening of the alliance systems, or the defense agreements among nations. In 1873 **Otto von Bismarck** created the Three Emperors' League, which united Germany, Austria-Hungary, and Russia. His purpose was to isolate France by attaching all of its possible friends to Germany. The Emperors' League, however, did not last very long because of Austrian-Russian rivalry in the Balkans. Bismarck then created a new and stronger alliance with Austria-Hungary.

In 1882 Italy joined the Austrian-German alliance, and it became known as the Triple Alliance. Italy joined because it wanted allies against France. The Italians were angry with the French for occupying Tunis, or present-day Tunisia, in North Africa. They also were afraid that the French might send an army to defend the pope, with whom they were having a dispute. The three powers of the Triple Alliance agreed that if any one member became involved in a war with two or more enemies, the others would provide support.

In 1890 another alliance began to evolve as Russia and France developed friendlier relations. In 1894 Russia and France signed a military alliance in which they agreed to come to each other's aid in case of an attack by either Germany or Austria-Hungary, or by both powers. This was followed in 1904 by the Entente Cordiale between France and Great Britain. The term *entente* refers to a friendly understanding between two nations that, at the same time, lacks the binding commitments of a full-fledged alliance. Three years later, Great Britain and Russia settled their conflicting ambitions in the Middle East and central Asia.

All of these agreements developed into the Triple Entente, a loose alliance between France, Russia, and Great Britain. Russia, an autocratic monarchy, and France, a democratic republic, were willing to ally out of a common fear of Germany and Austria-Hungary. Great Britain, a democratic monarchy, was willing to join because it was alarmed by Germany's naval-building program. It felt hard pressed to protect its empire on its own.

Thus, by 1907, the great powers of Europe had aligned themselves in two opposing combinations. On one side stood the Triple Alliance. On the other stood the Triple Entente. Instead of making their members more secure, however, these alliances threatened the peace of the continent. Given the conditions of the Triple Alliance and the Triple Entente, a minor conflict between rival nations had the potential to involve all major European powers in war.

Recall
1. **Define** militarism, conscription, alliance system, *entente*.
2. **Identify** Otto von Bismarck, Triple Alliance, Triple Entente.
3. **Locate** Germany on the map on page 742. Why was Germany at a disadvantage in fighting an all-European war?

Critical Thinking
4. **Evaluating Information** What were the factors that led to alliances before the outbreak of World War I?

Understanding Themes
5. **Cooperation** Given the conditions that existed in Europe before 1914, could the nations of that continent have avoided a major war? If so, how?

JUNE 28, 1914 Slav nationalist assassinates Austria's Archduke Francis Ferdinand.

JULY 28, 1914 Austria-Hungary declares war on Serbia.

AUGUST 1, 1914 Germany declares war on Russia.

AUGUST 4, 1914 Great Britain declares war on Germany.

Section 2

The Spark

Setting the Scene

▶ **Terms to Define**
   ultimatum, mobilization

▶ **People to Meet**
   Francis Ferdinand, Gavrilo Princip, William II, Nicholas II

▶ **Places to Locate**
   Sarajevo, Serbia

Find Out ▶ What series of events provided the spark that ignited World War I?

The Storyteller

Nearly one month after Archduke Francis Ferdinand was assassinated at the Bosnian capital of Sarajevo, some European leaders suspected that the crisis would pass. Newspaper headlines carried other stories. Cabinet minister Lloyd George of Britain told the House of Commons: "I cannot help thinking that civilization which is able to deal with disputes among individuals and small communities … should be able to extend its operations to the larger sphere of disputes among states." Before he finished his address, Austria had delivered an ultimatum to Serbia. World War I was about to begin.

Assassination at Sarajevo

—adapted from *The Modern World*, edited by Esmond Wright, 1979

Until 1914, a false optimism prevailed in Europe. Although military buildups continued, most Europeans did not really think there would be a major war. Almost a century of relative peace had followed the Congress of Vienna. The absence of a major war for so long a period had lulled many Europeans into believing that such a war would not ever happen again.

Major social reforms and important scientific advances during the 1800s reinforced the belief that the world was improving steadily and that people had outgrown the need for war to solve their problems. Most countries were enjoying economic prosperity. A war would destroy what had been built up over the years. Despite this optimism, war did come, triggered by the assassination in the Balkans. That event set in motion the diplomatic moves that ended in war.

Trouble in the Balkans

On June 28, 1914, Archduke **Francis Ferdinand**, nephew and heir to Austro-Hungarian Emperor Francis Joseph, paid a visit to **Sarajevo** (SAR•uh•YAY•voh), the capital of Bosnia-Herzegovina. Francis Ferdinand planned, upon becoming emperor, to give the Slavs of Bosnia-Herzegovina and other parts of the empire a voice in the government equal to that of the Austrians and Hungarians. This political action might have defused the movement for a separate Slavic state.

Before the archduke and his wife, Sophie, began their ride through the streets of Sarajevo in an open car, seven young assassins had already taken their places along the route. All were members of a secret nationalist group based in **Serbia** known as the Black Hand, or Union of Death. Although the archduke and Sophie survived the first assassin's attempt, their luck did not hold.

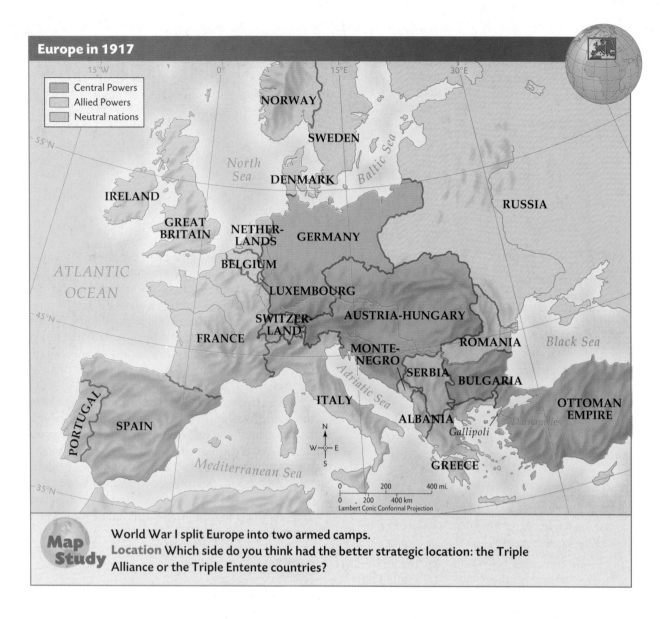

Europe in 1917

Legend:
- Central Powers
- Allied Powers
- Neutral nations

NORWAY
SWEDEN
DENMARK
North Sea
Baltic Sea
IRELAND
GREAT BRITAIN
NETHER-LANDS
GERMANY
RUSSIA
BELGIUM
ATLANTIC OCEAN
LUXEMBOURG
SWITZER-LAND
AUSTRIA-HUNGARY
FRANCE
MONTE-NEGRO
ROMANIA
Black Sea
Adriatic Sea
SERBIA
BULGARIA
PORTUGAL
SPAIN
ITALY
ALBANIA
Gallipoli
Dardanelles
OTTOMAN EMPIRE
Mediterranean Sea
GREECE

0   200   400 mi.
0   200   400 km
Lambert Conic Conformal Projection

Map Study World War I split Europe into two armed camps.
Location Which side do you think had the better strategic location: the Triple Alliance or the Triple Entente countries?

When the couple's car took a wrong turn, 19-year-old **Gavrilo Princip** (gah•VREE•loh PREEN•seep) fired his gun, fatally wounding them both.

German Support

Although the assassination had not occurred in Serbia, Austro-Hungarian leaders held the Serbians responsible. They were encouraged in this line of thinking by their German allies and by Count Leopold Berchtold, the Austro-Hungarian foreign minister. On July 5, Berchtold sent an envoy to Berlin to talk to the German emperor, **William II**. William assured the envoy that Germany would give its full support to any actions Austria-Hungary might take against Serbia. The next day, the German chancellor officially repeated this promise to the Austro-Hungarian government. In effect, Germany gave Austria-Hungary permission to do with Serbia as it pleased.

Declaration of War

On July 23, Austria-Hungary gave Serbia an ultimatum, a set of final conditions that must be accepted to avoid severe consequences. The ultimatum demanded that Serbia allow Austro-Hungarian officials into the country to suppress all subversive movements there and to lead an investigation into the archduke's murder. Austria-Hungary gave Serbia 48 hours to agree to these terms or face war. Berchtold knew, however, that the ultimatum "would be wholly impossible for the Serbs to accept."

Although the ultimatum outraged Serbian leaders, they knew that their nation was not ready for war with Austria-Hungary. Therefore, on July 25, they responded in a conciliatory manner. They rejected, however, the demand that Austro-Hungarian officials take part in the investigation and trial of those involved in the assassination.

The Serbian answer did not satisfy Austria-Hungary. Consequently, on July 28, 1914, exactly one month after the assassination of Archduke Ferdinand, Austria-Hungary declared war on Serbia. Both countries immediately issued general orders for mobilization, the gathering and transport of military troops and fighting equipment in preparation for war. News of these mobilizations spread quickly across the European continent.

A European War

Many Europeans still believed war could be avoided. The major European powers pushed each other to the brink of war, believing that the other side would back down at the last minute. They were tragically mistaken.

Russia was the first to act once Austria-Hungary declared war. Knowing it had lost face often in the past, the Russian government had to support Serbia now or risk the bitter hatred of all the Slavs in the Balkan region. Although the czar was convinced that Germany would fight, he had also been assured through diplomatic channels that France would support Russia.

Consequently, on July 30, Czar **Nicholas II** ordered a general mobilization of his armed forces against both Austria-Hungary and Germany. Austria-Hungary mobilized against Russia the following day. Once Russia's intentions were clear, France and Great Britain showed their hands.

On July 31, Germany issued Russia an ultimatum to cancel its mobilization order or face war. On the same day, Germany also delivered an ultimatum to France. France had 18 hours to decide whether or not it would remain neutral if Germany went to war with Russia. France's answer was to give its support to Russia. When Czar Nicholas did not even reply to Germany's ultimatum, Germany declared war on Russia on August 1. Two days later, Germany declared war on France as well.

The British, meanwhile, were divided on the question of going to war. They still hoped to avoid conflict through negotiations. They did not make it clear whether or not they would support France and Russia. Germany hoped that Great Britain would stay neutral.

The same day that Germany declared war on Russia, however, the German army marched into Luxembourg. The Germans then demanded passage across Belgium, claiming that France intended to invade that country at any moment. Belgium was a neutral country whose borders and neutrality had been guaranteed in an 1839 treaty signed by Great Britain, Russia, France, and Germany.

The Belgians refused the Germans entry into their territory and appealed to Great Britain for help. When the Germans went ahead and invaded Belgium on August 3, Britain protested and sent an ultimatum to the German government that demanded withdrawal of German forces from Belgium. The German chancellor responded by calling the 1839 treaty "a scrap of paper." This left the British little choice. On August 4, Britain declared war on Germany.

The outbreak of war in August 1914 was generally greeted with confidence and rejoicing by the peoples of Europe. In an outburst of patriotic enthusiasm, crowds gathered in the streets, squares, and railway stations of European cities to cheer on the military forces of their respective nations. As the conflict unfolded, most Europeans believed in the war as a matter of defending their country's honor or upholding "right against might."

Few people, however, imagined how long or how devastating a war between the powers of Europe could be. Designed to protect nations against their enemies, the European alliance systems instead dragged a whole continent into war. What began as a local dispute between Austria-Hungary and Serbia eventually became a global conflict that had no clear, limited objective.

SECTION 2 REVIEW

Recall
1. **Define** ultimatum, mobilization.
2. **Identify** Francis Ferdinand, Gavrilo Princip, William II, Nicholas II.
3. **Locate** Serbia on the map on page 742. How did Serbia's location affect its relations with Austria-Hungary?

Critical Thinking
4. **Evaluating Information** Historians have long argued over which European nation was most responsible for the start of World War I. Using examples to support your statements, explain which country you think was most responsible for the war.

Understanding Themes
5. **Conflict** Why do you think World War I came as a surprise to many Europeans?

Section 3

The War

Setting the Scene

▶ **Terms to Define**

belligerent, propaganda, war of attrition, trench, contraband

▶ **People to Meet**

Alfred von Schlieffen, Helmuth von Moltke, Joseph Jacques Joffre, Henri-Philippe Pétain, Winston Churchill, Woodrow Wilson

▶ **Places to Locate**

Paris, Tannenberg, Verdun, Gallipoli

 Where and how was World War I fought?

The Storyteller

François was only 8 years old when war's realities entered his small French village. Gendarmes delivered the official notice of death on the field of honor to the towns, villages, and farms. A hush fell when the names were read. Then the word spread. "Gustave was killed, the little clerk who had looked so handsome in his cavalryman's uniform. Alcide, Jules, Léon, Maurice, Rèmi, Raoul—all killed." In horror, François watched his neighbors' grief. Childhood playmates, cousins, the only sons of families, and brothers all perished in battle. "They remained on their battlefields in the great military cemeteries, neat and orderly, hidden forever."

—adapted from "World War I: A Frenchman's Recollections," reprinted in *The Global Experience*, vol. 2, 1987

French soldiers in the trenches

By August 1914 the major powers of Europe had lined up against each other. Germany and Austria-Hungary, joined by the Ottoman Empire and Bulgaria, became known as the Central Powers. Great Britain, France, Russia, Serbia, Belgium, and, later, Japan and Montenegro, became known as the Allied Powers, or Allies. Claiming that Austria-Hungary and Germany had acted aggressively rather than defensively, Italy remained neutral.

In spite of their military buildups, none of the European powers was fully prepared for what lay ahead. For example, cavalry and horse-drawn vehicles still played an important role in each nation's army—traditions that were quickly discarded. Nations from both sides also seriously underestimated the length of the war. No country had stockpiled enough war materials or ammunition to last more than six months. The widespread feeling among Europeans was that the war would be over by Christmas.

The Schlieffen Plan

Germany's invasion of Belgium on August 3 had been part of the Schlieffen Plan, a war strategy that German General **Alfred von Schlieffen** (SHLEE•fuhn) drew up in 1905. Germany's main problem was that it had enemies in both the east and the west. Schlieffen assumed, however, that Russia would be slow to mobilize. As a result, Schlieffen believed that the Germans could reach Paris and defeat the French in six weeks and then move on to the Eastern Front and fight against Russian forces.

Schlieffen's plan ran into problems from the beginning. First, German Commander **Helmuth von Moltke** led his troops through an area of Belgium that proved to be heavily fortified. Second, Moltke encountered far stronger resistance than anyone had expected; the German advance was delayed until August 20. Third, the Russian army mobilized far more quickly than Schlieffen had estimated, necessitating the movement of two German divisions to the Eastern Front.

The Germans were held up further when they met British forces in the north of France. British troops eventually had to retreat, but they fought expertly and inflicted heavy losses on the Germans. At the same time, the French attacked another wing of the German army in Alsace-Lorraine. The French offensive eventually collapsed but not before delaying the German advance yet again.

The Battle of the Marne

France struggled to recover after the defeat at Alsace-Lorraine. The French chief of command, General **Joseph Jacques Joffre**, pulled back his troops to protect **Paris**. While many Parisians fled the city, General Joseph Simon Gallieni strengthened the army in Paris to the point that it was able to launch a counterattack. To speed troops into position, the French army requisitioned several hundred Parisian taxis.

On September 5 the French and German armies collided in northeastern France in the Battle of the Marne. After four days of shelling, the French finally pushed the Germans back a distance of about 50 miles (80 km) from Paris. The attack saved Paris from the Germans and boosted French morale. Although German forces continued to hold much of France's heavily industrialized areas, the German retreat from the Battle of the Marne signified the abandonment of the Schlieffen Plan. It also made it clear that neither side was capable of defeating the other quickly or easily.

A Russian Disaster

Russia, meanwhile, kept its word to the French and sent troops into battle even before its military was fully mobilized. The speed with which the Russians moved surprised Germany and Austria-Hungary. By August 13 the Russians had invaded East Prussia from the south and from the east. This attack diverted German troops from the attack against the French and British during the first critical weeks of the war.

Russia's success did not last long. At the end of August, Russian and German troops met at **Tannenberg** in present-day Poland. There the Russians suffered a disastrous defeat from which they never fully recovered. At Tannenberg, the Germans were able to encircle and destroy the Russian army. They killed more than 30,000 Russian soldiers and took 92,000 prisoners. German casualties numbered only about 13,000.

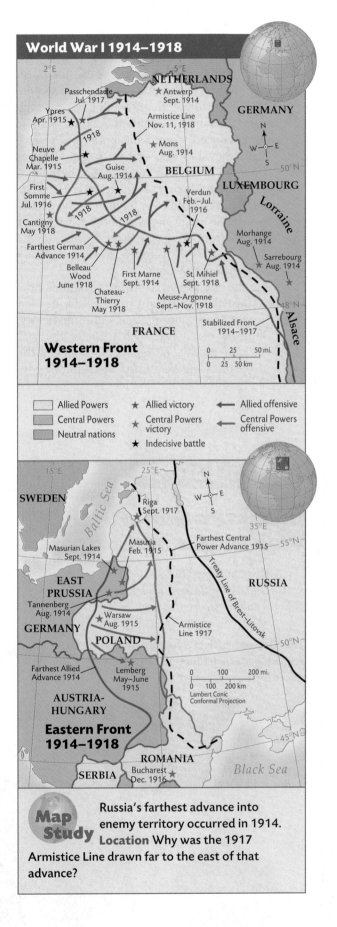

World War I 1914–1918

Western Front 1914–1918

Passchendaele Jul. 1917
Antwerp Sept. 1914
Ypres Apr. 1915
Armistice Line Nov. 11, 1918
Neuve Chapelle Mar. 1915
Mons Aug. 1914
Guise Aug. 1914
BELGIUM
First Somme Jul. 1916
Verdun Feb.–Jul. 1916
LUXEMBOURG
Cantigny May 1918
Farthest German Advance 1914
Belleau Wood June 1918
First Marne Sept. 1914
St. Mihiel Sept. 1918
Morhange Aug. 1914
Sarrebourg Aug. 1914
Chateau-Thierry May 1918
Meuse-Argonne Sept.–Nov. 1918
FRANCE
Stabilized Front 1914–1917
Lorraine
Alsace

0 25 50 mi.
0 25 50 km

Allied Powers — Allied victory ★ — Allied offensive ←
Central Powers — Central Powers victory ★ — Central Powers offensive ←
Neutral nations — Indecisive battle ★

Eastern Front 1914–1918

SWEDEN
Baltic Sea
Riga Sept. 1917
Masurian Lakes Sept. 1914
Masuria Feb. 1915
Farthest Central Power Advance 1915
EAST PRUSSIA
RUSSIA
Tannenberg Aug. 1914
Warsaw Aug. 1915
Armistice Line 1917
GERMANY
POLAND
Treaty Line of Brest-Litovsk
Farthest Allied Advance 1914
Lemberg May–June 1915
AUSTRIA-HUNGARY
0 100 200 mi.
0 100 200 km
Lambert Conic Conformal Projection
ROMANIA
Bucharest Dec. 1916
SERBIA
Black Sea

Map Study Russia's farthest advance into enemy territory occurred in 1914. **Location** Why was the 1917 Armistice Line drawn far to the east of that advance?

Years of Deadlock

After the Battle of the Marne, the Germans and the Allies began a series of battles known as "the race to the sea," with each attempting to reach the North Sea first and outflank the other. As the Germans advanced toward the ports of Dunkirk and Calais, they ran into British troops at Ypres (EEPR), a town in western Belgium. The battle that followed brought high casualties to both sides. Despite the heavy sacrifices, there were no breakthroughs. At this point the war in the west settled into a stable front from the Swiss border to the North Sea coast. By November 1914 the war had already reached a stalemate.

All of the belligerent, or warring, nations now had to adjust their plans. To produce the needed ships, guns, food, ammunition, and medicines, large numbers of civilians had to enter the war effort. To raise morale, newspapers gave even the smallest victories big headlines. In addition, governments used propaganda—ideas or rumors used to harm an opposing cause—to portray the enemy as beastly and inhuman. Making peace with such an enemy seemed unthinkable.

Trench Warfare

By early 1915 the war on the Western Front had turned into a deadly war of attrition, in which each side tried to wear down the other side by constant attacks. To protect themselves, soldiers on both

> **Footnotes to History**
>
> **Holiday Cheer**
> On Christmas Day, 1914, fighting stopped, and British and German soldiers met in "no-man's-land" to chat, play soccer, and pose for photographs! Officers, however, quickly ended these goodwill meetings, and the soldiers returned to their positions to take up firing at one another again.

Images of the Times

Industry Generates War Materials

More than any previous war, World War I demanded large-scale industrial production of military and transportation equipment.

This German officer's helmet and the English gas mask and pack were produced by their respective war industries.

sides dug trenches, or ditches. Eventually, two parallel trenches stretched for about 500 miles (805 km) in an unbroken line from Switzerland to the North Sea. Land mines and barbed wire protected the area in front of each trench. The desolate area that separated the two sides, which could vary from a half a mile to a few yards, was known as "no-man's-land."

Soldiers lived in the trenches for weeks at a time, fighting boredom and terror. They endured cold, mud, rats, and disease. To attack, the soldiers charged "over the top" of their own trenches and ran across "no man's land" to the enemy's trenches. As attackers struggled through the barbed wire, their opponents mowed them down with heavy artillery and machine guns.

Throughout 1915, battle followed battle, and casualties mounted. At the battle of Ypres, the Germans introduced a new weapon—poison gas. From cylinders in their trenches, they released yellow-green chlorine gas. The wind carried the gas into French trenches, causing blindness, choking, vomiting, torn lungs, and death. Wilfred

Owen, an English poet and soldier, described the horrors of poison gas in his poem "Dulce et Decorum Est" (1916):

> **66** Gas! Gas! Quick, boys!—An ecstasy of
> fumbling,
> Fitting the clumsy helmets just in time;
> But someone still was yelling out and
> stumbling
> And flound'ring like a man in fire or lime …
> Dim, through the misty panes and thick
> green light,
> As under a green sea, I saw him drowning. **99**

Verdun and the Somme

The year 1916 opened with the war on the Western Front still stalemated. Although Italy had denounced the Central Powers six months earlier and entered the war on the side of the Allies, it had gained little ground after four battles against the Austro-Hungarians. Then in February 1916, the Germans made a move. They staged a surprise

Return to the Front by Richard Jack illustrates the importance of rail transportation in moving British soldiers and equipment.

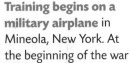

Training begins on a military airplane in Mineola, New York. At the beginning of the war Germany had more planes than did the United States. Most American pilots flew French and English planes.

REFLECTING ON THE TIMES

1. What changes in production take place in industrial nations during war?
2. How does developing technology affect the training of a nation's armed forces?

attack against French forces at **Verdun**, a massive fortress in northeastern France on the Meuse River. The French, under General **Henri-Philippe Pétain** (PAY•TAN), rallied to the cry "They shall not pass." After six months, the French still held firm, and the Germans finally abandoned the attack. The Battle of Verdun was one of the bloodiest of the war. Before the struggle ended, both sides had suffered more than a half million casualties.

Later that year, the British, aided by a small French force, launched a similar offensive against the Germans in the Somme River valley in northern France. The Battle of the Somme turned out to be as terrible and inconclusive as the one at Verdun, costing the Germans about 500,000 men, the British 400,000, and the French 200,000. Although the British introduced another new weapon during this battle—an armored vehicle called the tank—it made little difference to the outcome of the struggle. Tanks were still too clumsy and slow to be an effective weapon, and the generals on both sides did not yet understand how best to use them.

The Eastern Front

The Eastern Front in Russia was less entrenched than the Western Front in France; the war there was far more mobile, involving constant changes in battlefield positions. Neither side, however, was able to achieve a complete victory.

In 1915 Germany and Austria-Hungary made determined efforts to remove Russia from the war. As the least industrialized of the European powers, Russia did not have the resources and skills to fight a modern conflict. By year's end, the Russians had been forced to give up territory greater than the whole of France. In addition to suffering a staggering number of casualties, they had lost ammunition and guns equal to the amount they had possessed when the war began. The Allies, however, had promised Russia control of Constantinople and the Dardanelles if their side won the war.

Inspired by this agreement, the Russians went to work rebuilding their army. In March 1916 they launched an offensive against the Germans but made little headway. A few months later, however, they fared much better against Austria-Hungary. In addition to capturing many cities, they took several hundred thousand prisoners. They paid a heavy toll in the process, however, losing more than a million men and most of their supplies.

Although morale in the Russian army suffered greatly as a result of the 1916 offenses, their efforts

CONNECTIONS
Science and Technology

Flaming Coffins

Airplanes added a new dimension to fighting in World War I. For the first time, combat took place not only on land and at sea but also in the air. Crude but operational, these noisy, pitching, and bucking machines were not built with the pilot's safety foremost in mind. The typical plane was made of thin wood reinforced by steel wire. Its body and wings were covered by cloth coated with a highly flammable liquid. The pilot sat on a seat directly over the fuel tank. Fire was such a constant danger that airplanes were often referred to as "flaming coffins."

Brakes did not exist on World War I-era planes. On takeoff, the crew had to hold the plane back while the pilot revved the engine. On landing, the pilot had to turn the engine off and on to slow the approach. Once the pilot was airborne, contact with the ground was possible only if an unwieldy Morse code transmitter was on board.

Today, military aircraft are safer, faster, and more maneuverable. For example, the development of jet engines has enabled planes to fly much faster than before. Other recent innovations increasing the speed and range of planes include the development of thinner and flatter wings and the use of more effective heat-resistant materials.

Battle between German and British planes

Linking Past and Present **ACTIVITY**

In what sense were World War I airplanes "crude" vehicles? Compare World War I-era military aircraft with that of today.

Visualizing History These heavy guns were not enough to overcome the resistance of the Turks at Gallipoli. *What were Churchill's three main goals in attacking Turkey?*

helped the Allies on the Western Front. The Germans had to transfer several divisions from the west to the east, hampering the effectiveness of their attack at Verdun.

Gallipoli Campaign

As the war dragged on and casualties soared, each side tried to find ways to turn the war in its favor. In Great Britain, First Lord of the Admiralty **Winston Churchill**—head of the British navy—asked, "Are there not other alternatives than sending our armies to chew barbed wire in Flanders?" Churchill favored opening an offensive on the Dardanelles strait, which Turkey controlled. This strait was the only practical means of supplying Russia and of strengthening Serbia. From there, the Allies could take Constantinople and possibly put the Ottoman Empire out of the war. This offensive, Churchill believed, might also lead to the collapse of Austria-Hungary.

Churchill's idea had merit. The Allies' initial offensive in early 1915 nearly succeeded, but a lack of coordination, planning, and reinforcements gave the Turks time to rearm. When the Allies followed up in April with a land attack on the peninsula of **Gallipoli** (guh•LIH•puh•lee), the Turks drove them back. On January 9, 1916, the Allies finally gave up the effort and withdrew the last of their troops from the area.

On the Seas

The British, meanwhile, had been using their naval superiority to dominate the seas. They were determined to keep the Germans from invading Great Britain and to keep war materials from reaching the Central Powers by sea. The Germans were just as determined to disrupt Allied shipping. Both Great Britain and Germany depended heavily on the seas for their food and war materials. Without those goods, neither country could continue the war.

Great Britain blockaded all ports under German control at the start of the war. The blockade was so effective that Germany had to receive most of its supplies through the neutral countries of Holland, Denmark, Sweden, and Norway. The

Hulton Picture Company

In the Trenches

In the Dardanelles Campaign of 1915 these soldiers of the British Empire fought to capture Gallipoli. Held by the Ottoman Empire, Gallipoli was a strategic location for supplying Russia and the Eastern Front of the war. These troops have hastily dug a trench on their way up a hillside. There they could make use of periscopes and wait for their officers to decide whether they should go "over the top." Three of the men in this photo are Australian. The heavy losses sustained by Australian troops in the Gallipoli Campaign fostered a new sense of Australian identity.

It was on the Western Front, however, in France and Belgium, that trench warfare was most gruesome. In ditches and tunnels called trenches the armies of the Allies and the Central Powers settled into a war of position. The units of horse cavalry that had pranced proudly into war were replaced by foot soldiers hunkered into trenches, facing the enemy across a no-man's-land of barbed wire. Stuck in mud and water, soldiers lived alongside lice and rats amid the smell of dead horses and dead men. It was a war, British poet Wilfred Owen wrote, "obscene as cancer" and "bitter as ... vile." ⊕

Germans protested that the blockade violated international law and called it "the hunger blockade." Ignoring these protests, the British also stopped ships they suspected of carrying contraband, or prohibited goods. They escorted these ships into port and seized their cargoes.

Submarine Warfare

To wear down British sea power, the Germans introduced submarine warfare. At first, German submarines, or U-boats, struck only warships. In 1915 they also began to strike civilian and commercial ships, many of which were carrying supplies to the Allies. In May 1915 a German U-boat torpedoed the British passenger liner *Lusitania*. About 1,200 people, including 128 Americans, were killed. The Germans justified the attack, arguing the *Lusitania* carried weapons.

By March 1916, German U-boats had sunk other British and French ships. This led President **Woodrow Wilson** to issue an ultimatum to the Germans. He threatened to sever diplomatic relations if Germany did not agree to stop attacking passenger and freight vessels. The Germans responded by ending unrestricted submarine warfare for a while.

In May 1916, the only major battle between the British and German fleets took place off the coast of Denmark. Both sides claimed victory, but the Battle of Jutland as it was called still left the British in control of the seas and the Germans bound by the British blockade.

United States Enters War

One of the most important events of 1917 was the decision of the United States to enter the war. Until this point, American public opinion was divided about the conflict in Europe. For example, many Irish Americans were staunchly anti-British, and many German Americans sided with the Central Powers. Many other Americans, mostly of English, Scottish, and Scots Irish descent, favored the Allies. The majority of Americans, however, agreed with President Woodrow Wilson that the war was strictly a European conflict. While incidents such as the sinking of the *Lusitania* in 1915 angered them, Americans were not ready to take an active part in the war.

Meanwhile, in Europe, the Germans did not want the Americans to enter the war. At the same time, they were determined to break the British blockade and end British control of the seas. They believed that the way to do this was by resuming a policy of unrestricted submarine warfare. As a result, Germany announced that beginning February 1, 1917, it would sink any merchant ships heading to British or western European ports. President Wilson responded by breaking off diplomatic relations with Germany.

Tensions between the two countries grew worse in March 1917 when American newspapers printed the Zimmermann telegram, a message from the German foreign minister, Arthur Zimmermann, to his ambassador in Mexico. Zimmermann promised that, in return for Mexican support, Germany would help Mexico to regain New Mexico, Texas, and Arizona. The British had passed on the Zimmermann telegram to the American government, and the message's publication heightened anti-German attitudes in the United States.

After the German sinking of four American merchant ships, President Wilson on April 2, 1917, asked Congress for a declaration of war and called upon Americans to help "make the world safe for democracy." American financial aid and military intervention would tip the scales in favor of an eventual Allied victory.

SECTION 3 REVIEW

Recall
1. **Define** belligerent, propaganda, war of attrition, trench, contraband.
2. **Identify** Alfred von Schlieffen, Helmuth von Moltke, Joseph Jacques Joffre, Henri-Philippe Pétain, Winston Churchill, Woodrow Wilson.

3. **Locate** Gallipoli and the Dardanelles on the map on page 742. Why was an Allied military campaign carried out there?

Critical Thinking
4. **Synthesizing Information** Create your own strategy for avoiding a stalemate in trench warfare. Determine the main factors working against a breakthrough in this type of warfare.

Understanding Themes
5. **Conflict** Explain how World War I was a new kind of war. Consider objectives, strategy, and technology in the course of your explanation.

Bettmann

The Lusitania

Passengers boarding the British liner R.M.S. *Lusitania* in New York on May 1, 1915, for the voyage to Liverpool, England, knew of Germany's threat to sink ships bound for the British Isles. England and Germany had been fighting for nine months. Still, few passengers imagined that a civilized nation would attack an unarmed passenger steamer without warning.

Built eight years earlier, the *Lusitania* was described as a "floating palace." German authorities, however, saw her as a threat. They accused the British government of using the *Lusitania* to carry ammunition and other war materials across the Atlantic.

With her four towering funnels, the liner looked invincible as she left New York on her last voyage. Six days later, at 2:10 p.m. on May 7, 1915, Walther Schwieger, the 30-year-old commander of the German submarine U 20, fired a single torpedo at the *Lusitania* from a range of about 750 yards.

Captain William Turner of the *Lusitania* saw the torpedo's wake from the navigation bridge just before impact. It sounded like a "million-ton hammer hitting a steam boiler a hundred feet high," one passenger said. A second, more powerful explosion followed, sending a geyser of water, coal, and debris high above the deck.

Listing to starboard, the liner began to sink rapidly at the bow, sending passengers tumbling down her slanted decks. Lifeboats on the port side were hanging too far inboard to be readily launched, while those on the starboard side

IRELAND

St. George's Channel

WALES

Cork

Cobh (Queenstown)

Kinsale

✕ **Candidate** sunk May 6

✕ **Centurion** sunk May 6

Galley Head

Old Head of Kinsale

✕ **Earl of Lathom** sunk May 5

Fastnet Rock   Cape Clear

U 20'S COURSE

LUSITANIA'S COURSE

Sunk 2:28 p.m. May 7, 1915

Celtic Sea

0   30
MILES
NGS CARTOGRAPHIC DIVISION

0   100
MILES

SCOTLAND

North Sea

Atlantic Ocean

UNITED

N. IRELAND

Dublin   ★   • Liverpool

IRELAND   WALES   ENGLAND

Cobh   KINGDOM

Celtic Sea   London ★

AREA ENLARGED   FRANCE

ENGLAND

NGS Cartographic Division

Boston Evening Globe   Evening Edition 1¢

EVENING EDITION—7:30 O'CLOCK—LATEST

LUSITANIA SUNK

Not Known How Many Passengers Saved

TORPEDOED BY GERMANS, REMAINED AFLOAT 12 HOURS

TORPEDOED OFF THE IRISH COAST

Left New York Last Saturday With 1253 Passengers.

Titanic Historical Society Inc.

were too far out to be easily boarded. Several overfilled lifeboats spilled occupants into the sea. The great liner disappeared under the waves in only 18 minutes, leaving behind a jumble of swimmers, corpses, deck chairs, and wreckage. Looking back upon the scene from his submarine, even German commander Schwieger was shocked. He later called it the most horrible sight he had ever seen.

News of the disaster raced across the Atlantic. Of 1,959 people aboard, only 764 were saved. The dead included 94 children and infants.

Questions were immediately raised. Did the British Admiralty

give the *Lusitania* adequate warning? How could one torpedo have sunk her? Why did she go down so fast? Was there any truth to the German claim that the *Lusitania* had been armed?

From the moment the *Lusitania* sank, she was surrounded by controversy. Americans were outraged by the attack, which claimed the lives of 128 U.S. citizens. Newspapers called the attack "deliberate murder" and a "foul deed," and former President Theodore Roosevelt demanded revenge against Germany. The attack on the *Lusitania* is often credited with drawing the United States into

🔲 **The** Lusitania *arrives in New York on her maiden voyage in 1907 (opposite page).*

🔲 *In the two days prior to the attack on the* Lusitania, *the German submarine U 20 had sunk three ships off Ireland's southern coast. Yet the captain of the Lusitania, who had received warnings by wireless from the British Admiralty, took only limited precautions as he approached the area. Headlines in Boston and New York report the terrible news of the sinking of the* Lusitania *on May 7, 1915 (above).*

World War I. President Woodrow Wilson—though he had vowed to hold Germany responsible for its submarine attacks—knew that the American people were not ready to go to war. It was almost two more years before the United States joined the conflict in Europe.

A British judge laid full blame on the German submarine commander, while the German government claimed that the British had deliberately made her a military target. Tragically, inquiries following the sinking of the *Lusitania* revealed that Captain Turner had received warnings by wireless from the British Admiralty, but took only limited precautions as he approached the area where U 20 was waiting.

Rumors of diamonds, gold, and valuables locked away in *Lusitania's* safes have prompted salvage attempts over the years. To date, no treasure has ever been reported.

Perhaps the biggest puzzle has been the hardest to solve: Why did the liner sink so fast? Newspapers speculated that the torpedo had struck ammunition in a cargo hold, causing the strong secondary explosion. Divers later reported a huge hole in the port side of the bow, opposite where munitions would have been stored.

HOPING TO SETTLE the issue, a team from the Woods Hole Oceanographic Institution, sponsored by the National Geographic Society, sent their robot vehicle Jason down to photograph the damage. Fitted with cameras and powerful lights, the robot sent video images of the wreck by fiber-optic cable to a control room on the surface ship, *Northern Horizon*. A pilot maneuvered Jason with a joystick, while an engineer relayed instructions to the robot's computers. Other team members watched for recognizable objects on the monitors. In addition to using Jason to make a visual survey of the *Lusitania*, the team of researchers and scientists also used sonar to create a computerized, three-dimensional diagram of how the wreck looks today.

From this data, it was discovered that the *Lusitania's* hull had been flattened—in part by the force of gravity—to half its original width. When Jason's cameras swept across the hold, looking for the hole reported by divers shortly after the sinking, there was none to be found. Indeed, no evidence was found that would indicate that the torpedo had detonated an explosion in a cargo hold, undermining one theory of why the liner sank.

Questions about her cargo have haunted the *Lusitania* since the day she went down. Was she carrying illegal munitions as the Germans have always claimed? In fact, she was. The manifest for her last voyage included wartime essentials such as motorcycle parts, metals, cotton goods, and food, as well as 4,200 cases of rifle ammunition, 1,250 cases of shrapnel (not explosive), and 18 boxes of percussion fuses. The investigation conducted by the Woods Hole team and Jason suggested that these munitions did not cause the secondary blast that sent the *Lusitania* to the bottom. So what did?

One likely possibility was a coal-dust explosion. The German torpedo struck the liner's starboard side about ten feet below the waterline, rupturing one of the long coal bunkers that stretched along both sides. If that bunker, mostly empty by the end of the voyage, contained explosive coal dust, the torpedo might have ignited it. That would explain all the coal found scattered on the seafloor near the wreck.

The *Lusitania's* giant funnels have long since turned to rust, an eerie

Brown Brothers

UPI/Bettmann

marine growth covers her hull, and her superstructure is ghostly wreckage. Yet the horror and fascination surrounding the sinking of the great liner live on. With today's high-technology tools, researchers and scientists at Woods Hole and the National Geographic Society have provided another look—and some new answers—to explain the chain of events that ended with the *Lusitania* at the bottom of the sea.

ENLIST

◈ Captain William Turner of the Lusitania, (opposite page, top); Walther Schwieger, commander of the German submarine U 20 (opposite page, bottom).

◈ Homer, a small robot, (left) explores a hole in the stern of the Lusitania that was cut by a salvage crew to recover silverware and other items.

◈ A provocative poster (left) depicted drowning innocents and urged Americans to enlist in the armed forces. For the women pictured above, the image was all too real. Alice Drury (above left) was a young nanny for an American couple on the Lusitania. She and another nanny were caring for the couple's children: Audrey, Stuart, Amy, and Susan. Alice was about to give Audrey a bottle when the torpedo hit. Alice wrapped Audrey in a shawl, grabbed Stuart, and headed for the lifeboats. A crewman loaded Stuart, but when Alice tried to board, the sailor told her it was full. Without a life jacket and with Audrey around her neck, Alice jumped into the water. A woman in the lifeboat grabbed her hair and pulled her aboard. Audrey's parents were rescued too, but Amy, Susan, and the other nanny were lost. Alice and Audrey Lawson Johnston (above right) have remained close ever since.

1917 Czar Nicholas II abdicates.

1918 Bolshevik Russia and Germany sign Treaty of Brest-Litovsk.

1919 Reds and Whites fight civil war.

Section 4

The Russian Revolution

Setting the Scene

▶ **Terms to Define**
   provisional government, communism

▶ **People to Meet**
   Nicholas II, Grigori Rasputin, Alexander Kerensky, Vladimir Ilyich Lenin, Leon Trotsky

▶ **Places to Locate**
   Petrograd, Siberia, Poland, Ukraine

 Find Out What events led to the Russian Revolution?

 **The Storyteller**

Thousands filled the hall, waiting for Trotsky's speech. The crowd was tense, waiting. When Trotsky appeared, they applauded, but briefly, so as to hear that much sooner what he would say. Trotsky spoke of current conditions, and then continued. "The Soviet government will give everything the country contains to the poor and the men in the trenches. You, bourgeois, have two fur caps!—give one of them to the soldier, who's freezing in the trenches." The crowd surrounding Trotsky was aroused almost to ecstasy. This, actually, was already an insurrection. A transformation had begun.

Leon Trotsky

—adapted from *The Russian Revolution*, N. N. Sukharov, translated by Joel Carmichael, 1917

World War I proved to be the breaking point for czarist rule in Russia. By 1917, morale in the Russian army had reached bottom. As many as one-fourth of the Russian soldiers, having no weapons of their own, had to pick up the guns of dead soldiers. Inadequate transport made grave food shortages even worse. Almost all of the country's resources went to supply the army, making the human and financial costs of war increasingly unbearable.

A nurse at the Russian front in 1917 described the situation that helped bring about the collapse of the autocracy and the establishment of a Communist state:

❝ Discontent among the masses in Russia is daily becoming more marked. Disparaging statements concerning the Government are being voiced…. "Bring the men home!" "Conclude peace!" "Finish this interminable war once and for all!" Cries such as these penetrate to the cold and hungry soldiers in their bleak earthworks, and begin to echo among them. Now that food has grown scarce in Petrograd (St. Petersburg) and Moscow, disorder takes the shape of riots and insurrections. We are told that mobs of the lower classes parade the streets shouting 'Peace and Bread!' ❞

Fall of the Czar

Events leading to the fall of the czar began to accelerate in the last half of 1916. Czar **Nicholas II** and his wife, Alexandra, had already become unpopular because of the czar's political incompetence and the couple's reliance on the mystic healer **Grigori Rasputin** (ra•SPYOO•tuhn). Wanting to save the monarchy, two relatives of the czar assisted in killing Rasputin in December 1916.

Rasputin's death did not solve the monarchy's problems. Public anger against the government mounted as a result of food and fuel shortages, and strikes erupted across the country. On March 8, 1917, and for the next few days, hundreds of thousands of men and women gathered in the streets of **Petrograd** (the Russian name given to St. Petersburg). Demanding food and an end to the war, the crowds shouted, "Down with the czar!" On March 11 and 12, the troops the government ordered to put down the riots refused to fire on the crowds. Many soldiers joined the protesters.

When the czar ordered his generals at the front to crush the rebellion, they told him that any troops they might send to the capital would also join the rioters. With the country sinking into chaos, the czar finally abdicated on March 15, ending the 300-year-old Romanov dynasty. The March revolution was a spontaneous uprising of working people and soldiers. It caused the loss of relatively few lives and took place, surprisingly, without the leadership of its revolutionary intellectuals, most of whom were living in exile abroad.

The Provisional Government

After Czar Nicholas II's abdication, political authority in Russia passed into the hands of a temporary central government known as the provisional government. This new regime called for elections later in the year to choose a constituent, or constitutional, assembly. The constituent assembly would then establish a permanent government.

The provisional government, which consisted of middle-class Duma representatives, soon had a rival for power—the Petrograd Soviet of Workers' and Soldiers' Deputies. Members of the Petrograd Soviet were workers and peasants belonging to different socialist groups. The majority were either Mensheviks or Social Revolutionaries, the political heirs of the Populists. A smaller, more radical group was the Bolsheviks.

One man who moved easily between the provisional government and the Petrograd Soviet was **Alexander Kerensky** (keh•REHN•skee). A moderate socialist, Kerensky served first as the provisional government's minister of justice and then as its prime minister. He also belonged to the executive committee of the Petrograd Soviet.

The Petrograd Soviet became a model for the founding of other soviets throughout Russia.

Together, the soviets called for an immediate peace, the transfer of land to the peasants, and the control of factories by workers. As the Russian economy continued to collapse under the war effort, this three-point program gained great popularity among the Russian masses.

In spite of the suffering and anger of the Russian people, however, the provisional government did not withdraw from the war. Desertion, worsening transportation problems, and a drop in already low armament production plagued the Russian army. Preoccupied with war policy, the provisional government could not carry out the social reforms proposed by the soviets. As a result, the government lost much of its popular support, a factor that contributed to its eventual downfall.

Lenin

As the provisional government struggled to maintain order, a variety of revolutionary groups vied to fill the power vacuum. Since their split into two factions in 1903, the Mensheviks and the Bolsheviks had competed for control of Russia's revolutionary movement. By 1917 the Mensheviks far outnumbered the Bolsheviks. Because they believed that a socialist revolution would be the work of the masses, however, the Mensheviks did not make concrete plans to seize control of the Russian government.

The more radical Bolsheviks, on the other hand, believed that a socialist society could be introduced immediately by force. They claimed that a small group of dedicated revolutionaries could carry out the revolution with the help of a relatively small working class and the peasants. They also believed that Russia's revolution would spread worldwide. Their leader, **Vladimir Ilyich Lenin**, urged them to make plans to topple the provisional government from power.

Born in 1870, Lenin came from a middle-class provincial background. When Lenin was in high school, his older brother, Alexander, became involved in a plot to assassinate Czar Alexander III, the father of Nicholas II. The attempt failed, however, and the government hanged Lenin's brother and four fellow conspirators in 1887. Alexander's death made a powerful impression on Lenin, who dedicated his life to promoting a revolution.

In 1895 the Russian government arrested Lenin for his activities and exiled him to **Siberia**. After his release, he went to Germany, Great Britain, and Switzerland, where he wrote revolutionary articles and kept a close eye on the political situation in

Russia. After hearing the news of the March 1917 revolution, he wanted to return to Russia as soon as possible. Since Germany wanted Russia out of the war and knew that Lenin would promote a withdrawal, it provided him with a special "sealed" train that allowed no one to enter or exit during the trip. Lenin's goal upon his arrival in Russia was to organize the Bolsheviks and seize power from the provisional government.

Lenin realized that the provisional government could not maintain the support of the soldiers, peasants, and workers. His slogan, "Peace, Land, and Bread," promised the Russian people that Russia would withdraw from the war, that the peasants would be given land, and that everyone would have enough to eat. Another point in Lenin's program was that the soviets should become the nation's only government. This goal was summed up in the slogan "All power to the soviets!"

The Bolshevik Revolution

During the summer of 1917, a number of demonstrations against the provisional government broke out across Russia. Blaming these demonstrations on the Bolsheviks and calling Lenin a German agent, the government issued arrest warrants for all Bolshevik leaders, forcing Lenin into hiding. By late August, however, the Bolsheviks started to show new strength in local elections, and by mid-September they had gained control of the Petrograd Soviet.

Two months later, in November 1917, the Bolsheviks staged a coup d'etat in Petrograd, overthrowing the provisional government in the name of the soviets. Bolshevik soldiers, workers, and sailors took over the main post office, the telephone system, electrical generating plants, and train stations. When the Bolsheviks turned the guns of the battleship *Aurora* against the Winter Palace, the former home of the czar, the ministers of the provisional government quickly surrendered. As a result, the revolution was relatively bloodless.

In spite of the Bolshevik coup, the election for the constituent assembly still took place in late November. Of those elected, 420 seats went to the Social Revolutionaries and only 225 to the Bolsheviks. When the assembly met in Petrograd in January 1918, however, the Bolsheviks dissolved it after only one day.

Claiming absolute power, the Bolsheviks laid the foundation of a socialist state—ending private ownership of property, distributing land among the peasants, and giving workers control of factories and mines. The Bolsheviks began calling themselves Communists and their political viewpoint, based on the ideas of Marx and Lenin, **communism**. The Communists and their supporters in other countries created an international movement to spread their revolution throughout the world.

Civil War

In addition to building a socialist state, Lenin also sought peace with Germany. At a heavy price, Russia in March 1918 signed the Treaty of Brest-Litovsk, losing much western territory and a third of the population. Meanwhile, the Bolsheviks faced challenges from within the former empire. Powerful nationalist movements set up independent governments in Estonia, Latvia, Lithuania, **Poland**, **Ukraine**, and the Caucasus lands of Armenia, Georgia, and Azerbaijan. Although in theory allowing these countries to break away from Russia, the Communists in practice used force to gain control in Ukraine and the Caucasus.

Reds and Whites

During the early months of 1918, Russia also slipped into a devastating civil war between the Communists and their political opponents. In this conflict, the Communists were called Reds, because they favored the red flag of revolution. Their opponents—royalists, liberal democrats, and moderate socialists—became known as the Whites.

Lenin's government was determined not to yield power. Under the Communist leader, **Leon Trotsky**, the Red Army was organized to defend the Communist state. Trotsky restored discipline to military ranks, using force and education to foster loyalty to communism.

The Whites promised to defeat the Reds quickly and get Russia back into World War I against the Central Powers. As a result, they received soldiers and military aid from the Allies and the United States. The foreign intervention did little to help the Whites, but it stirred Russian nationalist support for the Communists and increased Communist distrust of the West.

For three grim years, the fighting raged across the vast landscape. Both sides burned villages and killed civilians. When the Whites captured an area, they killed all suspected Communists. The Reds did the same to "counter-revolutionaries," or those believed to be opposed to communism. In the meantime, workers and peasants were starving and the nation's economy was crumbling.

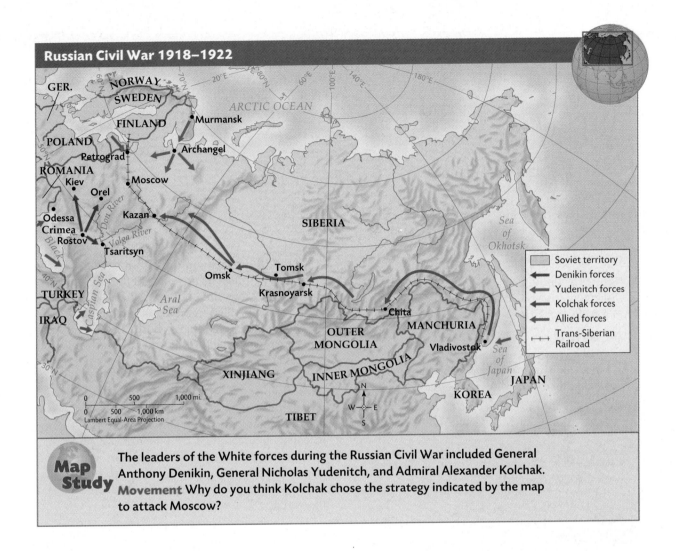

Russian Civil War 1918–1922

Map Study The leaders of the White forces during the Russian Civil War included General Anthony Denikin, General Nicholas Yudenitch, and Admiral Alexander Kolchak. **Movement** Why do you think Kolchak chose the strategy indicated by the map to attack Moscow?

The Terror

During the upheaval, the Communists further tightened their hold on Russia. They imposed a policy called "war communism"—taking direct control of industry and forcing peasants to send food to the starving cities. Lenin also used terror as a weapon against his opponents. In 1918 Communist soldiers killed the imprisoned czar and his family. A secret police force, the Cheka, arrested anyone considered an "enemy of the revolution." In keeping with communism's anti-religious viewpoint, Lenin placed severe restrictions on the Russian Orthodox Church.

Many Socialists who had backed Lenin's revolution now withdrew their support and fled Russia. At the same time, the Whites suffered from a lack of unity among their royalist, liberal, and moderate socialist supporters. Outnumbered, disorganized, and poorly equipped, the White armies finally admitted defeat. By 1921 Lenin had extended Communist control throughout the war-ravaged country.

SECTION 4 REVIEW

Recall

1. **Define** provisional government, communism.
2. **Identify** Nicholas II, Grigori Rasputin, Alexander Kerensky, Vladimir Ilyich Lenin, Leon Trotsky.
3. **Discuss** the main differences that separated the Mensheviks and the Bolsheviks.

Critical Thinking

4. **Evaluating Information** Do you think Lenin was justified in closing down the democratically elected constituent assembly in January 1918? Why or why not?

Understanding Themes

5. **Revolution** Why was the Russian Revolution a significant turning point in world history? What impact did it have on Russian and global affairs?

Section 5

Peace at Last

Setting the Scene

▶ **Terms to Define**

convoy, armistice, reparation, mandate, cordon sanitaire

▶ **People to Meet**

T.E. Lawrence, Ferdinand Foch, Woodrow Wilson, Georges Clemenceau, David Lloyd George, Vittorio Orlando

▶ **Places to Locate**

Fiume

Find Out Why was the Treaty of Versailles ultimately unsuccessful?

The Storyteller

Four officers of France, Great Britain, America, and Italy marched into the Palace of Versailles to sign the treaty ending World War I. Harold Nicholson described the ceremony in his diary: "And then, isolated and pitiable, come the two German delegates, Dr. Muller and Dr. Bell. The silence is terrifying…. They keep their eyes fixed away from those two thousand staring eyes, fixed upon the ceiling. They are deathly pale…. Suddenly from outside comes the crash of guns thundering a salute. It announces to Paris that the second Treaty of Versailles had been signed….

We kept our seats while the Germans were conducted like prisoners from the dock, their eyes still fixed upon some distant point of the horizon."

—adapted from *Peacemaking,* Harold Nicholson, reprinted in *Western Civilization, an Urban Perspective,* F. Roy Willis, 1973

German officer's helmet

Russia's withdrawal from the war was offset by the entry of the United States into the conflict. American intervention boosted Allied morale and gave the Allies much needed resources, both industrial and human. It took time for the Americans to build and train an army, but the American navy was of immediate help. United States Admiral William S. Sims introduced the idea of the convoy to guard Allied ships from German U-boats. Under the successful convoy system, merchant ships crossed the Atlantic in clusters surrounded by warships for protection. At the same time, improvements in mines and underwater explosives—as well as the use of the airplane for air surveying and bombing—changed the way the war was being fought.

Turning the Tide

Until American forces arrived, the fighting along the trench lines in the Western Front continued without lasting gains for either side. In April 1917 a French offensive stalled, leading to losses so great that French forces mutinied. The British, in order to keep the Germans from taking advantage of French weakness, launched an offensive into Flanders, a coastal region of northern France and southwestern Belgium. Heavy rains, however, made the clay soil of Flanders an impassable expanse of mud. In November, the fighting finally came to an end at Passchendaele (PAH•shehn•dayl). Casualties were so enormous that both the British and the Germans were reaching the end of their reserves.

Total War

By 1917, the pressures of war had brought notable changes to the societies of fighting countries. The demands of a large-scale mechanized war required the efficient use of human and natural resources. Governments therefore carried out the principle of total war, directing all people and resources to the war effort. Greatly increasing their powers, governments on both sides recruited, drafted, trained, and supplied large armies. They raised taxes and borrowed vast sums of money. They also placed controls on capitalist economies, setting prices and wages, rationing goods, and banning strikes. Even in democratic countries, censorship of the press and other media was imposed in an effort to control public opinion and to keep morale high.

Women also played an important role in the war effort. As millions of men went to the battlefields, many women took their places in factories making weapons and supplies. Other women became military nurses or joined special branches of the armed forces. War work proved the abilities of women in areas once limited to men. Although women had to leave many jobs after the war, their contributions had boosted their self-confidence and in the long term aided the ongoing struggle for women's rights. By war's end, many countries were ready to grant the vote to women.

Global War

World War I reached beyond Europe to other parts of the world. European imperialist nations obtained badly needed resources from their empires. They also turned to recruits from their overseas possessions to fight on the Western Front. Meanwhile, in parts of Asia and Africa, Allied forces, including those of Japan, won victories that enabled them to take control of German colonies.

For their services, colonial Asians and Africans expected citizenship or independence at war's end; however, they were often disappointed when European empires were not only preserved but often extended at their expense. In the Middle East, the Arabs, seeking freedom from Ottoman rule, backed the Allied cause. While the war on the Western Front was deadlocked, they helped the British advance in the Middle East and finally conquer the Ottoman Turks. For example, Arab guerilla fighters, led by **T.E. Lawrence**, a young British officer, harassed the Ottoman Turks and gave the British information about important Turkish military positions. Unknown to the Arabs, however, the British and the French had in the 1916 Sykes-Picot Agreement already determined to divide the defeated Ottoman Empire among themselves.

End of Fighting

In July 1918 an Allied breakthrough on the Western Front finally came. Under the unified command of French General **Ferdinand Foch** (FAWSH), Allied forces stopped a huge German offensive that had moved them back to within 40 miles (60 km) of

Visualizing History More than 2 million American soldiers made up of 42 infantry divisions served in France before the war ended in 1918. *How did the arrival of American troops affect the war's outcome?*

Paris. Aided by the arrival of American forces, the Allies then launched a counterattack that pushed the exhausted Germans back to the border of Germany. In September, German generals told Kaiser Wilhelm II that the war could not be won.

The collapse of other Central Powers followed. The Ottoman Turks asked for peace after an Allied drive through the Balkans, and the Austro-Hungarians surrendered following their defeat by the Italians at Vittorio Veneto in northern Italy. The Austro-Hungarian military collapse led to the revolt of the empire's many nationalities and the end of the Hapsburg monarchy.

Although the German army stood firm, morale in Germany gave way. On November 9, 1918, the kaiser abdicated, and a German republic was proclaimed. On November 11, the Germans signed an armistice, or agreement to end the fighting.

Effects of the War

The war shattered Europe's aristocratic order and increased political and social instability. Boundaries had to be redrawn in various parts of the world. Human misery also had become commonplace. Nearly 9 million soldiers were dead, and another 21 million of them were wounded.

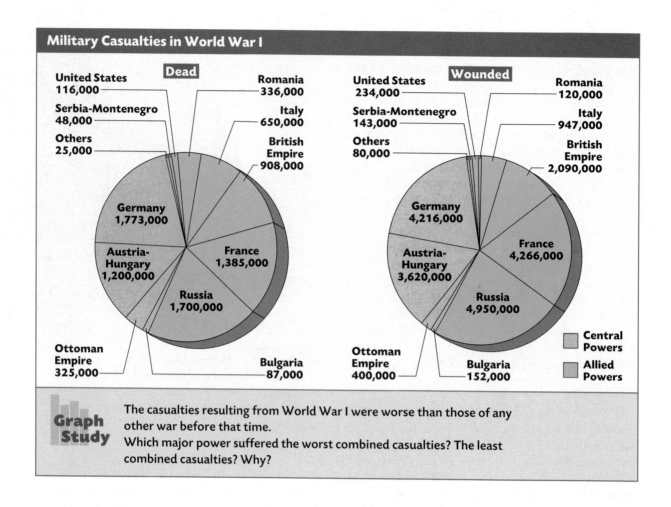

Military Casualties in World War I

Dead

United States 116,000
Serbia-Montenegro 48,000
Others 25,000
Germany 1,773,000
Austria-Hungary 1,200,000
Russia 1,700,000
Ottoman Empire 325,000
Romania 336,000
Italy 650,000
British Empire 908,000
France 1,385,000
Bulgaria 87,000

Wounded

United States 234,000
Serbia-Montenegro 143,000
Others 80,000
Germany 4,216,000
Austria-Hungary 3,620,000
Russia 4,950,000
Ottoman Empire 400,000
Romania 120,000
Italy 947,000
British Empire 2,090,000
France 4,266,000
Bulgaria 152,000

Central Powers
Allied Powers

Graph Study

The casualties resulting from World War I were worse than those of any other war before that time.
Which major power suffered the worst combined casualties? The least combined casualties? Why?

In addition, about 13 million civilians were dead of disease and starvation. Mass deaths or killings on a grand scale, such as those of the Armenians under the rule of the Ottoman Turks in 1915, added to the list of horrors.

Angry at Armenian support for the Allies and fearful of Armenian nationalism, the Turkish government decided to use the war as an excuse to end the long history of animosity between Turks and Armenians. The Turkish army first removed all Armenian soldiers from its ranks and deported them to labor camps. Then they rounded up Armenian civilians, roped them together, and drove them into the desert to starve. In other cases they destroyed whole Armenian villages and shot the inhabitants. Some historians have estimated that more than 1 million Armenians lost their lives in this slaughter.

Restoring the Peace

The hopes of many Europeans and North Americans focused on United States President **Woodrow Wilson**. Even before the war ended,

Wilson had put forth his Fourteen Points, a peace plan whose terms included international recognition of freedom of the seas and of trade, limitations on arms, and an end to all secret alliances. Wilson's plan also called for just settlements of colonial claims, the right of self-rule for all nations, and the establishment of a "general assembly of nations" to settle future problems peacefully. It was these points that Germany thought would be the basis of peace negotiations.

For the most part, everyone seemed to agree that Wilson's points should be the guiding framework for the peace settlement. There were only two major reservations—one was Great Britain's. Control of the seas had been a major British war aim vital to British interests. Great Britain depended on foreign trade for its survival and still ruled a vast overseas empire. The British, therefore, objected to the idea of open seas. The other reservation was held by France. Wilson had stated that there should be "no annexations, no contributions, and no punitive damages" as a result of the war. France believed that some statement demanding reparations, or payments for damages, should be included in any peace settlement.

The Paris Peace Conference

In January 1919, delegates from 27 nations gathered in Paris to work out 5 separate peace treaties known as the Peace of Paris. The Allies did not invite representatives from the defeated Central Powers or Russia. In a break with tradition, heads of state attended the conference. President Wilson represented the United States; Prime Minister **Georges Clemenceau** (KLEH•muhn•SOH), France; Prime Minister **David Lloyd George**, Britain; and Prime Minister **Vittorio Orlando**, Italy. Most of the decisions were made by these "Big Four."

It soon became clear that there was a large gap between the idealistic goals of Wilson and the nationalistic goals of the French, British, and Italian leaders. Lloyd George and Clemenceau wanted to make Germany pay for the war. Wilson's chief aim was to win support for his idea of an international assembly of nations. The League of Nations, as Wilson called it, became a bargaining point. Again and again, Wilson gave in on other issues to ensure the acceptance of the League of Nations.

The Treaty of Versailles

The Treaty of Versailles, the most important treaty of the Peace of Paris, spelled out the details of the Allied settlement with Germany. Lloyd George and Clemenceau prevailed in their goal to punish Germany. Militarily, the treaty reduced the German army and banned conscription and the manufacture of major war weapons.

The treaty reduced Germany in size as well. Germany had to return Alsace-Lorraine, seized in the Franco-Prussian War of 1870, to France. For a period of 15 years, France would also control the coal-rich Saar Basin, while Allied forces together would occupy the Rhineland region of Germany.

In the east, Germany had to renounce the Treaty of Brest-Litovsk. The Allies also reestablished an independent Poland out of lands held by Germany, Austria-Hungary, and Russia. So that it had access to the Baltic Sea, Poland received the Polish Corridor, a strip of land separating East Prussia from the rest of Germany.

The Treaty of Versailles stripped Germany of all of its overseas colonies as well. The Allies received all of Germany's overseas possessions as mandates, territories administered by other countries. Great Britain and France divided Germany's African colonies, Australia and New Zealand split the German Pacific islands south of the Equator, and Japan took the German Pacific islands north of the Equator.

Although these terms were harsh, France and Great Britain were still not satisfied. The Allies also demanded that Germany accept blame for causing the war and that it pay reparations for Allied war costs and damages.

The Allies signed the treaty at the Palace of Versailles on June 28, 1919. Only four of Wilson's Fourteen Points and nine supplementary principles emerged intact in the treaty. The most important of these was the Covenant of the League of Nations.

Other Settlements

The Allied Powers signed separate peace agreements with Austria, Bulgaria, Hungary, and Turkey. In them, the greatest attention was given to territorial matters. The Allies recognized the breakup of Austria-Hungary. Austria was left a small, economically weak country. Italy received from Austria German-speaking areas near the Brenner Pass in the Alps. Italy also wanted the port of **Fiume** on the Adriatic, but Wilson refused to agree.

New nations emerged in eastern Europe from the ashes of the old German, Russian, and Austro-Hungarian empires. These included Finland, Estonia, Latvia, Lithuania, Poland, Czechoslovakia, and Yugoslavia. The Allies, particularly France, regarded these countries as a cordon sanitaire (kawr•DOHN sah•nee•TEHR), or quarantine line, that would serve as a buffer against any potential threat from Russia or Germany. In creating Yugoslavia, the Serbs achieved their goal of forming a nation of South Slavic peoples. Hungary lost territory to Yugoslavia, Czechoslovakia, and Romania, while Bulgaria lost land to Yugoslavia, Greece, and Romania.

In the Middle East, the Allies divided what was left of the Ottoman Empire. The Arabs did not receive the independence that Great Britain had promised them. Instead, Palestine, Transjordan, and Iraq became British mandates. At the same time, Lebanon and Syria became French mandates.

Bitter Fruits

A general disillusionment set in after World War I. Slogans such as "the war to end all wars" and "to make the world safe for democracy" rang hollow after years of slaughter. In addition to killing millions of people, the war destroyed the homes and lives of millions more. Many people suddenly found themselves to be minorities within newly formed nations. Others who believed they would become the citizens of independent nations found their hopes dashed by the settlements. Those whose lands were defeated were embittered by the loss of territory and prestige.

Territories lost
- by Russia
- by Austria-Hungary
- by Bulgaria
- by Germany

FINLAND

NORWAY SWEDEN

ESTONIA

LATVIA

DENMARK LITHUANIA

IRELAND

EAST
PRUSSIA
(Germany)

SOVIET
RUSSIA

GREAT
BRITAIN NETHERLANDS

POLAND

ATLANTIC
OCEAN

BELGIUM GERMANY

LUXEMBOURG CZECHOSLOVAKIA

FRANCE SWITZER- AUSTRIA
LAND HUNGARY ROMANIA

Black Sea

YUGOSLAVIA

PORTUGAL ITALY BULGARIA

SPAIN ALBANIA

GREECE TURKEY

Mediterranean Sea

0   200   400 mi.
0   200   400 km
Lambert Conic Conformal Projection

North
Sea

Baltic Sea

Adriatic Sea

Map Study The map of Europe changed considerably after World War I. Some nations disappeared, while other nations emerged.
Region Which major power lost the most territory as a result of the war?

The Germans felt an especially deep sense of resentment about their loss in World War I. Because they had fought mostly on foreign territory and used resources from other countries to supplement their own, German economic strength remained largely intact. The harsh provisions of the Treaty of Versailles, however, left Germany weakened and humiliated as well as deprived of great-power status. This made reconciliation with the Allies very difficult. The Germans' festering resentment burst forth upon the world with an even greater violence two decades later in the form of Nazism.

SECTION 5 REVIEW

Recall
1. **Define** convoy, armistice, reparation, mandate, cordon sanitaire.
2. **Identify** T. E. Lawrence, Ferdinand Foch, Woodrow Wilson, the Fourteen Points, Georges Clemenceau, David Lloyd George, Vittorio Orlando.

3. **Discuss** the effect of Ottoman Turkish policies on the Armenian population.

Critical Thinking
4. **Analyzing Information** How do you think a German citizen in 1919 would have felt about the provisions of the Treaty of Versailles?

Understanding Themes
5. **Internationalism** Explain some of the problems created by the Treaty of Versailles. How did this treaty lay the foundation for another international conflict? How could it have been written to prevent this?

Interpreting Military Movements on Maps

Although wars begin over many different issues, they all end up as fights to control territory. Because wars are basically fought over land, maps are particularly good tools for seeing the "big picture" of a war.

Learning the Skill

The map key is essential in interpreting military maps. The key explains what the map's colors and symbols represent. Use the following steps to study the key:

- Determine what color scheme appears on the map. Usually, colors represent different sides in the conflict.
- Identify all symbols. These may include symbols for battle sites, victories, types of military units and equipment, fortifications, and so on.
- Study the arrows, which show the direction of military movements. Because these movements occur over periods of time, some maps give dates showing when and where the troops advanced and retreated.

Once you have carefully studied the key and the map, try to follow the progress of the battle or campaign that is shown. Notice where each side began, in which direction it moved, where the two sides met and fought, and which side claimed victory.

Practicing the Skill

The map on this page shows the Middle East front during World War I. Study the map and then answer the following questions.

1. On which side did Arabia and Egypt fight?
2. Which side won the crucial battle of the Dardanelles?
3. Describe the movement of the Central Powers offensive.
4. When did the Allied Powers win the most battles in the Middle East?

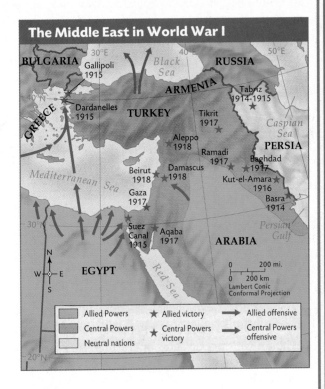

The Middle East in World War I

Applying the Skill

Choose one of the maps (showing the Western Front and the Eastern Front of World War I) on page 745. Study your map selection carefully. Then write a paragraph answering the following questions.

1. Where did most of the fighting occur?
2. Which side made the most significant advance in 1914?
3. How did each side progress on this front as the war continued?
4. Did either side win a decisive victory on this front?

For More Practice

Turn to the Skill Practice in the Chapter Review on page 767 for more practice in interpreting military movements on maps.

Connections Across Time

Historical Significance World War I brought weapons of mass destruction. The resulting slaughter on the battlefields destroyed the image of war as a heroic undertaking.

Many people also became disillusioned about the war's aftermath. World War I swept away the old order in Europe and redrew the map of the continent. It caused widespread economic suffering and ended in a controversial peace settlement that sowed the seeds for another, even more destructive, war. After World War I, Europe's global power began to ebb.

Using Key Terms

Write the key term that completes each sentence. Then write a sentence for each term not chosen.

a. armistice
b. contraband
c. convoy
d. entente
e. propaganda
f. mobilization
g. trenches
h. alliance system
i. provisional government
j. reparations
k. communism
l. ultimatum

1. After Czar Nicholas's abdication, political authority in Russia passed into the hands of a _____.
2. In 1904, Great Britain and France signed an _____ that settled key colonial disputes.
3. The British stopped ships on the high seas that they suspected carried _____ , or prohibited goods.
4. The Bolsheviks founded an international revolutionary movement based on _____ , the political viewpoint stemming from the ideas of Marx and Lenin.
5. Warring countries issued general orders for _____ , the gathering and transport of military troops and fighting equipment.

Technology Activity

Using E-mail Use your local library or access the Internet to locate an E-mail address for an organization that deals with World War I. Compose a letter requesting information about World War I submarine warfare. Using your response, create a bulletin board of the history of the American submarine during the Great War. Provide pictures and captions showing different types of submarines.

Using Your History Journal

Take the role of a parent and answer the letter you wrote as a first-person account of the war. Include words of encouragement and try to explain the significance of the war effort.

Reviewing Facts

1. **History** State the significance of the following dates: 1914, 1917, and 1918.
2. **History** Explain how Germany's war strategy changed after the Battle of the Marne.
3. **History** State how many soldiers were killed or wounded in World War I. How many civilians died of disease or starvation?
4. **Culture** Explain the social changes promised by the Bolshevik slogans.
5. **History** List five of the Fourteen Points that United States President Woodrow Wilson presented at the Paris peace conference in 1919.
6. **Culture** State the role and contributions of women during World War I. What was their standing in society after the war?

Critical Thinking

1. **Evaluate** How did Lenin's beliefs and goals differ from those of Wilson? Which leader has had the greater impact on world history?
2. **Apply** How did sea power have a major effect on the outcome of World War I?
3. **Analyze** How were technological advances in weaponry most responsible for the military stalemate during much of World War I?

Understanding Themes

1. **Cooperation** Why do you think Great Britain, France, and Russia put aside their differences to form the Triple Entente?
2. **Conflict** Name a war goal for each of these countries: Serbia, Austria-Hungary, Russia, and France. Discuss a situation today where a conflict over national goals might lead to war.
3. **Conflict** What were the causes of World War I? What key events affected its outcome? How did World War I affect global affairs?
4. **Revolution** Name the main causes of the Russian Revolution of 1917. How did the Russian Revolution differ from the American Revolution in its causes and global impact?
5. **Internationalism** Do you think the peace settlement after World War I promoted the success of the League of Nations? Explain.

Skill Practice

Study the map "Russian Civil War 1918–1922" and answer the questions that follow.

1. From which direction did the Allied forces invade Russia?

2. Where did Denikin's forces begin and in what direction did they move?
3. Why do you think Kolchak chose his route to Moscow?
4. Which military group advanced on Russian territory from an area near Poland?

Geography in History

1. **Place** Refer to the map below. What five European nations had built up the largest standing armies during World War I?
2. **Location** How do you think Germany's location affected its military strategy?
3. **Movement** When war broke out, which side had the more challenging task of moving troops and materials, the Allies or the Central Powers? Why?

Russian Civil War 1918–1922

GERMANY · NORWAY · SWEDEN · ARCTIC OCEAN · FINLAND · Murmansk · POLAND · Petrograd · Archangel · ROMANIA · Kiev · Moscow · Orel · Odessa · Kazan · SIBERIA · Crimea · Rostov · Tsaritsyn · Omsk · Tomsk · Krasnoyarsk · TURKEY · Aral Sea · IRAQ · Don River · Volga River · Black Sea · Caspian Sea

Soviet territory
Denikin forces
Yudenitch forces
Kolchak forces
Allied forces
Trans-Siberian Railroad

0   500   1,000 mi.
0   500   1,000 km
Lambert Equal-Area Projection

Mobilized Forces During World War I

GREAT BRITAIN 9,500,000 · NORWAY · SWEDEN · DENMARK · RUSSIAN EMPIRE 13,000,000 · GERMANY 13,250,000 · HOLLAND · BELGIUM 380,000 · LUXEMBOURG · AUSTRIA-HUNGARY 9,000,000 · FRANCE 8,200,000 · SWITZERLAND · ROMANIA 1,000,000 · ITALY 5,600,000 · SERBIA 1,000,000 · PORTUGAL 100,000 · MONTENEGRO 50,000 · BULGARIA 950,000 · SPAIN · ALBANIA · OTTOMAN EMPIRE 2,850,000 · GREECE 200,000

Central Powers
Allied Powers
Neutral nations
Neutral nations who later joined the Central Powers
Neutral nations who later joined the Allied Powers

2 million troops

Linking Past and Present

1. How do conflicts in the Balkans before World War I compare with those in the region today?
2. The ideal of self-determination was not granted to European colonies after World War I. Where do struggles for self-determination continue today? How are they faring?

Between Two Fires

Chapter Themes

▶ **Innovation** The period after World War I brings revolutionary changes in science, the arts, and popular culture. *Section 1*

▶ **Change** The Great Depression forces governments in Europe and North America to increase their involvement in social and economic affairs. *Section 2*

▶ **Uniformity** Fascist governments in Italy and Germany limit individual liberties and stress loyalty to the state. *Section 3*

▶ **Uniformity** Communist leaders in the Soviet Union impose state control on society and crush opposition. *Section 4*

The Storyteller

From early evening until long past midnight, Nazi stormtroopers and youth groups marched in disciplined columns through Berlin. For many of the young people in that torchlight parade in the 1930s, their marching was only a beginning. They looked forward to a bright future, playing important roles in creating a new Germany out of the confusion and trouble that surrounded them. To them, Hitler seemed like a deliverer who would restore Germany's greatness.

Years later, a number of them looked back on that night, appalled at how little they really knew about the Nazis. But the economic and political chaos caused by World War I and the Great Depression led many Europeans to support powerful dictators during the 1920s and 1930s.

Historical Significance

What factors led to the rise of dictatorships in Europe after World War I? How were democratic nations affected by the social and economic crises that came after the end of World War I?

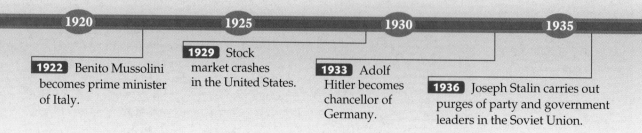

1920   **1925**   **1930**   **1935**

1922 Benito Mussolini becomes prime minister of Italy.

1929 Stock market crashes in the United States.

1933 Adolf Hitler becomes chancellor of Germany.

1936 Joseph Stalin carries out purges of party and government leaders in the Soviet Union.

Automat, Edward Hopper, 1927. Des Moines Art Center Permanent Collection, Des Moines, Iowa

Your History Journal

Interview an older person about his or her feelings and perceptions in the period between 1930 and 1941. Use the chapter to formulate questions about events. Take notes during the interview, or write down your impressions soon afterward.

Section 1

The Postwar World

Setting the Scene

▶ **Terms to Define**
cubism, surrealism, jazz, choreographer

▶ **People to Meet**
Albert Einstein, Sigmund Freud, T.S. Eliot, Pablo Picasso, Sergey Prokofiev, Walter Gropius

▶ **Places to Locate**
Hollywood

**ind Out** What trends dominated the arts and popular culture from 1919 to 1939?

The Storyteller

There was trouble in Hollywood. One of Tinseltown's biggest names, with a bigger screen following than 90 percent of the stars, according to columnist Louella Parsons, had "fallen afoul of the censors in a big way." Censor boards throughout the nation were receiving vigorous complaints about the "devilish, naughty" behavior of this national celebrity. Terry Ramsaye wrote in the Motion Picture Herald, "It's the old, old story. If nobody knows you, you can do anything, and if everybody knows you, you can't do anything—except what everyone approves." The star was Mickey Mouse.

Hollywood landmark

—adapted from *Of Mice and Magic*, Leonard Maltin, 1987

"A RMISTICE SIGNED, END OF THE WAR!" proclaimed *The New York Times* headline on November 11, 1918. In the United States and Europe, people exploded in a frenzy of celebration. The critic and author Malcolm Cowley wrote later of the feeling of euphoria that marked the end of the war: "We danced in the streets, embraced old women and pretty girls, swore blood brotherhood with soldiers in little bars...." But the excitement did not last. "On the next day," continued Cowley, "...we didn't know what to do."

World War I marked the great divide between the old and the new. The war changed the way many people looked at the world, and the disillusionment it caused led artists and intellectuals on a restless search for something new. The postwar period was a time for breaking with tradition and experimenting with new styles in politics and culture.

Changing Patterns of Life

Warren Harding was elected President of the United States in 1920, promising a "return to normalcy." But there was no going back to the past. The war had changed the world too much for that to be possible. Instead, people in both North America and Europe began to experiment with new customs and ways of life.

New Trends in Culture and Style

In the postwar era, women gained a new level of independence. With the ratification of the Nineteenth Amendment in 1920, women in the United States won the right to vote at last. Women also won the vote in most other Western countries following the war.

Many women now demanded other freedoms as well. Throwing off the inhibitions of the prewar era, some women in the United States and western

Europe began to use rouge and lipstick openly. Their skirts rose from a few inches above the ankle to an inch above the knee. They cropped their hair to a shingle bob and aimed for a carefree, little-boy look. Thus attired, the "flapper" created a revolution in manners and morals.

In the postwar era, not only the flapper but people in general disdained the familiar and the commonplace. They wanted heroes who were larger than life. Babe Ruth, the "Sultan of Swat," was the king of baseball. Tennis champions Big Bill Tilden and Helen Wills Moody became national heroes. When Gertrude Ederle swam the English Channel and Charles Lindbergh flew nonstop from Long Island to Paris, the public saluted them with tumultuous ticker-tape parades on Broadway.

Amid all the hoopla, bankers and business leaders were having a heyday. The war had opened new prospects for economic development. President Calvin Coolidge neatly summed up the nation's focus in the 1920s when he said, "The business of America is business."

The Impact of Technology

New forms of technology altered people's lifestyles and brought people closer together in the 1920s. The decade following World War I witnessed a revolution in transportation and communication throughout the world.

The automobile had perhaps the greatest impact on European and American society. A network of highways began to crisscross Europe and the United States. People could now move easily from place to place, and move they did. The United States, in particular, became an increasingly mobile society. Americans traveled farther afield on vacations and moved from rural areas to cities.

Radio also brought about dramatic changes. By exposing millions of people to the same news and entertainment shows, radio helped to produce a more homogeneous, or uniform, culture. Through its advertisements, radio also stimulated the public's desire for consumer goods. Advertisers learned the art of motivation, and ads now played on people's insecurities and self-doubts. "Why had he changed so in his attentions?" queried a forlorn-looking woman in an ad for a leading mouthwash.

Many products of the new technology eased the burden of the homemaker. With the advent of packaged foods, refrigerators, vacuum cleaners, and electric irons, people had more leisure time. Instead of working at home, they could take a drive, listen to the radio, or go out dancing. Millions spent their idle moments with another new product of technology: the movies.

A Revolution in Ideas

New inventions had an enormous impact on people's daily lives in the postwar period. At the same time, exciting new ideas in physics and psychology transformed the way people looked at themselves and the world.

Physics

In 1905 German physicist **Albert Einstein** introduced his theories of relativity, shattering Newton's view of the universe as a machine that operated by universal laws. According to Einstein, there are no absolutes in measuring time and space. Time and space instead depend on the relative motion of bodies in space. For example, the speed of two trains appears differently to bystanders on the station platform than it does to passengers on the trains.

Einstein also held that the speed of light is constant, and that all matter has energy. If matter could be broken down and changed into energy, the amount of energy would be enormous. Einstein's formula $E=MC^2$ was finally supported in 1945 when scientists tested the first atomic bomb in New Mexico.

Although too difficult for the average person to understand, Einstein's views had an impact beyond physics. To many people, his views seemed to reinforce the idea that there were no absolutes in any field of knowledge or in moral values.

Psychology

The Austrian physician **Sigmund Freud** (FROYD) revolutionized people's ideas about how the human mind works. After observing many patients, Freud concluded that the unconscious mind plays a major role in shaping behavior. The unconscious, he said, is full of memories of events from early childhood. If the memories are especially painful, people sometimes suppress them. Such suppression may lead to a variety of mental disorders.

When Freud first introduced his theories in the late 1800s, many people ridiculed or attacked them. By the 1920s, however, his ideas about human

Footnotes to History

Fads
The 1920s was a time when many fads swept the United States. These ranged from crossword puzzles, to stunts, such as sitting on the top of flagpoles for days at a time, to parlor games, such as mah-jongg, a Chinese version of rummy played with tiles.

Gertrude Stein by Pablo Picasso, 1906. The Metropolitan Museum of Art, New York, New York **The Spanish painter Pablo Picasso and the American writer Gertrude Stein were two of the major cultural figures of the 1920s and 1930s.** *What were two major characteristics of the arts during the period between the world wars?*

psychology had become more accepted and influential. Freud's theories eventually led to new approaches in the treatment of mental illness, in child rearing, and in education.

Upheaval in the Arts

The break between old and new following World War I was perhaps most sharply defined in the arts. In painting, music, literature, and dance, artists abandoned long-accepted traditions. The avant-garde experimented with new styles, media, and subject matter. Often the public greeted their pioneering efforts with cries of shock and protest.

Literature

Many of the period's writers had been disillusioned by World War I and its aftermath. The war had destroyed their belief in the traditional values of middle-class society. In expressing that disillusionment, they broke new literary ground.

In his poems *The Waste Land* and "The Hollow Men," for example, American-born poet **T.S. Eliot** used a patchwork style that juxtaposed different literary, religious, and historical references to convey a sense of despair about life. German novelist Thomas Mann, Czech novelist Franz Kafka, and British novelist Virginia Woolf also experimented

with new literary techniques. Both in terms of their style and content, all of these writers represented a sharp break with the literature of the past.

While they echoed Eliot's sense of disenchantment, American writers such as Ernest Hemingway and F. Scott Fitzgerald developed markedly different literary styles. For instance, in his 1926 novel *The Sun Also Rises*, Hemingway used a lean, straightforward style to tell the tale of Americans and Britons who roamed France and Spain, living for the moment while trying to find meaning in their lives. In contrast, Fitzgerald used a more elaborate poetic style in his 1925 novel *The Great Gatsby* to explore the atmosphere and excesses of the Roaring Twenties.

Several years earlier, in 1922, Irish novelist James Joyce had published *Ulysses*, an in-depth account of a day in the lives of three ordinary people in Dublin. *Ulysses* was a landmark in the development of the modern novel. Influenced by Freud's theories, Joyce developed a style known as "stream of consciousness" in which he presented the inner thoughts—rather than just the external actions—of his characters. Joyce's psychological emphasis and his earthy language caused a storm of protest, which led to a number of court battles over the publication of his novel.

In the late 1920s and the 1930s, many writers became interested in important social issues of the day. Langston Hughes, Claude McKay, and Zora Neale Hurston, who belonged to an African American literary movement known as the Harlem Renaissance, explored the African American experience in America. In *The Grapes of Wrath*, John Steinbeck described the plight of Oklahoma farmers who, in the midst of a severe drought, abandoned their farms and moved to California. John Dos Passos's *U.S.A.* trilogy was a broader social criticism of conditions in American society during the postwar period.

Painting

The postwar world also saw a revolution in the visual arts. Artists no longer tried to be realistic in their works. Instead they developed radical new styles and redefined the nature of painting. In 1907, the Spanish painter **Pablo Picasso** created an uproar in the art world when he painted *Les Demoiselles d'Avignon*. The painting was the earliest example of cubism, an abstract art form that uses intersecting geometric shapes. Cubist painters transform their subjects by flattening them, cutting them up, rearranging different portions of them, and altering shapes and colors to fit their own vision. As Picasso explained: "Art is a lie that makes us realize the truth."

Another development was Dada, an art form that aimed to shock middle-class viewers. Dada stressed absurdity and the role of the unpredictable in life. For example, the paintings and poems of Dada consisted of meaningless and random arrangements of objects and words. Dada's reliance on the imagination led to surrealism, an art form that used dreamlike images and unnatural combinations of objects. Influenced by Freud, surrealist painters tried to find a new reality by exploring the unconscious mind. The Spanish painter Salvador Dali created such realistically impossible images as limp watches set in bleak landscapes.

In the tradition of Steinbeck and Dos Passos, other artists used their talents to attack social problems. In their paintings and photographs, social realists such as Ben Shahn, Peter Blume, and Dorothea Lange showed the human suffering caused by the Depression of the 1930s. Although not a realist, Pablo Picasso protested the horrors of Spain's civil war in his symbolic painting *Guernica*.

Music and Dance

Composers also broke new ground after the war. Several eastern European composers transformed the classical form. **Sergey Prokofiev**

(sehr•GAY pruh•KAWF•yuhf), a Russian, composed driving and dissonant music that lacked the familiar harmonies of traditional forms. Critics dubbed him the "age of steel composer." Prokofiev, however, later composed more pleasant sounding symphonies and operas.

Arnold Schoenberg (SHUHN•BUHRG), a self-taught Austrian composer, made radical changes in music theory. Instead of harmonies based on the traditional eight-note scale, he proposed new musical arrangements based on 12 equally valued notes. In his groundbreaking composition, *Pierrot Lunaire* (1912), Schoenberg used harsh, dissonant music to express what he regarded as the decay of Western civilization. His composition outraged conservative audiences.

Meanwhile, in the United States, musicians were creating their own distinctive sound. The 1920s was "the golden age of jazz." What some have called the only art form to originate in the United States, jazz is a mixture of American folk songs, West African rhythms, harmonies from European classical music, and work songs from the days of slavery. Trumpet player Louis Armstrong, blues singer Bessie Smith, and pianist Jelly Roll Morton popularized the new music which soon spread throughout the world.

The postwar era also saw a transformation in the art of dance. Performing barefoot in a loose tunic, the American dancer Isadora Duncan changed people's ideas about dance. Another American, Martha Graham, expanded on Duncan's style and turned modern dance into a striking new art form.

Visualizing History Pablo Picasso's mural painting *Guernica* expresses the horror of the bombing of the town of Guernica during the civil war that devastated Spain in the 1930s. *What changes developed in the visual arts after World War I?*

Brown Brothers

Flying High

Racing down a dark road, the young men and women in this photograph enjoy a new freedom. Cars were important throughout the industrialized world of Europe and North America, and the American auto industry led the global market. The automobile brought mobility to many Americans during the years following World War I. It was all part of a new lifestyle called the Roaring Twenties.

Behind the gaiety and frivolity, however, the 1920s was a decade in which a new urban style of living came into conflict with an older rural way of life. In the United States this conflict was played out again and again: Politician and orator William Jennings Bryan battled lawyer Clarence Darrow in the famous Scopes trial over whether or not public schools should teach Darwinian science. Farms failed and farmers lost their land, while the sounds of the new prosperity played on radios in their living rooms. The new city slickers were jazz age flappers, like the ones here, racing along unpaved roads in a fancy new Stutz Bearcat. ⊕

Sergey Diaghilev (dee•AH•guh•LEHF), the Russian impresario, or sponsor, developed modern ballet, which blended modern dance with classical ballet. When Russian composer Igor Stravinsky wrote *The Rite of Spring* (1913) for Diaghilev and his company of dancers, the Ballets Russes, it was a turning point for ballet. The leaping dance steps that ballet star Vaslav Nijinsky (VAHT•slahv nuh •ZHIHN•skee) performed to Stravinsky's music created a sensation. George Balanchine, who had been a choreographer, or dance arranger, with the Ballets Russes, expanded on Diaghilev's work after moving from the Soviet Union to the United States.

Architecture

The 1920s and 1930s saw striking new designs in buildings and furnishings. **Walter Gropius** founded the Bauhaus (BOW•HOWS) school of design in Weimar (VY•MAHR), Germany. He and his followers created a simple, unornamented style of design. Linking beauty to practicality, Gropius pioneered geometric concrete and glass structures in both Germany and the United States.

In the United States, Frank Lloyd Wright blended his structures with their natural surroundings. Because of their low horizontal form, his houses seem to grow out of the ground. Instead of creating boxlike rooms, Wright reduced the number of walls so that one room flowed into another.

Popular Culture

While the revolutionary developments taking place in art and music may not have had an immediate effect on the lives of ordinary people, films and big bands did. In the postwar era, **Hollywood** productions dominated the movie screens of the world. The movies reflected the new morality of the "Jazz Age" and the doctrine of living for the moment. During the 1930s the public flocked to movie theaters, where for 10 cents they could escape the harsh realities of hard economic times.

In the early part of the century, the creative use of the camera elevated the motion picture to an art form. In *The Last Laugh*, a silent film directed by German filmmaker F.W. Murnau, the camera work is so expressive that the story is told entirely without subtitles. British actor and director Charlie Chaplin also broke new ground in his films while delighting millions of moviegoers with his humor.

But in 1927 motion pictures found their voice. *The Jazz Singer*, starring American actor Al Jolson, changed motion pictures overnight and signaled the beginning of the end of the era of silent films. During the early 1930s American musicals, gangster movies, and horror movies were popular. However, some filmmakers tried to educate as well as entertain their audiences. *I Am a Fugitive From a Chain Gang* (1932) was a forceful indictment of the Southern penal system, while *Mr. Smith Goes to Washington* (1939) showed the effects of political corruption.

The public also sought escape from their troubles on the ballroom floor. In the 1930s and 1940s, dance bands reached their greatest popularity. Tommy Dorsey, Count Basie, Benny Goodman, Duke Ellington, Artie Shaw, and their swing bands performed in ballrooms and hotels all across America. Swing was the new word for music played with a happy, relaxed jazz beat. But if swing was not everyone's cup of tea, there were alternatives. The bands of Guy Lombardo and Sammy Kaye played traditional waltzes and fox-trots.

Obviously, the social upheavals and economic hardships that World War I created did not dampen the creative spirit following the war. During this era artists introduced new styles in every major art form. They took little interest in politics and reform. Many cried out against conformity and retreated into individualism. At times it seemed as if they were transforming the world with their radical new visions of life. But the euphoria did not last. The stock market crash that took place on Wall Street in late October 1929 signaled for the United States and much of the world an economic depression that had devastating and deadly consequences.

SECTION 1 REVIEW

Recall
1. **Define** cubism, surrealism, jazz, choreographer.
2. **Identify** Albert Einstein, Sigmund Freud, T.S. Eliot, Pablo Picasso, Sergey Prokofiev, Walter Gropius.
3. **Explain** how women shaped many of the changes that came to Western societies after World War I.

Critical Thinking
4. **Analyzing Information** The era after World War I was a time for breaking with tradition. How could abandoning traditions help a society? How might it harm a society?

Understanding Themes
5. **Innovation** What impact did technological advances in transportation and communication have on American culture in the 1920s?

Section 2

The Western Democracies

Setting the Scene

▶ **Terms to Define**
disarmament, general strike, coalition

▶ **People to Meet**
Franklin D. Roosevelt, Ramsay MacDonald, Eamon De Valera, Léon Blum

▶ **Places to Locate**
Washington, D.C., Irish Free State

ind Out Why did democratic government survive in the United States, Great Britain, and France during the post-World War I era?

The Storyteller

Throughout 1932 the lines had grown. They formed at banks, as investors tried to withdraw their savings before the bank collapsed. They formed at factory gates and employment offices. Men lost their jobs, lost their homes. They swallowed their pride and formed another line—for relief. If there was none to be found, another line waited. As one eyewitness reported, "We saw a crowd of some 50 men fighting over a barrel of garbage which had been set outside the back door of a restaurant."

Depression-era food line

—adapted from *Since Yesterday,* Frederick Lewis Allen, 1939

Peace brought neither stability nor lasting prosperity to the Western democracies, which paid a heavy price for their victory in World War I. Although the United States suffered comparatively minor financial losses, huge war debts threatened the economic and political stability of Great Britain and France. The West did enjoy a brief period of prosperity in the 1920s, but a global economic depression soon followed. This depression further weakened the Western democracies in the 1930s, making it difficult for them to counter the rising totalitarian threat in Italy and Germany.

The United States

The United States emerged from World War I in better shape than its allies. No battles were fought on American soil, and because of its late entry into the conflict, America suffered far fewer casualties than the other nations. Moreover, unlike the economies of many European countries, the American economy remained strong until 1929.

Cutting Foreign Ties

President Woodrow Wilson wanted the United States to assume a greater role in world affairs following the war. Americans, however, were weary of war and of the foreign entanglements that had dragged the nation into war. They wanted to return to a life of isolation, free from international problems.

An idealistic man, Wilson had seized on the notion of a League of Nations as the cornerstone of a lasting peace. But the newly elected Republican majorities in Congress had no wish to accommodate the Democratic President. When Congress failed to ratify the Treaty of Versailles in 1919, it also rejected American membership in the League. The absence of the United States significantly weakened the

League's effectiveness as a strong international peacekeeping organization.

Meanwhile, many Americans feared the effects of communism on the United States. In 1919 and 1920 this "red scare" led to the expulsion of suspected foreign-born radicals. Some native-born Americans also opposed immigration from southern and eastern Europe. In response, Congress enacted limits to immigration from Europe. Earlier laws had already excluded or limited Asian immigration.

From Boom to Depression

Unlike Europe, the United States emerged from the war with a dynamic industrial economy. It was now a nation lending, instead of borrowing, money. American industries produced a major share of the world's manufactured goods, and many industrial workers earned higher wages. As a result of this prosperity, more Americans were willing to take risks. Some bought expensive goods on credit. Others entered the stock market, buying stocks on margin, that is, they paid only part of the cost and borrowed the rest from brokers.

Despite the soaring "bull market," the economy had underlying weaknesses. Most farmers faced hardships because of falling farm prices. Also, in certain industries, workers did not see their wages rise as fast as the production of goods. As a result, many people held back from buying goods that factories were rapidly turning out. This combination of slow demand and overproduction paved the way for an economic crisis.

In late October 1929, concern about the economy led brokers to call in loans. When investors were unable to pay, a financial panic began. Stock prices tumbled, wiping out the fortunes of many investors. This stock market crash sparked the Great Depression of the 1930s. In the three years after the crash, prices fell and many businesses and banks closed. Sales dropped off, forcing a production slump. Salaries and wages also fell, and many workers lost their jobs. By 1933 more than 13 million American workers were unemployed—nearly one-fourth of the nation's workforce.

Many Americans believed that direct relief for the needy was the responsibility of the individual, the family, and the local community. Government-funded relief, they held, would destroy American self-reliance and lead to socialism. However, in these desperate times, not everyone agreed.

Geography

The Dust Bowl

American farmers in the 1930s suffered greatly from the Great Depression, but their hardships also came from a devastating drought that afflicted the central United States from 1933 to 1937. As the Great Plains became powder-dry, winds lifted vital topsoil in clouds of dust that turned day into night. Dust storms had swept over the area before, but never on such a large and destructive scale.

The roots of this disaster lay well in the past. Ranchers' cattle overgrazed an area that experienced scant rainfall. The ranchers were followed by farmers, who planted wheat. These early settlers plowed land that should never have been cultivated, and they farmed it badly. They did not use contour plowing to check erosion, rotate their crops, or plant trees as windbreaks to hold the soil.

Ruined by drought, about 200,000 farm families headed West, especially to California. They found little relief in their new home—only low-paying jobs and the resentments of local residents opposed to their coming. It took many years of normal rainfall and improved farming methods to transform the Great Plains into productive land again. In addition to agriculture, the region today prospers from petroleum and coal mining.

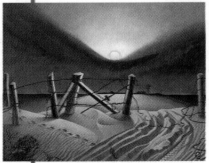

Dust Bowl scene

Linking Past and Present ACTIVITY

Describe the factors that created the Dust Bowl. What did many Dust Bowl farmers do in the 1930s? How has the region developed since that time?

During the 1920s and 1930s, economic downturns led to labor unrest in many western democracies. British workers especially carried out strikes for better wages. *What was Great Britain's economic standing after World War I?*

The New Deal

In 1932 voters elected a new President, former New York governor **Franklin D. Roosevelt.** Roosevelt had campaigned on the promise of "a new deal" for the American people. He believed that the federal government had to aid the stricken economy and provide relief for the unemployed.

In the first 100 days of his administration, in the spring and early summer of 1933, Roosevelt sent a number of bills to Congress that quickly became laws. These measures regulated the banks and stock market and established production guidelines for industry and agriculture. To put people back to work, the government established public works projects to build roads, dams, bridges, homes, and parks. Later New Deal legislation provided for social security and unemployment insurance. Although Roosevelt's New Deal policies were not entirely successful in ending the Depression, they did much to restore the confidence of the nation.

Foreign Affairs

The American government was concerned with more than just domestic affairs during the 1920s and 1930s. Despite its rejection of the League of Nations and binding alliances, the United States did take steps to prevent a future world war. In 1922 it played host in **Washington, D.C.,** to an international conference on disarmament, the reduction of military weapons. At this conference, the United States signed a treaty with Japan and Great Britain limiting the number of naval warships each could stockpile. The leading powers at the conference also agreed to seek peaceful rather than military solutions to disagreements.

In 1928 the United States and France signed the Kellogg-Briand Pact, which denounced war as a means of settling disputes. Eventually, nearly all the nations of the world signed this agreement. Unfortunately, it was nothing more than a statement of intentions and had no powers of enforcement.

Great Britain

Although World War I increased the United States's economic and political influence, it cost Great Britain its position as a leading economic power in the world. Before the war British banks lent money to nations all over the globe. But the war was costly, and Great Britain was forced to borrow heavily from the United States. As a result, Great Britain became a debtor instead of a creditor nation.

The war also cost Great Britain its privileged position in world trade. American and Japanese companies captured many British overseas markets during the war. In addition, Great Britain's factories were old and the equipment outdated. Countries like the United States and Japan, which had industrialized later, had newer factories and more modern equipment. Consequently, they could produce goods at a lower cost. Many factories in Great Britain closed or cut back production after the war. By 1921 more than 2 million workers had lost their jobs.

The General Strike

Great Britain's economic woes reached a crisis point in 1926. Coal miners were engaged in a bitter strike for higher wages that year. For months the coal companies had refused to give in to their demands. In an effort to end the stalemate, the coal miners convinced many other trade union workers to join in a general strike, a strike involving all or a large number of a nation's workers. On May 4 all transport workers, dockers, public utility employees, and workers in the building trades and heavy industry walked off their jobs. The government declared a state of emergency and called out the troops to run essential services.

In the end, the General Strike was a failure. By December 1926 the coal strike had also collapsed. In 1927 Parliament passed the Trade Disputes Act, which made general strikes illegal.

Rise of the Labour Party

Despite the failure of the General Strike, British workers gained political strength during the 1920s. During this decade the Labour party became the second leading party in the country after the Conservatives. In 1924 and again in 1929, Labour governments were elected to office. Each time, King George V named Scottish Labour leader **Ramsay MacDonald** prime minister. Because the Labour party supported Socialist policies, its rise to power alarmed the Conservatives and their wealthy supporters. However, once in power, MacDonald and other Labour leaders tempered many of their radical demands.

The Dominions and Ireland

During the 1920s and 1930s, Great Britain still held on to most of its empire. However, dominions, such as Canada and Australia, became completely independent states. In 1931 Parliament passed the Statute of Westminister, which established the

Irish nationalist leader Michael Collins, speaking here to crowds in the Irish capital of Dublin, negotiated a 1921 treaty with the British. *What changes did the treaty bring to Ireland?*

Commonwealth of Nations, a voluntary association linking Great Britain and its former colonies on an equal basis.

One of Great Britain's major problems was its relationship with Ireland. Unwilling to wait for home rule, militant Irish nationalists on Easter 1916 had revolted against the British. The brutal crushing of the Easter Uprising by British forces increased Irish support for full independence. In 1921 moderate leaders in Ireland and Great Britain signed a compromise agreement. The Catholic southern part of Ireland became a dominion known as the **Irish Free State**. The largely Protestant northern counties remained joined to Great Britain as Northern Ireland.

Wanting full independence for all of Ireland, Irish radicals, led by **Eamon De Valera**, revolted against the Irish Free State. The Irish government suppressed this uprising, but Irish elections in 1932 brought De Valera to power. Five years later, the country's name was changed to Eire, and a president replaced the British monarch as head of state.

France

World War I had an even more devastating effect on France than on Great Britain. In the four years of fighting, the combatants had destroyed thousands of square miles of farmland and forests and reduced villages and cities to rubble. French casualties were enormous. Half of the males

AROUND THE WORLD

Jordan Gains Independence

Jordan, 1921

After World War I, lands east and west of the Jordan River were administered by Great Britain. In 1921 the territory east of the Jordan gained partial self-government. This land—then called Transjordan—won full independence in 1946 as a monarchy under King Abdullah. The country was renamed Jordan after it annexed the West Bank of the Jordan River following the 1948–1949 Arab-Israeli war.

between the ages of 18 and 32 were killed in the fighting.

Troubled Years

Like Great Britain, France faced severe economic problems after the war. High unemployment and soaring inflation caused terrible hardships. The French government was nearly bankrupt, and its war debts were staggering. As a result of these financial problems, France's factories, railways, and canals could not be quickly rebuilt.

The political picture was as bleak as the economic one. Many political parties competed for votes. Since each party received seats in the national legislature according to its percentage of the vote, no party ever won a majority of seats. In order to form a government, several parties had to band together into a coalition, or alliance of factions, but the coalition governments often fell apart soon after they were formed.

Extremist groups on both the left and the right also threatened the political stability of the nation. Communists and Socialists struggled for power against Fascists, extreme nationalists favoring a strong government, and outbreaks of violence were common.

The Popular Front

In 1934 the political crisis reached a head. Fascist groups rioted in Paris, killing several people. Fearing a Fascist takeover, the Communists appealed to leaders of the Socialist party for "a broad Popular Front to combat fascism and for work, liberty, and peace."

The new coalition won enough votes in a 1936 election to form a government. **Léon Blum**, the Socialist leader, became prime minister. The Popular Front was in power for about a year, but in that short time it passed many new laws that benefited workers and farmers.

Foreign Policy

Exhausted and drained by World War I, France wanted, above all else, to prevent another war. Consequently, the French government supported the League of Nations in the postwar years and worked to create a series of alliances to contain Germany. But it also sought friendly ties with Germany's new democratic Weimar Republic. In 1925 France signed the Locarno Treaties with Germany, Italy, Belgium, and Great Britain that appeared to ensure a lasting peace.

As added insurance against a future German invasion, France built a series of fortifications that were 200 miles (320 km) long called the Maginot (MA•zhuh•NOH) Line. This stretch of concrete bunkers and trenches extended along France's border with Germany. French military leaders boasted that the Maginot Line could never be crossed. What they failed to consider was that past German invasions had come through Belgium, whose border with France remained virtually undefended.

SECTION 2 REVIEW

Recall

1. **Define** disarmament, general strike, coalition.
2. **Identify** Franklin D. Roosevelt, Ramsay MacDonald, Commonwealth of Nations, Eamon De Valera, Léon Blum.
3. **Explain** how World War I affected the economies of the United States, Great Britain, and France.

Critical Thinking

4. **Evaluating Information** Why do you think the democracies of the United States, Great Britain, and France survived despite postwar political, economic, and social problems?

Understanding Themes

5. **Change** How did President Franklin D. Roosevelt's New Deal change the role the federal government played in American society after 1933?

Section 3

Fascist Dictatorships

Setting the Scene

▶ **Terms to Define**
totalitarianism, fascism, corporate state, syndicate, *Kristallnacht*, concentration camp

▶ **People to Meet**
Benito Mussolini, Adolf Hitler

▶ **Places to Locate**
Weimar

Find Out What factors led to the rise of Fascist dictatorships in Italy and Germany?

The Storyteller

Alice Hamilton was dismayed. Twenty-five years earlier, she had spent a year in Frankfurt as a student. She now returned to visit the city only to find the lovely Römer Platz draped with Nazi flags. The city's children and young people also had changed. Formerly they played games; now they marched in regular ranks. Where tuneful songs had been sung in public houses, militant music blared forth. Mrs. Hamilton understood why this transformation had taken place. Hitler was inspiring Germany's impoverished, hopeless youth to believe they were the elect of the earth.

—adapted from "The Youth Who Are Hitler's Strength," *New York Times Magazine*, October 8, 1933. Alice Hamilton. Reprinted in *Sources of the Western Tradition*, Marvin Perry, 1991

Nazi poster

After World War I, political, economic, and social strife engulfed many Western nations. Long-established democracies remained strong in the United States and Great Britain, but in Italy, Germany, and Russia, a new form of dictatorship known as totalitarianism emerged. Totalitarian governments aimed at total control over every aspect of citizens' lives. Under totalitarianism, the individual was viewed as a servant of the state and was allowed few personal freedoms. Books, radio, films, the arts, and the schools were used to promote the government's political philosophy.

Totalitarianism grew out of World War I. To fight a total war, democratic and autocratic governments alike had temporarily assumed sweeping powers. After the war, totalitarian dictatorships extended such powers further, using their vast authority to remodel entire societies and conquer other lands. In seeking these goals, totalitarian governments came into conflict with each other and with the Western democracies. Their actions set the stage for the beginning of another world war.

Rise of Fascism in Italy

After World War I, a general mood of dissatisfaction gripped the people of Italy. Italian nationalists were outraged that the Paris peace treaties had not given Italy huge portions of territory from the Central Powers. Returning veterans found no work, workers went on strike or took over factories, and peasants seized land. Reeling from an economic downturn, the government was unable to relieve the mounting discontent.

These chaotic conditions favored the rise of **Benito Mussolini** (MOO•suh•LEE•nee). Born in 1883, Mussolini came from a working-class family. As a young journalist, he was active in Socialist politics; but during the war, he switched loyalties and became an ardent nationalist.

Italian dictator Benito Mussolini salutes soldiers at a military parade. He dreamed of making Italy a great nation and reviving the Roman Empire. *How did Mussolini come to power in Italy?*

declined steadily, the price of bread rose, and a shortage of coal hampered industrial production. To express their dissatisfaction, workers staged a series of strikes that paralyzed the country. In September 1920, workers in Lombardy and Piedmont took over the factories. Mussolini showed his support for the strikers in a speech at Trieste:

> **❝** I demand that the factories increase their production. If this is guaranteed to me by the workers in place of the industrialists, I shall declare without hesitation that the former have the right to substitute themselves … [for] the latter. **❞**

The unrest spread to rural Italy. Peasants seized land from wealthy landowners, and tenant farmers refused to pay their rents. The situation was so chaotic that the middle and upper classes feared a Communist revolution. Ever the politician, Mussolini offered "a little something to everyone." To appease the landowners, he vowed to end the unrest and protect private property. To woo the workers, he promised full employment and workers' benefits. He pleased nationalists by pledging to restore Italy to its former greatness.

By 1922 the Fascists were ready to use force in a bid for power. The Blackshirts, as Mussolini's followers were called, did not rely on verbal assaults alone to achieve their goals. They physically attacked political opponents in the streets and drove elected officials from office.

Believing that fascism was a useful way of controlling the Socialists and workers, the democratic government did nothing to stop the Blackshirts. As a result, Mussolini grew even bolder. In October 1922 the Fascists staged a march on Rome. Mussolini waited in Milan to see how the government would react. Believing that the Fascists were planning to seize power, the cabinet asked King Victor Emmanuel III to declare martial law. The king refused, and the cabinet resigned. Instead of calling for new elections, the monarch named Mussolini prime minister.

Mussolini's Dictatorship

Mussolini quickly put an end to democratic rule in Italy. In a 1924 election, Blackshirts used their now familiar brutal tactics to make sure that Italians voted for Fascist candidates. As a result, Fascists won a majority of seats in the Italian parliament. The Fascist-controlled parliament gave Mussolini sweeping new powers. After this election Mussolini began calling himself *Il Duce* (eel DOO•chay), "The Leader."

Mussolini formed a new political party in 1919 called the *Fasci di Combattimento*, or Fascist party. Fascism (FA•SHIH•zuhm) is a political philosophy that advocates the glorification of the state, a single-party system with a strong ruler, and an aggressive form of nationalism. Like communism, fascism gave the state absolute authority. But fascism defended private property, although with some government regulation, and the class structure. According to its principles, the nation's cause was to be advanced at all cost even by war.

Mussolini's Road to Power

Conditions in Italy continued to deteriorate in the months following the war. The value of the lira

To consolidate his power, Mussolini reorganized the Italian government and established a **corporate state**. Under the corporate state, Mussolini hoped to bring workers and employers together and consequently to end the political quarreling that he associated with a democratic, multiparty system. To this end, he banned non-Fascist parties and ordered that **syndicates**, or corporations of workers and employers, be formed in each industry. Each syndicate sent representatives to a legislature in Rome that set policies on wages, production, and distribution. In theory, the corporate state was a new form of democracy; in practice, it was a political tool expressly designed for strengthening Mussolini's power.

Many Italians bitterly opposed fascism. They mourned the loss of democracy and individual freedoms. The Fascists arrested, assaulted, and murdered any who dared speak out against the abuses. "The masses must obey," thundered Mussolini. "They cannot afford to waste time searching for truth."

A majority of Italians, however, supported Mussolini. They believed he had done Italy a great service by preventing a Communist revolution and had brought order to the nation. After all, they said, he "made the trains run on time."

By building up Italy's armed forces, Mussolini did solve the unemployment problem. Even more important, he rekindled the feelings of patriotism and nationalism that had lain dormant in the Italian people. He made it clear to Italians that it was in their destiny to recapture all the greatness that had made the glory of ancient Rome. He would use all the economic and human resources available to make Italy a great power again.

The Weimar Republic

While Mussolini was establishing fascism in Italy, the Allies were preoccupied with ensuring that Germany would never again threaten peace. As a result, the Treaty of Versailles limited the size of Germany's armed forces and required the Germans to form a democratic government. While many Germans believed that democracy had become inevitable after the breakdown of the monarchy, few really believed in it.

In early 1919 Germans went to the polls and elected delegates to a national assembly. Meeting in **Weimar**, the assembly drafted a constitution for Germany establishing a democratic republic. The republic, which lasted from 1919 to 1933, was called the Weimar Republic.

Soon after the Weimar Republic became a reality, political instability and violence threatened to overwhelm it. In 1920 nationalist army officers tried to overthrow the government in a coup d'état. Like many other Germans, they claimed that Weimar leaders had betrayed the nation by accepting the Treaty of Versailles. Although the revolt was suppressed, the government failed to overcome widespread opposition to its policies.

Reparations

More than just political problems threatened Germany. Great Britain and France promised their citizens that the German government would pay reparations for the full cost of the war. The Allies set this cost at $35 billion. Already beset by serious economic problems, the German government in 1922

Visualizing History The blockade of Germany in World War I and postwar reparations on Germany brought hardships to many German citizens. These women in Berlin are searching in a garbage pile for food. *What form of government did Germany have between 1919 and 1933?*

announced that it could not under present circumstances meet its obligations.

France, however, insisted that Germany pay its debt. To ensure this result, French troops marched into Germany's industrial Ruhr Valley in 1923 and took control of the coal mines and steel mills. Angered at the French invasion, German workers went on strike while their government paid them. With income from Ruhr industries going to France, Germany had lost an important asset.

Inflation

To meet expenses, the German government printed more and more paper money. As a result, inflation soared. Before the war, 4 marks equaled 1 American dollar. By late 1923, it took 4 trillion marks to equal 1 dollar. Inflation wiped out the savings of many middle-class Germans.

In the mid-1920s, Germany finally saw some relief ahead from its troubles. The French reached a compromise with the Germans that eased payments, and they left the Ruhr. Freed of debt and strengthened by American loans, Germany entered a five-year period of relative prosperity. But the seeds of discontent had already been sown.

Rise of Nazism

Among the political parties challenging the Weimar Republic was the National Socialist Workers' party, or Nazi party. One of its first recruits was World War I veteran **Adolf Hitler**. Born in Austria in 1889, Hitler failed in his efforts to become a successful artist. After the war, he settled in Munich and joined the Nazi party.

Hitler soon formed the Brownshirts, a private army of young veterans and street thugs. During the inflationary crisis of 1923, Hitler made an attempt to seize power. With armed Brownshirts outside, Hitler jumped on a table in a Munich beer hall and announced, "The revolution has begun!"

Images of the Times

Life in Nazi Germany

During the 1930s, Hitler's National Socialist party ruled Germany with an iron hand. Many Germans accepted the Nazi dictatorship, believing that it would solve the country's problems. Other Germans, however, suffered under Hitler's rule.

Adolf Hitler at a Nazi rally accepts flowers from a German child. German children were taught in schools to honor Hitler as Germany's savior.

German young people joined Nazi youth groups where they participated in parades and athletics and learned Nazi ideas.

When the police intervened and arrested Hitler, however, the revolt quickly collapsed.

While in prison, Hitler wrote his autobiography, *Mein Kampf* (My Struggle). In Hitler's view, the Germans were not responsible for losing the war. He blamed the Jews and the Communists for the German defeat. He also declared that the Germans were a "master race" whose destiny was to rule the world. Hitler saw himself as the leader who would unite all German-speaking people into a new empire that would dominate other groups.

After his release from prison, Hitler resumed his activities. When the Great Depression struck in 1929, he appealed to German workers and industrialists alike with his promise to end unemployment and restore Germany's military might. In the early 1930s, the Nazis won a large number of seats in the multiparty Reichstag, or legislative lower house. With the government paralyzed by divisions, conservative politicians decided to back Hitler and use him for their own ends. In 1933 Hitler became chancellor. Through entirely legal means, the Nazis had come to power.

Hitler in Power

Hitler's goal all along was the creation of a totalitarian state. Because the Nazis were still a minority in the Reichstag, however, he planned to hold a new election. But a week before it was to be held, the Reichstag building mysteriously caught fire and burned to the ground. Hoping to reduce Communist support among the workers, Hitler blamed the Communists for the fire. In the election, the Brownshirts forced German voters to back the Nazis. When the Nazi-dominated Reichstag met after the election, it voted Hitler emergency powers to deal with the "Communist threat."

Hitler used his new powers to crush his opponents and consolidate his rule. All political parties, except the Nazi party were banned, and constitutional guarantees of freedom of speech, assembly, press and religion were ended. The Nazi government took over the labor unions and regulated production and wages. It also tried to control the Christian churches and silence clergy who opposed Nazi policies.

The Jews of Germany were persecuted by the Nazis. Nazi groups often terrorized Jewish people and vandalized Jewish-owned businesses.

REFLECTING ON THE TIMES

1. How were Germany's young people influenced by the Nazis?
2. How did Nazi rule affect Germany's Jews?

After becoming dictator of Germany in 1933, Adolf Hitler often held large rallies to inspire the loyalty of Germans. Hitler also adopted the slogan *Ein Volk, Ein Reich, Ein Führer* (One People, One Empire, One Leader). *What ambitions did Adolf Hitler have for Germany?*

Attacks on the Jews

Hitler directed his most bitter attacks against the Jews. In 1935 the Nuremberg Laws stripped Jews of their citizenship and their right to hold public office. The laws barred Jewish students from schools and destroyed Jewish businesses. In the *Kristallnacht* of November 9 and 10, 1938, members of the Nazi party attacked Jews on the streets and vandalized Jewish businesses, homes, and synagogues. Hitler's secret police, the Gestapo, arrested Jews and other opponents of the government by the thousands. Many of these opponents were shot. Others were sent to concentration camps, large prison camps where political prisoners or refugees were confined.

Hitler was suspicious of even his closest supporters. He particularly feared radical members among the Brownshirts and set out to weaken their ranks. On June 30, 1934, the "Night of Long Knives," Hitler had hundreds of Brownshirts and their leaders shot.

The Third Reich

Assured of absolute power, Hitler took the title of *der Führer* (duhr FYUR•uhr), "the Leader." He called his government the Third Reich (RYK), or Third Empire, and boasted it would last 1,000 years. To reach this end, he set about restoring Germany's military might. He ignored the provisions of the Versailles Treaty, which limited the size of the German army, and ordered German factories to begin turning out guns, ammunition, airplanes, tanks, and other weapons. He made no secret of his ambitions to expand Germany's territory: "Today, Germany; tomorrow, the world!"

Hitler also brought all intellectual and artistic activity in Germany under his control and imposed his own ideas on the arts. To glorify Nazism, he made plans to rebuild Berlin in the style of monumental classical architecture. He discouraged the artistic experimentation that had flourished during the 1920s. As a result, many of Germany's most talented artists and scientists—among whom were Walter Gropius, Arnold Schoenberg, Sigmund Freud, and Albert Einstein—fled the country.

Hitler actively used the press, radio, and movies to flood Germany with propaganda praising the Nazi cause. In its propaganda, the government stressed the importance of a strong military and devotion to the nation and its leader. Hitler also set up organizations for young people between the ages of 6 and 18. These organizations aimed to mold German youth to accept Nazi ideas.

SECTION 3 REVIEW

Recall
1. **Define** totalitarianism, fascism, corporate state, syndicate, *Kristallnacht*, concentration camp.
2. **Identify** Benito Mussolini, Weimar, Adolf Hitler.

3. **Explain** how Italians differed regarding Mussolini.

Critical Thinking
4. **Analyzing Information** Why did fascism appeal to many Italians and Germans in the decade following World War I?

Understanding Themes
5. **Uniformity** Analyze the type of government Germany had under the Nazis. What were its goals?

Analyzing Political Cartoons

Do you enjoy reading the comics section in the newspaper? Most people enjoy reading comic strips. Cartoons, however, also appear on the editorial page. These are opinions on political issues. Political cartoons are good sources of historical information because they reflect opinions on current affairs.

Learning the Skill

A political cartoonist relies mostly on images to communicate a message. Using caricature and symbols, political cartoons help readers see relationships and draw conclusions about events. A caricature exaggerates a detail in a drawing such as a subject's features. Cartoonists use caricature to create a positive or negative impression of a subject. For example, if a cartoon shows one figure three times larger than another, it implies that one figure is more powerful than the other.

A symbol is an image or object that represents something else. For example, a cartoonist may use a crown to represent monarchy. Symbols often represent nations or political parties. The bald eagle and Uncle Sam are common symbols for the United States. A bear often stands for Russia. A dragon might be used to stand for China.

To analyze a political cartoon, first identify the topic and principal characters. Read labels and messages. Note relationships between the figures and symbols. Review your knowledge of the cartoon's topic to determine the cartoonist's viewpoint and message.

Practicing the Skill

The political cartoon on this page, published in 1938, makes a statement about the dictatorships that developed in Europe after World War I and the reaction of the Western democracies toward the newly formed dictatorships. Study the cartoon and then answer these questions.

1. What do the figures represent?
2. Why is the standing figure so large?
3. What is the standing figure holding and what is it attached to?
4. What is the message of the cartoon?

Applying the Skill

Choose a current issue on which you hold a strong opinion. It can be a school, local, national, or international issue. Draw a political cartoon expressing your opinion on this issue. Show it to a friend to find out if the message is clear. If not, revise the cartoon to clarify its point.

For More Practice

Turn to the Skill Practice in the Chapter Review on page 793 for more practice in analyzing a political cartoon.

WOULD YOU OBLIGE ME WITH A MATCH PLEASE ?

Section 4

The Soviet Union

Setting the Scene

▶ **Terms to Define**
nationalization, dictatorship of the proletariat, collectivization, kulak, purge, Socialist realism

▶ **People to Meet**
Vladimir Ilyich Ulyanov (Lenin), Leon Trotsky, Joseph Stalin, Maksim Gorky

▶ **Places to Locate**
Georgia, Ukraine

**ind Out** How did Joseph Stalin's rule transform the Soviet Union?

The Storyteller

It was 35 degrees below zero when the team set out for work at Magnitogorsk. They would weld fittings to the blast furnaces 100 feet off the ground. It was hazardous work, for ice coated every surface. Three hours into the day a rigger fell off the scaffolding. Badly injured, he was carried to the first-aid station. His shaken companions talked of the need to improve the scaffolding. The foreman, however, blamed the workers. "You ploughboys don't know how to be careful. You don't pay as much attention as you should. People will fall, but we are building blast furnaces all the same, aren't we?"

Soviet construction project, 1930s

—adapted from *Behind the Urals: An American Worker in Russia's City of Steel*, John Scott, reprinted in *The Global Experience*, Volume 2, 1987

By 1921 Russia had endured the horrors of world war, revolution, and civil war. In the course of seven years of conflict, 27 million people had perished. Most had died on the battlefields and in countless guerrilla engagements, but millions had died of disease and starvation as well. In addition, the nation's transport system was in ruins, the peasants were in open revolt, and the economy was plunging toward collapse. At the Tenth Party Congress, Red Army director Leon Trotsky proclaimed: "We have destroyed the country in order to defeat the Whites."

Lenin in Power

In their struggle for survival during the civil war, **Vladimir Ilyich Ulyanov** (ool•YAH•nuhf), also known as **Lenin**, and the Bolsheviks had introduced an economic policy called war communism in 1918. Under war communism, the government carried out a policy of nationalization, in which it brought under state control all major industries. Applying the principle that those who would eat must work, the government required everyone between the ages of 16 and 50 to hold a job. It also erected a huge bureaucratic administration that wielded tremendous power but was extremely inefficient.

In 1921 Lenin tried to bring order out of the chaos that both war and government policy had caused. He announced a plan called the New Economic Policy, or NEP. Major industries such as steel, railroads, and large-scale manufacturing remained under government control. But in an attempt to stimulate the economy, Lenin allowed some private businesses to operate. In a startling departure from Marxist theory, NEP permitted small manufacturers and farmers to own their own businesses and to sell what they produced for a profit.

In 1922 the Communists changed the official name of the country from Russia to the Union of

Soviet Socialist Republics (USSR), or the Soviet Union. During this time, Lenin and other Communist leaders also completed a new constitution. This constitution stated that the USSR was a Socialist state, meaning that the government controlled the means of production.

In theory this state, called the dictatorship of the proletariat, was controlled by workers. But in practice the leadership of the Communist party controlled the workers. It was, as German Communist party member Rosa Luxemburg observed: "… a dictatorship, to be sure, not the dictatorship of the proletariat, however, but only the dictatorship of a handful of politicians." The classless society envisioned by Marx was, in the Soviet Union, a pyramid, with the party boss at the top and the peasants at the bottom.

The non-Russian nationalities in the USSR did not fare much better than the peasants. Because Lenin did not want to break up the old Russian Empire into independent states, he gave each major nationality its own republic with its own bureaucracy. In reality, however, the central government in Moscow still made the important decisions for these republics. In spite of the government's talk about equality for all nationalities, the Russians remained the dominant group in the Soviet Union and largely determined its policies.

Trotsky and Stalin

In 1922 Lenin suffered two strokes that left him permanently disabled. He died two years later at the age of 54.

The struggle to succeed Lenin began during his final illness. The two main contenders for the position were **Leon Trotsky** and **Joseph Stalin**. Next to Lenin, Trotsky had been the most important person in the Communist party. He had played a key role in the Bolshevik Revolution and had built the Red Army into a powerful fighting force. Trotsky came from a middle-class background and was a scholar who contributed many new ideas to the Marxist movement. He was also a speaker of great power and eloquence.

Born in **Georgia**, a territory south of Russia, Stalin was the son of artisans. A seminary student in his youth, Stalin was punished for reading books about revolution and social conditions, including novels such as *Les Misérables*. Stalin later renounced Russian Orthodoxy and became a Marxist revolutionary. Unlike Trotsky, Stalin was a skilled administrator. In 1922 he rose to the post of general secretary of the Communist party.

Visualizing History Lenin's New Economic Policy (NEP) helped put the Soviet Union's economy back on its feet in the early 1920s. *In what way did NEP depart from Marxist theory?*

Trotsky and Stalin held fundamentally different views about the path the Soviet Union should follow. Like Lenin, Trotsky believed in the theory of a "permanent revolution." He believed that only when the Russian Revolution had touched off uprisings all over the world could Socialists build an ideal society in the Soviet Union. Stalin, in contrast, declared it possible and necessary to "build socialism in a single country." By this he meant that the Soviet Union should concentrate on growing strong first, before it tried to spread revolution around the world.

Trotsky was better known than Stalin, both at home and in the Comintern (Communist International), an organization of Communist parties from all over the world. Moreover, Trotsky had been closer to Lenin. Nevertheless, Stalin managed to outmaneuver Trotsky politically. As general secretary, Stalin had the authority to appoint and remove officials. He gradually gained control of the party bureaucracy. As soon as he was securely in power, Stalin exiled Trotsky to Siberia and then expelled him from the Soviet Union. Trotsky eventually settled in Mexico City, where he continued to write about communism and the Soviet Union. An assassin acting on Stalin's orders murdered Trotsky in 1940.

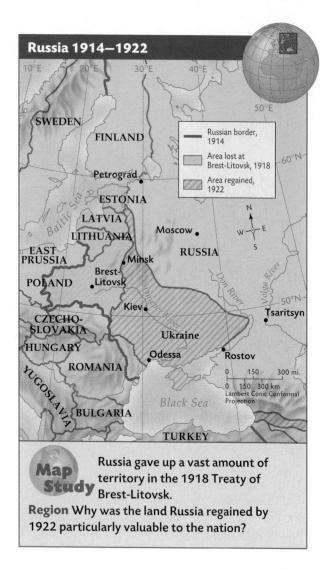

Russia 1914–1922

Russian border, 1914

Area lost at Brest-Litovsk, 1918

Area regained, 1922

SWEDEN

FINLAND

Petrograd

ESTONIA

LATVIA

LITHUANIA

Moscow

EAST PRUSSIA

Minsk

RUSSIA

Brest-Litovsk

POLAND

Kiev

CZECHO-SLOVAKIA

Ukraine

Tsaritsyn

HUNGARY

Odessa

Rostov

ROMANIA

YUGOSLAVIA

Black Sea

BULGARIA

TURKEY

Baltic Sea

Don River

Volga River

Dnieper River

0   150   300 mi.

0   150 300 km
Lambert Conic Conformal Projection

Map Study Russia gave up a vast amount of territory in the 1918 Treaty of Brest-Litovsk.

Region Why was the land Russia regained by 1922 particularly valuable to the nation?

Five-Year Plans

Fearing war with the West, Stalin wanted to rapidly transform the Soviet Union into an industrial power. In 1928 he declared an end to NEP and announced the first of his Five-Year Plans, a program that set economic goals for a five-year period. The plan brought all industrial and agricultural production under government control. It also provided for housing, health care, and other services.

While promising a better future, Stalin demanded sacrifices from the Soviet people. The first Five-Year Plan concentrated on building heavy industry. Consumer goods were produced in small amounts and were of inferior quality.

Responsibility for administering the plan lay in the hands of bureaucrats in Moscow. Theirs was a difficult task requiring tight control and careful planning. Not surprisingly, they made plenty of mistakes. For example, one Soviet enterprise purchased its nail supply from a nail factory many miles away, while a nail factory across the street was shipping its goods a similar distance. Despite the mistakes, the first Five-Year Plan was a success in spurring industrial growth.

Collective Farms

In agriculture, Stalin's plan called for collectivization, a system of farming in which the government owned the land and used peasants to farm it. Stalin believed that collective farms would be more efficient. They would not only produce food for the Soviet people but produce it for export as well. By increasing agricultural exports, Stalin hoped to pay for Soviet industrialization without borrowing from the capitalist West.

Stalin also planned to use collectivization to intimidate the Soviet Union's peasant majority, most of whom were fiercely anti-Communist. Kulaks, or the most prosperous peasants, especially opposed collectivization. They had prospered under NEP and did not want to give up their land, livestock, and machinery. Fighting broke out in the countryside when the government tried to impose its plans. Thousands of peasants and their families were killed or arrested and sent to labor camps in Siberia. Stalin also took measures to crush anti-Communist resistance in Ukraine. By seizing the region's grain during the terrible winter of 1932, Stalin promoted a "terror famine," causing the deaths of millions of Ukrainian peasants.

Results

The first Five-Year Plan transformed the Soviet Union into an industrial power, but the human cost of the plan was enormous. Industrial workers received low wages, or none at all, and food was often limited in quantity. Millions of people died because of rural unrest, and collective farms were often unable to provide enough grain to feed the nation's population.

POINT

Stalin's Dictatorship

Stalin ruled the Soviet Union from the mid-1920s until his death in 1953. During this period he established one of the most brutal dictatorships the world has ever seen. Stalin demanded complete obedience from the people he ruled and got it through an effective use of terror. He granted the secret police immense power, which they used to scrutinize every aspect of the nation's social and political life. Agents of the secret police encouraged workers to spy on each other and children to spy on their parents. Those accused of disloyalty were either shot or sent to labor camps in Siberia. The secret police and their activities helped to create a climate of fear in Soviet society.

Purges

In the 1930s Stalin began a methodical attack upon his potential enemies. Even members of the Communist party did not escape the reach of Stalin and his secret police. In 1934 an unknown assailant, probably acting on Stalin's orders, assassinated a high party official. Stalin used the event to rid himself of opponents and strengthen his hold on the party. He had millions of Communist party members expelled from the party, arrested and put in labor camps, or shot.

Stalin then turned against the Old Bolsheviks. These officials had been associates of Lenin and Stalin in the early days of the movement. Because some of them had sided with Trotsky, Stalin moved in 1936 to purge, or remove, them from any position where they could threaten his leadership. He had them arrested and put on trial. In open court in Moscow, with foreign reporters looking on, they pleaded guilty to false charges of treason, murder, and other crimes. Although these prisoners showed no signs of mistreatment, many Western experts have since concluded that the secret police used psychological torture to break their wills.

The Arts

Stalin also set out to put all artistic and cultural activities under the Communist party's control. In

Visualizing History The Soviet government used posters to glorify Soviet achievements and to urge people to carry out the goals of the Communist party. *How did Stalin strengthen his hold on the Soviet Union and the Communist party?*

1934 he put **Maksim Gorky**, one of the Soviet Union's leading writers, in charge of all Soviet culture. Gorky promoted a new literary style that soon became obligatory in the arts: Socialist realism. Writers and artists created a "new reality" by glorifying Soviet heroes and achievements, while denouncing the rumors about forced labor and terror. Artists who violated these dictates faced exile or imprisonment in labor camps.

Stalin's restrictions had a chilling effect on Soviet artists. Although talented writers and artists struggled to survive, most official artistic works were predictable and uninspiring.

The Comintern

In 1919 Lenin had established the Communist International, or Comintern. The goal of the Comintern was to encourage Communist parties in other countries to overthrow their governments by legal or illegal means and to establish Soviet-style regimes. While Stalin at first gave low priority to Comintern affairs, he later took more seriously the relations of the Soviet Union to the Communist parties in other countries. Stalin eventually decided to dissolve the Comintern in 1943, to win the favor and approval of the Western Allies during World War II.

SECTION 4 REVIEW

Recall
1. **Define** nationalization, dictatorship of the proletariat, collectivization, kulak, purge, Socialist realism.
2. **Identify** Vladimir Ilyich Ulyanov (Lenin), Leon Trotsky, Joseph Stalin, Georgia, Ukraine, Maksim Gorky.
3. **Describe** how the communists governed the Soviet Union.

Critical Thinking
4. **Analyzing Information** How did Stalin transform the Soviet Union? What effects did Stalin's policies have on the Soviet people? Are these effects still felt today? Explain.

Understanding Themes
5. **Uniformity** Predict what might have happened if Trotsky—and not Stalin—had succeeded Lenin.

Connections Across Time

Historical Significance After World War I, scientists and artists in the West broke with old traditions and sought a "new reality." Meanwhile, economic and political instability posed challenges to democratic societies, which took emergency steps to save their economies. In lands where democracy was weak, such as Italy and Germany, social and economic upheaval led to the rise of Fascist governments. At the same time, a brutal Communist dictatorship emerged in the Soviet Union. Tensions between totalitarian and democratic nations paved the way for a new global conflict.

Using Key Terms

Write the key term that completes each sentence. Then write a sentence for each term not chosen.

a. cubism
b. coalition
c. surrealism
d. fascism
e. purge
f. kulaks
g. concentration camps
h. disarmament
i. corporate state
j. nationalization
k. *Kristallnacht*
l. general strike

1. Under the _____, Mussolini hoped to bring workers and employers together.
2. Because there were numerous political parties, the formation of a government in France required a _____ of several parties.
3. _____ is a political philosophy that glorifies the state, supports a single-party system under a strong leader, and promotes an aggressive form of nationalism.
4. In the _____, members of the Nazi party attacked Jews on the streets and vandalized Jewish businesses, homes, and synagogues.
5. The art form of _____ used dreamlike images and unnatural combinations of objects.

Technology Activity

Developing a Multimedia Presentation Search the Internet or your local library for sources on World War I. Based on your research, create a multimedia presentation about the economic effects of World War I on Western countries. Use images from the Internet in your presentation. Include a plan describing the type of presentation you would like to develop and the steps you will take to ensure a successful presentation.

Using Your History Journal

Use your notes from the interview of a person who lived through the period between the wars. Write an account of how events affected ordinary people's lives.

Reviewing Facts

1. **Technology** List the technological advances in the 1920s and 1930s that impacted people.
2. **Culture** Identify three artists who produced changes in literature, art, music, or architecture. Describe the contributions each made.
3. **History** Explain why the United States retreated into isolationism after World War I.
4. **Culture** Explain the rise of fascism in Italy.
5. **Culture** Discuss how Hitler rose to power.
6. **Government** Explain how Hitler and Mussolini strengthened their political power.
7. **Economics** Identify Lenin's NEP.
8. **Government** Describe how Stalin defeated Trotsky.

Critical Thinking

1. **Apply** Why was World War I a watershed event in the twentieth century?
2. **Apply** How did Einstein's theories affect twentieth-century science and culture?
3. **Analyze** Compare totalitarianism and democracy. Why did totalitarian governments rise to power after World War I?
4. **Analyze** How does the term "Night of Terror" describe *Kristallnacht*?

5. **Synthesize** To aid Germany's economic recovery after World War I, how might the Allies have structured the peace settlements?
6. **Compare** How does fascism differ from communism? How do both differ from capitalism?
7. **Analyze** Salvador Dali was influenced by Sigmund Freud. How is Freud's influence evident in *The Persistence of Memory* (1931)?

The Persistence of Memory, *Salvador Dali.*
Museum of Modern Art, New York, New York

Understanding Themes

1. **Innovation** How did new movements in literature and the arts reflect changes after World War I?
2. **Change** How was Roosevelt's New Deal similar to Stalin's Five-Year Plan? How was it different?
3. **Uniformity** Why did the Nazis try to control labor unions and the Christian churches? Why did they mistreat Germany's Jewish population?
4. **Uniformity** How did Lenin try to unify all non-Russian republics under one government?

Linking Past and Present

During the 1920s and 1930s the automobile, motion pictures, and the radio transformed the way Americans lived. What technological advances shape our lives today? Are they negative or positive? Explain.

Skill Practice

Study the cartoon and answer the questions.

1. Who is the figure in the cartoon?
2. What country does the flag represent?
3. What is the message of the cartoon?

Geography in History

1. **Place** In which countries did Fascist governments come to power during the 1930s?
2. **Region** In what region of Europe were 10 of the 11 democracies in the 1930s?

Politics of Europe 1930s

1919–1939
Nationalism in Asia, Africa, and Latin America

Chapter Themes

▶ **Nationalism** Hope for a new world after World War I leads to the rise of nationalism in the Middle East and Africa. *Section 1*

▶ **Change** Gandhi calls for nonviolence in India's struggle for independence from British rule. *Section 2*

▶ **Conflict** Nationalists, Communists, and the Japanese compete for control of China. *Section 3*

▶ **Conflict** Japan's militarism and expansionism place it on a collision course with the West. *Section 4*

▶ **Change** Nationalist forces in Latin America oppose increased American intervention in the region. *Section 5*

S*The* toryteller

"I swear before country and history that my sword will defend our nation's dignity, that it will be a sword for the oppressed. I accept the invitation to fight.... The last of my soldiers, the soldiers of freedom for Nicaragua, may die; but before that, more than a battalion of your blond invaders will have bitten the dust of my wild mountains."

With these fighting words, General Augusto César Sandino challenged the United States Marines in 1927. Sandino was trying to drive out the "blond invaders" who had occupied Nicaragua for 15 years. In the years following World War I, nationalist leaders such as Sandino struggled to end foreign control and win independence for their countries around the globe.

Historical Significance

What factors led to the growth of nationalist and independence movements in Asia, Africa, and Latin America between 1919 and 1939?

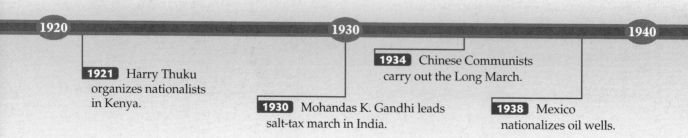

1920

1921 Harry Thuku organizes nationalists in Kenya.

1930

1930 Mohandas K. Gandhi leads salt-tax march in India.

1934 Chinese Communists carry out the Long March.

1938 Mexico nationalizes oil wells.

1940

History & Art *The Destruction of the Old Order* by José Clemente Orozco. National Preparatory School, Mexico City, Mexico

Your History Journal

Choose a major event that occurred after 1930 in one of the nations featured in this chapter. Write a short radio news report describing the event for broadcast in the United States.

1917   1927   1937

1917 The British issue
    the Balfour Declaration.

1929 Nigerian women
    oppose British tax.

1936 Egypt becomes
    independent.

Section 1

New Forces in the Middle East and Africa

Setting the Scene

▶ **Terms to Define**
    self-determination, fez, shah

▶ **People to Meet**
    Kemal Atatürk, Reza Shah Pahlavi, Theodor
    Herzl, Saad Zaghlul, Harry Thuku, Jomo
    Kenyatta, Nnamdi Azikiwe

▶ **Places to Locate**
    Turkey, Iran, Palestine, Egypt, Kenya, Nigeria

 **Find Out** How did the forces of nationalism
affect events in the Middle East and Africa after
World War I?

The Storyteller

*Fawaz Khourey listened as a delegate at the
Arab Students Congress in Paris read the committee report. "I am an Arab.
I believe Arabs constitute one
nation. This nation's sacred
right is to be sovereign in her
own affairs. Her ardent
nationalism drives her to lib-
erate our homeland, uniting
all parts, and finding political, economic, and social
institutions more sound and
more compatible than existing
ones."*

Paris mosque

—adapted from *Arab
Nationalism: An Anthology,*
edited by Sylvia G. Haim,
reprinted in *Documents in
World History,* Volume 2, 1988

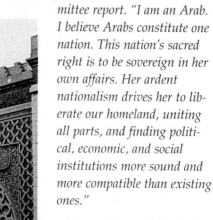

t the end of World War I, European
powers continued to control most of
the Middle East and Africa. Many
colonies had assisted the Allies during the war,
hoping to gain their independence as a reward.
President Woodrow Wilson of the United States
raised their hopes in 1918 by endorsing the concept
of **self-determination**: the right of national groups
to set up independent nations.

But instead of relaxing their grip, the European
powers tightened it. Nationalists prepared to fight
for independence and organized political demonstrations. They were eager to establish modern
countries where their own cultures could flourish.

Turkey

For nearly 500 years, Turkish emperors called
sultans ruled the vast Ottoman Empire, which at
one time included parts of eastern Europe, the
Middle East, and North Africa. During the 1800s,
however, large sections of this empire broke away
or were conquered. When World War I began, the
Ottomans joined forces with Germany, hoping to
save their remaining lands.

War With Greece

The Allied victory in World War I dashed
Ottoman hopes. The Ottoman sultan, or ruler, lost
all of his lands except the area of present-day
Turkey. In 1919 the Greeks invaded Turkey in an
attempt to complete the destruction of the Ottoman
Empire. Turkish general Mustafa Kemal, however,
rallied forces to his country's defense. Kemal led a
political group known as the Young Turks who
wanted reforms to modernize Turkey. Turkish
armies under Kemal counterattacked and defeated
the Greeks in 1922.

The Turkish victory led to dramatic changes. The sultan gave up his throne, and the Turks formed a new country, the Republic of Turkey. Kemal became its first president. The new government moved the capital from Istanbul to Ankara, a city near the center of the country. Believing that Turkey needed to industrialize in order to assert its role in world affairs, Kemal's government established industries and planned their growth. Tariffs on imports were raised to protect the new industries from foreign competition and to reduce dependence on foreign countries.

Kemal's Reforms

Kemal carried out a number of radical reforms in Turkish society. As a result of Kemal's policies, Turkey adopted a Western way of life. The Turks began using the Western calendar, the Latin alphabet, and the metric system. Kemal ordered men to stop wearing the fez, a traditional hat, and he tried to rid the country of the custom of veiling among women. He also urged Turks to use Western-style last names. To Westernize the government, he reformed the legal code and separated government and religion.

Some of Kemal's changes were designed to promote national pride among the Turks. For example, he urged Turks to "purify" their language by ridding it of all words that had Persian or Arabic origins. He also changed his own name to **Kemal Atatürk** (keh•MAHL AT•uh•TUHRK), which means "father of the Turks."

In defense of his reforms, Kemal said: "We have suffered much. This is because we have failed to understand the world. Our thoughts and our mentality will become civilized from head to toe." Kemal ruled Turkey with an iron fist until his death in 1938. His policies were not always popular, but he changed Turkey from an ancient empire into a modern nation.

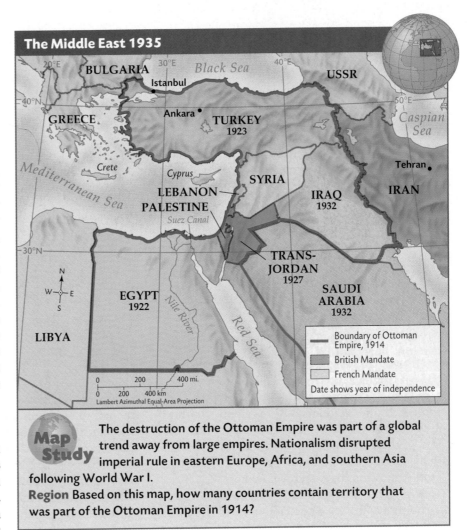

The Middle East 1935

Boundary of Ottoman Empire, 1914
British Mandate
French Mandate
Date shows year of independence

Map Study The destruction of the Ottoman Empire was part of a global trend away from large empires. Nationalism disrupted imperial rule in eastern Europe, Africa, and southern Asia following World War I.

Region Based on this map, how many countries contain territory that was part of the Ottoman Empire in 1914?

Iran

Located between Turkey and Pakistan, **Iran** is a land of mountains, deserts, and oil. At the end of World War I this land, known by its historic name of Persia, was ruled by a shah, or king. However, Great Britain and the Soviet Union each had controlling interests in Persia's oil fields.

In 1921 nationalist forces led by Reza Khan, an army officer, wanted to cut back the foreign influence on their government and economy. The nationalists overthrew the shah and set up a new government. Like Atatürk, Reza Khan built schools, roads, and hospitals, and he allowed women more freedom. Improved communications helped unite the diverse groups in the country. Although adopting many Western ways, he tried to reduce Western political influence in Persia.

Reza wanted to change the Persian monarchy into a republic. However, traditional Muslim leaders opposed this change, so Reza ruled as a dictator. Later, in 1925, he declared himself shah and

adopted the new name **Reza Shah Pahlavi** (rih•ZAH SHAH PAL•uh•vee). Pahlavi was the name of the ancient Persian language. Reza Shah Pahlavi earned money from Persia's oil fields and factories and from his vast royal estates.

During the 1930s, Reza Shah Pahlavi aligned his country with Germany. He admired Hitler, in part because he believed that Germans and Persians shared a common ancestry in the ancient Aryan, or Indo-European, peoples. In 1935 he changed the country's name from Persia to Iran, a variation of the word *Aryan*. In 1941, when Great Britain and the Soviet Union were at war with Germany, British and Soviet forces deposed Reza Shah Pahlavi and replaced him with his son, Mohammad Reza Pahlavi. The new ruler permitted British and Soviet troops to remain in Iran.

Palestine

While Iran was trying to free itself from European control, another Middle Eastern region was just coming under British domination. After World War I, the newly formed League of Nations gave Great Britain a mandate over **Palestine**. This region had been part of the Ottoman Empire. Britain was eager to benefit from control of Palestine's strategic location at the eastern end of the Mediterranean Sea.

In Palestine, the nationalism of two groups—Jews and Arabs—came into conflict. The Jews claimed the land on the basis of their biblical heritage and the continuing presence of Jews in the area since ancient times. Arabs pointed out that their ancestors had lived there for many centuries also. During this period, Palestine's small number of Jews and large number of Arabs lived together peacefully most of the time.

Beginning in the late 1800s, the number of Jews in Palestine began increasing. European Jews, facing harsh anti-Jewish pogroms in Russia and stirred by a growing sense of nationalism, believed they should reestablish a Jewish national homeland in Palestine. This movement, known as Zionism, became an organized political force in the late 1890s under the leadership of **Theodor Herzl**, a prominent Austrian Jewish writer and journalist. By World War I, about 500,000 Arabs and 85,000 Jews lived in Palestine.

During World War I, the British government promised independence to the Arabs in return for their help against the Ottoman Turks and also promised a homeland to the Jews. The Balfour Declaration—a letter from British Foreign Secretary Arthur Balfour in 1917 to the English Zionist Federation—promised Great Britain's help in establishing "a national home for the Jewish people" in Palestine. Great Britain's pledge of support, however, was on the condition that the civil and religious rights of other communities be protected. In September 1923, the British mandate officially came into force in Palestine in spite of Great Britain's conflicting promises to the area's Jewish and Arab communities.

Under the British mandate, tensions heightened between Arabs and Jews. As the persecution of Jews in Nazi Germany increased, so did Jewish immigration to Palestine. As more Jews moved into a region long inhabited by Arabs, the two groups clashed. Riots broke out, resulting in hundreds of casualties. When Great Britain tried to limit Jewish immigration, Zionists responded in anger. By the end of the 1930s, Great Britain's ambiguous promises had angered both Jews and Arabs, and the conflict in Palestine was worsening.

Egypt

Palestine's neighbor **Egypt** also confronted troubles after World War I. Under British occupation since 1882, Egypt was beginning to feel the power of nationalism. **Saad Zaghlul** (zag•LOOL) led the nationalist forces in Egypt demanding independence. The British tried to weaken the nationalist cause by arresting Zaghlul, but their action only sparked riots and violence. Finally, in 1922, Great Britain granted Egypt limited independence. However, the British kept control of the Suez Canal.

Tensions continued over the next decade between Egypt and Great Britain. But when Italy invaded Ethiopia in 1935, the British decided they needed Egypt's help to prevent further Italian aggression. As a result, the British government granted Egypt its complete independence in 1936 and helped it become a member of the League of Nations the following year. Great Britain also withdrew all British troops from Egypt, except for those in the Suez Canal zone.

Kenya

South of Egypt, in central East Africa, lay another part of Great Britain's empire: **Kenya**. During World War I, about 45,000 Kenyans died while helping the British fight the Germans in East Africa. The survivors returned home after the war with dreams of independence and a new life. However, instead of granting Kenya its independence, the British allowed European settlers to seize the land of many Kenyans in order to start large coffee plantations and other agricultural operations. The settlers hired Kenyans at low wages and made them work under harsh conditions. Resentment of British rule in Kenya gave rise to a

---

CONNECTIONS

Geography

Imperialist Boundaries

Nigerian nationalist Nnamdi Azikiwe

During the late 1800s, European powers carved up Africa without respect to the continent's historic ethnic boundaries. Colonial boundary lines split groups of people and joined them to other groups with different religious beliefs, customs, and languages. This often led to unwanted rivalries and hostilities. Nowhere was this problem more evident than in Nigeria.

Nigeria is home to more than 250 separate ethnic groups. The three largest are the Hausa, the Yoruba, and the Ibo. In the days before colonial rule, each group controlled its own territory. When the British united the region in 1914, Hausa, Yoruba, and Ibo peoples were part of the same country for the first time. They eyed each other with suspicion.

After independence arrived in 1960, the struggle for unity continued in Nigeria. However, hostilities flared into warfare in 1967. Eastern Nigeria seceded and established the independent state of Biafra. The Nigerian government eventually won the war and reclaimed Biafra, but the country remains haunted by the prophetic words that nationalist leader Obafemi Awolowo spoke in 1947: "Nigeria is not a nation. It is a mere geographical expression."

Linking Past and Present ACTIVITY

Explain the statement: "Nigeria is not a nation. It is a mere geographical expression." Why have Nigerians been reluctant to unite?

protest movement in 1921 led by **Harry Thuku** (THOO•koo). The protesters complained about high colonial taxes and strict British labor laws. Colonial officials promptly arrested Thuku, and in the riot that followed, British troops killed about 25 Kenyans. The British government then exiled Thuku from Kenya.

In Thuku's absence, **Jomo Kenyatta** took over the growing nationalist movement. Instead of fighting the British in Kenya for independence, Kenyatta took his struggle to the center of British power in London. By meeting with government officials in the 1920s and 1930s, he succeeded in making progress—but at a very slow pace. He later recalled his frustrations:

> **❝** By driving [the African] off his ancestral lands, the Europeans have robbed him of the material foundations of his culture, and reduced him to a state of serfdom incompatible with human happiness.... It is not in his nature to accept serfdom forever. He realizes that he must fight unceasingly for his own complete emancipation; for without this he is doomed to remain the prey of rival imperialisms. **❞**
>
> —Jomo Kenyatta, *Facing Mount Kenya*, 1938

In spite of Kenyatta's efforts for independence, when World War II began in 1939, Kenya remained firmly in British hands.

Nigeria

Across the continent from Kenya, on the west coast of Africa, lies **Nigeria**. The British controlled this region of Africa as well, and they made large fortunes from Nigeria's rubber, oil, and tin. As in Kenya, the British imposed heavy taxes on men and strict labor laws.

In 1929 Nigerian women learned that they too

Visualizing History Jomo Kenyatta wrote a book, *Facing Mount Kenya*, that explained how British rule had disrupted his country's culture. *How did Kenyatta try to obtain Kenya's independence?*

would be taxed. When a group of unarmed women protested by attacking British goods and property, police fired on them, killing 50.

The violent ending of the women's uprising drove many Nigerians to adopt nonviolent methods in their struggle for independence. One of these Nigerian nationalists was **Nnamdi Azikiwe** (eh •nahm•dee ah•zee•KEE•WEE), who started the newspaper *The West African Pilot* in 1937. He wrote many articles in favor of independence, not only for Nigeria but for all of Africa. "Africa needs a pilot," he wrote once. "Those who follow the true pilot, believing they are on the right track, will find their way to their destination."

SECTION 1 REVIEW

Recall
1. **Define** self-determination, fez, shah.
2. **Identify** Kemal Atatürk, Reza Shah Pahlavi, Theodor Herzl, Saad Zaghlul, the Balfour Declaration, Harry Thuku, Jomo Kenyatta, Nnamdi Azikiwe.
3. **State** the goal of the reforms introduced by Kemal Atatürk.

Critical Thinking
4. **Evaluating Information** The British in Kenya said they were "exercising a trust on behalf of the African population." What does that phrase imply about

Great Britain's attitude toward Africans?

Understanding Themes
5. **Nationalism** What were the reasons for the rise of nationalism in the Middle East and Africa at the end of World War I?

1919   1929   1939

1919 The Amritsar Massacre heightens anti-British feeling in India.

1930 Mohandas K. Gandhi leads protest against British rule.

1935 The British Parliament passes the Government of India Act.

Section 2

India's Struggle for Independence

Setting the Scene

▶ **Terms to Define**

pacifist, civil disobedience, satyagraha

▶ **People to Meet**

Mohandas K. Gandhi, Mohammed Ali Jinnah, Jawaharlal Nehru

▶ **Places to Locate**

India, Amritsar, Ahmadabad

Find Out What methods did Gandhi use in India's struggle for independence from British rule?

The Storyteller

Riswati and Kamala, once friendly neighbors in Bombay, had not spoken to each other for months—since relations between Muslims and Hindus had deteriorated. The British could use the problem as an excuse for delaying Indian independence. The two women had argued over which group, Muslims or Hindus, was more to blame. Kamala recalled the example of Mohandas Gandhi and resolved to visit Riswati and renew their friendship. Perhaps she could quote Gandhi saying, "It does not matter to me that we see things from different angles of vision." Kamala caught sight of Riswati at the market. Quickly she crossed the square toward her old friend.

—adapted from *Communal Unity*, M.K. Gandhi, reprinted in *World Civilizations*, Volume 2, 1994

Mohandas Gandhi

When World War I began, the most important territory in the British Empire was **India**. As in the Middle East and Africa, nationalism was spreading in India. Some Indians wanted independence. Many were willing to remain in the British Empire but demanded home rule. Two of the largest nationalist organizations were the Indian National Congress and the Muslim League.

During World War I, Indian nationalists supported Great Britain and its allies. More than a million Indian soldiers fought on the battlefields of the Middle East and Africa. Indian wheat fed the Allied troops, and Indian cotton kept them clothed. In return for this aid, Great Britain promised in 1917 to support eventual self-rule for India.

The Amritsar Massacre

Independence did not come easily to India. After the war, the Indian National Congress staged demonstrations to protest British rule. The nationalist movement, however, was divided by religion. The Hindu majority and the Muslim minority did not trust each other. The British authorities in India encouraged that distrust.

A second difficulty was British opposition. Many Britons were unwilling to see their empire's power reduced and staunchly opposed freeing India. In 1919 Great Britain imposed on India harsh laws intended to stifle opposition to British rule. British officials could arrest nationalists without cause and jail them without trial.

British repression reached an extreme in the Punjabi city of **Amritsar** in April 1919. The British had outlawed all large gatherings and declared that they would respond to any violation with force. When 10,000 unarmed Indians assembled in a

During the 1920s and 1930s, Gandhi was India's leading nationalist. He worked to promote unity between Hindus and Muslims in the Indian National Congress party. *Where did Gandhi first use nonviolent methods to protest injustices?*

walled garden in Amritsar for a political meeting, the local commander decided that the British needed to demonstrate their authority. Without warning, British troops blocked the only entrance to the garden and began firing into the trapped crowd. When the firing ceased, nearly 400 people, including many children, lay dead. Another 1,200 people were wounded. Criticized for his action, the British commander declared:

> 66 I fired and continued to fire until the crowd dispersed, and I consider this is the least amount of firing which would produce the necessary moral effect.... If more troops had been at hand, the casualties would have been greater. 99

Footnotes to History

Gandhi and the West

Mohandas K. Gandhi has had a profound influence on people in the West. He served as a model for Martin Luther King, Jr. King led the African American civil rights struggle until his assassination in 1968. Like Gandhi, King protested injustice with nonviolent boycotts and marches.

Indians across the country were shocked by the brutal massacre and the general's justification of it. In large numbers, they came together in meeting after meeting, more determined than ever to drive the British out of their land. However, they needed a strong leader to spearhead their struggle.

Gandhi's Campaign

In the months following the Amritsar Massacre, **Mohandas K. Gandhi** became the leading Indian nationalist. Born in India of middle-class parents in 1869, Gandhi had been educated in England. He later practiced law in South Africa, where he and other Indians experienced mistreatment because of their dark skin.

Until 1914 Gandhi lived in South Africa and led protests against racial discrimination. He was a pacifist, a person opposed to using war and other violence to settle disputes. In keeping with his beliefs, Gandhi used protest methods based on civil disobedience, or the refusal to obey laws that are considered unjust.

When Gandhi returned to India, he began working with the Indian National Congress and led a nonviolent movement for self-government and for greater tolerance among the country's many social and religious groups. Gandhi urged Indians to reject much of Western civilization for its use of brute force, its worship of money, and its prejudicial attitudes toward non-Western peoples. Gandhi's understanding of India's problems made him popular throughout the country. The Indian people called Gandhi *Mahatma*, meaning "great soul."

Gandhi's doctrine of moral nonviolent protest won him international attention. He believed that one could force an evil person or government to change by challenging it directly, but without violence. Gandhi used the term satyagraha (suh•TYAH•gruh•huh), which means "truth force," to describe the nonviolent protests he led after the Amritsar Massacre. One effective form of protest was the boycott, in which Indians refused to buy British cloth and other manufactured goods. As a step toward independence, Gandhi urged Indians to begin spinning their own cloth.

Gandhi practiced what he preached by spinning cloth for a half hour every day. He made the spinning wheel the symbol of the National Congress, and he wore nothing but simple homespun clothes for the rest of his life.

Gandhi's courage inspired millions of Indians to join in protests. In 1922, however, the British arrested Gandhi, and he disappeared from active protest for the rest of the decade. Undaunted, the Indian National Congress continued to protest, but it achieved very little success until Gandhi's return in 1930.

Toward Independence

Gandhi planned his next major protest around salt. In India's hot climate, the millions of people who worked in fields and factories needed salt to replace what they lost daily in sweat. The British controlled the salt mines and the ocean salt fields. They taxed every grain of salt they sold and jailed Indians who gathered salt on their own.

In 1930 Gandhi protested the salt tax. First he led thousands of his followers on a 200-mile (322-km) march from **Ahmadabad** to the sea, where they made salt from sea water. One month later, Gandhi openly defied British authority by wading into the sea and picking up a lump of salt. The British did not dare arrest him, but they did arrest thousands who followed his example. To quell the mounting protests, they arrested him a month later, but the protests only increased. Webb Miller, a British journalist, described one such protest, in which a group of Indians marched on a heavily guarded salt mine: "Although every one knew that within a few minutes he would be beaten down, perhaps killed, I could detect no signs of wavering or fear.... There was no fight, no struggle; the marchers simply walked forward until struck down."

This pattern continued throughout the 1930s. As Indians protested, the British responded with guns and clubs. Their violence could not stop the millions of people motivated by nationalism.

Limited Self-Rule

Under pressure from the nationalist movement, the British began to give Indians more political power. In 1935 the British Parliament passed the Government of India Act, which created a constitution for India. This measure gave provincial legislatures control over the making of law in the provinces. Areas such as agriculture, education, public health, and public works came under the control of the provincial governments. The British government retained control of national lawmaking, finance, defense, and foreign affairs.

The majority of Indian nationalists rejected the act, wanting complete independence. However, the Indian National Congress, at the insistence of Gandhi, finally accepted it as the first step toward self-rule. The Indian historian K.M. Panikkar states that with the Government of India Act, "British authority in India was in full retreat, in the administrative field no less than in the political and economic fields." Nevertheless, independence was not yet won.

Hindu-Muslim Relations

Even as India moved toward independence in the 1930s, conflicts among Indians increased. For every Muslim, India had three Hindus. As independence approached, the Muslims began worrying about their future treatment by the Hindus, and many joined the Muslim League.

In 1937 the Indian National Congress, controlled by Hindus, won election majorities in 7 out of 11 provinces. Muslims came to power in the others. This heightened bitter feelings. The Muslim League, headed by **Mohammed Ali Jinnah**, split with the Congress party. It demanded a separate Muslim nation for the millions of Muslims in India. The Hindus, led by **Jawaharlal Nehru**, a follower of Gandhi, wanted a united India.

Although a Hindu, Gandhi was concerned about the deepening rift between Hindus and Muslims. His pleas for toleration were largely ignored by both groups. As 1939 ended, India continued its long struggle for freedom. But now the nationalist movement had split in two, and not even Gandhi could put it together again.

SECTION 2 REVIEW

Recall
1. **Define** pacifist, civil disobedience, satyagraha.
2. **Identify** Mohandas K. Gandhi, Mohammed Ali Jinnah, Jawaharlal Nehru.
3. **List** the three countries

in which Gandhi spent most of his life. Locate these countries on the Atlas map on page A-5.

Critical Thinking
4. **Synthesizing Information** What could Hindus have done

to keep Muslims united with them against the British?

Understanding Themes
5. **Change** What nonviolent methods did Mohandas K. Gandhi use to bring about change?

Section 3

China's Drive for Modernization

Setting the Scene

▶ **Terms to Define**
warlord

▶ **People to Meet**
Sun Yat-sen, Yuan Shigai, Chiang Kai-shek, Mao Zedong

▶ **Places to Locate**
Nanjing, Guangzhou, Manchuria

ind Out ▶ What divided nationalist forces in China, and what united them?

The Storyteller

Wai Zhou watched a small man addressing a group in the square. "China has become a colony of all the Powers," he proclaimed. This was nothing new, Wai Zhou thought, just another agitator seeking an audience. But the man continued, "Foreigners often refer to the Chinese nation as a bowl of loose sand. To revive nationalism we must expand our small group loyalty to a very large group. The people must learn to read and write. China must become a democracy. Those who till the soil should own it." The speaker outlined a plan for Chinese independence. Completely won over, Wai Zhou asked a bystander who the speaker was. "I heard him called Sun Yat-sen," the man replied.

—adapted from *Lectures on Nationalism*, Sun Yat-sen, reprinted in *Lives and Times*, James P. Holoka and Jiu-Hwa Lo Upshur, 1995

Sun Yat-sen

Unlike India, China was never entirely controlled by a European country. However, despite its independence and population size, China did not have the military power to command respect. That they lacked the respect of Europeans was shown by the final terms of the Versailles peace conference that followed World War I. The Versailles Treaty had a provision granting Japan economic control of the Shandong (SHON•DOONG) Peninsula of northeastern China. This provision was a humiliating and surprising blow to the Chinese. During and after World War I, China was torn apart by internal divisions, and the foreign powers took advantage of China's weakness.

The Chinese Republic

As you read in Chapter 27, the Chinese revolutionary leader **Sun Yat-sen** formally declared China a republic in January 1912. Sun dreamed of a free, democratic society. However, just two months after taking office, he was ousted by a military strongman, **Yuan Shigai** (YOO•AHN SHUR•GIE). Yuan quickly turned the new republic into a dictatorship. Meanwhile, Sun organized and formed the nationalist Guomindang (KWOH•MIHN•DAHNG) party, tried and failed to overthrow Yuan, and then fled to Japan.

When Yuan died in 1916, China slipped into chaos. Local military leaders called warlords divided the vast country among themselves. An almost continual state of civil war followed.

Sun Yat-sen returned to China in 1917 and tried in vain to restore strong central government to China and rebuild the Guomindang party. Then in 1923, with aid from the Soviet Union and an ambitious young officer named **Chiang Kai-shek**

Chiang Kai-shek was appointed commander of the National Revolutionary Army in 1926. By the end of 1928 the last major faction of warlords pledged obedience to the National Government. *What other party opposed the warlords?*

(JEE•AHNG KY•SHEHK), the Guomindang army grew rapidly in strength. Sun Yat-sen died in 1925. Three years later, Chiang led the army to victory over the warlords and established a government in the city of **Nanjing**.

Though undemocratic, government under the Guomindang promoted economic development by building schools, roads, and railways. However, the Guomindang did very little to raise the living standards of the peasants who comprised the vast majority of the population of China.

Rivalry With the Communists

Many peasants, along with intellectuals and urban workers, supported another party that opposed the warlords: the Communists. During Chiang's drive against the warlords, Communist soldiers provided him with crucial military support. But in 1927 the Communists attempted to take over the Guomindang party and failed. Chiang turned against the Communists and tried to wipe them out. In Shanghai, **Guangzhou**, and other cities, Guomindang soldiers killed tens of thousands of Communists.

As Chiang began his purge, tens of thousands of Communists fled to the mountains in the southern province of Jiangxi (jee•AHNG•SHEE). Here they gathered their strength and formed the Red Army, led by the son of a prosperous peasant family, **Mao Zedong** (MOW DZUH•DOONG). Mao believed that the Communists could still triumph with the help of China's millions of peasants:

> ❝ In a very short time, in China's central, southern, and northern provinces, several hundred million peasants will rise like a mighty storm, like a hurricane, a force so swift and violent that no power, however great, will be able to hold it back. ❞
>
> —Mao Zedong, *Report on an Investigation*, 1926

Living conditions for China's peasants had changed little over the centuries. They worked small plots of land and turned over most of their crops to wealthy landlords. The Red Army gained popular support in rural areas of the country by overthrowing local landlords and distributing their land to the peasants. Before long, the Red Army included nearly 30,000 peasant troops.

The success of the Red Army worried Chiang. In the early 1930s he ordered a series of "extermination campaigns" in an attempt to destroy this rival army. Mao fought back, however, using his own strategies: "The enemy advances, we retreat; the enemy camps, we harass; the enemy tires, we attack; the enemy retreats, we pursue."

Mao's military plans worked at times, but by October 1934, the Guomindang had nearly surrounded the Communists with a million troops. Mao decided to retreat once again, leading about 100,000 followers out of Jiangxi Province in a desperate gamble for survival.

being chased by Guomindang military forces. The Chinese Communists called the arduous undertaking the Long March.

At times the line of marching Communist soldiers stretched out for nearly 50 miles (80 km). One of these soldiers later recalled the march:

❝ If it was a black night and the enemy far away, we made torches from pine branches or frayed bamboo, and then it was truly beautiful. At the foot of a mountain, we could look up and see a long column of lights coiling like a fiery dragon up the mountainside. From the summit we could look in both directions and see miles of torches moving forward like a wave of fire. A rosy glow hung over the whole route of the march. ❞

Conditions on the Long March were far from rosy, however. Thousands of soldiers froze or starved to death, and others died in battle. Of the original 100,000 troops, fewer than 8,000 remained at the end of the march in 1935.

Threat From Japan

While Chiang and Mao battled each other in 1931, the Japanese had conquered the large section of northeast China known as **Manchuria**. Now it appeared that Japan wanted even more land, and Chiang's advisers urged him to confront the Japanese. Mao offered assistance but was rejected by Chiang. Manchurian forces then kidnapped Chiang and held him prisoner until he finally agreed to end his war with the Communists.

However, unity between Chiang and Mao could not stop the Japanese invasion that came eight months later. By 1939 Japan controlled most of eastern China. Chiang withdrew to the interior of the country, where Mao was awaiting the proper moment to strike back. Before that moment arrived, the entire world was at war.

Visualizing History Mao Zedong led the Communist retreat known as the Long March. Some Communists survived the ordeal in spite of harsh weather and rugged terrain. *From what Chinese force were the Communists fleeing?*

The Long March

Mao's retreat from Jiangxi lasted for one year and covered about 6,000 miles (9,600 km). During that time the Red Army marched an average of 16 miles (26 km) a day, across rivers and mountains, and defeated 10 provincial armies—all the while

---

SECTION 3 REVIEW

Recall
1. **Define** warlord.
2. **Identify** Sun Yat-sen, Yuan Shigai, Chiang Kai-shek, Mao Zedong.
3. **List** the groups of Chinese who supported the Communists most strongly.

Critical Thinking
4. **Analyzing Information** Why do you think Mao decided to undertake the Long March?

What other choices did he have?

Understanding Themes
5. **Conflict** What conflicts kept China in turmoil after World War I?

1915   1925   1935

1915 Japan forces China to accept the Twenty-One Demands.

1925 Japanese parliament grants vote to all males.

1932 Army officers assassinate Japanese prime minister.

Section 4

Militarism in Japan

Setting the Scene

▶ **Terms to Define**
population explosion, heavy industry, *zaibatsu*

▶ **People to Meet**
Hirohito

▶ **Places to Locate**
Manchuria

Find Out How did militarism shape Japan during the period after World War I?

The Storyteller

Japan's Total War Research Institute drafted a secret strategy for the Japanese government. Called the "Greater East Asia Co-Prosperity Sphere," the plan outlined the establishment of a "zone of peaceful living and common prosperity for the peoples of East Asia." Japan would be the stabilizing power. The influence of all other nations would be driven out. The "New Order of East Asia" was an idea that did not include independence based on national self-determination. Instead, Japan would establish a new morality whose basic principle would be the Imperial Way.

—adapted from *Sources of the Japanese Tradition*, edited by W.T. deBary, reprinted in *Sources of World Civilization*, Volume 2, 1994

Japanese cavalry in China

Like China, Japan, an independent country, had fought on the side of the Allies in World War I. During the conflict, the Japanese supplied weapons to their European partners, particularly to Russia. At the same time, they took advantage of the war to expand their economic and political influence in East Asia. In addition to ruling Korea and Taiwan, Japan pressed for an enlargement of its role in China. In 1915 Japanese diplomats forced the Chinese government to accept a list of terms known as the Twenty-One Demands. The Twenty-One Demands, in effect, made China a Japanese protectorate.

Japan and the West

When World War I ended, Japan received Germany's Pacific islands north of the Equator as mandates from the League of Nations. The Japanese also entered into a series of military and commercial agreements with the Western powers. A disarmament conference held in Washington, D.C., in 1922 led to a five-power agreement among Japan, Great Britain, the United States, Italy, and France that allowed Japan to become the world's third-largest naval power after Great Britain and the United States. Yet, in spite of this and other gains, the Japanese were bitter toward the West.

First, Japan felt that the West did not accept it as an equal. In 1919 the League of Nations, dominated by Western powers, refused to accept Japan's demand for a statement on racial equality in the League's charter. The Japanese regarded this rejection as a humiliation. In 1924 the United States banned further Japanese immigration to its shores. In response, the Japanese staged demonstrations and boycotted American goods.

The Japanese were angered further by the West's refusal to support Japanese policy in China. Japan wanted to tie China closer to itself; the West wanted to retain the Open Door policy. As a result

Young Japanese students celebrate the fall of Nanjing to Japanese forces in 1938. *Why was Emperor Hirohito unable to thwart the spread of militarism in Japan?*

of Western pressure, Japan had to abandon the Twenty-One Demands and recognize Western interests in China.

Social and Political Tensions

After World War I, Japan faced social and economic challenges at home. Of major concern was a **population explosion**, or dramatic increase in population. Japan's population had increased from nearly 35 million in 1872 to about 60 million in 1925. This rate of increase was a challenge because of the already high density of population on the Japanese islands.

Japan's Industrial Growth

Since emigration was cut off to such places as the United States, the Japanese looked for other ways to cope. They placed new emphasis on manufacturing and foreign trade. It was hoped that new factories and markets would provide employment for large numbers of people.

Government-controlled banks provided the needed capital to encourage the expansion of **heavy industry**, or the manufacture of machinery and equipment needed for factories and mines. Industries important to national defense, especially steel and the railroads, were owned by the government, but most of the Japanese economy was in the hands of large privately owned businesses known together as the *zaibatsu* (zy•BAHT•soo).

During the 1920s and 1930s Japan's industry grew rapidly, and Japanese manufactured goods began to flood world markets. Increased manufacturing, however, stimulated the desire for raw materials. Since Japan had few mineral resources of its own, it was forced to look overseas for them.

Social and Political Changes

Meanwhile, Japan's working class increased in importance. Because of overpopulation in the countryside, land already scarce was continually subdivided among farmers. Rural economic woes enabled farm villages to provide the bulk of labor for the new urban industries. Along with male workers, many young women from rural areas found jobs in the factories.

Labor unions became more powerful and increased their membership to more than 300,000 members by the end of the 1920s. The growth of the urban, working-class population produced movements demanding social changes. Several efforts by intellectuals to organize Socialist groups, however, were speedily met with police repression.

During this period, the urban middle class expanded as well. Japanese cities became great metropolitan areas and centers of middle-class culture. The Tokyo-Yokohama area, devastated by a terrible earthquake in 1923, took on a new appearance as Western influences increasingly shaped the tempo of urban life. American music, dancing, and sports especially became popular, and rising standards of living and expectations produced the need for more and better higher education.

With the growth of the working and middle classes, steps were taken toward greater political democracy. In 1925 the Japanese parliament granted universal male suffrage; voters increased from 3 million to 14 million. Japanese women, however, did not receive the right to vote until 1947.

Political Weaknesses

In spite of these gains, democracy remained very limited in Japan. Political power was actually in the hands of nobles and urban industrialists. The emperor, **Hirohito**, was a constitutional monarch. However, he was a powerful symbol of traditional authority. Behind the emperor was an influential group of military leaders, who were opposed to democratic reforms.

The appeal of antidemocratic nationalist groups increased as the economy deteriorated in the 1930s. A worldwide fall in prices caused by the Great Depression devastated Japan's silk factories and other industries. Millions of workers lost their jobs and could not find new ones. Some began to starve, and children went begging in the streets. In November 1930 an assassin from a secret society shot Prime Minister Osachi Hamaguchi (oh•SAH•chee hah•mah•GOO•chee). Teetering on the brink of economic chaos, many impoverished farmers and workers in Japan looked to strong-minded military leaders such as Hashimoto Kingoro (hah•shee•MOH•toh keen•GOH•roh) for answers:

> 66 We are like a great crowd of people packed into a small and narrow room, and there are only three doors through which we might escape, namely emigration, advance into world markets, and expansion of territory. The first door … has been barred to us by the anti-Japanese immigration policies of other countries. The second door … is being pushed shut by tariff barriers.… Japan should rush upon the last door [expansion of territory]. 99
>
> —Hashimoto Kingoro, *Addresses to Young Men*

Militarism and Daily Life

During the 1930s, militarism began to influence all aspects of Japanese life—from foreign policy to education. Supporters of the military program opposed the spread of Western lifestyles in Japan and favored traditional Japanese ways. Military dress, including items such as the samurai swords, appealed to nationalist sentiments. Young children even carried out military drills in schools and participated in parades.

Military Expansion

In September 1931 the Japanese military demonstrated just how powerful it had become.

Without seeking approval from the government, army leaders decided to invade the northeastern region of China known as **Manchuria**. In short order, they launched an invasion. It was clear that the Japanese government could no longer control its own army. In five months the powerful Japanese army had conquered Manchuria.

The conquest of Manchuria was a clear sign of the plans of the military to dominate the Japanese government at home and expand Japanese influence abroad. The principal opposition to democratic government came from young military officers. Largely from rural backgrounds, they opposed the urban luxuries of the politicians and readily accepted extremist ideas.

By the early 1930s extremist groups in the military were ready to use violence to bend the government to their will. In 1932 army officers assassinated a prime minister who dared to oppose their views. Then, in 1936, another group of officers led an armed revolt against the government. Although the revolt collapsed, it did not halt the steady takeover of government policy making by the military. By early 1937 the army and the government had become one and the same.

Many democratically minded Japanese hoped that Emperor Hirohito would try to thwart the spread of militarism. As a crown prince, the emperor had traveled in the West and had a keen appreciation of Western ways. Palace advisers, however, feared that any strong stand by the emperor would only increase the extremism of the military leaders. Above all, they feared that the emperor would be removed from office and that the Japanese monarchy would be abolished.

As international criticism of Japan's expansion grew, many Japanese rallied to the support of their soldiers and the military leaders. With no powerful political opposition at home, Japan's military leaders looked forward to conquering all of Asia. Their dreams of a mighty Japanese empire—like the dreams of German and Italian rulers—brought the world to war.

SECTION 4 REVIEW

Recall
1. **Define** population explosion, heavy industry, *zaibatsu*.
2. **Identify** Hirohito.
3. **Locate** the Manchurian Plain on the map on pages A16 and A17 of the Atlas. Explain why the location of this region made it valuable to the Japanese.

Critical Thinking
4. **Synthesizing Information** Imagine you are an unemployed worker in Japan in the 1930s. Would you support the new military powers? Why or why not?

Understanding Themes
5. **Conflict** What steps did the military take to increase its hold on the Japanese government?

Critical Thinking SKILLS

Identifying an Argument

Have you ever argued with someone about a political or social issue? In everyday conversation, the word *argument* refers to a conflict involving two or more opinions. However, in writing and in formal debate, an argument is the full presentation of a single opinion. It is important to learn how to identify a writer's or speaker's argument to fully understand and evaluate the position.

Learning the Skill

The main idea of an argument is its thesis, or the writer's basic position or viewpoint on the subject. In some arguments the thesis is stated explicitly. In others, you must read carefully to determine the writer's position.

The writer supports the thesis with reasons and supports the reasons with examples or facts. For instance, suppose your parents have said that it would be better if you did not have a car to drive until after your 18th birthday. They support their thesis with these reasons: 1) other forms of transportation are available; and 2) you will be a more mature and better driver by that age. They support the first reason with these facts: you live in a city with good public transportation; your best friend has a car and frequently drives you to school. They support the second reason with accident statistics of younger and older drivers.

Before accepting or rejecting an argument, evaluate its strengths and weaknesses. Determine the validity of each reason. How well is each reason supported by facts and examples? Does the author's bias invalidate the argument? In the above example, your parents may be biased; they may want to protect your safety and keep their car insurance rates low for another year. Despite this bias, however, they still may have a strong argument if the supporting facts are true.

Practicing the Skill

Read the quotation from Jomo Kenyatta below, and review the discussion of Kenya in Section 1, pages 799-800. Then answer the following questions.

1. What is Kenyatta's thesis in this quotation?
2. What reasons does Kenyatta give to support this thesis?
3. What facts support Kenyatta's statement that Europeans have robbed Africans of their birthright?
4. What bias does Kenyatta show in his statement? Do the facts outweigh his bias? Why or why not?

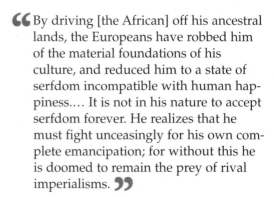

By driving [the African] off his ancestral lands, the Europeans have robbed him of the material foundations of his culture, and reduced him to a state of serfdom incompatible with human happiness.... It is not in his nature to accept serfdom forever. He realizes that he must fight unceasingly for his own complete emancipation; for without this he is doomed to remain the prey of rival imperialisms.

—Jomo Kenyatta, *Facing Mount Kenya*, 1938

Applying the Skill

Find an article in a recent newspaper or magazine that states an argument about a political or historical issue. Identify the thesis of the argument and major reasons and evidence supporting it. Decide whether you accept or reject this argument and explain why.

For More Practice

Turn to the Skill Practice in the Chapter Review on page 823 for more practice in identifying an argument.

Section 5

Nationalism in Latin America

Setting the Scene

▶ **Terms to Define**
cooperatives, nationalization

▶ **People to Meet**
Lázaro Cárdenas, Juan Vicente Gómez, Hipólito Irigoyen, José F. Uriburu, Getúlio Vargas, Augusto César Sandino

▶ **Places to Locate**
Mexico, Venezuela, Argentina, Brazil, Nicaragua

Find Out Why did nationalism in Latin America bring conflict with the United States?

The Storyteller

"Let us forget the marble of the Acropolis and the towers of the Gothic cathedrals. We are the sons of the hills and the forests. Stop thinking of Europe. Think of America!" The words of Ronald de Carvallo, a Brazilian nationalist, rang in Lucio Costa's ears. He resolved to break with traditional forms and create architecture appropriate for Brazil. He visualized a style integrating art and nature—murals, sculptures, and tiles with gardens and decorative painting.

—adapted from *Latin America, A Concise Interpretive History,* E. Bradford Burns, 1994

Palacio Do Ilamarati, Brasilia

After World War I, economic change and nationalism swept Latin America. Although the region's economy remained basically agricultural, the oil and mineral industries became increasingly important. Much of the investment that developed these resources was from the United States, Great Britain, France, Germany, and Italy. Anger at foreign influence led to growing nationalism among Latin Americans of all backgrounds. Rubén Darío, a noted Nicaraguan writer, had expressed the view of many Latin Americans:

❝ The United States is grand and powerful.
Whenever it trembles, a profound shudder
runs down the enormous backbone of the
  Andes.
If it shouts, the sound is like the roar of a
  lion....
But our own America, which has had poets
  since the ancient times ...
and has lived, since the earliest moments
  of its life,
in light, in fire, in fragrance, and in love—
the America of Moctezuma and Atahualpa,
the aromatic America of Columbus,
Catholic America, Spanish America ...
our America lives. And dreams. And loves.
And it is the daughter of the Sun. Be
  careful.
Long live Spanish America! ❞
—Rubén Darío, "To Roosevelt," 1903

Economic Changes

In the 20 years following World War I, Latin Americans continued to grow coffee, bananas, wheat, corn, beans, sugarcane, and other crops in large amounts. However, industrial growth—particularly in the United States and western Europe—increased the demand for tin, copper, silver, oil, and other raw materials from Latin America. As mineral exports increased, Latin Americans had more cash with which to buy imports. More and more of the Latin American economy became tied to global markets.

When world prices for raw materials increased, Latin American economies improved. However, in the 1920s, prices for coffee, sugar, and other raw materials plunged. The price declines foretold the global economic depression that was soon to occur. Like much of the world, Latin America suffered high unemployment and low prices for its products in the decade of the Great Depression, 1929–1939.

Mexico's Oil Economy

Oil was one of the vital resources for growing industries, and **Mexico** was an important source of oil. Mexico entered the postwar era, still reeling

from its own bloody and divisive revolution that had begun in 1910. However, a stable, one-party system was evolving that seemed able to maintain order and unity. Mexico's constitution, ratified in 1917, authorized the government to protect workers from exploitation and to require private property owners to act in the public interest.

Despite the constitution, reforms came slowly until 1934. In that year, **Lázaro Cárdenas** (KAHR•duhn•AHS) was elected to the presidency. Over the next six years, his government carried out other reforms in the spirit of the 1910 revolution. First, Cárdenas directed the redistribution of vast tracts of land to landless peasants. To increase agricultural production, the Mexican government also encouraged the formation of cooperatives, farm organizations operated by and for the peasants. By 1940 more than half of all Mexicans farmed land they could finally call their own.

Cárdenas's main goal, however, was to make Mexico economically independent of foreign countries. His government especially wanted to bring

Images of the Times

Mexican Murals

During the 1930s, Mexican artists painted colorful murals showing key themes and events in Mexico's history. Many of these murals still decorate outer and inner walls of government buildings, theaters, universities, and hospitals throughout the country.

Distribution of the Land by Diego Rivera. Court of Fiestas, Secretaria de Educacion Publica, Mexico City, Mexico

the industrial economy under Mexican control. In 1937 Cárdenas supported an oil workers' strike. At the time, many Mexican workers had gone on strike against their British and American employers, demanding higher wages and better working conditions. Cárdenas urged the oil companies to meet their demands, but the companies refused. After a year of futile negotiations, Cárdenas carried out a policy of nationalization of foreign-owned oil wells on March 18, 1938, declaring them the property of the government. He explained his actions by reaching all the way back to a colonial law written by the Spanish king in 1783, which had been retained in the new constitution: "The Mines are the property of My Royal Crown, [including] all bitumens [minerals] and juices of the earth."

The British and American companies were furious, but the Mexican people were ecstatic. They celebrated March 18 as the day of their "Declaration of Economic Independence." Cárdenas, meanwhile, defused the crisis by offering to pay a fair price for

the oil wells. With World War II looming on the horizon, Great Britain and the United States soon accepted this offer. They did not want an angry Mexico to sell its oil to Japan and Germany.

The nationalization of Mexico's oil fields signaled the arrival of economic nationalism in Latin America. For Mexico it was a clean break from the economic dependence of the past.

Changes in Venezuela

Another oil-rich country, **Venezuela**, followed a course unlike that of Mexico, but more like that of other Latin American countries that had a single source of wealth. Between 1908 and 1935, President **Juan Vicente Gómez** ruled Venezuela as a dictator. During this period, engineers discovered oil along Venezuela's Caribbean coast. By the late 1930s Venezuela was the third-largest oil-producing country in the world. However, British, Dutch, and American oil companies controlled the Venezuelan oil industry. Gómez, instead of nationalizing the oil companies, worked closely with them. He, his

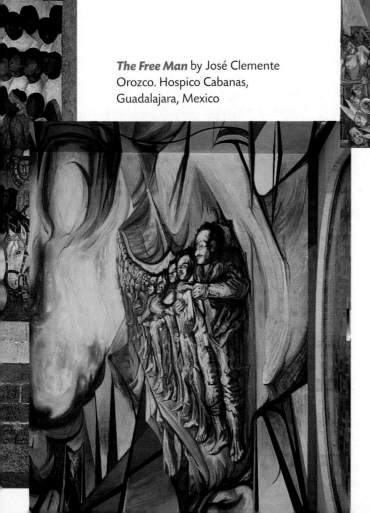

The Free Man by José Clemente Orozco. Hospico Cabanas, Guadalajara, Mexico

From Porfirio's Dictatorship to the Revolution (detail with Martyrs) by David Alfaro Siqueiros. Museo Nacional de Historia, Castillo de Chapultepec, Mexico City, Mexico

REFLECTING ON THE TIMES

1. What three leading Mexican artists painted murals during the 1930s?
2. Based on the murals, what do you think are some major themes in Mexican history?

813

By the 1930s, Buenos Aires had become a city of wide avenues and public buildings. Its prosperity rested on the export of beef and other agricultural products. *How did the Great Depression affect Argentina's political life during the 1930s?*

political allies, and oil companies prospered, but most Venezuelans did not.

Gómez used the oil profits to strengthen his government. He paid off his country's huge national debt to European bankers and created a strong army. He also used some of the profits for his personal benefit.

After Gómez died in 1935, workers and students around the country rioted to protest the domination of their country by foreign oil companies and their Venezuelan partners. The army intervened to stop the protests and remained in charge of the country for the next several decades.

Democracy and the Military

Venezuela was one of many Latin American countries in which a small group of people prospered from the natural wealth found in the country. It was also typical in that the military intervened to put down protests that threatened business interests. Argentina and Brazil are two of the other countries in which democracy failed to take hold.

Argentina Becomes Fascist

In 1916 **Argentina** held its first open presidential election in which every male could vote. The winner, **Hipólito Irigoyen** (ee•PAW•lee•TOH IHR •ih•GOH•YEHN), obtained most of his support from urban workers and the middle class. They elected him because of his party's success in

achieving electoral reforms. During his first administration, Irigoyen carried through social reforms that improved factory conditions, boosted workers' wages, and regulated working hours. He advocated other democratic reforms and efforts to help the poor. After serving six years as president, Irigoyen proudly claimed:

> ❝ We have held public office in obedience to the popular mandate and inspired by the duty to make reparation … for all the injustices, moral and political, collective and individual, that have long dishonored the country. ❞

In 1928 Irigoyen was again elected president. His second term, however, aroused widespread opposition, and he did not complete his term in office. Although he was personally popular, his government had often been ineffective. He was slow to make decisions, so that official documents needing his attention piled up on his desk awaiting action. More important, corrupt aides stole money from the national treasury. In addition, few Argentinians believed any more in the democratic process by which Irigoyen had won office.

Angered by inefficiency and corruption and opposed to democracy, General **José F. Uriburu** led a successful coup against Irigoyen in 1930. With the coming of the Great Depression, Argentina was divided between Socialist and Fascist political

National Archives

Sending in the Marines

National Archives

American marines in Nicaragua unload a cannon to help defend their military position. The United States has a history of military intervention in the Central American nation of Nicaragua. In the early years of the 1900s American interest in Nicaragua increased with the building of the Panama Canal, with growing pressure to defend the hemisphere against British and German threats, and with expanding United States involvement in Central American trade.

In 1912, U.S Marines landed in Nicaragua to ensure the payment of its debts and remained there for the next 13 years. In 1927, American forces again intervened to put down an uprising by nationalist leader Augusto César Sandino (left, center figure). Sandino fought American involvement in his country's domestic affairs—and failed. American forces remained in Nicaragua until 1933.

During the years between the two world wars the empires of Europe began to crumble. In the Western Hemisphere President Hoover pulled American troops out of Nicaragua, and President Franklin D. Roosevelt declared a Good Neighbor policy with Latin America. Nevertheless, imperialism endured until after World War II. ⊕

AROUND THE WORLD

Major Oil Discovery

Saudi Arabia, 1938

In 1933 the government of Ibn Saud granted an American oil company the right to explore for oil in the newly united kingdom of Saudi Arabia. After a major oil deposit was discovered on the Arabian Peninsula, other oil companies joined to form the Arabian American Oil Company (Aramco) in 1944. After World War II, large-scale oil production brought immense wealth to Saudi Arabia and enabled Ibn Saud's government to build roads, schools, and hospitals throughout the country.

Saudi Arabia

movements. To maintain social order, the army began to assume an important role in the Argentine government.

Uriburu, like Italy's Mussolini, believed in fascism. He cancelled elections and tried to abolish the congress. For the remainder of the 1930s, military men and their sympathizers ruled Argentina. They faked elections, suppressed their opponents, and consolidated their power. Democracy was dead in Argentina, destroyed by the military.

Brazil's Popular Dictator

Brazil, like Argentina, fell under an authoritarian government. In 1930 President **Getúlio Vargas** took power. Seven years later, Vargas proclaimed a new constitution that made him a virtual dictator. He strengthened the government by transferring powers from the cities and states to the national government. He won support from many Brazilians for his willingness to oppose the interests of large businesses. To gain working-class support, Vargas's administration increased wages, shortened working hours, and gave unions the right to organize. Vargas's supporters called him "father of the poor" for these efforts.

Vargas, with the support of the military, was able to keep Brazil united and stable until 1945. In that year, a democratic revolt threw him out of power. When Vargas refused to leave office, military leaders stepped in and forced Vargas out of office. Although the military did not actually rule in Brazil, their support was crucial in deciding who did.

Ties With the United States

During the 1920s and 1930s, the mineral wealth of Latin America attracted American businesses, which invested heavily in the region. To protect American economic interests, the United States intervened militarily in Central America and the Caribbean countries.

Increased American Intervention

In 1912 United States Marines had invaded **Nicaragua** when the country failed to pay its debts. American forces landed again during the 1920s to protect United States interests. Rebel forces led by General **Augusto César Sandino** resisted the Americans and tried to force a United States withdrawal. To help the American soldiers, the United States government trained a loyal Nicaraguan army called the National Guard. By the mid-1930s the National Guard was able to defeat the rebels. Its leader, Anastasio Somoza, seized power in 1936. From that time until 1979, the Somoza family ruled Nicaragua with American support.

During the early 1900s, American troops also occupied Haiti and the Dominican Republic as well as Nicaragua. This American military intervention, as well as the growth of American economic influence, was deeply resented by many Latin Americans. Latin American nationalists particularly opposed the Roosevelt Corollary. They stated that no country had the right to intervene in the affairs of another. They also claimed that, while the United States was exploiting their raw materials, Latin America was getting few economic benefits in return. Anti-Americanism was especially strong during the Great Depression. At this time, world market prices for raw materials fell sharply. This decline increased hardships among Latin Americans dependent on trade with North America and Europe.

Good Neighbor Policy

Aware of growing resentment, the United States tried to improve relations with its southern neighbors. Following his election in 1928, United States President Herbert Hoover went on a goodwill tour of Latin America. He hoped to show that the United States regarded its Latin American neighbors as equals. At the same time, Undersecretary of State Joshua Reuben Clark began to restate the meaning of the Monroe Doctrine. In a memorandum issued in December 1928, Clark held that the Monroe Doctrine's warning that European powers could not interfere in Latin America did not mean that the United States had the right to interfere.

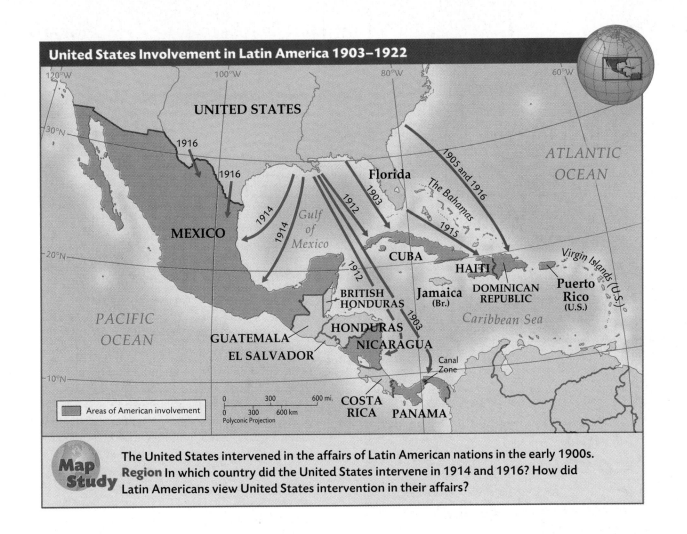

United States Involvement in Latin America 1903–1922

UNITED STATES

1916

1916

1914

1914

Gulf of Mexico

MEXICO

Florida

1912

1903

The Bahamas

1905 and 1916

ATLANTIC OCEAN

1915

CUBA

HAITI

Virgin Islands (U.S.)

1912

BRITISH HONDURAS

Jamaica (Br.)

DOMINICAN REPUBLIC

Puerto Rico (U.S.)

Caribbean Sea

PACIFIC OCEAN

GUATEMALA

EL SALVADOR

HONDURAS

1903

NICARAGUA

Canal Zone

COSTA RICA

PANAMA

Areas of American involvement

0   300   600 mi.
0   300   600 km
Polyconic Projection

Map Study The United States intervened in the affairs of Latin American nations in the early 1900s. **Region** In which country did the United States intervene in 1914 and 1916? How did Latin Americans view United States intervention in their affairs?

In 1933 President Franklin D. Roosevelt, Hoover's successor, announced the Good Neighbor policy toward Latin America. He declared, "I would dedicate this nation to the policy of the good neighbor—the neighbor who resolutely respects himself, and because he does so, respects the rights of others." The Good Neighbor policy renounced past United States military intervention in the region. To prove his good intentions, Roosevelt ended American restrictions on the sovereignty of Cuba. He also ordered the withdrawal of American troops from Haiti and Nicaragua.

In 1933 the United States took another step toward improving its relationship with Latin America. Diplomats from the United States joined with their Latin American counterparts at the Pan American conference in Montevideo, Uruguay. After much discussion, all parties signed an agreement stating: "No state has the right to intervene in the internal or external affairs of another."

SECTION 5 REVIEW

Recall
1. **Define** cooperatives, nationalization.
2. **Identify** Lázaro Cárdenas, Juan Vicente Gómez, Hipólito Irigoyen, José F. Uriburu, Getúlio Vargas, Augusto César Sandino, the Good Neighbor policy.

3. **Describe** major political and economic trends in Latin America during the period between the world wars.

Critical Thinking
4. **Making Comparisons** How did Mexico and Venezuela differ in their response to European

and American control of their oil industries?

Understanding Themes
5. **Change** Does the United States have the right to intervene in the affairs of other countries? Explain, using recent examples.

from

Gifts of Passage

by Santha Rama Rau

Santha Rama Rau, born in Madras, India, in 1923, spent her childhood in India, England, and South Africa. In each place, she closely watched the way people from different backgrounds related with one another. Advances in transportation and communication have sharply increased the interactions of people from different cultures. Today these interactions shape the world more than ever before. In the following excerpt, Rau recalls her early experiences at a school for English and Indian children in India.

At the Anglo-Indian day school in Zorinabad to which my sister and I were sent when she was eight and I was five and a half, they changed our names. On the first day of school, a hot, windless morning of a north Indian September, we stood in the head-mistress's study and she said, "Now you're the *new* girls. What are your names?"

My sister answered for us. "I am Premila, and she"—nodding in my direction—"is Santha."

The headmistress had been in India, I suppose, fifteen years or so, but she still smiled her helpless inability to cope with Indian names. Her rimless half-glasses glittered, and the precarious bun on the top of her head trembled as she shook her head. "Oh, my dears, those are much too hard for me. Suppose we give you pretty English names. Wouldn't that be more jolly? Let's see, now—Pamela for you, I think." She shrugged in a baffled way at my sister. "That's as close as I can get. And for *you*," she said to me, "how about Cynthia? Isn't that nice?"

My sister was always less intimidated than I was, and while she kept a stubborn silence, I said "Thank you," in a very tiny voice....

That first day at school is still, when I think of it, a remarkable one. At that age, if one's name is changed, one develops a curious form of dual personality. I remember having a certain detached and disbelieving concern in the actions of "Cynthia," but certainly no responsibility. ...

Visualizing History During the years of British rule, the Indian subcontinent had a wealthy upper class of princes and their families. This upper-class Indian family of the 1940s practiced traditional ways but was also familiar with the customs of the British aristocracy. *What are the British teachers' attitudes toward ordinary Indians in the story by Santha Rama Rau?*

Accordingly, I followed the thin, erect back of the headmistress down the veranda [porch] to my classroom feeling, at most, a passing interest in what was going to happen to me in this strange, new atmosphere of School....

I can't remember too much about the proceedings in class that day, except for the beginning. The teacher pointed to me and asked me to stand up. "Now, dear, tell the class your name."

I said nothing.

"Come along," she said, frowning slightly. "What's your name, dear?"

"I don't know," I said, finally.

The English children in the front of the class—there were about eight or ten of them—giggled and twisted around in their chairs to look at me. I sat down quickly and opened my

eyes very wide, hoping in that way to dry them off. The little girl with the braids put out her hand and very lightly touched my arm. She still didn't smile.

Most of the morning I was rather bored. I looked briefly at the children's drawings pinned to the wall, and then concentrated on a lizard clinging to the ledge of the high, barred window behind the teacher's head. Occasionally it would shoot out its long yellow tongue for a fly, and then it would rest, with its eyes closed and its belly palpitating, as though it were swallowing several times quickly. The lessons were mostly concerned with reading and writing and simple numbers—things that my mother had already taught me—and I paid very little attention. The teacher wrote on the easel blackboard words like "bat" and "cat," which seemed babyish to me; only "apple" was new and incomprehensible.

When it was time for the lunch recess, I followed the girl with braids out onto the veranda. There the children from the other classes were assembled. I saw Premila at once and ran over to her, as she had charge of our lunchbox. The children were all opening packages and sitting down to eat sandwiches. Premila and I were the only ones who had Indian food—thin wheat chapatties [a type of bread], some vegetable curry, and a bottle of buttermilk. Premila thrust half of it into my hand and whispered fiercely that I should go and sit with my class, because that was what the others seemed to be doing.…

I had never really grasped the system of competitive games. At home, whenever we played tag or guessing games, I was always allowed to "win"—"because," Mother used to tell Premila, "she is the youngest, and we have to allow for that." I had often heard her say it, and it seemed quite reasonable to me, but the result was that I had no clear idea of what "winning" meant.

When we played twos-and-threes that afternoon at school, in accordance with my training, I let one of the small English boys catch me, but was naturally rather puzzled when the other children did not return the courtesy. I ran about for what seemed like hours without ever catching anyone, until it was time for school to close. Much later I learned that my attitude was called "not being a good sport," and I stopped allowing myself to be caught, but it was not for years that I really learned the spirit of the thing.…

It was a week later, the day of Premila's first test, that our lives changed rather abruptly. I was sitting at the back of the class, in my usual inattentive way, only half listening to the teacher. I had started a rather guarded friendship with the girl with the braids, whose name turned out to be Nalini (Nancy, in school). The three other Indian children were already fast friends. Even at that age it was apparent to all of us that friendship with the English or Anglo-Indian children was out of the question. Occasionally, during the class, my new friend and I would draw pictures and show them to each other secretly.

The door opened sharply and Premila marched in. At first, the teacher smiled at her in a kindly and encouraging way and said, "Now, you're little Cynthia's sister?"

Premila didn't even look at her. She stood with her feet planted firmly apart and her shoulders rigid, and addressed herself directly to me. "Get up," she said. "We're going home."

I didn't know what happened, but I was aware that it was a crisis of some sort. I rose obediently and started to walk toward my sister.

"Bring your pencils and your notebook," she said.

I went back for them, and together we left the room. The teacher started to say something just as Premila closed the door, but we didn't wait to hear what it was.

In complete silence we left the school grounds and started to walk home. Then I asked Premila what the matter was. All she would say was "We're going home for good."…

When we got to our house the ayah [maid] was just taking a tray of lunch into Mother's room. She immediately started a long, worried questioning about what are you children doing back here at this hour of the day.

Mother looked very startled and very concerned, and asked Premila what had happened.

Premila said, "We had our test today, and she made me and the other Indians sit at the back of the room, with a desk between each one."

Mother said, "Why was that, darling?"

"She said it was because Indians cheat," Premila added. "So I don't think we should go back to that school."

Mother looked very distant, and was silent a long time. At last she said, "Of course not, darling." She sounded displeased.

We all shared the curry she was having for lunch, and afterward I was sent off to the beautifully familiar bedroom for my siesta. I could hear Mother and Premila talking through the open door.

Mother said, "Do you suppose she understood all that?"

Visualizing History These Indian women are dressed in the sari, a garment of several yards of material draped so that one end forms a skirt and the other a shoulder or head covering. *How do you think the two Indian girls in the story dressed for their classes at the British school?*

Premila said, "I shouldn't think so. She's a baby."

Mother said, "Well, I hope it won't bother her."

Of course, they were both wrong. I understood it perfectly, and I remember it all very clearly. But I put it happily away, because it had all happened to a girl called Cynthia, and I never was really particularly interested in her.

RESPONDING TO LITERATURE

1. Why did Santha and her sister leave school?
2. Explain why Santha was unable to tell the class her name.
3. When the headmistress gives Santha and her sister new names, what can you determine the headmistress thought of Indian culture?
4. **Demonstrating Reasoned Judgment** Explain why Santha's mother would or would not keep her children home permanently from the Anglo-Indian school.

Connections Across Time

Historical Significance World War I shattered the old order in Europe and stirred nationalist feelings in lands under Western colonial rule. During the 1900s dozens of new nations in Asia, Africa, and the Americas either emerged from the ashes of old empires or asserted their independence from powerful neighbors. In addition, newly developing countries began to follow economic policies based on nationalism. Governments in these lands sometimes took over foreign-owned industries and limited foreign investment when national sovereignty seemed threatened.

Using Key Terms

Write the key term that completes each sentence. Then write a sentence for each term not chosen.

a. warlords
b. nationalization
c. pacifist
d. *zaibatsu*
e. cooperatives
f. heavy industry
g. shah
h. population explosion
i. self-determination
j. civil disobedience

1. After Yuan Shigai's death in 1916, local military leaders called _____ divided China among themselves.
2. United States President Woodrow Wilson raised the hopes of colonial peoples by endorsing the principle of _____.
3. In 1938 the Mexican government carried out a policy of _____ in which it took over the foreign-owned oil industries.
4. Mohandas K. Gandhi was a _____, a person opposed to using war and other means of violence to settle disputes.
5. The privately owned part of the Japanese economy in the 1920s and 1930s was largely in the hands of large companies known as _____.

Technology Activity

Using a Computerized Card Catalog Use a computerized card catalog to locate information about nationalism in Asia, Africa, and Latin America after World War I. Using your research, create a bulletin board focusing on the themes of "global nationalism." Include time lines for each region, showing significant events related to nationalism. List similarities and differences you see among the nationalist movements.

Using Your History Journal

Write a three-minute radio news feature about the setting and causes of the event you described in Your History Journal news report at the beginning of the chapter.

Reviewing Facts

1. **History** Name the contributions that India made to the war effort in World War I. What did Great Britain promise India in return?
2. **Government** Identify three leaders who would agree with the statement "Political power grows out of the barrel of a gun."
3. **History** Describe the influence of Gandhi on India's struggle for freedom.
4. **History** List the reforms introduced by Kemal Atatürk in Turkey and Reza Shah in Iran.
5. **Culture** Discuss the role of women in the nationalist movement in Nigeria after World War I.
6. **History** Identify the major event in 1938 that marked the arrival of economic nationalism in the countries of Latin America.

Critical Thinking

1. **Apply** How does political control relate to economic control? Give examples from Egypt or India.
2. **Apply** How did religious differences hamper the Indian independence movement? Give examples to support your opinion.

3. **Analyze** In 1939 most of Africa and much of Asia were European colonies. What conditions needed to change before self-determination could be achieved by all countries? Give examples to support your answer.

4. **Synthesize** Name a 1930s Mexican mural and state its theme. Could artists of other cultures and eras have also used this theme? Explain.

5. **Evaluate** Did the global influence of the West become more or less widespread in the two decades after World War I? Give examples to support your opinion.

Geography in History

1. **Location** Refer to the map below. What is the relative location of the Sea of Japan?

2. **Movement** Approximately how many miles would the Japanese military have had to transport troops across the Sea of Japan to invade Manchuria (Northeast Plain) in 1931?

3. **Region** Along what major rivers might the Japanese have traveled to gain access to central China? What obstacles would they have faced?

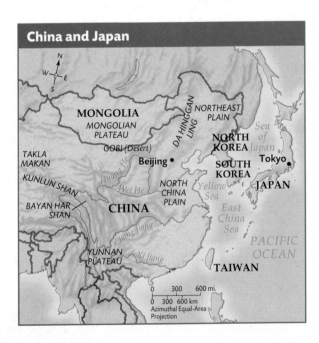

China and Japan

Understanding Themes

1. **Nationalism** In what countries of Africa and the Middle East did nationalism lead to self-

determination in the period 1919 to 1939?

2. **Change** How did the British respond to Gandhi's campaign for Indian independence?

3. **Conflict** Do you think Mao Zedong and Chiang Kai-shek were wise to put aside their differences and unite against Japan? Explain.

4. **Conflict** What were the main areas of disagreement that resulted in conflict between Japan and the West after World War I?

5. **Change** How did nationalism change Latin America following World War I?

Linking Past and Present

1. Review Gandhi's major criticisms of Western civilization. Were they accurate? Do they apply today?

2. Do you think nationalism is stronger or weaker throughout the world today than it was in the 1920s and 1930s? Give examples from current events that support your opinion.

Skill Practice

Read the quotation below by Hashimoto Kingoro and review the discussion of Japan in Section 4, pages 807–809. Then answer the questions below.

    ❝We are like a great crowd of people packed into a small and narrow room, and there are only three doors through which we might escape, namely emigration, advance into world markets, and expansion of territory. The first door … has been barred to us by the anti-Japanese immigration policies of other countries. The second door … is being pushed shut by tariff barriers … Japan should rush upon the last door [expansion of territory].❞

    —Hashimoto Kingoro, *Addresses to Young Men*

1. What is Kingoro's thesis in this argument?

2. What reasons does he give to support this thesis?

3. What evidence in Section 4 supports Kingoro's thesis?

4. Do you accept or reject Kingoro's argument? Explain your answer.

World War II

Chapter Themes

▶ **Movement** Japan, Italy, and Germany carry out expansionist policies. *Section 1*

▶ **Cooperation** The United States and Great Britain move slowly toward an alliance, while Germany and Italy make major territorial gains in Europe and the Mediterranean. *Section 2*

▶ **Conflict** Two separate and opposing alliances, the Allies and the Axis, wage a worldwide war. *Section 3*

▶ **Conflict** The Allies make major gains against the Axis Powers. *Section 4*

▶ **Innovation** New military technologies, such as the atomic bomb, affect the outcome of World War II. *Section 5*

The Storyteller

On June 6, 1944, the Allies mounted an all-out attack against German forces in Normandy, France. Years later an American soldier named Elliott Johnson could still vividly recall the events of the day:

"I remember going up to the highest part of that ship and watching the panorama around me unfold. In my mind's eye, I see one of our ships take a direct hit and go up in a huge ball of flames. There were big geysers coming up where the shells were landing and there were bodies floating, face down, face up."

The invasion of Normandy was one of the key events of World War II. Although the war began in 1939, it had its roots in the peace treaties that settled World War I.

Historical Significance

How did World War II affect the world balance of power? What nations emerged from conflict as world powers?

1930   1935   1940   1945

1931 Japanese forces invade Manchuria.

1936 The Spanish Civil War begins.

1939 Germany invades Poland; World War II begins.

1945 Germany and Japan surrender; World War II ends.

Visualizing History Allied forces led by the United States land in the Pacific island of Bougainville, the largest of the Solomon Islands.

Your History Journal

Create a two-column chart that shows the significance of ten key events in World War II. In column one list the event and date. In column two write a short statement of why the event was important to the outcome of the war.

Section 1

The Path to War

Setting the Scene

▶ **Terms to Define**
collective security, sanctions, appeasement

▶ **People to Meet**
Chiang Kai-shek, Benito Mussolini, Haile Selassie, Francisco Franco, Adolf Hitler, Joseph Stalin, Neville Chamberlain

▶ **Places to Locate**
Manchuria, Ethiopia, Spain, the Rhineland, Austria, Czechoslovakia

 **Find Out** In what sense was World War II a product of World War I?

The Storyteller

Joseph Stalin sent an invitation to formal negotiations to Adolf Hitler, the Nazi dictator. Hitler read the note and drummed both fists against the wall, exclaiming, "Now I have the world in my pocket." German Foreign Minister Joachim von Ribbentrop and Stalin arranged the division of Europe and agreed never to attack each other, then celebrated with an elaborate dinner. Each side toasted the other and told jokes the other side did not find funny. After dinner, in a final show of hospitality, Stalin drew the German foreign minister aside and told him that he personally could guarantee, on his word of honor, that the Soviet Union would not betray its partner.

Joseph Stalin

—adapted from *Joseph Stalin: Man and Legend*, Ronald Hingley, 1974

In the 1930s the Western democracies watched uneasily as militaristic dictatorships came to power in Europe and Asia. Despite their fears, Britain, France, and the United States could not agree on what steps to take to ensure their collective security, or what was needed to defend their common interests against enemy attack. Much of the unrest in Europe and Asia can be traced to the peace settlements made at the end of World War I. Great Britain, France, and the United States were substantially satisfied with these settlements; however, Japan, Italy, and Germany were not.

Japan's Expansion in Asia

Japan was the first of the nondemocratic powers to reveal its territorial ambitions in the interwar period. With limited natural resources of its own, Japan depended heavily on foreign sources for raw materials and on foreign markets for finished goods. To acquire more of these materials and markets, Japan sought new territories for conquest.

The Japanese military used a bomb explosion on the South Manchurian Railway in September 1931 as an excuse to overrun **Manchuria**. The following year Japan established Manchuria as an independent state, renamed it Manchukuo, and set up former Chinese emperor Pu Yi as puppet ruler.

When China protested in the League of Nations about Japan's actions, the League ordered a commission under British statesman Lord Lytton to investigate the affair. Lytton's commission laid the blame squarely on Japan and ordered the Japanese government to return Manchuria to China. The League voted overwhelmingly in favor of this recommendation, to which Japan responded in March 1933 by withdrawing from the League. The Manchurian incident not only revealed that the League of Nations was powerless, but also boosted the expansionist ambitions of Italy and Germany.

In the early 1930s, the Japanese military wanted to acquire the rich oil reserves of the East Indies to supply its ships and airplanes. But to control the East Indies, Japan needed Chinese ports. Consequently, in the summer of 1937, Japanese forces invaded China and captured major eastern and southern cities. In the capital of Nanjing, they engaged in mass brutality, killing over 200,000 civilians. Meanwhile, the Nationalist government of **Chiang Kai-shek** retreated inland and later allied with the Western powers. From 1937 to 1945, the Nationalists, the Chinese Communists, and the Japanese fought each other for control of China.

Visualizing History Haile Selassie (center) appealed to the League of Nations for action against Italian aggression in Ethiopia. The League's failure to halt Axis expansion led to its own downfall. *Why were the League's sanctions against Italy ineffective?*

Italy's Conquest of Ethiopia

The relative ease with which Japan acquired Manchuria encouraged Italy to make a similar move. Italy's goal was to secure control of the ancient kingdom of **Ethiopia** in eastern Africa. In 1934 Italian and Ethiopian forces clashed in a disputed zone on the border of Ethiopia and Italian Somaliland. When the Italian dictator, **Benito Mussolini**, demanded an apology and reparations, the Ethiopians responded by asking the League of Nations to investigate the matter. The League decided that because each side viewed the area where the incident took place as its own territory, neither side was to blame.

The League's decision did not satisfy Mussolini, who thought an Ethiopian colony would enhance Italy's image as a world power. Consequently, in October 1935, Mussolini ordered the Italian army to invade Ethiopia. In a dramatic appearance at the League of Nations, Ethiopian Emperor **Haile Selassie** appealed for help. This time the League condemned the action and voted to impose economic sanctions, measures designed to stop trade and other economic contacts, against Italy. The League forbade its members to sell Italy arms and certain raw materials. But the sanctions did not include oil, coal, and iron, all vital to Italy's war efforts.

Once again the League's actions were ineffective. Mussolini completed his conquest of Ethiopia, and in May 1936 he formally annexed the African nation.

Spanish Civil War

A civil war in **Spain** further inflamed the international situation in the 1930s. After presiding over years of social and economic chaos, King Alfonso XIII abdicated in 1931, and Spain became a republic. The new republican government immediately began a program of social reforms. It ended the Catholic Church's role in educating Spanish youth and redistributed land from nobles to peasants.

As a result of these and other reforms, many right-wing groups in Spain opposed the republic and wished to restore the old order. In July 1936 right-wing army chiefs staged an uprising in Spanish Morocco that soon spread to Spain. For three years the conservative Spanish Nationalists, led by General **Francisco Franco**, and the left-wing Loyalists, or Spanish Republicans, battled for control of Spain.

Early in the fighting several foreign powers intervened in the Spanish war. The Soviets supported the Loyalists, while the Germans and Italians aided the Nationalists. Volunteers from Britain, France, the United States, and other countries around the world flocked to Spain to join the International Brigade and fight for the Republican cause against fascism. The governments of the Western democracies, however, refused to intervene because they feared a general European war.

Germany's dictator, **Adolf Hitler**, viewed German participation in the Spanish Civil War as a way to strengthen ties with Italy and to secure a vital supply of Spanish iron ore and magnesium. Hermann Goering, head of the Luftwaffe—or German air force—saw an opportunity "firstly, to prevent the further spread of Communism; secondly, to test my young Luftwaffe in this or that technical aspect." To accomplish these goals, Goering formed the Condor Legion, an all-German air and ground force. They used Spanish towns and cities as testing grounds for new weapons and military tactics, such as the combined use of fire and high-explosive bombs.

By the summer of 1936, the Nationalists had taken most of western Spain. When the Soviets stopped sending aid to the Loyalists in 1938, Franco launched his final offensive. In March 1939 Franco entered Madrid, the last of the Loyalist strongholds. The civil war had ended, but more than half a million Spaniards had died, and much of the country lay in ruins. Although Spain joined Italy and Germany as countries headed by fascist dictators, Franco did not ally himself with Italy and Germany.

Hitler on the Offensive

The same year the Spanish Civil War broke out, Hitler made his move in Germany. The German dictator was convinced that Germany needed more *lebensraum*, or living space, for its expanding population. In his book, *Mein Kampf (My Struggle)*, Hitler wrote:

> **“** Only an adequate large space on this earth assures a nation freedom of existence....We must hold unflinchingly to our aim ... to secure for the German people the land and soil to which they are entitled.... **”**

Footnotes to History

Writers at War
The Spanish Civil War became a crusade for many writers. In *For Whom the Bell Tolls*, American writer Ernest Hemingway describes an idealistic American fighting the Fascist forces in Spain. The English novelist George Orwell, in *Homage to Catalonia*, presents his experiences on the Aragon front and his nearly fatal gunshot wound.

Occupying the Rhineland

Since 1919, the Versailles Treaty had forbidden German troops in **the Rhineland**, a German region between the Rhine and the French border. This ban was designed to provide security to France. Hitler gambled that if he violated the treaty, France and Great Britain would do nothing to stop him. In March 1936, therefore, Hitler sent troops into the Rhineland. France had the right to take military action, and Britain had the obligation to back France with its own armed forces. Neither country acted, however, because neither was willing to risk a war.

In October 1936, Hitler and Mussolini agreed to the Rome-Berlin Axis, an alliance that they hoped would be the "axis" around which world affairs would turn. Known thereafter as the Axis Powers, Italy and Germany later joined Japan in the Anti-Comintern Pact, an alliance against Soviet communism. Viewing the Pact as a threat to his country, the Soviet dictator **Joseph Stalin** urged the West to unite against the Axis. But the West, fearing war and distrusting Stalin, refused.

Seizing Austria

Hitler, meanwhile, grew bolder. For a long time he had dreamed of *Anschluss* (ANSH•luhs)—the joining of **Austria** to Germany. "German-Austria must return to the great mother country," he wrote. "One blood demands one Reich."

In 1934 Hitler had tried to take over Austria but backed down when Mussolini responded by mobilizing Italy's troops. In 1938, now that Germany and Italy were allies, Hitler tried again. He invited the Austrian chancellor to Berchtesgaden, his mountain retreat in the German Alps, and bullied him into appointing Nazis to key posts in Austria. The Austrian chancellor appealed to Britain and France for help, but once more the two major democracies in Europe did nothing. In March 1938 Hitler sent German troops into Austria and then proclaimed it part of Germany. He insisted that he was only promoting political stability in central Europe by uniting German-speaking peoples into one country. The Western democracies, however, refused to take military action.

Tension Builds in Europe

Austria was the first victim of Hitler's policy of expansion. **Czechoslovakia** was the next. In the late 1930s, Czechoslovakia was the only democratic nation in central Europe. It held a key strategic position in the region. Its standard of living was second only to that of

Germany. Czechoslovakia also had a strong army and alliances with France and the Soviet Union.

The nation of Czechoslovakia was created by treaty at the end of World War I. In addition to Czechs and Slovaks, it had 1 million Hungarians, half a million Ruthenians, and more than 3 million Germans. During the 1930s these minorities began to demand more freedom than they had received under the terms of the treaties, creating serious problems for the Czechoslovak government. Hitler took advantage of Czechoslovakia's ethnic problems to destroy the country.

Sudeten Crisis

On September 12, 1938, Hitler demanded that the Germans of the Sudetenland, a heavily fortified region in northwestern Czechoslovakia, be given the right of self-determination. Czechoslovak leaders responded by proclaiming martial law. In an effort to avert an international crisis, British Prime Minister **Neville Chamberlain** suggested to Hitler that they meet to discuss the matter. France supported his request.

Chamberlain met with Hitler in Germany on September 15, 1938. There Hitler demanded that the Sudetenland be given to Germany. At a second meeting a week later, Chamberlain accepted Hitler's demands. He thought that a policy of appeasement, granting concessions to maintain peace, would stabilize Europe. As the British and their French allies searched for a peaceful solution, Hitler raised his demands. The Sudetenland, he stated, must be united with Germany.

The Munich Conference

On September 29, Chamberlain met with Hitler a third time in Munich, Germany. Also attending were French Premier Édouard Daladier and Italy's dictator Benito Mussolini. Czechoslovakia and the Soviet Union were not represented.

Mussolini offered a "compromise" that gave Germany control over the Sudetenland. In return, Hitler promised to respect Czechoslovakia's sovereignty. He also promised not to take any more European territory and to settle future disputes by peaceful negotiation. Still hoping to avoid war,

 **Visualizing History** In May 1938 Adolf Hitler (left) visited Rome, Italy, to meet with his Italian ally Benito Mussolini (right). The visit was designed to demonstrate the unity of the Rome-Berlin Axis. *What role did Mussolini play in the Czech crisis later that year?*

Great Britain and France accepted the terms. On September 30, Czechoslovakia reluctantly accepted the Munich Agreement.

Chamberlain returned home to cheering crowds, proclaiming that he had ensured "peace in our time." He trusted Hitler and believed that the Nazis would cause no more trouble. Events soon proved him wrong. On March 15, 1939, Hitler sent his armies into Czechoslovakia and took control of the western part of the country. The eastern part, Slovakia, became a German puppet state. After the takeover the Western democracies could no longer maintain their illusions about Hitler's plans and began to prepare for war.

TURNING POINT

The Coming of War

More German demands followed the Munich agreement. In March 1939 Hitler turned his attention to eastern Europe. He forced Lithuania to give up the German-speaking city of Memel. Next the German dictator put pressure on Poland, threatening to take over the Baltic port of Danzig and the Polish Corridor, a narrow strip of Polish land that separated the German region of East Prussia from the rest of Germany. Great Britain and France promised to help Poland defend its borders if it became necessary. The Polish government accepted the support of the Western democracies and firmly rejected Hitler's demands.

The West and the Soviets

To defend Poland, the democracies had to consider the Soviet Union, Poland's neighbor but also its traditional enemy. During the late 1930s, Stalin had urged the Western powers to do something about Hitler. He suspected that the Munich Agreement was an attempt by the British and the French to turn Hitler's attention away from the West and toward the Soviet Union. Chamberlain, on the other hand, did not trust Stalin. He suspected that the Soviet leader wanted to extend his influence in eastern Europe. This confusion as to whether the Fascists or the Communists were the greater enemy contributed to the coolness of the British and the French toward Stalin.

Despite Chamberlain's suspicions and his lack of faith in the fighting ability of the Soviet army, he asked the Soviets to join Britain and France in an alliance to contain Nazism. Stalin agreed on the condition that the Western powers acknowledge the Soviet right to occupy a broad zone stretching from Finland to Bulgaria. Chamberlain refused Stalin's request, deepening Stalin's suspicion that the West would like nothing better than to see Germany and the Soviet Union destroy each other.

Nazi-Soviet Talks

Stalin believed that Hitler's desire for "living space" would eventually lead the German dictator to move into the rich agricultural areas of eastern Europe. Because he doubted that the West would come to his country's aid if Germany threatened it, Stalin began secret talks with the Germans. On August 23, 1939, the Soviet Union and Germany signed the Nazi-Soviet Nonaggression Pact.

According to the agreement, Germany and the Soviet Union pledged that they would never attack each other. Moreover, each would remain neutral if the other became involved in a war. Stalin and Hitler also secretly agreed to create spheres of influence in eastern Europe. Germany would occupy the western part of Poland, while the Soviet Union would govern the eastern part. They agreed to include Finland, part of Romania, and the Baltic republics of Estonia, Latvia, and Lithuania in the Soviet sphere of influence.

Neither Stalin nor Hitler had any illusions about their agreement. They were long-term enemies who, for their own purposes, needed a short-term arrangement. Stalin still believed that war with Germany was inevitable. But he thought that the pact would improve Soviet security. If nothing else, it would buy the Soviets time to prepare for war. Hitler saw the pact as a means of securing Germany's eastern border. If he did not have to worry about fighting the Soviets, he would be free to act as he wanted.

The pact shocked Western leaders, who realized that it destroyed the last barrier to war. The West had also lost a potential ally, and Hitler had won a pledge of neutrality that freed him to pursue his military objectives regarding Poland. Hitler remained convinced, however, that the West would do nothing if he moved against Poland. "The men of Munich," he said, "will not take the risk." With this thought in mind, Hitler sent his armies across the Polish frontier on September 1, 1939. However, he had finally misjudged what the Western leaders would do. Two days after Hitler's invasion of Poland, Great Britain and France declared war on Germany. World War II had begun.

SECTION 1 REVIEW

Recall
1. **Define** collective security, sanctions, appeasement.
2. **Identify** Chiang Kai-shek, Benito Mussolini, Haile Selassie, Francisco Franco, Adolf Hitler, Joseph Stalin, Neville Chamberlain.
3. **Locate** Czechoslovakia on the map on page 832. What about this country's location gave it such strategic value in Hitler's eyes?

Critical Thinking
4. **Evaluating Information** What major factors do you think contributed to the outbreak of World War II?

Understanding Themes
5. **Movement** How was the response by the League of Nations to Japanese expansion in 1933 similar to the response by the Western democracies to German expansion in 1938? How was it different? Explain your response.

1939 The Soviet Union fights Finland.

1940 France surrenders to Germany; the Battle of Britain begins.

1941 Franklin D. Roosevelt and Winston Churchill issue the Atlantic Charter.

Section 2

War in Europe

Setting the Scene

▶ **Terms to Define**
blitzkrieg, blitz, cash-and-carry policy, lend-lease

▶ **People to Meet**
Winston Churchill, Charles de Gaulle, Franklin D. Roosevelt

▶ **Places to Locate**
Finland, Norway, London, Libya

Find Out How did Hitler take over most of Europe, and what was the response of Great Britain and the United States to German expansion?

The Storyteller

Saturday night, August 24th, 1940, the first German bombs fell on London. That September, bombing became more frequent and deadly as waves of planes came over the city. For hours bombers would attack; then, to fight the fires, thousands of firefighters went into action. Many Londoners lost their homes. An observer reported that boats normally used by tourists on vacation became evacuation boats "chugging along the riverside ... defying high explosive and incendiary bombs, walls of flame, and clouds of choking fumes.... With a few bundles of clothes the refugees climbed aboard and were taken by river to the safety zone or ferried across to the opposite bank."

—adapted from *The Lost Treasures of London*, William Kent, 1947

German bombers

On September 1, 1939, the German Luftwaffe roared toward its targets in Poland, spreading panic and confusion with its bombs. At the same time, armored tank divisions known as panzers swept across the Polish border. Next came the infantry, a million and a half strong, in motorized vehicles. This was blitzkrieg, or "lightning war," a new German strategy aimed at taking the enemy by surprise.

The blitzkrieg worked with speed and efficiency, devastating Poland in a few weeks. Great Britain and France could not move fast enough to send troops to Poland. The Soviet Union, meanwhile, quickly moved its forces to occupy the eastern half of that nation.

Stalin also forced the Baltic republics of Latvia, Lithuania, and Estonia to accept Soviet military bases. When he tried to do the same with **Finland**, war broke out. The Finns held out heroically until March before the Soviets forced them to surrender. As a result of their victory, the Soviets moved their frontier 70 miles (112 km) to the west, making the city of Leningrad less vulnerable to German attack.

Hitler Looks to the West

All through the winter and spring of 1939–1940, the western front was quiet. The Germans called this period the "sit-down war," or *Sitzkrieg*, while the West dubbed it the "phony war." Many hoped that an all-out war could still be avoided.

When Finland capitulated to the Soviets, however, the British took steps to ensure that the same fate would not befall **Norway**. In early April 1940, they mined Norwegian waters to block any ships trading with Germany. Hitler used the mining to support his claim that the Allies were about to invade Scandinavia. He delivered an ultimatum to Norway and Denmark, demanding that they accept the "protection of the Reich." The Danes accepted his demands; the Norwegians did not.

Axis Expansion Into Europe 1935–1941

Legend:
- Allied nations
- Neutral nations
- Axis nations
- Occupied by Germany
- Occupied by Italy
- Vichy France and colonies
- → Axis offensive
- --- Siegfried Line
- --- Maginot Line

NORWAY 1940
FINLAND 1941
SWEDEN
DENMARK 1940
ESTONIA 1941
LATVIA 1941
Memel Territory 1939
LITHUANIA 1941
Line of Dec. 5, 1941
USSR
NORTHERN IRELAND
IRELAND
GREAT BRITAIN
NETHERLANDS 1940
GERMANY
Sudetenland 1938
EAST PRUSSIA (Ger.)
POLAND 1939
BELGIUM 1940
LUXEMBOURG 1940
CZECHO-SLOVAKIA 1939
Line of June 21, 1941
FRANCE Invaded May 10, 1940 Surrendered June 22, 1940
Rhineland 1936
SWITZER-LAND
AUSTRIA 1938
HUNGARY 1940
VICHY FRANCE
ROMANIA 1940
Black Sea
PORTUGAL
SPAIN Civil War 1936–39
ITALY
YUGOSLAVIA 1941
BULGARIA 1941
Corsica
ALBANIA 1939
TURKEY
Sardinia
Spanish Morocco
Sicily
Italy invades Ethiopia 1935
GREECE 1941
Cyprus
Rhodes
Crete
SYRIA (Fr.)
French Morocco
Mediterranean Sea
LEBANON (Br.-Fr.)
PALESTINE (Br.)
TRANS-JORDAN (Br.)
TUNISIA
ALGERIA
LIBYA
EGYPT

0 200 400 mi.
0 200 400 km
Lambert Conic Conformal Projection

Map Study By the end of 1941, Germany had seized control of much of Europe.
Location Which European nations chose to remain neutral during the war?

The Invasion of Scandinavia

In the early morning hours of April 9, three small German transports steamed into the harbor of Copenhagen, the Danish capital. After meeting little resistance, the Germans took control of Denmark. That same morning, German forces also landed along the coast of Norway. British forces had been busy laying mines in Norwegian waters in an effort to cut off German shipment of iron ore from neighboring Sweden. Within hours, however, the Germans had seized Norway's major cities, including the capital of Oslo.

Although Germany now controlled Norway, the Norwegian invasion proved costly. Germany lost a large number of destroyers and cruisers. On the other hand, Hitler won the outlet to the Atlantic that he needed to ensure that the German navy would not be bottled up in the Baltic Sea like it had in World War I.

News of the fall of Norway and Denmark caused an uproar in the British House of Commons. The Labour and Liberal opposition strongly attacked Prime Minister Neville Chamberlain and his policies. Knowing that he had lost the confidence of his own Conservative party as well, Chamberlain stepped down. On May 10, 1940, King George VI summoned **Winston Churchill** to Buckingham Palace and asked him to form a new government. Churchill, one of the few politicians to warn of the Nazi danger in the 1930s, was now prime minister.

The Fall of France

On that same momentous date, the war began in earnest on the western front. Along the Maginot Line, the British and French watched and waited. The Maginot Line was impressive, but it had one major flaw. It had a 50-mile (80-km) gap in the Ardennes. Although the Germans had invaded through Belgium and the Ardennes during World War I, the French still believed that the forests, swamps, and hills of that region were a sufficient barrier. A French tank commander, **Charles de Gaulle**, pleaded for more tanks and planes, but the French command insisted that the Maginot Line was impenetrable.

Hitler, meanwhile, carried out a massive attack on the Low Countries—Luxembourg, the Netherlands, and Belgium. Before dawn on May 10, 1940, German troops parachuted into the Netherlands. It was the first large-scale airborne attack in the history of warfare and caught the Dutch by surprise. Five days after the start of the invasion, the Dutch capitulated.

On the same day that Germany invaded the Netherlands, Britain and France moved their best troops into Belgium. German panzers swept into the Ardennes and began to encircle them. Other panzer divisions drove through Luxembourg and raced toward France.

Dunkirk

Although the Belgian forces fought valiantly, they did not hold out as long as had been expected. The Germans were now rolling through undefended open country. They pushed westward toward the English Channel, trapping the Belgian, British, and French forces in the northwest corner of France. The only hope for the Allies was an evacuation by sea from the French port of Dunkirk. With German forces within sight of the coast, the rescue of 300,000 Allied soldiers seemed impossible. But for reasons never entirely understood, Hitler ordered his forces to halt.

The British Admiralty began a desperate rescue operation at Dunkirk on May 26. A ragtag armada of 850 vessels, ranging from destroyers and cruisers to trawlers, tugs, yachts, and fishing boats, left England and set sail for Dunkirk. Civilians operated many of the smaller boats. Over the next nine days, under fierce air and ground attack, this hastily assembled fleet rescued the Allied armies.

The evacuation of Dunkirk was a stunning military achievement, but as Churchill said, "wars are not won by evacuations." Faced with an unprepared French army and a confused French government, the Germans continued their sweep into France and on June 14 entered Paris. A week later France signed an armistice with Germany.

Vichy and the Free French

By the terms of the armistice, the Germans occupied all of northern France and the Atlantic coastline to the Spanish border. In southern France, the Nazis set up a puppet government in the city of Vichy under French Marshal Henri Pétain. Pétain and other officials in the so-called Vichy government collaborated with the Germans. Many French citizens, on the other hand, continued to fight for freedom. In Britain, de Gaulle organized a Free French government, while in France many joined the French Resistance, an underground movement that opposed the German occupation.

Battle of Britain

All that stood between Hitler and German domination of western Europe was Winston Churchill and the determined British people. Hitler expected that Britain would seek peace with Germany, but he misjudged the resolve of the British. Alone and only partially prepared, Britain faced the mightiest military machine the world had ever seen.

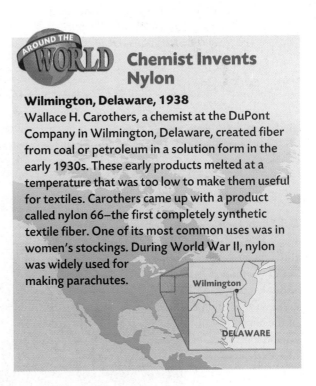

AROUND THE WORLD Chemist Invents Nylon

Wilmington, Delaware, 1938
Wallace H. Carothers, a chemist at the DuPont Company in Wilmington, Delaware, created fiber from coal or petroleum in a solution form in the early 1930s. These early products melted at a temperature that was too low to make them useful for textiles. Carothers came up with a product called nylon 66–the first completely synthetic textile fiber. One of its most common uses was in women's stockings. During World War II, nylon was widely used for making parachutes.

On May 13, 1940, Churchill delivered his first speech before the House of Commons. He told the Commons that he had "nothing to offer but blood, toil, tears, and sweat." He ended the speech with these words:

❝ You ask, what is our policy? I will say: it is to wage war, by sea, land, and air, with all our might and with all the strength that God can give us: to wage war against a monstrous tyranny, never surpassed in the dark, lamentable catalogue of human crime. That is our policy. You ask, what is our aim? I can answer in one word: Victory—victory at all costs, victory in spite of all terror, victory, however hard and long the road may be; for without victory, there is no survival. ❞

Immediately after France fell, Hitler began making plans to invade Great Britain. Hitler and the German High Command soon realized that this invasion depended on winning air supremacy over the English Channel and destroying British airfields and vital industries. To accomplish this goal, the Luftwaffe began bombing the southern coast of Britain in early August 1940. The bombings damaged four aircraft factories and five Royal Air Force (RAF) airfields, but British fighter planes known as Hurricanes and Spitfires shot down 75 German planes. From then on, Hermann Goering, head of the German air force, focused his attacks on the RAF. From August 24 to September 6, Goering sent over 1,000 planes a day. The RAF lost 466 fighters and 103 pilots, but it inflicted even heavier losses on the Germans.

Seeking to do better, the Luftwaffe changed tactics once again, switching its attack to massive night bombings of **London**. For 57 consecutive nights, from September 7 to November 3, German bombers pounded London in its great blitz, or series of air raids. In one night alone, the Luftwaffe dropped 70,000 fire bombs on Britain's capital. The devastation was enormous, killing and injuring thousands of

Images *of the* Times

The Blitz

During World War II, German bombers rained destruction on London and strategic targets in an attempt to knock out Great Britain's defenses and force the British to surrender.

Many London school children were evacuated to safer parts of Great Britain and even overseas to escape the bombing.

Public shelters were set up throughout London in subway tunnels and other protected areas. At the height of the blitz, 1 out of 7 Londoners slept in a shelter.

civilians, damaging light, power, and gas lines and destroying buildings, roads, and railways. But the bombings did not break the British people's morale.

The Luftwaffe never did gain air supremacy over Britain. While incurring heavy losses of its own, the RAF downed more than 1,700 German aircraft during the Battle of Britain, and in so doing, blocked Hitler's invasion. Churchill spoke for all Britons when he said of the RAF pilots: "Never in the field of human conflict was so much owed by so many to so few."

Anglo–American Cooperation

Throughout the early phase of the war, the United States expressed its determination to remain neutral. Even before the fighting began, the United States Congress had enacted laws designed to prevent American involvement in the war. The Neutrality Acts, passed in 1937, prohibited arms shipments, loans, and credit to belligerent nations. Congress later banned the export of armaments, "for the use of either of the opposing forces" in the Spanish Civil War.

President **Franklin D. Roosevelt,** however, became convinced that Germany's expansion endangered American security and that Britain and France could not stop Hitler without American aid. Throughout his campaign for the presidency in 1940, Roosevelt tried to rally national opinion. And as they listened to news reports of German aggression, Americans became more sympathetic to Britain's plight.

After Dunkirk, Churchill appealed to the United States for help. Roosevelt gave the British 50 old American naval destroyers in return for the right to maintain American bases in Newfoundland, Bermuda, and the British West Indies. He also convinced Congress that a cash-and-carry policy—a program in which Great Britain traded cash for desperately needed supplies—would allow the United States to supply the British without risking the loss

The Royal Air Force (RAF) won the Battle of Britain, the first battle ever fought to control the air. RAF pilots intercepted German planes with the help of ground radar stations that warned of the German planes' approach.

The bombing of London, which lasted nightly beginning in September 1940, caused much ruin, but failed to break the determined spirit of the British people.

REFLECTING ON THE TIMES

1. What did the Germans achieve by bombing London during World War II?
2. How did the British people respond to the German attacks?

Visualizing History In the spring of 1941, Erwin Rommel, "The Desert Fox" drove the British out of Libya into Egypt. *Why had Churchill diverted some troops from Africa to southeast Europe?*

of American neutrality. Throughout 1940 this policy enabled the British to import American food and armaments. They paid cash and transported the goods in their own ships.

But the cost of the war drained the British treasury. Britain ordered 12,000 airplanes from the United States in 1940 but could not pay for them. On Roosevelt's urging, Congress approved a policy of lend-lease. It authorized the President to lend war equipment to any country whose defense he deemed vital to the national security of the United States.

On August 9, 1941, Churchill met with Roosevelt on a British battleship off the Newfoundland coast to discuss war aims. The leaders issued a joint declaration called the Atlantic Charter. It upheld freedom of trade and the right of people to choose their own government. But it also called for the "final destruction of Nazi tyranny."

Eastern Europe and Africa

While Hitler was conquering much of western Europe, Mussolini was dreaming of building a Mediterranean empire for his own country—Italy. On June 10, 1940, Mussolini declared war on France and Britain. Italy's armies in **Libya** were poised for an attack on the British forces guarding Egypt and the Sudan. Although vastly outnumbered, the British attacked the Italians on December 9. In the following weeks they scored victory after victory against the Italians stationed along Libya's north coast.

Churchill, however, halted this advance and diverted some of the troops to stop a German advance in southeast Europe that had already claimed Romania, Bulgaria, and Hungary. It was a fatal decision. German forces, sweeping through Yugoslavia and Greece in April 1941, forced the British into a second Dunkirk. Although most British troops escaped by sea, they left behind their tanks and 12,000 men. Meanwhile, Hitler sent Erwin Rommel, a brilliant general who had led the 7th Panzer Division in France, to take command of a tank force in Libya and rescue the Italians. By April 11, Rommel had pushed the British out of northern Libya, except for a small force at Tobruk.

SECTION 2 REVIEW

Recall
1. **Define** blitzkrieg, blitz, cash-and-carry policy, lend-lease.
2. **Identify** Winston Churchill, Charles de Gaulle, Franklin D. Roosevelt.
3. **Explain** why Neville Chamberlain stepped down as British prime minister in 1940.

Critical Thinking
4. **Analyzing Information** What mistakes did French military leaders make that led to the fall of France?

Understanding Themes
5. **Cooperation** How did the United States government in the early 1940s move from a policy of isolationism to a policy of openly assisting the British in the war effort against the Nazis?

Critical Thinking SKILLS

Synthesizing Information

If you want to play the guitar, you must learn different skills: how to hold the instrument, play various chords, and read music. By putting together, or synthesizing, this information, you will learn to play the guitar.

Learning the Skill

When synthesizing information, we combine information obtained from separate sources. To write a research report, for example, you study the topic in several sources—encyclopedias, books, articles, and so on. Eventually, you synthesize this information and write the report.

Before synthesizing information, first analyze each source separately. Determine the value and reliability of each source. Then, look for connections and relationships among the different sources. Some information may conflict with your existing knowledge, or may present exceptions to the general rule.

Practicing the Skill

Study the passage and the map on this page. Then answer the following questions.
1. What is the main idea of the passage?
2. What information does the map add to your knowledge of this topic?
3. By synthesizing the two sources, what conclusion can you draw about the extent of the Nazis' "final solution."

❝ I have received a report which is of the greatest importance.... It is stated in this report that very large numbers of … Jews first deported to Poland or directly sent to [Auschwitz-] Birkenau in the well-known cattle-trucks from Germany, France, Belgium, Holland, Greece, etc. have been killed in these establishments. The bodies have been burnt in specially constructed stoves and the ashes have been used as fertilizers. All those who died by starvation or ill-treatment in the various labour-camps nearby were also burned in these stoves. ❞
—Letter from Richard Lichtheim of the Jewish Agency, June 19, 1944

Applying the Skill

Find two sources of information on the same topic and write a short report. In your report, answer these questions: What kinds of sources did you use—primary or secondary? What are the main ideas in these sources? How does each source add to your understanding of the topic? Do the sources support or contradict each other?

For More Practice

Turn to the Skill Practice in the Chapter Review on page 853 for more practice in synthesizing information.

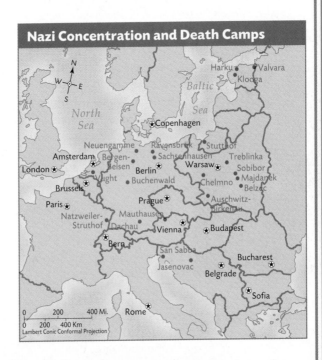

Nazi Concentration and Death Camps

MAY 1941	AUG. 1941	NOV. 1941	FEB. 1942

JUNE 1941 German forces invade the Soviet Union.

JULY 1941 The Nazis order the mass killing of Europe's Jews.

NOV. 1941 German forces reach the outskirts of Moscow.

DEC. 1941 Japan stages surprise attack on Pearl Harbor; the United States enters World War II.

Section 3

A Global Conflict

Setting the Scene

▶ **Terms to Define**
  scorched-earth policy, Holocaust, genocide

▶ **People to Meet**
  Isoroku Yamamoto

▶ **Places to Locate**
  Moscow, Kiev, Leningrad, Dachau, Warsaw, Auschwitz, Pearl Harbor

 **ind Out** How did the Soviet Union and the United States enter World War II?

The Storyteller

In 1942 a young Jewish woman wrote: "Of course, it is our complete destruction they want! But let us bear it with grace.... And a camp needs a poet, one who experiences life there, even there ... and is able to sing about it.... At night, as I lay in the camp on my plank bed ... I was sometimes filled with an infinite tenderness, and lay awake for hours letting all the many, too many impressions of a much too long day wash over me, and I prayed, 'Let me be the thinking heart of these barracks.' And that is what I want to be again. The thinking heart of a whole concentration camp."

Surviving in a concentration camp

—from *An Interrupted Life, the Diaries of Etty Hillesum, 1941–1943*, translated by Arno Pomerans, 1983

In the spring of 1941, Great Britain stood alone against Nazi Germany, which now controlled almost all of western Europe. In Africa, the Nazi General Erwin Rommel had succeeded in pushing the British back and had taken control of most of Libya. In Asia, meanwhile, the Japanese held Manchuria and controlled much of China. By the end of 1941, the expansive war would grow even larger. Events since June drew two more major powers into the conflict: the Soviet Union and the United States.

Invasion of the Soviet Union

Having failed in his attempt to defeat Great Britain, Hitler now turned his attention to the Soviet Union. Only by conquering the vast Soviet steppe, Hitler reasoned, could the "living space" believed vital to Germany's future be gained. He also wanted the wheat of Ukraine and the oil reserves of the Caucasus region.

On June 22, 1941, Hitler launched Operation Barbarossa, a massive attack on the Soviet Union. Despite British warnings and the massing of German troops along the border, the invasion took Stalin by surprise. In the first few days of fighting, the Germans destroyed the greater part of the Soviet air force, disabled thousands of Soviet tanks, and captured half a million Soviet soldiers. As German divisions advanced deeper into Soviet territory, Stalin appealed to his people to resist the invasion and issued his famous scorched-earth policy. If the Germans forced Soviet forces to retreat, Stalin ordered, Soviet citizens should destroy everything that could be of use to the invaders.

By November 1941 German armies had pushed 600 miles (960 km) inside the Soviet Union to the outskirts of **Moscow**. In addition to controlling 40 percent of the Soviet population, the Germans had captured **Kiev** and begun the siege of **Leningrad**. Yet the Soviets refused to surrender. Young Soviet soldiers rallied to the cry, "Behind us is Moscow—there is no room left for retreat!" The Germans faced not only a steely Soviet resistance but another equally formidable foe—the Russian winter. A German soldier described the conditions:

> ❝ We had no gloves. We had no winter shoes. We had no equipment whatsoever to fight or withstand the cold…. We lost a considerable part of our equipment…. Due to the cold we lost a lot of people who got frost-bitten, and we had not even the necessary amount of ointments, or the most simple and primitive things to fight in…. Guns didn't fire anymore. Even our wireless equipment didn't work properly anymore because the batteries were frozen hard…. ❞

On December 2, 1941, German troops began an assault on Moscow, and in just one day they drew within sight of the city's center. It was as far as they ever got. When all seemed lost, the Soviets staged a counterattack and forced a German retreat.

The Nazi Order

Hitler wanted to conquer the Soviet Union as part of his plan to create a "New Order" in Europe. In the new world that Hitler envisioned, the Nazis would rule Europe and exploit its resources. In addition to enslaving the conquered peoples and forcing them to work for the German "master race," the Nazis would exterminate "undesirable elements" such as the Jews and the Slavs.

The Nazis began to implement Hitler's plan by plundering the occupied countries. They seized art treasures, raw materials, and factory equipment. At the same time, the Nazis drove millions into forced labor and concentration camps and massacred millions more. Between 1939 and 1944, about 7.5 million people were deported to Germany and put to work in factories, fields, and mines. Many people in the occupied countries, however, joined underground resistance movements to combat the Nazis.

The Holocaust

Beginning in 1941, Nazi leaders carried out a plan that aimed at the complete extermination of all Jews in Europe. During the next four years, the

Visualizing History The powerful German panzers were no match for the harsh Soviet winter of 1941. The intense cold froze lubricating oil and cracked engine blocks. *What other problems did the German invaders encounter during that winter?*

Nazis murdered more than 6 million Jews. This mass destruction of the Jewish people based on racial grounds has become known as the Holocaust. Another 6 million people, including the Slavs and Gypsies, also were killed by the Nazis.

Beginnings

In mid-1940, the Nazis began to persecute Jews in the lands they had conquered. They expelled Jews from jobs and schools and forced them to wear yellow badges showing the Star of David, an ancient Jewish symbol. Some Jews managed to flee Nazi-occupied Europe; others went into hiding; but many more failed to escape and were sent to concentration camps, such as **Dachau** (DAH•KOW) in southern Germany.

The largest number of Jews in Nazi-occupied Europe lived in areas of Poland and the Soviet Union. To control this sizable Jewish population, the Nazis at first forced the Jews into specially designated areas of towns and cities called ghettos. The largest ghetto was in **Warsaw**, where almost half a million Jews were kept.

Life in the ghettos was unbearable. Families had to crowd into unsanitary housing, and contagious diseases spread rapidly. The Nazis deliberately tried to starve residents by allowing only small amounts of food. As a result, tens of thousands died in the ghettos from hunger, disease, and the cold. Despite their suffering, many people courageously tried to live as normally as possible. For example, many young people carried out their education by attending secret classes organized and taught by adults.

The Killing Squads

The German invasion of the Soviet Union in June 1941, proved to be a turning point in the Nazi mistreatment of the Jews. At that time, the Nazis turned from the forced emigration and imprisonment of Jews to the mass murder of them. Special units of Nazi soldiers known as the SS moving with the German army acted quickly to kill any Jews they could find in occupied Soviet territory. Captured Jews had to surrender their valuables and were forcibly marched to open areas on the outskirts of captured towns and cities. There they were shot, and their bodies dumped into mass graves. The killing squads murdered more than a million Jews and hundreds of thousands of other innocent people. At Babi Yar, near Kiev in Ukraine, about 35,000 Jews were murdered in two days of shooting.

The Final Solution

In January 1942, Nazi party and German government leaders secretly agreed to what they called "the final solution to the Jewish question in Europe." The "final solution" was the Nazi code word for the destruction of all European Jews. Never before had a modern state set out on a campaign of genocide, the deliberate, carefully planned killing of an entire people on the basis of race, politics, or culture.

Beginning in the summer of 1942, the Nazis arrested and rounded up Jews throughout occupied Europe by the hundreds of thousands. The Jews then were transported by train or trucks to death camps, such as **Auschwitz** (AUSH•VIHTS) in Poland, where most eventually died. Many of the people in the camps were murdered in poison gas chambers. Others died of starvation or were the victims of cruel experiments carried out by Nazi doctors.

Response and Resistance

The Nazis tried to keep the killings and death camps secret from the world. Even European Jews at first had been unaware of the fate in store for them. But once they became aware of Nazi intentions, Jews fought back in Warsaw and other European ghettos. However, Jewish resistance groups in the ghettos were outnumbered and lacked the arms to fight the Germans. In spite of their heroic efforts, Jewish resistors were easily defeated.

Some Jews who succeeded in escaping from the ghettos formed fighting units in densely forested areas of eastern Europe. Others joined regular

Let Us Never Forget

Concentration camp survivors

From 1941 to 1945, Jewish artists, musicians, and writers in the Theresienstadt concentration camp created moving artistic expressions of their Holocaust experiences. Since World War II, their works—and those of others—have stirred hearts and consciences of people everywhere about one of the most horrifying events of our century.

In his memoir called *Night* (1958), the Romanian-born writer Elie Wiesel (vee•ZEHL), a Holocaust survivor, described the horrors he witnessed in the Auschwitz and Buchenwald camps. Another writer, the Australian Thomas Keneally, in his 1982 novel

Schindler's List, tells a powerful true story about Oskar Schindler, a German manufacturer who saved his Jewish workers from the Holocaust. The American filmmaker Steven Spielberg later turned Keneally's novel into an Oscar Award-winning movie in 1993.

Another 1993 event relating to the Holocaust was the opening of the United States Holocaust Memorial Museum in Washington, D.C. Through exhibits, videos, and special lectures, the museum commemorates the millions of Jews and others murdered by the Nazis during World War II.

Linking Past and Present ACTIVITY

Explain how people in the Theresienstadt concentration camp tried to cope with their ordeal. How has the Holocaust been artistically commemorated since World War II?

When the Nazis advanced throughout Europe in 1939 and 1940, they rounded up Jews—such as these residents of Warsaw, Poland—and forced them to work as slave laborers. Later, the Nazis killed or imprisoned millions of Jews. *How did the Allies react to the Nazi persecution and killing of Europe's Jews?*

Allied forces fighting the Nazis. One Jewish resistance fighter was Hannah Senesh, a Hungarian Jew who had emigrated to Palestine in 1939. Allied forces dropped her and other parachutists into German-controlled Hungary to organize resistance efforts. Before she could accomplish her mission, she was captured and executed.

A major factor hindering Jewish resistance both in the ghettos and the forests was the widespread lack of support for the Jews. Anti-Semitic Europeans in occupied areas helped the Nazis hunt down Jews, and pro-Nazi governments, such as those of France, Italy, and Hungary, sent tens of thousands of Jews to the death camps. Even banks in neutral Switzerland accepted and profited from the money and valuables stolen from Jews by the Nazis. Even as late as the 1990s, much of this wealth had yet to be returned to the families of the rightful owners.

Most people in occupied areas, however, did nothing, thinking that the plight of the Jews did not concern them or fearing punishment if they got involved. Despite dangers, a small number of courageous people did provide help to the Jews and other persecuted people. Denmark, alone among the occupied countries, actively resisted the Nazi regime's efforts to remove its Jewish citizens.

During the Holocaust, evidence reached the outside world about the Nazi mistreatment of Jews and other groups. However, little action was taken.

Allied governments believed that fighting the war and defeating the Nazis was the only way they could help those suffering from Nazi injustices. The full horror of the Holocaust was not realized until Allied forces had liberated the concentration camps and death camps in 1945.

Japanese Expansion

After seizing much of China in the 1930s, Japan shifted its attention to the European colonies in East and Southeast Asia and their stores of raw materials. Taking advantage of Hitler's offensive in Europe, the Japanese acquired many of these territories. The collapse of France and the Low Countries left French Indochina and the Dutch East Indies virtually defenseless. And when the Germans threatened to invade Great Britain, the British withdrew their fleet from Singapore, leaving that colony open to attack as well.

In July 1940 the Japanese government announced its plan to create a "new order in greater East Asia." Proclaiming "Asia for the Asiatics," Japan moved to establish the "Greater East Asia Co-prosperity Sphere," an appeal to Asians who wanted to rid their lands of European rule. First, it asked France for the right to build airfields and station troops in northern Indochina. After gaining this foothold, Japan invaded southern Indochina.

SOLD by WHITE & POLLARD

GROCERY WANTO

FRUITS AND VEGETABLES

I AM AN AMERICAN

WANTO CO. WANTO CO.

National Archives

Japanese Americans

During World War II Japanese Americans were feared and hated by many other Americans, especially those living on the West Coast. In Oakland, California, the Japanese American owner of this small store—in an attempt to prevent its burning or looting—put up a sign asserting his loyalty: "I am an American." This very American scene emphasizes the cruelty of persecuting Japanese American businessmen. After the Japanese bombed Pearl Harbor, U.S. politicians spoke with fiery rhetoric, and newspapers ran hate stories that fanned the fear and antagonism against Japanese Americans.

This campaign of hate was a symptom of the brutality of the war in the Pacific. Both sides, Japanese and American, found it necessary to demonize the enemy so that their own soldiers could fight a long and hard war, and their own civilian populations could fully support their country's war effort, despite wartime shortages, extra-long working hours, or family members killed in the war. ⊕

The United States retaliated by placing an embargo, or ban, on the sale of scrap iron to Japan. In response, Japan signed the Tripartite Pact with Germany and Italy on September 27, 1940. Under this pact, the three powers affirmed the right of every nation to "receive the space to which it is entitled" and pledged to cooperate to reach that goal as well as to come to one another's aid if attacked.

Pearl Harbor

When the Japanese invaded southern Indochina on July 24, 1941, President Roosevelt demanded that they withdraw—not only from Indochina but also from China. To back up his demands, Congress placed an embargo on oil and froze all Japanese assets in the United States. Negotiations with the Japanese government continued during the summer and fall.

Japan decided to go to war with the United States because it believed the United States stood in the way of its plans for expansion in the East. To defeat American military forces, however, Japanese leaders knew they had to destroy the American Pacific fleet based at **Pearl Harbor** in Hawaii. Although most American and Japanese leaders believed that Pearl Harbor was safe from attack, Admiral **Isoroku Yamamoto**, the commander of the Japanese navy, did not agree. He convinced Japanese leaders that bombers taking off from aircraft carriers and equipped with newly designed torpedos for use in shallow water could effect a successful surprise attack on Pearl Harbor. In November 1941 Yamamoto's plan was put into effect, and the Japanese fleet set sail for Hawaii.

Meanwhile, negotiations between the United States and Japan had broken down. By now Roosevelt knew that the Japanese were "poised for attack," but was convinced that Japan's move would be in Southeast Asia. As a precaution, United States military leaders sent all aircraft carriers and half the army's planes from Pearl Harbor.

On the morning of December 7, the Japanese attack squadron took off from their carrier decks and began the attack on Pearl Harbor. Within the first 25 minutes of the attack, they sank or damaged the battleships *Arizona*, *Utah*, *Oklahoma*, *West Virginia*, and *California*. The Japanese success was even greater than they had hoped. In all, they sank or disabled 19 American ships and destroyed 188 airplanes. They also killed more than 2,400 people and wounded 1,100. Fortunately for the United States, its aircraft carriers were at sea and escaped the attack. Calling December 7 "a date which will live in infamy," President Roosevelt, in an appearance before Congress the next day, asked for and received a declaration of war against Japan.

The Allies

The United States was now officially at war. On December 11, 1941, Germany and Italy honored their pledge to Japan in the Tripartite Pact by declaring war on the United States. Great Britain, backing the United States, declared war on Japan.

Although mistrust still lingered between the Western democracies and the Soviet Union, they put aside their differences in their resolve to defeat their common enemy. Meanwhile, the fighting in the Soviet Union remained fierce. Vast areas of the country were under German occupation. The Germans had completely surrounded Leningrad, trapping 3 million people. Within two years, nearly 1 million of its people died from cold, hunger, and starvation.

Stalin urged the Allies to open a "second front" in Europe as quickly as possible. Although President Roosevelt favored a second front, Winston Churchill was opposed to it. He knew that Great Britain would have to bear the brunt of any second-front operation. Consequently, the two Allied leaders postponed plans for an invasion of Europe. Instead, they laid plans for military campaigns in North Africa and the Mediterranean area.

SECTION 3 REVIEW

Recall
1. **Define** scorched-earth policy, Holocaust, genocide.
2. **Identify** Isoroku Yamamoto.
3. **Explain** Adolf Hitler's reasons for attacking the Soviet Union

in June 1941.
Critical Thinking
4. **Analyzing Information** How did the "New Order" that Germany's Adolf Hitler wanted to create in Europe affect differ-

ent groups of people living on that continent?
Understanding Themes
5. **Conflict** How did World War II turn into a large-scale global conflict?

1941   1942   1943

MAY 1941 British naval forces sink German battleship *Bismarck*.

October 1942 British halt German advance in North Africa at El Alamein, Egypt.

FEB. 1943 German forces at Stalingrad surrender to the Soviets.

Section 4

Turning Points

Setting the Scene

▶ **Terms to Define**
   kamikaze

▶ **People to Meet**
   Erwin Rommel, Bernard Montgomery, Dwight D. Eisenhower, Douglas MacArthur, Chester W. Nimitz

▶ **Places to Locate**
   Stalingrad, Casablanca, Sicily, Guadalcanal

ind Out   How did the tide of war turn in favor of the Allies during 1942 and 1943?

The Storyteller

A kamikaze attack on an American aircraft carrier, the Hornet, *was recorded in photographs and by eyewitness accounts such as this one: "His [plane] already with flame blossoming on its underside, appeared high above the* Hornet's *starboard quarter. Perhaps dead or dying, [the pilot] did not release his bomb but kept coming directly at the carrier. He did not miss.... Ruptured fuel tanks sprayed the signal bridge with burning gasoline, while the wrecked airplane smashed into the flight deck...." The impact and burning fuel killed and maimed many men, and fires blazed for two hours.*

—adapted from *The First Team and the Guadalcanal Campaign,* John B. Lundstrom, 1994

Japanese kamikaze pilot

In the early months of 1942, the war was going badly for the Allies. By destroying much of the American fleet at Pearl Harbor, Japan had gained control of the Pacific Ocean and cleared the way for a seaborne invasion of American, British, and Dutch territories in that region. In December 1941 Japanese forces had captured the British colony of Hong Kong and invaded the Malay Peninsula. In the West, meanwhile, Rommel controlled a large area of North Africa, and German forces held the upper hand in the Soviet Union as well.

Despite these successes, the Axis powers would never again enjoy such a strong position. By the end of 1942, the tide of the war had begun to turn in favor of the Allies.

Sea and Air Battles

Even before the United States entered the war, it was shipping food and war supplies to Britain under the Lend-Lease Act. But German submarines, or U-boats, threatened this vital lifeline across the Atlantic. By the end of 1939, U-boats had already sunk 114 Allied and neutral ships. German air attacks also took their toll.

To make matters worse for the Allies, the new German battleship *Bismarck,* accompanied by the new cruiser *Prinz Eugen,* entered the fight in May 1941. With 11 Allied convoys either at sea or about to sail, the British hastily dispatched several ships to intercept the Nazis. On May 23 they sighted the two German ships in the Denmark Strait between Iceland and Greenland and opened fire. In the battle that followed, the *Bismarck* sank the British battle cruiser *Hood* and damaged a new British battleship before slipping away to safety.

Three days later, on May 26, a British patrol plane spotted the *Bismarck* about 600 miles (965 km) off the French coast. In the battle that followed, the *Bismarck* sustained at least eight torpedo hits before it finally sank. With this crucial victory, the British put an end to German efforts to win the Battle of the Atlantic with surface ships. Gradually, the Allies devised new methods for protecting their convoys against U-boats as well.

As they fought for control of the Atlantic, the Allies carried out an air offensive against Germany. These attacks were directed at factories, railroads, dockyards, and cities and towns. Their purpose was to destroy German war industries and weaken the will of the civilian population to continue the war.

Stalingrad

In July 1942 the military situation in the Soviet Union looked desperate. With the Soviet army in full retreat, the Germans were approaching **Stalingrad**, a major industrial center on the Volga River. In angry exchanges with Churchill, Stalin continued to press for a second front in the West to take some of the military pressure off his nation. But in August Churchill went to Moscow to tell Stalin that there would be no second front in 1942.

On August 22 the Germans attacked Stalingrad. Because it was named after Stalin, losing the city would have been a blow to Soviet morale. As determined to protect Stalingrad as Hitler was to take it, Stalin ordered that the city be held at all costs.

The Soviets launched a counterattack in September and encircled the German troops threatening the city. They cut off German supply lines. Although the Soviets and the frigid winter weather were closing in on the Germans, Hitler refused to allow his troops to retreat. By the time German officers finally surrendered in February 1943, the German army had lost the best of its troops. Many historians now view the Soviet victory at Stalingrad as the major turning point of World War II. By killing about 100,000 German soldiers, capturing 80,000 more, and seizing large quantities of German military equipment, the Soviet Union broke the back of the Nazi military machine.

War in the Desert

In January 1942 Allied forces in North Africa were struggling to regain ground lost to the Germans. They faced a formidable foe. **Erwin Rommel,** commander of the Afrika Korps, applied blitzkrieg tactics to warfare in the desert. His exploits earned him the nickname "the Desert Fox."

Eastern Front 1941–1944

Map Study Some of the fiercest battles of World War II took place on the eastern front in the Soviet Union.
Place How did the German offensive affect the city of Leningrad?

In the spring of 1942, Rommel pushed the British two-thirds of the way back to the Egyptian frontier. He struck again at the end of May, but the British, under General **Bernard Montgomery**, stopped him two months later at El Alamein (EL A•luh•MAYN), a railway junction about 70 miles (112 km) from Alexandria. In October Montgomery launched a counterattack that forced the Germans back across the Egyptian-Libyan frontier and ended with the British capture of Tripoli, the capital of Libya, in January 1943.

As Montgomery was advancing westward, the Allies were landing troops in Morocco and Algeria as part of a planned offensive against Rommel. By advancing from the east and from the west, the Allies hoped to trap Rommel with their "pincers" strategy. But the Allied landings met with heavy resistance from the Vichy French, who governed French North Africa. To end the fighting, Allied commander **Dwight D. Eisenhower** struck a deal with Admiral François Darlan, a Vichy official. In

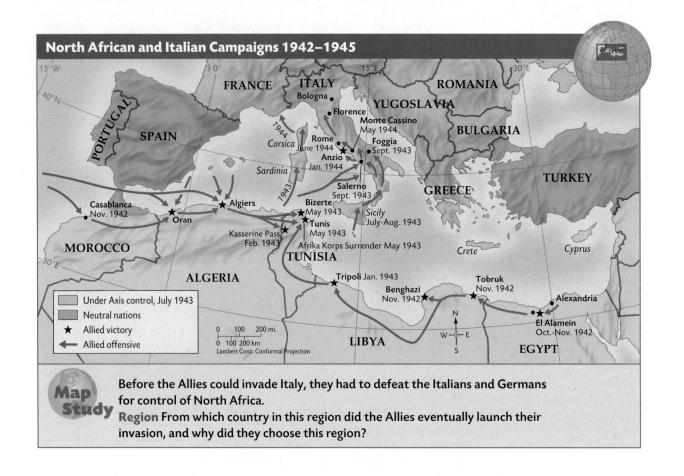

Map Study

Before the Allies could invade Italy, they had to defeat the Italians and Germans for control of North Africa.

Region From which country in this region did the Allies eventually launch their invasion, and why did they choose this region?

return for Allied support of his claim to French North Africa, Darlan ordered an end to the resistance. With the armistice concluded in November 1942, the Free French, under Charles de Gaulle, joined the Allies in Africa. Meanwhile, in a series of powerful attacks, the Allies began closing the pincers. When Rommel flew to Berlin to tell Hitler that the situation was hopeless, the Nazi dictator rejected his general's assessment and barred Rommel from returning to Africa. But Rommel was right. In May 1943, General von Arnim, the new commander of the German forces in Tunisia, surrendered. The Allies now controlled all of North Africa.

Invasion of Italy

In early 1943, the American and British chiefs of staff and political leaders met at **Casablanca** in Morocco to discuss their next move. Because they wanted to secure communications in the Mediterranean and intensify the pressure on Italy, they decided to invade **Sicily**, the large island near the southern tip of the Italian Peninsula.

Under the command of General Eisenhower, the Allies began a combined air and sea attack on **Sicily** in July 1943. The seaborne landings met little

resistance at first, but when the Allies approached Messina, on the extreme northeastern tip of the island, the Germans put up a stronger fight to cover their withdrawal across the Strait of Messina. In six days nearly 40,000 German and 70,000 Italian troops escaped to Italy.

The conquest of Sicily led quickly to Mussolini's downfall. On July 25, King Victor Emmanuel III, pressed into action by antiwar factions, fired Mussolini and had him arrested. The new prime minister, Marshal Pietro Badoglio, soon dissolved the Fascist party and on September 3 signed a secret act of surrender.

That same day, Allied forces crossed the Strait of Messina and landed in Calabria on the Italian mainland. The broadcast announcement of Badoglio's unconditional surrender caught the Germans by surprise, but they recovered in time to occupy Rome two days later, forcing the king and Badoglio to withdraw to the south. The Germans later rescued Mussolini and put him in control of northern Italy.

For the remaining months of 1943 and early months of 1944, the Allies fought their way up the Italian Peninsula. Allied troops could not penetrate the German defenses at Monte Cassino, a sixth-century monastery located on a mountaintop that dominated the road to Rome. In the end it took a massive artillery bombardment and almost five months for the Allies to dislodge the Germans in May 1944. One month later, on June 4, Allied forces entered Rome.

Pacific War

While war raged in Europe, Japan took over much of Southeast Asia and the Pacific. At first welcomed as liberators, the Japanese soon were hated by local peoples for their killing of civilians and taking of property. Resistance groups arose to fight Japanese forces.

Meanwhile, the Allies were able to make some gains. In May 1942, in the Battle of the Coral Sea, the Allies claimed a victory. And in June, at the Battle of Midway, the Americans defeated the Japanese navy and ended Japanese naval superiority in the Pacific.

Japanese Empire 1910–1945

Legend:
- Area held by Japan in 1910
- To 1931
- To 1941
- To 1942
- Anglo-American advances, 1943–1945
- Soviet advances, 1945
- ★ Allied victory

0 500 1,000 mi.
0 500 1,000 km
Mercator Projection

Map Study

Between 1910 and 1942, Japan took over large areas of East Asia, Southeast Asia, and the Pacific.
Region Why were the Japanese able to seize the European colonies in this region so easily in 1941 and 1942?

To follow up this victory, the Americans launched an attack against the Pacific island of **Guadalcanal** in early August. While troops under General **Douglas MacArthur** attacked the Japanese on land, naval forces under Admiral **Chester W. Nimitz** confronted them at sea. The six-month land, sea, and air battle for control of the island ended in victory for the Allies. Guadalcanal was the first in a series of island battles the Americans fought as they leapfrogged their way north to Japan. Their strategy was to capture some

islands and bypass others. Those bypassed would be cut off from supplies and made to "wither on the vine."

After Guadalcanal, the Americans paused to build up their Pacific forces. When the American advance resumed in November 1943, Japanese leaders called upon their soldiers to die for their homeland. Japanese pilots known as kamikazes volunteered for suicide missions, crashing their bomb-laden aircraft into Allied bases and ships. The Japanese were far from ready to surrender.

SECTION 4 REVIEW

Recall
1. **Define** kamikaze.
2. **Identify** Erwin Rommel, Bernard Montgomery, Dwight D. Eisenhower, Douglas MacArthur, Chester W. Nimitz.
3. **Locate** Stalingrad on the map on page 845. Why was the Battle of Stalingrad a major turning point in World War II?

Critical Thinking
4. **Synthesizing Information** How did Hitler's decisions contribute to Germany's defeats in both Stalingrad and North Africa?

Understanding Themes
5. **Conflict** Why did the Allies decide to "leapfrog" their way to Japan rather than launch a direct attack?

JUNE 1944	DEC. 1944	JUNE 1945	DEC. 1945

JUNE 6, 1944 (D-Day) Allies land in Normandy.

DEC. 16, 1944 Battle of the Bulge begins.

MAY 8, 9, 1945 V-E (Victory in Europe) Day celebrated in Allied countries.

AUG. 6, 1945 The United States drops atomic bomb on Hiroshima, Japan.

Section 5

Allied Victories

Setting the Scene

▶ **Terms to Define**
   D-Day, partisan

▶ **People to Meet**
   George Patton, Harry S Truman, Clement Attlee

▶ **Places to Locate**
   Rhine River, Berlin, Yalta, Potsdam, Hiroshima, Nagasaki

ind Out   How did new technology affect the conduct and outcome of World War II?

toryteller

An American woman, living in Russia, later recalled how hope for Allied rescue was everywhere in Russia during the spring of 1944:

"They knew it must come this summer, for the war was already in Europe.... On a day in early June the air was split by a radio announcement: 'Stand by for a special broadcast at 1:45.' We knew what it would be. Everybody knew. 'Today, June 6, 1944, early in the morning, General Eisenhower's forces began landing operations on the northern coast of France.'" The long-awaited second front was a reality. People laughed and slapped each other on the back.

—adapted from *Fifty Russian Winters, An American Woman's Life in the Soviet Union*, Margaret Wettlin, 1992

American troops land in Normandy

To fight the Axis, Allied democracies geared their economies for war production, rationed goods, and regulated prices and wages. The wartime emergency limited citizens' rights , but unemployment ended as factories turned out weapons and supplies. With men joining the military, women in large numbers entered industry and served in supporting roles in the armed forces. Outside of the democracies, women supported the Allied cause by fighting in the resistance forces of occupied Europe; in the Soviet Union, they saw combat as ground soldiers and pilots.

TURNING POINT

D-Day

At a 1943 conference in Tehran, Iran, Roosevelt and Churchill told Stalin about their plan to open a second front the following spring. Meanwhile, General Eisenhower assembled a force of 176,000 soldiers, 600 warships, and 10,000 aircraft in England for Operation Overlord, the invasion of France. On June 6, 1944, **D-Day**, or the day of attack, convoys carrying troops and equipment sailed across the English Channel to the French province of Normandy. British bombers attacked German coastal defenses, and Allied airborne troops parachuted into France to assist the invasion. As battleship guns pounded German positions, Allied soldiers moved from their landing craft onto the beaches, fighting their way forward amid German machine-gun fire.

Despite the battle's confusion and the heavy German resistance, the invasion was a success. From their Normandy foothold, the Allies launched an offensive against the Germans. By early August, American tank commander General **George Patton** and his forces were racing across northern France. At the same time, in Paris, French resistance fighters rose up against the occupying Germans.

Allied Offensive in Europe June 1944–May 1945

Legend:
- Allied offensive
- German offensive
- Land held by Allies, Sept. 1944
- Land held by Allies, Jan. 1945
- Land held by Allies, May 1945
- Land held by Germans, May 1945

Map labels: FINLAND, NORWAY, SWEDEN, ESTONIA, LATVIA, LITHUANIA, Baltic Sea, North Sea, IRELAND, GREAT BRITAIN, DENMARK, Antwerp Sept. 4, Brussels Sept. 3, Bremen Apr. 26, Hamburg May 3, GERMANY, Berlin Apr. 22–May 2, Torgau Apr. 25, POLAND, Rouen Aug. 30, Cologne Mar. 7, D-Day June 6, Battle of the Bulge Dec. 16–Jan. 16, Brest Sept. 18, Paris Aug. 25, Nuremberg Apr. 20, Metz Nov. 22, CZECHOSLOVAKIA, ATLANTIC OCEAN, Orléans Aug. 16, Munich Apr. 30, Vienna Apr. 13, SWITZERLAND, AUSTRIA, HUNGARY, Budapest Feb. 13, FRANCE, ROMANIA, The Rhine River, PORTUGAL, SPAIN, Corsica, ITALY, YUGOSLAVIA, Adriatic Sea, BULGARIA, Black Sea, Sardinia, ALBANIA, Spanish Morocco, Sicily, GREECE, TURKEY, Mediterranean Sea, Crete

Scale: 0 150 300 mi. / 0 150 300 km / Lambert Conic Conformal Projection

Map Study From D-Day in June 1944 to its surrender in May 1945, Germany was in full retreat on both the western and eastern fronts.
Location Where did the one German offensive occur during this period?

Pressured on all sides, German forces retreated, and on August 25, Allied troops, led by Free French forces, entered Paris.

Victory Over Germany

Months before D-Day, Soviet forces advanced steadily toward Germany from the east. By the summer of 1944, they had pushed the Germans out of Soviet territory and were moving into eastern Europe. Despite the Allied gains, Hitler was convinced that a surprise offensive in the west might still reverse the Allied advance. In December 1944, the Germans cut through the center of the American forces, creating a bulge in the Allied line of troops. The Allies finally checked the German drive at Bastogne, Belgium, and in March 1945, stormed across the **Rhine River**, Germany's historic defense barrier. By this time, Germany's cities had undergone repeated Allied air attacks, which destroyed industrial centers and killed hundreds of thousands of people.

Meanwhile, from the east, the Soviets inflicted a savage revenge on the German population and fought their way into the city of **Berlin**. In late April, American and Soviet troops met on the Elbe

River. On May 7, the Germans surrendered unconditionally, and the next day was proclaimed V-E (Victory in Europe) Day in the Allied democracies; May 9 was celebrated as V-E Day in the Soviet Union. With the German surrender, the war in Europe had finally ended. The end also came for the Fascist dictators. Italian partisans, or resistance fighters, had shot Mussolini, and Hitler had committed suicide in an underground chamber in Berlin.

Yalta and Potsdam

In February 1945, Roosevelt, Churchill, and Stalin had met at **Yalta**, a Black Sea resort in the Soviet Union, to discuss issues affecting the postwar world. The Allied leaders proposed that France and China join their countries in forming the United Nations, a permanent international organization to maintain peace after the war. They also agreed to divide Germany, as well as the city of Berlin, into four zones that Great Britain, France, the United States, and the Soviet Union would occupy.

Celebrating the Red Army's capture of Berlin, a group of Soviet troops unfurl the Soviet flag over the ruins of the German parliament building. *What advances were made by the Western Allies during the spring of 1945?*

Roosevelt and Churchill obtained from Stalin a promise to hold free elections in Soviet-occupied eastern Europe. In return, they gave Stalin the eastern part of Poland. Poland would receive German land in return for yielding its eastern territory.

To hasten the end of the Pacific conflict, the Western leaders sought and received Stalin's promise to declare war on Japan. In return, Stalin gained the Kuril Islands and the southern part of Sakhalin Island. These islands, located off the coast of Siberia in the northern Pacific Ocean, were ruled by Japan.

Six months later, the Allies met in **Potsdam** in Germany, but by this time some of the key participants had changed. After Franklin D. Roosevelt died in April, **Harry S Truman** succeeded him as President. Although Churchill was there at the opening, his Conservative party lost the general election, and **Clement Attlee** of the Labour party replaced him as prime minister halfway through the conference.

The atmosphere at Potsdam was also quite different from that at Yalta. The Allies made plans for the occupation of Germany and issued an ultimatum to Japan demanding unconditional surrender. However, more issues were raised than were settled. New tensions over the future of Europe were beginning to pull apart the wartime alliance.

Victory Over Japan

By end of 1944, an Allied victory over Japan seemed inevitable. American planes bombed Japanese cities, and General Douglas MacArthur regained the Philippines. In early 1945, the Americans defeated the Japanese in bloody battles on the Pacific islands of Iwo Jima and Okinawa, and the British completed the destruction of Japanese forces in Southeast Asia. Despite setbacks, Japan's military leaders, such as General Hideki Tojo, refused to surrender.

When Japan rejected an American ultimatum in July, President Truman decided to use a new secret weapon—the atomic bomb. His stated reason for using the bomb against Japan was to end the war swiftly and to avoid the enormous loss of life that would have resulted from an American invasion of the Japanese home islands. Concerned about growing Soviet-American rivalry, Truman also may have used the bomb to impress the Soviets with American military might.

On August 6, 1945, an American plane dropped an atomic bomb on **Hiroshima**, a munitions center. The blast leveled most of the city. When no response

Visualizing History In February 1945, Allied leaders Winston Churchill, Franklin D. Roosevelt, and Joseph Stalin met at Yalta on the USSR's Crimean Peninsula. They discussed a number of issues related to the postwar Europe. *What major agreement was made at Yalta regarding the war against Japan?*

came from Japan, three days later the Americans dropped a second atomic bomb on the port city of **Nagasaki**. Altogether, about 200,000 Japanese died in both cities. In the following months, many more would die from the blasts' radioactivity.

On August 14, 1945, Japan finally surrendered. A few weeks later, on September 2 (proclaimed V-J— or Victory over Japan—Day by the Allies) Japanese officials signed the official surrender document on board the American battleship *Missouri* anchored in Tokyo Bay. World War II was over.

Effects of the War

More than 70 million people fought in World War II. The casualties were staggering. Altogether, some 55 million people perished because of the conflict. The Soviet Union lost 22 million people, Germany almost 8 million, Japan 2 million, and the United States almost 300,000. In addition, millions of people in Europe and Asia died in campaigns of genocide.

After the war the Allies began to address the wrongs committed by the Axis Powers. Between November 1945 and September 1946, trials held at Nuremburg, Germany, brought many Nazi leaders to justice for pursuing "aggressive war" and for "committing crimes against humanity." Similar war crimes trials were held in Japan and Italy.

In addition to the casualties, many areas of Europe and Asia lay in ruins. The use of deadly new weapons made World War II the most destructive war in history. Heavy aerial bombing and shifting battlelines left as many as 12 million people homeless. Food, medicine, and clothing, were in short supply. One Japanese student recalls life after the war:

> ❝ When winter came we were really miserable. We had neither food nor clothing.... We were told to go to the countryside and find food wherever we could. There was nothing in Tokyo. ❞

For millions of people the suffering and hardships lasted long after the war's end.

SECTION 5 REVIEW

Recall
1. **Define** D-Day , partisan.
2. **Identify** George Patton, Harry S Truman, Clement Attlee.
3. **Explain** why Operation Overlord has been called "unmatched in history."

Critical Thinking
4. **Analyzing Information** War crimes trials after World War II held Axis leaders responsible for actions in wartime. Give examples of similar trials after recent conflicts. Why were these trials held?

Understanding Themes
5. **Innovation** World War II was even more costly in the destruction of human life and property than World War I. What factors made World War II the most destructive war in the history of the world?

Connections Across Time

Historical Significance World War II dramatically shifted the world balance of power. Weakened by the conflict, European nations lost their empires and their dominance of world affairs. In their place emerged the United States and the Soviet Union—superpowers and rivals with nuclear arsenals capable of unleashing global mass destruction. Meanwhile, scores of newly independent nations arose from the ashes of the European empires and presented their own distinct outlooks on world affairs. One hopeful development in the postwar world was the United Nations, an international body dedicated to world peace. Another was the increased attention given to human rights as a result of the horrors of the Holocaust and Japanese atrocities in Asia.

Using Key Terms

Write the key term that completes each sentence. Then write a sentence for each term not chosen.

a. blitzkrieg
b. sanctions
c. lend-lease
d. appeasement
e. kamikazes
f. partisan
g. D-Day
h. scorched-earth policy
i. genocide
j. Holocaust
k. collective security
l. cash-and-carry policy

1. British Prime Minister Chamberlain pursued _____ with Nazi Germany in hopes of stabilizing Europe.
2. In the _____, the Nazis murdered almost 6 million Jews during the war.
3. The _____ allowed the United States to supply the British in return for payment without risking American neutrality.
4. Joseph Stalin tried to thwart the German invasion of his country by a _____.
5. During the 1930s, the Western democracies were unable to agree on what steps to take to ensure their _____.

Using Your History Journal

Select one event from your chart about important events in World War II. Write a paragraph showing how the event affected other developments in the war.

Reviewing Facts

1. **Citizenship** Explain why the League of Nations could not stop Japan's expansion. How did Japan treat its conquered peoples?
2. **History** List the countries that Germany occupied before the outbreak of war.
3. **History** Identify the causes and effects of World War II.
4. **History** Explain Japan's attack on Pearl Harbor.
5. **Citizenship** Identify the Holocaust and discuss the different stages of its implementation.

Technology Activity

Using the Internet Search the Internet for a World War II Web site that includes memoirs or excerpts from Holocaust survivors. Copy or print a part of the memoirs that you find especially moving. Create a bulletin board about the Holocaust. Post the excerpts on the bulletin board under the heading "Voices of World War II." Include pictures of the Holocaust with captions underneath providing explanations.

Critical Thinking

1. **Apply** Why did the Western democracies let Hitler overrun much of Europe before trying to stop him?
2. **Analyze** What factors account for the response the world gave to the Holocaust?
3. **Synthesize** If the Japanese had not bombed Pearl Harbor, would the United States have entered the war? Explain your position.
4. **Evaluate** Was the United States justified in using the atomic bomb to end the war with Japan?

Understanding Themes

1. **Movement** What were Hitler's objectives in Europe? What were Japan's objectives in Asia?
2. **Cooperation** What assistance did the United States provide to Great Britain before American entry into the conflict?
3. **Conflict** Why did Stalin press the Allies to establish a second front in Europe?
4. **Conflict** Why did the Western Allies at Yalta agree to give Stalin the Kuril Islands and the southern part of Sakhalin Island?
5. **Innovation** What effect did new technology have on the war?

Geography in History

1. **Location** Refer to the map below. What were the relative locations of territories held in France by the Allies in September 1944?
2. **Region** What areas touching the Mediterranean Sea were in Allied control by September 1944?
3. **Movement** Beginning in June 1944, the Allied strategy was to pressure Germany on two fronts —East and West. How does the map show that the plan was a successful way to end the war?
4. **Location** Where did Soviet and American forces meet in April 1945?

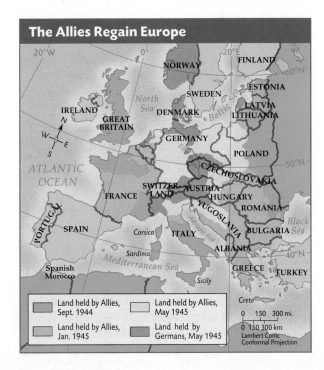

The Allies Regain Europe

Land held by Allies, Sept. 1944
Land held by Allies, Jan. 1945
Land held by Allies, May 1945
Land held by Germans, May 1945

0   150   300 mi.
0 150 300 km
Lambert Conic
Conformal Projection

Linking Past and Present

1. To avert war with Germany, the European democracies allowed Hitler to occupy Czechoslovakia. How did the United Nations react to Iraq's occupation of Kuwait in 1990? Do you think the United Nations made the correct decision? Explain.
2. In the 1940s, several publications called Churchill "Man of the Century." Do you think he still deserves the title? Explain.

Skill Practice

Reread the section of Chapter 31 that describes the bombing on Hiroshima, pages 850–851. Then read the passage on this page written six years later by a survivor. Use the two sources to answer the questions below.

“ I was eating breakfast … when there was bright light in front of my eyes and an indescribable orange light surged in.… It must have been ten or fifteen minutes later when I recovered consciousness.… but I could see nothing because the place was filled with white smoke.… I tried to stand up and fell again.… What on earth had happened? …

  I looked over my shoulder and saw our house was a flattened wreck, and at the back waves of swirling flames were threatening to sweep down on us at any moment.… I suddenly heard my sister's voice calling, 'Someone help me! …' She was my own sister but the sight of her was horrifying. Her dark hair which reached her shoulders, that hair was now pure white. At the side of her mouth was a crescent-shaped gash through which her gums were pitifully exposed, and from which bright red blood flowed… When I saw this figure my sister had been transformed into, for a fleeting moment, I just couldn't think that it was her. I was afraid even to go near her. ”

—Eiko Matsunaga, 11th grade girl, 1951

1. What is the topic of the two sources?
2. What information does the textbook give about this topic?
3. How does the passage add to your understanding of this topic?

Turning Points in World History

The Holocaust

Setting up the Video

Work with a group of your classmates to view "The Holocaust" on the videodisc *Turning Points in World History*. The Holocaust was a horrific period in history when the Nazi regime was responsible for murders and crimes against 6 million Jews. This program examines the impact on those who experienced Nazi control during the 1930s and 1940s.

Hands-On Activity

Using the Holocaust theme, create a haiku. The Japanese haiku is one of the shortest types of lyric poetry. The haiku is made up of 17 syllables arranged in three lines. The first line has 5 syllables, the second 7, and the third 5.

Side Two, Chapter 6

View the video by scanning the bar code or by entering the chapter number on your keypad and pressing Search. (Also available in VHS format.)

Surfing the "Net"

Mohandas K. Gandhi and India

The early 1900s brought a great struggle for India concerning the issue of independence from Great Britain. Mohandas K. Gandhi provided leadership for independence by practicing active nonviolence. To learn more about Gandhi and the nonviolent movement, access the Internet.

3. The search engine should provide you with a number of links to follow. Links are "pointers" to different sites on the Internet and commonly appear as blue underlined words.

Getting There

Follow these steps to gather information about Mohandas Gandhi.
1. Go to a search engine. Type in the phrase *mohandas gandhi.*
2. After typing in the phrase, enter words such as these to focus your search:
   - *india*
   - *soulforce*
   - *independence*

What to Do When You Are There

Click on the links to navigate through the information and gather your findings. Organize into cooperative groups of three. Design large banners promoting peace and nonviolence for today's world. Share your banner with the other groups. Be sure to explain why you chose particular symbols, language, or colors for your banner.

Two destructive wars engulfed the world in the first half of the 1900s. World War I brought about the collapse of European monarchies, triggered a Communist revolution in Russia, and left many countries in chaos. This turmoil, the bitterness created by the peace treaties ending the war, and a worldwide economic depression that started in 1929 led to the rise of dictatorships in Germany, Italy, and Japan.

During the 1930s, the world once again was set on a course toward war. When it arrived, World War II proved to be the most destructive in history. At its end, European dominance of world affairs had ended, with many new nations arising from the ashes of the overseas European empires. Above all, two superpowers—the United States and the Soviet Union—were extending their power and struggling for global influence.

Chapter 28
World War I

In the late 1800s and early 1900s, nationalism and imperialism led the nations of Europe to form two rival alliances: the Triple Alliance, made up of Germany, Austria-Hungary, and Italy, and the Triple Entente (later, the Allies), consisting of France, Great Britain, and Russia. Conflict between the two armed camps broke out following the assassination of the heir to the Austrian throne in June 1914. For four years, the belligerents fought on land, at sea, and in the air, using new weapons, such as machine guns, tanks, airplanes, and poison gas. In western Europe the war quickly settled into a stalemate along two parallel lines of trenches stretching from Switzerland to the North Sea. In eastern Europe and the Middle East, constant changes occurred in battlefield positions, but neither side was able to achieve a speedy total victory.

To try to cut off Germany's supply lines, Great Britain blockaded German ports. The Germans struck back with U-boats, or submarines. German sinking of American merchant ships eventually brought the neutral United States into the war on the side of the Allies. The United States gave the Allies much-needed human and material resources; and in November 1918, Germany finally surrendered.

The war brought sweeping changes. The Ottoman, Russian, and Austro-Hungarian empires collapsed, and new nations emerged from the breakup. The peace settlement at Versailles, France, made Germany responsible for the war and imposed a heavy financial penalty on its people. The war also increased human misery on a large scale, with millions of soldiers and civilians dead or wounded. Mass killings, such as those of the Armenians under Ottoman rule, added to the list of horrors. Finally, revolution in Russia led to the rise of communism as a force in world affairs.

Chapter 29
Between Two Fires

World War I destroyed the West's belief in progress and created feelings of disillusionment. In the postwar era, European and American artists and writers rejected the past and experimented with new styles and subject matter. Innovative forms of technology, such as the automobile and the radio, transformed people's lives and brought the world closer together.

The United States came out of the war in far better shape than its allies. The 1920s were boom years for the American economy, but the general prosperity hid the fact that farmers and workers were worse off than before the war. Finally, in 1929, wild speculation led to a stock market crash, and the nation fell into a major economic depression that had worldwide effects.

Although war and depression had a terrible effect on Great Britain and France, democracy managed to survive in these nations. Germany and Italy also faced setbacks, but these countries did not have strong democratic traditions. Amid political and economic chaos in Italy, Benito Mussolini in 1922 set up a Fascist dictatorship that stressed nationalism and military strength. In Germany Nazi party leader Adolf Hitler came to power in 1933 with a similar program that also included persecution of the Jews, whom he blamed for Germany's economic woes.

Dramatic changes were also occurring in the Soviet Union. After seizing power, Lenin and the Bolsheviks, renamed Communists, tried to quickly

Lenin guided the affairs of the Soviet state through civil war and economic collapse until his death in January 1924. *What changes did Lenin's successor, Joseph Stalin, bring to the Soviet Union?*

impose a new socialist order but faced widespread opposition. In 1921 Lenin strengthened Communist power by allowing limited capitalism. After Lenin's death in 1924, Joseph Stalin won a political power struggle with his rival, Leon Trotsky. Beginning in the late 1920s, Stalin brought all Soviet industry and agriculture under state control. He also removed suspected opponents from leadership positions, and promoted a famine that cost many lives in Ukraine, a stronghold of anti-Communist nationalism. Other Soviet citizens also suffered imprisonment, exile, and death under Stalin's grim rule.

Chapter 30
Nationalism in Asia, Africa, and Latin America

After World War I, the European powers retained control of their colonies. But in the years following the conflict, nationalist groups arose in Asia and Africa that challenged continued European rule in these areas.

Weakened by internal discord, the Ottoman Empire crumbled during the war. After halting a Greek invasion in 1922, the Turks removed their Ottoman ruler and formed the Republic of Turkey. Persians, too, asserted their independence and gave Persia a new name—Iran.

Although Great Britain granted Egypt independence in 1936, it controlled neighboring Palestine and continued to rule African colonies such as Kenya and Nigeria. Despite India's contribution to the British war effort, Great Britain refused to grant the Indians independence. Mohandas K. Gandhi and other Indian nationalists organized nonviolent protests against British rule, including strikes and a refusal to buy British goods.

In China, the nationalist Guomindang army led by Chiang Kai-shek gained power. During the late 1920s, Chiang turned on his Chinese Communist allies, many of whom fled to the mountainous inte-

rior of China. When the Japanese invaded China in the 1930s, however, Chiang again joined with the Communists in an effort to repulse the invaders.

In Japan military leaders became a powerful force in the 1920s and 1930s. They believed that Japan could solve the problems of a growing population and limited resources by conquering new territories. By the late 1930s, the military had won complete control of the government and embarked on a collision course with the United States and Western powers.

Although most Latin American countries had won political independence before the 1920s, they remained economically dependent on the United States. They also faced American military intervention whenever internal unrest threatened American interests. In the early 1930s, United States President Franklin D. Roosevelt worked for good relations with Latin America. He proclaimed the Good Neighbor policy, in which the United States would refrain from intervention.

Chapter 31
World War II

The desire of Fascist dictatorships for more territory increasingly threatened world peace during the 1930s. The League of Nations, which had been formed after World War I to preserve peace, proved powerless to stop the drift toward war.

Adolf Hitler aimed to bring much of Europe under Nazi control. When the German leader threatened to invade Czechoslovakia in 1938, Great Britain and France negotiated the Munich Agreement that gave Hitler the part of Czechoslovakia that he demanded. This policy of appeasement—or compromise with the dictatorships—to avoid war only increased Hitler's expansionism. In early 1939, Hitler took over all of Czechoslovakia, and in September of that year secured the help of the Soviet Union in attacking Poland. The Nazi assault on Poland led Great Britain and France to declare war on Germany.

After Pearl Harbor, San Francisco prepared for possible Japanese air attacks by sandbagging buildings. *Why was the Japanese attack on Pearl Harbor a significant event?*

In the spring of 1940, German forces took control of Norway and Denmark, and then invaded the Low Countries and France, pushing British and French forces to the English Channel. France surrendered in June, leaving the British to fight Hitler alone. In the summer and fall of 1940, Great Britain, under the leadership of Winston Churchill, fought and won a crucial victory over Germany in the air conflict known as the Battle of Britain. By 1941, however, Nazi Germany had conquered large areas of Europe, and in June of that year, launched a large-scale invasion of the Soviet Union.

Meanwhile, the United States remained neutral in the conflict, although it supplied the British with equipment to fight the war. To prevent the Americans from interfering with its expansionist thrust in East Asia and the Pacific, Japan attacked the United States fleet at Pearl Harbor, Hawaii. The Pearl Harbor attack brought the United States into the war on the side of the Allies—Great Britain, the Soviet Union, the Free French, and other anti-Fascist governments and nations.

Not until 1942 did the tide begin to turn in favor of the Allies. Americans defeated Japanese naval forces at the Battle of Midway in the Pacific Ocean. In 1943, Soviet forces threw back a German offensive at Stalingrad, and British and American forces pushed the Germans out of North Africa. From there, the Allies launched an invasion of Sicily and the Italian Peninsula.

In June 1944, Western Allied forces invaded Normandy in France and pushed toward Germany as Soviet troops advanced from the east. In April 1945 Western and Soviet allies met at the Elbe River, and the following month Germany surrendered. When Japan refused to surrender, the United States dropped its new secret weapon, the atomic bomb, on Hiroshima and Nagasaki in August. Days later Japan surrendered.

World War II was over, but much of Europe lay in ruins, and millions of people had died. The most shocking horror in a war filled with atrocities was the Holocaust, the killing of over 6 million Jews by the Nazis in a campaign of genocide, or the deliberate killing of a racial, political, or cultural group. Among the political changes brought by the war was the division of Europe into Communist and non-Communist areas.

SURVEYING UNIT 7

1. **Chapter 28** What general factors led to the outbreak of World War I?
2. **Chapter 29** What common problems did many nations face in the 1920s and 1930s? Why did democracy survive in Great Britain and France, while it collapsed in Italy and Germany?
3. **Chapter 30** How did nationalism in Latin America during the 1920s and 1930s differ from nationalism in Asia and Africa?
4. **Chapter 31** How were the causes of World Wars I and II different? How were they similar?

Unit

8

1945–Present

The Contemporary World

Then & Now

International tension continued after World War II. Two blocs of nations aligned themselves behind the United States and the Soviet Union to dominate world politics. The two sides fought a cold war using economic powers, diplomacy, espionage, and the threat of nuclear war. When the cold war ended, leaders struggled to address the long-standing problems of nationalism, poverty in the developing nations, distribution of resources, and environmental damage.

The pace of scientific and technological change quickened. Satellite communications and computers linked in a global network offered undreamed of challenges and opportunities. When you turn on your computer, remember that it has been just a few years since this technology was invented. No one can guess the nature or degree of change it will bring to your future.

A Global Chronology

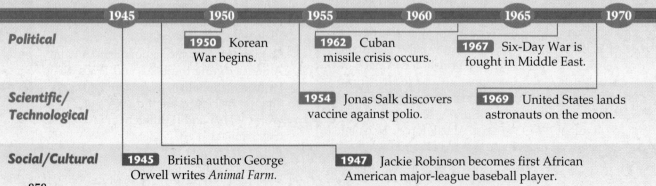

	1945	1950	1955	1960	1965	1970
Political		**1950** Korean War begins.	**1962** Cuban missile crisis occurs.		**1967** Six-Day War is fought in Middle East.	
Scientific/ Technological			**1954** Jonas Salk discovers vaccine against polio.		**1969** United States lands astronauts on the moon.	
Social/Cultural	**1945** British author George Orwell writes *Animal Farm.*		**1947** Jackie Robinson becomes first African American major-league baseball player.			

Computer Pentium chip

Choose an ongoing worldwide problem or situation such as ethnic wars or rivalries, the conflict between Arabs and Israelis, economic difficulties in former Soviet states, population growth in overcrowded cities, oil or other resource shortages, debt in developing nations, the spread of arms, hunger and homelessness, or terrorism. Collect and study news articles about this subject. Write a one-page essay offering suggestions for dealing with the issue.

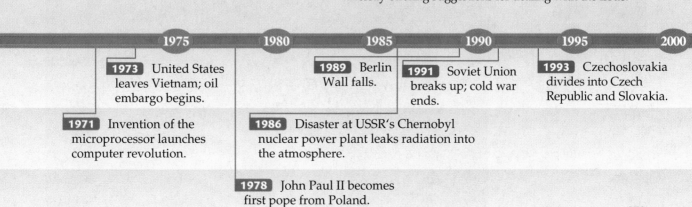

1975   **1980**   **1985**   **1990**   **1995**   **2000**

1973 United States leaves Vietnam; oil embargo begins.

1989 Berlin Wall falls.

1991 Soviet Union breaks up; cold war ends.

1993 Czechoslovakia divides into Czech Republic and Slovakia.

1971 Invention of the microprocessor launches computer revolution.

1986 Disaster at USSR's Chernobyl nuclear power plant leaks radiation into the atmosphere.

1978 John Paul II becomes first pope from Poland.

The Spread of Ideas

Communications

*T*he invention of writing reshaped history. So did Johannes Gutenberg's use of movable type. Today, however, electronics technology is moving communications forward at a startling rate. Two of the biggest changes have been the linking of people around the world via satellite broadcasts and the creation of a vast computer network known as the "information highway."

The United States
Satellite Communications

In October 1957, a special announcement interrupted radio broadcasts across the United States. "Listen now … for the sound which forever separates the old from the new," said the broadcaster. Then a voice from outer space—and eerie beep … beep … beep.

The former Soviet Union had taken the lead in space exploration by launching a tiny communications satellite named *Sputnik I.* A crudely simple device by today's standards, the first satellite could do little more than beam back radio signals. In the cold war era, however, it sent shock waves through American society.

Three years later, the United States launched *Echo* and *Courier.* Instead of beeps, these satellites relayed telephone calls between Europe and the United States. In 1962, the United States launched *Telstar*—the first satellite to relay live television programs from one place to another. By the 1980s people around the world with satellite dish antennas could tune in to hundreds of television programs. The effect was revolutionary. Repressive governments in Eastern Europe and elsewhere could not legislate against free speech beamed down from the skies.

Telstar

Scientist and Soviet Sputnik I

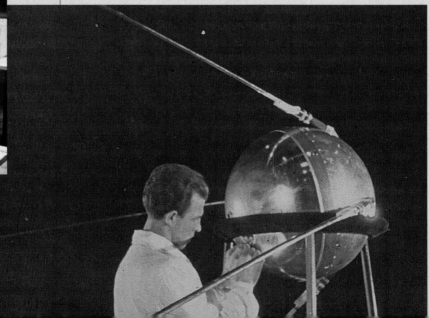

China
Satellite Dishes

In the 1990s, satellite dishes sprouted like mushrooms across the People's Republic of China. Star TV, a pan-Asian satellite service, boomed down Mandarin-speaking rappers out of Hong Kong, English broadcasts of CNN News, NFL football games, and movies from Japan. The uncensored broadcasts enraged government officials. However, a 1993 ban against satellite dishes proved nearly impossible to enforce. Even while officials tried to dismantle the thousands of large dishes, kits for smaller dishes were being smuggled into the country.

The example of China was repeated in other repressive nations. Iran, Myanmar (Burma), and other countries tried and failed to ban satellite reception. Even free governments, such as India, expressed concern about the "cultural invasion," but satellite television, a part of the information age, was here to stay.

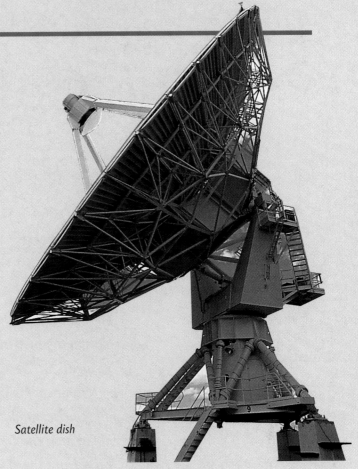

Satellite dish

Africa
The Internet

A telephone line and a personal computer—that is all someone needs to jump on the information highway. Internet Web sites exist globally, putting individuals in touch with databases and other computer users on every continent.

In Africa, the least electronic continent, UNESCO is helping the Pan-African News Agency to link up with the Internet. The project will help Africans overcome one of the legacies of imperialism—a communications system that linked African nations with European capitals rather than with each other. The driving force behind the project, a Senegalese journalist named Babacar Fall, sees the Internet as one of the keys to unlocking Africa's economic potential. "Without information," explained Fall, "there can be no development."

High school students on the Internet

LINKING THE IDEAS

1. How did the revolution in satellite communications get its start?
2. How has this revolution affected nondemocratic political systems?

Critical Thinking

3. **Drawing Conclusions** How has the revolution in communications made our world more interdependent?

Chapter Themes

▶ **Conflict** A cold war develops between the United States and the Soviet Union, the two superpowers that emerged after World War II. *Section 1*

▶ **Change** The Soviet Union tries to move away from the legacy of Stalin while maintaining its control over Eastern Europe. *Section 2*

▶ **Regionalism** Western European democracies develop closer regional unity. *Section 3*

▶ **Cooperation** The United States and Canada build strong economies and forge closer ties. *Section 4*

The Storyteller

In 1948 the city of West Berlin was an island in the middle of a hostile sea. The Soviets had cut off all land routes into the German city in the hope of driving out the Western Allies. For 11 months the United States airlifted food to 2 million stranded residents in West Berlin.

One day while his plane was on the ground in West Berlin, an American pilot, Lieutenant Gale S. Halvorsen, met a group of German children. Although they had received few sweets to eat during the blockade, they did not beg. He told them to wait for his plane at the end of the airport runway the next day. The children came, and, to their delight, packets of gum and chocolate showered down from Halvorsen's plane.

Soon other pilots joined "Operation Little Vittles," and the crowds of children grew. The children named Halvorsen "the Chocolate Pilot."

Historical Significance

What developments led to a cold war between the Western democracies and the Soviet Union? How did this East-West split affect world affairs during the next 40 years?

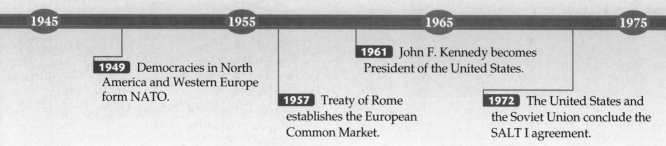

1945	1955	1965	1975

1949 Democracies in North America and Western Europe form NATO.

1957 Treaty of Rome establishes the European Common Market.

1961 John F. Kennedy becomes President of the United States.

1972 The United States and the Soviet Union conclude the SALT I agreement.

Visualizing History During the Soviet era, vast numbers of military vehicles and marchers paraded past Soviet leaders in Moscow's famous Red Square to celebrate May Day (May 1st), the Communist workers' holiday.

Your History Journal

Interview people who can remember the early period of the cold war. Evaluate the reliability of their accounts by analyzing their background, biases, and closeness to the events.

1947 The United States announces the Truman Doctrine and the Marshall Plan.

1955 West Germany joins NATO.

1961 Soviets and East Germans build the Berlin Wall.

Section 1

The East-West Split

Setting the Scene

▶ **Terms to Define**
   superpower, cold war, satellite, iron curtain, containment, arms race, ideology, bloc

▶ **People to Meet**
   Joseph Stalin, Harry S Truman, George C. Marshall

▶ **Places to Locate**
   San Francisco, Greece, West Berlin

 **ind Out** What key events caused and heightened the cold war?

Storyteller

Nikita Khrushchev recalled the beginning of the arms race: "We are surrounded by American air bases.... For many years after the war, bombers were to represent the major threat in our enemy's arsenal of weapons. It took time and a great deal of work for us to develop a bomber force on our own.... Two of our famous designers ... developed the MiG-15, which in time was acknowledged as the best jet fighter in the world.... However, our superiority was short-lived. During the Korean War the U.S. started making a jet fighter that was better than the MiG-15, and soon the Americans ruled the air over Korea."

—from *Khrushchev Remembers, The Last Testament,* translated and edited by Strobe Talbott, 1974

Nikita Khrushchev

The United States and the Soviet Union emerged from World War II as the world's two **superpowers**. No other countries were equal to them in military power or political influence. Differences in political beliefs and policies soon pulled the two superpowers apart and led to a struggle between them known as the **cold war**. In the cold war, each superpower sought world influence by means short of total war. This was because the possibility of nuclear war made the costs of a "hot" war too high. The "weapons" used in the cold war included the threat of force, the use of propaganda, and the sending of military and economic aid to weaker nations.

The United Nations

In the closing months of World War II, the Allies started planning for the postwar world. To handle future global problems, they had agreed at Yalta to replace the League of Nations with the United Nations, a new, permanent international organization. The purpose of the United Nations (UN) was to maintain peace by guaranteeing the security of member nations. It would foster good relations among nations based on the principles of equal rights and self-determination. It would also encourage cooperation on economic, cultural, and humanitarian problems.

In April 1945, representatives from 50 nations gathered in **San Francisco** to draft the Charter of the United Nations, which was completed and signed in June. The United Nations, headquartered in New York City, held its first sessions in 1946.

Although the UN Charter provided for six major bodies, it assigned the bulk of power to only two of them—the Security Council and the General Assembly. The Security Council, which decided diplomatic, political, and military disputes, was made up of 11 members. The five permanent members were Great Britain, China, France, the

All seemed well when American and Soviet forces met at the Elbe River in April 1945. *What events in Eastern Europe changed the American attitude toward the Soviet Union?*

United States, and the Soviet Union. Each was given the right to veto any Security Council decision. The other six members served two-year terms. The General Assembly, the policy-making body, was made up of representatives from all UN member nations. Each nation had one vote.

The third body, the Economic and Social Council, oversaw the fights against poverty, ignorance, and disease. The fourth, the International Court of Justice, handled international legal disputes. The fifth, the Trusteeship Council, promoted the welfare of people in colonial territories and helped them toward self-rule. The sixth, the Secretariat, handled the UN's administrative work.

During the postwar period, the UN effectively resolved many crises. However, the right of veto granted the Security Council's permanent members made the UN powerless to resolve any dispute involving the United States and the Soviet Union. The United Nations became deadlocked. It was criticized as being a "debating society"—far from what the signers of the Charter had hoped it would be.

From Allies to Arch Enemies

After World War II, the Western Allies—the United States, Great Britain, and France—believed the best way to achieve security was to strengthen democracy and to build prosperous economies in Europe. The Soviets, however, had different goals. Historically, they had well-justified fears of invasion and had lost more than 20 million people in World War II. The Soviet dictator **Joseph Stalin** wanted to establish pro-Soviet governments in Eastern Europe not only to prevent any future attacks but also to expand his empire. He made sure Eastern Europe's Communist parties were loyal to him and worked to strengthen their position throughout the region.

President Franklin D. Roosevelt had believed that postwar cooperation with Stalin was possible, although he was starting to change his mind shortly before his death in April 1945. In the months afterward, Roosevelt's successor, President **Harry S Truman**, and other leaders adopted a much darker view of Stalin. They concluded that the Soviet dictator wanted to control Eastern Europe with the same ruthlessness that he used to govern the Soviet Union.

The Iron Curtain

Eastern Europe thus became the first region where Soviet and Western interests came into conflict. In Albania and Yugoslavia, local Communist parties, which had led the resistance against Axis forces in their countries, took control with little help from the Soviets. In Poland, Romania, and Bulgaria, where Soviet troops were in full command, the Soviet Union made sure that government ministries included Communists. Later, breaking his promise made at Yalta, Stalin refused to allow free elections. Non-Communists were ousted from governments, and Communists took charge. By 1947, most of the nations of the region had become Soviet satellites, controlled by the Soviet Union.

Warsaw Pact member
Communist nation outside Soviet bloc
Neutral nation
NATO member

ICELAND

NORWAY

FINLAND

SWEDEN

North Sea

Baltic Sea

DENMARK

REPUBLIC OF IRELAND

BRITAIN

NETHER-LANDS

GERMAN DEMOCRATIC REPUBLIC

BELGIUM

POLAND

LUXEMBOURG

FEDERAL REPUBLIC OF GERMANY

CZECHOSLOVAKIA

ATLANTIC OCEAN

FRANCE

AUSTRIA

HUNGARY

SWITZER-LAND

YUGOSLAVIA

ROMANIA

Adriatic Sea

Black Sea

Corsica

ITALY

BULGARIA

PORTUGAL

SPAIN

ALBANIA

TURKEY

Sardinia

GREECE

UNION OF SOVIET SOCIALIST REPUBLICS

Caspian Sea

NORTH AFRICA

Crete

Cyprus

Mediterranean Sea

0   250   500 mi.
0   250   500 km
Lambert Conic Conformal Projection

Map Study   After World War II, Europe became divided between the Soviet and Western spheres of influence.
Place What nations of Europe remained neutral?

Stalin's actions in Eastern Europe convinced President Truman that the United States had to resist further Soviet moves. Truman was backed by British statesman Winston Churchill. In March 1946, Churchill had first used the phrase "iron curtain" in a speech in Fulton, Missouri: "From Stettin in the Baltic to Trieste in the Adriatic an iron curtain has descended across the continent of Europe." Thereafter, iron curtain referred to the Soviet-made barrier that split Europe into non-Communist Western Europe and Communist Eastern Europe.

Containing Communism

To counter any expansionist threat from the Soviet Union, the United States developed a new

foreign policy in 1947. The idea for the new policy was presented in early 1947 by George Kennan, a State Department expert on the Soviet Union. Believing that the Soviets sought to expand their territory without war, he suggested a policy of containment—holding back the spread of communism. By standing firm, the United States hoped to keep communism inside its existing borders.

The Truman Doctrine

In the spring of 1947, President Truman applied the containment policy for the first time in the eastern Mediterranean. In **Greece**, local Communists were fighting a guerrilla war against the pro-Western monarchy. They were aided by Communists from neighboring Yugoslavia and Albania. The West feared that the fall of Greece to

Cornell Capa. Magnum.

Cold War

In 1961 Soviet Premier Nikita Khrushchev (left) and United States President John F. Kennedy held a cold war meeting. Khrushchev insisted that troops of the Soviet Union's former World War II Allies—France, Great Britain, and the United States—must leave West Berlin. The Allies' sector of Berlin was entirely inside East Germany, a separate nation from West Germany and an ally of the Soviet Union. Kennedy refused, believing that the Soviets would take control over West Berlin if the Allies departed. Two months later the Soviets shocked the people of both Berlins—and the world—by building the Berlin Wall.

The Berlin Wall became an important symbol of the cold war. For nearly a half century after the end of World War II the world's two superpowers, the United States and the Union of Soviet Socialist Republics, dominated the world and fought a "cold" war. In fact, it was not always cold. The two powers fought a number of regional conflicts either directly or through allies, including the Korean and Vietnam Wars. In 1989 the Berlin Wall was torn down; in 1991, the Soviet Union crumbled and the cold war came to an end. ⊕

communism would endanger Western influence in the eastern Mediterranean region.

Great Britain was the traditional defender of the eastern Mediterranean. Economic weaknesses at home, however, prevented the British from continuing their commitment. In February 1947, Great Britain informed President Truman of this fact and asked the United States to assume British responsibilities in the area. A month later, Truman asked Congress for a $400 million aid program for Greece and Turkey. In asking Congress for support, Truman made a new statement of foreign policy that became known as the Truman Doctrine. He stated:

> **❝** I believe that it must be the policy of the United States to support free peoples who are resisting attempted subjugation by armed minorities or by outside pressures.... [W]e must assist free peoples to work out their own destiny in their own way. **❞**

Congress approved Truman's aid request. With the acceptance of the Truman Doctrine, the United States took on international responsibilities as the leader of the Western world. American military aid would now be available to any nation threatened by communism. As a result of American assistance, Greece was able to defeat the Communist guerrillas and the spread of communism in the eastern Mediterranean was blocked.

The Marshall Plan

Conditions in Europe posed immediate and long-term challenges for the United States. World War II had severely weakened European economies. The Truman administration feared that a European economic collapse would open Europe to communism. It believed that the military and economic security of the United States depended on a strong and democratic Europe.

Therefore, the United States government devised a new approach to provide aid to Europe. Speaking at Harvard University on June 5, 1947,

Images of the Times

Rebuilding Europe

Fearing the spread of communism, the United States adopted strong economic programs to rebuild Europe after World War II. The Soviets responded with a rival plan in Eastern Europe.

Devastation in the divided city of Berlin challenged the resolve of the West to restore not only the structures but the spirit of the people.

ΑΓΑΘΑ ΤΟΥ ΑΜΕΡΙΚΑΝΙΚΟΥ ΣΧΕΔΙΟΥ ΜΑΡΣΑΛΛ ΔΙΑ ΤΗΝ ΕΛΛΑΔΑ

ΤΟ ΦΟΡΤΙΟΝ ΑΥΤΟ ΜΕΤΑΦΕΡΕΤΑΙ ΔΙΑ ΤΗΣ ΣΙΔΗΡΟΔΡΟΜΙΚΗΣ ΓΡΑΜΜΗΣ ΑΘΗΝΩΝ - ΘΕΣΣΑΛΟΝΙΚΗΣ ΤΩΝ ΣΕΚ ΜΗΚΟΥΣ 512 ΧΙΛΙΟΜΕΤΡΩΝ. ΤΩΡΑ ΑΙ ΔΥΟ ΜΕΓΑΛΕΙΤΕΡΑΙ ΠΟΛΕΙΣ ΤΗΣ ΑΔΟΣ ΣΥΝΔΕΟΝΤΑΙ ΚΑΙ ΠΑΛΙΝ ΣΙΔΗΡΟΔΡΟΜΙΚΩΣ ΔΙΑ ΣΤΗΝ ΦΟΡΑΝ ΑΠΟ ΤΟ 1944

●

AMERICAN MARSHALL PLAN GOODS FOR GREECE

S FREIGHT IS BEING TRANSPORTED OVER THE 3-MILE ATHENS-SALONIKA RAILROAD LINE OF K-RR. GREECE'S TWO LARGEST CITIES ARE NOW KED BY RAIL FOR THE FIRST TIME SINCE 1944

Secretary of State **George C. Marshall** proposed a European aid program that became known as the Marshall Plan. Its purpose, he said, was to restore "the confidence of European people in the economic future of their own countries." For the plan to work, Marshall urged a united effort to determine where Europe's economic needs lay and how the United States could help.

Western European countries responded enthusiastically to the Marshall Plan; however, the Soviet Union refused to participate in the plan and forced its Eastern European allies to do the same. Despite their great need for economic aid, the Soviets felt they could not afford to give out information about their economy. They also opposed linking their Communist economy with the largely capitalist ones of Western Europe.

The Marshall Plan was a great success. Western European nations worked together to boost productivity, reduce trade barriers, and use resources efficiently. They received about $13 billion in aid from the United States during the next four years.

By 1951, Western Europe's economies were prospering, and Communist prospects in these countries had declined.

The Marshall Plan extended American influence in Western Europe and helped unite the region into a single economic group to counter the Soviets. In reaction to the Marshall Plan, in 1949 the Soviet Union set up a rival plan known as the Council for Mutual Economic Assistance, or COMECON. Eastern Europe was thus formed into a competing economic group led by the Soviet Union.

Germany Divided

In 1945, Germany had been divided into four zones, controlled by Great Britain, France, the United States, and the Soviet Union. The zones of the Western Allies included the western part of Germany, while the Soviet zone encompassed eastern Germany. The city of Berlin, deep within the Soviet zone, was also divided into four sectors.

Modern Warsaw finally emerged from behind the iron curtain when Poland overthrew its Communist government in 1989.

Threatened by revolt, Greece received economic aid under the Truman Doctrine until the Marshall Plan went into effect.

REFLECTING ON THE TIMES

1. Why was it difficult for the United States to send supplies into Berlin in 1948?
2. What is the purpose of the large sign on the railway car delivering goods in Greece?
3. Why did the Soviet Union prevent its allies from participating in the Marshall Plan?

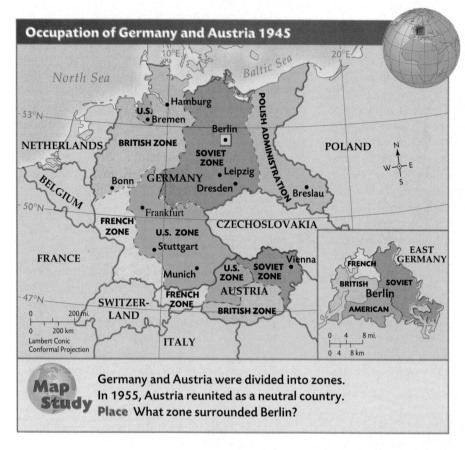

Map Study

Germany and Austria were divided into zones. In 1955, Austria reunited as a neutral country.

Place What zone surrounded Berlin?

Zones of Occupation

The Western Allies and the Soviets could not reach agreement on a final peace treaty for Germany. As relations with Stalin soured, the United States, Great Britain, and France decided to include their zones in the Marshall Plan as means to contain communism.

While the Soviets stripped their German zone of its industrial resources and equipment, the three Western powers aided their zones toward economic recovery. Free elections for local governments were held in the Western zones. The United States, Great Britain, and France also agreed to combine their sectors of Berlin to form what became known as the city of **West Berlin**. They also planned to form an independent West German state by joining their zones of occupation.

The Berlin Blockade

In June 1948, the Soviets tried to block this merger plan by cutting all land access from the West into West Berlin. Two million Berliners depended on the Western Allies for all their food, fuel, and other needs. The United States and other Western countries considered and rejected the idea of using force to regain access to Berlin. Instead, they came up with a plan to airlift needed supplies to the isolated city.

To keep the city alive, at least 4,000 tons of supplies were needed every day. Airplanes surpassed this goal by landing every 3 minutes at West Berlin's 2 airports. At the peak of the airlift, 13,000 tons were landed in one day. The airlift would continue for 11 months. Its success finally forced the Soviets to lift the blockade in May 1949.

That same month, the Western Allies went ahead with their plans to form an independent West German state. A constitution was approved that set up a federal system of 10 states. In the fall of 1949, the Federal Republic of Germany, or West Germany, was proclaimed. Its capital was at Bonn. The Soviets then set up the German Democratic Republic, or East Germany, with its capital at East Berlin. Thus, Germany was divided into 2 separate countries.

New Alliances

Just before the Berlin blockade, another crisis had occurred in Europe. In February 1948, Czechoslovakia was taken over by Communists and incorporated into the Soviet alliance system. The Czechoslovak and Berlin crises heightened Western concerns about military defense. In April 1949, shortly before the end of the Berlin blockade, the North Atlantic Treaty Organization (NATO) was formed by the United States, Great Britain, France, Belgium, the Netherlands, Luxembourg, Italy, Portugal, Denmark, Iceland, Norway, and Canada. NATO expanded to include Greece and Turkey in 1952 and West Germany in 1955. Members of this military alliance agreed that an attack on one would be considered an attack on all. In response to NATO, the Soviet Union and its Eastern European allies signed a military agreement known as the Warsaw Pact in 1955.

Later events showed that the purpose of the Warsaw Pact was as much to strengthen the Soviet hold on Eastern Europe as to defend it. Soviet troops stationed in Hungary under the terms of the Warsaw Pact were used to suppress a 1956 uprising there. In 1968 the Soviet Union appealed to the treaty to justify its invasion of Czechoslovakia, which had introduced a liberal form of communism.

Worldwide Struggle

The cold war soon turned into a global struggle. In 1949, the Soviets successfully exploded their first atomic bomb. International tensions further increased as the two superpowers engaged in an arms race, or a competition to strengthen their armed forces and weapons systems.

Meanwhile, communism made rapid advances in Asia. In the late 1940s, Communist governments came to power in China and North Korea. In 1950, the North Koreans, allied to the Soviet Union and Communist-ruled China, attacked South Korea, a pro-Western republic. Although the North Koreans were forced back to their territory, the Korean conflict fed Western fears that in communism, it faced a single, powerful enemy seeking world conquest.

Beginning in the 1950s, the cold war also came to be not only a test of military strength, but also a test of the superpowers' competing ideologies, or political and economic philosophies—democratic capitalism on the part of the United States, and communism on the part of the Soviet Union. Military buildups, space exploration, and local and regional conflicts around the globe became entangled in the cold war as the two superpowers sought to win support and to block gains by the other.

Germany

Germany became a critical flash point in the cold war during the 1950s and 1960s. Nikita Khrushchev (krush•CHAWF), who became Soviet leader in the mid-1950s, set out to test the resolve of the new United States President John F. Kennedy in 1961 by threatening to force the Allies out of West Berlin. Stating that the West would defend West Berlin's freedom, Kennedy bolstered the United States military presence, and Khrushchev did not act on his threats.

Meanwhile, large numbers of East Germans were fleeing to West Berlin, which was easily accessible to them. In an effort to halt the drain of its workforce, the East German government, with Soviet backing, built a concrete wall across the divided city in August 1961. The Berlin Wall stemmed the flow of East Germans fleeing communism and raised East-West tensions. It became a symbol of the cold war and the hostile confrontation between democracy and communism.

The Developing World

After the early 1960s, superpower competition directly affected developing nations in Asia, Africa, and Latin America. In most areas, such as in Africa and the Caribbean area, the superpowers provided aid to their allies in the particular region. Sometimes—as in the case of the Soviet Union in Afghanistan and the United States in Vietnam—they became militarily involved themselves.

By the late 1970s, however, the division of the world into two blocs, or groups of nations, each headed by a superpower, was coming to an end. The United States, wary of military involvements, faced growing challenges to its hold on world markets. Western Europe and Japan, less dependent on the United States, were prosperous economic powers in their own right. The Soviet Union, faltering economically, was facing internal pressures for change. Finally, many smaller nations, aligned with neither superpower, were following their own paths of development. All of these events marked the move away from a world dominated by the superpowers to one in which there were many competing groups of countries. ▬

SECTION 1 REVIEW

Recall
1. **Define** superpower, cold war, satellite, iron curtain, containment, arms race, ideology, bloc.
2. **Identify** Joseph Stalin, Harry S Truman, George C. Marshall, the Marshall Plan, NATO,

Warsaw Pact.
3. **Use** the map on page 866 to name the European nations under Soviet control.

Critical Thinking
4. **Analyzing Information** What geographic factor made it possible for Stalin to impose

the Berlin blockade?

Understanding Themes
5. **Conflict** What were some of the political and economic "weapons" of the cold war? What goals did the superpowers hope to accomplish using these varying strategies?

1955	1965	1975

1955 Nikita Khrushchev becomes the dominant leader in the Soviet Union.

1968 The Soviets invade Czechoslovakia.

1972 Soviet and American leaders hold summit meeting in Moscow.

Section 2

The Communist Bloc

Setting the Scene

▶ **Terms to Define**

peaceful coexistence, intercontinental ballistic missile (ICBM), dissident, detente

▶ **People to Meet**

Nikita Khrushchev, Leonid Brezhnev, Josip Broz Tito, Alexander Dubček

▶ **Places to Locate**

Yugoslavia, East Germany, Poland, Hungary, Czechoslovakia

Find Out How did the Soviet Union carry out Communist policies after the death of Stalin?

The Storyteller

Peter Hauptman and Willi Pfeiffer had been best friends since childhood. Although their homes were only two blocks apart, they lived in different sectors of Berlin. Now, literally overnight, their frequent visits ended. The Soviet sector was walled off. Not just a barricade or a lowered gate, it was a wall, protected by barbed wire and concrete blocks. Peter stood on the western side of the wall, straining to catch a glimpse of Willi. But it was to no avail. Everyone living near the wall's eastern side had been forcibly relocated, and the nearby apartment doors and windows were sealed shut.

—adapted from People and Politics: The Years 1960–1975, translated and edited by Strobe Talbott, 1974

Children play near the Berlin Wall

The cold war affected the internal policies of the Soviet Union and its Eastern European satellites. During the late 1940s and early 1950s, Joseph Stalin believed that a full-scale conflict with the West was inevitable. To confront the West, the Soviet leader increased his control over the Soviet Union and Eastern Europe. He purged Communist parties of officials suspected of disloyalty. He also forbade writers and artists to use Western ideas in their works.

The Soviet Union

After World War II, Stalin worked to rebuild the Soviet Union's heavy industry and to boost its military strength. The Soviet Union surpassed its prewar rates of production in several major products, including coal, steel, and oil. It continued a high level of military spending and exploded its first nuclear bomb. In spite of the country's military prestige, life for the average Soviet citizen was difficult. Towns and cities destroyed by the war were rebuilt. Consumer goods, food, and clothing, however, remained in short supply because of high military spending.

Stalin died in March 1953. He was succeeded by a collective leadership of top Communist officials. **Nikita Khrushchev**, who served as Communist party secretary, emerged as the dominant leader in 1955.

De-Stalinization

In the following year, the 20th Congress of the Soviet Communist Party was held in Moscow. At a secret session, Nikita Khrushchev gave a controversial speech about Stalin. He denounced the Soviet dictator for the purges in the 1930s, in which thousands of loyal party members had been tortured

Visualizing History President Eisenhower hosts Premier Nikita Khrushchev in Washington, D.C., in 1959. *What prevented the four-power summit meeting planned for May 1960 from taking place?*

by improving working conditions. He sought to improve housing and to increase the production of consumer goods. The Soviet leader also put new emphasis on technological research. This paid off in 1957 with the launch of *Sputnik I*, the world's first space satellite. *Sputnik* stunned the United States and boosted the prestige of the Soviet Union and its leader.

Despite the cold war "thaw," both superpowers continued a massive military buildup. In the late 1950s, the Americans and Soviets successfully tested long-range rockets known as intercontinental ballistic missiles, or ICBMs, and added them to their arsenals. ICBMs for the first time could target locations in both countries. A nuclear war would result in what was known as mutual assured destruction—that is, the certain destruction of both nations.

Even as they pursued this deadly race, United States and Soviet leaders sought to maintain peace. Summit meetings were the most visible of many contacts between Soviets and the United States. United States President Dwight Eisenhower and Soviet Premier Khrushchev met in Geneva, Switzerland, in 1955 and again in 1959 at Camp David, in Maryland. They recognized the deadly threat of nuclear war and agreed on the need to end the arms race. They planned a four-power summit for Paris in May 1960 and Khrushchev invited Eisenhower to visit the Soviet Union later in the year. But shortly before the Paris summit, the Soviets shot down an American U-2 spy plane over their territory and captured its pilot. Facing criticism from the Soviet military, Khrushchev strongly

and condemned to death or sent to labor camps. He also accused Stalin of creating a "cult of personality," in which he boosted his own image at the expense of the Communist party.

Khrushchev's anti-Stalin speech was part of a broader program of de-Stalinization, which he undertook from 1956 to 1964 to reverse some of the policies that had existed under Stalin. Khrushchev understood that many Soviet citizens wanted a relaxation of government controls and an improved standard of living. While keeping Stalin's Five-Year Plans and collective farms, he promised better wages and more consumer goods. He gave artists and intellectuals more freedom. He also reduced the terror of the secret police and freed many political prisoners from labor camps.

Cold War "Thaw"

By the mid-1950s, both American and Soviet leaders were interested in reducing cold-war tensions. Khrushchev called for a policy of peaceful coexistence in which the Soviets would compete with the West but avoid war. He stated the Soviet Union would surpass the West economically and encouraged other countries to follow the Communist model.

To make the Soviet Union more economically competitive, Khrushchev tried to boost production

The Kitchen Debate

In 1959, Vice President Richard M. Nixon, on a tour of the Soviet Union, visited an exhibition of American products with Soviet leader Nikita Khrushchev. The two leaders soon got into a heated argument on the merits of capitalism versus communism. The argument became known as the "kitchen debate" because the two men were standing in front of a model kitchen display.

denounced the United States and canceled Eisenhower's visit. Relations soon worsened further.

The Cuban Missile Crisis

The Soviet Union and the United States came to the brink of nuclear war in 1962. In 1961, Eisenhower was succeeded as United States President by John F. Kennedy, who adopted a dynamic foreign policy to impress the Soviets with American strength and boost American prestige abroad. Testing Kennedy's resolve, Khrushchev used pressure to try to remove the Allies from Berlin. Then in 1962 he secretly began to install nuclear missiles on Cuba 90 miles (145 km) from Florida. In his gamble, the Soviet leader hoped to offset American missiles based in Turkey that were aimed at the Soviet Union. He also wanted to get from Kennedy a promise not to overthrow Cuba's Communist government. Devising a strong response short of attack, Kennedy blockaded Cuba. Khrushchev then agreed to withdraw the missiles; and in return, Kennedy pledged not to invade Cuba.

The Cuban missile crisis was one of the most significant events in the cold war. Having come so close to nuclear conflict, the superpowers decided to establish a better relationship. In 1963, a telephone "hot line" linked Washington and Moscow to provide instant communication. That same year, the Soviets and the Western Allies also signed a treaty banning nuclear weapons tests in the atmosphere.

Meanwhile, Khrushchev's position within the Soviet Union weakened. In addition to his poor handling of the Cuban missile crisis, relations with China had soured, and Khrushchev's economic policies were in trouble. Heavy spending on technology, defense, and heavy industry had left little for improving agriculture and consumer goods. Far from surpassing the United States, the Soviet Union was forced to import grain from the United States. Sharply rising meat and butter prices provoked angry public demonstrations. In October 1964, Khrushchev was removed from office.

The Brezhnev Era

The Communist party chose a new collective leadership: Aleksei Kosygin (kuh•SEE•guhn) was premier and **Leonid Brezhnev** (BREHZH•NEHF) was general secretary of the party. By the mid-1970s, Brezhnev emerged as the dominant leader. He remained in control until his death in 1982.

Cautious and traditional, Brezhnev reversed Khrushchev's de-Stalinization policies. He clamped down again on intellectuals and dissidents—those who criticized the party or regime. Two prominent dissidents refused to be silenced. Alexander Solzhenitsyn (SOHL•zhuh•NEET•suhn), author of many works including *The Gulag Archipelago*, an account of the horrors of Soviet prison camps, was eventually deported and settled in the United States. Dr. Andrei Sakharov (SAH•kuh•RAWF), scientist and developer of the Soviet hydrogen bomb, later denounced the arms race and was sentenced to internal exile in Gorki.

Brezhnev's military and economic policies were similar to Khrushchev's. Concerned that there was a missile gap with the United States, he greatly increased the Soviet nuclear arsenal and its supplies of conventional weapons. He felt that military power gave the Soviet Union a stronger position in world diplomacy.

Under Brezhnev, economic conditions, however, worsened in the Soviet Union. Heavy military spending stifled growth in other sectors of the economy. Soviet workers had to make do with outdated equipment. Technologically, many industries were at least 20 years behind the times. Consumer goods were shoddy and in short supply. Farmers were only one-sixth as productive as their American counterparts. Poor harvests forced the Soviet Union to again import grain from the West.

Detente

By 1972, Brezhnev was ready to reduce tensions with the West. He hoped to find a way to cut military spending without falling behind the United States militarily. He also needed access to Western technology, grain, and consumer goods.

The United States was ready for Brezhnev's policy of detente. Derived from the French word meaning "relaxation," detente referred to an improvement of American-Soviet relations. A 1972 summit meeting between Brezhnev and United States President Richard Nixon in Moscow began a period of detente that lasted seven years. The Brezhnev-Nixon summit led to the signing of the Strategic Arms Limitation Agreement (SALT) Treaty, under which both sides agreed to limit the number of nuclear warheads and missiles each country could maintain. SALT did not reduce the number of weapons or end the arms race; it did slow it significantly.

Detente did not end the rivalry between the United States and the Soviet Union. The countries continued to compete for influence in various parts of the world. In 1979, the Soviets invaded neighboring Afghanistan to reinforce local Communist control. The move shocked the West and marked the end of detente. It also drew the Soviet Union into a 10-year guerrilla war against tough Afghan

Visualizing History While the Soviets constructed the Berlin Wall in 1961, Russian and American tanks maneuvered within sight of each other.

What was the real purpose of the wall?

nationalists. The occupation of Afghanistan drained the national treasury, brought about the deaths of thousands of young Soviet soldiers, and became extremely unpopular at home.

Soviet Satellites

For most of the cold war, the Soviet Union maintained tight control over its Eastern European satellites. The peoples of these nations resented Soviet domination, but were largely powerless against the secret police and Soviet troops.

Yugoslavia

After World War II, **Yugoslavia** became the only large Communist state in Eastern Europe to resist Soviet control. Its leader, **Josip Broz Tito**, had participated in the resistance against the Nazis. As much a nationalist as a Communist, Tito insisted on developing his own national policies. Angered by Tito's independence, Stalin expelled Yugoslavia from the international Communist movement. Throughout Eastern Europe, Stalin waged a propaganda war against what he called Titoism, or the

tendency of some Communists to place their national interests above those of the Soviet Union. With the support of his people, Tito resisted Soviet pressure, developed his own form of communism, held together the different religious and ethnic groups of the country, and won aid from the West. He led Yugoslavia until his death in 1980.

East Germany

Although it recovered from World War II more slowly than West Germany, **East Germany** became the most prosperous of the Soviet satellites. Its people deeply resented Soviet controls, however. In the aftermath of Stalin's death in 1953, East German workers went on strike and rioted when the government tried to lengthen the work day without an increase in wages. Soviet troops and tanks easily put down the revolt.

In the years that followed, nearly 3 million East Germans migrated to West Germany, by way of West Berlin, the only safe access available once the Soviets sealed the East German-West German border. A large percentage of the migrants were well-educated professionals who were attracted by West Germany's higher standard of living and greater freedoms. This "brain drain" was an embarrassment to the Soviets and an economic blow to the nation.

East Germany's problems contributed to a new cold war crisis in 1959. By then, West Germany had recovered from the war and was fully armed with tanks, bombs, and guns. It also had nuclear weapons on its soil under the control of NATO command. Alarmed at this development, Khrushchev called for negotiations on European security and on a nuclear-free Germany. He also demanded that the Western powers withdraw from Berlin.

Frustrated by the lack of a settlement and the continuing flight of East Germans, Khrushchev ordered the construction of what became the notorious Berlin Wall. In 1961, East German soldiers began work on the wall, a massive concrete structure 26 miles (42 km) long and up to 15 feet (4.6 m) high, topped with electrified wire.

The stated purpose of the wall was to keep Westerners out, but its true purpose was to halt the exodus of East Germans from East Berlin. To escape to West Berlin, people now had to survive mined trenches, guard dogs, and self-activating guns. Then they had to scale the wall itself. Stories reached the West of heroic escapes, but scores of East Germans died trying to run to freedom. Although the Berlin Wall did halt the flow of East German refugees, it became the most visible and powerful physical symbol of the iron curtain.

Poland

Under Communist rule, **Poland** industrialized and, among the satellites, became second in manufacturing only to East Germany. Poles, however, resented Soviet controls. They were angered by the government's efforts to collectivize farms and by its anti-Catholic policies. In June 1956 workers demanding better wages rioted in the city of Poznan. Upheavals in other cities forced Poland's Communist leaders to remove hard-line officials from office.

Poland's new leader was Wladyslaw Gomulka (VLAH•dee•slah goh•MUL•kuh), a popular Communist who had been accused of anti-Soviet activities and jailed during the late 1940s. Gomulka freed political prisoners, ended forced collectivization, and eased relations with the Catholic Church. He retained close ties with the Soviet Union, however. By the mid-1960s many of the Polish freedoms had again been lost.

In the 1970s, there was a new wave of anti-government strikes, with workers demanding better living conditions, and political and economic reforms. Gomulka resigned under the pressure.

Continued economic problems led to food riots in 1976 and the growth of an underground anti-Soviet movement, aided by the Catholic Church.

Hungary

Hungary, a largely agricultural nation, experienced harsh Communist rule after 1947. The Hungarian government required peasants to join collective farms, and nationalized banking, trade and industry. Central planners emphasized heavy industry, at the expense of consumer goods. The Communist leadership silenced or disbanded potential opposition groups, such as trade unions or other political parties. Catholic Church property was seized, and Church schools taken over by the government. Opponents within the Communist party were purged and executed.

After Stalin's death in 1953, Hungary's Communist leaders eased controls for two years and then reimposed them when the economy did not reach its goals. Bitter opposition turned into full revolt in the fall of 1956. As in Poland, worker uprisings brought a liberal Communist government to power. However, Imre Nagy, the new Hungarian prime minister, went further than the Polish leaders. He announced Hungary's neutrality and its withdrawal from the Warsaw Pact. This raised the danger the Soviet Union feared most—the loss of Soviet control over Eastern Europe.

Two days after Nagy's announcement, Soviet tanks and troops poured into Hungary to crush the revolt. Realizing that intervention could cause World War III, the West sympathized with the Hungarians, but did nothing to help. Order in Hungary was restored under a Soviet-controlled government led by János Kádár. More than 200,000 Hungarian refugees fled to the West.

During the 1960s and 1970s, Hungary's Communist government tried to increase production, sometimes tightening controls, while at other times encouraging initiative through small private enterprises. Support of economic reform would eventually spur political reform efforts in the 1980s.

Czechoslovakia

Czechoslovakia, with its developed industry and democratic traditions, was the last Eastern European country to become Communist. After the Communist takeover in 1948, the country was forced to conform to the Soviet model, like Hungary. Purges against officials in Czechoslovakia were the bloodiest outside of the Soviet Union. The Czechoslovak leader, Antonin Novotny, kept the country under such rigid control that

Visualizing History Czech citizens reacted in anger and defiance when Soviet and other Warsaw Pact troops invaded Prague. *How did the Soviets justify the invasion?*

de-Stalinization did not begin in Czechoslovakia until the 1960s.

At this time, public pressure for reform finally gained strength because of Czechoslovakia's economic stagnation. A liberal Communist reformer, **Alexander Dubček** (DOOB•chehk), replaced Novotny as leader in 1968 when Brezhnev signaled his approval. For a brief time, known as "the Prague spring," reform was allowed. Dubček eased press censorship and began to allow some political groups to meet freely.

Although Dubček assured the Soviets that Czechoslovakia was still loyal to the Warsaw Pact and to communism, the Soviets became alarmed at the direction the reform movement was taking. Many Czechoslovak thinkers wanted more freedom, and there were hints that opposition parties might

be allowed to operate. To the Soviets, their hold on Eastern Europe again seemed threatened.

On August 20, 1968, about 500,000 troops from the Soviet Union and its Warsaw Pact allies invaded Czechoslovakia. They took control of Prague and sent Dubček and other Czechoslovak leaders to Moscow. Most of Dubček's reforms were withdrawn and a new constitution put into effect. In April 1969, Dubček was replaced as party leader. In 1970 he was expelled from the party entirely.

The Soviet Union declared its right to intervene in Communist states to counter any opposition that threatened communism or the unity of the Soviet bloc. This principle, called the Brezhnev Doctrine, was the basis for relations between the Soviet Union and its Eastern European satellites for the next 20 years.

SECTION 2 REVIEW

Recall
1. **Define** peaceful coexistence, intercontinental ballistic missile (ICBM), dissident, detente.
2. **Identify** Nikita Khrushchev, Leonid Brezhnev, Josip Broz Tito, Alexander Dubček, the Brezhnev Doctrine.

3. **Explain** why the Soviet Union and East Germany built the Berlin Wall.

Critical Thinking
4. **Analyzing Information** Analyze church-government relations in Eastern Europe during the cold war. How did

Communist rule affect religion in the region?

Understanding Themes
5. **Change** What impact do you think Nikita Khrushchev's 1956 de-Stalinization speech had in the satellites of Eastern Europe?

Section 3

Western Europe

Setting the Scene

▶ **Terms to Define**
welfare state, coalition

▶ **People to Meet**
Clement Attlee, Charles de Gaulle, Valéry Giscard d'Estaing, Konrad Adenauer, Willy Brandt

▶ **Places to Locate**
Rome

ind Out How did Western Europe move toward greater political and economic unity during the period of the cold war?

The Storyteller

Jacques LeMoine nervously held the rifle issued to him just that morning. Like many other citizens of Paris, the 17-year-old had been pressed into service, guarding the city's perimeter. President de Gaulle's announced plans to guide

Paris street disturbance

Algeria to independence had aroused furious opposition. In reaction to the independence policy for Algeria, a threat had been received: Paris would be invaded. Paratroopers under the leadership of four retired French generals had seized key overseas bases and planned to bring citizens like Jacques LeMoine to defend the city.

—adapted from *The 1962 World Year Book*, "France," Fred J. Pannwitt, 1962

After World War II, the non-Communist nations of Western Europe were concerned about two major issues: economic recovery and military security. They came to realize that only through united action would they be able to improve their economies, strengthen the Western Alliance, and contribute to world affairs.

Great Britain

After World War II, Great Britain's position as a world power further declined. The British had bankrupted themselves to win the war. Therefore, they had to sharply reduce their worldwide military, political, and economic role.

A Reduced Role

Even with financial cutbacks, Great Britain's recovery was slow. Many British industries were too inefficient and outdated to compete successfully in world markets that were increasingly dominated by the United States, Japan, and other Western European nations.

Because of economic weakness, the British passed on many of their international obligations to the United States. To maintain its pride and a level of independent security, Great Britain, however, developed its own nuclear force. It also maintained a close relationship with other members of the Western Alliance.

Loss of Empire

The British also could no longer afford to support a vast global empire. During the 1950s and 1960s, many of Great Britain's important Asian and African colonies became independent. Most of these new nations joined as equals with Great Britain in the Commonwealth of Nations, an organization that promoted cooperation among the nations of the former British Empire.

The Welfare State

Internally, Great Britain underwent many changes after World War II. In 1945 Churchill and the Conservatives were voted out of office. They were replaced by the Labour party, which appealed to many Britons who wanted greater economic equality. Under Prime Minister **Clement Attlee**, the Labour government continued wartime restrictions to improve the economy. However, it also promised a better standard of living for all British citizens.

Carrying out a moderate Socialist program, the Labour government nationalized the coal, steel, and transportation industries. Greater freedom was given to labor unions to strike and to participate in political activities. Like many other Western European governments, Britain's Labour government created a welfare state, a system in which the national government provides programs for the well-being of its citizens. Social security was expanded to provide lifetime benefits for the needy. Free education was provided to all children up to the age of 16. The government also introduced a national health service that provided free medical care for everyone.

As the economic situation improved in the early 1950s, the Conservatives returned to power and ruled until 1964. Although they ended many government controls over the economy, Conservative prime ministers, such as Winston Churchill, Anthony Eden, and Harold Macmillan did not eliminate the social welfare programs introduced by the Labour party.

The Monarchy

In 1952, the popular wartime monarch, George VI, died and was succeeded by his elder daughter, Elizabeth. As queen, Elizabeth II had little, if any, power. But, for many Britons, she served as a reassuring symbol of traditional British values during a period of rapid, and sometimes discouraging, change. For other Britons, however, the monarchy represented all that they believed was wrong with Great Britain—its preoccupation with past imperial glories and its failure to discard the trappings of an outdated class system.

France

Germany's occupation of France during World War II had ended the Third French Republic created in 1870. After the war, a new constitution established the Fourth French Republic. Like the Third Republic, it, too, had a strong legislature and a weak presidency.

Visualizing History Riots between Hindus and Muslims led to the division of British India in 1947 into two nations: India and Pakistan. Both joined the Commonwealth of Nations. *What was the Commonwealth of Nations?*

The Fourth French Republic

In spite of economic growth, France in the 1950s was plagued with domestic and international problems. The existence of many political parties undermined hopes for a stable government. No single political party was strong enough to obtain a working majority in the National Assembly. Cabinets were formed by coalitions, or temporary alliances, of several parties. When one of the parties disagreed with policy, the cabinet members had to resign and form a new government.

Overseas, France's Asian and African colonies demanded their independence. Unlike Great Britain, France at first clung to its empire. It fought, and lost, expensive and bloody wars in Indochina and North Africa.

The Fifth French Republic

In 1958, the threat of civil war in the North African colony of Algeria resulted in the downfall of France's ineffective Fourth Republic. **Charles de Gaulle**, leader of the French Resistance during World War II, was called from retirement to head an emergency government. De Gaulle asked the

French people to approve a new constitution providing for a strong presidency. French voters overwhelmingly responded to de Gaulle's appeal. Thus, the Fifth French Republic was born.

De Gaulle became the first president of the Fifth Republic. His political party, the Gaullist Union, formed a working majority in the National Assembly. As president, de Gaulle recognized that France could not stubbornly hold on to its empire against strong nationalist opposition. In the early 1960s, he allowed France's African colonies, including Algeria, to become independent.

With the loss of France's empire, de Gaulle worked to strengthen French cultural and economic influence in Europe and throughout the rest of the world. His strongly nationalistic policies angered France's allies, especially Great Britain and the United States. In 1963, de Gaulle blocked Great Britain's application for membership in the European Common Market. Three years later, the French president decided to withdraw all French troops from NATO's military command and requested that all NATO bases and headquarters be removed from French soil. At the same time, he insisted on maintaining France's political ties to NATO. De Gaulle's ultimate expression of nationalism was the building of an independent French nuclear force.

De Gaulle's successor, Georges Pompidou (PAHM•pih•DOO), by contrast, worked to build closer relations with Great Britain and the United States. He also focused on economic growth rather than on nationalistic projects. After Pompidou's death in 1974, **Valéry Giscard d'Estaing** (zhihs •KAHR dehs•TAN) was elected president. Giscard continued Pompidou's domestic and international policies. He set out to lessen state economic controls and to encourage the expansion of French private enterprise. Giscard's pro-business policies, however, were crippled by the worldwide economic downturn of the 1970s.

Germany

During the postwar years, West Germany rebuilt its economy and became Western Europe's leading industrial nation. Many experts called West Germany's reconstruction an "economic miracle." New industries used the latest in modern equipment, and industrial production more than tripled in the 1950s. Prosperity enabled West Germany to create a welfare state closely resembling that in Great Britain and France. West Germany also absorbed 10 million refugees from Eastern Europe. Another 1 million people settled in Germany from other parts of the continent.

The Adenauer Years

West Germany's democratic political system was dominated by two parties: the Christian Democrats and the Social Democrats. In 1949, the Christian Democrats, led by **Konrad Adenauer** (A•duhn•OWR), formed the first West German government. They created a capitalist economy with close ties to the West. In 1955 West Germany joined NATO and developed its own armed forces.

As chancellor, Adenauer was known as a strong leader devoted to the Western Alliance, European unity, and the reunification of Germany under a democratic government. During his tenure, West Germany became one of the world's most stable democracies. Adenauer retired in 1963. He was succeeded as chancellor by the economic minister Ludwig Erhard, who served until 1966.

Willy Brandt

During the 1960s, the Christian Democrats lost support to the Social Democrats, a moderate socialist party led by West Berlin's mayor, **Willy Brandt**. The Social Democrats maintained strong support for NATO while seeking improved relations with the Soviet bloc.

Brandt became chancellor of Germany in 1969. During the 1970s, he worked to reduce tensions

Visualizing History France gave Charles de Gaulle broad presidential powers and election by direct popular vote. *How did de Gaulle solve the problem of nationalist opposition in Algeria?*

between West Germany and the Soviet bloc. This policy, known as *Ostpolitik* (German for "Eastern policy") led West Germany to reach agreements to normalize relations with the Soviet Union and Poland in 1972. Brandt's initiative eventually led to the establishment of diplomatic ties between West Germany and East Germany a year later.

European Unity

Throughout Europe's history, local disputes between two or more nations often drew the entire continent into war. In the twentieth century, developments in technology, such as nuclear weapons, made it clear that future wars could lead to global catastrophe. This possibility prompted leaders to seek regional solutions to European issues.

As World War II ended, European leaders discussed plans for the postwar unification of European countries. These plans included organizations for economic cooperation and the resolution of disputes. Some even raised the idea of a United States of Europe. Others proposed that each nation retain its national identity but hand over control of defense and foreign policy to an all-European government. This arrangement, it was felt, would prevent European nations from waging war on each other.

To coordinate economic policies, six nations—France, Italy, West Germany, Belgium, the Netherlands, and Luxembourg established the European Coal and Steel Community in 1952. The organization's goal was to create a tariff-free market for European coal and steel products. By ending trade barriers and developing uniform standards, the European Coal and Steel Community would further European industrial growth.

The Community was so successful that the same countries decided to bring together the rest of their economies. In 1957, representatives of the six nations meeting in **Rome**, Italy, signed the Treaty of

Edmund Hillary Climbs Mount Everest

Nepal-Tibet, 1953
Located in the Himalayas, on the Nepal-Tibet border, Mount Everest is the world's highest peak. A British expedition set out in 1953 to scale the south slope, which was considered unclimbable. The climbers established a series of camps as they advanced up the mountain. The last camp was set up by Edmund Hillary of New Zealand and Tenzing Norgay of Nepal. On May 29, 1953, they became the first climbers to reach the top of Mount Everest. Queen Elizabeth II knighted Hillary for his achievement.

Rome. This agreement created the European Economic Community, also known as the Common Market. The six members of the Common Market planned to abolish all tariffs among themselves and form a single economic market by 1970. During the 1960s and 1970s, Great Britain, attracted by the Common Market's success, ended its traditional aloofness from European affairs and sought membership in the European organization.

The Common Market benefited Western Europe in several ways. By promoting economic cooperation among individual European nations, it reduced the threat of conflict and contributed to European prosperity. It also enabled Western Europe to pursue cooperative technological programs in fields such as space research and nuclear energy. These programs were too expensive for any one nation to pursue on its own. Finally, it enabled Europe to compete on an equal basis with North America and East Asia in world markets.

SECTION 3 REVIEW

Recall
1. **Define** welfare state, coalition.
2. **Identify** Clement Attlee, Charles de Gaulle, Valéry Giscard d'Estaing, Konrad Adenauer, Willy Brandt, *Ostpolitik*, European Economic Community (Common Market).

3. **Explain** why Charles de Gaulle of France was considered an independent leader.

Critical Thinking
4. **Synthesizing Information** Why was a strong European economy vital to world peace after World War II? What fac-

tors contributed to the economic recovery of Western Europe during the postwar years?

Understanding Themes
5. **Regionalism** What do you think would be the advantages and disadvantages of a United States of Europe?

1947 U.S. Congress conducts hearings on Communist influence in American life.

1955 Martin Luther King, Jr., begins nonviolent civil rights campaign for African Americans.

1967 Canada celebrates 100th anniversary of nationhood.

1974 Richard M. Nixon becomes the first United States President to resign his office.

Section 4

The United States and Canada

Setting the Scene

▶ **Terms to Define**

automation, racial segregation, imperial presidency, stagflation, embargo, double-digit inflation, trade deficit, middle power, multicultural, separatism

▶ **People to Meet**

Dwight D. Eisenhower, John F. Kennedy, Lyndon B. Johnson, Richard M. Nixon, Martin Luther King, Jr., Gerald R. Ford, Jimmy Carter, Lester B. Pearson, Pierre Elliott Trudeau

▶ **Places to Locate**

Vietnam, Cambodia, Washington, D.C., St. Lawrence Seaway, Toronto, Montreal, Quebec

Find Out What political and social changes did the people of the United States and Canada experience during the cold war years?

The Storyteller

By the time President Eisenhower began his first term, 33,629 Americans had been killed in the Korean War. Then on March 5, 1953, Joseph Stalin died. Hearing of Stalin's death, Eisenhower asked his associates, "Well, what do you think we can do about this?" He was advised to seek improved relations with Russia. The new Soviet leaders also wanted reduced tensions. As a result, a truce ending the war in Korea was signed on July 28th.

—adapted from *The Glorious Burden*, Stefan Lorant, 1968

President Dwight D. Eisenhower

B ecause they were spared the destruction of their territory in World War II, the United States and Canada emerged from the war with prosperous economies. During the postwar era, the stunning technological achievements of the United States, its high standard of living, and business success were admired and envied around the globe.

In the 1960s and the 1970s, however, the United States was shaken by domestic political crises, economic difficulties, and its involvement in the Vietnam War. By the 1980s other nations were catching up economically, but the United States retained its role as the leader of the non-Communist world.

During this time, the United States's northern neighbor, Canada, sought to maintain unity between its French-speaking and English-speaking populations. It also attracted immigrants from all parts of the world. Moving away from its traditional British connection, Canada sought a new identity in international affairs and developed closer economic ties with the United States.

American Prosperity

After World War II, the United States entered an era of economic growth that brought material wealth to a larger group of Americans. Demand for American goods was high, and business responded to meet this need. Production soared, and new industries appeared. Higher wages and better benefits gave Americans more money to spend. American shoppers pushed up demand as they eagerly purchased consumer goods that had been scarce during the war. Future prospects were also bright. The postwar "baby boom," or soaring birthrate, added to the potential number of consumers and promised increased economic growth.

Science and Technology

During the postwar years, the United States made spectacular leaps in the field of science and technology. With more money to spend, an increase in the number of university-trained scientists, and a growing commitment to the future, the United States led the world in new technological developments.

During the 1950s and 1960s, American factories and industries began to use automation, the technique of operating a production system using mechanical or electronic devices. With automated methods of production, goods could be produced more efficiently than with human workers.

Beginning in the 1950s, the use of computers began to revolutionize American industry. Businesses used computers for many purposes, including billing and inventory control. Computers were also used for such things as making hotel reservations, sorting bank checks, tracking space satellites, forecasting weather conditions, and setting type for printing. Automation and computers in the workplace caused many workers to lose their jobs. In the long run, however, computers and automation created more jobs than they eliminated. In addition, the new jobs usually demanded a higher level of education.

American technological skills brought the United States into competition with the Soviet Union in space exploration and missile development. The two superpowers experimented with moon probes, weather and communications satellites, and extended flights of humans orbiting the earth. The grand prize of the "space race" was putting a human on the moon. United States astronaut Neil Armstrong won that honor on July 20, 1969.

Social Changes

Many social changes came to the United States during the period from the late 1940s to the late 1970s. In the 1950s the automobile changed the face of America. No longer did people have to live near their places of work. Those who lived and worked in the city could move to less-crowded places. This migration of city residents caused the rapid growth of suburbs.

In the years after World War II, American cities became ringed by seemingly endless housing developments carved out of the less densely settled country land. Shopping centers with vast parking lots were built to serve the new suburban population. Businesses and factories also began relocating from the cities to the suburbs, where their workers now lived. The Highway Act of 1956 contributed to the growth of the suburbs by adding 41,000 miles (66,000 km) to the interstate highway system.

Visualizing History Cold war tensions and fear of nuclear attack led to "duck and cover" drills in public schools. *How did the government react to the fear of the "enemy within"?*

In addition to the automobile, another symbol of American prosperity was the television set. In 1945, fewer than 1 in every 20,000 people had a television. But within a few years, televisions were everywhere, and they were almost as common as telephones. Some critics worried that television would make Americans desire entertainment more than solid information. However, other experts pointed out the positive impact of television in making people directly aware of national and international events.

The Cold War at Home

Despite this time of prosperity, the cold war created deep political divisions in the United States. During the late 1940s and early 1950s, conservatives blamed President Harry S Truman and State Department officials for allowing the Communists to make gains in Eastern Europe and Asia. They also charged that Communists were serving in high government positions. A "red scare" swept the country. The growing fear of the "enemy within"— of subversion within the United States government and society—helped to launch a controversial anti-Communist crusade to discover and expose suspected Communists. The search focused on diplomats, intellectuals, labor leaders, and entertainers believed to be tolerant of communism.

Congressional Investigations

A congressional body, the House Committee on Un-American Activities, investigated Communist influences. Alger Hiss, a former government official, denied that he had tried to pass secrets to the Soviets in the 1930s. Brought to trial, Hiss was not prosecuted because too much time had passed since the events had occurred. However, he was found guilty of lying and was sent to prison. Later, Julius and Ethel Rosenberg, both Communists, were accused of spying. They claimed innocence but were tried, convicted, and executed.

In the early 1950s, Senator Joseph McCarthy of Wisconsin charged that Communists were conspiring within the federal government. The Senate Committee on Investigation, which McCarthy headed, called government workers to testify. McCarthy never proved his charges, but the public mood was such that even the accusation alone was enough to label someone a Communist, and many lost their jobs. The term *McCarthyism* came to mean making charges of disloyalty without regard to evidence.

Forming Alliances

Between the 1950s and the 1980s, the cold war influenced national political campaigns, and many aspects of domestic policy, as well as most major foreign policy decisions of the United States. In its dealings with Eastern Europe, Africa, the Middle East, Latin America, and Asia, the United States saw its diplomacy as an extension of the struggle against communism.

During the 1950s, the United States expanded the nation's network of alliances in order to contain communism. In Western Europe, the Americans took a leading role in NATO. In Southeast Asia, the United States helped to create the Southeast Asia Treaty Organization (SEATO). In the Middle East, the United States counted on the cooperation of the Central Treaty Organization (CENTO), and in Latin America, the United States promoted the Organization of American States (OAS). These alliances created a formidable counterbalance to the influence of the Soviet Union.

Military Buildup

When necessary, American Presidents also used espionage and military power to fight the cold war. During the 1950s, the effort to contain

CONNECTIONS
The Arts

Abstract Painting

Abstract expressionism was a movement in American painting that flourished from the mid-1940s to the mid-1950s. Abstract expressionist artists rejected many of the rules of earlier art. Instead of showing recognizable subject matter in their works, they emphasized the techniques or basic elements of painting, such as color, brushstrokes, lines, and shapes.

One of the important

Out of the Web *by Jackson Pollock*

abstract expressionist painters was Jackson Pollock. His usual painting technique involved placing a huge canvas on the floor and then dripping paint from above onto it. The drippings formed sweeping, rhythmic

patterns that seemed to move across the surface. About his highly unusual method of painting, Pollock said, "I feel nearer, more a part of the painting, since this way I can walk around it, work from the four sides, and literally be in the painting."

Although abstract expressionist styles differed, all of the artists in the movement believed that art should express immediate personal feelings and attitudes toward life. Their nontraditional, revolutionary approach to art has influenced painters throughout the world.

Linking Past and Present ACTIVITY

Explain how abstract expressionist painting differs from traditional forms of art. Why do you think abstract expressionist art developed in the United States during the cold war era?

communism, strongly backed by the American public, caused the United States to send troops to fight Communist forces in Korea. It also led President **Dwight D. Eisenhower** in 1954 to agree to shoulder France's efforts to stop Communist military activity in **Vietnam**. The United States engaged in an unprecedented military buildup during this time, even during the cold war "thaw" in the late 1950s.

By the closing months of his presidency, Dwight D. Eisenhower, though a proponent of a strong military, was deeply concerned about the global arms race, or the competition between the superpowers for new and better weapons. On leaving office in 1961, he warned of a growing "military-industrial complex" in the United States. According to Eisenhower, the superpower rivalry, the competition for sophisticated weapons, and the role of arms production in supporting economic growth had created a built-in incentive to increase military spending.

Battle of Ideas

John F. Kennedy, a young senator from Massachusetts, succeeded Eisenhower as President in 1961. During the 1960 presidential race, Kennedy had campaigned on the theme of restoring the strength and prestige the United States had lost after the embarrassments of the U-2 spying incident and *Sputnik*.

Kennedy engaged in cold-war maneuvering on several fronts. He acted quickly to create the Peace Corps, a program that sent young American volunteers overseas to help impoverished countries that were open to Communist influence. Kennedy's cold-war views influenced his actions in several major foreign policy crises, including the building of the Berlin Wall and the Cuban missile crisis.

The Vietnam War

Kennedy's assassination in 1963 brought **Lyndon B. Johnson** to the White House. Johnson supported civil rights laws and reforms in education and social welfare to achieve what he

Nuclear Battlefield

By the 1980s the United States and the Soviet Union each had more than 12,000 ICBMs aimed at the other. The Distant Early Warning Line (DEW Line) was a radar system built in 1957 to detect incoming missiles. It was replaced in 1994 with a more sophisticated North Warning System.

Region Why were DEW Line radars placed in northern Canada rather than along the east and west coasts of the United States?

called the Great Society. However, the consuming issue during Johnson's five years in office became the Vietnam War, in which the United States assisted South Vietnam in resisting a Communist takeover.

American involvement in Vietnam, described in Chapter 33, began under Presidents Eisenhower and Kennedy and grew out of their desire to keep communism from spreading throughout Southeast Asia. During the Eisenhower and Kennedy years, American civilian and military advisers had arrived in Vietnam to aid the South Vietnamese. The role of the United States in the Southeast Asian nation was later expanded into full-scale participation by President Johnson. During Johnson's administration, large numbers of American combat soldiers were sent to fight in Vietnam.

Opposition to the War

By 1968, large-scale American intervention had not been able to overcome the Communist Vietnamese forces. As a result, domestic opposition to the war became widespread, and Vietnam became the central issue in the presidential race of that year. President Johnson, condemned for his handling of the lengthy, costly, and indecisive war, decided not to run for reelection. Former Vice President **Richard M. Nixon**, a strong anti-Communist, won the election with his pledge to stop the war and bring the American people together.

President Nixon soon found that ending the war was difficult. As he struggled to find a politically acceptable solution, his administration was besieged by the antiwar forces that had overwhelmed Johnson's presidency.

Although many young Americans believed that it was their duty to serve in the military if they were called, others stated that they would refuse to serve. Some young men eligible for the draft—the mandatory enrollment in the United States armed forces—burned their draft cards, which was an illegal act. Others fled to Canada to avoid the draft, choosing to spend years in exile from their country rather than fight in the war. Demonstrators marched in front of the White House, carrying signs and shouting antiwar slogans. College professors cancelled classes and held antiwar protests called "teach-ins." Most protests across the country were peaceful, but many incidents of violence occurred, including the bombing of military facilities and other institutions that symbolized America's political and military power.

Ending the War

President Nixon's plans for ending the war for the United States was called "Vietnamization"—a gradual withdrawal of American troops while handing over control of war operations to South Vietnam. In a November 1969 speech, the President tried to counter the antiwar protests by appealing to what he called the silent majority of Americans whom he said supported his policies.

Simultaneously with the American withdrawal from Vietnam, Nixon ordered fierce bombing raids on neighboring **Cambodia**. The bombings prompted renewed protests, creating a superheated atmosphere of anger and distrust between supporters and opponents of the war. The situation exploded tragically in May 1970, when National Guard soldiers fired into a crowd of demonstrators at Kent State University in Ohio, killing four students.

In 1973, the last of the active American forces withdrew from Vietnam, and the Paris Accords were signed. Of the 2,700,000 Americans who served in Vietnam, about 58,000 died and more than 300,000 were wounded. The war cost the United States $150 billion. In addition, it made the nation more cautious of foreign involvement.

Struggle for Civil Rights

Despite the general economic prosperity of the United States after World War II, millions of Americans continued to live in poverty. The poor included members of all ethnic groups, but the plight of the nation's poor in the African American community seemed especially critical. Ever since emancipation in the 1860s, African Americans in both the North and the South had faced discrimination in jobs, housing, education, and other areas. After World War II, an increasing number of Americans realized that continuing poverty and racial discrimination were at odds with the basic American values of equality and justice for all. A civil rights movement begun by African Americans in the early 1900s gained momentum and affected many areas of American life.

Changing Social Attitudes

Changing social attitudes helped civil rights advances. The war against Germany played a part. The horrifying racism of the Nazis helped to make some Americans more sensitive to racism in their own country. They began to realize that not only African Americans, but also Asian Americans, Hispanic Americans, and other ethnic groups had been treated unfairly and denied social and educational opportunities.

Court Decisions

During the 1940s and 1950s, African Americans worked hard to gain civil rights. The war years saw the membership of the National Association for the Advancement of Colored People (NAACP) increase from 100,000 to 351,000. In the late 1940s, the NAACP hired teams of able lawyers to bring a series of lawsuits to the federal courts to end violations of the constitutional rights of African American citizens.

This effort resulted in several United States Supreme Court decisions that attacked discrimination. In the best known case, *Brown* v. *Board of Education of Topeka, Kansas* (1954), the United States Supreme Court ruled that racial segregation, or the separation of the races, in public schools was illegal. President Eisenhower used federal agencies to enforce the Court's decision.

Martin Luther King, Jr.

In the following years, the civil rights movement broadened and changed tactics. **Martin Luther King, Jr.**, a Baptist minister, advocated the use of nonviolent sit-ins and marches to focus attention on discrimination in housing, public facilities, and voting. Media coverage of the segregationist opposition to the movement's efforts helped convince many Americans of the injustice of discrimination.

In 1963, more than 200,000 African Americans, whites, and people of other ethnic groups converged on Washington, D.C., for the largest civil rights demonstration in the nation's history. At the Lincoln Memorial, the marchers heard eloquent speeches, especially from Martin Luther King, Jr., who, in a famous address, described his dream of freedom and equality for all people:

“ I have a dream that one day this nation will rise up and live out the true meaning of its creed: 'We hold these truths to be self-evident; that all men are created equal'…. And when this happens, and when we allow freedom to ring, when we let it ring from every village and hamlet, from every state and every city, we will be able to speed up that day when all God's children … [will] join hands and sing in the words of the old … spiritual: 'Free at last, Free at last, Thank God Almighty, we're free at last.' ”

The civil rights movement peaked in the 1960s with the passage of major civil rights laws under President Johnson. These measures banned discrimination in public places and education as well as strengthened the right to vote. In addition to helping African Americans, the civil rights legislation also advanced opportunities for other groups, such as Hispanic Americans.

After Martin Luther King, Jr.'s assassination in 1968, the civil rights movement faced the loss or delay of some of its hard-won gains. Beginning in the late 1960s, much of the United States government's social policies shifted to the right, away from earlier liberal policies. However, despite the setback, the movement for civil rights continued. It strongly influenced other groups in the United States—women, Hispanic Americans, and Native Americans—that wanted better opportunities and social equality. It also was an inspiration to civil rights groups in other parts of the world.

Visualizing History Dr. Martin Luther King, Jr., spoke to more than 200,000 people on the 100th anniversary of the Emancipation Proclamation. *What civil rights did legislation in the 1960s address?*

Visualizing History Long lines formed at gasoline stations because of shortages when OPEC placed an embargo on oil exports. *How did the embargo affect the prices of other goods?*

The Changing Presidency

During the cold war, United States Presidents gradually began to exercise powers beyond those spelled out in the United States Constitution. Claiming a need for a quick military response to counter communism, Presidents began to assume the war-making powers of Congress, committing American military forces to combat without congressional approval. The two largest commitments to undeclared wars were in Korea and Vietnam.

The Imperial Presidency

As the cold war continued into the 1960s and 1970s, many people felt that the increased presidential power was subject to abuses and a violation of the Constitution. The term imperial presidency came into use, reflecting this concern.

The term was most often applied to Presidents Lyndon B. Johnson and Richard M. Nixon, both of whom expanded the conflict in Vietnam without a congressional declaration of war, as called for in the Constitution, and often kept their actions secret from Congress. In 1973 Congress overrode Nixon's veto to pass the War Powers Limitation Act. The measure required the President to consult Congress before committing United States troops to combat.

The Watergate Scandal

Political scandals rocked the United States during the 1970s. Investigations revealed many cases of corruption in local and state government, but the country's attention focused primarily on charges of corruption in the federal government. Early in President Nixon's second term, scandal engulfed his administration. Vice President Spiro Agnew was accused of taking bribes when he was governor of Maryland and was forced to resign. Then the President himself came under fire in a scandal that became known as Watergate.

The Watergate scandal began on June 17, 1972, when five men were caught trying to plant electronic listening devices in the offices of the Democratic National Committee, located in the Watergate building in downtown **Washington, D.C.** The break-in was traced to Nixon's reelection committee.

A congressional probe revealed that the White House knew of the burglary and tried to cover it up. The President denied the charges at first, but tape recordings of Oval Office conversations proved that he had participated in the cover-up. Under the threat of impeachment, Nixon resigned on August 9, 1974. He was the first United States President ever to do so.

Gerald R. Ford, the Republican congressman from Michigan who had replaced Spiro Agnew as Vice President, became President when Nixon stepped down. Ford was the first United States President not to have been elected to either of the nation's top two offices. He assumed a presidency that had been weakened and tarnished. Watergate had shaken public confidence in the American political system. In addition, Ford had no personal mandate from the voters, since he had not been elected. As a former congressman, Ford maintained close ties with Congress. That, coupled with his acknowledged personal integrity, enabled him to function effectively. Both Ford and his Democratic successor, **Jimmy Carter**, a former governor of Georgia, worked to restore ethics to the presidency. In addition, as a result of Watergate, the media became far more vigilant in pursuing wrong-doing of public officials.

The Economy

During the late 1960s and 1970s, the United States economy was buffeted by the effects of the cold war and a changing world economy. The country suffered serious inflation in the 1970s as a result of the costs of the Vietnam War and increased government spending for social programs. Administrations and congressional leaders were reluctant to offset spiraling costs with either cuts in programs or tax increases. Meanwhile, inflation combined with high unemployment to produce an economic trend called stagflation. Low productivity in factories and increased competition from foreign companies also slowed the American economy.

Soaring gas prices were part of an energy crisis that crippled economies around the world during the 1970s. In the United States, rapid economic growth had been dependent on cheap, abundant oil. Wanting to gain from increased world oil prices, OPEC (Organization of Petroleum Exporting Countries) countries in 1973 refused to ship oil to foreign customers. This oil embargo was damaging to American—and world—economic stability because it increased the cost of producing a wide range of goods.

Sharp rises in the price of oil and gasoline contributed to double-digit inflation, or a rise in the general level of prices of 10 percent or more. By 1980 it cost more than $200 to purchase the same goods that $100 would have bought only 10 years earlier. At the same time, the United States government raised interest rates to all-time highs in an effort to discourage borrowing and bring the economy under control. These policies helped reduce inflation but caused a severe recession.

During the 1970s, the United States also experienced a trade deficit, or importing more goods than it was exporting, and the steady loss of American jobs. As other nations in the world became more industrialized, they began to compete with American companies for sales to American consumers. In the late 1970s for example, rising gasoline prices led Americans to buy more fuel efficient Japanese cars rather than larger American cars. The shift of American factories abroad to take advantage of cheaper, talented labor also had a chilling impact on the employment situation in the United States.

Canada

Canada thrived economically after World War II. By 1960, it had changed from a primarily agricultural country to one of the world's most important industrial nations. Like the United States, production in Canada boomed after World War II as consumers demanded household goods and new homes. The exploitation of Canada's rich mineral resources also enabled the Canadian economy to flourish. Foreign investors, mainly from the neighboring United States, financed the development of many new industries.

Improved communications and transportation strengthened Canada's trade links with the United States. One significant joint venture of both countries in the 1950s was the completion of the **St. Lawrence Seaway**, a system of locks and canals that allows ships to travel between the Great Lakes and the Atlantic Ocean.

Canada's World Role

Traditionally linked to Great Britain, Canada's loyalties to the parent country gradually diminished as British global influence plummeted after World War II. Meanwhile, Canada's new and growing economic strength convinced many Canadians that their country needed to play a more active, independent role in world affairs. In 1945, Canada became a founding member of the United Nations and sent troops to Korea as part of the UN forces in 1950. Canada also joined NATO when it was formed in 1949. During the 1950s, cold-war tensions brought the United States and Canada into a close defensive partnership.

In pursuing their foreign policy, Canadians were suspicious of a world dominated by superpowers. Over time, Canada advanced a role for itself as a middle power—that is, one that is strong economically, if not militarily. The Canadians used what military strength they had to promote peace. In 1956, Canada helped to bring about peace in the Middle East after Great Britain, France, and Israel had invaded Egypt. **Lester B. Pearson**, Canada's secretary of state for external affairs, won the 1957 Nobel Peace Prize for proposing and organizing a UN peacekeeping force for the troubled area.

A National Identity

In internal affairs, Canada struggled to find its own national identity during the period after World War II. While breaking many of their traditional ties to Europe, Canadians found themselves increasingly influenced by American ideas and practices. Most Canadians favored a continued close relationship to the United States. However, there were growing concerns that the "Americanization" of Canada posed a threat to Canada's newly emerging culture. In 1963, Pearson became Canada's prime minister. His administration expanded the country's social welfare programs and worked to strengthen Canadian national identity. Pearson achieved a personal goal when the Canadian parliament in 1965 adopted a new national flag, one that featured a red maple leaf as a symbol of Canada. The maple leaf soon became very popular

however, were still people of British descent, who make up about 35 percent of the population, and those of French descent, who make up about 30 percent.

Separatism

While celebrating their nationhood, Canadians also faced a growing challenge to their country's unity. During the 1960s, French Canadians began a movement to defend their rights throughout Canada. They also wanted English-speaking Canadians to recognize and respect their culture in the province of **Quebec**, where 80 percent of the people are French-speaking.

A growing debate arose over the issue of separatism, a movement favoring the establishment of Quebec as an independent country. The issue gave rise to the Parti Quebecois (kay•beh•KWAH), or Quebec party, sometimes known as the Separatist party. Opposing the separatist drive for Quebec independence was Canadian Prime Minister **Pierre Elliott Trudeau**, himself a French Canadian, who had been elected to office in 1968. Trudeau promised to protect French Canadian language and cultural rights while supporting a strong united Canada. In 1969, he had the Canadian parliament pass the Official Languages Act. This law required federal government offices to provide service in both French and English if 10 percent of the people in a particular area spoke either language.

The Official Languages Act brought many changes to Canada's government. However, it had little effect on the growing separatist movement. In 1976, the Parti Quebecois won control of Quebec's government and declared French the province's official language. It also promised to hold an election to decide Quebec's future.

Visualizing History The movement for an independent Quebec continued to gain strength through the 1990s. *How ethnically diverse is the population of Canada?*

among Canadians, who for years had honored some form of the Union Jack, or the British flag, as their national flag.

In 1967, Pearson presided over celebrations marking Canada's 100th anniversary of its nationhood. Many Canadians were especially proud of the fact that Canada had become a multicultural country, made up of people from many different ethnic groups. From 1945 to 1956, more than a million people from Germany, Italy, and other war-torn European countries had moved to farms or to **Toronto**, **Montreal**, and other large Canadian cities. In addition, other Canadians claimed Native American, Asian, African, or Latin American ancestry. Canada's two major ethnic groups,

---

SECTION 4 REVIEW

Recall

1. **Define** automation, racial segregation, imperial presidency, stagflation, embargo, double-digit inflation, trade deficit, middle power, multicultural, separatism.

2. **Identify** Dwight D. Eisenhower, John F. Kennedy, Lyndon B. Johnson, Richard M. Nixon, Martin Luther King, Jr., Gerald R. Ford, Jimmy Carter, Lester B. Pearson, Pierre Elliott Trudeau.

3. **Describe** the Supreme Court ruling in *Brown* v. *Board of Education of Topeka, Kansas.*

Critical Thinking

4. **Analyzing Information** Why did President Eisenhower believe that the military-industrial complex was dangerous? Has his warning been borne out by history?

Understanding Themes

5. **Cooperation** Why did the United States and Canada develop close ties after 1945?

Understanding World Time Zones

Imagine that you work in an office in New Jersey. Your boss asks you to place a telephone call to a client in London. At 2:00 P.M. you place the call, but no one answers. Why? When it is 2:00 P.M. in New Jersey, it is already 7:00 P.M. in London. The times differ because the world is divided into time zones.

Learning the Skill

In 1884 an international conference established standard time zones around the world. The Prime Meridian (0° longitude), which runs through Greenwich, England, became the reference point for measuring time. The conference divided the world into 24 time zones, each 15° of longitude apart. Traveling east from Greenwich, the time is one hour later in each time zone. Traveling west from Greenwich, the time is one hour earlier.

The conference also established the International Date Line at 180° longitude. When crossing this line from west to east, you lose one day; when crossing in the opposite direction, you gain a day.

The map on this page illustrates the world time zones. To use this map, locate a reference point and note its time. Then locate the place for which you wish to know the time. Determine whether this place lies east or west of the reference point. Then count the number of time zones and add or subtract as needed. If the International Date Line lies between two points, add or subtract a day.

Practicing the Skill

Use the map to calculate these times.
1. If it is 3:00 P.M. in Greenwich, what time is it in Moscow?
2. If it is 9:00 A.M. in Cape Town, what time is it in Washington, D.C.?
3. If it is Tuesday, 4:30 P.M. in Japan, what day and time is it in Honolulu?
4. If it is Friday, 8:15 A.M. in Rio de Janeiro, what day and time is it in Beijing?

Applying the Skill

Make up four time zone problems and compute the answers. Exchange your problems with a friend. See who can answer them most quickly.

For More Practice

Turn to the Skill Practice in the Chapter Review on page 893 for more practice in understanding world time zones.

Time Zones of the World

4 pm 5 pm 6 pm 7 pm 8 pm 9 pm 10 pm 11 pm 12 am 1 am 2 am 3 am 4 am 5 am 6 am 7 am 8 am 9 am 10 am 11 am 12 pm 1 pm 2 pm 3 pm 4 pm

P.M.   A.M.   P.M.

Non-standard time

RUSSIA
Alaska
CANADA
Beijing
CHINA JAPAN
INDIA
Mumbai
Los Angeles
UNITED STATES
New York
Washington, D.C.
Honolulu
Hawaii
MEXICO
London Greenwich Moscow
Rome
Cocos Islands
International Date Line
Cook Islands
BRAZIL
Rio de Janeiro
ARGENTINA
Cape Town
Prime Meridian
NEW ZEALAND

60° 75° 90° 105° 120° 135° 150° 165° 180° 165° 150° 135° 120° 105° 90° 75° 60° 45°W 30° 15° 0° 15° 30° 45°E 60°

Connections Across Time

Historical Significance The cold war between the United States and the Soviet Union divided Europe and the large areas of the rest of the world into two camps. Long-range nuclear weapons made the superpowers' quarrel dangerous because of the threat of nuclear war that would destroy civilization.

Gradually, this realization compelled the superpowers to seek ways of reducing tensions. Ultimately, the economic strength and democratic principles of the United States and Western Europe undermined communism and stimulated demands for change within the Communist bloc. Meanwhile, nationalism replaced ideology as a source of conflict.

Using Key Terms

Write the key term that completes each sentence. Then write a sentence for each term not chosen.

a. cold war
b. containment
c. ICBMs
d. iron curtain
e. welfare states
f. stagflation
g. dissidents
h. separatism
i. racial segregation
j. imperial presidency
k. peaceful coexistence
l. middle power

1. The term _____ referred to the Soviet-made barrier that divided Europe into non-Communist and Communist areas.
2. To counter any expansionist threat from the Soviet Union, the Truman administration in 1947 developed a policy known as _____.
3. In the 1970s, inflation combined with high unemployment to produce _____.
4. Soviet leader Leonid Brezhnev applied harsh measures to _____ who criticized the Communist party or the Soviet government.
5. In *Brown* v. *Board of Education of Topeka, Kansas*, the United States Supreme Court ruled that _____ in public schools was illegal.

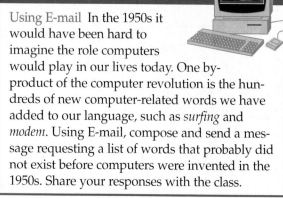

Technology Activity

Using E-mail In the 1950s it would have been hard to imagine the role computers would play in our lives today. One by-product of the computer revolution is the hundreds of new computer-related words we have added to our language, such as *surfing* and *modem*. Using E-mail, compose and send a message requesting a list of words that probably did not exist before computers were invented in the 1950s. Share your responses with the class.

Using Your History Journal

From your notes on the interviews with the people who remember the events of the 1950s or early 1960s, write a newspaper feature piece titled "Living Through the Cold War."

Reviewing Facts

1. **History** Explain the purpose of the Marshall Plan. In what ways was the plan effective?
2. **History** Explain why Joseph Stalin ordered the Berlin blockade.
3. **Government** Describe how Communists came to power in Eastern Europe. How did they govern?
4. **History** Identify the reforms that Dubček introduced in Czechoslovakia.
5. **History** Explain the meaning of *McCarthyism*.
6. **Citizenship** Identify the role of Martin Luther King, Jr., in the civil rights struggle.

Critical Thinking

1. **Apply** What postwar developments launched the cold war?
2. **Analyze** In your view, why did the United States assume global responsibility for containing communism?
3. **Synthesize** Create a time line showing major events in the spread of communism from 1945 to 1979. What effect did Communist expansion have on global affairs during this period?
4. **Evaluate** Was Americans' fear of communism during the 1950s justified? Do you think the actions that Congress took to counter

communism were appropriate? Explain your reasoning.

5. **Apply** How do you think the cold war affected politics in Western European countries?

6. **Synthesize** Compare the economic systems of the United States, Great Britain, and the Soviet Union during the cold war era.

7. **Apply** Is the United States presidency today an imperial presidency? Why or why not?

8. **Apply** What was the major source of tension that led to French Canadian separatism?

Understanding Themes

1. **Conflict** By the 1950s the superpowers had enough nuclear weapons to eliminate each other. What effect did this power have on super-power relations during the cold war?

2. **Change** What might have happened if the Soviet Union had not used force to keep its Eastern European satellite countries under control?

3. **Regionalism** How did the European Common Market benefit member countries?

4. **Cooperation** How did the foreign policy of Canada compare and contrast with that of the United States during the cold war era?

1. Key cold war issues continued until about 1989, when they reached a dramatic conclusion. Name these issues and explain their link to recent events.

2. Name a previous period in history when Europe was united. When did the continent become fragmented again?

3. Is containment an important or pressing issue in American foreign policy today? Explain your reasoning.

Geography in History

1. **Location** Refer to the map of Berlin on this page. What side of the city of Berlin became the Soviet sector after World War II?

2. **Place** What nations maintained army headquarters in Berlin following the war?

Berlin After World War II

0 2.5 5 mi.
0 2.5 5 km

French HQ

FRENCH

Spree River

SOVIET

BRITISH

British HQ

AMERICAN

American HQ

Soviet HQ

EAST GERMANY

EAST GERMANY

N
W—E
S

— Berlin Wall
○ Control points
▮ Army HQ 1945–1949
— Main roads
+++ International railways

3. **Movement** Approximately how long was the wall that the Soviets built to keep East Germans from crossing to the West?

4. **Location** How many control points were located along the Berlin Wall?

Skill Practice

Refer to the map of World Time Zones on page 891 to answer the following questions.

1. Name some areas of the world in which you find non-standard time.

2. You are in New York and you want to call someone in Rome, Italy, at noon Rome time. When would you call?

3. Assume that flying from New York to London requires 6 hours. When would a flight leaving New York on a Wednesday at 6:00 P.M. arrive in London?

4. You are flying from Los Angeles to Moscow. You leave Los Angeles at 10:00 A.M. on Saturday and you arrive in Moscow on Sunday at 9:00 A.M. How many hours did you actually spend flying?

5. You are planning a flight from Mumbai, India, to Washington, D.C., that must connect through several cities. You will leave Mumbai on August 2, at 8:00 A.M., and will continue directly through Beijing and Los Angeles to Washington, D.C. What time is it in Washington, D.C., when you begin your trip? What will be the date when you arrive in Washington, D.C.?

33

1945–Present

Asia and the Pacific

Chapter Themes

▶ **Change** Japan builds a democracy and becomes a global economic power. *Section 1*

▶ **Revolution** Communists in China introduce socialist measures, and then promote a limited free enterprise economy. *Section 2*

▶ **Regionalism** After decades of conflict and cold war tensions, North Korea and South Korea take first steps toward unification. *Section 3*

▶ **Conflict** The rise of nationalism and cold war competition leads to conflict in post-World War II Southeast Asia. *Section 4*

▶ **Diversity** A diversity of religious and ethnic groups challenges the unity in South Asia. *Section 5*

▶ **Cultural Diffusion** Changing political and economic roles open the nations of the Pacific to other parts of the globe. *Section 6*

The Storyteller

"My methods are old, " declares Japanese artist Kako Muriguchi, "but my designs are new." Muriguchi designs innovative patterns for kimonos, the traditional Japanese garment for women. The people of Japan have such respect for his contributions to their heritage that they have declared him a "living national treasure." As a result of this designation, Muriguchi is entitled to lifetime national support for his art. Like Muriguchi, Japan and other countries in Asia have found success by combining old and new. Traditional values that encourage education and hard work, combined with modern developments, such as computer technology, have brought prosperity to many countries in Asia since the end of World War II.

Historical Significance

What role do the countries of Asia and the Pacific play in the contemporary world? How have they contributed to the world's economy, culture, and politics since 1945?

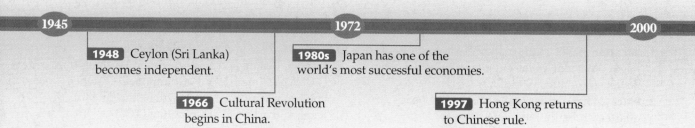

1945 ・ **1972** ・ **2000**

1948 Ceylon (Sri Lanka) becomes independent.

1980s Japan has one of the world's most successful economies.

1966 Cultural Revolution begins in China.

1997 Hong Kong returns to Chinese rule.

Visualizing History Hong Kong's skyline is aglow with lights in celebration of the territory's return to Chinese rule on June 30, 1997.

Your History Journal

Interview someone who migrated to the United States from an Asian or Pacific nation, or research the culture of an Asian or Pacific nation. Write a short report on the cultural adjustments a person from that nation would make to live in the United States.

1947 Japan adopts democratic constitution.

1980s Japan has one of the world's most successful economies.

1995 Severe earthquake strikes Kobe area.

Section 1

Japan's Economic Rise

Setting the Scene

▶ **Terms to Define**
   gross domestic product, pollution, sect, quota

▶ **People to Meet**
   Douglas MacArthur, Hirohito

▶ **Places to Locate**
   Tokyo, Kobe

Find Out ▶ What factors have contributed to the economic success of Japan?

The Storyteller

   Kyoichi Tabuchi's plane landed in Bangkok, the city he would now call home. He had accepted a position as manager of an industrial complex. The Thai government eagerly received Tabuchi and his fellow Japanese for establishing economic opportunities. The age of Heisei, or peaceful achievement, had begun. Japan's economy was booming; her industry was welcomed throughout the region she had occupied militarily just 50 years earlier. As Tabuchi drove to the Japanese district, he heard the radio play a song that clearly defined the beneficial situation: "The Samurai Are Here."

   —adapted from "Japan's Sun Rises Over the Pacific," National Geographic, November, 1995, Arthur Zich

Ascendant electronics

The end of World War II brought dramatic changes to Asia; Japan was stripped of the lands it had conquered. Great Britain, France, and the Netherlands were forced to withdraw from their Asian colonies, and new nations arose. Communists won control in China and North Korea, and the cold war affected the entire region. Out of the turmoil, vigorous industrial powers have emerged. Japan's transformation into a global economic giant has been one of the most important changes of the post-World War II era.

Occupation and Reform

   Japan, a proud nation with a long history of self-reliance, ended World War II with its pride crushed, its economy wrecked, and its people demoralized by the humiliating defeat. The victorious countries established an occupation government, the Supreme Command of the Allied Powers (SCAP), to govern Japan after the war. Although planned as a joint venture of the Allies, the occupation government became entirely a United States enterprise, headed by General **Douglas MacArthur**. The general was determined not to plant the seeds of future war by imposing an unjust and unworkable system on the Japanese. MacArthur's reform policies affected Japan's political and economic spheres, and Japan made a remarkable recovery.

A New Constitution

   SCAP required Japan to adopt a new constitution in 1947. The constitution stripped the imperial family of its political power and gave it to the Japanese citizens. No longer could Japanese emperors rule by their claim to divine authority. Instead, Emperor **Hirohito** remained in office as a symbol of the state. The constitution also established a cabinet based on the British model. Both houses of the Diet, or legislature, were made elective, and citizens over the age of 20 could vote. A bill of rights guaranteed basic freedoms.

The new constitution included an unusual provision. Article 9 barred Japan from all warfare except for defense—"The Japanese people forever renounce war as a sovereign right of the nation.... Land, sea, and air forces, as well as other war potential, will never be maintained." SCAP hoped that this would prevent Japan from ever threatening its neighbors again. The United States agreed to protect Japan militarily. In the late 1990s, the United States still had troops—47,000 in all—stationed on Japanese territory, most of them on the island of Okinawa. This military arrangement enabled Japan to concentrate more of its resources on consumer goods than on military equipment. It also reassured other nations of the region who feared the revival of a militarily strong Japan.

Economic Reform

SCAP also set out to decentralize Japanese agriculture and industry. Landlords not living on their property could own only 2.5 acres (1.1 ha) of land. The law required them to sell off holdings above this figure at very low prices. Those who actually farmed the soil were permitted to own up to 7.5 acres (3.1 ha). Decentralization changed the face of Japanese agriculture, resulting in the transfer of more than 5 million acres (2 million ha). Although Japanese farmers have prospered, small-scale farming has been costly and inefficient. Today, the Japanese government subsidizes farmers by buying their crops at high prices to cover farmers' costs and then resells the crops to consumers at a loss.

SCAP took steps to decentralize the *zaibatsu*, the giant industrial and banking organizations that controlled Japanese industry. General MacArthur believed that removal of *zaibatsu* control would prevent Japan from rearming. The Korean War, however, led the United States to change this policy and gave renewed life to Japan's large industrial organizations. It was hoped by the United States that a strong Japanese economy would help contain the spread of communism in Asia.

Japan's Dramatic Recovery

Japan's shattered economy recovered quickly in the early 1950s with assistance from the United States. The Korean War created a vast need for all kinds of war supplies, ranging from trucks to uniforms and medical supplies. To have sources of supply close at hand, the United States poured $3.5 billion into Japan—an amount nearly equal to what

Visualizing History Japan's Emperor Hirohito (center) reigned from 1926 until his death in 1989. His son, Akihito, succeeded him. *What changes came to Japan's government during the late 1940s?*

the United States gave Germany under the Marshall Plan. The United States also provided training in management skills so that Japan was able to rebuild its factories to the latest standards. Japanese shipbuilders, car manufacturers, electronics and pharmaceutical industries all benefited from American aid and later became major leaders in the global economy.

As part of its recognition of Japan's support to the United States during the Korean War, a formal peace treaty with Japan was reached in 1951 and the American occupation of Japan ended.

Government-Business Cooperation

The Japanese government and Japan's well-educated workforce took advantage of the boom created by the United States. Although Japan had to import most of its raw materials, the Japanese economy expanded quickly. Japan's engineers, managers, and laborers worked hard to boost the country's prosperity. The Japanese government worked closely with large corporations to plan and promote industrial growth. They brought vision to long-range planning and then followed through on their

Visualizing History Production of automobiles became the heart of Japan's industrial expansion in the 1960s. *How fast did Japanese auto production grow?*

decisions. For example, in the late 1950s government and industry agreed to invest heavily in research and development in the home electronics field. By the early 1970s, Japanese radios, televisions, stereos, and other items were challenging American dominance in the world market.

Similarly, the Japanese government and industrial leaders targeted the automobile industry as one they thought could help bring prosperity to Japan. The government helped fund researchers who developed dependable, high-mileage automobiles. Managers and laborers worked together to develop newer and more efficient production techniques. As a result of these innovations, Japan began producing high-quality cars at competitive prices, and sales of Japanese automobiles around the world soared. Japan increased its share of world automobile production from 3 percent in 1960 to a full 29 percent in 1980.

By 1980 Japan had one of the world's most successful economies. Although only as big as California, Japan's **gross domestic product** (GDP)—the sum value of all goods and services it produced—was about half that of the United States. Its per capita GDP, the amount of production per individual, was among the highest in the industrialized world.

Japan's rapid growth continued through the 1980s. Between 1988 and 1992, the annual growth rate was 5 percent, one of the highest rates in the world. Japanese businesses invested heavily overseas in real estate, banks, and factories.

In 1997, a severe economic slump affected Japan and several other Asian nations. Because of Japan's role as a major lending nation, Japanese banks were especially hard hit. Japanese companies also faced losses, and unemployment increased. Concerned about the global impact of the economic crisis, the United States and other industrial nations urged Japan to stimulate its economy by cutting taxes and ending regulations that restricted production and trade.

Side Effects of Growth

Like many other industrialized countries, postwar Japan had solid economic growth that raised the standard of living of its citizens. However, the spread of industry also caused environmental damage. Japan's industries clustered along a narrow coastal belt between the city of **Tokyo** and the southernmost Japanese island, Kyushu. Along with industry came a dense concentration of people and automobiles and pollution, or the release of impure or poisonous substances into land, water, and air. In addition, rapid industrial development had created severe housing shortages in urban areas. Government and business leaders began to take steps to balance industrial growth with environmental protection.

Politics and Government

Until recently, Japan's economic growth had been bolstered by an extraordinary level of political stability. From 1955 to 1993, one political party dominated the Japanese government. Despite its name, the Liberal Democratic Party (LDP) is a conservative, pro-business party that has had broad Japanese support. The LDP has traditionally been strong among Japan's farming population, but it also receives heavy financial support from the country's large corporations. Voters liked the party's dependability, especially during the uncertainty of the cold war.

In 1993, Japanese voters defeated the scandal-weakened LDP. With the collapse of the Soviet Union, and the end of the cold war, it seemed safe to support the chief opposition party, the Social Democratic Party of Japan (SDPJ). The splintered SDPJ was forced to form a coalition government and to include many LDP leaders in the cabinet.

Because of its political diversity, the new government had difficulty steering Japan through a number of crises. In January 1995, a severe earthquake struck the area around the port city of **Kobe**. It was one of the deadliest natural disasters to hit Japan in the twentieth century. Political opponents criticized the government for not responding rapidly to provide relief to the quake victims. In addition many SDPJ members, unhappy about their party's linkage to the LDP, were leaving the party to form another political party: the New Democratic League.

Japan also encountered the ugly face of terrorism. In March 1995, a Japanese sect, or small religious group, carried out a nerve gas attack in Tokyo's subway system, leaving 12 people dead and 5,000 injured. A month later, another gas attack in a railroad station in the city of Yokohama injured more than 300 people. The two attacks stunned most Japanese, who considered their society violence-free, and heightened security concerns among government officials and business leaders.

In early 1996, the LDP regained its influence over Japanese politics. A new prime minister, Ryutaro Hashimoto (ree•you•TAH•roh hah•shee•MOH•toh), promised to rid Japan's government of corruption and promote economic growth.

Japan in World Affairs

As a result of its economic growth since World War II, once self-reliant and isolated Japan became tightly interwoven into the world economy. Economic power has made Japan a world political leader as well, but the Japanese have been unsure how to use their power in world affairs.

Trade Tensions

Japan's economic prosperity has created tensions with other countries in the area of trade. Japan today exports more products than it imports. It therefore has trade surpluses with many countries. By contrast, Japan's major trading partners—the United States, Europe, and neighboring Asian

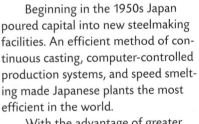
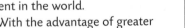

CONNECTIONS
Economics

Japan's Steel Industry

Japanese steel mill

Japan's steel industry was devastated by World War II. Steel, like other Japanese industries, needed a major rebuilding effort.

Beginning in the 1950s Japan poured capital into new steelmaking facilities. An efficient method of continuous casting, computer-controlled production systems, and speed smelting made Japanese plants the most efficient in the world.

With the advantage of greater productivity, Japan began to sell steel at lower prices on the world market. By the 1980s, American steelmakers who had dominated world production were complaining that the Japanese were dumping underpriced steel on the market.

The United States responded with voluntary restraint agreements to hold imported steel to 20 percent of its domestic market. Japanese companies began to buy into United States steel companies, partially owning several by the 1990s.

By the 1990s, however, American steel companies had regained the lead in productivity. Then Japanese and American steelmakers started joint ventures to find even more efficient methods of making steel.

Linking Past and Present ACTIVITY

Discuss three methods that enabled Japan to become the world's most efficient steel producer. How did competition in the making of steel change from the 1980s to the 1990s?

lands—have trade deficits with Japan. That is, they import more goods from Japan than they export to it. Because of this trade imbalance, other industrialized countries have pressured Japan to change its trade laws to make it easier for their companies to sell their products to Japanese consumers.

Japanese government regulations limit the ability of foreign companies to sell goods in Japan. Japanese retailers have long-standing ties with local producers that they want to maintain. Japanese farmers want to continue trade protection for their crops and livestock rather than face competition with lower-priced imports. Japanese consumers prefer to purchase goods made in Japan because the goods are well made and because they wish to protect the jobs of Japanese citizens.

Overcoming Japanese trade barriers has been difficult and frustrating for foreigners. In 1995 a trade war between the United States and Japan was prevented by a compromise agreement. In the accord, the United States agreed not to impose trade quotas, or specified restrictions, on Japanese goods. In return, Japan agreed to encourage its auto companies to increase purchases of American car parts and to step up production at their plants in the United States. In 1997 the United States urged Japan to make further changes that would open the Japanese home market to foreign goods.

Military Issues

Since the early 1950s, Japan has relied on the United States for its national security. However, the fall of Soviet communism in 1991 greatly reduced Japanese fears of an attack from the Russians. Today most Japanese still expect American help in any emergency, but many of them question the need for large numbers of American troops in their country. Tensions have flared on Okinawa between local residents and American troops. In 1996 Japan and the United States agreed that some of the American military sites on Okinawa would be returned to Japan by 2003. In the meantime, American troop strength would remain the same.

Japan also faces the issue of taking on more responsibility for its own defense and that of other parts of Asia. Some American leaders claim that Japan's low defense budget gives Japan an economic advantage in non-defense industries. They also believe that Japan's economic strength requires that it play a part in maintaining peace in Asia. Many Japanese, however, oppose an expansion of the country's military role. In 1990, when the Middle Eastern country of Iraq invaded its neighbor Kuwait, the United States called upon Japan to help force Iraq out of Kuwait. The Japanese government responded with a financial contribution to the military effort but refused to send troops. Two years later, however, Japan did send troops overseas as part of a United Nations peacekeeping mission in war-torn Cambodia.

In 1997 Japan cautiously took steps to increase its role in the military alliance with the United States. It stated that, in any emergency, the Japanese military would support American forces with sea operations, facilities, equipment, and fuel. In return for changes in the alliance, Japan wants a permanent seat on the UN Security Council.

Japan and Its Neighbors

With the most advanced economy in East Asia, Japan since the 1970s has increased its influence in the region. Beginning in 1978, Japan improved relations and forged new trading links with China. Today large amounts of Japanese aid and investment flow to the Chinese. Japan also has developed ties with South Korea, but is more hesitant with Communist North Korea because of concerns that North Korea is intent on pursuing aggressive policies in Asia. Since the late 1970s, the Japanese have greatly expanded trade and investment links with Southeast Asia, one of their fastest growing markets. Still Japan's past continues to trouble relations with its neighbors. Many people in China, Korea, and Southeast Asia recall with bitterness Japan's harsh occupation of their lands during World War II. They fear a renewal of Japanese power in East Asia, whether economic or military.

SECTION 1 REVIEW

Recall
1. **Define** gross domestic product, pollution, sect, quota.
2. **Identify** Douglas MacArthur, Hirohito, Liberal Democratic Party.
3. **Describe** two major reforms

instituted during the Allied occupation of Japan after World War II.

Critical Thinking
4. **Synthesizing Information** Imagine how Japan's modern history might have been

different if General MacArthur had wanted to punish Japan for its actions in World War II.

Understanding Themes
5. **Change** What economic policies have promoted Japan's prosperity since World War II?

1949 Communists proclaim the People's Republic of China.

1972 United States President Richard M. Nixon visits China.

1989 Chinese students in Beijing call for democracy.

Section 2

China in Revolution

Setting the Scene

▶ **Terms to Define**
   communes, pragmatists, special economic zone

▶ **People to Meet**
   Chiang Kai-shek, Mao Zedong, Deng Xiaoping, Jiang Jing, Zhou Enlai, Jiang Zemin, Dalai Lama

▶ **Places to Locate**
   Beijing, Taiwan, Taipei, Shanghai, Tibet, Hong Kong

Find Out How has communism affected the domestic and international affairs of China since the late 1940s?

The Storyteller

Wang Xin had heard his father and grandfather talk about the old days in China. As peasants, they owned no land. If someone was unable to work, he was dismissed by the landlord and had to beg or live off his family. But when Wang was a small boy, things changed. The peasants became masters, receiving shares of farmland. They were no longer starving. Wang's family of 10 people moved from a three-room house to one with seven rooms and a tile roof. For the rest of his life, Wang Xin would remember how happy the peasants were that spring of 1950.

—adapted from "A Peasant Maps His Road to Wealth," *Beijing Review*, reprinted in *Documents in World History*, Peter Stearns, 1988

Chinese peasant's house

After World War II, the Nationalists under **Chiang Kai-shek** and the Communists led by **Mao Zedong** fought a bitter civil war in China. By 1949, Mao's Communist forces had defeated the Nationalists. That year, the Communists proclaimed the People's Republic of China, with **Beijing** as the capital. The defeated Nationalists fled to the offshore island of **Taiwan**, where they set up the new capital of the Republic of China at **Taipei**.

Mao's revolution was one of the major upheavals of the century. It succeeded in part because the Communists' self-proclaimed patriotism and sense of duty appealed to many Chinese citizens disgusted with foreign controls and the corruption of Chiang's officials. Above all, Mao won over China's peasants with his promises of land reform and an end to oppression by landlords.

TURNING POINT

The Mao Era

After coming to power, the Chinese Communists worked to remake Chinese society along totalitarian Communist lines. Having absolute control of the Chinese government, the Communist party set out to impose its will on the country. Its leaders were determined to uproot both traditional Chinese and Western attitudes in the process.

In theory, the Chinese Communists promoted equality. Women, for example, were made equal with men under the law and benefited from social reforms, such as state-run nurseries that provided child care. They also were expected to enter the workplace alongside men; however, few women were freed from traditional household chores, and even fewer gained top positions in government and industry.

Building a New Economy

One of the major Communist goals was China's transformation into a modern industrial and agricultural nation. In rural areas, the Communists drove landlords from their property and distributed land to the peasants. Several million people may have died in this often bloody struggle.

Once in power, the Communists worked to improve living conditions and education in the countryside. Health workers and teachers loyal to communism set up clinics and schools in rural villages. Despite limited training, they helped to reduce disease and to increase literacy.

China's Communist government also set out to establish a state-controlled economy that would advance industrial and agricultural development. In 1953 it launched its first Soviet-style Five-Year Plan, which stressed heavy industry and agricultural efficiency. The Plan brought private industries under government control and had peasants merge their individual landholdings into large cooperatives. With Soviet help, the Chinese Communists built roads, railroads, factories, and canals. While industrial output rose significantly under this first Plan, agricultural production improved more slowly.

The Great Leap Forward

In 1958 the Chinese launched an ambitious economic plan known as the Great Leap Forward. Under this plan the cooperatives were merged into larger government-controlled units called communes. In producing goods, the Great Leap Forward stressed human labor over complex technology. Members of communes worked in production brigades on tasks ranging from farming to making steel in small backyard furnaces.

Within two years it was clear that the Great Leap Forward was a disaster. Food shortages, mismanagement, and peasant resistance to communes brought the program to a halt. While it lasted, the Great Leap Forward caused massive suffering—as many as 20 million people died of starvation.

The Cultural Revolution

After the Great Leap Forward, a deep division occurred within the Chinese Communist party. Pragmatists, headed by **Deng Xiaoping** (DUNG SHOW•PIHNG), party general secretary, wanted practical reforms. Radicals, led by Mao and his wife **Jiang Jing**, insisted on strict obedience to revolutionary principles.

To end the influence of the pragmatists, Mao in 1966 launched the Cultural Revolution. In response to Mao's direction, young people formed bands of Red Guards. Waving copies of the "Little Red Book" of Mao's sayings, the Red Guards attacked local politicians, teachers, and other leaders for betraying Mao and the revolution. The accused were denounced, publicly humiliated, and sometimes killed.

The Cultural Revolution was a time of disorder and confusion. Schools closed, factory production dropped, and violence erupted. Finally, in 1968, Mao called on the army to restore order. By the time Mao acted, however, the lives of millions of people had been disrupted, and tens of thousands of people had died.

China's Foreign Policy

After the Communist victory in 1949, Mao Zedong followed the Soviet example and opposed the United States and other capitalist countries. In the early 1950s, China actively supported Communist North Korea in its war against American-backed South Korea. In 1954 Chinese Premier **Zhou Enlai** (joh ehn•LY) took part in talks that ended French rule in Indochina and paved the way for a Communist state in northern Vietnam.

During the late 1950s, Chinese-Soviet relations soured and led to an open split. Mao's version of Marxism, based on Chinese experience, held that peasants, rather than workers, were the leaders of revolutions in largely agricultural societies. The Soviets viewed Mao's ideas as a threat to their leadership of world communism. Mao, for his part, demanded that the Soviets take a firmer line against the West. The two Communist powers soon became rivals for influence in the developing

AROUND THE WORLD
Free Speech Movement

Berkeley, California, 1964

In 1964 officials at the University of California at Berkeley prohibited political activities on campus, including the distribution of literature promoting various causes near the school's main gate. The Free Speech Movement was a reaction against these restrictions. In December, students took over the college administration building, then proclaimed a strike. More than 800 students were arrested, but the movement succeeded in forcing the school's president and chancellor out of office.

Berkeley

CALIFORNIA

world. They also had disputes over their long border, with China wanting back the territory seized from it by the Russians in the late 1600s. In 1960 the Soviets finally withdrew their advisers from China, and the alliance came to an end.

During the 1960s, internal upheavals largely isolated China from the rest of the world. The Chinese, however, were able in 1964 to explode their first atomic bomb. By the 1970s the desire for advanced technology made the Chinese reach out to other countries, especially the United States. Since 1949, the United States had regarded China as an aggressive Communist power and maintained ties with the Nationalist government on Taiwan. But the Chinese-Soviet split gave the United States and China an opportunity to improve relations. In 1972 United States President Richard Nixon made a historic visit to China, and seven years later the United States and China established diplomatic ties.

Students at a commune perform a play supporting Mao Zedong. *What was the role of the Red Guards in the Cultural Revolution?*

The Deng Era

After Mao's death in 1976, the pragmatists under Deng Xiaoping gained power. They arrested the Gang of Four, the name given to Jiang Jing and three of her radical supporters. Deng then began to move China in a new direction. Under Deng, the Communist party remained in firm control of political affairs. In making economic policy, however, Deng was willing to learn from the capitalist West if it could contribute to China's well-being.

The Four Modernizations

Deng backed a plan called the Four Modernizations that stressed the need for improvements in agriculture, industry, science, and defense. To boost food production, the government replaced the communes with the rural "responsibility system," in which families farmed individual plots. The government received some of the produce; the family could keep or sell the rest.

Although the government still controlled major industries, factory managers were encouraged to make plants more efficient. They could now base production on supply and demand rather than by government decree. In addition, economic reforms allowed some privately owned small businesses and private property.

Deng also welcomed foreign businesses and technology to China. European, American, and Japanese investment flowed into the country, and the Chinese set up special economic zones where foreigners could own and operate businesses with little government interference.

The Four Modernizations sparked economic growth and raised standards of living. For the first time, many Chinese were able to buy consumer goods, such as televisions and household appliances. The reforms, however, had created a social gap between a new wealthy class and the rest of the Chinese population. Other problems included increased crime and corruption, more unemployment, and rising prices. By the late 1980s, discontent was stirring in China despite the progress that had been made.

Tiananmen Square Massacre

While Deng encouraged some free enterprise, he refused to grant political freedoms. By the late 1980s, students and intellectuals in Beijing, **Shanghai**, and other Chinese cities had organized movements to demand a more open political system. In May and June 1989, more than 100,000 people rallied for democracy and other reforms in Beijing's Tiananmen Square. Determined to maintain control, government

Footnotes to History

Chinese Students Abroad

In the spirit of improving and expanding relations with Western countries, the Chinese government allowed more students to study in foreign countries. By the early 1900s there were about 40,000 Chinese students studying in American universities.

Demonstrating for more freedoms, students carry a hastily constructed model of the Statue of Liberty through Tiananmen Square. *How was this demonstration broken up?*

leaders sent in troops and tanks when the demonstrators refused to disperse. Thousands of demonstrators were killed or wounded. Throughout the country, those who supported political change were shot, imprisoned, tortured, or silenced.

The Tiananmen Square massacre damaged China's prestige abroad. The United States and other democratic nations condemned Deng's use of force. Fearing political instability, foreign investors backed off from doing business with the Chinese. Later, they resumed dealings when the Chinese government continued with economic reforms.

China After Deng

Following the Tiananmen Square massacre, Deng Xiaoping, elderly and in poor health, named Chinese President **Jiang Zemin** as his successor. Deng, however, retained power from behind the scenes until his death in 1997. Deng at that time was hailed worldwide for his free enterprise reforms, but he was criticized for his use of force against the pro-democracy movement.

The Economy

Since Deng's death, China's economic growth has remained strong, but uneven. A gap has widened between prosperous industrial areas on the coast and less wealthy agricultural regions of the interior. Since the 1980s, millions of peasants have moved to the cities seeking work. This mass migration has put pressure on housing and various city social services.

Deng's successors have continued his emphasis on capitalist-style economic reforms. In 1997 Jiang Zemin allowed ailing state-run industries to sell stock, although the government would hold the majority of shares. Chinese authorities also moved ahead with the world's largest public works project: the Three Gorges Dam on the Chang Jiang in central China. When completed in 2009, the dam is expected to prevent dangerous flooding and will provide electricity for new commercial ventures. Almost 2 million people will be relocated before the dam's giant reservoir covers up farms, villages, and canyons. Critics charge that the project is destroying one of the world's most scenic areas.

Human Rights

China's leaders continue to affirm Communist party control over government and the military. However, they have also raised the possibility that they might consider some political reforms. One of the challenges faced by Chinese leaders is growing unrest among China's many ethnic groups. Of every 100 people in China, 93 are Chinese; the remainder are from at least 55 other groups, including Kazakhstanis, Mongols, Uyghurs, and Tibetans. Opposition to Chinese Communist rule is particularly strong in **Tibet**, a mountainous region in the southwestern part of the country. Once an independent Buddhist kingdom, Tibet came under direct Chinese control in 1950. Since an unsuccessful Tibetan rebellion in 1959, the **Dalai Lama**, the spiritual leader of Tibet, has led a worldwide movement in support of Tibetan rights from his place of exile in India.

International Relations

During most of the 1990s, China's relations with the West have been strained. China wants Western trade and investment but resents Western pressures on human rights issues and continuing American support for the Nationalists on Taiwan. The United States especially opposes Chinese sales of missiles and nuclear technology to countries in the Middle East and South Asia. In spite of differences, China and the West have tried to stress the positive aspects of their relationship.

China also expanded contacts with its neighbors in East Asia. Although some Chinese remain bitter about Japan's harsh occupation policies in World War II, Japan now ranks as one of China's major trade partners. China has ties to both North Korea and South Korea, and has developed friendly relations with Russia since the fall of the Soviet Union. It also has expanded trade with various countries in Southeast Asia.

Hong Kong and Taiwan

Economic growth has increased Chinese national pride. In recent years, China's leaders have set as their goal the return of all separated territories to the Chinese homeland. In 1997, they regained **Hong Kong** from the British; in 1999, they will acquire the port of Macao from the Portuguese. Their most controversial demand, however, is the reuniting of Taiwan with the People's Republic of China.

Hong Kong

In 1997 Hong Kong, one of the world's major ports and financial centers, became part of China after 156 years of British rule. Under a "one country, two systems" plan, Hong Kong keeps its capitalist system and some of its freedoms for 50 years after its return to China. Many Hong Kong residents, however, are concerned about their territory's future under Communist control.

During the early 1990s, Great Britain introduced democratic reforms such as a freely elected legislative council. The Chinese Communists, however, opposed these reforms and developed their own institutions for the territory. On June 30, 1997, the date of transfer, Tung Chee-hwa, a local businessman favored by Beijing, became Hong Kong's leader. A China-backed provisional legislature replaced the democratically-elected legislative council. Although China promises to respect Hong Kong's unique status, many Hong Kong residents resent the limits on their political rights.

Taiwan

The status of Taiwan has been a prominent issue in Chinese affairs since 1949. Both the Chinese Nationalists and the Chinese Communists believe that Taiwan is a province of China. Each government claims to be the legal ruler of all of China.

Under Chiang Kai-shek and his son Chiang Ching-kuo, Taiwan prospered from the export of manufactured goods. In 1988 Lee Teng-hui became president of the country. He moved Taiwan toward democracy by allowing other political parties to challenge the Nationalists. Popular with voters, Lee Teng-hui in 1997 was reelected in Taiwan's first democratic presidential race.

Today, Taiwan's economy remains strong, but its political future is uncertain. In recent years, many Taiwanese have come to accept separation from China as a fact and want to declare Taiwan an independent country. The Chinese government in Beijing, however, opposes such a move and has threatened to use force against Taiwan if the island declares its independence.

SECTION 2 REVIEW

Recall

1. **Define** communes, pragmatists, special economic zone.
2. **Identify** Chiang Kai-shek, Mao Zedong, Great Leap Forward, Cultural Revolution, Deng Xiaoping, Jiang Jing, Zhou Enlai, Tiananmen Square, Jiang Zemin, Dalai Lama.

3. **Describe** the changes that occurred in China's relations with the United States and with the Soviet Union between 1949 and 1973.

Critical Thinking

4. **Making Comparisons** How did Mao's policies for the economic development of China

differ with those of MacArthur in Japan?

Understanding Themes

5. **Revolution** Can political struggles within a country always be viewed as a battle between pragmatists and radicals? In your answer use different historical examples.

1945 Soviets and Americans divide Korea at the 38th parallel.

1950 North Koreans invade South Korea.

1953 Korean War ends.

1997 North Korea and South Korea participa in preliminary peace talk

Section 3

A Divided Korea

Setting the Scene

▶ **Terms to Define**
  stalemate, referendum

▶ **People to Meet**
  Kim Il Sung, Kim Young Sam, Kim Jong Il

▶ **Places to Locate**
  Pyongyang, Seoul

Find Out How have South Korea and North Korea differed in their political and economic development?

The Storyteller

South Korean government officials watched as teams from 161 nations marched into the stadium. It was a proud day for South Korea, host of the 1988 Olympic games. North Korea had called for a boycott, had even threatened violence, but only 6 national teams had chosen to stay at home. In fact, most communist states had openly supported the Seoul Olympics. Even now, as the torch entered the stadium, American, Japanese, and Soviet ships off the peninsula kept North Korea under surveillance. As South Koreans watched 300 of China's finest athletes in the opening ceremonies, they wondered, was it a sign of a new era dawning?

—adapted from "The Politics of the Olympics," *The World and I,* October 1988

1988 Olympics in Seoul

Korea's modern history has been heavily shaped by international politics. In 1910 the Korean Peninsula was annexed by the Japanese, who ruled it as a colony until the end of World War II, when Japan was stripped of its territorial possessions.

During the war, the Allied powers had agreed that Korea was to be temporarily occupied. In 1945 Soviet troops moved into the northern part of Korea down to the 38th parallel. United States forces occupied the southern area. The occupation was to end as soon as a Korean government could be freely elected. The Soviets and Americans, however, could not agree on procedures for the election.

By 1948, two separate governments had emerged, each claiming to be the legal ruler of all of Korea. North Korea, officially called the Democratic People's Republic of Korea, with its capital at **Pyongyang**, kept close ties with the Soviet Union and China. South Korea, officially the Republic of Korea, established its capital at **Seoul**. It maintained links with the United States. The Soviets withdrew their troops from North Korea in late 1948, and the United States withdrew their troops from South Korea in mid-1949.

The Korean War

In June 1950, North Korea, hoping to unify the country under a Communist government, invaded South Korea. The United Nations Security Council immediately voted to condemn the invasion and organized an army to oppose it. At that time the Soviets could not use their veto because of their absence from the Council in protest at the United Nations' refusal to recognize Communist China. While 16 countries contributed troops to the UN force, more than 90 percent of the soldiers came from the United States.

In the first months of the war, the North Koreans swept southward, conquering almost all of South Korea. However, in September 1950, the UN troops led by United States General Douglas MacArthur counterattacked. MacArthur launched a surprise invasion at Inchon, along Korea's west coast and far behind North Korean lines. The daring move gave UN forces the offensive they needed. Within six weeks, the UN forces had pushed the North Koreans out of South Korea and had advanced into North Korea, reaching the Yalu River at the Chinese border.

At this point in the war, Communist China came to the aid of North Korea. Chinese forces crossed into Korea in such large numbers that the UN forces were forced to retreat southward. By mid-1951, each army dug in along a line near the 38th parallel. There the fighting reached a stalemate, a situation in which two opponents are unable to move significantly or make further gains. Talks between the two sides began in July 1951 and lasted until July 1953, when a truce was signed. After the deaths of nearly 5 million people and the devastation of much of Korea, the fighting ended with Korea once again divided near the 38th parallel.

Korea Since 1953

The stalemate in the Korean War for a long time was matched by a stalemate in diplomacy. The two Koreas continued to draw economic and military aid from their respective sponsors, the United States and China.

North Korea

From 1948 to 1994, North Korea was led by the Communist dictator **Kim Il Sung**. A cult of personality developed around Kim, and North Koreans revered him as a god-like figure. Called the "Great Leader," Kim established a repressive and tightly controlled government that largely isolated North Korea from the rest of the world.

Like the Soviet Union and China, North Korea implemented a Communist program of economic development. Under Kim's direction, all of the country's farmland was organized into collective farms between 1953 and 1956. In 1954 the North Korean government announced the first Five-Year Plan for building an industrial economy. North Korea stressed the growth of heavy industry and built up its military power.

Until the early 1990s, North Korea made some progress in developing its economy, but it did not match South Korea's growth. About 20 percent of North Korea's gross domestic product (GDP) was

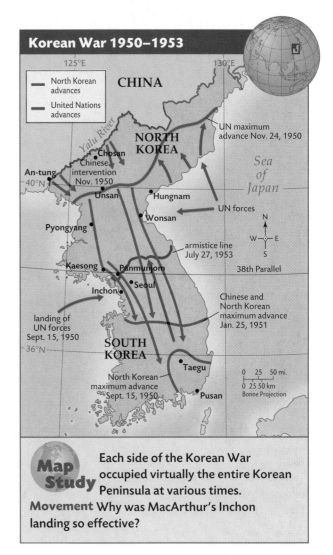

Korean War 1950–1953

Legend:
— North Korean advances
— United Nations advances

CHINA
NORTH KOREA
Yalu River
An-tung
Chosan
Chinese intervention Nov. 1950
Unsan
Hungnam
Wonsan
UN forces
UN maximum advance Nov. 24, 1950
Sea of Japan
Pyongyang
Kaesong
Panmunjom
armistice line July 27, 1953
38th Parallel
Seoul
Inchon
Chinese and North Korean maximum advance Jan. 25, 1951
landing of UN forces Sept. 15, 1950
SOUTH KOREA
Taegu
North Korean maximum advance Sept. 15, 1950
Pusan

0   25   50 mi.
0 25 50 km
Bonne Projection

Map Study Each side of the Korean War occupied virtually the entire Korean Peninsula at various times.
Movement Why was MacArthur's Inchon landing so effective?

annually devoted to military expenditures, including the development of nuclear capabilities. Improvements in the standard of living were limited by this heavy military spending.

In the mid-1990s, another factor limiting North Korea's growth was widespread crop failure. This agricultural collapse was due to floods, drought, and government policies that provided few incentives for farmers to produce. The resulting food shortages brought starvation to many of North Korea's people. As catastrophe loomed on the horizon, the Communist government reluctantly admitted its need for foreign aid. In 1997 relief organizations in the United States and other countries began sending food to North Korea.

South Korea

In contrast, South Korea after the mid-1960s enjoyed tremendous economic success. By the mid-1980s, the South Korean economy was growing at the remarkable rate of 10 percent a year. To promote

The central area of Seoul, South Korea, reflects the city's economic prosperity in recent years. *What challenges face South Korea as it approaches the year 2000?*

During the 1980s, massive student protests led to greater democracy. In 1987 a new constitution allowing almost complete political freedoms was adopted by referendum, an election in which all voters approve or disapprove a measure. That same year, South Korean voters for the first time elected a new president—Roh Tae Woo—by direct vote instead of indirectly by an electoral college. Six years later, the same method was used to select **Kim Young Sam** as president.

During Kim's term, South Korea was plagued by strikes, political scandals, and economic setbacks. When a number of leading companies and banks collapsed, the South Korean government turned to the International Monetary Fund (IMF), an international lending agency, for a $57 billion bailout. Under IMF controls, the South Koreans were forced to reform their economy. In the short term, this meant industrial cutbacks, lower wages, and higher unemployment. As discontent mounted, South Korean voters in December 1997 elected Kim Dae Jung, a leading government opponent, as president.

North-South Relations

The end of the cold war in the early 1990s raised hopes for uniting the two Koreas. North Korea and South Korea took halting steps toward better relations, but continuing resentments on both sides hampered progress. The death of Kim Il Sung in 1994 and uncertainty about the intentions of his son and successor, **Kim Jong Il**, further delayed any movement toward peace.

By the late 1990s, however, North Korea's food crisis had forced the North Korean government to increase its contacts with the outside world. Hoping to get commitments for food aid, North Korea in 1997 entered into talks with South Korea, the United States, and China. The purpose of the talks was to prepare for further discussions on a peace treaty ending the state of war that still exists between the two Koreas.

prosperity, the South Korean government strongly encouraged the export of electronics products, textiles, ships, trucks, automobiles, and other industrial goods.

South Korea's economic boom, however, was achieved under repressive governments. Beginning in the early 1960s, the military used the Communist threat to play a strong role in the government. Despite elections, South Korea's president was essentially a military-backed dictator, limiting speech, press, and opposition.

SECTION 3 REVIEW

Recall
1. **Define** stalemate, referendum.
2. **Identify** Inchon, Kim Il Sung, Kim Young Sam, Kim Jong Il.
3. **Explain** the political significance of the 38th parallel

in the history of modern Korea.
Critical Thinking
4. **Making Comparisons** How are North Korea and South Korea similar? In what ways are the two Koreas different?

Understanding Themes
5. **Regionalism** How might the two Koreas' futures be influenced by recent global events such as the end of the cold war?

1945   1972   2000

1949 Indonesia wins its independence from Dutch rule.

1954 Vietminh defeats French forces at Dien Bien Phu.

1965 U.S. President Johnson sends first American ground troops to Vietnam.

1994 Cambodia establishes a democracy.

Section 4

Southeast Asia

Setting the Scene

▶ **Terms to Define**
   domino theory, refugee

▶ **People to Meet**
   Ho Chi Minh, Norodom Sihanouk, Pol Pot, Aung San Suu Kyi, Achmed Sukarno, Suharto, Lee Kuan Yew

▶ **Places to Locate**
   Vietnam, Cambodia, Laos, Thailand, Myanmar, Indonesia, Malaysia, Singapore

Find Out How have nationalism, the cold war, and the rise of a global economy affected Southeast Asia?

The Storyteller

Once again it was Tet. Tran Van Dinh could recall when that most joyous of Vietnamese holidays was the background for twenty-six days of bloody fighting between American and Viet Cong forces. Thousands had died. But throughout Vietnam's history, whether independent or under foreign domination, Tet was an occasion to meditate on the past, enjoy the present, and contemplate the future. Tran, who had made his life in France since 1968, bought flowers from the street vendor to mark the new beginning. It was deeply satisfying to return to his native city of Hue for the celebration.

—adapted from "Hue: My City, Myself," *National Geographic*, November, 1989, Tran Van Dinh.

Celebrating Tet

During the cold war years, Southeast Asia was thrust into the middle of the superpower contest and also suffered because of regional hostilities. The ongoing struggle between Communists and anti-Communists brought instability and war to much of the region of Southeast Asia known as Indochina. Only in recent years have Indochinese countries such as **Vietnam** and **Cambodia** begun to recover from earlier conflicts.

Struggle for Indochina

Before Japan conquered Southeast Asia in World War II, France ruled most of Indochina as a colony. When Japanese forces withdrew following the war, France attempted to reestablish its control. By then, however, nationalist movements demanding independence had gained strength. Vietnamese nationalists in the Indochinese Communist party, later known as the Vietminh, declared the formation of the independent Democratic Republic of Vietnam in 1945. The Vietminh were supported by the Soviet Union and the Communist Chinese.

The Vietminh, under the leadership of **Ho Chi Minh**, and the French could not reach an agreement on how to share power. In 1946 the two sides went to war. The United States, fearing Ho's Communist ties and wanting to support its ally France, provided military and financial aid to France to subdue the Vietminh. Despite American aid, the French could not win a military victory. In May 1954 the Vietminh defeated French forces in the decisive battle at Dien Bien Phu. After their loss, the French agreed to a cease-fire and decided to pull out of Vietnam completely.

A month before the battle, the Vietminh, the French, the United States, and several other countries had agreed to meet in Geneva, Switzerland, to negotiate a settlement to the Vietnam conflict. Negotiators divided Vietnam along the 17th parallel, creating a Communist North Vietnam and a pro-Western South Vietnam. This arrangement was to last only until elections could be held in 1956. With United States approval, Ngo Dinh Diem, South Vietnam's leader, rejected the proposed elections. He claimed that the Communists would not allow fair elections in North Vietnam. Diem also may have feared that elections would reveal Ho's popularity. Guerrillas in South Vietnam, known as the Viet Cong, fought Diem in hope of uniting Vietnam under Ho. The United States sent financial aid and several hundred advisers to help Diem.

However, Diem was a weak and unpopular leader. In 1963 the South Vietnamese military, despairing of Diem's leadership and fearing that the South would fall to the Communists, staged a coup in which Diem was killed. This was done with the quiet approval of the United States government and President John F. Kennedy.

Reflecting on France's earlier troubles in Vietnam, French President Charles de Gaulle urged Kennedy to withdraw. "I predict you will sink step by step into a bottomless quagmire," he warned.

The Vietnam War

Since the early 1950s, American officials had accepted the domino theory—that if one Southeast Asian land fell to communism, its neighbors would fall as well. To halt communism, the United States moved deeper into the conflict. By late 1963, 16,000 American advisers were in Vietnam.

In 1964 the United States approved secret South Vietnamese naval raids against North Vietnam. On August 2, 1964, United States President Lyndon Johnson announced that North Vietnam had fired on two American destroyers off the coast of Vietnam. Although the incident could not be confirmed, Johnson used it to increase American involvement in the war. He ordered air strikes on North Vietnam. At his request Congress passed the Gulf of Tonkin Resolution, which gave the

Images of the Times

Vietnam War, 1964–1975

Americans, forced to consider the cost of war in terms of human and economic sacrifice, debated for years before withdrawing troops in 1973.

United States troops searched the hills and rice paddies for Viet Cong guerrillas, the hidden enemy.

President broad war powers. In March 1965 Johnson sent the first ground troops to Vietnam.

By 1968, American forces numbered more than 500,000, and United States planes were bombing Vietnam heavily. The South Vietnamese army was about 800,000; the Viet Cong and their North Vietnamese allies had about 300,000. The Soviet Union and China sent aid but no troops to help North Vietnam. North Vietnam sent troops and supplies southward over the Ho Chi Minh Trail. Despite greater numbers and advanced technology, the Americans could not defeat the Communists, who relied on surprise and mobility and avoided open battle. As the war intensified, antiwar attitudes spread within the United States and overseas.

The Tet Offensive

The turning point in the war came in early 1968. The Viet Cong launched a major military offensive during the Vietnamese New Year holiday, Tet. Although they failed to capture any major cities, the bitter fighting made more and more Americans real-ize that several years of United States involvement had failed to significantly weaken the Viet Cong. Opposition to Johnson's war policy became so fierce that Johnson decided not to seek reelection in 1968.

Ending the War

Opposition to the war grew rapidly during the Nixon presidency. As a result, the United States began withdrawing its troops. With the war becoming costly to both sides, South Vietnam, the United States, and the Communists in 1973 agreed to a cease-fire, and the last United States troops left Vietnam. The war resumed in 1975, however, when North Vietnamese and Viet Cong forces defeated the South Vietnamese.

After more than 20 years of fighting, Vietnam was reunited under the Communists. However, at least 2 million people, including 58,000 Americans, had died in the conflict. About 10 million South Vietnamese were refugees, people who flee to another country for safety from danger or disaster. In addition, large areas of Vietnam lay devastated.

Student war protest demonstrations on United States college campuses became common in the early 1970s.

South Vietnamese villagers from Quang Tri Province assemble at a refugee camp. Many hope to leave Vietnam.

REFLECTING ON THE TIMES

1. Why did college students play a significant role in the antiwar protest movement?
2. Why was the war so difficult for a powerful nation like the United States to win?

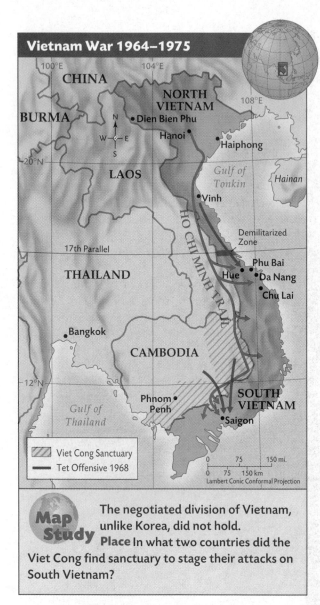

CHINA

BURMA

NORTH VIETNAM

Dien Bien Phu

Hanoi

Haiphong

LAOS

Gulf of Tonkin

Hainan

Vinh

17th Parallel

THAILAND

Demilitarized Zone

Phu Bai

Hue • Da Nang

Chu Lai

Bangkok

CAMBODIA

Phnom Penh

SOUTH VIETNAM

Saigon

Gulf of Thailand

Viet Cong Sanctuary

Tet Offensive 1968

0   75   150 mi.

0   75   150 km

Lambert Conic Conformal Projection

Map Study The negotiated division of Vietnam, unlike Korea, did not hold.
Place In what two countries did the Viet Cong find sanctuary to stage their attacks on South Vietnam?

Vietnam's Relations with the West

Since the war, Vietnam has faced economic difficulties. To improve the economy, the government in the late 1980s encouraged limited private enterprise and sought contacts with the West.

In recent years, relations between the United States and Vietnam have begun to improve. The Vietnamese government has helped locate and return many of the bodies of American soldiers killed in Vietnam. Unfortunately, the remains of many United States soldiers have not been found. Some former American soldiers have returned to Vietnam to help disarm land mines they planted during the war.

A major step toward normal relations was made in 1995 when the United States and Vietnam established diplomatic ties. Vietnam also moved to improve its relations and trade with the industrial-

ized nations of western Europe as a way to gain funds to rebuild and strengthen its desperately poor economy.

A Legacy of Violence

The Vietnam War affected many areas of Southeast Asia other than Vietnam. Fighting and civil war engulfed Vietnam's neighbors, Laos and Cambodia. Other countries of Southeast Asia, such as Thailand, escaped combat but were flooded by refugees. Since the late 1970s, the region has slowly recovered from the effects of conflict.

Cambodia

In 1953 Cambodia won its independence from France. The country became a constitutional monarchy led by King **Norodom Sihanouk** (noo•roh•DAHM SEE•ah•nuk), a member of Cambodia's historic ruling family. In 1955 Sihanouk abdicated the Cambodian throne in order to become prime minister.

Sihanouk refused to take sides in cold war power struggles. However, as the war intensified in Vietnam, Cambodia became an unwilling participant. In 1969 American planes began to bomb Cambodia in an effort to destroy Viet Cong bases there. The bombings were also intended to stop the flow of supplies and troops moving through Cambodia from North Vietnam to South Vietnam.

The bombing failed to achieve its objectives but did intensify the conflict between Cambodian Communists and Sihanouk's government. In 1970 an American-backed army officer, Lon Nol, ousted Sihanouk. Lon Nol charged that Sihanouk was not battling the Communists aggressively enough.

Civil war broke out after the American bombings and Lon Nol's seizure of power. Cambodian Communists, known as the Khmer Rouge, finally defeated Lon Nol's forces in 1975. Khmer Rouge troops, under the leadership of **Pol Pot**, took control of Cambodia's capital, Phnom Penh.

The Khmer Rouge wanted Cambodia, which they renamed Kampuchea, to become an independent, self-sufficient agricultural country. In the attempt to achieve this goal, the Khmer Rouge devastated the country. They destroyed all money and books. Soldiers forced city residents into the countryside to work on farms. Troops murdered civil servants, teachers, and students who may have supported the old system. Starvation, torture, and executions by the brutal government killed more than 3 million people—nearly one-third of the entire Cambodian population.

National Geographic photographer Jodi Cobb

Boat People

Two decades after the Vietnam War, Vietnamese refugees waiting to go elsewhere remained stranded in Hong Kong. In this photograph, Vietnamese refugees in Hong Kong live inside huge concrete-and-metal dormitories where whole families sleep together in shelf-like bunks.

Vietnam suffered decades of war. In the 1800s the area was colonized by the French, who often proved to be brutal masters of rubber plantations and tin works. By the beginning of the 1900s an independence movement had begun in Vietnam. Not until 1975 did Vietnam free itself from foreign interference. But the price was high: economic devastation and domination of South Vietnam by North Vietnam. During the second half of the 1970s—years of poverty and political persecution—hundreds of thousands of Vietnamese left their country, many by boat. Untold numbers died. Some came to the United States; others scattered across Asia. By 1996, international pressure had forced Vietnam to increase its efforts to bring home the boat people. ⊕

Aung San Suu Kyi addresses a pro-democracy rally in Yangon, Myanmar's capital. *What group rules Myanmar?*

In 1978, after a series of border incidents, Vietnam invaded Cambodia and ousted Pol Pot. Cambodian Communists friendly to Vietnam took control of the government, but other Communist groups continued the civil war. In October 1991, representatives of the four major political groups in Cambodia signed an agreement that ended the civil war and called for an election under UN peacekeeping forces.

Cambodian voters in 1993 elected a government under Prince Norodom Ranariddh. However, Hun Sen, a political rival, demanded a role in the government. He gradually forced his way into power, finally removing the prince in July 1997. At that time, Cambodia began still another round of civil war. Continuing political instability has hindered growth of Cambodia's largely agricultural economy.

Laos

Laos became independent of France in 1954. While war raged in neighboring Vietnam, Laos had its own civil war between Laotian Communists and the American-backed government.

After United States forces withdrew from the region, Laos fell under the domination of Vietnam in 1975. A Communist government was formed, and the economy was reorganized along socialist lines. The Lao People's Revolutionary party abandoned those policies 20 years later after the collapse of the Soviet Union. They have reintroduced private land ownership and free markets. With investments from Thailand, Australia, and other foreign countries, the Lao government has built new roads, bridges, and railroads to advance regional trade and to gain access to timber and mineral resources.

Thailand

Thailand's post-World War II history was less violent than that of its neighbors because it had not been a European colony. It did not have to fight a war of national independence or struggle to forge a new national identity. The monarchy continued as a stabilizing force in Thai society, but the real power was often held by top military leaders.

During the Vietnam War, Thailand held to a firm anti-Communist policy, aligning itself decisively with the United States. In recent years, Thailand has adopted a more relaxed policy toward China and its neighbors, while remaining an ally of the United States.

During the 1980s, Thailand had one of Southeast Asia's fast-growing "tiger" economies, with a yearly growth rate of 8 percent. By 1997, high foreign borrowing and slow export growth had cast a dark shadow over the Thai economy. As hardships mounted for the Thai people, the government devalued its currency to make Thai exports cheaper and relied on an international loan. Its economic woes threatened to spill over into neighboring Southeast Asian lands with similar problems.

Myanmar

Myanmar is the northernmost country of Southeast Asia. Once called Burma, it was for many years part of British India but became a separate independent republic in 1948. The new Burmese government faced opposition from Communists and various ethnic groups. To restore order, military leaders took control of the country in 1962.

During the 1960s and 1970s, the military leadership turned Myanmar into a dictatorship. The government took control of the economy and forbade any criticism of its policies. It also limited Myanmar's contacts with the outside world.

During the late 1980s, large numbers of Burmese began to protest the government's policies and call for democracy. Military leaders finally promised free elections in 1990, but before the voting took place they arrested the leader of the main opposition party, **Aung San Suu Kyi** (AWNG SAHN SOO SHE). In spite of her arrest, her party won the elections.

The military leaders refused to accept the election results, but Aung San Suu Kyi won increased international support. While under house arrest, she received the 1991 Nobel Peace Prize. Released in 1995, she has continued efforts to achieve democracy in Myanmar.

Rim of Southeast Asia

Indonesia, Malaysia, Singapore, and the Philippines won their independence following World War II. They went through periods of turmoil and have emerged 50 years later with stable, booming economies. Their people and leaders are optimistic about the future of their countries.

Indonesia

Under Dutch rule for nearly 350 years, **Indonesia** won its freedom in 1949. Largely Muslim in religion, the new nation was very diverse in other ways. It consisted of a string of 14,000 islands stretching 3,000 miles (4,827 km) as well as nearly 80 million people of many cultures and languages. Therefore, forging a national identity was an early goal. Indonesia's first president, **Achmed Sukarno**, did much to unite the country. He ensured the adoption of a national language that put all Indonesians on an equal footing.

In 1965 Indonesia's Communists tried to seize power. In a bloody crackdown, the army killed about 300,000 allegedly pro-Communist ethnic Chinese. The anti-Communist General **Suharto** then replaced Sukarno as ruler.

Suharto at first brought economic growth to Indonesia. By the late 1990s, however, his long dictatorial rule had led to a staggering national debt and political corruption. In 1998 the collapse of Indonesia's economy sparked protests that finally drove Suharto from office.

Suharto's rule also was known for its human rights abuses. In 1975 Indonesia had seized the former Portuguese colony of East Timor. Wanting independence, the largely Roman Catholic East Timorans resisted Indonesian rule. By the late 1990s, about 200,000 of them had died as a result of Indonesia's use of force. In 1997 East Timoran human rights advocates José Ramos Horta and Bishop Carlos Belo received the Nobel Peace Prize.

Malaysia

Created by the merger of several former British colonies in 1963, **Malaysia** is made up of territory on the Malay Peninsula and on the island of Borneo. Conflict between Malays and Chinese—the country's two largest ethnic groups—has been a frequent source of tension.

Since the early 1970s, however, Malaysia has been relatively stable. Like other nations on the rim of Southeast Asia, Malaysia has enjoyed an economic boom. Its well-educated labor force, good transportation networks, and tax incentives have helped attract foreign investment. Large public-works projects, however, have greatly increased the country's debt.

Singapore

Singapore is a small island republic off the tip of the Malay Peninsula. Independent since 1965, Singapore is a leading international port and commercial center, involved in shipping, banking, insurance, and telecommunications. Today, Singapore's people are well-educated and prosperous. Their standard of living is second only to Japan's in Asia.

Singapore's modern economic growth occurred under the authoritarian leadership of **Lee Kuan Yew** (lee kwahn yoo), who was prime minister from 1965 to 1990. Closely involved with Singapore's economic development, the government focused on encouraging high-technology industries and welcomed foreign business investment. A prosperous economy and the high rate of savings by Singapore citizens helped finance quality housing, health care, and education. In spite of having these benefits, Singapore's people have had limits placed on their freedom of speech and other rights.

1945		1972		2000

1947 India and Pakistan become independent nations.

1971 Civil war in Pakistan leads to independence of Bangladesh.

1984 Sikh unrest leads to assassination of Indira Gandhi.

Section 5

South Asia

Setting the Scene

▶ **Terms to Define**
nonaligned

▶ **People to Meet**
Muhammad Ali Jinnah, Jawaharlal Nehru, Indira Gandhi, Benazir Ali Bhutto

▶ **Places to Locate**
India, Pakistan, Kashmir, Bangladesh, Sri Lanka

Find Out What challenges have the countries of South Asia faced since independence?

The Storyteller

Pradeep Bandhari was deeply shaken. Yet another Indian leader had been assassinated. Confused and distressed, he asked his professor to explain why visionary leaders were repeatedly struck down. "I have no immediate answer to give," replied the professor. "However, you might find some meaning in the eulogy for Mohandas Gandhi written by Jawaharlal Nehru." Pradeep was struck by the timeliness of the message:

> *"Long ages afterwards history will judge of this period we have passed through. We are too near to be proper judges and to understand what has happened and what has not happened."*

—adapted from Independence and After, "A Glory Has Departed," Jawaharlal Nehru, reprinted in Great Speeches from Pericles to Kennedy, 1965

Nehru and Mohandas Gandhi

British rule of South Asia came to an end after World War II. The creation of independent states in the region, however, was marred by religious and ethnic conflicts. The cold war also had an impact. In recent years, dramatic changes in the world have made South Asian nations rethink their policies and relationships.

TURNING POINT

Dividing the Subcontinent

After World War II, the British finally agreed to give **India** its freedom. Growing political disunity, however, divided the subcontinent. **Muhammad Ali Jinnah**, leader of the Muslim League, wanted Muslims to have their own state named **Pakistan**. Riots between Hindus and Muslims finally convinced the British to partition, or divide, India. In early 1947, Lord Louis Mountbatten, a World War II military hero, became British India's last viceroy. He and other officials quickly drew borders for two separate states, a difficult task because many Hindus and Muslims lived side by side. Heavily Muslim areas in the far west and far east became Pakistan. The vast area in between, where most of the people were Hindus, became India.

On August 15, 1947, independence came to both countries, but not peace. The division of the subcontinent led to one of the largest single mass movements of people in history. About 12 million Hindus and Muslims crossed the borders of India and Pakistan in both directions. Centuries of mistrust between religious groups led to violence that resulted in the deaths of a million or more people. Tragically, another casualty of the conflict was Mohandas Gandhi, killed in January 1948 by a Hindu extremist who was angered at Gandhi's call for peace and reconciliation.

The migrations and the killings did not end the conflicts between Hindus and Muslims. More than

60 million Muslims remained in India, ensuring future tensions. Bitter hostilities between India and Pakistan would also continue.

India

India's first prime minister was **Jawaharlal Nehru** (jah•wah•HAR•lahl NAY•roo), a British-educated lawyer who had led the fight for freedom along with Gandhi. Nehru headed India's government from 1947 until his death in 1964.

The Nehru "Dynasty"

For forty years after independence, India was ruled by a member of the Nehru family. Jawaharlal Nehru aimed to make India a modern, industrialized state based on secular ideas. His government worked for religious freedom and greater social equality. India's constitution granted universal suffrage, and aimed to ban caste distinctions and improve the status of women.

Nehru favored a mixed economy of privately owned and government-run businesses. Attention was also given to raising food production. Increased food supplies, however, were accompanied by rapid population growth and the increased migration of people from rural areas to the cities.

Under Nehru, India became a leader among the new nations of Asia and Africa. Nehru argued that recently independent countries such as India should not participate in the cold war. By remaining nonaligned—that is, tied to neither superpower—the less powerful countries of the world could forge their own way in global affairs. In the early 1960s, however, tense relations with China helped bring India into a closer relationship with China's new rival, the Soviet Union.

Two years after Nehru's death in 1964, his daughter **Indira Gandhi** became prime minister. An energetic leader, Gandhi continued her father's policies; however, her crackdown on political opponents in 1977 made her unpopular and eventually swept her from office.

When Gandhi returned to power in 1980, India faced growing religious and ethnic unrest. In the Punjab region of northern India, some Sikhs wanted their own state. Sikh separatists occupied the Golden Temple of Amritsar, Sikhism's holiest shrine. When talks failed, Indira Gandhi in 1984 drove out the separatists with troops and tanks. Outraged at the shrine's violation, two of Gandhi's bodyguards, themselves Sikhs, later assassinated her.

Gandhi's son, Rajiv Gandhi, served as prime minister from 1984 to 1989. In 1991 he was assassi-

Visualizing History Indira Gandhi had been a leader in the Congress party and minister of information and broadcasting in India before becoming prime minister. *Why did she lose the 1977 election?*

nated while campaigning to become prime minister again. Rajiv's death seemed to mark the end of the Nehru "dynasty" in politics.

A New Course

In the 1990s India's prime ministers have not had the influence or power of the Nehru "dynasty." However, with workable parliamentary institutions, India's democracy may have been strengthened. Although India still struggles with poverty, disease, and illiteracy, recent reforms have improved its economy by promoting free enterprise, less government regulation, and increased trade.

A major challenge still facing India is religious and ethnic conflict. Uncertainties caused by modernization have led to a revival of traditional Hinduism mixed with modern politics. In the early 1990s, the Hindu nationalist party increased its support. Its desire to promote Hindu principles has disturbed many non-Hindu Indians who view it as a threat to India's secular government. Violence has also erupted between religious groups. In 1992 fierce battles broke out between Hindus and Muslims over the ownership of a religious site at Ayodhya.

Since 1947, India has faced periodic conflicts with Pakistan. A major source of hostility between the two countries has been the disputed northern territory of **Kashmir**. Although most of Kashmir's people are Muslim, two-thirds of the territory is governed by India. Since the 1980s, Muslims in the

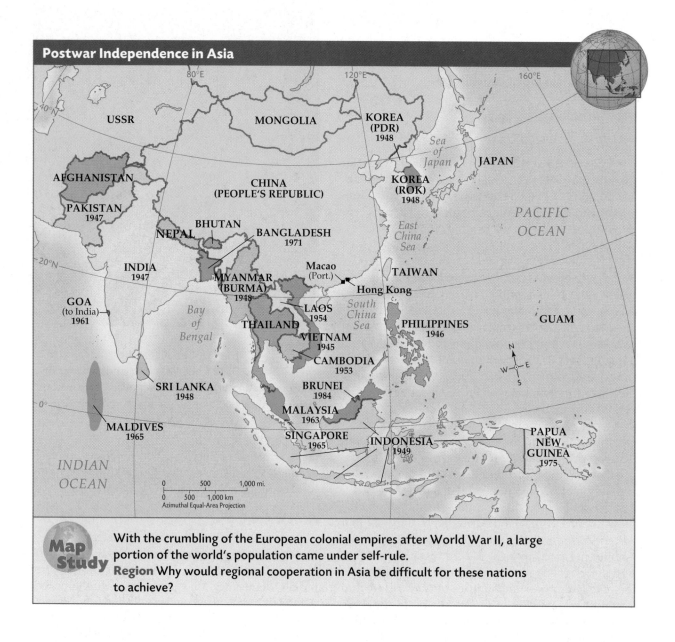

USSR

MONGOLIA

KOREA
(PDR)
1948

*Sea
of
Japan*

JAPAN

AFGHANISTAN

CHINA
(PEOPLE'S REPUBLIC)

KOREA
(ROK)
1948

PAKISTAN
1947

BHUTAN

NEPAL

BANGLADESH
1971

*East
China
Sea*

PACIFIC
OCEAN

INDIA
1947

Macao
(Port.)

TAIWAN

MYANMAR
(BURMA)
1948

Hong Kong

GOA
(to India)
1961

*Bay
of
Bengal*

LAOS
1954

THAILAND

*South
China
Sea*

PHILIPPINES
1946

GUAM

VIETNAM
1945

CAMBODIA
1953

SRI LANKA
1948

BRUNEI
1984

MALDIVES
1965

MALAYSIA
1963

SINGAPORE
1965

INDONESIA
1949

PAPUA
NEW
GUINEA
1975

*INDIAN
OCEAN*

0   500   1,000 mi.
0   500   1,000 km
Azimuthal Equal-Area Projection

Map Study

With the crumbling of the European colonial empires after World War II, a large portion of the world's population came under self-rule.
Region Why would regional cooperation in Asia be difficult for these nations to achieve?

Indian section of Kashmir have organized to oppose Indian rule.

In the 1990s, a nuclear arms race developed between India and Pakistan. India has had nuclear weapons since the 1970s. In 1998, Pakistan for the first time tested nuclear devices in response to nuclear testing by India. International efforts are underway to halt the race before it leads to a nuclear conflict in South Asia.

Pakistan and Bangladesh

After independence in 1947, Pakistan faced difficulties in joining two distinct regions separated by over 1,000 miles (1,609 km) of Indian territory. West Pakistan was a dry, mountainous region in which most people spoke Urdu. East Pakistan was a wet lowlands region in which most people spoke Bengali. The religion of Islam was their only common bond.

In March 1971, a fierce civil war broke out between the two regions of Pakistan. In December 1971, India joined the war in support of East Pakistan. This military action spread the fighting to West Pakistan and Kashmir. The war ended quickly, and East Pakistan won its independence as the republic of Bangladesh.

Bangladesh

Bangladesh is one of the most densely populated nations of the world. More than 125 million people live in an area about the size of New York State. Most people are located in rural areas where illiteracy and the birthrate are high and the life expectancy is low.

Achieving stable rule has been difficult in Bangladesh. Since independence, two leaders of the country have been assassinated, and military officials often have controlled the government. Beginning in 1991, free elections have been held, however, and political power has alternated between the female leaders of the two major parties. In 1996 Sheik Hasina Wazid became prime minister.

In spite of economic growth and substantial foreign aid, the future of Bangladesh remains uncertain. The average annual per capita (per person) income of $150 is one of the world's lowest. The country also is subject to intense summer storms and flooding.

Pakistan Since 1971

Pakistan suffered from political instability and military rule after 1971. A move toward a stable democracy seemed likely in 1993 when **Benazir Ali Bhutto** became prime minister. In 1996, however, her government fell as a result of corruption charges. Elections brought to power the opposition party under Nawaz Sharif. Sharif's government promised to reduce government regulations over the economy.

During the 1970s and 1980s, Pakistan allied with the United States in order to counter India's ties with the Soviet Union. The Pakistani government allowed the Americans to channel military arms to anti-Soviet rebels in neighboring Afghanistan. It also permitted Afghani fighters to use Pakistan as a base of operations, and sheltered 3 million Afghani refugees. Despite United States aid, the presence of so many refugees was costly and worsened ethnic tensions within Pakistan.

Military spending has taken a large share of Pakistan's budget because of tensions with India. This has drained resources that could have been used for the economic development of the country. Pakistan's efforts to develop nuclear weapons have raised international concern about a South Asian arms race.

Visualizing History Sheik Hasina Wazid became prime minister of Bangladesh in 1996. Her father, Sheik Mujibar Rahman, is regarded as Bangladesh's founder. *What challenges does Bangladesh face?*

Sri Lanka

In 1948, the year after the partition of India, Great Britain granted independence to Ceylon, known since 1972 as **Sri Lanka**. This beautiful island off the southeast coast of India has been the site of ethnic civil war since the 1980s. The Sinhalese, who make up about about 75 percent of the population, are Buddhists. The Tamils, who make up about 20 percent, are Hindus. In recent years the Tamils, complaining of discrimination against them by the Sinhalese, have demanded their own state within Sri Lanka. Hundreds of people have died in conflicts between government troops and Tamil guerrillas. Efforts to improve the economy have been helped by developing privately owned businesses and by attracting foreign investments.

SECTION 5 REVIEW

Recall
1. **Define** nonaligned.
2. **Identify** Muhammad Ali Jinnah, Jawaharlal Nehru, Indira Gandhi, Benazir Ali Bhutto.
3. **Explain** the consequences of Great Britain's withdrawal from South Asia.

Critical Thinking
4. **Analyzing Information** What do you think are the underlying causes of continuing political strife in India?

Understanding Themes
5. **Diversity** Has the division of the Indian subcontinent into separate countries been beneficial? Explain your answer.

1945   1972   2000

1946 The Philippines wins independence from the United States.

1970s Australia admits non-British European and Asian immigrants for the first time.

1995 Pacific nations protest French nuclear testing.

Section 6

The Pacific

Setting the Scene

▶ **Terms to Define**
archipelago

▶ **People to Meet**
Ferdinand Marcos, Corazon Aquino, Paul Keating, David Lange, Jim Bolger

▶ **Places to Locate**
The Philippines, Australia, New Zealand, Papua New Guinea

Find Out What factors have helped Pacific nations develop prosperous economies and new national identities since World War II?

The Storyteller

Toby Doust knew what to expect between the Great Sandy Desert and the Gibson Desert in northwestern Australia—and it wasn't water. Earlier explorers had expected water, but Lake Disappointment had water only when a rare inland cyclone brought a spattering shower to the dry bed. Toby, however, was prospecting for more commercial materials—iron, zinc, bauxite—to sell throughout the Pacific Basin. Perhaps there was even gold or uranium. One thing Toby never lacked was nerve. Nearing a remote outcrop, he unstrapped his bag and got out his metal detector, ready to strike it rich.

—adapted from "Journey into the Daytime," *National Geographic*, January 1991

Australia's Uluru (Ayers Rock)

The Pacific region east and south of Asia contains Australia, the world's only island continent, and numerous other islands that spread out across millions of miles of the Pacific Ocean. Until recently, long distances and rugged landscapes kept many parts of the region isolated from each other and the rest of the world. Beginning in the 1700s, Western powers exercised a strong influence in the region. Since World War II, the Pacific countries, now mostly independent, have forged new identities from a mix of European, traditional Pacific, and Asian cultures. Many of them have close trading ties to Japan, Singapore, and other nations of the Pacific Rim, a region of economically prosperous countries bordering the Pacific Ocean.

The Philippines

The Philippines is an archipelago, or group of islands, in the Pacific Ocean east of Vietnam. The Philippines faced severe challenges when it became independent from the United States in 1946. Philippine Communists, known as the Huks, pressed for land reform and tried to take over the government. The Philippine army defeated them in 1954, but the Huks have arisen periodically to challenge later leaders.

Between 1965 and 1986, the Philippines was led by President **Ferdinand Marcos**. Marcos at first was popular because he tried to improve education and transportation. Evidence of corruption later fueled bitter protests against him. Marcos's downfall finally came about as a result of his suspected involvement in the killing of the political opposition leader, Benigno Aquino, Jr.

A massive public outcry over the assassination forced new elections, which Marcos won by fraud. Popular outrage at his deceit forced Marcos to flee the country. **Corazon Aquino**, the widow of the assassinated opposition leader, became the new president.

President Corazon Aquino pledged to restore democracy to the Philippines under a new constitution in 1987. *What four groups opposed her rule?*

Hopes for reform faded, however, as Aquino faced opposition from Marcos supporters, the Huks, the military, and nationalists opposed to American military bases in the country. An attempt to overthrow Aquino failed due to American support. In the 1990s her successors, Fidel Ramos and later, Joseph Estrada, worked to promote economic growth and to reduce crime.

In 1992 the United States withdrew from its last military base in the Philippines. Although this was the desire of the Philippine government, the loss of revenue to the Philippine economy was substantial. Japan has since become the foreign country with the most economic influence in the Philippines.

Australia

Before World War II, **Australia** was a largely agricultural country dependent on Great Britain. Beef, wool, wheat, and dairy products were the country's main exports. Since 1945, Australia has changed to an industrial economy with close links to the United States and Asian countries. With the help of foreign investment, Australians have developed assembly and manufacturing plants for consumer goods, processed foods, paper, textiles, and transportation equipment.

Since the 1970s, Australia has strengthened ties with Japan and Southeast Asia. Today more than 60 percent of Australia's trade is with Asian countries. Meanwhile, Australia is gradually ending its links

to Great Britain and the monarchy. **Paul Keating**, who was prime minister in the early 1990s, pushed for the creation of an Australian republic by the year 2000.

Australia's shift from Great Britain to its Asian and Pacific neighbors has been influenced by the country's changing population. After World War II, large numbers of southern and eastern Europeans—Greeks, Italians, and Slavs—made new homes in Australia. Then, in the 1970s, the Australian government liberalized its immigration laws and allowed Asian immigrants into the country. Today, about 50 percent of immigrants to Australia each year come from neighboring Asian countries. By the 1990s, only about 35 percent of Australians were of British descent; this was down from 75 percent in 1949.

On the World Stage

Since World War II Australia has also sought a greater role in world affairs. It became a founding member of the United Nations in 1945. Five years later, Australian troops joined the UN forces fighting in the Korean War. In 1951 Australia signed the ANZUS treaty, which linked Australia, New Zealand, and the United States in a mutual defense pact. As part of the effort to contain communism, Australia sent forces to fight alongside the United States in the Vietnam War. It later backed the UN effort against Iraq in 1990 by sending Australian warships to the Persian Gulf.

Australians continue to support close military ties with the United States but are concerned about the presence of nuclear weapons in the Pacific region. Australia has been a major sponsor of a South Pacific Nuclear-Free Zone. Even so, it sided with the United States in the United States's dispute with New Zealand about American nuclear-armed vessels entering into New Zealand waters.

New Zealand

Consisting of two major islands and many small ones, **New Zealand** lies about 1,000 miles (1,600 km) to the southeast of Australia. Most of New Zealand's 3.5 million people are of British, other European, or Maori descent. Like Australia, New Zealand traditionally was joined by trade, politics, and culture to Great Britain. After World War II, it began to ally itself more closely with the United States and Asian countries.

New Zealand also added more variety to its economy. While agriculture—mainly sheep and dairy farming—remain important, New Zealand now has many manufacturing and service industries. It trades with Japan, Australia, the United States, and the countries of Western Europe.

Fear of Japanese attack during World War II made New Zealand turn to the United States for defense when the war was over. In 1951, New Zealand welcomed the creation of the ANZUS alliance and participated in the Korean and Vietnam conflicts.

Since the 1980s, however, New Zealand's opposition to nuclear weapons has strained its relationship with the United States and has drawn it closer to other Pacific countries that also oppose nuclear weapons. In 1985, New Zealand Prime Minister **David Lange** announced that ships carrying nuclear weapons, including those from the United States, could no longer enter New Zealand ports. In the early 1990s, Lange's successor as prime minister, **Jim Bolger**, worked to improve relations with the United States on the nuclear issue.

South Pacific Island Countries

Thousands of islands dot the Pacific Ocean. Many are small and uninhabited. Others were first settled thousands of years ago by various Asian and Pacific peoples. Their descendants today belong to three major groups: Melanesians, Micronesians, and Polynesians.

Nations and Colonies

Since World War II, some of the islands—such as Fiji—have become independent of Western rule. Other islands—such as Tahiti—continue to be held by Western powers as colonial territories valued for military reasons. France, for example, in 1995 conducted nuclear tests on an atoll, or ring-shaped coral island, in French Polynesia. French actions aroused antinuclear protests. The international outcry led to an early end of the tests.

Papua New Guinea

Among the larger island countries in the Pacific region is **Papua New Guinea**. Made up of 700 islands, Papua New Guinea has most of its territory on the eastern half of the island of New Guinea. Formerly held by Germany and Great Britain, and later by Australia, Papua New Guinea became independent in 1975.

Papua New Guinea faces many challenges in its efforts to achieve national unity. Its population is made up of many ethnic groups that speak nearly 700 different languages. Because of this ethnic diversity, Papua New Guinea has little sense of nationhood. Tensions and conflict between ethnic groups is common.

In addition, most of Papua New Guinea's people are poor and illiterate. Copper and gold mining has boosted the economy since the 1980s, but other economic sectors remain to be developed. The government of Papua New Guinea is working to interest companies in Japan, the United States, Hong Kong, and Singapore to invest in the country.

SECTION 6 REVIEW

Recall
1. **Define** archipelago.
2. **Identify** Ferdinand Marcos, Corazon Aquino, Paul Keating, ANZUS, David Lange, Jim Bolger.

3. **Explain** what events led to Marcos's downfall in the Philippines.

Critical Thinking
4. **Analyzing Information** How has the economy of Australia

changed since World War II?
Understanding Themes
5. **Cultural Diffusion** What cultural influences have affected the development of South Pacific island countries?

Using a Spreadsheet

Electronic spreadsheets can help people manage numbers quickly and easily. You can use a spreadsheet any time a problem involves numbers that can be arranged in rows and columns.

Learning the Skill

A spreadsheet is an electronic worksheet. All spreadsheets follow a basic design of rows and columns. Each *column* (vertical) is assigned a letter or number. Each *row* (horizontal) is assigned a number. Each point where a column and row intersect is called a *cell*. The cell's position on the spreadsheet is labeled according to its corresponding column and row—Column A, Row 1 (A1); Column B, Row 2 (B2); and so on.

Spreadsheets use *standard formulas* to calculate the numbers. You create a simple mathematical equation that uses these standard formulas and the computer does the calculations for you.

Practicing the Skill

Suppose you want to know the population densities (population per square mile) of the countries in South Asia. Use these steps to create a spreadsheet that will provide this information.

1. In cell A1 type *Country*, in cell B1 type *Population*, in cell C1 type *Land Area (square miles)*, and in cell D1 type *Population per square mile*.
2. In cells A2-A5 respectively, type one of the following country's name: *India*, *Pakistan*, *Bangladesh*, and *Sri Lanka*. In cell A6, type the words *Total for South Asia*.
3. In cells B2-B5, enter the population area of each country shown in cells A2-A5.
4. In cells C2-C5, enter the land area (square miles) of each country shown in cells A2-A5.
5. In cell D2, create a formula to calculate the population per square mile. The formula for the equation tells what cells (B1 ÷ C1) to divide. Copy this formula into cells D3-D5.

6. Use the process in step 5 to create and copy a formula to calculate the total population of South Asia (B2 + B3 + B4 + B5) for cell B6; to calculate the total Land Area of South Asia (C2 + C3 + C4 + C5) for cell C6.
7. Use the process in step 5 to create and copy a formula to calculate the population per square mile of South Asia (B6 ÷ C6) for cell D6.

Applying the Skill

Use a spreadsheet to enter your test scores and your homework grades. At the end of the grading period, the spreadsheet can calculate your average grade.

For More Practice

Turn to the Skill Practice in the Chapter Review on page 925 for more practice in using a spreadsheet.

Connections Across Time

Historical Significance The most dramatic change in Asia since 1945 is the dazzling economic achievements of Japan, South Korea, Hong Kong, Taiwan, and Singapore. In these nations, stable governments have worked with private companies to foster economic growth and high standards of living. Experts from around the world study Japan and other prosperous Asian countries to learn the reasons for their success.

Meanwhile, India and other Asian countries are developing their agriculture and industries. While the gap between rich and poor remains wide in many areas, standards of living are rising.

Using Key Terms

Write the key term that completes each sentence. Then write a sentence for each term not chosen.

a. referendum
b. stalemate
c. archipelago
d. refugee
e. quota
f. pragmatists
g. sect
h. special economic zones
i. domino theory
j. nonaligned
k. pollution
l. gross domestic product

1. In the 1960s the growing American role in Vietnam was justified by those who accepted the _____.
2. Jawaharlal Nehru believed if India and other less powerful countries remained _____ in the cold war, they could provide alternatives to the superpowers.
3. In China, a group known as _____ favored modernizing China through increased trade and contacts with the West.
4. The Chinese government has allowed foreign privately owned businesses to flourish in _____ located in southeastern China.
5. In a _____, voters are asked to accept or reject a measure.

Technology Activity

Using a Word Processor Locate sources about present-day North Korea and South Korea. Organize your findings by creating a fact sheet comparing the two countries. Use a word processor to create a chart. Headings to include are population, type of economy, GDP, type of government, currency, infant mortality rate, literacy rate, and official religion. Provide a map of each country that shows political boundaries, major cities, and natural resources.

Using Your History Journal

Imagine that you and your family have moved to an Asian country. Write a letter back to your friends in the United States about your experiences during the first year in your new country.

Reviewing Facts

1. **Culture** Identify examples of women who have been successful in Asian politics.
2. **Culture** Explain the role of the Dalai Lama.
3. **History** Discuss the policies of Mao Zedong and Deng Xiaoping, and describe their effects on the Chinese people.
4. **Citizenship** Identify examples of how human rights have advanced and how they have been violated in Asia since World War II.
5. **History** Identify the causes and outcome of the Korean War.
6. **History** Describe the impact of the Vietnam War on Southeast Asia and the United States.

Critical Thinking

1. **Apply** Using examples from Asia, explain whether a country's economic progress is related to its form of government.
2. **Analyze** What impact has Japan's recovery since World War II had on global affairs?
3. **Synthesize** Explain how events in Asia since 1945 have influenced the population profile of the people of the United States.
4. **Analyze** How do you think the return of Hong Kong to China will affect China and Hong Kong?

5. Analyze United States President Richard Nixon visited China in 1972. What historic change in United States policy did this visit signal?

Understanding Themes

1. **Change** What factors account for Japan's economic recovery and prosperity since World War II?
2. **Revolution** What changes did the Communist takeover of 1949 bring to China during the 1950s? How have policies changed since the 1970s?
3. **Regionalism** What basic reason keeps Korea divided into two nations?
4. **Conflict** How did the United States get involved in the war in Vietnam?
5. **Diversity** Why was India partitioned in 1947? Why did Pakistan later split into two separate nations?
6. **Cultural Diffusion** What new national and ethnic groups have come to once predominately British Australia as a result of changes in immigration since World War II?

Linking Past and Present

1. The era from about 1950 to the present and on into the twenty-first century has been called the Asian Century. Explain what name you would give to the 100 years prior to 1950.
2. The involvement by the United States in Vietnam was based on the domino theory and the Truman Doctrine, both of which declared the United States commitment to containing communism. What circumstances, if any, do you think would justify United States involvement overseas today?

Geography in History

1. **Region** Refer to the map on this page. What generalization describes the diverse economies of East Asia and the Pacific?
2. **Place** What nations make up the middle-income economies group?
3. **Region** What do the economies of Japan and Australia have in common according to the map?

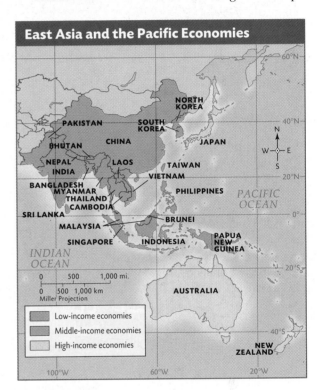

East Asia and the Pacific Economies

Low-income economies
Middle-income economies
High-income economies

Skill Practice

Look at the weather page in a newspaper or on the Internet. Choose a city in Asia or the Pacific that is listed in the weather report for international cities. Using an electronic spreadsheet over a 4-week period, note both the high and low temperature for each day. Insert an equation to calculate the average temperature for the first day. Copy the equation to calculate the average temperature for each day. Using your spreadsheet software, create a line graph showing the daily high, daily low, and the daily average temperature for this 4-week period.

Chapter Themes

▶ **Nationalism** European empires crumble, and independent nations emerge in Africa. *Section 1*

▶ **Change** Some African nations move toward democracy and free enterprise economies. *Section 2*

▶ **Change** Ethnic, cultural, environmental, and economic challenges face newly independent African nations. *Section 3*

The Storyteller

From April 26 to 29, 1994, South Africa held its first election in which all of its citizens, regardless of race, could vote. The outcome was a landslide victory for nationalist leader Nelson Mandela and his African National Congress party.

On May 10, during his inauguration as South Africa's first black president, Mandela declared, "The people of South Africa … want change…. Our plan is to create jobs, promote peace and reconciliation and to guarantee freedom for all South Africans." Mandela's rise to office signaled a joyous dawn of freedom after decades of white-minority rule and racial discrimination in South Africa.

By the 1990s nearly 700 million people in more than 50 African countries had thrown off various forms of colonial rule and were charting new courses as independent nations.

Historical Significance

What sweeping changes came to Africa after World War II? What role does Africa play in world affairs today?

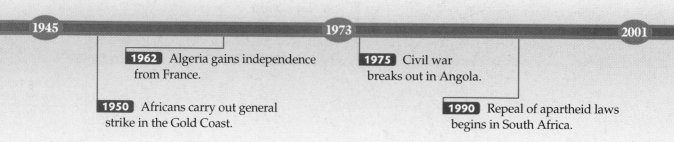

1945   1973   2001

1962 Algeria gains independence from France.

1950 Africans carry out general strike in the Gold Coast.

1975 Civil war breaks out in Angola.

1990 Repeal of apartheid laws begins in South Africa.

Children in Somalia, like this student, were doing their daily schoolwork in the midst of civil war, when United Nations troops arrived in 1992.

Your History Journal

Watch for current articles about African nations in newspapers and magazines. Clip and paste or write headlines and paraphrase short excerpts from these articles in your History Journal.

Section 1

African Independence

Setting the Scene

▶ **Terms to Define**
colons, general strike, apartheid

▶ **People to Meet**
Muammar al-Qaddafi, Kwame Nkrumah, Ahmed Sékou Touré, Jomo Kenyatta, Nelson Mandela, Desmond Tutu

▶ **Places to Locate**
Sudan, Algeria, Ghana, Nigeria, Congo (Zaire), Kenya, Angola, Mozambique, Malawi, Zambia, Zimbabwe, South Africa

 How did African nations win their independence after World War II?

The Storyteller

Meeting in an open field at Kliptown, South Africa, 3,000 delegates adopted the Freedom Charter in 1955. The Charter held out hope for a democratic nation: "We the people of South Africa, declare for all our country and the world to know: that South Africa belongs to all who live in it, black and white, and that no government can claim authority unless it is based on the will of all the people ... that our country will never be prosperous and free until all people live in brotherhood, enjoying equal rights and opportunities."

—from *South Africa, Challenge and Hope,* American Friends Service Committee, Lyle Tatum, editor, 1987

First free election in South Africa

After World War II, the desire for liberation that found expression in Asia also spread to Africa. On the vast African continent in 1945, only Egypt, Ethiopia, and Liberia were independent states. South Africa, although independent, was governed by a white minority that withheld freedom from most of the country's population. In other areas, Great Britain, France, Portugal, Spain, and Belgium still exercised direct colonial rule.

By the mid-1960s, these European countries had freed most of their African colonies. The southern part of Africa remained the only area of the continent where liberation movements encountered obstacles—in this case, from sizable European settler populations. The path to independence in Africa was often bloody, and once free, the new nations faced the enormous task of building modern societies.

POINT

A Changing Africa

Since the beginning of the colonial era, nationalist groups in Africa had resisted European rule, often violently. But following World War II, these relatively small efforts for freedom swelled into powerful mass movements.

Opposition to Empire

The democratic ideals for which the Allies fought in the war—self-rule and freedom from tyranny—inspired Africans, many of whom had fought in the Allied armies. "[We] overseas soldiers are coming back home with new ideas," wrote Nigerian Theo Ayoola, stationed with British troops in India. "We have been told what we fought for. That is freedom! We want freedom, nothing but freedom!"

Many people throughout the world were recognizing the hypocrisy and injustice of European nations continuing to rule African populations while professing democratic values. In addition to the moral argument against colonialism, European nations faced political and economic changes that made it impractical to retain their African possessions. The European continent itself was devastated by World War II, and debt-ridden Europeans could scarcely afford to maintain empires abroad. Even so, the imperial nations of Europe as a matter of pride clung stubbornly to the idea of empire, making the inevitable changes more painful.

African Nationalism

What European imperial nations did not recognize were the changes occurring throughout Africa. In many colonies, nationalism was growing among the European-educated African elite who worked in colonial governments and in businesses. In the late 1940s, leaders emerged among this group, and rallied support for African independence.

Nationalist leaders found a ready audience for their ideas among workers in the fields, mines, and factories owned by overseas investors. World demand for African minerals and crops boomed after World War II, but Africa's European-owned industries appropriated the profits. Africans saw little change in their conditions, and their resentment of foreign rule grew.

North Africa

The movement for independence from European rule saw its first successes in North Africa. Italy ruled Libya, a large country west of Egypt, under a UN trusteeship. France owned colonial possessions—Tunisia, Algeria, and Morocco—in the rest of North Africa. All of the territories of North

Africa were Muslim and shared in a common Arab culture.

The only exception was **Sudan**—ruled jointly by Great Britain and Egypt—which had a large non-Muslim African population in its southern part. Sudan eventually became independent in 1956.

Libya

In 1951, Libya, once an Italian colony, became an independent monarchy. The discovery of oil in Libya in 1959 transformed the country from a poor, desert nation into one of the wealthiest in the world. Widespread discontent against the monarchy and the ruling class owning the oil wealth led to a military takeover in 1969 under Colonel **Muammar al-Qaddafi** (kuh•DAH•fee). Qaddafi established a socialist government to redistribute the national wealth. He also sought to spread his radical brand of nationalism to other parts of Africa and the Arab world.

African Independence

Map with dates of African independence.

MOROCCO 1956
TUNISIA 1956
ALGERIA 1962
LIBYA 1951
EGYPT 1922
Western Sahara (Disputed Territory)
MAURITANIA 1960
SENEGAL 1960
GAMBIA 1965
MALI 1960
BURKINA FASO 1960
NIGER 1960
CHAD 1960
SUDAN 1956
ERITREA 1993
DJIBOUTI 1977
GUINEA-BISSAU 1974
GUINEA 1958
BENIN 1960
TOGO 1960
GHANA 1957
NIGERIA 1960
CENTRAL AFRICAN REPUBLIC 1960
ETHIOPIA*
SIERRA LEONE 1961
CÔTE D'IVOIRE 1960
CAMEROON 1960
SOMALIA 1960
LIBERIA 1847
EQUATORIAL GUINEA 1968
GABON 1960
CONGO 1960
RWANDA 1962
UGANDA 1962
KENYA 1963
SÃO TOMÉ AND PRÍNCIPE 1975
DEMOCRATIC REPUBLIC OF THE CONGO 1960
BURUNDI 1962
TANZANIA 1961
SEYCHELLES 1976
Cabinda (Angola)
MALAWI 1964
COMOROS 1975
ANGOLA 1975
ZAMBIA 1964
MOZAMBIQUE 1975
MADAGASCAR 1960
ZIMBABWE 1980
NAMIBIA 1990
BOTSWANA 1966
MAURITIUS 1968
SWAZILAND 1968
SOUTH AFRICA 1931
LESOTHO 1966
CAPE VERDE 1975

*Ethiopia was invaded by Italy in 1935 but regained independence in 1941.

Map Study Between 1951 and 1993 more than 50 African colonies achieved independence.
Place What four African nations were independent before 1950?

Michael Kirtley

Africa and Independence

This mother in Banjul, capital of The Gambia, combines something old and something new. She wears a traditional West African dress stamped with the colors of Africa: red, black, yellow, and green. Printed on the fabric is a portrait of two of Africa's independence leaders. On the left is Sir Dawda Jawara, who led The Gambia to independence in 1965. He remained president until 1994, when Captain Yahya Ajj Jammeh took power. On the right is President Abdou Diouf, who succeeded Senegal's great independence leader Léopold Sédar Senghor in 1981.

Keeping local traditions and languages—the pride in being African—while discarding the years of colonial rule and white supremacy became the task of the new leaders of West Africa. Where once there were 3 colonial empires, today there are 14 sovereign states in the region.

Independence from France, Great Britain, and Portugal was won peacefully. The task that now remains is to create and to sustain expanding economies. This is the hope of all West Africans, including this young mother and her children on Perseverance Street in The Gambia's capital. ⊕

Algeria

The French colonies of Morocco, Tunisia, and Algeria also wanted independence. France reluctantly granted independence to Morocco and Tunisia in 1956, but refused to do so in the case of Algeria.

Freedom for **Algeria** came only after one of the most costly wars in African colonial history. French settlers, called colons, had been coming to Algeria since the 1830s. By 1940 nearly 1 million colons had taken the best land and jobs in Algeria, ignoring the needs of 9 million Muslim Algerians.

Backed by Egypt, Morocco, and Tunisia, Algerian guerrilla fighters launched a war for independence in 1954. In response to guerrilla raids, French troops destroyed Algerian property, herded people into concentration camps, and used helicopters and heavy artillery to hunt down the rebels.

Despite French firepower, the guerrillas fought on. The controversial war forced the collapse of France's government, the Fourth Republic. After General Charles de Gaulle became president in May 1958, he promised self-determination for Algeria. Despite fierce resistance from the colons, de Gaulle arranged talks with the rebels that led to independence on July 3, 1962. The price of freedom had been eight years of warfare and more than 1 million deaths.

Ghana

In Africa south of the Sahara, mass independence movements pressured the colonial powers to relinquish control. Great Britain's richest colony, the Gold Coast, traveled a relatively easy road to independence, raising the hopes of other African nations for a smooth transition.

Before World War II ended, the British had begun to give the Africans of the Gold Coast more political rights. By then, well-educated African leaders had organized an independence movement. In 1947 the group asked the political activist **Kwame Nkrumah** (kwah•may ehn•KROO•muh) to lead them. Three years later, Nkrumah led a general strike, in which a large number of workers pressured the British for independence.

For his role in the strike, Nkrumah was jailed, but his efforts were effective. He soon moved from his jail cell to head a new government. In 1957 the

Visualizing History Kwame Nkrumah celebrates independence. Ten years of struggle had won freedom for Ghana and inspired other African nations to form national movements. *What led to Nkrumah's loss of power in Ghana?*

Gold Coast, now renamed **Ghana**, became the first African nation south of the Sahara to gain full independence after World War II.

The Nkrumah years came to represent the best and the worst in African leadership after independence. Ghana got off to a strong start, exporting cocoa, gold, and diamonds. It also had a skilled labor force. The Nkrumah government, however, mismanaged the economy. After Nkrumah was ousted by the army in 1966, one regime after another ruled Ghana, forcing the nation into a slow decline.

Guinea

Nationalist movements also took hold in France's African colonies south of the Sahara. Seeking to head off another "Algeria-like" conflict, France's President de Gaulle in 1958 proposed the creation of a French Community. Under this plan, France's African colonies south of the Sahara could choose to remain linked to France, with their foreign and economic policies under French control. The other option was for them to become completely

Crowds in eastern Nigeria celebrate Nigeria's independence in 1960 with a folk-dancing and sports festival. *Why was the path to Nigerian independence easier than that of other African countries?*

independent—with no economic support from France.

Only Guinea (GIH•nee) under its nationalist leader, **Ahmed Sékou Touré** (ah•MEHD SEH•koo TOO•ray), wanted full independence. De Gaulle swiftly ordered all French officials out of Guinea and vowed not to help the new nation. The Soviet Union, however, promised aid to the new nation.

In a world dominated by the cold war, Sékou Touré's link to the Soviets angered de Gaulle, who feared that other African colonies would follow suit. To prevent this, France gave its remaining African colonies independence in 1960, this time with French help.

Nigeria

In the West African country of **Nigeria**, Africa's most populous nation, few Europeans had settled during the period of British colonial rule. The path to independence was therefore easier there than in the colonies that had sizable European minorities. With little resistance, the Nigerians won independence from Great Britain in 1960. Creating

a stable democratic nation was far more difficult, however.

Because Nigeria was contained within old colonial boundaries, the country's population consisted of 250 ethnic groups speaking 395 languages, as well as 3 major religious groups. Muslims dominated the north, followers of traditional African religions the east, and Christians the west. From 1960 to 1965, first one group, then another seized control of the central government.

By the mid-1960s, ethnic conflict drove the Ibo to set up the independent Republic of Biafra in the eastern part of Nigeria. After the creation of Biafra, civil war ravaged Nigeria for three years, killing more than 600,000. About 2 million Biafrans died of hunger as a result of the fighting. Biafra surrendered in January 1970. The Nigerian government then turned to rebuilding the country, developing the nation's rich oil reserves.

Congo

By the late 1950s the vast Belgian Congo in central Africa was ready for change. Belgian authorities, however, responded slowly to the independence movement and imprisoned nationalist leaders who demanded radical changes. Following riots in 1959, however, Belgium hastily granted independence in June 1960. The new country was called **Congo**. In the 1970s, it became known as **Zaire**.

Civil war broke out in Congo following independence between rival political groups and different regions. The rich copper-mining province of Katanga (now the Shaba region) seceded from the new nation in July 1960. UN peacekeeping forces arrived in Congo to prevent the superpowers from becoming involved. After settling differences with the central government, Katanga finally returned to Congolese rule, and UN forces withdrew in 1964. However, conflicts among rival political and ethnic groups continued to divide the country. Not until General Joseph D. Mobutu became dictator in 1965 was order restored.

East Africa

After World War II, nationalism also swept the East African countries of Uganda, Tanzania, and Kenya, all ruled by Great Britain. Uganda, which won independence in 1962, fell prey to ethnic conflicts and brutal military dictatorship.

By contrast, Tanzania, independent in 1961, developed a stable government that followed socialist principles. **Kenya**, however, attracted considerable global attention because of a combination of unique geographic and political characteristics.

Under British colonial rule, Kenya was dominated by European settlers who held control of the fertile highlands of central Kenya. The Kikuyu, the local African ethnic group, regarded this region as their homeland. Moreover, the Europeans banned all Africans from owning land. This discrimination fanned the flames of nationalism in Kenya.

During the postwar period, the nationalist leader **Jomo Kenyatta**, who had been living in Great Britain, brought his battle for independence home to Kenya. By this time, nationalist feelings in Kenya had become intense. A political movement for independence—the Kenya African Union—was formed, and it chose Kenyatta as its president in 1947.

Meanwhile, some Kenyans had formed an underground freedom movement, which the Europeans called the Mau Mau. The movement sought to unite Kenya's many African ethnic groups against British rule. In the early 1950s, it carried out attacks on European settlers, and the British government took military action against the movement. British authorities jailed thousands of nationalists, including Kenyatta, whom they accused of leading the rebellion. By 1956, the uprising had been crushed, but calls for freedom continued. The British finally granted Kenya its independence in 1963.

Kenyatta was elected Kenya's first president in 1964 and held office until 1978. He maintained a free market economy and made Kenya a popular spot for tourists and international businesses.

Angola and Mozambique

Portugal ruled the southern African countries of **Angola** and **Mozambique** with an iron hand. The Portuguese, governed by a dictatorship at home, refused to listen to nationalist demands and created conditions for brutal uprisings.

Starting in 1961 in Angola and 1964 in Mozambique, rebel groups waged guerrilla wars against Portugal. For over a decade, Portuguese troops were able to suppress the guerrillas. In 1974, however, Portugal itself underwent a revolution that overthrew the dictatorship. The new democratic Portuguese government, facing many problems at home, freed Angola and Mozambique in 1975. Both African countries eventually came under Marxist governments that took complete control of their economies.

Malawi, Zambia, and Zimbabwe

Throughout the late 1950s and early 1960s, Great Britain slowly gave up control of its other African colonies. In 1964, Nyasaland became **Malawi** (mah•LAH•wee), and Northern Rhodesia became **Zambia**. The future, however, remained uncertain for Rhodesia, with 4 million Africans and 250,000 Europeans.

As European Rhodesians saw new African nations coming into existence in the 1960s, they formed a party called the Rhodesian Front. Two years later, the Front took control of Rhodesian politics to keep Africans from gaining power.

Great Britain opposed the Front's goals and asked that Africans be given a greater share of political power. White Rhodesians were enraged. In 1965 Rhodesian Prime Minister Ian Smith declared Rhodesia independent. Although most of the world refused to recognize or trade with Rhodesia, the country did get support from South Africa, where a white minority also ruled.

In the 1970s, bands of guerrilla fighters began attacking Rhodesia's Europeans. European settlers began to flee, and the nation's economy was disrupted. In 1979 Smith agreed to negotiate with the African majority, and in 1980, Rhodesia—renamed **Zimbabwe**—won its freedom.

South Africa

After World War II, independent **South Africa** was governed by a white minority—most of British and Afrikaner descent—that denied basic freedoms to other minorities and the majority African population. British and pro-British Afrikaner South Africans controlled the government until elections in 1948 brought to power the nationalist Afrikaners. The nationalist Afrikaner government opposed

Footnotes to History

The Great Zimbabwe Once winning freedom, many African nations took new names with great meaning for their people. Zimbabwe, for example, refers to the 1,000-year-old city of Great Zimbabwe. Massive, protective stone walls gave the city its name—*zimbabwe*—which means "stone enclosure."

Smoke rises from a burning tanker, set aflame by rioting students in Soweto, outside Johannesburg, South Africa. *What conditions in Soweto led to student protests and riots?*

South Africa's remaining ties to Great Britain and had a strong belief in its divine right to rule the country. Committed to white supremacy, the nationalist Afrikaners legalized and strengthened a policy of racial separation between blacks and whites called apartheid.

Enforcement of Apartheid

Under apartheid—meaning "apartness"—white, black, and mixed races were strictly segregated. Black South Africans suffered the worst under this legalized segregation. Apartheid laws defined whom blacks could marry and where they could travel, eat, and go to school. Blacks could not vote or own property. To enforce separation of the races, the government moved thousands of blacks to desolate rural areas that it called "homelands," where jobs and food were scarce. Those who were able to get low-paying jobs in the cities were forced to live in wretched, fenced-in townships like Soweto, on the outskirts of Johannesburg. Blacks had to carry identity cards at all times. Under the repressive police state, blacks could be jailed indefinitely without cause.

African Resistance

Black nationalist groups, such as the African National Congress (ANC), peacefully demanded reforms, but the government moved against the resistance. By the 1960s ANC leader **Nelson Mandela** was leading a military operation to press for change. In 1962 he was jailed on charges of treason, becoming a symbol of the struggle for freedom in South Africa.

International criticism of apartheid led to South Africa's increasing political isolation from the 1960s to the 1980s. South Africa, for example, was not welcome in the Commonwealth of Nations, the United Nations, and the Olympics. Many nations eventually imposed sanctions on South Africa, moves designed to hurt South Africa's economy. Within South Africa itself, massive protests developed after police fired on a student march in the black township of Soweto in 1976. During the 1980s, Archbishop **Desmond Tutu**, the head of South Africa's Anglican Church, emerged as a major advocate of nonviolence and interracial reconciliation in the struggle against apartheid. In 1984 he was awarded the Nobel Peace Prize.

SECTION I REVIEW

Recall

1. **Define** colon, general strike, apartheid.
2. **Identify** Muammar al-Qaddafi, Kwame Nkrumah, Ahmed Sékou Touré, Jomo Kenyatta, Nelson Mandela, Desmond Tutu.

3. **Explain** How did Ghana serve as a model for nationalists in other African countries?

Critical Thinking

4. **Applying Information** How did the presence of large populations of European descent in Algeria, Kenya, Zimbabwe, and South Africa affect African nationalist movements?

Understanding Themes

5. **Nationalism** What impact did nationalist movements have on Africa after World War II?

1970   1980   1990   2000

1978 Daniel T. arap Moi becomes president of Kenya.

1994 African National Congress wins South Africa's first open, multiracial elections.

Section 2

Africa Today

Setting the Scene

▶ **Terms to Define**
genocide, clan

▶ **People to Meet**
Muammar al-Qaddafi, Mobutu Sese Seko, Daniel T. arap Moi, F.W. de Klerk, Nelson Mandela

▶ **Places to Locate**
Namibia, Eritrea, Libya, Democratic Republic of the Congo, Rwanda, Burundi, Somalia

Find Out What kinds of governments ruled in Africa from the 1970s to the 1990s?

The Storyteller

Fidele Nshogoza had been monitoring gorillas for 18 years. In the gorilla parks of the Virunga volcano range of east central Africa, he worked to prevent war and poaching from wiping out the animals he loved. "Gorillas are better than us," he explained. "They are peaceful. They have no tribes. When they fight it is for good reason." Fidele knew the horror of warfare. An ethnic Hutu, he fled over the volcanoes after the 1994 Tutsi victory. Two of his children almost died in a refugee camp—one of seven huge camps in Zaire [now the Democratic Republic of the Congo] that sheltered more than 700,000 ethnic Hutu.

Hutu children in a refugee camp

—adapted from "Gorillas and Humans: An Uneasy Truce," by Paul F. Salopek in *National Geographic*, October 1995.

By the late 1990s, Africa had experienced both setbacks and gains. Beginning in the early 1980s, devastating droughts ravaged large areas of the continent. The ups and downs of the world economy as well as political and ethnic conflict also negatively affected African nations.

Still there were reasons for celebration. Since the late 1970s, three new nations had emerged—Zimbabwe and **Namibia** in southern Africa (1980 and 1990), and **Eritrea** in the northeastern part of the continent (1993). Progress also was made in settling some of the civil wars that ravaged the continent. The most remarkable achievement was the dismantling of apartheid in the Republic of South Africa.

North Africa

The 1980s and 1990s saw widespread economic and political unrest in the North African countries of Algeria, Morocco, and Tunisia. A soaring population and increased industrialization led to the growth of the cities. Urban growth rates were further heightened as people from the countryside crowded into urban areas in hope of finding food, shelter, and work. When governments proved unable to provide decent housing and steady jobs, many people turned to a strict practice of Islam or to radical political movements in an effort to solve their problems.

Algeria

The greatest challenge to established government in the region took place in Algeria. In a free election in 1992, the people of Algeria elected to the national legislature a majority of members who favored greater recognition of Islamic laws and values. The more moderate government, however, ignored the election results and dissolved the legislature. Military leaders then took control of Algeria.

Chapter 34 *Africa* **935**

They banned the Islamic movement and arrested many of its members.

Armed conflict soon developed between the government and the Islamic opposition. By 1997, the unrest had claimed more than 60,000 lives. That year, the government claimed victory in a legislative election, but opposition groups questioned the election's fairness. Meanwhile, conflict continued to rage between government forces and the Islamic guerrillas.

Libya

During the 1980s, Colonel **Muammar al-Qaddafi** of **Libya** aroused great resentment among Western countries because of his foreign policy. The United States, accusing Qaddafi of aiding international terrorists, broke economic ties with Libya in 1986. Qaddafi in turn charged the United States with attempting to overthrow his government. Military encounters in the air between aircraft of the two countries were accompanied by United States bombing of Libyan military installations. Since the mid-1980s, declining oil revenue and a worsening Libyan economy have prompted Qaddafi to improve his relations with neighboring countries. Libya's suspected involvement with terrorist bombings of civilian airlines, however, has kept Libya isolated from the international community.

Nigeria

After independence, Nigeria and other nations in West Africa faced political conflicts and economic hardships. Some relied on military leaders or one-party systems to maintain order. By the late 1980s, a trend toward democracy and stability had emerged in the region. However, in the 1990s, some countries, such as Liberia and Sierra Leone, were torn by fierce conflicts between rival political and military groups.

Nigeria, the most populous West African country, continued to remain under military rule. After the Biafran war of the 1960s, Nigeria's military

Images *of the* Times

Toward a New Africa

Beyond independence, African nations work to promote economic growth, while preserving cultural traditions and developing democracy.

An earth satellite station 30 miles (48 km) from Nairobi, Kenya, signals Africa's connection to the telecommunications revolution.

leaders worked to rebuild the country. They relied on oil for the country's economic prosperity. As oil prices rose in the 1970s, Nigeria grew wealthy. Its military leaders set as their goals industrial development, new schools, improved transportation, and development programs to raise the standard of living of all Nigerians.

Hopes for progress, however, were dashed by instability in the global oil market and government mismanagement of the economy. During the 1980s and 1990s, pro-democracy groups called for an end to military rule. Although promising to work for reform, Nigeria's military rulers instead ignored election results and cracked down on their opponents. In 1997, they even brought treason charges against exiled writer Wole Soyinka, winner of the Nobel Prize for Literature.

The international community responded by imposing economic sanctions on Nigeria. When a new military leadership in 1998 released some political prisoners, many Nigerians hoped that democratic reforms would follow.

Democratic Republic of the Congo

From the 1970s to the 1990s Congo continued under the rule of Mobutu, who took the name **Mobutu Sese Seko** and changed the country's name to Zaire. During his rule, copper prices rose and fell, bringing a boom and then a decline to Zaire's economy. Meanwhile, Mobutu ruled as a dictator, stole from the country's resources, and banned rival political groups.

Angered by Mobutu's misrule, guerrilla forces led by Laurent Kabila began a rebellion in late 1996. During the next several months, they took control of most of Zaire with little opposition from demoralized government forces. In May 1997, Mobutu gave up power and fled abroad. Kabila's forces then entered the capital, Kinshasa, where he named himself the new leader and changed the country's name to the **Democratic Republic of the Congo**. Kabila promised eventual elections, but his com-

Modern office buildings rise above a newly built monument and public garden in Pretoria, South Africa.

Tea pickers toil on a plantation in Kenya. Tea is one of Kenya's chief cash crops and a major export.

REFLECTING ON THE TIMES

1. In what ways could the connection to global telecommunications affect African economies? Cultural traditions?
2. Why are export products key to economic development?

937

Visualizing History South African President Nelson Mandela arrives in Paris, France, on a 1996 state visit with French President Jacques Chirac. *What event in 1994 was a turning point in South Africa's history?*

mitment to democracy was questioned when he banned political parties.

East Africa

In East Africa, ethnic unrest tore apart the inland countries of **Rwanda** and **Burundi**. Some countries in the region, however, enjoyed political stability. Uganda, after a period of harsh rule in the 1970s under dictator Idi Amin, moved toward a one-party system that at the same time encouraged free enterprise. Uganda's southern neighbor, Tanzania, combined a tradition of stable government with socialism. Economic difficulties in the 1990s, however, moved Tanzania toward free enterprise.

Kenya

From the early 1960s to the late 1970s, Kenya enjoyed political stability and economic prosperity under a one-party system. After President Kenyatta's death in 1978, **Daniel T. arap Moi** became the leader. In the 1980s Moi dealt harshly with political opponents wanting a multiparty system. A decade later, he allowed a multiparty election in which he won endorsement. However, critics charged that the elections were not free or fair. In 1997 a powerful reform movement led by opposition politicians, human rights activists, and Christian and Muslim religious leaders pressured Moi to carry out genuine democratic reforms. At the same time, European governments threatened to cut aid to Kenya if Moi resisted change.

Rwanda and Burundi

During the 1990s, ethnic tensions in Rwanda and Burundi led to violent conflict. Most people in Rwanda and Burundi belong to the Hutu and the Tutsi ethnic groups. The Hutu are the largest group in both countries. Under Belgian colonial rule, the Tutsi were favored over the Hutu. Since the independence of Rwanda and Burundi in 1962, the Hutu have worked to regain power.

In 1994 the Hutu-led Rwandan government battled Tutsi-led guerrillas. In a genocide, or the deliberate killing of a racial or cultural group, Hutu forces killed some 500,000 people, mostly Tutsi, before the Tutsi guerrillas declared victory. Another 2 million people fled Rwanda and settled in camps on the border of Zaire and neighboring countries.

In 1996, conflict broke out in Burundi between the Tutsi-led government and Hutu rebels. Meanwhile, about 1.2 million Rwandan Hutu refugees in eastern Zaire faced mass starvation as ethnic and political conflict erupted in that country. A human catastrophe was avoided when hundreds of thousands of refugees voluntarily returned to Rwanda. In early 1997, tribunals in Tanzania and Rwanda began bringing to justice people accused of participating in the 1994 genocide.

Ethiopia and Somalia

In Ethiopia, military leaders in 1974 ousted the ancient monarchy of Emperor Haile Selassie I and replaced it with a Marxist dictatorship. While implementing land reforms, the new government persecuted and killed many of its opponents. These policies led to civil war. Movements for independence arose in the regions of Tigre and Eritrea.

By the early 1990s, widespread suffering caused by drought and civil war led to the fall of the military dictatorship. In 1991, rebel forces took control of the government and moved Ethiopia onto the path toward democracy. As a result of their victory, Eritrea became independent in 1993.

Drought and civil war also ravaged Ethiopia's neighbor, **Somalia**. There, in the 1980s, rival clans, or groups of people related to one another, fought for control of the government. When a drought struck a few years later, many Somalis starved. Other countries sent food, but the fierce fighting kept much of it from reaching the starving.

In 1992, a UN-sponsored coalition of military forces led by the United States arrived in Somalia to protect relief organizations that were distributing food to needy Somalis. A year later, UN forces replaced most of the coalition troops. Tensions heightened when fighting broke out between the UN soldiers and the forces of one of the Somali clan leaders. By 1995, foreign troops, including United States forces, had withdrawn from Somalia after the worst of the famine had ended, and rival clan leaders had signed a peace settlement. Continued fighting, however, delayed progress toward stability.

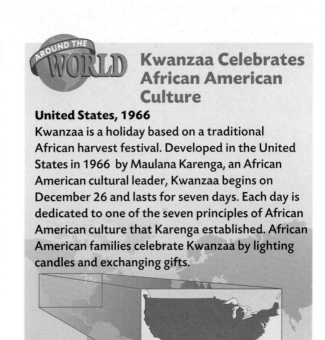

Kwanzaa Celebrates African American Culture

United States, 1966

Kwanzaa is a holiday based on a traditional African harvest festival. Developed in the United States in 1966 by Maulana Karenga, an African American cultural leader, Kwanzaa begins on December 26 and lasts for seven days. Each day is dedicated to one of the seven principles of African American culture that Karenga established. African American families celebrate Kwanzaa by lighting candles and exchanging gifts.

South Africa

From the 1970s to the 1990s, South Africa and its neighbors Mozambique, Angola, and Zimbabwe experienced many sweeping changes. After a period of civil wars between Marxist and non-Marxist groups, Mozambique, Angola, and Zimbabwe moved toward peace and gradually abandoned socialism for free enterprise.

In South Africa, mounting pressure from the antiapartheid movement and from foreign countries brought a gradual end to apartheid. During the 1980s, the white-dominated South African government lifted the ban on interracial marriage, and the nation's sizable population of Asian and mixed-race people won voting rights.

In February 1990, South African President **F. W. de Klerk** surprised the world by releasing the black nationalist leader **Nelson Mandela** from prison. During the next few years, the South African government repealed the remaining apartheid laws. Talks began in 1992 between white and black political groups that paved the way for a constitution, ending apartheid, and granting political equality to all South Africans regardless of race. A year later, black South Africans won full voting rights.

In April 1994, South Africa held its first election open to all races. The African National Congress won nearly two-thirds of the seats in the national legislature, and the legislature then elected Nelson Mandela president. Mandela recognized the importance of reconciling racial and ethnic groups and bridging the social and economic gap that separated white and nonwhite South Africans. He faced the challenge of raising the standard of living of disadvantaged South Africans while maintaining economic growth.

In 1997 South Africa began to prepare for a transition of power from Mandela to his successor. The likely person to become president of South Africa after the 1999 general election is the current deputy president, Thabo Mbeki.

SECTION 2 REVIEW

Recall
1. **Define** genocide, clan.
2. **Identify** Muammar al-Qaddafi, Mobutu Sese Seko, Daniel T. arap Moi, F.W. de Klerk, Nelson Mandela.
3. **State** the causes and effects of the civil war in Rwanda.

Critical Thinking
4. **Synthesize** If you were a citizen of South Africa today, how would you describe recent changes there?

Understanding Themes
5. **Change** What worldwide factors do you think account for the recent trend toward democracy in Africa?

Writing a Research Report

Writing a research report is similar to most other complex tasks. There are tools to use, skills to master, and steps to follow.

Learning the Skill

Select a topic that interests you. Brainstorming, skimming books and magazines, and talking with classmates can help.

Do preliminary research to determine whether your topic is too broad or too specific. Suppose you've chosen "Problems Facing Africa Today." The library's computers list more than 100 books on this topic. A more manageable topic might be: "Environmental Problems in the Sahara."

As early as possible, write a statement defining what you want to prove, discover, or illustrate in your report. For this topic, your statement might be: "Deforestation is the greatest environmental threat to North Africa."

- **Prepare to do research**. Formulate a list of main idea questions.
- **Research your topic and take notes**. At the library, use the computerized referral service to find suitable research sources. Note cards are a great tool for preparing a research report. They let you record and combine related facts and ideas from several sources. Prepare note cards on each main idea question listing the source information. Keep all the facts for each main idea together.
- **Organize your information**. Build an outline or another kind of organizer. Follow your outline or organizer in writing a rough draft.
- **Write a rough draft**. A research report should have three main parts: the introduction, the body, and the conclusion. The introduction briefly presents the topic and gives your thesis statement. In the body, follow your outline to develop the important ideas in your argument. Connect

these ideas with transitions. The conclusion summarizes and restates your findings.

In writing the rough draft write as quickly as possible without editing. Imagine that you are explaining your findings and ideas to an interested listener.

Revise the draft into a final report. Put it away for a day or so; then reread it with the cold, clear eye of an editor. Does the report have a clear structure—an introduction, a body, and a conclusion? Does the body contain all the main ideas arranged logically? Are there transitions to lead the reader from one thought to the next? If not, revise it and repeat the writing process. Correct spelling, punctuation, and grammar. Finally, make a clean copy.

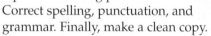

Practicing the Skill

Suppose you are writing a report on recent changes in South Africa. Answer the following questions about the writing process.

1. How could you narrow this topic?
2. What are three main idea questions to use?
3. Name three possible sources of information.
4. What are the next two steps in the process of writing a research report?

Applying the Skill

Choose a topic and prepare note cards. Continue your research on this topic, organize your information, and write a short report.

For More Practice

Turn to the Skill Practice in the Chapter Review on page 947 for more practice in writing a research report.

1963 African nations form Organization of African Unity (OAU).

1980s Famine ravages Ethiopia, Somalia, and other areas of Africa.

1990s A trend develops in Africa toward democracy and free enterprise.

Section 3

Africa's Challenge

Setting the Scene

▶ **Terms to Define**
Pan-Africanism, cash crop, subsistence farmer, desertification, literacy rate, negritude

▶ **People to Meet**
Kofi Annan, Léopold Sédar Senghor

▶ **Places to Locate**
the Sahel

**ind Out** What challenges have modern African nations faced in their quest for political and economic development?

The Storyteller

The Sahara has its own voices. The abrupt changes from darkness to daylight are often accompanied by the shattering of the desert rocks, with a grating sound or a loud noise. Even the sand dunes talk: wind or even the pressure of a human foot will cause shocks and tremblings; then the countless grains of sand, rubbing gently together, will make a strange snoring noise.

According to legend, these mysterious noises are the bursts of laughter of a genie named Rul—the bad angel of strayed travelers. When the wanderer has lost his way, when fatigue and thirst begin to confuse the mind, then the traveler is tormented by "the laughter of Rul."

—adapted from *Sahara, the Great Desert*, Emile Felix Gautier, 1935

Desert oasis

African nations have seen enormous changes in less than half a century. In that short time, a largely rural continent has become increasingly urban, with ties to all parts of the globe. By the mid-1990s, African economies were growing at an average rate of nearly 5 percent, faster than for two decades. Africa also has become an international force, wielding more than a third of the votes in the United Nations General Assembly. In 1997 **Kofi Annan**, a career diplomat from the West African nation of Ghana, became secretary-general of the United Nations. He was the first African from south of the Sahara to serve in the post.

Search for Unity

After the excitement of independence celebrations had passed, Africa's new nations entered a difficult period. Many of them adopted the political borders that had been drawn by the colonial powers. These boundaries divided people with similar customs and faiths. Old ruling families and ethnic groups began to struggle for power, and civil wars often erupted.

National Unity

African politicians and parliaments were unable to stop the violence that sprang from these ethnic divisions. At first, many leaders in Africa governed through political systems inherited from their colonial predecessors—systems that were unfamiliar to many Africans. Often these systems did not work for African countries in the postindependence years. All too often, a nation's most powerful group, the military, stepped in to restore order.

By the 1970s, military leaders or one-party dictatorships ruled about half of Africa's newly freed nations. In some, like Nigeria, dividing strong regional groups into smaller states helped to break down some regional rivalry. By the late 1980s, however, military rule and one-party political systems

The Kenyatta Conference Center, named after Jomo Kenyatta—Kenya's first president, reflects the rapid growth and modernity of Nairobi, Kenya's capital. Founded in the late 1890s as a small railway settlement, Nairobi today is a busy metropolis of more than 1.5 million people. *What major goal has been set by the Organization of African Unity?*

had failed to fulfill their promises of order and economic progress. They were in decline in certain countries of Africa. Meanwhile, the end of the cold war and the collapse of the Soviet Union discredited the socialist economic model once popular among many African leaders. By the mid-1990s, some African countries had adopted multiparty systems and free enterprise approaches to economic development.

Pan-Africanism

Through a movement called Pan-Africanism, African leaders have sought to promote cooperation among all nations of the continent. In 1963, 32 African nations formed the Organization of African Unity (OAU) in Addis Ababa, Ethiopia. Although the original vision of creating a United States of Africa failed, the OAU did help to build a strong African identity and to coordinate national defense, health, and other policies.

Since its founding, the OAU has increased its influence in African and global affairs. During the 1970s and 1980s, member nations of the OAU pledged to remain neutral in cold war politics. To rid Africa of colonialism, the OAU backed nationalist movements in Angola, Mozambique, and Zimbabwe. As part of this undertaking, OAU members put pressure on

white-ruled South Africa to end apartheid. A major achievement of the OAU during this period was the settlement of border disputes among member states.

In addition to working through the OAU, African states have cooperated on a regional level. In 1996, the Economic Community of West African States (ECOWAS) provided a 10,000-strong peacekeeping force to implement a cease-fire between warring groups in the West African nation of Liberia. Their efforts helped end a 7-year civil war that had killed 150,000 of Liberia's 2.4 million people and had left the country in ruins.

As they look to the twenty-first century, the OAU and other African organizations have set as their major goal Africa's economic growth and development. Member states of the OAU eventually plan to create an all-African free trade area.

Economic Development

In addition to creating a united continent, post-independence leaders of Africa worked to build strong economies in their nations. To move Africa's rural economies into the world of mining, manufacturing, and service industries, millions of people had to learn to read and write. Workers who made a living with their hands had to learn to operate machines in factories. Governments had to repair aging phone lines, railroads, and highways. Tanzania's President Julius Nyerere in the 1960s stated "while the great powers are trying to get to the moon, we are trying to get to the village."

Legacy of Colonialism

After independence, most African countries suffered from the economies created by colonial rule. As you remember from Chapter 27, Europeans obtained raw materials in Africa for their home industries and developed little industry in Africa. Under colonial rule, some Africans worked on European-owned plantations that produced cash crops, or crops grown for profit and exported. Most, however, were subsistence farmers, who grew only enough food to meet the needs of a family or village.

After independence, African leaders tried to remedy the imbalance between farming and industry. Many African countries were rich in one or two key resources or crops, but their economies could not provide the basic needs of their populations.

One-product economies, such as Ghana with cocoa and Burundi with coffee, were constantly at the mercy of changing prices for products on world markets. In addition, internal conflicts left some countries with ruined land and heavy war debts.

Economic Challenges

To bring economic advancement, African leaders decided to push the export of cash crops and raw materials while promoting industrialization. A lack of capital, skilled workers, and transportation systems, however, stood in the way of industrial growth. Seeking to overcome these obstacles, African countries turned to foreign governments and banks for loans to build factories, airports, harbors, and roads.

Reliance on foreign aid, however, provoked different reactions among Africans. Some nations followed a capitalist model and developed close ties with the West. Resource-rich nations, such as Nigeria with its oil wealth, tried to fund development from their exports of minerals and other raw materials. To assert their sovereignty, other nations decided to organize various kinds of

Geography

The Moving Sahara

Deep in the Sahara, ancient rock paintings show grazing cattle and grasses where now there is only rock and sand. In recent times, farmers also grazed cattle in areas bordering the Sahara. But now those grasslands too are giving way to desert.

Before Africa was colonized, farmers cultivated fields until the soil was exhausted. When they moved to new plots of land, they let the old ones lie fallow, replenishing the soil. Under colonialism, better medical care caused a population boom and a growing demand for food. Europeans pushed Africans to grow big cash crops for export.

The encroaching desert

Destruction of the land increased. Farmers cut down trees to open up new fields and farmed land year after year without allowing the fields to lie fallow. Droughts in the 1980s brought disaster. People had to use grains for food instead of for seed. Without plants to anchor the soil, tons of topsoil disappeared. The mixture of overfarming, overgrazing, cutting trees, and drought pushed the Sahara south as fast as 90 miles (145 km) a year.

The solution to this problem lies with individual farmers. By planting trees, terracing fields, and fertilizing the soil, they may be able to slow the shifting of the Sahara.

 **ACTIVITY**

Examine what is causing the Sahara to spread south. Why do you think it is difficult to get individual farmers to change their agricultural practices?

The education of children like these kindergarten students in Angola is the key to the nation's future. *What is happening with literacy rates in Africa?*

In the case of Africa in the 1980s, growing populations, a lack of capital, and overdependence on cash crops all contributed to this problem.

Another factor was the expansion of desert into formerly fertile areas. Countries crossed by the Sahara, Africa's largest desert, particularly faced the effects of desertification, or the transformation of fertile land into desert land. The worst occurrence of desertification took place in **the Sahel**, a West African grassland area bordering the Sahara. In addition to the ravages of nature, human activities, such as grazing livestock, planting, and the harvesting of trees, left the land in this environmentally fragile area dangerously exposed to erosion.

Signs of Hope

In the 1980s, Africa was a continent in crisis. A World Bank study showed that 21 of the world's 34 poorest countries were in Africa. More than 60 percent of all Africans received too little food each day, and more than 5 million children died every year. Relying on foreign help to remedy these problems, sub-Saharan African nations by the mid-1980s were $130 billion in debt.

As the year 2000 approaches, the problems of inadequate food, growing populations, and foreign debt still plague Africa, but some hopeful signs exist. More Africans than ever are attending school. Literacy rates, or the percentages of people who can read and write, have risen. Through education, many Africans are developing the skills needed to improve their standard of living.

In various parts of the continent, Africans are cooperating to improve their economies. To break their dependency on foreign countries, some African nations have formed regional associations that promote trade and economic contacts. An example of this type of organization is the Economic Community of West African States (ECOWAS), in which a number of West African nations have agreed to barter among themselves, trading products for oil instead of for scarce cash. In late 1992 Ugandan President Yoweri Museveni expressed a viewpoint that had become increasingly widespread throughout Africa: "We have to go back to the year 1500 [prior to colonialism], where we left off building an African economy, able to produce its own food, its own tools, its own weapons.... In short, we have to rely on ourselves."

government-controlled economies. This turn to socialism pleased many nationalists, who equated capitalism with colonialism.

No matter how they organized their economies, however, many countries failed to develop agriculture in their push to industrialize. Soon food crops for the domestic markets began to suffer and thousands of unskilled rural people moved to the cities, searching in vain for jobs. With many people out of work and unable to buy the products of new African industries, economies suffered.

Africa's soaring population also caused problems for economic growth. With economies geared for export, not enough food was produced for domestic needs. Governments had to increase borrowing from foreign sources, often to buy food, and their debts grew. As a result, not enough money was available to develop health care, food production, and industry necessary to improve overall standards of living.

Famine

Severe droughts in Africa also hindered economic development, causing food shortages and starvation in various parts of western, central, and eastern Africa. The causes of famine in Africa, as in other parts of the world, are complex and varied.

 **Visualizing History** African American children celebrate Kwanzaa, a festival held in late December since 1966. *What is the purpose of such poems as "My Africa"?*

African Identity

> I love a world,
> This priceless world,
> Sweet home of haunting melodies
> And roll of tom-toms—
> My Africa.
>
> —Michael Dei-Anang,
> from the poem "My Africa"

In 1963 the African American poet Langston Hughes gathered nearly 100 African poems into a collection called *Poems from Black Africa*. It includes this one by Dei-Anang, a poet and government official in Ghana.

"Usually," Hughes wrote in the foreword, "poets have their fingers on the emotional pulse of their peoples." The poetry of Dei-Anang, like that of other Africans, had begun to rekindle a deep pride among Africans in their heritage.

During the colonial era, Africans had learned much, both good and bad, from Europeans. There remained the idea, although not accepted by all Africans, that European culture was superior to African culture in art, music, literature, and technology.

As independent nations emerged on the continent, many African leaders stressed the need to take pride in Africa. In Senegal, a former French colony, President **Léopold Sédar Senghor** published poems that expressed his love of Africa. Because Africans had never lost touch with nature, he thought, they could help restore "a world that has died of machines and cannons." Senghor helped found a poetry movement called negritude, an effort to recapture black Africa's past dignity.

During the decades since independence, African artists and writers have built on this foundation of pride. Theater groups, filmmakers, novelists, painters, and others have explored the pain of colonialism as well as the modern problems of corruption and hunger. Music, in particular, developed as a form of social protest in countries such as South Africa.

Open now to influences from around the globe, Africans have also created exciting new art forms. Congolese music, for instance, a mix of African, Latin American, and Caribbean styles, brings pleasure and delight to people in all of Africa and around the world.

SECTION 3 REVIEW

Recall

1. **Define** Pan-Africanism, cash crop, subsistence farmer, desertification, literacy rate, negritude.
2. **Identify** Kofi Annan, Organization of African Unity, Economic Community of West African States, Léopold Sédar Senghor.
3. **Discuss** the goal the OAU has for the future development of African economies.

Critical Thinking

4. **Evaluating Information** What might have happened if African nations had spent funds producing more food for their people instead of growing cash crops and industrializing their economies?

Understanding Themes

5. **Change** What trend influenced African political systems by the early 1990s? How do you think this will affect the political future of African nations?

Connections Across Time

Historical Significance The nations of Africa are very old—and very new. They have ancient cultures, but their political systems are still young. Most have been independent for only a generation. Their efforts to forge effective governments are complicated by debt, hunger, and ethnic strife.

Despite difficulties, Africans have made progress. Nations, such as Angola, South Africa, and Zimbabwe, have developed peaceful ways of dealing with their challenges. Also, education and a higher standard of living are being enjoyed by more people now than in the past.

Using Key Terms

Write the key term that completes each sentence. Then write a sentence for each term not chosen.

a. general strike
b. colons
c. clans
d. negritude
e. Pan-Africanism
f. desertification
g. cash crops
h. apartheid
i. genocide
j. literacy rate

1. Through the movement of _____, African nations seek to promote oneness and cooperation throughout the continent.
2. _____, or the transformation of fertile land into desert land, affected countries near the Sahara.
3. In 1948, the South African government began legalizing and strengthening a policy of racial separation known as _____.
4. The deliberate killing of a racial, ethnic, or national group is known as _____.
5. _____, the percentage of people who can read and write, has increased in Africa in recent years.

Technology Activity

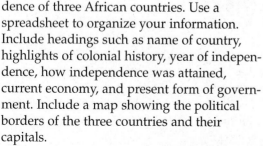

Using a Spreadsheet Search the Internet or a library for sources about the independence of three African countries. Use a spreadsheet to organize your information. Include headings such as name of country, highlights of colonial history, year of independence, how independence was attained, current economy, and present form of government. Include a map showing the political borders of the three countries and their capitals.

Using Your History Journal

Review your news clippings on Africa. Write a short essay on the future of an African nation. What are the challenges that your chosen nation faces? What are the prospects for peace and progress?

Reviewing Facts

1. **History** Discuss the reasons for the growth of nationalism in Africa after 1945.
2. **Culture** Identify the groups that pressed for reform in Kenya during the 1990s.
3. **Economics** Explain the reason for Libya's postwar economic prosperity.
4. **History** Discuss the events leading to Zimbabwe's late independence in 1980.
5. **History/Culture** Describe the roles of Nelson Mandela and Desmond Tutu in South Africa from the 1960s to the 1990s. What was the outcome of their efforts?
6. **History** Discuss developments in Somalia during the 1980s and early 1990s.
7. **Culture** Identify the changes that are occurring in African culture.

Critical Thinking

1. **Analyze** What are the benefits and drawbacks of Africa's cultural and ethnic diversity?
2. **Apply** How would you solve the problem of food shortages in various parts of Africa?
3. **Analyze** How did the political boundaries drawn by European colonial powers cause

problems for many African nations after they gained independence?

4. **Synthesize** How would you respond if you had lived under the system of apartheid?

5. **Apply** How has migration of people from the countryside to cities affected many African countries?

6. **Analyze** In the photograph below Nigerian farmers irrigate a field. How does this show the transition to a new Africa?

Understanding Themes

1. **Nationalism** What was the purpose of the African National Congress (ANC) in South Africa? How has its role changed since 1994?

2. **Change** What political changes came to Angola and Mozambique between the 1970s and 1990s?

3. **Change** How has the Organization of African Unity (OAU) affected African affairs since its founding in 1963?

Skill Practice

Exchange with another student the research reports you completed in "Applying the Skill" for this chapter. Critique the reports using the following questions. For each question, find examples in the report and present them to the author.

1. Does the report have an introduction, body, and conclusion?

2. Does the introduction define the writer's thesis or main point of the report?

3. Is the body of the report organized in a logical way?

4. Are there clear transitions between ideas? Give an example of a good transition and a weak one.

5. Does the conclusion restate and summarize the thesis of the report?

Geography in History

1. **Region** Refer to the map below. What is the largest uninhabited region of Africa?

2. **Human/Environment Interaction** Why is a narrow strip of land in northeast Africa heavily populated?

3. **Location** Near what city in South Africa is the heaviest population?

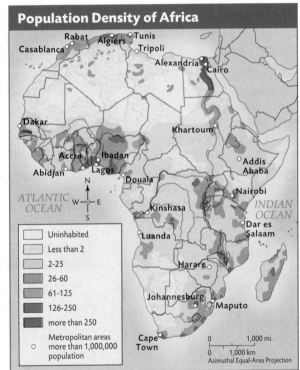

Linking Past and Present

1. In the 1980s, droughts brought widespread famine to Africa. What efforts to relieve food shortages continue there today?

2. In 1994, power passed relatively peacefully from the white minority government of South Africa to an all-racial government that includes black South Africans. How might the South African solution serve as a model for solving political problems in other countries that are torn by ethnic unrest?

Chapter
35

1945–Present
The Middle East

Chapter Themes

▶ **Nationalism** The cold war and rival nationalisms affect the politics of the Middle East. *Section 1*

▶ **Cooperation** Middle Eastern nations take steps toward peace after years of conflict. *Section 2*

▶ **Cultural Diffusion** Middle Eastern countries search for a reconciliation between traditional and modern values. *Section 3*

Storyteller

In the fall of 1993, a remarkable event occurred that, to many people, seemed like a miracle. Yitzhak Rabin, the prime minister of Israel, and Yasir Arafat, the chairman of the Palestine Liberation Organization (PLO) signed an agreement to end the decades-long conflict between Israel and the Arabs, known as Palestinians.

In 1995, Rabin's assassination stunned Israel and the world, revealing that the quest for peace is often an uphill struggle marked by tragedy. Since 1945, the Middle East has shown itself to be a complex region where violence has been a constant feature of life but where hopes for peace remain unquenchable.

Historical Significance

How have Middle Eastern developments affected world affairs since 1945? What steps have the nations of the Middle East taken to resolve their differences?

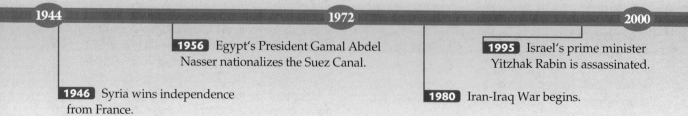

| 1944 | 1972 | 2000 |

1956 Egypt's President Gamal Abdel Nasser nationalizes the Suez Canal.

1995 Israel's prime minister Yitzhak Rabin is assassinated.

1946 Syria wins independence from France.

1980 Iran-Iraq War begins.

Istanbul (formerly Constantinople) is Turkey's largest city and one of the busiest ports in the Middle East.

Your History Journal

Create an illustrated time line of conflicts and peace conferences or accords in the Middle East beginning in 1948 and ending at the present. Illustrate your time line with symbols of peace and war.

Section 1

Nationalism in the Middle East

Setting the Scene

▶ **Terms to Define**

Pan-Arabism, kibbutzim, nationalize, pact

▶ **People to Meet**

David Ben-Gurion, Gamal Abdel Nasser, Hussein I, Mohammad Reza Pahlavi, Mohammad Mossadeg

▶ **Places to Locate**

Egypt, Iraq, Lebanon, Syria, Jordan, Saudi Arabia, Yemen, Israel, Suez Canal, Turkey, Iran

Find Out How did nationalism establish independent nations and create conflict in the Middle East after World War II?

The Storyteller

In spite of the separate living arrangements, members of a kibbutz family do not become strangers to one another.... Kibbutz parents spend a great deal of their free time with their children.... Parents and children enjoy each other all the more when they meet just for fun and companionship. Kibbutz-niks [residents of a kibbutz] take good care of their elderly parents, too. There is less friction among kibbutz grandparents, parents, and children.... There is less divorce—fewer marriage problems.

—adapted from *Israel Today*, Harry Essrig and Abraham Segal, 1977

Children in a kibbutz

$\mathcal{I}$n the decades after World War II, nationalist movements took hold in the Middle East. For more than 20 years, Great Britain and France had governed much of the area under the terms of post–World War I agreements. Gradually the presence of foreign officials and troops on Middle Eastern soil revived the desire for independence, as it did in Asia and Africa.

While most Middle Eastern countries shook off European control in the postwar years, foreign influence in the region remained strong. With its valuable waterways and oil reserves, the Middle East became the scene of superpower maneuvering for influence during the cold war.

Arab Independence

Several Arab countries, such as **Egypt** and **Iraq**, had achieved independence before World War II. During the 1940s, other European-ruled Arab territories followed. The Mediterranean coastal lands of **Lebanon** and **Syria** won their freedom from France. In Lebanon, Christian and Muslim leaders agreed to share power under a new constitution, while Syria elected its first parliamentary government. The largely desert kingdom of Transjordan (present-day **Jordan**) gained its independence from Great Britain. In all of these new states, however, Western influences remained strong after independence.

As independent Arab states emerged, Pan-Arabism, a movement aimed at building closer cultural and political ties among Arabs, grew stronger, especially among the educated urban middle class. In 1945, leaders of Egypt, Iraq, Transjordan, Syria, Lebanon, **Saudi Arabia**, and **Yemen** formed the Arab League. Its mission was to unify the Arab world.

Formation of Israel

By 1947, Palestine remained the only significant European-ruled territory in the region. Arabs, who had lived in Palestine for centuries, wanted the British to honor their promise of freedom made in the early 1900s. Zionist Jews wanted to build a Jewish state on the same land—land that their ancestors had claimed since Biblical times and that the British had also promised to them.

The Holocaust in Nazi-occupied Europe had boosted support in Western countries for the Zionist movement. Fearing that the British would allow increased Jewish immigration, Arabs in Palestine increased attacks on Jewish settlers. Many of Palestine's Jews lived on kibbutzim, or collective farms, where they struggled to turn swamps and boulder-strewn hillsides into productive farms. To defend themselves, Jewish settlements relied on a military force called the Haganah. Meanwhile, Jewish underground forces carried out attacks on British soldiers and Palestinian Arabs. As hostilities mounted, Great Britain admitted its inability to keep the peace and turned Palestine over to the United Nations in 1947.

For months, world leaders debated the future of Palestine. The United States and much of the West wanted to divide Palestine into a Jewish and an Arab state. Arab nations, along with several European and Pacific nations, rejected the idea and called for a single Palestinian state. At a meeting of the General Assembly on November 29, 1947, the United Nations voted to partition Palestine and to place Jerusalem under UN administration.

Jewish leaders were quick to accept the UN partition plan, while embittered Arab leaders rejected it. Great Britain relinquished control of Palestine on May 14, 1948, as Prime Minister **David Ben-Gurion** proclaimed the new state of **Israel**. Within 24 hours, the armies of Syria, Lebanon, Iraq, Egypt, and Transjordan attacked the new Jewish state. With foreign aid and effective civilian and military organization, the Israelis defeated the Arab forces in nine months.

When the fighting ended in early 1949, Israel held more territory. Jerusalem was divided, with the eastern part of the city in Arab hands. Transjordan annexed East Jerusalem and the West Bank of the Jordan River. Egypt held the Gaza Strip. The war was a resounding victory for Israel. To the Arabs, the war spelled disaster. As a result of partition, more than 700,000 Palestinians became homeless. Many fled to neighboring Arab lands, where a large number settled in refugee camps hoping to eventually return home.

Visualizing History Despite British restrictions on immigration, Jews aboard the *Exodus* tried to migrate to Palestine in 1947. *Why did Great Britain turn Palestine over to the United Nations in 1947?*

Arab Unity

The 1948–1949 war had other serious consequences for the Arab world. In Egypt, many people blamed rich, corrupt King Farouk for the Arab defeat and the country's weak economy. In 1952 army officers seized control of the government and proclaimed a republic. Within a year, Colonel **Gamal Abdel Nasser**, a leader of the coup, took over as president.

Nasser profoundly disliked Western influence in the Middle East, and quickly launched new policies through which he hoped Egypt would lead the Arab world to greatness. In an extremely popular move, Nasser broke up the estates of wealthy Egyptian landowners and gave plots of land to the peasants. Then he negotiated the British withdrawal from the **Suez Canal**. Finally, he set out to modernize Egypt and build up its military muscle to confront Israel.

The Suez Crisis

Nasser wanted to help Egypt by building a dam at Aswan in the Upper Nile River valley. Known as the Aswan High Dam, the massive structure—36 stories high and more than 2 miles (3 km) wide—would end flooding, increase irrigation, and give farmers two extra harvests a year. Electricity generated by the dam would power new industries.

Seeking political influence in the economic development of Egypt, the United States offered Egypt a $270 million loan to build the dam. However, Nasser's growing Soviet leanings, including a major arms deal with the Soviet Union, caused the United States to angrily withdraw

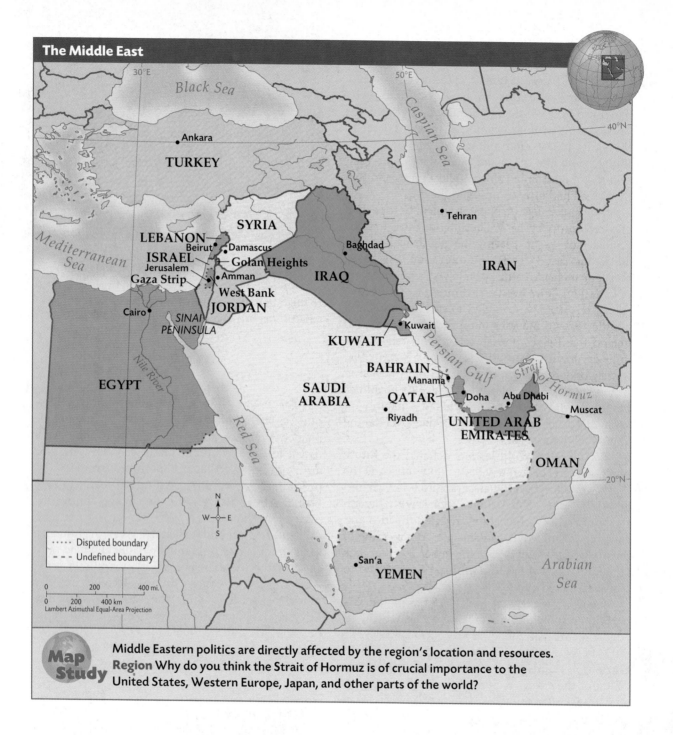

30°E 50°E

40°N

Black Sea

Caspian Sea

•Ankara

TURKEY

•Tehran

SYRIA

LEBANON—
Beirut •Damascus Baghdad• IRAN

ISRAEL ──Golan Heights
Jerusalem•   IRAQ
Gaza Strip• •Amman

Mediterranean Sea

West Bank
Cairo•   JORDAN

SINAI
PENINSULA   •Kuwait

KUWAIT

EGYPT   BAHRAIN—   Persian Gulf   Strait of Hormuz

SAUDI   Manama•
ARABIA   QATAR   •Doha Abu Dhabi•
         •Riyadh   UNITED ARAB   •Muscat
                   EMIRATES

Nile River

Red Sea

OMAN

20°N

N
W—◇—E
S

······ Disputed boundary
– – – Undefined boundary

0   200   400 mi.
0   200   400 km
Lambert Azimuthal Equal-Area Projection

San'a•
YEMEN

Arabian
Sea

Map Study Middle Eastern politics are directly affected by the region's location and resources.
Region Why do you think the Strait of Hormuz is of crucial importance to the
United States, Western Europe, Japan, and other parts of the world?

its offer. In July 1956 Nasser retaliated against the Western powers by nationalizing, or bringing under government control, the Suez Canal. He vowed to use millions of dollars in canal fees to finance the building of the dam.

President Eisenhower was opposed to Western intervention, and the United States tried to negotiate an end to the crisis. Great Britain and France, however, feared that Nasser might close the canal and cut off shipments of oil between the Middle East and Western Europe. In October, the two European powers joined Israel in invading Egypt. Great Britain and

France hoped to overthrow Nasser and seize the canal. Israel wanted to end Egyptian guerrilla attacks on its borders. The United States immediately sponsored a United Nations resolution calling for British and French withdrawal from Egypt. The Russians threatened rocket attacks on British and French cities. Eisenhower, opposed to Soviet interference, put the Strategic Air Command on alert. In face of this pressure, the three nations pulled out of Egypt. United Nations forces were sent to patrol the Egyptian-Israeli border. Nasser then accepted the Soviet offer to build the Aswan High Dam.

Middle East Crises

Nasser emerged from the Suez crisis as a powerful Arab leader. He had embarrassed Great Britain and France, won control of the Suez Canal, and had stopped Israel from taking more territory. Pro-Nasser parties began forming throughout the Arab world. It seemed that Nasser might rise to lead a unified Arab world.

In early 1958 Syria and Egypt merged to form a Nasser-led state called the United Arab Republic (UAR). The union lasted about three years. At that point, Syrian leaders had grown resentful of the loss of their power, and Syria withdrew from the UAR.

That same year, Nasser's brand of Arab nationalism seemed to be taking hold in Iraq. There, King Faisal II, Nasser's strongest Arab opponent and a friend of the West, was killed by radical political and military forces in his country. They set up a one-party regime like Nasser's and broke ties with the West.

In the face of pro-Nasser pressure, some Arab leaders turned to the West for support. Jordan's **Hussein I** asked for British and American help when pro-Nasser forces threatened his government. In Lebanon, violence broke out between the Christians, who dominated the nation, and a huge Muslim population that sympathized with Nasser and the UAR. Christian President Camille Chamoun, a supporter of the West, sought election to a new term. Anti-Western elements revolted, and a civil war followed. Chamoun asked for Western help to stop the violence. At first, Eisenhower refused. However, when an unexpected coup overthrew the government of Iraq, Eisenhower decided to uphold political stability in the region. He sent 15,000 Marines to Lebanon in July 1958. When order was restored that fall, the troops pulled out.

By 1960 Arab nationalism had made gains, but the Middle East was in a state of uncertainty. A fragile truce held between Arabs and Israelis; competing Arab groups were at an impasse; and neither superpower had managed to achieve dominance in the region.

Pro-Western Tier

Two other Middle Eastern countries, **Turkey** and **Iran**, experienced the upheaval of nationalism and rapid modernization. Both bordered the Soviet Union, making them pawns in cold war struggles.

Turkey

At the end of World War II, Turkey received American aid to modernize its economy and to ward off Soviet advances. During the 1950s, the Turks joined NATO and the Baghdad Pact, alliances aimed at blocking Soviet expansion. Turkey also made strides toward democracy, encouraged foreign investment, and strengthened its capitalist economy. By the 1960s, however, government corruption, inflation, and a huge international debt discredited Turkey's ruling politicians and increased the political influence of the military.

Iran

By contrast, Western influence in oil-rich Iran was shaken after World War II. The young shah, **Mohammad Reza Pahlavi**, relied on Western help to block Soviet influence. Many Iranian people, however, resented the West. For decades, the British had grown rich on Iranian oil at Iran's expense.

In 1951, a wealthy politician, **Mohammad Mossadeg**, became prime minister. He nationalized the British-owned oil industry and declared that all oil money would be used for social and economic reforms. Great Britain called for a world boycott of Iranian oil. As Iranians began to suffer, their hatred of the West and the shah grew.

In 1953 growing support for Mossadeg forced the shah to flee the country. He returned after a military coup—promoted by the United States—deposed Mossadeg. The shah increased his ties to the United States and signed the Baghdad Pact. A pact is a treaty between two or more nations. He also signed an agreement with Western oil companies. Backed by the army and Western powers, the shah was firmly in control by the 1960s.

SECTION 1 REVIEW

Recall
1. **Define** Pan-Arabism, kibbutzim, nationalize, pact.
2. **Identify** David Ben-Gurion, Gamal Abdel Nasser, United Arab Republic, Hussein I, Mohammad Reza Pahlavi, Mohammad Mossadeg.
3. **Explain** why the United Nations divided Palestine into an Arab and a Jewish state.

Critical Thinking
4. **Applying Information** How did the Holocaust in Europe contribute to the development of the Jewish state in Palestine?

Understanding Themes
5. **Nationalism** How was Nasser viewed by the Arab world after his nationalization of the Suez Canal?

Section 2

War and Peace in the Middle East

Setting the Scene

▶ **Terms to Define**

disengagement, cartel, *intifada*, embargo

▶ **People to Meet**

Yasir Arafat, Anwar el-Sadat, Menachem Begin, Hosni Mubarak, Yitzhak Rabin, Shimon Peres, Benjamin Netanyahu, Ayatollah Ruhollah Khomeini, Saddam Hussein

▶ **Places to Locate**

Gaza Strip, Golan Heights, West Bank, Beirut, Strait of Hormuz, Kuwait

 **ind Out** How have issues of peace and war been decided in the Middle East since the mid-1960s?

The Storyteller

When Shah Mohammad Reza Pahlavi was overthrown in 1979, Iran had male tailors fitting women's clothes and male teachers in girls' classrooms. The revolutionaries, however, refused to allow unrelated men and women to work closely together. The result: many more job opportunities for women. In the media, for example, the need for women to cover women's sports opened jobs for directors and reporters.

—adapted from *Nine Parts of Desire, The Hidden World of Islamic Women*, Geraldine Brooks, 1995

Shah Mohammad Reza Pahlavi

From the 1960s to the 1990s, many sweeping changes came to the Middle East. Wars broke out between various nations and groups in the region, but hopes for peace were also high, especially in the early 1990s.

As the 1960s opened, the most prolonged and bitter dispute was between Israel, its Arab neighbors, and the Palestinians. In their struggle for nationhood, the Palestinians in 1964 formed the Palestine Liberation Organization (PLO) to eliminate Israel and to create a Palestinian state. Later, however, many Palestinians and Israelis came to accept a two-state solution: a state for Israelis and a state for Palestinians.

 **POINT**

Arab-Israeli Conflict

The cease-fire between Israel and its Arab neighbors fell apart during the 1960s. A new radical regime in Syria sought the end of Israel and the creation of an Arab Palestine. Syrian and Israeli troops engaged in border clashes in early 1967. Egypt's President Nasser aided Syria by closing the Gulf of Aqaba to Israel and by having United Nations forces removed from the Israeli-Egyptian border.

Six-Day War

Fearing possible attack, Israel responded with force on June 5, 1967. At 8:45 A.M., Israeli fighter jets bore down on 17 Egyptian airfields, destroying 300 of Egypt's 350 warplanes. Hundreds of miles away, Israeli jets also demolished the air forces of Iraq, Jordan, and Syria.

In the Six-Day War, Israeli forces tripled Israel's land holdings, seizing the Sinai Peninsula and the **Gaza Strip** from Egypt, and the **Golan Heights** from Syria. When Jordan entered the war, Israeli troops also took East Jerusalem.

In a move that spawned decades of upheaval, Israel occupied the **West Bank** of the Jordan River. The West Bank was land that had been designated as part of Arab Palestine in the United Nations partition plan in 1947. Palestinian Arabs had never achieved self-rule, however; they had been under Jordanian rule ever since 1949, when Jordan annexed the West Bank. Now, as a result of the Six-Day War, the area's more than 1 million Palestinians found themselves under Israeli military occupation.

Thousands more Palestinians fled to neighboring countries such as Lebanon. They turned more than ever to the PLO and its militant leader, **Yasir Arafat**, who vowed to use armed struggle to establish a Palestinian state.

The United Nations asked Israel to pull out of occupied territories and asked Arab nations to recognize Israel's right to exist. Both sides refused. Terrorist attacks and border raids continued for many years.

Oil and Conflict

Nasser died in 1970. His successor, President **Anwar el-Sadat**, led Arab forces in a new war against Israel. On October 6, 1973, Egyptian and Syrian forces launched a surprise attack on Israel on the Jewish holy day of Yom Kippur and during the Muslim holy month of Ramadan. In early battles, many Israeli planes were shot down. Egyptian troops crossed over into the Sinai, and Syria moved into the Golan Heights. With an American airlift of weapons, Israel struck back. Israeli troops crossed the Suez Canal and occupied Egyptian territory. The fighting raged until the UN negotiated a ceasefire. Secretary of State Henry Kissinger negotiated a disengagement, or military withdrawal, agreement in early 1974.

American support of Israel during the 1973 war angered Arab countries. Attempting to halt Western support, Arab oil countries imposed an embargo on oil sales to Israel's allies in 1973. Additional pressure came from the Organization of Petroleum Exporting Countries (OPEC), a cartel, or group of businesses formed to regulate production and prices among its members. OPEC, which included Arab and non-Arab oil producers, quadrupled the price of oil. However, the embargo threatened such dire economic problems for the world, including Arab countries, that it was lifted in 1974.

The Camp David Accords

In 1977, Egypt's President Sadat acted independently to break the deadlock. He accepted an invitation to visit Israel, becoming the first Arab

Visualizing History Yasir Arafat became chairman of the Palestine Liberation Organization (PLO) in 1969. The PLO, formed in 1964, is a confederation of various Palestinian Arab groups. *Why was the PLO formed?*

leader to step in peace on Israeli soil. In a speech before Israel's parliament, Sadat called for Arab acceptance of Israel, a just solution to the Palestinian problem, and an end to hostilities between Israelis and Arabs.

The next year Sadat accepted an invitation from United States President Jimmy Carter to meet with Israeli Prime Minister **Menachem Begin** (BAY•gihn). The 12 days of meetings at Camp David in Maryland resulted in the Camp David Accords, the basis for an Arab-Israeli peace treaty.

Sadat and Begin signed the treaty in March 1979—the first time an Arab nation recognized Israel's right to exist. In return, Israel gave up the Sinai Peninsula. Many nations applauded Sadat's actions, but several Arab states broke ties with Egypt. Sadat's separate peace with Israel, they said, threatened Arab unity.

In 1981 Muslim extremists assassinated Sadat, and **Hosni Mubarak** succeeded him as president. Mubarak supported Egypt's peace with Israel but also worked to improve Egypt's relations with other Arab nations in the region. At home, he faced economic pressures caused by Egypt's soaring population and lack of resources. Another challenge to Mubarak came from a growing opposition movement led by Islamic groups that wanted to end Western influences in Egypt.

The Palestinian Issue

For 20 years after the 1967 war, Arabs and Israelis could not agree on the future of the West Bank and Gaza Strip. Resenting Israeli rule, Palestinians lived in a smoldering rage. Most could get only low-paying jobs; those who protested could be arrested. During this time, the PLO staged hijackings and bombings in Israel and in foreign countries.

In 1987 the Palestinians carried out an *intifada*, or uprising, against the Israelis. The uprising spread from the Gaza Strip to the West Bank. Workers went on strike, and protesters hurled stones at Israeli soldiers and civilians. The *intifada* focused world attention on the Palestinian issue.

In 1988 the PLO's leader Arafat stated that he would renounce terrorism and accept Israel's right to exist. However, believing that Arafat would not be true to his word, Israel refused to hold talks with the PLO and to halt the growth of Jewish settlements in the West Bank.

The Peace Process

Despite continuing tensions in the Middle East, the United States pressed the Arabs and Israelis to hold peace talks beginning in 1991. The Israeli Prime Minister **Yitzhak Rabin** (YIHT•zahk rah•BEEN), elected in 1992, agreed in principle to exchange some of the occupied land for security guarantees and to accept self-rule by the Palestinians. Many Arab leaders also showed a new flexibility in their positions.

In 1993, Israel and the PLO recognized each other and agreed to eventual self-rule for Palestinians in the West Bank and the Gaza Strip. The Israelis also stated they would gradually withdraw militarily from both areas. By mid-1996, the Palestinians had gained significant self-rule with Yasir Arafat as their first president.

The peace process also reached out to Israel's Arab neighbors: Jordan and Syria. In 1994, Israel and Jordan signed a peace treaty, the first such agreement between Israel and an Arab country since the Israeli-Egyptian peace treaty of 1979. Syria

Images *of the* Times

Living in the Middle East

Daily life in the Middle East today is a blend of modern and traditional ways as well as urban and rural lifestyles.

Beirut, Lebanon, is rebuilding its neighborhoods after a long period of civil war.

Jiddah, Saudi Arabia, is a modern port city on the Red Sea that has prospered from the country's oil wealth.

and Israel began talks, but a major obstacle between them was the future status of the Golan Heights, occupied by Israel since the 1967 war.

Increased Tensions

Although many Israelis and Palestinians supported the peace process, a large number on both sides opposed it. Some Palestinians feared that peace would lead to a less-than-independent Palestinian state subject to Israeli restrictions. Israeli opponents of the process feared that a self-governing Palestinian state could threaten Israel.

Tragically, in November 1995, Rabin was shot to death by an Israeli student who opposed the peace process. Rabin's successor, **Shimon Peres** (shee•MOHN PEHR•ehs), pledged to continue efforts toward peace, and Yasir Arafat made the same commitment. However, events followed that heightened tensions and hardened positions on both sides.

Opposed to the peace process, the militant Palestinian group Hamas in early 1996 began a series of suicide bombings that killed a number of Israelis. Shocked by the violence, Israeli voters that May narrowly elected **Benjamin Netanyahu** (neh•tahn•YAH•hoo), leader of the conservative Likud party, over Peres and the Labor party. As a candidate and later as prime minister, Netanyahu stressed Israel's security needs over peace with the Palestinians.

After the Israeli elections, Hamas stepped up its bombings and attacks on Israeli citizens. Although Arafat publicly denounced Hamas's actions, Prime Minister Netanyahu and many Israelis believed that Arafat was unable or unwilling to control the militants. To keep would-be bombers out of Israeli cities, Netanyahu closed off Palestinian areas from Israel. These closings kept tens of thousands of Palestinian workers from jobs in Israel and restricted travel between West Bank cities and villages. The Israelis also refused to carry out promises to withdraw military forces from remaining Palestinian areas (except for the town of Hebron) until the bombings stopped.

Kuwait on the Persian Gulf has an economy based on oil. An increasing number of women in the Middle East, as in other areas of the world, earn university degrees and work in businesses.

The Galilee region of Israel has areas where swamps and lakes have been drained to create productive farmlands.

REFLECTING ON THE TIMES

1. What impact has oil had on various countries of the Middle East?
2. What country in the Middle East is rebuilding after a long period of civil war?

Educated in the United States, Israeli Prime Minister Benjamin Netanyahu favored strengthening free enterprise in Israel. *What was Netanyahu's position in dealing with the Palestinians?*

During the late 1990s, Israelis feared continued attacks, while Palestinians protested what they felt were Israeli efforts to block progress toward their freedom. Palestinians especially opposed Jewish settlements in the West Bank. As turmoil threatened, the United States engaged in an uphill struggle to get the two sides together. With the help of Jordan's King Hussein, talks held outside of Washington, D.C., in late 1998 moved the peace process forward. However, in early 1999, the "peacemaker" king's death and uncertainty about the policies of his successor, King Abdullah, seemed to again impede the peace process.

Lebanon

The Palestinian issue also affected neighboring Lebanon. In 1975 a civil war broke out between Lebanon's Christian and Muslim groups. As the Muslim population grew to outnumber Christians, unrest had spread. Adding to these tensions was the presence of armed PLO forces in the country. Most Lebanese Muslims supported the PLO; most Lebanese Christians did not.

As fighting erupted, the weakened Lebanese government asked Syria to send in troops to keep order. In 1982 the Israelis invaded southern Lebanon to wipe out PLO bases that had been attacking Israel. A multinational peacekeeping force finally arranged a PLO withdrawal to other Arab countries; however, private armies continued fighting among themselves. After foreign troops became victims of terrorist bombings, the peacekeeping force departed by 1985.

In the early 1990s, some signs of hope appeared. Lebanon agreed to give Muslims an equitable say in the political process, and the various private armies in **Beirut** pulled out of the city, which made rapid strides in rebuilding. By the mid-1990s, Lebanon had made progress toward stability. Tensions remained, however, and both Syria and Israel kept troops in the country.

Iran's Revolution

During the 1960s and 1970s, Iran became a major military power in the Persian Gulf area. Shah Mohammad Reza Pahlavi worked to build a modern industrial economy based on oil. Shiite Muslim religious leaders, however, disliked the influx of Western values into Iran and called for a return to Muslim traditions. The shah silenced all protests and dissent.

In the late 1970s, anti-shah forces rallied around **Ayatollah Ruhollah Khomeini** (ko•MAY•nee), a powerful Shiite Muslim leader, living in exile in France. Khomeini had long preached the overthrow of the shah and the creation of an Islamic republic. By January 1979, widespread unrest forced the shah to flee Iran. Khomeini returned to form a government based on Muslim values.

Iranian hatred for the shah was also directed at the United States. The Americans had long supported the shah, valuing Iran as a major supplier of oil and a reliable buffer against Soviet expansion. Anti-American feelings were so strong that on November 4, 1979, militants stormed the American embassy in Tehran, the capital, and took 52 Americans hostage. United States President Carter's efforts to free the hostages were unsuccessful, thus sealing his defeat in the 1980 presidential election. Only after his successor, Ronald Reagan, was sworn in on January 20, 1981, did Iran release the Americans.

During most of the 1980s, Iran fought a devastating war with neighboring Iraq. The Iraqis first seized a disputed border area and then pushed into Iran. The Iranians, hoping to spread their revolution into Iraq, responded with a fierce counter-

Steve McCurry, Magnum

Mohsen Shandiz, SYGMA

Mortal Enemies

This giant portrait of Iraqi President Saddam Hussein (left) overlooks a Baghdad street. An inscription under the portrait in red Arabic characters praises the Arab forces in Iraq's struggle with its Islamic but non-Arab enemy neighbor, Iran. In Iran the stern gaze of the Ayatollah Ruhollah Khomeini peers from a mural behind women attending the departure of soldiers for the battlefront in September 1988. With his zealous view of Islam, Khomeini, who died in 1989, regarded the secular Saddam Hussein as both an enemy and an infidel.

The Middle East has changed profoundly since World War II. What was once an area largely held by the Ottoman Empire and then by European colonial powers is now a region of independent nations. With the end of imperialism came the rise of nationalism. At the same time parts of the Islamic world have witnessed the rise of a fiercely held fundamentalism that views the secular world, even the Muslim secular world, as evil and corrupt. In this context Iran and Iraq fought a long and devastating war that lasted from 1980 to 1988. ⊕

attack. The Iraqis had superior weapons and used poison gas; the Iranians, however, relied on larger numbers of troops. When both sides targeted commercial vessels in the Persian Gulf, the United States sent naval forces to protect the vital shipping lanes running through the **Strait of Hormuz**. In 1988 Iran and Iraq, both exhausted, agreed to end the fighting.

After Khomeini's death a year later, his successors worked to rebuild Iran's crippled economy. In 1997 a moderate religious leader, Mohammad Khatami, became president. Khatami supported a reduction in press censorship and closer economic ties with the West. Observers, however, did not expect a significant improvement in Iran's relations with the West. The United States, for example, still was concerned about Iran's use of nuclear technology and linked Iran to terrorist attacks in other countries.

Iraq's Bid for Power

The war with Iran left Iraq near collapse and in debt to its small, but oil-rich, neighbor, **Kuwait**. In August 1990, Iraq's President **Saddam Hussein** sent Iraqi forces into Kuwait, claiming that the country was a historic part of Iraq. In occupying Kuwait, Hussein also wanted to expand Iraq's influence in the Persian Gulf region.

The Persian Gulf War

Fearing an Iraqi attack, oil-rich Saudi Arabia asked the United States for protection. United States President George Bush responded by sending troops to the Saudi desert. Eight Arab nations also sent forces to Saudi Arabia. At the urging of the UN, Western nations, the Soviet Union, and Japan imposed a trade embargo, or a ban on the export of goods, against Iraq.

In January 1991, after a UN deadline for an Iraqi withdrawal expired, the United States rained medium-range missiles on the Iraqi capital of Baghdad. During the next month, coalition forces from the United States, Great Britain, France, Syria, Saudi Arabia, Egypt, and Kuwait conducted a massive air war against Iraq. Iraq responded by launching missiles against Saudi Arabia and Israel. Iraqi forces in Kuwait also set fire to oil fields. When Iraq still refused to withdraw, coalition land forces moved into Iraq and Kuwait, defeating the Iraqis after 100 hours of fighting. With Kuwait freed, a cease-fire went into effect. Allied war deaths totaled just over 100, with tens of thousands of Iraqi soldiers believed killed.

Iraq After the War

After their victory, coalition forces withdrew from Iraq. Saddam Hussein, however, remained in power. He brutally crushed Kurdish and Shiite groups in Iraq that used the war to rebel against his authority. World public opinion condemned Hussein's attacks on his civilian population.

Meanwhile, the UN trade embargo continued in an effort to force Iraq to end its chemical and nuclear weapons program. The embargo caused much hardship to Iraqis. In December 1996, the UN allowed Iraq to resume oil exports on a limited basis to pay for badly needed food and medical supplies. Iraq, however, placed limits on the work of UN teams assigned to inspect Iraqi weapons sites. In February 1998, an agreement between the UN and Iraq finally cleared the way for the inspections to resume without interference.

SECTION 2 REVIEW

Recall
1. **Define** disengagement, cartel, *intifada*, embargo.
2. **Identify** PLO, Yasir Arafat, Anwar el-Sadat, OPEC, Menachem Begin, Camp David Accords, Hosni Mubarak, Yitzhak Rabin, Shimon Peres, Benjamin Netanyahu, Ayatollah Ruhollah Khomeini, Saddam Hussein.
3. **Explain** the outcome of the Six-Day War.

Critical Thinking
4. **Analyzing Information** How has the Persian Gulf War affected the Middle East?

Understanding Themes
5. **Cooperation** What were the major points of the 1993 agreement between Israel and the Palestinians?

Preparing a Bibliography

In the last chapter, you wrote a research report on some topic of interest. To complete your report, you have one more step—preparing a bibliography.

Learning the Skill

A bibliography is a list of sources used in a research report. These sources include: books; articles from newspapers, magazines, and journals; interviews; films, videotapes, audiotapes, and compact discs. Why do you need a bibliography? What purpose does it serve?

There are two main reasons to write a bibliography. First, those who read your report may want to learn more about the topic. Second, a bibliography supports the reliability of your report.

A bibliography should follow a definite format. The entry for each source must contain all the information needed to find that source: author, title, publisher information, and publication date. You should have this information already on note cards. If you neglected this step earlier, you must return to the library to find the sources again.

In a bibliography, arrange entries alphabetically by the author's last name. The following are accepted formats for bibliography entries, followed by sample entries. Note the form of punctuation used between parts of the entry.

Books
Author's last name, first name. <u>Full Title</u>. Place of publication: publisher, copyright date.
Hay, Peter. <u>Ordinary Heroes: The Life and Death of Chana Szenes, Israel's National Heroine</u>. New York: Paragon House, 1986.

Articles
Author's last name, first name. "Title of Article." <u>Name of Periodical</u> in which article appears, Volume number (date of issue): page numbers.
Watson, Bruce. "The New Peace Corps in the New Kazakhstan." <u>Smithsonian</u>, Vol. 25 (August 1994): pp. 26–35.

Other Sources
For other kinds of sources, adapt the format for book entries.

Practicing the Skill

Review the sample bibliography below for a report on Mexico. Then answer the questions that follow.

Castañeda, Jorge G. <u>The Mexican Shock: Its Meaning for the United States</u>. New York: The New Press, 1995.
Marquez, Viviane Brachet de. The Dynamics of Domination: State, Class and Social Reform in Mexico, 1910–1990. Pittsburgh, Penn., University of Pittsburgh Press, 1994.
Cockburn, A., "The Fire This Time." <u>Condé Nast Traveller</u>, Vol. 30 (June 1995): pp. 104–113.
Smith, G. "The Brave New World of Mexican Politics." Business Week (August 28, 1995) pp. 42–44.

1. Are the bibliography entries in the correct order? Why or why not?
2. What is missing from the second book listing?
3. What is missing from the second article listing?

Applying the Skill

Compile a bibliography for your research report. Include at least five sources, preferably a mix of books and articles. Exchange bibliographies with another student and check each other for proper format and arrangement.

For More Practice

Turn to the Skill Practice in the Chapter Review on page 971 for more practice in preparing a bibliography.

1944   1972   2000

1945 Arab nations form
the Arab League.

1979 Israel and Egypt
sign peace treaty.

1994 Jordan and Israel
end their state of war.

Section 3

Challenges Facing the Middle East

Setting the Scene

▶ **Terms to Define**
   sovereignty, desalination, fundamentalism

▶ **People to Meet**
   Shimon Peres, Hafez al-Assad, Benjamin Netanyahu, Golda Meir, Tansu Çiller

▶ **Places to Locate**
   West Bank, Gaza Strip, Jerusalem, Golan Heights, Saudi Arabia, Cairo, Turkey, Euphrates River

Find Out How have people in the Middle East handled the conflict between traditional ways and modern values?

The Storyteller

An Israeli observer records the expulsion of Arabs from Israeli-held territory: "Masses of people marched on behind the next. Women bore bundles and sacks on their heads; mothers dragged children after them. From close up it was sad to watch this trek of thousands going into exile. As soon as they left the city, they began to divest themselves of things ... and the roads were cluttered with the belongings that people had abandoned to make their walk easier."

—from *The People of Nowhere,* Danny Rubenstein, 1991

Palestinian Arabs in exile

The tragic cycle of violence, wars between nations, and civil wars within nations have brought much suffering to the people of the Middle East since the end of World War II. Besides the lost lives, billions of dollars of precious resources are spent each year on weapons. If you speak to Middle Easterners about their hopes for the future, they consistently include peace and stability. But peace and stability have been hard to achieve.

War and Peace

Since Egypt and Israel agreed to peace in 1979, major steps have been taken in ending the state of war between Israel and the rest of the Arab world. In 1993, the Israelis and the Palestinians came to an agreement, and a year later, Jordan and Israel finally ended their conflict. Contacts also began between Israel and Syria for the settlement of issues stemming from the Six-Day War of 1967.

West Bank and Gaza Strip

After successful efforts toward peace in the early 1990s, Israeli-Palestinian relations worsened by 1997. Hamas bombings and the tougher position of Israel's conservative government both threatened to derail the peace process. Increasing tensions delayed indefinitely any resolution of the major issues dividing Israelis and Palestinians. These issues include the timing of Israeli military withdrawals from Palestinian areas in the **West Bank** and **Gaza Strip**, the ownership of **Jerusalem**, and the status and security of Israeli Jewish settlers on the West Bank.

Still another major issue is the resettlement of Palestinians who fled their homes beginning in the 1948 Arab-Israeli conflict. Today, more than 6 million Palestinian Arabs live in the Middle East, North Africa, Europe, and the Americas. About 2 million Palestinians live in the West Bank and Gaza Strip. In addition, about 850,000 Israeli Arabs live inside Israel itself and try to combine Israeli citizenship with their Arab heritage.

Golan Heights and Lebanon

Relations between Israel and its northern neighbor, Syria, also need to improve before a general peace can be achieved. The **Golan Heights**, which has been in Israeli hands since 1967, is a major area of dispute. Israeli Prime Minister **Shimon Peres** and Syrian President **Hafez al-Assad** committed themselves to settling this issue, but talks between Israel and Syria have been deadlocked since the election of Israeli Prime Minister **Benjamin Netanyahu** in 1996.

In neighboring Lebanon, the civil war has ended, but Israeli and Syrian troops remain. Some Israelis would like their troops to withdraw, but the Netanyahu government believes an Israeli military presence in Lebanon is vital for Israel's security. In Lebanon, Israeli forces are opposed by Shiite Muslim guerrillas. Attacks repeatedly occur between the two sides. In 1997 Netanyahu called on Syria, the major power in Lebanon, to restrain the guerrillas.

The Elusive Dream

Unity among Arab people has long been a powerful desire. For many centuries, millions of people throughout the Arab world have shared strong cultural ties, such as the Arabic language, traditions, religious beliefs, and a common history. British and French imperialism in the 1800s and 1900s increased division among the Arabs and created numerous states with artificial boundaries. Many Arabs thought that with independence from foreign powers they would be able to achieve unity. They began to take steps to strengthen the common links among them.

In 1945 political unity seemed within reach when Egypt, Transjordan (present-day Jordan), Syria, Lebanon, Iraq, **Saudi Arabia**, and Yemen formed the Arab League, a step toward unity. By 1995 membership in the Arab League had grown to 22 participants (including the PLO) covering an area larger than the United States, with a population of about 200 million. But disagreements among governments and the unwillingness of some Arab nations to give up their sovereignty, or independent decision-making powers, frustrated any move toward further unity.

Visualizing History Banking and financial services are important to the economies of many Middle Eastern countries. *In what other ways have Middle Eastern economies changed in the past 40 years?*

Some political leaders and government officials have advocated a cautious move toward unity. They formed cooperative councils among their countries to coordinate trade, economic development, and travel. Peoples' aspirations and political realities, in time, may lead to some type of loose union in which each state would retain independence and contribute to stability in the region.

Economic Developments

In the past 40 years the Middle East has seen greatly changed economic and social conditions. Light and heavy industry has been developed in most countries of the region. Irrigation for agriculture spread as hydroelectric projects were constructed on major rivers, such as the Nile and the Euphrates. At the same time as production rose and jobs became available, the region's population grew rapidly. If the current rate of increase continues, the population will double in the next 25 years. The increase has been most apparent in major urban centers. By the mid-1990s, more than 6 cities had populations exceeding 3 million each. The largest is **Cairo**, Egypt's capital, with 12 million people. It is also the largest in the whole African continent. The needs and the challenges of rapidly growing populations are on the minds of every major leader in the Middle East.

Oil and Water

Oil-producing countries of the Middle East have built wealthy and highly developed societies in recent years. The region's highest per capita incomes, or the total national incomes divided by the number of people in each nation, are found in the Persian Gulf countries. Their prosperity, however, contrasts sharply with the poverty of some other countries in the region. Hoping to lessen the gap between rich and poor nations, oil-producing countries have invested in and loaned large sums of money to the non-oil producing countries.

Another valuable, but scarce, resource in the Middle East is water. The region has long had critical water shortages caused by an unequal distribution of water. However, as Middle Eastern countries develop industrially and face population increases, they are working to meet their water needs. For example, **Turkey** has built dams and other water facilities on the **Euphrates River** to irrigate fertile, but dry, areas.

Other countries with water shortages include Israel, Syria, and Jordan. If all three countries settle their political differences, they will be able to coordinate their water resources and build plants for desalination, the removal of salt from sea water to make it usable for drinking and farming. In 1997 Israel and Jordan settled a dispute about the sharing of water. At present, both countries are constructing dams on the Yarmuk River, which serves as part of the Jordanian-Israeli border.

Social Change

Throughout the Middle East, modernization has turned traditional societies upside down. With the discovery of oil, desert cities bloomed and new industrial areas were created. Urban areas now contain high-rise offices, shopping centers, and freeways. Foreign investment has created new jobs and raised living standards. New wealth has led to better education and health care. In addition, women in the region have made a growing impact on business and politics. In politics, for example, **Golda Meir** (meh•IHR), who served as Israeli prime min-

CONNECTIONS

Science and Technology

Water From the Euphrates

Like their ancient ancestors, people in the Middle East today rely on the Euphrates River for water. The technology used to obtain the water, however, has changed considerably over the centuries. To ensure their water supply, the people of Turkey today rely on a series of huge dams on the Euphrates. The dams' reservoirs provide water for Turkey's expanding industries and urban centers.

Turkey's solution for its water problem, however, deprives Syria and Iraq of water from the same river. Iraq would be especially worse off because it is the last country that is situated along the river.

The Turks claim they need the river to better their economy. They hope to turn more of the Anatolian Peninsula into farmland. Crops grown there are needed to feed Turkey's growing population, they say.

Syria and Iraq claim that Turkey does not own the entire Euphrates River. They point out that not only will they lose water from the reduced flow, but that more will be lost through evaporation from the Turkish reservoirs.

Experts state that this crisis can be eased by all three countries repairing existing equipment, improving irrigation and water conservation methods, and expanding water recycling. The countries also need to grow some crops that do not require so much water. Above all, experts state that the countries need to better manage their population growth.

Turkish dam on the Euphrates River

Linking Past and Present ACTIVITY

Compare water technology today with that used in the past. What peoples relied on the Euphrates in ancient times? What lands depend on the Euphrates today? Does Turkey have a right to build dams on the river?

ister from 1969 to 1974, was the modern Middle East's first female head of government. In early 1990s **Tansu Çiller** (TAHN•soo see•LAHR) of Turkey became the first female prime minister to govern a Middle Eastern Muslim country.

Challenges

As in other parts of the world, the rapid pace of change in the Middle East also had its negative side. Cities experienced rising crime, and there was a growing gap between the rich and the poor. The greater independence of family members led to a loosening of traditional family ties. The availability of cars, TVs, VCRs, and personal computers brought a new materialism to daily life. Many people in the Middle East blamed the West for the new social trends.

Saudi Arabia

In Saudi Arabia, the birthplace of Islam, most people have fiercely resisted undesirable Western cultural influences. For hundreds of years, the land that is now Saudi Arabia was divided among many tribes. During the early 1900s, these groups joined together under the Saud family to form the kingdom of Saudi Arabia. Beginning in the mid-1900s, the Saudi royal family used income from the oil industry to support modernization programs. As a result, many Saudis have developed skills for management and technical jobs. However, the Saudi royal family, which still maintains a close hold on the country's affairs, has used tight censorship to shield Saudis from exposure to many Western ideas and practices. By contrast, more liberal lifestyles are permitted in Iraq, Lebanon, Syria, Jordan, Egypt, and Israel.

A Return to Religion

In recent years many Middle Easterners have sought solutions to their problems in fundamentalism, or adherence to traditional religious values. This development has also occurred, although in different ways, in other parts of the world. For example, in the United States, conservative Protestantism has flourished and has expressed itself politically; in India, Hindu nationalists have won widespread support.

Some observers view support for fundamentalism as a natural reaction by people who are overwhelmed by massive change and desire to seek security in long-valued traditions. Other experts, however, point out that the continued growth of religious fundamentalism deepens mistrust and hardens divisions at a time when the world's peoples need to develop greater understanding and cooperation.

In the Middle East, the revival of traditional religion has increased the political influence of Islam in many countries. Since 1979, Shiite Muslim religious leaders have ruled Iran. In Turkey, Egypt, and Jordan, the political power of Islam poses a serious challenge to secular forms of government. Israel's Jewish right-wing religious parties, although small in size, have contributed to the rising strength of political conservatism and nationalism there.

The most direct confrontation in the Middle East between traditional religion and secularism has occurred in Turkey. In 1996 Necmettin Erbakan became Turkey's first prime minister from an Islamic party. Military leaders, however, saw Erbakan's pro-Islamic policies as a threat to Turkey's secular political traditions. They forced Erbakan from power in 1997, and secular politicians then formed a new government. Many of the new leaders believe that the country's Islamic schools promote militancy among students. They have proposed a plan that would force the closing of many Islamic schools. Devout Muslims have protested this plan as a violation of their religious freedom.

Egypt also has seen religious conflict. Since 1992, Muslims in southern Egypt have sought to oust President Hosni Mubarak's secular government and establish a government based on Islamic principles. By late 1997, more than 1,150 people had been killed in battles between Muslim supporters and the police.

SECTION 3 REVIEW

Recall
1. **Define** sovereignty, desalination, fundamentalism.
2. **Identify** Shimon Peres, Hafez al-Assad, Benjamin Netanyahu, Arab League, Golda Meir, Tansu Çiller.
3. **Explain** three challenges to stability in the Middle East today.

Critical Thinking
4. **Applying Information** What impact has religious fundamentalism had on the Middle East?

Understanding Themes
5. **Cultural Diffusion** In what ways have foreign influences affected modern Middle Eastern society?

Bridge to the Past

Literature

from

Modern Poems

by
Jaime Torres Bodet,
Nazim Hikmet, and
Gabriel Okara

Modern poets have continued to explore both universal themes, such as friendship and loneliness, as well as individual preferences for a particular place or group of people.

The following poem was written by one of Mexico's greatest writers, Jaime Torres Bodet, who was born in 1902 and was active in politics. Bodet served the government as an administrator and diplomat. In this poem, Bodet urges people to take risks in their lives. Bodet died in 1974.

The Window

Translated from Spanish by George Kearns

You closed the window, And it was the world,
the world that wanted to enter, all at once,
the world that gave that great shout,
that great, deep, rough cry
you did not want to hear—and now
will never call to you again as it called today,
asking your mercy!

The whole of life was in that cry:
the wind, the sea, the land
with its poles and its tropics,
the unreachable skies,
the ripened grain in the resounding wheat field,
the thick heat above the wine presses,
dawn on the mountains, shadowy woods,
parched lips stuck together longing for
cool water condensed in pools,
and all pleasures, all sufferings,
all loves, all hates,
were in this day, anxiously
asking your mercy …

But you were afraid of life,
And you remained alone,
behind the closed and silent window,
not understanding that the world calls to a man
only once that way, and with that kind of cry,
with that great, rough, hoarse cry!

Nazim Hikmet, who lived from 1902 to 1963, often criticized the government of his native Turkey for serving only the wealthy. In 1951 he left Turkey, never to return, and settled in Europe. His sympathy for the peasants of his country, his love of nature, and his hope for humanity are all suggested in the following poem.

The World, My Friends, My Enemies, You, and the Earth

Translated from Turkish by
Randy Blasing and Mutlu Konuk

I'm wonderfully happy I came into the world,
I love its earth, its light, its struggle, and its bread.
Even though I know its dimensions from pole to pole to the
  centimeter,
and while I'm not unaware that it's a mere toy next to the sun,
the world for me is unbelievably big.
I would have liked to go around the world
and see the fish, the fruits, and the stars that I haven't seen.
However,
I made my European trip only in books and pictures.
In all my life I never got one letter
               with its blue stamp canceled in Asia.
Me and our corner grocer,
we're both mightily unknown in America.
Nevertheless,
from China to Spain, from the Cape of Good Hope to Alaska,
in every nautical mile, in every kilometer, I have friends and
    enemies.
Such friends that we haven't met even once—
we can die for the same bread, the same freedom, the same dream.
And such enemies that they're thirsty for my blood,
              I am thirsty for their blood.
My strength
is that I'm not alone in this big world.
The world and its people are no secret in my heart,
        no mystery in my science.
Calmly and openly
        I took my place
              in the great struggle.
And without it,
       you and the earth
          are not enough for me.
And yet you are astonishingly beautiful,
         the earth is warm and beautiful.

Nazim Hikmet

*G*abriel Okara, born in 1921, is one of many Nigerian writers to achieve international acclaim since the 1960s. Others include Chinua Achebe,
Christopher Okigbo, and Wole Soyinka. Some of Okara's poems deal with the problems of living in a country that is influenced by European culture. Others deal with
family, friends, and daily life.

Once Upon a Time

Once upon a time, son,
they used to laugh with their hearts
and laugh with their eyes;
but now they only laugh with their teeth,
while their ice-block-cold eyes
search behind my shadow.

There was a time indeed
they used to shake hands with their hearts;
but that's gone, son.
Now they shake hands without hearts
while their left hands search
my empty pockets.

"Feel at home," "Come again,"
they say, and when I come
again and feel
at home, once, twice,
there will be no thrice—
for then I find doors shut on me.

So I have learned many things, son.
I have learned to wear many faces
like dresses—homeface,
officeface, streetface, hostface, cock-
tailface, with all their conforming smiles
like a fixed portrait smile.

And I have learned, too,
to laugh with only my teeth
and shake hands without my heart.
I have also learned to say, "Goodbye,"
when I mean, "Good-riddance";
to say "Glad to meet you,"
without being glad; and to say "It's been
nice talking to you," after being bored.

Visualizing History National unity has been difficult for Nigeria to achieve because of its diverse ethnic groups. *How does the author remember his childhood years before strife divided the country?*

But believe me, son.
I want to be what I used to be
when I was like you. I want
to unlearn all these muting things.
Most of all, I want to relearn
how to laugh, for my laugh in the mirror
shows only my teeth like a snake's bare fangs!

So show me, son,
how to laugh; show me how
I used to laugh and smile
once upon a time when I was like you.

RESPONDING TO LITERATURE

1. In your own words, define "the great struggle" that Hikmet refers to near the end of his poem.
2. Explain whether you think the poem by Bodet is written just to the people of Mexico or whether it applies to people throughout the world.
3. What is the main point of the poem by Okara?
4. **Demonstrating Reasoned Judgment** How does each poet view individuals who are willing to act boldly?

Connections Across Time

Historical Significance The nations of the Middle East have ancient cultures, but their political systems are still being developed. This undertaking has often been complicated by conflicts among themselves and by the great difficulties of reconciling traditional and modern ways of life.

Solutions for the challenges facing the Middle East often seem elusive, and progress has to be measured in gradual steps. An example is the complicated peace process among Israel and its Arab neighbors. In spite of setbacks, some factors weigh on the side of progress and peace. The end of the cold war has made cooperation among Middle Eastern nations a greater possibility.

Using Key Terms

Write the key term that completes each sentence. Then write a sentence for each term not chosen.

a. disengagement
b. nationalized
c. fundamentalism
d. *intifada*
e. kibbutzim
f. embargo
g. sovereignty
h. Pan-Arabism
i. pact
j. desalination
k. cartel

1. In 1974 United States Secretary of State Henry Kissinger negotiated a _____, or military withdrawal, agreement between Egypt and Israel.
2. In the quest for regional unity, some Arab nations refuse to yield their _____ to an international body.
3. Some Jewish immigrants to Palestine settled on _____, or collective farms.
4. In recent years, some Middle Easterners have supported religious _____ in their efforts to defend traditional values and to oppose governments they dislike.
5. In 1987, Palestinians in the West Bank and Gaza Strip carried out an _____ to oppose Israeli rule of their areas.

Technology Activity

Using the Internet Use the Internet to search for an online newspaper with current articles about the Middle East. Find a recent article pertaining to any news from the Middle East. Evaluate your findings by writing a report that contains the source of information, title, date, and summary of the article. Include an opinion of whether or not this particular current event impacts your life.

Using Your History Journal

Write an essay about an unresolved Middle Eastern issue shown on your time line. Gather information about the issue, consider ways of solving the problems it poses, and evaluate which resolution you believe is most effective.

Reviewing Facts

1. **Geography** Discuss how geography helped make the Middle East a scene of cold war rivalry.
2. **History** Explain the link between the Aswan High Dam and the Suez crisis of 1956.
3. **History** Describe United States President Jimmy Carter's role in improving relations between Israel and Egypt.
4. **Geography** Explain the importance of the West Bank, the Gaza Strip, and the Golan Heights.
5. **History** Explain why the United States gave support to Turkey and to Iran.
6. **History** State the reasons for Saddam Hussein's invasion of Kuwait in 1990.
7. **Citizenship** Discuss why Iran's Muslim leaders opposed the rule of the shah.
8. **Citizenship** Describe the factors that sparked the outbreak of the Palestinian *intifada*.

Critical Thinking

1. **Evaluate** Do you think that terrorism can be justified as a means of attaining political goals? Why or why not?

2. **Apply** How have women's roles changed in the Middle East in recent years? Compare the position of women in the Middle East today with those of women in other parts of the world.

3. **Evaluate** To what degree do you think human rights and democratic government have made advances in the Middle East since 1945?

4. **Evaluate** Saddam Hussein justified Iraq's invasion of Kuwait, in part, on the grounds of nationalism and Arab unity. Analyze this reasoning. Do you think it is justified?

Geography in History

1. **Place** Refer to the map below. What country of the Middle East produced the most oil?

2. **Location** The four main producers of oil in the Middle East all border what body of water?

3. **Region** What correlation is there between the size, in area, and the amount of oil produced in the countries shown?

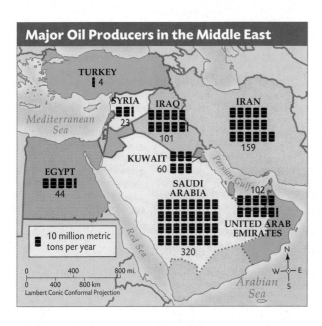

Major Oil Producers in the Middle East

TURKEY 4
SYRIA 23
IRAQ 101
IRAN 159
EGYPT 44
KUWAIT 60
SAUDI ARABIA 320
UNITED ARAB EMIRATES 102

Mediterranean Sea
Persian Gulf
Red Sea
Arabian Sea

10 million metric tons per year

0 400 800 mi.
0 400 800 km
Lambert Conic Conformal Projection

Understanding Themes

1. **Nationalism** How did the cold war contribute to the development of the Suez crisis in 1956?

2. **Cooperation** Why can the Camp David Accords be considered a turning point in the history of the modern Middle East?

3. **Cultural Diffusion** Do you think Saudi Arabia

will succeed in resisting unwanted foreign influences while developing its economy and society? Explain.

Linking Past and Present

1. When the state of Israel was founded in 1948, Israelis and Palestinians were bitter enemies. What was the basic issue that divided them in 1948? By 1995, how had their relationship changed? What issues continue to divide them?

2. Religion continues to influence life in the Middle East. What recent developments reflect this influence? How have religious ideas and movements shaped events in other parts of the world since World War II? What impact will they have in the future?

Skill Practice

Review the sample bibliography below for a report on the South American country of Brazil. Then answer the questions that follow.

Page, Joseph A. The Brazilians. Addison-Wesley Publishing Company, 1995.

Kirch, John. Why is This Country Dancing: One-Man Samba to the Beat of Brazil. New York: Simon & Schuster, 1993.

Rambali, Paul. In the cities and the Jungles of Brazil. New York, 1994.

J. F. Hage, "Fulfilling Brazil's Promise: a Conversation with President Cardoso." Foreign Affairs, Vol. 74, July–August 1995: pp. 62–75.

Levine, J. "The Dance Drink: Brazil's Samba Soft Drink to be Marketed in the U.S." Vol. 154: p. 232.

1. The entries presented above are not listed in the correct order. What author do you think should be listed first?

2. What is missing from the Joseph A. Page book listing?

3. What is wrong or missing in the Paul Rambali book listing?

4. Rewrite the J.F. Hage article listing correctly.

5. What do you think is missing from the J. Levine listing?

Latin America

Chapter Themes

▶ **Cooperation** New organizations promote economic ties in Latin America. *Section 1*
▶ **Revolution** The overthrow of dictatorial government in Cuba opens the door to communism in the Western Hemisphere. *Section 2*
▶ **Conflict** Calls for land reform and political freedom lead to civil wars in Latin America. *Section 3*
▶ **Change** Latin American countries work to develop their struggling economies and to establish democracies. *Section 4*

The Storyteller

On New Year's Day, 1959, the island of Cuba went mad with joy. Tall, bearded Fidel Castro, a lawyer turned soldier, and his band of guerrillas had overthrown dictator Fulgencio Batista.

Along the road to Santiago, crowds of people waved and cheered as Castro's ragtag troops passed by in battered jeeps and trucks. "Viva, Fidel! Viva la revolución!" they cried. So delirious were the throngs, so swept away by the power of the moment, that a friend of Castro's later recalled, "It was like a messiah arriving. We were walking on a cloud."

Castro's revolution was not the first in Latin America, nor the last. Over the next few decades, tensions between rich and poor would erupt in violence repeatedly as the nations of Latin America struggled toward economic and political development.

Historical Significance

How have Latin American countries worked toward political reform and economic growth? What changes have come to Latin America since the end of the cold war?

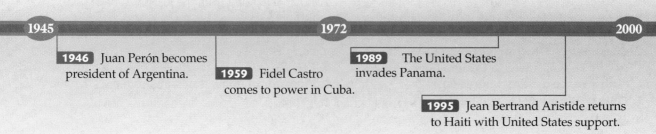

1945

1972

2000

1946 Juan Perón becomes president of Argentina.

1959 Fidel Castro comes to power in Cuba.

1989 The United States invades Panama.

1995 Jean Bertrand Aristide returns to Haiti with United States support.

Visualizing History Amid the glow of night lights, Sugarloaf Mountain overlooks the city of Rio de Janeiro, Brazil.

Your History Journal

Research population statistics of either Central or South American nations. Draw a cartogram that shows the relative population sizes of these nations today.

1948 The United States and Latin American nations form the Organization of American States (OAS).

1968 Catholic clergy in Latin America support social reform efforts.

1990s Civilian democratic governments begin to replace military rule throughout Latin America.

Section 1

Latin American Challenges

Setting the Scene

▶ **Terms to Define**
campesino, elite, liberation theology, free trade

▶ **People to Meet**
Luis Echeverría, Javier Pérez de Cuéllar, Jacobo Arbenz Guzmán

▶ **Places to Locate**
Mexico City, Brazil, Rio de Janeiro

 **Find Out** What social and political challenges did Latin America face after World War II?

The Storyteller

The university student volunteers reached the Guatemalan Indian village after nightfall. Eating tortillas and drinking fresh milk around the fire came first; then the cursillo *began—city and mountain people coming together to talk about liberation. The program included talks about the common good, the right of people to organize, and how to organize for greater strength. Standing before the gathering, Juan took a stick and snapped it. "Alone we are like this," he said. Then he picked up a bundle of sticks that he could not break. "Together we are like this. You and I and your children."*

—adapted from *Guerrillas of Peace, Liberation Theology and the Central America Revolution*, Blase Bonpane, 1985

Guatemalan village

In the years after World War II, powerful changes began to reshape Latin America. Between 1940 and 1970, many Latin American nations industrialized as rapidly as did the United States in the late 1800s. Social changes followed this economic transformation. For example, schools and health-care facilities spread, and women won the right to vote.

Yet a dark cloud hung over these bright and hopeful achievements. Much of the region's new-found wealth flowed into the hands of the well-to-do, leaving millions of farmers and workers in the grip of desperate poverty. As the gap between rich and poor widened, the huge peasant class grew hungry and angry. Communism, with its appeal to the oppressed and its promise of social and economic equality, won many converts. As the peasants' demands increased, strong military dictators emerged to quell political upheaval through repression and terror.

These military leaders, in turn, were unable to solve mounting political and economic problems during the 1970s, and their failures inspired calls for democratic reform. By the early 1990s, new civilian democratic governments had replaced many of the old, harsh regimes in a number of Latin American countries.

Population Growth

Since World War II, Latin America's population has skyrocketed. In 1940 Latin America's population was 126 million. With a growth rate of about 2.3 percent a year—about three times the rate of the United States and other industrialized countries—the region's population may expand to nearly 600 million by the year 2000.

Rapid growth has resulted from a combination

Visualizing History Deforestation by slash-and-burn methods and by excessive logging threatens the rainforests of Latin America. Despite increased agricultural acreage, there are not enough jobs in rural areas. *Where do people from these areas go to find work?*

of tradition and progress. Traditionally, families had many children. But because so many died in infancy, the population grew slowly. Latin American women still have many children. The average number of births per 1,000 Latin American women is twice the number in the United States, but improved health care has sharply lowered the infant mortality rate.

The rate of infant deaths, though five times that in the United States, is lower than in the past. Thus, more babies live to adulthood, and Latin America's population is increasing.

The population growth of Latin America has strained its economic and political systems. The expanding population requires increased supplies of food, clean drinking water, housing, schools, health care, jobs, and transportation.

Urbanization

As the population of rural areas expanded, the poor farmers—known as campesinos—headed to cities in search of work in factories or stores and of better living conditions. With more schools, medical facilities, and other social services than rural areas have, larger cities continue to attract many rural people. In the 1950s about 10 percent of Latin Americans lived in a city of at least 1 million people. Today, over 25 percent do; another 45 percent live in smaller cities.

Cities, however, could not absorb easily the heavy flow of campesinos. The new residents clustered in sprawling, dilapidated shantytowns, many with no electricity, running water, or sanitary

facilities. In his 1969 book *A Death in the Sanchez Family*, Oscar Lewis captured the bleakness of life in one such **Mexico City** slum:

❝ The [place] where she [Guadalupe] lived consisted of a row of 14 one-room adobe huts about 10 feet by 15 feet, built along the left side and across the back of a 30-foot-wide bare lot.... Five of the dwellings had makeshift sheds, constructed by setting up two poles and extending the kitchen roofs of tarpaper, tin, and corrugated metal over the low front doorways.... Toward the rear of the yard, two large cement water troughs, each with a faucet, were the sole sources of water for the 84 inhabitants. ❞

Such miserable surroundings offered little comfort or hope for the future. Even so, thousands of campesinos kept coming. The president of Venezuela observed, "The poor country peasant would rather come to the city and try to make a living selling lottery tickets than remain in the [countryside] where he has absolutely nothing."

Social Inequalities

Latin America's social structure—masses of poor people dominated by a small but wealthy class of elite—was established during the colonial period. Today the elite includes large landowners, industrialists, top church officials, and military leaders. Many of the elite in Latin America today

Chapter 36 *Latin America* **975**

are the descendants of the Europeans who colonized the region centuries ago. The increase in wealth brought by industrialization in this century simply made these families richer. By the late 1980s, 50 percent of the newly generated wealth in **Brazil** flowed into the hands of the wealthiest 10 percent of the people. As of 1992, 33 million Brazilians, about 21 percent of the population, lived in extreme poverty.

The majority of Latin America's population consists of poor people: peasants, landless farm workers, and factory workers. Many countries in recent decades have a small but growing middle class consisting of professionals, managers, clerks, and government workers.

A more important change has been in the development of the role of women in Latin America. Traditionally women had important but restricted roles in society. They were expected to work at home and raise children. In the late 1800s, women established their right to get an education and to enter a variety of careers. However, not until the mid-1960s did all Latin American women win the right to vote.

Economic Development

In recent decades many Latin American leaders pushed for increased industrialization. They hoped that their countries could manufacture their own products instead of importing them, thereby reducing their trade deficits. In just a few decades, Latin American steel production grew by 20 percent, while the production of metals, machines, and energy rose by 10 percent. Manufacturers flooded the markets with consumer products aimed at the upper and middle classes—fashions, sports cars, toys, and appliances. Since industrialization did little to increase the buying power of the poor, the market for consumer goods was limited to the small elite. Latin American firms quickly produced more than they could sell at home, so they turned to exporting goods to stay in business.

The efforts at industrialization brought results. Between 1950 and 1995, Latin America achieved a remarkable economic growth rate. Much of the money to finance industrial growth, however, came from large multinational corporations and banks. For every dollar they invested in Latin America,

CONNECTIONS

Geography

Booming Buenos Aires

Latin America is one of the world's most rapidly urbanizing continents. For example, today more than 12 million people—well over one-third of all Argentinians—live in the port city and capital of Buenos Aires. One attractive feature of the city is the pleasant, temperate climate. The people of Buenos Aires, called *porteños*, or port dwellers, are descendants of immigrants from all over the world—Spain, Italy, England, France, Poland, and the Middle East.

In the mid-1800s, British and Argentinian investors built a network of rail lines spreading outward from Buenos Aires. On these rail lines, wheat, corn, cattle, and

Downtown Buenos Aires

sheep are now sent to Buenos Aires for export. Building on its foundation of trade in agricultural products, Buenos Aires grew into a prosperous industrial center. Among the major industries are food processing and textiles.

Buenos Aires' rapid growth typifies the recent expansion of cities throughout the region. In 1909 Buenos Aires topped the 1 million mark. Immigration from overseas and from rural areas in Argentina added to the population in the succeeding decades. During the 1940s, Buenos Aires had 4.5 million people, and in forty years the population had nearly tripled, reaching over 12 million.

Linking Past and Present ACTIVITY

Discuss the features of Buenos Aires that have attracted immigrants. What effects do you think continued growth will have on Buenos Aires' future?

these business and banking enterprises took out more than three dollars in profits and dividends.

Agricultural growth did not match industrial growth. More land was allocated for growing cash crops for export, such as coffee, bananas, and coca, which is used to make cocaine. But as farmers converted more land to growing cash crops, they grew less food for the local population. Although the landowners prospered from selling their crops abroad, local people had to pay more to buy food from farther away. Most campesinos remained poor.

Hoping to stimulate economic growth, many Latin American leaders borrowed heavily from large banks in the United States and other countries. Between 1975 and 1985, Latin American debt to other parts of the world rose 318 percent. By the 1980s, a worldwide recession made matters worse—cutting global demand for Latin American products and further raising interest rates and Latin American debts. By 1984, the region's debt totaled $350 billion; by 1993, it had climbed to over $465 billion.

In spite of economic improvements in the 1990s, Latin American debt remains a major problem for the region. If debts are not paid, banks may fail, threatening the stability of the global economy. In the mid-1990s, a political and economic crisis in Mexico nearly led to Mexico's failure to meet its international debt payments. The United States came to Mexico's rescue with an aid package to bolster the Mexican economy. The United States government has also worked with Latin American countries to reschedule international loan payments to avoid potential crises.

Another economic area in which the United States and Latin America work together is the war on drugs. Powerful dealers profit from international trading in illegal drugs made from certain crops grown in Latin America. The United States and Latin American governments both aim to end the illegal drug trade, but difficulties often hamper cooperation. The United States often expresses concern about the corrupt influence drug dealers have on Latin American governments, while Latin American countries claim the United States needs to take stronger measures at home to lessen the demand for drugs.

Growth of Democracy

The economic problems of Latin America made the growth of democracy almost impossible. In most countries, the elite controlled the government as well as the economy. The elite did not trust the masses enough to allow any form of majority rule to take hold. The majority of people, long dominat-

Visualizing History Workers load bananas for shipment in Ecuador, where petroleum and agricultural products are the main exports. *How did the emphasis on production of cash crops affect the campesinos?*

ed by a few powerful leaders, had little experience in making decisions or choosing leaders.

Political conflicts in most of Latin America were between liberals and conservatives. Liberals tried to help the masses through land and tax reforms. Conservatives wanted to maintain the traditional social structure and opposed any redistribution of wealth. Clashes between liberals and conservatives have often been bloody.

The failure of democracy and social reform prompted calls for more radical change. Armed guerrilla movements, that sought to change society by force, emerged in many countries. These groups often relied on the support and protection of campesinos. Many guerrilla organizations included at least some Communists. In countries such as Cuba and Nicaragua, guerrilla movements successfully overthrew governments and took power themselves.

Fear of communism combined with outrage at the poverty of so many people caused changes in the Catholic Church. Since colonial times, the Church had generally supported rule by elites in most Latin American countries. Individual priests sometimes called for reforms to help the poor, but they were exceptions. After a meeting of Latin American bishops in Colombia in 1968, however, an increasing number of Catholic clergy began supporting land reform, democracy, and other changes that campesinos and workers had long demanded. They began emphasizing the role of Christianity in liberating people from oppression. Their beliefs became known as liberation theology. One Latin American religious worker explained the new movement this way:

> 66 For example, if, as the book of Genesis teaches, human beings have been created in God's image, they have a great dignity; hence, to torture another human being is to disfigure God's image. If the Lord gave the Earth to Adam and Eve, he meant it for all—not just a few plantation owners. 99
> —Philip Berryman, *Inside Central America*, 1985

The combined pressure of guerrillas, liberal Catholic clergy, and organized citizens began to bring changes in the 1980s. Argentina, Brazil, Chile, and other countries threw off their dictators and adopted democratic governments. However, these young democracies inherited international debts, widespread poverty, and social unrest. The most controversial issue in many countries has been land reform, which is still opposed by the military and wealthy landowners.

International Relations

Since the end of World War II, Latin America has become involved with the rest of the world. Latin American nations have forged new trading relationships with Western Europe, Asia, Africa, and Japan. In addition, many Latin American leaders have taken leadership positions in world diplomacy. For example, in the 1970s Mexico's president, **Luis Echeverría** (AY•chuh•vuh•REE•uh), was a leader in the nonaligned movement. Peruvian diplomat **Javier Pérez de Cuéllar** (kway•YAHR) served as the secretary general of the United Nations from 1982 to 1991.

The most important relations of Latin American nations, however, have been with each other and with the United States. In **Rio de Janeiro**, Brazil, in 1947, representatives of the United States and most of the Latin American nations signed the Rio Treaty. This defense pact provided that any attack on one member would be considered an attack on all members.

A year later, the Organization of American States (OAS) was set up to develop political and economic ties among the nations of the Western Hemisphere. One of its most important successes was in 1995, when OAS members Brazil, the United States, Argentina, and Chile intervened to stop a war between Peru and Ecuador.

Relations between Latin America and the United States were shaped by the cold war. The United States often provided military aid to conservative regimes while undermining left-wing governments. In 1954 the U.S. CIA helped overthrow a left-wing government in Guatemala led by **Jacobo Arbenz Guzmán**. Guzmán's efforts to redistribute land to the peasants was viewed as a threat to American business interests.

Another way to fight communism was through financial assistance. In 1961 President John F. Kennedy launched the Alliance for Progress. It provided $10 billion for Latin American industry, housing, medical care, and military development. However, much of the money sent to Latin America was used to buy American-made goods.

As the cold war ended in the 1980s nations in the Americas began working toward free trade, or the elimination of trade barriers among countries. Throughout the Western Hemisphere, groups of countries formed regional economic pacts, such as the North American Free Trade Agreement (NAFTA), the Andean Pact, the Southern Common Market (Mercosur), the Caribbean Community and Common Market (Caricom), and the Central American Common Market.

Western Hemisphere governments also took steps to bring together all of the region's free trade organizations. In 1994 leaders from 34 Western Hemisphere nations planned for a free trade area by the year 2005.

SECTION 1 REVIEW

Recall
1. **Define** campesino, elite, liberation theology, free trade.
2. **Identify** Luis Echeverría, Javier Pérez de Cuéllar, Jacobo Arbenz Guzmán, Alliance for Progress, NAFTA.

3. **State** how the role of the Roman Catholic Church in Latin America has changed since World War II.

Critical Thinking
4. **Evaluating Information** Has the cause of human rights advanced in Latin America since the 1980s? Explain.

Understanding Themes
5. **Cooperation** How might increased United States–Latin American trade affect the campesinos of Latin America?

1961 U.S.-trained exiles stage Bay of Pigs invasion in Cuba.

1971 The first Duvalier presidency ends in Haiti.

1993 United States, Mexico, and Canada enact NAFTA.

Section 2

Mexico and the Caribbean

Setting the Scene

▶ **Terms to Define**
standard of living, privatization

▶ **People to Meet**
Carlos Salinas de Gortari, Zapatistas, Ernesto Zedillo Ponce de León, Fidel Castro, Jean Bertrand Aristide

▶ **Places to Locate**
Mexico, Cuba, Dominican Republic, Haiti

 **Find Out** How did Mexico and the Caribbean face political and economic crises after World War II?

The Storyteller

The revolutionary leader Fidel Castro spoke of revolutionaries: "Whoever stops to wait for ideas to triumph among the majority of the masses before initiating revolutionary action will never be a revolutionary.... It is obvious that in Latin America there are already in many places a number of men who ... have started revolutionary action. And what distinguished the true revolutionary from the false revolutionary is precisely this: one acts to move the masses, the other waits for the masses to have a conscience already before starting to act."

—*Fidel Castro Speaks*, edited by Martin Kenner and James Petras, 1969

Castro as a young rebel fighter

After World War II, Mexico and the Caribbean nations of Cuba, the Dominican Republic, and Haiti were ruled frequently by either a single political party or by dictators. Mexico's single-party government controlled much of its economy, while American businesses played an important role in the Caribbean economies. In Cuba, a Communist government took power in 1959, bringing the cold war to the Western Hemisphere. In recent decades, Mexico and the Caribbean countries have tried to reform their political systems and develop their economies. Growing populations and political turmoil, however, have made these goals difficult to reach.

Mexico

Of all the countries in Latin America, **Mexico** was among the most stable after World War II. Since 1929, it had been dominated by one political party, the Institutional Revolutionary Party (PRI). Restricted by the constitution to single, six-year terms, strong PRI presidents, using their appointment powers, kept tight control over national and local governments. State-controlled businesses produced rapid industrialization and a growing middle class.

From the late 1940s to the 1960s, Mexico's standard of living—the overall wealth of its people—increased. Industrial growth was concentrated in the central region of the country around Mexico City. There, more goods and services were available to a growing number of people. Rural areas, especially in the south, lagged far behind, and millions of peasants remained desperately poor. Today 40 percent of Mexico's population lives in poverty.

Economic Problems

In the 1970s, oil seemed to offer Mexico a way to prosperity. New oil discoveries and rising world oil prices brought profits to the state-owned Mexican oil industry and boosted the Mexican economy. The government borrowed money from foreign sources to finance economic development, assuming that oil revenues would make repaying the loans easy.

Global recession in the early 1980s and increased oil supplies caused world oil prices to drop. The Mexican government was forced to cut back jobs and services to save money. To boost exports, the value of the peso, the Mexican unit of currency, was cut by nearly half. Some wealthy Mexicans responded by fleeing the country with their money.

Mexico soon faced an economic crisis, owing foreign investors $100 billion, one of the highest national debts in the developing world. The gap between rich and poor widened, as the population continued to grow rapidly. The growing demand for jobs, goods, and services could not be met. Then in 1985, a devastating earthquake hit Mexico City, the capital, killing thousands of people and causing billions of dollars in damages.

Relations worsened with the United States during this period, too, as a result of differences over drug smuggling and illegal immigration. The United States wanted the Mexican government to do more to stop the flow of illegal drugs into United States territory. In addition, growing numbers of Mexicans and Central Americans were crossing the United States-Mexico border without visas in hopes of finding work.

The Salinas Era

In 1988 Mexican president **Carlos Salinas de Gortari** promised broad reforms. To improve relations with the United States, he pledged to crack down on drug smuggling and illegal immigration. He also rolled back the policy of government ownership of major industries. With privatization, or a shift to private ownership of businesses, Salinas

Images of the Times

Mexico Today

Mexico faces economic, social, and political change as the nation attempts to provide a better living for its growing population.

Native Mexican crafts delight shoppers in the Sunday craft market in Oaxaca.

Petroleum and petroleum products play an important role in Mexico's trade. World oil prices affect the nation's economy.

hoped that Mexican industries would be run more efficiently.

Salinas also sought to create jobs for Mexicans by attracting more foreign investment. The centerpiece of his effort was NAFTA, the North American Free Trade Agreement. Begun in 1993, NAFTA committed Mexico, Canada, and the United States to removing trade barriers among all three countries over a 15-year period.

While Salinas's reforms were expected to succeed in the long run, Mexico at first faced setbacks. Economic benefits were slow to reach the poorest Mexicans. In addition, there was growing opposition to the PRI's hold on political power. In 1994 a guerrilla army of Native American peasants in the southern Mexican state of Chiapas rebelled against the government. Calling themselves the **Zapatistas**, after the revolutionary leader Emiliano Zapata, they demanded that the government aid the poor and advance democracy. They also vehemently opposed NAFTA, which they feared would hand their lands over to large corporations.

Zedillo and Reform

Also in 1994, the PRI candidate for president was assassinated during the campaign. **Ernesto Zedillo Ponce de León**, the new PRI candidate, won easily, but there was widespread dissatisfaction about the extent of government corruption, which allegedly reached even to the Salinas family.

As president, Zedillo continued free enterprise reforms, while promising to improve the lot of the poor. In late 1994, however, he faced a trade deficit that forced him to devalue the peso, a move that shook international business confidence in Mexico. American financial aid helped support Mexico's economy, but Mexican government cutbacks in jobs and services imposed hardships on many Mexicans.

To counter growing public discontent, Zedillo held talks with the Zapatistas and opened up the political system to other political parties. In 1997 elections, the PRI, for the first time since 1929, lost its majority in the lower house of the Mexican legislature. The two major opposition parties—the

Mexico City, home to more than 20 million people and one of the world's most rapidly growing cities, faces pollution, crime, and inadequate housing.

Ballet Folklórico enhances the cultural life of Mexico City, the nation's leading business, industrial, and cultural center.

REFLECTING ON THE TIMES

1. How do world oil prices affect Mexico's economy?
2. What challenges does Mexico City face because of its rapidly growing population?

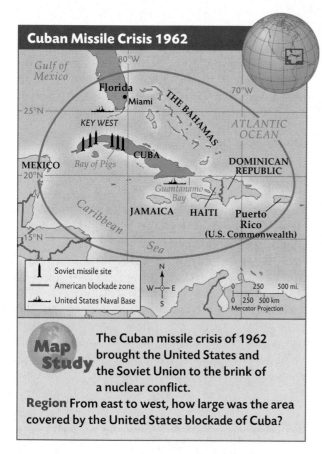

Cuban Missile Crisis 1962

Soviet missile site
American blockade zone
United States Naval Base

Map Study

The Cuban missile crisis of 1962 brought the United States and the Soviet Union to the brink of a nuclear conflict.

Region From east to west, how large was the area covered by the United States blockade of Cuba?

conservative National Action Party (PAN) and the leftist Democratic Revolutionary Party (PRD) gained a significant influence in national politics.

Meanwhile, United States-Mexican relations remained strained over the drug trade and illegal immigration. Mexican nationalists were angered by American doubts about Mexico's commitment to the war against drugs. They also opposed a new United States law that sought to crack down on illegal immigration.

Cuba

From 1952 to 1959, the Caribbean island nation of **Cuba** was ruled by the dictator Fulgencio Batista. Batista's government—often accused of employing corrupt practices—allowed American corporations to dominate the Cuban economy. By the early 1950s, United States companies, taking full advantage of this policy, owned or controlled many of Cuba's mines and ranches as well as much of the oil and sugar industries.

In 1956 a young lawyer named **Fidel Castro** began a guerrilla movement against Batista. Castro opposed Batista's repressive and corrupt practices and called for political reforms. For three years, he

and his soldiers carried out attacks on Batista's forces. On January 1, 1959, Batista fled the country, and Castro took control. Many former political officials and army officers were tried and executed. Independent newspapers were closed. Many Cubans who opposed Castro left the country and settled in the United States.

Castro's Domestic Policies

Castro promised democratic reforms and a better standard of living for the Cuban people. Instead of establishing a democracy, however, Castro suspended elections. He did push through reforms to improve wages, health care, and basic education. He took control of the land and nationalized plantations and major industries. Castro's seizure of American-owned property and his disregard of Cuban civil liberties angered the United States.

In retaliation, the United States cut off all sugar imports from Cuba in 1960. Castro meanwhile allied Cuba with the Soviet Union. Soviet Premier Nikita Khrushchev agreed to buy Cuban sugar and to sell arms to Cuba. Castro's dictatorship was openly Communist two years after the revolution.

TURNING POINT

Cuba and the Cold War

Castro's friendship with the Soviet Union made Cuba the focal point of the cold war in the Western Hemisphere. Castro supported revolutions in Latin America and Africa by supplying military aid and troops and by urging people to join the cause:

66 The revolution will triumph in America and throughout the world, but it is not for revolutionaries to sit in the doorways of their houses waiting for the corpse of imperialism to pass by. 99

—From a 1962 speech by Fidel Castro

Castro's defiance of the United States put him in danger. During this period the Central Intelligence Agency (CIA), the intelligence-gathering agency of the United States government, made many attempts to assassinate Castro.

In April 1961 the United States tried and failed to overthrow Castro in a secretly planned invasion. About 1,500 anti-Castro exiles trained by the CIA landed in Cuba at the Bay of Pigs, hoping to rally the Cubans to revolt and topple Castro. At the last moment, United States President John F. Kennedy barred open American military support for the

James L. Stanfield

Rich Heritage

Havana, the capital city of Cuba, dates to the 1500s. The Old City has endured, essentially unchanged for four centuries. Today more than 900 buildings—including palaces, churches, mansions, and humble dwellings—remain so uniquely preserved that the United Nations has classified Old Havana as a world heritage site. This palace, being restored from the ground up, reveals the faded grandeur and splendor of the colonial era. Once home to a Spanish conquistador's widow and later to orphans, the building now houses one of the few restaurants in Old Havana.

In 1959 Fidel Castro led a successful Cuban Revolution. After the United States rejected Castro, he turned to the Soviet Union, and for the next 30 years Cuba was a critical stronghold of communism in the Western Hemisphere. Castro's revolution kept out modern developers—along with tourist dollars. But it is partly as a result of Cuba's poverty and relative isolation that the island has preserved its heritage of architectural wonders like the building above. ⊕

effort. The Cuban people failed to revolt, and Castro's forces captured or killed most of the invaders within a few days. Kennedy's new presidency and the global image of the United States were badly damaged by the disaster.

A year later, the Cuban missile crisis brought the world to the brink of nuclear war. Soviet leader Khrushchev's installation of nuclear missiles on Cuba met with stiff American opposition. President Kennedy ordered nearly 200 American warships to blockade Cuba and stop military shipments from the Soviet Union. American B-52 bombers with nuclear warheads took to the skies, and American forces worldwide went on full alert. As Soviet ships steamed toward Cuba, a tense world waited.

Four days later, after tense negotiations, the crisis ended. Khrushchev agreed to dismantle the bases and withdraw the missiles, if the United States promised never to attack Cuba again. Separately the United States agreed to remove American missiles in Turkey aimed at the Soviet Union. The most dangerous confrontation of the cold war left the world shaken but relieved. Castro, however, was outraged at Khrushchev's yielding to American pressure.

United States-Cuban relations also continued to be icy. In 1962, the United States imposed an economic embargo on Cuba. Travel between the two countries was tightly restricted. Due to its ties with the Communist world, Cuba was isolated by other countries in the Western Hemisphere.

For brief periods, in 1980 and 1994, Castro allowed thousands of Cubans to sail to the United States. Most of these people were opponents of Castro's authoritarian rule. Others were criminals, mentally ill, or impoverished peasants.

Cuba After the Cold War

In the 1970s, Cuba sent troops to Africa to aid Marxists in Angola. With the fall of Soviet communism two decades later, the Cubans could no longer export revolution. Due to loss of Soviet aid, poor sugar harvests, and the American embargo, they had to devote primary attention to their devastated economy.

Despite setbacks, Castro still clung to communism. However, he allowed limited free enterprise to obtain foreign investment. He also permitted some religious freedom after a 1998 visit by Pope John Paul II. Although Castro's system appeared to be softening, the United States refused to end the embargo. As a result, Cuba remained the last remnant of the cold war.

Haiti

East of Cuba is the large, mountainous island of Hispaniola, which is divided into two nations. The eastern two-thirds of the island is the **Dominican Republic**, a Spanish-speaking country. The western third is French-speaking **Haiti**. The two countries are among the poorest in the Western Hemisphere. Relations between the two countries have often been tense because of their cultural differences.

Economically poorer than the Dominican Republic, Haiti has been ruled by dictatorships during much of its recent history. The dictator François Duvalier (du•VAL•YAY) ruled Haiti from 1957 to 1971. His son, Jean-Claude Duvalier, then became Haiti's leader but was overthrown in 1986. After four years of strife, **Jean Bertrand Aristide** (ah•reh•STEED), a popular reform-minded priest, was elected president. A military coup forced Aristide to flee the country in 1991. With broad international support, and the intervention of American military forces, Aristide returned to power in 1994. A United Nations peacekeeping mission helped in the country's transition from military rule to democracy. Mistrust and violence among rival political groups, however, slowed progress toward stable government and economic recovery. In December 1995, however, a peacefully conducted election brought René Preval to power as Aristide's successor to the presidency.

SECTION 2 REVIEW

Recall
1. **Define** standard of living, privatization.
2. **Identify** Carlos Salinas de Gortari, Zapatistas, Ernesto Zedillo Ponce de León, Fidel Castro, Jean Bertrand Aristide.

3. **Locate** Cuba on the map on page 982. Why might Americans have felt threatened by a Soviet military presence there?

Critical Thinking
4. **Analyzing Information** How was citizens' participation in government advanced in Mexico during the 1990s?

Understanding Themes
5. **Revolution** Explain why revolutions have been so common in the Caribbean and in other parts of Latin America since 1945.

1970	1980	1990	2000

1979 The Sandinistas overthrow Somoza rule in Nicaragua.

1981 United States begins aid to the contras in Nicaragua.

1999 U.S.-owned Panama Canal to come under Panamanian control.

Section 3

Central America

Setting the Scene

▶ **Terms to Define**
covert, death squad

▶ **People to Meet**
Anastasio Somoza Debayle, Sandinistas, contras, Oscar Arias, Violeta Chamorro, Oscar Romero, Manuel Noriega

▶ **Places to Locate**
Nicaragua, El Salvador, Panama

 **Find Out** What factors led to conflicts in Central America from the 1970s to the 1990s?

The Storyteller

An American journalist interviewed a Nicaraguan mother whose daughter, a school-teacher, had been killed. The teacher, who had volunteered to help young children in a small remote village in the war zone, was ambushed by the contras. "My daughter gave her life fighting for freedom, like my son who died in the insurrection. Losing a child is like losing your life." She stopped for a moment to wipe her cheeks, and then looked up again. "My children were my whole life," she said. "My daughter never hurt anyone. All she was doing was teaching poor children in the mountains how to read."

—adapted from *Blood of Brothers, Life and War in Nicaragua,* Stephen Kinzer, 1991

Contra soldiers

A lthough independent since the 1800s, the nations of Central America have suffered from wars, civil unrest, and interference by foreign powers. Ruled by wealthy elites, several nations were gripped by revolution and civil war from the late 1970s. Only in the early 1990s was some stability restored to the region. This achievement gave hope that the desperate needs of the people could finally be addressed.

Nicaragua

Nowhere was the hold of the wealthy elite tighter than it was in **Nicaragua**. There the Somoza family took power in 1937, and, with the exception of one four-year period, remained in control, backed by the American-trained army known as the National Guard until 1979. By 1967, when **Anastasio Somoza Debayle** took over the presidency, the Somoza family owned one-quarter of the land in Nicaragua and most of the country's industries, banks, and businesses.

The Somozas' rule of Nicaragua caused increasing resentment; and by the late 1970s, the United States had ended its support. In 1978 peasants, Catholic priests, business people, and Marxists united to challenge Somoza. Leading the anti-Somoza alliance was the Sandinista National Liberation Front (FSLN). The **Sandinistas** took their name from Augustino Sandino, the popular hero who had waged guerrilla attacks on American occupation forces in Nicaragua in the 1920s. Sandino had been killed by the father of Anastasio Somoza in 1934.

After the Revolution

The rebel alliance succeeded in overthrowing Somoza in 1979. Although the majority of Nicaraguans cheered the revolution, they differed on how the new government should operate. Some Nicaraguans believed in capitalism and wanted to

Chapter 36 *Latin America* **985**

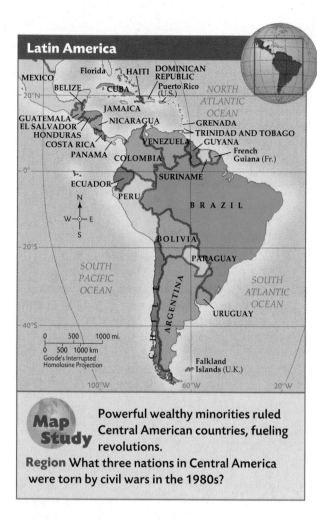

Map Study

Powerful wealthy minorities ruled Central American countries, fueling revolutions.

Region What three nations in Central America were torn by civil wars in the 1980s?

many western European countries. However, the United States, fearing the influence of the Soviets and the Cubans, decided to support the contras. In 1981 the United States government sent $19.5 million to the contras, the first official aid to the rebels. By 1985 contra forces numbered approximately 12,000 soldiers. From bases in Honduras and Costa Rica, they attacked Nicaraguan military bases and businesses.

By 1985 the American public began to fear that the United States would be drawn into another conflict like that in Vietnam. The United States Congress banned military aid to the contras. Despite the ban, members of President Ronald Reagan's staff continued to send covert, or secret, funds to the contras. This illegal use of funds was part of the so-called Iran-Contra scandal that became public in 1987, embarrassing the Reagan administration and leading to indictments of some of the President's staff. Critics charged that an undercover foreign policy was being carried out against the express will of Congress.

Through negotiations, which were led by Costa Rican president **Oscar Arias**, the contras and the Nicaraguan government agreed to a cease-fire and to hold presidential elections in 1990. With American financial and political backing, **Violeta Chamorro**, the widow of a popular newspaper editor killed by Somoza in 1978, won the election. Chamorro led a wide-ranging coalition of parties. After her victory, she faced immense challenges. Her inclusion of key Sandinistas in her government cost her support among the conservative opposition. Despite efforts to introduce reforms, Nicaragua by the mid-1990s had a staggering foreign debt, high inflation, and massive unemployment. In 1996 Arnoldo Aleman, a conservative, was elected president over his Sandinista challenger Daniel Ortega. After a campaign marked by bitter political rivalry, the new president called for national unity to solve Nicaragua's problems.

maintain close ties with the United States. Others called for socialism and a lessening of dependence on the United States.

The Sandinistas, many of whom were Socialists or Communists, held control and began a series of popular reforms. They seized land that belonged to Somoza supporters and turned it over to peasant groups. With Castro's help, they taught people to read and write and improved rural health care.

Within a year after taking power, however, the new Nicaraguan government faced growing opposition. Upper- and middle-class Nicaraguans who had lost property to the Sandinistas opposed the creation of what they saw as a socialist dictatorship. Many of them fled to the United States. Meanwhile, disgruntled former allies of the Sandinistas joined forces with former Somoza supporters to try to overthrow the government. These opponents were called the **contras**, from the Spanish word meaning "against."

Civil War

The Nicaraguan government received financial and military aid from Cuba, the Soviet Union, and

Footnotes to History

Nicaragua's Literacy Campaign

In 1980 over one-half of adult Nicaraguans were unable to read or write. The Nicaraguan government decided that those who were literate must help those who were not literate. Over the next 5 months, almost 100,000 students helped teach 500,000 people, most of whom were peasants. At the end of the period, Nicaragua's illiteracy rate was less than 15 percent.

El Salvador

By the early 1970s, **El Salvador** was one of the most industrialized countries in Central America, boasting modern highways, railroads, airports, and office buildings. However, nearly 90 percent of the country's wealth was held by a small group of landowning families. About 40 percent of the population consisted of landless peasants.

The unequal distribution of wealth led to demands for change. Fearing a revolution, wealthy landowners hired death squads—bands of killers who murdered their political opponents. As many as 1,000 people were being killed a month. One of the leading critics of the murder of innocent civilians was Roman Catholic archbishop **Oscar Romero**. When a death squad killed him as he celebrated Mass on March 24, 1980, the country erupted into a civil war. In her poem, "Because I Want," Claribel Alegría described the feelings of many Salvadorans:

> **❝** Because there are clandestine
> cemeteries
> and Squadrons of Death
> drug-crazed killers
> who torture
> who maim
> who assassinate
> I want to keep on fighting....
> Because there are liberated
> territories
> where people
> learn how to read
> and the sick are cured
> and the fruits of the soil
> belong to all
> I have to keep on fighting.
> Because I want peace
> and not war. **❞**

Moderates in the El Salvadoran government supported land reform but were powerless to stop the death squads. As the killing continued, the Farabundo Martí National Liberation Front (FMLN),—a coalition of leftist guerrilla groups—won greater popular support. The United States, fearing Communist influence within the FMLN, gave military aid to the El Salvadoran government. In 1992 the government and the FMLN finally agreed to a peace settlement. Over 70,000 people had died in the 12-year civil war. Another 1.5 million became refugees. Since the end of fighting, the government has made progress toward economic recovery and cooperation with its Central American neighbors.

Visualizing History Civil war in El Salvador claimed more than 70,000 lives before the 12-year war ended in 1992. *What was the FMLN?*

Guatemala

In recent decades Guatemala, the northernmost Central American country, has been torn by conflict arising from deep-rooted ethnic and social divisions. Most Guatemalans are rural Native Americans, but political and economic power has long been held by Spanish-speaking urban dwellers. Beginning in the 1960s, the wide social gap between rich and poor contributed to tensions between these two groups. A small number of Europeanized families owned most of the nation's wealth, while the majority of the Native American population were landless and faced discrimination.

In the early 1960s, leftist guerrillas supporting land reform took up arms against the Guatemalan government. The conflict heightened in the 1970s

Rigoberta Menchú received the 1992 Nobel Peace Prize for her work on behalf of Native American rights in Guatemala. *Why was Guatemala engulfed in civil war from about 1960 to 1996?*

and 1980s as the guerrillas strengthened their hold on the countryside. In response, the military harshly treated rural villagers, whom it suspected of aiding the guerrillas.

In the late 1980s, the government and the guerrillas agreed to talks. The 36-year civil war finally ended with a peace agreement in 1996. Although making no promises about land reform, the government agreed to reduce the military's size and to end discrimination against Native Americans. The guerrillas in turn agreed to disarm and return to their homes. As a result of the conflict, more than 100,000 people had died, 46,000 others were missing, and about 1 million civilians were refugees.

Panama

Despite periods of dictatorship, **Panama** was relatively prosperous and peaceful after World War II. Much of this prosperity came from the American-owned Panama Canal. Many Panamanians, however, resented what they saw as foreign domination. In 1977 United States President Jimmy Carter and Panamanian President Omar Torrijos (toh•REE•hohs) signed the Panama Canal Treaties. According to the agreements, Panama would take control of the canal by December 31, 1999, the canal would remain open to the ships of all nations, and the United States would have the right to protect the canal's neutrality.

In 1988 General **Manuel Noriega** took power as president. Despite Noriega's former position as a CIA agent, his role in drug smuggling increased tensions with the United States. When Noriega arrested Americans in Panama, United States President George Bush sent American troops into the country in December 1989. Noriega was seized a month later and taken to Florida, where in 1992 he was tried and convicted of drug smuggling. Panama's new President Ernesto Pérez Balladares worked to attract foreign investors and to end the legacy of the drug trade.

SECTION 3 REVIEW

Recall
1. **Define** covert, death squad.
2. **Identify** Anastasio Somoza Debayle, Sandinistas, contras, Oscar Arias, Violeta Chamorro, Oscar Romero, Manuel Noriega.
3. **List** the terms of the 1977 Panama Canal Treaty.

Critical Thinking
4. **Applying Information** President Kennedy once said of Central America: "Those who make peaceful change impossible make violent change inevitable." Show how events in El Salvador supported this observation.

Understanding Themes
5. **Conflict** What role do you think the United States should play in Central America? What role do you think other countries should play?

Developing a Database

Do you have a collection of sports cards or CDs? Have you ever kept a list of the names, addresses, and phone numbers of friends and relatives? If you have collected information and kept some sort of list or file, then you have created a database.

Learning the Skill

An electronic database is a collection of facts that are stored in a file on the computer. The information is organized in fields.

A database can be organized and reorganized in any way that is useful to you. By using a database management system (DBMS)—special software developed for record keeping—you can easily add, delete, change, or update information. You give commands to the computer telling it what to do with the information, and it follows your commands. When you want to retrieve information, the computer searches through the file, finds the information, and displays it on the screen.

Practicing the Skill

Fidel Castro is one of the Latin American leaders discussed in this chapter. Follow these steps to build a database of the political events that have taken place during his years as Cuba's leader.

1. Determine what facts you want to include in your database.
2. Follow instructions in the DBMS that you are using to set up fields. Then enter each item of data in its assigned field.
3. Determine how you want to organize the facts in the database—chronologically by the date of the event, or alphabetically by the name of the event.
4. Follow the instructions in your computer program to place the information in order of importance.

5. Check that the information in your database is all correct. If necessary, add, delete, or change information or fields.

Applying the Skill

Bring to class current newspapers. Using the steps just described, build a database of current political events in Latin American countries. Explain to a partner why the database is organized the way it is and how it might be used in this class.

For More Practice

Turn to the Skill Practice in the Chapter Review on page 995 for more practice in developing a database.

1973 Military forces overthrow Allende presidency in Chile.

1982 Argentina and Great Britain fight the Falkland Islands War.

Section 4

South America

Setting the Scene

▶ **Terms to Define**
hyperinflation, cartel

▶ **People to Meet**
Juan Perón, Eva Perón, Carlos Menem, Salvador Allende, Augusto Pinochet, Alberto Fujimori

▶ **Places to Locate**
Argentina, Falkland Islands, Chile, Colombia, Peru, Brazil

Find Out How has democracy advanced in South America since the late 1980s?

The Storyteller

Eva Perón expressed herself about many topics, including feminismo, *the women's movement in Argentina: "I felt that the women's movement in my country and all over the world had a sublime mission to fulfill ... and everything I knew about feminism seemed to me ridiculous. For, not led by women but by those who aspired to be men, it ceased to be womanly and was nothing: feminism had taken the step from the sublime to the ridiculous. And that is the step I always try to avoid taking."*

—from *Feminismo!* by Marifran Carlson, 1988

Eva Perón

Since the end of World War II, South America has become a region of sharp contrasts. Rapidly growing cities have sprawling slum areas as well as suburbs for the well-to-do and glamorous tourist resorts. While new industries have developed in the coastal urban areas, traditional forms of agriculture still dominate much of the interior of the continent. Despite areas of modernization and prosperity, widespread poverty continues to shape the politics and social structures of South American nations.

Argentina

Before a world depression and the rise of fascism in **Argentina** in the 1930s, the country was one of the 10 wealthiest in the world. Since then, the country has often been under military rule, and its prosperity has declined.

The Perón Era

The dominant political figure in Argentina from the 1940s to the 1970s was Colonel **Juan Perón** (pay•ROHN). When he was first elected president in 1946, Perón enjoyed great popularity, even though he was an authoritarian ruler. Perón and his glamorous wife, **Eva Perón**, a former film and radio star, became the heroes of the downtrodden. By increasing the military budget and supporting pay raises for union members, Perón won the loyalty of soldiers and workers. By nationalizing foreign-owned industries, he appealed to Argentinian pride over controlling its own resources. Eva supported construction of hospitals, schools, clinics, and nursing homes and distributed millions of shoes, sewing machines, and other household goods to the poor.

However, Perón's popularity began to wane in the 1950s. The much-loved Eva died in 1952. Perón's policy of taxing agriculture to fuel industrial growth led to a decline in food production. As the economy declined, anti-Perón protests increased.

More than 100,000 people rally in Buenos Aires, Argentina, in support of democratic government in 1987. The nation has had long periods of military rule interrupted by brief intervals of constitutional government. *Why has the military often seized power?*

In 1973, after almost 20 years of military rule, Perón returned briefly to power. When he died in 1974, his new wife Isabel took over, becoming the first woman president in the Americas. Economic problems led the military to oust her in 1976.

Argentina's military leaders sparked an economic recovery but ruled brutally. Death squads roamed the country, torturing and killing those who dissented. About 20,000 people simply disappeared. Mothers of missing children brought these human rights abuses to the world's attention through their weekly silent protest in Buenos Aires.

Toward Democracy

In 1982, in an effort to unite Argentina and to end one of the last outposts of colonialism, the military leadership sent Argentinian troops to seize the **Falkland Islands**, also known as the Malvinas. These islands off the coast of Argentina had been controlled by the British since 1833. Seventy-four days later, the Argentinians returned home defeated by the British forces.

After the Falklands humiliation, the military was discredited, and democracy was gradually restored. Economically, Argentina came dangerous-ly close to collapse. In 1988 inflation reached 388 percent. This hyperinflation—extremely sharp and rapid price increases—caused a severe depression, and much of the middle class fell into poverty.

In 1989 Argentinians elected **Carlos Menem** as president and in 1995 reelected him. Menem has brought inflation under control, attracted foreign investment, and sold off inefficient state-owned industries. Despite a growing economy, many Argentinians worry about high unemployment, deteriorating public education, and government corruption. Regionally, Argentina has joined with Brazil, Paraguay, and Uruguay to form Mercosur, a free trade area. Internationally, its role has been enhanced by joining in UN peacekeeping missions.

Chile

The long coastal country of **Chile** has one of the strongest traditions of democracy in Latin America. In 1970 the voters elected socialist **Salvador Allende** (ah•YEHN•day) to the presidency. He was the first Marxist in the Western Hemisphere to come to power through peaceful means.

To stimulate the faltering economy, Allende nationalized businesses, including American copper-mining companies, and distributed land to the poor. He also boosted wages and put a ceiling on prices. In two years, the economy grew 13.5 percent and unemployment was cut in half.

Not all of Allende's policies were successful, however. For example, the breakup of big farms resulted in a decline in food production, which in turn caused food shortages. And the increased wages led to inflation.

More important, though, Allende's policies made him powerful enemies. Wealthy Chileans, frightened by Allende's ties to Castro's Cuba, took their money out of Chile and invested it in other countries. In addition, the United States decided to undermine the Allende government by funding opposition candidates, promoting strikes and protests, and convincing the World Bank to halt loans to Chile. By 1972 Chile's economy was near collapse.

In 1973 Chilean military leaders who had worked closely with the CIA led a coup against Allende. After the successful uprising, Allende was found dead in his office. The military leaders claimed Allende had killed himself with a machine gun that Castro had given him as a gift. It was reported that thousands of people died during and after the coup.

The new government was led by a ruthless and powerful dictator, General **Augusto Pinochet** (PEE •noh•CHEHT). Immediately, Pinochet put an end to Chile's long-standing democracy. He dissolved the congress, censored the press, canceled civil liberties, and issued a new constitution. He killed or imprisoned as many as 1 in every 100 Chileans.

To improve the Chilean economy, Pinochet imposed higher taxes and encouraged foreign investment. Inflation, which had reached 600 percent in 1973, fell to 10 percent by 1981. Soon, store shelves were filled with consumer goods.

Popular opposition to Pinochet, however, remained strong. Many Catholic leaders continued to risk arrest, torture, and death by protesting against Pinochet's cruelty. In 1988, at long last Pinochet gave in to mounting pressure and allowed the people to have elections, which brought Patricio Aylwin to power. With the threat of another military coup still strong, Aylwin tried to revive Chile's democratic tradition.

In 1993, Eduardo Frei Ruiz-Tagle succeeded Aylwin as Chile's president. He has continued many of Aylwin's policies: decreasing the number of people in poverty by increased spending on education, health, and housing; and achieving steady economic growth. By 1997, Chile had one of the strongest economies in Latin America and prepared to join NAFTA.

Colombia

Since World War II, **Colombia** has had long periods of instability. Between the late 1940s and the mid-1960s, battles between liberals and conservatives caused the deaths of about 200,000 people. Colombians refer to this period as *La Violencia*, or the Violence.

During the 1970s and 1980s, the ever-growing power of drug dealers infected Colombian politics. Drugs, including marijuana and cocaine, became Colombia's largest export. Drug dealers in the city of Medellín amassed tremendous fortunes. They murdered more than 350 judges and prosecutors who tried to stop the drug business. By the mid-1990s, some progress was made in curtailing the power of the Colombian drug cartels, associations formed to establish an international monopoly by price fixing and regulating production. Yet, the illegal trade continued to flourish. In 1996, President Ernest Samper and other government officials faced charges that they had accepted campaign contributions from drug dealers.

Peru

Since World War II, **Peru** has experienced both military and civilian rule. In the early 1970s, military leaders distributed land to peasants, nationalized foreign-owned industries, and aided the urban poor. However, inflation and unemployment remained high. By the early 1980s, democracy had been restored under a new constitution.

In 1990, and again in 1995, Peruvians elected **Alberto Fujimori**, the son of Japanese immigrants, as president. Although criticized for his dictatorial ways, Fujimori worked to improve government effiency and increase free enterprise. During Fujimori's term, Peru has increased economic links with other Pacific countries, especially Japan.

In 1995 Fujimori succeeded in ending a 15-year civil war with a Marxist guerrilla group known as the Shining Path. A year later, militant leftists seized the Japanese ambassador's residence in Lima, the capital, and took a number of hostages. Four months later, Fujimori had Peruvian troops storm the residence to rescue the hostages. The successful outcome of the crisis boosted Fujimori's popularity and increased business confidence in Peru's stability.

Brazil

From the late 1940s to the early 1960s, **Brazil** was generally a democracy. During this period, Brazil's economy expanded as foreign investors opened steel plants and auto factories. In the early 1960s, labor unions helped elect leaders

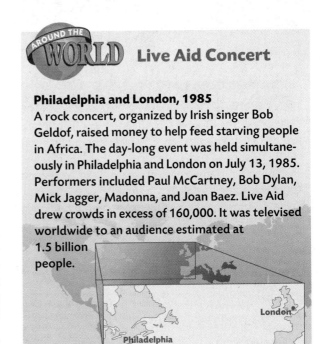

AROUND THE WORLD **Live Aid Concert**

Philadelphia and London, 1985
A rock concert, organized by Irish singer Bob Geldof, raised money to help feed starving people in Africa. The day-long event was held simultaneously in Philadelphia and London on July 13, 1985. Performers included Paul McCartney, Bob Dylan, Mick Jagger, Madonna, and Joan Baez. Live Aid drew crowds in excess of 160,000. It was televised worldwide to an audience estimated at 1.5 billion people.

London

Philadelphia

who promoted social reforms as well. However, military leaders, fearing that the reforms would lead to communism, took control of the government in 1964.

In the late 1960s, Brazil's military rulers pressed for greater industrial growth. They reduced social programs, increased foreign investment, and weakened labor unions. Although the economy prospered, workers' wages remained low, and poverty remained widespread.

By the late 1980s, increasing opposition at home and abroad forced the military to gradually return Brazil to democracy. Hopes for both economic growth and social reforms were raised with the election of Fernando Collor de Mello as president in 1990. Collor's concern for the environment, including efforts to slow the destruction of the Amazon rain forest, won him international support. However, in 1992 Collor faced charges of corruption and resigned. The new president, Fernando Henrique Cardoso, faced many economic challenges, among them reducing inflation and government waste.

SECTION 4 REVIEW

Recall
1. **Define** hyperinflation, cartel.
2. **Identify** Juan Perón, Eva Perón, Carlos Menem, Salvador Allende, Augusto Pinochet, Alberto Fujimori.

3. **Describe** major developments in Peru under the presidency of Alberto Fujimori.
Critical Thinking
4. **Making Comparisons** How do the economies of Chile and

Cuba differ?
Understanding Themes
5. **Change** How did military governments both improve and damage various South American nations?

Connections Across Time

Historical Significance The history of Latin America since World War II shows the challenge of establishing democracy in societies traditionally ruled by a small elite. In most countries, the bitter conflict between the rich and the poor has limited the development of stable democracies.

A second significant challenge in Latin America is economic development. Increasing agricultural exports and building industry have brought increases in total national wealth. However, the majority of the population has not always benefited from these changes.

Using Key Terms

Write the key term that completes each sentence. Then write a sentence for each term not chosen.

a. campesinos
b. death squads
c. elite
d. privatization
e. standard of living
f. free trade
g. liberation theology
h. covert
i. cartels
j. hyperinflation

1. Since colonial times, Latin American society has consisted of masses of poor people dominated by a small but wealthy _____.
2. From 1945 to the 1960s, Mexico's _____—the overall wealth of its people—increased.
3. Beginning in the 1960s, many Catholics in Latin America supported social change and promoted the ideas of _____.
4. Since the 1970s, Colombia has been affected by the drug _____, who control the illegal drug trade by fixing prices and regulating production.
5. By the mid-1980s, Mexico and other Latin American countries were supporting programs of _____, shifting control of industry from governments to private owners.

Technology Activity

Creating a Multimedia Presentation Locate information about the history of colonialism in Central America. Create a multimedia presentation about an individual country from that region. Include information about the history of colonialism, cultural influences of colonial powers and how that country achieved its independence. Before you begin, plan the type of multimedia presentation you would like to develop and the steps you will need to take. Cite all electronic resources used.

Using Your History Journal

Research statistics about the gross national (or gross domestic) product of Central American or South American nations. Draw a cartogram that shows the relative economic strength of these nations.

Reviewing Facts

1. **Government/Economics** List various political and economic challenges that confront Latin American countries.
2. **Government** Describe Mexico's political and economic system since the 1980s.
3. **History** List the causes of the civil wars in Nicaragua and El Salvador.
4. **History** Discuss political developments in Haiti since the fall of the Duvaliers.
5. **History** Explain how the Soviet collapse affected Cuba.
6. **History** Explain the purpose of the Organization of American States (OAS).
7. **Culture** Discuss the role of women in the struggle for human rights in Argentina.
8. **History** State why Juan and Eva Perón were popular in Argentina.

Critical Thinking

1. **Evaluate** How did the policies of the United States and Canada differ in the mid–1990s regarding Cuba? Which country do you think had the better approach in dealing with Castro?
2. **Apply** How would you solve the problem of the illegal drug trade between Colombia and criminals in the United States?

3. **Synthesize** Imagine that you were a citizen of Nicaragua in the 1970s and 1980s. How would you feel about the Somoza government? The Sandinistas? The contras?

4. **Synthesize** Describe the goal of NAFTA. What are the advantages and disadvantages of NAFTA to Mexico and the United States?

Geography in History

1. **Region** Refer to the map below. What large area of South America has an economy largely based on hunting, fishing, and gathering?

2. **Movement** Why are most manufacturing and commercial areas located along the seacoast?

3. **Place** Judging from the type of economic activity, where are South America's largest plains?

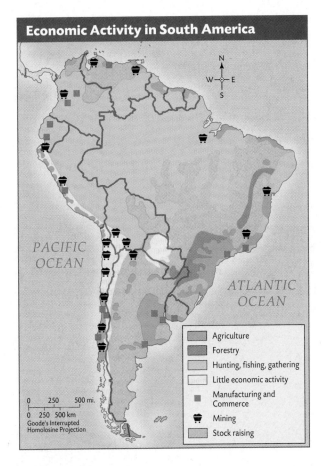

Economic Activity in South America

PACIFIC OCEAN

ATLANTIC OCEAN

▨	Agriculture
▨	Forestry
▨	Hunting, fishing, gathering
☐	Little economic activity
■	Manufacturing and Commerce
⛏	Mining
▨	Stock raising

0   250   500 mi.
0   250   500 km
Goode's Interrupted Homolosine Projection

Understanding Themes

1. **Cooperation** How has Latin America's interdependence with global and hemispheric

markets affected its ability to develop economically?

2. **Revolution** How did Cuba's revolution affect the United States and the Soviet Union?

3. **Conflict** How did the cold war affect revolutions and civil wars in Central America?

4. **Change** How have South American countries changed politically and economically since the late 1980s and early 1990s?

Linking Past and Present

1. How have American responses to Latin American crises today differed from American responses a century ago? How do you think the United States might respond in years to come?

2. In both the Monroe Doctrine and the Rio Treaty of 1947, the United States pledged to protect Latin American nations from outside powers. In the Falkland Islands War, however, the United States supported Great Britain. How do you think Latin Americans responded to this?

Skill Practice

Prepare a database of the major political events in South America from the 1970s to the 1990s. Include the following information in your database.
- Year
- Country
- Event

Be sure to follow these steps to build your database.

1. Determine what facts to include.

2. Follow instructions in the DBMS that you are using. Then enter each item in its assigned field.

3. Determine how you want to organize the facts in the database.

4. Place the information in order of importance.

5. Check the accuracy of the information. Make necessary changes.

The World in Transition

Chapter Themes

▶ **Change** The end of the cold war and the collapse of communism transform the relationship of the United States and the Soviet Union. *Section 1*

▶ **Change** The weakening of the Soviet Union and the rise of reform movements bring an end to Soviet control in Eastern Europe. *Section 2*

▶ **Cooperation** The European Union works to create a united Europe that will be a major economic power. *Section 3*

▶ **Conflict** National and ethnic conflicts intensify worldwide after the end of the cold war. *Section 4*

▶ **Cultural Diffusion** New technology and an integrated world communications system speed the transfer of ideas and practices throughout the world. *Section 5*

ᔓtoryteller

On December 25, 1991, Soviet President Mikhail Gorbachev resigned his office in a speech on national television:

"We live in a new world. The Cold War has ended, the arms race has stopped, as has the insane militarization that mutilated our economy, public psyche and morals. The threat of world war has been removed….

We opened ourselves to the rest of the world, abandoned the practices of interfering in others' internal affairs …, and we were reciprocated with trust, solidarity, and respect…. "

With these words, Gorbachev pronounced the end of the cold war. The road that had led to the end of this war was long and dangerous. The last ten years were no exception. Now, amid the jubilation and hope, the question was raised: "Where do we go from here?"

Historical Significance

What developments brought about the end of the cold war? How has the world changed politically and economically since the beginning of the 1980s?

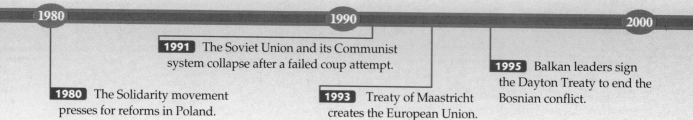

| 1980 | 1990 | 2000 |

1991 The Soviet Union and its Communist system collapse after a failed coup attempt.

1980 The Solidarity movement presses for reforms in Poland.

1993 Treaty of Maastricht creates the European Union.

1995 Balkan leaders sign the Dayton Treaty to end the Bosnian conflict.

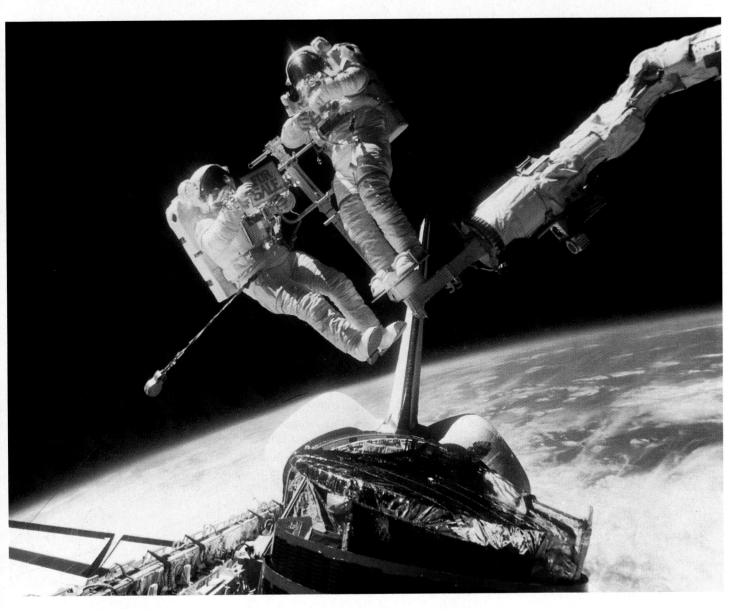

Visualizing History New technology has helped advance space exploration. The earth's people now can view the earth as a single unit with a shared environment.

Your History Journal

Choose a region of the world that is having difficulty keeping peace. Imagine that you are part of a delegation of diplomats from the United Nations who have been sent to the region to talk with leaders. Write your opening statement.

1980	1990	2000

1980 Ronald Reagan is elected President of the United States.

1985 Mikhail Gorbachev becomes leader of the Soviet Union.

1991 Former Soviet republics form the CIS.

1995 Russian and American soldiers take part in NATO-led Bosnian peacekeeping mission.

Section 1

The End of the Cold War

Setting the Scene

▶ **Terms to Define**

trade deficit, budget deficit, glasnost, perestroika, privatization

▶ **People to Meet**

Ronald Reagan, George Bush, Bill Clinton, Madeleine Albright, Mikhail Gorbachev, Boris Yeltsin

▶ **Places to Locate**

Moscow, Latvia, Lithuania, Estonia, Russia, Ukraine, Belarus, Kazakhstan, Georgia, Armenia, Azerbaijan, Uzbekistan, Tajikistan, Turkmenistan

Find Out What developments changed superpower relations by the mid-1990s?

The Storyteller

As the U.S. government's deficit soared out of control, the budget became the focus of debate.

U.S. group protesting budget cuts

Aaron Wildavsky explained what may be the heart of the problem: *"There are times when an agency wishes to cut its budget…. If the agency [has] effective clientele groups (special interests), however, it may not only fail in this purpose but may actually see the appropriation increased as this threat mobilizes the affected interests."*

—from "Political Implications of Budgetary Reform," Aaron Wildavsky in *Classic Readings in American Politics,* 1986

In the early 1980s, cold war tensions between the United States and the Soviet Union increased dramatically. However, the world had changed since the 1950s when the superpowers competed alone in the arena of world affairs. Now other blocs of nations, with their own separate concerns, were influencing global developments. In addition, the two superpowers faced growing political and economic problems at home. Together, domestic and international changes would lead to the end of the cold war.

The United States

By the early 1980s, the United States was losing its dominance of the global market. It had changed from a lending nation to a borrowing nation. America also experienced trade deficits, buying more from foreign nations than it sold in foreign markets. As other industrialized lands developed powerful economies, their industries competed with American industries in sales to American consumers.

Reinventing Government

Meanwhile, the United States government found it difficult to live within its means. In 1980 Republican **Ronald Reagan** won the presidency partly on his promise to reduce the budget deficit, or the difference between the amount of money the government collects in revenues and what it spends. As President, Reagan cut spending on social programs and lowered taxes to stimulate economic growth. During his two terms, inflation slowed and the economy improved. However, increased military spending by Reagan and his Republican successor, **George Bush**, pushed the budget deficit to new heights.

In 1992, Democrat **Bill Clinton** was elected President. Clinton supported both moderate deficit reduction and increased spending. Attacking Clinton for favoring costly government programs, Republicans in 1994 won control of both houses of Congress. Despite disagreement, Clinton and Congress finally worked out a plan to balance the budget and to move people from welfare to jobs. Meanwhile, new technology and increased efficiency boosted the American economy. This success enabled Clinton to win reelection in 1996 over his Republican opponent, Robert Dole, and Reform party candidate Ross Perot.

Accusations about his personal ethics, however, posed challenges for Clinton well into his second term. In 1998, the House of Representatives determined that Clinton had lied under oath and had obstructed justice in trying to cover up improper behavior. The House passed two articles of impeachment, or formal charges of misconduct in office, against the President. Clinton became the first President in 130 years to be impeached. In January 1999, Clinton's case went to the Senate for trial.

American Foreign Policy

During the 1980s and 1990s, sweeping changes in the world affected American foreign policy. In the early 1980s, tensions heightened between the United States and the Soviet Union. Both superpowers engaged in military buildups, and the Soviet army continued to occupy Afghanistan. By mid-decade, however, relations had improved as the Soviets undertook reforms. With the collapse of the Soviet Union in 1991, George Bush, and later Bill Clinton, supported the growth of democracy in Russia and other former Communist nations.

In the 1990s, the United States sought to develop a new foreign policy for the postwar world. Cuts were made in defense spending, and both Bush and Clinton generally conducted foreign policy through diplomacy or by using economic pressures. However, as the world's only superpower, the United States also joined in multinational military operations in such trouble spots as the Persian Gulf, Somalia, Haiti, and the Balkans. One of the architects of the new foreign policy was **Madeleine Albright**, who in 1997 became the first woman to serve as Secretary of State. Previously the American ambassador to the UN, Albright supported United States efforts to strengthen democracy in Europe, advance peace in the Middle East, and establish effective partnerships with Latin American and Asian countries.

American Society

As the twentieth century draws to a close, opportunities and challenges face the United States. The technological revolution has created opportunities for workers trained in new skills. However, workers without such training have not always benefited. In 1996, the income gap between rich and poor was wider than at any time since the 1930s. As a result, Americans now recognize the need for more effective ways to improve education and provide people with relevant job skills.

Crime and violence is another challenge. In 1995 the bombing of a federal office building in Oklahoma City claimed the lives of 168 people and focused national attention on the violent anti-government feelings of private American militia groups. To combat terrorism, the government has sought new powers, such as increased wiretapping, but this raises the question of whether Americans would accept limits on their civil liberties.

In the 1990s there were increased risks to the health of Americans. Diseases such as AIDS (acquired immunodeficiency syndrome) have killed thousands in the United States. Drug addiction continues to be a concern, which causes many to demand more government involvement to halt the problem.

Immigration became a pressing issue in the 1990s, when economic and political ills around the world brought a new tide of immigrants to the United States. Some newcomers were illegal aliens, people who enter a country without a permit. Many Americans blamed increased immigration for loss of jobs and higher taxes. In 1996 Congress passed legislation that imposed new restrictions on both legal and illegal immigrants. The new rules, however, were opposed by civil rights groups.

Related to immigration is the question of diversity. Some Americans believe that the different peoples who make up the United States should retain their individual cultural heritages. Others believe that the United States should be a melting-pot society in which immigrants from around the world blend into one unique people.

Gorbachev's USSR

In the mid-1980s, **Mikhail Gorbachev**, a reform-minded leader, came to power in the Soviet Union. To transform the inefficient, state-run economy and halt the decay of Soviet society, Gorbachev was willing to make drastic changes. Under his policy of glasnost, meaning "openness," Gorbachev allowed freedom of expression for Soviet citizens and eased harsh measures against critics of the Soviet system.

Soviet leader Mikhail Gorbachev (right) and his wife Raisa (center) greet Soviet citizens at a public meeting. *What changes did Gorbachev want to make in 1985?*

Departing from rigid state controls, Gorbachev also pushed for a rebuilding of the Soviet economy, a policy the Soviets called perestroika (PEHR•uh•STROY•kuh). Gorbachev encouraged limited moves toward free enterprise. He began to dismantle the national bureaucracy that controlled industrial production, allowing more decision making at local levels.

Gorbachev's Foreign Policy

Facing the enormous American military buildup under President Reagan, Gorbachev needed to negotiate new arms-reduction agreements with the United States. Since Soviet economic progress depended on military cutbacks, Gorbachev made large concessions to settle long-stalled treaty negotiations. His offers to cancel nuclear tests and to withdraw Soviet missiles from Eastern Europe were so sweeping that they took Western leaders by surprise. To further ease global tensions, Gorbachev withdrew Soviet troops from Afghanistan.

Gorbachev also encouraged Eastern European Communist leaders to carry out reforms. His policies inspired discontented majorities in these repressed countries. Scattered demands for democracy grew into a wave of anti-Communist protest that eventually brought down the Iron Curtain.

New Challenges

Gorbachev's fresh outlook and friendly personality made him popular in the Western countries he visited. At home, however, Gorbachev was increasingly criticized. Economic problems continued, and even worsened, while reforms stalled. At the same time, the conservative bureaucracy and military resisted change, fearing the loss of jobs and the weakening of Soviet might. To maintain control, Gorbachev zigzagged between reformist and hard-line positions, creating uncertainty throughout government and business.

By 1990, perestroika's slow pace had brought forward rivals to Gorbachev's leadership. The most powerful of these challengers was **Boris Yeltsin**, a former Gorbachev ally. Wanting to increase the pace of reforms, Yeltsin took his case to the people, winning election to the presidency of the Russian Republic, the largest of the Soviet republics. As an elected leader, Yeltsin had a stronger base of support than did Gorbachev.

The Soviet Breakup

While Gorbachev faced mounting opposition from political rivals, nationalist and ethnic unrest began to sweep the Soviet Union. As its name reflected, the Union of Soviet Socialist Republics (USSR) was a union of 15 separate republics, or states. The largest was Russia, which included the Soviet capital, **Moscow**. The non-Russian republics resented the dominance of the Russians over their affairs. A strong Soviet secret police and army had long kept opposition and nationalist groups under control. But in the relaxed atmosphere of glasnost, old hatreds resurfaced. Throughout the republics there were strong demands for self-rule, if not outright secession. In 1990 **Latvia**, **Lithuania**, and **Estonia** became the first republics to declare their independence from the Soviet Union.

A Dangerous Course

To appease the conservatives who feared a breakup of the Soviet Union, Gorbachev began a rollback of glasnost in the early 1990s and adopted new hard-line positions. Among them were the tightening of controls on the Soviet press to curb dissent and the restoration of powers to the secret police. Some of Gorbachev's reform-minded political aides resigned in protest, and Soviet citizens, led by Yeltsin, called for Gorbachev to step down.

The Coup Attempt

In August 1991 events in the Soviet Union finally reached a climax. Hard-liners in the military and secret police staged a coup to remove Gorbachev from power and to restore the old order. In three tense days the coup unraveled. Early support for the coup evaporated in the face of the heroic leadership of Boris Yeltsin in Moscow. Resistance spread to other parts of the country. Military units refused to carry out the orders of the coup leaders.

The coup turned out to be the turning point for the Soviet Union. Gorbachev was seen as unable to solve the country's problems and unable to shake off his Communist roots. Yeltsin became the real leader of the Soviet Union. Popular anger at the Communist party and the secret police swept the land, and the party dissolved. Statues of party leaders were torn down; many cities chose to return to their pre-1917 names. One such city was Leningrad, which had given birth to the 1917 Bolshevik Revolution. It took back its historic name —St. Petersburg.

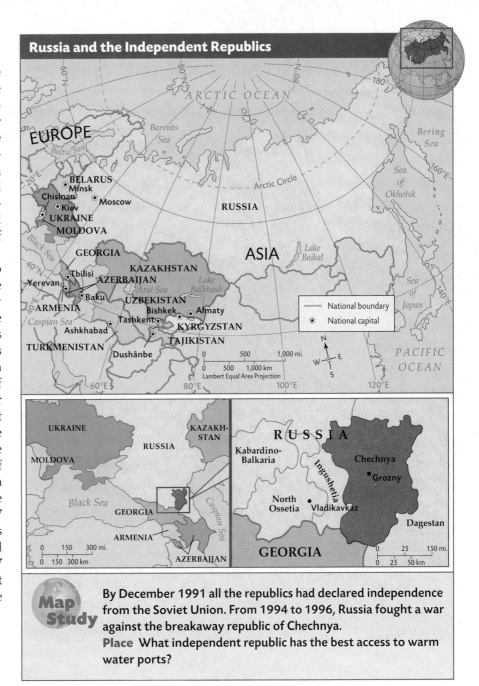

Russia and the Independent Republics

By December 1991 all the republics had declared independence from the Soviet Union. From 1994 to 1996, Russia fought a war against the breakaway republic of Chechnya.

Place What independent republic has the best access to warm water ports?

Independent Republics

By late September all the Soviet republics had announced their independence from the Soviet Union. Gorbachev failed to win their support for a Union Treaty guaranteeing the republics greater self-rule within the old Soviet framework. Yeltsin, however, chose another plan to maintain some form of unity among the republics. In December 1991, the three Slavic republics—**Russia**, **Ukraine**, and **Belarus**—announced the formation of the Commonwealth of Independent States (CIS), a loose association of republics to take the place of the Soviet Union. Other republics quickly joined. Mikhail Gorbachev, now a man without a country to govern, resigned the Soviet presidency.

Foreign Policy

After the Soviet breakup, Russian president Yeltsin moved to ensure the security of the Soviet nuclear arsenal. He and the leaders of the other republics holding nuclear weapons—Ukraine, Belarus, and **Kazakhstan**—agreed that Russia would assume command of the weapons. Ukraine later declared itself a nuclear-free zone and dismantled its arsenal of nuclear warheads. A further agreement between Russia and the United States was reached. The two nations agreed on a mutual reduction in the number of nuclear weapons that each had. By 1997, Russia and the United States no

Steve Raymer

Seeing Red

Traitor! A flag-waving Russian colonel shouts at a demonstrator who wants to end the 70-year-long rule of communism in the Soviet Union. Opposing visions divided the Russian people as they faced their uncertain future in the spring of 1990. Would their children live in the Union of Soviet Socialist Republics where they had grown up? Would communism prevail, after all the sacrifices made in the name of Lenin or Stalin? Would the state plan a national economy, or would the forces of the market prevail? Who would win and who would lose?

Communism first began to crumble in the satellite nations of Eastern Europe. As early as 1956 the Hungarians revolted, and in 1968 the Czechs rebelled. In these early years of the cold war the Communist regime was strong enough to withstand those assaults. In 1989 Germany's Berlin Wall crumbled. In 1990 the Soviet Union itself began to fall apart, first in the Baltic States and then throughout the country as the various republics proclaimed their independence. No wonder anger and fear line the faces of the two men pictured above, as they confront the end of the world they know. ⊕

longer targeted nuclear warheads at each other; however, mounting disorder in Russia increased Western concerns about foreign dictators and terrorists buying or stealing Soviet-era nuclear technology.

During the 1990s, Russia at first opposed the West's effort to turn NATO into a collective security alliance embracing much of Europe, including Eastern European countries formerly under Soviet control. To allay Russian security fears, the West pledged not to place nuclear weapons in Eastern Europe. Russia then agreed to the plan, while promising to continue its partnership with NATO in peacekeeping ventures. It also strengthened economic and political ties with the West by joining the leading free enterprise democracies in periodic discussions that became known as the Group of Eight.

Soviet President Boris Yeltsin tried to promote free enterprise reforms but faced powerful opposition. *What two groups opposed Yeltsin's reforms?*

Economic and Social Changes

At home, Yeltsin introduced reforms to move Russia's economy from government control to free enterprise. These measures included removing price controls, closing inefficient factories, and promoting privatization, the setting up of privately owned businesses. The immediate result, however, was an increase in both prices and unemployment, causing much discontent. Many of the other CIS countries—for example, Ukraine, **Georgia**, **Armenia**, **Azerbaijan**, **Uzbekistan**, **Tajikistan**, and **Turkmenistan**—pushed similar economic reforms while facing unrest among their populations.

By the mid-1990s, some progress had been made in stabilizing prices, and new businesses and a new middle class were growing in the former Soviet republics. Yet many reforms were stalled or had little immediate impact. In Russia, production fell sharply, and the government lacked funds to meets its obligations, mainly due to mismanagement, corruption, and difficulty in collecting taxes. To receive badly needed financial aid from abroad, Yeltsin had to cut spending for the military .

Russia also faced mounting social problems. Workers, the elderly, and the poor suffered economic hardships. Street violence, organized crime, and ethnic unrest increased public fears about the collapse of law and order. Pollution caused by Soviet-era industrialization presented a major health risk.

Taking advantage of widespread dissatisfaction, nationalists and Communists in Russia tried to block Yeltsin's reforms. Despite this opposition and his poor health, Yeltsin in 1996 defeated his Communist rival in presidential elections. To win nationalist voters, he had brought a popular general, Alexander Lebed, into his government; but after several months, Yeltsin fired Lebed when the general criticized his policies. During his second term, Yeltsin pressed ahead with reforms, naming a cabinet made up of free enterprise supporters.

SECTION 1 REVIEW

Recall
1. **Define** trade deficit, budget deficit, glasnost, perestroika, privatization.
2. **Identify** Ronald Reagan, George Bush, Bill Clinton, Madeleine Albright, Mikhail Gorbachev, Boris Yeltsin.

3. **State** the major issues facing the United States during the 1980s and 1990s.

Critical Thinking
4. **Applying Information** Why do you think the transition from communism to free enterprise has been difficult in the former Soviet republics?

Understanding Themes
5. **Change** How did Gorbachev's policy of glasnost contribute to ethnic unrest in the former Soviet republics and open the way for independence movements there?

1983 Polish labor leader Lech Walesa is awarded the Nobel Peace Prize.

1989 Uprisings topple Communist governments in Eastern Europe.

1993 Czechoslovakia divides into the Czech Republic and the Republic of Slovakia.

Section 2

The Crumbling Wall

Setting the Scene

▶ **Terms to Define**
autonomy

▶ **People to Meet**
Pope John Paul II, Lech Walesa, Nicolae Ceauşescu, Václav Havel, Aleksander Kwasniewski, Slobodan Milosevic

▶ **Places to Locate**
Poland, Gdansk, East Germany, Hungary, Romania, Bulgaria, Berlin, the Czech Republic, Slovakia, Albania, Bosnia-Herzegovina, Croatia, Macedonia, Slovenia, Serbia, Montenegro, Dayton

 **ind Out** How did Soviet Communist controls come to an end in Eastern Europe?

The Storyteller

The wall was coming down. West Berliners chipped away at it with hammers and chisels, while impatient East Berliners used heavy equipment. Finally a gap opened and a crowd of people surged through. Young people who had never visited the West sampled the goods of a market economy. Older people looked for friends whom they had not seen for nearly three decades. "It's been so long, it's a wonder we recognized each other!" With joyful exclamations, two old friends met by the ruins of the wall that had separated them as teenagers.

—adapted from "Berlin's Ode to Joy," Prit J. Vesilind in *National Geographic*, April 1990

Fall of the Berlin Wall

During the 1980s, the Communist nations of Eastern Europe, like the Soviet Union, faced massive problems. Their government-controlled economies failed to produce high-quality consumer goods and had fallen far behind the economies of the West. Reform had to be tried, but the Communist system was too flawed. When the Soviet Union began to change and signaled that it would not object to changes in Eastern Europe, the Communist systems collapsed.

The Rise of Solidarity

The final round of unrest in Eastern Europe began in the 1970s and continued into the 1980s. In **Poland**, the antigovernment movement had received a strong boost in 1978, when the Roman Catholic Church selected a Polish church leader, Karol Wojtyla (voy•TEE•wah), as its pope. The elevation of **Pope John Paul II**, a staunch anti-Communist, inspired confidence among the largely Catholic Poles and enabled them to take further steps toward liberation from Communist control.

In 1980 Polish workers in the Baltic port of **Gdansk** organized a trade union called Solidarity. **Lech Walesa** (lehk vah•LEHN•suh), an electrical worker at the Lenin Shipyard in Gdansk, was a founder and leader of Solidarity.

Solidarity backed up its demands for better living and working conditions with strikes, including one led by Walesa at the Gdansk shipyards. In a remarkable victory, the strikers forced the Polish government to recognize Solidarity in October 1980. Until this time, self-governing trade unions independent of Communist control had not been allowed to exist in Communist countries.

Under Walesa's leadership, Solidarity demanded free elections and a voice for workers in forming government policy. The Polish government responded by demanding that strikes and other "antistate" activities be ended. Under pressure

Lech Walesa began his career as an electrician and eventually became Poland's first democratically elected president of the post-Communist era. *What role did Walesa have in Polish affairs during the early 1980s?*

from the Soviet Union, Polish authorities outlawed the union 16 months later and jailed many of its leaders. Despite this, Walesa and others continued their activities underground.

Although Solidarity's activities were not immediately successful, the courage of its members inspired people in other Eastern European countries. Walesa became a symbol of freedom and an international hero. He was awarded the Nobel Peace Prize in 1983. By the end of the decade, the Soviet Union itself was changing under Gorbachev, and unrest had spread across Eastern Europe.

TURNING POINT

1989: A Year of Miracles

By the late 1980s, reduced production, decreases in labor productivity, high inflation, and trade deficits had virtually paralyzed the economies of Eastern Europe. This meant fewer goods at ever-increasing prices. The highly centralized economies, out of touch with consumer needs, caused widespread food shortages. Dissent against communism reached its peak in 1989.

Soviet Policies

As democratic movements gathered force across Eastern Europe during the late 1980s, many people wondered: Would Mikhail Gorbachev exer-

cise the terms of the Brezhnev Doctrine and put down rebellions? In a speech in January 1989, Gorbachev announced that he had ordered a cutback of 500,000 troops in the Soviet army—about half of that number to come from troops stationed in Eastern Europe. The troops had been put there to keep the Soviet satellites in line.

In March he pledged not to interfere with democratic reforms in Hungary. Referring to the 1956 and 1968 invasions of Hungary and Czechoslovakia, Gorbachev declared that "all possible safeguards should be provided so that no external force can interfere in the domestic affairs of socialist countries."

Gorbachev decided that most Eastern-bloc governments—which lacked popular support—would continue to provoke opposition. The Soviet Union would be forced to intervene militarily at great cost. Soviet interests would be better served if he simply let these governments fall. Gorbachev would then establish friendly relations with new governments.

Collapse of Communism

In 1989 Communist governments in Eastern Europe crumbled under the weight of staggering problems. All the satellite countries had ruined economies. Many had terrible environmental damage that had been ignored in the push to industrialize. Other countries, such as Yugoslavia, were being shaken by internal ethnic conflicts.

As economic and political instability increased, Communist regimes either resigned or were overturned in **East Germany**, Czechoslovakia, **Hungary**, Poland, **Romania**, and **Bulgaria**. Throughout this remarkable year of 1989, Gorbachev astounded the world by not only refusing to intervene in democratic uprisings, but actually encouraging reform in the region.

In mid-1989 Hungary, which had been quietly moving toward democratic reform for more than a decade, opened its sealed borders. A flood of East German refugees poured through this new "hole" in the Iron Curtain, seeking sanctuary in the West. The exodus called attention to the failed government of East Germany's leader, Erich Honecker.

The Wall's Fall

Amid mass demonstrations and calls for democratic reform, Honecker's government was toppled in October and replaced by a more moderate Communist administration. The move did not satisfy the reform movement but made its supporters bolder and more demanding. The next month, in an attempt to defuse the situation, the government lifted all travel restrictions between East and West. It hoped the refugees would remain in East Germany under a reformed but still Communist government.

On the evening of November 9, 1989, the famous Brandenburg Gate at the **Berlin** Wall was opened. All through the night East Germans and West Germans, hearing the wall had been opened, rushed there to see for themselves, overwhelming the guards and passing through the gate in both directions. Others swarmed over the wall, dancing and singing atop it.

In the following days, people on both sides of the wall attacked it with picks and shovels, opening huge holes—even selling chunks as souvenirs. More gates were opened, and the flow of people increased. Families and friends who had not seen each other in decades were reunited. The government, helpless before this popular uprising, ordered the rest of the wall torn down.

Violence in Romania

The overthrow of Communist governments in Eastern Europe was, for the most part, nonviolent.

The one grim chapter in the story took place in Romania, where dictator **Nicolae Ceauşescu** (NEE•koh•lay chow•SHEHS•koo) had ruled for 24 years. Ceauşescu's methods had become increasingly brutal over the years, and his reaction to freedom protests in his country was violent. Hundreds of people were killed before the Romanians revolted and ousted the dictator in December 1989. Ceauşescu and his wife, Elena, were tried and shot.

Throughout Europe and the West, crowds celebrated the fall of Ceauşescu. They were also celebrating the end of Soviet control in Eastern Europe and, in a larger sense, the end of the cold war.

New Leaders in a New Age

Following the downfall of Communist governments, reformers looked for new leaders to bring democracy and stability to their countries. They wanted leaders who had not been tainted by collaboration or membership in the Communist

Images of the Times

A New Era

A wave of unrest swept Eastern Europe in the late 1980s, leading to the fall of hard-line Communist governments. By the mid-1990s, some countries in the region had become sound democracies; others, plagued by economic uncertainties, turned to nationalist or former Communist leaders.

Solidarity led the movement for democracy in Poland. The labor union began in the shipyards of the Baltic port of Gdansk and soon spread to other parts of the country.

party—a particularly difficult task in East Germany and Romania.

In East Germany, the fall of the Berlin Wall quickly led to calls for the reunification of Germany. On December 2, 1990, Helmut Kohl, riding a wave of pro-unification sentiment, was elected in a landslide as the first chancellor of a reunited Germany. Other countries looked to their national heroes to lead their new regimes. Czechoslovakia elected a dissident playwright, **Václav Havel** (VAHT•SLAHF HAH•vehl), who had been in jail only months before. Then, in 1992, Czech and Slovak leaders agreed to split Czechoslovakia into two separate nations. **The Czech Republic** and the Republic of **Slovakia** became separate sovereign nations in January 1993. The countries maintain close economic and political ties. In Poland, voters made a choice that surprised no one: Lech Walesa was elected president in 1990.

Even staunchly Communist **Albania**, the lone holdout against the reforms of 1989, was finally swept up in the wave of protests. It opened its sealed borders, allowed opposition parties to form, and held elections in 1991. Other nations, such as Romania, organized coalition governments from a multitude of political parties.

Facing Challenges

After coming to power, new Eastern European governments faced the awesome task of shifting from communism to democracy and free enterprise. State-run economies were in shambles, and new governments inherited a host of problems. These included inefficient or outdated industries, huge national debts, workforces paid regardless of the quality of their work, artificially low prices for basic goods, and currencies considered worthless by the rest of the world. In addition, little investment was available in Eastern Europe to modernize old industries or fund new ones. To attract foreign investment and financial aid, new governments had to reform their economies by cutting spending,

Refugees push across the border from Hungary into Austria after Hungary in 1989 became the first Communist state to open its sealed borders.

A reunited Germany was celebrated by throngs of people near Berlin's Brandenburg Gate on October 3, 1990.

REFLECTING ON THE TIMES

1. How did the fall of communism in Eastern Europe affect Germany?
2. What movement rallied public support for democracy in Poland?

balancing budgets, closing or selling off inefficient state-run firms, and training workers in new skills.

Reforms and Stability

With their strong industrial bases, the Czech Republic, Hungary, and Poland seemed the most likely to succeed in the transition from communism to capitalism. However, even in these lands, economic reforms imposed hardships on citizens, with many workers facing unemployment and reductions in social benefits. In Hungary and Poland, dissatisfied voters in the mid-1990s returned ex-Communists to power. For example, a 41-year-old former Communist, **Aleksander Kwasniewski** (kvash•NYEHF•skee) defeated Lech Walesa for Poland's presidency. Eastern Europe's reformed communists, however, supported democracy and favored their countries joining NATO, although they wanted a slower pace to privatization and opposed radical cuts in social welfare programs. Yet by decade's end, voters seemed to be moving back toward the political center. In 1997 Solidarity and other non-Communist candidates triumphed over their ex-Communist opponents in Poland's parliamentary elections. Encouraging this trend was the decision of NATO to admit Poland, Hungary, and the Czech Republic in 1999.

Upheavals

The post-Communist era not only brought economic hardships but political instability and widespread violence to countries in the southern part of Eastern Europe. There, democratic traditions were not as strong, and economies had only recently been industrialized. In Bulgaria, ex-Communist leaders poorly managed the state-run economy and rejected any reforms until the country was hit by a grain shortage and severe inflation. In 1997 citizen protests finally forced the government to call elections, which brought anti-Communists to power. Bulgaria's new leaders promised to introduce free enterprise and won international financial help.

In Albania, Eastern Europe's poorest country, democracy and free enterprise were nearly engulfed in chaos. During the early 1990s, almost every Albanian family had put money in investment schemes, which abruptly collapsed in 1997. With their life savings wiped out, Albanians rioted throughout the country, blaming the government for the collapse and demanding payment. Rebel groups took control of southern Albania, and many Albanians in other areas fought each other with weapons looted from the country's arsenals. A UN-sponsored peacekeeping force finally restored order, and new elections were held. The new government stated that it could not pay back investors but that it would work to revive the economy.

War in the Balkans

After communism's fall, Eastern Europe experienced a rebirth of nationalist feeling. The most serious outbreak of nationalist conflict occurred in Yugoslavia. For centuries, tensions had existed among Yugoslavia's many ethnic groups. However, these hatreds were muted under the Communist leadership of Josip Broz Tito. After Tito's death in 1980, Communist controls gradually weakened, and in 1990, opposition political parties were allowed to form.

Multiparty elections in Yugoslavia were held later that year. Non-Communist parties won most seats in the parliaments of **Bosnia-Herzegovina**, **Croatia**, **Macedonia**, and **Slovenia**. In **Serbia** and **Montenegro**, the former Communist parties, renamed as Socialist parties, won majorities. The leader of Serbia, **Slobodan Milosevic** (swoh •boh•dahn mee•LAH•soh•veech), renounced communism but was intent on expanding his power. After the elections, the most industrialized republics—Croatia and Slovenia—charged that Serbia sought to dominate the rest of the country. In 1991, when Serbia opposed any restructuring of Yugoslavia that would give the other republics more autonomy, or self-rule, Slovenia and Croatia declared their independence.

Fighting in Croatia

Fighting then broke out in Croatia between the Croat army and ethnic Serbs who refused to be under Croat rule. Serbia and Montenegro, which together became known as Yugoslavia, backed the ethnic Serbs of Croatia. With this aid, ethnic Serb forces gained control of one-third of Croatia's territory.

A cease-fire in 1992 finally ended much of the fighting in Croatia, and UN peacekeeping forces patrolled the borders between Serb-held and Croat-held areas. A Croat offensive in 1995 finally brought the Serb-held territory back into Croatia. Since then, international human rights groups have accused the Croat government of abuses in its treatment of the ethnic Serbs in Croatia.

Bosnia-Herzegovina

In the fall of 1991, another republic, Macedonia, declared its independence. The following year, most of the Muslim population and the ethnic Croats in still another republic—Bosnia-Herzegovina—voted for independence from Serb-controlled

Visualizing History On November 21, 1995, the leaders of Serbia, Bosnia-Herzegovina, and Croatia joined U.S. Secretary of State Warren Christopher in initialing an accord. *What decision was reached at the Dayton peace talks?*

Yugoslavia. Ethnic Serbs living in Bosnia-Herzegovina opposed the election and its outcome.

Fighting then broke out between the ethnic Serbs in Bosnia-Herzegovina and the rest of the population—the Bosnian Muslims and the Croats. Yugoslavia, Serbia and Montenegro provided aid to the Bosnian Serbs, who soon controlled most of Bosnia-Herzegovina.

In 1994 the exhausted Bosnian Muslims and Croats formed a federation, and the United States asked the Bosnian Serbs to end the fighting and join as well. After military pressure from Croatia's land forces and NATO air strikes, the Bosnian Serbs accepted a cease-fire and American-sponsored peace talks. In 1995 the leaders of Bosnia-Herzegovina, Yugoslavia (Serbia and Montenegro), and Croatia met at **Dayton**, Ohio, and agreed to set up a Bosnian state divided into separate Croat-Muslim and Serb regions.

Milosevic's Serbia

Dissatisfaction with Slobodan Milosevic led to discord in Serbia. In 1996 Milosevic tried to block opposition wins in local elections. Protests later forced him to accept the results, but Milosevic continued to strengthen his power. In 1998 he sent forces into Kosovo province to crack down on ethnic Albanians demanding independence. The Serbian president ignored international calls for a cease-fire and pullback of forces.

SECTION 2 REVIEW

Recall

1. **Define** autonomy.
2. **Identify** Pope John Paul II, Solidarity, Lech Walesa, Nicolae Ceauşescu, Václav Havel, Aleksander Kwasniewski, Slobodan Milosevic.

3. **Explain** Why were some of the revolutions in Eastern Europe more violent than others?

Critical Thinking

4. **Applying Information** What kinds of changes have occurred rapidly in Eastern European countries? Which changes are occurring slowly?

Understanding Themes

5. **Change** What changes came to the Yugoslav area with the fall of communism in the late 1980s and early 1990s?

1980 .... 1990 2000

1981 France elects its first Socialist president.

1986 Spain and Portugal join the European Community.

1990 East Germany and West Germany reunite.

1995 The British and Irish governments announce talks to resolve Northern Ireland's future.

Section 3

Toward a European Union

Setting the Scene

▶ **Terms to Define**
referendum, collective security

▶ **People to Meet**
Margaret Thatcher, John Major, Tony Blair, François Mitterrand, Jacques Chirac, Helmut Kohl, Juan Carlos I, Felipe González, Andreas Papandreou

▶ **Places to Locate**
Northern Ireland, Cyprus

ind Out   What steps have Western European nations taken to unify their governments and economies?

The **Storyteller**

Paddy Ashdown believed in the European Union. As a businessman and a member of Parliament, he saw the benefits of Britain's participation. Already he had seen imports and exports move more freely, unhampered by restrictive tariffs. The last remaining hurdle was that of a common currency. Ashdown took the floor of Parliament to argue for the proposition. "We face the prospect of either joining an imperfect monetary union at a later date, or staying out altogether. This is exactly what happened over the EU itself. We must not make the same mistake twice."

European Union Currency

—adapted from "The Case for a Single Currency," Paddy Ashdown, in *The Economist Newspaper, Ltd.*, March 4, 1995

Since the 1970s, Western European nations have faced economic recession, budget deficits, and high unemployment. However, they also have worked to modernize their societies and to balance economic growth with the social needs of their peoples. By 1995, Western Europe as a whole had made great strides toward full economic and political unity. Yet it faced a number of economic and political challenges resulting from economic restructuring, increasing immigration, the reunification of Germany, the collapse of the Soviet bloc, and the outbreak of fierce ethnic conflict in the Balkans.

Great Britain

During the 1970s, Great Britain's economic woes continued under Labour governments. In 1979 voters, dissatisfied with a weak economy, high taxes, and trade union strikes, brought the Conservative party into a long period of power.

From Thatcher to Blair

As Great Britain's first woman prime minister, Conservative party leader **Margaret Thatcher** aggressively introduced free market measures. She privatized state-owned industries, scaled back welfare programs, and limited trade union powers. Although Thatcher's policies aided business growth, they created high unemployment. Declining popularity and the loss of Conservative support led to her resignation in 1990.

Thatcher's successor, **John Major**, led a Conservative party increasingly divided over Great Britain's ties to Europe. Some Conservatives wanted British participation in a united Europe, while others feared a future European union would mean a loss of British independence.

Political murals cover buildings in both Protestant and Catholic Northern Ireland neighborhoods. *What issue has led to conflict in Northern Ireland?*

During the 1990s, the British economy continued to grow, with falling unemployment and relatively low inflation. However, after nearly 18 years of Conservative rule, voters wanted a change and in 1997 brought the Labour party to power. Known for his youthful, energetic style, the new prime minister, **Tony Blair**, moved away from Labour's traditional socialism and favored low taxes, tightly controlled social spending, and closer ties to Europe.

The most innovative of Blair's plans was the reform of British government. In response to growing nationalism in Scotland and Wales, Blair favored home rule for these parts of Great Britain.

In 1997 Scottish voters approved creation of their own parliament to tax and legislate on local issues, and Welsh voters backed plans for a less powerful assembly that would spend funds provided by the British Parliament. Blair also pressured the long-established but scandal-plagued monarchy to be more in touch with the people.

Ireland

A major European issue from the 1970s to the 1990s was the status of **Northern Ireland**, the British-ruled province torn by divisions between Protestants and Catholics. The Protestant majority wanted to remain British, while the Catholic minority wanted to be part of the Republic of Ireland. Long-standing Protestant discrimination of Roman Catholics in the province had led to civil rights protests during the 1960s. As clashes between the two communities increased, the British government sent troops to Northern Ireland and imposed direct rule during the early 1970s. Meanwhile, the outlawed Irish Republican Army (IRA) fought British rule by attacking British military forces and civilians in the province and in Great Britain.

After heightened violence and crackdowns in the 1980s, all sides in the Northern Irish dispute agreed to a cease-fire and talks a decade later. A peace agreement made in 1998 continued British rule in Northern Ireland, but also set up an elected assembly and an executive council made up of Protestants and Catholics. The new government was to cooperate with the Republic of Ireland, which for the first time had a share in governing Northern Ireland.

France

France enjoyed political stability from the 1970s to the 1990s. In 1981 French voters elected **François Mitterrand** as France's first Socialist president. Mitterrand nationalized major industries and funded new social programs. His measures, however, increased inflation, and he eventually was forced to make cutbacks. By the mid-1990s, Mitterrand also had to work with a largely conservative legislature. Meanwhile, voter concerns about government corruption, unemployment, high taxes, and increasing immigration from northern Africa and Asia remained high.

In 1995 **Jacques Chirac**, the conservative mayor of Paris, was elected president of France. Chirac promised a referendum, or popular vote, on France's future relationship with a united Europe. He also tried to balance the budget by further cuts in government spending. To protest Chirac's economic policies, workers and students staged nationwide strikes and demonstrations. In 1997 a majority of voters rebuffed Chirac and elected Socialists and other leftists to France's legislature. A period of difficult relations began between the conservative president and the leftist legislature. Chirac pushed for less spending and more business growth, while his Socialist opponents stressed jobs for unemployed workers and the protection of social benefits.

Germany

During the 1970s West Germany, under Chancellor Willy Brandt and his successor, Helmut Schmidt, enjoyed prosperity. But the early 1980s saw a growth of inflation and unemployment. Promising better times, a conservative chancellor, **Helmut Kohl**, came to power. In 1990 Kohl presided over the reunification of Germany following the collapse of communism in Eastern Europe. He made preparations for the transfer of the German capital from Bonn to Berlin by the year 2000.

When the excitement of reunification wore off, Germans realized that the economic costs of reunification were far higher than anyone had foreseen. Eastern Germany's economic rebuilding after years of Communist rule required vast expenditures, and Germans in the western part had to pay higher taxes to support this restructuring. In eastern Germany, the closing of inefficient industries caused unemployment to soar, although economic rebuilding in the long term would provide eastern Germany with the most modern technology in Europe.

By 1997, unemployment was at its highest level throughout Germany since the 1930s. Meanwhile, the government faced the dilemma of trying to maintain generous welfare programs while controlling its budget deficit. Further progress toward greater European economic unity required Germany to keep its deficit under control, but workers opposed any government effort to roll back price supports for certain goods.

Social and political unrest accompanied economic difficulties throughout Germany. Neo-Nazis and other right-wing Germans protested against immigration from southern Europe and the Middle East. Some of them attacked foreigners, resulting in a number of deaths. Large numbers of Germans protested the attacks, but the German parliament in 1993 amended the constitution to reduce the flow of immigrants into Germany.

That same year, Germany's highest court ruled that German troops could take part in international peacekeeping missions. Until then, the constitution had banned all military activities except those related to collective security, or joint agreement by nations to protect themselves from attack.

Mediterranean Europe

Mediterranean Europe made great strides in political and economic development from the 1970s to the 1990s. Dictatorships fell and democracies arose in Spain and Portugal. Economic recession, however, hurt the Mediterranean countries.

Italy

From the 1970s to the 1990s, a variety of economic, social, and political problems plagued Italy. Among these were the uneven distribution of wealth, especially between north and south, an inefficient government bureaucracy, and constantly changing governments.

During the 1970s, Italy had the largest Communist party in western Europe. The party was popular in part because it promoted a less authoritarian view of communism. It sought to share power with the ruling conservative Christian Democrats. Many conservative Italians, however, were alarmed at this prospect. Adding to the political uncertainty was a wave of murders, kidnappings, and bombings by leftist groups.

Christian Democrats, later renamed the Populists, controlled the government during the late 1980s and early 1990s. During this time, the leftist parties—Communists and Socialists—suffered from policy disputes and political scandals. By the late 1990s, government power shifted back and forth between conservative and leftist coalitions. The leaders of these governments faced the challenge of shrinking Italy's enormous budget deficit.

Spain and Portugal

After nearly 35 years of dictatorship under Francisco Franco, Spain in the late 1970s entered a new era of democracy guided by its new king, **Juan Carlos I**. For most of the 1980s and 1990s, Spain's democratic government was in the hands of the Socialists and their leader, **Felipe González**. In 1996 Spanish voters replaced the Socialists with a conservative government under José Maria Aznar.

Since the restoration of democracy, the Spanish government has granted the Basque Provinces and other regions of Spain increased self-rule after years of repression under Franco. Nevertheless, it has been unable to stop terrorist attacks by Basques wanting full independence for their region. In foreign affairs, Spain has strengthened its links to the

Footnotes to History

The Chunnel
In 1994 Great Britain and France, separated for thousands of years by the English Channel, were once again joined. The Channel Tunnel, nicknamed the Chunnel, linked the island country to mainland Europe. By the year 2003 the Chunnel is expected to carry more than 120,000 people between Great Britain and France each day. At night, tons of freight will now move through the Chunnel.

rest of Europe after joining NATO and the European Community in the 1980s.

A turn toward democracy also occurred in Portugal. There, dictatorship ended with a military coup in 1974, and two years later the nation held its first free elections in 50 years. During this time, Portugal freed most of its African and Asian colonies and in 1986 joined the European Community.

Greece

From the mid-1960s to the early 1970s, Greece was ruled by a repressive military government. In 1974 democracy was restored, and for the next two decades the country was ruled by either conservatives or Socialists. In 1981 the Socialists under Premier **Andreas Papandreou** (pah•pahn•DRAY•yoo) brought Greece into the European Community.

In recent years, Greece has had differences with neighboring Turkey over **Cyprus**, a Mediterranean island republic divided between feuding Greek and Turkish communities. Since 1974, Turkish forces have occupied northern Cyprus, while the southern part of the island remains under an internationally recognized government led by Greek Cypriots.

A United Europe

During the 1980s and 1990s, the Common Market broadened its activities to include political and financial affairs and became known as the European Community. In 1992 European Community members met in Maastricht, the Netherlands, and signed the Treaty of Maastricht, setting up the European Union (EU). This new body aimed to extend cooperation among members.

In 1993 another measure—the Single Europe Act—ended most obstacles to trade among EU members. Two years later, seven EU nations allowed their citizens to freely travel from one member country to another without a passport. The year 1995 also saw the admission of Austria, Finland, and Sweden to the EU.

The EU looks ahead to even closer unity among its members. Plans are underway to include Eastern European countries and to create an Economic and Monetary Union (EMU) by the year 1999. The principal features of the EMU will be a common currency known as the euro and a central bank.

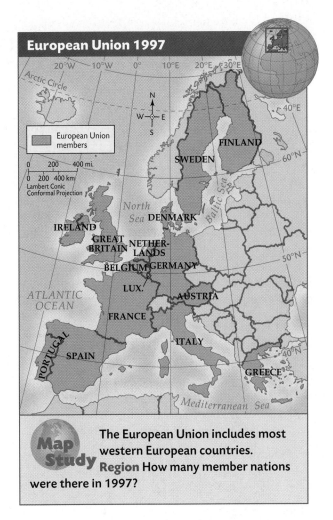

European Union 1997

European Union members

0   200   400 mi.

0 200 400 km
Lambert Conic
Conformal Projection

FINLAND

SWEDEN

North Sea DENMARK

IRELAND

GREAT BRITAIN NETHER-LANDS

BELGIUM GERMANY

LUX. AUSTRIA

ATLANTIC OCEAN

FRANCE

PORTUGAL SPAIN

ITALY

GREECE

Mediterranean Sea

Map Study The European Union includes most western European countries. **Region** How many member nations were there in 1997?

SECTION 3 REVIEW

Recall
1. **Define** referendum, collective security.
2. **Identify** Margaret Thatcher, John Major, Tony Blair, the Irish Republican Army, François Mitterrand, Jacques Chirac, Helmut Kohl, Juan Carlos I, Felipe González, Andreas Papandreou, Treaty of Maastricht.
3. **Explain** the purpose of the European Union.

Critical Thinking
4. **Applying Information** Explain why Great Britain has shown reluctance to fully participate in plans for full European unity.

Understanding Themes
5. **Cooperation** How do relationships among countries in the European Union compare with those among states in the United States?

Section 4

National and Ethnic Conflicts

Setting the Scene

▶ **Terms to Define**

ethnic cleansing, atrocity, embargo, enclave

▶ **People to Meet**

Slobodan Milosevic, Alija Izetbegovic, Franjo Tudjman, the Chechens, the Ossetians, the Abkhazians, the Kurds, the Sinhalese, the Tamils, Brian Mulroney, Jean Chretien

▶ **Places to Locate**

Sarajevo, Dayton, Chechnya, Nagorno-Karabakh, Sri Lanka, Quebec

 **Find Out** What areas of the world have been in ethnic discord since the end of the cold war?

The Storyteller

Zahid Olorcic remembered how things had been just a few years ago. People in Sarajevo had gotten along with their neighbors. Even though coming from diverse backgrounds, the city's multiethnic population lived in harmony. Then the situation changed as radical groups stirred up ethnic hatred. Zahid recalled earlier times:

"Funerals, weddings, birthdays, we never counted how many Muslims were there, how many Serbs, how many Croats. The only important thing was to be together...."

—adapted from "Bosnians Recall Karadzic, a Neighbor Turned Enemy," Tracy Wilkinson, in *The Los Angeles Times,* July 23, 1995

War damage in Sarajevo

The end of the cold war brought about communism's fall and the triumph of democracy. A new world was at hand— or so it seemed. The aftermath has proven to be more complex. During the cold war, even regional conflicts were often linked to the East-West struggle. Now that the superpower rivalry was over, each issue stood on its own terms, and predictability and stability had given way to uncertainty and confusion.

During the 1990s, long-hidden national and ethnic rivalries flared into violence in various parts of the world. The threats to peace included not only fighting, but also human tragedies such as starvation and the flow of refugees. Often, the global community, through the United Nations and other organizations, seemed helpless in dealing with these crises. However, there were bright spots—for example, South Africa, the Balkans, and the Middle East. In all three places, the 1990s saw efforts, either fulfilled or in progress, to peacefully resolve disputes or deeply rooted injustices.

Fighting in Bosnia

The most serious ethnic fighting in Europe took place in Bosnia-Herzegovina, where the creation of an independent state led to conflict among Croats, Muslims, and Serbs in the early 1990s. With the support of neighboring Serbia and Montenegro, the Bosnian Serbs conquered most of Bosnia-Herzegovina. In April 1992, they began a siege of **Sarajevo**, the Bosnian capital, which was largely controlled by Muslims. Following a policy called ethnic cleansing, the Serbs ruthlessly expelled rival ethnic groups from the areas taken by their army. The Croats and Muslims also carried out atrocities, or cruel actions, against the Serbs.

The UN imposed an embargo, a ban on trade, against Serbia in 1992, hoping to get the Serbs to stop supplying the ethnic Serbs in Bosnia. UN peacekeeping forces also arrived in the war-torn republic to protect food and medicine sent to the Bosnian people. Since the war began, thousands of Bosnians had been killed, and hundreds of thousands left homeless.

The United States and other UN members also reported human rights abuses in Bosnia. The reports indicated that Bosnian Serbs had tortured and killed Bosnian Muslims and Croats in detention camps. In 1995 an international court charged Bosnian Serb leaders with genocide for operating thousands of Nazi-style concentration camps and ruthlessly attacking civilian populations.

Steps Toward Peace

In 1994 Serbia, hurting from the effects of the UN embargo, called on Bosnian Serbs to cease fighting. Later that year, the United States offered a peace plan that proposed dividing Bosnia between the Serbs and a new Muslim-Croat federation. Hostilities, however, continued into 1995. When Bosnian Serbs stepped up their attacks on Sarajevo, NATO responded with air attacks on Serb positions around the city. Meanwhile, Croatia completed a land offensive to regain land held by its own Serb minority. With a possible defeat looming, the Bosnian Serbs finally decided to negotiate.

In November 1995, three presidents—**Slobodan Milosevic** (swoh•boh•dahn mee •LAH•soh•veech) of Serbia, **Alija Izetbegovic** (ah•LEE•hah ee•zeht•BEH•goh•veech) of Bosnia-Herzegovina, and **Franjo Tudjman** (FRAHN•hoh TOOZH•mahn) of Croatia—met in **Dayton**, Ohio, and agreed to the partition of Bosnia into distinct Serb and Muslim-Croat areas. In December the Dayton Treaty was signed in Paris, ending the Bosnian conflict. In response to the agreement, the UN Security Council voted to lift the embargo on Serbia. By the time of the Dayton agreement, the Bosnian conflict had resulted in the deaths of 200,000 people and the forced removal of 3 million people from their homes.

Keeping the Peace

To safeguard the peace, a 60,000-strong NATO-led force arrived in Bosnia to replace the exhausted UN troops. American and Russian troops served as part of the peacekeeping force. In 1996 Bosnian voters elected Muslim, Serb, and Croat leaders to serve on a three-person panel that would govern the country. Despite these steps toward peace, the three Bosnian communities disputed territory and blocked refugees from returning to their homes. Another problem was the difficulty in bringing indicted war criminals to justice. However, in 1997 as conflicts erupted between moderate and extremist Bosnian Serbs, NATO forces began attacks against positions held by the war criminals and their supporters.

Unrest in the CIS

With the collapse of communism, fierce ethnic hatreds boiled to the surface in Russia and the other CIS republics. During the Soviet era, the Russian-dominated government in Moscow had repressed the nationalism of non-Russian ethnic groups. This policy increased resentment among many peoples.

Russia and the CIS

Even after the Soviet collapse, relations among the Commonwealth republics were strained. Russia was clearly the most powerful nation, and European republics, such as Ukraine, were reluctant to concede their hard-won independence to a Russian-dominated federation. During the late 1990s, however, Russia worked to improve relations with these countries in order to offset NATO's eastward expansion. In 1997 Russia and Ukraine signed a treaty that recognized Ukrainian rule over the Crimea and divided the disputed Black Sea naval fleet between them. Also that year, Russia and Belarus forged a close union, allowing Russian and Belarussian citizens to move freely between the two countries, own property in either country, and vote in each other's local elections.

Wary of Russia, the Central Asian republics and those in the Caucasus region balanced ties to Russia with new links to Middle Eastern and Western countries. Largely Muslim in religious background, the Caucasus republic of Azerbaijan and the Central Asian republics rediscovered the spiritual and cultural traditions they shared with the Middle East. Rich in oil deposits awaiting development, these lands also were eager to attract Western businesses.

Although Commonwealth ties were often weak, the CIS remained intact as member nations worked together to resolve conflicts between them and within their territories. For example, the CIS backed peacekeeping forces in the Central Asian republic of Tajikistan, which until 1997 had been torn apart by a civil war between its ex-Communist leadership and Muslim opposition forces. Since the Soviet collapse, ethnic unrest had also arisen within some of the individual CIS republics. Each republic had dominant ethnic groups and many smaller ones. Many of

In December 1994, Russian soldiers with tanks (above) attacked Chechen fighters (left), some of whom were dressed in traditional Chechen clothing. *Why did Yeltsin send troops to Chechnya?*

these groups were concentrated in a particular area and had their own local governments. With the collapse of Soviet power, they asserted pride in their traditions and demanded greater self-rule.

The Chechens

The Chechens are among the ethnic groups of Russia. Their territory, **Chechnya** (chehch•NYA), lies in southern Russia near the Caspian Sea. In 1994 the Chechens declared their independence from Russia. Fearing Russia's breakup if other groups did the same, Russian leader Boris Yeltsin sent Russian troops into Chechnya. He was widely criticized at home and abroad for the invasion, in which hundreds of civilians were killed in bombing attacks.

The Chechens fought extremely well against poorly trained and disheartened Russian forces. At the same time, the conflict divided Russian public opinion and further strained the economy. In 1996, when Chechen forces took back their capital from the Russians, Yeltsin sent his aide General Alexander Lebed to Chechnya to work out an agreement to end the conflict. Russia and Chechnya soon signed a peace treaty in which both pledged to renounce force in any future disputes. Although the treaty avoided mention of independence, the Chechens claimed victory and proceeded to build an independent state.

The Caucasus Republics

Ethnic conflicts troubled other republics in the CIS. In the Caucasus region, Armenia and Azerbaijan both claimed ownership of the enclave of **Nagorno-Karabakh**. An **enclave** is a small territory entirely surrounded by another territory.

Nagorno-Karabakh lies entirely within Azerbaijan, but its majority population of Armenians wanted it to separate from Azerbaijan and join Armenia. In 1993 Armenia and Azerbaijan went to war over Nagorno-Karabakh. Armenian forces made significant advances and took control of much of the disputed territory.

Neighboring Georgia has faced separatist uprisings by minority ethnic groups, such as **the Ossetians** and **the Abkhazians**. In 1994 the Abkhazians declared their region an independent republic. Meanwhile, Georgia has received support from Russia in the effort to preserve its national unity. The Russians hold three military bases in Georgia and train and equip the Georgian army.

Africa and Asia

During the 1990s, ethnic conflicts erupted in various parts of Africa and Asia. In Africa, full-scale fighting broke out between Hutu and Tutsi peoples in the East African republics of Rwanda and Burundi. The unleashed hatreds led to genocides within these nations, and the violence spilled over into neighboring Zaire, later called the Democratic Republic of the Congo. Other ethnic divisions contributed to civil wars in West Africa, especially in the nations of Sierra Leone and Liberia.

The Kurds

In the Middle East, one of the most divisive ethnic disputes was between **the Kurds** and the governments of Iraq and Turkey. The 20 million Kurds are Sunni Muslims and live mostly in Armenia, Iran, Iraq, Syria, and Turkey. They have never had their own nation but have long sought their freedom. This goal has been thwarted by divisions among themselves and by the scheming of the governments that rule them. In the 1980s and 1990s, the Kurds of Turkey and Iraq carried out separate revolts against their respective governments. Before and after the Persian Gulf War, Iraqi forces used bombings and poison gas to put down Kurdish uprisings, which left over 1 million Kurds as refugees. Turkish forces have staged offensives against Turkish Kurdish bases in remote mountain areas along the border of Turkey and Iran.

Sri Lanka

Another place torn by ethnic discord was the Indian Ocean island republic of **Sri Lanka**. Sri Lanka's 18 million people largely belong to two ethnic groups, **the Sinhalese** and **the Tamils**. The Sinhalese, who make up about 75 percent of the population, are Buddhist. The Tamils, most of whom are Hindus, form about 18 percent of the population and live in northern and eastern areas of Sri Lanka.

For decades, the Tamils had resented discrimination by the Sinhalese-controlled government. In 1983 fighting broke out between Tamil guerrillas and Sinhalese government troops. Despite peace efforts, the fighting continued into the 1990s. Nearly 40,000 were killed, and hundreds of thousands of Tamil refugees fled to India.

Canada's Fragile Unity

During the 1980s and 1990s, Canada faced growing uncertainty about its future. Many French-speaking people in the province of **Quebec** wanted independence from English-speaking Canada. When Quebec voters in 1980 narrowly defeated an independence proposal, the Canadian federal government worked to strengthen national unity while respecting regional differences. In 1982 a new Canadian constitution was enacted that granted more power to the provinces and guaranteed the language and cultural rights of all Canadians.

Quebec, however, rejected the constitution because it did not allow individual provinces to veto future amendments. Prime Minister **Brian Mulroney**, whose Conservative party came to power in 1984, tried in vain to get English-speaking Canada to accept a special status for Quebec. Ten years later, the Liberal party won parliamentary elections, and **Jean Chretien** (cray•TYEHN) became prime minister. Although a French-speaking Quebecer, Chretien was a firm believer in national unity and opposed Quebec separatism.

In 1995 Quebec voters again turned down independence for the province, but only by a margin of a little over 1 percent. In addition, nearly 60 percent of French-speaking Quebecers had voted for the proposal. Canada in theory remained united, but the Quebec referendum left Canada's people deeply divided.

In June 1997 Canadian voters elected a new parliament, splitting their vote along regional lines. Running on its record of reducing government spending, Prime Minister Jean Chretien's Liberal party captured a majority of seats—19 less than it held in parliament before the vote. Most Liberals were elected in Ontario, Canada's most populous province, and in the Atlantic provinces of Prince Edward Island and Newfoundland.

In second place was the Reform party, a conservative group that had strong support in the western Canadian provinces. There, opposition to a special status for Quebec was strongest in Canada. The Bloc Quebeçois, the Quebec separatist party, was third. Because of divisions within its ranks, however, the Bloc's total number of party seats went down from 50 before the vote.

SECTION 4 REVIEW

Recall
1. **Define** ethnic cleansing, atrocity, embargo, enclave.
2. **Identify** Slobodan Milosevic, Alija Izetbegovic, Franjo Tudjman, the Chechens, the Ossetians, the Abkhazians, the Kurds, the Sinhalese, the Tamils, Brian Mulroney, Jean Chretien.

3. **List** the nations involved in the Nagorno-Karabakh dispute. What geographic factor makes any settlement difficult to achieve?

Critical Thinking
4. **Making Comparisons** How was Quebec's expression of dissatisfaction with Canada different from that of the Tamils with Sri Lanka? What do you think accounts for the differences between the two disputes?

Understanding Themes
5. **Conflict** Why did the Bosnian Serbs in 1992 oppose the creation of an independent Bosnia? Why did they agree to peace talks in 1995?

1987 The Montreal Protocol calls for global reduction of chemical pollutants.

1992 The first Earth Summit is held in Rio de Janeiro, Brazil.

1995 The United States space shuttle *Atlantis* docks with the Russian space station *Mir*.

Section 5

Global Interdependence

Setting the Scene

▶ **Terms to Define**
interdependent, developing nations, developed nations, deforestation, Internet, genetic engineering

▶ **People to Meet**
Neil Armstrong, Jean Paul Sartre, Mother Teresa

▶ **Places to Locate**
Montreal, Rio de Janeiro

Find Out How have recent advances in technology affected the world's cultures?

The Storyteller

Robert "Hoot" Gibson, the American astronaut, carefully maneuvered Atlantis closer to Mir, the Russian space station. Finally, just after 9:00 A.M. eastern standard time, June 29, 1995, Gibson gently docked the 100-ton shuttle with the Mir's central docking port. On Earth, at the Russian mission control, NASA chief Dan Goldin leaped from his seat to hug his Russian counterpart, Yuri Koptev. When the hatch was opened, Gibson floated along the pathway into the Russian ship. After decades of competition, American and Russian space programs had launched a promising partnership.

—adapted from "Mir Reflections," Frank Sietzen, in *Final Frontier*, November/December 1995

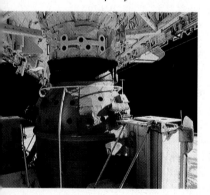

Partnership in space

In 1900 most of the world's people knew little about other people in distant places on the planet. As the year 2000 approaches, however, people communicate instantly with others thousands of miles away and access vast amounts of information with their fingertips. Today, we share in a technological and communications revolution that has made people increasingly interdependent, or reliant on each other.

The Global Community

Today's nations have become economically interdependent through world trade, which now exceeds $8 trillion per year. Since World War II, technological advances and the removal of tariff and other barriers to free trade have led to a tremendous increase in the global exchange of goods and services. The forging of new trade links among different regions has ensured that an economic boom or bust in one region will impact economies in other parts of the world.

The world's economic superpowers include the United States, the European Union, and Japan. These areas, along with South Korea, Taiwan, and other countries of Asia's Pacific Rim, are the leading competitors in international markets and will probably remain so into the next century.

Developing and Developed Nations

With the rise of the global economy, some observers claim that the nation-state is no longer the key economic and political institution it was a hundred years ago. They point out that large multinational organizations and corporations now have greater control over international flows of people, goods, funds, and technology. Others, while recognizing the growing importance of international bodies such as the EU, believe that nation-states are still crucial in making and carrying out basic economic policies.

One of the major global issues involving nations is the gap between rich and poor countries. Developing nations in Asia, Africa, and Latin America are newly industrializing countries, and many of their people still follow traditional ways of life. These developing nations are dependent on developed nations, such as the United States, that have long been industrialized and have the technology to produce a great quantity and variety of goods.

Building Strong Economies

To raise standards of living, developing nations often try to diversify, or increase the variety of, the goods they supply to the world. This enables them to avoid relying on a single crop or product. The transition to a diversified economy, however, can be difficult because of lack of funds and skilled workers. Developing countries often rely on outside lending sources for funding. The World Bank and the International Monetary Fund (IMF) were set up after World War II to assist global economic development. Private banks and international corporations also invest in developing nations.

Borrowing funds for economic growth has placed many countries in monumental debt. When loans cannot be paid, banks suffer huge losses that hurt businesses. Many strategies have been tried to solve international debt problems. In some cases, the banks involved have issued new loans to enable developing countries to pay off old debts. While such practices have helped to offset immediate concerns, the debt question remains a threat to the world's economic health.

Population Growth

The number of people on our planet affects both human well-being and the environment. Developed nations point to the rapid growth of population in developing countries as a major cause in straining world resources. As much as 97 percent of the world's population growth occurs in the developing world. Families are large in very poor countries because many children are needed to help earn money and to assist parents in their old age. At the present rate of growth, the world's population is expected to increase from the present 5.8 billion to more than 6 billion by 2000 and about 12 billion by 2050.

People in developing countries consume far less per person than do people in developed countries. However, the large populations in the developing world are exhausting the resources of many areas. In Africa and Asia, for example, population pressures have forced farmers to make a living on

Visualizing History **Hong Kong is one of the busiest ports of Asia's Pacific Rim.** *In addition to Asia's Pacific Rim, what other prosperous area of the world trades extensively with the United States?*

fragile, poorly productive lands. In some places erosion and landslides have caused irreversible environmental damage. Throughout the developing world, millions of people leave the countryside each year and crowd into cities in the hope of improving their lives. Urban growth has been so rapid that cities cannot keep up with the needs for shelter, food, and jobs. To remedy these problems, developing countries are working to link population, development, and environmental needs in their planning.

The Environment

Protecting the environment is another challenge facing the planet. For much of human history, the abundance of the earth's resources was taken for granted. Today, however, human use and abuse of resources—especially the high consumption of resources in the developed world—has reached such levels that the planet may no longer be able to heal itself. Damage to the atmosphere, land, water, and air, has an impact on all living things.

Land and Water

Vast areas of the earth's land have been destroyed by overgrazing, pesticides, and deforestation, the widespread clearing of forests for logging or farming. Particularly at risk are semi-arid areas near the edge of deserts. Between 1970 and 1990, developing countries lost 40 percent of their farmland. This loss will make it increasingly difficult for poorer countries to raise enough food for their growing populations.

The oceans and freshwater supplies of the planet also are showing signs of overuse and abuse. Coastal waters are heavily polluted with chemicals and litter. The bulk of contamination comes from poisonous industrial wastes, municipal sewage, and runoffs of fertilizers, pesticides, and salts. Instead of being swept out to sea, most of this contamination settles into the coastal soil. Environmental damage is reflected in epidemics spread by contaminated fish, in increasing numbers of diseased wildlife, and in the decay of coral reefs.

Meanwhile, demand for fresh water has grown. Conflicts over the distribution of limited water supplies have already developed in the southwestern United States, the Middle East, and North Africa. Efforts are underway to achieve some fair distribution of scarce water supplies among countries, as well as between rural and urban areas.

Environmental Awareness

Since the 1970s, the world's people have become increasingly aware of environmental issues, and a number of international gatherings have stressed the urgency of dealing with the environmental crisis. In 1987 delegates from 46 countries met in **Montreal**, Canada, and signed the Montreal Protocol, which called for reductions in the use of chemicals damaging to the earth's atmosphere. Other important gatherings were the 1992 Earth Summit in **Rio de Janeiro**, Brazil and the follow-up 1997 Earth Summit+5 in New York City. These UN-sponsored conferences called on nations to plan economic growth to meet present global needs without sacrificing the environmental needs of future generations.

CONNECTIONS

Economics

Global Economy

Since 1945, many of the world's nations have joined together to create large regional economic markets. The goal of each of these markets is to increase trade and to coordinate economic growth among member nations.

In North America the United States, Canada, and Mexico have implemented the North American Free Trade Agreement (NAFTA). In southern South America several nations participate in the Southern Common Market (Mercosur), while in the Caribbean region a number of countries form the Association of Caribbean States (ACS).

Western European nations have not only promoted economic interdependence among themselves. In the 1993 Treaty of Maastricht, they also took steps toward political unity by creating the European Union.

The creation of large economic blocs in the Americas and in Europe in part stems from the increasing competition these two regions have faced from the growing economic might of the countries of Asia's Pacific Rim. During the past few decades Japan, South Korea, Taiwan, and Hong Kong have become economic giants and are very active in world trade. In the near future, China, (now including Hong Kong) and the Association of Southeast Asian Nations (ASEAN) will powerfully impact the global economy.

Linking Past and Present ACTIVITY

Explain why individual countries have joined in forming large regional economic markets. Do you think regional economic blocs benefit or hinder the global economy?

Japanese cars for export

The Technological Revolution

Since 1945, the world has undergone a technological revolution as significant as the Industrial Revolution of the early 1800s. Computers are at the heart of this transformation. They process information that can analyze a nation's economy, forecast the weather, interpret public opinion polls, or calculate the flight path of a rocket. Nations that can afford the latest computer technology gain a distinct advantage—whether through increased productivity or ultimately a higher standard of living—over those still struggling with outdated equipment.

The applications of computer technology are varied. The "brain" driving the computer is the microchip, a mesh of circuits etched on a silicon wafer. In medicine, doctors use these chips to power artificial limbs worn by people who need them. Industrial robots programmed to assemble machines and perform tasks such as welding and painting represent another application of microchip technology.

The Internet

Computers are playing an important role in the expansion of global communications. The most dramatic leap in communications in recent years has been the development of the Internet, a massive number of computers linked together through a worldwide, high-speed, telecommunications network. Using a computer and a modem, a device linking two compatible computers together by a direct connection to the telephone line, a user can research and share information with millions of other participants around the globe. One can create a World Wide Web page to present research results or send a message through E-mail, or electronic mail, to any place in the world in seconds.

Space Exploration

Computer and other new technologies have made space exploration possible. Since the Soviet launching of *Sputnik*, the first satellite into orbit, in 1957, the Americans and Russians have sent hundreds of satellites and human-operated spacecraft into outer space. In July 1969 American astronaut **Neil Armstrong** became the first human to step on the moon's surface. In the early 1980s, American scientists developed the space shuttle, a reusable spacecraft that takes off like a rocket and lands like an airplane. From the shuttle, astronauts can launch, retrieve, and repair satellites. In the mid-

Visualizing History Air pollution from factories is a problem in industrialized countries. In this scene, clouds containing industrial pollutants cover an area in Germany. *How has pollution affected the planet's water?*

1990s the American space shuttle *Atlantis* docked with the Russian space station *Mir*. Symbolizing a new era of space cooperation, this linkage prepared the way for the building of an internationally operated space station.

Medical Advances

Medical science also has benefited from technological progress. Lasers, or devices that emit narrow, powerful beams of light, allow doctors to perform delicate surgery with minimal discomfort to patients. Current medicines can even correct chemical imbalances in the brain, thereby treating the severe depression that can cripple some people's lives. Organ transplants have become possible with new technologies. Kidneys and livers are among the most commonly transplanted organs, and many people now live for years with transplanted hearts as well.

Recent DNA (deoxyribonucleic acid) technology has led to the new field of genetic engineering, a process that involves the alteration of cells to produce new life-forms. Further molecular research may yield insights into the origins and cure of diseases such as cancer and AIDS that affect millions of people worldwide.

The Global Culture

Technological advances have hastened the growth of a global culture. Jet travel, television, and communications satellites have spread ideas and practices from one part of the globe to another. Today the cultures of various regions meet and blend. American rock music now echoes in clubs around the world. Asian folk dancers perform their artistry on tour in Europe, while Latin American poets recite their works before audiences in Japan.

The Search for Life's Meaning

Today's rapid and often complex changes have sent many people on a search for life's meaning. After World War II, the French thinker **Jean Paul Sartre** stated a viewpoint known as existentialism that became popular among intellectuals in the West. According to Sartre, each person is essentially alone, but free to choose his or her path in life.

Individual freedom has become a key goal during the last half of the twentieth century. Civil rights movements have advanced racial equality in the United States and South Africa; and in many countries, the women's movement has altered traditional female roles and opened new career opportunities for women.

While secular viewpoints have spread, religious individuals and groups have sought to meet society's needs. For example, the Vatican Council II (1962–1965) related Roman Catholic teaching to modern life and simplified many church practices. The Roman Catholic nun **Mother Teresa** inspired many people with her care of the needy in the slums of Calcutta, India. Also, the Dalai Lama, Tibet's Buddhist leader, and Desmond Tutu, South African Anglican archbishop, spoke out for human rights. Within Islam and Protestant Christianity, powerful conservative movements have attracted many followers. Although religious hostilities persist in areas such as the Balkans and South Asia, efforts have increased to promote understanding among global religions.

Human Rights

In recent decades, the issue of human rights has captured world attention. According to human rights groups, despite democratic advances since the 1980s, many governments still imprison and abuse people for speaking their minds. Among the countries accused of human rights violations are China, Indonesia, Nigeria, Saudi Arabia, Afghanistan, and Myanmar. Others, such as Iran, Iraq, Cuba, Libya, North Korea, Sudan, and Syria have also been charged with sponsoring terrorist acts outside of their borders.

The good news is that human rights abuses are more carefully monitored than they were. In South Africa, Haiti, and El Salvador, for example, national truth commissions have investigated abuses of past governments, and international tribunals for Bosnia and Rwanda have called individuals to account for their war crimes. The increased visibility of each government's actions and the accompanying accountability that many nations and groups feel is showing results.

In 1948 the United Nations adopted what has become the most important human-rights document of the postwar years—the Universal Declaration of Human Rights. Addressing social and economic as well as political rights, the Declaration is a statement not of the way things are, but of the way they should be. As new technologies develop, more will have to be done to provide the basic needs and a decent quality of life for the planet's inhabitants. As the year 2000 approaches, the Universal Declaration of Human Rights gives the world's people a common goal and ideal for the twenty-first century.

SECTION 5 REVIEW

Recall
1. **Define** interdependent, developing nations, developed nations, deforestation, Internet, genetic engineering.
2. **Identify** NAFTA, ASEAN, Montreal Protocol, Neil Armstrong, Jean Paul Sartre, Mother Teresa
3. **Explain** how population changes have affected lifestyles in developing countries.

Critical Thinking
4. **Analyze** Why do environmental dangers to the planet require global solutions?

Understanding Themes
5. **Cultural Diffusion** What is the most powerful source of cultural diffusion today? Explain the reasoning behind your answer.

Interpreting Statistics

Statistics seem to support a claim or an opinion with a ring of authority. We have heard that statistics can be misleading, but do we really understand how to interpret statistics?

Learning the Skill

Statistics are sets of tabulated information that may be gathered through surveys and other sources. When studying statistics, consider each of the following:

Biased sample A sample, or group of the total population surveyed, may affect the results. A sample that does not represent the entire population is called a biased sample. An unbiased sample is called a representative sample.

Correlation Two sets of data may be related or unrelated. If they are related, we say that there is a correlation between them. For example, there is a positive correlation between academic achievement and wages. There is a negative correlation, however, between smoking and life expectancy. Statistics may seem to show a correlation when none exists. For example, a report that "people who go fishing are less likely to get cancer" may be statistically true but lack any correlation.

Statistical Significance Using statistics, researchers determine whether the data support a generalization or whether the results are due to chance. If the probability that the results were due to chance is less than 5 percent, researchers say that the result is statistically significant.

Practicing the Skill

Study the table below (the amount of economic freedom is shown on a scale from 0–8, with 8 being most free). Then answer the questions that follow.

1. Is there a correlation between wage rates and the percentage of government employees? Explain.
2. What statistics deny a correlation between the percentage of government employees and the index of economic freedom?

Applying the Skill

Create a survey with two questions for which you believe the answers may show a correlation. For example, "How many hours of television do you watch per day?" and "How many hours of sleep do you average per night?" Gather a representative sample of responses. Tabulate and evaluate your statistics.

For More Practice

Turn to the Skill Practice in the Chapter Review on page 1025 for more practice in interpreting statistics.

Wages, Government Employment, and Economic Freedom

Nation	Hourly Wage Rate (1994)	Government employees as percent of total	Index of Economic Freedom 1993–1995*
Germany	$27	16.2	6.5
Japan	$21	8.4	7.0
Sweden	$19	33.2	5.5
United States	$17	15.4	7.5
Great Britain	$14	18.1	7.0
New Zealand	$10	15.3	8.0
South Korea	$6	na	7.0
Mexico	$5	31.8	5.5

* Index compiled by survey of economists for "Economic Freedom of the World: 1975–1995," James Gwartney, Robert Lawson, and Walter Block.

Connections Across Time

Historical Significance Since World War II, the world has undergone tremendous changes. The cold war between the United States and the Soviet Union was resolved peacefully, and the global supremacy of the super-powers has given way to a world of regional blocs. Capitalist economies have triumphed over Communist ones, and efforts toward democracy are yielding results in many parts of the world. New technology also has linked world regions more close-ly together, creating a global economy and culture. The planet, however, faces complex political, economic, and environmental challenges. The world's nations must learn to cooperate to find solutions and to meet the needs of all people.

Using Key Terms

Write the key term that completes each sentence. Then write a sentence for each term not chosen.

a. interdependent
b. glasnost
c. privatization
d. genetic engineering
e. developing nations
f. ethnic cleansing
g. Internet
h. referendum
i. perestroika
j. trade deficit
k. enclave
l. deforestation

1. The growth of technology, communications, and transportation since 1945 has made the regions of the world increasingly _____.
2. In the war in Bosnia, ethnic Serb forces carried out _____, a policy of forcibly remov-ing rival ethnic groups.
3. Through _____, scientists can now alter cells to produce new life-forms.
4. _____ have established new industries, but many of their people still follow traditional ways of earning a living.
5. The territory of Nagorno-Karabakh is an _____ completely surrounded by Azerbaijan.

Technology Activity

Using the Internet Search the Internet for information about the latest technological innovations that are influencing our global culture. Use a search engine to focus your search by using phrases such as *information technology innovations*, *global communications* and *technology revolution*. Create a bulletin board using the information retrieved on the Internet. Include illustrations or pictures of the latest technological innovations.

Using Your History Journal

How will world events affect your future? Write an essay entitled "The World's Future and My Own" identify-ing important international issues and explaining how events could affect your life.

Reviewing Facts

1. **Economics** Describe the economic challenges faced by Americans and Soviets during the 1980s.
2. **History** Explain how Mikhail Gorbachev dif-fered from earlier Soviet leaders.
3. **History** List in chronological order, the signifi-cant events that led to the fall of communism.
4. **Economics** Discuss Boris Yeltsin's economic pol-icy and its effects on Russia.
5. **History** Describe how the Soviet collapse and the fall of communism affected global affairs.
6. **Culture** Explain the role of religion in the anti-Communist movements of Eastern Europe dur-ing the late 1970s and early 1980s.
7. **Geography** Explain how developed and devel-oping nations affect the environment.
8. **History** Describe the roles of Pope John Paul II, the Dalai Lama, and Mother Teresa.
9. **Citizenship** Discuss the advances made in human rights since World War II. How has the UN dealt with this issue?
10. **Science/Technology** Explain how the cold war affected space exploration.

Critical Thinking

1. **Analyze** Is Europe less stable now than it was during the cold war? Why or why not?
2. **Analyze** How would you identify the era after 1989? What are its major features?
3. **Evaluate** How does a global economy affect developing nations?
4. **Analyze** How have recent developments in medical technology affected humans?

Geography in History

1. **Region** Refer to the map below. What continent has the largest population?
2. **Place** Why do economists believe that the Pacific Rim is likely to become the world's fastest-growing market in the next decades?
3. **Human/Environment Interaction** How does this map help to identify regions of extreme climate and unsuitable living conditions?

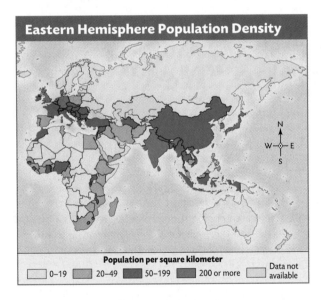

Eastern Hemisphere Population Density

Population per square kilometer
0–19 | 20–49 | 50–199 | 200 or more | Data not available

Understanding Themes

1. **Change** What factors do you think led both superpowers to seek an end to the cold war?
2. **Change** Evaluate Mikhail Gorbachev's response to the uprisings in Eastern Europe. What might have happened if he had tried to stop the changes? How were changes in the Soviet Union and its satellites linked?

3. **Cooperation** What are two future goals of the European Union that was created by the 1993 Treaty of Maastricht?
4. **Conflict** How did the Dayton peace settlement attempt to bring peace to Bosnia?
5. **Cultural Diffusion** What factors have led to the emergence of a global culture?

Linking Past and Present

1. How have many people's attitudes toward natural resources and their use changed over the past fifty years?
2. Placing a person on the moon was the primary goal of the space race between the United States and the Soviet Union. Has a new goal for the space programs of the United States and Russia emerged? Explain.

Skill Practice

Study the statistics in the chart below and answer the questions that follow.

1. Is there a correlation between energy consumed and per capita GDP?
2. What factors may explain the correlation between energy consumption and GDP?
3. Is the sample of countries used in the chart statistically significant? Explain.

Energy Use and Per Capita GDP		
Country	**Energy Consumed* per capita (kilograms)**	**GDP** per capita**
Bahrain	15,608	$12,000
United States	10,798	$24,000
Netherlands	7,248	$9,700
New Zealand	5,838	$15,700
Poland	3,167	$4,400
Argentina	1,977	$5,500
Thailand	833	$5,500
India	336	$1,300
Sudan	62	$750

* figures for 1991
** Gross Domestic Product: the sum of all goods and services produced within the country (1993).

ABCNEWS INTERACTIVE™

Turning Points in World History

Fall of the Berlin Wall

Setting up the Video

Work with a group of your classmates to view "Fall of the Berlin Wall" on the videodisc Turning Points in World History. On New Year's Eve, 1990, the two Germanys celebrated reunification. Afterward, Germany was faced with many economic problems to address—such as high unemployment and the arrival of refugees from Eastern Europe that placed a strain on social services.

Hands-On Activity

Create an economic fact sheet about Germany's present economic status. Include information such as GDP, unemployment rate, imports, exports, rate of currency, and other related information.

Side Two,
Chapter 9

View the video by scanning the bar code or by entering the chapter number on your keypad and pressing Search. (Also available in VHS format.)

Surfing the "Net"

Human Rights

The protection of human rights has been a major priority for the United Nations since its creation in 1945. In 1948, the United Nations adopted an important human-rights document known as the Universal Declaration of Human Rights. This document addresses economic, social, and political rights. To find out about the content of the United Nations Universal Declaration of Human Rights document, look on the Internet.

Getting There

Follow these steps to gather in-depth information about the content of the Universal Declaration of Human Rights.

1. Go to a search engine. Type in *united nations*.

2. After typing in the phrase, enter terms such as the following to focus your search.
   • *human rights document*   • *peace*
3. The search engine should provide you with a number of links to follow. Links are "pointers" to different sites on the Internet and commonly appear as blue underlined words.

What to Do When You Are There

Click on the links to navigate through the pages of information and gather your findings. Design a poster illustrating the different articles of the United Nations Declaration of Human Rights. Hang posters around your classroom.

Unit 8 Digest

From 1945 to the present, major political shifts have occurred throughout the world. During most of this period, the United States—promoting democracy—and the Soviet Union—promoting communism—were locked in the cold war, a struggle for global dominance short of total war. Meanwhile, Europe's imperial powers, weakened by World War II and facing nationalist upheavals, withdrew from Asia and Africa. New nations emerged from the remains of the European empires to establish their roles in the global community.

By the 1980s, the United States and Soviet Union no longer dominated the world scene. New groups of nations—especially those located on Asia's Pacific Rim—began to influence world trade and economics. The United States began to adjust to this challenge, but the Soviet Union and the Eastern European nations under its sway faced severe economic difficulties. Communism proved incapable of reform; and as Soviet controls loosened, popular uprisings toppled Communist governments in Eastern Europe. The collapse of the Soviet Union itself and the emergence of new republics in 1991 signaled both the end of communism and the cold war. Hope for a new era of global cooperation faded, however, as ethnic rivalries led to bloody conflicts in various parts of the world.

Chapter 32
The Cold War

After World War II, Europe was divided into the Eastern bloc, dominated by the Soviet Union, and the Western bloc, tied to the United States. To maintain control of Eastern Europe, the Soviets in 1955 created the Warsaw Pact and later used force against uprisings in Hungary and Czechoslovakia. The United States, as the leader of the non-Communist world, developed the Truman Doctrine to aid countries threatened by Communist takeover. Under the American-sponsored Marshall Plan, Western Europe's democratic nations rebuilt their economies and soon enjoyed economic prosperity. With the United States and Canada, they formed the NATO alliance in 1949 for mutual defense against Soviet attack.

The United States and Canada developed strong, closely-linked economies after World War II. The cold war affected American politics during the 1950s, when concern arose about Communist influences in American government and society. During the 1960s women, African Americans, Hispanic Americans, and Native Americans began to make advances in civil rights. The Vietnam War divided American society and led to a questioning of the United States's military role in world trouble spots.

Chapter 33
Asia and the Pacific

The era after World War II brought profound changes to Asian and Pacific nations. Japan went from defeat to become a major world economic power. A Communist victory in 1949 established the People's Republic of China on the Chinese

Visualizing History The cold war led to an arms race between the United States and the Soviet Union. This Soviet rocket launcher was based in Ukraine. *What major step did the Western allies take in 1949 to contain communism?*

mainland, with the Nationalist government based on the island of Taiwan. Beginning in the 1970s, China combined its Communist system with free enterprise and contacts with the West. In South Asia, nationalist movements created four new nations: India, Pakistan, Sri Lanka, and later, Bangladesh. In spite of economic progress, ethnic and religious rivalries hampered unity within and among these countries.

Korea and Vietnam, both divided into Communist and non-Communist parts, became cold war hot spots. During the Korean War, fought from 1950 to 1953, American-led United Nations forces fought back a Communist advance, but the conflict ended in a stalemate, with Korea returning to its divided status. In Vietnam, however, Communist forces defeated American and anti-Communist Vietnamese forces and united the entire country under Communist rule. The Vietnam conflict lasted from the 1950s to the mid-1970s, with direct American military involvement beginning in the mid-1960s.

Since the Korean and Vietnam conflicts, economic prosperity has come to the nations along Asia's Pacific Rim, stretching from South Korea through Japan and Taiwan to Southeast Asia. Australia, New Zealand, and other South Pacific nations are increasingly involved in trade with their Asian neighbors.

Visualizing History Since the 1960s, Taiwan has developed a booming economy that exports goods to other parts of the world. *How was Taiwan affected by events in China during the late 1940s?*

Chapter 34
Africa

The collapse of European colonialism from the mid-1950s to the mid-1990s led to the rise of new nations throughout Africa. Newly independent African nations worked to build stable governments, resolve ethnic conflicts, and create modern economies. The colonial legacy, however, often interfered with these efforts. Some African countries, forced by European colonial rulers to rely on a single product, had difficulty protecting their economies from sharp declines in world commodity prices. Others, based on boundaries set up by the European powers without regard to ethnic loyalties, faced internal unrest.

In other ways, Africa's future seemed full of promise. Many Africans were reestablishing their cultural identities by throwing off reminders of the colonial past. A movement for African unity created new political and economic links among the nations on the continent. Meanwhile, after years of struggle against racial separation, South Africa in the mid-1990s became a full democracy open to all its races, especially the black majority.

Chapter 35
The Middle East

After 1945, fully independent nations arose in the Middle East as European influence declined. Huge oil reserves brought economic growth to some Middle Eastern nations; but they also drew the Middle East into the cold war struggle between the superpowers the United States and the Soviet Union.

Arabs united in opposing the formation of the Jewish state of Israel in 1948. During the years of the Arab-Israeli conflict, the Israelis were able to preserve their independence and even extend their territory. A major issue related to the fighting was the status of the Palestinian Arabs, who claimed the land that Israel occupied.

After years of struggle, Israel and its Arab neighbors began to make peace in the 1970s and 1980s. With the end of the cold war, this task became less complicated. By the early 1990s, Israel had agreed to give back some of the territory it had taken in the 1967 war in return for guarantees of peace and security from the Arabs. The peace process, however, moved slowly. It was often marred by violence from opponents of peace on both sides.

Chapter 36
Latin America

Latin American nations faced many challenges during the postwar era. Rapid industrialization brought new wealth to the region, but the sharp divide between rich and poor often led to political unrest. In the late 1950s, Fidel Castro's revolution in Cuba brought communism to the Western Hemisphere. To contain communism's spread, the United States often supported military dictatorships in various Latin American countries.

During the 1980s and 1990s, pro-democracy movements overturned dictatorships in several Latin American countries. A new generation of political leaders began to encourage free enterprise, free trade, and a limited role for government. In spite of economic advances, the region still faced rapid population growth, heavy foreign debt, and deep divisions between rich and poor.

Visualizing History This leftist mural in Bolivia reflects the political conflicts dividing many **Latin American countries.** *What two groups fought civil wars in Latin America during the 1970s and 1980s?*

Chapter 37
The World in Transition

During the 1980s and 1990s, superpower relations warmed considerably, signaling the end of the cold war. Under Republican Presidents Ronald Reagan and George Bush and Democratic President Bill Clinton, the United States carried out a military role in world trouble spots while reducing government spending on social programs at home. In the Soviet Union, leader Mikhail Gorbachev introduced sweeping economic and social changes that led to the collapse of the Soviet Union and its Communist system. Russia's leader Boris Yeltsin and the other leaders of the now independent republics moved toward free enterprise, but the transition from communism to capitalism brought hardships to many citizens accustomed to government controls.

The reform movement spread to Eastern European countries, which broke free of the Soviet grip and launched new governments. Meanwhile, the nations of Western Europe moved forward toward economic and political unity as members of the European Union (EU).

During the mid-1990s, ethnic and national divisions affected peoples and governments in various parts of the world. In places such as Yugoslavia, Czechoslovakia, and Canada, disputes split or nearly split countries in two. The bloodiest encounters took place along the southern borders of the former Soviet Union and in the Balkans.

As the world heads into the twenty-first century, the interdependence and common purpose of nations and peoples are being recognized. Advances in technology have enabled instantaneous communication around the globe, creating an electronic neighborhood of the world's peoples. Such advances, however, are offset by rapid increases in world population and industrial growth. These trends have created critical environmental problems that affect the entire world. It is apparent that global cooperation is essential to protecting the future of the planet.

SURVEYING UNIT 8

1. **Chapter 32** How did the cold war affect the continent of Europe? How has Europe changed since the end of the cold war?
2. **Chapter 33** What area of Asia is entering a new era of economic prosperity? How has its economic growth affected global affairs?
3. **Chapter 34** How has the colonial legacy affected Africa? In what ways have Africans overcome this legacy?
4. **Chapter 35** How has the relationship between Israelis and Arabs evolved since 1948?
5. **Chapter 36** What changes have come to Latin America since the 1980s?
6. **Chapter 37** How have global environmental problems changed people's thinking about political relationships among nations?

APPENDIX

GLOSSARY

abbess – belligerent

abbess the director of a convent (p. 305)

abbot the head of a monastery (p. 304)

absolutism political system in which a monarch (or group) holds supreme, unlimited power or theory that supports such a system (p. 482)

acupuncture traditional technique of Chinese medicine using thin needles at vital body points (p. 232)

age set in traditional Africa, a group of males or females of similar age who learn skills and go through life stages together (p. 188)

ahimsa (uh•HIHM•sah) Hindu doctrine of nonviolence toward all living things (p. 207)

alchemist person who practiced alchemy, an early form of chemistry emphasizing changes in substances, such as lead into gold (p. 520)

alliance system series of defense agreements involving two or more nations (p. 740)

alphabet system of symbols or characters that represent the sounds of a language (p. 82)

amphora a tall, two-handled Greek vase (p. 131)

anarchy absence of political authority (p. 692)

animism belief that spirits are found in both living and nonliving things (pp. 351, 476)

anthropologist (an•thruh•PAH•luh•jihst) scientist who studies physical and cultural characteristics of humans and their ancestors (p. 20)

apartheid official policy of strict racial separation and discrimination practiced in South Africa from 1948 to the early 1990s (p. 934)

appeasement policy of granting concessions to a potential enemy in order to maintain peace (p. 829)

apportion to divide into assigned shares (p. 648)

apprentice person who works for a master to learn a trade, art, or business (p. 325)

aqueduct a channel built to carry water (p. 168)

arabesque (ar•uh•BEHSK) complex designs typical of Islamic art, combining intertwining plants and geometric patterns (p. 286)

"Arabic numerals" counting symbols (1-9) devised by mathematicians in Gupta India (p. 214)

arbitration process of settling a dispute by submitting it to an impartial third party (p. 722)

archaeologist (ahr•kee•AHL•uh•jihst) scientist who studies earlier peoples and cultures (p. 20)

archipelago a group or chain of islands (pp. 351, 920)

aristocrat member of the nobility or the upper class (p. 113)

armada (ahr•MAH•duh) a fleet of warships (p. 483)

armistice an agreement to stop fighting (p. 761)

arms race the cold war competition between the U.S. and Soviet Union to build up their respective armed forces and weapons (p. 871)

artifact a historic object made or used by humans, such as a tool, ornament, or pottery (p. 20)

artisan person skilled in a craft (p. 33)

atomic theory scientific idea that all matter is made up of tiny particles called atoms (p. 628)

atrocity a cruel and evil action, such as torture (p. 1015)

autocracy government ruled by one person with unlimited authority (p. 690)

automation process in which electronic devices or machines do work once done by humans (p. 883)

autonomy self-government (p. 1008)

balance of power the distribution of power among rival nations so that no one is dominant (p. 489)

balance of trade difference in value between what a nation imports and what it exports over a period of time (p. 448)

bard a poet who tells stories by singing (p. 108)

baroque (buh•ROHK) ornate, dramatic artistic style developed in Europe in the 1550s (p. 424)

barter a system of trade in which goods, not money, are exchanged (p. 82)

bazaar marketplace in an Islamic city (p. 284)

belligerent engaged in fighting or war (p. 746)

bishop a regional leader of the early Christian Church, with authority over a diocese and other clergy (p. 174)

blitz a series of intensive air raids (p. 834)

blitzkrieg (German, "lightning war") a swift, sudden Nazi offensive (p. 831)

bloc a group of political factions or nations acting together (p. 871)

bourgeoisie (boorzh•wah•ZEE) the middle class, between aristocrats and workers (pp. 561, 625)

boyar a landowning noble of early Russia (pp. 260, 499)

boycott a refusal to buy or use certain goods as a protest against an action (p. 548)

budget deficit the amount by which government spending exceeds government income (p. 998)

buffer state neutral territory between rival powers, intended to prevent conflict (p. 582)

bullion gold or silver in the form of bars or plate (p. 448)

bureaucracy a group of government officials headed by an administrator (p. 48)

C

cabinet group of advisers to a ruler or head of state (p. 544)

calculus system of mathematics developed by Newton to analyze changing quantities (p. 519)

caliph (KAY•lihf) supreme leader of Islam, chosen as the "successor" of Muhammad (p. 277)

calligraphy the art of beautiful handwriting (p. 286)

campesino (kahm•puh•SEE•noh) a poor Latin American farm worker (p. 975)

capital money available to invest in business (p. 604)

cardinal high-ranking official of Roman Catholic Church, appointed by the pope (p. 306)

cartel (kahr•TELL) an association of businesses supplying the same product that regulates its members' prices and production (pp. 955, 993)

cartographer person who makes maps (p. 436)

cash-and-carry policy World War II program allowing Great Britain to pay cash and transport needed supplies from the U.S. (p. 835)

cash crop farm product grown to be sold or traded, not used by the farmer (p. 943)

cavalry soldiers mounted on horseback (p. 221)

cell theory scientific theory that small units called cells make up all living things (p. 626)

chancellor title of the chief minister of some European countries (p. 685)

charter formal document granting the right of self-rule (p. 326)

châteaux (sing., chateau [Fr.]) castles (p. 413)

chinampas artificial islands built by the Aztecs for use as gardens (p. 388)

chivalry code of conduct for medieval knights, based on ideals of honor and courtesy (p. 301)

choreographer person who creates dances (p. 775)

chronicle an account that records events in the order in which they happened (p. 288)

circumnavigation sailing completely around something, such as the world (p. 439)

citizen in ancient Greece, a person who took part in the government of a city-state (p. 112)

city-state an independent state consisting of a city and the surrounding land and villages (p. 59)

civil disobedience nonviolent refusal to obey a law or practice thought unjust (p. 802)

civil service system by which government offices are given on the basis of examinations (p. 224)

civilization highly organized society marked by advanced knowledge of trade, government, arts, science, and often written language (p. 32)

clan group based on family ties (pp. 342, 939)

classical describing the artistic style of ancient Greece and Rome, characterized by balance, elegance, and simplicity (p. 130)

classicism style and attitudes derived from the ideals of ancient Greece and Rome (p. 528)

clergy persons, such as priests, given authority to conduct religious services (p. 249)

coalition a temporary alliance of differing political factions (pp. 780, 879)

cold war era of political tension in which the United States and the Soviet Union competed for world influence without actual armed conflict (p. 864)

collective bargaining negotiations between union representatives and employers (p. 616)

collective security the common defense interests of several nations against an enemy (pp. 826, 1012)

collectivization under Stalin, a system to combine land into large farms owned by the government and worked by peasants (p. 790)

colon (koh•LOHN) a French settler in the colony of Algeria (p. 931)

colony a settlement of people outside their homeland, linked with the parent country by trade and direct government control (pp. 82, 475, 706)

comedy story or play intended to entertain and amuse, usually with a happy ending (p. 134)

common law body of English law based on tradition and court decisions, not specific laws (p. 309)

commonwealth a nation or state governed by the people or their representatives (p. 539)

commune people who live communally, with collective ownership and use of property (p. 902)

communism in the theories of Marx and Engels, a society without class distinctions or private property (pp. 625, 758)

concentration camp prison camp where political prisoners or refugees are held (p. 786)

confederation a loose alliance or union of several states or groups (pp. 82, 378, 554)

conquistador (kon•KEES•tuh•dohr) a Spanish "conqueror" or soldier in the Americas (p. 441)

conscription compulsory call to military service; the draft (pp. 569, 740)

constitution plan of government (p. 117)

constitutional monarchy state in which a monarch's power is limited by a constitution (p. 541)

consul in ancient Rome, one of two officials who headed the executive branch (p. 157)

containment U.S. policy designed to prevent the spread of communism (p. 866)

contraband goods that may not legally be transported, particularly during wartime (p. 751)

convoy group of merchant ships traveling together with warships for safety (p. 760)

cooperative a farm organization owned and managed by members, who share profits (p. 812)

cordon sanitaire (kawr•dahn sah•nee•TEHR) a line of "quarantine" or buffer states (p. 763)

corporate state Mussolini's concept of a government with representation by industrial corporations, not political parties (p. 783)

corporation business organization that is owned by stockholders who buy shares, and is run by professional managers (p. 609)

cortes (KOR•tays) assembly of nobles, clergy, and town officials in medieval Spain; also, the parliament of modern Spain (p. 332)

count a noble who acted as a local official within the Frankish empire (p. 295)

coup d'état (koo day•TAH) sudden overthrow of government leaders by a small group (pp. 573, 657)

covenant a solemn pledge or agreement (p. 83)

covert (KOH•vert) secret (p. 986)

Creole a person of European ancestry born in colonial Latin America (p. 667)

Crusades military expeditions by European Christians in the 11th–13th centuries to regain the Holy Land from the Muslims (p. 318)

cubism 20th-century art style that abstracts natural forms into geometric shapes (p. 773)

cultural diffusion the exchange of goods, ideas, and customs among different cultures (p. 34)

culture the way of life of a given people at a given time, including language, behavior, and beliefs (p. 24)

culture system in Dutch colonies in Asia, a system of forced labor to get raw materials (p. 718)

cuneiform (kyoo•NEE•uh•fawrm) Sumerian system of writing using wedge-shaped markings (p. 60)

czar (from "caesar") title taken by rulers of Russia beginning in the late 1400s (p. 264)

D

D-Day the day of the Allied invasion of Normandy, France (June 6, 1944)(p. 846)

daimyo (DY•mee•oh) a powerful local noble in feudal Japan (p. 363)

datus local rulers in the Philippines (p. 475)

death squad in Central America, a band of killers hired by landowners to murder political opponents (p. 987)

deforestation process of cutting trees and clearing forests on large areas of land (p. 1020)

deism religious philosophy of the 1700s based on reason and the idea of natural law (p. 523)

deity a god or goddess (p. 31)

democracy form of government in which the citizens hold power (p. 114)

depression economic situation characterized by a business slump and unemployment (p. 609)

desalination process of removing salt from seawater to produce drinkable water (p. 964)

desertification process of fertile land becoming desert (p. 944)

détente (day•TAHNT) the relaxing of tensions between the United States and the Soviet Union in the 1970s (p. 874)

developed nation an industrialized nation with advanced technology (p. 1019)

developing nation a country in the process of industrializing, where people often follow traditional lifestyles (p. 1019)

dharma duties and rights of members of each class in traditional Hindu society (p. 205)

Diaspora (dye•AS•pur•uh) term for the scattering of communities of Jews outside their original homeland after the Babylonian captivity (p. 86)

dictator in ancient Rome, a leader given temporary absolute power during a crisis (p. 157)

dictatorship government headed by a ruler with absolute authority (p. 574)

dictatorship of the proletariat in the former Soviet Union, theoretical control of the state by the working class (p. 789)

direct tax a tax paid directly to the government (p. 548)

disarmament limiting or reducing military forces and weapons (p. 778)

disciple an active follower of a teacher (p. 172)

disenfranchised denied the right to vote (p. 649)

disengagement act of freeing oneself or withdrawing from a situation (p. 955)

dissident a person who openly criticizes the policies of his or her government (p. 874)

divine right political theory that a ruler derives his or her power directly from God and is accountable only to God (pp. 482, 536)

division of labor production technique in which each worker does one specialized task (p. 609)

doge (DOHJ) the elected leader of the republic in the city-states of Venice and Genoa (p. 408)

domain territory held by a ruler (p. 142)

domesticate to tame animals or plants to serve human needs (p. 30)

domestic system early industrial labor system in which workers produced goods at home (p. 602)

dominion a self-governing nation within the British Empire, later the Commonwealth (p. 653)

domino theory cold war belief that if one nation became Communist, its neighbors would follow (p. 910)

double-digit inflation a quick rise in prices of 10 percent or more (p. 889)

dual monarchy two states with one monarch (p.696)

duma the Russian national legislature (p. 694)

duty a tax on imports (p. 546)

dvorianie (dvoh•ree•YAH•nee•yuh) new class of Russian landed nobility established by Peter the Great (p. 501)

dynasty a line of rulers who belong to the same family (p. 47)

E

economy system by which goods and services are produced and distributed to meet people's needs (p. 33)

elite a select group of people (p. 975)

ellipse an oval (not round) closed curve (p. 517)

emancipation legally granting freedom (p. 691)

embargo an order restricting trade (pp. 889, 960, 1015)

emigration leaving one's home country or region to settle elsewhere (p. 630)

émigré (EH•mih•GRAY) person who fled France during the Revolution (p. 566)

empire group of territories or nations ruled by a single ruler or government (p. 49)

enclave (EHN•klayv) a small territory entirely surrounded by the territory of another country or group (p. 1016)

enclosure movement the trend for large landowners gradually to fence and include public and private common lands in their own estates (p. 603)

enlightened despot a monarch who began social changes based on Enlightenment ideas (p. 527)

entente (ahn•TAHNT) an agreement, but not a formal alliance, between nations (p. 740)

entrepreneur person who undertakes risks to establish a business (pp. 448, 604)

epic long poem celebrating the deeds of a legendary or historical hero (p. 203)

estate one of three distinct social classes in France during the 1700s: clergy, nobility, and commoners (the Third Estate) (p. 560)

ethics a system of moral principles that guide behavior (p. 225)

ethnic cleansing term used in the Bosnian conflict for a policy of forcibly removing or killing members of another ethnic group (pp. 1014-15)

evolution theory that species of living things change over long periods of time (p. 626)

excommunication formal exclusion from membership or participation in a church (p. 306)

exodus the departure of a large group of people (p. 84)

extended family family group including several generations as well as other relatives (p. 229)

F

factory system method of production in which goods are made by workers and machines in one location (a factory) outside their homes (p. 606)

fascism (FASH•ihz•uhm) political philosophy based on nationalism and an all-powerful state (p. 782)

federal system form of government in which power is divided between a central authority and its political subdivisions (p. 534)

feudalism medieval political system in which monarchs and lesser nobles made alliances based on exchanging land grants for loyalty (p. 298)

fez traditional hat worn by Turkish men (p. 797)

fief under feudalism, an estate with its peasant workers granted to a noble in exchange for loyalty and military help (p. 298)

filial piety children's respect for their parents, an important principle in Confucian ethics (p. 226)

free trade the elimination of trade barriers between nations (p. 978)

friar member of a Catholic order who preached in towns and practiced poverty (p. 307)

fundamentalism movement emphasizing adherence to traditional religious laws and practices (p. 965)

G

geisha Japanese woman trained as a professional entertainer (p. 472)

general strike a strike involving workers from many parts of a nation's economy (pp. 779, 931)

genetic engineering scientific field in which cell structures can be altered to produce new or different organisms (p. 1022)

genetics the study of biological heredity (p. 627)

genocide deliberate attempt to kill all members of a racial, cultural, or ethnic group (pp. 840, 938)

gentry in Elizabethan England, the social group including minor nobility and landowners (p. 488)

ghana title of the ruler of a region in ancient Africa, later applied to the kingdom (p. 189)

glasnost Russian term for the policy of "openness" and free expression introduced by Mikhail Gorbachev (p. 999)

grand jury in English law, group of people who decide whether the evidence of a crime justifies bringing a person to trial (p. 309)

grand vizier (vih•ZEER) prime minister to the sultan of a Muslim country (p. 457)

gross domestic product (GDP) total value of goods and services produced within a country in a year (p. 898)

guerrilla warfare method of fighting in which small groups strike unexpectedly (p. 679)

guild medieval business association of merchants or craftsworkers (p. 324)

H

habeas corpus legal principle that requires authorities to show reasons why a person should be held in custody and to provide a speedy trial (p. 542)

haiku (HY•koo) Japanese poetry form with 17 syllables, usually in three lines (p. 472)

hajj pilgrimage to Makkah that every able-bodied Muslim is expected to make at least once (p. 276)

heavy industry the manufacture of machines and equipment for factories and mines (p. 808)

heresy disagreement with or denial of the basic teachings of a religion (p. 306)

hierarchy group of people organized according to levels of rank or importance (pp. 228, 389)

hieroglyphics ancient Egyptian writing system using picture symbols for ideas or sounds (p. 52)

Holocaust name given to the Nazis' mass murder of European Jews in World War II (p. 839)

homage formal ceremony establishing feudal ties between a lord and a vassal (p. 299)

home rule self-government, especially when granted to a dependent country (p. 651)

hominid (HAH•muh•nihd) member of the group that includes human beings and earlier human-like creatures (p. 20)

humanism Renaissance movement based on the literature and ideas of ancient Greece and Rome, such as the worth of each individual (p. 404)

hygiene the science of good health (p. 138)

hyperinflation an extreme form of inflation, with sharp, rapid price increases (p. 991)

hypothesis solution proposed to explain a set of facts, which can be tested (p. 517)

I

icon a Christian religious image or picture (p. 249)

iconoclast ("image breaker") an opponent of the use of icons in Byzantine churches, who thought they encouraged the worship of idols (p. 250)

ideology the system of beliefs and attitudes that guides the actions of a group or nation (p. 871)

illuminated manuscript book page decorated by hand with elaborate designs, beautiful lettering, or miniature paintings (p. 253)

imam (ih•MAM) a Muslim prayer leader (p. 276)

immigration entering a new country or region to settle permanently there (p. 630)

imperialism policy of building an empire (p. 704)

imperial presidency term for a President and executive branch who assume powers beyond those defined in the Constitution (p. 888)

impressionism artistic style of the late 1800s in which painters tried to capture quick impressions and the effects of light (p. 638)

indemnity payment for damages or losses (p. 160)

individualism emphasis on the dignity and worth of the individual person (p. 404-05)

indulgence pardon sold by the Catholic Church to reduce one's punishment for sins (p. 416)

industrial capitalism economic system in which individuals continually reinvest profits and expand their businesses (p. 608)

inflation situation in which prices rise quickly while the value of money decreases (pp. 176, 484)

intendant an agent representing the king of France in local government (p. 491)

interchangeable parts production method using identical, easy-to-assemble parts (p. 609)

intercontinental ballistic missile (ICBM) a long-range rocket carrying a warhead (p. 873)

interdependent relying on one another (p. 1018)

Internet popular term for the advanced communications network linking people and computers around the world (p. 1021)

intifada the 1987 uprising by Palestinians against Israeli occupation (p. 956)

iron curtain term coined by Winston Churchill for the political barrier isolating Soviet-dominated Eastern Europe from Western Europe (p. 866)

J

jaguar spotted wild cat of Mesoamerica (p. 380)

janissary member of an elite corps of soldiers in the Ottoman Empire (p. 457)

jati groups based on occupation formed within larger social classes (varna) in ancient India, each with its own rules and customs (p. 204)

jazz American musical style incorporating African rhythms with American and European sounds (p. 773)

jihad (jih•HAHD) Muslim struggle to introduce Islam to other lands (p. 278)

jingoism attitude of extreme patriotism, usually directed toward a foreign power (p. 698)

joint-stock company trading venture that sold shares to divide costs and profits (p. 447)

journeyman craftsworker who has finished an apprenticeship and works for pay (p. 325)

junk a Chinese sailing ship (p. 464)

justification by faith Martin Luther's concept that faith alone is enough to bring salvation (p. 415)

K

kaiser title of the German emperor (p. 685)

kamikaze in World War II, the Japanese pilots who crashed bomb-filled planes in suicide attacks on Allied targets (p. 845)

karma in Hinduism, the idea that one's actions in life determine one's destiny and future (p. 207)

khan an absolute ruler of the Mongols (p. 344)

kibbutz (pl. kibbutzim) a collective farm community in Israel (p. 951)

Kristallnacht ("night of broken glass") Nazi terrorist attacks, November 9-10, 1938, on Jewish property in Germany and Austria (p. 786)

kulak a well-to-do peasant in the USSR (p. 790)

L

labor-intensive farming agriculture that relies on human labor, not animals or machines (p. 466)

labor union organization of workers formed to pressure business owners to improve wages and working conditions (p. 616)

labyrinth a complex, confusing series of connected passages (p. 107)

laissez-faire (leh•say•FAYR) economic principle that government should not regulate businesses (p. 622)

laity church members who are not clergy (p. 249)

lay investiture medieval practice in which secular rulers appointed and inaugurated church officials such as bishops (p. 306)

lend-lease World War II policy allowing the loan of equipment to friendly countries (p. 836)

liberalism political philosophy that promotes social change and individual freedoms (p. 582)

liberation theology movement led by Catholic clergy in Latin America emphasizing the Church's role in improving people's lives (p. 978)

line of demarcation imaginary line in the Atlantic Ocean, drawn by the pope in 1493 to divide the world's lands between Spain and Portugal (p. 439)

literacy rate the percentage of a country's adult population who can read and write (p. 944)

logic the science of reasoning and establishing proof for arguments (p. 135)

M

madrasa Muslim school of theology and law (p. 283)

maize corn native to the Americas (p. 374)

mandarin member of the elite class of civil servants in Chinese government (pp. 224, 348)

mandate (1) in ancient China, authority granted by heaven to deserving rulers, called the Mandate of Heaven (p. 71); (2) a territory administered by another nation before independence (p. 763)

manorialism medieval economic system linking nobles and the peasants on their land (p. 301)

martial law temporary military rule, limiting rights such as free speech (p. 537)

martyr person who suffers and dies for a belief (p. 173)

master skilled artisan who owned a shop and employed other craftsworkers (p. 325)

matrilineal tracing family descent through the mother and her ancestors (p. 187)

mayor of the palace Frankish official who, by A.D. 700, held real power in government (p. 294)

mercantilism economic policy of European nations in the 1600s, equating wealth and power (p. 448)

mercenary a soldier who serves a foreign country for pay (p. 124)

meritocracy system in which people gain success on the basis of ability and performance (p. 347)

messiah in Judaism, a savior promised by the Hebrew prophets, who would bring peace (p. 171)

mestizo (meh•STEE•zoh) in Latin America, a person of Native American and European ancestry (p. 667)

metaphysics aspects of philosophy dealing with basic questions of existence and reality (p. 530)

metsuke group of officials who gathered information for the Tokugawa shoguns (p. 469)

middle class class of society that originally fell between nobility and peasants, earning their income from business and trade (p. 310)

Middle Passage middle section of the triangular trade, in which enslaved Africans were brought by ship to the Americas (p. 445)

middle power a nation that is economically strong but not a military power (p. 889)

militarism national policy based on military strength and glorification of war (pp. 689, 740)

millet community of non-Muslims within the Ottoman Empire (p. 458)

missionary person who travels to carry the ideas of a religion to others (p. 254)

mobilization act of assembling and preparing troops and equipment for war (p. 743)

monarchy rule by a king or a queen (p. 47)

monastery a community of men who have taken religious vows (p. 254)

money economy economic system in which money (not barter) is used to buy and sell (p. 323)

monopoly control of all (or almost all) trade or production of a given good (p. 194)

monotheism belief in one God (pp. 83, 189)

monsoon seasonal wind that affects climates and ways of life in southern Asia (p. 66)

mosaic picture made up of tiny pieces of colored glass, tile, or stone set in mortar (p. 253)

mosque a Muslim house of worship (pp. 191, 276)

multicultural representing several different cultural and ethnic groups (pp. 195, 890)

myth a traditional story that explains natural events (p. 35)

N

nationalism pride in one's own nation; desire for independence (pp. 576, 676)

nationalization placing a privately owned business under government ownership (p. 813)

nationalize to bring a private industry under government control (p. 952)

nation-state a political state whose people also share the same language and culture (p. 677)

natural law a universal truth or principle that 17th-century thinkers believed could be found through reason (p. 521)

natural rights rights belonging to all persons from birth (p. 523)

negritude a literary movement that emphasizes and takes pride in Africa's cultural heritage (p. 945)

nihilist member of a Russian political movement of the late 1800s that rejected all authority and advocated terrorism (p. 692)

nirvana in Buddhism, a state of oneness with the universe, the end of the cycle of rebirth (p. 210)

nomad member of a group of people with no fixed home, who travel constantly to find food and water (p. 22)

nonaligned not taking sides with either of the superpowers in the cold war (p. 917)

nuclear family family group consisting only of parents and children (p. 229)

O

obsidian black volcanic glass (p. 383)

oligarchy form of government in which a small group holds political power (p. 114)

oral tradition the legends and history of a culture preserved by word of mouth (p. 184)

P

pacifism opposition to war or violence as a way to settle disputes (p. 523)

pacifist a believer in pacifism (p. 802)

pact a treaty between several nations (p. 953)

paleontologist (pay•lee•ahn•TAH•luh•jihst) scientist who studies fossil remains (p. 20)

Pan-Africanism movement encouraging unity and cooperation among African nations (p. 942)

Pan-Arabism movement intended to build cultural and political ties among Arabs (p. 950)

papal infallibility Roman Catholic doctrine that the pope cannot make an error in speaking about faith and morals (p. 686)

partisan World War II term for an underground resistance fighter, especially in Italy and Yugoslavia (p. 848)

partition to divide a region (p. 707)

partnership business owned by two or more entrepreneurs who share management, profits, and losses (p. 609)

patriarch in the early Christian Church, one of five powerful bishops in major cities (p. 174)

patrician a member of the wealthy aristocratic class of ancient Rome (p. 156)

peaceful coexistence Soviet policy of competing with the United States while avoiding war (p. 873)

peninsulares officials born in Spain or Portugal who led society in colonial Latin America (p. 667)

perestroika (pehr•uh•STROY•kuh) Russian term for "restructuring," the changes in the Soviet economy begun by Mikhail Gorbachev (p. 1000)

perspective an artistic technique for showing relationships and space between objects (p. 131)

petit jury group of people who determine the guilt or innocence of a person on trial (p. 309)

phalanx in ancient Greece, a military formation in which foot soldiers stood so that their shields overlapped (p. 114)

pharaoh title of rulers of ancient Egypt (p. 49)

philosophe (fee•luh•ZAWF) a social or political thinker of the Enlightenment (p. 524)

philosopher a thinker or lover of wisdom (p. 135)

pilgrimage journey to a holy place (p. 334)

plateau a relatively flat region of land higher than the surrounding area (p. 185)

plebeian (plih•BEE•uhn) a citizen of ancient Rome who was not an aristocrat (p. 156)

plebiscite (PLEB•uh•syt) a direct popular vote on a program or issue (pp. 575, 657)

pogrom organized persecution of a minority group, usually Jews, in czarist Russia (p. 693)

polis city-state of ancient Greece (p. 112)

pollution putting toxic or impure substances into the air, land, or water (p. 898)

polytheism worship of many gods (p. 52)

pope the bishop of Rome, later the head of the Roman Catholic Church (p. 174)

population explosion a large, sudden increase in the human population (p. 808)

Postimpressionism artistic movement whose members experimented with form and color (p. 639)

potlatch feast held by Native Americans of the Pacific Northwest to display their wealth (p. 376)

pragmatic sanction decree issued by a ruler on an important question (p. 495)

pragmatist in China, a moderate who advocated economic reform and trade with the West (p. 902)

predestination doctrine of John Calvin that each person's fate is predetermined by God (p. 419)

prehistory time before written history (p. 20)

prime minister the chief executive of a parliamentary government (p. 544)

principality territory ruled by a prince (p. 260)

privatization the return of government-owned industries to private owners (pp. 980-81, 1003)

proletariat in Marxist theory, the working class (p. 625)

propaganda news and information intended to influence people's feelings about a cause (p. 746)

prophet a person who preaches or interprets what are thought to be messages from God (p. 83)

protectorate a country whose policies are guided by a foreign nation (p. 706)

provisional government a temporary government set up while waiting for elections (p. 757)

psychology study of behavior and its causes (p. 628)

purge an official effort to remove people that a government considers undesirable (p. 791)

Q

queue (KYOO) single braid of hair at the back of the head (p. 466)

quinoa grain grown in the Andes (p. 390)

quota a specified number or amount (p. 900)

R

racial segregation the social separation of people according to their race (p. 887)

radiocarbon dating modern scientific method for telling the age of once-living material by measuring the amount of radioactive carbon remaining in it (p. 21)

rajah an Aryan tribal chief in ancient India; later the ruler of an Indian state (p. 202)

ratify to give formal approval (p. 665)

reactionary one who opposes progress or change and wants to return to earlier ways (p. 582)

realism artistic and literary style of the mid-1800s that pictured the realities of everyday life (p. 636)

realpolitik political theory that national success justifies the use of any means (p. 682)

referendum a direct popular vote on a measure or proposed law (pp. 908, 1011)

refugee person who must leave his or her home and flee elsewhere for safety (p. 911)

regent person who acts as a temporary ruler (p. 251)

reincarnation the rebirth of the soul or spirit in different bodies over time (p. 206)

reparation compensation for war damage (p. 763)

republic a government in which citizens elect the leaders (p. 156)

revelation a vision of divine truth, such as those attributed to Muhammad (p. 272)

revolution a sudden, radical change; change of government by force (p. 554)

rhetoric art of effective public speaking (p. 119)

romanticism artistic movement of the early 1800s emphasizing individuality and emotion (pp. 530, 635)

royalist person who supports a monarchy (p. 539)

Russification policy of imposing Russian language and customs on other peoples (p. 692)

S

sacrament one of the established formal rituals of the Roman Catholic Church, such as baptism, holy communion, or matrimony (p. 303)

salon in France, a gathering where Enlightenment intellectuals met for conversation (p. 525)

samurai class of landowning warriors in feudal Japan, who pledged loyalty to a daimyo (p. 363)

sanctions penalties and restrictions imposed on a nation for breaking international law (p. 827)

sanctuary building used for worship (p. 130)

sankin-kotai ("alternate attendance") in feudal Japan, system in which a daimyo had to spend every other year at the shogun's court (p. 469)

satellite a country politically dominated by a nearby power (p. 865)

satrap governor of a Persian province (p. 91)

satyagraha ("truth force") term for nonviolent protests led by Gandhi (p. 802)

savanna a flat grassland, with few trees, in tropical or subtropical regions (p. 185)

schism (SIH•zuhm) the division of the Christian Church in 1054 that separated the Roman Catholic Church and the Eastern Orthodox Church (p. 250)

scholasticism medieval school of thought that tried to bring together Aristotle's philosophy and the teachings of Church scholars (p. 326)

scientific method steps to find scientific truth through observation and experiments (p. 518)

scorched-earth policy Stalin's order for the Soviet people to destroy buildings, land, and anything that Nazi invaders could use (p. 838)

secede to withdraw formally from membership in a political organization (p. 663)

sect a subgroup with distinct beliefs within a larger religious group (pp. 171, 899)

sectionalism overemphasis on the political and economic interests of one's own region (p. 663)

secular worldly, not overtly or specifically religious (p. 404)

self-determination the right of a people to decide their own political status or government (p. 796)

seminary school for educating priests, as ordered by the Council of Trent (p. 423)

separatism in Canada, a political movement favoring the independence of Quebec (p. 890)

sepoy an Indian soldier in the British army (p. 713)

serf a peasant laborer legally bound to the lands of a noble (pp. 302, 501)

shah the ruler of a Middle Eastern country (p. 797)

shamanism belief that spirits inhabit living and nonliving things, communicating with humans through priests called shamans (p. 358)

shari'ah (shuh•REE•uh) Islamic code of law that includes rules for all aspects of life (p. 275)

sheikh (SHAYK) chief of a bedouin tribe (p. 271)

shogun military ruler of feudal Japan (p. 363)

shogunate government established by a shogun's family and followers in feudal Japan (p. 363)

simony the selling of official positions in the medieval Roman Catholic Church (p. 335)

slash-and-burn farming farming method in which land for crops is cleared by cutting and burning trees to fertilize the soil (p. 380)

socialism political theory that society as a whole should control the means of production, such as factories and land (p. 624)

Socialist realism under Stalin, an artistic style that glorified the Soviet way of life (p. 791)

sociology study of human group behavior (p. 628)

sonnet poetry form with 14 lines and a fixed pattern of rhyme and meter (p. 405)

sovereignty the independent decision-making power of a group or nation (p. 963)

soviet a workers' council formed early in the Russian Revolution; later, a unit of government in the Soviet Union (p. 694)

special economic zone areas of China where foreign businesses and a free market were allowed to operate in the 1990s (p. 903)

sphere of influence area in a country where a foreign power has exclusive rights to trade or invest (pp. 706, 715)

stagflation slow growth with high inflation and unemployment (p. 889)

stalemate a deadlock, or situation in which neither of two opponents can move further (p. 907)

standard of living a general measure of people's overall wealth and quality of life (p. 979)

steppe wide, grassy, semiarid plains of Eurasia, from the Black Sea to the Altai Mountains (p. 258)

stupa a dome-shaped Buddhist shrine built over relics or bones of a holy person (p. 210)

subcontinent landmass that is part of a continent but distinct from it, such as India (p. 66)

subsistence farmer farmer who grows only enough to supply a family or village (p. 943)

suffragette woman who actively worked to win voting rights for women (p. 651)

sultan political leader with absolute authority over a Muslim country (p. 457)

superpower a powerful, influential nation with a bloc of allies; specifically, the United States and the Soviet Union during the cold war (p. 864)

surrealism 20th-century art movement using distorted, surprising images (p. 773)

symbolism antirealism artistic movement that focused on dreamlike images and symbols (p. 638)

symposium in ancient Athens, a gathering of men that featured eating, drinking, entertainment, and intellectual discussions (p. 123)

syndicate under fascism, an organization of workers and employers in an industry (p. 783)

T

technology the skills and knowledge used by people to make tools and do work (p. 24)

theocracy government headed by religious leaders or a leader regarded as a god (pp. 48, 418)

theology study of religious questions (p. 251)

tithe a 10 percent tax on income, paid to the clergy (p. 561)

totalitarianism idea that a dictatorial government should control all aspects of citizens' lives (p. 781)

tournament medieval sport in which knights competed to show their fighting skills (p. 299)

trade deficit the economic imbalance when a country's imports exceeds its exports (pp. 889, 998)

tragedy story or play in which the central character struggles against destiny but meets an unhappy end (p. 132)

trench a ditch dug to protect soldiers (p. 747)

triangular trade three-directional trade route between Europe, Africa, and America in the 1600s (p. 444)

tribune in ancient Rome, an official who represented the plebeians (p. 157)

triumvirate in ancient Rome, a three-person ruling group (p. 162)

troubadour poet-musician of the Middle Ages, who traveled from court to court (p. 327)

tyrant in ancient Greece, a person who seized power and established one-man rule (p. 114)

U V

ultimatum a final demand or statement of terms, implying a threat of serious penalties (p. 742)

ultraroyalist an extremely conservative aristocrat in France in the 1820s (p. 655)

unicameral legislature assembly or lawmaking body with one house (p. 565)

urbanization the spread of cities and city living (p. 631)

utilitarianism economic philosophy, developed by Jeremy Bentham, that social and political actions should be useful and helpful to humanity (p. 624)

varna one of four main social classes in Aryan society of ancient India (p. 203)

vassal in feudalism, a noble who held land from and served a higher-ranking lord (p. 299)

vernacular the language of everyday speech, not of scholars, in a country or region (p. 328)

viceroy governor representing a monarch (p. 714)

vocation a calling from God to take up certain work (p. 417)

W X Y Z

war of attrition conflict in which each side tries to win by wearing down the other (p. 747)

warlord local military leader in China (p. 804)

weir net or trap placed across a river to catch fish (p. 376)

welfare state government system in which the state provides programs to protect people's social and economic well-being (p. 879)

westernization the spread of European culture (p. 718)

yasa Mongol law code of Genghis Khan (p. 344)

yeoman (YOH•mun) in English society, a farmer who owned land (p. 488)

yin and yang in Chinese thinking, the opposing principles present in all nature (p. 227)

yurt large, round, portable tent used by nomads of central Asia (p. 343)

zaibatsu (zy•BAHT•soo) large Japanese industrial firms owned by a few families (p. 808)

zemstvo local assembly in czarist Russia (p. 692)

Italicized page numbers refer to illustrations. Preceding the page number, abbreviations refer to a map (m), chart (c) photograph or other picture (p), graph (g), cartoon (crt), painting (ptg). Quoted material is referenced with the abbreviation (q) before the page number.

A

Abbas, Shah, 459
Abbasid dynasty, *m284,* 274, 280–81; cultural life, 282, 285; establishment, 277, 280; Turk mercenaries, 342
abbesses, 305
abbots, 304
Abdul-Aziz, 458
Abdul-Hamid II, 458
Abdul-Mejid I, 458
á Becket, Thomas, 309
Aborigines, 654
Abraham, 83, 84, 275
absolutism, 482, 492; end of, in England, 539; in France, 655
abstract expressionism, 884
Abu Bakr, 273, 277
Abu'l-'Abbas, 280
Achebe, Chinua, 968
acid rain. *See* pollution
Acropolis, *p116–17,* 112, 130
Actium, 163
Act of Seclusion, 468, 471
Act of Settlement, 543, 544
Act of Supremacy. *See* Church of England
Act of Union, 540, 543, 651
acupuncture, *p228,* 232
Adams, John, *q548*
Adams, John Quincy, 722
Adams, Samuel, 550
Adena culture, *p376,* 377
Adenauer, Konrad, 878, 880
adobe, 377
Adowa, Battle of, 707, 710
Adrianople, *m177*
Adulis, 186
advertising, 771
Aegean civilizations, *m107;* culture, 108–10; deities, 110–11; festivals, 111; Minoan civilization, 107–11; Mycenaean civilization, 107–08; religion, 110–11
Aeneid, 170
Aeschylus, 132
Aesop's fables, 229
Affonso I, ruler of Kongo, 445
Afghanistan; Pakistan, relations with, 919; Seleucus, rule of, 143; Soviet invasion of, 871, 874–75
Africa, *m199,* 184–96; agriculture, 17, 943–44; arts, 945; climate, 184–85; cold war, 871; colonialism, 928–29; colonialism, legacy of, 943; common market, 942; digest, 238; economic development, 942–43; exploration, 434, 436, 707; food production, 944; foreign aid, 943–944; future challenges, 941–45; geography, 184–85; human prehistory, 20; imperialism, social effects, 799; independence, 928–29; Internet, 861; kingdoms, *m193;* military rulers, 941–42; national borders, 942; nationalism, 856, 929; national unity, 941–42; Pan-Africanism, 942; population growth, 944; post-World War II period, 1027; pride, 930, 941–45; regional economic cooperatives, 944; religion, 190–91; social-

ism, 944; Southern Africa. *See* East Africa, North Africa, Southern Africa, West Africa. *See also* individual countries
African Americans; citizenship, 664; civil rights movement, 886–87; literature, 773; identity, 945; music, 401
African National Congress (ANC), 712, 926, 934, 935, 939
Afrika Korps, 845
Afrikaners, 711, 933
Afro-Caribbean music, 401
After Naseby, 1645, *ptg535*
Agamemnon, 132
age sets, 187–88
Agincourt, Battle of, 329
Agnew, Spiro, 888
Agni, 206
agora, 112, 119
agriculture; as a business, 603; cash crops, 943; civilization, influence on, 31; collectivization, 790; development of, 16–17, 18, 30; enclosure movement, 603; food distribution, 34; labor-intensive farming, 466; in Middle Ages, 302; pre-Industrial Revolution, 601–02; rotation of crops, 298; slash–and–burn, 380; subsistence farming, 467, 943
Aguateca, 386
Aquinaldo Emilio, 719
ahimsa, 207
Ahmose, 49
Ahriman, 92–93
Ahura Mazda, 92–93
AIDS, 999, 1022
airplanes, 611; in cold war, 864; first flight, 598; reconnaissance aircraft, 760; in World War I, 748
Aix-la-Chapelle, Treaty of, 497
Ajanta caves, *p214*
Akan culture, *p191*
Akbar, 461
Akbar Hunting Tigers Near Gwalior, *ptg461*
Akhenaton, 51
Akkadian Empire, *m60,* 62
Aladdin and His Lamp, 287
Alaric, 178
Alaska, 724; Native Americans, 375
Albania, 739; communism, 865; communism, end of, 1007; post communist riots in, 1008
Alberta, Canada, 653
Albigensians, 306–07
Albright, Madeleine, 999
alchemy, 285, 520
Alcuin, 295, 303
Alegría, Claribel, *q987*
Alejandro of Alva, 482
Aleman, Arnoldo, 986
Alemanni, 175
Alexander I, czar, 576, 580, 582, 690–91
Alexander II, czar, *p690,* 674, 691–92
Alexander III, czar, 692–93, 757
Alexander the Great, *p141, p142,* 141–42, 237; becomes king of Macedonia, 128; empire, *m141, m151;* invasion of Indus River valley, 211; Pachacuti, compared to, 389; Persepolis, destruction of, 90; Persian Empire, conquest of, 93, 256. *See also* Macedonian Empire
Alexander VI, pope, 408, 428
Alexandra, empress, 692, 693, 756–57
Alexandria, Egypt, 100, 142, 143–44
Alexis, son of Czar Nicholas II, 692
Alexius I Comnenus, 343
Alfonso XIII, king of Spain, 827
Alfred of Wessex, 308

Alfred the Great, 308
algebra, 243, 285
Algeria, 708; French imperialism, 697, 704, 705; independence, 879–80, 926, 931; Islamic state, 936; in the 1990s, 935–36
Algiers, 708
Alhambra, *p279*
Ali, Muhammad, 708
Ali, son-in-law of Muhammad, 277, 278
Ali, Sunni, 193
Ali Baba and the Forty Thieves, 287
al-jabr w'al-muqabalah, 243
Allah, 272, 275
Allen, Douglas, 721
Allen, Frederick Lewis, 776
Allende, Salvador, 991
Alliance for Progress, 978
alliance systems; as a cause of World War I, 740, 743; defined, 740
Allied Powers (World War I), 744–751
alloys, 34
All Quiet on the Western Front, 736
Almoravids, 190
alms, 276
alphabet, 78, 82; Cyrillic, 255; Ionians, use by, 108; Japanese, 250
Alps; Hannibal's crossing, 160
Alsace-Lorraine, 739, 763
Alsace province, 658
al Tabari, 282, 288
Amaterasu, 360, 361
Amazon River, 421
Amen-hir-khopshef, 55
Amenhotep, 49, 51
America; Cro-Magnon migration into, 35; name derivation, 438. *See also* North America. *See also* South America
American colonies. *See* English colonies
American Revolution; anthems, 578; battles, *m557;* Boston Massacre, 548; Boston Tea Party, 550, 552; British view; 549; causes of, 545–550; Continental Congress, First, 550; Continental Congress, Second, 553; Declaration of Independence, 553–54; effects of, 555–56; events leading to, 545–50; French Revolution, influence on, 560, 562; Revolutionary War. *See* Revolutionary War; women, 552
American Tragedy, An, 638
Amiens, Treaty of, 574, 576
Amin, Idi, 938
Amon, 52
Amon-Ra, 52
Amorites, 63
amphora, 131
Amritsar Massacre, 801–02
Amsterdam, Netherlands, 442
Anabaptists, 419
Analects, 226, 231
anarchy, defined, 692
Anasazi. *See* Pueblo
Anatolia, 88
anatomy, 519
ANC; *See* African National Congress (ANC)
Ancient Records of Assyria and Babylonia, *q69, q88*
Andean South America. *See* Inca Empire, Moche
Andean Pact, 978
Andes Mountains, 389
Andrea, Alfred J., 277, 456, 462, 468, 498, 524
Angkor, 351, 352
Angkor Wat, *p352–53,* 353, 476
Angles, 178, 308

A

abbess/abadesa superiora de un convento (pág. 305)

abbot/abad superior de un monasterio (pág. 304)

absolutism/absolutismo sistema político en el cual un monarca (o grupo) tiene poder supremo e ilimitado, o teoría que sustenta tal sistema (pág. 482)

acupuncture/acupuntura técnica tradicional de la medicina china que utiliza agujas finas en puntos vitales del cuerpo (pág. 232)

age set/grupo etario en el África tradicional, un grupo de varones o hembras de edad semejante que adquieren destrezas y siguen juntos a través de las distintas etapas de la vida (pág. 188)

ahimsa/ahimsa doctrina hindú de no-violencia hacia todo lo que tiene vida (pág. 207)

alchemist/alquimista persona que practica la alquimia, forma primitiva de la química, que enfatizaba cambios en las sustancias, como la conversión del plomo en oro (pág. 520)

alliance system/sistema de alianzas serie de acuerdos sobre la defensa en que participan dos o más naciones (pág. 740)

alphabet/alfabeto sistema de símbolos o caracteres que representan los sonidos de un lenguaje (pág. 82)

amphora/ánfora jarrón griego alto, de dos asas (pág. 131)

anarchy/anarquía ausencia de autoridad política (pág. 692)

animism/animismo creencia de que los espíritus residen tanto en los seres vivos como en las cosas inanimadas (págs. 351, 476)

anthropologist/antropólogo científico que estudia las características físicas y culturales de los seres humanos y sus antecesores (pág. 20)

apartheid/apartheid política oficial de estricta segregación y discriminación racial practicada en África del Sur desde 1948 hasta principios de la década de 1990 (pág. 934)

appeasement/apaciguamiento la política de hacer concesiones a un enemigo en potencia a fin de mantener la paz (pág. 829)

apportion/prorratear dividir en partes proporcionales (pág. 648)

apprentice/aprendiz persona que trabaja para un maestro a fin de aprender un oficio, arte o negocio (pág. 325)

aqueduct/acueducto canal construido para conducir las aguas (pág. 168)

arabesque/arabesco complejos diseños típicos del arte islámico que combinaban plantas entrelazadas y patrones geométricos (pág. 286)

"Arabic numerals"/números arábigos símbolos de numeración diseñados por matemáticos en Gupta, India (pág. 214)

arbitration/arbitraje proceso de poner fin a una disputa sometiéndola a una tercera parte imparcial (pág. 722)

archaeologist/arqueólogo científico que estudia pueblos y culturas de la Antigüedad (pág. 20)

archipelago/archipiélago grupo o cadena de islas (págs. 351, 920)

aristocrat/aristócrata miembro de la nobleza o de la clase alta (pág. 113)

armada/armada escuadra de buques de guerra (pág. 483)

armistice/armisticio acuerdo para dar fin a una guerra (pág. 761)

arms race/carrera armamentista la competencia durante la Guerra Fría entre Estados Unidos y la Unión Soviética para fortalecer sus respectivas fuerzas militares y armamentos (pág. 871)

artifact/artefacto histórico objeto fabricado o usado por los humanos, tal como una herramienta, adorno o artículo de alfarería (pág. 20)

artisan/artesano persona diestra en un arte manual (pág. 33)

atomic theory/teoría atómica idea científica de que la materia está hecha de partículas pequeñas llamadas átomos (pág. 628)

atrocity/atrocidad acción cruel y maligna, tal como la tortura (pág. 1015)

autocracy/autocracia gobierno regido por una persona con poder ilimitado (pág. 690)

automation/automatización proceso por el cual dispositivos electrónicos o máquinas hacen el trabajo antes realizado por humanos (pág. 883)

autonomy/autonomía gobierno propio (pág. 1008)

B

balance of power/equilibrio de poder la distribución del poder entra naciones rivales de modo que ninguna predomine (pág. 489)

balance of trade/equilibrio comercial diferencia en valor entre lo que una nación importa y lo que exporta durante un período de tiempo (pág. 448)

bard/bardo poeta que narra cuentos por medio del canto (pág. 108)

baroque/barroco estilo artístico recargado y dramático, desarrollado en Europa a mediados del siglo XVI (pág. 424)

barter/trueque sistema de comercio en el cual se

intercambiaban bienes y no dinero (pág. 82)

bazaar/bazar mercado público en una ciudad islámica (pág. 284)

belligerent/beligerante enfrascado en una guerra (pág. 746)

bishop/obispo jefe regional de la Iglesia Cristiana primitiva, con autoridad sobre una diócesis y otros miembros del clero (pág. 174)

blitz/ataque relámpago serie de ataques aéreos intensos (pág. 834)

blitzkrieg/guerra relámpago ofensiva nazi rápida e inesperada (pág. 831)

bloc/bloque grupo de facciones políticas o agrupación de naciones que actúan conjuntamente (pág. 871)

bourgeoisie/burguesía la clase media, entre los aristócratas y los trabajadores (págs. 561, 625)

boyar/boyardo un noble propietario de tierras en la Rusia primitiva (págs. 260, 499)

boycott/boicot rechazo a comprar ciertos productos como protesta por alguna acción (pág. 548)

budget deficit/déficit presupuestario la cantidad por la cual los gastos del gobierno exceden a sus ingresos (pág. 998)

buffer state/estado parachoques territorio neutral entre potencias rivales, destinado a prevenir un conflicto (pág. 582)

bullion/lingote oro o plata en forma de barras o planchas (pág. 448)

bureaucracy/burocracia un grupo de funcionarios del gobierno encabezado por un administrador (pág. 48)

C

cabinet/gabinete grupo de consejeros de un gobernante o jefe de estado (pág. 544)

calculus/cálculo sistema de matemáticas desarrollado por Newton para analizar cantidades variables (pág. 519)

caliph/califa líder supremo de Islam, escogido como sucesor de Mahoma (pág. 277)

calligraphy/caligrafía el arte de escribir con letra hermosa (pág. 286)

campesino/campesino agricultor pobre de Latinoamérica que trabaja en una finca (pág. 975)

capital/capital dinero disponible para invertir en negocios (pág. 604)

cardinal/cardenal eclesiástico de alto rango en la Iglesia Católica designado por el Papa (pág. 306)

cartel/cartel convenio entre empresas que ofrecen el mismo producto, que regula los precios de sus

miembros y su producción (págs. 955, 993)

cartographer/cartógrafo persona que dibuja mapas (pág. 436)

cash-and-carry policy/política de compra al contado programa de la Segunda Guerra Mundial que permitía a Gran Bretaña pagar en efectivo y transportar desde los Estados Unidos las mercancías que necesitara (pág. 835)

cash crop/cosecha comercial producto agrícola cultivado para la venta o el intercambio, no usado por el agricultor (pág. 943)

cavalry/caballería cuerpo de soldados a caballo (pág. 221)

cell theory/teoría celular teoría científica que sostiene que las pequeñas unidades llamadas células constituyen todas las cosas vivas (pág. 626)

chancellor/canciller título del primer ministro en algunos países europeos (pág. 685)

charter/carta constitucional documento formal que concede el derecho al gobierno propio (pág. 326)

chateaux/castillos un tipo de fortaleza (pág. 413)

chinampas/chinampas islas artificiales construidas por los aztecas para utilizar como jardines (pág. 388)

chivalry/caballería código de conducta de los caballeros medievales basado en ideales de honor y cortesía (pág. 301)

choreographer/coreógrafo persona que crea bailes (pág. 775)

chronicle/crónica relación que registra eventos en el orden en que éstos sucedieron (pág. 288)

circumnavigation/circunnavegación viaje marítimo completamente alrededor de algo, como por ejemplo, el mundo (pág. 439)

citizen/ciudadano en la antigua Gracia, persona que participaba del gobierno en una ciudad-estado (pág. 112)

city-state/ciudad-estado un estado independiente que consistía en una ciudad y las tierras y aldeas que la rodeaban (pág. 59)

civil disobedience/desobediencia civil rechazo sin violencia a obedecer una ley o práctica considerada injusta (pág. 802)

civil service/servicio civil sistema mediante el cual puestos del gobierno son concedidos mediante exámenes (pág. 224)

civilization/civilización sociedad altamente organizada caracterizada por el conocimiento avanzado del comercio, gobierno, artes, ciencia y a menudo, lenguaje escrito (pág. 32)

clan/clan grupo unido por lazos familiares (págs. 342, 939)

classical/clásico que describe el estilo artístico de las antiguas Gracia y Roma, caracterizado por el equilibrio, la elegancia y la simpleza (pág. 130)

classicism/clasicismo estilo y actitudes derivadas de los ideales de las antiguas Gracia y Roma (pág. 528)

clergy/clero personas, tales como los sacerdotes, que tienen autoridad para conducir servicios religiosos (pág. 249)

coalition/coalición alianza temporal de facciones políticas en desacuerdo (págs. 780, 879)

cold war/Guerra Fría período de tensión política en el que Estados Unidos y la Unión Soviética rivalizaron por obtener el dominio mundial sin llegar a un conflicto armado real (pág 864)

collective bargaining/convenios colectivos negociaciones entre los delegados sindicales y los patronos acerca de asuntos (pág. 616)

collective security/seguridad colectiva los intereses de defensa comunes a varias naciones frente a un enemigo (págs. 826, 1012)

collectivization/colectivización bajo Stalin, sistema de unificar tierras en grandes fincas que pertenecían al gobierno y las trabajaban los campesinos (pág. 790)

colon/colon colonizador francés en la colonia de Algeria (pág. 931)

colony/colonia establecimiento de personas que están fuera de su país, enlazado a la madre patria por el comercio y el control directo del gobierno (págs. 82, 475, 706)

comedy/comedia historia o representación que se propone entretener y divertir usualmente con un desenlace feliz (pág. 134)

common law/derecho consuetudinario sistema de leyes inglesas basadas en la tradición y decisiones de la corte, no en leyes específicas (pág. 309)

commonwealth/mancomunidad nación o estado gobernado por el pueblo o representantes del mismo (pág. 539)

commune/comuna Un grupo de personas que viven en comuna, con posesión y uso colectivo de la sociedad (pág. 902)

communism/comunismo según las teorías de Marx y Engels, una sociedad sin distinciones de clases ni propiedad privada (págs. 625, 758)

concentration camp/campo de concentración recinto donde se encierra a prisioneros políticos o a refugiados (pág. 786)

confederation/confederación alianza flexible o unión de varios estados o grupos (págs. 82, 378, 554)

conquistador/conquistador aventurero o soldado

español en las Américas (pág. 441)

conscription/reclutamiento llamado obligatorio al servicio militar (págs. 569, 740)

constitution/constitución plan de gobierno (pág. 117)

constitutional monarchy/monarquía constitucional estado en el cual el poder del monarca está limitado por una constitución (pág. 541)

consul/cónsul en la antigua Roma, uno de los dos magistrados que dirigían al poder ejecutivo (pág. 157)

containment/contención política de Estados Unidos proyectada para prevenir la propagación del comunismo (pág. 866)

contraband/contrabando mercancías que no pueden ser transportadas legalmente, particularmente en tiempo de guerra (pág. 751)

convoy/convoy grupo de naves mercantes que viajan junto a buques de guerra para su seguridad (pág. 760)

cooperative/cooperativa sociedad de fincas que pertenece y es administrada por sus miembros, los cuales comparten sus ganancias (pág. 812)

cordon sanitaire/cordón sanitario línea de cuarentena o estados "parachoques" (pág. 763)

corporate state/estado corporativo concepto de Mussolini de un gobierno con representación de corporaciones, y no de partidos políticos (pág. 783)

corporation/corporación organización de empresas que es propiedad de socios que compran acciones y que es dirigida por administradores profesionales (pág. 609)

cortes/cortes asamblea de los nobles, el clero y los funcionarios del pueblo en la España medieval; también, el parlamento en la España moderna (pág. 332)

count/conde noble que actuaba como funcionario local dentro del imperio de los francos (pág. 295)

coup d'état/golpe de estado derrocamiento repentino de líderes del gobierno por un pequeño grupo (págs. 573, 657)

covenant/convenio pacto o acuerdo solemne (pág. 83)

covert/encubierto secreto (pág. 986)

Creole/criollo persona de ascendencia europea nacida en la América Latina colonial (pág. 667)

Crusades/Cruzadas expediciones militares por cristianos europeos en los siglos XI al XIII para conquistar la Tierra Santa de manos de los musulmanes (pág. 318)

cubism/cubismo estilo artístico del siglo XX que representa las formas naturales por medio de formas geométricas (pág. 773)

cultural diffusion/difusión cultural intercambio de bienes, ideas y costumbres entre diferentes culturas (pág. 34)

culture/cultura modo de vida de un pueblo en un tiempo determinado, que incluye su lenguaje, conducta y creencias (pág. 24)

culture system/sistema de cultivo en las colonias holandesas en Asia, sistema de trabajos forzados para obtener materias primas (pág. 718)

cuneiform/cuneiforme sistema de escritura sumerio que utilizaba símbolos en forma de cuña (pág. 60)

czar/zar (de "caesar") título adoptado por los gobernantes de Rusia desde finales del siglo XV (pág. 264)

D

D-Day/Día D día de la invasión de Normandía, Francia por los Aliados (junio 6 de 1944)(pág. 846)

daimyo/daimyo poderoso noble local en el Japón feudal (pág. 363)

datus/datus gobernantes locales en las Filipinas (pág. 475)

death squad/escuadrón de la muerte en la América Central, una banda de asesinos contratados por terratenientes para asesinar a sus contrincantes políticos (pág. 987)

deforestation/deforestación proceso de talar los árboles y desmontar los bosques en grandes extensiones de tierra (pág. 1020)

deism/deísmo filosofía religiosa del siglo XVIII basada en la razón y en la idea de leyes naturales (pág. 523)

deity/deidad un dios o diosa (pág. 31)

democracy/democracia forma de gobierno en la cual los ciudadanos ejercen el poder (pág. 114)

depression/depresión situación económica caracterizada por la quiebra de los negocios y el desempleo (pág. 609)

desalination/desalinización proceso de extraer la sal del agua de mar para producir agua potable (pág.964)

desertification/desertización proceso por el cual una tierra fértil se convierte en un desierto (pág. 944)

détente/detente la relajación de las tensiones entre los Estados Unidos y la Unión Soviética en la década de 1970 (pág. 874)

developed nation/nación desarrollado nación industrializada, con una tecnología avanzada (pág. 1019)

developing nation/nación en desarrollo nación en proceso de industrialización, donde el pueblo mantiene frecuentemente los estilos de vida tradicionales (pág. 1019)

dharma/dharma deberes y derechos de los miembros de cada clase en la sociedad hindú tradicional (pág. 205)

Diaspora/Diáspora término que se refiere a la dispersión de las comunidades judías fuera de su patria original después de la Cautividad de Babilonia (pág. 86)

dictator/dictador en la antigua Roma, líder a quien se daba poder temporal absoluto durante una crisis (pág. 157)

dictatorship/dictadura gobierno encabezado por un gobernante con poder absoluto (pág. 574)

dictatorship of the proletariat/dictadura del proletariado en la antigua Unión Soviética, control teórico del estado por la clase trabajadora (pág. 789)

direct tax/impuesto directo impuesto pagado directamente al gobierno (pág. 548)

disarmament/desarme limitación o reducción de las fuerzas militares y de las armas (pág. 778)

disciple/discípulo activo seguidor de un maestro (pág. 172)

disenfranchised/privado del derecho al sufragio negado el derecho al voto (pág. 649)

disengagement/desembarazo acto de liberarse o retirarse uno mismo de una situación (pág. 955)

dissident/disidente persona que critica abiertamente las maneras de actuar de su gobierno (pág. 874)

divine right/derecho divino teoría politica que mantiene que un gobernante deriva su autoridad directamente de Dios y es responsable de sus actos sólo ante Dios (págs. 482, 536)

division of labor/división del trabajo técnica de producción en la cual cada obrero realiza un trabajo especializado (pág. 609)

doge/dux líder electo de la república en las ciudades-estados de Venecia y Génova (pág. 408)

domain/dominio territorio perteneciente a un gobernante (pág. 142)

domesticate/domesticar adiestrar animales o adaptar plantas para satisfacer necesidades humanas (pág. 30)

domestic system/sistema doméstico sistema primitivo de trabajo industrial en el cual los obreros producían los bienes en sus hogares (pág. 602)

dominion/dominio nación de gobierno propio dentro del Imperio Británico; más tarde, mancomunidad (pág. 653)

domino theory/teoría del dominó creencia de la época de la Guerra Fría por la que si una nación se hacía comunista, sus vecinos seguirían el ejemplo (pág. 910)

double-digit inflation/inflación de dos dígitos rápida elevación de los precios en un diez por ciento o más (pag. 889)

dual monarchy/monarquía dual dos estados con un solo monarca (pág. 696)

duma/duma legislatura nacional rusa (pág. 694)

duty/arancel de aduana impuesto sobre productos importados (pág. 546)

dvorianie/dvorianie nueva clase de nobleza rusa dueña de tierras, establecida por Pedro I el Grande (pág. 501)

dynasty/dinastía sucesión de gobernantes que pertenecen a la misma familia (pág. 47)

E

economy/economía sistema por el cual bienes y servicios son producidos y distribuidos para satisfacer las necesidades del pueblo (pág. 33)

elite/elite un grupo de personas selecto (pág. 975)

ellipse/elipse curva cerrada ovalada (no redonda) (pág. 517)

emancipation/emancipación acción de conceder la libertad legalmente (pág. 691)

embargo/embargo orden restringiendo el tráfico comercial (págs. 889, 960, 1015)

emigration/emigración abandono del país o región natal para establecerse en otro lugar (pág. 630)

émigré/émigré emigrado o persona que huyó de Francia durante la Revolución (pág. 566)

empire/imperio grupo de territorios o naciones regidos por un solo emperador o gobierno (pág. 49)

enclave/enclave pequeño territorio completamente rodeado por el territorio de otro país o grupo (pag. 1016)

enclosure movement/expansión por apropiación tendencia de los grandes terratenientes a cercar e incluir tierras comunes públicas y privadas en sus propios terrenos (pág. 603)

enlightened despot/déspota iluminista monarca que comenzaba cambios sociales basados en las ideas del iluminismo (pág. 527)

entente/entente acuerdo, pero no alianza formal, entre naciones (pág. 740)

entrepreneur/empresario persona que corre riesgos para fundar un negocio (págs. 448, 604)

epic/poema épico poema extenso que celebraba las hazañas de un héroe legendario o histórico (pág. 203)

estate/estado una de las tres clases sociales distintas en Francia durante el Siglo XVIII: el clero, la nobleza y los plebeyos (el Tercer Estado) (pág. 560)

ethics/ética sistema de principios morales que guían la conducta (pág. 225)

ethnic cleansing/limpieza étnica término usado en el conflicto de Bosnia, para referirse a una política de traslado forzoso o de dar muerte a los miembros de otro grupo étnico (págs. 1014-15)

evolution/evolución teoría de que las especies de seres vivos se transforman a través de largos períodos de tiempo (pág. 626)

excommunication/excomunión exclusión formal de la membresía o de su participación en una iglesia (pág. 306)

exodus/éxodo emigración de un grupo numeroso de personas (pag. 84)

extended family/familia completa grupo familiar que incluye a varias generaciones así como a otros parientes (pág. 229)

F

factory system/sistema de fábrica método de producción en el cual los bienes son producidos por obreros y máquinas en un local (una fábrica) fuera de sus hogares (pág. 606)

fascism/fascismo filosofía política basada en el nacionalismo y en un estado todopoderoso (pág. 782)

federal system/sistema federal forma de gobierno en la cual el poder se halla dividido entre la autoridad central y sus subdivisiones políticas (pág. 534)

feudalism/feudalismo sistema político medieval en el cual los monarcas y los nobles menores hacían alianzas basadas en el intercambio de concesiones de tierras por lealtad (pág. 298)

fez/fez sombrero tradicional usado por los hombres turcos (pág. 797)

fief/feudo bajo el feudalismo, una tierra con sus labriegos concedida a un noble a cambio de lealtad y ayuda militar (pág. 298)

filial piety/piedad filial respeto de los hijos hacia sus padres, un principio importante en la filosofía moral de Confucio (pág. 226)

free trade/comercio libre la eliminación de barreras comerciales entre naciones (pág. 978)

friar/fraile miembro de una orden religiosa católica que predicaba en los pueblos y practicaba la pobreza (pág. 307)

fundamentalism/fundamentalismo movimiento que enfatiza el cumplimiento de las leyes y prácticas religiosas tradicionales (pág. 965)

geisha/geisha mujer japonesa adiestrada profesionalmente para entretener (pág. 472)

general strike/huelga general huelga en que participan obreros de muchas áreas de la economía de la nación (págs. 779, 931)

genetic engineering/ingeniería genética campo científico en el cual la estructura de las células puede ser alterada para producir organismos nuevos o distintos (pág. 1022)

genetics/genética el estudio de la herencia biológica (pág. 627)

genocide/genocidio intento deliberado de matar a todos los miembros de un grupo racial, cultural o étnico (págs. 840, 938)

gentry/gentry en la Inglaterra isabelina, el grupo social que incluía a la nobleza menor y a los terratenientes (pág. 488)

ghana/ghana título del gobernante de una región en el África antigua, que más tarde fue aplicado al reinado (pág. 189)

glasnost/glasnost palabra rusa aplicada a la política de "apertura" o "transparencia" y de libre expresión, introducida por Mijail Gorbachov (pág. 999)

grand jury/gran jurado en la ley inglesa, grupo de personas que deciden si la evidencia de un crimen justifica llevar a una persona a juicio (pag. 309)

grand vizier/gran visir primer ministro del sultán de un país musulmán (pág. 457)

gross domestic product/producto territorial bruto valor total de las mercancías y los servicios producidos en un país en un año (pág. 898)

guerrilla warfare/guerra de guerrillas método de lucha en el cual pequeños grupos atacan de modo inesperado (pág. 679)

guild/gremio asociación comercial medieval de mercaderes o artesanos (pág. 324)

habeas corpus/hábeas corpus principio legal que requiere que las autoridades muestren las razones por las cuales una persona debe ser detenida y garanticen un juicio rápido (pág. 542)

haiku/hai kai forma de poesía japonesa generalmente con tres versos de 17 sílabas (pág. 472)

hajj/hajj peregrinación a La Meca que todo musulmán en buenas condiciones físicas se supone realice por lo menos una vez en su vida (pág. 276)

heavy industry/industria pesada la manufactura de máquinas y equipo para fábricas y minas (pág. 808)

heresy/herejía desacuerdo con la enseñanzas básicas de una religión o negación de las mismas (pág. 306)

hierarchy/jerarquía grupo de personas organizadas de acuerdo con niveles de rango o importancia (págs. 228, 389)

hieroglyphics/jeroglíficos sistema egipcio antiguo de escritura que utilizaba símbolos pictóricos para representar ideas o sonidos (pág. 52)

Holocaust/Holocausto nombre dado al asesinato en masa de judíos europeos por los nazis en la Segunda Guerra Mundial (pág. 839)

homage/homenaje ceremonia formal que establecía lazos feudales entre un señor y un vasallo (pág. 299)

home rule/autonomía local gobierno propio, especialmente cuando se concede a un país dependiente (pág. 651)

hominid/homínido miembro del grupo que incluye a los seres humanos y a las criaturas primates primitivas (pág. 20)

humanism/Humanismo movimiento renacentista basado en la literatura e ideas de las antiguas Grecia y Roma, tales como el valor de cada individuo (pág. 404)

hygiene/higiene la ciencia de la buena salud (pág. 138)

hyperinflation/hiperinflación forma extrema de inflación, con aumentos violentos y rápidos de los precios (pág. 991)

hypothesis/hipótesis solución propuesta para explicar una serie de hechos, que puede ser probada (pág. 517)

icon/ícono imagen religiosa cristiana o cuadro que representa a un santo u otra persona sagrada (pág. 249)

iconoclast/iconoclasta ("destructor de imágenes") un opositor al uso de íconos en las iglesias bizantinas, que pensaba que éstos estimulaban la adoración de ídolos (pág. 250)

ideology/ideología sistema de creencias y actitudes que guían las acciones de un grupo o nación (pág. 871)

illuminated manuscript/manuscrito iluminado página de un libro, decorada con elaborados diseños, hermosas letras, o pinturas en miniatura (pág. 253)

imam/imán un guía de oraciones musulmanas (pág. 276)

immigration/inmigración entrada a un nuevo país o región para asentarse allí permanentemente (pág. 630)

imperialism/imperialismo política de erigir un imperio para extender el poderío y el territorio de una nación (pág. 704)

imperial presidency/presidencia imperial término aplicado a un presidente y al poder ejecutivo que asumen poderes que van más allá de los estipulados en la Constitución (pág. 888)

impressionism/impresionismo estilo artístico del Siglo XIX en el cual los pintores trataban de captar impresiones rápidas y los efectos de la luz (pág. 638)

indemnity/indemnización pago por daños y pérdidas (pág. 160)

individualism/individualismo énfasis en la aignidad de la persona (pág. 404–05)

indulgence/indulgencia perdón vendido por la Iglesia Católica para reducir el castigo de pecados (pág. 416)

industrial capitalism/capitalismo industrial sistema económico en en cual individuos continuamente reinvierten sus ganancias y expanden sus negocios (pág. 608)

inflation/inflación situación en la cual los precios suben rápidamente mientras que el valor del dinero disminuye (págs. 176, 484)

intendant/intendente agente que representaba al rey de Francia en el gobierno local (pág. 491)

interchangeable parts/piezas intercambiables método de producción que utiliza piezas idénticas, fáciles de ensamblar (pág. 609)

intercontinental ballistic missile (ICBM)/misil balístico intercontinental un cohete de combate de largo alcance que lleva una carga explosiva en la punta (pág. 873)

interdependent/interdependiente confianza mutua (pág. 1018)

Internet/Internet término popular para la red avanzada de comunicación que vincula a personas y computadoras a nivel mundial (pág. 1021)

intifada/intifada el levantamiento de los palestinos contra la ocupación israelita (pág. 956)

iron curtain/Cortina de Hierro término acuñado por Winston Churchill para referirse a la barrera política que aislaba a la Europa Oriental dominada por los soviéticos de la Europa Occidental (pág. 866)

jaguar/jaguar gato salvaje con manchas en la piel, de América Central (pág. 380)

janissary/jenízaro miembro del cuerpo más selecto de soldados del Imperio Otomano (pág. 457)

jati/jati grupos formados dentro de las mayores clases sociales *(varna)* en la antigua India según las ocupaciones de sus miembros y con sus propias reglas y costumbres (pág. 204)

jazz/jazz estilo de música de Estados Unidos que incorpora ritmos africanos a sonidos estadounidenses y europeos (pág. 773)

jihad/jihad lucha mahometana para introducir el islamismo en otras tierras (pág. 278)

jingoism/jingoísmo actitud de patriotismo extremo, usualmente dirigida hacia un poder extranjero (pág. 698)

joint-stock company/compañía por acciones empresa comercial que vende acciones para dividir entre los participantes los costos y las ganancias (pág. 447)

journeyman/jornalero artesano que ha terminado su aprendizaje y trabaja por un jornal (pág. 325)

junk/junco embarcación china (pág. 464)

justification by faith/justificación por la fe concepto de Martín Lutero de que la fe por sí sola es suficiente para alcanzar la salvación (pág. 415)

kaiser/káiser título del emperador de Alemania (pág. 685)

kamikaze/kamikaze en la Segunda Guerra Mundial, pilotos japoneses que hacían estallar aviones llenos de bombas en ataques suicidas contra objetivos Aliados (pág. 845)

karma/karma en el hinduismo, la idea de que las acciones de los hombres en la vida determinaban sus destinos y sus futuros (pág. 207)

khan/kan gobernante absoluto de los mongoles (pág. 344)

kibbutz/kibbutz comunidad de granjas colectivas en Israel (pág. 951)

Kristallnacht/la noche de las vidrieras rotas ataques terroristas nazis en noviembre 9 y 10 de 1938, contra propiedades judías en Alemania y Austria (pág. 786)

kulak/kulak labriego en la Unión Soviética que vivía holgadamente (pág. 790)

labor-intensive farming/agricultura manual intensiva agricultura que confía en el trabajo humano, no en animales o máquinas (pág. 466)

SPANISH GLOSSARY

labor union — *millet*

labor union/sindicato obrero organización de obreros formada para presionar a los dueños de los negocios a que mejoren los salarios y las condiciones en el trabajo (pág. 616)

labyrinth/laberinto conjunto complejo y confuso de pasajes que se conectan (pág. 107)

laissez-faire/laissez-faire doctrina económica según la cual el gobierno no debe regular los negocios (pág. 622)

laity/el estado seglar miembros de una iglesia que no pertenecen al clero (pág. 249)

lay investiture/investidura seglar práctica medieval en la cual las autoridades seglares designaban e investían a funcionarios de la iglesia tales como los obispos (pág. 306)

lend-lease/préstamo-arriendo política de la Segunda Guerra Mundial de permitir el préstamo de equipo a países amigos (pág. 836)

liberalism/liberalismo filosofía política que promueve el cambio social y las libertades individuales (pág. 582)

liberation theology/teología de la liberación movimiento dirigido por el clero católico en la América Latina que enfatizaba el papel de la Iglesia en el mejoramiento de las vidas humanas (pág. 978)

line of demarcation/línea de demarcación línea imaginaria en el Océano Atlántico, trazada por el papa en 1493 para dividir las tierras del mundo entre España y Portugal (pág. 439)

literacy rate/tasa de alfabetización el porcentaje de población adulta de un país que sabe leer y escribir (pág. 944)

logic/lógica la ciencia del razonamiento y del establecimiento de pruebas en los debates (pág. 135)

madrasa/madrasa escuela musulmana de teología y leyes (pág. 283)

maize/maíz el maíz nativo de la América (pág. 374)

mandarin/mandarín miembro de la clase más selecta de funcionarios en el gobierno chino (págs. 224, 348)

mandate/mandato (1) en la antigua China, la autoridad concedida por el cielo a gobernantes merecedores de ello, llamada el Mandato del Cielo (pág. 71); (2) territorio administrado por otra nación antes de su independencia (pág. 763)

manorialism/economía feudal sistema económico medieval que ataba a los nobles y a los campesinos a su tierra (pág. 301)

martial law/ley marcial ley militar temporal, que limita derechos tales como la libertad de expresión (pág. 537)

martyr/mártir persona que sufre y muere por una creencia (pág. 173)

master/maestro artesano hábil que era el propietario de un taller y empleaba a otros artesanos (pág. 325)

matrilineal/línea materna que traza el origen de una familia a través de la madre y los ancestros de ésta (pág. 187)

mayor of the palace/jefe del palacio dignatario franco que, alrededor del siglo VIII d.C. tenía poder en el gobierno (pág. 294)

mercantilism/mercantilismo política económica de las naciones europeas en el Siglo XVII, que igualaba la riqueza al poder (pág. 448)

mercenary/mercenario soldado que sirve a un país extranjero por dinero (pág. 124)

meritocracy/sistema de ascenso por méritos sistema en el cual las personas obtienen éxito a base de su habilidad y actuación (pág. 347)

messiah/mesías en el judaísmo, el salvador prometido por los profetas hebreos, quien traería la paz (pág. 171)

mestizo/mestizo en América Latina, persona de ancestro indígena americano y europeo (pág. 667)

metaphysics/metafísica aspectos de la filosofía relativos a los problemas básicos de la existencia y la realidad (pág. 530)

metsuke/metsuke grupo de funcionarios que recolectaban información para los shogúnes de Tokugawa (pag. 469)

middle class/clase media clase social que originalmente estaba entre la nobleza y el campesinado, y que se ganaba la vida por medio de actividades comerciales (pág. 310)

Middle Passage/Paso Central sección intermedia del comercio triangular, en el cual los africanos esclavizados eran traídos a la América por barco (pág. 445)

middle power/potencia mediana nación que es fuerte económicamente pero que no es una potencia militar (pág. 889)

militarism/militarismo política nacional basada en la fuerza militar y la glorificación de la guerra (págs. 689, 740)

millet/millet comunidad de los no-musulmanes dentro del imperio otomano (pág. 458)

missionary/misionero persona que viaja para llevar las principios de una religión a otras personas (pág. 254)

mobilization/movilización acción de reunir y preparar tropas y equipo para la guerra (pág. 743)

monarchy/monarquía gobierno de un rey o una reina (pág. 47)

monastery/monasterio comunidad de hombres que han tomado votos religiosos (pág. 254)

money economy/economía monetaria sistema económico en el cual se usa el dinero y no el trueque para comprar y vender (pág. 323)

monopoly/monopolio control de todo (o casi todo) el comercio o la producción de un producto determinado (pág. 194)

monotheism/monoteísmo creencia en un solo dios (págs. 83, 189)

monsoon/monzón viento periódico que afecta el clima y las formas de vida en el sur de Asia (pág. 66)

mosaic/mosaico cuadro hecho de pedazos de vidrio de colores, barro cocido o piedra unidos con mortero (pág. 253)

mosque/mezquita templo mahometano (págs. 191, 276)

multicultural/multicultural que representa varios grupos culturales y étnicos diferentes (págs. 195, 890)

myth/mito relato tradicional que explica sucesos naturales (pág. 35)

nationalism/nacionalismo orgullo en la nación o grupo propios y sus tradiciones; deseo de independencia de un gobierno extranjero (págs. 576, 676)

nationalization/nacionalización traspaso de un negocio de propiedad privada al gobierno (pág. 813)

nationalize/nacionalizar traspasar una industria privada al control del gobierno (pág. 952)

nation-state/estado-nación un estado político cuyos habitantes comparten también el mismo idioma y la misma cultura (pág. 677)

natural law/ley natural verdad o principio universal que los pensadores del Siglo XVII creían podía ser hallado mediante la razón (pág. 521)

natural rights/dereches naturales derechas que poseen todas las personas al nacer (pág. 521)

negritude/negritud movimiento literario que enfatiza y se enorgullece de la herencia cultural del África (pág. 945)

nihilist/nihilista miembro de un movimiento político ruso de finales del Siglo XIX que rechazaba toda autoridad y abogaba a favor del terrorismo (pág. 692)

nirvana/nirvana en el budismo, estado de unidad con el universo; el final del ciclo de renacimiento (pág. 210)

nomad/nómada miembro de un grupo de personas sin hogar fijo, que viajan constantemente para buscar comida y agua (pág. 22)

nonaligned/no alineado que no toma partido con ninguna de las superpotencias en una guerra fría (pág. 917)

nuclear family/núcleo familiar grupo familiar que incluye sólo a padres e hijos (pág. 229)

O

obsidian/obsidiana cristal volcánico negro (pág. 383)

oligarchy/oligarquía forma de gobierno en la cual un grupo pequeño ejerce el poder político (pág. 114)

oral tradition/tradición oral las leyendas e historia de una cultura preservada de viva voz (pág. 184)

P

pacifism/pacifismo oposición a la guerra o a la violencia como medio de resolver disputas (pág. 523)

pacifist/pacifista creyente en el pacifismo (pág. 802)

pact/pacto tratado entre varias naciones (pág. 953)

paleontologist/paleontólogo científico que estudia los fósiles (pág. 20)

Pan-Africanism/Panafricanismo movimiento que aboga por la unidad y la cooperación entre las naciones africanas (pág. 942)

Pan-Arabism/Panarabismo movimiento de mediados del siglo XX que pretendía construir lazos culturales y políticos entre los árabes (pág. 950)

papal infallibility/infalibilidad papal doctrina católica romana que sostiene que el papa no puede cometer un error al hablar acerca de la fe y la moral (pág. 686)

partisan/partisano en la Segunda Guerra Mundial, término aplicado a un guerrillero de la resistencia clandestina, especialmente en Italia y Yugoeslavia (pág. 848)

partition/partición división de una región (pág. 707)

partnership/sociedad negocio que es propiedad de dos o más empresarios que comparten el manejo, las ganancias y las pérdidas (pág. 609)

patriarch/patriarca en la Iglesia cristiana primitiva, uno de los cinco obispos poderosos en las ciudades importantes (pág. 174)

patrician/patricio miembro de una clase aristocrática acaudalada en la antigua Roma (pág. 156)

peaceful coexistence/coexistencia pacífica política soviética de competir con los Estados unidos para evitar la guerra (pág. 873)

peninsulares/peninsulares funcionarios nacidos en España o Portugal que dirigían la sociedad en la América Latina colonial (pág. 667)

perestroika/perestroika término ruso que significa "reestructuración"; los cambios en la economía soviética iniciados por Mikhail Gorbachev (pág. 1000)

perspective/perspectiva técnica artística que muestra las relaciones y el espacio entre los objetos (pág. 131)

petit jury/jurado menor grupo de personas que determinan la culpabilidad o la inocencia de una persona procesada (pág. 309)

phalanx/falange en la antigua Grecia, una formación militar en la cual soldados de infantería se colocaban de tal modo que sus escudos quedaban superpuestos (pág. 114)

pharaoh/faraón título de los gobernadores del antiguo Egipto (pág. 49)

philosophe/filósofo pensador social o político del Siglo de las Luces (pág. 524)

philosopher/filósofo un pensador o un amante de la sabiduría (pág. 135)

pilgrimage/peregrinación viaje a un lugar sagrado (pág. 334)

plateau/altiplanicie región relativamente llana más elevada que el área circundante (pág. 185)

plebeian/plebeyo ciudadano de la antigua Roma que no era un aristócrata (pág. 156)

plebiscite/plebiscito voto popular directo sobre un programa o asunto (págs. 575, 657)

pogrom/pogrom persecución organizada de un grupo minoritario, usualmente judíos, en la Rusia de los zares (pág. 693)

polis/polis ciudad-estado de la antigua Grecia (pág. 112)

pollution/contaminación incorporación de sustancias tóxicas o impuras en el aire, tierra o agua (pág. 898)

polytheism/politeísmo adoración de varios dioses (pág. 52)

pope/papa el obispo de Roma, más tarde el jefe de la Iglesia Católica Romana (pág. 174)

population explosion/explosión demográfica aumento grande y repentino de la población humana (pág. 808)

Postimpressionism/Posimpresionismo movimiento artístico cuyos miembros experimentaban con la forma y el color (pág. 639)

potlatch festín celebrado por los americanos nativos del Noroeste del Pacífico (pág. 376)

pragmatic sanction/sanción pragmática decreto emitido por un gobernante sobre un asunto importante (pág. 495)

pragmatist/pragmatista en China, una persona moderada que abogaba por reformas económicas y por el comercio con Occidente (pág. 902)

predestination/predestinación doctrina de John Calvin (fundador del calvinismo) que predicaba que el destino de una persona estaba predeterminado por Dios (pág. 419)

prehistory/prehistoria tiempo anterior a la historia escrita (pág. 20)

prime minister/primer ministro jefe ejecutivo de un gobierno parlamentario (pág. 544)

principality/principado territorio gobernado por un príncipe (pág. 260)

privatization/privatización la devolución de industrias que eran propiedad del gobierno, a dueños privados (págs. 980-81, 1003)

proletariat/proletariado según la teoría marxista, la clase trabajadora (pág. 625)

propaganda/propaganda noticias e información destinadas a influir en los sentimientos de las personas hacia una causa (pág. 746)

prophet/profeta persona que predica o interpreta lo que se cree son mensajes de Dios (pág. 83)

protectorate/protectorado país cuya política es dirigida por una nación extranjera (pág. 706)

provisional government/gobierno provisional gobierno temporal establecido mientras se espera por un proceso electoral (pág. 757)

psychology/psicología estudio del comportamiento y sus causas (pág. 628)

purge/purga esfuerzo oficial para eliminar a las personas que un gobierno considera indeseables (pág. 791)

Q

queue/coleta trenza de pelo única en la parte posterior de la cabeza (pág. 466)

quinoa/quinua grano cultivado en los Andes (pág. 390)

quota/cuota número o cantidad específica (pág. 900)

R

racial segregation/segregación racial separación social de las personas de acuerdo a su raza (pág. 887)

radiocarbon dating/datación de carbono radioactivo método científico moderno para determinar la edad de un sustancia que tuvo vida, midiendo la cantidad de carbono que permanece en ella (pág. 21)

rajah/rajá jefe tribal ario en la antigua India; más tarde el gobernante de un estado indio (pág. 202)

ratify/ratificar dar aprobación oficial (pág. 665)

reactionary/reaccionario el individuo que se opone al progreso o al cambio y desea retornar a costumbres antiguas (pág. 582)

realism/realismo estilo y literatura de mediados del Siglo XIX, que reflejaba las realidades de la vida cotidiana (pág. 636)

realpolitik/realpolitik teoría política según la cual el éxito nacional justifica el uso de cualquier medio (pág. 682)

referendum/referéndum voto popular directo para ratificar una disposición o una ley propuesta (págs. 908, 1011)

refugee/refugiado persona que tiene que abandonar su patria y escapar a otro lugar buscando seguridad (pág. 911)

regent/regente persona que actúa como gobernante temporal (pág. 251)

reincarnation/reencarnación el renacimiento del alma o el espíritu en diferentes cuerpos a través del tiempo (pág. 206)

reparation/indemnización de guerra compensación por daños producidos durante una guerra (pág. 763)

republic/república gobierno en el cual los ciudadanos eligen a sus dirigentes (pág. 156)

revelation/revelación visión de una realidad divina, como las atribuidas a Mahoma (pág. 272)

revolution/revolución cambio de gobierno mediante la fuerza (pág. 554)

rhetoric/retórica el arte de hablar en público de manera efectiva (pág. 119)

romanticism/romanticismo movimiento artístico de principios del siglo XIX, que enfatizaba la individualidad y la emoción (págs. 530, 635)

royalist/realista persona que apoya una monarquía (pág. 539)

Russification/rusificación política de imponer la lengua y costumbres rusas a otros pueblos (pág. 692)

S

sacrament/sacramento uno de los rituales formales establecidos por la Iglesia Católica Romana, tales como el bautismo, la sagrada comunión o el matrimonio (pág. 303)

salon/salón en Francia, tertulia donde los intelectuales del Siglo de las Luces se reunían para conversar (pág. 525)

samurai/samurai clase de guerreros terratenientes en el Japón feudal que juraban lealtad a un *daimyo* (pág. 363)

sanctions/sanciones penalidades y restricciones impuestas a una nación por haber infringido la ley internacional (pág. 827)

sanctuary/santuario edificio considerado sagrado, usado para la adoración (pág. 130)

sankin-kotai/sankin-kotai ("presencia alterna") en el Japón feudal, el sistema en el cual un *daimyo* tenía que residir en años alternos en la corte de un shogún (pág. 469)

satellite/satélite país dominado políticamente por un poder vecino (pág. 865)

satrap/sátrapa el gobernador de una provincia persa (pág. 91)

satyagraha/satyagraha ("fuerza de la verdad") término para referirse a las protestas no violentas guiadas por Ghandi (pág. 802)

savanna/sabana llanura cubierta de vegetación, con pocos árboles, en las regiones tropicales o subtropicales (pág. 185)

schism/Cisma de Oriente la división de la Iglesia cristiana en 1054, que separó a la Iglesia Católica Romana de la Iglesia Ortodoxa Oriental (pág. 250)

scholasticism/escolasticismo enseñanza medieval que trataba de combinar la filosofía de Aristóteles con las enseñanzas de los sabios de la Iglesia (pág. 326)

scientific method/método científico pasos para descubrir la verdad científica por medio de la observación y la experimentación (pág. 518)

scorched-earth policy/política de tierra arrasada orden dada por Stalin para que el pueblo soviético destruyera edificios, tierras y cualquier cosa que pudiera ser usada por los invasores nazis (pág. 838)

secede/separarse retirarse formalmente de la membresía de una organización política (pág. 663)

sect/secta subgrupo con sus propias creencias dentro de un grupo religioso mayor (págs. 171, 899)

sectionalism/regionalismo énfasis exagerado en los intereses políticos y económicos de la región propia (pág. 663)

secular/seglar mundano, que no es abierta o específicamente religioso (pág. 404)

self-determination/autodeterminación el derecho de un pueblo de decidir su propio gobierno o estado político (pág. 796)

seminary/seminario escuela destinada para la enseñanza de los sacerdotes, según ordenó el Concilio de Trento (pág. 423)

separatism/separatismo en el Canadá, movimiento político que favorecía la independencia de Quebec (pág. 890)

sepoy/cipayo soldado natural de la India en el ejército británico (pág. 713)

serf/siervo campesino labrador que dependía de las tierras de un noble (págs. 302, 501)

shah/sha el soberano de un país del Oriente Medio (pág. 797)

shamanism/chamanismo creencia de que los espíritus habitan en cosas vivas y muertas, y que se comunican con los humanos a través de unos sacerdotes llamados chamanes (pág. 358)

shari'ah/shari ah código islámico de leyes que contiene reglas para todos los aspectos de la vida (pág. 275)

sheikh/jeque jefe de una tribu beduina (pág. 271)

shogun/shogún gobernador militar en el Japón feudal (pág. 363)

shogunate/shogunado gobierno fundado por la familia de un shogún y sus seguidores en el Japón feudal (pág. 363)

simony/simonía venta de cargos oficiales en la Iglesia Católica Romana medieval (pág. 335)

slash-and-burn farming/sistema de quema y siembra método de labranza en el cual la tierra cosechable se limpia talando y quemando los árboles para fertilizar el terreno (pág. 380)

socialism/socialismo teoría política que propugna que la sociedad como un todo debe tener el control de los medios de producción, tales como las fábricas y la tierra (pág. 624)

Socialist realism/realismo socialista bajo Stalin, un estilo artístico que glorificaba el modo de vida soviético (pág. 791)

sociology/sociología el estudio del comportamiento de grupos humanos (pág. 628)

sonnet/soneto composición poética de 14 versos y con un patrón de rima y métrica (pág. 405)

sovereignty/soberanía el poder independiente de un grupo o nación de tomar sus propias decisiones (pág. 963)

soviet/soviet un consejo de trabajadores formado al principio de la Revolución Rusa; más tarde, una unidad del gobierno en la Unión Soviética (pág. 694)

special economic zone/zona económica especial áreas de China donde se han permitido que negocios extranjeros y un mercado libre desarrollaran sus actividades en la década de 1990 (pág. 903)

sphere of influence/esfera de influencia área de un país donde una potencia extranjera tiene derechos exclusivos para comerciar o hacer inversiones (págs. 706, 715)

stagflation/estanflación tendencia económica que combina el estancamiento con la elevada inflación y el desempleo (pág. 889)

stalemate/estancamiento una detención o una situación en la que ninguna de las dos partes opuestas pueden avanzar (pág. 907)

standard of living/nivel de vida la medida general de la riqueza global de las personas y su calidad de vida (pág. 979)

steppe/estepa llanuras de Eurasia, extensas, herbáceas, semiáridas, que se extienden desde el Mar Negro hasta los montes Altai (pág. 258)

stupa/estupa capilla budista con bóveda semiesférica, construida sobre las reliquias o los huesos de un santo (pág. 210)

subcontinent/subcontinente porción de tierra que es parte de un continente pero bien diferenciada del mismo, tal como la India (pág. 66)

subsistence farmer/agricultor de subsistencia campesino que cultiva sólo lo suficiente para mantener a su familia o a una aldea (pág. 943)

suffragette/sufragista mujer que trabajaba activamente para obtener el derecho al voto femenino (pág. 651)

sultan/sultán líder político con autoridad absoluta sobre un país mahometano (pág. 457)

superpower/superpotencia nación poderosa e influyente, con un bloque de aliados, específicamente, los Estados Unidos y la Unión Soviética durante la Guerra Fría (pág. 864)

surrealism/surrealismo movimiento artístico que utilizaba sorpresivas imágenes distorsionadas (pág. 773)

symbolism/simbolismo movimiento artístico antirrealista que se centraba alrededor de imágenes y símbolos fantásticos (pág. 638)

symposium/simposio en la antigua Atenas, reunión que se celebraba con banquetes, entretenimiento y discusiones literarias (pág. 123)

syndicate/sindicato bajo el fascismo, agrupación de obreros y patronos en una industria (pág. 783)

T

technology/tecnología las habilidades y conocimientos empleados por las personas para fabricar herramientas y trabajar (pág. 24)

theocracy/teocracia gobierno encabezado por líderes religiosos o por un líder considerado como un dios (págs. 48, 418)

theology/teología el estudio de temas religiosos (pág. 251)

tithe/diezmo contribución de un 10 por ciento de los ingresos que se pagaba al clero (pág. 561)

totalitarianism/totalitarismo idea en que un gobierno dictatorial debe controlar todos los aspectos de la vida de los ciudadanos (pág. 781)

tournament/torneo deporte medieval en el cual los caballeros competían para mostrar sus habilidades en la lucha (pág. 299)

trade deficit/déficit comercial el desequilibrio económico que ocurre cuando el valor de las importaciones excede el valor de las exportaciones (págs. 889, 998)

tragedy/tragedia historia o representación teatral en la que el personaje central lucha contra el destino pero que desemboca en un final trágico (pág. 132)

trench/trinchera zanja cavada para dar protección a los soldados (pág. 747)

triangular trade/comercio triangular ruta de tres direcciones entre Europa, África y América en el Siglo XVII (pág. 444)

tribune/tribuna en la antigua Roma, magistrado que representaba a los plebeyos (pág. 157)

triumvirate/triunvirato en la antigua Roma, grupo de tres personas gobernando (pág. 162)

troubadour/trovador músico y poeta de la Edad Media que viajaba de corte en corte (pág. 327)

tyrant/tirano en la antigua Grecia, persona que usurpaba el poder y establecía un gobierno unipersonal (pág. 114)

U V

ultimatum/ultimátum última disposición o declaración de condiciones, que implica una amenaza de penalidades severas (pág. 742)

ultraroyalist/ultrarrealista aristócrata extremadamente conservador en la Francia de principios del Siglo XIX (pág. 655)

unicameral legislature/legislatura unicameral asamblea o cuerpo legislativo de una sola cámara (pág. 565)

urbanization/urbanización la expansión de las ciudades y la vida citadina (pág. 631)

utilitarianism/utilitarismo filosofía económica desarrollada por Jeremy Bentham que considera que las acciones sociales y políticas deben ser de utilidad y ayuda a la humanidad (pág. 624)

varna/varna una de las cuatro clases sociales principales en la sociedad aria de la antigua India (pág. 203)

vassal/vasallo en el feudalismo, noble que ocupaba la tierra de un señor de más alto rango y le servía (pág. 299)

vernacular/vernáculo el lenguaje del habla diaria, no de los eruditos, en un país o región (pág. 328)

viceroy/virrey gobernante que representa a un monarca (pág. 714)

vocation/vocación llamado de Dios para asumir cierto trabajo (pág. 417)

W X Y Z

war of attrition/guerra de desgaste conflicto en el cual cada bando trata de ganar agotando al contrario (pág. 747)

warlord/señor de la guerra líder militar local en China (pág. 804)

weir/nasa red o trampa colocada a lo ancho de un río para coger peces (pág. 376)

welfare state/estado de proteccionismo social sistema de gobierno en el cual el estado provee programas para proteger el bienestar económico y social del pueblo (pág. 879)

westernization/occidentalización la expansión de la cultura europea (pág. 718)

yasa/yasa código de leyes de Gengis Kan (pág. 344)

yeoman/campesino propietario en la sociedad inglesa, un campesino que poseía tierras (pág. 488)

yin and yang/yin y yan en el pensamiento chino, los principios opuestos presentes en toda naturaleza (pág. 227)

yurt/yurta tienda de campaña portátil grande y redonda que usaban los nómadas del Asia central (pág. 343)

zaibatsu/zaibatsu grandes firmas industriales japonesas que pertenecían a varias familias (pág. 808)

zemstvo/zemstvo asamblea local en la Rusia zarista (pág. 692)

Text

Grateful acknowledgment is given authors and publishers for permission to reprint the following copyrighted material.
58 W.G. Lambert, Shamash Hymn from Babylonian Wisdom Literature, Copyright © 1960. Reprinted by permission Oxford University Press; **72** Reprinted by permission of Houghton Mifflin Co. All rights reserved; **146** From "Antigone" in *Sophocles, the Oedipus Cycle: An English Version* by Dudley Fitts and Robert Fitzgerald, copyright 1939 by Harcourt Brace & Company and renewed 1967 by Dudley Fitts and Robert Fitzgerald, reprinted by permission of Harcourt Brace & Company. CAUTION: All rights, including professional, amateur, motion picture, recitation, lecturing, performance, public reading, radio broadcasting, and television are strictly reserved. Inquiries on all rights should be addressed to Harcourt Brace & Company, Permissions Dept., Orlando, FL 32887; **366** Li Bo, "On a Quiet Night" from The Works of Li Bo the Chinese Poet, translated by Shigeyoshi Obata. Published in 1965 by Paragon Book Reprint Corp.; **366** Li Bo, "Taking Leave of a Friend" from Personae by Ezra Pound. Copyright 1926 by Ezra Pound. Reprinted by permission of New Directions Publishing Corporation; **367** "Hard Is the Journey" and **368** Li Bo, "Letter to His Two Small Children Staying in Eastern Lu at Wen Yang Village Under Turtle Mountain" from Li Bo and Tu Fu, translated by Arthur Cooper. Translation copyright © 1973 by Arthur Cooper. Reprinted by permission of Viking-Dutton, Inc.; **388** from "The Broken Spears" by Miguel Leon-Portilla, Copyright © 1962, 1990 by Beacon Press, Reprinted by permission of Beacon Press; **426** Niccolò Machiavelli, The Prince, translated and edited by Thomas G. Bergin. Copyright © 1947 by F. S. Crofts & Co. Inc. Reprinted by permission of Viking-Dutton, Inc.; **584** From *Les Misérables* by Victor Hugo, translated by Lee Fahnestock and Norman MacAfee. Translation copyright © 1987 by Lee Fahnestock and Norman MacAfee. Used by permission of Dutton Signet, a division of Penguin Books USA Inc.; **640** "The Beggar" from *The Short Stories of Anton Chekhov* by Anton Chekhov, edited with introduction by Robert Linscott. Copyright © 1932 and renewed 1960 by The Modern Library, Inc. Reprinted by permission of Random House, Inc.; **747** "Dulce et Decorum Est" by Wilfred Owen, from *The Collected Poems of Wilfred Owen*. Copyright © 1963 by Chatto & Windus. Reprinted by permission of New Directions Publishing Corp.; **818** From "By Any Other Name" from *Gifts of Passage* by Santha Rama Rau. Copyright © 1951 by Vasanthi Rama Rau Bowers. Copyright renewed. Reprinted by permission of HarperCollins Publishers, Inc. "By Any Other Name" originally appeared in The New Yorker; **837** From *Central Zionist Archives, Jerusalem 1939–1945*, edited by Francis R. Nicosia, Volume 4 of the *Archives of the Holocaust*, Garland Publishing, 1990; **945** Michael Dei-Anang, "My Africa" from Poems from Black Africa, edited by Langston Hughes. Copyright © 1963 by Langston Hughes. Reprinted by permission of Indiana University Press; **966** Jaime Torres Bodet, "The Window," translated by George Kearns. Translation copyright © 1974, 1963 by the McGraw-Hill Book Company, Inc.; **967** "The World, My Friends, My Enemies, You, and the Earth" from *Things I Didn't Know I Loved* by Nazim Hikmet, translated by Randy Blasing and Mutlu Konuk, copyright © 1975 by Randy Blasing and Mutlu Konuk. Reprinted by permission of Persea Books, Inc.; **968** Gabriel Okara, "Once Upon a Time," from African Voices, edited by Howard Sergeant. Copyright © 1973 by Howard Sergeant. Used by permission of Evans Brothers Ltd, London; **987** "Because I Want Peace" by Claribel Alegría, from *El Salvador: Testament of Terror*, edited by Joe Fish and Cristina Sganga. Copyright © 1988. Reprinted by permission of Interlink Publishing Group, Inc.

Maps

Cartographic Services provided by Ortelius Design, and GeoSystems Global Corp.

Photographs

Cover i Mark D. Phillips/Photo Researchers; **iv** Erich Lessing/Art Resource, NY; **v** (t)Palazzo Ducale, Mantua, Italy/M. Magliari/SuperStock, (b)National Gallery of Art, Washington DC; **vi** (t)Scala/Art Resource, NY, (b)Christies, London/SuperStock; **vii** AFP/Bettmann; **viii** (l)David David Gallery, Philadelphia/SuperStock, (r)Heraklion Museum, Crete/Kurt Scholz/SuperStock; **ix** Scala/Art Resource, NY; **x** Mark Burnett; **0** Lauros-Giraudon/Art Resource, NY;

2 NASA; **8** Simon Fraser/Science Photo Library/Photo Researchers; **10** (t)NASA, (b)Edna Douthout; **11** (t)Bosvieux/Explorer/Photo Researchers, (c)David R. Frazier, (b)Jeff Greenberg/Photo Researchers; **12** (tl) Robert Harding Picture Library, (tr)Fred Maroon/Photo Researchers, (cl, cr)Musee de Petit Palais, Paris/Bridgeman Art Library/SuperStock, (b) NASA; **13** The Metropolitan Museum of Art, The Michael C. Rockefeller Collection, Gift of Nelson A. Rockefeller, 1972 (1978.412.310); **15** National Museum, Belgrade/E.T. Archives, London/SuperStock; **16-17** Anthony Howard/Woodfin Camp & Associates; **16** Heraklion Museum, Crete/Kurt Scholz/SuperStock; **17** (t)David David Gallery, Philadelphia/SuperStock, (b)National Museum, Lagos, Nigeria/Kurt Scholz/SuperStock; **19** Jean Clottes/Sygma; **20** Esias Baitel/Gamma-Liaison; **26** Boltin Picture Library; **27** John Reader/Science Photo Library/Photo Researchers; **28-29** Erich Lessing/Art Resource, NY; **28** Boltin Picture Library; **29** Scala/Art Resource, NY; **31** Ara Guler/Magnum; **32** Scala/Art Resource, NY; **33** Borromeo/Art Resource, NY; **35** Ira Block/The Image Bank; **36** Scala/Art Resource, NY; **45** The British Museum, London/Bridgeman Art Library/SuperStock; **46** Giraudon/Art Resource, NY; **47** (t)Sylvain Grandadam/Photo Researchers, (b)Erich Lessing/Magnum; **49** John Heaton/Westlight; **51** Michael Holford; **52** Boltin Picture Library; **58** Boltin Picture Library; **59** Ancient Art & Architecture Collection Ltd.; **60 through 62** Boltin Picture Library; **63** (l)Aleppo Museum, Syria/E.T. Archives, London/SuperStock, (r)Museum of Baghdad, Iraq/Silvio Fiore/SuperStock; **64** Musee de Louvre, Paris/E.T. Archives, London/SuperStock; **66** Borromeo/Art Resource, NY; **68** Scala/Art Resource, NY; **69** Courtesy the Institute of History and Philology; **70-71** Bridgeman/Art Resource, NY; **72 74 79** Michael Holford; **80** Giraudon/Art Resource, NY; **83** Laura Zito/Photo Researchers; **85** David Forbert/SuperStock; **86** SuperStock; **87** Brent Turner; **88** Boltin Picture Library; **90-91** SEF/Art Resource, NY; **90 91** Erich Lessing/Art Resource, NY; **93** H. Linke/SuperStock; **97** Jerry Bergman/Gamma-Liaison; **98** Scala/Art Resource, NY; **99** Laurie Platt Winfrey, Inc.; **101** Scala/Art Resource, NY; **102-103** Bettmann Archive; **103** Joseph Nettis/Photo Researchers; **105** Scala/Art Resource, NY; **106** Erich Lessing/Art Resource, NY; **107** SuperStock; **108** Alberto Incrocci/The Image Bank; **110** Museo Capitolino, Rome/E.T. Archives, London/SuperStock; **111** House of Masks, Delos, Greece/Bridgeman Art Library/SuperStock; **112** William Katz/Photo Researchers; **113** Giraudon/Art Resource, NY; **115** Michael Holford; **116-117** Bill Bachmann/Photo Researchers; **116** Nimatallah/Art Resource, NY; **117** Art Resource, NY; **118** The Brooklyn Museum, Charles Wilbour Fund; **120 122** Scala/Art Resource, NY; **123** Foto Marberg/Art Resource, NY; **127** Bettmann Archive; **129** Scala/Art Resource, NY; **130** Scala/Art Resource, NY; **131** Werner Forman Archive/Art Resource, NY; **134** Museo Delle Terme, Rome/E.T. Archives, London/SuperStock; **135** Scala/Art Resource, NY; **136** Museo Capitolino, Rome/E.T. Archives, London/SuperStock; **138** Erich Lessing/Art Resource, NY; **140** Scala/Art Resource, NY; **141** Musee du Louvre, Paris/E.T. Archives, London/SuperStock; **142-143** Erich Lessing/Art Resource, NY; **142** (r)Staatliche Antikensammlung, Munich/Bridgeman Art Library/Art Resource, NY, (l)The Metropolitan Museum of Art, Bequest of Walter C. Backer, 1972 (1972.118.95); **143** (l)Art Resource, NY, (r)Giraudon/Art Resource, NY; **144** Boltin Picture Library; **145** Eric Lessing/Art Resource; **146 147 148** Art Resource, NY; **153** Erich Lessing/Art Resource, NY; **154 through 159** Scala/Art Resource, NY; **160** Prenestino Museum, Rome/E.T. Archives, London/SuperStock; **161** Scala/Art Resource, NY; **162** Archaeological Museum, Venice/E.T. Archives, London/SuperStock; **164** Robert Emmett Bright/Photo Researchers; **166-167** Scala/Art Resource, NY; **166** (c)Villa of the Mysteries, Pompeii/Euramax/SuperStock, (l)The Metropolitan Museum of Art, Rogers Fund, 1903 (03.14.5); **167** Alinari/Art Resource, NY; **168 171** Scala/Art Resource, NY; **172** Erich Lessing/Art Resource, NY; **173** Werner Forman/Art Resource, NY; **174** Scala/Art Resource, NY; **175** Robert Frerck/Tony Stone Images; **176** (l)Erich Lessing/Art Resource, NY; **179** Scala/Art Resource, NY; **181** The Metropolitan Museum of Art, Fletcher Fund, 1924 (24/97.21ab) **183** Tassili N'Ajjer Plateau, Algeria/Holton Collection/SuperStock; **184** Roger K. Burnard; **185** Egyptian Expedition of The Metropolitan Museum of Art, The Rogers Fund, 1930 (30.4.21); **186** file photo; **189** The Metropolitan Museum of Art, The Michael C. Rockefeller Collection, Gift of Nelson A. Rockefeller, 1972 (1978.412.310); **190** The British

Museum, London/Bridgeman Art Library/SuperStock; **190-191** The Elliott Elisofon Archives, Museum of African Art, The Smithsonian Institution; **191** The Metropolitan Museum of Art, The Michael C. Rockefeller Memorial Collection, Gift of Nelson A. Rockefeller, 1964 (1978.412.352). Photo by Schecter Lee; **194** H. von Meiss/Photo Researchers; **195** Dave G. Houser; **196** M.P. Kahl/Photo Researchers; **197** Mark Burnett; **199** The Metropolitan Museum of Art, The Michael C. Rockefeller Collection, Gift of Nelson A. Rockefeller, 1972 (1978.412.310); **201** Scala/Art Resource, NY; **202** Toby Molenaar/The Image Bank; **204** Robert Harding Picture Library; **204-205** B. Kapbor/SuperStock; **205** Art Resource, NY; **207** Victoria & Albert Museum, London/Art Resource, NY; **208** Christies, London/Bridgeman Art Library/SuperStock; **211** Ancient Art & Architecture Collection; **213** Gueorgui Pinkhassov/Magnum Photos, Inc.; **214** James P. Blair/National Geographic Image Collection; **215** Borromeo/Art Resource, NY; **217** Jon Gardey/Robert Harding Picture Library Ltd.; **219** Tony Stone Images; **220** Bettmann Archive; **225** Bibliotheque Nationale, Paris/Bridgeman Art Library/SuperStock; **226** Michael Holford; **227** Giraudon/Art Resource, NY; **228** Paul Biddle & Tim Malyon/Science Photo Library/Photo Researchers; **230** Bibliotheque Nationale, Paris; **231** (l)Giraudon/Art Resource, NY, (r)Bettmann Archive; **232** Bettmann Archive; **233** Mark Burnett; **237** SuperStock; **238** Robert Emmett Bright/Photo Researchers; **239** Robert Harding Picture Library; **241** Jacksonville Museum of Contemporary Art, FL/SuperStock; **242** Erich Lessing/Art Resource; **243** (l)The Smithsonian Institution, (c)Archive Photos, (r)Ancient Art & Architecture Collection, **245 246 248** Scala/Art Resource, NY; **249** SuperStock; **251** Hagia Sophia, Istanbul, Turkey/E.T. Archives, London/SuperStock; **252** (l)Michael Holford, (r)Ancient Art & Architecture Collection; **253 255** Ancient Art & Architecture Collection; **256** SEF/Art Resource, NY; **258** Roy/Explorer/Photo Researchers; **260** Art Wolfe/Tony Stone Images; **262 263** Bettmann Archive; **264** Richard Bergman/Photo Researchers; **265** Michael Holford; **267** Ancient Art & Architecture Collection; **269** Bettmann Archive; **270** British Library, London/Bridgeman Art Library International Ltd; **272** AKG Berlin/SuperStock; **273** Ancient Art & Architecture Collection; **275** Werner Forman/Art Resource, NY; **276** Michael Holford; **277** Bibliotheque Nationale, Paris/The Bridgeman Art Library International Ltd; **278-279** Lerner Fine Art Collection/SuperStock; **278** Courtesy of the Arthur M. Sackler Gallery, Smithsonian Institution, Washington, D.C.; **279** Ancient Art & Architecture Collection; **282 286** Bettmann Archive; **287** Michael Holford; **288** SuperStock; **293** San Francesco, Assisi/Canali PhotoBank, Milan/SuperStock; **294** Bettmann Archive; **295** Scala/Art Resource, NY; **298** British Library, London/Bridgeman Art Library/SuperStock; **299** Ancient Art & Architecture Collection; **301** The Metropolitan Museum of Art, Munsey Fund, 1932(32.130.6); **303** Robert Smith/Ancient Art & Architecture Collection; **304-305** Art Resource, NY; **304** (l)Ronald Sheridan/Ancient Art & Architecture, (r)Abbey of Monteoliveto Maggiore, Sienna/E.T. Archives, London/SuperStock; **304-305** Art Resource, NY; **305 306** Ronald Sheridan/Ancient Art & Architecture Collection; **307** Museo del Prado, Madrid/E.T. Archives, London/SuperStock; **308** Ronald Sheridan/Ancient Art & Architecture Collection; **309** Erich Lessing/Art Resource, NY; **313** Robert Smith/Ancient Art & Architecture Collection; **317** Scala/Art Resource, NY; **318** Ancient Art & Architecture Collection; **319** Giraudon/Art Resource, NY; **321** Erich Lessing/Art Resource, NY; **322** O. Troisfontaines/SuperStock; **323** The British Library, London/Bridgeman Art Library/SuperStock; **324-325** Scala/Art Resource, NY; **325** Ancient Art & Architecture Collection; **327** Giraudon/Art Resource, NY; **328** Scala/Art Resource, NY; **329** British Library, London/E.T. Archives, London/SuperStock; **330** Erich Lessing/Art Resource, NY; **334** Ancient Art & Architecture Collection; **336** Bridgeman Art Library/Art Resource, NY; **341** Bibliotheque Nationale, Paris/AKG Berlin/SuperStock; **342** Laurie Platt Winfrey, Inc.; **344** J. Bertrand/Photo Researchers; **345** SEF/Art Resource, NY; **346** Naomi Duguid/Asia Access; **347** Laurie Platt Winfrey, Inc.; **351** Wolfgang Kaehler; **352-353** Ernest Manewal/SuperStock; **352** (l)George Holton/Photo Researchers, (r)Frederick Ayer/Photo Researchers; **353** R. Rowan/Photo Researchers; **355** A. Hubrich/H. Armstrong Roberts; **356** Jim Steinberg/Photo Researchers; **358** T. Iwamiya/Photo Researchers; **359** Rick Browne/Photo Researchers; **360** Masao Hayashi/Dunq/Photo Researchers; **361** Bettmann Archive; **363** Private Collection/Bridgeman Art Library/SuperStock; **364** Freer Gallery; **365** Paul Chesley/Tony Stone Images; **366** Mary Evans Picture Library; **367** The Metropolitan Museum of Art, Edward Elliott Family Collection. Purchase, the Dillon Fund Gift, 1982. !982.2.2; **368 369** Bettmann Archive; **371** file photo; **373** Boltin Picture Library; **374** Steve Smith/Westlight; **376-377** Mark Burnett; **376** Georgia Department of Natural Resources; **377** (l)Cranbrook Institute of Science, (r)Bettmann Archive; **378** J. Warden/SuperStock; **379** S. Vidler/SuperStock; **380** Museum of Mankind/E.T. Archives, London/SuperStock; **381** W. Bertsch/H. Armstrong Roberts; **383** Jacksonville Museum of Contemporary Art, FL/SuperStock; **388** Michael Zabe/Art Resource, NY; **391** Woodfin Camp & Associates; **393** Loren McIntyre/Woodfin Camp & Associates; **394** Mark Burnett; **395** Werner Forman/Art Resource, NY; **397** Giraudon/Art Resource, NY; **399** Scala/Art Resource, NY; **400** The British Museum; **401-402** Scala/Art Resource, NY; **401** Wolfgang Kaehler; **403** Palazzo Ducale, Mantua, Italy/M. Magliari/SuperStock; **404** Sistine Chapel, Vatican, Rome/Bridgeman Art Library/SuperStock; **406-407** Vatican Museums & Galleries, Rome/Fratelli Alinari/SuperStock; **406** Galleria Dell'Academia, Florence/Scala/SuperStock; **407** Erich Lessing/Art Resource, NY; **408** Scala/Art Resource, NY; **410** Victor R. Boswell, Jr.; **411** Vatican Museums & Galleries, Rome/Canali PhotoBank, Milan/SuperStock; **412** AKG, Berlin/SuperStock; **413** Scala/Art Resource, NY; **414** Erich Lessing/Art Resource, NY; **415** SuperStock; **416** Erich Lessing/Art Resource, NY; **417** (l)Erich Lessing/Art Resource, NY, (r)National Museum, Copenhagen/E.T. Archives, London/SuperStock; **418** Mary Evans Picture Library/Photo Researchers; **420** Scala/Art Resource, NY; **421** Erich Lessing/Art Resource, NY; **422** Michael Holford; **423** Giraudon/Art Resource, NY; **425** Werner Forman Archive/Art Institute of Chicago/Art Resource, NY; **426 through 429** Scala/Art Resource, NY; **431** Erich Lessing/Art Resource, NY; **433** National Maritime Museum; **434** Karen Kasmauski/Woodfin Camp & Associates; **436** (l)SuperStock, (r)Michael Holford; **438** National Museum of American Art, Washington DC/Art Resource, NY; **439 440** AKG, Berlin/SuperStock; **442-443** Alinari/Art Resource, NY; **442** Erich Lessing/Art Resource, NY; **443** (t)Scala/Art Resource, NY, (b)Brent Turner/BLT Productions; **445** Bettmann Archive; **446 447** SuperStock; **448** Bridgeman/Art Resource, NY; **449** Michael Holford; **450** Bridgeman/Art Resource, NY; **455 456** Giraudon/Art Resource, NY; **458** Art Resource, NY; **459** Adam Woolfitt/Woodfin Camp & Associates; **461** by courtesy of the Board of Trustees of the Victoria & Albert Museum, London/Bridgeman Art Library/SuperStock; **462** Bibliotheque Nationale, Paris; **463** Dallas & John Heaton/Westlight; **464-465** Philadelphia Free Library/AKG, Berlin/SuperStock; **464** G. Hunter/SuperStock; **465** (l)Art Trade, Bonhams, London/Bridgeman Art Library/SuperStock, (r)SEF/Art Resource, NY; **466** D.E. Cox/Tony Stone Images; **468** Werner Forman Archive/Art Resource, NY; **469** Culver Pictures Inc./SuperStock; **470** Kita-In Saitumi/Werner Foreman Archive/Art Resource, NY; **471** Michael Holford; **473** Doug Martin; **474** George Holton/Photo Researchers; **475** SuperStock; **476** Scala/Art Resource, NY; **477** Bettmann Archive; **481** Giraudon/Art Resource, NY; **482** Bridgeman Art Library, London/SuperStock; **483** Bettmann Archive; **485** Victoria & Albert Museum/Art Resource, NY; **486** Michael Holford; **487** (l)Bridgeman/Art Resource, NY, (r)National Portrait Gallery, London; **488 489** National Portrait Gallery, London/SuperStock; **490** Giraudon/Art Resource, NY; **491** Lauros-Giraudon/Art Resource, NY; **492** A&F Pears Ltd., London/SuperStock; **494** Museum of Art History, Vienna/AKG, Berlin/SuperStock; **496** AKG, Berlin/SuperStock; **498** Novosti from Sovfoto; **499** Michael Holford; **502** Giraudon/Art Resource, NY; **505** Bridgeman/Art Resource, NY; **507** National Gallery, London/SuperStock; **508** Bridgeman/Art Resource, NY; **509** Giraudon/Art Resource, NY; **511** Scala/Art Resource, NY; **512** Architect of the Capitol, Washington D.C.; **513** Bettmann Archive; **515** Giraudon/Art Resource, NY; **516** Royal Society of London **517** Private Collection/Bridgeman Art Library/SuperStock; **519** Bettmann Archive; **521** (detail)Erich Lessing/Art Resource, NY; **524** Giraudon/Art Resource, NY; **525** Derby Museum and Art Gallery, England/Bridgeman Art Library/SuperStock; **526** Christies, London/SuperStock; **526-527** Erich Lessing/Art Resource, NY; **527** Bettmann Archive; **528 529** Ronald Sheridan/Ancient Art & Architecture Collection; **530 531** Archive Photos; **535** Bridgeman/Art Resource, NY; **536** Ronald Sheridan/Ancient Art & Architecture Collection; **537** Bettmann Archive; **538** courtesy The Pilgrim Society; **540** National

Portrait Gallery, London/SuperStock; **541 543** Ronald Sheridan/ Ancient Art & Architecture Collection; **544** Bettmann Archive; **545** Scala/Art Resource, NY; **546-547** Bettmann Archive; **546** Historic Deerfield Inc.: photo by Amanda Merullo; **547** (l)John Carter Brown Library, Brown University, (r)Massachusetts Historical Society; **548** Bettmann Archive; **550** Archive Photos; **551** Ronald Sheridan/ Ancient Art & Architecture Collection; **552** Chicago Historical Society; **553** Yale University Art Gallery; **559** AKG, Berlin/SuperStock; **560** Bettmann Archive; **561** Scala/Art Resource, NY; **563** Mary Evans Picture Library/Photo Researchers; **564** Bettmann Archive; **565** Giraudon/Art Resource, NY; **567** Photo Researchers; **568** AKG, Berlin/ SuperStock; **570-571** Stock Montage; **570** Photo Researchers; **571** Archiv/Photo Researchers; **573** Erich Lessing/Art Resource, NY; **574** Bettmann Archive; **575 578** Giraudon/Art Resource, NY; **580** Photo Researchers; **582 583** Bettmann Archive; **584** Giraudon/Art Resource, NY; **585** The Metropolitan Museum of Art, Gift of Mrs. Herbert N. Straus, 1942(42.203.1) Photo by Derry Moore; **586** Mary Evans Picture Library/Photo Researchers; **591** (l)Stock Montage, (r)Scala/Art Resource, NY; **592** (t)Bettmann Archive, (b)Original painting hangs in the Selectmen's Meeting Room, Abbot Hall, Marblehead MA; **593** Scala/Art Resource, NY; **595** L. Berger/SuperStock; **596** Stock Montage; **597** (t)Library of Congress, (b)Laurie Platt Winfrey, Inc.; **599** The Science Museum, London; **600** Waterhouse and Dodd, London/Bridgeman Art Library/SuperStock; **601** Christies, London/SuperStock; **603** Archive Photos; **604** Ronald Sheridan/ Ancient Art & Architecture Collection; **605** file photo; **606 607** The Smithsonian Institution; **608** Royal Museum of Fine Arts, Copenhagen/Bridgeman Art Library/SuperStock; **612** International Museum of Photography/George Eastman House; **613 614** Collection of Picture Research Consultants; **614-615** Snark/Art Resource, NY; **615** Library of Congress; **616** Courtesy Labor Archives and Research Center, San Francisco State University; **621 622** Giraudon/Art Resource, NY; **623** Library of Congress; **624** file photo; **626** Bettmann Archive; **627** Erich Lessing/Art Resource, NY; **629** National Portrait Gallery, London/SuperStock; **630-631** Christies, London/SuperStock; **630** Library of Congress; **631** Missouri Historical Society; **633** Tate Gallery, London/Art Resource, NY; **635** Gemaldegalerie, Dresden, Germany/A.K.G., Berlin/SuperStock; **636** Christies, London/SuperStock; **639** Erich Lessing/Art Resource, NY; **640** Archive Photos; **641** Scala/Art Resource, NY; **642** Russian Sate Museum, St. Petersburg/Bourkatouskey/SuperStock; **645** National Portrait Gallery, London/SuperStock; **647** Giraudon/Art Resource, NY; **648** Library of Congress; **649** Snark/Art Resource, NY; **651 652** Bettmann Archive; **653** Archive Photos; **655** Erich Lessing/Art Resource, NY; **656** Stock Montage; **657** Giraudon/Art Resource, NY; **658 660 662** Bettmann Archive; **662-663** Scala/Art Resource, NY; **663** Mark Burnett; **665** Library of Congress; **666** Bettmann Archive; **668** Schalkwijk/Art Resource, NY; **675 676** Scala/Art Resource, NY; **678-679** Giraudon/Art Resource, NY; **679** (l)Scala/Art Resource, NY, (r)Vince Streano/Tony Stone Images; **680** Bettmann Archive; **681** Archive for Art & History, Berlin/AKG, Berlin/SuperStock; **683** Bryan F. Peterson/The Stock Market; **685** Erich Lessing/Art Resource, NY; **686** FPG International; **687** SuperStock; **689** Bettmann Archive; **690** FPG International; **693** Bettmann Archive; **695** Corbis-Bettmann; **696** SEF/ Art Resource, NY; **701** Mark Burnett; **703** Bridgeman/Art Resource, NY; **704** Laurie Platt Winfrey, Inc.; **705** Bettmann Archive; **707** Archive Photos/Popperfoto; **708** Bettmann Archive; **709** Werner Forman Archive/Art Resource, NY; **711** Bettmann Archive; **712** Thierry Prat/Sygma; **713** Stock Concepts; **716-717** Bridgeman/Art Resource, NY; **717** (l)Bettmann Archive, (r)Bridgeman Art Library/Art Resource, NY; **719** Bettmann Archive; **720** file photo; **721 722** Bettmann Archive; **727** Historical Picture Service; **729** Musee de Petit Palais, Paris/Bridgeman Art Library/SuperStock; **731** Stock Montage; **733** Aaron Haupt; **734** UPI/Bettmann Archive; **735** (t)AP/Wide World Photos, (b)Lena Kara/SIPA; **737** West Point Museum/Joshua Nefsky; **738** SuperStock; **741** Bettmann Archive; **744** Archive Photos; **746-747** Bridgeman/Art Resource, NY; **746** Collection of Colonel Stuart S. Corning. Photo: Rob Huntley: Lightstream; **747** UPI/Bettmann Archive; **748** Erich Lessing/Art Resource, NY; **749** Bettmann Archive; **756** Snark/Art Resource, NY; **757** AP/Wide World Photos; **760** Collection of Colonel Stuart S. Corning. Photo: Rob Huntley:Lightstream; **761** Bettmann Archive; **769** Des Moines Art Center Permanent Collection, 1958.2. Photo:

Craig Anderson; **770** Archive Photos; **772** The Metropolitan Museum of Art, bequest of Gertrude Stein, 1946(47.106); **773** Centro de Arte Reina Sofia, Madrid, Spain/Giraudon, Paris/SuperStock; **776** Archive Photos; **777** National Museum of American Art/Art Resource, NY; **778** Bettmann Archive; **779** UPI/Bettmann; **781** AKG, Berlin/SuperStock; **782** L'Illustration/Sygma; **783 784** Bettmann Archive; **784-785** AP/Wide World Photos; **785** Bettmann Archive; **786** Hugo Jaeger/LIFE Magazine, Time Inc.; **787** David Low/London Evening Standard/Solo Syndication Limited; **788** Sovfoto; **789 791** Bettmann Archive; **793** (l) Museum of Modern Art, New York/ Bridegeman Art Library/SuperStock, Demart Pro Arte, Geneva/ Artists' Rights Society, NY; (r) Stock Montage, Inc.; **795** Schalkwijk/ Art Resource, NY; **796** Archive Photos; **798** UPI/Bettmann; **799** Eliot Elisofon National Museum of African Art, Eliot Elisofon Archives, Smithsonian Institution; **800** John Moss/Black Star; **801** Bridgeman/ Art Resource, NY; **802** file photo; **804** Keystone, Paris/Sygma; **805** AP/Wide World Photos; **806** SIPA Press; **807 808** Bettmann Archive; **810** John Moss/Black Star; **811** SuperStock; **812 813** Schalkwijk/Art Resource, NY; **814 818** UPI/Bettmann; **819** Laurie Platt Winfrey, Inc.; **821** Rudi Von Briel; **825** U.S. Naval Photographic Center; **826** UPI/Bettmann; **827** AP/Wide World Photos; **829** Sygma; **831** Archive Photos; **834-835** UPI/Bettmann; **834** AP/Wide World Photos; **835** (l)Bettmann Archive, (r)Archive Photos; **836** Popperfoto/Archive Photos; **838 839 842** UPI/Bettmann; **846** Archive Photos; **848** RIA-Novosti/Sovphoto; **849** UPI/Bettmann; **850** Archive Photos; **851** UPI/Bettmann; **856** B. Swersey/Gamma-Liaison; **857** AP/Wide World Photos; **859** Chuck O'Rear/Westlight; **860** (l)UPI/Corbis-Bettmann, (r)Sovfoto/Eastfoto; **861** (l)T. Rosenthal/SuperStock; (r)The Granger Collection; **863** Sovfoto/Eastfoto; **864** Archive Photos; **865** SuperStock; **868-869** AP/Wide World Photos; **868** UPI/Bettmann; **869** S. Vidler/SuperStock; **872** Archive Photos; **873** UPI/Bettmann; **875** Black Star; **877** UPI/Bettmann; **878** Roger-Viollet; **879** AP/Wide World Photos; **880** UPI/Bettmann; **882** Bettmann Archive; **883** UPI/Bettmann; **884** SIPA Press; **887** AP/Wide World Photos; **888** UPI/Corbis-Bettmann; **890** Reuters/Bettmann; **895** M. Setboun/ Sygma; **896** P. Amranand/SuperStock; **897** T. Matsumoto/Sygma; **898** Tom Wagner/SABA; **899** Michael Yamashita/Westlight; **901** George Matchneer; **903** Bettmann Archive; **904** Langevin/Sygma; **906** Duclos/Guichard/Gouver/Gamma-Liaison; **908** R. Ian Lloyd/ The Stock Market; **909** UPI/Bettmann; **910-911** file photo; **911** UPI/Bettmann; **914** Howard/Spooner/Gamma; **916** Sygma; **917** UPI/Bettmann; **919** V. Miladinovic/Sygma; **920** G.R. Robert; **921 925** Sygma; **927** Klaus Reisinger/Black Star; **928** Louis Gubb/JB Pictures; **931** UPI/Bettmann; **932** Archive Photos/Express News/D.E.1; **934** David Keith Jones/Images of Africa Photobank; **935** Haviv/SABA; **936 937** (l)David Keith Jones/Images of Africa Photobank; **938** Alain Buu/Gamma Liaison Network; **940** Mark Burnett; **941** J.M. Bertrand/SuperStock; **942** David Travers/The Stock Market; **943** Doug Menuez/SABA; **944** P. Schmidt/SuperStock; **945** Lawrence Migdale/Tony Stone Images; **947** Betty Press/Woodfin Camp & Associates; **949** Robert Frerck/Woodfin Camp & Associates; **950** Jesse Nemerofsky/Photoreporters; **951** Sygma; **954** L. de Raemy/Sygma; **955** UPPA/Photoreporters; **956 957** Barry Iverson/Woodfin Camp & Associates; **957** (l)Penny Tweedie/Woodfin Camp & Associates, (r)Esaias Baitel/Gamma-Liaison; **958** Terry Ashe/The Gamma Liaison Network; **962** Reuters/Bettmann; **963** Tony Stone Images; **964** Ed Kashi; **967** AP/Wide World Photos; **969** Dennis Stock/ Magnum; **973** Ary Diesendruck/Tony Stone Images; **974** Alain Keler/Sygma; **975** David L. Perry; **976** Neil Beer/Tony Stone Images; **977** Carrion/Sygma; **979** Bettmann Archive; **980-981** Sergio Dorantes/Sygma; **980** Robert Frerck/Tony Stone Images; **981** (l)Robert Frerck/Woodfin Camp & Associates, (r)Russell Cheyne/ Tony Stone Images; **985** Javier Bauluz/SABA; **987** Sygma; **988** Sergio Dorantes/Sygma; **989** Gary Payne/Gamma Liaison; **990** UPI/ Bettmann; **991** Reuters/Bettmann; **992** David L. Perry; **997** NASA; **998** Les Stone/Sygma; **1000** Novosti/Gamma-Liaison; **1003 1004** Reuters/Bettmann; **1005** AP/Wide World Photos; **1006 1007** Reuters/Bettmann; **1009** AFP/Bettmann; **1010** AP/Wide World Photos; **1011** Peter Turnley/Black Star; **1014** AP/Wide World Photos; **1016** (l)AP/Wide World Photos, (r)Reuters/Bettmann; **1018** NASA/ Gamma-Liaison; **1019** SuperStock; **1020** J.L. Atlan/Sygma; **1021** Hans Peter Merten/Tony Stone Images; **1027** Epix/Sygma; **1028** Adrian Bradshaw/SABA; **1029** David L. Perry.